Criminal Psychology

Criminal Psychology

Volume 1: Theory and Research

Jacqueline B. Helfgott, PhD, Editor

Foreword by J. Reid Meloy

PRAEGER

AN IMPRINT OF ABC-CLIO, LLC
Santa Barbara, California • Denver, Colorado • Oxford, England

Library of Congress Cataloging-in-Publication Data

Criminal psychology / Jacqueline B. Helfgott, PhD, editor ; foreword by J. Reid Meloy.
volumes ; cm
Includes bibliographical references and index.
ISBN 978–0–313–39607–6 (hbk. : alk. paper) — ISBN 978–0–313–39608–3 (ebk.)
1. Criminal psychology. I. Helfgott, Jacqueline B.
HV6080.C7335 2013
364.3—dc23 2012051076

ISBN: 978–0–313–39607–6
EISBN: 978–0–313–39608–3

17 16 15 14 3 4 5

This book is also available on the World Wide Web as an eBook.
Visit www.abc-clio.com for details.

Praeger
An Imprint of ABC-CLIO, LLC

ABC-CLIO, LLC
130 Cremona Drive, P.O. Box 1911
Santa Barbara, California 93116-1911

This book is printed on acid-free paper ∞

Manufactured in the United States of America

For my parents, Esther & Oscar

Contents

Foreword by J. Reid Meloy ix

Preface by Jacqueline B. Helfgott xiii

SECTION I: CRIMINAL PSYCHOLOGY: AN OVERVIEW

Chapter One: Criminal Psychology and Criminal Behavior 3
Jacqueline B. Helfgott

Chapter Two: Education and Training Models in Forensic Psychology 43
David DeMatteo, Geoffrey Marczyk, Daniel A. Krauss, and Jeffrey Burl

SECTION II: THEORETICAL PERSPECTIVES

Chapter Three: Becoming Criminal: Theoretical Perspectives on the Development and Desistance of Criminality 63
Nahanni Pollard

Chapter Four: The Psychophysiology and Neuroanatomy of Antisocial Behavior 89
Max M. Loomans, Joke H. M. Tulen, and Hjalmar J. C. van Marle

Chapter Five: Perspectives on Neurocriminology 117
Benjamin R. Nordstrom, Yu Gao, Andrea L. Glenn, Melissa Peskin, Anna S. Rudo-Hutt, Robert A. Schug, Yaling Yang, and Adrian Raine

Chapter Six: Two Sides of the Same Coin: The Sociological and Psychological Social Psychology of Crime 163
Mark Cohan and Kathleen E. Cook

Chapter Seven: Personality and Antisocial Behavior: Theoretical Perspectives 189
Shayne Jones

Chapter Eight: The Criminal Personality 209
Stanton E. Samenow

SECTION III: KEY RESEARCH FINDINGS

Chapter Nine: Predatory and Affective Aggression: Calculated and Explosive Pathways to Violence 229
Stacey L. Shipley and Jennifer L. Russell

Chapter Ten: Psychological Theories and Research on Female Criminal Behavior 261
Elaine Gunnison

Chapter Eleven: The Phenomenology of Addiction and the Artifact of Criminal Behavior 299
David Polizzi

Chapter Twelve: Criminality and Co-Occurring Psychiatric and Substance Use Disorders 321
Arthur J. Lurigio and Thomas Lyons

About the Editor and Contributors *341*

Index *351*

Foreword

J. Reid Meloy

Ever since the eighteenth and nineteenth centuries—when Franz Gall and Cesare Lombroso, in phrenological leaps of faith, studied the shape of criminal skulls, and Ernst Kretschmer and William Sheldon, in morphological moments of insight, kindled an interest in the physical habitus of the criminal's body—philosophers, biologists, theologians, and psychologists have attempted to discern the criminal's mind. Introducing the unconscious world of psychodynamics shortly thereafter—and challenging a pure biological determinism—Sigmund Freud wrote at the beginning of the twentieth century:

> Two traits are essential in a criminal: a boundless egoism and a strong destructive urge. Common to both of these, and a necessary condition for their expression, is the absence of love, the lack of an emotional appreciation of (human) objects. (Standard Edition, Vol. XXI, p. 178)

None of these pioneers would have imagined the enormity and complexity of criminal psychology at the dawn of the twenty-first century. Jacqueline Helfgott did, and undertook what others might perceive as a Sisyphean task for which she was clearly capable: assemble a multivolume understanding of criminal psychology based upon contemporary theory and empirical research, with the breadth and depth it both required and deserved. She has achieved this remarkable goal with the help of over 100 very accomplished, and in some cases internationally known, contributors.

Dr. Helfgott is a professor and chair of the Criminal Justice Department at Seattle University. We first met in 1989 when she was a young doctoral student at Pennsylvania State University, and had taken an interest in some of our early writing on conscious cognitive processes and psychopathy. She readily understood that there are both unconscious psychodynamics and neurobiological processes that may shape the criminal's conscious thinking—a perspective often lost in some psychology professionals' treatment of choice for criminals, such as a heavy reliance on just cognitive behavioral therapy. To avoid the fundamental attribution error, our tendency to overweight the contribution of personality to motivation and underweight the contribution of the environment, she also paid close attention to both criminology and social psychology. But to really leave a footprint in her profession, she embraced the dynamic interplay between theory and research. Without theory, empirical research is just counting; and without empirical research, theory is just speculation. Or as the British astrophysicist Arthur Eddington once wrote, "No experiment should be believed until it has been confirmed by theory." Dr. Helfgott's early work resulted in two important papers (Helfgott, 1997, 2004) which empirically tested the theory of the relationship between conscious cognitive processes and unconscious psychodynamics in psychopaths, and also applied such findings to the field of forensic psychology practice.

She continues to recognize the importance of engaging both the ivory tower and the street. She has managed the authors and guided in the production of these scholarly volumes; and at the same time, she continues her work on other applied research projects, advisory boards, and various boards of directors concerning treatment of both perpetrators and victims of crime in the Seattle and surrounding Washington State.

When I open a professional or technical book for the first time, I conduct a test that consists of three parts. First, I read something from the book I know a lot about to see how accurate and well referenced it is. Second, I then read something I know nothing about to see if I will learn something new. Finally, I check to see if the writing style delivers the content in a pleasurable manner, or if it is an impediment to learning. In other words, do I have to struggle with poor grammatical choices, moments of illogic, occasional meandering thinking, and awkward syntax to glean something useful from the text? Are there any sentences that approach, for instance, the most elegant and poetic understanding of transference ever written: "So we beat on, boats against the current, borne back ceaselessly into the past"? Probably not, but textbooks should not drive us away, longing for the novels of F. Scott Fitzgerald.

I remember once hearing a well-known forensic psychiatrist testify in a criminal case. His testimony followed a psychiatrist for the defense who had talked in detail about the defendant's propensity to sexually assault his victims only late at night, and his habit of sleeping, instead, throughout the day. He went on with great erudition, his technical use of terms, such as the circadian rhythm sleep disorder of this defendant, superseded only by his boring delivery. When the opposing psychiatrist took the stand and was asked the same question, he responded, "the defendant is a nocturnal predator." Clarity of thought; luminescence in the mind of the listener.

Criminal Psychology, if measured by my admittedly simple yardstick, is a resounding success. The readers of this four-volume set, whether graduate student or seasoned professional, practitioner or academic, will be assured of their existing knowledge, learn much that is new, creative, and scientifically sound, and find it a pleasure to deepen their own thinking.

References

Helfgott, J. (1997). The unconscious defensive process/conscious cognitive style relationship in psychopaths. *Criminal Justice and Behavior, 24*, 278–293.

Helfgott, J. (2004). Primitive defenses in the language of the psychopath: Considerations for forensic practice. *Journal of Forensic Psychology Practice, 4*, 1–29.

J. Reid Meloy is a clinical professor of psychiatry at UC San Diego School of Medicine, and a faculty member of the San Diego Psychoanalytic Institute.

Preface

Jacqueline B. Helfgott

My interest in criminal psychology began sometime around the late 1970s/early 1980s. I'm not sure if I can identify exactly what led me to willingly want to spend the majority of my adult life and most of my waking hours reading, writing, thinking about crime, violence, and psychopathy, and conducting research and programs inside prisons and other criminal justice contexts. When I think back, I guess it was probably a mix of popular culture and personal experiences that made me so interested in the intersection of psychology and criminology/criminal justice. I grew up in the Northwest with a single mother in graduate school, a social activist grandmother, and two younger brothers. I watched a good amount of TV (mostly *I Dream of Jeannie* and *The Brady Bunch*, and shows my brothers wanted to watch such as *Speed Racer*), but not a lot of crime shows. The crime shows on TV at the time were nothing like they are today. Most of the pop cultural crime and violence I was exposed to growing up was on Saturday morning superhero cartoons such as *Wonder Woman* and *Batman*, *ABC After-School Specials*, or shows such as *Charlie's Angels*, *The Six Million Dollar Man*, and *The Bionic Woman* and in the *Hardy Boys* and *Nancy Drew* books. It was well before the era of the serial murder film, and the most memorable depiction of film violence I was allowed to see as a kid was Sissy Spacek's character in *Carrie* when she unleashed her torment on her classmates at the prom after being publicly doused with pig's blood.

One of my earliest memories of being aware of real-life crime was at the breakfast table sometime in the 1970s while eating cereal with my brothers. The little kid on the back of the milk carton was missing, and there had been a lot of stuff in the news around that time about missing children. A couple of years later, my youngest brother's five-year-old friend was found dead, hung in his mother's closet, murdered by a man who was renting a room from his mom. I knew people growing up who shoplifted, used drugs, did time in juvenile detention, and dropped out of school. At my high school graduation, when everyone threw up their hats to hug their friends, I looked around and realized that everyone I knew had dropped out. I wondered why I continued on to college while all of my close friends from that time did not, and a few of them even ended up spending time in jail or prison. I attributed my own trajectory of academic success and crime desistance to the fact that I grew up seeing my mom studying and reading all the time and my grandma fighting for this or that social cause. But I wondered if it could be that simple.

At the time I graduated from high school, my old high school boyfriend came home to find his mother stabbed to death multiple times—the guy who did it was a drug dealer she knew who was caught shortly after. A couple of years later, I bumped into a neighbor friend who lived across the street, who told me that his younger sister was missing and was determined by police to be a victim of the Green River killer. Some years after that, an 83-year-old woman I knew was attacked with lawn sheers and butcher knives by her schizophrenic son who had gone off his meds. He attacked her for hours, stabbed her in the head, and cut her throat from ear to ear. I helped clean the mess that remained after the police and medics left. She survived the attack, and her son was sent to Western State Hospital upon a "Not Guilty by Reason of Insanity" verdict. He was released to his mother's—his victim's—care five years later. These and other incidents and experiences have made criminal behavior and its response in both the mental health and criminal justice systems very real for me.

I decided to study criminal justice and psychology in college after starting out as an art major and deciding that I would not be able to draw under pressure and that it would probably be more realistic to do something else for a living. I waited tables through college and got to know police officers who came into the restaurants where I worked and who took me on ride-alongs. I completed an internship in community corrections working with an officer in charge of a sex-offender caseload and read case files filled with accounts of bizarre acts of sexual deviancy. I went on tours of prisons and halfway houses and on work releases. I took courses from inspirational faculty, many of whom were leading-edge scholars at the forefront of forensic psychology and criminology, some of the most prominent scholars in the field—cognitive psychologist Elizabeth Loftus, now one of the most cited psychologists in history; Dale Smith, a psychologist who had published work with Hans Toch on inmate adjustment; and criminology and criminal justice with George Bridges, whose lecture style of story after story made academic criminology seem like one of the most important callings. I took a tour of the Washington State Penitentiary in Walla Walla, where I saw Kevin Coe, the subject of Jack Olsen's book *Son: A Psychopath and His Victims*, soon after he was convicted, standing only feet away from me. I conducted a study on psychologists' views on psychopathy and had the opportunity to interview Seattle-area psychologists who worked in the intersection of criminal justice and mental health, including psychologists who later would go on to evaluate infamous serial killers such as Wesley Dodd. My personal experiences learning about crime from people I knew who were victims or offenders were shaped and explained in a new way through learning from practitioners in the field and academic research.

In my senior year of college in the late 1980s, while finishing up my undergraduate degrees in psychology and society and justice, I read books that to this day I have not been able to get out of my head—Wambaugh's (1987) *The Onion Field*; Olsen's (1983) *Son: A Psychopath and His Victims*; Rule's (1987) *Small Sacrifices*; Cleckley's (1941) *The Mask of Sanity*; Lindner's (1945) *Rebel without a Cause*; McCoy's (1981) *Concrete Mama: Prison Profiles from Walla Walla*; Hare's (1970) *Psychopathy: Theory and Research*; Yochelson and Samenow's (1977) *The Criminal Personality, Volumes 1–3*; Goffman's (1963) *Stigma*; Meloy's (1988) *The Psychopathic Mind*; and Johnson's (1987) *Hard Time: Understanding and Reforming the Prison*. These and other works I read at the time created great intrigue for me, raising question after question at the nexus of psychology and criminology/criminal justice—*What makes a person a law-abiding citizen versus a home invasion robber or a rapist or a murderer? How do police and corrections officers mentally process their jobs and their interactions with offenders? How do the mental health and criminal justice systems work together to respond to criminal behavior? How do victims of crime move on in the aftermath of criminal behavior? What makes a person incapable of feeling and able to hurt other people without feeling any guilt or concern for their welfare? What kinds of things go on in people's minds when they steal, vandalize, kidnap, rape, and murder? How do prison inmates adjust to long-term confinement? Where do fantasies about hurting other people come from in the first place? What is a psychopath, and how do you tell who is and who is not one? If psychopaths and other persistent offenders are so impervious to treatment, what should be done with them? How were psychologists so certain they could tell the difference between a criminal psychopath and a criminal who was just down on his luck? What mental mechanisms are at work when people commit minor crimes like shoplifting and major crimes like child abduction and serial murder? Once a person develops a deviant or criminal identity, what hope is there that the person can change to be a law-abiding citizen?*

In the late 1980s, there were few quick or definitive answers to most of these questions. Forensic psychology did not yet exist in the form of formal academic programs (beyond a few joint psychology and law programs). Computers were just becoming accessible on college campuses, and there was no Internet or Google. I typed my graduate school applications on a typewriter and picked schools I thought sounded good in places I thought I might like to go. I had read Bob Hare's book *Psychopathy*, but as a naïve undergraduate who was working three waitress jobs while going to school full time, it somehow eluded me (until a couple of years later when across the country in graduate school) that he was only 150 miles away at the University of British Columbia. I recall calling and speaking with Stanton Samenow on the phone as I prepared my graduate applications. I don't remember what I asked him or what we discussed, but he was nice enough to speak to a know-nothing college student just starting out. I had no idea where to apply to graduate school. All I knew was that I wanted to study psychopaths and the intersection of criminal justice and psychology. I applied to programs in psychology and criminal justice and landed at Penn State. I had applied to the Psychology Department there but had written a cover letter about wanting to study psychopathy and the intersection of mental health and criminal justice. The Psychology Department called and asked if I minded if they sent my file to the Administration of Justice Department. I got a call the next day with an enthusiastic offer of a research and teaching assistantship in administration of justice with a graduate minor in psychology that would allow me to pursue my research interests, which I gladly accepted.

I did my master's thesis and dissertation in the early 1990s on the unconscious defensive process/conscious cognitive style relationship in psychopaths. When I got to graduate school and started doing research for my master's thesis, I came across Gacono and Meloy's (1988) article, "The Relationship between Conscious Cognitive Style and Unconscious Defensive Process in the Psychopath," published in *Criminal Justice and Behavior*. I still remember the day I got my hands on the article and sat in the library reading it. I was so enthralled that soon after, I began the process of pulling together my thesis and dissertation committee and developing a study to empirically test the hypothetical rape scenario and levels hypothesis on the UDP/CCS relationship in psychopaths proposed in the article. My dissertation committee consisted of two psychologists (Lynne Goodstein, who had done work on inmate adjustment and long-term imprisonment, and Juris Draguns, whose research focused on cross-cultural psychology and personality), a lawyer (Daniel Katkin), and a former probation officer turned professor (William Parsonage). I took courses with Philip Jenkins (who some years later went on to write highly influential work on moral panic theory), Fran Bernat (now the editor of *Women and Criminal Justice*), and was fortunate to have assistance from Bob Hare, Carl Gacono, and Reid Meloy during the process of completing my dissertation. I received training in administering the PCL-R through the old-school method, which involved receiving large cardboard boxes in the mail from Bob Hare and colleagues containing videotapes and files that I was to review, score, and mail back for interrater reliability scores. Juris Draguns taught me how to administer the Rorschach. In my graduate school years, Faith Lutze, who went on to do important work in corrections and offender reentry, and Bruce Arrigo (now editor of the *Journal of Forensic Psychology Practice*), who has made prolific and key contributions in forensic psychology, were classmates; and I had the opportunity to meet other scholars whose work I admired at conferences, such as Adrian Raine, Robert Johnson, Kathleen Heide, and many others. Later, as a newly minted assistant professor, I invited my favorite true crime authors Jack Olsen and Ann Rule to campus to speak and had the opportunity to get to know them as well, especially Jack Olsen, who I consider the greatest true crime writer of all time.

Since those early years that shaped my academic career, I have had the opportunity to engage in research in law enforcement and corrections that has further shaped my perspective and academic pursuits. I have spent a good part of my career teaching courses and conducting research at the intersection of psychology and criminal justice. I have also been fortunate to be able to combine some of my other interests into my work. I have coordinated art and other programs in prisons for most of my career, which has allowed me to spend great amounts of time working directly with people who have committed crimes and who have served long sentences, both in and out of confinement. I have been involved in applied research that has kept me constantly aware of the real issues confronting practitioners and the responsibility academics have to make theory and research accessible to practice. I have worked with truly amazing students, from whom I have learned and who have helped me to expand my views and the questions I ask. Through some of these experiences, I have had been able to learn about the psychology of crime and criminal justice in ways that more formal research endeavors have not allowed. It has always been a bit surprising to me how much more I have learned about crime while painting a mural with a group of Lifers or riding around town with police officers than by analyzing data from psychometric tests and self-reports.

I sometimes find myself envious of the opportunities my students have today for the great many academic programs in forensic psychology. In the

1980s, the field of forensic psychology did not yet exist in the form of established academic programs, scholarly journals, or professional organizations. The academic discipline of criminal justice/criminology was only a generation old, if that. Library research on topics such as "psychopaths," "criminal psychology," or "criminal profiling" at that time resulted in a confusing absence of consensus and muddled terminology that had the potential to generate more frustration than new ideas or frameworks for empirical research. Today, there are a range of opportunities to study the intersection of psychology and crime, with many academic programs in forensic psychology and criminology/criminal justice, and there is disciplinary integration that did not exist 20 years ago.

However, I feel fortunate to have learned from, worked with, and/or gone to school with some of the brightest minds in the field responsible for shaping the study of criminal and forensic psychology today. Many of these scholars have contributed their work to this reference set. The study of criminal psychology and criminal behavior has come incredibly far in a very short time. Theory and anecdote have been tested by empirical research; forensic assessment tools have been developed, standardized, and validated; and much of the important theoretical and empirical work that has been done in the intersection of psychology and criminology/criminal justice is now making its way into practice in law enforcement agencies, courts, prisons and halfway houses, juvenile detention facilities, schools, victim services, and communities.

The volumes and chapters included in *Criminal Psychology, Volumes 1–4* reflect the state of the science of criminal psychology and criminal behavior written by the best and brightest minds in the academic criminology and forensic psychology, practitioners at the front end of the criminal justice and forensic settings, and scholars engaged in creative cutting-edge work. The work is organized into four volumes: Volume 1: Theory and Research; Volume 2: Typologies, Mental Disorders, and Profiles; Volume 3: Implications for Forensic Assessment, Policing, and the Courts; and Volume 4: Implications for Juvenile Justice, Corrections, and Reentry. Volume 1 offers an overview of theory, research, and key findings on criminal psychology and criminal behavior. Volume 2 addresses the utility of criminal typologies and profiles, presents research on specific crime types and psychopathy. The chapters included in Volumes 3 and 4 illustrate how theory and research on criminal psychology enter the criminal justice system in forensic assessment and prediction of dangerousness, law enforcement, criminal law, the courts, and sentencing, juvenile justice, institutional and community corrections, and offender reentry. I am proud of this mix of key and prominent researchers and theorists, whose work is the brick and mortar of today's criminal psychology joined by scholars just starting out in the field and practitioners who have a front-line vantage point. I am grateful to their willingness to contribute their work in this comprehensive, timely, and important collection on criminal psychology and criminal behavior. We have seen an unprecedented amount of attention to criminal psychology in the last 20 years, in all realms—academic, popular culture, and real-world practice. I hope the work contained in this set raises new questions and helps set the stage for what promises to be an era of greater refinement of theory, research, and practice that will provide answers that will help whittle away at the complex underpinnings and sometime tragic effects of criminal behavior.

A project like this is an enormous undertaking that requires the collaboration of many people. I am grateful to the many authors who have contributed their work and would like to thank each one of them individually. There are a number of people who deserve special acknowledgment. First and foremost, my research assistant Teneshia Thurman, who corresponded with over 100 authors, edited 61 chapters, and assisted with all aspects of the project. Teneshia's contributions to this project were enormous and invaluable and required extraordinary patience and attention. I could not have completed the project without her. I would also like to thank Praeger/ABC-CLIO senior editor Debbie Carvalko for her assistance with the project and her advice, contributions, and good humor at key points in the process, and Praeger/ABC-CLIO acquisitions editor Alicia Merritt for inviting me to serve as editor for this set. Special thanks to the energetic and supportive faculty and students I work with in the Criminal Justice Department at Seattle University; to George Palermo (editor of the *International Journal of Offender Therapy and Comparative Criminology*), Carl Gacono and Kathleen Heide, who, in addition to contributing their own work, were instrumental in linking me to other authors; and to Reid Meloy for both contributing work and for writing the foreword. I don't think a single student has completed one of my courses during the course of my career who hasn't heard me say that I think Reid Meloy is the most brilliant theorist that has ever written in the field of criminal psychology. To have him write the foreword for this set is an incredible honor, and I can't think of a more perfect way to introduce to the subject of criminal psychology and the work and authors contained in this collection.

Finally, I would like to thank my family and friends who provided a huge amount of support in the three years it took to complete this project, especially: my daughter Zalia, who saves me from embarrassing myself on a daily basis and has spent many more hours than I would have liked talking to me behind a computer screen; my brothers Ian and Scott; and my parents Esther Helfgott and Oscar Feit, to whom this work is dedicated. My mom is a never-ending source of inspiration. She is my flagger at the fork at the end of the road and the reason I took the right turn instead of the wrong one. My dad died during the course of this project. Even after he had a heart attack and was struggling to recuperate, he was always trying to send me on my way, saying, "Go write your books . . ." He died sitting in his living room chair. When we cleaned out his apartment, there were three books in the little cabinet right next to his chair—a Bible, my dissertation, and the *Criminal Behavior* textbook I wrote a few years ago (Helfgott, 2008). I think he would have enjoyed reading this.

References

Cleckley, H. (1941, 1976, 1988). *The mask of sanity*. St. Louis, MO: Mosby.

Goffman, E. (1963). *Stigma: Notes on the management of spoiled identity*. Englewood Cliffs, NJ: Prentice-Hall.

Hare, R. D. (1970). *Psychopathy: Theory and research*. New York/London: John Wiley & Sons.

Helfgott, J. B. (2008). *Criminal behavior: Theories, typologies, and criminal justice*. Thousand Oaks, CA: Sage.

Johnson, R. (1987) *Hard time: Understanding and reforming the prison*. Belmont, CA: Brooks/Cole.

Lindner, R. M. (1945). *Rebel without a cause*. London: Research Books.

McCoy, J. (1981). *Concrete mama: Prison profiles from Walla Walla*. Columbia, MO: University of Missouri Press.

Meloy, J. R. (1988). *The psychopathic mind: Origins, dynamics, and treatment*. New Jersey/London: Jason Aronson.

Olsen, J. (1983). *Son: A psychopath and his victims*. New York: Macmillan Press.

Rule, A. (1987). *Small sacrifices: A true story of passion and murder*. New York: New American Library.

Wambaugh, J. (1987). *The onion field*. New York: Dell.

Yochelson, S., & Samenow, S. E. (1977). *The criminal personality: Volumes 1–3*. New York: Jason Aronson.

SECTION I

Criminal Psychology: An Overview

CHAPTER ONE

Criminal Psychology and Criminal Behavior

Jacqueline B. Helfgott

Introduction

The study of the criminal mind and the motivations and nature of criminal behavior has puzzled theorists and scholars for centuries. Particularly heinous and violent crimes that appear to involve offenders who show no remorse are difficult to understand. Some crimes are so unusual and the motivations so obscure, they boggle the mind. More mundane crimes that may seem at first glance easier to understand are sometimes even more perplexing because they involve people who are willing to take unusual risks to engage in crime. TV shows and films often depict characters who engage in fascinating and frightening behaviors that reflect extreme and rare forms of human behavior. These individuals are usually psychologically complex and raise questions such as: *What would make a person think about, let alone do, something like that?*

Advances in computer and mass media technology have put high-profile criminal behaviors at the forefront of people's minds with a click of a button and on a global scale. Disproportionate and widespread media attention to extreme types of crimes have created a situation in which the average citizen may be more likely to be able to rattle off the names of historical serial killers more easily than they can presidents. High-profile crimes that have occurred over the past century—such as the Lindbergh kidnapping; the Manson family murders; the Patty Hearst kidnapping; the John Hinckley assassination attempt on Ronald Reagan; the Mark David Chapman murder of John Lennon; the Ted Bundy, Jeffrey Dahmer, John Wayne Gacy, Gary Ridgway, Dennis Rader, and Aileen Wuornos serial killer cases; the Polly Klaas and Elizabeth Smart abductions; school shootings in Columbine and Virginia Tech; the Armin Meiwes sexual homicide/cannibalism case; the Amanda Knox case; the fetus theft/cesarean abduction of Bobbie Jo Stinnett; the Benjamin Darras/Sarah Edmondson Natural Born Killer and Devin Moore Grand Theft Auto copycat cases; and large-scale domestic and international terrorism such as acts committed by the Animal Liberation Front and Earth Liberation Front (ALF and ELF), and 9/11—have brought great fascination and attention to the criminal mind and the psychology of criminal behavior.

Historical changes over the past 50 years have culminated in complex and sometimes contradictory notions of criminal behavior that has directed attention to both aberrant and everyday forms of criminal behavior. Socio-cultural-political changes in the United States and Britain have culminated in late modern "culture of control" characterized by competing criminologies that drive ideas about and responses to crime (Garland, 2001). The "criminology of everyday life," made prominent by research and practice involving routine activity theory and Crime Prevention through Environmental Design (CPTED), suggests that crime is a normal everyday behavior determined by an interaction between individual-level self-control and environmental temptations and controls. The competing "criminology of the other" views crime as the product of a monster-human who must be controlled, profiled, and forensically identified by actuarial tools (Garland, 2001; Harcourt, 2007).

What Is Criminal Psychology?

The term "criminal psychology" is commonly used in the public and popular discourse in reference to the criminal mind, the psychology of criminal behavior, and practices in the criminal justice system such as criminal profiling and prediction of dangerousness. While psychological theories of crime are only part of the picture in terms of the body of research focusing on crime, the more extreme forms of criminal behavior are often understood within the context of psychological theories that explain behavior in terms of psychopathology. Popular television shows such as *Criminal Minds* and *Dexter* and classic films such as *Taxi Driver*, *Silence of the Lambs*, *Natural Born Killers*, *Henry: Portrait of a Serial Killer*, and *Se7en* have brought attention to the inner workings of the criminal mind and of law enforcement, mental health, and forensic professionals who try to understand and apprehend them.

Historical Origins and Contemporary Interest in Criminal Psychology

In 1991, the film *Silence of the Lambs* was released on the heels of highly publicized serial murder investigation cases involving the FBI Behavioral Sciences Unit in the 1970s and 1980s. The film, based on Thomas Harris's (1988) novel (a sequel to his 1981 book *Red Dragon*), was based on the work of FBI profilers who served as consultants for the film (Jenkins, 1994). The *Crime Classification Manual* (Douglas et al., 2006) and *Sexual Homicide: Patterns and Motives* (Ressler, Burgess, & Douglas, 1992) were published, and FBI profilers such as John Douglas, Robert Ressler, and Roy Hazelton and authors such as Jack Olsen and Ann Rule published true crime novels such as *Son: A Psychopath and His Victims* (Olsen, 1983) and *Small Sacrifices: A True Story of Passion and Murder* (Rule, 1987) that became wildly popular and were made into made-for-TV movies.[1] The number of films, TV programs, memorabilia, and true crime novels depicting serial killers and profiling in the 1980s disproportionately surpassed the actual number of serial murder cases and embellished the effectiveness and role of criminal profilers in serial murder investigations (Jenkins, 1994).

The birth of modern criminology in the mid-1700s marks the early origins of the study of criminal behavior and the psychology of crime. The evolution of the classical and positivist schools of criminology (Jones, 1986), recognition and evolution of the construct of psychopathy (Arrigo & Shipley, 2001; Shipley & Arrigo, 2001), the law of insanity and discourse about the demarcation of madness from badness (Elliott, 1996), and correctional reform (Barnes, 1972; Foucault, 1977) represent multidisciplinary stepping stones to the state of the research and practice in criminal psychology today.

The psychology of crime and criminal behavior has gained increased attention over the past century. Hervey Cleckley's seminal 1941 work *The Mask of Sanity*, Krafft-Ebing's (1927) *Psychopathia Sexualis*, Robert Lindner's (1945) *Rebel without a Cause*, Karpan's (1941, 1946, 1948) work on subtypes of psychopathy, and McCord and McCord's (1964) *The Psychopath: An Essay on the Criminal Mind* set the foundation for discourse and debate over the terminology and classification criteria for sociopathy, antisocial personality disorder, and psychopathy in the 1952, 1968, 1980, 1987, and 2000 editions of the American Psychiatric Association's *Diagnostic and Statistical Manual of Mental Disorders*. Later works—including Menninger's (1968)

The Crime of Punishment; Yochelson and Samenow's (1977) *Criminal Personality*; Groth's (1979) *Men Who Rape*; Kernberg's (1984) *Severe Personality Disorders*; Meloy's (1988) *The Psychopathic Mind*; Marshall, Laws, and Barbaree's (1990) *Handbook of Sexual Assault*; Raine's (1993) *The Psychopathology of Crime*; Blackburn's (1993) *Psychology of Criminal Conduct*; Robert Johnson's (1995) *Hardtime*; and correctional psychology scholars including Paul Gendreau, Susan Turner, Doris MacKenzie, Ed Latessa, Frank Cullen, Patricia Van Voorhis, and others (Cullen, 2005)—were among those responsible for reviving empirical interest in psychological theories of crime that had been criticized during the anti-psychology/psychiatry movement of the 1960s and 1970s spurred by writers such as Szasz (1963) and Kittrie (1971) and the demise of the correctional rehabilitation era originating in part from Martinson's (1974) article in *The Public Interest*, "What Works?—Questions and Answers about Prison Reform."

These scholars and works were instrumental in laying the foundation for increasingly sophisticated empirical research in criminal psychology and criminal behavior and growth of the field. The work of these and other scholars led to the development of established formal academic programs in forensic psychology and forensic psychiatry and renewed interest and attention to integrated theories and research in criminology and criminal justice that put criminal psychology back into the more traditional sociology-oriented criminology and criminal justice programs after years of suspicion regarding ethics and justice issues associated with locating criminal behavior in the criminal mind rather than external, environmental forces.

Forensic assessment tools published and made available for widespread use in the 1990s contributed to an explosion of empirical research on forensic assessment of dangerousness. Robert Hare's publication of the *Psychopathy Checklist–Revised (PCL-R)* (1991, 2003); Andrews and Bonta's (1994, 1998, 2003, 2006, 2010) *The Psychology of Criminal Conduct* and the *Level of Service Inventory-Revised (LSI-R)*; Quinsey et al.'s (1998) *Violent Offenders: Appraising and Managing Risk* and the *Violence Risk Appraisal Guide (VRAG)* and *Sex Offender Risk Appraisal Guide (SORAG)*; Hanson and Thornton's (1998) *Static 99*; and Webster, Douglas, Eaves, and Hart's (1997) *Historical, Clinical, Risk-20 (HCR-20)* and other assessment tools brought research and practice in the intersection of psychology and criminal justice to a new level providing a means for researchers to arrive at consensus on the construct of psychopathy and to provide criminal justice practitioners with tools to make critical risk assessment decisions at all stages of the criminal justice process.

Media depictions of psychopaths and criminal profilers have been instrumental in generating increased interest in the study of the criminal mind and criminal psychology. The term "criminal psychology" is used to a lesser extent in the academic realm and is captured within the intersection of psychology and criminology and, in recent years, as a component of forensic psychology, a relatively new sub-discipline within professional psychology (DeMatteo et al., 2009). Theory, research, and insight into the criminal mind and the understanding of criminal behavior is the business of scholars and researchers in the behavioral and social sciences including forensic psychology and psychiatry and the entire range of subfields in psychology—clinical psychology, neuropsychology, experimental psychology, cognitive psychology, developmental psychology, social psychology, evolutionary psychology, school psychology, neuropsychology, and neuroscience, as well as scholars and researchers in the disciplines of criminology/criminal justice, sociology, social work, anthropology, cultural studies, and other disciplines beyond psychology.

Criminal Psychology and Forensic Psychology: Definitional Issues, Training, and Academic Programs

Investigation into the available knowledge base on the criminal mind and theories and empirical research on criminal behavior and the application of this knowledge to the criminal justice system require straddling multiple disciplines and sub-disciplines within the broad scope of the social and behavioral sciences. Definitional issues have emerged with respect to whether or not forensic psychology should be narrowly defined to include application and practice of psychology in the legal system or, more broadly, to include research and theory in the intersection of psychology, criminology, criminal justice, and law (Bartol & Bartol, 2012; Packer, 2008).

The range of disciplines and subdisciplines involved in the study of criminal behavior and discussions regarding terminology, definitions, and subfields involved in forensic psychology as well as narrow and broad definitions of forensic psychology make it difficult to situate the topic of criminal psychology within a single discipline or training program. For example, some have suggested that there should be distinction between the terms "forensic psychology" and "legal psychology," with the former referring to psychologists who practice in the legal arena from legal psychology, and the latter to include theorists and scholars who engage in research and writing in the intersection of psychology, criminal justice, and law (Packer, 2008). Complicating the issue further, much of the theory, empirical research, and development of forensic assessment tools that have been responsible for the proliferation of need for forensic psychologists in the criminal and civil justice systems has been produced by scholars who hold doctorates in experimental criminology, cognitive psychology, neuropsychology, social psychology, criminology/criminal justice, and sociology who would not fit the narrow definition of the term forensic psychologist, but whose work is squarely within the crux of the psychology–criminal justice nexus.

Advances in theory, research, and development of specialized forensic assessment instruments have led to the founding of interdisciplinary professional organizations and journals, growth in research and practice-related literature, and increased availability of training programs and educational opportunities that focus specifically on forensic psychology at the undergraduate, graduate, and postdoctoral levels (DeMatteo et al., 2009). However, there has been a proliferation of need for psychology practitioners to provide services to the criminal justice system and availability of formal forensic psychology graduate training and discourse regarding the type of necessary training for different roles in the field has not kept up with strong student interest in the topic (Heilbrun & Annis, 1988; Olver, 2011; Packer, 2008).

Psychological Theories and Integrative and Interdisciplinary Approaches to the Study of Criminial Behavior

Throughout the over-200-year history of the study of crime, scholars have been divided into two camps: psychologically trained or oriented scholars who examine individual-level influences (biology, psychology); and sociologically trained or oriented scholars who focus on environmental influences (family, neighborhood, society, culture). A large body of work has accumulated on criminal behavior. This dichotomous framework has been somewhat resistant to change over time and has resulted in a divide in the literature that continues today into "sociological criminology" and "psychological criminology" (Wortley, 2011). Sociologically oriented scholars have historically minimized, overlooked, or have not had the training to examine individual-level factors such as biological predisposition and personality (Schmidl, 1946), while psychologists have published in a vacuum without acknowledging contextual realities and social infrastructures that surround individuals (Adler & Gray, 2010). However, in recent years, there has been revived attention to biological and psychological theories, a call for attention to situational specificity in the study of criminal behavior that examines details of individual-environment/situation interaction (Horney, 2006) and increasingly integrative and interdisciplinary approaches to the study of crime. Advances in the academic fields of criminology, criminal justice, and forensic psychology have led to recognition that theory and empirical research from a range of disciplines is critical to effective and efficient use of social resources to respond to crime.

Crime scholars have amassed a body of theoretical work, empirical findings, and critical questions for future research that have taken us closer than ever before to understanding why people commit crime (Agnew, 2005; Andrews & Bonta, 2010; Gottfredson & Hirschi, 1990; Robinson, 2004). Contemporary theories of criminal behavior integrate etiological theories that explain the biological and early childhood origins of criminal behavior with risk factor approaches that focus on risk and protective factors that increase or decrease an individual's likelihood of engaging in different types of criminal behavior in different situations. Integrative theories have been developed to explain how biological, developmental, personality, social, and situational factors and forces converge to produce criminal behavior (e.g., Agnew, 2005; Barak, 1998; Elliott, Ageton, & Canter, 1979; Gottfredson & Hirschi, 1990; Moffitt, 1993; Thornberry, 1987; Tittle, 1995; Robinson, 2004).

Why Do People Commit Crime?

Thus the question "*Why do people commit crime?*" is more complex than it may seem requiring the expertise and contributions of psychologists, psychiatrists, sociologists, criminology/criminal justice scholars, and others to provide answers that together may answer parts of the question for some people some of the time. Criminal behavior is the product of chain of events influenced by an infinite possibility of variables and individual-environment interactions that can be closely examined and deliberately interrupted (Helfgott, 2008). People who engage in criminal behavior are a heterogeneous group that may include generally law-abiding people who commit an isolated act, people who commit different types of crimes for a period of time and then desist, people who engage in low-level criminal activity throughout their lives, people who specialize in particular types of crime, people who engage in frequent and serious crimes throughout their lives, and people who commit extreme and rare forms of criminal behavior. Pathways to criminal behavior are just as diverse, the precise mix of causes differing for each offender (Wortley, 2001).

If every criminal act were to be retrospectively analyzed, we would likely find that most crime is preventable—that if one link in the chain had been missing, the crime would not have occurred. While some suggest that "specificity in the extreme is incompatible with the scientific objective of general understandings of human psychology" (Andrews & Bonta, 2010, p. 3) and that it is a strength of science to discovering uniformity under diverse conditions, identifying how to prevent and respond to crime requires detailed analysis of criminal events while at the same time recognizing the importance of understanding the variability of criminal behavior within the context of human behavior. Simultaneous focus on aggregate-level factors (e.g., which factors are statistically associated with criminal behavior across large groups of offenders) and individual-level factors (the unique influences and chain of events in an individual's life that can be attributed to the individual's criminal behavior) is critical. Theory and research directed toward identifying correlates of crime at the aggregate level as well as detailed analysis of individual-level offenses are necessary to explain why crime occurs. For example, research shows that gender, age, and social class are highly correlated with criminal behavior, with young males with lower socioeconomic status more likely to commit crime. However, knowing that a person is young, male, and poor tells us very little about why a particular person decides to engage in an individual criminal behavior or a lifestyle of crime, nor can these factors be used to predict or clearly explain the dynamics of individual-level criminal acts.

The Continuum of Criminal Behavior

Crime that makes it into the news often distorts the range of criminal behavior that human beings are known to engage in. Extreme and rare crimes such as serial murder, mass or spree murder, genocide, suicide bombing, or terrorist acts, or bizarre crimes such as sexual homicide involving dismemberment and cannibalism or fetus theft[2] that involve mutilation, torture, or unusual fantasies or ways of thinking often dominate media attention and popular interest. However, human beings commit all sorts of crimes from the bizarre to the mundane. If it were possible to produce a complete catalogue of human criminal behavior over time and around the world, such a document would likely be one of the most fascinating reads of all time.

Crimes that fall on the more "normal" side of the continuum of criminal behavior may be even more interesting than rare and extreme sorts of crime because they involve regular people in usual settings making decisions (some spontaneous, some not) about violating the law. The nature and dynamics of these sorts of everyday crimes provide a great deal of information about what lies at the root of criminal behavior—in fact, probably more so than can be said for the more extreme forms of criminal behavior that can

Normal →	Everyday Problems in Living →	Pathological
Behavior resulting from: - Poor judgment - Bad decisions - Situational factors - Environmental context	*Behavior resulting from:* - Minor medical or mental health condition - Drug or alcohol addiction - Severe poverty and deprivation	*Behavior resulting from:* - Severe medical of mental health condition - Long term development of deviant identity and behavioral conditioning processes involving interaction of some combination of biological predisposition, childhood trauma, and environmental-cultural facilitators.

Figure 1.1 Criminal Behavior Continuum.

often be explained in terms of severe psychopathology or social or political conflict (see Figure 1.1, Criminal Behavior Continuum).

On one end of the continuum, there are regular people who sometimes use poor judgment and make bad choices that, when mixed with particular situational factors and circumstances, may result in behavior that violates the law. On the extreme end of the continuum are severely disturbed individuals who commit statistically rare and/or extreme forms of criminal behavior. The study of criminal behavior is a fascinating look at the continuum of behavior that violates the law from the mundane to the bizarre.

Psychological Theories of Crime

Psychologists have been interested in criminal behavior since the advent of psychology as a discipline (Blackburn, 1993). Psychological theories of crime have been the dominant theories to offer explanation for crimes on the extreme end of the continuum of criminal behavior. Psychological theories are micro-level theories that attribute criminal behavior to individual differences resulting from early psychodynamic development, information processing and cognition, and conditioning processes that result in criminal behavior. Much of the psychological research on criminal behavior has focused on the relationship between personality, mental disorder, and crime. Research at the intersection of psychology and criminology has emphasized integration of cognitive, behavioral, and psychodynamic perspectives in the development of functional concepts of psychopathy and criminality (Meloy, 1988; Walters, 1990). Because crime is a social construct, and criminal behavior is a behavioral symptom that may or may not be a manifestation of a psychological condition, psychological research on criminal behavior involves study of internal psychological conditions that produce behaviors and conditions associated with crime, such as antisocial behavior, psychopathy, aggression, and impulsivity.

Psychodynamic and Personality Theories

Psychodynamic theories of criminal behavior focus on development of the psyche in infancy. Motivation for criminal behavior is rooted in an individual's psychodynamic structure and development. Contemporary psychodynamic theories of criminal behavior are rooted in Freud's theory of the *Id*, *Ego*, and *Superego*. Freud postulated that behavior is the product of the interaction between the Id, the Ego, the Superego, and the environment. The Id represents the human drive for pleasure, the Ego regulates the Id in accordance with the demands of the external environment, and the Superego reflects the conscience and ego ideal or the parental voice inside one's head that says "Do the right thing."

Offender Types in Psychodynamic Theory

Many theories and typologies have been developed from the psychoanalytic perspective suggesting that there are different developmental routes to criminal behavior. Andrews and Bonta (2010) review four offender types that have emerged from psychodynamic theory: (1) the Weak Superego Type; (2) the Weak Ego Type; (3) the "Normal" Antisocial Offender; and (4) the Neurotic Offender. The *Weak Superego Type* needs immediate gratification and does not hear or respond to that "voice inside the head." The *Weak Ego Type* is immature with poorly developed social skills, gullibility, and dependence whereby criminal behavior is produced through misreading the external environment and stumbling into crime (e.g., following the leader). The *"Normal" Antisocial Offender Type* passes through normal stages of development as a fully functioning adult but possesses a pro-criminal superego as a result of identification with a criminal parent and ego-mastery of criminal skills. The *Neurotic Offender Type* has an overactive superego that results in criminal behavior to fulfill the wish to be punished for "past sins."

The Weak Superego theory is the most popular of the theories in the psychodynamic literature and was the topic of much discourse and discussion in the 1940s, 1950s, and 1960s. Behavioral indicators of a weak superego include: reckless disregard for conventional rules, lack of conscience and antisocial cognitions, weak ambition, absence of guilt, early conduct problems, expressions of bravado, authority conflicts, and isolation (Andrews & Bonta, 2003). These features have been consistently associated with antisocial personality disorder, psychopathy, and criminal behavior. An example of the Weak Superego theory is the classic work *The Mask of Sanity* by Hervey Cleckley (1941), which, though not solely focused on criminal behavior, offers case-study illustration of criminal and noncriminal psychopaths. According to Cleckley, psychopaths have a "defect in affect" that enables them to harm and manipulate others without remorse. Psychopaths delight in shocking others and have no interest in engaging in conformist behaviors. Cleckley identified 16 characteristics of the psychopath (discussed in Chapter 4) such as unreliability, lack or remorse or shame, and failure to learn from experience reflecting defect in interpersonal relations and unwillingness or inability to adhere to social (and superego) norms, rules, and values.

Kernberg's Theory of Borderline Personality Organization

Another prominent superego pathology theory is *Kernberg's Theory of Borderline Personality Organization (BPO)*. BPO theory is particularly helpful in terms of understanding how internal conditions across the continuum of personality produce a tendency toward criminal behavior. According to Kernberg (1966, 1967, 1984, 1985a, 1985b, 1992), personality is organized along a continuum from "psychotic" to "borderline" to "neurotic" and defined by capacity for reality testing and unconscious defensive process. Psychotic personality organization is characterized by absence of reality testing and the use of primitive defenses, borderline personality organization by capacity for reality testing and use of primitive defenses, and neurotic by capacity for reality testing and use of higher-level defenses (see Figure 1.2, Borderline Personality Organization).

Kernberg's "primitive defenses" center around the lower-level mechanism of *splitting*, and the related mechanisms of *primitive idealization*, *projective identification*, *denial*, *omnipotence*, and *devaluation*. Splitting is a genotypic defensive operation that is expressed through the phenotypic defensive process of dissociation. This defensive operation is pathognomonic of general borderline ego functioning, particularly in the psychopath (Meloy, 1988). Kernberg (1976) views splitting as alternating ego states, each consisting of completely separate complex psychic manifestations, a fundamental feature of the borderline ego functioning experienced by the narcissistic, histrionic, borderline, and psychopathic personalities. Splitting is a defensive process exemplified by lack of personality integration, and the continual existence of cohesive personality attitudes with

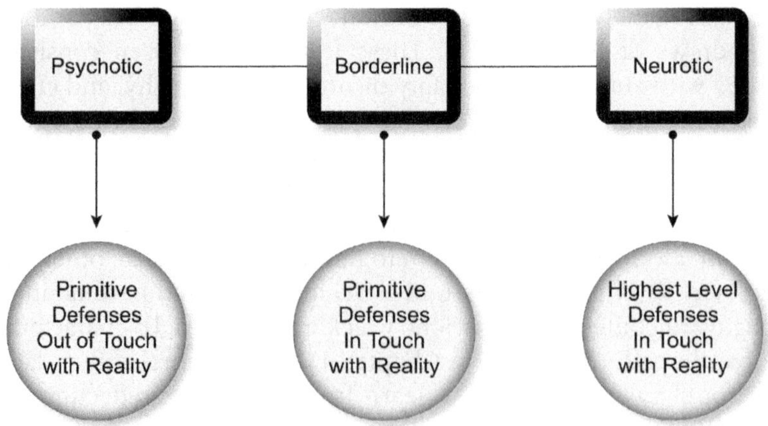

Figure 1.2 Kernberg's Theory of Borderline Personality Organization.

different aims, goals, and moral and aesthetic values (Kohut, 1971). Put simply, splitting is the view of oneself and others as all good or all bad, with an inability to reconcile the two identities.

The subsidiary defenses of primitive idealization, projective identification, omnipotence, devaluation, and denial protect the ego from conflict by dissociating or actively separating contradictory experiences of the self and of others. As a result, the contradictory ego states (e.g., good/bad) are alternatively activated, and as long as they are kept apart, anxiety related to these conflicts is controlled or prevented. Although these defenses protect the individual from intrapsychic conflict, they do so at a cost of weakening the person's ego functioning, reducing adaptive effectiveness and flexibility (Kernberg, 1985b). This "lower level" of the borderline personality organization differs from "higher level" functioning that centers around repression and other higher-level operations such as reaction formation, intellectualization, rationalization, and isolation, all of which protect the ego from intrapsychic conflict. The lower-level defenses are shared by the psychotic and the borderline personality, while the neurotic utilizes higher-level operations. Borderline disorders are set apart from the psychotic by their capacity for reality testing, which is not present in psychotic organization (Kernberg, 1985b).

Kernberg (1985a) views borderline personality organization as an intermediary stage between psychosis and neurosis. Primitive defenses facilitate criminal behavior because they enable an individual to objectify and harm other human beings while maintaining an image of themselves as all-good. By definition, crime requires *mens rea* (a guilty mind); thus individuals who are psychotic may commit criminal behavior, but if they are determined to be out of touch with reality, they are not legally responsible for their behavior. On the continuum from psychotic to borderline to neurotic, individuals with personalities organized at the borderline level of functioning are most susceptible to criminal behavior by the very nature of their defensive structure.

Antisocial Personality Disorder and Psychopathy

A personality disorder is an "enduring pattern of inner experience and behavior that deviates markedly from the expectations of the individual's culture" (American Psychiatric Association, 2000, p. 686). To be diagnosed with a personality disorder, an individual must manifest the disorder in two or more of the following areas: cognitions (ways of perceiving the world), affectivity (emotional response), interpersonal functioning, and impulse control. The enduring pattern must also be inflexible and pervasive across a range of circumstances and situations, lead to clinically significant impairment or distress, and is stable having originated in adolescence or early adulthood.

Of the personality disorders defined in the DSM-IV-TR, the *Axis II, Cluster B* disorders are most relevant to the study of criminal behavior. The Axis II, Cluster B disorders include: *Antisocial Personality Disorder*, *Borderline Personality Disorder*, *Histrionic Personality Disorder*, and *Narcissistic Personality Disorder*. These four disorders share common behavioral features such as impulsive acting out, unpredictable behavior, and dramatic presentation, as well as a common intrapsychic structure centered around a lower-level defensive organization that utilizes primitive defenses. Wulach (1988) suggests that features of each of these disorders comprise the "criminal personality" and there is evidence to suggest that each may represent distinct behavioral expressions of psychopathy. Much of the psychological research on criminal behavior has focused on *Antisocial Personality Disorder* (ASPD) and *Psychopathy*.[3] In fact, the concepts of criminality, insanity, antisocial personality, and psychopathy have been so historically intertwined over the past two centuries that much of the research, particularly in the discipline of psychology, has failed to clearly differentiate between mental disorder (an internal condition) and crime (a behavioral symptom and social construct). Researchers have spent the last 20 years trying to sort out the conceptual differences and in recent years there has been rapid advancement in our understanding of the relationship between antisocial personality disorder, psychopathy, and crime.

According to the DSM-IV-TR, the essential feature of ASPD is "a pervasive pattern of disregard for, and violation of, the rights of others that begins in childhood or early adolescence and continues into adulthood" (p. 701). The DSM-IV-TR definition goes on to say that "Antisocial Personality Disorder must be distinguished from criminal behavior undertaken for gain that is not accompanied by the personality features characteristic of this disorder" (p. 705). While the DSM-IV-TR states that "this pattern has also been referred to as psychopathy, sociopathy, and dyssocial personality disorder" (p. 702), researchers have criticized the ASPD classification because it is not able to differentiate between criminal behavior (again, a social construction and symptom) and personality features of the disorder. In other words, 50%–75% of offenders in prisons' forensic populations can be diagnosed as ASPD because the criteria upon which the classification is based are predominantly antisocial and criminal behaviors. Psychopathy, in contrast, is characterized by specific personality characteristics, with only 15%–25% in forensic populations meeting the criteria. According to Robert Hare, foremost researcher on psychopathy, "Although my colleagues and I have taken great pains to differentiate between psychopathy and ASPD, some clinicians and investigators use the labels as if the constructs they measure were interchangeable. They are not, and the failure to recognize this results in confusion and misleading conclusions" (Hare, 1998, p. 193).

Psychopathy is now considered to be one of the most important clinical constructs in the criminal justice system (Hare, 1998). A large body of research has accumulated linking psychopathy and criminal recidivism, violence, and dangerousness. The Psychopathy Checklist–Revised (PCL-R) (Hare, 1991, 2003), a 20-item checklist that measures the affective, interpersonal, and behavioral features of the disorder, has gained widespread attention and is a popular tool in used research, clinical assessment, and criminal justice practice in the criminal justice systems in Canada and the United States (Hare, 1998) and around the world (Sullivan & Kosson, 2006). The PCL-R is a valid and reliable measure of psychopathy that is a strong predictor of violent recidivism, dangerousness (Gacono, 2000; Hare, 2001, 2003; Harris, Rice, & Cormier, 1991; Hart, 1998; Hemphill et al., 1998; Hodgins, 1997; Litwack & Schlesinger, 1998; Salekin, Rogers, & Sewell, 1996; Serin & Amos, 1995) and determinant of high criminogenic offender risk/needs (Simourd & Hodge, 2000).

Cognition and Information Processing Theories

Cognitive theories focus on the thinking errors and information processing anomalies that lead to and are associated with criminal behavior. From this perspective, criminal behavior is the product of cognitive defects and cognitive schemas that facilitate and support criminal behavior. Cognitive theories of criminal behavior include "rational choice theories," which suggest that crime is a conscious, freely chosen activity produced by thinking errors and particular cognitive style; and information-processing theories, which identify specific cognitive deficits that contribute to a tendency to commit criminal behavior.

The Criminal Personality–Cognitive Distortion

According to the "*criminal personality theory*" (Yochelson & Samenow, 1977), a subset of chronic offenders possess a "criminal personality." These offenders engage in chronic criminal behavior across their lifespan as a result of a unique pattern of thinking and use of specific thinking errors. From this perspective, offenders consciously choose to commit crime and maintain a criminal lifestyle through the use of a cognitive style that enables them to "cut-off" deterrents and feelings of remorse and guilt that would otherwise stop them from committing crime. Offenders with "criminal personalities" utilize thinking errors such as "uniqueness," "ownership," "concrete thinking," "lying," "victim stance," "fragmentation," and "power thrust." These thinking errors are used and practiced from childhood, forming a unique cognitive style. These offenders engage in the conscious mechanisms of "corrosion" and "cut-off"—slowly eliminating external deterrents (corrosion) until feelings of guilt are quickly "cut-off" in the moment before committing a criminal act.

Information Processing–Cognitive Deficit

Cognitive/information-processing studies have focused on information-processing deficits in antisocial personality–disordered offenders and, more recently, psychopaths. Researchers have attempted to empirically explore Cleckley's (1976) "*semantic dementia*"—the psychopath's attempt to mimic emotion and manipulate meaning through language. Reiber and Vetter (1995) suggest that the language of the psychopath reflects underlying personality dynamics, in particular the ability to dissociate feelings of guilt. Other researchers have found that psychopaths use fewer cohesive ties when telling stories (Brinkley et al., 1999a; 1999b), and extract less information from affective words than nonpsychopaths (Williamson et al., 1991). Research by Blair et al. (1995) suggests that psychopathy is the result of early dysfunction within the Violence Inhibition Mechanism (VIM), a cognitive mechanism that reduces the likelihood of aggressive attack when the aggressor is faced with the display of distress cues. When psychopaths are asked to identify with protagonists in stories in which someone is harmed, their dominant attribution to story protagonists is indifference and happiness, in striking contrast to the guilt and regret attributed by the controls.

Other studies suggest that crime is the product of culturally supported cognitive schemas and "techniques of neutralization" (Sykes & Matza, 1957).[4] People use a range of neutralization techniques to rationalize their behavior and maintain a positive self-image. The neutralization techniques include: Condemnation of the condemners, appeal to higher loyalties, denial of injury, denial of victim, and denial of responsibility (Sykes & Matza, 1957). Acceptance of neutralizations has a positive effect on violence (Agnew, 1994). For example, Stermac, Segal, and Gillis (1989) found that rape is the product of traditional male sex-role stereotypes, and that rapists (seen as having an excess of stereotypical maleness) express more positive attitudes toward women and less endorsement of rape myths than controls. Rapists excuse or deny their behavior by employing distinct excuses and justifications that reflect cognitive schemas that allow them to rationalize their behaviors. Rape "Excusers" maintain a positive image of themselves by attributing their behavior to alcohol and drug use, emotional problems, or compartmentalizing their rape behavior by presenting themselves as "good guys" in other areas of their lives. Rape "Deniers" utilize cognitive schema such as "nice girls don't get raped," "women mean yes when they say no," "women are seductresses," etc. (Scully & Marolla,1984). These cognitive distortions allow rapists to neutralize (and continue) their behavior.

Recent findings by Wallace et al. (2000) suggest that individuals who score above 30 on the PCL-R likely have a *cognitive deficit* characterized by failure in the response modulation process. These individuals are unable to attend to nonsalient stimuli and alter their behavioral sequence accordingly. They are inclined to engage in criminal behavior because they are unable to "pause" once they begin a behavioral course as a result of this deficit in response modulation. Individuals who score below 30 on the PCL-R do not have this deficit, but may employ *cognitive distortions* that may provide justification and excuses that will enable criminal behavior—the higher the PCL-R score up to 30, the more likely the individual will experience cognitive distortions conducive to antisocial and criminal behavior. This research makes room for the notion of a categorically distinct group of individuals whose behavior is the product of a cognitive deficit (primary psychopaths), while at the same time acknowledging that most people (nonpsychopaths) use cognitive distortions that may increase their likelihood of antisocial and criminal behavior along a continuum of severity.

Behavioral Theories

Operant and Classical Conditioning

Conditioning theories explain crime in terms of the ways in which behaviors are shaped through stimulus pairing (classical conditioning) and reinforcement and punishment (operant conditioning). *Operant conditioning* involves the increase of behaviors through reinforcements and decrease of behaviors through punishments. *Classical ("Pavlovian") conditioning* involves the increase or decrease of behaviors through pairing and removal of stimuli. Conditioning theories are based on the work of early behavioral theorists B. F. Skinner (operant conditioning) and Ivan Pavlov (classical conditioning). Skinner believed that behavior could be changed by altering environmental stimuli (i.e., reinforcers, punishments) while Pavlov found that behavior could be conditioned by pairing primary and secondary stimuli based on his famous salivating dog experiment. Pavlov found that after feeding his dogs following the ringing of a bell, the dogs began to salivate when they heard the bell even when food was not presented. The dog's primary or unconditioned stimulus was the food, which caused a primary physiological response. The secondary or conditioned stimulus was the ringing of the bell, which, by itself, would not cause salivation. The dogs learned to salivate at the sound of the bell with or without the presentation of food. This is classical conditioning.

Applying operant and classical conditioning theory to criminal behavior, crime (a behavior) can increase or decrease through exposure to various stimuli. For example, criminal behavior can increase through operant conditioning when such behaviors are immediately followed by positive or negative reinforcement. Positive reinforcement involves delivering a reward, while negative reinforcement involves withholding something. Criminal behavior can also be classically conditioned when such behavior is associated with a secondary or conditioned stimulus. A simple example: A teen runaway who has been living on the streets for some time finds a gun and decides to commit an armed robbery to acquire money to live. Immediately following the robbery, the offender is rewarded with a wallet full of cash. The offender discovers that the anxiety he had been experiencing over having no financial resources is immediately alleviated. In this case, the offender's robbery behavior is positively reinforced by acquiring the cash and negatively reinforced by the alleviation of anxiety. However, what if immediately following the robbery, a bystander intervenes by tackling and severely beating the offender? Rather than receiving reinforcements (money, decreased anxiety), the offender receives punishment (attack/beating), and the likelihood of repeating the behavior is reduced. This is an example of *operant conditioning*. Classical conditioning is somewhat different in that behavior increases through pairing of stimuli. When the offender commits the robbery, he finds that the act of robbing someone at gunpoint generates feelings of exhilaration. After committing a number of subsequent robberies and experiencing this physiological arousal each time, the offender begins to associate armed robbery with feeling good. This "pairing" of an unconditioned or secondary stimulus (the act of robbing someone) with unconditioned or primary stimuli (physiological arousal produced by fear and uncertainty) increases the likelihood of future robbery behavior.

Learning Theory

Skinner's and Pavlov's early behavioral theories were based on experiments with animals. Though strict behaviorists support the application of conditioning theories to human behavior, many contend that these theories do not take into account human agency. Learning theories deal with this problem by taking into consideration how individual human beings interpret, perceive, and make decisions in response to environmental cues. Learning theorists contend that behavior is learned through a combination of environmental influences and individual interpretation and response to those influences. For the learning theorist, crime is a product of social learning, whereby an individual's decision to commit crime is a product of observation and association.

Returning to the armed robber example, when the teenager found the gun, where did he get the idea to rob someone with it instead of turning it in to the police? Learning theory offers the missing piece not answered by operant and classical conditioning theories. Perhaps the teen was an avid *Criminal Minds*, *Law and Order*, or *CSI* fan and had seen countless television accounts of armed robbery. Or maybe he had been hanging out with other homeless teens, whom he regularly watched commit these sorts of acts. Or maybe prior to running away he came from a family or community in which the act of armed robbery was seen a common means to obtain resources.

There are a number of variations on learning theory, including expectancy theory, imitation or modeling, and differential association (a sociological theory discussed in the following section). Expectancy theory suggests that people act on the basis of what they expect will happen as a result of a particular act. In other words, people act based on what they perceive the consequences and benefits will be. Imitation or modeling theories suggest that people imitate or model what they see. Imitation theories are based on the work of Albert Bandura, whose famous 1960s study showed that preschool-aged children who viewed a film of an adult assaulting a rubber "Bobo" doll behaved more aggressively after viewing the film than did a control group of children who viewed a film depicting more passive behavior. Differential association theory suggests that individuals act on the basis of who they associate with. People learn criminal behavior through interaction with friends and family members who engage in such behavior. Burgess and Akers's (1966) differential association-reinforcement theory combines differential association with conditioning theories to suggest that people learn to engage in crime through differential association, but then criminal behavior is maintained through operant and classical conditioning.

A great deal of research has accumulated applying social learning theory to the analysis of the impact of crime and violence in media and pop culture. Early studies (called the "Payne Fund Studies") conducted in the 1930s found that many in a sample of 2,000 respondents were conscious of having directly imitated acts of violence they saw in films. This research spawned decades of controversy and research on the subject of media violence (Sparks & Sparks, 2002). A more recent study found that 25% of juvenile offenders obtained ideas about how to commit their crimes from popular culture (Surette, 2002). From the perspective of social learning theory, expectations and ideas are conveyed through television, film, music, computer games, and other forms of popular culture and are mimicked particularly by youth. While there is some disagreement in the literature about whether or not media violence is criminogenic (crime producing) or cathartic (crime reducing), or both, there is a large and growing body of research suggesting that media violence triggers the occurrence of criminal behavior and shapes its form (Surette, 1998). However, most of the studies on the effects of TV and computer game violence have been conducted in laboratory settings and have measured level of aggression in response to violent stimuli (rather than actual criminal behavior), which is problematic for drawing conclusions.

Beyond anecdotal accounts of media-mediated violence, there is little empirical research to support a direct criminalizing effect of violent media. Findings suggest that media depictions of violence are more likely to shape criminal behavior rather than trigger it (Surette, 1998). People already inclined to commit a crime get ideas about how to commit the crime from media images, but few otherwise law-abiding citizens will be influenced by media to commit a crime. On the other hand, there is compelling case-study evidence to suggest that the behavior of a small group of "media junkies" may be unduly influenced by media violence, though the potential for violent media to trigger criminal behavior is very small.[5]

Interdisciplinary Perspectives in the Study of Criminal Behavior

Knowledge about what factors are associated with criminal behavior, the situational contexts and circumstances under which certain crimes are more or less likely to occur, the characteristics of offender types, and the "causes" of crime is critical to control and respond to crime. The study of criminal behavior has been approached from a broad range of disciplinary perspectives including criminology and criminal justice, sociology, psychology, psychiatry, neuroscience, biology, social work, law, anthropology, political science, economics, cultural and media studies, women's studies, philosophy, and others. Historical competition between macro-level sociological theories and micro-level psychological theories and inability to come up with a general theory to explain all types of criminal behavior have called into question how much criminologists really know about crime. In recent years, there has been recognition among crime scholars that comprehensive and accurate understanding and prediction of criminal behavior requires theoretical and disciplinary integration. While no unified theory or model yet exists that can be considered truly integrative (Fishbein, 2001; Schmalleger, 2004), promising integrative models have emerged (Barak, 1998; Hickey, 2009; Robinson & Beaver, 2010).

Two schools of thought have dominated the study of criminal behavior—positivist criminology and classical criminology. Positivist criminology locates the root of criminal behavior in identifiable factors such as biological, psychological, and environmental forces, while classical criminology identifies free will as the root of criminal behavior with the notion that human beings make choices about the behaviors in which they engage. Contemporary criminal behavior scholars recognize that a clear line cannot be drawn between classical and positivist thought (Barak, 1998), and that criminal behavior involves both free will and deterministic forces, and they have called for integration of the many different theories and perspectives that operate on a continuum between classical and positivist criminology. Many now argue that no single discipline can explain crime alone, that criminal behavior is so complex that most theories have something to offer or explain part of the picture for at least some types of crimes, and that what is needed is an interdisciplinary approach to the study of crime that integrates the natural sciences, social sciences, and humanities (Barak, 1998; Colvin, 2000; Ferrell & Sanders, 1995; Robinson, 2004; Walsh & Ellis, 2007).

Integrating Theories of Criminal Behavior

Crime is the end-product of a complex interplay between individual and environmental forces. Most crimes are adaptive, normal, and easy to understand, and (in legalistic terms) all crime can be explained by the fact that a criminal law exists prohibiting such behavior (Robinson, 2004). The historical lack of theory integration has obscured the fact that many theories of crime, antisocial behavior, and deviance overlap and cannot be neatly separated by discipline. Some crimes are more difficult to understand and explain. Multiple theoretical perspectives can be used to explain criminal behavior with recognition that no single discipline is capable of offering the "answer." Disciplinary perspectives and knowledge bases can be broken down into six general areas and related research questions (Helfgott, 2008):

1) Biological—*What are the biological roots of criminal behavior?*
2) Psychological—*What psychological factors contributed to this behavior?*
3) Sociological—*What sociological forces contributed to this behavior?*
4) Routine Activity/Opportunity/Ecological—*What situational, contextual, environmental factors provided the setting and opportunity for this crime to occur?*
5) Cultural—*What cultural forces provided the context in which this crime could occur?*
6) Phenomenological—*What personal meaning does the crime hold for the offender?*

Full review of these six theoretical perspectives and knowledge bases is beyond the scope of this chapter. Key features of each of these perspectives are listed in Table 1.1.[6]

While there is much disciplinary and theoretical overlap,[7] these six bodies of knowledge represent unique ways of looking at crime and offer specific theories and research findings with which to understand and explain criminal behavior. To make sense of criminal behavior, it is important to identify the many factors and forces that provide the impetus and ingredients for a particular crime to occur. The different theories and knowledge bases can be thought of as distinct tools that can explain converging parts of the whole story. According to Bartol and Bartol (2011), "Criminology needs all the interdisciplinary help it can get to explain and control criminal behavior. An integration of the data, theories, and general viewpoints of each discipline is crucial" (p. 2). Figure 1.3 shows

Table 1.1 Disciplinary Perspectives and Knowledge Bases in the Study of Criminal Behavior

Disciplinary Perspective	Central Question	Key Theories
Biological	*What are the biological roots of criminal behavior?*	• Evolution and genetics • Brain Chemistry and function • Hormones • Psychophysiology
Psychological	*What psychological factors contributed to this behavior?*	• Psychodynamic and personality • Cognitive • Behavioral
Sociological	*What sociological forces contributed to this behavior?*	• Structural • Subcultural • Interactionist
Routine Activity	*What situational, contextual, environmental factors provided the setting and opportunity for this crime to occur?*	• Rational choice • Opportunity • Environmental/ecological • Situational
Cultural	*What cultural forces provided the context in which this crime could occur?*	• Cultural criminology • Crime and popular culture • Criminological *Verstehen*
Phenomenological	*What personal meaning does the crime hold for the offender?*	• Phenomenology • Existentialism • Criminological *Verstehen*

Source: Helfgott (2008).

the factors contributing to crime that can be explained by different theoretical perspectives, knowledge bases.

Each of these perspectives can explain aspects of criminal behavior. Some crimes may be better explained by biological theories, while others may be better explained by psychological theories, and so on. Given the complexity of crime, all theoretical perspectives have something to offer in terms of understanding and explaining a piece of each and every criminal event.

A number of theories have emerged that attempt to incorporate multiple theories and perspectives in explaining crime. Some are more integrated than others in the sense that they incorporate a wider range of theories. Examples of (partially) integrated theories include: A General

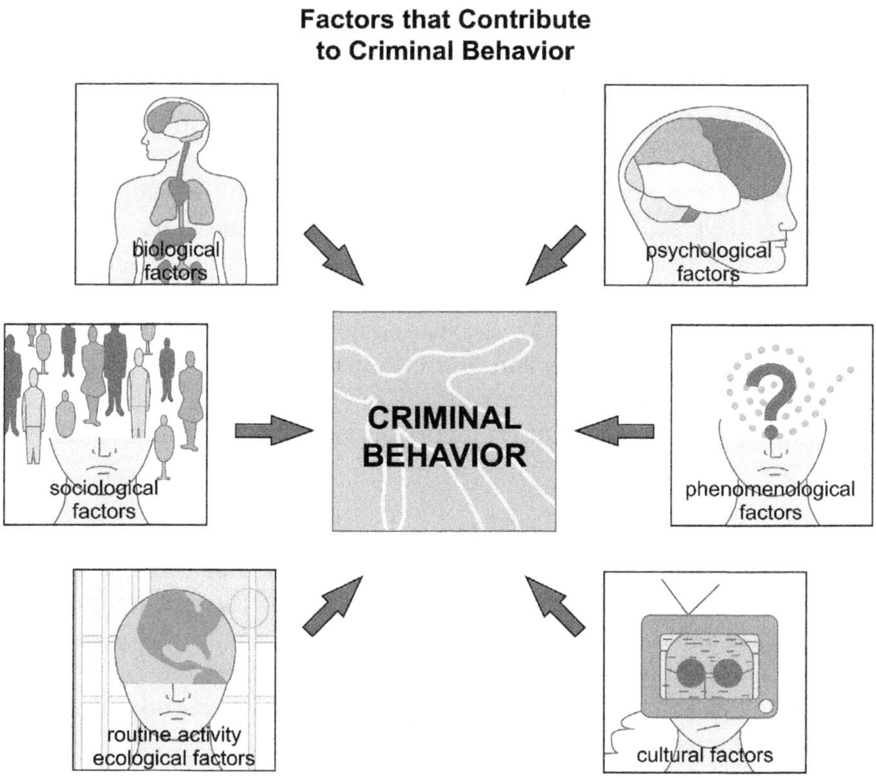

Figure 1.3 Factors That Influence Criminal Behavior.
Source: Helfgott (2008)

Theory of Crime (Gottfredson & Hirschi, 1990) and Developmental (Moffitt, 1993) and Life-Course Criminology (Farrington, 2003),[8] Integrated Systems Theory (Robinson, 2004), Control Balance Theory (Tittle, 2003), Integrated Theory of Delinquency (Elliot, Ageton, & Canter, 2003) and Interdisciplinary Criminology (Barak, 1998). Descriptions of some of the leading partially integrated theories of crime provide illustration of criminologists' attempt to address complexities of criminal behavior that cannot be explained by single-perspectives.

Gottfredson and Hirschi's General Theory of Crime

Gottfredson and Hirschi (1990) developed the "general theory of crime" that explains criminal behavior in all places at all times as a failure in self-control. The general theory of crime is commonly viewed as a sociological theory. However, it can be considered a partially integrative theory in that it utilizes both sociological and psychological concepts.

For example, the authors state that self control is an "enduring tendency well within the meaning of 'personality trait'" (Gottfredson & Hirschi, 1990, p. 109), but that self-control is largely the product of child-rearing practices and influenced by a range of social forces. Self-control is conceptualized along a continuum of low/immediate gratification on one end to high/deferred gratification on the other and attempts to explain both the stability and versatility of crime over time. Social bonds are subsumed under the umbrella of self-control (i.e., individuals with low self-control are likely to be less attached, committed, involved, and connected to community beliefs). Research suggests that learning processes may link social bonds, self-control, and deviant and criminal behavior. This theory has generated a great deal of interest and, some argue, may supplant social bond theory as the major control theory of crime (Akers & Sellers, 2004).

Developmental and Life-Course Theories

Developmental theories of crime focus on how individual offenders' lives unfold to influence crime patterns across the life course. Crime is seen as a dynamic developmental process that begins in childhood and occurs across the life course. Developmental theories are now "center stage in criminology" (Cullen & Agnew, 2006, p. 492). Like Gottfredson and Hirschi's General Theory of Crime, developmental and life-course theories synthesize psychological and sociological concepts and can be considered partially integrative. Life-course criminology emerged from recent developments in sociology and psychology focusing on critical life events and the interaction between the individual and their social environments in connection with life events, transitions, and turning points. The life-course perspective addresses criminological controversies such as the age-crime curve (the unimodal distribution of crime peaking in adolescence and declining dramatically in adulthood), career criminality, juvenile delinquency and adult criminality, as well as the pushes and pulls toward and from criminality and the persistence and desistance in crime for different populations at different times and situations across the life course (Cullen & Agnew, 2006; Piquero & Mazerolle, 2001).

The most exciting thing about developmental and life-course theories is that they represent a historically rare attempt to connect the dots between sociological, psychological, and biological theories of crime. Life-course criminologists (Sampson & Laub, 1993, Laub & Sampson, 2003; Moffitt, 1993, and others) recognize research in psychology that has consistently shown that childhood antisocial behavior is empirically linked to juvenile delinquency and persistent adult criminality. At the same time, life-course criminology addresses social and situational contexts and changes over time that influence individual criminal behavior with attention to differences across individuals and subsets of offenders in terms of continuity and change.

Sampson and Laub's (1993) *Crime in the Making* is considered one of the early classics in life-course criminology. The authors offered a theory of criminal behavior that explained crime across the life course in terms of changing social controls. Their theory combined Hirschi's social bond theory with developmental theories. They hypothesized that people can be caught in life trajectories that involve crime and that can extend to childhood, but that people experience turning points and changes in their attachment, commitment, involvement, and beliefs that may influence their propensity to continue crime over the course of their lives. The authors revised their theory in 2003 (Laub & Sampson, 2003) retaining their core thesis that structural turning points such as marriage, employment, military service and so on serve as sources of social control, but they broadened their theory to better explain the multiple processes that characterize informal social controls across the life-course.

Moffitt's *Adolescent-Limited and Life-Course Persistent Theory of Antisocial Behavior* is one of the most well known of the developmental theories of crime. Moffitt's theory has been described as "one of the best attempts to integrate biological, psychological, and sociological variables in the recent literature" (Cullen & Agnew, 2006, p. 502). The theory identifies two qualitatively distinct groups of offenders who differ in terms of their developmental pathways into crime. "Life-course-persistent" offenders represent a small group of offenders who engage in antisocial behavior at a high rate throughout their lives. "Adolescent-limited" offenders are a larger group that limits their antisocial behavior to adolescent years (Moffitt, 1993). The antisocial and criminal behavior of these two groups can be explained by fundamentally different causal influences. A theory of antisocial behavior in life-course-persistent offenders must locate causal factors in early childhood and explain the continuity of crime over time. The antisocial behavior of adolescent-limited offenders may be specific to situations and events in adolescence and must account for the discontinuity of crime in their lives. Moffitt's theory is compatible with much of the literature on antisocial behavior and has received empirical support.

Barak's (1998) vision of interdisciplinary criminology provides a framework for attempting the complex task of integrating theories to explain and predict criminal behavior. The task of interdisciplinary criminology is to discuss and articulate the ways in which constitutive elements interact to generally coproduce criminal behavior and its control. Integrative theories that have emerged over the past 15 years have made considerable gains in terms of linking critical and complementary findings from different perspectives. However, criminologists are still faced with the task of integrating a much wider range of theoretical perspectives. Few if any theories, integrative or not, can explain all forms of criminal behavior, criminal events, and/or all individuals or groups who engage in crime. Some scholars are skeptical that a true integrative theory of crime is possible at all. However, it is unlikely that any criminal behavior can be explained by a single theory.

Concluding Comments—Successes and Challenges

The job of criminal behavior scholars, criminologists, and forensic psychologists who study criminal behavior is to make sense of both rare and everyday crimes through the scientific method with the goals of *prevention*, *explanation*, and *prediction*. Almost 70 years ago, Schmidl wrote:

> At the present stage of the development of criminology and the related sciences of psychology and psychiatry, the cooperation of these disciplines is not satisfactory. Psychologists and psychiatrists have failed to arrive at general and reliable statements about crime and criminals because some of the specific problems involved have escaped their attention. Criminologists have made disputable statements on the psychological causation of crime because of insufficient familiarity with psychology and psychiatry. (Schmidl, 1946, p. 37)

To some extent, little has changed. Psychologists, sociologists, and criminology/criminal justice scholars often operate in their own circles, attend their own conferences within their own professional organizations, publish in their own journals, and find little time to read each other's work. Since the eighteenth-century origins of the study of crime, the pendulum has swung back and forth, from individual/psychological explanations to environmental/sociological explanations of crime, and back again.

However, great progress has also been made. We are in an unprecedented time of interdisciplinary scholarship and evidence-based practice. Academic programs in forensic psychology and criminal justice that provide interdisciplinary training are becoming increasingly available, and researchers are engaging in creative interdisciplinary collaboration in developing theories and research agendas that cannot be characterized as purely psychological or sociological. Major advances in the study of criminal behavior include: the development of forensic assessment tools such as the PCL-R; the revival of correctional psychology and creative and widespread application of theory to practice such as statistically based offender profiling and crime analysis; risk assessment and the prediction of dangerousness; crime prevention through environmental design and crisis intervention and hostage negotiation teams in law enforcement; specialized courts for the mentally ill and substance abusers. All of these are examples of the considerable theoretical and empirical advances that have been made in the study of criminal behavior and offer great promise for future research and theoretical developments to come.

Evidence-Based Practice in Criminal Justice and Forensic Settings

Linking theory to practice is crucial at all stages of the criminal justice process. Theory and research on criminal behavior is used to inform policy, legislation, and practice in criminal justice and forensic settings. Police strategy is informed by theories about offender motivation and offense patterns. Crime prevention policy is dependent upon knowledge about situational and opportunity factors that increase and decrease the likelihood for an offense to occur. Juries and attorneys rely on expert testimony involving research on offender motivation and the nature and types of criminal behavior in reaching adjudication and sentencing decisions. Effective correctional management and treatment is developed based on theory and knowledge about the needs and risk levels of different types of offenders in correctional populations. Victim services can be enhanced and improved with attention to offender typologies and theory and research on victim-offender dynamics and the ways in which offense characteristics influence victim impact and recovery in the aftermath of crime. Determination of when and in what situation juvenile offenders should be adjudicated as adults is guided by theory and research on how offender patterns develop across the life course. At all stages of the criminal justice system—from arrest to release, from crime prevention strategy to victim services, theory and research play a primary role in the administration of justice.

While it has long been recognized that criminal justice practice must be informed by theory and research, accumulation of empirical research on criminal behavior in the last 50 years has given new meaning to the term "applied criminology."[9] One notable example is in the area of psychopathy and violent risk prediction. The advent and standardization of the Psychopathy Checklist–Revised (Hare 1991, 2003) made it possible for research to be conducted utilizing a common definition. Prior to the 1990s, the term "psychopath" was considered a wastebasket category with minimal utility in the criminal justice system. The concept of psychopathy has been discussed in the criminal justice and mental health literature since the early 1800s, but lack of empirical research and consensus on the meaning of the concept made it problematic to apply the concept to criminal justice practice.[10] Today, there is a vast and growing body of research linking psychopathy to violent recidivism (Blair, et al., 2005; Gacono, 2000; Hare, 2007; Patrick, 2006) and recognition that psychopathy research has led to the beginnings of a *mini-theory of crime of human predatory violence* (Report of the Committee on Serious Violence and Sex Offenders, 2000). Theory and research on psychopathy is used by law enforcement agencies in hostage negotiation training (Greenstone, Kosson, & Gacono, 2000), criminal profiling (Turvey, 2011) and crime scene analysis (O'Toole, 2007), in adjudication and sentencing decisions (Edens, 2001; Freeman, 2001), and in correctional classification, management, treatment, and release decisions (Wong & Hare, 2005) and critical issues have been raised regarding legal and public policy questions associated with psychopathy and its intersection with law, psychiatry, and philosophy (Malatesti & McMillan, 2010).

Psychopathy research is just one of many examples of lines of criminological inquiry that have been applied on a widespread scale to criminal justice practice. Theories and research from psychological, sociological, biological, routine activity, and other perspectives have been applied to criminal justice practice with greater frequency with the accumulation of methodologically sound and theoretically rich research and closer nexus between academics and practitioners. Criminal typologies play a particular role in law enforcement, judicial, and correctional response to specific types of offenders and offense situations.

Understanding the connection between criminological theory and criminal justice practice is the foundation of theoretically grounded evidence-based initiatives. While identifying and understanding the factors and forces that influence criminal behavior is a worthy endeavor in and of itself, explaining and discussing criminal behavior in a textbook, college classroom, or academic article does little to ensure that criminal justice initiatives do not repeat past mistakes and/or expend tax dollars on interventions that have no theoretical or empirical basis. A number of authors have noted the wasted efforts that have occurred in the history of criminal justice when policy and practice is blindly initiated without attention to theory and empirical research (Clements, 1996; Gendreau, 1996; Hengeller, 1996; Van Voorhis, Cullen, & Applegate, 1995). Societal response to criminal behavior at all stages of the criminal justice process, from law enforcement and public safety to courts and law to corrections and offender reentry, depends on what is known about the causes, nature, extent, types, and subtypes of criminal behavior.

Challenges for the Future in the Study of Criminal Psychology and Criminal Behavior

With the explosion of research in key areas in the study of criminal psychology and criminal behavior and the move to integrative and interdisciplinary scholarship and application has come recognition of areas for improvement and future study. Five key considerations for future directions in criminal behavior research and its application to criminal justice practice rise to the top (Helfgott, 2008):

1) *Applied Criminology*: Obstacles continue to hinder successful application of theory and research to criminal justice practice, including *theoreticism* (the tendency of researchers to accept or reject knowledge bases outside of their own discipline, affiliation, or framework), *technology transfer* (the transfer of information from researchers to administrators to linestaff), and *training* that is evidence-based and current (Gendreau, 1996).
2) *Interdisciplinary Perspectives and Theory Integration*: Interdisciplinary criminology is in its infancy. Much work needs to be done to synthesize and integrate perspectives, theories, and empirical research in ways that help answer specific questions about criminal behavior that bridge gaps between the psychological theories of criminal behavior and other disciplinary perspectives. Questions need to be asked, connections need to be made, and key insights need to be synthesized to pull the best works together into a cohesive megatheory of crime that addresses the need for both a general theory of crime and situational specificity that examines criminal typologies and the differences between crime types and individual-environment interactions.
3) *Technology*: Much of the available theory and research has been based on secondary datasets that are decades or more old. Rapid technological advances have the potential to shape the nature and extent of criminal behavior across all categories of crime as well as the criminal justice response to crime. Criminologists have ignored the phenomenology of modern teenagers (Moffitt, 2001) and important work has been done by media effects psychologists, cultural criminologists, and media & crime scholars (e.g., Anderson & Dill, 2000; Anderson et al., 2003; Black, 1990; Bryant & Zillman, 2002; Coleman, 2004; Ferrell et al., 2008; Ferrell & Sanders, 1995; Harvey, 2002; Katz, 1988; Katz, 2002; Lloyd, 2002; Manning, 1998; Newman; 1998; Pers, 2001; Preiss et al., 2007; Rafter, 1996; Surette, 1990, 1998, 2002) that offers an interdisciplinary framework to develop theory and conduct empirical research on the role of mass media and computer technology in shaping criminal behavior.

4) *Imbedded stereotypes: Stereotypes about gender, race, social class, and age are historically imbedded in law and in theories and typologies of crime and criminal behavior*. Feminist criminologists have said that there is one thing that would significantly reduce crime—to socialize little boys as if they were little girls and to "make men think and act more like women" (Pollock, 1999). Future research is needed incorporating works by feminist and other scholars (e.g., Adler, 1975; Allen, 1987; Balfour, 2006; Bjorkqvist & Niemela, 1992; Boyle, 2001; Burgess-Proctor, 2006; Campbell, 1994; Chesney-Lind, 1997; Daly, 1995; Daly & Chesney-Lind, 1988; Gerbner, 1994; Kirsta, 1994; Naffine, 1996) to identify the ways in which gender, race, class, and age stereotypes continue to be imbedded in criminological theory and applied to criminal justice practice.
5) *Methodological Creativity*: Traditional and nontraditional methods need to be incorporated into research designs in new ways to capture data areas missing in current literature. If researchers were to attempt to match traditional research designs with more creative attempts to collect primary data from difficult-to-obtain samples using both qualitative and quantitative data collection strategies, such as primary data collection and incorporation of ethnographic accounts (Ferrell & Hamm, 1998), we may be able to get closer to capturing some of the nuances of criminal behavior that will help answer questions about individual-situation interactions, differences in criminal behavior across time periods, gender, race/ethnicity, cultures, subcultures, etc, and findings that are more rooted in and relevant to real life and real people in the here and now.

With historical successes and challenges in mind, criminal psychology has a great deal to offer the study of criminal behavior in contributing to interdisciplinary theory. The importance of individual-situation interaction in the study of criminal behavior calls for situational data in longitudinal studies that would allow researchers to examine change across different types of situations. Acknowledgment that situation plays an important role in when and whether an individual will commit a criminal act can be extended to analysis of cultural-individual interactions and the ways in which societal changes such as technology, economics, and shifts in power interact with individual-level characteristics. The explosion of research in all subfields of psychology, criminology and criminal justice, and the social and behavioral sciences offers great promise for future theory and research in criminal behavior.

Notes

1. Jack Olsen's (1983) book *Son: A psychopath and his victims* about the Spokane, Washington, South Hill rapist Kevin Coe was made into a 1991 made-for-TV movie called *The sins of the mother*, starring Dale Midkiff as Coe and Elizabeth

Montgomery as his mother. Ann Rule's (1987) book *Small sacrifices: A true story of passion and murder*, about Diane Downs, an Oregon mother who shot her three children, was made into a made-for-TV movie called *Small sacrifices: A true story*, starring Farrah Fawcett as Diane Downs in 1989. Over 25 years later, both Kevin Coe and Diane Downs continue to make the news. In August 2006, the Washington State attorney general filed a petition for civil commitment of Kevin Coe as a sexually violent predator, blocking his September release date after serving almost 30 years in prison. Coe was civilly committed in 2008 (see: http://www.spokesmanreview.com/sections/coe). In 2010, the Oregon parole board denied Diane Downs parole, for a second time, after over 25 years in prison, stating that she will not be reviewed again for another 10 years (see: http://m.youtube.com/#/watch?v=fsV1u25eXR4&desktop_uri=%2Fwatch%3Fv%3DfsV1u25eXR4).

2. One of the most unusual types of crime in recent years has involved cases in which pregnant women have been attacked and their fetus has been stolen. Also referred to as "cesarean kidnapping" or "fetal abduction," these cases represent a statistically rare and exceptionally vicious type of criminal behavior. To date, all but one of the known cases of fetus theft have been committed by women. See: Baker et al. (2002); Geberth (2006).

3. Also sometimes referred to as APD. In recent years the preferred acronym ASPD has been used to avoid confusion with Avoidant Personality Disorder.

4. Sykes and Matza's "Techniques of Neutralization" theory is generally viewed as a sociological theory. The theory, though sociological, is discussed here because it focuses on the ways in which cognitive processes enable criminal behavior.

5. Black (1991) offers a comprehensive analysis of media-mediated violence and the criminogenic and cathartic effects of depictions of violence in art, literature, film, TV, and pop culture, including case study examples of copycat offenders such as John Hinckley and Mark David Chapman. However for most people, rather than providing role models for criminal behavior, violent media primes violent events, exacerbates fear of crime, and creates and reinforces a "mean world" view (Gerbner, 1994).

6. See Helfgott (2008) for a more comprehensive review of the six theoretical perspectives.

7. For example, many scholars who approach crime from the routine activity, cultural, and phenomenological perspectives are sociology-trained criminologists, and some texts address these perspectives under the heading of "sociological theories." Some criminology/criminal justice-trained scholars engage in psychological or biological-based research, and many sociological and psychological theories arrive at similar conclusions, predictions, and policy implications using their own disciplinary jargon.

8. Gottfredson and Hirschi's General Theory of Crime and Life Course Criminology are not generally classified as "integrated theories" in criminological texts because they are primarily sociological theories. I include them here because they integrate psychological and sociological concepts such as "self-control" and "antisocial propensity" (though they do not specifically address the psychological literature encompassing these concepts).

9. Some use the term "applied criminology" to refer to the application of criminological theory to law enforcement practice. This is likely rooted in the FBI's use of the term as a title for a course in the Behavioral Science Unit since the 1970s. There is a long history of the use of the term to refer to the general application of criminological theory to criminal justice policy and practice, but little consistency in terms of how the term is used today. For example, some academic programs that emphasize the intersection of theory and practice use the term as a program or department title, while others use the term to apply to programs that focus on emergency management and security-oriented areas.

10. Application of the concept of psychopathy to criminal justice prior to the 1990s was problematic because the term psychopath meant different things to different researchers and practitioners. However, the concept of psychopathy has been part of the discourse in criminal justice for over 200 years and has been used as the dividing line between insanity and criminality and as a notion upon which old and new habitual offender and civil commitment laws have been based.

References

Adler, F. (1975). *Sisters in crime*. New York: McGraw-Hill.

Adler, J. R., & Gray, J. M. (2010). *Forensic psychology: Concepts, debates, and practice*. New York: Willan Publishing.

Agnew, R. (1994). The techniques of neutralization and violence. *Criminology, 32* (4), 555–580.

Agnew, R. (2005). *Why do criminals offend? A general theory of crime and delinquency*. Los Angeles: Roxbury.

Allen, H. (1987). *Justice unbalanced*. Milton Keynes, England: Open University Press.

American Psychiatric Association (1952). *Diagnostic and statistical manual of mental disorders* [DSM-I]. Washington, DC: Author.

American Psychiatric Association (1968). *Diagnostic and statistical manual of mental disorders* (2nd ed. [DSM-II]). Washington, DC: Author.

American Psychiatric Association (1980). *Diagnostic and statistical manual of mental disorders*, (3rd ed. [DSM-III]). Washington, DC: Author.

American Psychiatric Association (1987). *Diagnostic and statistical manual of mental disorders*, (3rd ed., rev. [DSM-III-R]). Washington, DC: Author.

American Psychiatric Association (2000). *Diagnostic and statistical manual of mental disorders*, (4th ed., text rev. [DSM-IV-TR]). Washington, DC: Author.

Anderson, C. A., Berkowitz, L., Donnerstein, E., Huesmann, L. R., Johnson, J. D., Linz, D., Malamuth, N. M., & Wartella, E. (2003). The influence of media violence on youth. *Psychological Science in the Public Interest, 4*(3), 81–110.

Anderson, C. A., & Dill, K. E. (2000). Video games and aggressive thoughts, feelings, and behavior in the laboratory and life. *Journal of Personality and Social Psychology, 78*, 772–790.

Andrews, D. A., & Bonta, J. (1994, 1998, 2003, 2006, 2010). *The psychology of criminal conduct*. Cincinnati, OH: Anderson Publishing.

Arrigo, B. A., & Shipley, S. (2001). The confusion over psychopathy (I): Historical considerations. *International Journal of Offender Therapy and Comparative Criminology*, *45*, 325–344.

Balfour, G. (2006, September). Re-imagining a feminist criminology. *Canadian Journal of Criminology and Criminal Justice*, 735–752.

Barbaree, H. E. (1990). Stimulus control of sexual arousal: Its role in sexual assault. In W. L. Marshall, D. R. Laws, & H. E. Barbaree (Eds.), *Handbook of sexual assault: Issues, theories, and treatment of the offender* (pp. 115–142). New York: Plenum.

Barak, G. (1998). *Integrating criminologies*. Needham Heights, MA: Allyn & Bacon

Barnes, H. E. (1972). *The story of punishment*. Montclaire, NJ: Patterson Smith.

Bartol, C. R., & Bartol, A. M. (2012). *Introduction to forensic psychology: Research and application*. Thousand Oaks, CA: Sage Publications.

Bartol, C. R., & Bartol, A. M. (2011). *Criminal behavior: A psychological approach*. Upper Saddle River, NJ: Prentice-Hall.

Belnap, J. (2010). "Offending women": A double entendre. *Journal of Criminal Law & Criminology, 100*(3).

Bjorkqvist, K., & Niemela, P. (1992). *Of mice and women: Aspects of female aggression*. New York: Academic Press.

Black, J. (1991). *The aesthetics of murder: A study in romantic literature and contemporary culture*. Baltimore, MD: Johns Hopkins University Press.

Blackburn, R. (1993). *The psychology of criminal conduct: Theory, research, and practice*. New York: John Wiley & Sons.

Blair, J., Mitchell, D., & Blair, K. (2005). *The psychopath: Emotion and the brain*. Oxford: Blackwell Publishing.

Blair, R. J. R., Sellars, C., Strickland, I., Clark, F., Williams, A. O., & Smith, M. (1995). Emotion attributions in the psychopath. *Personality and Individual Differences*, *19*, 431–437.

Brinkley, C. A., Bernstein, A., & Newman, J. P. (1999). Coherence in the narratives of psychopathic and nonpsychopathic criminal offenders. *Personality and Individual Differences, 27*, 519–530.

Brinkley, C. A., Newman, J. P., Harpur, T. J., & Johnson M. M. (1999). Cohesion in texts produced by psychopathic and nonpsychopathic criminal inmates. *Personality and Individual Differences, 26*, 873–885.

Bryant, J., & Zillman, D. (Eds.) (2002). *Media effects: Advances in theory and research*. Mahwah, NJ: Lawrence Erlbaum Associates.

Boyle, K. (2001). What's natural about killing? Gender, copycat violence and *Natural born killers*. *Journal of Gender Studies, 10*(3), 311–321.

Burgess, R., & Akers, R. L. (1966). A differential association-reinforcement theory of criminal behavior. *Social Problems, 14*, 363–383.

Burgess-Proctor, A. (2006). Intersections of race, gender, and crime: New directions for feminist criminology. *Feminist Criminology, 1*(1), 27–47.

Campbell, A. (1994) *Men, women, & aggression*. New York: Basic Books.

Chesney-Lind, M. (1997). *The female offender: Girls, women, and crime*. Thousand Oaks, CA: Sage.

Cleckley, H. (1941, 1976, 1988). *The mask of sanity*. St. Louis, MO: Mosby.

Clements, C. B. (1996). Offender classification: Two decades of progress. *Criminal Justice and Behavior, 23*(1), 121–143.

Coleman, L. (2004). *The copycat effect: How the media and popular culture trigger mayhem in tomorrow's headlines*. New York: Paraview Pocket Books.

Colvin, M. (2000) *Crime and coercion: An integrated theory of chronic criminality*. New York: St. Martin's Press.

Cullen, D. (2004, April 20). "The depressive and the psychopath: At last we know why the Columbine killers did it." *Slate*. Retrieved October 19, 2005, from http://slate.msn.com/id/2099203.

Cullen, F. T. (2005) "The Twelve People Who Saved Rehabilitation: How The Science of Criminology Made a Difference" *Criminology*, 43(1), 1–42.

Cullen, F. T. and Agnew, R. (2006). *Criminological theory: Past to present*. New York: Oxford University Press.

Daly, K. (1995). *Gender, crime, and punishment*. New Haven, CT: Yale University Press.

Daly, K., & M. Chesney-Lind. (1988). Feminism and criminology. *Justice Quarterly, 5*(4), 101–143.

DeMatteo, D., Marczyk, G., Krauss, D. A., & Burl, J. (2009). Education and training models in forensic psychology. *Training and Education in Professional Psychology*, 3(3), 184–191.

Douglas, K. S., Vincent, G. M., & Edens, J. F. (2006). Risk for criminal recidivism: The role of psychopathy. In C. J. Patrick (Ed.), *The handbook of psychopathy* (pp. 533–554). New York: Guilford Press.

Edens, J.F. (2001). Misuses of the Hare Psychopathy Checklist-Revised in court. *Journal of Interpersonal Violence, 16*(10), 1082–1093.

Elliot, D. S., Ageton, S. S., & Canter, R. J. (1979). An integrative theoretical perspective on delinquent behavior. *Journal of Research in Crime and Delinquency, 16*(1), 3–27.

Elliott, C. (1996). *The rules of insanity: Moral responsibility and the mentally ill offender*. Albany: State University of New York Press.

Farrington, D. P. Developmental and life-course criminology: Key theoretical and empirical issues. *Criminology, 41*(2), 221–225.

Ferrell, J., & Hamm, M. S. (1998). *Ethnography at the edge: Crime, deviance, and field research*. Belmont, CA: Wadsworth.

Ferrell, J., Hayworth, K., & Young, J. (2008). *Cultural criminology*. Thousand Oaks, CA: Sage.

Ferrell, J., & Sanders, C. R. (1995). *Cultural criminology*. Boston, MA: Northeastern University Press.

Fishbein, D. (2001). *Biobehavioral perspectives in criminology*. Belmont, CA: Wadsworth.

Foucault, M. (1995). *Discipline and punish: The birth of the prison*. New York: Vintage. (Original work published 1977).

Gacono, C. B. (Ed.) (2000). *The clinical and forensic assessment of psychopathy: A Practitioner's Guide*. Mahwah, NJ: Lawrence Erlbaum Associates.

Garland, D. (Ed.) (2001). *Mass imprisonment: Social causes and consequences*. Thousand Oaks, CA: Sage.

Gendreau, P. (1996). Offender rehabilitation: What we know and what needs to be done. *Criminal Justice and Behavior, 23*(1), 144–161.

Gerbner, G. (1994). Reclaiming our cultural mythology: Television's global marketing strategy creates a damaging and alienated window on the world. *The Ecology of Justice, 38*. Retrieved February 28, 2004, from http://www.context.org/ICLIB/IC38/Gerbner.htm.

Gottfredson, M. R., & Hirschi, T. (1990). *A general theory of crime*. Palo Alto, CA: Stanford University Press.

Greenstone, J. L., Kosson, D. S., & Gacono, C. B. (2000). Psychopathy and hostage negotiations: some preliminary thoughts and findings. In Carl B. Gacono (Ed.), *The clinical and forensic assessment of psychopathy: A practitioner's guide* (pp. 385–404). Mahwah, NJ: Lawrence Erlbaum Associates.

Groth, N. A. (1979). *Men who rape: The psychology of the offender*. New York: Plenum Press.

Hanson, R. K., & Thornton, D. (1999). *Static-99: Improving actuarial risk assessment for sexual offenders*. Ottawa: Solicitor General of Canada (Corrections Research User Report 199-02).

Hare, R. D. (1991, 2003). *Manual for the Psychopathy Checklist–Revised*. Toronto, Ontario, Canada: Multi-Health Systems.

Hare, R. D. (1993). *Without conscience: The disturbing world of psychopaths among us*. New York: Pocket Books.

Hare, R. D. (1998). Psychopaths and their nature: Implications for the mental health and criminal justice systems. In: T. Millon, E. Simonsen, E. Birket-Smith, & R. D. Davis (Eds.), *Psychopathy: Antisocial, criminal, and violent behavior* (pp. 188–212). New York: Guilford Press.

Hare, R. D. (2001). Psychopaths and their nature: Some implications for understanding human predatory violence. In A. Raine & J. Sanmartin (Eds.), *Violence and psychopathy* (pp. 5–34). New York: Kluwer/Plenum.

Hare, R. D. (2003). *Hare Psychopathy Checklist–Revised* (2nd ed.). Toronto, Ontario, Canada: Multi-Health Systems.

Harcourt, B. E. (2007). *Against prediction: Profiling, policing, and punishing in an actuarial age*. Chicago: University of Chicago Press.

Harris, G. T., Rice, M. E., & Cormier, C. A. (1991). Psychopathy and violent recidivism. *Law and Human Behavior, 15*(6), 625–637.

Harris, T. (1981). *Red dragon*. New York: G. P. Putnam's Sons.

Harris, T. (1988). *The silence of the lambs*. New York: St. Martin's Press.

Hart, S. D. (1998). Psychopathy and risk for violence. In D. J. Cooke et al. (Eds.), *Psychopathy: Theory, research, and implications for society* (pp. 355–357). Netherlands: Kluwer.

Harvey, D. (2002). *Obsession: Celebrities and their stalkers*. Dublin, Ireland: Merlin Publishing.

Heilbrun, K. S., & Annis, L. V. (1988). Research and training in forensic psychology: National survey of forensic facilities. *Professional Psychology: Research and Practice, 19*, 211–215.

Helfgott, J. B. (2008). *Criminal behavior: Theories, typologies, and criminal justice*. Thousand Oaks, CA: Sage Publications.

Hemphill, J. F., Templeman, R., Wong, S., & Hare, R. D. (1998). Psychopathy and crime: Recidivism and criminal careers. In D. J. Cooke et al. (Eds.), *Psychopathy: Theory, research, and implications for society* (pp. 375–399). Netherlands: Kluwer.

Hickey, E. W. (2009). *Serial murderers and their victims*. Belmont, CA: Wadsworth.

Hodgins, S. (1997). An overview of research on the prediction of dangerousness. *Nordic Journal of Psychiatry, 51*, 33–38.

Horney, J. (2006). An alternative psychology of criminal behavior. *Criminology, 44*(1), 1–16.

Jenkins, P. (1994). *Using murder: The social construction of serial homicide*. New York: Aldine de Gruyter.

Johnson, R. (1995). *Hardtime: Understanding and reforming the prison*. Belmont, CA: Wadsworth.

Jones, D. A. (1986). *History of criminology*. New York/London: Greenwood Press.

Karpman, B. (1941). On the need of separating psychopathy into two distinct clinical types: The symptomatic and the ideopathic. *Journal of Criminal Psychopathology, 3*, 112–137.

Karpman, B. (1946). Psychopathy in the scheme of human typology. *Journal of Nervous and Mental Disease, 103*, 276–288.

Karpman, B. (1948). The myth of the psychopathic personality. *American Journal of Psychiatry, 104*, 523–534.

Katz, J. (2006). *Macho Paradox: Why some men hurt women and how all men can help*. Naperville, IL: Sourcebooks

Katz, J. (1988). *Seductions of crime: Moral and sensual attractions in doing evil*. New York: Basic Books.

Kernberg O. F. (1966). Structural derivatives of object relationships. *International Journal of Psychoanalysis, 47*, 236–253.

Kernberg, O. F. (1967). Borderline personality organization. *Journal of the American Psychoanalytic Association, 15*, 641–685.

Kernberg, O. F. (1976). *Object relations theory and clinical psychoanalysis*. New York: Jason Aronson.

Kernberg, O. F. (1984). *Severe personality disorders: Psychotherapeutic strategies*. New Haven, CT: Yale University Press.

Kernberg, O. F. (1985a). *Borderline conditions and pathological narcissism*. New York: Jason Aronson.

Kernberg, O. F. (1985b). *Internal world and external reality*. New York: Jason Aronson.

Kernberg O. F. (1992). *Aggression in personality disorders and perversions*. New Haven, CT: Yale University Press.

Kirsta, A. (1994). *Deadlier than the male: Violence and aggression in women*. Hammersmith, London: HarperCollins.

Kittrie, N. N. (1971). *The right to be different: Deviance and enforced therapy*. Baltimore, MD: Johns Hopkins University Press.

Kohut, H. (1971). *Analysis of the self*. New York: International Universities Press.

Krafft-Ebing, R. V. (1929). *Psychopathia sexualis*. Chicago: Login Brothers.

Laub, J. H., & Sampson, R. J. (2003). *Shared beginnings, divergent lives: Delinquent boys to age 70*. Cambridge, MA: Harvard University Press.

Lindner, R. M. (1945). *Rebel without a cause*. London: Research Books, Ltd.

Litwack, T. R., & Schlesinger L. B. (1998). Dangerous risk assessments: Research, legal, and clinical considerations. In A. K. Hess and I. B. Weiner (Eds.), *Handbook of forensic psychology* (pp. 171–217). New York: John Wiley.

Lloyd, B. T. (2002). A conceptual framework for examining adolescent identity, media influence, and social development. *Review of General Psychology, 6*(1), 73–91.

Malatesti, L., & McMillan, J. (Eds.) (2010). *Responsibility and psychopathy: Interfacing law, psychiatry, and philosophy*. New York Oxford University Press.

Manning, P. (1998). Media loops. In F. Bailey & D. Hale (Eds.), *Popular culture, crime, and justice* (pp. 25–39). Belmont, CA: Wadsworth.

Martinson, R. (1974). What works?—Questions and answers about prison reform. *The Public Interest, 35*, 22–54.

Meloy, J. R. (1988). *The psychopathic mind: Origins, dynamics, and treatment*. New York: Jason Aronson.

Menninger, K. (1968). *The crime of punishment*. New York: Viking Press.

McCord, W., & McCord, J. (1964). *The psychopath: An essay on the criminal mind*. New York: Van Nostrand Reinhold.

Moffitt, T. E. (1993). Adolescent-limited and life-course-persistent antisocial behavior: A developmental taxonomy. *Psychological Review, 100*(4), 674–701.

Naffine, N. (1996). *Feminism and criminology*. Philadelphia: Temple University Press.

Newman, G. (1998). Popular culture and violence: Decoding the violence of popular movies. In F. Bailey & D. Hale (Eds.), *Popular culture, crime, and justice* (pp. 40–56). Belmont, CA: Wadsworth.

Olsen, J. (1983). *Son: A psychopath and his victims*. New York: Macmillan Press.

Olver, M. E. (2011). Forensic psychology opportunities in Canadian graduate programs: Update of Simourd and Wormith's (1995) survey. *Canadian Psychology, 52*(2), 122–127.

O'Toole, M. E. (1999). Psychopathy as a behavior classification system for violent and serial crime scenes. In H. Herve & J. Yuille (Eds.) The psychopath: Theory, research, and practice (pp. 301–325). Mahwah, NJ: Lawrence Erlbaum Associates.

Packer, I. K. (2008). Specialized practice in forensic psychology: Opportunities and obstacles. *Professional Psychology: Research and Practice, 39*(2), 245–249.

Pers, E. M. *Media effects and society*. Mahwah, NJ: Lawrence Erlbaum.

Piquero, A., & Mazerolle, P. (2001). Introduction. *Life-course criminology: Contemporary and classic readings*.

Pollock, J. M. (1999). *Criminal women*. Cincinnati, OH: Anderson Publishing.

Preiss, R. W., Gayle, B. M., Burrell, N., Allen, M., & Bryant, J. (Eds.) (2007). *Mass media effects research*. Mahwah, NJ: Lawrence Erlbaum.

Quinsey, V. L., Harris, G. T., Rice, M. E., & Cormier, C. A. (1998). *Violent offenders: Appraising and managing risk*. Washington, DC: American Psychological Association.

Radzinowicz, L. (1966). *Ideology and crime*. New York: Columbia University Press.

Rafter, N. (2006). *Shots in the mirror: Crime films and society*. Oxford: Oxford University Press.

Raine, A. (1993). *The psychopathology of crime: Criminal behavior as a clinical disorder*. New York: Academic Press.

Reiber, R. W. & Vetter, H. J. (1995). The language of the psychopath. In R. W. Reiber (Ed.), *The psychopathology of language and cognition*. New York: Plenum Press.

Ressler, R. K., Burgess, A. W., & Douglas, J. E. (1992). *Sexual Homicide: Patterns and Motives*. New York: Simon & Schuster.

Robinson, M. B. (2004). *Why crime?: An integrated systems theory of antisocial behavior*. Upper Saddle River, NJ: Pearson/Prentice-Hall.

Robinson, M. B., & Beaver, K. M. (2009). *Why crime?: An interdisciplinary approach to explaining criminal behavior*. Durham, NC: Carolina Academic Press.

Rule, A. (1987). *Small sacrifices: A true story of passion and murder*. New York: New American Library.

Salekin, R. T., Rogers R., & Sewell K. W. (1996). A review and meta-analysis of the Psychopathy Checklist and Psychopathy Checklist-Revised: Predictive validity of dangerousness. *Clinical Psychology: Science and Practice, 3*, 203–215.

Sampson, R. J., & Laub, J. H. (1993). *Crime in the making: Pathways and turning points through life*. Cambridge, MA: Harvard University Press.

Schmalleger, F. (2004). *Criminology today: An integrative introduction*. Upper Saddle River, NJ: Pearson/Prentice-Hall.

Schmidle, F. (1946). Psychological and psychiatric concepts in criminology. *Journal of Criminal Law and Criminology*.

Scully, D., & Marolla, J. (1984). Convicted rapists' vocabulary of motives: Excuses and justifications. *Social Problems, 31*, 530–544.

Serin, R. C., & Amos, N. L. (1995). The role of psychopathy in the assessment of dangerousness. *International Journal of Law and Psychiatry, 18*(2), 231–238.

Shelden, R. G. (2001). *Controlling the dangerous classes: A critical introduction to the history of criminal justice*. Needham Heights, MA: Allyn & Bacon.

Shipley, S., & Arrigo, B. A. (2001, August). The confusion over psychopathy (II): Implications for forensic (correctional) practice. *International Journal of Offender Therapy and Comparative Criminology, 45*, 407–420.

Simourd, D. J., & Hodge, R. D. (2000). Criminal psychopathy: A risk-and-need perspective. *Criminal Justice and Behavior, 27*, 256–272.

Sparks, C. G., & Sparks, C. W. (2002). Effects of media violence. In J. Bryant & D. Zillman (Eds.), *Media effects: Advances in theory and research* (pp. 269–285). Mahwah, NJ: Lawrence Erlbaum Associates, Publishers.

Stermac, L. E., Segal Z. V., & Gillis R. (1990). Social and cultural factors in sexual assault. In W. L. Marshall, D. R. Laws, & H. E. Barbaree (Eds.), *Handbook of sexual assault: Issues, theories, and treatment of the offender* (pp. 143–159). New York: Plenum.

Surette, R. (1990). Estimating the magnitude and mechanisms of copycat crime. In R. Surette (Ed.), *The media and criminal justice policy: Recent research and social effects*. Springfield, IL: CC Thomas Publishers.

Surette, R. (1998). *Media, crime, and criminal justice: Images and realities*. Belmont, CA: Wadsworth.

Surette, R. (2002). Self-reported copycat crime among a population of serious and violent juvenile offenders. *Crime & Delinquency, 48*(1), 46–69.

Sullivan, E. A., & Kosson, D. S. (2006). Ethnic and cultural variations in psychopathy. In C. J. Patrick (Ed.), *Handbook of psychopathy*. New York: Guilford Press.

Sykes, G. M., & Matza, D. (1957). Techniques of neutralization: A theory of delinquency. *American Sociological Review, 22*, 664–670.

Szasz, T. S. (1961). *The myth of mental illness: Foundations of a theory of personal conduct*. New York: Hoeber-Harper.

Thornberry, T. P. (1987). Toward an interactional theory of delinquency. *Criminology, 25*(4), 865–891.

Tittle, C. R. (1995). *Control Balance: Towards a general theory of deviance*. Boulder, CO: Westview Press.

Tunnell, K. D. (1992). *Choosing crime: The criminal calculus of property offenders*. Chicago: Nelson-Hall Publishers.

Turvey, B. E. (2011). *Criminal profiling: An introduction to behavioral evidence analysis*. San Diego, CA: Academic Press.

Van Voorhis, P., Cullen, F. T., & Applegate, B. (1995). Evaluating interventions with violent offenders: A guide for practitioners and policymakers. *Federal Probation, 59*(2), 17–27.

Walsh, A., & Ellis, L. (2007). *Criminology: An interdisciplinary approach*. Thousand Oaks, CA: Sage.

Walters, G. D. (1990). *The criminal lifestyle: Patterns of serious criminal conduct*. Newbury Park, CA: Sage.

Webster, C. D., Douglas, K. S., Eaves, D., & Hart, S. D. (1997). *HCR-20: Assessing risk for violence* (version 2). Burnaby, British Columbia, Canada: The Mental Health, Law, and Policy Institute of Simon Fraser University.

Williamson, S., Harpur T. J., & Hare, R. D. (1991). Abnormal processing of affective words by psychopaths. *Psychophysiology, 29*, 260–273.

Wortley, R. (2011). *Psychological criminology*. New York: Routledge.

Wong, S., & Hare, R. D. (2005). *Guidelines for a psychopathy treatment program*. Toronto, Ontario, Canada: Multi-Health Systems.

Wulach, J. S. (1988). The criminal personality as a DSMIII-R antisocial, narcissistic, borderline, and histrionic personality disorder. *International Journal of Offender Counseling and Comparative Criminology, 33*(3), 185–199.

Yochelson, S., & Samenow, S. E. (1976). *The criminal personality. Volumes 1–3*. New York: Jason Aronson.

CHAPTER TWO

Education and Training Models in Forensic Psychology*

David DeMatteo, Geoffrey Marczyk, Daniel A. Krauss, and Jeffrey Burl

The field of forensic psychology has quite recently emerged as a distinct subdiscipline within professional psychology. Despite a historical lineage dating back to the early 1900s and the influential publication of Hugo Munsterberg's (1908) *On the Witness Stand*, the American Psychological Association (APA) did not formally recognize forensic psychology as a discrete specialization until 2001 (Otto & Heilbrun, 2002). Although specialty recognition by APA in any area of psychology other than clinical, counseling, school, or industrial-organizational is a relatively recent development, the recent recognition of forensic psychology as a specialty area was arguably overdue in light of the field's long history and rapid growth over the past 30 years.

One indicator of the growth of forensic psychology is the number and range of educational and training opportunities available to students and practitioners. The development of the first joint-degree law-psychology graduate training program in 1973 at the University of Nebraska marked the beginning of a paradigm shift in how forensic practitioners are educated and trained (Bersoff, 1999). A number of law-psychology and forensic psychology programs have been developed since that time, and students and practitioners interested in forensic psychology now have a range of educational and training options from which to choose.

Despite the increased availability of forensic psychology training programs, there is little consensus regarding the core educational components of these programs. Given the rapid growth of the field of forensic psychology, it is critical that training programs provide students with the necessary breadth of knowledge, skills, and experiences. Ensuring proper training takes on additional importance because of the increasingly varied roles being assumed by forensic psychologists in the areas of assessment, treatment, and consultation (Marczyk, DeMatteo, Kutinsky, & Heilbrun, 2008).

This article will first review the divergent and expanding roles assumed by forensic psychologists. We will then examine the educational and training models currently used in forensic psychology programs and consider whether these training models are adequately preparing students for forensic practice. Finally, we will offer a substantive training curriculum that emphasizes the core competencies that arguably should be included in doctoral-level forensic psychology training programs. It is important to note that a model curriculum for doctoral-level forensic psychology graduate programs has not yet been developed, and we hope that our proposed model will stimulate further discourse on this important topic. Although this article may primarily benefit training directors from doctoral-level programs that offer forensic psychology training, we believe this article will also prove useful for those who are less familiar with specialized training opportunities in forensic psychology. As student interest in forensic psychology continues to increase, it is becoming increasingly more important for nonforensic professionals to be able to educate their students about available training opportunities.

Defining the Role of the Modern Forensic Psychologist

Psychologists have a long tradition of providing services to the legal system (see Bartol & Bartol, 2006, and Otto & Heilbrun, 2002, for comprehensive summaries). Initial interaction between psychologists and the legal system, beginning in the early 1900s, consisted of the provision of clinical services to incarcerated adult offenders and juvenile offenders in detention centers (Otto & Heilbrun, 2002). Other early activities of psychologists providing services to criminal justice and the legal system included psychological fitness testing of law enforcement personnel and the pretrial evaluation of criminal offenders (Bartol & Bartol, 2006). These early efforts helped to cement the relationship between psychologists and the legal system, and the use of psychologists for evaluating law enforcement personnel, criminal offenders, and civil litigants has now become commonplace (Melton, Petrila, Poythress, & Slobogin, 2007). The U.S. Court of Appeals for the District of Columbia Circuit decision in *Jenkins v. United States* (1962), which held that appropriately qualified psychologists could testify in court as experts in psychiatric disorders and that psychological measures could be introduced in court to support their expert opinions, further expanded psychological practitioners, interactions within the courts. Following this decision, the use of psychologists as expert witnesses in judicial proceedings has increased dramatically, with thousands of forensic evaluations conducted each year on a variety of psycholegal issues (Otto & Heilbrun, 2002).

Although forensic psychologists now assume a prominent role within the forensic mental health and criminal justice systems, there is a vigorous debate within the parent field of law and psychology regarding the definition of forensic psychology and roles that may be appropriately assumed by forensic psychologists (Brigham, 1999; Hess, 2006). It is generally understood that forensic psychology is one specialty area within the broader rubric of law and psychology research and practice (Hess, 2006), but there is less agreement regarding the precise definition and scope of forensic psychology. At its basic level, forensic psychology can be conceptualized as the application of the science and profession of psychology to questions and issues relating to the law and the legal system. This is the definition of forensic psychology adopted by the American Board of Forensic Psychology (ABFP, 2006). Although most practitioners would likely agree, at least in principle, with the core components of this definition, there is considerable disagreement over the scope of forensic psychology and what activities (i.e., research, assessment, and treatment) and roles should appropriately be considered the exclusive province of forensic psychology.

On the one hand, forensic psychology could be narrowly defined as only encompassing clinical psychology, counseling psychology, school psychology, or another specialty recognized by the APA, and consisting only of activities that provide clinical psychological expertise to the judicial system. This was the definition of forensic psychology endorsed by the American Psychology-Law Society, which is Division 41 of the APA, when it initially pursued formal specialty recognition for forensic psychology from the APA (Heilbrun, 2000; see Forensic Specialty Council, 2007). This definition only encompasses clinically based areas of psychology and therefore excludes practitioners without clinical degrees. Under this narrow and restrictive definition, research psychologists in the fields of social, experimental, and cognitive psychology would not be considered forensic psychologists, despite the obvious contribution that these researchers can make in certain legal contexts (e.g., reliability of eyewitness testimony, perceptions of jurors). It is important to note that this narrow definition may have been chosen for both practical and legal reasons. Practically, specialty recognition from APA is generally reserved for clinically based subspecialties, while legally many states prohibit the term "psychologist" from being used by psychological professionals who are not licensed by the state. It is rare that nonclinical practitioners would seek state licensure in such a jurisdiction and, as a result, research psychologists who study law-psychology issues could not legally refer to themselves as forensic "psychologists," nor would they likely meet the requirements for specialty certification imposed by APA.

Dissatisfaction with narrow conceptualizations of forensic psychology soon emerged, which led to the proposal of several broader definitions. For example, the Committee on the Revision of the Specialty Guidelines for Forensic Psychology (2006) recently adopted a broader definition of forensic psychology, which was subsequently endorsed by the American Psychology-Law Society. Under this definition, forensic psychology includes "all professional practice by any psychologist working within any subdiscipline of psychology . . . when the intended purpose of the service is to apply the scientific, technical, or specialized knowledge of psychology to the law and to use that knowledge to assist in solving legal, contractual, and administrative problems" (1.03). This more expansive definition of forensic psychology reflects the widely varying roles that can be assumed by forensic professionals in terms of both clinical practice and research. This definition encompasses the clinically based activities of forensic psychologists, including policy psychology (i.e., application of clinical skills to law enforcement and public safety), correctional psychology (i.e., provision of assessment and treatment services in correctional settings), and forensic mental health assessment (i.e., assessment of criminal offenders and civil litigants to assist courts in answering legal questions) (Bartol & Bartol, 2006), while also recognizing that nonclinical/research psychologists are engaging in forensic psychology research if their research interfaces with some aspect of the legal system.

Several prominent researchers and commentators have also offered broader definitions of forensic psychology that include both clinical and nonclinical aspects. For example, Grisso (1987) defined a forensic psychologist as "any psychologist, experimental or clinical, who specializes in producing or communicating psychological research or assessment information intended for application to legal issues" (p. 831). Bartol and Bartol (2006) offered a similarly broad definition when they defined forensic psychology as "both (1) the *research endeavor* that examines aspects of human behavior directly related to the legal process ... and (2) the *professional practice* of psychology within or in consultation with a legal system that embraces both civil and criminal law and the numerous areas where they intersect" (pp. 3–4). Finally, Goldstein (2007) recently defined forensic psychology as "the application of psychological research, theory, practice, and traditional and specialized methodology ... to provide information relevant to a legal question" (p. 5).

Educational and Training Opportunities in Forensic Psychology

Regardless of the precise definition, it is clear that the field of forensic psychology has experienced remarkable conceptual and empirical advances in the past three decades (Grisso, 2003; Heilbrun, 2001; Melton et al., 2007). These advances have been fueled by increased attention to the law's demands (Melton et al., 2007); the development of specialized forensic assessment instruments (e.g., Grisso, 1998; Grisso & Appelbaum, 1998; Monahan et al., 2005; Quinsey, Harris, Rice, & Cormier, 2006); the founding of interdisciplinary professional organizations and journals (Otto & Heilbrun, 2002); and substantial growth in research, scholarship, and practice-related literature (e.g., Goldstein, 2007; Heilbrun, 2001; Heilbrun, Marczyk, & DeMatteo, 2002). As a result of this growth, psychologists are being called upon with increasing frequency to conduct forensic mental health assessments, provide treatment, and serve as consultants in a variety of criminal and civil contexts. Changes in the health care reimbursement system for psychologists have also caused forensic practice to become particularly appealing to more general clinical practitioners because forensic services are often not financially constrained by managed care (Melton et al., 2007). Because of this increase in interest, it is important that forensic psychology training programs adequately prepare students to engage in high-quality forensic practice, and more general clinical training programs should also be advised to supplement their basic training with forensically oriented courses and training opportunities to more fully meet the needs of their students. The growth and development of forensic psychology is perhaps best evidenced by looking at the number and diversity of educational and training opportunities available to students and practitioners (Krauss & Sales, 2006; Marczyk et al., 2008). These opportunities range from undergraduate survey courses examining the broad intersection of law and psychology to joint-degree graduate programs offering terminal degrees in both law (JD) and psychology (PhD or PsyD). Moreover, opportunities for continuing education and postdoctoral specialization in forensic psychology are becoming increasingly more available.

As the popularity of forensic psychology has increased in recent years, the availability of forensic psychology training programs has increased almost commensurately. Forensic psychology training programs, or more general programs that offer a forensic psychology track or concentration, have proliferated rapidly in the past two decades. As will be discussed, a variety of educational and training opportunities in forensic psychology now exist at the undergraduate, graduate, and postdoctoral levels, and they offer a wide variety of educational and training opportunities in both clinical and nonclinical (i.e., research-based) forensic psychology. Even beyond the doctoral degrees, there are opportunities for advanced credentialing (i.e., board certification) for forensic practitioners who wish to distinguish themselves as having specific expertise in forensic psychology.

Despite the remarkable growth in educational and training opportunities in forensic psychology, there is little consensus regarding appropriate training models, curricula, and training goals (see Bersoff et al., 1997, and Krauss & Sales, 2006, for discussions of this problem). The field of forensic psychology continues to broaden in scope and diversity, and it encompasses a wide range of knowledge and skills (e.g., knowledge of legal standards; research skills; assessment, intervention, and consultation skills). As such, training programs must consider the varied roles that may be assumed by forensic psychologists. Although forensic psychology training programs have increased in number, scope, and sophistication in recent years, important questions remain regarding the structure, focus, and goals of these programs.

The following sections will examine the educational and training opportunities available to students and practitioners interested in forensic psychology. After discussing the various training models employed in these programs, we will discuss a proposed model curriculum for doctoral-level programs that would serve to adequately prepare students to become forensic practitioners. Rather than ending the debate regarding appropriate training models, we hope that our proposed curriculum will stimulate further discussion of this important topic.

Undergraduate Training in Forensic Psychology

Many colleges and universities currently offer at least one undergraduate course that covers some aspect of law-psychology, including forensic psychology. Several surveys conducted in the 1990s revealed an increase in the number of undergraduate law-psychology courses being offered

(Ogloff, Tomkins, & Bersoff, 1996), with many high-ranked psychology departments offering at least one law-psychology course (see Bersoff et al., 1997, for a review of this research). Anecdotally, law-psychology courses, particularly courses on forensic psychology, are among the most popular course offerings at the undergraduate level.

Recent years have witnessed an increase in the number and diversity of undergraduate law-psychology courses. Whereas most undergraduate courses offered in years past were survey courses that focused broadly on the intersection between law and psychology, newer courses offer a more detailed and sophisticated examination of circumscribed aspects of law and psychology. For example, undergraduate courses are being offered on child witnesses, the role of psychology in the legal process, and social science applications to the law (see the American Psychology-Law Society Web site [www.ap-ls.org] for a listing of available courses). A more recent development is the offering of undergraduate degrees in forensic psychology. John Jay College of Criminal Justice now offers a Bachelor of Arts in Forensic Psychology that provides training in psychological theory, research methods, and the application of psychological principles to specific areas in the legal system. Of note, employment opportunities are somewhat restricted for those with bachelor-level training in forensic psychology. Although some graduates may find employment in various agencies or institutions, such as police departments, social service agencies, or court systems, these programs typically function to prepare students for additional education/training.

Graduate Training in Forensic Psychology

Despite recent advances in course offerings and curricula in forensic psychology at the undergraduate level, educational and training opportunities for undergraduates interested in forensic psychology are still quite limited. There are considerably more educational and training opportunities in forensic psychology for students in graduate training programs. Depending on one's academic and professional interests, various options are available at both the master's and doctoral levels, and there are also several clinical and nonclinical joint-degree programs available for those who wish to obtain formal training in both law and psychology (see Krauss & Sales, 2006).

According to the *Guide to Graduate Programs in Forensic and Legal Psychology (2007–2008)* [hereinafter referred to as the "*Guide to Graduate Programs*"], which was created by the Teaching, Training, and Careers Committee of the American Psychology-Law Society, there are nearly

50 programs that offer graduate training in forensic psychology (see also Burl, Shah, & DeMatteo, 2008). Broadly speaking, these programs can be categorized by program focus (e.g., clinical forensic psychology, nonclinical legal psychology), training models (e.g., clinical scientist-practitioner, nonclinical scientist-scholar), and degrees awarded (e.g., masters, doctorate, joint-degree) (Krauss & Sales, 2006). On a more practical level, graduate programs in law and psychology, and forensic psychology more specifically, differ quite considerably in terms of length of training. These programs can range from 2 to 7 years postbachelor's degree, with many students taking closer to 10 years to complete joint-degree programs. As the following discussion illustrates, those interested in forensic psychology have a rich variety of graduate training programs from which to choose.

There are roughly 12 programs that offer a master's degree in forensic psychology. Identifying the exact number of programs is difficult, because some programs do not admit students on a regular basis and other programs use terminology that makes it difficult to determine the exact nature of the training. Some of these programs are clinical in nature, while others are nonclinical. In terms of program goals, some programs are designed to prepare students for research or clinical positions within various institutions and professional agencies, such as prisons, juvenile facilities, social service agencies, police departments, probation and parole departments, court systems, and community mental health centers. Other programs seek to prepare students for continued training in PhD programs, with the recognition that graduates of doctoral programs typically have more employment opportunities (see Morgan, Kuther, & Habben, 2004).

There are a variety of educational and training opportunities available in forensic psychology in doctoral programs. A review of published program descriptions and the *Guide to Graduate Programs* reveals that there are approximately 10 programs in which students can obtain a PhD in clinical psychology with a formal concentration (focus or specialty track) in forensic psychology, and there are roughly the same number of PsyD programs that have a formal programmatic emphasis in forensic psychology. In addition, another approximately 10 programs offer a PhD in other areas of psychology, such as social or experimental, with a formal concentration in forensic psychology, legal psychology, or psychology and law. Several of these programs offer a PhD specifically in forensic psychology or legal psychology. Using a less formal approach, students in programs in which forensic psychology is not a core component can obtain relevant training and experience by working with faculty with forensic interests who offer relevant courses and practical experience.

Finally, there are several joint-degree programs (JD/PhD or JD/PsyD) for those students interested in obtaining formal training in both law and psychology. As of this writing, six programs offered JD/PhD (or JD/PsyD) programs in law and psychology: Drexel University, Pacific Graduate School of Psychology in cooperation with Golden Gate Law School, Simon Fraser University in cooperation with the University of British Columbia, University of Arizona, University of Nebraska, and Widener University (JD/ PsyD). In some of these programs, students can pursue clinical or nonclinical psychology training. Of particular note is the University of Nebraska, which offers several joint-degree options, including JD/PhD, JD/MA, and PhD/MLS (i.e., Master's of Legal Studies, which is a nonpractitioner degree requiring the student to complete the equivalent of 1 year of law school education). There are also several schools that permit students to pursue a JD and PhD concurrently, but that offer no formal or coordinated/ integrated curricula in law and psychology.

Students pursuing a PhD or PsyD in clinical psychology (or other applied areas of psychology, such as counseling and school psychology) must complete a 1-year APA-accredited predoctoral internship prior to receiving their degree. A substantial number of internships offer training and clinical/research experience in forensic psychology. A review of the internship programs listed in the Association of Psychology Postdoctoral and Internship Centers (APPIC) directory indicates that 209 (47.1%) of the 444 APA-accredited internship programs in the U.S. report offering a minor rotation in forensic/correctional psychology, and 74 (16.7%) of the 444 programs report offering a major rotation. As these numbers demonstrate, it has become commonplace for clinical internships to offer at least some experience in forensic settings. These internships differ greatly in terms of the range and depth of forensic experiences that are offered. A student interested in general clinical practice might benefit from completing a minor forensic rotation. This clinical experience would, at the very least, offer the beginnings of the knowledge and training necessary to pursue (if desired) later forensic practice and training. Other internships provide students with a forensic rotation with more expansive but still limited forensic activities (e.g., conducting assessments of criminal offenders), while still other internships, such as those offered by the Federal Bureau of Prisons, are entirely forensically focused and provide students with a range of clinical experiences that are specifically directed at forensic assessment, treatment, and consultation among correctional populations. These specialized internships are ideal for those seeking to build upon an existing base of forensic knowledge, experience, and skills. Completing a forensic-focused internship is an effective way to broaden and refine one's repertoire of forensic knowledge and skills, and it can serve as a stepping-stone for obtaining employment in a specific area of forensic psychology. A forensic-focused internship is also useful for those students without significant forensic experience who are seeking to specialize in forensic psychology.

Postdoctoral Training and Continuing Education in Forensic Psychology

There are several forensic psychology training opportunities available at the postdoctoral level, including formal postdoctoral fellowships and Continuing Education programs. Indeed, much of the specialty training in forensic psychology occurs after completion of the doctorate degree (Otto & Heilbrun, 2002). A postdoctoral fellowship in forensic psychology provides intensive, supervised research and/or practical experience. These types of fellowships are ideal for those with previous forensic experience seeking to specialize in a particular area of forensic psychology, or for individuals trained in nonclinical programs seeking to obtain respecialization training in clinical psychology with a forensic emphasis. For those with forensic experience, a forensic postdoctoral fellowship will provide highly intensive, specialized forensic experience (typically 1 or 2 years), and it may serve as a useful way of obtaining employment working with specific forensic populations. Furthermore, postdoctoral fellowships are useful for those seeking licensure as a psychologist because states typically require licensure candidates to obtain a set amount of postdoctoral supervised experience after receiving their doctorate. These fellowships will also meet one component of the training requirements for achieving board certification in forensic psychology (this issue is discussed more fully in the section entitled "Credentialing in Forensic Psychology"). Individuals trained in nonclinical areas of psychology seeking to pursue a career in forensic psychology can use a postdoctoral fellowship to respecialize in clinical psychology with a forensic emphasis. The respecialization process typically requires additional educational and experiential requirements, and it can take several years to complete.

Practitioners can also enhance their forensic knowledge and skills by attending Continuing Education (CE) seminars. CE programs are available on a wide variety of topics within forensic psychology, and they are appropriate for practitioners with varying levels of forensic skills and experience. While some CE programs are one-time 3-hr sessions that provide an introduction to a broad topic area within forensic psychology, other CE programs consist of intensive 3-day workshops that provide highly specific training on a particular assessment instrument or intervention approach. It is important to note that a growing number of states require (either by statute or regulation) that professionals obtain certification through additional training, examination, or both before they can begin conducting forensic evaluations. According to a survey conducted by Farkas, DeLeon, and Newman (1997), nine states required training for certification and 14 states offered or planned to offer formalized training (see Otto & Heilbrun, 2002). Without a doubt, many more states today are likely to require standardized training for professionals to provide a wide array of forensic services.

Credentialing in Forensic Psychology

After obtaining a doctorate and working in the field for several years, individuals seeking to distinguish themselves as having advanced expertise in forensic psychology can seek board certification. Although several boards offer certifications, the most highly respected is the American Board of Professional Psychology (ABPP), which has been incorporated since 1947. Board certification by ABPP is the only post-doctoral specialty certification recognized by the APA Directory (ABFP, 2006). The ABPP offers certification in 13 specialty areas of psychology, including clinical psychology, neuropsychology, and forensic psychology. The credential identifying the highest level of competence in forensic psychology is the Diplomate in Forensic Psychology awarded by the ABFP, which operates as an affiliated member of ABPP. The ABFP awarded the first Diploma in Forensic Psychology in 1978. Eligibility criteria to apply for Diplomate status include the following: a doctoral degree in professional psychology from a program accredited by the APA or Canadian Psychological Association (or listed in the *Doctoral Psychology Programs Meeting Designation Criteria);* licensure or certification at the independent practice level as a psychologist in the State, Province, or Territory in which the psychologist practices; a minimum of 100 hours of formal education, direct supervision, or continuing education in forensic psychology; and a minimum of 1,000 hours of experience in forensic psychology obtained by either the completion of a full-time (at least 1-year) postdoctoral training program in forensic psychology (approved by the American Board of Forensic Psychology) or practice over a minimum period of 4 postdoctoral years. The examination process involves a written and oral examination, with the latter being based on the submission of two practice samples.

Basic Competencies and Training Models in Forensic Psychology

Although forensic psychology training programs have increased in both number and popularity in recent years, there is little consensus regarding which training models are most appropriate. It is important to note that the debate over appropriate training models in forensic psychology is not new (Bersoff, 1999; Bersoff et al., 1997; Freeman & Roesch, 1992; Otto, Heilbrun, & Grisso, 1990; Poythress, 1979). It is also likely that the continuing increase in forensic psychology programs and the increases in interest for forensic training will force the field to reexamine current training models and, perhaps, develop new ones as the field continues to expand. Moreover, as the roles of forensic psychologists continue to expand into new areas of research and practice, it is important that training programs properly prepare future researchers and practitioners by incorporating educational, training, and practical experiences that provide a solid foundation of forensic-related knowledge and skills.

The lack of consensus regarding appropriate training models for forensic psychology may in part reflect the lack of consensus regarding the definition of forensic psychology and the roles that forensic psychologists may properly assume. As previously discussed, some definitions of forensic psychology focus almost exclusively on the clinical aspects of the profession, while other definitions are broader and consider areas of law-psychology research that are not exclusively clinical in nature. For example, although few would dispute that forensic mental health assessments of criminal offenders (e.g., competence to stand trial, mental state at the time of the offense) fall within the scope of forensic psychology, there is less agreement regarding whether psycholegal research conducted by cognitive, social, and experimental psychologists should be considered forensic psychology (e.g., reliability of expert testimony, perceptions of jurors). For the purposes of this article, we will use a broad definition of forensic psychology that encompasses both research and practice.

There are several training goals that may be appropriate in doctoral-level forensic psychology programs (Krauss & Sales, 2006). On the broadest level, students can be trained to become clinicians (i.e., applied forensic psychology), researchers (clinical or nonclinical), or both. Using this broad categorization, we will summarize the three training models predominantly used in doctoral-level psychology and forensic psychology programs.

Some programs train students to become *scientist–practitioners* using the Boulder model. Students in these programs are trained in the science and practice of clinical and forensic psychology, and graduates are particularly well suited for careers in research, academia, and practice. Because a key goal of scientist–practitioner training is scientifically based clinical practice, this model is only employed in clinical and counseling programs. Other clinically based programs follow a *practitioner–scientist* model of training. These programs focus less on research and more on the clinical/ applied aspects of psychology (e.g., PsyD programs). Students in these programs typically receive a heavy dose of practice-focused coursework and experiential training. Finally, some forensic psychology programs prepare students to become *scientist–scholars*, with either a clinical or nonclinical focus. Many of these programs are in areas other than clinical psychology, such as cognitive, developmental, and social psychology, and they train students to engage in empirical research designed to increase our forensic knowledge base and inform public policy. These three categories of training models are admittedly broad and not necessarily mutually exclusive or exhaustive, but they provide some indication of the types of training available in forensic psychology programs.

Given the expanding roles of forensic psychologists, it is admittedly challenging to design a graduate program that provides all of the educational, training, and experiential components needed to properly prepare students for a forensic career. This is particularly true given the time-limited nature of graduate training and differences between clinical and nonclinical forensic psychologists. Nevertheless, we believe it is possible to identify a core set of basic competencies that should be emphasized in doctoral-level forensic psychology training programs. We recognize that the APA Committee on Accreditation (2008) provides programs with considerable leeway when developing training models, provided that the training models cover the core areas identified by the Committee on Accreditation and have curricula designed to achieve their stated goals and objectives. As such, we are not arguing that all programs should blindly adopt our proposed curricula. With that said, we believe our proposed curricula is a solid starting point in terms of identifying core competencies in forensic training programs, and we hope it is useful in stimulating continued discussion on this issue.

Although most specialty training in forensic psychology takes place at the postdoctoral level (Otto & Heilbrun, 2002), we chose to focus on doctoral-level training programs because our proposed curriculum is designed to offer foundational skills that will prepare graduates to (1) engage in practice without additional training (after obtaining licensure, if needed), or (2) seek more advanced training and experience at the postdoctoral level. At a minimum, it would seem that forensic practitioners should obtain training and experience in the following areas:

1) *Substantive psychology*, including core knowledge of basic areas of psychology central to one's major area of study (e.g., clinical, developmental, experimental, cognitive);

2) *Research design/methodology and statistics*, designed to prepare students to conduct research and/or be informed consumers of research;
3) *Conducting research*, consisting of performing original empirical research that culminates in a doctoral dissertation (except in PsyD programs);
4) *Legal knowledge*, including foundations of the legal system, sources of law, legal research, relevant civil and criminal case law, criminal and civil procedures relevant to forensic practice, legal rules and professional guidelines relating to expert testimony, and substantive law in relevant areas (e.g., competence to stand trial, mental state at the time of the offense);
5) *Integrative law-psychology knowledge*, including introductory/overview foundational courses on forensic psychology, and knowledge of research in psycholegal areas such as eyewitness testimony, jury decision-making, admissibility of scientific testimony, forensic assessment measures and techniques, and the treatment of offender populations;
6) *Ethics and professional issues*, relating to general research and practice (e.g., *Ethical Principles of Psychologists and Code of Conduct* (APA, 2002)), and forensic research and practice (e.g., *Specialty Guidelines for Forensic Psychologists* (Committee on the Revision of the Specialty Guidelines for Forensic Psychology, 2006)); and
7) *Clinical forensic training* (for those in clinical training programs), including forensic mental health assessments, forensically based interventions, and/or forensic consultation.

We believe that a focus on these core areas would adequately prepare doctoral-level students for basic forensic practice. These training elements were identified through several means, including a review of the *Guidelines and Principles for Accreditation of Programs in Professional Psychology* (2008) promulgated by the APA's Committee on Accreditation, which informed the broad and general training components of the curriculum, a review of existing forensic psychology training curricula, and a review of relevant literature and guidelines on forensic training. The forensic components overlap to some extent with the training goals identified by the Forensic Specialty Council (2007) in its educational and training guidelines, although the elements in the above proposal are narrower in scope and designed to train graduate students as opposed to residents.

Of note, the first three elements would likely fall under the "broad and general" rubric identified by the APA's Committee on Accreditation (2008), meaning that they are foundational skills not specific to forensic psychology. According to the Committee on Accreditation (2008), broad and general training provides students with knowledge in scientific psychology and the foundations of practice, which prepares them for entry-level practice in professional psychology. As such, forensic psychology training programs would typically need to focus on adding the remaining four elements to their curricula. If these topic areas are covered through a combination of course work (required and elective), research experience, and practical experience, the inclusion of these elements should not lengthen the overall course of study for doctoral students.

We reviewed the curricula for the roughly 35 doctoral or joint degree programs that offer training in forensic psychology to get an idea of how many programs incorporate the forensic components of the proposed curricula (i.e., not elements 1, 2, and 3, which fall under the "broad and general" rubric). Unfortunately, outdated posted curricula, ambiguous course titles and descriptions, and unclear training foci complicated this task, so the results should be treated with caution. Our review reveals that roughly 40% of the programs report offering one or more courses that would fall under the "Legal Knowledge" component, which includes courses on legal procedures, civil or criminal law, and mental health law. All of the programs report offering courses that would fall under the "Integrated Law-Psychology Knowledge" component, which includes introductory/overview foundational courses on forensic psychology and courses on forensic assessment and intervention. Of note, however, most of these programs offer introductory courses, with roughly 60% offering a forensic assessment course and 30% offering a forensic intervention course. Although all programs report offering a general ethics course, only three programs report offering a course on "Ethics and Professional Issues" specifically related to forensic psychology. The descriptions of the practical training were often unclear, but it appears that nearly all clinical PhD and PsyD programs offer practical experience in forensic psychology, which would satisfy the "Clinical Forensic Training" component.

Overall, these findings suggest that most programs offer course work that would satisfy the forensic components of the proposed curricula. However, less than half of the programs report offering legal knowledge coursework, and a large number of programs satisfy the integrated law-psychology component by offering an introductory course. Finally, only three programs have curricula that would satisfy all four forensic components of the proposed curricula (mostly due to the small number of programs that report offering ethics courses in forensic psychology).

It is important to note that only those forensic psychology training programs that are housed within clinical, counseling, or school psychology programs are eligible for APA accreditation. Stand-alone forensic programs are not currently accredited by the APA, and it remains an open empirical question whether such accreditation would serve to increase the quality of training that students receive and resulting forensic practice.

A recent development, however, is the accreditation of postdoctoral fellowships in forensic psychology. A set of educational and training guidelines prepared by the Forensic Specialty Council (which includes representatives from the American Psychology-Law Society, American Board of Forensic Psychology, and American Academy of Forensic Psychology) in 2007 were recently endorsed by the Council of Specialties in Professional Psychology. As such, postdoctoral fellowships in forensic psychology can apply for APA accreditation.

Conclusion

Given the increasing involvement of forensic psychologists in the civil and criminal justice systems, and the increasing numbers of students who are studying forensic psychology, it is critical that existing training programs adequately prepare future practitioners to assume a variety of roles. Just as traditional PhD programs in clinical psychology (at least those that adhere to the Boulder model) prepare students to function in a variety of roles (e.g., researcher, clinician, academic), it is essential that forensic psychology training programs prepare students to assume several different roles. Rather than creating specialists, forensic psychology training programs would be better advised to provide students with a foundational level of competence in a variety of core component areas, which is consistent with the guidelines promulgated by the APA's Committee on Accreditation (2008) in terms of preparing students for entry-level practice in professional psychology. Specialization in a particular area of forensic psychology would seem to be best achieved at the postdoctoral level after the student has obtained a core set of competencies.

References

American Board of Forensic Psychology. (2006). *ABFP brochure*. Retrieved May 8, 2008, from http://www.abfp.com/brochure.asp.

American Psychological Association. (2002). Ethical principles of psychologists and code of conduct. *American Psychologist, 57*, 1060–1073.

American Psychological Association Committee on Accreditation. (2008). *Guidelines and principles for accreditation of programs in professional psychology*. Washington, DC: Author.

American Psychology-Law Society. (2008). *Guide to graduate programs in forensic and legal psychology (2007–2008)*. Southport, NC: Author.

Bartol, C., & Bartol, A. (2006). History of forensic psychology. In I. B. Weiner & A. K. Hess (Eds.), *The handbook of forensic psychology* (3rd ed.) (pp. 3–27). Hoboken, NJ: Wiley.

Bersoff, D. N. (1999). Preparing for two cultures: Education and training in law and psychology. In R. Roesch, S. D. Hart, & J. R. P. Ogloff (Eds.), *Psychology and law: The state of the discipline* (pp. 375–401). New York: Kluwer Academic/Plenum Publishers.

Bersoff, D. N., Goodman-Delahunty, J., Grisso, J. T., Hans, V. P., Poythress, N. G., & Roesch, R. G. (1997). Training in law and psychology: Models from the Villanova conference. *American Psychologist, 52*, 1301–1310.

Brigham, J. (1999). What is forensic psychology anyway? *Law & Human Behavior, 23*, 273–298.

Burl, J., Shah, S. B., & DeMatteo, D. (2008, August). *Graduate training in forensic psychology: A survey of training models*. Poster session to be presented at the 116th Annual Convention of the American Psychological Association (APA), Boston, MA.

Committee on the Revision of the Specialty Guidelines for Forensic Psychology. (2006). *Specialty guidelines for forensic psychologists* (second official draft). Retrieved December 13, 2006, from http://www.ap-ls.org/links/SGFP%20 January%202006.pdf.

Farkas, G. M., DeLeon, P. H., & Newman, R. (1997). Sanity examiner certification: An evolving national agenda. *Professional Psychology: Research & Practice, 28*, 73–76.

Forensic Specialty Council. (2007). *Education and training guidelines for forensic psychology*. Available at http://umassmed.edu/uploadedFiles/ET%20Guidelines %20final.pdf.

Freeman, R. J., & Roesch, R. (1992). Psycholegal education: Training for forum and function. In D. K. Kagehiro & W. S. Laufer (Eds.), *Handbook of psychology and law* (pp. 567–576). New York: Springer-Verlag.

Goldstein, A. M. (2007). Forensic psychology: Toward a standard of care. In A. M. Goldstein (Ed.), *Forensic psychology: Emerging topics and expanding roles* (pp. 3–41). Hoboken, NJ: Wiley.

Grisso, T. (1987). The economic and scientific future of forensic psychological assessment. *American Psychologist, 9*, 831–839.

Grisso, T. (1998). *Instruments for assessing understanding and appreciation of Miranda rights*. Sarasota, FL: Professional Resource Press.

Grisso, T. (2003). Advances in assessments for legal competencies. In T. Grisso (Ed.), *Evaluating competencies: Forensic assessments and instruments* (2nd ed.) (pp. 1–20). New York: Kluwer.

Grisso, T., & Appelbaum, P. S. (1998). *MacArthur Competence Assessment Tool for Treatment (MacCAT-T)*. Sarasota, FL: Professional Resource Press.

Heilbrun, K. (2001). *Principles of forensic mental health assessment*. New York: Kluwer Academic/Plenum Press.

Heilbrun, K. (2000). *Petition for the recognition for a specialty in professional psychology*. Submitted on behalf of the American Board of Forensic Psychology and the American Psychology-Law Society to the American Psychological Association.

Heilbrun, K., Marczyk, G. R., & DeMatteo, D. (2002). *Forensic mental health assessment: A casebook*. New York: Oxford University Press.

Hess, A. K. (2006). Defining forensic psychology. In I. B. Weiner & A. K. Hess (Eds.), *The handbook of forensic psychology* (3rd ed.) (pp. 28–58). Hoboken, NJ: John Wiley & Sons.

Jenkins v. United States, 307 F.2d 637 (D.C. Cir. 1962).

Krauss, D. A., & Sales, B. D. (2006). Training in forensic psychology: Training for what goal? In I. B. Weiner & A. K. Hess (Eds.), *The handbook of forensic psychology* (3rd ed.) (pp. 851–871). New York: Wiley.

Marczyk, G., DeMatteo, D., Kutinsky, J., & Heilbrun, K. (2008). Training in forensic assessment and intervention: Implications for principles-based models. In R. Jackson (Ed.), *Learning forensic assessment* (pp. 3–31). New York: Routledge (Taylor & Francis Group).

Melton, G., Petrila, J., Poythress, N., & Slobogin, C. (2007). *Psychological evaluations for the courts: A handbook for mental health professionals and lawyers* (3rd ed.). New York: Guilford.

Monahan, J., Steadman, H., Appelbaum, P., Grisso, T., Mulvey, E., Roth, L., et al. (2005). *Classification of violence risk (COVR)*. Lutz, FL: Psychological Assessment Resources.

Morgan, R. D., Kuther, T. L., & Habben, C. J. (Eds.) (2004). *Life after graduate school in psychology: Insider's advice from new psychologists*. New York: Psychology Press.

Munsterberg, H. (1908). *On the witness stand: Essays on psychology and crime*. New York: Doubleday.

Ogloff, J. R. P., Tomkins, A. J., & Bersoff, D. N. (1996). Education and training in law/criminal justice: Historical foundations, present structures, and future developments. *Criminal Justice & Behavior, 23*, 200–235.

Otto, R. K., & Heilbrun, K. (2002). The practice of forensic psychology: A look toward the future in light of the past. *American Psychologist, 57*, 5–18.

Otto, R. K., Heilbrun, K., & Grisso, T. (1990). Training and credentialing in forensic psychology. *Behavioral Sciences & the Law, 8*, 217–231.

Poythress, N. G. (1979). A proposal for training in forensic psychology. *American Psychologist, 34*, 612–621.

Quinsey, V. L, Harris, G. T., Rice, M. E., & Cormier, C. A. (2006). *Violent offenders: Appraising and managing risk* (2nd ed.). Washington, DC: American Psychological Association.

SECTION II

Theoretical Perspectives

CHAPTER THREE

Becoming Criminal: Theoretical Perspectives on the Development and Desistance of Criminality

Nahanni Pollard

Becoming Criminal

Why do some individuals become criminals? What factors in their development lead to persistence or desistance from crime? The developmental approach to criminality seeks to answer questions regarding the development of offending behavior with age, and whether causal factors can be identified that influence an individual's antisocial or criminal progression. Most developmental theories observe offending behavior as a dynamic process over the life course, influenced by the interplay between psychological, social, and biological factors. Seeing the development, persistence, and desistance of offending behavior on a trajectory allow theorists to identify and isolate those factors that appear to solidify an individual's propensity toward crime, or protect one against it. Although a relatively new approach in criminology, it has strong intersections with developmental psychology and the primary tenets of many of the prominent theories. From the legacy of the psychological approach to development rose the criminological focus on how behaviors develop over time, the role of cognition and attachment, and the psychological development and desistance of criminal behavior. This chapter will introduce the reader to some of the primary themes and theorists in developmental psychology and then explore their contribution toward the newer conceptions of the developmental approach to criminality.

Developmental Psychology

The evolution of the developmental approach to criminality shares its origins with developmental psychology. This branch of psychology concerned itself primarily with examining the roots of human development, and the unique psychological changes that may occur in individuals over their life span. This perspective began with studies aimed at examining childhood and infant development, but has gone on to expand into adolescent and adult developmental stages. Numerous perspectives and research foci are encompassed within the developmental approach, such as cognitive development, moral development, and how the social, personality, and emotional development of individuals influence other areas of their life and change over their lifetime. Although not initially focused solely on delinquent or criminal development, this is increasingly becoming a concentration for psychologists involved in this area. Many early theories pointed to the features that may influence aggression or antisocial behavior, and how psychological processes influence this. Using the perspectives and theories from developmental psychology, criminal psychology began to examine the science behind how criminal behavior is acquired, maintained, modified, and ended. Like developmental psychology, criminal psychology examined these facets through the lens of cognitive, learning, moral, and psychoanalytic theories.

Many of the classical developmental theories that formed the basis for the developmental approach to criminality sought to explain development in children by examining the stages wherein they acquire knowledge, morality, cognitive functioning, and social development. Among the most prominent in this area are Jean Piaget's Stage Theory, and more narrow approaches such as Kohlberg's stages of moral reasoning and Bowlby's Attachment Theory. Psychoanalytic theory is often cited as one of the precursors to the theoretical development of the field and, along with other cognitive and learning theories, is often considered a "grand theory."

The theories that form the base for developmental psychology often propose a stage-like development to personality, morality, and cognitive aptitude, as well as antisocial behavior. These stages, when examined as per criminality, started to show some distinctive patterns of pathways or trajectories to criminality, with some offenders starting in early childhood and others beginning in adolescence or later. These trajectories appeared to support the notion that the pathways would dictate the direction that the individual would take in their criminal development, and as such, remain true to many of the earlier theories of developmental psychology, which focus on the progression through stages of human development. This expansion of the developmental approach has led the psychological study of crime somewhat away from a sole focus on personality traits and more toward an interactive cognitive focus and the changes therein over the life span (Bartol & Bartol, 2008).

Theoretical Base

Psychoanalytic Theories

One of the earliest examples of the developmental approach is attributed to the work of Sigmund Freud. His work focused primarily on the development of personality and how early experiences and development influenced behavior later on in life. Freud believed that an individual's personality was largely developed by the age of five and was formed through a serious of childhood stages whereby the child would work through fixations on certain erogenous areas and battle their unconscious desires and conscious notions of reality. Central to his theory were the concepts of the Id, Ego, and Superego (Elliott, 2002).

The Id represented the innate pleasure-seeking center of the individual, from which the Ego and Superego formed. The Id focused on primary purposes such as eating, drinking, and eliminating wastes. The Ego, on the other hand, represented reasonable and sensible thinking, which developed as the child learned they could always simply operate according to their Id. Through punishment or other consequences of Id-driven behavior, the reality of the child is slowly brought into focus by the Ego, which regulates behavior and determines when and where certain behavior is appropriate. The Superego represents the third stage of development, whereby the child starts to internalize moral standards of behavior and conceptions of right and wrong (Elliott, 2002).

Freud conceptualized the early personality as being largely led by the Id, which was the pleasure-seeking energy of the individual and a largely unconscious "drive." The ego, on the other hand, developed slowly through the constant conflict of the Id and the Superego. Much of Freud's ideas regarding adult personality and certain psychological dysfunctions could be traced back to "fixation" in any particular stage of development.

For example, a person who may have become fixated at the oral stage of development by not resolving the conflict between the Id and Superego at that stage may manifest that conflict by seeking oral stimulation such as eating, drinking, or smoking. Alternatively, if the individual was able to successfully resolve the conflict between their conscious rationality and unconscious desires, then a healthy personality would develop (Elliott, 2002). Although psychoanalysis is often used as an example of the first developmental theories, modern conceptions eschew the notion that developmental theories are really psychoanalytic in nature (Gilmore, 2008).

Cognitive Theories

Two of the most prominent theorists focusing on cognitive development were Jean Piaget and Lawrence Kohlberg. Similarly to other developmental approaches, they examined the trajectory or pathways toward intellectual maturity and moral reasoning in children, and proposed specific stages through which infants, children, and adults would travel over their life span to reach full cognitive development.

Piaget's primary focus was on uncovering the process of cognitive development in infants and children. As one of the most well-known theorists in the area, his work contributed enormously to developmental theory in general. He hypothesized four stages of cognitive development, starting in infancy and carrying on through adolescence and adulthood. The first stage, termed "sensorimotor," had six sub-stages, and focused primarily on motor skills as demonstrative of intelligence. As infants and children do not yet hold symbols or speech, Piaget posited that their interactions with their world were largely physical, and knowledge and intelligence developed through this physical interaction. By the end of this stage, basic verbal communication was beginning to develop, and heralded the child into the second stage, or "pre-operational" stage. This stage encompassed development from toddlerhood through to young children. Language was being developed and allowed children to start to understand and create symbols and other schema for their experiences. However, although imagination was developing, thinking was done in a largely nonlogical way and was focused on the personal needs of the child (ego-centered). In the concrete operational stage (elementary and early adolescence), the child's ego-driven thinking diminished, and logic and operational thinking further developed. Children were able to grasp more abstract concepts and began to be able to empathize. The formal operational stage represented the final stage in cognitive development, whereby individuals were capable of the logical use of symbols to demonstrate abstract concepts. Intellectual grasp of the nuances of concepts also symbolized this final stage of development (Huitt & Hummel, 2003). While Piaget did conceptualize the development of moral thinking, his typology tended to place that particular aspect of cognitive development into one of two stages. Prior to the concrete operational stage, he asserted that children tended to view moral decisions as unchangeable and absolute. Once the ability to think abstractly developed (after about the age of 11), this thinking became somewhat more malleable as children began to understand that rules could be broken or changed. This recognition changed children's moral thinking to incorporate notions of intention into their consideration, rather than simply rule breaking (Crain, 1985). The conceptions of the development of morality became more expansive under the work of Kohlberg.

Kohlberg's contribution focused on how morality is acquired and developed in childhood, and how an individual's development at different stages of their life will inform how they make moral decisions and what information is considered in the process of those decision (Crain, 1985). Similarly to Piaget, Kohlberg presented a series of moral stages of development that children go through. The first level, preconventional morality, presumes that children see rules (and thus morality) as fixed and unchanging, and identify what is moral or immoral according to what is likely to be punished. Although encompassing two stages whereby children may start to see some nuances to what is right or wrong, the binding principle in preconventional morality is the limited ability to see beyond the individual scenario. The second level, or conventional morality, also is comprised of two sublevels that see children move their moral thinking, from concrete notions of right and wrong to a finer appreciation of people's intentions as being what determines moral versus immoral behavior. The viewpoint expands beyond the individual, first to the family and/or community, then on to society as a whole. Level three, or post-conventional morality, represents the highest level of moral development. The notion of basic human rights and social morality enters into the individual's conceptions, and an understanding of what it takes to keep society functioning is factored into decisions (Crain, 1985).

Unlike some later developmental psychologists who asserted various pathways and stages, Kohlberg's conceptions suggested that the development through the moral stages was unidirectional and invariant. Work building on Kohlberg's ideas, most notably from his student Carol Gilligan (1987), would clarify how these conceptions may need to be modified for gender differences, and how the original schemas were biased toward male moral development. Although many of her claims were not supported in later research, Kohlberg's theory was expanded, and a sixth stage ("respect for persons") was incorporated in an attempt to incorporate the ethic of care that was primarily thought as a representation of female moral development (Crain, 1985).

Attachment Theory

Originally developed by John Bowlby and continued by Mary Ainsworth, the theory of attachment focuses on the role that early relationships between child and caregiver can have on ongoing emotional and psychological development. The central tenets see the child's need for attachment to a caregiver as being essential for both physical survival and intellectual and emotional development. Children with a secure attachment to a caregiver will develop the ability to explore and learn from their environment, as the base (caregiver) gives them the confidence and security from which to do so. However, establishing a secure attachment relies heavily on parental affection, support, and interaction. Children whose experiences with their parents are missing some or all of those elements may develop one of several subtypes of an insecure attachment. Children who experience an avoidant or ambivalent attachment style from their caregiver will often be subject to inconsistent or nonexistent comfort from that caregiver, and may develop reactions such as rebelliousness or anxiety in future situations (Ainsworth, Blehar, Waters, & Wall, 1978). These children may become isolated emotionally, or they may demonstrate an unhealthy need for the caregiver in all situations, showing their lack of confidence and self-esteem. The role of attachment may arguably be one of the most important developments in a child's life, and can have devastating effects on future behavior, personality, and delinquency. A dismissive, or avoidant, attachment style can be extremely detrimental to development in children, and has been shown to be related to an impairment in the development of a positive empathic affect toward others (Mikulincer et al., 2001), and significant overlap with personality disorders (Brennan & Shaver, 1998). This may have dire consequences for the nature and type of offending as well, as it was shown that an insecure attachment style was significantly associated with sexual offending (Lyn & Burton, 2004), the development of dysfunctional anger, and served as a predictor of trait anger in adolescence and adulthood (Troisi & D'Argenio, 2004).

While insecure attachment alone has not been shown to be the sole determinant of deviant behavior later on, combined with a myriad of other negative psychological and social variables, it can serve as an initiator along the pathway to future psychopathological aggression (Sroufe, Carlson, Levy, & Egeland, 1999). In particular, neglected or abused children are at a greater risk of suffering from antisocial behavior, sustained suspicion of others, and social withdrawal in adolescence, thereby exacerbating the chance of positive social and interpersonal bonding and attachment (Finzi, Cohen, Sapir, & Weizman, 2000). These behavioral problems have been shown to persist from childhood to adolescence (Moss, St-Laurent, Rousseau, & Parent, 1999). Children from families with a history of alcoholism also appear to be at a greater risk of developing an insecure and/or avoidant attachment style and, in turn, put them at greater risk for development of an alcohol use disorder themselves (Vungkhanching, Sher, Jackson, & Parra, 2004).

Developmental Factors in Delinquency and Criminality

The theories surrounding the development of criminality are relatively recent in conception, owing much of their lineage to the early perspectives on cognitive and moral development in children. One of the more important lessons taken from developmental psychology was the importance of viewing the life span of the individual when attempting to explain the reasons behind behaviors. Rather than simply focusing on the act or immediate behavior, the tenets behind the developmental approach prompted researchers to try to isolate factors that may be present far earlier in development that could shed light on later development. Much as developmental psychologists saw early experiences and development as crucial to the end result in adulthood, early criminological theorists began to view childhood and adolescence as invaluable to the study of the development of criminality. This interest in the development of criminality and criminal careers owes much to the early work of Eleanor and Sheldon Glueck.

The Gluecks' study focused on comparing the criminal activity of a matched sample of 500 delinquent and 500 nondelinquent boys who were born in Massachusetts in the 1930s. A key finding in their work identified a number of traits associated with antisocial behavior in the individuals, including ambivalence, defiance, destructiveness, distrust of authority, extraversion, impulsiveness, inadequate social skills, mental instability, narcissism, sadism, self-assertiveness, and suspicion. Generally, they asserted that families with lax discipline combined with erratic/threatening punishment, poor supervision, and weak emotional ties between parent and child generated the highest probability of persistent delinquency. This early observation that key psychological traits developed in childhood could be predictive of adult antisocial behavior prompted a great deal of research on what additional psychological variables may be associated with future delinquency, but also how those develop in children.

This observation, coupled with the understandings from developmental psychology, has led to the proliferation of concepts of risk factors for future antisocial behavior in children. Figuring prominently in both psychological and criminology theories are childhood psychological disorders such as Conduct Disorder and Attention-Deficit Hyperactivity Disorder, and the influence seen on antisocial, delinquent, or criminal behavior later on in life. Conduct Disorder, when linked to disrupted neural development, has shown to manifest as significant impairments to several executive functioning measures (Toupin, Dery, Pauze, Mercier, & Fortin, 2000). Of specific concern is that research has found a link between conduct disorders in childhood or adolescence and antisocial personality disorder in adult life (Dowson, Sussams, Grounds, & Taylor, 2001; Mannuzza, Klein, Abikoff, & Moulton, 2004). This association has held even independently of associated adverse family and social factors (Hill, 2003) and in the absence of a diagnosis of ADHD (Martens, 2000). Mental disorders and crime were also strongly associated among males with a history of childhood conduct problems (Kratzer & Hodgins, 1997). Even in the absence of a diagnosis of CD, a diagnosis of ADHD can lead to a diagnosis of adult antisocial personality disorders (Mannuzza et al., 2004). However, this link is even stronger when there is the presence of both disorders, even when controlling for intervening variables (Simonoff et al., 2004). While ADHD and CD are separate constructs, the presence of both in childhood or adolescence has shown a greater risk of development of antisocial behaviors, substance abuse, and psychopathy (Abramowitz, Kosson, & Seidenberg, 2004; Cote, Tremblay, Nagin, Zoccolillo, & Vitaro, 2002; Flory & Lynam, 2003).

Evolution of Developmental Approaches to Criminality

Developmental psychology and its primary theories attempt to explain the evolution of human personality, morality, and cognition through several lenses. Some approaches attest that development progresses through a stage-like development, while others focus on whether children are born with innate mental structures or whether they are shaped and refined through systems of learning, experience, and moral development. Developmental approaches to criminality have shared many of these perspectives and applied these psychological theories to the specific development of criminal behavior. "Developmentally inclined criminologists take as their null hypothesis that antisocial behavior has to develop and is not simply the manifestation of some underlying or primordial condition" (deLisi, 2005, p. 52).

One of the most well-known typologies for the development of criminal behavior is Terrie Moffitt's dual-taxonomy approach. Similar to other developmental psychology perspectives, this theory examines trajectories of behavior from early adolescence through to adulthood and the factors that appear to be influential in the development of long-term criminality. Other perspectives within the developmental approach to criminality examine the development of criminal behavior as adhering to one of two notions, either a state-dependence approach or a population heterogeneity viewpoint. Developmental theories, according to Siegel (2004) are either "latent-trait" theories, also known as population heterogeneity approaches, or "life-course" theories, or state-dependence approaches. *State-dependence* theories view an individual's propensity for criminal offending as highly dependent upon their individual attachment to society by way of prosocial bonds that develop over the life course. The dynamic nature of these theories acknowledges that social and life circumstances, however, may solidify or break these bonds, thereby inducing the continuance or desistance of criminality over time. A principal theory that represents this approach is the *Age-Graded Theory of Informal Social Control*, developed by Robert Sampson and John Laub. The alternate approach, the *population heterogeneity* perspective, views criminality as due to a "master" or latent trait identifiable in an individual generally soon after birth. This latent trait will dictate the propensity the individual has for offending, and may present a risk factor for criminality throughout the individual's development unless tempered with appropriate protective factors within the family or social circle. However, even with ample protective factors, theories in this area posit that this master trait will always be present within the individual, and thus will always be a factor in their decision to engage in criminal activity. The principal theory under this approach is the *General Theory of Crime*, proposed by Michael Gottfredson and Travis Hirschi.

Pathways and Trajectories

Moffitt's Dual Taxonomy

The Dunedin Multidisciplinary Health and Human Development Study, a cohort study led by Terrie Moffitt and Avshalom Caspi, followed more than 1,000 children born in Dunedin, New Zealand, between 1972 and 1973. The results of this study led Moffitt to develop the dual-taxonomic theory, which asserted that there were two primary groups of offenders, and two distinct offending trajectories. The first group of offenders, the life-course persisters, was hypothesized to engage in antisocial behavior early in life, offend more while active, and be unlikely to desist. Moffitt (1993) contended that this group should be more versatile in the types of crimes they commit, will offend on their own more often than within a group, and whose criminality will include increased participation in crimes of violence and/or fraud. The cause of their involvement, according to Moffitt, lies in the interaction between neuropsychological deficits and disadvantaged familial and socioeconomic environments.

The second group of offenders, the adolescent-limited, is hypothesized to concentrate their involvement in antisocial behavior to the adolescent period. Limited to acts that symbolize adult privilege and prestige (i.e., smoking, vandalism, alcohol and drug use, minor theft, status offenses), adolescent-limited antisocial behavior is caused by the modeling of deviant peer affiliations and the maturity gap (i.e., strain) experienced throughout the teenage years. According to Moffitt, the two groups of offenders are discernible according to one feature: the age of onset. For Moffitt, life-course persisters experience onset at an earlier age in the life course than do their adolescent-limited counterparts, such that age of onset becomes the defining feature of the two groups (Moffitt, 1993).

Moffitt examined the development of both groups with a particular focus on what factors appear in early childhood and adolescence that lead to their particular "style" of offending. Those who Moffitt (1993) identifies as the life-course persisters often present with severe neurological and/or psychological impairments, and are often considered very difficult children. These neuropsychological impairments can affect psychological traits and higher-order functioning, resulting in hyperactivity, inattention, conduct disorder, and aggression. These traits, understandably, may lead these children to have difficulty with familial social relations and discipline, or worse, their negative familial influences (or even abuse) may exacerbate these problems. This may then lead to rejection by peers and poor school performance, and may ultimately leave the child with few avenues with which to learn prosocial bonds. Recognizing their rejection and poor performance both at home and in social situations may leave the child feeling powerless or without control, as their neuropsychological deficits may make academic achievement feel impossible, as well as social performance exceedingly difficult. The second factor necessary in deviance is that the individual must be provoked to experience a negative emotion, likely one of shame, humility, or embarrassment, such that the thought of deviance is thought to be sufficient to rebut against the rebuff. Perhaps this may explain the early onset of deviance for those LCP offenders, as they may feel they have few cognitive options for successful mediation of instances of childhood teasing, ridicule, or punishment, and may experience more situations such as this due to their poor social skills and low academic achievement. Adolescent-limited offenders, on the other hand, may have the cognitive skills to ward off internalizing ridicule or rejection, and therefore, may succumb to criminality during those years only when rebellion and rejection of adult control become the norm (Moffitt, 1993).

In general, Moffitt's position that early onset is the defining feature between two distinct groups has met with a certain amount of support. Farrington & West (1993) agree that early onset is very important to the examination of chronic offending, and they assert that those criminals who begin their offending careers early on (in childhood or adolescence) will often become socially isolated, and will continue in their involvement in crime and live unsuccessful lives. Many studies now accept that this pivotal dissection between early onset and late onset occurs at the age of 14. Those initiating offending prior to this age showed a pattern of multiple offenses, high rates of imprisonment, and a great deal of variety in offense types (less specialization) relative to late-onset offenders (Mazerolle, Brame, Paternoster, Piquero, & Dean, 2000). In addition, statistical analysis showed that age 14 was significant in predicting how chronic the individuals were, how dangerous they were, and how often they would offend (deLisi, 2006).

However, some examinations revealed that more specificity may be warranted in Moffitt's taxonomy. Although the results from one study supported the assertion that early-onset offenders received higher overall seriousness scores for their offenses, there appeared to be gender differences insofar as these patterns held for males, but not for females. This led the researchers to question whether Moffitt's taxonomy is really a theory about boys, and that it does not hold very well for girls (Piquero & Chung, 2001). The assertion that life-course-persistent offenders may more appropriately be limited to boys was supported by research conducted decades earlier, which indicated that boys showed a similar pattern insofar as earlier convictions tended to translate into higher rates of offending (West & Farrington, 1973). Even subsequent research by Moffitt and others has supported this assertion somewhat, as they found early aggressive or violent behavior to be predictive of later antisocial behavior for boys, but not for girls (Broidy et al., 2003). Silverthorn and Frick (1999), finding a similar pattern, concluding that girls instead showed a similar pattern to early-onset boys, but only later on in adolescence, which led them to label this trajectory as a "delayed-onset" pathway.

A more strong refutation comes from Gottfredson (2005), who holds that even the most serious offenders eventually desist from crime and will "age out" with the rest of the offending population. As Moffitt (1993) attests that age is unrelated to offending for highly active offenders, Gottfredson (2005) takes the recognition of the "aging out" as direct evidence against Moffitt's taxonomy. In no uncertain terms, he asserts, "It now seems that we can safely dispense with the notion of the 'lifecourse persisters' in our theories of criminality" (Gottfredson, 2005, p. 53). However, despite a recognition that overall desistance may be high for the majority of individuals, some researchers have found a small yet distinct group that do not appear to be on the pathway to desistance (Piquero et al., 2001). In this study, only 7% of the population showed such a trend, but this group was identified as an obvious class of non-desisters—or, chronic offenders. This finding was also supported by a recent study that identified a small group of persistent offenders, making up less than 2% of the sampled population, whose offending trajectory remain relatively flat, at about 2 to 2.5 convictions per year from age 30 onward (Blokland & Nieuwbeerta, 2005).

Current conceptions of Moffitt's approach have demonstrated the utility in theorizing four trajectories rather than the classic dual approach. Others have explored trajectories from a slightly different angle, and proposed different trajectories or pathways to the development of criminality, which will be discussed below.

Further Pathways and Taxonomies

Several other theories have discussed the development of criminality with specific focus on the pathways that children and youth follow, and the resultant impact on the severity and duration of delinquent or criminal behavior. Many of the observations are similar to those of Moffitt, although not necessarily based on her work. Specifically, this grouping of theories tends to organize according to risk factors that are present early on in a child's life, and to discuss whether those risk factors will propel that child onto a pathway leading to more serious and/or long-term offending.

Similarly to Moffitt's taxonomy is Patterson's Coercion Theory, which also suggested that the development of criminality could be isolated into one of two trajectories. The differentiation was largely due to the age of onset, much like Moffitt's conception, and saw the early-starters as more likely to be exposed to negative or authoritarian parenting and thereby more likely to develop poor self-esteem, suffer peer rejection, and harbor anger and other mental health problems such as depression. Patterson asserted these individuals could generally be identified as early as grade four, and would often experience an arrest or police contact by age 14 (deLisi, 2005). Alternatively, late starters exhibited delinquent or criminal behavior primarily in response to peer influence or the lack of parental supervision. These individuals, according to Patterson, would generally not develop into long-term or prolific offenders as their early-onset peers were more prone to do (deLisi, 2005).

West and Farrington's Cambridge Study in Delinquent Development became the basis for Farrington's later conception of criminal development. This longitudinal study focused on examining criminality over the life course while attempting to isolate those predictive and risk factors that may explain an individual's criminality. Many psychological factors were found to be influential in the development of criminality, including the existence of impulsivity and low intelligence, which were often exacerbated by more social factors such as their family environment, parental supervision, and general social environment (West, 1969; West & Farrington, 1973). Farrington termed his theory the Integrated Cognitive Antisocial Potential model, and focused on the concept of Antisocial Potential (AP), which assumes the translation from antisocial potential to antisocial behavior to depend on cognitive processes that take into account situations and targets (Farrington, 2005). This model placed individuals into one of two categories—those with long-term AP, and those with short-term AP. The group with long-term AP tended to come from poor families who exhibited poor socialization. In addition, these individuals often had lower IQ and tended to show more school failure. Short-term AP individuals may not suffer from the same deficits, but may increase their AP temporarily in response to certain situational factors or provocations.

Unlike Moffitt's two-pathway model, Loeber and his colleagues formulated a three-pathway model to examine the development of delinquency and antisocial behavior. The three categories include children and adolescents with overt behavior problems, those with covert behavior problems, and those with authority figure problems. The overt pathway sees a trajectory toward serious violent offenses, with the initiation of more minor offenses exhibiting aggression such as bullying, followed by more overt aggression and violence toward others as the individual develops. Alternatively, the covert pathway sees an individual use deceit and surreptitious behavior on an increasingly serious scale to obtain goods or property. These individuals may start with some relatively minor behaviors, such as lying or shoplifting, and progress to more serious forms of theft, such as fraud or burglary. The authority avoidance pathway, unlike the other two, is more attributed to defiant behaviors to those in an authority position, such as parents or teachers, and may primarily manifest as truancy or running away without serious criminal activity (Blanc & Loeber, 1998). Generally all three pathways share a similarity insofar as the behaviors unique to each tend to develop along a sequence that increases in severity. However, youth may present behavior on more than one pathway, and some may even demonstrate behaviors present in all three pathways. Those individuals who display behaviors along multiple pathways are thought to develop into the most frequent offenders, particularly when the behavior includes both overt and covert behaviors (Blanc & Loeber, 1998).

Life-Course/State-Dependence Theories

Developmental theories in this group adhere to similar central notions, notably that criminality is influenced by individual characteristics, social experiences, and economic and environmental factors. All postulate that criminal involvement changes over time as a result of these changes in circumstances, and life transitions often dictate whether individuals will participate, persist, or desist in offending. A theme resonant in these and others that may reasonably fit within this category is that of attachment. Attaching to prosocial groups, institutions, and subsequently ideas may be the basis for whether an individual turns down a path of delinquency and offending, or whether that individual follows a prosocial path and avoids these negative pitfalls. Sampson and Laub's theory focuses on the changing importance of attaching to prosocial institutions throughout the life course, beginning with the family and moving through school, work, and peer groups. Milestones, such as marriage and a career, may provide the social control necessary for many to desist from offending, as the investment in these institutions may provide the necessary deterrence to engage in offending. Similarly, Thornberry's theory also espouses the importance of the development of prosocial bonds to family, school, and peer groups. However, his theory seeks to explain how antisocial behaviors may be internalized early on, thereby influencing the peer and social attachments that an individual has. Should these attachments be antisocial in nature, the individual's already-internalized antisocial sentiments are reinforced, thereby making it far more difficult to reinvigorate prosocial bonds later in life (Sampson & Laub, 1993).

Sampson and Laub's Age-Graded Theory of Informal Social Control

Sampson and Laub's state-dependence theory is a framework that explains childhood antisocial behavior, adolescent delinquency, and crime in early adulthood, and that incorporates the notion of "life events" or milestones in development that are thought to be relevant to offending trajectories (Sampson & Laub, 1993). These milestones in life, according to the theory, have the ability to exert informal social control on an individual, thereby steering them away from crime when the bonds are strong. Life events such as marriage and steady employment are thought to be two of the factors that may inhibit crime, by increasing commitment to these prosocial institutions and a crime-free lifestyle (Laub & Sampson, 2001). In particular, Sampson and Laub attest to the impact of early development on the individual's bond to society prior to any of these life events. They focused on parenting styles, advocating for steady supervision, warmth and affection, and consistent discipline—features analogous to attachment theories in general. They also attested to the importance of emotional attachment to parents in childhood, attachment to school and peers in adolescence, and attachment to institutions of marriage, military service, and employment in adulthood (Sampson & Laub, 1993). However, participation in crime and deviance may weaken or sever these bonds to society, and the informal social controls that they exhibited will no longer protect the individual. Changing life events, therefore, are thought to be the driving force behind offending, and are marked by changes to the informal social control structure and thus changes in offending participation, frequency, and duration.

One of the strongest correlates of desistance and support for the state-dependence perspective was found to be "relationship quality." The researchers (Massoglia and Uggen, 2007) found that a quality relationship increases the odds of subjective desistance (whereby the offender deems himself as moving toward desistance) by 72%, reference group desistance (whereby the offender deems himself as desisting in comparison to his peers) by 89%, behavioral desistance (self-report) by 102%, and official desistance (official records) by more than 250%. "The estimate for relationship quality is thus the strongest in magnitude and the most consistent predictor across the measures of desistance considered in our analysis" (Massoglia & Uggen, 2007, p. 98). How these turning points affect the trajectory of offending in general, and desistance specifically, include psychological and structural change to the offenders' lives. These correlates, such as marriage, the military, reform school, and neighborhood, change all work to provide a point of dissection (or "knifing off") between the past and the present; provide supervision, monitoring, and opportunities for social support and growth; bring structure to activities; and provide an opportunity for identity transformation (Sampson & Laub, 2003; Sampson & Laub, 2005a, 2005b). However, subsequent research has cautioned that it is not simply the effect of marriage per se on desistance, but rather the effect that life event has on peer associations. Instead, with either psychological or personal changes, Warr (1998) suggested that marriage takes away from the amount of time an offender has to spend with peers, and therefore it lowers the opportunities for offending. It is furthered argued that these life events, such that they provide this "knifing off," should be viewed on a continuum rather than a strict amputation. "For instance, a new spouse may impede one's ability to go to one's favored drinking establishments on a Friday night, but marriage does not sever this possibility completely or permanently" (Maruna & Roy, 2007, p. 120).

Later reflections on their own work produced some slight modifications on their theory, particularly in reference to marriage. Instead of conceiving of marriage as a single turning point in life, they reiterated the milestone of marriage as being far more malleable and dynamic, in order to reflect the reality that people enter and exit marriage through time—often several times (Sampson & Laub, 2005a).

Further Development of State-Dependence and Interaction Theories

Terrence Thornberry's Interaction Theory focuses on an individual's interactions with social groups and institutions and how those interactions shape behavior, and it shares perspectives from social learning theories of development and attachments to social and familial institutions such as Sampson and Laub. Thornberry outlined this perspective as one that espouses the importance of attachment—both to other people, such as parents and peers, and to social institutions, such as school or work. However, these attachments will be significant during different stages of an individual's life. In early years, attachment to parents will provide the most important avenue for the development of prosocial bonds, thereby protecting the individual from delinquent or antisocial behavior, similarly to what Bowlby and Ainsworth have posited. As the child develops, the attachment to family will become less central, and influences from peers and their social world will begin to supersede the familial bonds in terms of importance and influence. By adulthood, the attachment to their conventional world, including their own family, will guide their behavioral choices (deLisi, 2005).

Delinquency, according to Thornberry, results from a weakening of the social constraints over the conduct of the individuals (Thornberry, 1987). This lack of constraint will result in the internalization and development of an antisocial belief system consistent to which they will subsequently seek out others who hold similar views. In this way, the interactions are bidirectional. By seeking out deviant peer groups, the individual who has already internalized delinquent values will thereby have those values reinforced and will reinforce those of the others in the peer group. This reinforcement will then have the effect of further weakening the social bonds acting as constraints on the individual, and thus will reinforce the further progression into delinquency. The return to conventional and prosocial networks then becomes very difficult later on in life, and the individuals continue to reinforce their deviant lifestyle over time. Life events are also important in this theory, as often stressful or distressing life events such as the separation of parents, family financial crises, or even the breakup of a meaningful relationship may motivate the individual to seek out deviant peer relationships and commit antisocial behaviors (deLisi, 2005; Thornberry, 1987).

Similar themes of the development of prosocial bonds over time are also present in the Social Development Model of Richard Catalano and J. David Hawkins (and later Weis). The central tenets of the model attempt to integrate social control, social learning, and structural models by examining a child's ability to develop attachment to others, commitment to conforming behavior, and belief in the conventional order. Similarly to Sampson and Laub's concepts, if these abilities are well developed in the child, they will be able to resist antisocial activity and prevent delinquent behavior. However, numerous risk factors within the family, the community, and other socializing institutions may inhibit this ability to form the necessary attachment and commitment within the child, and therefore will not be able to resist delinquency. Areas that have low income, high levels of disorganization, inadequate educational institutions, and families under stress are at a significant disadvantagewhen it comes to adequate socialization and attachment formation, similar to the risk factors identified through Farrington's theory. Their theory also asserts that both antisocial and prosocial opportunities for socialization will be present during the child's life, and the development of both will come from the same socializing agents. In this way, youth that have been primarily exposed to prosocial behaviors from agents are more likely to exhibit those prosocial behaviors later on in life. The same holds for the alternative, whereby children and youth primarily exposed to negative or antisocial agents and behaviors will be more likely to exhibit those behaviors later in life. Therefore, it is the opportunities that are present in a child's life for prosocial bonding that become vitally important to the avoidance of delinquent or criminal behavior later on (Catalano & Hawkins, 1996).

Latent Trait

The "latent trait" view holds that there is some personal attribute or characteristic present in all people that controls their inclination or propensity to commit crime. Gottfredson and Hirschi (1990) argued that "low self-control" was the "master" trait, the root cause of which was inadequate child-rearing. Although widely considered a general theory rather than a developmental theory of crime, the inclusion of the psychological variable of self-control and the appearance of attachment early on in life makes this theory relevant to the examination of developmental psychological approaches.

Gottfredson and Hirschi's General Theory of Crime

The General Theory of Crime (Gottfredson & Hirschi, 1990) proposes a theory of offending that hypothesizes that one's self-control will be the principal barrier to involvement in crime. As they define it, self-control is a trait that is established in early childhood and, once established, is stable over time. Self-control in their conception includes such elements as impulsivity, self-centeredness, inability to persevere in a line of activity, and an inclination to participate in risky/thrilling activities. A fundamental prediction of Gottfredson and Hirschi's theory is that low self-control will manifest itself in a number of ways, including participation in crime. Specifically, they hypothesize that individuals with low levels of self-control will be more likely to begin offending early in life (i.e., early onset), offend more frequently while active, and desist later in life than their high-self-control counterparts (Gottfredson & Hirschi, 1990). The child's level of self-control, according to the theory, is evident through specific characteristics such as their propensity to engage in risk-taking behavior, the inability to delay gratification, and a very low tolerance for frustration. Of particular interest is the cause of this low self-control. As the theory recognizes that there will be wide variations in individuals' levels of self-control, these can be primarily attributed to parenting practices that do not provide the kind of supervision and discipline that is required in order for the child to learn self-modulation of control. Gottfredson and Hirschi squarely place the blame on what they consider ineffective child-rearing. They assert that in order to be effective and teach the child self-control, parents must, "(1) monitor the child's behavior; (2) recognize deviant behavior when it occurs; and (3) punish such behavior" (Gottfredson & Hirschi, 1990, p. 97).

Recent studies have found support for Gottfredson and Hirschi's (1990) model, demonstrating that variables relating to levels of disinhibition, such as egotism, callous hostility, impulsiveness, authority opposition, and societal skepticism, were all considered in line with constructs of low self-control. These variables were shown to significantly hinder desistance and predict desistance in the sample (Morizot & Le Blanc,

2007). More support for Gottfredson and Hirschi's (1990) theory came from Moffitt herself in a recent work. Her group's objective was to directly test self-control on all aspects of the criminal career—participation, frequency, persistence, and desistance. Self-control was significantly associated with all of these aspects and, perhaps most importantly, was able to distinguish between desisters and persisters, with desisters exhibiting higher levels of self-control (Piquero, Moffitt, & Wright, 2007).

By Gottfredson and Hirschi's own admission, their theory has left much to be explored; but the soul of their argument has been the source of much debate. While some studies have supported their view of self-control as the defining feature of criminality, others have found that the population heterogeneity hypothesis simply does not stand up to rigorous testing. Some have found that a single attribute, such as self-control, does not account for the entirely of an individual's offending experience (Golub, 1990; Sullivan, McGloin, Pratt, & Piquero, 2006). Others have added that although self-control may play a part in offending, there also appears to be a significant contribution by state-dependence theorists, such as demonstrated in the tenets of Sampson and Laub (Bushway, Brame, & Paternoster, 1999).

From Initiation to Desistance

One area that has not been well explored until very recently in either the developmental psychology approach or developmental theories of crime has been the process of desistance. Many of the psychological theories of development focused on early childhood and adolescence, with an emphasis on what started children down a path of delinquency and problem behavior. However, little was done on the opposite end of the spectrum to investigate how and why they ever stepped off the path. Developmental theorists in criminology have started to examine what explains this, and they continue to use their conceptions of stages or trajectories of development to guide propositions. Research into desistance has examined what factors may influence an offender's decision to exit the criminal realm, either by choice or by duress. The examination of the correlates of desistance may provide useful insights into the onset of offending, as it has been found that often the risk factors for offending are the opposite of the correlates of desistance (Armstrong & Britt, 2002; Loeber & LeBlanc, 1990).

The existence of research appears to be increasing in recent years, possibly due to the influence of the criminal careers approach (Brame, Bushway, & Paternoster, 2003; Kazemian, 2007; Laub & Sampson, 2001; Sampson & Laub, 2003). Part of the prior absence in the literature may have been due in part to the difficulty with both defining and measuring the phenomenon. The definition of desistance is variable at best, haphazard at worst, and measuring the existence of a concept that is marked by the absence of the activity under examination is exceedingly difficult. In addition to the logistical challenges in investigating this phenomenon, there are also differing theoretical perspectives that rule the desistance forum; namely Gottfredson and Hirschi's (1990) population heterogeneity view, Sampson and Laub's (2003) state-dependence perspective, and Moffitt's (1993) dual-taxonomy approach.

A primary assertion of Moffitt's taxonomy is that for the life-course persisters, their offending will show a pattern of persistence, rather than desistance. Some research did not support this hypothesis and found that "desistance processes are at work even among active offenders and predicted life-course persisters" (Sampson & Laub, 2003, p. 301). This conclusion was also reached in work done the year prior, which called into question the existence of Moffitt's LCP group, as the evidence pointed toward a trajectory of desistance for all offenders under study (Piquero, Brame, Mazerolle, & Haapanen, 2002). The evidence appears to support the notion that aging out of crime is still considered the norm, with even the most active offenders desisting or reducing their offending at a certain point (Blokland & Nieuwbeerta, 2005). However, although the rates of overall desistance are high—as much as 92% of the sample population (Piquero et al., 2001), that still leaves a small percentage that may not be on the trajectory to desistance. Notably, this study found that 7.2% of the population did not appear to be on a trajectory toward zero offenses, and asserted that this was the only obvious class of non-desisters in their sample. This finding was also supported by a recent study that identified a small group of persistent offenders, making up less than 2% of the sampled population, whose offending trajectory remain relatively flat, at about 2 to 2.5 convictions per year from age 30 onward (Blokland & Nieuwbeerta, 2005). Moffitt's conception of the life-course persistent offender as coming from some severe psychological and/or neurological deficits may point to the persistence hypothesis, as without resolution, those preceptors to criminality would most likely continue to be at play.

To support Gottfredson and Hirschi's population-heterogeneity approach, some research indeed found that a singular feature—self-control—predicts all aspects of criminal development, including desistance; however, the researchers caution that this does not mean it is the only predictor, but should be considered impactful across all dimensions (Piquero et al., 2007). Aging, or maturation, tends to be the strongest correlate with desistance from offending (Rand, 1987; Shover & Thompson, 1992), as the age-crime curve clearly shows a steady decline in offending for older age groups.

Sampson and Laub's theory discussed the nature of desistance fairly openly, whereby the life events were hypothesized to "knife off" offending at different points in one's development. Therefore, their theory in essence is one more of desistance than initiation. These life events, however, are not always static and can illicit change in either direction—from offending to desistance, or vice versa. These changes in life circumstances, such as employment, marriage, and substance abuse, can alter the direction of offending trajectories (Piquero et al., 2002), and being divorced, for instance, can boost offending behavior (Blokland & Nieuwbeerta, 2005). These changes, in combination with persistent individual differences, are related to crime over the life course.

Interestingly, other studies have found that the correlates such as fatherhood and college education showed no effect on desistance. Contradictory to Sampson and Laub (2003), military service was not found to have any effect on desistance, either (Rand, 1987). The effects of these correlates appears to continually change as the research emerges (Morizot & Le Blanc, 2007), however, as even Sampson and Laub have modified their position on the effect of marriage such that they do not view it as a static turning point, but rather as a potential causal force that operates dynamically (Sampson & Laub, 2005a). Moderate support was found for social control variables akin to those espoused by Laub and Sampson (1993), although these were primarily age-dependent. For instance, employment was a significant predictor of desistance, but only emerging adulthood. Affiliation with prosocial friends was also found to be significant, but this effect was exhibited only in adolescence (Morizot & Le Blanc, 2007).

Some research has expressly showed support for state dependence while forwarding evidence that rejects population heterogeneity, such as the work of Bushway, Brame, and Paternoster (1999), who found that their models did not uncover any evidence that stable individual differences were the primary source of variation in offending and desistance over the life span; rather, they conclude that some kind of state-dependence process is at work (Bushway et al., 1999). Ezel (2007) also came to a similar conclusion, as his results indicated that events in early adulthood played a more important role in prediction of risk in later adulthood, rather than individual differences that were identifiable in the juvenile years.

The knowledge about the desistance process is limited and often contradictory. Both developmental psychology and developmental criminology have focused on creating theories to explain initiation of behavior and the early development of lifetime patterns, but have not turned that focus toward the end of the cycle and what factors may influence psychological or personality changes later in life. If the same processes are at work for both initiation and desistance, then theories may be modified to become more holistic and to have better explanatory power. However, if the processes or underlying psychology behind desistance is shown to be subject to a completely different set of assumptions, then developmental theories must be expanded beyond the childhood and adolescent years to explain that development continues later on in life.

Concluding Considerations

Developmental criminology continues to examine those features that appear to determine whether an individual will develop antisocial or criminal tendencies over their life span. As evidenced in their propositions about human development, they borrow heavily from the developmental psychology approach with the incorporation of cognition, morality, attachment, modeling, and learning from childhood to adolescence and beyond. Both disciplines have aided in the explanation for why some individuals become criminal, and why some develop antisocial or delinquent behavior patterns. The challenge now will be to examine why some stop displaying those behavior patterns, and what processes are at work. If theorists posit only a set number of stages that are linear in nature, then what can explain movement through stages or a reversion to earlier stages if that is shown to be the case? For instance, does morality ever backslide? Is it possible for an individual to have a strong moral center, thereby theoretically protecting them from criminal offending, but then experience a life event that causes them to revert to previous levels of moral understanding? If long-term trajectories of antisocial behavior may be attributable to psychological or neurological deficits early in life, what occurs when those are addressed or resolved? The developmental approach, in both psychology and criminology, may benefit from further appreciation of the changing nature of human development over the entire life span. While some propensities and likelihoods may be observable in early childhood or adolescence, further research may highlight that this is neither concrete nor immutable.

References

Abramowitz, C., Kosson, D., & Seidenberg, M. (2004). The relationship between childhood attention deficit hyperactivity disorder and conduct problems and adult psychopathy in male inmates. *Personality and Individual Differences, 36*(5), 1031–1047.

Ainsworth, M. D., Blehar, M., Waters, E., & Wall, S. (1978). *Patterns of attachment: A psychological study of the strange situation*. Hillsdale, NJ: Lawrence Erlbaum Associates.

Armstrong, T. A., & Britt, C. L. (2002). *Exploration of the correlates of specialization and escalation: Final report*. U.S. Department of Justice. Washington, DC: National Institute of Justice.

Bartol, C. R., & Bartol, A. M. (2008). *Introduction to forensic psychology: Research and application* (2nd ed.). New York: Sage Publications.

Blanc, M. L., & Loeber, R. (1998). Developmental criminology updated. *Crime and Justice, 23*, 115–198.

Blokland, A. J., & Nieuwbeerta, P. (2005). The effects of life circumstances on longitudinal trajectories of offending. *Criminology, 43*(4), 1203–1240.

Brame, R., Bushway, S. D., & Paternoster, R. (2003). Examining the prevalence of criminal desistance. *Criminology, 41*(2), 423–448.

Brennan, K., & Shaver, P. (1998). Attachment styles and personality disorders: Their connections to each other and to parental divorce, parental death and perceptions of parental caregiving. *Journal of Personality, 66*(5), 835–878.

Broidy, L. M., Nagin, D. S., Tremblay, R. E., Bates, J. E., Brame, B., Dodge, K. A., et al. (2003). Developmental trajectories of childhood disruptive behaviors and adolescent delinquency: A six-site, cross-national study. *Developmental Psychology, 39*(2), 222–245.

Bushway, S., Brame, R., & Paternoster, R. (1999). Assessing stability and change in criminal offending: A comparison of random effects, semiparametric, and fixed effects modeling strategies. *Journal of Quantitative Criminology, 15*(1), 23–61.

Catalano, R. F., & Hawkins, J. D. (1996). The social development model: A theory of antisocial behavior. In J. D. Hawkins (Ed.), *Delinquency and crime: Current theories* (pp. 149–197). New York: Cambridge University Press.

Cote, S., Tremblay, R., Nagin, D., Zoccolillo, M., & Vitaro, F. (2002). Childhood behavioral profiles leading to adolescent conduct disorder: Risk trajectories for boys and girls. *Journal of the American Academy of Child and Adolescent Psychiatry, 41*(9), 1086–1094.

Crain, W. (1985). Kohlberg's stages of moral development. In *Theories of Development* (pp. 118–136). New York: Prentice Hall.

deLisi, M. (2005). *Career criminals in society*. Thousand Oaks, CA: Sage Publications.

deLisi, M. (2006). Zeroing in on early arrest onset: Results from a population of extreme career criminals. *Journal of Criminal Justice, 34*, 17–26.

Dowson, J., Sussams, P., Grounds, A., & Taylor, J. (2001). Associations of past conduct disorder and personality disorders in "non-psychotic" psychiatric inpatients. *European Psychiatry, 16*(1), 49–56.

Elliott, A. (2002). *Psychoanalytic theory: An introduction* (2nd ed.). Durham, NC: Duke University Press.

Ezel, M. (2007). The effect of criminal history variables on the process of desistance in adulthood among serious youthful offenders. *Journal of Contemporary Criminal Justice, 23*(1), 28–49.

Farrington, D. (2005). *Integrated developmental and life-course theories of offending*. New Brunswick, NJ: Transaction Publishers.

Farrington, D. P., & West, D. J. (1993). Criminal, penal and life histories of chronic offenders: Risk and protective factors and early identification. *Criminal Behavior and Mental Health, 3*, 492–523.

Finzi, R., Cohen, O., Sapir, Y., & Weizman, A. (2000). Attachment styles in maltreated children: A comparative study. *Child Psychiatry & Human Development, 31*(2), 113–128.

Flory, K., & Lynam, D. (2003). The relation between attention deficit hyperactivity disorder and substance abuse: What role does conduct disorder play? *Child and Family Psychology Review, 6*(1), 1–16.

Gilligan, C. (1987). Moral orientation and moral development. In E. Kittay & D. Meyers (Eds.), *Women and moral theory* (pp. 19–33). Totowa, NJ: Rowman & Littlefield.

Gilmore, K. (2008). Psychoanalytic development theory: A contemporary reconsideration. *Journal of the American Psychoanalytic Association, 56*(3), 885–907.

Golub, A. (1990). *The termination rate of adult criminal careers*. School of Urban and Public Affairs. Pittsburgh, PA: Carnegie-Mellon University.

Gottfredson, M. R. (2005). Offender classifications and treatment effects in developmental criminology: A propensity/event consideration. *The Annals of the American Academy of Political and Social Science, 602*, 46–56.

Gottfredson, M. R., & Hirschi, T. (1990). *A general theory of crime*. Stanford, CA: Stanford University Press.

Hill, J. (2003). Early identification of individuals at risk for antisocial personality disorder. *British Journal of Psychiatry, 182*, S11–S14.

Huitt, W., & Hummel, J. (2003). Piaget's theory of cognitive development. In *Educational Psychology Interactive*. Valdosta, GA: Valdosta State University.

Kazemian, L. (2007). Desistance from crime: Theoretical, empirical, methodological, and policy considerations. *Journal of Contemporary Criminal Justice, 23*(1), 5–27.

Kratzer, L., & Hodgins, S. (1997). Adult outcomes of child conduct problems: A cohort study. *Journal of Abnormal Child Psychology, 25*(1), 65–81.

Laub, J. H., & Sampson, R. J. (2001). Understanding Desistance from Crime. In M. Tonry (Ed.), *Crime and justice: A review of the research* (Vol. 28, pp. 1–69). Chicago: University of Chicago Press.

Loeber, R., & LeBlanc, M. (1990). Toward a developmental criminology. In M. Tonry & N. Morris (Eds.), *Crime and justice: A review of research* (Vol. 12). Chicago: University of Chicago Press.

Lyn, T., & Burton, D. (2004). Adult attachment and sexual offender status. *American Journal of Orthopsychiatry, 74*(2), 150–159.

Mannuzza, S., Klein, R., Abikoff, H., & Moulton, J. (2004). Significance of childhood conduct problems to later development of conduct disorder among children with ADHD: A prospective follow-up study. *Journal of Abnormal Child Psychology, 32*(5), 565–573.

Martens, W. H. (2000). Antisocial and psychopathic personality disorders: Causes, course, and remission—a review article. *International Journal of Offender Therapy and Comparative Criminology, 44*(4), 406–430.

Maruna, S., & Roy, K. (2007). Amputation or reconstruction? Notes on the concept of "knifing off" and desistance from crime. *Journal of Contemporary Criminal Justice, 23*(1), 104–124.

Massoglia, M., & Uggen, C. (2007). Subjective desistance and the transition to adulthood. *Journal of Contemporary Criminal Justice, 23*(1), 90–103.

Mazerolle, P., Brame, R., Paternoster, R., Piquero, A., & Dean, C. (2000). Onset age, persistence, and offending versatility: Comparisons across gender. *Criminology, 38*(4), 1143–1172.

Mikulincer, M., Gillath, O., Halevy, V., Avihou, N., Avidan, S., & & Eshkoli, N. (2001). Attachment theory and reactions to others' needs: Evidence that activation of the sense of attachment security promotes empathic responses. *Journal of Personality and Social Psychology, 81*(6), 1205–1224.

Moffitt, T. E. (1993). Adolescence-limited and life-course persistent antisocial behavior: A developmental taxonomy. *Psychological Review, 100*, 674–701.

Morizot, J., & Le Blanc, M. (2007). Behavior, self, and social control predictors of desistance from crime: A test of launch and contemporaneous effect models. *Journal of Contemporary Criminal Justice, 23*(1), 50–71.

Moss, E., St-Laurent, D., Rousseau, D., & Parent, S. (1999). Attachment of school age children and the development of behavioral troubles. *Canadian Journal of Behavioural Science–Revue Canadienne des Sciences du Comportement, 31*(2), 107–118.

Piquero, A. R., Blumstein, A., Brame, R., Haapanen, R., Mulvey, E. P., & Nagin, D. S. (2001). Assessing the impact of exposure time and incapacitation on longitudinal trajectories of criminal offending. *Journal of Adolescent Research, 16*(1), 54–74.

Piquero, A. R., Brame, R., Mazerolle, P., & Haapanen, R. (2002). Crime in emerging adulthood. *Criminology, 40*(1), 137–168.

Piquero, A. R., & Chung, H. L. (2001). On the relationships between gender, early onset and the seriousness of offending. *Journal of Criminal Justice, 29*, 189–206.

Piquero, A. R., Moffitt, T. E., & Wright, B. E. (2007). Self-control and criminal career dimensions. *Journal of Contemporary Criminal Justice, 23*(1), 72–89.

Rand, A. (1987). Transitional life events and desistance from delinquency and crime. In M. E. Wolfgang, T. P. Thornberry, & R. M. Figlio, *From boy to man, from delinquency to crime* (pp. 134–161). Chicago: University of Chicago Press.

Sampson, R. J., & Laub, J. H. (1993). *Crime in the making: Pathways and turning points through life*. Cambridge, MA: Harvard University Press.

Sampson, R. J., & Laub, J. H. (2003). Life-course desisters? Trajectories of crime among delinquent boys followed to age 70. *Criminology, 41*(3), 301–337.

Sampson, R. J., & Laub, J. H. (2005a). A life-course view of the development of crime. *Annals of the American Academy of Political and Social Science, 602*, 12–45.

Sampson, R. J., & Laub, J. H. (2005b). When prediction fails: From crime-prone boys to heterogeneity in adulthood. *The Annals of the American Academy of Political and Social Science, 602*, 73–79.

Shover, N., & Thompson, C. Y. (1992). Age, differential expectations and crime desistance. *Criminology, 30* (1), 89–104.

Siegel, L. (2006). *Criminology* (9th ed.). Belmont, CA: Thomson-Wadsworth.

Silverthorn, P., & Frick, P. J. (1999). Developmental pathways to antisocial behavior: The delayed-onset pathway in girls. *Development and Psychopathology, 11*, 101–126.

Simonoff, E., Elander, J., Holmshaw, J., Pickles, A., Murray, R., & & Rutter, M. (2004). Predictors of antisocial personality—continuities from childhood to adult life. *British Journal of Psychiatry, 184*, 118–127.

Sroufe, L., Carlson, E., Levy, A., & Egeland, B. (1999). Implications of attachment theory for developmental psychopathology. *Development and Psychopathology, 11*(1), 1–13.

Sullivan, C. J., McGloin, J. M., Pratt, T. C., & Piquero, A. R. (2006). Rethinking the "norm" of offender generality: Investigating specialization in the short-term. *Criminology, 44*(1), 199–233.

Thornberry, T. P. (1987). Toward an interactional theory of delinquency. *Criminology, 25*(4), 863–892.

Toupin, J., Dery, M., Pauze, R., Mercier, H., & Fortin, L. (2000). Cognitive and familial contributions to conduct disorder in children. *Journal of Child Psychology and Psychiatry and Allied Disciplines, 41*(3), 333–344.

Troisi, A., & D'Argenio, A. (2004). The relationship between anger and depression in a clinical sample of young men: The role of insecure attachment. *Journal of Affective Disorders, 79*(1–3), 269–272.

Vungkhanching, M., Sher, K. J., Jackson, K. A., & Parra, G. R. (2004). Relation of attachment style to family history of alcoholism and alcohol use disorders in early adulthood. *Drug and Alcohol Dependence, 75*(1), 47–53.

Warr, M. (1998). Life-course transitions and desistance from crime. *Criminology, 36*(2), 183–216.

West, D. (1969). *Present conduct and future delinquency: First report of the Cambridge Study in Delinquent Development*. New York: International Universities Press.

West, D. J., & Farrington, D. P. (1973). *Who becomes delinquent? Second report of the Cambridge Study in Delinquent Development*. London: Heinemann Educational Books.

CHAPTER FOUR

The Psychophysiology and Neuroanatomy of Antisocial Behavior

Max M. Loomans, Joke H. M. Tulen, and Hjalmar J. C. van Marle

Introduction

For a better understanding of the concepts of psychopathy and antisocial personality disorder (ASPD), we need to find an explanation for the behavioral symptoms these disorders exhibit. Psychophysiological measurements are frequently used as peripheral indices of central brain processes that are thought to be ultimately responsible for behavior (Lorber, 2004). In this chapter, behavioral symptoms of psychopathy and ASPD will be explained in terms of psychophysiological and brain-related (neuro-imaging) research findings.

At present, a simple integration of research findings is difficult because most of the available psychophysiological and neuro-imaging studies are found to be heterogeneous in their use of research populations. The subjects studied mostly consisted of convicted offenders with either psychopathy or ASPD, or persons with high aggression levels. Also, various definitions of psychopathy, different psychopathy characteristics, different indicators of aggression, and ASPD-diagnostic criteria have been used, making an integration of findings a challenge. Yet, the advantage of such an integrated approach is clear, since this will provide us with information about the similarities, but also on the differences in etiology between the ASPD and the psychopathy concept.

In the following paragraphs, we will first present the relevant behavioral issues involved in ASPD and psychopathy. We will then describe several theories that integrate psychophysiological and neuroanatomical findings in relation to behavior, briefly summarize psychophysiological research findings related to ASPD and psychopathy, and subsequently review the studies about the different brain areas correlated with aggressive, antisocial, and psychopathic behavior, resulting in an integrated view of antisocial behavior as a final common pathway of different cognitive and affective brain functions.

Antisocial Personality Disorder and Psychopathy

ASPD and psychopathy uniquely stand together in the toll they exact on society. For this reason, these syndromes have long been the focus of many researchers in the scientific field to shed light on the underlying principles. Over 200 years ago, Philippe Pinel (1801) gave an account on patients "who at no period gave evidence of any lesion of understanding, but who were under the dominion of instinctive and abstract fury, as if the faculties of affect alone had sustained injury" (Patrick, 2007). Pinel named this syndrome *manie sans delire* ("insanity without delirium"). In the years to follow, many researchers made an account on this syndrome (e.g., Rush, 1812; Pritchard, 1835; Koch, 1891; and Kraepelin, 1904). The construct was, however, further defined by Cleckley (1941) in his *The Mask of Sanity*. Cleckley presented a variety of patients to illustrate the personality and behavioral characteristics of patients he viewed as psychopathic. Cleckley considered psychopathy to be a highly distinctive clinical syndrome with a unique underlying etiology. Cleckley described 16 criteria on which our recent insights on psychopathy are still based, with an affective deficiency as a main component. Cleckley's construct served as the basis for Hare's Psychopathy Checklist–Revised (PCL-R; Hare, 1991, 2003). The PCL-R is now the dominantly used assessment instrument for psychopathy in research studies as well as in clinical assessments.

The ASPD construct initially followed Cleckley's construct of psychopathy (second edition of the *Diagnostic and Statistical Manual of Mental Disorders*; DSM-II; APA, 1968). In search for a higher reliability, the ASPD construct focused more and more on behavioral indicators such as delinquency, stealing, aggressiveness, and impulsivity in childhood and adulthood. The result was a highly reliable diagnostic tool, but without the key affective criteria in Cleckley's construct of psychopathy. Although the construct of the ASPD was revised in the DSM-IV, no effort was made to increase the representation of the core affective-interpersonal features of psychopathy. Since the publication of the DSM-III (APA, 1980), the relationship between the ASPD and psychopathy has been controversial (Hare, Hart, & Harpur, 1991).

In behavioral aspects, psychopathy predicts many of the same negative outcomes as ASPD, including treatment failure (Reiss, Meux, & Grubin, 2000; Shine & Hobson, 2000), involvement in violent and nonviolent offenses (Hare & McPherson, 1984), recidivism (Harris, Rice, & Cormier, 1991) and substance abuse or dependence (Smith & Newman, 1990). However, in clinical and research populations most individuals who meet diagnostic criteria for ASPD do not meet current criteria for psychopathy (Hare, 2003; Hildebrand & de Ruiter, 2004).

Theories: Integrating Psychophysiology, Neuroanatomy, and Antisocial Behavior

Two main models are generally used to explain the deviant neural systems in antisocial behavior: the somatic marker hypothesis, based on the work of Damasio (1996) and the violence inhibition mechanism, based on the work of Blair (1995) and Weber, Habel, Amunts, and Schneider (2008). The somatic marker hypothesis suggests that prefrontal damage leads to impaired decision-making abilities and an incapability of activating autonomic somatic states linked to the anticipation of reward and punishment. The neurobiological equivalent of this theory is the ventromedial prefrontal cortex (Critchley, Elliott, Mathias, & Dolan, 2000) and is based on a person's capabilities to generate and experience emotions, which present themselves as changes in the present physiological condition. These changes are recorded in the brain as alterations ("markers") in somato-sensory structure activation (Bechara, Damasio, Damasio, & Lee, 1999). Damasio (1996) stated that these changes in physiological state help us in decision making by taking previous negative experiences into account. The person will remember the conditioned unpleasant feeling in prior experiences and will eliminate this choice as an option. This results in a reduction of the number of options and an efficient availability of the necessary resources to evaluate the remaining choices. In regard to antisocial behavior, the processing of the number of options will be disrupted. Negative outcomes of antisocial behavior will not be integrated as a somatic marker and will remain a viable option. A known physiological parameter like the low resting heart rate in antisocial subjects compared to controls (Ortiz & Raine, 2004) could represent this incapability to activate an autonomic somatic state. The somatic marker theory also includes other brain structures involved in regulating emotion and psychophysiological responses such as the amygdala (Bechara et al., 1999), hypothalamus, cingulated cortex, and insula (Davidson, Putnam, & Larson, 2000).

The violence inhibition system is based on generating an aversive emotional reaction when confronted with a distress cue. It is based on the principles of empathy, and the neurobiological equivalent of this theory is the amygdala (Weber, Habel, Amunts, & Schneider, 2008). For example, the viewing of a sad, distressed face will be seen as a submissive sign and will stop the aggressive behavior. The violence inhibition mechanism is proposed to be activated when a distress cue is present. This will trigger autonomic arousal and an empathic response, which inhibits the distressing behavior. In psychopathy, the violence inhibition model is malfunctioning. Dolan and Fullam (2006) showed an impairment in the processing of sad and fearful faces in psychopathic adults. When a distress cue is not processed, the behavior will not be inhibited.

These two theories are explanatory models, which help to explain antisocial behavior, but cannot be seen as an all-embracing model. Weber et al. (2008) state that psychopathy is associated with brain abnormalities in a prefrontal-temporo-limbic system (prefrontal cortex, amygdala, hippocampus, superior temporal gyrus, and corpus callosum) and that the ventromedial prefrontal cortex and the amygdale are highly interconnected. Psychopathy is suggested to be associated with multiple neurobiological dysfunctions (Mitchell et al., 2006).

A third different model proposed by Thayer and Lane (2000) is not an explanatory model for antisocial behavior, but sheds more light on the interaction between the neuro-anatomy, psychophysiology, and psychopathy/ASPD. It links psychological processes with peripheral physiological responses via a set of common neural structures. In this model, the link between heart rate variability (HRV) and the central nervous system (CNS), specifically the central autonomic network (CAN), is considered. Porges (2007) has emphasized the role of HRV in relation to attentional and emotional regulation, and suggested that a higher HRV is associated with more flexible adaptation to environmental challenges. Regarding psychopathy, Ishikawa, Raine, Lencz, Bihrle, & LaCasse (2001) showed that successful psychopaths who had never been convicted showed HR acceleration in a social anxiety task, but unsuccessful, convicted psychopaths did not. Unsuccessful psychopaths might lack this adaptivity to environmental challenges. Structurally, the CAN includes brain structures as a network consisting of the anterior cingulated cortex;

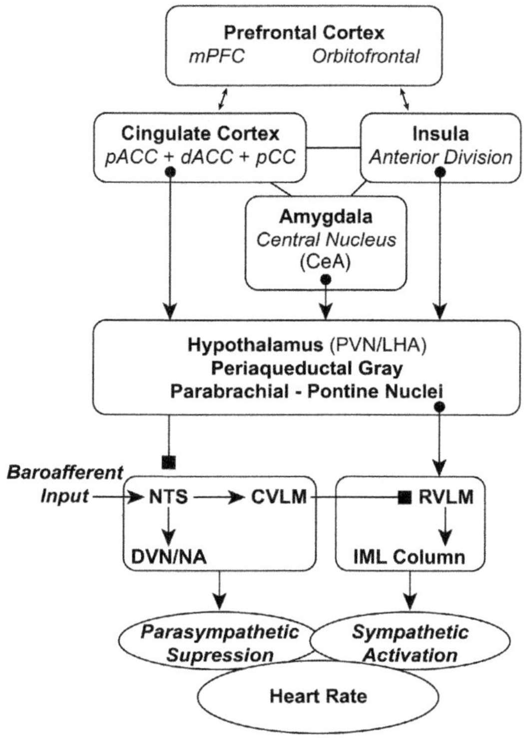

Figure 4.1 A composite schematic diagram showing the pathways by which the prefrontal cortex might influence control of heart rate (CeA: central nucleus of the amygdala, NTS: nucleus of the solitary tract, CVLM: caudal ventrolateral medullary, RVLM: rostral ventrolateral medullary, NA: nucleus ambiguous, DVN: dorsal vagal motor nucleus). (Adapted from Thayer et al. (2000), *Annual Behavioral Medicine*, 2009, pp. 37, 141–153.)

the insula, orbitofrontal, and ventromedial prefrontal cortices; and brain stem motor outputs such as the nucleus ambiguous (Figure 4.1). These structures are reciprocally interconnected, making it possible for both bottom-up and top-down modulation of environmental inputs (Thayer & Siegel, 2002). The primary output of the CAN is mediated through the preganglionic sympathetic neurons that innervate the heart via the stellate ganglia and the parasympathetic neurons via the vagus nerve. Sensory information from the periphery, such as the heart and the immune system, is fed back to the CAN. The CAN can be seen as an integrated part of a regulatory system, which allows the brain to control responses that are critical for goal-directed behavior and adaptability. The model emphasizes the importance of inhibitory processes in the regulation of behavior. Thayer and Siegel (2002) argued that inhibitory processes can be viewed as negative feedback circuits that allow for the interruption of ongoing behavior. An interruption in these negative feedback circuits might explain the tendency toward antisocial behavior.

Behavioral Symptoms and Psychophysiological Deficiencies

Two basic survival systems are considered to be the foundation on which motivational states are based. One system is defensive, and the other system is appetitive in nature (Lang, Bradley, & Cuthbert, 1990). The survival system on which we will focus our main attention is the defensive system that is triggered in situations in which a person is under threat or in danger. Applying threatening stimuli to animals has shown that there is an activation in the subcortical circuitry in the brain including the basolateral and central nuclei of the amygdala (Campeau & Davis 1995). The central nucleus of the amygdala orgistrates, depending on the kind of threatening stimulus, stimulates activity in other brain areas that produces varying defensive responses, including freezing, fear bradycardia (Kapp, Frysinger, Gallagher, & Haselton, 1979), blood pressure increase (LeDoux, 1990), and potentiation of the startle response (Davis, 2000). In the following section, we will briefly present the different physiological mechanisms and the observed differences between PCL-R psychopaths and the antisocial individuals.

Heart Rate and Skin Conductance Level

Many of the psychophysiological studies have been conducted with incarcerated men (Levenston, Patrick, Bradley, & Lang, 2000; Verona, Patrick, Curtin, Bradley, & Lang, 2004). Heart rate (HR) and electrodermal activity (skin conductance level; SCL) are variables of central interest in many theories on the physiology of antisocial spectrum behavior and have historically been the most popular measures of psychophysiological response (Lorber 2004).

Heart Rate

The heart is innervated by the sympathetic (SNS) and parasympathetic (PNS) branches of the autonomic nervous system, and it is subject to neuroendocrine influences. Cardiac effects on the heart rate (chonotropic) are controlled primarily by the PNS, whereas effects such as contractile force and stroke volume (inotropic) are controlled primarily by the SNS.

A documented physiological finding in ASPD is the low resting HR. Twin studies of HR have repeatedly found substantial heritability for resting HR, with heritabilities in the 0.65 to 0.82 range (Boomsma, van den Bree, & Orlebeke, 1989). Some studies claim to have found that resting HR is significantly lower in antisocial children compared to controls (e.g., Herpertz et al., 2001; Raine, 1997a; van Goozen, Matthys, Cohan-Kettenis, Buitelarr, & van England, 2000), and that the effect is found in girls as well as in boys (Maliphant, Hume, & Furnham, 1990). Nevertheless, other studies have failed to observe such effects (Pine et al., 1998; Van Hulle, Corley, Zahn-Waxler, Kagan, & Hewitt, 2000), leading to the possibility that this effect cannot be generalized. Ortiz and Raine (2004), however, showed in their meta-analysis that a low resting HR appears to be diagnostically specific for antisocial behavior. Antisocial children were found to have a significantly lower HR compared to psychiatric controls as well as to normal controls. In comparison, Lorber (2004) showed in his meta-analysis that a low resting HR was associated with aggression, but not associated with PCL-R psychopathy.

The HR indexes the interaction of valence and arousal (e.g., Lang, Greenwald, Bradley, & Hamm, 1993; Ritz, Alatupa, Thöns, & Dahme, 2002) in contrast to SCL, which is a measure of emotional arousal. Subjects who exhibit antisocial behavior generally showed a smaller HR reactivity than those with low tendencies toward antisocial behavior (Patrick, Cuthbert, & Lang, 1994). The HR data is inconsistent for psychopathy. Arnett (1997) shows that psychopaths have smaller HR stress reactions than controls. Other studies, however, show that psychopaths have a normal or even greater HR acceleration compared with nonpsychopaths while anticipating aversive stimuli (Hare & Quinn, 1971; Ogloff & Wong, 1990). With regard to successful psychopathy, Ishikawa et al. (2001) reported that psychopaths who had never been convicted showed HR acceleration in a social anxiety task, but convicted psychopaths did not.

Skin Conductance Level

The SCL is viewed as a psychophysiological measure that represents the allocation of attentional resources to the processing of a stimulus (Dawson, 1990), and is frequently used as an indicator of arousal and SNS activity. It is measured by the activity of eccrine sweat glands that are innervated by cholinergic fibers of the sympathetic nervous system (Blascovich & Kelsey, 1990). Most studies of SCL and antisocial behavior have focused specifically on the psychopathic group.

Compared to controls, individuals identified with global ratings of Cleckley's psychopathy syndrome exhibited deficient SCL responses to conditioned stimuli in aversive conditioning tasks—for example, during shock anticipation (Hare, 1965, 1978; Hare & Craigen, 1974; Lykken, 1957) and loud noise bursts (Hare, Frazelle, & Cox, 1978). Moreover, Lorber's (2004) meta-analysis found that psychopathy was consistently inversely related to a variety of SCL measures (e.g., Raine, 1997a). The findings of these studies indicate that individuals with psychopathy are less electrodermally aroused by aversive stimuli, consistent with the notion that such individuals are relatively fearless (Lykken, 1957, 1995). This could reflect a disability in anticipating punishment. More recent insight tells us that attention has a moderating effect on the capability to avoid punishment in psychopaths (Baskin-Sommers, Zeier, & Newman, 2009).

However, increases in SCL magnitude in normal controls are not specific to aversive stimuli. SCL also increases with exposure to pleasant arousing stimuli (Bradley, Codispoti, Cuthbert, & Lang, 2001; Lang et al., 1993), indicating that it acts as a nonspecific measure of SNS activation. In fact, there is evidence that individuals with psychopathy show global deficits in SCL magnitudes to all emotional pictures (Benning, Patrick, & Iacono, 2005; Herpertz et al., 2001; Pastor, Moltó, Vils, & Lang, 2003). Interestingly, there is a lower skin conductance response in psychopathy in response to adrenalin infusions compared to nonpsychopaths (Hare, 1972). This might account for a different response to hormonal influence.

Overall, we state that there is a decreased functioning of the skin conductance on a variety of measures in psychopathy and antisocial behavior. Since the skin conductance can be seen as an indicator of the activity of the sympathetic nervous system, this supports the notion that there is a general level of underactivation of the sympathetic nervous system in reaction to an aversive event, but also a lack of activation to emotional stimuli in general.

The Eye Blink Startle Reflex

The startle reflex potentiation is a paradigm for indexing fear reactivity and especially the defensive reactivity in humans and animals. The involved pathway (Figure 4.2) leads from the central nucleus of the amygdala to the pontine reticular node of the basic startle circuit (Davis, 1989).

The startle paradigm is based on a fear-potentiated startle to a sudden noise. It has been shown that in healthy controls, the startle eye blink

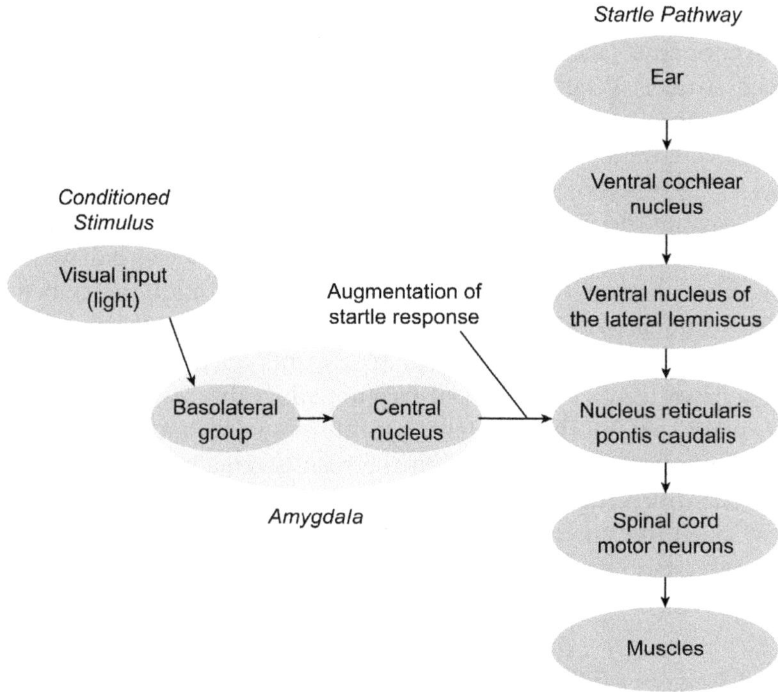

Figure 4.2 Neural circuits responsible for an auditory startle response with a visual input. (Adapted from: Davis, M. [1992], *Trends in Pharmacological Sciences*, pp. 13, 35–41.)

response is potentiated during viewing of aversive pictures compared to neutral pictures (Lang et al., 1990), and that blink potentiation is highest while viewing threatening images like a gun pointed at the viewer (Levenston et al., 2000; Bernat, Patrick, Benning, & Tellegen 2006). Patrick, Bradley, and Lang (1993) have demonstrated that PCL-R psychopaths have a deficient startle potentiation, reflecting a reduced potentiation during aversive pictures. This deficiency is mainly linked to factor 1 scores in PCL-R psychopathy, the affective-interpersonal component (Patrick, 2007). Participants who scored high on factor 2 of the PCL-R, the antisocial deviance features, but low on the factor 1, did not show the same deficiency in the startle reflex (Patrick et al., 1994). Because PCL-R factor 2 has the highest correlation with ASPD, we may expect the same outcome in an ASPD sample. Thus, eye blink startle data suggest that there is a deficiency in fear and defensive reactivity in PCL-R psychopaths and not in the ASPD patients, which is prominently based on the factor I aspects of psychopathy.

To summarize the psychophysiological deficiencies, we can state that for psychopathic individuals, the HR reactivity data is inconsistent between studies. Whereas evidence can be found for a normal or even greater HR acceleration compared with non-psychopaths while anticipating aversive stimuli, other studies have reported that psychopaths have smaller HR stress reactions. This second notion would be in accordance with the overall decreased functioning of the skin conductance found in a variety of measures in psychopathy as well as antisocial behavior. The eye blink startle data, however, suggest that there is a difference between PCL-R psychopaths and ASPD patients. This is prominently based on the factor I aspects of psychopathy, which accounts for the deficiency in fear and defensive reactivity in PCL-R psychopaths. The psychophysiological data explain some of the differences in physiological and behavioral data within the antisocial spectrum, but the results remain inconclusive for a permanent differentiation between PCL-R psychopathy and ASPD. For this, we need to examine the neuro-imaging research developments for a better understanding of the fundamental anatomical aspects of the antisocial spectrum.

Behavioral Symptoms and Underlying Neuroanatomical Deficiencies

Blair, in his review on the construct of psychopathy (2006), summarized structural and functional imaging studies as well as more indirect measurements of specific cerebral area functioning. He concluded that psychopathy manifests in at least two main cortical systems: the amygdala and orbital/ventrolateral frontal cortex (FC). Orbital and ventrolateral FC dysfunction is stated to be a risk factor specifically for reactive aggression. Amygdala dysfunction disrupts the ability of the individual to become socialized.

Kiehl (2006) showed that psychopathy, defined by high PCL-R scores, is associated with paralimbic system dysfunction. His model is formed by a review of studies of behavioral changes following lesions or damage to the paralimbic system, findings from analog studies, and the cognitive neuroscience literature in psychopathy. The particular neural regions included the orbital frontal cortex, insula, amygdala, parahippocampal regions, anterior superior temporal gyrus, and rostral, caudal, and posterior cingulate. Weber et al. (2008) reviewed studies of structural neuro-imaging of men diagnosed with psychopathy and ASPD. He supported the findings of Kiehl and concluded that psychopathy is associated with brain abnormalities in a prefrontal-temporo-limbic system (prefrontal cortex, amygdala, hippocampus, superior temporal gyrus and corpus callosum).

The Prefrontal Cortex

Raine, Lencz, Bihrle, LaCasse, and Colletti (2000) showed that there is a reduction of prefrontal gray matter volume in ASPD-diagnosed young men compared to other psychiatric patients and healthy controls. Low prefrontal gray volume was associated with high total PCL-R scores. The relationship between psychopathy and prefrontal gray volume was non-specific in that it was found for all psychopathy factors. Tiihonen et al. (2008) made a difference between ASPD only and psychopathy based on PCL-R combined with ASPD. They found larger white matter volume in the right and left parietal lobes, right and left occipital lobes, and left cerebellum, and more gray matter volume in the right cerebral hemisphere in men diagnosed with ASPD and men with psychopathy. This was combined with findings of symmetrical, bilateral areas of gray matter atrophy in the post central gyri, frontopolar cortex and orbitofrontal cortex and right insula. This atrophy was present even more in men with PCL-R psychopathy, than in men with ASPD only. Both groups differed significantly compared to healthy controls. It is interesting to see that this difference was only seen in unsuccessful—i.e., incarcerated—psychopaths, but not in successful psychopaths, who did not have a reduction in prefrontal gray matter volumes compared with control subjects (Yang et al., 2005).

The orbital frontal cortex is one of the areas in the prefrontal cortex that are most often associated with psychopathy. The orbitofrontal cortex appears to elicit behaviors and deficiencies of psychopathy, including symptoms of impulsivity, irresponsibility, and stimulation seeking, as well as a general lack of empathy. Items that score on the interpersonal PCL-R factor 1 (superficial charm, grandiose sense of self-worth, and pathological lying) are sometimes associated with acquired head injury in the orbital frontal area (Blumer & Benson, 1975). The orbital frontal cortex is furthermore involved in the modulation of reactive aggression and less obviously involved in the modulation of instrumental aggression (Blair, 2004). Blair (2004) also concluded that the orbital frontal cortex is involved in response reversal and that impairments in response reversal are seen in psychopathic individuals (Budhani & Blair 2005; Budhani, Richell, & Blair, 2006).

The orbital prefrontal cortex and dorsolateral prefrontal cortex interact with the hypothalamus, hippocampus, and/or amygdala to regulate electrodermal and cardiovascular reactivity (Critchley, Elliott, et al., 2000; Raine, Reynolds, & Sheard, 1991). However, the influences of the human frontal cortex on autonomic activity are most relevant for psychological processes such as effortful information processing and classical conditioning (Tranel & Damasio, 1994; Zahn, Grafman, & Tranel, 1999), rather than to basic functions such as thermoregulation or unconditioned responses to aversive stimuli (Grueninger, Kimble, Grueninger, & Levine, 1965).

The prefrontal cortex and, specifically, the orbital/ventromedial prefrontal cortex are involved in the regulation of emotion, control of impulsive behavior, and the acquisition of reward/punishment associations, which are crucial to the social and moral development into adulthood. In his extensive review, Kiehl (2006) stated that damage to other regions of the frontal cortex (i.e., superior frontal or dorsolateral prefrontal), parietal cortex, or occipital cortex, are not known to lead to behavioral symptoms or cognitive abnormalities consistent with psychopathy.

The Temporal Lobe

The temporal lobe is a neurobiological substrate for typical symptoms of psychopathy such as a lack of empathy, disturbed interpersonal relationships, and instrumental aggression. PCL-R psychopathy was associated with gray matter loss in the right superior temporal gyrus compared to healthy controls (Muller et al., 2008). Wong, Lumsden, Fenton, and Fenwick (1994) reported that 41% of the patients in a maximum-security mental hospital showed dilatation of the temporal horn in combination with or separate from a reduced size of the temporal lobe. The prevalence of symptoms of psychopathy is reported in up to 70% of the patients with anterior temporal lobe epilepsy, according to detailed psychological and personality assessments (Hill, Pond, Mitchell, & Falconer, 1957).

The Anterior Cingulate Cortex

The rostral region of the anterior cingulate cortex (ACC) is known to be involved in pain perception and affect regulation (Bush, Luu, & Posner, 2000). The dorsal region is known to be involved in error monitoring, task switching, and response conflict (Kiehl, Liddle, & Hopfinger, 2000). Patients with deficits to bilateral ACC are exhibiting disturbances in personality functioning similar to patients with orbital frontal lesions (Hornak et al., 2003). Hornak et al. (2003) also gave evidence that those deficits in the ACC explain difficulties in affective face and voice identification. This is also seen for error monitoring (Swick & Jovanovic, 2002; Swick & Turken, 2002) and response inhibition abnormalities (Tekin & Cummings, 2002). These are all items and processes associated with psychopathy (e.g., Blair, Jones, Clark, & Smith, 1997; Kosson, Suchy, Myer, & Libby, 2002).

The affective division of the ACC has been shown to correlate with autonomic responses during execution of cognitive functions of the Stroop task in healthy controls (Critchley, Tang, Glaser, Butterworth, & Dolan, 2005). The ACC also interacts with the hypothalamus, hippocampus, and/or amygdala to regulate electrodermal and cardiovascular reactivity together with the orbital PFC and dorsolateral PFC (Critchley, Elliott, et al., 2000; Raine et al., 1991).

Insula

Birbaumer et al. (2005) studied criminal psychopaths during a classical aversive conditioning task. The participants were asked to perform three conditioning phases (habituation, acquisition, and extinction) during which photos of faces were used as the CS and painful pressure was the US. The antisocial group failed to show the appropriate differential activation in the amygdala, orbitofrontal cortex, insula, and ACC during the acquisition of fear and successful conditioning.

It appeared that the left and right posterior insula are associated with regulation of parasympathetic and sympathetic cardiovascular function, respectively (Oppenheimer, Gelb, et al., 1992). In addition, there is mounting evidence that the posterior insular cortex, which innervates the lateral hypothalamus (Allen and Cechetto, 1992), plays an important role in mediating cardiovascular function (Critchley, Corfield, Chandler, Mathias, & Dolan, 2000; Zhang, Dougherty, & Oppenheimer, 1999).

The Corpus Callosum

Raine (1997b) used positron emission tomography brain imaging during a continuous performance challenge task conducted on 41 murderer's pleading not guilty by reason of insanity and 41 age- and sex-matched controls. He showed that the murderers were characterized by reduced glucose metabolism in the corpus callosum as well as the prefrontal cortex, superior parietal gyrus and the left angular gyrus, while abnormal asymmetries of activity (left hemisphere lower than right) were also found in the amygdala, thalamus, and medial temporal lobe. Raine et al. (2003) later showed that the deficiencies in the corpus callosum which are related to psychopathy in comparison to healthy controls are an increase in estimated callosal white matter volume, an increase in callosal length and a reduction in callosal thickness. The volume of the callosal white matter was significantly related to the deficient affect factor of psychopathy. To a lesser extent, it was related to the impulsive lifestyle factor, but not to the interpersonal factor (Raine et al., 2003).

The Amygdalae

The amygdalae are known to play an important role in the top-down and bottom-up processes in the emergence and regulation of aggressive behavior. Blair (2004) stated that structural changes of the amygdalae can both increase and decrease the probability of aggressive behavior. Bilateral amygdalotomy reduces the accounts of aggressive behavior in severity as well as in frequency (Bagshaw, Mackworth, & Pribram, 1972; Lee et al., 1998). On the other hand van Elst et al. (2000) associated temporal lobe epilepsy and aggressive behavior with a severe atrophy of the amygdalae.

The research of Tiihonen et al. (2000) showed that the PCL-R scores were negatively correlated with the right amygdaloidal volume. Furthermore, different studies have shown that amygdala damage is involved in the processing of different affective stimuli known to be disrupted in psychopathy. The medial temporal lobe regions appear to be involved with affective face-processing difficulties (Anderson, Spencer, Fulbright, & Phelps, 2000) and with the fear-potentiated startle during emotional processing in pictures (Angrilli et al., 1996) as well as with verbal stimuli (Funayama, Grillon, Davis, & Phelps, 2001).

The antero-lateral temporal lobe regions are implicated with certain symptoms of psychopathy, including aggression, impulsivity and poor behavioral control, and empathy and emotional unconcern. The right amygdala is also involved with affective face-processing (Anderson et al., 2000). The left amygdala is considered to be involved in aversive conditioning (Bechara et al., 1995; Funayama et al., 2001). It appears that damage to the amygdalae and regions of the antero-lateral temporal lobe are involved in certain symptoms of psychopathy, including aggression, impulsivity and poor behavioral control, and empathy and emotional unconcern.

The amygdalae, located within the temporal lobe, assist in the regulation of autonomic functions. In animals, stimulation of the amygdalae and temporal cortex consistently elicits the cardiac vigilance response. Similarly, the amygdalae exert an excitatory influence on electrodermal activity (Sequeira & Roy, 1997). In humans, size of the temporal area (including the amygdalae) relates to skin conductance responses to novel stimuli (Raine et al., 1991). Damage to the amygdalae and/or medio-basal temporal lobes frequently (Bechara et al., 1999), but not always (Tranel & Damasio, 1989), disrupts the generation of skin conductance responses. Amygdalae damage is also associated with deficiencies in the startle response. Funayama et al. (2001) showed that a deficient startle response after a lesion of the temporal lobe with a visual stimulus is due to a lesion in the right temporal lobe.

The Hippocampus

There is evidence for structural abnormalities in the hippocampal region in psychopathy (Ishikawa et al., 2001; Laakso et al., 2001; Raine et al., 2004). The degree of psychopathy assessed by the PCL-R was correlated with MRI-derived regional hippocampus volumes in a group of incarcerated male, habitually violent offenders with ASPD and type 2 alcoholism (Laakso et al., 2001). They found a strong negative correlation between the volume of the posterior half of the hippocampus bilaterally and the psychopathy scores.

Lesions of the hippocampus are known to be involved with processes strongly associated with psychopathy such as impaired associative learning and poor contextual fear conditioning (Laakso et al., 2001; LeDoux, 1996). The hippocampus is also implicated in contextual fear conditioning. As in the prefrontal cortex, there is a difference between successful and unsuccessful psychopaths, wherein the latter show a structural asymmetry in the anterior hippocampus (R > L) compared to both successful psychopaths and normal control subjects (Raine et al., 2004).

The hippocampus, located within the temporal lobe, assists in the regulation of autonomic functions. Studies of the hippocampus in animals and humans using electrical stimulation have produced opposing results on electrodermal activity, suggesting both an inhibitory and excitatory influence (Frederickson et al., 1998). Moreover, it appears that the influence of the hippocampus on electrodermal activity is controlled by higher cortical structures (Ishikawa et al., 2001).

To summarize the neuroanatomical deficiencies, we can state that abnormalities in the prefrontal cortex, amygdala, hippocampus, superior temporal gyrus, corpus callosum, and anterior cingulate cortex explain a great part of the symptomatology in psychopathy and ASPD (e.g., aggression, impulsivity, and poor behavioral control). Deviations within the anterior cingulate cortex are found in ASPD. The concept of psychopathy is primarily associated with abnormalities in the prefrontal-temporo-limbic system. The differences in neuro-anatomical structure and functioning also give us more information on the origin of the psychophysiological deficiencies found in the antisocial spectrum.

Discussion: Toward an Integrated View of Antisocial Behavior

It has been proposed that psychopathy is featured by emotional and, in some cases, cognitive deficits that do not distinguish inmates with ASPD from those without ASPD (Patrick, 1994). Recent evidence indicates that psychopathy explains variance in hippocampal volume even among individuals with ASPD (Laakso et al., 2001). Patients with ASPD, on the other hand, display cardiovascular anomalies (Raine et al., 2000) that are not associated with psychopathy (Raine, 1997a). Similarly, ASPD and life-course-persistent offenders have been reported to exhibit neuropsychological deficits (Moffitt, 1993; Stevens, Kaplan, & Hasselbrock, 2003) that are not seen in psychopathic offenders (Hart, Forth, & Hare, 1990). Differences such as these raise the question that the syndrome of ASPD with psychopathy is fundamentally and etiologically different from the syndrome of ASPD without psychopathy (Hare, 1999). In this perspective, psychopathy can be seen as an etiologically distinct subgroup in the ASPD spectrum (Lykken, 1995).

On the other hand, it may be argued that the ASPD with or without psychopathy and psychopathy as such are based on the same pathological biological and developmental pathways. This would mean that diagnostic criteria for ASPD and psychopathy assess different parameters of the same underlying syndrome.

The heterogeneity in study populations in different studies and, for this research question, the inadequate capabilities for neuro-imaging do not allow a straightforward answer to these questions. Only few studies directly elucidate the difference between psychopathy and ASPD. A ruling on specific neurobiological differences between psychopathy and ASPD is therefore not possible. However, there is growing evidence that this distinction in neurobiological function indeed exists. Tiihonen et al. (2008), for example, found a clearly significant difference between one group of patients who met the criteria for ASPD with high levels of psychopathy and an antisocial group without high levels of psychopathy. There was a greater atrophy of the gray matter in the orbitofrontal cortex in patients with a high degree of psychopathy.

One answer might be found within the limits of the psychophysiological research findings. In studies with patients with acquired brain damage, lesions of discrete brain areas may also modulate autonomic responsivity. Thus, orbitofrontal damage can reduce anticipatory arousal to emotive stimuli (Damasio, Tranel, & Damasio, 1990), while lesions of the amygdala may block the autonomic responses that accompany conditioning (Bechara et al., 1995). Overall, our psychophysiological and neuro-anatomical findings indicate the appearance of an overlap in functioning between the brain areas that regulate psychophysiological signals such as SCL, HR, or eye blink startle response (e.g., amygdala, cingulate cortex, orbitofrontal and ventromedial frontal cortex), and the cortical and limbic regions associated with psychopathy and ASPD. Therefore, if there are deficiencies in the cortical and limbic areas in patients diagnosed with psychopathy and ASPD, it can be expected that the psychophysiological functioning of these patients is also different.

These differences are prominently seen in the differentiation between heart rate, skin conductance, and eye blink reflex. Especially, the eye blink reflex suggests that there is a nuancy between PCL-R psychopaths and ASPD patients. This is prominently based on the factor I aspects of psychopathy. The psychophysiological data explain some of the differences in physiological and behavioral data within the antisocial spectrum, but the results remain inconclusive for a differentiation between PCL-R psychopathy and ASPD.

The neurobiological and psychophysiological findings that emerge in the physiological, structural, and functional imaging studies that we highlighted, and the neurobiological findings in the reviews of Blair, Peschardt, Budhani, Mitchell, and Pine (2006), Kiehl (2006), and Weber et al. (2008), support both the "violence inhibition" model of Blair (1995) and the "somatic marker" hypothesis of Damasio (1996). The models themselves offer no comprehensive explanation for the variety of abnormalities and give no definitive explanation for the origin and nature of antisocial behavior.

Because of the diversity of the affected brain structures, it is plausible that not only are the specific dysfunctions in individual brain structures of importance, but that especially the combinations of dysfunctions in several brain regions play a crucial role. Also, the communication between different brain structures will most likely take a critical position, since the brain is considered to be a complex network of interconnected structures (Crick & Jones, 1993). In this context, psychopathy can be seen as a dysregulated and deficient functional connectivity of emotion-related brain areas (Muller et al., 2003). Imaging studies that map the connectivity of the affected structures are not yet available. Additional research specifically focused on this connectivity will be necessary to ensure the development of a comprehensive explanatory model, which is very likely to integrate existing models such as the "violence inhibition" model and the "somatic marker" model.

With the discussion of the neurobiological research, some critical remarks have to be made. The discussed imaging studies appear to be heterogeneous in their study populations. Some studies, for example, looked specifically at murderers (Raine et al., 1994), and in another study to aggression in patients with an epileptic condition (Woermann et al., 2000). It was not possible to specify the different degrees of psychopathy in the research groups. In addition, there are various imaging techniques being used, combined or not combined with a variety of physiological or psychological tests. In an attempt to make the research more broadly applicable, the designs are focused on the disorders at symptom level, such as aggression or impulsivity, which in itself is again difficult to define. It is therefore advisable to strictly define and publish the diagnosis and the selection of subjects used in neuroimaging and psychophysiological studies.

Conclusion

Many brain structures play a role in antisocial behavior, as is shown by a broad variety of neuro-anatomical research findings. Three models are condensed from the neuro-biological findings: the somatic marker hypothesis in the ventromedial prefrontal cortex, the violence inhibition system with the amygdalae as the main loci of control, and the central autonomic network in the PFC, insula, and brain stem. Not one of these models can explain by itself the origin and types of antisocial behavior. Also, it is hard to understand that these three models are working as an isolated part of the brain, because by recent neuro-scientific knowledge, the brain is seen as a complex interconnected system (Kandel, 2005). So deficiencies in the communication between brain structures seem to play a more important role than deficiencies in isolated brain structures. It cannot be excluded that with regard to these deficiencies, there exists an underlying common etiology—for instance, the genetic expression of genes (Kandel, 2005)—caused by different criminogenic factors such as child abuse or malnutrition, which may be the key to the complexities of antisocial behavior. In this context, Weber et al. (2008) concluded that the emergence of psychopathy and antisocial behavior can be seen as the result of interaction of various factors best summed up in a bio-psycho-social model (Engel, 1980).

Until now, research has not been able to develop a model to hypothesize and measure antisocial behavior as the result of a fixed set of deficient brain functions. This review strongly suggests that future directions in research point at looking at the brain as an integrated system. The psychophysiological findings may serve as a bridge between the neuro-anatomical findings and the behavioral abnormalities within an integrated view of the antisocial spectrum.

References

Allen, G. V., & Cechetto, D. F. (1992). Functional and anatomical organization of cardiovascular pressor and depressor sites in the lateral hypothalamic area: I. Descending projections. *Journal of Comparative Neurology, 315*(3), 313–332. doi:10.1002/cne.903150307.

Anderson, A. K., Spencer, D. D., Fulbright, R. K., & Phelps, E. A. (2000). Contribution of the anteromedial temporal lobes to the evaluation of facial emotion. *Neuropsychology, 14*(4), 526–536.

Angrilli, A., Mauri, A., Palomba, D., Flor, H., Birbaumer, N., Sartori, G., & di Paola, F. (1996). Startle reflex and emotion modulation impairment after a right amygdala lesion. *Brain, 119*(6), 1991–2000.

Arnett, P. A. (1997). Autonomic responsivity in psychopaths: A critical review and theoretical proposal. *Clinical Psychology Review, 17*(8), 903–936.

Bagshaw, M. H., Mackworth, N. H., & Pribram, K. H. (1972). The effect of resections of the inferotemporal cortex or the amygdala on visual orienting and habituation. *Neuropsychologia, 10*(2), 153–162.

Baskin-Sommers, A. R., Zeier, J. D., & Newman, J. P. (2009). Self-reported attentional control differentiates the major factors of psychopathy. *Personality and Individual Differences, 47*(6), 626–630. doi:10.1016/j.paid.2009.05.027.

Bechara, A., Damasio, H., Damasio, A. R., & Lee, G. P. (1999). Different contributions of the human amygdala and ventromedial prefrontal cortex to decision-making. *Journal of Neuroscience, 19*(13), 5473–5481.

Bechara, A., Tranel, D., Damasio, H., Adolphs, R., Rockland, C., & Damasio, A. R. (1995). Double dissociation of conditioning and declarative knowledge relative to the amygdala and hippocampus in humans. *Science, 269*(5227), 1115–1118.

Benning, S. D., Patrick, C. J., & Iacono, W. G. (2005). Psychopathy, startle blink modulation, and electrodermal reactivity in twin men. *Psychophysiology, 42*(6), 753–762.

Bernat, E., Patrick, C. J., Benning, S. T., & Tellegen, A. (2006). Effects of picture content and intensity on affective physiological response. *Psychophysiology 43*(1), 93–103.

Birbaumer, N., Veit, R., Lotze, M., Erb, M., Hermann, C., Grodd, W., & Flor, H. (2005). Deficient fear conditioning in psychopathy: A functional magnetic resonance imaging study. *Archives of General Psychiatry, 62*(7), 799–805.

Blair, R. J. (1995). A cognitive developmental approach to mortality: investigating the psychopath. *Cognition, 57*(1), 1–29.

Blair, R. J. (2004). The roles of orbital frontal cortex in the modulation of antisocial behavior. *Brain and Cognition, 55*(1), 198–208.

Blair, R. J. (2006). The emergence of psychopathy: Implications for the neuropsychological approach to developmental disorders. *Cognition, 101*(2), 414–442.

Blair, R. J., Colledge, E., Murray, L., & Mitchell, D. G. (2001). A selective impairment in the processing of sad and fearful expressions in children with psychopathic tendencies. *Journal of Abnormal Child Psychology, 29*(6), 491–498.

Blair, R. J., Jones, L., Clark, F., & Smith, M. (1997). The psychopathic individual: A lack of responsiveness to distress cues? *Psychophysiology, 34*(2), 192–198.

Blair, R. J., Peschardt, K. S., Budhani, S., Mitchell, D. G. V., & Pine, D. S. (2006). The development of psychopathy. *Journal of Child Psychology and Psychiatry, 47* (3–4), 262–275.

Blascovich, J., & Kelsey, R. M. (1990). Using electrodermal and cardiovascular measures of arousal in social psychological research. In C. A. Hendricks & M. A. Clark (Eds.), *Research methods in personality and social psychology* (pp. 45–73). Newbury Park, CA: Sage Publications.

Blumer, D., & Benson, D. F. (1975). Personality changes with frontal and temporal lobe lesions. In D. F. Benson & D. Blumer (Eds.), *Psychiatric aspects of neurological disease* (pp. 151–170). New York: Grune and Stratton.

Boomsma, D. I., van den Bree, M. B., & Orlebeke, J. F. (1989). Resemblances of parents and twins in sports participation and heart rate. *Behavior Genetics, 19* (1), 123–141.

Bradley, M. M., Codispoti, M., Cuthbert, B. N., & Lang, P. J. (2001). Emotion and motivation I: Defensive and appetitive reactions in picture processing. *Emotion, 1*(3), 276–298.

Budhani, S., & Blair, R. J. (2005). Response reversal and children with psychopathic tendencies: Success is a function of salience of contingency change. *Journal of Child Psychology and Psychiatry, 46*(9), 972–981.

Budhani, S., Richell, R. A., & Blair, R. J. (2006). Impaired reversal but intact acquisition: Probabilistic response reversal deficits in adult individuals with psychopathy.*Journal of Abnormal Psychology, 115*(3), 552–558.

Bush, G., Luu., P., & Posner, M. I. (2000). Cognitive and emotional influences in anterior cingulate cortex. *Trends in Cognitive Science, 4*(6), 215–222.

Campeau, S., & Davis, M. (1995). Involvement of the central nucleus and basolateral complex of the amygdala in fear conditioning measured with fear-potentiated startle in rats trained concurrently with auditory and visual conditioned stimuli. *Journal of Neuroscience, 15*(3 Pt. 2), 2301–2311.

Crick, F., & Jones, E. (1993). Backwardness of human neuroanatomy. *Nature, 361*(6408), 109–110. doi:10.1038/361109a0.

Critchley, H. D., Corfield, D. R., Chandler, M. P., Mathias, C. J., & Dolan, R. J. (2000). Cerebral correlates of autonomic cardiovascular arousal: A functional neuroimaging investigation in humans. *Journal of Physiology, 523*(Pt. 1), 259–270.

Critchley, H. D., Elliott, R., Mathias, C. J., & Dolan, R. J. (2000). Neural activity relating to generation and representation of galvanic skin conductance responses: A functional magnetic resonance imaging study. *Journal of Neuroscience, 20*(8), 3033–3040.

Critchley, H. D., Tang, J., Glaser, D., Butterworth, B., & Dolan, R. (2005). Anterior cingulate activity during error and autonomic response. *Neuroimage, 27*(4), 885–895.

Damasio, A. R. (1996). The somatic marker hypothesis and the possible functions of the prefrontal cortex. *Philosophical Transactions of the Royal Society of London, 351*(1346), 1413–1420. doi:10.1098/rstb.1996.0125.

Damasio, A. R., Tranel, D., & Damasio, H. (1990). Individuals with sociopathic behavior caused by frontal damage fail to respond autonomically to social stimuli. *Behavioural Brain Research, 41*(2), 81–94. doi:0166-4328(90)90144-4 [pii].

Davis, M. (1989). Neural systems involved in fear-potentiated startle. *Annals of the New York Academy of Science, 563*, 165–183.

Davis, M. (2000). The role of the amygdala in conditioned and unconditioned fear and anxiety. In J. P. Aggleton (Ed.), *The amygdala* (2nd ed., pp. 213–287). Oxford: Oxford University Press.

Dawson, M. E. (1990). Psychophysiology at the interface of clinical science, cognitive science, and neuroscience. *Psychophysiology, 27*(3), 243–255.

Davidson, R. J., Putnam, K. M., & Larson, C. L. (2000). Dysfunction in the neural circuitry of emotion regulation—a possible prelude to violence. *Science, 289* (5479), 591–594. doi:8703 [pii].

Dolan, M., & Fullam, R. (2006). Face affect recognition deficits in personality-disordered offenders: Association with psychopathy. *Psychological Medicine, 36*(11), 1563–1569.

Engel, G. L. (1980). The clinical application of the biopsychosocial model. *American Journal of Psychiatry, 137*(5), 535–544.

Frederickson, M., Furmark, T., Olsson, M. T., Fischer, H., Anderson, J., & Langstrom, B. (1998). Functional neuroanatomical correlates of electrodermal activity: A positron emission tomographic study. *Psychophysiology, 35*, 179–185.

Funayama, E. S., Grillon, C., Davis, M., & Phelps, E. A. (2001). A double dissociation in the affective modulation of startle in humans: Effects of unilateral temporal lobectomy. *Journal of Cognitive Neuroscience, 13*(6), 721–729.

Grueninger, W. W., Kimble, D. P., Grueninger, J., & Levine, S. (1965). GSR and corticosteroid response in monkeys with frontal ablations. *Neuropsychologia, 3*, 205–216.

Hare, R. D. (1965). Temporal gradient of fear arousal in psychopaths. *Journal of Abnormal Psychology, 70*(6), 442–445.

Hare, R. D. (1972). Psychopathy and physiological responses to adrenalin. *Journal of Abnormal Psychology, 79*(2), 138–147.

Hare, R. D. (1978). Psychopathy and electrodermal responses to nonsignal stimulation. *Biological Psychology, 6*(4), 237–246.

Hare, R. D. (1999). Psychopathy as a risk factor for violence. *Psychiatric Quarterly, 70*(3), 181–197.

Hare, R. D. (2003). *The Hare Psychopathy Checklist—Revised* (2nd ed.). Toronto, Ontario, Canada: Multi-Health Systems.

Hare, R. D., & Craigen, D. (1974). Psychopathy and physiological activity in a mixed-motive game situation. *Psychophysiology, 11*(2), 197–206.

Hare, R. D., Frazelle, J., & Cox, D. N. (1978). Psychopathy and physiological responses to threat of an aversive stimulus. *Psychophysiology, 15*(2), 165–172.

Hare, R. D., Hart, S. D., & Harpur, T. J. (1991). Psychopathy and the DSM-IV criteria for antisocial personality disorder. *Journal of Abnormal Psychology, 100*(3), 391–398.

Hare, R. D., & McPherson, L. M. (1984). Psychopathy and perceptual asymmetry during verbal dichotic listening. *Journal of Abnormal Psychology, 93*(2), 141–149.

Hare, R. D., & Quinn, M. J. (1971). Psychopathy and autonomic conditioning. *Journal of Abnormal Psychology, 77*(3), 223–235.

Harris G. T., Rice M. E., & Cormier C. A. (1991). Psychopathy and violent recidivism. *Law and Human Behavior, 15*, 625–637.

Hart, S. D., Forth, A. E., & Hare, R. D. (1990). Performance of criminal psychopaths on selected neuropsychological tests. *Journal of Abnormal Psychology, 99*(4), 374–379.

Herpertz, S. C., Wenning, B., Mueller, B., Qunaibi, M., Sass, H., & Herpertz-Dahlmann, B. (2001). Psychophysiological responses in ADHD boys with and without conduct disorder: Implications for adult antisocial behavior. *Journal of American Academy of Child Adolescent Psychiatry, 40*(10), 1222–1230.

Hildebrand, M., & de Ruiter, C. (2004). PCL-R psychopathy and its relation to DSM-IV Axis I and II disorders in a sample of male forensic psychiatric patients in the Netherlands. *International Journal of Law and Psychiatry, 27*(3), 233–248.

Hill, D., Pond, D. A., Mitchell, W., & Falconer, M. A. (1957). Personality changes following temporal lobectomy for epilepsy. *British Journal of Psychiatry, 103* (430), 18–27.

Hornak, J., Bramham, J., Rolls, E. T., Morris, R. G., O'Doherty, J. O., Bullock, P. R., & Polkey, C. E. (2003). Changes in emotion after circumscribed surgical lesions of the orbitofrontal and cingulate cortices. *Brain, 126*, 1691–1712.

Ishikawa, S. S., Raine, A., Lencz, T., Bihrle, S., & LaCasse, L. (2001). Autonomic stress reactivity and executive functions in successful and unsuccessful criminal psychopaths from the community. *Journal of Abnormal Psychology, 110*(3), 423–432.

Kandel, E. R. (2005). Eric Kandel: A life in learning and memory. [Interview]. *Drug Discovery Today, 10*(5), 302–304. doi:10.1016/S1359-6446(04)03331-8.

Kapp, B. S., Frysinger, R. C., Gallagher, M., & Haselton, J. R. (1979). Amygdala central nucleus lesions: Effect on heart rate conditioning in the rabbit. *Physiology & Behavior, 23*(6), 1109–1117.

Kiehl, K. A. (2006). A cognitive neuroscience perspective on psychopathy: Evidence for paralimbic system dysfunction. *Psychiatry Research, 142*(2–3), 107–128.

Kiehl, K. A., Liddle, P. F., & Hopfinger, J. B. (2000). Error processing and the rostral anterior cingulate: An event-related fMRI study. *Psychophysiology, 37*(2), 216–223.

Kosson, D. S., Suchy, Y., Myer, A. R., & Libby, J. (2002). Facial affect recognition in criminal psychopaths. *Emotion, 2*(4), 398–411.

Laakso, M. P., Vaurio, O., Koivisto, E., Savolainen, L., Eronen, M., Aronen, H. J., ... Tiihonen, J. (2001). Psychopathy and the posterior hippocampus. *Behavioral Brain Research, 118*(2), 187–193.

Lang, P. J., Bradley, M. M., & Cuthbert, B. N. (1990). Emotion, attention, and the startle reflex. *Psychological Review, 97*(3), 377–395.

Lang, P. J., Greenwald, M. K., Bradley, M. M., & Hamm, A. O. (1993). Looking at pictures: Affective, facial, visceral, and behavioral reactions. *Psychophysiology, 30*(3), 261–273.

LeDoux, J. (1996). Emotional networks and motor control: a fearful view. *Progress in Brain Research, 107*, 437–446.

LeDoux, J. E. (1990). Information flow from sensation to emotion plasticity in the neural computation of stimulus values. In M. Gabriel, & J. Moore (Eds.), *Learning and computational neuroscience: Foundations of adaptive networks* (pp. 3–52). Cambridge, MA: MIT Press.

Lee, G. P., Bechara, A., Adolphs, R., Arena, J., Meador, K. J., Loring, D. W., & Smith, J. R. (1998). Clinical and physiological effects of stereotaxic bilateral amygdalotomy for intractable aggression. *Journal of Neuropsychiatry and Clinical Neurosciences, 10*(4), 413–420.

Levenston, G. K., Patrick, C. J., Bradley, M. M., & Lang, P. J. (2000). The psychopath as observer: Emotion and attention in picture processing. *Journal of Abnormal Psychology, 109*(3), 373–385.

Lorber, M. F. (2004). Psychophysiology of aggression, psychopathy, and conduct problems: A meta-analysis. *Psychological Bulletin, 130*(4), 531–552.

Lykken, D. T. (1957). A study of anxiety in the sociopathic personality. *Journal of Abnormal Psychology, 55*(1), 6–10.

Lykken, D. T. (1995). *The antisocial personalities*. Hillsdale, NJ: Erlbaum.

Maliphant, R., Hume, F., & Furnham, A. (1990). Autonomic nervous system (ANS) activity, personality characteristics and disruptive behavior in girls. *Journal of Child Psychology and Psychiatry, 31*(4), 619–628.

Mitchell, D. G., Fine, C., Richell, R. A., Newman, C., Lumsden, J., Blair, K. S., & Blair, R. J. (2006). Instrumental learning and relearning in individuals with psychopathy and in patients with lesions involving the amygdala or orbitofrontal cortex. *Neuropsychology, 20*(3), 280–289.

Moffitt, T. E. (1993). Adolescence-limited and life-course-persistent antisocial behavior: A developmental taxonomy. *Psychological Review, 100*(4), 674–701.

Muller, J. L., Ganssbauer, S., Sommer, M., Döhnel, K., Weber, T., Schmidt-Wilcke, T., & Hajak, G. (2008). Gray matter changes in right superior temporal gyrus in criminal psychopaths. Evidence from voxel-based morphometry. *Psychiatry Research, 163*(3), 213–222.

Muller, J. L., Sommer, M., Wagner, V., Lange, K., Taschler, H., Roder, C. H., . . . Hajak, G. (2003). Abnormalities in emotion processing within cortical and subcortical regions in criminal psychopaths: evidence from a functional magnetic resonance imaging study using pictures with emotional content. *Biological Psychiatry, 54*(2), 152–162. doi:S0006322302017493 [pii]

Ogloff, J. R., & Wong, S. (1990). Electrodermal and cardiovascular evidence of a coping response in psychopaths. *Criminal Justice and Behavior, 17*, 231–245.

Oppenheimer, S. M., Gelb, A., Girvin, J. P., & Hachinski, V. C. (1992). Cardiovascular effects of human insular cortex stimulation. *Neurology, 42*(9), 1727–1732.

Ortiz, J., & Raine, A. (2004). Heart rate level and antisocial behavior in children and adolescents: A meta-analysis. *Journal of the American Academy of Child and Adolescent Psychiatry, 43*(2), 154–162.

Pastor, M. C., Moltó, J., Vila, J., & Lang, P. J. (2003). Startle reflex modulation, affective ratings and autonomic reactivity in incarcerated Spanish psychopaths. *Psychophysiology, 40*(6), 934–938.

Patrick, C. J. (1994). Emotion and psychopathy: Startling new insights. *Psychophysiology, 31*(4), 319–330.

Patrick, C. J. (2007). Getting to the heart of psychopathy. In H. Hervé & J. C. Yuille (Eds.), *The psychopath: Theory, research, and social implications* (pp. 207–252). Hillsdale, NJ: Lawrence Erlbaum Associates.

Patrick, C. J., Bradley, M. M., & Lang, P. J. (1993). Emotion in the criminal psychopath: Startle reflex modulation. *Journal of Abnormal Psychology, 102*(1), 82–92.

Patrick, C. J., Cuthbert, B. N., & Lang, P. J. (1994). Emotion in the criminal psychopath: Fear image processing. *Journal of Abnormal Psychology, 103*(3), 523–534.

Pine, D. S., Wasserman, G. A., Miller, L., Coplan, J. D., Bagiella, E., Kovelenku, P., . . . Sloan, R. P. (1998). Heart period variability and psychopathology in urban boys at risk for delinquency. *Psychophysiology, 35*(5), 521–529.

Porges, S. W. (2007). The polyvagal perspective. [Research Support, NIH, Extramural Review]. *Biological Psychology, 74*(2), 116–143. doi:10.1016/j.biopsycho.2006.06.009.

Raine, A. (1997a). Antisocial behavior and psychophysiology: A biosocial perspective and a prefrontal dysfunction hypothesis. In J. B. D. M. Stoff & J. D. Maser (Eds.), *Handbook of antisocial behavior* (pp. 289–304). New York: Wiley.

Raine, A. (1997b). Classical conditioning, arousal, and crime: a biosocial perspective. In *The scientific study of human nature: Tribute to Hans J. Eysenck at 80* (pp. 122–141). N. H. Amsterdam: Pergamon/Elsevier Science.

Raine, A., Buchsbaum, M. S., Stanley, J., Lottenberg, S., Abel, L., & Stoddard, J. (1994). Selective reductions in prefrontal glucose metabolism in murderers. *Biological Psychiatry, 36*(6), 365–373. doi:0006-3223(94)91211-4 [pii]

Raine, A., Ishikawa, S. S., Arce, E., Lencz, T., Knuth, K. H., Bihrle, S., . . . Colletti, P. (2004). Hippocampal structural asymmetry in unsuccessful psychopaths. *Biological Psychiatry, 55*(2), 185–191.

Raine, A., Lencz, T., Bihrle, S., LaCasse, L., & Colletti, P. (2000). Reduced prefrontal gray matter volume and reduced autonomic activity in antisocial personality disorder. *Archives of General Psychiatry, 57*(2), 119–127.

Raine, A., Lencz, T., Taylor, K., Hellige, J., Bihrle, S., Lacasse., L., . . . Colletti, P. (2003). Corpus callosum abnormalities in psychopathic antisocial individuals. *Archives of General Psychiatry, 60*(11), 1134–1142.

Raine, A., Reynolds, G. P., & Sheard, C. (1991). Neuroanatomical correlates of skin conductance orienting in normal humans: A magnetic resonance imaging study. *Psychophysiology, 28*(5), 548–558.

Reiss, D., Meux, C., & Grubin, D. (2000). The effect of psychopathy on outcome in high security patients. *Journal of American Academy of Psychiatry and the Law, 28*(3), 309–314.

Ritz, T., Alatupa, S., Thöns, M., & Dahme, B. (2002). Effects of affective picture viewing and imagery on respiratory resistance in nonasthmatic individuals. *Psychophysiology 39*(1), 86–94.

Sequeira, H., & Roy, J. C. (1997). Neural control of electrodermal activity. In D. Jordan (Ed.), *Central Nervous Control of Autonomic Function, Vol. 11* (pp. 259–293). Amsterdam: Harwood Academic Publishers,

Shine, J., & Hobson, J. (2000). Institutional behaviour and time in treatment among psychopaths admitted to a prison-based therapeutic community. *Medicine, Science and the Law, 40*(4), 327–335.

Smith, S. S., & Newman, J. P. (1990). Alcohol and drug abuse-dependence disorders in psychopathic and nonpsychopathic criminal offenders. *Journal of Abnormal Psychology, 99*, 430–439.

Stevens, M. C., Kaplan, R. F., & Hasselbrock, V. M. (2003). Executive-cognitive functioning in the development of antisocial personality disorder. *Addictive Behaviors, 28*(2), 285–300.

Swick, D., & Jovanovic, J. (2002). Anterior cingulate cortex and the Stroop task: Neuropsychological evidence for topographic specificity. *Neuropsychologia, 40*(8), 1240–1253.

Swick, D., & Turken, A. U. (2002). Dissociation between conflict detection and error monitoring in the human anterior cingulate cortex. *Proceedings of the National Academy of Sciences of the United States of America, 99*(25), 16354–16359.

Tekin, S., & Cummings, J. L. (2002). Frontal-subcortical neuronal circuits and clinical neuropsychiatry: An update. *Journal of Psychosomatic Research, 53*(2), 647–654.

Thayer, J. F., & Lane, R. D. (2000). A model of neurovisceral integration in emotion regulation and dysregulation. [Review]. *Journal of Affect Disorder, 61*(3), 201–216.

Thayer, J. F., & Siegel, G. J. (2002). Neurovisceral integration in cardiac and emotional regulation, *IEEE Engineering in Medicine and Biology, 21*, 24–29.

Tiihonen, J., Hodgins, S., Vaurio, O., Laakso, M., Repo, E., Soininen, H., . . . Savolainen, L. (2000). Amygdaloid volume loss in psychopathy [Abstract]. *Society for Neuroscience Abstracts*, 2017.

Tiihonen, J., Rossi, R., Laakso, M. P., Hodgins, S., Testa, C., Perez, J., . . . Frisoni, G. B. (2008). Brain anatomy of persistent violent offenders: More rather than less. *Psychiatry Research, 163*(3), 201–212.

Tranel, D., & Damasio, H. (1989). Intact electrodermal skin conductance responses after bilateral amygdala damage. *Neuropsychologia, 27*(4), 381–390. doi:0028-3932(89)90046-8 [pii]

Tranel, D., & Damasio, H. (1994). Neuroanatomical correlates of electrodermal skin conductance responses. *Psychophysiology, 31*(5), 427–438.

van Elst, L. T., Woermann, F. G., Lemieux, L., Thompson, P. J., & Trimble, M. R. (2000). Affective aggression in patients with temporal lobe epilepsy: A quantitative MRI study of the amygdala. *Brain, 123*(2), 234–243.

van Goozen, S. H., Matthys, W., Cohan-Kettenis, P. T., Buitelarr, J. K., & van England, H. (2000). Hypothalamic-pituitary-adrenal axis and autonomic nervous system activity in disruptive children and matched controls. *Journal of American Academy of Child Adolescent Psychiatry, 39*(11), 1438–1445.

van Honk, J., Hermans, E. J., Putman, P., Montagne, B., & Schutter, D. J. (2002). Defective somatic markers in sub-clinical psychopathy. *Neuroreport, 13*(8), 1025–1027.

Van Hulle, C. A., Corley, R., Zahn-Waxler, C., Kagan, J., & Hewitt, J. (2000). Early childhood heart rate does not predict externalizing behavior problems at age 7 years. *Journal of the American Academy of Child Adolescent Psychiatry, 39*(10), 1238–1244.

Verona, E., Patrick, C. J., Curtin, J. J., Bradley, M. M., & Lang, P. J. (2004). Psychopathy and physiological response to emotionally evocative sounds. *Journal of Abnormal Psychology, 113*(1), 99–108.

Verschuere, B., Crombez, G., De Clercq, A., & Koster, E. H. W. (2005). Psychopathic traits and autonomic responding to concealed information in a prison sample. *Psychophysiology, 42*(2), 239–245.

Weber, S., Habel, U., Amunts, K., & Schneider, F. (2008). Structural brain abnormalities in psychopaths—a review. *Behavioral Sciences and the Law 26*(1), 7–28.

Woermann, F. G., van Elst, L. T., Koepp, M. J., Free, S. L., Thompson, P. J., Trimble, M. R., & Duncan, J. S. (2000). Reduction of frontal neocortical grey matter associated with affective aggression in patients with temporal lobe epilepsy: an objective voxel by voxel analysis of automatically segmented MRI. *Journal of Neurology, Neurosurgery and Psychiatry, 68*(2), 162–169.

Wong, M. T., Lumsden, J., Fenton, G. W., & Fenwick, P. B. C. (1994). Electroencephalography, computed tomography and violence ratings of male patients in a maximum-security mental hospital. *Acta Psychiatrica Scandinavica, 90*(2), 97–101.

Yang, Y., Raine, A., Lencz, T., Bihrle, S., LaCasse, L., & Colletti, P. (2005). Volume reduction in prefrontal gray matter in unsuccessful criminal psychopaths. *Biological Psychiatry, 57*(10), 1103–1108.

Zahn, T. P., Grafman, J., & Tranel, D. (1999). Frontal lobe lesions and electrodermal activity: Effects of significance. *Neuropsychologia, 37*(11), 1227–1241. doi: S0028393299000202 [pii].

Zhang, Z. H., Dougherty, P. M., & Oppenheimer, S. M. (1999). Monkey insular cortex neurons respond to baroreceptive and somatosensory convergent inputs. *Neuroscience, 94*(2), 351–360.

CHAPTER FIVE

Perspectives on Neurocriminology

Benjamin R. Nordstrom, Yu Gao, Andrea L. Glenn, Melissa Peskin, Anna S. Rudo-Hutt, Robert A. Schug, Yaling Yang, and Adrian Raine

Introduction

In recent decades, there has been an explosion of research into the biological correlates of criminal behavior. New technologies have allowed researchers to produce high-resolution images of the brain's structure, and even of its function. At the same time, more has been learned about how genetic, biological, and environmental risk factors act alone and in concert to produce antisocial behavior. The objective of this chapter is to summarize the state of current research into the biological correlates of criminal behavior. We will cover psychodynamic models of explanation of criminality, and then consider biological aspects of antisocial behavior as well. We will discuss structural and functional brain imaging data, neuropsychological studies, genetic research, and electrophysiological data and how they pertain to criminality.

Psychoanalytic Models of Crime

Psychoanalytic theory is actually a group of theories (ego psychology, object relations theory, self psychology, and attachment theory) that emphasize the effects of unconscious processes on both normal and abnormal human behavior (Gabbard, 2005). Sigmund Freud, the pioneer of psychoanalysis and originator of ego psychology, speculated that the true meaning of much of our thoughts, feelings, and behaviors is determined outside of our awareness, in the realm of the unconscious (Mitchell & Black, 1995). In the past several decades, a significant number of investigations (i.e., studies of implicit memory, neurological data from brain-damaged patients, and conditioning experiments) have produced evidence supporting the existence of unconscious cognitive, affective, and motivational processes (Westen, 1999).

Psychoanalytic theorists were among the first to offer formalized psychological theories of criminality. The lion's share of these theories are based in ego psychology (e.g., Freud, Hartmann, Anna Freud, Mahler—focusing on unconscious conflicts between sexual and aggressive instincts and the moral/realistic constraints of society), and contributions to criminological theory from object relations (e.g., Klein, Kernberg, Fairburn, Winnicott—emphasizing the later effects of early internalized self-object relationships) and self psychology (e.g., Kohut—stressing how external relationships maintain self-esteem and self-cohesion) are somewhat less common.

Toward the first half of the twentieth century, psychoanalytic interpretations of crime and/or criminality (Holmes & Holmes, 1998; Wittels, 1937), cases of murder (Abrahamsen, 1973; Arieti & Schreiber, 1981; Bromberg, 1951; Cassity, 1941; Evseef & Wisniewski, 1972; Karpman, 1951a, 1951b; Lehrman, 1939; Morrison, 1979; Revitch & Schlesinger, 1981, 1989; Wertham, 1949, 1950; Wittels, 1937), and even homicide wound patterns (DeRiver, 1951) began appearing in the psychiatric literature. One common thread of psychoanalytic criminological theory centers on *unconscious processes* (i.e., drives, instincts, and motivations, and the defense mechanisms used to control them), which are maladaptive and lead to antisocial and criminal behavior. Being unconscious, the causal mechanisms for crime occur outside of the offender's awareness—thus he or she may not be able to fully articulate explanations for the criminal behavior (Alexander & Staub, 1931). One example would be unconscious aggressive and even homicidal impulses (Freud, 1950). Another would be unconscious guilt. Freud proposed that crime is committed to provide the offender with a sense of psychological relief from an "oppressive feeling of guilt" that is reduced after the commission of the crime—thus, the guilt precedes the crime and not vice versa (Freud, 1961). Freud interpreted this preexisting guilt as stemming from the Oedipus complex (the normative developmental phase in childhood wherein a boy develops sexual desires for his mother and rivalries with his father, with the actual offense representing this forbidden Oedipal "crime" in disguised form (Alexander & Staub, 1931)). Thus, the criminal commits the crime *in order to be caught and punished*—the crime becomes an actual physical act to which the unconscious guilt may "attach" and subsequently be punished for. Some (e.g., Indira, 1987) have even speculated that unconsciously motivated errors in criminal behavior serve as clues for law enforcement.

Unconscious aggressive impulses and Oedipal guilt are not the only motivational factors discussed in psychoanalytic criminological theory. For example, Alexander and Healy interpret the significant history of property theft by Richard, a 20-year-old male, as being unconsciously motivated by: (1) overcompensation for a sense of inferiority (giving him feelings of bravery, self-reliance, toughness, and aggressiveness, which hide his inner weakness and insecurities—common in many cases, according to these authors); (2) relief of guilt (as above, though in this case guilt derived from resentment toward his stronger brother, who is the focus of his mother's interest and love); (3) spite toward his mother (revenge by disgrace for denying him interest and love); and (4) the need for gratification of dependency wishes in a carefree, incarcerated setting (i.e., prison) (Alexander & Healy, 1969). Other unconscious motivational processes mentioned in the literature include masculine protest reactions against female identification or passivity (Alexander & Healy, 1969); a need to be apprehended and protected, in order to receive containment or holding functions similar to the self-object functions provided by a therapist in treatment (Adler, 1982); or a regression to the phallic phase of psychosexual development (Wittels, 1937). Later in Freud's career (1961), he proposed aggression as an instinctual drive and discussed opposing death and life instincts (Thanatos and Eros)—with the goal of the former being the return of the individual to the inorganic state (i.e., death). Finally, Freud proposed that every suicide simultaneously and unconsciously represented the murder of another person; and others have speculated that the reverse was also true, i.e., that many neurotic murders represented disguised suicides (Alexander & Straub, 1931).

Self psychologist Heinz Kohut described responses to narcissistic injury (i.e., a psychological "assault"—such as disapproval, betrayal, frustration, or manipulation—which results in the fragmentation or loss of one's sense of self) that were destructive, violent, and homicidal; and in which aggression serves to preserve the self. Others have also discussed rageful and violent outbursts resulting from ego function breakdown or dyscontrol (i.e., the unsuccessful restraining, diverting, or neutralizing by the ego of dangerous impulses, or its suspended efforts to control aggression in the interests of self-preservation). These rage responses can be made worse when weapons are available to the narcissistically injured person. Coupled with a disregard for behavioral consequences (which enhance the individual's sense of potency and capacity to respond), these can result in acts of extreme violence such as mass homicidal attacks (Menninger, 2007).

Attachment theorists (Bowlby, 1969, 1973, 1980; Freud, 1964) have proposed detrimental effects of failed infant-mother attachments (e.g., social isolation, emotional coldness, or a sense of weakness, insignificance, unimportance, and lacking in worth). In fact, in a study of the character and home life of 44 juvenile thieves, John Bowlby (1944) indicated that prolonged early separation from the mother precluded one from forming later emotional attachments with others, and coined the term "affectionless psychopathy" for this condition. Many researchers have since identified factors related to failed early attachments and bond formation in psychopaths, which may explain the impulsivity, stimulation seeking, lack of remorse, and emotional superficiality of this potentially criminogenic disorder. Later writers have even speculated that failed infant-mother attachments may explain the psychological dynamics of serial homicide (Whitman & Akutagawa, 2004). Lastly, object relations theorists have proposed that the aggressive/destructive elements of the early mother-child relationship are introjected (mentally internalized) as "unmetabolized" (dissociated or separated) elements in homicidal individuals, who subsequently split the internalized "badness" from their self and unconsciously project it onto the female victim (Liebert, 1972).

While a fair amount of psychoanalytic criminological theory has been dedicated to the influences of unconscious processes on crime, other writers have focused on criminality caused by *defective psychological equipment* (i.e., what would amount to "structural" deficits in the Ego and Superego—though these are theoretical concepts and not actual physical components). For example, August Aichhorn, in his pioneering work on the application of psychoanalytic theory to juvenile delinquency, emphasized how maladaptive parenting practices may contribute to the development of a psychological apparatus that is prone to delinquent behavior (Aichhorn, 1935). Exposed to excess parental love or severity during development, the resulting ego may be unable to repress instinctual (aggressive or sexual) urges. Bernabeu later proposed that delinquency is rooted in a constricted ego (with a limited repertoire of defense mechanisms, i.e., reversal and projection) that has developed in response to unmet unconscious dependency needs (Bernabeu, 1958). The delinquent sees the world as hostile (because of past experiences and projection), has had infantile and unnurturing parents (i.e., bad objects) as models, and has felt severe deprivation. Unable to give up his only safeguard—a fantasy of omnipotence—he has not psychologically delegated omnipotence to parental figures or substitutes. Thus, external controls are not internalized, and acting out behaviors causes a continuing lack of socialization and subsequently a constricted ego that is ill equipped to produce realistic gratifications of sexual and aggressive instincts or wishes. Furthermore, identification with a parent who is antisocial may facilitate the development of a Superego which functions normally yet is characterized by an antisocial value system; or, alternatively, a weak and defective Superego may result from early childhood deprivations (Friedlander, 1947).

Finally, Alexander and Straub (1931) proposed a biopsychosocial typology of offenders based upon the structural integrity of the psychological apparatus. First, the *normal criminal* possesses normal psychological equipment—Id, Ego, and Superego—yet identifies with criminal prototypes (i.e., a sociological etiology). Second, the *organic criminal* is characterized by organic brain damage from which criminal behavior was derived (i.e., a biological etiology). Lastly, the *neurotic criminal* is characterized by an unconscious sense of guilt and an excessively strong Superego (i.e., a psychological etiology). These authors propose the neurotic type utilizes atonement (suffering/punishment) as a license for criminal behavior, as it commonly only serves to lift moral inhibitions. Hence, this type of criminal is not frightened away, inhibited, or made a better person by punishment; for punishment in neurotics acts as a temptation to crime, which perpetuates rather than ceases criminality.

Behavioral Models of Crime

Behavioral theory in general is based on the assumption that both normal and abnormal behavior is caused by learning experiences, involving conditions that precede rewards and punishments that follow behavior (i.e., operant conditioning, pioneered by Thorndike and Skinner) or the psychological/physiological pairing of various sensations or emotions with situations and events (i.e., classical conditioning, introduced by Pavlov). The latter may be somewhat less applicable to crime in general, though perhaps relevant in specific criminological applications situations such as the initiation and maintenance of illegal substance use. For example, drug-induced euphoria (unconditioned stimulus) may over time become associated with drug paraphernalia, locations, behavior, and individuals present during the euphoric state (conditioned stimuli). After continued pairings, these associated stimuli may produce intense urges or cravings to use the substance (Tapert, Tate, & Brown, 2001). Similar processes have been discussed in the development of sadistic and violent paraphilic behaviors (i.e., an orgasmic conditioning process involving increasingly violent fantasies and pornography (Arrigo & Purcell, 2001); and incidental sexual arousal associated with nonhuman objects (e.g., shoes or undergarments)) may lead to fetishistic behavior and subsequent property crimes (e.g., burglaries) to obtain fetish items.

Behavioral criminological theories have centered largely upon social learning, proposing that crime is initially acquired through observations of individuals around us, and subsequently maintained through reinforcements. One key contributor—particularly in the area of aggression—is Alfred Bandura, who conducted a series of studies on the social learning of aggression (Bandura & Huston, 1961; Bandura, Ross, & Ross, 1961, 1963). These studies demonstrated how young schoolchildren learned to imitate aggressive behaviors, such as assaulting inflatable or rubber dolls, by observing adults (on film or in person) engaged in the same activity.

Eron (1987) provides additional examples. In his 22-year longitudinal study of over 600 children, this author found decreased parental nurturance and acceptance at home (frustration), increased punishment for aggression at home, and decreased identification with parents all to be associated with increased aggression at school. From an operant conditioning perspective, a general lack of favorable parental support may have instigated children's aggression and reduced the effectiveness of any punishment administered to deter aggressive behavior; while from a social learning perspective, parental punitiveness may have provided a model of aggressive behavior for children to emulate. The aforementioned illegal substance use example also illustrates how operant conditioning can facilitate the initiation and maintenance of other criminal behaviors. More specifically, pharmacological impact (e.g., euphoria, relief from aversive states) and social/environmental factors (social approval) associated with substance use may produce rewards following drug self-administration, which increase the chance that drug use will recur (Tapert et al., 2001). Other positive reinforcers might include financial gain (i.e., for property crimes), sexual arousal (for sexual offenses), and increased self-esteem (for violent assaults).

Genetics

Advances in the field of molecular genetics, in addition to increased use of sophisticated behavioral genetics designs, have provided greater insight into the role of genes in the intergenerational transmission of criminal behavior. Adoption studies and research comparing monozygotic and dizygotic twins reared together and apart have revealed considerable genetic influences on crime (Beaver, DeLisi, Wright, & Vaughn, 2009; Popma & Raine, 2006). These studies have reported heritability estimates that range substantially, although the vast majority of studies find heritability estimates that fall between 40% and 60% (Arsenault et al., 2003; Beaver et al., 2009; Jaffee et al., 2005; Jaffee, Caspi, Moffitt, & Taylor, 2004; Lyons et al., 1995; Moffitt, 2005; Rhee & Waldman, 2002; Slutske et al., 1997). Numerous methodological differences between studies are probably responsible for this variation in heritability estimates. These differences include sample age, age of offending onset, inclusion of both sexes versus only one, and how criminal behavior is defined; for example, as the violation of legal or social norms, the presence of a psychiatric disorder such as conduct disorder or antisocial personality disorder, or the degree of violence and aggression individuals exhibit.

Several factors have been shown to moderate the extent of genetic and environmental contributions to criminality, including sample age. Research has revealed variation across the life span in the relative importance of genes and environment in the etiology of crime (Goldman & Ducci, 2007). Most studies find that heritability estimates for antisocial behavior are lower, and shared environmental effects on antisocial behavior are higher in childhood than in adolescence (Jacobson, Prescott, & Kendler, 2002; Lyons et al., 1995; Miles & Carey, 1997). This is in keeping with research that suggests that genetic contributions to criminal behavior appear to increase with age while shared environmental influences appear to decrease (Goldman & Ducci, 2007). Greater heritability has also been found for early-onset and persistent antisocial behavior than for childhood-limited antisocial behavior. Differences have also been reported in the length of time in which certain genes influence criminal behavior; for example, some genes have been found to impact criminality throughout life, while others only influence criminal behavior during adolescence or adulthood (Goldman & Ducci, 2007).

In addition to sample age, type of offending appears to moderate the magnitude of genetic influences on criminality. In this respect, the most important distinction is between aggressive and nonaggressive crime, because research suggests that heritability estimates for aggressive offending are higher than those for nonaggressive offending, such as rule breaking and theft (Eley, Lichtenstein, & Moffitt, 2003). The converse appears to be true for non-aggressive offending, which may be influenced more by shared environmental factors such as family criminality, family poverty, and poor parenting, although research suggests that genetic influences also affect several of these risk factors (Moffitt, 2005).

The search for candidate genes involved in the etiology of antisocial behavior has led to a number of insights. While several candidate genes have been implicated, they have not been found to account for a large proportion of the phenotypic variance in offending (Goldman & Ducci, 2007). This suggests, first, that multiple genes are involved in increasing risk for criminal behavior; and second, that gene-environment interactions are involved in the etiology of antisocial behavior. A seminal study highlighting the importance of examining how environmental risk interacts with genotype in the cycle of violence (Caspi et al., 2002) paved the way for future research in this area and led to a burgeoning of research on measured gene-environment interactions. This study examined whether individuals with a functional polymorphism in the gene encoding monoamine oxidase A (MAOA; a neurotransmitter-metabolizing enzyme) differed in their response to childhood maltreatment. These researchers found that maltreated children with a genotype conferring high levels of MAOA expression were less likely to develop conduct disorder in adolescence or engage in violent crime in adulthood than maltreated children with a genotype conferring low levels of MAOA expression. By demonstrating that genotype can moderate children's vulnerability to environmental insults, this study offers insight into why adverse experiences affect some individuals differently from others and offers an explanation for the fact that not all children who experience maltreatment or abuse become violent perpetrators themselves. Thus, both molecular and behavioral genetics research has provided compelling evidence for genetic influences on criminal behavior.

Early Health Risks

Over the past 20 years, great progress has been made in uncovering various biological risk factors that predispose to criminality. One area in particular that has received increasing attention has been the role of early health risk factors in contributing to crime and violence. Extensive evidence suggests that a number of early health risk factors, including minor physical anomalies (MPAs), prenatal nicotine exposure, birth complications, and malnutrition significantly elevate risk for antisocial and criminal behavior across the life span.

MPAs, which consist of congenital malformations such as adherent ear lobes, a single palmar crease, and a furrowed tongue, are viewed as indirect indicators of fetal neurodevelopment toward the end of the first three months of pregnancy (Firestone & Peters, 1983). The shared embryological origins of the epidermis and central nervous system (CNS) have led researchers to view MPAs as biomarkers of atypical CNS and brain development. Studies have not only documented relationships between the number of MPAs and the extent of antisocial behavior in children, adolescents, and adults (Raine, 1993), but have also repeatedly found associations between MPAs and violent offending in particular (Arsenault, Tremblay, Boulerice, Seguin, & Saucier, 2000; Kandel, Brennan, Mednick, & Michelson, 1989). Other studies have found that MPAs moderate the relationship between familial risk factors and violent crime (Brennan, Mednick, & Raine, 1997; Mednick & Kandel, 1988) and conduct disorder (Pine, Shaffer, Schonfeld, & Davies, 1997). These studies suggest that subtle neurological impairments such as MPAs may heighten vulnerability to family adversity and other environmental risk factors for crime and violence.

Research on the relationship between prenatal smoking exposure and criminality adds to the growing recognition that the prenatal environment has a significant impact on offspring behavior in a diverse number of domains. This research is similar to that on MPAs in that studies have not only found main effects of maternal prenatal smoking on offspring conduct disorder, delinquency, and crime (Brennan, Grekin, & Mednick, 1999; Brennan, Grekin, Mortensen, & Mednick, 2002; Fergusson, Woodward, & Horwood, 1998; Rantakallio, Laara, Isohanni, & Moilanen, 1992; Wakschlag et al., 1997; Weissman, Warner, Wickramarante, & Kandel, 1999), but have also found biosocial interactions between prenatal smoking and psychosocial risk factors in predisposing to violence (Gibson & Tibbetts, 1998; Ransen et al., 1999). Other studies have found interactions between prenatal smoking and delivery complications in relation to violent offending (Brennan et al., 1999). Further evidence for the link between prenatal smoking exposure and antisocial behavior comes from three studies that have found a dose-response relationship between the extent of maternal pregnancy smoking and the extent of offspring antisocial behavior (Brennan et al., 1999; Maughan, Taylor, Caspi, & Moffitt, 2004; Maughan, Taylor, Taylor, Butler, & Bynner, 2001). Thus, an extensive literature strongly suggests that individuals exposed to maternal smoking during pregnancy are at greater risk for criminal and violent behavior.

In addition to MPAs and prenatal smoking, research has examined the relationship between birth complications and crime. Birth complications, which consist of such delivery problems as premature birth, low birth weight, placement in a neonatal intensive care unit, forceps delivery, Cesarean section, anoxia, resuscitation after delivery, pre-eclampsia in the mother, and low Apgar score, are believed to negatively impact brain function (Liu, 2004; Liu & Wuerker, 2005). Several studies have revealed interactions between birth complications and various psychosocial risk factors in predisposing to delinquency and violent crime (Raine, Brennan, & Mednick, 1997; Raine, Brennan, & Mednick, 1994; Werner,

1987). Similar findings have been replicated in large samples around the world (Arsenault, Tremblay, Boulerice, & Saucier, 2002; Brennan, Mednick, & Mednick, 1993; Hodgins, Kratzer, & McNeil, 2001; Piquero & Tibbetts, 1999), highlighting the importance of investigating interactions between biological and psychosocial risk factors.

Another early health risk factor that has been shown to contribute to criminal and antisocial behavior is malnutrition. In addition to epidemiological studies that show a relationship between vitamin and mineral deficiency and aggression (Breakey, 1997; Werbach, 1995) research has found micronutrient deficiencies in incarcerated juvenile delinquents (Rosen et al., 1985) and violence-prone, assaultive young males (Walsh, Isaacson, Rehman, & Hall, 1997). Other studies have found that violent offenders are deficient in omega-3 essential fatty acids (Corrigan et al., 1994) and have abnormalities in essential fatty acid metabolism (Hibbeln et al., 1998; Vikkunen, Horrobin, Jenkins, & Manku, 1987), which is consistent with research linking higher consumption of fish rich in omega-3 essential fatty acids to lower levels of violent and aggressive behavior (Hallahan, Hibbeln, Davis, & Garland, 2007). Further support for the relationship between malnutrition during childhood and antisocial behavior in later life comes from a prospective longitudinal study, which found that children with iron, zinc, or protein deficiencies at age 3 exhibited more aggression at age 8, more externalizing behavior at age 11, and more conduct disorder at age 17 (Liu, Raine, Venables, & Mednick, 2004).

Nutritional interventions and randomized controlled trials also provide persuasive evidence that malnutrition relates to criminal behavior. For example, a large randomized, double-blind, placebo-controlled trial revealed that public-school children given a daily vitamin and mineral supplement showed a reduction of 47% in antisocial behavior after four months compared with children given the placebo (Schoenthaler & Bier, 2000). Another randomized, double-blind, placebo-controlled trial found that young adult prisoners who received nutritional supplements committed significantly fewer violent and antisocial offenses than those who received placebos (Gesch, Hammond, Eves, & Crowder, 2002). Supplementation with omega-3 essential fatty acids has also been associated with significant reductions in conduct disorder symptoms, (Stevens et al., 2003) although findings have not always been consistent (Hirayama, Hamazaki, & Terasawa, 2004). Perhaps the best evidence for a possible causal role of early malnutrition in subsequent criminal behavior comes from a randomized controlled trial, which found that an enrichment program from ages 3 to 5 significantly reduced antisocial behavior at age 17 and criminal behavior at age 23 (Raine, Mellingen, Liu, Venables, & Mednick, 2003).

While the enrichment program consisted of nutrition, education, and physical exercise, Raine et al. (2003) demonstrated that the intervention was most beneficial for children who exhibited signs of malnutrition at age 3, implying that the nutritional components of the intervention were the active ingredients in the enrichment program.

Research from several domains thus suggests that a number of early health risks, including MPAs, prenatal nicotine exposure, birth complications, and malnutrition predispose to adult crime and violence.

Structural Brain Abnormalities

In recent years, neurobiological predispositions for antisocial behavior and psychopathic traits have been a focus of research interest in the understanding of personal characteristics of criminal offenders. Findings from lesion studies have long been suggesting a plausible relationship between brain structural impairments and antisocial criminal behavior. For example, several case studies have linked frontal lesions, particularly in the orbitofrontal cortex, to the development of elevated antisocial behavior and impaired social and emotional functioning (e.g., poor insight, lack of empathy). One such case was the famous Phineas Gage, an unfortunate railway foreman who suffered damage to his frontal lobe (most severely to the orbitofrontal cortex) in an accident involving explosives. Despite surviving such injury and proceeding to have a full recovery physically and intellectually, his personality changed dramatically, and he became irresponsible, impulsive, and "psychopathic-like" (Harlow, 1848). Similar increase in antisocial tendency was observed in several subsequent reports of other patients with frontal damage (Damasio, Grabowski, Frank, Galaburda, & Damasio, 1994; Damasio, Trabel, & Damasio, 1990). Furthermore, antisocial characteristics, violence in particular, seem to develop when the lesion damaged the medial section of the orbitofrontal cortex. For example, Grafman et al. examined a large group of Vietnam War veterans and found that aggressive attitudes were heightened in veterans who had suffered lesions to the ventromedial prefrontal cortex when compared to controls and individuals with damage to other brain regions (Grafman et al., 1996).

Another line of evidence linking brain damage to antisocial behavior has come largely from studies of traumatic brain injuries (TBIs). TBIs, ranging from subclinical to fatal in severity, are one of the leading causes of morbidity and mortality in children and adolescents in the United States (Hayman-Abello, Rourke, & Fuerst, 2003). Most TBIs were suffered during a fall, motor vehicle accident, assault, or suicide attempt (Langlois, Rutland-Brown, & Wald, 2006), and put the individuals at higher risk for developing functional impairments. Evidence has been accumulated suggesting a high correlation between violent crime and TBIs. For example, Lewis et al., in a study of 15 death-row inmates, found that all of these violent offenders had a history of severe head injury, and five had major neurological impairment (Lewis, Pincus, Feldman, Jackson, & Bard, 1986). Hux, Bond, Skinner, Belau, and Sanger (1998) also reported that half of the delinquents they studied had experienced a TBI (defined as having ever received a "blow to the head"), while one-third of delinquents with TBIs were thought (by their parents) to have suffered adverse, long-term behavioral problems including diminished attentional capacity, impaired interpersonal skills, and poor school performance. Similarly, another study conducted by Craswell, Maughan, Davis, Davenport, and Goddard (2004) found that 27.7% of the delinquents had TBIs (defined as a "significant head injury involving loss of consciousness/amnesia with ongoing cognitive or social impairment"). Several longitudinal studies using large samples have also consistently showed an elevated incidence of delinquency among children and adolescents and criminal offending in adults who had experienced brain trauma (Asarnow, Satz, Light, Lewis, & Neumann, 1991; Bloom et al., 2001; Butler, Chadwick, Shaffer, Rutter, & Traub, 1997; McAllister, 1992; Perron & Howard, 2008; Rantakallio, Koiranen, & Mottonen, 1992; Rimel, Giordani, & Barth, 1981; Rivera et al., 1994). Interestingly, the severity of antisocial criminal behavior in individuals with TBIs not only fails to improve, but becomes greater over time. For example, in a longitudinal study, Hall et al. (1994) found that the frequency of aggressive behavior and severity of temper bursts in a group of patients with TBIs increased over time, and the aggressiveness was reported by caregivers as moderate or severe in 31% of cases by two years post injury. Similar patterns were documented by Brooks, Campsie, Symington, Beattie, and McKinlay (1986) in a five-year study following 42 patients with severe TBIs, and found a significant increase in threats of violence at five years after the injury (54%) compared to 15% at one year post injury. They also noted that 7% of their sample had been in trouble with the law during the first year post injury, and the rate increased to 31% at five years post injury. The arrest and conviction rates of individuals with TBIs were especially alarming when compared to the rate of 2% of the general population arrested annually. In addition, the increasing arrest and incarceration rates over the years post injury raise concerns about the long-term effects of traumatic brain injuries.

Recent development in brain imaging technique has allowed researchers to understand the neurobiological basis of antisocial, criminal behavior by identifying global and regional alterations in brain morphology and connectivity in individuals with delinquent behavior using structural magnetic resonance imaging (sMRI) and diffusion tensor imaging (DTI). The strongest evidence has been found for the prefrontal cortex, a result not surprising considering findings from lesion studies and the key function of this region, which is to inhibit behavioral impulses and regulate emotion generated by subcortical structures such as the amygdala. Specifically, several sMRI studies to date have found volumetric and morphological abnormalities in the prefrontal regions in individuals with antisocial, aggressive behavior. For example, Raine and colleagues found that individuals with antisocial personality disorders (ASPD) show a significant gray matter volume reduction in the prefrontal cortex compared with controls, particularly the middle and orbitofrontal cortex (Raine, Lee, Yang, & Colletti, 2010; Raine, Lencz, Bihrle, LaCasse, & Colletti, 2000). Similarly, Laakso et al. (2002) reported reduced gray matter volume in dorsolateral prefrontal, medial frontal, and orbitofrontal cortex in alcoholics with ASPD compared with normal controls. Furthermore, Yang and colleagues (2009) revealed reduced cortical gray matter thickness in the frontal and temporal regions in psychopaths compared to normal controls. In support of these findings, Yang and colleagues found a volume reduction in prefrontal gray matter, particularly in the dorsolateral prefrontal and orbitofrontal cortex, in psychopaths with prior convictions (i.e., unsuccessful psychopaths) compared to both those without convictions (i.e., successful psychopaths) and also non-psychopathic controls (Yang, Raine, Colletti, Toga, & Narr, 2010; Yang et al., 2005). Similar neuropathology has been observed in children and adolescents with conduct disorder (Huebner et al., 2008; Kruesi, Casanova, Mannheim, & Jonson-Bilder, 2004) and several other independent adult samples with psychopathy, antisocial personality disorder, and criminal behavior (Boccardi et al., 2011; Muller et al., 2008). Thus, the results suggest that reduced volume/thickness in the frontal regions may predispose one to impaired decision-making and poor impulse control, which result in various degrees of antisocial, psychopathic behavior as well as criminal offending and violence.

Although the majority of the studies have focused on the frontal cortex, converging evidence is beginning to shade light on the involvement of other cortical and subcortical structures in association with criminal behavior. For example, violent offenders and criminal psychopaths have been found to show increased callosal volume and length (Raine et al., 2003), reduced amygdala volume/surface shape (Boccardi et al., 2011; Tiihonen, Hodgins, & Vaurio, 2000; Yang et al., 2009, 2010) and increased striatal volume (Glenn, Raine, Yaralian, & Yang, 2010) compared to normal controls. Furthermore, Raine et al. (2010) showed that individuals with cavum septum pellucidum (CSP; a marker of limbic neural maldevelopment) have significantly higher levels of antisocial personality, psychopathy, arrests, and convictions compared with controls. Furthermore, subjects who were charged or convicted for an offense but without a diagnosis of antisocial personality disorders had a more extensive CSP than non-antisocial controls. In an independent sample, Yang et al. reported reduced hippocampal and parahippocampal volumes in Chinese murderers with schizophrenia and reduced parahippocampal volumes in murderers compared to normal controls (Yang, Raine, Han, et al., 2010). The findings were consistent with reports showing abnormal hippocampal volume and shape in offenders with psychopathy (Boccardi et al., 2010; Laakso et al., 2001). Studies of children and adolescents with conduct disorders (CD) have also revealed a similar pattern of neuropathology underlying antisocial, criminal behavior. For example, Sterzer and colleagues found reduced gray matter volumes in the amygdala and insula in adolescents with conduct disorder compared to healthy controls (Sterzer, Stadler, Poutska, & Kleinschmidt, 2007). In addition, Huebner and colleagues showed reduced gray matter volumes in the amygdala and the hippocampus (in addition to reduced frontal volumes) in children with conduct disorders compared with healthy controls (Huebner et al., 2008). Although the structural integrity of these regions remains to be further examined, these findings provided initial evidence suggesting that disturbances in the fronto-limbic network may also contribute to the development of disruptive behavior in children and adolescents and may lead to antisocial, criminal behavior in adulthood.

The relatively new imaging technique of DTI is promising in providing information regarding white matter development in the brain and the mapping of neuronal connectivity. This technique has been used in examining the microstructural integrity of white matter in various populations; however, very few studies have applied it to criminal or antisocial samples. One of the very few studies was conducted by Li and colleagues, which showed reduced fractional anisotropy (FA; a measure of the directional diffusivity of water within fiber tracts) in the fronto-temporal regions in adolescents with disruptive behavior disorder compared to normal controls (Li, Mathews, Wang, Dunn, & Kronenberger, 2005). Findings are consistent with a recent report by Graig et al. (2009) revealing reduced FA in the uncinate fasciculus (a major fiber tract connecting the amygdala and the orbitofrontal cortex) in adult psychopaths with criminal convictions compared to healthy controls. These studies provided initial evidence suggesting that disturbed structural integrity in the morphometry and connectivity of the fronto-temporal regions plays a crucial role in the development of disruptive behavior and emotional deficiency that, especially in the presence of environmental and/or social risk factors, may escalate into delinquency and ultimately a lifetime of persistent criminal, violent offending. Overall, the increasing evidence from lesion and brain imaging studies has confirmed that morphological abnormalities in the brain, particularly the frontal, temporal, and limbic regions, and alterations in neural connectivity between these regions may contribute to disturbances in decision making, emotional regulation, and moral judgment and ultimately predispose to criminal, violent behavior.

Functional Imaging

Brain imaging studies are beginning to provide evidence of abnormalities in brain functioning in individuals with antisocial behavior and psychopathic-like traits. Numerous brain regions involved in social processes have been identified. Most commonly, brain abnormalities have been identified in the amygdala and orbitofrontal/ventromedial prefrontal cortex, which play key roles in fear conditioning, socialization, and the integration of emotion into decision making. Additional regions involved in the process of moral judgment have also been implicated.

The best-replicated abnormality across a wide range of antisocial groups is in the prefrontal cortex. Regions of the prefrontal cortex have been found to be involved in several processes that may lead to antisocial behavior or psychopathic traits when disrupted. The disruptions of the ventromedial/orbitofrontal and medial/frontopolar regions may affect processes that are important to moral decision-making, such as processing social and emotional information. Disruptions to the dorsolateral prefrontal cortex may affect executive functioning.

Early studies used positron emission tomography (PET), which involved injecting the participant with a short-lived radioactive tracer to detect abnormalities in the brain. Several studies observed reduced metabolism in frontal regions of the brain in antisocial and aggressive populations (New et al., 2002; Raine, Buchsbaum, & LaCasse, 1997; Volkow et al., 1995). Researchers have also used a similar technique, single photon emission computed tomography (SPECT), to show that violent offenders and individuals with antisocial personality demonstrate reduced blood flow in the prefrontal cortex (Soderstrom, Tullberg, Wikkelso, Ekholm, & Forsman, 2000; Kuruoglu, Arikan, Vural, & Karatas, 1996). More recently, functional MRI studies have found reduced activity specifically in the orbitofrontal cortex of antisocial individuals during inhibitory control (Vollm et al., 2004) and in patients with intermittent explosive disorder when viewing angry faces (Coccaro, McCloskey, Fitzgerald, & Phan, 2007). Reduced blood flow in the dorsolateral region of the prefrontal cortex has been found in aggressive patients (Hirono, Mega, Dinov, Mishkin, & Cummings, 2000) and in two fMRI studies of individuals with ASPD (Schneider et al., 2000; Vollm et al., 2004).

In psychopathic individuals, reduced functioning has been observed in several regions of the prefrontal cortex during both cognitive and emotional tasks. For example, in a semantic task using fMRI, Kiehl and colleagues (2004) found that compared to controls, psychopaths fail to show the appropriate neural differentiation between abstract and concrete stimuli in the left ventrolateral prefrontal cortex and anterior cingulate cortex. In another study using SPECT, Soderstrom et al. (2002) found significant negative correlations between psychopathy scores (particularly the interpersonal factor) and frontotemporal perfusion. Also, fMRI studies have observed reduced activity associated with psychopathy in the orbitofrontal cortex during fear conditioning (Birbaumer et al., 2005), during a socially interactive game involving cooperating with or defecting against another player to earn money (Rilling et al., 2007).

Additionally, by using affective pictures as stimuli, a growing number of fMRI studies have reported abnormal affect-related activation in several frontal regions including the dorsolateral prefrontal cortex, orbitofrontal cortex, and ventrolateral prefrontal cortex in psychopaths (Gordon, Baird, & End, 2004; Kiehl et al., 2001; Müller et al., 2003; Schneider et al., 2000; Viet et al., 2002). Reduced activity in the ventromedial prefrontal cortex has also been observed in criminal psychopaths when evaluating pictures of moral violations (Harenski, Harenski, Shane, & Kiehl, 2010).

Also in the frontal lobe, functional imaging studies have revealed reduced activity in the anterior cingulate region in psychopathic individuals (Birbaumer et al., 2005; Kiehl et al., 2001; Müller et al., 2003; Rilling et al., 2007; Viet et al., 2002). The anterior cingulate serves as a relay station of information and is densely interconnected to regions such as the amygdala and orbitofrontal cortex, both of which are consistently implicated in psychopathy.

It should be noted that abnormal functioning in the prefrontal cortex has not been observed in all subgroups of psychopathic or antisocial individuals. Raine et al. (1998) conducted a PET study comparing predatory (planned, instrumental) murderers with affective (heat of the moment) murders. They found that prefrontal glucose metabolism of predatory murderers was similar to controls; in contrast, glucose metabolism in affective murderers was significantly reduced. It was hypothesized that murderers who engage in more premeditated planned crimes may require good prefrontal functioning, which would help them to regulate their impulses and carefully plan their actions.

Some evidence suggests that increased prefrontal functioning observed in some psychopathic individuals may be primarily in the dorsolateral prefrontal cortex. Although several studies mentioned above have found reduced functioning in the dorsolateral prefrontal cortex (e.g., Hirono et al., 2000; Schneider et al., 2000; Vollm et al., 2004), several functional imaging studies of psychopathy have observed increased activation in this region during tasks that involve emotional processing (Gordon et al., 2004; Intrator et al., 1997; Kiehl et al., 2001; Rilling et al., 2007). Since the dorsolateral prefrontal cortex is involved in higher cognition, it has been suggested that some psychopaths may use more cognitive resources to process affective information than non-psychopaths, due to an absence of appropriate limbic input (Kiehl et al., 2001).

Overall, reductions in the orbitofrontal and medial prefrontal cortex appear to contribute to the emotional deficits and poor decision-making in antisocial individuals, whereas reductions in the dorsolateral prefrontal cortex may contribute to the antisocial features of impulsivity and poor behavioral control.

The amygdala is another region that has been implicated in psychopathy and antisocial behavior. The amygdala is thought to be important in normal socialization and the development of appropriate social behavior. Dysfunction in the amygdala is associated with impaired classical conditioning (LeDoux, 2000) (i.e., the formation of stimulus-reinforcement associations). These processes are important in the development of conscience (i.e., the feelings of guilt that accompany wrongdoings) and the anticipatory fear that normally deters individuals from committing antisocial acts (Blair, 2004).

In a sample of murderers, Raine et al. (1997) found that activity in the amygdala was asymmetrical, in that there was reduced activity in the left amygdala and increased activity in the right amygdala in murders compared to controls. In both criminal psychopaths, and healthy individuals scoring high in psychopathic traits, fMRI studies have revealed reduced activity in the amygdala during various tasks, including the processing of emotional stimuli (Gordon et al., 2004; Kiehl et al., 2001), during fear conditioning (Birbaumer et al., 2005; Viet et al., 2002), and during a socially interactive game (Rilling et al., 2007). Reduced amygdala activity has also been observed during moral decision-making about emotional moral dilemmas (Glenn, Raine, & Schug, 2009). However, two studies have reported increased amygdala activation in antisocial individuals while viewing negative visual content (Müller et al., 2003) and during aversive conditioning (Schneider et al., 2000).

The amygdala is thought to be important in moral judgment (Greene, Nystrom, Engell, Darley, & Cohen, 2004) and the experience of moral emotions such as guilt and empathy (Moll et al., 2002). It is active when judging one's own moral violations (Berthoz, Grezes, Armony, Passingham, & Dolan, 2006), suggesting that functioning in the amygdala is important for affective responsiveness to one's own transgressions. The finding of reduced amygdala activation associated with psychopathy during a moral decision task (Glenn et al., 2009) supports the idea that dysfunction in the amygdala may partly underlie deficits in moral behavior in psychopathic individuals.

The angular gyrus and posterior cingulate are also implicated in moral decision-making and have also been associated with antisocial behavior. Deficits in the angular gyrus have been observed in murderers (Raine, Buchsbaum, et al., 1997) impulsive, violent criminals (Soderstrom et al., 2000), and in psychopathic individuals during a semantic processing task (Kiehl et al., 2004). The angular gyrus has been found to be active during the experience of social emotions such as guilt and embarrassment—emotions that may motivate individuals to avoid antisocial actions (Takahashi et al., 2004). The posterior cingulate is involved in emotional processing, such as the recall of emotional memories (Maratos, Dolan, Morris, Henson, & Rugg, 2001) and the experience of emotion (Mayberg et al., 1999). It also appears to be important in relating information to the self, as it has been found to be active during self-referencing (Ochsner et al., 2005) and reflecting on one's duties and obligations (Johnson et al., 2006). One study of criminal psychopaths has observed reduced functioning in the posterior cingulate during an affective memory task (Kiehl et al., 2001).

Neuropsychology

Neuropsychological impairments have long been hypothesized to be a cause of criminal and antisocial behavior. Moffitt postulated that neuropsychological impairment interacts with a criminogenic environment to produce life-course-persistent criminal behavior, in contrast to adolescence-limited offending, which was theorized to be the result of social mimicry (Moffitt, 1993a). Many areas of functioning have been found to be impaired in criminal populations, most strikingly overall cognitive ability (especially verbal abilities) as well as executive functioning.

Intelligence

Evidence for decreased cognitive ability (as measured by IQ) in association with antisocial behavior has been found by many researchers. In fact, at a very broad level, estimates of the average U.S. state IQ have been found to be significantly and negatively correlated with FBI crime statistics in each state (Bartels, Ryan, Urban, & Glass, 2010), and this relationship has been replicated at the county level using county crime statistics (Beaver & Wright, 2011). Furthermore, a large number of studies have documented an association between low IQ and antisocial behavior (Finn et al., 2009; Goodman, Simonoff, & Stevenson, 1995; Lipsitt, Buka, & Lipsitt, 1990; Lussier, Farrington, & Moffitt, 2009; Stattin & Klackenberg-Larsson, 1993). This association is not merely due to increased detection of cognitively impaired offenders, as it has been shown to persist even when considering undocumented delinquency (Moffitt & Silva, 1988). Cognitive ability has also been conceptualized as a protective, rather than risk, factor. Boys (but not girls) who were at high risk for later offending, due to high levels of antisocial behavior by age five, were found to be protected from later delinquency by above-average IQ (White, Moffitt, & Silva, 1989). Similarly, Piquero and White found that higher levels of cognitive ability at age seven, as measured by digit span (a verbal test of short-term memory), protected against life-course-persistent offending in an African American sample (Piquero, 2003). High IQ has also been found to be protective in the context of environmental adversity, such that children and adolescents with high intellectual functioning do not show the typical increase in antisociality in risky environments (Masten et al., 1999; Vanderbilt-Adriance & Shaw, 2008).

In addition to an overall lower IQ, much research on intellectual functioning in antisocial populations has highlighted a discrepancy between Verbal IQ and Performance IQ. Measures of Verbal IQ include tests that require participants to answer orally and often cover fact-based or crystallized knowledge, such as defining words or solving math problems aloud. Performance IQ tasks, in contrast, involve measures of spatial and nonverbal reasoning, such as manipulating blocks or searching for symbols on a page. Researchers have found decreased Verbal IQ compared to Performance IQ in children (Loney, Frick, Ellis, & McCoy, 1998; McHale, Obrzut, & Sabers, 2003), adolescents (Archwamety & Katsiyannis, 2000; Dougherty et al., 2007), and adults with antisocial behavior (Kirkpatrick et al., 2007; Vitacco, Neumann, & Wodushek, 2008). However, some studies have found no relative deficit in Verbal IQ in antisocial populations (Cadesky, Mota, & Schachar, 2000; Rispens et al., 1997) and another found deficits in spatial, but not verbal, abilities (Raine, Yaralian, Reynolds, Venables, & Mednick, 2002). A recent meta-analysis of this Performance > Verbal discrepancy found that, while the results were statistically significant for all age groups, the effect size of reduced Verbal IQ was negligible in children and small in adults (Isen, 2010). In contrast, the effect size for the discrepancy in antisocial adolescents was closer to medium in size, and reflected a six-point difference on average between Verbal and Performance IQ in delinquent adolescents (Isen, 2010). Therefore, the deficit in Verbal compared to Performance IQ appears to characterize antisocial populations, especially during adolescence.

In addition to these age-based differences in the discrepancy between Verbal and Performance IQ measures, there appear to be some differences based on race or type of antisocial behavior. For example, Isen (2010) reported that effect sizes for black participants were smaller than for white or mixed-race samples. Additionally, in one sample, the highest rates of violent delinquency were found in those adolescents who were both high in callous-unemotional (psychopathic-like) traits and high in verbal abilities (Munoz, Frick, Kimonis, & Aucoin, 2008). Similarly, in a group of boys with conduct disorder, those who had a biological parent with antisocial personality disorder and who had Verbal IQ scores above 100 had the highest number of conduct disorder symptoms three years later (Lahey et al., 1995). Thus, it is likely that the Performance > Verbal IQ pattern is not found in all antisocial groups. Indeed, the finding of overall lowered intelligence was found to apply to single, but not multiple, murderers in one study (Hanlon, Rubin, Jensen, & Daoust, 2010). Further research is needed to clarify these findings.

Several hypotheses have been advanced to explain the discrepancy between verbal and nonverbal measures of ability in antisocial populations. One prominent theory is that preexisting deficits in verbal ability lead to underachievement in school, which is, in turn, a risk factor for antisocial behavior (Moffitt, Lynam, & Silva, 1994). Others argue that antisocial behavior in childhood and adolescence often includes school refusal or gaps in education due to suspensions or incarceration, and these gaps in education are what account for deficits in Verbal IQ scores (Isen, 2010). That is, Verbal IQ tests often tap knowledge learned in school (e.g., word definitions), whereas Performance IQ tests are less reliant on education. Yet another hypothesis is that verbal deficits may lead to socialization failure (Eriksson, Hodgins, & Tengstrom, 2005) by affecting the development of self-control (Luria, 1996). Thus, it is unclear what underlies the relationship between Verbal IQ deficits and antisocial behavior, but researchers are continuing to probe this question.

Executive Function

In comprehensive neuropsychological batteries, executive functioning (EF) is also often found to be impaired in antisocial populations. EF is conceptualized as those cognitive processes which maintain representations of and allow the achievement of goals, and these processes are believed to be controlled largely by the prefrontal cortex (Miller & Cohen, 2001). Tasks commonly used to measure EF usually require mental flexibility, strategy formation, selective attention, and suppression of habitual responses, and they are often used to identify patients with frontal lobe damage.

Thus far, research has supported the hypothesis that antisocial populations have impaired scores on tests of EF. A meta-analysis of this literature found that the effect size for EF deficits in antisocial populations was in the medium to large range, and this relationship held across all ages and all EF tests included (Morgan & Lilienfeld, 2000). More recent studies have supported these results, in adult male, (Dolan & Park, 2002; Kavanagh, Rowe, Hersch, Barnett, & Reznik, 2010) as well as female offenders, (Giancola, Shoal, & Mezzich, 2001) and in relation to violent, (Hancock, Tapscott, & Hoaken, 2010) but not nonviolent (Barker et al., 2007; Hancock et al., 2010; Levi, Nussbaum, & Rich, 2010), offending. Although not all the evidence for EF impairment in youths with conduct problems is consistent (Nigg et al., 2004) the same deficit has generally been found in recent studies of antisocial children and adolescents (Beaver, DeLisi, Vaughn, & Wright, 2010; Hughes, Zagar, Busch, Grove, & Arbit, 2009; Raine et al., 2005; Syngelaki, Moore, Savage, Fairchild, & Van Goozen, 2009).

To some extent, the EF deficits seen in antisocial populations may reflect the high comorbidity between attention-deficit hyperactivity disorder (ADHD) and crime. One study of prisoners found that 50% had met criteria for ADHD in childhood, and many were still symptomatic as adults (Einarsson, Sigurdsson, Gudjonsson, Newton, & Bragason, 2009). The tasks used to measure EF are often precisely those abilities which would be expected to be impaired in people with ADHD. For example, Kavanagh et al. reported four tasks on which inmates were impaired, and two of these tasks (Continuous Performance Test and Verbal Interference) primarily measure attention and impulsivity (Kavanagh et al., 2010). Notably, the EF measure with the strongest effect size in Morgan and Lilienfeld's meta-analysis was the Porteus Maze Test, which is thought to assess impulsivity (Morgan & Lilienfeld, 2000). These findings may suggest that EF impairments cause ADHD, which happens to be highly comorbid with antisocial behavior, but that EF impairments are not directly related to antisocial behavior. However, Moffitt frames this relationship in a different light, arguing that the underlying neuropsychological impairment can manifest as *both* ADHD and persistent antisocial behavior (Moffitt, 1993b). More research is needed in order to disentangle the relationship between EF and ADHD versus that between EF and antisocial behavior.

Biosocial Interactions

A number of studies have found interactions between neuropsychological deficits and social risk factors in the prediction of antisocial behavior, especially in children and adolescents. Lewis, Lovely, Yeager, and Femina (1989) found that adult offending was better predicted using neuropsychological measures and abuse history than by juvenile offending alone. School attendance and self-regulation were found to interact in the prediction of crime such that attending school decreased the risk of later offending in males, even after controlling for familial disruption (Henry, Caspi, Moffitt, Harrington, & Silva, 1999). Adverse environmental factors, such as neighborhood violence, have been found to negatively impact children's intellectual functioning (Sharkey, 2010), and the relationship between neighborhood violence and crime may be mediated by this decrease in cognitive functioning. One piece of support for this hypothesis is the strong relationship between exposure to violent media and poor EF that has been found in children with disruptive behavior disorders (Kronenberger et al., 2005).

Parent traits have also been found to interact with neuropsychological functioning. Grekin, Brennan, and Hammen (2005) found that the relationship between parental alcohol use disorders (AUD) and offspring violent delinquency was mediated by the child's executive functioning, such that parental AUD leads to poor EF in the child, thereby increasing violence in the child. Furthermore, Lahey et al. (1995) found that (relatively) high IQ was only protective for conduct disorder in those children who did not have a biological parent with antisocial personality disorder. One longitudinal study of women followed from childhood into adulthood and motherhood found that the women who were aggressive as children provided poorer cognitive stimulation of their own children, who in turn had poorer verbal and abstract/visual abilities (Saltaris et al., 2004). Cigarette smoke in the home, shorter duration of breastfeeding, low income, and less maternal involvement have also been found to increase the rate of neuropsychological deficits (Beaver, Vaughn, DeLisi, & Higgins, 2010). Given the link between neuropsychological impairment and crime, these studies suggest several mechanisms by which parents may pass on antisocial behavior to the next generation.

Electrophysiological Studies

Electrophysiological studies are also used to investigate the link between neurobiology and criminal behavior. Excellent and extensive reviews are available of both the methodologies used (Cacioppo, Tassinary, & Berntson, 2007) and the results produced by the techniques (Patrick, 2008).

Numerous studies have demonstrated that antisocial individuals are characterized by autonomic underarousal. This underarousal can be measured by decreased skin conductance, low resting heart rate, and slow rhythms as measured by electroencephalogram.

Skin conductance activity is controlled by the sympathetic nervous system and reflects sweating. This can measure both baseline arousal (or activity) and responsivity (or reactivity) to neutral or emotionally charged cues. The change in conductance from increased sweating is measured by electrodes placed on the fingers or palm of the hand. Heart rate measures the number of heartbeats per minute and reflects the complex interactions between sympathetic and parasympathetic nervous system activity.

Low skin conductance has been shown to be associated with conduct problems in children (Lorber, 2004). Boys with conduct disorder have been shown to have reduced fluctuations in skin conductance and impairments in conditioned fear responses (Fairchild, Van Goozen, Strollery, & Goodyer, 2008; Herpertz et al., 2005). Longitudinal studies have demonstrated that reduced skin conductance arousal at age 15 has been associated with criminal offending at age 24 (Raine, Venables, & Williams, 1995) and that low skin conductance at age 11 predicts institutionalization at age 13 (Kruesi et al., 1992).

Low sympathetic reactivity has been shown in psychopathy-prone adolescents and in children with conduct disorder and callous-unemotional traits (Anastassiou-Hadjichara & Warden, 2008; Kimonis, Frick, Fazekas, & Loney, 2006; Loney, Frick, Clements, Ellis, & Kerlin, 2003). It has been demonstrated that individuals having an abnormal skin conductance response to unpleasant stimuli at age three years are at significantly increased risk for displaying psychopathy in adulthood (Glenn, Raine, Venables, & Mednick, 2007).

Low resting heart rate is the most replicated biological correlate of antisocial behavior in juvenile samples (Ortiz & Raine, 2004). In a meta-analytic review of 29 samples, the average effect size was 0.56 (Raine, 1996). This relationship is not artifactual, as confounding variables such as height, weight, body composition, muscle tone, poor school performance, low IQ, hyperactivity, low attention, drug and alcohol use, participation in sports and exercise, social class, and family size and composition have all been ruled out (Farrington, 1997; Raine, Venables, & Mednick, 1997; Raine, Venables, & Williams, 1990b; Wadsworth, 1976).

The finding that low resting heart rate predicts later crime has been replicated in the United States, Germany, England, Canada, Mauritius, and New Zealand (Farrington, 1997; Mezzacappa et al., 1997; Moffitt & Caspi, 2001; Raine, Venables, et al., 1997; Rogeness, Cepeda, Macedo, Fischer, & Harris, 1990; Schmeck & Poustra, 1993). In longitudinal studies, low resting heart rate has been shown to accurately identify individuals who are at risk for later developing antisocial behavior. This finding is specific for antisocial behavior (Rogeness et al., 1990) and has not been shown in other psychiatric syndromes.

In the Cambridge Study in Delinquent Development, only two risk factors, low resting heart rate and poor concentration, were found, independently of all other risk factors, to predict violence. This same study found evidence of an interaction between low resting heart rate and several environmental risk factors (e.g., coming from a large family, having a teenaged mother, being of low socioeconomic status) in producing violent behavior (Farrington, 1997). Conversely, it has also been demonstrated that a high resting heart rate is protective against developing later criminal behavior (Raine et al., 1995).

This pattern of underarousal has implications for the treatment of antisocial populations as well. Studies have shown that interventions targeted at children with behavior problems are less useful in subgroups with lower resting heart rates (Stadler et al., 2008) and deficits in skin conductance (Fishbein, Hyde, Coe, & Paschall, 2004).

The autonomic underarousal and hyporesponsivity noted in these studies have given rise to fearlessness theory. This theory posits that the low level of arousal noted in testing situations can be taken as evidence of a lack of normal fear (Raine, 1993, 1997). An alternative to fearlessness theory is the stimulation-seeking theory, which presumes that the observed hypoarousal is experienced by affected individuals as unpleasant, and is compensated for with risk-taking/thrill-seeking behaviors. Supporting this hypothesis is the observation that three-year-old children who show high levels of sensation seeking and lower levels of fearlessness demonstrate increased levels of aggression at age 11 (Raine, Reynolds, Venables, Mednick, & Farrington, 1998).

It is likely that stimulation seeking and fearlessness explain some part of the low resting heart rate shown in antisocial youth, but a causal link between the low resting heart rate and criminal behavior is more elusive (Raine, 2002). Another, the prefrontal deficit theory, argues that the low arousal seen arises from abnormalities in the prefrontal cortical-subcortical circuits involved with arousal and stress response (Raine, 2002).

Poor Fear Conditioning

Fear conditioning is a form of classical, or Pavlovian, conditioning. Fear conditioning is the process through which individuals learn the social significance of previously neutral stimuli through a process of associative learning. For example, individuals learn that certain behaviors (e.g., aggression, impulsive sensation-seeking) lead to aversive consequences (e.g., anger from others, physical pain). Deficits in such conditioning may lead to the failure to associate punishment with disruptive behavior and thus predispose individuals to antisocial acts. Studies have consistently shown that diminished fear conditioning (as measured by reduced changes in skin conductance in response to aversive stimuli) is associated with aggressive, psychopathic, and antisocial behavior. Specifically, one longitudinal study revealed that poor skin conductance conditioning evidenced at age 3 years predisposes individuals to criminal offending at age 23 years (Gao, Raine, Venables, Dawson, & Mednick, 2010).

Reduced fear conditioning has been a key concept in theories of about the development of antisocial behavior and crime. Hans Eysenck framed the concept of one's conscience as a set of classically conditioned emotional responses that is developed early in childhood. Eysenck hypothesized that individuals with intact fear conditioning develop a conscience that deters them from antisocial and aggressive behavior (Eysenck, 1977).

Slow-Wave EEG and Underarousal

Electroencephalogram (EEG) data measure electrical activity in the brain and are collected via a standardized array of surface electrodes placed on an individual's scalp (Hugdahl, 2001). A large number of studies have implicated EEG abnormalities in criminal individuals. The most commonly reported findings are more slow-wave (i.e., theta and delta) EEG—reflecting underarousal—especially in frontal and temporal regions of the brain (Mednick, Volavka, Gabrielli, & Itil, 1981; Petersen, Matousek, Mednick, Volkava, & Pollock, 1982). Specifically, evidence has emerged that increased slow-wave EEG activity in adolescence predicts official criminal convictions later in life (Raine, Venables, & Williams, 1990a). It is possible that, given that the dominant frequencies in the brain increase with age (Dustman, Shearer, & Emmerson, 1999), these slower rhythms are evidence of cortical immaturity (Volavka, 1987). This immaturity may result in impaired inhibitory control. Alternatively, these slower patterns are evidence of cortical underarousal that predisposes toward compensatory stimulation seeking, which in turn leads to problematic and disruptive behaviors.

Frontal EEG Asymmetry

Another line of evidence using EEG data in the study of antisocial individuals concerns asymmetry in the activity of the right and left frontal lobes. This frontal asymmetry is used as a measure of underlying affective styles and tendencies to approach- or withdrawal-related behavior in individuals. In general, relatively greater left frontal activity is thought to be associated with positive affect and/or approach motivation and behavior, whereas relatively greater right frontal activity is related to negative affect and/or withdrawal motivation and behavioral patterns.

Some studies have associated atypical frontal asymmetry with externalizing behavior in children and with anger proneness and aggressive traits in adults (for a review of this work, see Harmon-Jones, 2003), although these associations may vary based on gender and social factors. In general, atypical frontal EEG asymmetry may indicate abnormal emotional reactivity and affective styles, which could give rise to the disruptive behavior seen in antisocials and criminals (Ishikawa & Raine, 2002; Santesso, Reker, Schmidt, & Segalowitz, 2006).

Atypical Event-Related Potentials

Event-related potentials (ERP) are averaged changes in the electrical activity of the brain in response to experimentally induced external stimuli. ERPs are thought to be electrical correlates of specific psychological processes and therefore may differentiate the brain activity of antisocials and non-antisocials.

The most consistent association between ERP and antisocial behavior has been found for the ERP referred to as P3, which is thought to represent deployment of neural resources to task-relevant or novel information. Although the findings on P3 and psychopathy have been inconsistent, reduced P3 amplitudes and longer P3 latencies have been found in aggressive and antisocial individuals, indicating information-processing deficits in this population (Gao & Raine, 2009). In fact, P3 deficits have also been associated with other externalizing behavior problem, including drug abuse, child conduct disorder, and attention deficit hyperactivity disorder, and this association appears to be mediated by genetic factors (Hicks et al., 2007). It is possible that abnormal P3 may be related to a broad behavioral phenotype of various externalizing behaviors.

Conclusion

Historically, biological and sociological forces within the field of criminology have sought to discredit one another. They have behaved as if discernment of the causes of criminality was a zero-sum game, in which a gain made by one perspective was a loss suffered by the other. The legacy of bigoted and sloppy positivism of such early thinkers as Lombroso has been a heavy albatross around the necks of modern researchers who have sought to elucidate the biological correlates of antisocial behavior. The memory of pseudoscientific disciplines such as phrenology and the misappropriation of evolutional theory into racist political thought such as social Darwinism have also affected how social scientists receive neurocriminological studies.

It is clear, however, that the mind is instantiated in the brain (Kendler, 2005) and that our subjective and objective experiences of self are, at a minimum, mediated by our biology. Insofar as there are meaningful differences in our mental lives and our manifest behavior, there are therefore also meaningful differences in the biological correlates of these thoughts and behaviors. It is important to bear in mind that these biological correlates are not necessarily related to the behaviors in a causal manner, lest we fall into the same biological positivism that plagued early efforts (Yang, Glenn, & Raine, 2008). That said, the more the biological aspects of problematic behavior are investigated and discerned, the richer our understanding will be of the roots of criminal behavior, and hopefully, and more opportunities for intervention and prevention will be discovered.

References

Abrahamsen, D. (1973). *The murdering mind.* New York: Harper & Row.

Adler, G. (1982). Recent psychoanalytic contributions to the understanding and treatment of criminal behavior. *International Journal of Offender Therapy and Comparative Criminology, 26*, 281–287.

Aichhorn, A. (1935). *Wayward youth.* New York: Viking Press.

Alexander, F., & Healy, W. (1969). *Roots of crime: Psychoanalytic studies.* Montclair, NJ: Patterson Smith.

Alexander, F., & Staub, H. (1931). *The criminal, the judge and the public: A psychological analysis* (G. Zilboorg, Trans.). New York: Macmillan Company.

Anastassiou-Hadjichara, X., & Warden, D. (2008). Physiologically-indexed and self-perceived affective empathy in conduct-disordered children high and low on callous-unemotional traits. *Child Psychiatry and Human Development, 39*, 503–517.

Archwamety, T., & Katsiyannis, A. (2000). Academic remediation, parole violations, and recidivism rates among delinquent youths. *Remedial and Special Education, 21*(3), 161–170.

Arieti, S., & Schreiber, F. R. (1981). Multiple murders of a schizophrenic patient: A psychodynamic interpretation. *Journal of the American Academy of Psychoanalysis, 9*(4), 501–524.

Arrigo, B. A., & Purcell, C. E. (2001). Explaining paraphilias and lust murder: Toward an integrated model. *International Journal of Offender Therapy and Comparative Criminology, 45*(1), 6–31.

Arsenault, L., Moffitt, T. E., Caspi, A., Taylor, A., Fruhlilng, A., Rijsdijk, F. V., . . . Measelle, J. R. (2003). Strong genetic effects on cross-situational antisocial behaviour among 5-year-old children according to mothers, teachers, examiners-observers, and twins' self-reports. *Journal of Child Psychology and Psychiatry, 44*(6), 832–848.

Arsenault, L., Tremblay, R. E., Boulerice, B., & Saucier, J. F. (2002). Obstetrical complications and violent delinquency: Testing two developmental pathways. *Child Development, 73*, 496–508.

Arsenault, L., Tremblay, R. E., Boulerice, B., Seguin, J. R., & Saucier, J. F. (2000). Minor physical anomalies and family adversity as risk factors for violent delinquency in adolescence. *American Journal of Psychiatry, 157*, 917–923.

Asarnow, R., Satz, P., Light, R., Lewis, R., & Neumann, E. (1991). Behavior problems and adaptive functioning in children with mild and severe closed head injury. *Journal of Pediatric Psychology, 16*, 543–555.

Bandura, A., & Huston, A. C. (1961). Identification as a process of incidental learning. *Journal of Abnormal and Social Psychology, 63*(2), 311–318.

Bandura, A., Ross, D., & Ross, S. A. (1961). Transmission of aggression through imitation of aggressive models. *Journal of Abnormal and Social Psychology, 63*(3), 575–582.

Bandura, A., Ross, D., & Ross, S. A. (1963). Vicarious reinforcement and imitative learning. *Journal of Abnormal and Social Psychology, 67*(6), 601–607.

Barker, E. D., Séguin, J. R., White, H. R., Bates, M. E., Lacourse, E., & Carbonneau, R. (2007). Developmental trajectories of male physical violence and theft: Relation to neurocognitive performance. *Archives of General Psychiatry, 64*, 592–599.

Bartels, J. M., Ryan, J. J., Urban, L. S., & Glass, L. A. (2010). Correlations between estimates of state IQ and FBI crime statistics. *Personality and Individual Differences, 48*(5), 579–583.

Beaver, K. M., DeLisi, M., Vaughn, M. G., & Wright, J. P. (2010). The intersection of genes and neuropsychological deficits in the prediction of adolescent delinquncy and low self-control. *International Journal of Offender Therapy and Comparative Criminology.*, *54*(1), 22–42.

Beaver, K. M., DeLisi, M., Wright, J. P., & Vaughn, M. G. (2009). Gene environment interplay and delinquent involvement: Evidence of direct and indirect, and interactive effects. *Journal of Adolescent Research, 24*, 147–168.

Beaver, K. M., Vaughn, M. G., DeLisi, M., & Higgins, G. E. (2010). The biosocial correlates of neuropsychological deficits: Results from the National Longitudinal Study of Adolescent Health. *International Journal of Offender Therapy and Comparative Criminology, 54*(6), 878–894.

Beaver, K. M., & Wright, J. P. (2011). The association between county-level IQ and county-level crime rates. *Intelligence, 39*(1), 22–26.

Bernabeu, E. P. (1958). Underlying ego mechanisms in delinquency, USA. *Psychoanalytic Quarterly, 27*(3), 383–396.

Berthoz, S., Grezes, J., Armony, J. L., Passingham, R. E., & Dolan, R. J. (2006). Affective response to one's own moral violations. *NeuroImage, 31*, 945–950.

Birbaumer, N., Viet, R., Lotze, M., Erb, M., Hermann, C., Grodd, W., & Flor, H. (2005). Deficient fear conditioning in psychopathy: A functional magnetic resonance imaging study. *Archives of General Psychiatry, 62*(7), 799–805.

Blair, R. J. (2004). The roles of the orbital frontal cortex in the modulation of antisocial behavior. *Brain and Cognition, 55*, 198–208.

Blair, R. J. (2006). Subcortical brain systems in psychopathy. In C. J. Patrick (Ed.), *Handbook of Psychopathy* (pp. 296–312). New York: Guilford.

Bloom, D. R., Levin, H. S., Ewing-Cobbs, L., Saunders, A. E., Song, J., Fletcher, J. M., & Kowatch, R. A. (2001). Lifetime and novel psychiatric disorders after pediatric brain injury. *Journal of the American Academy of Child and Adolescent Psychiatry, 40*, 572–579.

Boccardi, M., Frisoni, G. B., Hare, R. D., Cavedo, E., Najt, P., Pievani, M., . . . Tiihonen, J. (2011). Cortex and amygdala morphology in psychopathy. *Psychiatry Research, 193*(2), 85–92.

Boccardi, M., Ganzola, R., Rossi, R., Sabattoli, F., Laakso, M. P., Repo-Tiihonen, E., . . . Tiihonen, J. (2010). Abnormal hippocampal shape in offenders with psychopathy. *Human Brain Mapping, 31*, 438–447.

Bowlby, J. (1944). Forty-four thieves: Their character and home life. *International Journal of Psychoanalysis, 25*, 19–52.

Bowlby, J. (1969). *Attachment and loss: Vol. 1. Attachment*. New York: Basic Books.

Bowlby, J. (1973). *Attachment and loss. Vol. 2. Separation: Anxiety and anger*. New York: Basic Books.

Bowlby, J. (1980). *Attachment and loss: Vol. 3. Loss: Sadness and depression.* New York: Basic Books.

Breakey, J. (1997). The role of diet and behaviour in childhood. *Journal of Paediatrics and Child Health, 33*, 190–194.

Brennan, P. A., Grekin, E. R., & Mednick, S. A. (1999). Maternal smoking during pregnancy and adult male criminal outcomes. *Archives of General Psychiatry, 56*, 215–219.

Brennan, P. A., Grekin, E. R., Mortensen, E. L., & Mednick, S. A. (2002). Relationship of maternal smoking during pregnancy with criminal arrest and hospitalization for substance abuse in male and female adult offspring. *American Journal of Psychiatry, 159*, 48–54.

Brennan, P. A., Mednick, B. R., & Mednick, S. A. (1993). Parental psychopathology, congenital factors, and violence. In S. Hodgins (Ed.), *Mental disorder and crime* (pp. 244–261). Thousand Oaks, CA: Sage.

Brennan, P. A., Mednick, S. A., & Raine, A. (1997). Biosocial interactions and violence: A focus on perinatal factors. In A. Raine, P. Brennan, D. P. Farrington & S. A. Mednick (Eds.), *Biosocial bases of violence*. New York: Plenum.

Bromberg, W. (1951). A psychological study of murder. *International Journal of Psychoanalysis, 32*, 117–127.

Brooks, N., Campsie, L., Symington, C., Beattie, A., & McKinlay, W. (1986). The five year outcome of severe blunt head injury: A relative view. *Journal of Neurology, Neurosurgery, and Psychiatry, 49*, 764–770.

Butler, G., Chadwick, O., Shaffer, D., Rutter, M., & Traub, M. (1997). A typology of psychosocial functioning in pediatric closed-head injury. *Child Neuropsychology, 3*, 98–133.

Cacioppo, J. T., Tassinary, L. G., & Berntson, G. (Eds.). (2007). *Handbook of Psychophysiology*. New York: Cambridge University Press.

Cadesky, E. B., Mota, V., & Schachar, R. J. (2000). Beyond words: How do problem children with ADHD and/or conduct problems process nonverbal information about affect? *Journal of the American Academy of Child and Adolescent Psychiatry, 39*(9), 1160–1167.

Caspi, A., McClay, J., Moffitt, T. E., Mill, J., Martin, J., Craig, I. W., . . . Poulton, R. (2002). Role of genotype in the cycle of violence in maltreated children. *Science, 297*(5582), 851–854.

Cassity, J. H. (1941). Personality study of 200 murderers. *Journal of Criminal Psychopathology, 2*, 296–304.

Coccaro, E. F., McCloskey, M. S., Fitzgerald, D. A., & Phan, K. L. (2007). Amygdala and orbitofrontal reactivity to social threat in individuals with impulsive aggression. *Biological Psychiatry, 62*, 168–178.

Corrigan, F., Gary, R., Strathdee, A., Skinner, R., Van Rhijn, A., & Horrobin, D. (1994). Fatty acid analysis of blood from violent offenders. *Journal of Forensic Psychiatry, 5*, 83–92.

Craswell, K., Maughan, B., Davis, H., Davenport, F., & Goddard, N. (2004). The psychosocial needs of young offenders and adolescents from an inner city area. *Journal of Adolescence, 27*, 415–428.

Damasio, A. R., Trabel, D., & Damasio, H. (1990). Individuals with sociopathic behavior caused by frontal damage fail to respond autonomically to social stimuli. *Behavioural Brain Research, 41*, 81–94.

Damasio, H., Grabowski, T., Frank, R., Galaburda, A. M., & Damasio, A. R. (1994). The return of Phineas Gage: clues about the brain from the skull of a famous patient. *Science, 264*(5162), 1102–1105.

DeRiver, J. P. (1951). *The sexual criminal: A psychoanalytic study.* (3rd ed.). Springfield, IL: Charles C. Thomas.

Dolan, M., & Park, I. (2002). The neuropsychology of antisocial personality disorder. *Psychological Medicine, 32*, 417–427.

Dougherty, D. M., Dew, R. E., Mathias, C. W., Marsh, D. M., Addicott, M. A., & Barratt, E. S. (2007). Impulsive and premeditated subtypes of aggression in conduct disorder: Differences in time estimation. *Aggressive Behavior, 33*(6), 574–582.

Dustman, R. E., Shearer, D. E., & Emmerson, R. Y. (1999). Life-span changes in EEG spectral amplitude, amplitude variability and mean frequency. *Clinical Neurophysiology, 110*, 1399–1409.

Einarsson, E., Sigurdsson, J. F., Gudjonsson, G. H., Newton, A. K., & Bragason, O. O. (2009). Screening for attention-deficit hyperactivity disorder and co-morbid mental disorders among prison inmates. *Nordic Journal of Psychiatry, 63*(5), 361–367.

Eley, T. C., Lichtenstein, P., & Moffitt, T. E. (2003). A longitudinal behavioral genetic analysis of the etiology of aggressive and nonaggressive antisocial behavior. *Development and Psychopathology, 15*(383–402).

Eriksson, A., Hodgins, S., & Tengstrom, A. (2005). Verbal intelligence and criminal offending among men with schizophrenia. *International Journal of Forensic Mental Health, 4*, 191–200.

Eron, L. D. (1987). The development of aggressive behavior from the perspective of developing behaviorism. *American Psychologist, 42*(5), 435–442.

Evseef, G. S., & Wisniewski, E. M. (1972). A psychiatric study of a violent mass murderer. *Journal of Forensic Sciences, 17*(3), 371–376.

Eysenck, Hans J. (1977). *Crime and personality* (3rd ed.). London: Routledge & Kegan Paul.

Fairchild, G., Van Goozen, S. H. M., Strollery, S. J., & Goodyer, I. M. (2008). Fear conditioning and affective modiulation of the startle reflex in male adolescents with early-onset or adolescence-onset conduct disorder and health control subjects. *Biological Psychiatry, 63*, 279–285.

Farrington, D. P. (1997). The relationship between low resting heart rate and violence. In A. Raine, P. A. Brennan, D. P. Farrington & S. A. Mednick (Eds.), *Biosocial bases of violence* (pp. 89–106). New York: Plenum Press.

Fergusson, D. M., Woodward, L. J., & Horwood, L. J. (1998). Maternal smoking during pregnancy and psychiatric adjustment in late adolescence. *Archives of General Psychiatry, 55*, 721–727.

Fiddick, L., Spampinato, M. V., & Grafman, J. (2005). Social contracts and precautions activate different neurological systems: an fMRI investigation of deontic reasoning. *NeuroImage, 28*(4), 778–786.

Finn, P. R., Rickert, M. E., Miller, M. A., Lucas, J., Bogg, T., Bobova, L., & Cantrell, H. (2009). Reduced cogntive ability in alcohol dependence: Examing the role of covarying externalizing psychopathology. *Journal of Abnormal Psychology, 118*(1), 100–116.

Firestone, P., & Peters, S. (1983). Minor physical anomalies and behavior in children: A review. *Journal of Autism and Developmental Disorders, 13*, 411–425.

Fishbein, D., Hyde, C., Coe, B., & Paschall, M. J. (2004). Neurocognitive and physiological prerequisites for prevention of adolescent drug abuse. *Journal of Primary Prevention, 24*, 471–495.

Freud, S. (1950). *Totem and taboo.* (J. Strachey, Trans.). New York: W. W. Norton & Company.

Freud, S. (1961). Some character-types met with in psychoanalytic work: Criminals from a sense of guilt. (J. Strachey, Trans.). In J. Strachey (Ed.), *The standard edition of the complete psychologocial works of Sigmund Freud* (Vol. 14, pp. 332–333). London: Hogarth Press.

Freud, S. (1964). New introductory lectures on psycho-analysis. (J. Strachey, Trans.). In J. Strachey (Ed.), *The standard edition of the complete psychological works of Sigmund Freud.* (Vol. 22, pp. 1–182). London: Hogarth Press.

Friedlander, K. (1947). *The psychoanalytic approach to juvenile delinquency.* New York: International Universities Press.

Gabbard, G. (2005). *Psychodynamic psychiatry in clinical practice* (4th ed.). Washington, DC: American Psychiatric Publishing.

Gao, Y., & Raine, A. (2009). P3 event-related potential impairments in antisocial and psychopathic individuals: A meta-analysis. *Biological Psychology, 82*, 199–210.

Gao, Y., Raine, A., Venables, P. H., Dawson, M. E., & Mednick, S. A. (2010). Association of poor childhood fear conditioning and adult crime. *American Journal of Psychiatry, 167*, 56–60.

Gesch, C. B., Hammond, S. M., Eves, A., & Crowder, M. J. (2002). Influence of supplemenatry vitamins, minerals and essential fatty acids on the antisocial behaviour of young adult prisoners: Randomised, placebo-controlled trial. *British Journal of Psychiatry, 181*, 22–28.

Giancola, P. R., Shoal, G. D., & Mezzich, A. C. (2001). Constructive thinking, executive functioning, antisocial behavior, and drug use involvement in adolescent females with a substance use disorder. *Experimental and Clinical Psychopharmacology, 9*(2), 215–227.

Gibson, C. L., & Tibbetts, S. G. (1998). Interaction between maternal cigarette smoking and Apgar scores in predicting offending behavior. *Psychological Reports, 83*, 579–586.

Glenn, A. L., Raine, A., & Schug, R. A. (2009). The neural correlates of moral decision-making in psychopathy. *Molecular Psychiatry, 14*, 5–6.

Glenn, A. L., Raine, A., Venables, P. H., & Mednick, S. A. (2007). Early temperamental and psychophysiological precursors of adult psychopathic personality. *Journal of Abnormal Psychology, 116*, 508–518.

Glenn, A. L., Raine, A., Yaralian, P. S., & Yang, Y. (2010). Increased volume of the striatum in psychopathic individuals. *Biological Psychiatry, 67*(1), 52–58.

Goldman, D., & Ducci, F. (2007). The genetics of psychopathic disorders. In A. R. Felthous & H. Sa (Eds.), *International handbook of psychopathic disorders and the law* (Vol. 1, pp. 149–169). West Sussex, England: John Wiley and Sons, Ltd.

Goodman, R., Simonoff, E., & Stevenson, J. (1995). The impact of child IQ, parent IQ and sibling IQ on child behavioural deviance scores. *Journal of Child Psychology and Psychiatry, 36*(3), 409–425.

Gordon, H. L., Baird, A. A., & End, A. (2004). Functional differences among those high and low on a trait measure of psychopathy. *Biological Psychiatry, 56*, 516–521.

Grafman, J., Schwab, K., Warden, D., Pridgen, A., Brown, H. R., & Salazar, A. M. (1996). Frontal lobe injuries, violence and aggression: A report of the Vietnam Head Injury Study. *Neurology, 46*(5), 1231–1238.

Graig, M. C., Catani, M., Deeley, Q., Robert, L., Daly, E., Kanaan, R. A. A., . . . Murphy, D. G. M. (2009). Altered connections on the road to psychopathy. *Molecular Psychiatry, 14*(10), 946–953.

Greene, J. D., Nystrom, L. E., Engell, A. D., Darley, J. M., & Cohen, J. (2004). The neural bases of cognitive conflict and control in moral judgment. *Neuron, 44*, 389–400.

Grekin, E. R., Brennan, P. A., & Hammen, C. (2005). Parental alcohol use disorders and child delinquency: The mediating effects of executive functioning and chronic family stress. *Journal of Studies on Alcohol, 66*, 14–22.

Hall, K. M., Karzmark, P., Stevens, M., Englander, J., O'Hare, P., & Wright, J. (1994). Family stressors in traumatic brain injury: A two year follow-up. *Archives of Physical Medicine and Rehabilitation, 75*, 876–884.

Hallahan, B., Hibbeln, J. R., Davis, J. M., & Garland, M. R. (2007). Omega-3 fatty acid supplementation in patients with recurrent self harm- Single centre double-blind randomised controlled trial. *British Journal of Psychiatry, 190*, 118–122.

Hancock, M., Tapscott, J. L., & Hoaken, P. N. S. (2010). Role of executive dysfunction in predicting frequency and severity of violence. *Aggressive Behavior, 36*(5), 338–349.

Hanlon, R. E., Rubin, L. H., Jensen, M., & Daoust, S. (2010). Neuropsychological features of indigent murder defendants and death row inmates in relation to homicidal aspects of their crimes. *Archives of Clinical Neuropsychology, 25*(1), 13.

Harenski, C. L., Harenski, K. A., Shane, M. S., & Kiehl, K. A. (2010). Aberrant neural processing of moral violations in criminal psychopaths. *Journal of Abnormal Psychology 119*, 863–874.

Harlow, J. M. (1848). Passage of an iron rod through the head. *Boston Medical and Surgical Journal, 39*, 389–393.

Harmon-Jones, E. (2003). Clarifying the emotive functions of asymmetrical frontal cortical activity. *Psychophysiology, 40*, 838–848.

Hayman-Abello, S. E., Rourke, B. P., & Fuerst, D. R. (2003). Psychosocial status after pediatric traumatic brain injury: A subtype analysis using the Child Behavior Checklist. *Journal of the International Neuropsychological Society, 9*, 887–898.

Henry, B., Caspi, A., Moffitt, T. E., Harrington, H., & Silva, P. A. (1999). Staying in school protects boys with poor self-regulation in childhood from later crime: A longitudinal study. *International Journal of Behavioral Development, 23*(4), 1049–1073.

Herpertz, S. C., Mueller, B., Qunaibi, M., Lichterfeld, C., Konrad, K., & Herpertz-Dahlmann, B. (2005). Emotional responses in boys with conduct disorder. *American Journal of Psychiatry, 162*, 1100–1107.

Hibbeln, J. R., Umhau, J. C., Linnoila, M., George, D. T., Ragan, P. W., Shoaf, S. E., . . . Salem, N. (1998). A replication study of violent and nonviolent subjects: Cerebrospinal fluid metabolites of serotonin and dopamine are predicted by plasma essential fatty acids. *Biological Psychiatry, 44*, 243–249.

Hicks, B. M., Bernat, E. M., Malone, S. M., Iacono, W. G., Patrick, C. J., Krueger, R. F., & McGue, M. (2007). Genes mediate the association between P3 amplitude and externalizing disorders. *Psychophysiology, 44*, 98–105.

Hirayama, S., Hamazaki, T., & Terasawa, K. (2004). Effect of docosahexaenoic acid-containing food administration on symptoms of attention-deficit/hyperactivity disorder—a placebo-controlled double-blind study. *European Journal of Clinical Nutrition, 58*, 467–473.

Hirono, N., Mega, M. S., Dinov, I. D., Mishkin, F., & Cummings, J. L. (2000). Left frontotemporal hypoperfusion is associated with aggression in patients with dementia. *Archives of Neurology, 57*, 861–866.

Hodgins, S., Kratzer, L., & McNeil, R. F. (2001). Obstetric complications, parenting, and risk of criminal behavior. *Archives of General Psychiatry, 58*, 746–752.

Holmes, R. M., & Holmes, S. T. (1998). *Serial murder* (2nd ed.). Thousand Oaks, CA: Sage.

Huebner, T., Vloet, T. D., Marx, I., Konrad, K., Fink, G. R., Herpertz, S. C., & Herpertz-Dahlmann, B. (2008). Morphometric brain abnormalities in boys with conduct disorder. *Journal of the American Academy of Child and Adolescent Psychiatry, 47*, 540–547.

Hugdahl, K. (2001). *Psychophysiology: The mind-body perspective.* Cambridge, MA: Harvard University Press.

Hughes, J. R., Zagar, R. J., Busch, K. G., Grove, W. M., & Arbit, J. (2009). Looking forward in records of youth abused as children: Risks for homicidal, violent, and delinquent offenses. *Psychological Reports, 104*(1), 77–101.

Hux, K., Bond, V., Skinner, S., Belau, D., & Sanger, D. (1998). Parental report of occurences and consequences of traumatic brain injury among delinquent and non-delinquent youth. *Brain Injury, 12*, 667–681.

Indira, R. (1987). The psychoanalytic theory as a basis for understanding criminal behavior. *Indian Journal of Behavior, 11*(1), 29–32.

Intrator, J., Hare, R. D., Stritzke, P., Brichtswein, K., Dorfman, D., & Harpur, T. (1997). A brain imaging (single photon emission computerized tomography) study of semantic and affective processing in psychopaths. *Biological Psychiatry, 42*, 96–103.

Isen, J. (2010). A meta-analytic assessment of Wechsler's P>V sign in antisocial populations. *Clinical Psychology Review, 30*, 423–435.

Ishikawa, S. S., & Raine, A. (2002). Psychophysiological correlates of antisocial behavior: A central control hypothesis. In J. Glicksohn (Ed.), *The neurobiology of criminal behavior* (pp. 187–229). Boston, MA: Kluwer.

Jacobson, K. C., Prescott, C. A., & Kendler, K. S. (2002). Sex differences in the genetic and environmental influences on the development of antisocial behavior. *Development and Psychopathology, 14*, 395–416.

Jaffee, S. R., Caspi, A., Moffitt, T. E., Dodge, K. A., Rutter, M., Taylor, A., & Tully, L. A. (2005). Nature x nurture: Genetic vulnerabilities interact with physical maltreatment to promote conduct problems. *Development and Psychopathology, 17*, 67–84.

Jaffee, S. R., Caspi, A., Moffitt, T. E., & Taylor, A. (2004). Physical maltreatment victim to antisocial child: Evidence of an environmentally-mediated process. *Journal of Abnormal Psychology, 113*, 44–55.

Johnson, M. K., Raye, C. R., Mitchell, K. J., Touryan, S. R., Greene, E. J., & Nolen-Hoeksema, S. (2006). Dissociating the medial frontal and posterior cingulate activity during self-reflection. *Social, Cognitive, and Affective Neuroscience, 1*, 64.

Kandel, E. S., Brennan, P. A., Mednick, S. A., & Michelson, N. M. (1989). Minor physical anomalies and recidivistic adult criminal behavior. *Acta Psychiatrica Scandinavica, 79*, 103–107.

Karpman, B. (1951a). A psychoanalytic study of a case of murder. *Psychoanalytic Review, 38*(2), 139–157.

Karpman, B. (1951b). A psychoanalytic study of a case of murder. *Psychoanalytic Review, 38*(2), 245–270.

Kavanagh, L., Rowe, D. C., Hersch, J., Barnett, K. J., & Reznik, R. (2010). Neurocognitive deficits and psychiatric disorders in a NSW prison population. *International Journal of Law and Psychiatry, 33*(1), 20–26.

Kendler, K. S. (2005). Toward a philosophical structure for psychiatry. *American Journal of Psychiatry, 162*, 433–440.

Kiehl, K. A., Smith, A. M., Hare, R. D., Mendrek, A., Forster, B. B., & Brink, J. (2001). Limbic abnormalities in affective processing by criminal psychopaths as revealed by functional magnetic resonance imaging. *Biological Psychiatry, 50*, 677–684.

Kiehl, K. A., Smith, A. M., Mendrek, A., Forster, B. B., Hare, R. D., & Liddle, P. F. (2004). Temporal lobe abnormalities in semantic processing by criminal psychopaths as revealed by functional magnetic resonance imaging. *Psychiatry Research, 130*, 27–42.

Kimonis, E. R., Frick, P. J., Fazekas, H., & Loney, B. R. (2006). Psychopathy, aggression, and the processing of emotional stimuli in non-referred girls and boys. *Behavioral Sciences and the Law, 24*, 21–37.

Kirkpatrick, T., Joyce, E., Milton, J., Duggan, C., Tyrer, P., & Rogers, R. D. (2007). Altered memory and affective instability in prisoners assessed for dangerous and severe personality disorder. *British Journal of Psychiatry, 190* (49), s20–s26.

Kronenberger, W., Mathews, V. P., Dunn, D., Wang, Y., Wood, E. A., Giauque, A. L., & Li, T. Q. (2005). Media violence exposure and executive functioning in aggressive and control adolescents. *Journal of Abnormal Psychology, 61*(6), 725–737.

Kruesi, M. J. P., Casanova, M. V., Mannheim, G., & Jonson-Bilder, A. (2004). Reduced temportal lobe volume in early-onset conduct disorder. *Psychiatry Research: Neuroimaging, 132*, 1–11.

Kruesi, M. J. P., Hibbs, E. D., Zahn, T. P., Keysor, C. S., Hamburger, S. D., Bartko, J. J., & Rapoport, J. L. (1992). A 2-year prospective follow-up study of children and adolescents with disruptive behavior disorders: Prediction by cerebrospinal fluid 5-hydroxyindoleacetic acid, homovanillic acid, and autonomic measures? *American Journal of Psychiatry, 49*(6), 429–435.

Kuruoglu, A. C., Arikan, Z., Vural, G., & Karatas, M. (1996). Single photon emission computerised tomography in chronic alcoholism: Antisocial personality disorder may be associated with decreased frontal perfusion. *British Journal of Psychiatry, 169*, 348–354.

Laakso, M. P., Gunning-Dixon, F., Vaurio, O., Repo, E., Soininen, H., & Tiihonen, J. (2002). Prefrontal volume in habitually violent subjects with antisocial personality disorder and type 2 alcoholism. *Psychiatry Research Neuroimaging, 114*, 95–102.

Laakso, M. P., Vaurio, O., Koivisto, E., Savolainen, L., Eronen, M., Aronen, H. J., . . . Tiihonen, J. (2001). Psychopathy and the posterior hippocampus. *Behavioral Brain Research, 118*(2), 187–193.

Lahey, B. B., Loeber, R., Hart, E. L., Frick, P. J., Applegate, B., Zhang, Q., & Russo, M. F. (1995). Four-year longitudinal study of conduct disorder in boys: Patterns and predictors of presistence. *Journal of Abnormal Psychology, 104*(1), 83–93.

Langlois, J. A., Rutland-Brown, W., & Wald, M. M. (2006). The epidemiology and impact of traumatic brain injury: A brief overview. *Journal of Head Trauma and Rehabilitation, 21*, 375–378.

LeDoux, J. E. (2000). Emotion circuits in the brain. *Annual Review of Neuroscience, 23*, 155–184.

Lehrman, P. R. (1939). Some unconscious determinants in homicide. *Psychoanalytic Quarterly, 13*(4), 606–621.

Levi, M. D., Nussbaum, D. S., & Rich, J. B. (2010). Neuropsychological and personality characteristics of predatory, irritable, and nonviolent offenders: Support for a typology of criminal human aggression. *Criminal Justice and Behavior, 37*(6), 633–655.

Lewis, D. O., Lovely, R., Yeager, C., & Femina, D. D. (1989). Toward a theory of the genesis of violence: A follow-up study of delinquents. *Journal of the American Academy of Child and Adolescent Psychiatry, 28*, 431–436.

Lewis, D. O., Pincus, J. H., Feldman, M., Jackson, L., & Bard, B. (1986). Psychiatric, neurological and psychoeduational characteristics of 15 death row inmates in the United States. *American Journal of Psychiatry, 143*, 838–845.

Li, T. Q., Mathews, V. P., Wang, Y., Dunn, D., & Kronenberger, W. (2005). Adolescents with disruptive behavior disorder investigated using an optimized MR diffusion tensor imaging protocol. *Annals of the New York Academy of Sciences, 1064*, 184–192.

Liebert, J. A. (1972). Contributions of psychiatric consultation in the investigation of serial murder. *International Journal of Offender Therapy and Comparative Criminology, 29*, 187–200.

Lipsitt, P. D., Buka, S. L., & Lipsitt, L. P. (1990). Early intelligence scores and subsequent delinquency: A prospective study. *American Journal of Family Therapy, 18*(2), 197–208.

Liu, J. (2004). Childhood externalizing behavior: Theory and implications. *Journal of Child and Adolescent Psychiatric Nursing, 17*, 93–103.

Liu, J., Raine, A., Venables, P. H., & Mednick, S. A. (2004). Malnutrition at age 3 years predisposes to externalizing behavior problems at ages 8, 11, and 17 years. *American Journal of Psychiatry, 161*, 2005–2013.

Liu, J., & Wuerker, A. (2005). Biosocial bases of aggressive and violent behavior —implications for nursing studies. *International Journal of Nursing Studies, 42*, 229–241.

Loney, B. R., Frick, P. J., Clements, C. B., Ellis, M. L., & Kerlin, K. (2003). Callous-unemotional traits, impulsivity and emotional processing in adolescents with antisocial behavior problems. *Journal of Clinical Child and Adolescent Psychology, 32*, 66–80.

Loney, B. R., Frick, P. J., Ellis, M. L., & McCoy, M. G. (1998). Intelligence, callous-unemotional traits, and antisocial behavior. *Journal of Psychopathology and Behavioral Assessment, 20*(3), 231–247.

Lorber, M. F. (2004). Psychophysiology of aggression, psychopathy, and conduct problems: A meta-analysis. *Psychological Bulletin, 130*, 531–552.

Luria, A. (1996). *Higher cortical functions in man*. New York: Basic Books.

Lussier, P., Farrington, D. P., & Moffitt, T. E. (2009). Is the antisocial child the father of the abusive man? A 40-year prospective longitudinal study on the developmental antecedents of intimate partner violence. *Criminology, 47*(3), 741–780.

Lyons, M. J., True, W. R., Eisen, S. A., Golberg, J., Meyer, J. M., Faraone, S. V., . . . Tsuang, M. T. (1995). Differential heritability of adult and juvenile traits. *Archives of General Psychiatry, 52*, 906–915.

Maratos, E. J., Dolan, R. J., Morris, J. S., Henson, R. N. A., & Rugg, M. D. (2001). Neural activity associated with episodic memory for emotional context. *Neuropsychologia, 39*, 910–920.

Masten, A. S., Hubbard, J. J., Gest, S. D., Tellegen, A., Garmezy, N., & Ramirez, M. (1999). Competence in the context of adversity: Pathways to resilience and maladaptation from childhood to late adolescence. *Development and Psychopathology, 11*(1), 143–169.

Maughan, B., Taylor, A., Caspi, A., & Moffitt, T. E. (2004). Prenatal smoking and early childhood conduct problems. *Archives of General Psychiatry, 61*, 836–843.

Maughan, B., Taylor, C., Taylor, A., Butler, N., & Bynner, J. (2001). Pregnancy smoking and childhood conduct problems: A causal association? *Journal of Child Psychology and Psychiatry, 42*, 1021–1028.

Mayberg, H. S., Liotti, M., Brannan, S. K., McGinnis, S., Mahurin, R. K., & Jerabek, P. A. (1999). Reciprocal limbic-cortical function and negative mood: Converging PET findings in depression and normal sadness. *American Journal of Psychiatry, 156*, 675–682.

McAllister, T. (1992). Neuropsychiatric sequelae of head injuries. *Psychiatric Clinics of North America, 15*, 661–665.

McHale, B. G., Obrzut, J. E., & Sabers, D. L. (2003). Relationship of cognitive functioning and aggressive behavior with emotionally disabled and specific learning disabled students. *Journal of Developmental and Physical Disabilities, 15*(2), 123–140.

Mednick, S. A., & Kandel, E. S. (1988). Congential determinants of violence. *Bulletin of the American Academy of Psychiatry and the Law, 16*, 101–109.

Mednick, S. A., Volavka, J., Gabrielli, W. F., & Itil, T. M. (1981). EEG as a predictor of antisocial behavior. *Criminology, 19*, 219–229.

Menninger, W. W. (2007). Uncontained rage: A psychoanalytic perspective on violence. *Bulletin of the Menninger Clinic, 71*(2), 115–131.

Mezzacappa, E., Tremblay, R. E., Kindlon, D., Saul, J. P., Arsenault, L., Seguin, J., . . . Earls, F. J. (1997). Anxiety, antisocial behavior and heart rate regulation in adolescent males. *Journal of Child Psychology and Psychiatry, 38*, 457–468.

Miles, D. R., & Carey, G. (1997). Genetic and environmental architecture of human aggression. *Journal of Personality and Social Psychology, 72*, 207–217.

Miller, E. K., & Cohen, J. D. (2001). An integrative theory of prefrontal cortex function. *Annual Review of Neuroscience, 24*(1), 167–202.

Mitchell, S. A., & Black, M. J. (1995). *Freud and beyond: A history of modern psychoanalytic thought.* New York: Basic Books.

Moffitt, T. E. (1993a). Adolescence-limited and life-course-persistent antisocial behavior: A developmental taxonomy. *Psychological Review, 100*(2), 674–701.

Moffitt, T. E. (1993b). The neuropsychology of conduct disorder. *Development and Psychopathology, 5*(1–2), 135–151.

Moffitt, T. E. (2005). The new look of behavioral genetics in developmental psychopathology: Gene-environment interplay in antisocial behaviors. *Psychological Bulletin, 131*(4), 533–554.

Moffitt, T. E., & Caspi, A. (2001). Childhood predictors differentiate life-course persistent and adolescence-limited antisocial pathways among males and females. *Development and Psychopathology, 13*, 355–375.

Moffitt, T. E., Lynam, D. R., & Silva, P. A. (1994). Neuropsychological tests predicting persistent male delinquency. *Criminology, 32*(2), 277–300.

Moffitt, T. E., & Silva, P. A. (1988). IQ and delinquency: A direct test of the differential detection hypothesis. *Journal of Abnormal Psychology, 97*(3), 330–333.

Moll, J., Oliveira-Souza, R., Eslinger, P. J., Bramati, I. E., Mourao-Miranda, J., Andreiuolo, P. A., & Pessoa, L. (2002). The neural correlates of moral sensitivity: A functional magnetic resonance imaging investigation of basic and moral emotions. *Journal of Neuroscience, 22*(7), 2730–2736.

Morgan, A. B., & Lilienfeld, S. O. (2000). A meta-analytic review of the relationship between antisocial behavior and neuropsychological measures of executive function. *Clinical Psychology Review, 20*, 113–136.

Morrison, H. L. (1979). Psychiatric observations and interpretations of bite mark evidence in multiple murders. *Journal of Forensic Sciences, 24*(2), 492–502.

Muller, J. L., Ganssbauer, S., Sommer, M., Dohnel, K., Weber, T., Schmidt-Wilcke, T., & Hajak, G. (2008). Gray matter changes in right superior temporal gyrus in criminal psychopaths. Evidence from voxel-based morphometry. *Psychiatry Research, 163*, 213–222.

Müller, J. L., Sommer, M., Wagner, V., Lange, K., Taschler, H., Roder, C. H., . . . Hajak, G. (2003). Abnormalities in emotion processing within cortical and subcortical regions in criminal psychopaths: Evidence from a functional magnetic resonance imaging study using pictures with emotional content. *Biological Psychiatry, 54*, 152–162.

Munoz, L. C., Frick, P. J., Kimonis, E. R., & Aucoin, K. J. (2008). Verbal ability and delinquency: Testing the moderating role of psychopathic traits. *Journal of Child Psychology and Psychiatry, 49*(4), 414–421.

New, A. S., Hazlett, E., Buchsbaum, M. S., Goodman, M., Reynolds, D., Mitropoulous, V., . . . Siever, L. J. (2002). Blunted prefrontal cortical 18-fluorodeoxyglucose positron emission tomography response to meta-chlorophenylpiperazine in impulsive aggression. *Archives of General Psychiatry, 59*, 621–629.

Nigg, J. T., Glass, J. M., Wong, M. M., Poon, E., Jester, J., Fitzgerald, H. E., . . . Zucker, R. A. (2004). Neuropsychological executive functioning in children at elevated risk for alcoholism: Findings in early adolescence. *Journal of Abnormal Psychology, 113*, 302–314.

Ochsner, K. N., Beer, J. S., Robertson, E. R., Cooper, J. C., Gabrieli, J. D. E., Kihsltrom, J. F., & D'Esposito, M. (2005). The neural correlates of direct and reflected self-knowledge. *NeuroImage, 28*(4), 797–814.

Ortiz, J., & Raine, A. (2004). Heart rate level and antisocial behavior in children and adolescents: A meta analysis. *Journal of American Academy of Child and Adolescent Psychiatry, 43*, 154–162.

Patrick, C. J. (2008). Psychophysiological correlates of aggression and violence: An integrative review. *Philosophical Transactions of the Royal Society, 363*, 2543–2555.

Perron, B. E., & Howard, M. O. (2008). Prevalence and correlates of traumatic brain injury among delinquent youths. *Criminal Behaviour and Mental Health, 18*(4), 243–255.

Petersen, K. G. I., Matousek, M., Mednick, S. A., Volkava, J., & Pollock, V. E. (1982). EEG antecedents of thievery. *Acta Psychiatrica Scandinavica, 65*, 331–338.

Pine, D. S., Shaffer, D., Schonfeld, I. S., & Davies, M. (1997). Minor physical anomolies: Modifiers of environmental risks for psychiatric impairment? *Journal of the American Academy of Child and Adolescent Psychiatry, 36*, 395–403.

Piquero, A. R. (2003). On the relationship between cognitive abilities and life-course persistent offending among a sample of African Americans: A longitudinal test of Moffitt's hypothesis. *Journal of Criminal Justice, 31*(5), 399–409.

Piquero, A. R., & Tibbetts, S. G. (1999). The impact of pre/perinatal disturbances and disadvantaged familial environment in predicting criminal offending. *Studies on Crime and Crime Prevention., 8*, 52–70.

Popma, A., & Raine, A. (2006). Will future forensic assessment be neurobiologic? *Child and Adolescent Clinics of North America, 36*, 395–444.

Raine, A. (1993). *The psychopathology of crime: Criminal behavior as a clinical disorder.* San Diego, CA: Academic Press.

Raine, A. (1996). Autonomic nervous system activity and violence. In D. M. Stoff & R. B. Cairns (Eds.), *Neurobiological approaches to clinical aggression research* (pp. 145–168). Mahwah, NJ: Lawrence Erlbaum.

Raine, A. (1997). Psychophysiology and antisocial behavior: A biosocial perspective an a prefrontal dysfunction hypothesis. In D. M. Stoff, J. Breiling, & J. D. Maser (Eds.), *Handbook of antisocial behavior* (pp. 289–304). New York: Wiley.

Raine, A. (2002). Annotation: the role of prefrontal deficits, low autonomic arousal and early health factors in the development of antisocial and aggressive behavior in children. *Journal of Child Psychology and Psychiatry and Allied Disciplines, 43*, 417–434.

Raine, A., Brennan, P., & Mednick, S. A. (1994). Birth complications combined with early maternal rejection at age 1 year predispose to violent crime at age 18 years. *Archives of General Psychiatry, 51*, 984–988.

Raine, A., Brennan, P., & Mednick, S. A. (1997). Interaction between birth complications and early maternal rejection in redisposing individuals to adult violence: Specificity to serious, early-onset violence. *American Journal of Psychiatry, 154*, 1265–1271.

Raine, A., Buchsbaum, M. S., & LaCasse, L. (1997). Brain abnormalities in murderers indicated by positron emission tomography. *Biological Psychiatry, 42*, 495–508.

Raine, A., Lee, L., Yang, Y., & Colletti, P. (2010). Neurodevelopmental marker for limbic maldevelopment in antisocial personality disorder and psychopathy. *British Journal of Psychiatry, 197*, 186–192.

Raine, A., Lencz, T., Bihrle, S., LaCasse, L., & Colletti, P. (2000). Reduced prefrontal gray matter volume and reduced autonomic activity in antisocial personality disorder. *Archives of General Psychiatry, 57*, 119–127.

Raine, A., Lencz, T., Taylor, K., Hellige, J. B., Bihrle, S., LaCasse, L., . . . Coletti, P. (2003). Corpus callosum abnormalities in psychopathic individuals. *Archives of General Psychiatry, 160*, 1627–1635.

Raine, A., Mellingen, K., Liu, J., Venables, P. H., & Mednick, S. A. (2003). Effects of environmental enrichment at ages 3–5 years on schizotypal personality and antisocial behavior at ages 17 and 23 years. *American Journal of Psychiatry, 160*, 1627–1635.

Raine, A., Meloy, J. R., Bihrle, S., Stoddard, J., LaCasse, L., & Buchsbaum, M. S. (1998). Reduced prefrontal and increased subcortical brain functioning assessed using positron emission tomography in predatory and affective murderers. *Behavioral Sciences and the Law, 16*, 319–332.

Raine, A., Moffitt, T. E., Caspi, A., Loeber, R., Stouthamer-Loeber, M., & Lynam, D. R. (2005). Neurocognitive impairments in boys on the life-course persistent antisocial path. *Journal of Abnormal Psychology, 114*, 38–49.

Raine, A., Reynolds, C., Venables, P. H., Mednick, S. A., & Farrington, D. P. (1998). Fearlessness, stimulation-seeking, and large body size at age 3 years as early predispositions to childhood aggression at age 11 years. *Archives of General Psychiatry, 55*, 745–751.

Raine, A., Venables, P. H., & Mednick, S. A. (1997). Low resting heart rate age 3 years predisposes to aggression at age 11 years: Evidence from the Mauritius Child Health Project. *Journal of American Academy of Child and Adolescent Psychiatry, 36*, 1457–1464.

Raine, A., Venables, P. H., & Williams, M. (1990a). Relationships between CNS and ANS measures of arousal at age 15 and criminality at age 24. *Archives of General Psychiatry, 47*, 1003–1007.

Raine, A., Venables, P. H., & Williams, M. (1990b). Relationships between CNS and ANS measures of arousal at age 15 years as protective factors against criminal behavior at age 29 years. *American Journal of Psychiatry, 152*, 1595–1600.

Raine, A., Venables, P. H., & Williams, M. (1995). High autonomic arousal and electrodermal orienting at age 15 years as protective factors against criminal behavior at age 29 years. *American Journal of Psychiatry, 152*, 1595–1600.

Raine, A., Yaralian, P. S., Reynolds, C., Venables, P. H., & Mednick, S. A. (2002). Spatial but not verbal cognitive deficits at age 3 years in persistently antisocial individuals. *Development and Psychopathology., 14*, 25–44.

Ransen, P., Hakko, H., Isohanni, M., Hodgins, S., Jarvelin, M. R., & Tiihonen, J. (1999). Maternal smoking during pregnancy and risk of criminal behavior among adult male offspring in the northern Finland 1996 birth cohort. *American Journal of Psychiatry, 156*, 857–862.

Rantakallio, P., Koiranen, M., & Mottonen, J. (1992). Association of prenatal events, epilepsy, and central nervous system trauma with juvenile delinquency. *Archives of Disease in Childhood, 67*, 1459–1461.

Rantakallio, P., Laara, E., Isohanni, M., & Moilanen, I. (1992). Maternal smoking during pregnancy and delinquency of the offspring: An association without causation? *International Journal of Epidemiology, 21*, 1106–1113.

Revitch, E., & Schlesinger, L. B. (1981). *The psychopathology of homicide*. Springfield, IL: Charles C. Thomas.

Revitch, E., & Schlesinger, L. B. (1989). *Sex murder and sex aggression: Phenomenology, psychopathology, psychodynamics and prognosis*. Springfield, IL: Charles C. Thomas.

Rhee, S. H., & Waldman, I. D. (2002). Genetic and evironmental influences on antisocial behvior: A meta-analysis of twin and adoption studies. *Psychological Bulletin, 128*, 490–529.

Rilling, J. K., Glenn, A. L., Jairam, M. R., Pagnoni, G., Goldsmith, D. R., Elfenbein, H. A., & Lilienfeld, S. O. (2007). Neural correlates of social cooperation and non-cooperation as a function of psychopathy. *Biological Psychiatry, 61*, 1260–1271.

Rimel, R., Giordani, B., & Barth, J. (1981). Disability caused by minor head injury. *Neurosurgery, 9*, 1459–1461.

Rispens, J., Swaab, H., van den Oord, E. J. C. G., Cohen-Kettenis, P. T., Van England, H., & van Yperen, T. (1997). WISC profiles in child psychiatric diagnosis: Sense or nonsense? *Journal of the American Academy of Child and Adolescent Psychiatry, 36*(11), 1587–1594.

Rivera, J., Jaffee, K., Polissar, N., Fay, G., Martin, K., Shurtleff, H., & Liao, S. (1994). Family functioning and children's academic performance and behavior problems in the year following brain injury. *Archives of Physical Medicine and Rehabilitation, 75*, 369–379.

Rogeness, G. A., Cepeda, C., Macedo, C. A., Fischer, C., & Harris, W. R. (1990). Differences in heart rate and blood pressure in children with conduct disorder, major depression and separation anxiety. *Psychiatry Research, 33*, 199–206.

Rosen, G. M., Deinard, A. S., Schwartz, S., Smith, C., Stephenson, B., & Grabenstein, B. (1985). Iron deficiency among incarcerated juvenile delinquents. *Journal of Adolescent Health Care, 6*, 419–423.

Saltaris, C., Serbin, L. A., Stack, D. M., Karp, J. A., Schwartzman, A. E., & Ledingham, J. E. (2004). Nurturing cognitive competence in preschoolers: A longitudinal study of intergenerational continuity and risk. *International Journal of Behavioral Development, 28*(2), 105–115.

Santesso, D. L., Reker, D. L., Schmidt, L. A., & Segalowitz, S. J. (2006). Frontal electroencephalogram activation asymmetry, emotional intelligence, and externalizing behaviors in 10-year-old children. *Child Psychiatry and Human Development, 36*, 311–328.

Schmeck, K., & Poustra, F. (1993). Psychophysiologische Reacktionsmuster und psychische auffalligkeiten im kindesalter. In P. Baumann (Ed.), *Bioloogische psychiatrie der gegenwart*. Wien: Springer-Verlag.

Schneider, F., Habel, U., Kessler, C., Posse, S., Grodd, W., & Muller-Gartner, H. W. (2000). Functional imaging of conditioned aversive emotional responses in antisocial personality disorder. *Neuropsychobiology, 42*, 192–201.

Schoenthaler, S. J., & Bier, I. D. (2000). The effect of vitamin-mineral supplementation on juvenile delinquency among American schoolchildren: a randomized double blind placebo-controlled trial. *Journal of Alternative and Complementary Medicine, 6*, 19–29.

Sharkey, P. (2010). The acute effect of local homicides on children's cognitive performance. *Proceedings of the National Academy of Sciences, 107*(26), 11733–11738.

Slutske, W. S., Heath, A. C., Dinwiddie, S. H., Madden, P. A., Bucholz, K. K., Dunne, M. P., . . . Martin, N. G. (1997). Modeling genetic and environmental influences in the etiology of conduct disorder: A study of 2,682 adult twin pairs. *Journal of Abnormal Psychology, 106*, 266–279.

Soderstrom, H., Hultin, L., Tullberg, M., Wikkelso, C., Ekholm, S., & Forsman, A. (2002). Reduced frontotemporal perfusion in psychopathic personality. *Psychiatry Research: Neuroimaging, 114*, 81–94.

Soderstrom, H., Tullberg, M., Wikkelso, C., Ekholm, S., & Forsman, A. (2000). Reduced regional cerebral blood flow in non-psychotic violent offenders. *Psychiatry Research: Neuroimaging, 98*, 29–41.

Stadler, C., Grasmann, D., Fegert, J. M., Holtmann, M., Poustka, F., & Schmeck, K. (2008). Heart rate and treatment effect in children with disruptive behavior disorders. *Child Psychiatry and Human Development, 39*, 299–309.

Stattin, H., & Klackenberg-Larsson, I. (1993). Early language and intelligence development and their relationship to future criminal behavior. *Journal of Abnormal Psychology, 102*(3), 369–378.

Sterzer, P., Stadler, C., Poutska, F., & Kleinschmidt, A. (2007). A structural neural deficit in adolescents with conduct disorder and its association with lack of empathy. *Neuroimage, 37*, 335–342.

Stevens, L., Zhang, W., Peck, L., Kuczek, T., Grevstad, N., Mahon, A., . . . Burgess, J. R. (2003). EFA supplementation in children with inattention, hyperactivity, and other disruptive behaviors. *Lipids, 38*, 1007–1021.

Syngelaki, E. M., Moore, S. C., Savage, J. C., Fairchild, G., & Van Goozen, S. H. M. (2009). Executive functioning and risky decision making in young male offenders. *Criminal Justice and Behavior, 36*(11), 1213–1227.

Takahashi, H., Yahata, N., Koeda, M., Matsuda, T., Asai, K., & Okubo, Y. (2004). Brain activation associated with evaluative processes of guilt and embarrassment: an fMRI study. *NeuroImage, 23*(3), 967–974.

Tapert, S. F., Tate, S. R., & Brown, S. A. (2001). Substance abuse: An overview. In P. B. Sutker & H. E. Adams (Eds.), *Comprehensive handbook of psychopathology*. (3rd ed., pp. 559–594). New York: Kluwer Academic/Plenum Publishers.

Tiihonen, J., Hodgins, S., & Vaurio, O. (2000). Amygdayloid volume loss in psychopathy. *Society for Neuroscience Abstracts*, 20017.

Vanderbilt-Adriance, E., & Shaw, D. S. (2008). Protective factors and the development of resilience in the context of neighborhood disadvantage. *Journal of Abnormal Child Psychology, 36*(6), 887–901.

Viet, R., Flor, H., Erb, M., Hermann, C., Lotze, M., Grodd, W., & Birbaumer, N. (2002). Brain circuits involved in emotional learning in antisocial behavior and social phobia in humans. *Neuroscience Letters, 328*, 233–236.

Vikkunen, M. E., Horrobin, D., Jenkins, D. K., & Manku, M. S. (1987). Plasma phospholipid essential fatty acids and prostaglandins in alcoholic, habitually violent, and impulsive offenders. *Biological Psychiatry, 22*, 1087–1096.

Vitacco, M. J., Neumann, C. S., & Wodushek, T. (2008). Differential relationships between the dimensions of psychopathy and intelligence: Replication with adult jail inmates. *Criminal Justice and Behavior, 35*(1), 48–55.

Volavka, J. (1987). Electroencephalogram among criminals. In S. A. Mednick, T. E. Moffitt, & S. Stack (Eds.), *The causes of crime: New biological approches* (pp. 137–145). Cambridge: Cambridge Universtiy Press.

Volkow, N. D., Tancredi, L. R., Grant, C., Gillespie, H., Valentine, A., Mullani, N., . . . Hollister, L. (1995). Brain glucose metabolism in violent psychiatric patients: A preliminary study. *Psychiatry Research Neuroimaging, 61*, 243–253.

Vollm, B., Richardson, P., Stirling, J., Elliot, R., Dolan, M., Chaudhry, I., . . . Deakin, B. (2004). Neurobiological substrates of antisocial and borderline personality disorders: Preliminary result of a functional MRI study. *Criminal Behavior and Mental Health, 14*, 39–54.

Wadsworth, M. E. J. (1976). Delinquency, pulse rate and early emotional deprivation. *British Journal of Criminology, 16*, 245–256.

Wakschlag, L. S., Lahey, B. B., Loeber, R., Green, S. M., Gordon, R., & Leventhal, B. L. (1997). Maternal smoking during pregnancy and the risk of conduct disorder in boys. *Archives of General Psychiatry, 54*, 670–676.

Walsh, W. J., Isaacson, H. R., Rehman, F., & Hall, A. (1997). Elevated blood copper/zinc ratios in assaultive young males. *Physiology and Behavior, 62*, 327–329.

Weissman, M. M., Warner, V., Wickramarante, P. J., & Kandel, D. B. (1999). Maternal smoking during pregnancy and psychopathology in offspring followed to adulthood. *Journal of the American Academy of Child and Adolescent Psychiatry, 38*, 892–899.

Werbach, M. (1995). Nutritional influences on aggressive behavior. *Journal of Orthomolecular Medicine, 7*, 45–51.

Werner, E. E. (1987). Vulnerability and resiliency in children at risk for delinquency: A longitudinal study from birth to young adulthood. In J. D. Burchard & S. N. Burchard (Eds.), *Primary prevention of psychopathology* (pp. 16–43). Newbury Park, CA: Sage.

Wertham, F. (1949). *The show of violence.* Garden City, NY: Doubleday & Company.

Wertham, F. (1950). *Dark legend.* Garden City, NY: Doubleday & Company.

Westen, D. (1999). The scientific status of unconscious processes: Is Freud really dead? *Journal of the American Psychoanalytic Association, 47*, 1061–1106.

White, J. L., Moffitt, T. E., & Silva, P. A. (1989). A prospective replication of the protective effects of IQ in subjects at high risk for juvenile delinquency. *Journal of Consulting and Clinical Psychology, 57*(6), 719–724.

Whitman, T. A., & Akutagawa, D. (2004). Riddles in serial murder: A synthesis. *Aggression and Violent Behavior, 9*, 693–703.

Wittels, F. (1937). The criminal psychopath in the psychoanalytic system. *Psychoanalytic Review, 24*(1), 276–291.

Yang, Y., Glenn, A. L., & Raine, A. (2008). Brain abnormalities in antisocial individuals: Implications for the law. *Behavioral Sciences and the Law, 26*, 65–83.

Yang, Y., Raine, A., Colletti, P., Toga, A. W., & Narr, K. L. (2010). Morphological alterations in the prefrontal cortex and the amygdala in unsuccessful psychopaths. *Journal of Abnormal Psychology, 119*, 546–554.

Yang, Y., Raine, A., Han, C., Schug, R. A., Toga, A. W., & Narr, K. L. (2010). Reduced hippocampal and parahippocampal volumes in murderers with schizophrenia. *Psychiatry Research: Neuroimaging, 182*(1), 9–13.

Yang, Y., Raine, A., Lencz, T., Bihrle, S., LaCasse, L., & Colletti, P. (2005). Volume reduction in prefrontal gray matter in unsuccessful criminal psychopaths. *Biological Psychiatry, 57*, 1103–1108.

Yang, Y., Raine, A., Narr, K. L., Colletti, P., & Toga, A. W. (2009). Localization of deformaties within the amygdala in individuals with psychopathy. *Archives of General Psychiatry, 66*, 986–994.

CHAPTER SIX

Two Sides of the Same Coin: The Sociological and Psychological Social Psychology of Crime

Mark Cohan and Kathleen E. Cook

Considered abstractly, social psychological theories of crime seem relatively easy to define and envision. Such theories would elucidate how individual psychology and social conditions interact to produce or shape criminal behavior. In reality, however, there are no neatly packaged theories that fit this description. Instead, trying to delineate social psychological theories of crime is as much a constructive as a descriptive exercise. It is a task that requires the writers, us, to make debatable decisions about what to include and what to exclude, and, in many cases, involves inferring how a theory with a broader focus than crime would relate to that specific case. This is true for a number of reasons.

First, social psychology is a catch-all term that is used (often indiscriminately) to refer to the intersection of the individual and the social environment as it is understood and studied both by psychologists and by sociologists. While there is overlap in the real-world phenomena that both types of scholars examine, differences in perspective, terminology, and theoretical and philosophical assumptions often overshadow similarities. For all practical purposes, sociological theories of social psychology (as they relate to crime or any other topic) occupy a different intellectual terrain from that of psychological theories of social psychology. Presenting a unified set of "social psychological theories of crime" is, thus, somewhat disingenuous, since no such canon exists. Perhaps the best-case scenario would be for a social psychologist trained in psychology and another trained in sociology to collaborate to bring together what their unique disciplines offer to the study of the social psychology of crime. This chapter offers that best-case scenario.

Another reason that summarizing "social psychological theories of crime" involves as much construction as description on our part relates to the nature of the theorizing that has been done. The theoretical work in each discipline relevant to the social psychology of crime often does not originate or get classified as such. Some sociologists theorize specifically about crime (Colvin, Cullen, & Vander Van, 2002; Sutherland, 1947), but it is more likely that the examination of crime falls within the larger purview of the sociology of deviance. Social psychologists in psychology do not study criminal behavior per se. Rather, they study "normal" behavior—behavior that anyone in similar situations might enact. In fact, as soon as an individual's behavior becomes deviant in an ongoing way, it becomes the purview of abnormal psychologists (as the three determinants of abnormal behavior are traditionally deviance, dysfunction, and distress). On balance, scholars in both traditions focus on broader psychological and interactional processes than strictly criminological ones. For example, sociologists and psychologists theorize about things such as prejudice and social labeling, each in their own way. Their theoretical formulations related to these concepts (and many others) may be applicable to the study of crime, but they do not begin as theories of crime, per se.

One final complicating factor is what constitutes a social psychological theory. While sociologists have the luxury of finding the theoretical work relevant to crime collected in the theories of deviance, their domain of interest spans social structures both large (e.g., entire societies, organizations) and small (e.g., families, individuals in social roles), and social processes, such as media influence, that are simultaneously community-wide and felt uniquely by the individual. Similarly, psychologists study these things, but always through the perspective of the individual. For example, a theory of aggression may serve as a theory of crime when it explains an individual's criminal behavior. In these contexts, it can be difficult to say definitively which perspectives belong under the rubric of "social psychological" theories of crime.

The upshot of these limitations is that to speak of "social psychological theories of crime," we have had to make judgments about the theories that are, by extrapolation, most relevant to the examination of crime. We make these judgments fully aware that other scholars might make different but equally defensible judgments in our place.

With these appropriate caveats in place, we offer our delineation of "social psychological theories of crime." Our purpose in this chapter is twofold. We want to identify and describe the key theories we believe belong under this banner, but we also want to offer readers a sense of the real-world value of each theory. We accomplish this second goal by explaining how each theory might be applied to a hypothetical scenario. The scenario will be described below. First, we want to provide a skeleton of the structure we have chosen to present our theoretical overview. We present the theories in two broad sections. The first focuses on long-term factors, specifically those addressed by learning theory, that may, ultimately, be said to contribute to a person's involvement in crime. In this section are psychological theories of classical and operant conditioning, as well as social learning from both the sociological and the psychological perspective. In the second section, we focus on more short-term or proximal factors. We begin this section with the psychological social factors. Here, we include excitation transfer theory and various theories of aggression. Into the discussion of the latter we incorporate attributions, schemas, the weapons effect, and the media. We continue with conformity, first briefly from a psychological perspective, and then more comprehensively from a sociological perspective with social bonding theory and its variants. We conclude with labeling theory from sociology and a psychological perspective of prejudice and related theories. It should be noted that the organization scheme is our own and has been devised to highlight similarities in the general focus of particular psychological and sociological theories. Where appropriate, we locate individual theories within their discipline-specific traditions throughout the text.

Our scenario, which is necessarily vague to accommodate the concerns of different theories, is this: Steve, who is black, and Randall, who is white, are both having a drink at a crowded sports bar. They are strangers to one another, though they are standing virtually shoulder to shoulder in the bar. At some point during the evening, Steve bumps Randall, causing Randall to spill his drink on himself. A fistfight ensues in which at least one of the two patrons could be considered guilty of criminal assault.

I. Long-Term Factors

Learning Theory

Learning theory, originating as behaviorism, has long been a fundamental theory across branches of psychology. Social psychology in particular has relied on learning theory to explain behaviors such as person perception, attitude formation, and aggression.

Learning theory refers to a class of mechanisms that lead to a relatively permanent change in behavior due to an experience with the environment. The mechanisms are classical conditioning (aka Pavlovian or association), operant conditioning (aka instrumental or reinforcement), and social learning theory (aka modeling). Through these mechanisms, we learn which persons or groups are appropriate targets for aggression, what actions by others merit aggression, and what situations are ones in which aggression is warranted. A brief examination of each mechanism is presented below. What is learned will be reflected in the included examples.

Classical conditioning. In classical conditioning, stimuli in our environments automatically elicit responses. By pairing other stimuli with these automatically eliciting stimuli, these other stimuli are able to elicit those same responses (Pavlov, 1927). That is, a stimulus can come to elicit a response that it does not normally elicit after being paired with a stimulus that does elicit that response.

Suppose that when Randall was a child, his mother was always anxious (tense and terse) around black people. Randall would have learned to associate this unpleasantness with the presence of black individuals, regardless of what his mother says about blacks (Castelli, De Dea, & Nesdale, 2008; Eskritt & Lee, 2003). After repeated pairings of Mom's anxiety and black skin, Randall will develop prejudicial attitudes. His mother no longer needs to be present. Randall is automatically tense around blacks, and that tension or arousal makes Randall ready to aggress (as will be discussed in Section II below). It is important to appreciate that these associations develop and often occur beyond people's awareness (Krosnick, Betz, Jussim, & Lynn, 1992; Staats & Staats, 1958).

Operant conditioning. In operant (instrumental) conditioning, we operate on the environment and as a result receive some sort of reward or punishment (Catania, 2003). Actions followed by pleasant or rewarding consequences are strengthened, whereas those followed by unpleasant consequences are weakened (i.e., Thorndike's Law of Effect; Thorndike, 1911). Thus, anything that increases the frequency/strength of a response is a reinforcer, and anything that decreases the frequency/strength of a response is a punishment. There are positive (applying something to the situation) and negative (taking something away from the situation) reinforcers and punishment.

For people, there are four major reinforcers. The first is to be right. People are motivated to repeat behavior that makes them feel that they are doing the right thing. For Randall, this could take the form of standing up for himself, or being manly. The second reinforcer is to be like others. People want to be like those they respect or admire, such as parents, celebrities, or powerful people. Perhaps Randall wants to be like his dad or a tough-guy celebrity. The third reinforcer is to be liked. People want to be liked by others, and will do much to garner or hold on to that esteem. Randall may think that his friends will like him more if he fights. The final reinforcer is to achieve instrumental ends. People may engage in crime for instrumental reasons—to get something they want or need, which often brings regard from particular others. Randall may feel better about himself if he hits Steve.

Imagine that Randall is in grade school and one of his friends tells an offensive "joke" about blacks. Randall does not even really understand the joke, but he repeats it at the dinner table all the same. And his family laughs and laughs. Randall is then reinforced for holding a prejudice attitude. (Furthermore, his family just modeled disrespectful attitudes toward blacks for Randall. See the "Social learning theory" subsection that follows.) Further illustrative examples of reinforcement and punishment for Randall are provided in Table 6.1.

Social learning theory (Sutherland and Akers). Within sociology, the theoretical tradition known as symbolic interaction encompasses theories that presume that social behavior and the social world are produced as humans exchange symbols that have come to have (at least some) shared meaning. In essence, our reality is shaped by the meaning things have for us, and this meaning is learned and transformed by social interaction (e.g., conversation) and our own thoughts (i.e., internal conversation) (Blumer, 1969).

Social learning theory is a symbolic interactionist theory that builds on the pioneering work of Sutherland (1947), who advanced the *differential association theory* of crime. Sutherland's basic argument was that people learn to commit crime through the same learning mechanisms by which they learn any other behavior. The theory predicts that the probability of someone committing a particular crime increases if, on balance, they have learned more meanings (called "definitions") that favor the criminal act than ones that inure against it. In the words of Sutherland's successor,

Table 6.1 Operant Conditioning: Examples of Positive and Negative Reinforcers and Punishments for Randall

	Reinforcement	Punishment
Positive (Added)	Randall obtains admiration from the crowd for his toughness.	Randall is given jail time for assault.
Negative (Taken away)	Randall gets Steve to back away	Randall loses time with his girlfriend.

Ronald Akers, "If the balance of definitions is favorable to law, the outcome is conformity; if violation definitions are in excess, criminal behavior is the result" (1973, p. 39).

Sutherland's theory of differential association (1947) drew much-needed attention to the connection between the company we keep and what we learn from it about criminality and conformity. But his work was criticized for not describing how definitions are learned and not providing a mechanism for determining when definitions favorable to crime exceed or overpower definitions favoring conformity.

Akers's social learning theory (1973) extends differential association theory and seeks to answer some of the criticisms of it. Social learning theory posits that the probability of an individual engaging in criminal behavior (or, more broadly, deviance) is increased when that person has learned techniques and definitions favorable to the behavior and, in a given context, those definitions become more associated with valued rewards (e.g., approval of others, monetary gains) than conforming behaviors. In the language of the theory, individuals learn definitions favorable to criminal behavior from others through operant conditioning. Two keys to this conditioning are reinforcement and reinforcement schedules. Reinforcement occurs when a person either receives something that they value or is able to avoid pain or punishment because of their behavior. The reinforcement schedule indicates with how much frequency and predictability reinforcement is received for a behavior. When an individual experiences differential reinforcement, such that he is receiving reinforcers for criminal behavior in greater amount, frequency, and probability than reinforcers for conformity, he is more likely to act criminally than to conform. The theory identifies definitions (essentially, verbal statements) as the most important type of reinforcer. Through differential reinforcement, definitions in favor of criminal behavior—for example, a statement that suggests that a potential victim "has it coming"—can become associated, in the mind of the actor, with reinforcement. When that happens, these definitions are said to be discriminative. At that point, the theory predicts criminal behavior to be more likely than conformity.

For Akers, then, Randall's physical aggression against Steve at the bar can have its origins years before the act. The theory indicates that definitions regarding criminal and conforming behavior most often come from primary groups, and it is from these sources that they have the greatest impact on the individual. So we can imagine that, growing up, Randall learned from his father that what you do when someone seems to disrespect you is hit them.

How did Randall learn this from his father? It is likely that reinforcement played a great role. When Randall attended a baseball game with his father, there was an opposing fan who jeered Randall's father in a very personal way. Randall's father felt disrespected and responded by hitting the other person. Randall's father may have received support from nearby patrons and gone on to tell Randall, "I don't accept being disrespected. If someone talks to me like that, they deserve what they get." This comment by Randall's father provides a definition favorable to the aggressive behavior because it blames the victim for the violence. Having learned that "people who disrespect me deserve to be hit," Randall now has a definition favorable to crime (if his action against the other bar patron is so defined). This definition could be offset by others in his primary group. For instance, his mother may reiterate to him that "you don't solve your problems with your fists." But social learning theory tells us that if Randall's father's definition wins out—if Randall feels greater social reward associated with this definition, it is reinforced more often and with more regularity than definitions to the contrary—we should not be surprised if he slugs the bar patron who, in Randall's eyes, has disrespected him.

Social learning theory (Bandura).[1] Psychology also has a theoretical formulation that carries the name social learning theory. Behaviorists observed that learning took place in animals for which classical and operant conditioning had no explanation. Tolman (1948), for example, found evidence of rats modeling behavior on what was observed. The study of observational learning was embraced. Other theorists such as Rotter (1945) and Miller and Dollard (1941; see also the "Frustration-Aggression Hypothesis" subsection below) developed social learning theories. It was Albert Bandura, however, who wrote about social learning theory's broad application in a definitive 1977 book and in a widely read and cited article. Bandura's social learning theory stated that behavior is learned through observation and the mental processing of information. He went on to establish four steps that are needed for this type of learning: (1) attention (one must attend to a model's actions); (2) retention (one must remember what was observed); (3) reproduction (one must be able to produce actions); and (4) motivation (one must be motivated to perform behavior). Bandura asserts that the presence of these four elements indicates that learning has taken place. If an element is missing, the result is merely performance.

Bandura further provides four factors that enhance observational learning. The first is the type of model. Learning is enhanced when the model is seen as warm, caring, competent, or of higher social status. The second is the type of observer. Learning is enhanced if the observer is in a dependent position in relation to the model. The third factor is the situation. If the learner is uncertain about the correct behavior, observational learning is enhanced. Finally, outcomes play a part. Learning is heightened if the model receives a reward for the observed behavior. This last element can be thought of as vicarious operant conditioning.

The most famous of Bandura's studies is his Bobo doll study (Bandura, Ross, & Ross, 1961). In these, adults modeled aggression toward an inflatable doll. Children imitated the verbal and physical actions almost identically. We can see something similar reflected in Randall and Steve's interaction. According to Bandura's social learning theory, because Randall observed his father handling personal affronts with aggression, Randall has learned that the "right" behavior in such situations is violence. Moreover, Randall observed that his father received admiration for his aggression. In this scenario, there are not only the four steps necessary for observational learning, but also the four factors that enhance observational learning.

Social learning theory underpins the *Cycle of Family Violence*. Children who have aggressive parents are more likely to treat others in aggressive ways (Heyman & Slep, 2002). Moreover, physically abused adolescents have a greater likelihood of committing both violent and nonviolent crime (Fagan, 2005). "Children who experience child abuse & neglect are 59% more likely to be arrested as a juvenile, 28% more likely to be arrested as an adult, and 30% more likely to commit violent crime" (http://www.childhelp.org/pages/statistics, n.d.). Parents serve as our models, and unless we strive to do otherwise, we will do as they did.

Another influential model of aggression is the media. Because of its many impacts, it will be discussed as its own topic under "Aggression" in Section II. Note, however, that the media makes our culture seem more violent than it actually is. Known as *Cultivation Theory* (Gerbner & Gross, 1976), this misrepresentation shows violence as both common and acceptable, modeling for people that volatile situations are "usually" handled with aggression.

II. Short-Term Social Factors

Excitation Transfer

Like learning theory, excitation transfer theory (Zillman, 1979) also often affects our behavior beyond our awareness. In excitation transfer, physiological arousal arising in one situation intensifies emotional responses in a subsequent situation. Our arousal—via exercise, caffeine, stress, threat, etc.—tapers off gradually over the ensuing minutes. Because we fail to appreciate this fact, we misattribute arousal from an earlier experience to the current situation. In his original work, Zillman (1979) showed that subjects who had exercised prior to being insulted behaved more aggressively than subjects who had not exercised (and were not insulted).

Many characteristics of the typical bar scene, such as alcohol, heat, crowds, smoke, etc., increase physiological arousal. Randall, like most people, fails to appreciate his arousal; in fact, because he is "relaxing" with a drink, he may even think his arousal is less than normal. When Steve bumps into Randall, Randall transfers his excitation to the moment. That is, Randall easily misattributes his arousal and discomfort to the present situation with Steve and is ready to aggress—to transform what may have been an accident into an altercation.

Frustration-Aggression Hypothesis

Another variable that leaves one ready to aggress is frustration. The frustration-aggression hypothesis has its origins in learning theory. In the language of learning theory, frustration can be thought of as the stimulus and aggression as the naturally occurring response. In Buss's (1963) studies, confederates frustrated subjects by having them lose money, fail at a task, or lose extra credit. Subjects who were in one of the frustration conditions were more aggressive toward the confederate than those in the control conditions. Frustration is affected by the following: unexpected events blocking one's goal, with unanticipated obstructions increasing one's frustration; by closeness to the goal, with the closer one is to the goal, the greater the likelihood of frustration; and by relative deprivation, with the perception that others are achieving one's desired goal increasing one's frustration.

Imagine that Randall has endured a lengthy queue at the bar to get his drink. He has seen others receive their drinks (relative deprivation), and at last he has his. As he is turning to pass a drink to a friend, Steve bumps into him, spilling Randall's fresh drink. Because Randall was very close to his goal of enjoying his drink, and he has been unexpectedly blocked from doing so, Randall's frustration is high, and according to the frustration-aggression hypothesis, he is likely to aggress.

This original frustration-aggression hypothesis is limited because frustration does not always lead to aggression, and aggression is not always the result of frustration. The frustration-aggression hypothesis was repeatedly modified, leading ultimately to the comprehensive theory of aggression called Cognitive Neoassociation Model of Aggression (Berkowitz, 1989, 1990, 1993).

Cognitive Neoassociation Model of Aggression

In the Cognitive Neoassociation Model of Aggression, Berkowitz explains that it is not frustration per se that leads to aggression, but rather it is the negative affect (e.g., anger, irritation, hostility) that frustration evokes that leads to aggression. More specifically, negative feelings activate a complex interplay of thoughts, memories, and physiological responses. All of these, in turn, affect the cognitive appraisal of the situation, and it is our cognitive appraisal of the situation that determines whether we aggress.

To explore this model, we must appreciate that our responses to environmental events (i.e., situations) may lead to negative emotions. These negative emotions may ready us to aggress, but whether we actually aggress is again determined by our responses in the situation (see Table 6.2).

In the following sections, we will look at some of the factors that lead to the negative emotions (responses to environmental events) and, in turn, at some of the responses to those negative emotions—both those that increase and decrease the likelihood of aggression.

Responses to environmental events. Whether negative emotion occurs depends on one's cognitive appraisal of the situation. What are Randall and Steve's attributions for the event?

The study of attributions is a long and vast area of study in psychological social psychology. In short, attributions are our *whys* for events—our

Table 6.2 Cognitive Neoassociation Model of Aggression and Relevant Responses

Environmental Events → Negative Emotion → Aggression
(Stimulus → Perception → Behavioral Response)

Perception	Disinhibitors	Inhibitors
1. Attributions	1. Releasers	1. Fear of retaliation
2. Personality	2. Anonymity	2. Strong cultural norms against aggression
3. Nonspecific Arousal (e.g., fear, drugs, fatigue, heat)	3. Nonspecific Arousal	3. Peaceable behaviors
	4. Sociopathy	

explanations. What makes attributions such a rich area of study is their phenomenology; attributions are subjective. We think that we see the *whys* in the behavior of others (and, indeed, in our own behavior), but we do not. We supply the attributions, and our interpretations are subject to error.

Some errors are so common that they are codified. The *Fundamental Attribution Error* (Ross, 1977) notes our tendency to make dispositional attributions—to say that people did what they did because of the kind of people they are—and to ignore the role of the situation. Randall is more likely to think that Steve bumped into him because Steve is careless or rude (dispositional characteristics) than to think that Steve bumped him because Steve slipped or was pushed (situational features).

This reliance on dispositional attributions does not hold when it comes to us. Rather, we subscribe to the *Self-Serving Bias* (Miller & Ross, 1975). We tend to take credit when things go well (i.e., make dispositional/internal attributions for our success) and to blame others when things do not go well (i.e., make situational/external attributions of failure). Thus, neither Randall nor Steve is predisposed to think the collision is his fault; both will blame the other.

These biases can be even more pronounced when race is involved. The *Ultimate Attribution Error* is the tendency to attribute a minority group member's negative behavior to dispositional characteristics and a minority group member's positive behavior to situational factors (Pettigrew, 1979). Duncan (1976) showed white subjects a videotape of an aggressor (black or white) attacking a victim (black or white). The black aggressor attacking a white victim was labeled violent or aggressive 75% of time, whereas the white aggressor attacking a black victim was labeled violent only 17% of time. The attribution was dispositional for blacks ("they are just like that"), and situational for whites ("he was provoked"). Randall is even more likely to think of Steve as rude and careless because Steve is black.

The meaning of Steve bumping into Randall is unclear, and both Steve's and Randall's responses to the situation are predicated on how they interpret the other's behavior. Furthermore, one or both of them may have a *Hostile Attribution Bias* (Baron & Richardson, 1994) leading them to perceive hostile intent in ambiguous situations. Does Randall or Steve automatically perceive hostile intent behind the actions of those around him?

Schemas also shape our responses to environmental events. Schemas are simply cognitive structures that organize information around themes or topics. They are our theories about how things go together in our social world. For example, we have schemas about the sort of people who hang out in bars and schemas about how to order a drink at a bar (schemas about actions are known as scripts). Schemas have functions or consequences in that they determine what we notice, shape how we interpret or explain ambiguous information, and affect what we remember. In other words, schemas affect what we think we see. Moreover, once we form a schema, we seek, interpret, and even create information that verifies our existing beliefs, and we disregard disconfirming information. This tendency is called *Confirmation Bias*.

As mentioned earlier, physiological arousal increases the likelihood of strong emotions such as frustration and anger. A wide array of situational variables such as exercise, fatigue, pain, losing, threats to self-esteem, threats to manhood (Bosson & Vandello, 2011), alcohol, caffeine, drugs, cigarette smoke, sex, crowding, noise, unpleasant odors, and heat have been shown to create arousal, and that arousal affects us beyond our awareness. For example, people honked more at a research assistant sitting in a car at a green light on a hot day (Kenrick & MacFarlane, 1986). Similarly, the number of violent crimes per day and the daily high temperature were tabulated for Houston, Texas. As temperature increased, so did violent crime (Anderson & Anderson, 1984).

In the bar where Steve and Randall have their altercation, there is cigarette smoke, crowding, noise, heat, and perhaps unpleasant odors. It is the end of the day; Steve and Randall are fatigued and have presumably consumed alcohol. They may be looking for sexual partners, potentially leading to arousal or rejection. Then Steve bumps Randall. The run-in may have hurt and/or threatened Steve. The scene is ripe for violence.

Responses to negative emotions. Being ready to aggress does not mean that we will aggress. There are environmental factors that encourage us to refrain from aggression, and factors that prompt us to aggress. Factors that inhibit aggression include awareness of strong cultural or personal norms and the potentially high costs of aggression (e.g., fear of retaliation). In contrast, anything that reduces one's inhibitions serves as a releaser for aggression. Many of the same variables that increase arousal, such as alcohol, drugs, smoke, crowding, noise, etc., also decrease inhibition.

Additionally, anything in the environment that signals violence is acceptable also serves as a releaser. An example of such an environmental signal is the presence of a weapon. Subjects exposed to a gun lying on a table, for example, were significantly more aggressive than those exposed to another object or nothing (*Weapons Effect*; Berkowitz & LePage, 1967). Male subjects who interacted with a gun rather than a toy for 15 minutes showed significant increases in testosterone and aggression (Klinesmith, Kasser, & McAndrew, 2006). If the bar sported symbols of aggression, like a gun hanging behind the bar, such symbols could implicitly prime Randall and Steve to fight.

"Broken Windows" is another well-known symbol that aggression is permissible (Kelling & Wilson, 1982; Zimbardo, 1969). The *Broken Windows Theory* is that a single broken window can signal that no one cares, and thus that antisocial behavior is tolerated. A well-kept sports bar invites less vandalism and antisocial behavior than a poorly maintained one.

Another variable that permits aggressive behavior is *anonymity*. We are more likely to behave aggressively when we can do so anonymously. For example, convertible drivers with their tops up behaved more aggressively than convertible drivers with their tops down (Ellison, Govern, Petri, & Figler, 1995) and children stole significantly more candy and money when anonymous (Diener, Fraser, Beaman, & Kelem, 1976). When our anonymity leads to a disconnection with self, deindividuation occurs. *Deindividuation* will be discussed further in connection with conformity.

Violent media. Violent media can serve both to arouse negative emotions and to signal that aggressive behavior is allowed (Bushman & Anderson, 2001). First, violent media is a source of physiological arousal (Anderson, 2004). Second, it primes violent situations; because of the availability heuristic (Tversky & Kahneman, 1986), we are more likely to perceive situations as violent because of our recent exposure to them. Third, thinking back to social learning theory, violent media provides models of how we should handle conflict and threats. And fourth, violent media, through cultivation and its ubiquity, indicates that aggressive behaviors are appropriate responses; in other words, violent media permits aggressive behavior (Wood, Wong, & Chachere, 1991).[2]

It is possible that Steve and Randall were watching a violent sporting event, such as a boxing match or hockey game on the bar's televisions. Viewing such events would set the stage for ensuing aggression.

Using the Cognitive Neoassociation Model of Aggression, we considered responses to situations that may lead to negative affect, such as attributions, schemas, and sources of physiological arousal. We also explored what happens should negative emotions arise: Whether we aggress is again determined by our responses to the situation. Some factors such as strong norms and fear of retaliation reduce the likelihood that we will aggress. Others, such as the presence of weapons or violent media and deindividuation, increase the likelihood of aggression. What is central throughout the Cognitive Neoassociation Model of Aggression is the complex interaction of our cognitions and our physiology in determining whether we aggress.

Conformity

In committing a crime, one breaks societal norms. Engaging in unacceptable behavior is easier when one is deindividuated (Singer, Brush, & Lublin, 1965). Zimbardo (1969) defined deindividuation as a "process in which a series of antecedent social conditions lead to a change in perception of self and others, and thereby to a lowered threshold of normally restrained behavior" (p. 251). In deindividuation, there is destruction of traditional social structures. Responsibility is diffused or surrendered; the present seems expanded (and the past and future distanced). Control emotions such as guilt, shame, or fear are weakened, as is the threshold for expressing inhibited (e.g., impulsive, irrational, or aggressive) behaviors. Behavior is intensified, self-reinforcing, and difficult to stop. People are hyper-responsive to those active and present; group liking and affiliation is increased as the group shares behavior. Perceptions may be distorted and even memory may be impaired. Zimbardo's model of deindividuation (1969) has been used to explain mob violence, riots, military rampages, police brutality, prison violence, and even spousal abuse (Dutton, Fehr, & McEwen, 1982).

Among the most (in)famous social psychology, and Philip Zimbardo, studies is the Stanford Prison Experiment (Haney, Banks, & Zimbardo, 1973). The study is construed in various ways—as a demonstration of the power of roles, as a lesson in obedience, as an example of what happens to normal people placed in an "evil" situation, and as a display of deindividuation. In the experiment, similar (based on pretesting) healthy, college-aged male volunteers were randomly assigned to be prisoners and guards. Along with their roles came uniforms. Guards were told to maintain enough order for the prison to effectively function but not to physically aggress against the prisoners (Haney et al., 1973). Although intended to last two weeks, the experiment was ended after six days. All guard-prisoner interactions had become hostile and dehumanizing. *Dehumanization* is at the root of much aggressive and violent behavior. If we do not see others as humans worthy of just treatment, we can aggress without guilt. Zimbardo (1974) considered this study evidence of the force of the situation, not individuals' personality, on behavior. When the situation is strong enough, it determines our behavior.

A dark bar where one is unknown provides a perfect backdrop for unacceptable behavior. Darkness, heat, anonymity, and packed crowds also affect the deindividuation of not only Randall and Steve, but also of the bystanders. In such situations, crowds often bait bad behavior (Mann, 1981). Steve and Randall, because of deindividuation or prejudice (discussed below), may see the other as less than human—as deserving aggression.

Social bonding theory. Social bonding theories of delinquency—and, by extension, crime—appeared in American criminology in the mid-20th century. Travis Hirschi's social bonding theory (1969; sometimes called *social control theory*) is the hallmark approach in this tradition, but a number of other theories—Reckless's *Containment Theory* (1961), Sykes and Matza's *Techniques of Neutralization* (1957), and Reiss's (1951) and Nye's (1958) *Theories of Internal and External Controls*—are recognized as predecessors that shaped it.

When social bonding theories were first proposed, they were hailed, at least by their creators, as an entirely new approach to crime because they asked a fundamentally different question. Rather than investigating why people commit delinquent or criminal acts, these theories asked the reverse: Why do people not violate social rules and norms? In other words, why do people conform? In subsequent years, the novelty of this approach has been challenged by some, however (Akers, 1997). These critics argue that placing the focus on people's adherence to social rules over their violation of them is primarily a semantic distinction. In the final analysis, social bonding theories, like other theories of crime, seek to explain why crime occurs. That said, the basic strategy of the tradition—relating individuals' propensity for crime to the strength or weakness of their social bonds—remains an important one.

The quintessential statement of social bonding theory by Hirschi (1969) begins with the proposition that an individual is more likely to commit a delinquent act, including a crime, when his or her ties (or bond) to society are weak or broken. Hirschi theorized that the individual's bond to society was formed with four observable elements, which he called attachment, commitment, involvement, and belief.

Attachment, which is often identified as the most important of the four elements, describes feelings of affection, affiliation, connection, and identification with others. For Hirschi, the importance of attachment is encapsulated in Durkheim's assertion that, "We are moral beings to the extent that we are social beings" (1961, p. 64), which Hirschi takes to mean that we follow social norms to the degree that we are sensitive to the opinions of others. Those who are attached strongly to others are more likely to conform (i.e., not commit crime) than those who lack such ties or are connected to others only weakly.

Interestingly, Hirschi contends that the character of those to whom one is attached is of little consequence; any attachment will serve as a barrier against norm violation. Thus, a young person who is attached to his parents, who happen to be career criminals, will be less likely to commit crime than if this same young person were disconnected from his criminal parents.

Commitment refers to the degree to which a person is invested in conventional activities. More than simply reflecting what the person may be doing day to day that is conventional, this concept asks: How heavily is the person's life structured such that opportunities, reputation, lifestyle, or other things they value would be jeopardized by deviant or criminal acts? In this context, seeking an education, getting ahead in business, or fostering the good opinion of others would reflect strong commitment to conventionality and thus mitigate against criminal behavior.

The relevance of involvement is predicated on the notion that to commit crime, one must have time available. People with high degrees of involvement in conventional or conforming activities are seen as less likely to offend, simply because they do not have the time to do so. Belief in the power of involvement to reduce criminality is at the heart of social programs, such as afterschool initiatives for youth that seek to "keep busy" those who, it is believed, might use idle time for delinquency.

Belief refers simply to the degree to which an individual believes he or she is bound by the rules of society. If a person believes that the rules of society are just and appropriate, and should be obeyed, that person is less likely to violate those rules than someone who does not endorse them. For Hirschi, the notion of belief is a general concept. He is not asking whether a person finds a particular rule just and worthy of allegiance; he is asking the extent to which that person believes he or she should obey social rules as a matter of general course.

Does Randall react violently when he is bumped by Steve in a way that Randall interprets as confrontational? The answer, according to Hirschi's social bonding theory, depends on the interplay of Randall's levels of attachment, involvement, commitment, and belief at the time of the incident. If Randall's life is filled with family and friends who love and care for him (high attachment), if he is pursuing a degree to facilitate career advancement or is a valued member of his local synagogue (high commitment), if his days are extremely busy with these activities (high involvement), and if he generally feels that he should "play by the rules" (high belief), social bonding theory would predict the probability of his aggressing against Steve to be low. On the other hand, if Randall has no living relatives, if he is recently divorced and new in town (low attachment), if he sees no value in or avenues for bettering himself (low commitment), if he has lots of free time on his hands (low involvement), and if he believes the rules do not apply to him, Steve might be wise to brace for impact.

A number of extensions, revisions, and reinterpretations of social bonding theory have been proposed in the decades following Hirschi's initial articulation of it. Hirschi, along with Michael Gottfredson, advanced *Self-Control Theory* (1990), which proposes that people with low self-control are more likely than those with high self-control to commit crimes. Charles Tittle (1995) offered *Control-Balance Theory*. This theory suggests that individuals have more or less control over others, depending on their social position and personal qualities. Those individuals on the extremes of the spectrum of control—that is, those with either a control surplus or a control deficit—are more likely to commit crime than those whose control ratios are in balance. People with a control deficit may commit crime to gain control, while those with a surplus may seek to increase their control and may feel like their high level of control makes criminal behavior low-risk for them. Finally, *Coercive Control and Social Support Theory* (Colvin et al., 2002) sees the possibility of crime as depending on the balance between the presence of (perceived) coercion on an individual and social support for the individual that may or may not be strong enough to counteract the coercion. Somewhat counterintuitively, the theory proposes that the key question is not how strong the coercion or social support is, but how predictable each is for the individual. It suggests that individuals are most at risk to offend when both coercion and social support are erratic.

Labeling Theory. Labeling theory, like social learning theory, is a perspective associated with sociology's symbolic interactionist (Blumer, 1969) tradition. The term "labeling theory" is somewhat misleading because it suggests formal propositions about the relationship between variables that can be empirically tested. The collection of concepts and suggested relationships associated with labeling do not provide such testable propositions, so labeling is best thought of as a perspective or an approach, rather than a theory (Becker, 1963). Nevertheless, it is worthy of inclusion in a discussion of social psychology and crime because it raises important questions about the relationship between individual criminal behavior, societal reaction, and recidivism.

The central dynamic of the labeling approach is the movement from primary to secondary deviance. Primary deviance refers to deviant acts (including criminal ones) that are normalized. In other words, these norm violations may bring societal reactions, but they are not severe because the behavior is treated as somehow anomalous, not indicative of the person committing them. Repeated instances of primary deviation, however, are likely to bring stronger and stronger sanctions; the social control apparatuses of society work to label the social actor a "criminal" more and more forcefully. The escalation of punishments and social stigmatization creates the potential that people committing the crimes react against those who are judging them. They wholeheartedly embrace the status of criminal that is being imposed on them and begin to organize their identities accordingly. This transition marks the actors as secondary deviants, and their subsequent criminal acts constitute secondary deviance. As Lemert puts it, a secondary deviant is a person "whose life and identity are organized around the facts of deviance" (Lemert, 1972, p. 63).

The primary architects of the labeling perspective, Edwin Lemert and Howard Becker, shared a belief in relativistic definitions of crime and deviance. As such, they believed that scholars had not given enough attention to societal responses to crime (e.g., ostracism, rites of degradation, punishments) as factors that might affect rule violators' sense of self and subsequent behavior. In other words, there had been little focus on social processes that might create crime and deviance. The concept of secondary deviance seeks to capture that process. However, Lemert and Becker emphasized different aspects of the dynamic between criminals and the application of social control, so their two articulations of the perspective have distinct flavors.

Lemert's (1972) discussion of labeling emphasizes the actions of those imposing the sanctions or stigmas. He proposes that social control agencies may inspire individuals to commit to deviant careers precisely because these agencies treat their subjects as people who are not normal. For instance, a person on parole may behave identically to a person who is not (e.g., leaving a certain geographical area), but in the case of the former, the behavior becomes a confirmation of his or her criminality. Becker's version (1963) shifts focus from the social control agencies to the dynamics of identity involved in the production of secondary deviants. He examines how the label of criminal or deviant, consistently applied, can become a person's central identifying characteristic, or their "master status." True to a relativist perspective on crime, Becker noted that labeling could cause both someone who had committed crimes (a "pure deviant") and someone who had been falsely accused to have "criminal" as their master status. In both cases, he expected secondary deviance to follow (Becker, 1963).

In our hypothetical bar scenario, how the labeling approach applies depends on the context. If this incident is the first in which Randall has acted violently, his behavior would constitute primary deviance. At this point, Randall does not see himself as a barroom brawler, and neither do his associates, the bar staff, or the authorities. The incident is likely to be normalized, with only light penalties imposed, if any. All concerned are likely to chalk the incident up to an otherwise stable person flying off the handle.

However, if for some reason the response of the bar staff or the police is much harsher, to the point that Randall and his associates see it as disproportionate to the crime, the results may be different. In this case, Randall may believe that even if he tries to do right, he is going to be seen as doing wrong (as in the parolee's situation described above). He may start to see that others consider him, first and foremost, as a barroom thug (his master status), and he may begin to act and think accordingly (secondary deviance).

The dynamic is somewhat different if the confrontation with Steve is not the first violent barroom confrontation for Randall, but the most recent of many. In that case, the labeling approach argues that Randall has accepted his master status as "barroom thug." He now sees himself as a barroom thug and organizes his behavior this way. Presented with a situation, like the one with Steve, that can be construed as confrontational, Randall can be expected to act with criminal violence because such action is consistent with his self-concept. In fact, he may now garner some things he sees as positive from his "negative" social identity. For instance, being expected to respond violently to confrontational situations absolves him of the challenge of resolving difficult interpersonal issues through talk and negotiation.

Prejudice

Prejudice from a psychological perspective can be thought of as an attitude toward members of some group based solely on their membership in that group. Prejudice as it relates to crime mostly concerns membership in different religious, ethnic, or racial groups, and sometimes socioeconomic groups. Like all attitudes, prejudice consists of thoughts or schemas (stereotypes), feelings (prejudices), and behaviors (discrimination). However, social scientists and lay people alike tend to think of prejudice, and attitudes in general, as feelings. Because expressing prejudice is no longer socially acceptable (or legal), it has become more subtle. This *Modern Racism* (often so-called regardless of the target) surfaces when it is safe, socially acceptable, and easy to rationalize (Dovidio, Gaertner, Kawakami, & Hodson, 2002). This term reminds us that the absence of blatant prejudice does not mean the absence of prejudice. Indeed, the situation at the sports bar may give Randall just the excuse he needs to express his discomfort with blacks.

Our prejudices tell us against whom it is safe to aggress. They tell us who to blame. According to Freud, *scapegoating* occurs when we blame others for our own negative outcomes or situations. If Randall considers himself disadvantaged—perhaps having lost a romantic partner or a promotion at work—he may blame Steve and his group. Another form of blame is *projection.* Projection occurs when we assume that others possess the negative qualities we unconsciously see in ourselves. If Randall fears he is not sufficiently manly, he may accuse everyone else, Steve included, of being that way.

Realistic Conflict Theory. Another explanation for prejudice and conflict is groups' competition for (perceived) scarce resources (LeVine & Campbell, 1972). One group poses a "realistic" threat to another group's welfare. These might be land, mates, jobs, etc. This threat creates hostility, which in turn creates prejudice. Again, Randall may perceive that blacks, and therefore Steve, are getting what Randall should.

Social Identity Theory. Henri Tajfel (Tajfel, Billig, Bundy, & Flament, 1971) did not believe that competition was necessary for group hostility to form. Tajfel began his research by giving people a group label, with the intent of adding other variables until he observed prejudice. He created his groups on the basis of patently trivial criteria—the flip of the coin, being dot overestimators or underestimators, preferring Klee or Kandinsky—when, in fact, his groups were always generated by random assignment. Reliably, subjects discriminated in favor of their own group. For example, members granted more money, more points, more opportunities, etc., to their own group members than to outgroup members. Furthermore, they evaluated their own group members more positively on all criteria than they evaluated members of other groups.

The work of Tajfel and others established that we naturally and spontaneously classify people as members of our group(s) (us, i.e., ingroups) or as members of other groups (them, i.e., outgroups), and we automatically think of "us" as better than "them." Merely being classified into groups is sufficient to produce prejudice, and once we have targets of prejudice, we have targets of aggression and crime.

Certain personality types are also more likely to stereotype more. The *Authoritarian Personality*, characterized by a general intolerance and hostility, a rigid adherence to conventional values, and an exaggerated need to submit to strong authority figures, holds more prejudicial attitudes (Adorno, Frenkel-Brunswik, Levinson, & Sanford, 1950/1993). Individuals who hold entity beliefs believe that people are unchangeable (Dweck & Leggett, 1988). Such individuals show more prejudice than individuals who hold incremental beliefs—beliefs that people can change (Levy, Stroessner, & Dweck, 1998).

Just World Hypothesis. We believe that people get what they deserve (Lerner & Miller, 1978). For those with advantages—education, jobs, safe housing, etc.—there is a desire to believe that such advantages are deserved, and a wish to believe that those who do not have such things somehow did something to deserve not having them. If the disadvantaged did not do something to deserve their lots, then the world is a random place, and we could end up like them or be responsible for them. Instead, we blame the victims for outcomes that may not be their fault.

Steve and Randall are from different racial groups. They may have authoritarian personalities or strong entity beliefs. One of them may blame his outgroup for deflating wages or usurping jobs. If either is dating outside his racial group, he may be accused of taking "their women." The one who possesses a good job or a good mate believes that he deserves such things—after all, the world is just. Thus, Randall and/or Steve may be prejudiced. Their stereotypes function as schemas, ensuring that they notice stereotype-consistent behavior and that they disregard stereotype-inconsistent behavior. Thus, before the incident even occurs, one or both may be ready to aggress against the other. Indeed, the bump provides a socially acceptable opportunity to express their feelings. The situation allows for the expression of aggression, and prejudice increases the likelihood of it occurring.

Conclusion

As should be evident from our review, the theories that can be collected under the banner of social psychological theories of crime have histories that date back at least a century, and they have a bifurcated lineage—one in psychology and one in sociology. Over the decades, there has not been much communication between these two traditions as it relates to the social psychology of crime. Left to their own devices, each has developed their unique points of focus and lexicon. And yet, it is still fair to say they are two sides of the same coin. This quality is especially evident with learning theory in psychology and social learning theory in sociology, where the principles of conditioning are central to both. On one side of the coin, sociology's social learning theory calls our attention to the ways in which reinforcement schedules relate to the meanings people attribute to criminal behaviors; while, on the other, psychologists emphasize the interpersonal circumstances that serve as reinforcers. But at other points, too, one can glimpse broad commonalities beyond the immediate differences. For instance, the fundamental attribution error, which we have presented in the context of psychology, is part of the language of sociological social psychology as well. And although it is not part of the language of sociology's labeling theory, the term certainly describes a social psychological dynamic that could spur secondary deviance. These examples suggest that, in the end, the social psychology of crime need not be as bifurcated as it has been historically. With a common concern for the ways in which environment, interpersonal dynamics, beliefs, attitudes, and perceptions contribute to the potential for crime, criminologists, sociologists, and psychologists have reason to work together to advance theoretical approaches to the social psychology of crime.

Notes

1. Bandura has expanded his social learning theory into social-cognitive learning theory (1979). The latter emphasizes the interaction between thoughts, beliefs, and expectations with behavior, and acknowledges that these internal processes play a role in learning. Because interacting situational and mental processes have a hand in behavior, behavior cannot be predicted based solely on past environmental experience.

2. There remains the popular misconception that viewing violent media reduces one's aggressive drive. This notion is based on Freud's hypothesis that we all have thanatos or a death wish. Freud saw aggression as our need to fulfill this death wish in socially acceptable ways. As the need to meet the wish builds, the tendency toward aggression or violence does, too. Freud further hypothesized that we could release the pressure of the aggressive drive through small acts of aggression such as wrestling or boxing (catharsis), or even through viewing others being aggressive (dramatic catharsis). Unfortunately, as established above, viewing violent media actually has the opposite effect.

References

Adorno, T. W., Frenkel-Brunswik, E., Levinson, D., & Sanford, N. (1950). *The authoritarian personality* (Studies in Prejudice Series, Vol. 1). New York: Harper & Row, 1950; W. W. Norton & Company, 1993.

Akers, R. L. (1973). *Deviant behavior: A social learning approach*. Belmont, CA: Wadsworth.

Akers, R. L. (1997). *Criminological theories: Introduction and evaluation*. Los Angeles, CA: Roxbury.

Anderson, C. A. (2004). An update on the effects of playing violent video games. *Journal of Adolescence, 27*, 113–122. doi:10.1016/j.adolescence.2003.10.009.

Anderson, C. A., & Anderson, D. C. (1984). Ambient temperature and violent crime: Tests of the linear and curvilinear hypotheses. *Journal of Personality and Social Psychology, 46*, 91–97.

Bandura, A. (1977). *Social learning theory*. New York: General Learning Press.

Bandura, A. (1979). Self-referent mechanisms in social learning theory. *American Psychologist, 34*, 439–441.

Bandura, A., Ross, D., & Ross, S. (1961). Transmission of aggression through imitation of aggressive models. *Journal of Abnormal and Social Psychology, 63*, 575–582.

Baron, R. A., & Richardson, D. R. (1994). *Human aggression*. New York: Plenum Press.

Becker, H. S. (1963). *Outsiders: Studies in the sociology of deviance*. New York: Free Press.

Berkowitz, L. (1989). Frustration-aggression hypothesis: Examination and reformulation. *Psychological Bulletin, 106*, 59–73. doi:10.1037/0033-2909.106.1.59.

Berkowitz, L. (1990). On the formation and regulation of anger and aggression: A cognitive-neoassociationistic analysis. *American Psychologist, 45*, 494–503. doi:10.1037/0003-066X.45.4.494.

Berkowitz, L. (1993). *Aggression: Its causes, consequences, and control*. New York: McGraw-Hill.

Berkowitz, L., & LePage, A. (1967). Weapons as aggression-eliciting stimuli. *Journal of Personality and Social Psychology, 7*, 202–207.

Blumer, H. (1969). *Symbolic interaction: Perspective and method*. Englewood Cliffs, NJ: Prentice-Hall.

Bosson, J. K., & Vandello, J. A. (2011). Precarious manhood and its links to action and aggression. *Current Directions in Psychological Science, 20*, 82–86.

Bushman, B. J., & Anderson, C. A. (2001). Media violence and the American public: Scientific facts versus media misinformation. *American Psychologist, 56*, 477–489. doi:10.1037/0003-066X.56.6-7.477.

Buss, A. H. (1963). Physical aggression in relation to different frustrations. *Journal of Abnormal and Social Psychology, 67*, 1–7. doi:10.1037/h0040505.

Castelli, L., De Dea, C., & Nesdale, D. (2008). Learning social attitudes: Children's sensitivity to the nonverbal behaviors of adult models during interracial interactions. *Personality and Social Psychology Bulletin, 34*, 1504–1513. doi:10.1177/0146167208322769.

Catania, A. C. (2003). B. F. Skinner's science and human behavior: Its antecedents and its consequences. *Journal of the Experimental Analysis of Behavior, 80*, 313–320.

Childhelp.org (n.d.). National child abuse statistics. Retrieved from http://www.childhelp.org/pages/statistics.

Colvin, M., Cullen, F. T., & Vander Van, T. (2002). Coercion, social support, and crime: An emerging theoretical consensus. *Criminology, 40*, 19–42.

Diener, E., Fraser, S. C., Beaman, A. L., & Kelem, R. T. (1976). Effects of deindividuation variables on stealing among Halloween trick-or-treaters. *Journal of Personality and Social Psychology, 33*, 178–183. doi:10.1037/0022-3514.33.2.178.

Dovidio, J. F., Gaertner, S. E., Kawakami, K., & Hodson, G. (2002). Why can't we just get along? Interpersonal biases and interracial distrust. *Cultural Diversity and Ethnic Minority Psychology, 8*, 88–102. doi:10.1037/1099-9809.8.2.88.

Duncan, B. L. (1976). Differential social perception and attribution of intergroup violence: Testing the lower limits of stereotyping of blacks. *Journal of Personality and Social Psychology, 34*, 590–598. doi:10.1037/0022-3514.34.4.590.

Durkheim, E. (1961). *Moral education: A study in the theory and application of the sociology of education* (E. K. Wilson & H. Schnurer, Trans.). New York: Free Press.

Dutton, D., Fehr, B., & McEwen, H. (1982). Severe wife battering as deindividuated violence. *Victimology, 7*(1–4), 13–23.

Dweck, C. S., & Leggett, E. L. (1988). A social-cognitive approach to motivation and personality. *Psychological Review, 95*, 256–273. doi:10.1037/0033-295X.95.2.256.

Ellison, P., Govern, J., Petri, H. L., & Figler, M. (1995). Anonymity and aggressive driving behavior: A field study. *Journal of Social Behavior and Personality, 10*, 265–271.

Eskritt, M., & Lee, K. (2003). Do actions speak louder than words? Preschool children's use of the verbal-nonverbal consistency principle during inconsistent communications. *Journal of Nonverbal Behavior, 27*(1), 25–41. doi:10.1023/A:1023614123081.

Fagan, A. A. (2005). The relationship between adolescent physical abuse and criminal offending: Support for an enduring and generalized cycle of violence. *Journal of Family Violence, 20*, 279–290, doi:10.1007/s10896-005-6604-7.

Gerbner, G., & Gross, L. (1976). Living with television: The violence profile. *Journal of Communication, 26*(2), 172–199. doi:10.1111/j.1460-2466.1976.tb01397.x.

Gottfredson, M., & Hirschi, T. (1990). *A general theory of crime*. Palo Alto, CA: Stanford University Press.

Haney, C., Banks, W. C., & Zimbardo, P. G. (1973). Interpersonal dynamics in a simulated prison. *International Journal of Criminology and Penology, 1*, 69–97.

Heyman, R. E., & Slep, A. M. S. (2002). Do child abuse and interparental violence lead to adulthood family violence? *Journal of Marriage and Family, 64*, 864–870. doi:10.1111/j.1741-3737.2002.00864.x.

Hirschi, T. (1969). *Causes of delinquency*. Berkeley, CA: University of California Press.

Kelling, G. L., & Wilson, J. Q. (1982, March). Broken windows: The police and neighborhood safety. *Atlantic Magazine*, Retrieved from http://www.theatlantic.com/magazine/archive/1982/03/broken-windows/304465/.

Kenrick, D. T., & MacFarlane, S. W. (1986). Ambient temperature and horn honking: A field study of the heat/aggression relationship. *Environment and Behavior, 18*, 179–191. doi:10.1177/0013916586182002.

Klinesmith, J., Kasser, T., & McAndrew, F. T. (2006). Guns, testosterone, and aggression: An experimental test of a mediational hypothesis. *Psychological Science, 17*, 568–571.

Krosnick, J. A., Betz, A. L., Jussim, L. J., & Lynn, A. R. (1992). Subliminal conditioning of attitudes. *Personality and Social Psychology Bulletin, 18*, 152–162.

Lemert, E. M. (1972). *Human deviance, social problems, and social control* (2nd ed.). Englewood Cliffs, NJ: Prentice-Hall.

Lerner, M. J., & Miller, D. T. (1978). Just world research and the attribution process: Looking back and ahead. *Psychological Bulletin, 85*, 1030–1051. doi:10.1037/0033-2909.85.5.1030.

LeVine, R. A., & Campbell, D. T. (1972). *Ethnocentrism: Theories of conflict, ethnic attitudes, and group behavior*. Oxford, England: John Wiley & Sons.

Levy, S. R., Stroessner, S. J., & Dweck, C. S. (1998). Stereotype formation and endorsement: The role of implicit theories. *Journal of Personality and Social Psychology, 74*, 1421–1436. doi:10.1037/0022-3514.74.6.1421.

Mann, L. (1981). The baiting crowd in episodes of threatened suicide. *Journal of Personality and Social Psychology, 41*, 703–709. doi:10.1037/0022-3514.41.4.703.

Miller, D. T., & Ross, M. (1975). Self-serving biases in the attribution of causality: Fact or fiction? *Psychological Bulletin, 82*, 213–225. doi:10.1037/h0076486.

Miller, N. E., & Dollard, J. (1941). *Social learning and imitation.* New Haven, CT: Yale University Press.

Nye, F. I. (1958). *Family relationships and delinquent behavior.* New York: Wiley.

Pavlov, I. P. (1927). *Conditioned reflexes: An investigation of the physiological activity of the cerebral cortex* (G. V. Anrep, Trans.). London: Oxford University Press.

Pettigrew, T. F. (1979). The ultimate attribution error: Extending Allport's cognitive analysis of prejudice. *Personality and Social Psychology Bulletin, 5*, 461–476.

Reckless, W. C. (1961). A new theory of delinquency and crime. *Federal Probation, 25*, 42–46.

Reiss, A. J. (1951). Delinquency as the failure of personal and social controls. *American Sociological Review*, 16, 196–207.

Ross, L. (1977). The intuitive psychologist and his shortcomings: Distortions in the attribution process. In L. Berkowitz (Ed.), *Advances in experimental social psychology* (Vol. 10, pp. 173–220). New York: Academic Press.

Rotter, J. B. (1945). *Social learning and clinical psychology.* New York: Prentice-Hall.

Singer, J. E., Brush, C. A., & Lublin, S. C. (1965). Some aspects of deindividuation: Identification and conformity. *Journal of Experimental Social Psychology, 1*, 356–378. doi:10.1016/0022-1031(65)90015-6.

Staats, A. W., & Staats, C. K. (1958). Attitudes established by classical conditioning. *Journal of Abnormal and Social Psychology, 57*, 37–40.

Sutherland, E. H. (1947). *Principles of criminology* (4th ed.). Philadelphia, PA: J. P. Lippincott.

Sykes, G. M., & Matza, D. (1957). Techniques of neutralization: A theory of delinquency. *American Sociological Review*, 22, 664–670.

Tajfel, H., Billig, M. G., Bundy, R. P., & Flament, C. (1971). Social categorization and intergroup behaviour. *European Journal of Social Psychology, 1*(2), 149–177.

Thorndike, E. L. (1911). *Animal intelligence.* Toronto, Ontario, Canada: University of Toronto Libraries.

Tittle, C. R. (1995). *Control balance: Toward a general theory of deviance.* Boulder, CO: Westview Press.

Tolman, E. C. (1948). Cognitive maps in rats and men. *Psychological Review, 55*, 189–208.

Tversky, A., & Kahneman, D. (1986). Judgment under uncertainty: Heuristics and biases. In H. R. Arkes & K. R. Hammond (Eds.), *Judgment and decision making: An interdisciplinary reader* (pp. 38–55). New York: Cambridge University Press.

Wood, W., Wong, F. Y., & Chachere, J. G. (1991). Effects of media violence on viewers' aggression in unconstrained social interaction. *Psychological Bulletin, 109*, 371–383. doi:10.1037/0033-2909.109.3.371.

Zillman, D. (1979). *Hostility and aggression*. Hillsdale, NJ: Erlbaum.

Zimbardo, P. G. (1969). The human choice: Individuation, reason, and order versus deindividuation, impulse, and chaos. *Nebraska Symposium on Motivation, 17*, 237–307.

Zimbardo, P. G. (1974). On "obedience to authority." *American Psychologist, 29*, 566–567.

CHAPTER SEVEN

Personality and Antisocial Behavior: Theoretical Perspectives

Shayne Jones

Personality refers to the characteristic ways in which individuals think, feel, and behave. As this definition indicates, there are cognitive, affective, and behavioral elements of personality. Personality is a commonly examined factor within psychology, and has received substantial conceptual and empirical attention (Pervin & John, 1999). It has been used as a means of understanding and explaining a diverse set of phenomenon, including juror decision-making (Lieberman & Sales, 2007), depression (Klein, Kotov, & Bufferd, 2011), and health-related behaviors (Caspi et al., 1997). Of particular interest in this chapter is the relationship between personality and antisocial behavior, with a specific focus on explaining this relationship. Antisocial behavior covers a phenotypically diverse set of behaviors, such as crime, violence, aggression, and substance use. However different these behaviors appear, they are recognized as being interrelated and having a common origin (Krueger et al., 2002). One such origin is personality.

Despite its influence within psychology, the notion of personality has not garnered as much interest within mainstream criminology. Caspi et al. (1994) and Miller and Lynam (2001) noted the historical factors that played a role in preventing personality from taking a firmer foothold in the criminological literature, which was based on methodological shortcomings. It is likely, however, that ideological forces have also influenced the literature, with sociological perspectives dominating much criminological theory and research. These issues notwithstanding, the relationship between personality and antisocial behavior is well established (Jones, Miller, & Lynam, 2011), and criminologists have recently devoted more attention to this relationship (Agnew, Brezina, Wright, & Cullen, 2002; DeLisi, 2009; Jones, Cauffman, & Piquero, 2007). What remains more elusive is why personality matters. That is, there are lingering questions surrounding how personality traits are translated into behavior (Miller & Lynam, 2001).

In this chapter, some of the most influential theories of personality will be reviewed. It is important to note at the outset what is, and is not, included in this chapter. What is included are some of the most well-validated, widely used models of personality, along with specific traits, that have been examined as correlates of antisocial behavior. What is not included is a review of all theories of personality. Other sources provide excellent reviews of a more inclusive range of theories of personality, their relations to other fields of study, and on a wider variety of outcomes (see Pervin & John, 1999). The chapter will begin by focusing on specific traits that can be conceptualized as influencing an individual's ability to self-regulate. Then, structural models of personality will be discussed, with an emphasis on the Five-Factor Model of personality (Costa & McCrae, 1992). Personality-based multidimensional constructs that are commonly employed in the study of antisocial behavior will be reviewed next. The chapter will conclude by noting some future directions in the study of personality and antisocial behavior.

Personality and Antisocial Behavior: A Focus on Inhibitory Traits

Like many externalizing disorders, antisocial behavior can be viewed as an inability (or unwillingness) to inhibit or regulate one's behavior. It is unsurprising that many of the traits used to understand and explain antisocial behavior are related to inhibitory deficits. Although there is some degree of conceptual overlap, the traits examined in this section are distinct. Furthermore, they each proffer a different theoretical basis. Accordingly, each will be reviewed separately.

Impulsivity

For those who study the relationship between personality and antisocial behavior, the notion of impulsivity is well known and often used. Yet, this "trait" is one of the most elusive and misunderstood, in large part because "impulsivity" is not a singular trait. Moreover, it has been conceptualized in numerous ways that are related, but distinct. For instance, Dickman (1990) suggests impulsivity can be either functional or dysfunctional.

Functional impulsivity refers to one's ability to act quickly without much forethought when such a response is optimal (e.g., reacting quickly in an emergency situation), while dysfunctional impulsivity is the tendency to react without considering the negative consequences. He found these different tendencies were largely unrelated. Other measures of impulsivity are more highly related to one another, but clearly tap into distinct domains. Barrett's impulsivity scales are widely used and assess attentional, motor, and nonplanning impulsiveness (Patton, Stanford, & Barratt, 1995). There are numerous other measures and conceptualizations of "impulsivity" replete throughout the literature. Yet even this brief examination of two theoretical models of impulsivity reveals that these researchers are not referring to the same thing.

The discrepancies across impulsivity models led Whiteside and Lynam (2001) to examine the most prominent notions of impulsivity in the literature and to explore how they were alike and different. Through exploratory and confirmatory factor analyses, four distinct variants of impulsivity emerged. Whiteside and Lynam labeled them as Urgency, Premeditation, Perseverance, and Sensation Seeking, and called this the UPPS model. Urgency describes the tendency to give into cravings and desires because of negative affect. (Lack of) Premeditation refers to acting without much forethought and consideration of the consequences. (Lack of) Perseverance pertains to having difficulty with staying focused on and completing tasks that are boring or challenging. Sensation seeking captures the notion of engaging in novel, exciting activities. Whiteside and Lynam suggest that instead of referring to "impulsivity" as a trait, there are four distinct pathways to impulsive behavior. That is, there are four specific traits that influence the likelihood of impulsive behavior.

The UPPS model is based, in part, on the Five-Factor Model (FFM). Thus, the theoretical basis for these traits, as well as their expression, can be linked to that model of personality. The FFM will be more thoroughly reviewed below (under "Structural Models of Personality"), but a brief discussion will be made here. The FFM indicates there are five basic tendencies. The UPPS models draws from three of them—neuroticism (urgency), extraversion (sensation seeking), and conscientiousness (premeditation and perseverance). These basic tendencies influence characteristic adaptations (which are shaped by external factors). Although not clearly defined, external factors include the broad notion of the situation (McCrae & Costa, 1999). For the current discussion of the UPPS model, it may be that perceived opportunities, or costs (i.e., external factors), are differentially valued by those who are low in premeditation versus those who are high. Some initial evidence corroborates this. Individuals who are low in premeditation and high in sensation seeking are more likely to offend when they perceive that informal social control is weak (Jones & Lynam, 2009). Other evidence indicates the effect of premeditation on substance use is primarily mediated through perceived rewards of substance use, while the influence of sensation seeking on substance use is mediated by perceived costs and rewards (Jones, Lynam, & Piquero, 2011). Future work is necessary to further specify the causal links and characteristic adaptations, especially in relation to the UPPS model.

Lynam and Miller (2004) assessed the relationship between the four UPPS traits and a variety of antisocial outcomes. Premeditation and sensation seeking demonstrated the most consistent relationships with the outcomes. Although preliminary, Lynam, Smith, Cyders, Fischer, and Whiteside (2007) proposed that impulsive behavior stemming from affective states can be either positive or negative. (Recall, urgency as described above focuses only on negative affect.) Zapolski, Cyders, and Smith (2009) found that positive urgency, premeditation, and sensation seeking predicted substance use and risky sexual behavior. Negative urgency and perseverance were not significant predictors. Future research is necessary to understand whether positive urgency is related to other antisocial outcomes.

The Behavioral Inhibition and Activation Systems

Although the relationships between the behavioral inhibition system (BIS) and behavioral activation system (BAS; also referred to as the behavioral approach system) and antisocial behavior have not been extensively studied, there are theoretical linkages that explain how these systems might influence antisocial behavior. Gray (1987) is most well-known for describing the neurological bases of the BIS and BAS. The BIS is responsible for inhibitory behavior, especially when there are cues for punishment. It is the neurological system responsible for attending to potential cues for punishment, and influencing an individual to stop and reflect before proceeding. In contrast, the BAS is a motivation system that is responsive to reward and affects the likelihood of approach behavior. The BAS, as measured by the Carver and White (1994) scale, is comprised of three lower-order traits; reward dependence, drive, and fun seeking. In terms of antisocial behavior, it is not difficult to see how both might be important. Some individuals likely readily perceive the benefits of intoxication, taking something of value, or aggressing against an antagonist. According to this model of personality, the BAS is responsible for this. However, many individuals also likely perceive the costs associated with such behavior. Intoxication, theft, or aggression can lead to arrest, losing a job, causing injury to another, or being socially ridiculed. Thus, there are competing neurological systems that draw individual attention to both the costs and benefits—the colloquial angel and demon speaking into the ears of individuals. Thus, what seems to be most important is which system is most dominant, and how one balances, or reconciles, conflicts when both punishment and reward are present.

Newman and colleagues (Newman & Wallace, 1993; Wallace, Newman & Bachorowski, 1991) have identified how the BIS, BAS, and the non-specific arousal system (NAS) work in conjunction to influence impulsive behavior. One path suggests a strong BAS (over BIS; the neurotic extravert), and a second path indicates a strong BIS (over BAS; neurotic introvert), both of which lead to a highly reactive NAS and to impulsive responding. A third path suggests that for a subset of individuals, once a dominant response is established (i.e., the BAS is activated), the BIS is ineffective and the cues for punishment are ignored. This third path is characteristic of individuals with psychopathic personality disorder.

Several theorists have suggested that subtypes of psychopathic personality may be influenced by the BIS and BAS. One of the most well-known theorists proposing such a perspective is Lykken (1995). He suggests that primary psychopathy is characterized by an underactive BIS, while secondary psychopathy is typified by an overactive BAS. There is some evidence to indicate this conceptualization is accurate. Newman, MacCoon, Vaughn, and Sadeh (2005) found that Lykken's predictions regarding primary psychopathy were accurate, although only partial support was garnered for the secondary typology. More specifically, the primary subtypes were characterized by low BIS, and by normal BAS scores across two measures of BIS and BAS. The secondary subtype did evince elevated BAS on both BAS measures, but inconsistent outcomes for the two BIS measures (with one being elevated, and one normal).

Beyond the role of BIS and BAS in understanding psychopathic behavior, much less is known in terms of how these two systems individually influence antisocial behavior. Smits and Kuppens (2005) found that both BIS and BAS were related to anger. Other studies found only BIS (O'Gorman & Baxter, 2002; higher BIS related to criminal intent) or BAS (Seibert, Miller, Pryor, Reidy, & Zeichner, 2010; BAS drive positively related to laboratory aggression) were related to antisocial outcomes. Muris, Meesters, de Kanter, and Timmerman (2005) found different relations depending on both the outcome and rater. Specifically, BIS and BAS were positively related to child reports of aggression, but not parental reports of aggression. Also, BIS and BAS were positively related to child reports of hyperactivity/conduct disorder, but only BAS was positively related to parental reports of hyperactivity/conduct disorder. Given the dearth of empirical findings, as well as the discrepancies across studies, more research is needed before reaching firmer conclusions. It is also important to consider that BIS and BAS may be relevant for only a subset of the population—those with psychopathic personality disorder.

Sensation Seeking

As mentioned above, sensation seeking has been identified as one trait in the UPPS that leads to impulsive behavior. Yet, sensation seeking (SS) as discussed by its leading theorist—Zuckerman—has its own theoretical foundation. Zuckerman (1994) defines sensation seeking as a trait related to the tendency to engage in new, different, and intense experiences. SS is a second-order trait, underlain by four first-order traits: thrill and adventure seeking (TAS), experience seeking (ES), disinhibition (DIS), and boredom susceptibility (BS). TAS refers to the tendency to engage in risky, exciting activities such as skydiving, bungee jumping, and extreme sports. ES denotes a desire to seek out unique, unusual experiences and sensations, such as trying new foods, taking exotic trips, and participating in non-mainstream social groups. Compared to the other facets of SS, DIS is most closely aligned with common conceptualization of impulsiveness. This trait describes a willingness to behave in an unrestrained manner, and is evidenced by behaviors such as partying, substance use, and risky sex. Finally, BS refers to inclination to become easily bored by routines and monotonous activities. Zuckerman's latest conceptualization, consistent in some respects with the UPPS model, is to combine sensation seeking and impulsivity into a superordinate trait referred to as impulsive-sensation seeking (Zuckerman & Kuhlman, 2000).

Zuckerman (1994) suggests that the origins of SS are found in one's biological makeup. Specifically, he suggests that those higher on SS have different cerebral, physiological, and cognitive reactions when confronted with novel stimuli. It is not that those high on SS are simply underaroused, and that therefore, such individuals seek experiences to circumvent this tendency. Instead, the brains and bodies of high sensation seekers react differently to stimuli. When confronted with unusual or unknown stimuli in the environment, high sensation seekers have a differential attendance to and evaluation of cues, neurological response (in terms of the release of neurotransmitters and hormones), and physiological reactions. More specifically, those with elevated SS traits appear to be much more likely to engage in approach behavior in the face of novel stimuli. New people, situations, and experiences are alluring to high sensation seekers, whereas such unfamiliarity is avoided by those lower in sensation seeking. In some respects, this theoretical explanation is similar to that noted above regarding the BIS and BAS.

Several studies have found sensation seeking is related to antisocial behaviors (see Zuckerman, 1994, 2007, for more comprehensive reviews). For instance, Maldonado-Molina, Piquero, Jennings, Bird, and Canino (2009) found that sensation seeking was able to distinguish between different developmental trajectories of offending. Specifically, the more antisocial groups were the highest in sensation seeking. Other studies demonstrate the importance of examining the specific facets of SS. Jones and colleagues found that TAS was related to offending (Jones & Lynam, 2009; Jones, Lynam, & Piquero., 2011). Knust and Stewart (2002) found that the subscales of BS and DIS, and ES to a lesser extent, were correlated with hostility. However, only DIS was significant in multivariate analyses. Another multivariate analysis found DIS, TAS, and BS were significantly related to antisocial behavior typical of college students (Levenson, Kiehl, & Fitzpatrick, 1995).

Structural Models of Personality

There are several structural models of personality that have been presented, including Eysenck's PEN model, Cloninger's model, and Tellegen's three-factor model. Yet, arguably the most influential structural model of personality in the current literature is the Five-Factor Model (FFM; Costa & McCrae, 1992). Moreover, as Miller and Lynam (2001) have argued, other structural models of personality can be subsumed within the FFM.

The FFM is an extension of the Big Five Model of personality. The Big Five is premised on the lexical hypothesis to identifying personality traits (John & Srivastava, 1999). This hypothesis states that all important personality traits can be found in natural language. That is, the basic dimensions of personality should be well represented within the language of people. Examinations of words that can be used to describe one's personality have consistently found that there are five broad factors. The FFM is a specific conceptualization of what those five domains are—neuroticism, extraversion, openness to experience, agreeableness, and conscientiousness. Neuroticism refers to the tendency to experience and ability to regulate negative affect. Extraversion describes one's desire to engage in affiliative and social behavior. Openness to experience taps into one's curiosity and attraction with ideas, art, and emotions. Agreeableness refers to how one negotiates interpersonal relationships and reacts to others. Conscientiousness relates to an individual's abilities in self-regulation. As noted above, these domains are broad indicators of personality. In order to more precisely describe the domains, the FFM contains six lower-order facets. For instance, conscientiousness is comprised of the following facets: competence, order, dutifulness, achievement striving, self-discipline, and deliberation. In total, the FFM, as operationalized in the NEO-PI-R (Costa & McCrae, 1992) has 30 facets mapping onto five domains.

The FFM is based on the notion that there are basic human tendencies that have evolved over time and have a biological basis. Although the precise biological mechanisms are not well understood, there is evidence that these traits demonstrate a relatively high degree of heritability (Jang, Livesley, & Vernon, 1996; Riemann, Angleitner, & Strelau, 1997). These five traits, according to McCrae and Costa (1999), are universal and present cross-culturally. This does not mean, however, that their expression is the same. These traits interact with external influences (e.g., culture, rearing environment) to create characteristic adaptations. For instance, extraversion (a basic tendency) will influence the likelihood one will belong to several social groups (a characteristic adaptation). Of course, one must have access to such social groups, and the specific type of social group will be based, in part, on the options that exist (an external influence). Thus, one's culture, situation, and life events will shape the expression (or characteristic adaptations) of their basic tendencies (McCrae & Costa, 1999).

The most compelling evidence for the utility of the FFM in understanding antisocial behavior stems from two meta-analyses. Miller and Lynam (2001) explored the relationships between various structural models of personality and antisocial behavior. Although elements from each model evinced some relationship with antisocial behavior, they argued that many of these relationships are captured by the FFM. For instance, psychoticism from Eysenck's model (which had an effect size of .39) is a blend of low agreeableness and conscientiousness. Tellegen's negative emotionality (effect size = .27) contains elements from agreeableness and neuroticism. For the FFM, agreeableness, conscientiousness, and neuroticism each demonstrated significant effect sizes. Specifically, low agreeableness demonstrated the most robust relationship with antisocial behavior (effect size = −.27). Conscientiousness was also negatively related (effect size = −.25). Neuroticism evinced a weaker and positive effect (effect size = .09). Part of the reason that neuroticism demonstrated a weaker effect (compared to agreeableness and conscientiousness) was likely because some of the facets within this domain (e.g., angry hostility) are (positively) related to antisocial behavior, whereas other facets are either negatively related (e.g., anxiety) or unrelated (e.g., self-consciousness). This latter suggestion indicates it is important to look beyond the domain level and explore the relations between the FFM facets and antisocial behavior.

As mentioned above, each domain is comprised of six facets. For instance, trust, straightforwardness, altruism, compliance, modesty, and tender-mindedness are the facets of agreeableness. As noted in the Miller and Lynam (2001) meta-analysis, some of these facet-level relations might bore differential relations to antisocial behavior. In an effort to replicate the previous meta-analysis and extend it, Jones, Miller, and Lynam (2011) examined the relationships between FFM domains and facets and antisocial behavior and aggression. At the domain level, the findings were largely replicated. Agreeableness demonstrated the most robust (negative) relationship with both antisocial and aggressive behavior. Conscientiousness was also negatively related, although more strongly to antisocial behavior compared to aggression. Neuroticism was positively related to both, but demonstrated a stronger relation to aggression than antisocial behavior. The more novel set of findings stemming from this meta-analysis was the relationships between the facets and the outcomes. All six facets from agreeableness and conscientiousness were negatively related to both outcomes. The facets of straightforwardness, altruism, and compliance were the strongest from agreeableness (all effect sizes > .20). Deliberation, dutifulness, and competence were the strongest from conscientiousness. From extraversion, warmth was negatively related (to both outcomes) and excitement seeking was positively related (to antisocial behavior). These countervailing effects, and the nonsignificant effects for many facets, are the reason that extraversion fails to demonstrate a significant relation at the domain level. Similarly, angry hostility from neuroticism was positively related to antisocial behavior and aggression (effect sizes .20 and .21, respectively). Also from neuroticism, depression and impulsiveness were positively related to both, while anxiety was negatively related to antisocial behavior and vulnerability was positively related to aggression. These findings help explain the significant, but weak relationship between neuroticism and antisocial behavior. Specifically, some facets exerted stronger influences than others, some were negatively related while others were positive, and the effects were not the same across outcomes. Collectively, the findings from this meta-analysis demonstrate the importance of examining traits at a narrower level than the broad domains.

Although the FFM has received more recent empirical attention than other structural models, it is important to discuss the findings from another influential study briefly. Caspi and colleagues (1994) assessed Tellegen's three-factor model across two samples. One sample was based on a New Zealand cohort that included females and males, while the other was a high-risk sample of boys from Pittsburgh, Pennsylvania. Across both samples, they found individuals high in negative emotionality and low in constraint were the most likely to have engaged in delinquent behavior. Positive emotionality was not related to delinquency. What makes this study so important is that these relations held across samples, countries, sex, race, and methods. More specifically, in the New Zealand study, personality was assessed using the self-report Multidimensional Personality Questionnaire, while delinquency was measured across several sources: self- and informant-reports of delinquency, police contacts, and court records. For both females and males, the patterns of relationships were consistent, regardless of how delinquency was measured. In the Pittsburgh sample, Tellegen's constructs were measured using the California Q-Sort, with caregivers describing the personality of the boys. Delinquency was measured using self-, parent-, and teacher-reports. Once again, negative emotionality and constraint demonstrated negative relations with each outcome, and for both black and white boys. The robustness of the findings demonstrates impressive support for the relationship between personality and offending.

Like others, Caspi et al. (1994) suggest there are biological and environmental factors that influence the existence and expression of negative emotionality and constraint. They suggest parenting behavior, in particular, as a source of both negative emotionality and constraint. It is likely that such influences reach well beyond the family environment. Caspi (1993; Caspi & Roberts, 1999) has suggested that there are gene-environment transactions that occur throughout the life course. Reactive gene-environment transactions reflect the notion that different individuals react to and perceive similar external factors differently. Evocative gene-environment transactions refer to the characteristic reactions others have to an individual's behavior. Active gene-environment transactions denote that individuals select environments that are consistent with their dispositions. To illustrate these effects and their relation to personality, consider an individual who is high in negative emotionality. They might be more likely to demonstrate a hostile attribution bias (Dodge & Crick, 1990), in which they interpret ambiguous stimuli in an aggressive manner (a reactive gene-environment transaction). They are more argumentative and confrontational, which can lead nonaggressive others to avoid the person (thereby minimizing opportunities to interact with prosocial others) or aggressive others to challenge and escalate the confrontation (evocative gene-environment transaction). Individuals high in negative emotionality are more inclined to socialize with other antisocial individuals, initiate and participate in aggressive acts, and choose environments that allow for these opportunities (active gene-environment transaction). Although some of the basis for negative emotionality is genetic (Tellegen et al., 1988), the continuity, development, and expression of this trait interacts with the environment in several ways to promote antisocial and aggressive behaviors.

Multidimensional Models

The preceding section described personality from a structural perspective and indicated the specific traits that appear to be the most consistently related to antisocial behavior. Another approach to understanding the role of personality in influencing antisocial behavior is to combine specific traits into one construct. Such compilations can be conceived of as multidimensional models of personality. Two specific multidimensional models that have received extensive attention in the psychological and criminological literature will be discussed here.

Psychopathy

A series of other chapters in this volume discuss psychopathic personality disorder, and this section will not duplicate those efforts. What will be discussed is how psychopathy can be viewed from the lens of normal personality. This, of course, is based on the notion that psychopathy can be conceptualized as dimensional in nature, as opposed to categorical. Although this debate is not settled, there are studies that support the dimensional view (Edens, Marcus, Lilienfeld, & Poythress, 2006).

Lynam and colleagues (Miller & Lynam, 2003; Miller, Lynam, Widiger, & Leukefeld, 2001; Widiger & Lynam, 1998) have suggested that the FFM (discussed above) can capture the construct of psychopathy. Widiger and Lynam offered a detailed comparison between the Psychopathy Checklist–Revised (PCL-R; Hare, 2003) items and specific facets contained within the FFM. Most of the facets are represented within the domains of agreeableness and conscientiousness. For instance, they indicate that the interpersonal and affective items of grandiose sense of self-worth, conning and manipulativeness, and callousness and lack of empathy are reflected in the FFM facets of modesty (versus arrogance), straightforwardness (versus manipulative) and altruism (versus exploitative), and tender-mindedness (versus tough-mindedness), respectively. Some lifestyle and behavioral items—impulsivity (FFM facet: deliberation) and irresponsibility (FFM facets: dutifulness and competence)—are captured in facets from conscientiousness. Other PCL-R items (e.g., parasitic lifestyle, poor behavioral controls) are captured by facets contained within both agreeableness and conscientiousness. Collectively, Widiger and Lynam suggest that Factor 1 of psychopathy is primarily low agreeableness (with some low neuroticism and extraversion), while Factor 2 is comprised of a mix of low agreeableness and conscientiousness (with minor representations of high neuroticism and extraversion).

Drawing from the work of Widiger and Lynam (1998), Miller et al. (2001) assessed whether the FFM representation of psychopathy was valid. They did this in two ways. First, they asked 15 psychopathy experts to rate (on a scale from 1 to 5) the prototypic psychopath on 30 traits' descriptions drawn from the NEO-PI-R. The resulting psychopathy resemblance index (PRI) was based on the average scores generated from these experts. Second, they compared the scores of 481 community members on each of the 30 facets from the NEO-PI-R to that of the PRI. Their findings supported the FFM representation. The PRI generated from the experts was consistent with the description offered by Widiger and Lynam. The prototypic psychopath was rated as low in all facets of agreeableness, and several facets of conscientiousness, neuroticism, and openness to experience, and higher on specific facets stemming from neuroticism, extraversion, openness, and conscientiousness. Each community participant was given a PRI score based on the expert profiles, and these profiles were significantly correlated with a wide variety of externalizing behaviors. Moreover, the relations were largely the same across females and males.

As can be deduced from this brief discussion, some theorists believe psychopathy can be reasonably represented by normal personality traits drawn from the FFM. That is, instead of viewing psychopathy as qualitatively different (i.e., as a typology), these perspectives suggest psychopathy is a specific compilation of extreme expressions of specific personality traits. This approach has garnered support and will likely play an influential role in future conceptualizations of the psychopathic personality.

Self-Control

Not altogether dissimilar to psychopathy (DeLisi, 2009; Wiebe, 2003), the notion of self-control has become a widely studied concept within the field of criminology. In fact, self-control, as elaborated by Gottfredson and Hirschi (1990), is the most studied multidimensional model of personality in criminology. Although these theorists do not explicitly rely on the literature from personality psychology, they do indicate that their notion of self-control is consistent with the notion of a personality trait. In fact, examining the constituent elements of self-control appears to confirm it is a personality trait. They suggest that low self-control is comprised of impulsivity, risk-taking, insensitivity toward others, temper, a preference for physical activities (as opposed to mental), and choosing simple tasks over complicated ones. Beyond this, however, there are notable differences in how they describe the origins and development of self-control compared to many other models of personality.

For instance, they do not endorse biological factors as influential in understanding self-control. Instead, they suggest that all individuals are born with low self-control. Through socialization efforts, one acquires self-control. They specifically posit parenting as the major influence. They indicate that parents must monitor their children, recognize when antisocial behavior occurs, and fairly and consistently punish such behavior. Over time, the external control exhibited by the parent is internalized (presumably between the ages of 8 and 10), and the individual becomes able to inhibit their behavior in accord with social expectations and norms. They also suggest that self-control is the definitive factor that influences offending behavior and remains relatively stable after acquired in early childhood.

The empirical evidence supports many of the claims advanced by these authors. For example, self-control is a robust correlate of antisocial behavior (Pratt & Cullen, 2000), has a unidimensional factor structure (Grasmick, Tittle, Bursik, & Arneklev (1993), is influenced by parenting (Perrone, Sullivan, Pratt, & Margaryan, 2004), and is relatively stable across time (Mitchell & McKenzie, 2006). Of course, there are also disconfirming findings. For instance, self-control is not the sole explanation of offending (Pratt & Cullen, 2000). Some have found other sources that influence the development of self-control, including schools (Turner, Piquero, & Pratt, 2005) and neighborhoods (Pratt, Turner, & Piquero, 2004; cf. Gibson, Sullivan, Jones, & Piquero, 2010). Others have found self-control is not unidimensional (Cochran, Wood, Sellers, Wilkerson, & Chamlin, 1998; Longshore, Turner, & Stein, 1996). Collectively, however, self-control appears to be an important construct in understanding antisocial behavior, and that resembles the basic notion of personality.

It is worth noting that Hirschi (2004) has recently attempted to distinguish (and distance) the concept of self-control from personality. He indicated that his initial efforts to describe the construct ventured too far into the realm of personality psychology, which he views now as a mistake. Despite this retreat, it would appear that the personality-based notion of self-control has taken a firm footing within criminology, and will not likely be dismissed.

Conclusions

The goals of this chapter were to examine the theoretical bases, and empirical findings, of personality. To that end, specific traits (e.g., impulsivity) were explored, as well as structural and multidimensional models of personality. What is evident is that personality is robustly related to a wide variety of antisocial behaviors. The influence of agreeableness and conscientiousness, in particular, has garnered compelling empirical support. Furthermore, there exists a rich set of theoretical models to explain the origins of personality, and some of the mechanisms that influence behavior. Many of the models reviewed suggest there is a biological basis for many traits and models. This is not to negate the impact of factors external to the individual. Most contemporary models of personality clearly underscore the importance of familial, peer, neighborhood, situational, and other environmental factors in shaping the expression of underlying traits. Despite what is known, there are numerous questions remaining that allow for a plethora of future research.

Perhaps one of the most important is explaining the mechanisms by which specific traits are translated into antisocial behavior. As mentioned above, some limited empirical evidence exists to address this. For instance, traits appear to influence individual perceptions of costs and benefits to antisocial behavior (Jones & Lynam, 2009; Jones, Lynam, and Piquero, 2011). There are important person-environment transactions that have been identified (Caspi & Roberts, 1999), but more work remains to better understand what additional factors are involved in such transactions.

In addition, there is burgeoning evidence of person-environment interactions. Wright, Caspi, Moffitt, & Silva (2001) have found that individuals low in self-control are more strongly influenced by prosocial and antisocial ties. More specifically, individuals low in self-control received greater crime-reducing benefits from having prosocial attachments to school, work, family, and romantic partners than those higher in self-control. Also, the criminogenic effect of antisocial peers was more pronounced among those lower in self-control. It is also worth noting that this study found support for selection effects, whereby those lower in self-control were less likely to have prosocial ties and more likely to have antisocial ties. Several studies have also noted that the effects of impulsivity on offending are moderated by neighborhood factors. The findings indicate that those higher in impulsivity are more susceptible to criminogenic neighborhood influences, and thus more crime-prone when such neighborhood factors exist (Jones & Lynam, 2009; Lynam et al., 2000; Meier,

Slutske, Arndt, & Cadoret, 2008). Yet, other evidence suggests that social learning factors (e.g., reinforcement, peers, definitions) operate similarly across levels of self-control (Yarbrough, Jones, Sullivan, Sellers, & Cochran, 2011). Some of the discrepancies may be due to the specific traits being examined, or how such traits are being conceptualized (Jones et al., 2007). Such methodological issues should be attended to in future efforts.

Finally, future research in personality needs to be more explicitly interdisciplinary, drawing from both psychology and criminology. Psychologists have developed a number of scales to assess personality, and the psychometric properties of these measures have demonstrated their validity. Criminologists have been less enamored by the notion of personality, but have a set of rich theoretical models that can be complimented and improved by inclusion of personality (Agnew et al., 2002). Such integrated endeavors hold promise in advancing not just the notion of personality and how it is mediated and moderated by external forces, but also in progressing our knowledge about the causes of antisocial behavior.

References

Agnew, R., Brezina, T., Wright, J. P., & Cullen, F. T. (2002). Strain, personality traits, and delinquency: Extending general strain theory. *Criminology, 40*, 43–72.

Avshalom, A. (1993). Why maladaptive behaviors persist: Sources of continuity and change across the life course. In D. C. Funder, R. D. Park, C. Tomlinson-Keasey, & K. Widaman (Eds.), *Studying lives through time: Personality and development* (pp. 343–376). Washington, DC: American Psychological Association.

Carver, C. S., & White, T. L. (1994). Behavioural inhibition, behavioural activation, and affective responses to impending reward and punishment: The BIS/BAS scales. *Journal of Personality and Social Psychology, 67*, 319–333.

Caspi, A. (1993). Why maladaptive behaviors persist: Sources of continuity and change across the life course. In D. C. Funder, R. D. Parke, C. Tomlinson-Keasey, & K. Widaman (Eds.), *Studying lives through time: Personality and development* (pp. 209–230). Washington, DC: APA.

Caspi, A., Begg, D., Dickson, N., Harrington, H., Langley, J., Moffitt, T. E., & Silva, P. A. (1997). Personality differences predict health-risk behaviors in young adulthood: Evidence from a longitudinal study. *Journal of Personality and Social Psychology, 73*, 1052–1063.

Caspi, A., Moffitt, T. E., Silva, P. A., Stouthamer-Loeber, M., Krueger, R. F., & Schmutte, P. S. (1994). Are some people crime-prone? Replications of the personality-crime relationship across countries, genders, races, and methods. *Criminology, 32*, 163–195.

Caspi, A., & Roberts, B. W. (1999). Personality continuity and change across the life course. In L. A. Pervin & O. P. John (Eds.), *Handbook of personality: Theory and research* (2nd ed., pp. 300–326). New York: Guilford Press.

Cochran, J. K., Wood, P. B., Sellers, C. S., Wilkerson, W., & Chamlin, M. B. (1998). Academic dishonesty and low self-control: An empirical test of a general theory of crime. *Deviant Behavior, 3*, 227–255.

Costa, P. T., & McCrae, R. R. (1992). *Revised NEO Personality Inventory (NEO-PI-R) and NEO Five-Factor Inventory (NEO-FFI) professional manual*. Odessa, FL: Psychological Assessment Resources, Inc.

DeLisi, M. (2009). Psychopathy is the unified theory of crime. *Youth Violence and Juvenile Justice, 7*, 256–273.

Dickman, S. J. (1990). Functional and dysfunctional impulsivity: Personality and cognitive correlates. *Journal of Personality and Social Psychology, 58*, 95–102.

Dodge, K. A., & Crick, N. R. (1990). Social information processing bases of aggressive behaviour in children. *Personality and Social Psychology Bulletin, 16*, 8–22.

Edens, J. F., Marcus, D. K., Lilienfeld, S. O., & Poythress, N. G., Jr. (2006). Psychopathic, not psychopath: Taxometric evidence for the dimensional structure of psychopathy. *Journal of Abnormal Psychology, 115*, 131–144.

Gibson, C., Sullivan, C. J., Jones, S., & Piquero, A. R. (2010). "Does it take a village?" Assessing neighborhood influences on children's self-control. *Journal of Research in Crime and Delinquency, 47*, 31–47.

Gottfredson, M. R., & Hirschi, T. (1990). *A general theory of crime*. Stanford, CA: Stanford University Press.

Grasmick, H. G., Tittle, C. R., Bursik, R. J., Jr., & Arneklev, B. J. (1993). Testing the core assumptions of Gottfredson and Hirschi's general theory of crime. *Journal of Research in Crime and Delinquency, 30*, 5–29.

Gray, J. A. (1987). *The psychology of fear and stress*. New York: Cambridge University Press.

Hare, R. D. (2003). *Manual for the Psychopathy Checklist–Revised* (2nd ed.). Toronto, Ontario, Canada: Multi-Health Systems.

Hirschi, T. (2004). Self-control and crime. In R. F. Baumeister & K. D. Vohs (Eds.), *Handbook of self-regulation: Research, theory, and application*. New York: Guilford Press.

Jang, K. L., Livesley, J., & Vernon, P. A. (1996). Heritability of the big five personality dimensions and their facets: A twin study. *Journal of Personality, 64*, 577–591.

John, O. P., & Srivastava, S. (1999). The big five trait taxonomy: History, measurement, and theoretical perspectives. In L. A. Pervin & O. P. John (Eds.), *Handbook of personality: Theory and research* (2nd ed., pp. 102–138). New York: Guilford Press.

Jones, S., Cauffman, E., & Piquero, A. (2007). The influence of parental support among incarcerated adolescent offenders: The conditioning effects of impulse control and empathy. *Criminal Justice and Behavior, 34*, 229–245.

Jones, S., & Lynam, D. R. (2009). In the eye of the impulsive beholder: The influences of neighborhood perceptions and impulsivity on offending behavior. *Criminal Justice and Behavior, 36*, 307–321.

Jones, S., Lynam, D. R., & Piquero, A. R. (2011). Substance use, personality, and inhibitors: Testing Hirschi's predictions about the reconceptualization of self-control. *Crime and Delinquency*.

Jones, S. E., Miller, J. D., & Lynam, D. R. (2011). Personality, antisocial behavior, and aggression: A meta-analytic review. *Journal of Criminal Justice*. doi:10.1016/j.jcrimjus.2011.03.004.

Klein, D. N., Kotov, R., & Bufferd, S. J. (2011). Personality and depression: Explanatory models and review of the evidence. *Annual Review of Clinical Psychology, 7*, 269–295.

Knust, S., & Stewart, A. L. (2002). Risk-taking behaviour and offending: An investigation of sensation seeking and the Eysenck Personality Questionnaire. *International Journal of Offender Therapy and Comparative Criminology, 46*, 586–602.

Krueger, R. F., Hicks, B. M., Patrick, C. J., Carlson, S. R., Iacono, W. G., & McGue, M. (2002). Etiological connections among substance dependence, antisocial behavior, and personality: Modeling the externalizing spectrum. *Journal of Abnormal Psychology, 111*, 411–424.

Levenson, M. R., Kiehl, K. A., & Fitzpatrick, C. M. (1995). Assessing psychopathic attributes in a noninstitutionalized population. *Journal of Personality and Social Psychology, 68*, 151–158.

Lieberman, J. D., & Sales, B. D. (2007). *Scientific jury selection*. Washington, DC: American Psychological Association.

Longshore, D., Turner, S., & Stein, J. A. (1996). Self-control in a criminal sample: An examination of construct validity. *Criminology, 34*, 209–228.

Lykken, D. T. (1995). *The antisocial personalities*. Hillsdale, NJ: Lawrence Erlbaum Associates.

Lynam, D., Smith, G. T., Cyders, M. A., Fischer, S., & Whiteside, S. A. (2007). The UPPS-P: A multidimensional measure of risk for impulsive behavior [Unpublished technical report].

Lynam, D. R., Caspi, A., Moffitt, T. E., Wikström, P. O. H., Loeber, R., & Novak, S. (2000). The interaction between impulsivity and neighborhood context on offending: The effects of impulsivity are stronger in poorer neighborhoods. *Journal of Abnormal Psychology, 109*, 563–574.

Lynam, D. R., & Miller, J. D. (2004). Personality pathways to impulsive behavior and their relations to deviance: Results from three samples. *Journal of Quantitative Criminology, 20*, 319–342.

Maldonado-Molina, M. M., Piquero, A. R., Jennings, W. G., Bird, H., & Canino, G. (2009). Trajectories of delinquency among Puerto Rican children and adolescents at two sites. *Journal of Research in Crime and Delinquency, 46*, 144–181.

McCrae, R. R., & Costa, P. T., Jr. (1999). A five-factor theory of personality. In L. A. Pervin & O. P. John (Eds.), *Handbook of personality: Theory and research* (2nd ed., pp. 139–153). New York: Guilford Press.

Meier, M. H., Slutske, W. S., Arndt, S., & Cadoret, R. J. (2008). Impulsive and callous traits are more strongly associated with delinquent behavior in higher risk neighborhoods among boys and girls. *Journal of Abnormal Psychology, 117*, 377–385.

Miller, J. D., & Lynam, D. R. (2001). Structural models of personality and their relation to antisocial behavior: A meta-analytic review. *Criminology, 39*, 765–795.

Miller, J. D., & Lynam, D. R. (2003). Psychopathy and the five-factor model of personality: A replication and extension. *Journal of Personality Assessment, 81*, 168–178.

Miller, J. D., Lynam, D. R., Widiger, T. A., & Leukefeld, C. (2001). Personality disorders as extreme variants of common personality dimensions: Can the five-factor model adequately represent psychopathy? *Journal of Personality, 69*, 253–276.

Mitchell, O., & Mackenzie, D. L. (2006). The stability and resiliency of self-control in a sample of incarcerated offenders. *Crime & Delinquency, 52*, 432–449.

Muris, P., Meesters, C., de Kanter, E., & Timmerman, P. E. (2005). Behavioural inhibition and behavioural activation scales for children: Relationships with Eysenck's personality traits and psychopathological symptoms. *Personality and Individual Differences, 38*, 831–841.

Newman, J. P., MacCoon, D. G., Vaughn, L. J., & Sadeh, N. (2005). Validating a distinction between primary and secondary psychopathy with measures of Gray's BIS and BAS constructs. *Journal of Abnormal Psychology, 114*, 319–323.

Newman, J. P., & Wallace, J. F. (1993). Divergent pathways to deficient self-regulation: Implications for disinhibitory psychopathology in children. *Clinical Psychology Review, 13*, 699–720.

O'Gorman, J. G., & Baxter, E. (2002). Self-control as a personality measure. *Personality and Individual Differences, 32*, 533–539.

Patton, J. H., Stanford, M. S., & Barratt, E. S. (1995). Factor structure of the Barratt impulsiveness scale. *Journal of Clinical Psychology, 51*, 768–774.

Perrone, D., Sullivan, C. J., Pratt, T. C., & Margaryan, S. (2004). Parental efficacy, self-control, and deviance: A test of a general theory of crime on a nationally representative sample of youth. *International Journal of Offender Therapy and Comparative Criminology, 48*, 298–312.

Pervin, L. A., & John, O. P. (1999). *Handbook of personality: Theory and research* (2nd ed.). New York: Guilford Press.

Pratt, T. C., & Cullen, F. T. (2000). The empirical status of Gottfredson and Hirschi's general theory of crime: A meta-analysis. *Criminology, 38*, 931–964.

Pratt, T. C., Turner, M. G., & Piquero, A. R. (2004). Parental socialization and community context: A longitudinal analysis of the structural sources of low self-control. *Journal of Research in Crime and Delinquency, 41*, 219–243.

Riemann, R., Angleitner, A., & Strelau, J. (1997). Genetic and environmental influences on personality: A study of twins reared together using the self- and peer reports NEO-FFI scales. *Journal of Personality*, *65*(3), 449–475.

Seibert, L. A., Miller, J. D., Pryor, L. R., Reidy, D. E., & Zeichner, A. (2010). Personality and laboratory-based aggression: Comparing the predictive power of the Five-Factor Model, BIS/BAS, and impulsivity across context. *Journal of Research in Personality, 44*, 13–21.

Smits, D. J. M., & Kuppens, P. (2005). The relations between anger, coping with anger, and aggression, and the BIS/BAS system. *Personality and Individual Differences, 39*, 783–793.

Tellegen, A., Lykken, D. T., Bouchard, T. J., Wilcox, K. J., Segal, N. L., & Rich, S. (1988). Personality similarity in twins reared apart and together. *Journal of Personality and Social Psychology, 36*, 1031–1039.

Turner, M. G., Piquero, A. R., & Pratt, T. C. (2005). The school context as a source of self-control. *Journal of Criminal Justice, 33*, 327–339.

Wallace, J. F., Newman, J. P., & Bachorowski, J. (1991). Failures of response modulation: Impulsive behavior in anxious and impulsive individuals. *Journal of Research in Personality, 25*, 23–44.

Whiteside, S. P., & Lynam, D. R. (2001). The Five Factor Model and impulsivity: Using a structural model of personality to understand impulsivity. *Personality and Individual Differences, 30*, 669–689.

Widiger, T. A., & Lynam, D. R. (1998). Psychopathy and the five-factor model of personality. In T. Millon, E. Simonsen, M. Birket-Smith, & R. D. Davis (Eds.), *Psychopathy: Antisocial, criminal, and violent behaviors* (pp. 171–187). New York: Guilford.

Wiebe, R. P. (2003). Reconciling psychopathy and low self-control. *Justice Quarterly, 20*, 297–336.

Wright, B., Caspi, A., Moffitt, T., & Silva, P. (2001). The effects of social ties on crime vary by criminal propensity: A life-course model of interdependence. *Criminology, 39*, 321–351.

Yarbrough, A., Jones, S., Sullivan, C., Sellers, C., & Cochran, J. (2011). Social learning and self-control: Assessing the moderating potential of criminal propensity. *International Journal of Offender Therapy and Comparative Criminology*. doi:10.1177/0306624X10396041.

Zapolski, T. C. B., Cyders, M. A., & Smith, G. T. (2009). Positive urgency predicts illegal drug use and risky sexual behavior. *Psychology of Addictive Behaviors, 23*, 348–354.

Zuckerman, M. (1994). *Behavioral expressions and biosocial bases of sensation seeking*. Cambridge: Cambridge University Press.

Zuckerman, M. (2007). *Sensation seeking and risky behavior*. Washington, DC: American Psychological Association.

Zuckerman, M., & Kuhlman, M. D. (2000). Personality and risk taking: Common biosocial factors. *Journal of Personality, 68*, 999–1030.

CHAPTER EIGHT

The Criminal Personality

Stanton E. Samenow

In 1961, at the age of 55, Samuel Yochelson, MD, PhD, began a second career in psychiatry. After a successful practice in Buffalo, New York, he moved to Washington, D.C., to direct the Program for the Investigation of Criminal Behavior at St. Elizabeths Hospital. Funded by the National Institute of Mental Health (NIMH), this would become the longest in-depth research-treatment study of offenders conducted in North America and remains so to the present date. Dr. Yochelson died at the age of 70 while on his first trip to present the findings of his study. I became his assistant as a clinical research psychologist in 1970 and concluded the study in 1978.

When Dr. Yochelson began his research, he had three objectives. The first was to understand the factors giving rise to criminal behavior. A second was to establish a protocol to help offenders change. The third was to develop a program for crime prevention. The participants in the study were male adults. Some were hospitalized, having been found by the courts to be legally insane. Under the Durham Rule in the District of Columbia, this meant that their crimes were considered to be the product of a mental disease or defect. Others who participated in the study never were in the hospital. Referred by a variety of sources, some had committed numerous crimes but were never apprehended. These men came from a broad spectrum of backgrounds—college graduates and grade school dropouts, from impoverished and affluent families, from rural, suburban, and urban areas, and men from stable families as well as those from highly disorganized and dysfunctional families. In terms of the types of crimes they had committed, the study's participants ran the gamut, including property, violent, sex, and drug-related offenses. Nearly all the men had engaged in criminal behavior since childhood.

With his psychoanalytic background, Dr. Yochelson was very much a determinist, believing that people turned to crime because of sociological factors (e.g., poverty, peer pressure), because of psychological factors stemming from childhood adversities (e.g., bad parenting), or because of a mental illness. He also considered the possibility that biological factors were contributory. During his investigation, Dr. Yochelson spent as many as 8,000 hours interviewing and treating some individuals. With others he spent considerably less time, as some of these men agreed to be interviewed extensively but eventually voiced no interest in changing their lives. All men in the study took part voluntarily and were promised nothing in exchange for their participation. Nonetheless, some had ulterior motives, believing it might look good to the authorities and thus be to their advantage to join the study. Dr. Yochelson played no role in legal or administrative procedures affecting their cases.

Dr. Yochelson eventually understood that a mentality was operative in these men that differed greatly from most of his psychotherapy patients during his years of practice in Buffalo. Each participant presented himself as a victim of someone or something. The alleged causes of their criminal behavior lay outside themselves—what someone did to them or failed to do for them. Toward the end of the first few years, Dr. Yochelson found that these men had acquired insight, but he spelled it "incite," meaning that they were even more inclined to blame others. As one man said in a moment of rare candor, "Doctor, if I didn't have enough excuses for crime before psychiatry, I have more than enough now." The men had functioned with Dr. Yochelson as they had with others in the past—case out a person, assess what he wanted to hear, then feed it to him.

Dr. Yochelson gradually changed his approach. Rather than focus on what happened *to* these men, he questioned how they dealt with their life circumstances. Many of the participants grew up in impoverished neighborhoods with parents who themselves had a variety of problems. What Dr. Yochelson realized was that the environment was less important than how the individual *chose* to deal with whatever life handed him. Every offender had a sibling or neighbor who grew up under similar circumstances, but they did not turn to crime. For example, the sister of a mugger and gang leader had been a Red Cross employee for 20 years and lived a highly responsible life. Both were from a family in which their father was in jail, another brother was in prison, and temptation was at the doorstep in their drug-infested neighborhood—what sociologists term a "criminogenic environment." Asked why she did not follow the path of her father and brothers, this woman replied simply, "I wasn't interested." As she grew up, she made a series of choices as to whom she wanted to emulate and those whom she saw in a negative light. Had she become a thief, prostitute, or drug user, the determinists would have said, "How could it be otherwise," given the poor role models and harsh environment? What Dr. Yochelson found to be true in this case applied to all. Everyone encounters adversity while growing up. The critical question is, how does the individual cope with adversity?

Dr. Yochelson focused less on environmental challenges and more on the individual's response to those challenges. When questioned extensively about their choices, participants in the study revealed that, no matter what problems they encountered, they complicated the situation and made it worse by their responses. Harsh parents became even more punitive as they responded to their offspring's defiance, aggressiveness, and deception. Often the parents were mischaracterized. Parents want to believe and trust their children. However, the criminal as a child exploited the trusting nature of his parents, repeatedly concealing where he was going, whom he was with, and what he was doing. Consequently, his parents became less trusting and more punitive. To their dismay, mothers and fathers found themselves acting more like detectives and jailors to restrain and protect their youngster who, in turn, became even more defiant.

Dr. Yochelson was discovering that the men in his study were very different from their peers at an early age. For example, young children characteristically are self-centered, perceiving the world as revolving around their needs. Gradually, they learn to share, to delay gratification, and to consider the feelings of others. As a child, the criminal becomes not less, but more self-centered, determined to prevail in every situation. What he wants is paramount, and he will utilize any means to overcome others and reach his objective, resorting to manipulation, deception, or violence.

In short, the widely held view of the child as a lump of clay haplessly molded by the environment was not only called into question, but was also refuted. Children bring up parents as well as vice versa. Parents respond differently to a secretive, defiant child than they do to an affable, compliant son or daughter. Chapter one of volume one of *The Criminal Personality* is titled "The Reluctant Converts." This does not refer to the criminal, but rather to Dr. Yochelson and myself, who were reluctant to lead our sacred theoretical cows to pasture and slaughter them. None of the conventional wisdom about causes of crime stood up. During many decades and up to the present time, nearly everything but the federal deficit has been cited as causative of crime. These theories have dismally failed to explain why some men and women embark from an early age on a criminal path. Moreover, such theories have not led to any solutions!

Dr. Yochelson abandoned the search to establish causation for two reasons. One was that, although the theories and conjecture are endless, conclusive evidence is lacking. Furthermore, knowing "why" does not guarantee remediation of the problem. The second point is that focusing on causes is counterproductive in helping criminals change. They latch onto "why" questions and use them to justify past, present, and even future irresponsible behavior. Once the quest for causes was set aside, a new vista opened—a study of thinking. Behavior is largely a product of patterns of thought. Dr. Yochelson went beyond describing "traits" or characteristics of criminals to provide a detailed anatomy of their thinking processes. His identification of what he termed "errors in thinking" predated the interest in cognitive therapy that later became mainstream.

When the first volume of *The Criminal Personality* was published, intense criticism arose from some quarters that Dr. Yochelson wrongly dismissed the formative role of the environment, going against established principles of sociology, social psychology, and academic criminology. Dr. Yochelson well understood that social factors can facilitate or deter criminal behavior. Posting police officers and security cameras can deter crime in a particular area. This does not change the criminal, who then operates elsewhere. Living in a neighborhood where gangs roam and drugs are as available as candy may facilitate criminal behavior. But most residents of such areas are not criminals. In fact, crime is yet another adversity with which they must contend. They want to be safe from the predators around them and do not join gangs or use drugs.

Another criticism of our work was our use of the word "criminal." Because crimes are specified by laws, criminality is relative. One could be a criminal in one jurisdiction but not another, depending on the laws at the time and their enforcement. In its scope, our work goes well beyond the laws in force at a particular time and, instead, considers the way people live their lives. There are people who would be "criminals" in any environment, engaging in acts that injure others. One offender commented, "If rape were legalized, I wouldn't rape, but I would do something else." As he saw it, to be "somebody" in this world entailed doing the forbidden, whatever that might be. In his eyes, to live a responsible life was a treadmill to oblivion. Being ordinary in any way meant being a "nobody."

We conceptualized 52 errors in thinking on the part of people who make crime a way of life. Our critics pointed out that people who are not criminals also make some of these very same errors. It is not only criminals who lie. A child lies when he claims the cat knocked over the milk. An employee lies when he calls in sick but just wants the day off to relax. A mother lies when she tells her toddler the medicine tastes good when she knows it is bitter. There is a considerable difference between the basically responsible person who occasionally lies and the individual for whom lying is a way of life. The criminal lies because he has much to conceal in order to avoid detection. He also lies in order to dig himself out of a jam and minimize the severity of the consequences. What puzzles others is his lying for no discernible reason. He will say he went to McDonald's when he ate at Burger King. He will say he saw a film at one theater when he went to another. Lies roll off his tongue as automatically as he breathes. Mental health professionals interpret this behavior as pathological or "compulsive" lying. However, there is nothing compulsive about it. The criminal tells the truth if it serves his purpose. Often, he will tell part of the truth but lead others to think they are hearing it all. The "purposeless" lies have a purpose. By lying, the criminal preserves a view of himself and the world. He derives a sense of power by lying—in believing that he has pulled the wool over the eyes of others. The criminal lies more by omission than he does by concocting stories on the spot.

Like lying, thinking errors exist along a continuum. From time to time, responsible people blame others rather than own up to their own misconduct. Criminals perpetually present themselves as victims of others when held accountable, rarely admitting culpability. People who are basically responsible can be insensitive as they selfishly pursue an objective. The criminal operates throughout his life as though he is the hub of a wheel around which others must revolve. He lacks a concept of injury to others as he relentlessly and ruthlessly pursues whatever he wants. The same is true with the other thinking errors; they all exist along a continuum. If a person is extreme in all of them, the whole equals more than the sum of the parts. An individual emerges who has a set of premises about life radically different from those of people who are basically responsible. The result is that he leaves a trail of carnage behind.

Dr. Yochelson and I took a phenomenological approach to understanding the personality of the criminal. To identify and understand the ramifications of these thinking errors, we had to suspend our own theories and preconceptions and endeavor to understand the criminal's point of view. Turning from a traditional, deterministic conceptualization of criminal behavior, we arrived at a detailed understanding of the criminal's psychological makeup and how he functions in his daily life.

Criminals pursue power and control for their own sake. If they achieve power in a legitimate fashion, they abuse it. White-collar criminals do not commit crimes because they need the money. They behave as they do out of a sense of uniqueness—that they are special, that they are superior to others, and that rules do not apply to them. They are able to insinuate themselves into others' lives, gain their trust, and prey upon them, enriching themselves. The bank robber derives his power by pointing a gun at a teller and making off with money that he spends as quickly as he acquires it, even giving some away. For neither offender is the desire for money the central motive. How much money a person obtains is an index of his skill. But excitement lies in the power and control and then in the buildup of having gotten away with the crime.

Offenders from a wide range of backgrounds make identical thinking errors. And the same thinking errors lie behind very different sorts of crimes. Criminals have tastes and preferences in terms of the type of crime they want to commit. Some use force. Others resort to elaborate confidence games. A person is known for the crime for which he is arrested. A rapist is known as a sex offender. A shoplifter is a perpetrator of a property crime. However, what a person is caught for represents the tip of an iceberg. Rapists commit nonsexual crimes. Most shoplifters are irresponsible or arrestable for other types of offenses. Thinking errors give rise to all types of crimes!

In addition to understanding mental processes of the criminal, we became familiar with the tactics criminals deploy when held accountable. During the early phase of the St. Elizabeths study, Dr. Yochelson experienced these firsthand as the participants endeavored to present themselves in the best light. Characteristically, the men did with Dr. Yochelson what they had done by habit throughout their lives when others held them accountable. They told him what they thought he wanted to hear. Rather than respond candidly, they were vague. They would, on occasion, remain silent—a powerful control tactic. And they would generalize a point to an absurdity. For example, one man who made a jewelry heist said he was no different from his mother, who kept an extra dollar in change given to her by a cashier. These and other tactics were utilized in a struggle to keep their masks on—so others would not know who they really were and what intentions they harbored.

Dr. Yochelson's criminals had conveyed to others that they were unique, powerful, superior, and generally above the daily struggles most people encounter. But there was another dimension to their personality, features they concealed lest others consider them weak, namely their sentimentality and fearfulness. Savage brutality and maudlin sentiment existed within the same individual. "I can change from tears to ice and back again," exclaimed one man. Dr. Yochelson encountered a murderer who refused to step on a bug, saying he was repulsed by the idea of killing a living creature. Then there was the man who claimed to be deeply religious. A regular churchgoer and reader of the Bible, he wore a cross around his neck, which he touched after he uttered a curse word. His religiosity consisted of a set of ritualistic acts, but religion was divorced from moral and ethical concepts. He would pray at 10:00, then go out breaking into homes.

We discovered that criminals know full well the potential consequences of their actions. They are aware of the occupational hazards of criminal behavior—getting caught, convicted, confined, injured, or killed in a high-risk crime. And although they fear all of these consequences, they shut off this fear as completely as someone switching off a light. They rid themselves of fear long enough to do whatever they intend with just enough fear returning so they remain vigilant for the police or others who might hold them accountable.

Contrary to appearance, we found that criminals have a conscience and can experience remorse. However, their conscience is not fully operational and can speedily be shut off. One man broke into a home and cleared out valuable antiques and jewelry. When he learned that the owner was suffering from a terminal illness, he was so conscience-stricken that he arranged to have all the items returned. But this experience did not deter him from other break-ins. Perversely, the fact that criminals are able to experience remorse contributes to their view that they are good people.

The most pervasive fear, however, is of being put down. Expecting others to accommodate their every whim, the criminal is constantly disappointed. Any detail of life that runs counter to his desire of the moment is comparable in its effect to sticking a pin in a balloon. His entire self-image is in danger of being shattered. Because he thinks in extremes, the criminal is either number one or a zero. There are no in-betweens. Thus, if a driver is discourteous or even innocently gets in his way, he takes it personally and responds with anger. That is the essence of "road rage." Most motorists would likely avoid interacting with an erratic or rude driver. Not the criminal!

The individual with a criminal personality is chronically angry at a world that does not give him what he believes he is due. He harbors expectations that are unrealistic. What he demands of others does not apply to him. He expects his partner to cater to his every need, to be available at any time, and to meet any demand promptly. However, he may fail to show up as promised, refuse to say where he has been, and then becomes incensed if he is questioned.

The criminal responds with anger toward anyone who disappoints him and toward any situation that he finds disagreeable. During the course of a day, most individuals encounter frustration or disappointment. An entire literature has emerged counseling people, "don't sweat the small stuff." For the criminal, small stuff is major, because it threatens his self-image. When much of life eludes his control and others do not regard him as the colossus he thinks he is, the criminal experiences a threat. At the core of his anger is a fear of not being in control. The anger is always present, simmering within, often not evident to others. What appears to be an insignificant incident can be the stimulus, the one thing too much, that triggers an outburst of temper. A man is saving a seat for his buddy. Someone else occupying that chair offends his entire view of life. The criminal has regarded that chair as his possession. The other person, in all innocence, challenged the criminal's sense of himself. A personal attack may ensue as the criminal reclaims what he regards as "his," thereby establishing that he is a force to be reckoned with. And that is how his life proceeds—initiating or reacting to an unending series of events, endeavoring to prop up his always precarious self-image.

A pervasive pattern in the criminal's thinking is his lack of a concept of injury to others. Most people would not find this surprising. However, this cognitive feature pervades his personality to an extent that it is beyond the comprehension of most responsible individuals. If a criminal is held accountable for an offense, he might glibly acknowledge that someone was hurt, especially if the crime results in a physical injury or significant monetary loss. However, the ripple effect of injury to direct and indirect victims (e.g., family, community, society) is totally outside the realm of his consideration. A vivid example is the young man who donned a ski mask, burst into the office of a former employer at closing time and, at gunpoint, grabbed the cash being readied for a night deposit, then fled. Asked about this crime when he was interviewed at a jail, he asserted, "No one was hurt. There was no blood, no broken bones." The perpetrator was oblivious that the robbed employee feared for her life during 20 minutes of terror, that she might suffer severe psychological trauma that could last for months, if not years. Nor did he fathom the impact on the victim's family, friends, and nearby businesses. To his way of thinking, he was the victim who now faced years of incarceration. Yet, this same individual would be outraged if someone robbed his girlfriend or mother. For the criminal, people are like pawns on a chessboard, objects to be maneuvered for his own purpose.

To understand this personality, it is necessary to bear in mind that the criminal's expectations and pretensions outstrip his efforts. As indicated above, he thinks in extremes; he is "number one" or a "zero." He expects others to treat him in line with his inflated self-image. There are those who believe that the core problem is his low self-esteem. These individuals are ultimately failures. They may have failed in school or at work and been shunned by family members. Eventually, they even fail at crime. Despite their lack of success, they have do not consider themselves failures at all. They have chosen to reject parents, school, working, and many other aspects of responsible living. While others regard them as failures, they are determined to overcome others, to establish themselves as "number one." Even while incarcerated, their view of themselves as unique and superior remains undiminished.

In the aftermath of a crime, there often is an attempt to assess the "underlying" motive—e.g., greed, jealousy, revenge. Often, the motive remains elusive. A woman shoplifts an item while having a wad of cash in her purse. A homeless man sitting on a park bench finds himself beset by a pack of youths and is beaten senseless. Two youths, strangers to each other, erupt into pummeling each other with their fists. A man has sex with his wife, then stalks and sexually attacks a woman in a park. Why these crimes occurred is not clear. The mentality of the thief, it turns out, is that stealing an item is far more exciting than purchasing it. The attack on the homeless man results from the emotional voltage of overcoming another human being and forcing him to plead for mercy. There was no monetary gain. The fight in the hallway was triggered by one student taking offense at what he interpreted as an insulting stare by the other. And the rape occurred not out of a desire for sex, but because the opportunity presented itself to subdue a female whom the perpetrator was certain would find him irresistible, forcing her to submit, and building his ego in the process. In short, the nature of the crime in and of itself may not reveal the motive. There is gratification at each phase—thinking about the crime, committing it, and the aftermath of getting away with it. Even if the offender is apprehended, unless it is for the first time, there are multiple challenges dealing with his lawyer, court personnel, and law enforcement officers. Anyone evaluating an offender must be aware that when a criminal is held accountable, what he tells others after the fact may give few, if any, clues as to what actually transpired in his mind.

During our lengthy study of criminal behavior, we thought that offenders who use drugs might differ significantly in personality from those who seldom use mind-altering substances. This turned out not to be the case. Many offenders claim that drug use is their main problem and ascribe their difficulties to drugs. Statements such as, "I didn't kill him; the drugs did," are not unusual, with the perpetrator alleging the crime would not have occurred were it not for drugs, almost as if the crime were alien to his personality.

Drugs bring out what already resides within the offender. If 10 men become intoxicated while drinking alcohol, not all 10 will commit crimes. There will be different reactions depending upon the personality of the individuals involved. A person who has never been physically violent is unlikely to become violent when he drinks. An individual unaccustomed to drinking heavily might become sleepy and quiet. Others may be boisterous and loud. Still others may become rude, aggressive, sexually more assertive, and so forth.

When held accountable, the user tends to emphasize that drugs offer escape from life's problems. He does not volunteer that what he is "escaping" is life as it is, with its requirements, disappointments, and frustration. No matter how harsh the environment, the drug-using criminal has siblings and neighbors who do not turn to drugs and crime. Irresponsible and arrestable behavior did not begin with drugs. For the individual with a criminal personality, drugs facilitate whatever he seeks. Drugs may facilitate greater daring and more serious crimes. On a drug of his choosing, the user becomes less fearful of the consequences and thus more emboldened to assume risks he might not otherwise take. One man told us that he had fantasized many times about holding up a particular store. Only on heroin did he have the "heart" to actually pick up a gun and do it.

The criminal wants to be number one at everything, including sex. However, he is far more focused on power and conquest than on sex per se. On his drug of choice, he is more forward in seeking a partner. Fears about performance vanish. And he may be less discriminating in his choice of partner and take greater risks in his sexual practices (e.g., pregnancy, disease). As one man remarked, "I didn't care if she was deaf, dumb, and blind. All I wanted was her body."

Drugs also enhance the criminal's overall sense of power, being in charge and in control. "On drugs, I felt as if I owned the world" and similar statements were frequently expressed by drug-using offenders. If the user is with a group, he may be less socially reticent, more the life of the party. Anything the criminal seeks, drugs may facilitate, depending on the particular drug, the amount used, and the setting he is in. If he seeks a "religious" experience, he may achieve that. However, the content of his thinking is that he becomes more godlike rather than in touch with God. And, if he is depressed, drugs may intensify the thinking that he would be better off dead. The "depression" is not because he regards himself as unsatisfactory in any way, but rather that the world around him is not satisfactory. There is blazing anger at a world that does not meet his expectations.

The "addiction" of habitual drug users is less about a substance than it is about maintaining a way of life. With some drugs, a tolerance effect occurs whereby the criminal requires increasing amounts of the drug to obtain the effect he desires. However, offenders regularly find that if they abstain from drug use, to their surprise, life is still fraught with problems. One man said that he thought he would have no significant problems once he ceased using cocaine. To his dismay, he discovered he had more problems than ever. He had to work every day, attend Narcotics Anonymous meetings, pay bills, and comply with a number of probation requirements. He found responsible living to entail endless tedium and frustration, quite unlike the world he previously inhabited—the exciting people, the dangerous places, the thrill of the deal, all the intrigue and excitement. What others called "responsible living" to him was boring—an insufferable treadmill. Consequently, he returned not just to cocaine, but to an entire way of life.

In short, the psychological makeup of the drug-using criminal and that of the criminal nonuser is the same. The important point is to focus on basic character, not on drugs and their effects. Even if the person ceases all drug use, the errors of thinking persist.

An extraordinary characteristic of criminals is that they believe they are good people. This is true no matter how much physical, emotional, or financial misery they inflict on others. "Just because I killed someone doesn't mean I'm a bad guy," claimed one man who shot a store clerk during a holdup. "If I thought of myself as evil, I couldn't live," remarked another. We found no exceptions—every offender believed in his inherent goodness.

How does a one-man crime wave maintain such a view? There are numerous components to this perception. Working, going to school, and doing good deeds all contribute. Many offenders are talented musically and artistically. They have skills such as being able to repair broken items or build things. They are creative and have numerous talents, even if they are undisciplined in using them. Engaging in religious practices supports their view of themselves as kind and compassionate. As mentioned above, criminals attend church, celebrate religious holidays, and engage in other types of religious observance. Many organized crime members profess to be religious. They donate money to legitimate charities and have shrines in their homes. This does not prevent their cold-blooded slaughter of adversaries.

An integral component to the view of the self as a good person is that each offender maintains, often self-righteously, that there are crimes he never would commit. He sets himself apart from the "bad guys" because their actions are anathema to them. Said one man, "Anyone who knocks a little old lady down on the street and grabs her purse should be strung up." Although he vowed he never would do such a thing, he had broken into a widow's home when she was there and made off with her valued heirlooms. But this was acceptable because he did not physically attack her in the process. In prison, many offenders try to keep their crimes a secret because they fear how others will react. This is especially true of pedophiles who are likely to receive the worst treatment by other inmates. Criminals have their preferences in crimes and look down on those who do not share them. A "white-collar" offender may disparage perpetrators of violence for being crude. Conversely, criminals who use physical force may regard white-collar criminals as weak, not real men.

Individuals who seek to counsel offenders and help them change must understand this feature of the criminal personality. Even offenders who boast about their crimes and what they got away with believe that, no matter what devastation they wrought, they are, at heart, good human beings. They offer a variety of after-the-fact rationalizations and may even acknowledge making a "mistake." (One perpetrator referred to a brutal rape that he committed as a mistake.) Their sense of themselves as good people is not in the least diminished by such admissions.

Nearly everything set forth above ran counter to what Dr. Yochelson and I believed when we began our work. We were indeed "the reluctant converts," forced to abandon our beliefs and theories about criminal behavior as we spent thousands of hours interviewing offenders. Our project became a hypothesis-generating study rather than proving what we already thought at the outset. We changed our perspective from seeing the criminal as a victim to understanding that he made a series of choices resulting in his becoming a victimizer.

Human nature does not change, but diagnostic labels do. There used to be the "psychopath," then the "sociopath"—terms no longer in use. Writers familiar with our work have pointed out that there is overlap of the criminal personality with the antisocial personality disorder, the borderline personality disorder, and the histrionic personality disorder. We did not attempt to introduce a new diagnostic label. In fact, we believed that labels conceal more than they reveal. The concept of a criminal personality emerged in what became a phenomenological study leading to an understanding of how the criminal's mind works, how he sees himself and the world.

Even highly competent mental health professionals confuse the criminal personality with a "bipolar" disorder. Criminals experience extremes in their moods. Their highs are very high, and their lows are very low.

They may be animated, speak rapidly, and show boundless energy. Brimming with self-confidence, no task is too daunting. Yet these same individuals, on other occasions, appear downcast and lethargic, taking no initiative. Despite appearances, this is not bipolar disorder, and it will not respond to medication. The "highs" occur as the person is prevailing at whatever he undertakes, sweeping aside any challenge. The lows occur when life is not meeting his expectations and he is not receiving the affirmation he believes he is due. An effective antidote to the "lows" is to engage in activity that is exciting and offers a buildup. No medicine yet exists that transforms an irresponsible person into a responsible human being.

Professionals who deal with criminals in nearly any capacity must understand how these individuals think in order to help make informed decisions about them, which they are often asked to do by courts and a variety of agencies and facilities. Whether criminals should be helped to change has long generated heated debate. There are those who espouse a "rehabilitative" ideal versus those who believe that offenders are virtually incapable of change and therefore should be incarcerated in order to remove them from society. During our study at St. Elizabeths, Dr. Yochelson and I found that the concept of "rehabilitation" as applied to criminals is flawed. To "rehabilitate" means to restore to a former, constructive condition. One rehabilitates an old house to make it livable again. One helps rehabilitate a stroke victim so she can regain functions she once had. There is nothing to which to "re-habilitate" criminals who never functioned responsibly in society. Rehabilitative measures that have been employed in the past focus on equipping the offender with new skills—furthering his education, helping him to earn a livelihood, teaching him financial management, and improving social skills. As worthwhile as these programs are, they are insufficient. If a criminal earns a diploma, he is an educated offender, but an offender nonetheless. If he becomes an accomplished carpenter, his skills are of little value if he fails to show up for work, steals from the job site, and cheats the customer. In fact, educating him, training him for a new job, and facilitating social skills may provide him with entree into new arenas to commit crimes.

The programs alluded to above do not result in responsible behavior as long as basic errors in thinking remain unaltered. The scope of the task of change extends beyond acquisition of skills to becoming aware that one in fact has errors in his thinking, understanding the ramifications of those errors, becoming fed up with oneself, and then learning and implementing corrective thought processes. "Habilitation" is possible, but it does not occur quickly or easily.

Sources for motivation to change may be external or internal. In the former instance, a criminal may be facing extremely unpalatable consequences of his behavior. He has been arrested and risks loss of his freedom or, perhaps equally distressing, the loss of family support. Upon experiencing the specific consequences of their behavior, some experience a collapse of their good opinion of themselves. Arrest alone may precipitate vulnerability, or it may take the slamming of the jail's door behind them. Some previously have experienced such low periods in their lives. However, they have responded by returning to their former lifestyle with its excitement, intrigues, and conquests. Men and women who counsel offenders (and there are thousands of them working in the community and in correctional institutions) can approach an offender at a potentially vulnerable point when he appears to have reached a new low.

Skeptics understandably will argue that when a criminal seems to bottom out, all he really seeks is to get out of a jam and minimize the penalty. This may be the case. It is not possible to gauge an offender's sincerity at any given time. Moreover, sincerity of the moment may not translate into lasting change. Nonetheless, an approach can and should be made.

In our work at St. Elizabeths Hospital, Dr. Yochelson and I not only developed a detailed description of the criminal's mental processes, but we also pioneered a format for helping the criminal transform his life so that he willingly gives up his criminality and, eventually, with intense struggle, embraces a way of life that he has both envied and scorned. While incarcerated, it is not unusual for a criminal to espouse a desire to live what he thinks is a responsible life. (I have yet to find a man or woman who likes prison.) Many offenders maintain that they want to "settle down"—have a family, hold a good job, live comfortably, and have nice things. The problem is that they yearn for the trappings of responsible living without have to work hard to obtain them. Their motivation to change, though genuine, is short-lived once they realize that nothing comes quickly or easily and without hard work. Others who have an advanced education and accomplished a great deal in their occupations and professions never were content with living by the rules. They abused the authority and status that they obtained. Believing they were more shrewd and clever than their contemporaries, they lied, cheated, and took shortcuts. They appeared to others to be living responsibly, but this was all a facade.

In this chapter, it is not feasible to set forth in detail the program for change that we developed. The core of the program involves teaching offenders to think about their thinking, a process alien to most people. Criminals become aware of thinking errors as they occur in their minds *before* they act on them. They then learn corrective concepts and how to utilize them in daily life.

For example, a man eyes a laptop computer briefly left on a table by its owner, who has gone to the bathroom. A thought flashes into his mind as to how he can whisk it away, conceal it, then peddle it to gain money for drugs. He then considers potential consequences. The most primitive level of deterrence is to think he will get caught and wind up in serious trouble. A second level of deterrence is to regard the thought as tantamount to drinking poison—shorthand for not only what may happen to him, but also a consideration of the reverberating impact upon his family if he is apprehended as well as the injury to the owner of the laptop. He erases the thought from his mind and focuses his thinking in a more positive direction. As the agent of change works with him, there is an examination of his character. Not only are potential consequences of a crime to be considered, but also what kind of person he wants to be. The thought about stealing the computer is a dot on the landscape of his irresponsibility. Does he want to spend his life victimizing others, destroying others' lives, and end up going in and out of police stations, courts, jails, and, eventually, prison? Numerous errors in thinking are involved in the thought about stealing the laptop—pretensions, a sense of ownership, his thirst for excitement, a search to build himself up at others' expense, and shutting off deterrents but later ruing the consequences. Corrective processes including examining his pretensions and unrealistic expectations, considering the ripple effect of injury to direct and indirect victims, and allowing fear (deterrents) to be a guide to responsible conduct rather than perceiving fear as the enemy.

Helping a criminal change requires teaching him to report his thinking phenomenologically—as it occurs in his mind without editing or justifying. This process requires disclosure, receptivity, and self-criticism from an individual who has been secretive, closed-minded, and ruthlessly critical of others. The impetus to change can arise out of a combination of fear, deepening self-disgust, and a leap of faith. A person cannot be expected to embrace a way of life that he has never lived. He must reach a point where he rejects his criminal way of life, having discovered the costs to himself and others to be intolerable. Unused to struggle and humility, he understandably has grave doubts about what others call responsible living. Some contemplate suicide. Crime, change, and suicide are the three options. Time and again, the criminal has believed in the viability of a fourth option—functioning on both sides of the street. This entails living what appears to be a responsible life while trying to get away with offenses on the side. This has not worked in the long run. The criminal's mounting desire for ever greater excitement has ultimately resulted in a return to major crimes and the disagreeable consequences that follow in their wake. The necessary leap of faith is that, ultimately, he will be better off if he is receptive to the efforts of others to help him change his thinking.

Living responsibly carries no guarantees of wealth or fame. The calisthenics of change require developing endurance and dealing with adversity patiently and conscientiously, while making the most of one's abilities and talents. Rewards are slow. However, if a criminal sticks with the program, he will discover that the responsible world offers self-respect not based on empty pretensions, but in response to achievements. He will earn the respect and trust of others and no longer will need to look over his shoulder for those who seek to hold him accountable for wrongdoing. As a responsible person, he will discover not only freedom from imprisonment, but also the freedom to explore a vast world that he has heretofore rejected—the opportunities that living responsibly affords.

Together, Dr. Yochelson and I have spent 57 years in the field of criminal psychology. We came to understand in detail the mental makeup of the individual with a criminal personality and piloted a program to help such an individual change. Although this work has been adapted in numerous agencies and facilities, controversy remains. Questions about the origins of this personality remain unanswered. I continue to take the position that it is better to say that we know little about the etiology of criminal behavior rather than continue to espouse a conventional wisdom that, for more than a half century, has not led to solutions. The argument has been made, particularly in an era of diminishing resources, that it is not financially viable to undertake with offenders the sort of work we did. Society has choices to make. Nearly every individual locked up today will eventually be released once he has served his time. With rare exception, confining a person does not in and of itself change a criminal's personality. The savings to society will be vast if at least some offenders can be worked with in a habilitative process in correctional facilities and in the community. Thousands of professionals remain employed to counsel offenders. Certainly, if their efforts are to bear fruit, it is indisputable that the key to lasting and meaningful change is to help offenders recognize and change their thinking errors of a lifetime.

References

Samenow, S. E. (1998). *Straight talk about criminals: Perspectives on antisocial behavior*. Laurel, MD: Rowman & Littlefield.

Samenow, S. E. (1999). *Before it's too late: Why some kids get into trouble and what parents can do about it*. New York: Three Rivers Press.

Samenow, S. E. (2004). *Inside the criminal mind*. New York: Crown.
Samenow, S. E. (2007). *The myth of the out of character crime*. Santa Barbara, CA: ABC-CLIO (paperback distributed through Amazon.com).
Yochelson, S., & Samenow, S. E. (1976). *The criminal personality: A profile for change*. Laurel, MD: Rowman & Littlefield.
Yochelson, S., & Samenow, S. E. (1977). *The criminal personality: The change process*. Laurel, MD: Rowman & Littlefield.
Yochelson, S., & Samenow, S. E. (1986). *The criminal personality: The drug user*. Laurel, MD: Rowman & Littlefield.

SECTION III

Key Research Findings

CHAPTER NINE

Predatory and Affective Aggression: Calculated and Explosive Pathways to Violence

Stacey L. Shipley and Jennifer L. Russell

Introduction

Violent offenders are among the most common type of offenders in the United States' prison population, accounting for approximately 49% of inmates (Jeglic, Maile, & Calkins-Mercado, 2011). Further, violent crime is on the rise in the United States. Violent offenders accounted for 53% of the growth in state prison populations for the 10-year period between 1990 and 2000 (Jeglic et al., 2011). Most violent offenders have a prior arrest record, and more than half of these offenders (56%) have previously been arrested for a violent felony (Jeglic et al., 2011). It has been noted that 5%–6% of the adult male inmate population are responsible for about 50% of crime (Skilling, Harris, Rice, & Quinsey, 2002). Understanding the motivations for violence crime, the nature of the violence, and how it manifests is critical in order to inform efforts to help prevent it. Treatment to reduce recidivism among this population is of utmost importance for public safety, as well as for the effectiveness of our penal system in protecting society via containment and rehabilitation efforts (Jeglic et al., 2011). Social scientists have long indicated that in order to effectively understand, manage, and treat violent offenders, characteristics of their violent behavior, as well as personality and historical features that may correspond to various types of violent behavior must be examined.

One of the most well-known distinctions regarding types of aggression is that of predatory versus affective aggression (Meloy, 1988, 2000b; Shipley & Arrigo, 2004; Vitiello, Behar, Hunt, Stoff, & Ricciuti, 1990). This distinction was initially observed in studies of aggression in nonhuman animals (Eichelman, 1987; Siegel & Pott, 1988), and is supported by studies indicating that different neurochemical substrates and anatomical pathways mediate the two types of aggression in nonhuman animals (Eichelman, 1987; Siegel & Pott, 1988). Within the animal kingdom, the cobra has exemplified predatory aggression, while the pit bull on the attack exhibits affective aggression. Cats demonstrate clearly defined episodes of predatory aggression (e.g., stalking a mouse), as well as affective aggression when they are startled or cornered by a perceived threatening object. The model has more recently been applied to the study of aggression in humans (Fontaine, 2007; Kempes, Matthys, de Vries, & van Engeland, 2005; Siegel & Victoroff, 2009; Vitaro, Brendgen, & Barker, 2006; Vitiello et al., 1990; Vitiello & Stoff, 1997).

According to this model, predatory aggression (also known as instrumental, proactive, or offensive aggression) is characterized by "cold-blooded physiology and affect, deliberation, and instrumental motives" (Fontaine, 2007, p. 144), and is goal-oriented and apparently planned (Vitiello et al., 1990). During acts of predatory aggression, the "animal maintains good control of its motor activity" (Vitiello et al., 1990, p. 189). Affective aggression (also known as reactive, defensive, or hostile aggression), in contrast, is induced by fear or anger, accompanied by high autonomic arousal and poor modulation of behavior, and is apparently unplanned (Vitiello et al., 1990). Affective aggression "results from an interpretation of a provocative, threatening, or unjust stimulus, heated anger, impulsivity, and an interest in hurting the perceived provocateur" (Fontaine, 2007, p. 144). The usefulness and applicability of this model has been reflected in the U.S. system of classification for homicides, which distinguishes the premeditated and deliberate killing of another (i.e., first-degree murder) from the killing of one another in response to provocation or in the context of extreme emotional disturbance (i.e., manslaughter) (Fontaine, 2007). The former (e.g., instances of killing for financial remuneration, killing a spouse or partner to access a life insurance policy, serial killers such as Ted Bundy who plan thoroughly and then execute their murders in a calm, collected, often ritualistic fashion) would be indicative of predatory aggression, while the latter (e.g., a person who kills their cheating spouse or partner, a person who becomes intoxicated and when angered or provoked responds in explosive and excessive violence) represents affective aggression (Bushman & Anderson, 2001; Fontaine, 2007; Kempes et al., 2005). The examples of each type of aggression provided illustrate the differences in personality traits, behavioral tendencies, and the propensity for future violence exhibited by aggressors of each type. The North American justice system has acknowledged and reflected these issues in its traditional tiered system of classification of homicides and associated penalties, with less severe penalties for aggression that is provoked and more affective in nature and the severest of penalties reserved for those who engage in calculated, premeditated, and predatory aggression (Fontaine, 2007). According to Fontaine (2008), these distinctions indicate our society's increased tolerance for lapses in behavioral control motivated by emotional responses, and decreased tolerance for violence by those with deficits in processes that are typically viewed as more cognitively mediated, such as errors in interpretation of threat or degree of insult.

The likelihood of rehabilitation, as well as the types of treatments that may be most effective for treating these types of violence, differ; it has historically been noted that pharmacological treatment and behavioral interventions may be most effective for reducing aggression that is explosive rather than for planned aggression (Campbell et al., 1995; Crick & Dodge, 1996). More recent findings regarding the treatment of these two types of violence will be discussed later in the Treatment Implications subsection.

Although it is possible for violent offenders to only display predatory or affective violence, the lines between the types of aggression are often blurred. Many aggressors display both types of violence at different points or even within the same incident as demonstrated by the vignette below, which discusses the case of serial killer Aileen Wuornos who was convicted and put to death in Florida for murdering seven men (Shipley & Arrigo, 2004):

> Aileen Wuornos was born on February 29, 1956. Until the age of 11, Aileen Wuornos and her brother Keith believed that Lauri and Britta Wuornos (her grandparents) were their parents. Aileen and Keith were only 11 months apart. There were three actual children (two girls and one boy) of Lauri and Britta, who Aileen and her brother initially believed were their siblings. Dianne, an older daughter and Aileen's biological mother, was no longer in the home as Aileen was growing up. She was estranged from her parents and they rarely mentioned her. Dianne abandoned her children for good, when Aileen was two and Keith was three. Their biological father, Leo, was physically abusive toward her mother, was extremely jealous and

controlling, had many affairs, and was an alcoholic. He had a lengthy criminal history to include charges such as breaking and entering and car theft, which culminated in a conviction of kidnapping and brutally raping a seven-year-old girl long after he had split from Dianne (Shipley & Arrigo, 2004). He committed suicide while serving a life sentence for this crime. Leo had left early in Dianne's pregnancy with Aileen and was never known to her. Despite being spared from being raised by their biological father, both Aileen and Keith experienced severe abuse at the hands of Lauri, their grandfather.

Aileen's grandfather was characterized by one of his daughters as having a frightening temper and a dogmatic presentation. He was a chronic drinker, and Aileen described sadistic abuse at the hands of her grandfather. She described numerous beatings with a leather strap on her bare buttocks and described being beaten on consecutive days while her skin was still raw from prior beatings. Her grandfather was verbally abusive as well and would refer to her as evil and worthless.

As cited in Shipley and Arrigo (2004, p. 97): "Aileen in no uncertain terms made it clear that she hated her 'parents.' The 'cat incident' left a horrible impression not only on Aileen and Keith but also for many of the children in the neighborhood. A family of wild kittens had been living in the attic of the Wuornos home. Lauri demanded that they all be taken to the pound but one. The remaining kitten had scratched young Aileen on the cheek. The next day he observed Aileen playing with the kitten, became enraged, ordered that she follow him into the sauna and made her watch him hold the kitten under the water until it drowned. The Wuornoses kept a sauna as part of their Finnish heritage."

It is reported that by the age of 11, she was exchanging intercourse and other sexual favors for cigarettes or loose change from older boys in her neighborhood, and was reportedly sexually abused by numerous men throughout her life. Aileen was described as easily angered and often unpredictable. As Aileen began abusing substances, particularly alcohol, her volatility worsened. She exhibited behavioral problems at school, was prone to boredom, and often stole from other children and businesses. Aileen was sent to juvenile hall after she ran away from home. Her callousness and disregard for the feelings of others were reflected in many of her adolescent and early childhood behaviors, including defiantly blowing smoke in the face of her deceased mother at her funeral. Her early adult life was marked by unstable and short-term relationships, substance abuse, her reliance on and taking advantage of individuals who took her in and cared for her, and violent rages, which often resulted in legal charges. It is reported that in one instance, she became intensely angry during a pool game at a bar and hurled a cue ball at the bar manager so hard that it reportedly was lodged into the wall. The manager had closed Aileen's pool table after she became belligerent and threatened other patrons, provoking Aileen into explosive violence. She was charged with assault and battery for the incident, and this incident is only one of many in Aileen's history demonstrating her explosive temper and propensity for affective aggression.

Aileen eventually began a homosexual relationship with Tyria (Ty) Moore, whom Aileen would later implicate as an accessory to her murders. These murders represent Aileen's most brutal acts of predatory violence. Aileen's first victim was Richard Mallory, a truck driver from Clearwater, Florida, who had previously served a prison sentence for assault with attempt to rape but otherwise had no criminal history or allegations that he attacked any of the many women he encountered. It was no secret that Mallory enjoyed the company of women; he "loved spending time in gentlemen's clubs and procuring the services of prostitutes, many of whom knew him by name," and none of whom ever alleged that he assaulted them (Shipley & Arrigo, 2004, p. 105). Although Aileen claimed that he raped her and provoked her, these claims are inconsistent with forensic evidence collected from the crime scene, indicating Aileen's propensity not only for predatory acts of aggression, but also her willingness and ability to use deception to conceal her acts of violence.

Mallory picked Aileen up a truck stop and agreed to take her to Daytona, Florida. Mallory suggested that they stop before their destination to talk, and he and Aileen began to discuss prices and went to a deserted wooded location. Aileen undressed, but Mallory left his clothes on. Aileen reached through the window of the truck and grabbed her bag, pulling a gun on Mallory. According to Aileen, she pointed it at him, accused him of wanting to rape her, and fired a shot that hit Mallory in the right arm and then struck him in the side. Mallory crawled from the cab of the truck and attempted to shield himself behind the body of the truck. Aileen chased the disabled Mallory and fired a second shot, which struck him in the torso and caused him to fall to the ground. She then fired two more shots, one of which struck Mallory in the lung, causing a massive and fatal hemorrhage.

Mallory struggled to survive for between 10 and 20 minutes, while Aileen watched him die. After he died, she took his identification and money from his body and attempted to conceal the body before fleeing the scene. When Aileen returned home after the murder, Ty reported that she was perfectly coherent and acting normal, and that there were no physical indications of a struggle of any kind. Later that evening, Aileen reported to Ty that she had killed a man, and described her disposal of his body and belongings, and did so in a matter-of-fact, unemotional way, without reporting to Ty that Mallory had raped or attacked her, though she did report this in later interviews. Her report of Mallory's supposed attack of her was inconsistent across time, and became more and more dramatic and inconsistent with objective forensic evidence as her trial progressed. When she was interviewed regarding the Mallory murder, Aileen stated, "I'd be better off [dead]. If I had a life sentence . . . as raped as I was, I'd probably kill again [laughs] . . . probably would. I'm so psyched about the rape jazz,

I would kill over and over and over again. It wouldn't work. I'd be better off dead ... I didn't have flashbacks or anything. I don't even have dreams about the things I did. I don't have no dreams or nothing about the incidents. I don't have no flashbacks or nothing. I don't have any imaginary friends and I don't see or hear no voices [laughing] or none of that jazz" (Court TV, 1999 as cited in Shipley & Arrigo, 2004).

After being sentenced to death for Mallory's murder, Aileen pled no contest to three other murders and guilty to two other murders, and received death sentences for each. In subsequent media interviews from death row, Aileen made statements that she would kill again if she were not executed, and denied that she experienced symptoms of mental illness, although her mental state appeared to deteriorate to some degree as her execution date approached. She blamed law enforcement for allowing her to continue to kill, and expressed her belief that they did so in order to profit from movies and books about her life and crimes. On October 9, 2002, she was executed by lethal injection at Broward Correctional Institution in Pembroke Pines, Florida (Shipley & Arrigo, 2004).

Literature Review

The distinction between predatory and affective aggression perpetrated by a psychopathic individual was, perhaps, best explained by Meloy (1988) in his classic text, *The Psychopathic Mind* (Shipley & Arrigo, 2004). Predatory violence is characterized by minimal or absent autonomic arousal, a lack of conscious experience of emotion, and violence that is both planned and purposeful and not in retaliation for an actual or perceived threat from the victim. Predatory violence is designed to fulfill multiple conscious and/or unconscious purposes (e.g., need for revenge, desire for stimulation and emotional excitation the aggressor experiences from the violent act[s], to draw attention to particular social or political issues), has a decreased likelihood that the target of predatory violence will be displaced or abandoned for an easier or more accessible victim, and has a time-unlimited behavioral sequence in which the aggressor's impulses do not fade with diminished emotion or the passage of time (Meloy, 1988; Shipley & Arrigo, 2004). Moreover, predatory violence can be characterized by the aggressor's engaging in ritualistic behaviors (e.g., taking personal items from the victim, a particular method of disposal of the body, binding or other ritualized forms of torture) before or after the act of aggression, the presence of rational and goal-directed thought processes, heightened and focused sensory awareness, and heightened self-esteem on the part of the aggressor (Shipley & Arrigo, 2004). In contrast, affective aggression, the most common type of aggression displayed by humans, occurs in response to an internal or external threatening stimuli and is accompanied by intense sympathetic arousal; in other words, the aggressor is frightened or angered into aggressive action (Meloy 1988; Shipley & Arrigo, 2004). As will be demonstrated in the following section, the psychopathic personality style has several characteristics that increase the propensity of such individuals for predatory acts of aggression (Shipley & Arrigo, 2004).

Psychopathy and Predatory Aggression

Aileen Wuornos's case demonstrates well the construct of psychopathy, which is often associated with predatory acts of aggression (see Cornell et al., 1996; Shipley & Arrigo, 2004; Vitacco, Neumann, Caldwell, Leistico, & Van Rybroek, 2006). Although Aileen's less extreme acts of violence were often provoked by perceived slights, her violence was extreme in relationship to the wrongs dealt her and her most serious acts of violence (i.e., the murders of Mallory and her other victims) were cold, calculating, and marked by emotional aloofness to the pain she caused (Shipley & Arrigo, 2004). It has been observed that, absent pathological personality and psychological factors, provocation is necessary to elicit aggression, and theorists have proposed that individuals like Aileen, who act aggressively without discernible provocation, exhibit a pathological or malignant personality style (Arrigo & Shipley, 2001; Fontaine, 2007). Originally conceptualized and described by Cleckley (1976), the construct of psychopathy was later operationalized by Robert Hare (1991, 2003), who identified it as a malignant constellation of personality and behavioral traits comprised of two factors: Factor 1, malignant narcissism/emotional detachment; and Factor 2, social deviance. Factor 1 is characterized by emotional and interpersonal aspects, including affective shallowness, absence of empathy, lack of remorse, superficial charm, and manipulative behavior; while Factor 2 is marked by impulsivity, aggression, high sensation seeking, low socialization, proneness to boredom, irresponsibility, lack of concern or plans for the future, and early-life behavioral problems and delinquency (Hare, 2003). Psychopathy is most frequently quantified or classified via assessment using the Psychopathy Checklist–Revised (PCL-R), allowing for the study of the relationship between degree of psychopathy and risk for future violence.

With regard to its relationship to aggression, psychopathy has been empirically supported as one of the strongest dispositional predictors of aggression and violence (Hare & Neumann, 2008; Skeem & Mulvey, 2001; Stadtland, Kleindienst, Kroner, Eidt, & Nedopil, 2005; Vitacco,

Neumann, & Jackson, 2005; Walsh & Kosson, 2008). Further, the relationship between aggression and psychopathy has been demonstrated in multiple studies of forensic, psychiatric, and youth populations (e.g., Doyle & Dolan, 2006b; Edens, Skeem, & Douglas, 2006; Harris, Rice, & Quinsey, 1993; Hart, Hare, & Forth, 1994; Porter & Woodworth, 2006; Walsh & Kosson, 2008). Given recent research suggesting that psychopathy is a dimensional, rather than categorical construct (e.g., Edens, Marcus, Lilienfeld, & Poythress, 2006; Guay, Ruscio, Knight, & Hare, 2007; Marcus, John, & Edens, 2004; Murrie et al., 2007), laboratory studies of subclinical, nonforensic populations (Miller & Lynam, 2003; Parrott & Zeichner, 2006; Reidy, Zeichner, Miller, & Martinez, 2007) have also shown the relationship between traits of psychopathy and violence. Specifically, individuals who exhibit callous and unemotional traits (associated with Hare's Factor 1) have been shown to demonstrate increased rates of violence (Enebrink, Andershed, & Langstrom, 2005; Frick, Cornell, Barry, Bodin, & Dane, 2003; Kruh, Frick, & Clements, 2005), while those with lower levels of these traits exhibit less aggression, overall; and, when they do behave aggressively, they tend to do so in affective ways (Frick et al., 2003; Kruh et al., 2005). Additionally, individuals showing only affective aggression typically experience distress related to their behavior, while those who score highly on the measure of callousness are not so impacted by their violent behavior or its effects on others.

Callousness has also been related to an increased risk of predatory aggression (Fanti, Frick, & Georgiou, 2009; Gupta, 2008). Psychopathy in general has also been related to some of the most violent and pathological forms of aggression, including homicides that are marked by gratuitous and sadistic forms of violence (Porter, Woodworth, Earle, Drugge, & Boer, 2003; Shipley & Arrigo, 2001, 2008). It has also been noted that approximately 30% of male homicide offenders and fewer than 10% of female homicide offenders are psychopathic (Weizmann-Henelius et al., 2010). Such findings suggest that the presence and severity of predatory aggression is related to and produced by psychopathic traits, particularly emotional callousness.

Although the terms are not synonymous, it has been noted that psychopathy and predatory aggression share many similar features: both are associated with behavioral attitudes and styles that are cold, emotionally shallow, self-motivated, and reward-driven (Fontaine, 2007). Additionally, it has been shown that inmates incarcerated for predatory acts of violence were more psychopathic than both violent affective offenders and nonviolent offenders (Cornell et al., 1996). Psychopaths exhibit cognitive deficits, particularly in information processing (Newman, 1998), and demonstrate personality attributes to include antagonism (Skeem, Miller, Mulvey,

Tiemann, & Monahan, 2005). Recent evidence also indicates the presence of abnormalities in the neural mechanisms of psychopaths that are related to the following: moral cognitive development, making appropriate moral distinctions in one's behavioral judgments, inhibiting violent impulses, and having the ability to take the perspective of others (Blair, 2001; Blair, 2005). Although these traits are intuitively and conceptually related to predatory, rather than affective aggression, other traits of psychopathy, such as impulsivity, may also make these individuals prone to affective aggression (Vitacco & Rogers, 2001). Indeed, recent laboratory findings have indicated that, regardless of whether there is external motivation, traits associated with Hare's Factor 1 place individuals at higher risk for aggression, suggesting a relationship between these traits and predatory aggression. Traits associated with Factor 2, however, only increase an individual's risk for (affective) violence in situations where the traits are "activated" by some form of provocation (Reidy et al., 2007, p. 1249).

The relationship between psychopathy and antisocial personality has also been extensively studied, as these concepts exhibit considerable overlap, and both are connected to aggressive behavior (Arrigo & Shipley, 2001; Shipley & Arrigo, 2001, 2004, 2011). According to the DSM-IV-TR, antisocial personality disorder is characterized by a failure to conform to the laws and social norms of society, frequent use of deception, impulsivity, irritability and aggressiveness, reckless disregard for the safety of self and/or others, consistent irresponsibility, and a lack of remorse (American Psychiatric Association, 2000). Although psychopaths may also demonstrate these traits, they are better described as "remorseless predators who use charm, intimidation, and, if necessary, impulsive and cold-blooded violence to attain their ends" (Hare, 1996, p. 39). According to a study by Woodworth and Porter in 2002, 15% to 25% of the U.S. offender population is psychopathic; although most of these individuals will meet criteria for antisocial personality disorder, most individuals with antisocial personality disorder are not psychopaths (Skilling et al., 2002). Thus, while the constructs may overlap, the terms should not be used synonymously (though they often are); and the types of aggressive acts exhibited by the two groups may differ qualitatively and quantitatively, with varying implications for predictions of future acts of violence (Arrigo & Shipley, 2001; Shipley & Arrigo, 2001, 2004).

Sadism and Aggression

The relationship between sadism and aggression has also been the focus of recent research. Sadism has been defined as "cognitions and behaviors associated with the derivation of pleasure from inflicting physical or emotional pain on another person" (Porter & Woodworth, 2006, p. 486), and may explain seemingly unprovoked acts of aggression, as, in sadistic individuals, the motivating may be the pursuit of intrinsic pleasure from behaving aggressively. As with other constructs previously discussed, evidence suggests that sadism and psychopathy overlap (Holt, Meloy, & Strack, 1999; Meloy, 2000a; Shipley & Arrigo, 2008, 2011). Moreover, among murderers, those identified as psychopaths evidenced more extreme and sadistic acts of violence while carrying out their crimes than non-psychopaths (Porter et al., 2003). Conceptually, sadism is more extreme than psychopathy, but both are along the same continuum of malignant, destructive, and violent personalities. For example, sadists are psychopathic, but not all psychopaths are sadists. Psychopaths may be extremely violent as a means to an end without guilt or remorse; however, sadists are aroused and derive pleasure from the actual suffering of the victim. They savor this experience; the torture of the victim is the means to the end, which is the pain, either emotional or physical, of that victim. Both can be exceptionally predatory in their violence toward others.

A 2011 study by Reidy, Zeichner, and Siebert found that, although Factor 1 traits and sadism were both associated with increased risk for unprovoked violence, psychopathy and sadism were not significantly correlated in a sample of college students. These results, while inconsistent with earlier research, may "suggest a nonlinear relationship causing the two variables [psychopathy and sadism] to demonstrate different relations in different populations. That is, sadism, like psychopathy, may be dimensional in nature but may only precipitate violence in populations of clinical psychopaths not present in [their] sample" (Reidy et al., 2011, p. 91). Thus, sadism, psychopathy, and violence, while they appear to be interconnected at this time, may only be connected in significant ways when clinical levels of psychopathy and sadism are present; this represents a small portion of even the violent offender population, and represents an area deserving of future study.

The distinction between predatory and affective forms of violence is also reflected in the typologies of serial rape and murder (Shipley & Arrigo, 2008). The distinction is, perhaps, most apparent in the contrast between the anger-retaliatory rapist and the anger-excitation rapist typologies originally identified by Hazelwood and Burgess (1987) (Shipley & Arrigo, 2008). These typologies classify rapists according to the behavioral, motivational, and personality features of serial rapists and are often utilized by law enforcement and investigative agencies to construct profiles of likely suspects. The behavioral and violence patterns of two of these types of serial rapists will be examined, as illustrative of the differences in types of aggression displayed by these individuals. The anger-retaliatory rapist is motivated by anger and rage to sexually offend, thus exhibiting affective aggression. The anger prompting the aggression is displayed by the brandishing of weapons such as knives and the projection of a macho façade (Shipley & Arrigo, 2008; Warren, Reboussin, Hazelwood, & Wright, 1991). The victims may be severely injured during the assault, which is not motivated by sadistic fantasies, but rather by views of women as dirty and those who are not to be trusted (National Center for Women and Policing, 2004; Shipley & Arrigo, 2008). This type of rapist may gain control over the victim by means of a blitz attack with a great deal of violence. Although the victim may not be the woman who originally prompted the anger, she becomes the target of the misplaced anger, nonetheless, and the attack becomes a representative expression of punishment of and disdain for all women (Shipley & Arrigo, 2008; Warren et al., 1991). Thus, the anger-retaliatory rapist's methods epitomize affective aggression.

The actions of the anger-excitation rapist or the sadistic rapist, on the other hand, are examples of predatory aggression (Shipley & Arrigo, 2008). This type of rapist incorporates sadistic behavior into his attacks and gleans pleasure via the pain and suffering inflicted on victim(s) (Shipley & Arrigo, 2008). He may maintain a detached interaction with his victim(s) by binding and transporting them, or terrorizing them by telling them the ways in which he plans to harm him before doing so (Shipley & Arrigo, 2008; Warren et al., 1991). The attacks are typically well planned and orchestrated, and may involve weapons of restraint and torture. The rapist is sexually gratified not by the act of sex itself, but by his victim's experience of physical and emotional suffering (Shipley & Arrigo, 2008; Warren et al., 1991). Victims may be lured by this rapist via verbal strategies designed to elicit confidence from and access to the victim. In contrast to the reactive and affective violence exhibited by the anger-retaliatory rapist, this rapist engages in acts of predatory violence (Shipley & Arrigo, 2008).

Affective Aggression: Research Findings

Affective aggression, as the most common form of aggression, and its correlates have been extensively studied. This type of aggression is characterized by sudden, significant increases in sympathetic activation, impulsivity, and lack of cortical activation (Siegel & Victoroff, 2009). Additionally, the target of such violence is typically not specific, and may be displaced to others within the environment, and such rage is designed to reduce or eliminate a threatening stimulus and reduce the tension experienced by the aggressor (Siegel & Victoroff, 2009). In comparison to predatory aggression, reactive aggression exhibits a stronger relationship to a history of physical abuse, early onset of symptoms, problems with attention and impulsivity, hostile attribution to peers, and poor social problem-solving skills (Crick & Dodge, 1996; Day, Bream, & Pal, 1992). Further, individuals who exhibit affective aggression are less likely to exhibit unprovoked aggression and, when provoked, are less violent than those who exhibit predatory aggression (Reidy et al., 2011).

Much research has focused on cognitive and attributional errors made by individuals who exhibit affective aggression. For example, it has been noted that adolescents who display affective aggression have perceptual biases in how they encode environmental cues and attributional biases in the interpretation of those cues in social situations (Fontaine, 2007). Specifically, these adolescents tend to attribute hostility and harmful intent to situations and others, and tend to show greater difficulty in organizing and interpreting incoming social information relative to their peers (Fontaine, 2007). Such findings have implications for etiological theories, discussed below. Additionally, researchers have focused on psychosocial correlates of aggression in children, and have found that a majority (i.e., 55%) of children with disorganized attachment (i.e., an attachment style characterized by confusion, apprehension, disorientation, and feelings of both warmth toward and fear of the parent, typically associated with inconsistent parenting styles and strategies) as infants and who had a mother with psychological difficulties were affectively aggressive in kindergarten, compared with only 5% of students with neither risk factor (Lyons-Ruth & Jacobvitz, 1999).

With regard to affective aggression in inpatient settings, Vitacco and colleagues (2009) found that affective aggression was predicted by anger and mental health symptoms, as was verbal aggression. The authors noted that other findings (e.g., Doyle & Dolan, 2006a; Nolan et al., 2005) suggested that individuals with psychotic symptoms display difficulties with behavioral control, and this may explain the relationship between current symptoms and inpatient aggression. With regard to violent acts among inpatients, cluster analyses have revealed two "clusters" of aggression types—one associated with more goal-directed, planned, hidden, or controlled acts, and the other associated with impulsive, unplanned, overt, or uncontrolled aggression, suggesting that the predatory/affective distinction is an accurate reflection of violence displayed by psychiatric patients (Vitiello et al., 1990). Furthermore, it has been noted that affective aggressors typically have lower IQs, are more likely to be receiving neuroleptics (i.e., a class of antipsychotic medications with tranquilizing effects often used to manage psychosis) or lithium (i.e., a mood stabilizing drug often used in the treatment of bipolar), and to be diagnosed with schizophrenia (Vitiello et al., 1990).

Diversity Issues

Currently, the body of research regarding the applicability of the predatory/affective aggression model to various cultural groups is fairly limited. With regard to the relationship between gender and development of psychopathy, present literature indicates that experiencing physical abuse is associated with an increased risk of psychopathy for male, but not female, homicide offenders; while experiencing sexual abuse places female, but not male, homicide offenders at increased risk for psychopathy (Weizmann-Henelius et al., 2010). Research examining the relationship between cognitive errors (i.e., distortions in thinking, such as over- or under-generalization, which often result in perceptual distortion, inaccurate judgment, or illogical interpretation) and affective aggression has yielded mixed results, although overall, the research in this area suggests a small but significant relationship between intent attributions and relational aggression in males, but not females (Nelson, Mitchell, & Yang, 2008). With regard to the construct of callousness, this personality trait predicts juvenile aggression in females (Frick et al., 2003), while sensitivity to rejection is predictive of violence for both genders (Ayduk, Downey, & Testa, 1999; Downey, Feldman, & Ayduk, 2000). Finally, research has shown that the relationship between callousness and aggression holds true in a population from Cyprus, Greece (Fanti et al., 2009). In summary, existing research suggests that nuances are present in the applicability of the predatory/affective aggression model to various cultures and subgroups, as well as in the development of the related construct of psychopathy.

Etiological Theories

In determining the origins and causes of violent behavior within and between individuals, multiple factors must be considered, including the methods the aggressor utilizes in perpetrating violence, their criminal history, the use of fantasy, paraphilias, psychiatric illness, psychopathy, and the role of sadism (Shipley & Arrigo, 2008). Theories that explain the development and maintenance of violent behavior have existed for decades. Devising theories of violent behavior is a cumbersome and tedious process, as violent behavior within and across individuals is the result of multiple converging factors (Shipley & Arrigo, 2008). One of the earliest models, routine activities theory, posited that violent crime occurs when motivated offenders and suitable targets intersect spatially and temporally, in the absence of agents of control (Cohen & Felson, 1979). Since that time, research findings have encouraged and informed the development of more complex theories regarding aggressive behavior. Some of the more recent theories have focused on the development of antisocial personality disorder specifically, and research in this area has progressed from a primary focus on identifying environmental risk factors to elucidating the interaction of genetic and biological factors (e.g., specific neuroanatomical and physiological differences among members of this population) with environmental factors (Moffitt, 2005; Raine et al., 2005; Taylor, Iacono, & McGue, 2000). These findings, which will be summarized below, have led many researchers to propose biologically based theories of the development of aggression, antisocial personality disorder, and psychopathy. The policy implications of such proposals are discussed in the policy section that follows.

As research regarding the development and maintenance of violent behavior evolved, the distinct neural and physiological pathways responsible for the manifestation of predatory and affective violence have also been examined. Researchers have identified the medial hypothalamus or the dorsolateral region of the midbrain periaqueductal gray (PAG) as involved in the expression of affective aggression (Siegel, 2005; see also Siegel & Douard, 2011, for a review), while the perifornical lateral hypothalamus, ventral part of the PAG, and dopamine-producing ventral tegmental region of the midbrain are involved in the expression of predatory aggression (Siegel, 2005). Finally, damage to the limbic structures can interfere with an individual's ability to control both forms of aggressive behavior (Siegel & Victoroff, 2009). Brain abnormalities have been found in those with psychopathy; specifically, research has demonstrated that psychopaths have reduced amygdala volume (Tiihonen, Hodgins, & Vaurio, 2000), and that lesions to the medial orbitofrontal cortex can result in violent and psychopathic behavior in individuals who did not previously demonstrate such behaviors (Blair, 2003). Such findings may be related to observed deficits in psychopaths' ability to learn from punishment and aversive experiences, as well as their ability to experience a normal range of emotions involving fear or sadness, which would otherwise reduce their likelihood to engage in violent behavior (LaBrode, 2007).

In addition, researchers have examined differences in autonomic arousal for predatory and affective aggression. For example, affective aggression is associated with increased heart rate (Jacobsen & Gottman, 1998; Pitts, 1997), while predatory aggression is associated with decreased heart rate (Jacobsen & Gottman, 1998). Furthermore, elevated skin conductance (a measure of autonomic arousal) is associated with affective aggression, but not predatory aggression (Hubbard et al., 2002). Thus, research supports the notion that affective aggression is associated with hyperarousal, while predatory aggression is associated with hypoarousal (Haller & Kruk, 2006).

Research has also discovered differences in neurotransmitter activity; for example, decreased serotonergic function is related to affective, but not predatory aggression (Coccaro & Kavoussi, 1997; New et al., 2002). However, this relationship may be mediated by the ratio of testosterone (i.e., a steroid hormone associated with the development of male sex organs, growth of muscle mass, and display of aggression) to cortisol (i.e., a steroid hormone produced in response to stress) (van Honk, Harmon-Jones, Morgan, & Shutter, 2010). The relationship between serotonin levels and aggression has been demonstrated in experimental studies, suggesting a causal relationship between the two variables (see Siegel & Douard, 2011, for a review). Overall, these results lend support to the qualitative differences in predatory and affective aggression and have implications for the development of further theories regarding their development and treatment. Although any etiological theory must also consider psychological and environmental factors that affect the expression of aggression (Siegel & Douard, 2011).

In considering findings such as those described above, van Honk and Schutter (2005, 2006) examined the applicability of the Triple Balance Hypothesis (TBH) to affective aggression. According to the TBH, the well-being of social animals (e.g., humans) is contingent upon their ability to respond to environmental rewards and punishments in socially acceptable ways and to balance their responses between approach and withdrawal. Individuals who are able to select appropriately whether to approach or withdraw from a situation based on the likelihood of a positive or negative outcome to them are considered healthy, and such behavior is adaptive for both the individual and the species as a whole (Ressler, 2004). Many psychological disorders and difficulties, including the expression of extreme social aggression, can be conceptualized as pathological imbalances in emotional approach and withdrawal according to this framework (van Honk, Peper, & Schutter, 2005). Van Honk, et al. (2010) extended this model, identifying a Triple Imbalance Hypothesis (TIH) of affective aggression. According to the TIH, neurochemical changes in the brain (specifically the amygdala) can influence the way in which organisms perceive and act in the presence of social threat and can lead to exaggerated perceptions of hostility in others. These exaggerated perceptions often result in aggressive responses to social threats, which represent an unbalanced and, therefore, pathological selection of approach and withdrawal responses, leading to affective aggression (van Honk et al., 2010). The preemptive aggression, or the "I have to get you before you get me" perception of the world and explosive temper possessed by Aileen Wuornos, may have been influenced by this neurochemical process; although her environmental circumstances growing up also cannot be ignored.

Another biologically based theory that has been applied to the expression of violence is the opponent-process theory (Solomon & Corbit, 1974). As applied to predatory aggression and sadism in particular, this theory suggests that any person is capable of sadistic traits (Baumeister & Campbell, 1999). For example, a healthy individual will loathe inflicting harm to another person and will have a negative response if they engage in such an act. In response, the body will automatically produce an opponent process (i.e., an opposing emotion that occurs simultaneously with or directly following another emotion) to end the aversive experience and return to homeostasis; such a response is likely to have a positive quality, and the experience of such response is pleasurable to the organism. For example, a person learning to skydive may initially experience the activity as terrifying, which will activate an opponent process as the body seeks to return to its original, balanced state. This opponent process may be experienced by the individual as exhilaration or pleasure, and as the activity is continued, the positive emotions will become more intense while the initial negative emotion of fear will be suppressed, causing the overall experience of skydiving to become pleasurable. This same concept has been used to explain the development of aggressive behavior, as initially, the opponent process (of joy or pleasure in response to the initial experience of disdain, remorse, or regret) will be weak and slight but will increase with every act of violence, causing the overall quality of violent acts to be experienced as pleasurable. The authors acknowledge that very few individuals become sadists, and indicate that this is because the opponent process is typically moderated by guilt in healthy individuals, such that only those incapable of empathy and/or guilt (e.g., psychopaths) will go on to develop sadism from such a process (Baumeister & Campbell, 1999). As applied to serial murderers such as Aileen, this concept is demonstrated by the escalating patterns of violence and brutality often displayed over time; without the intervening process of guilt or remorse, the intensity of the pleasure experienced from violent acts continues to increase, leading to further and more sadistic acts.

In addition to research investigating the biological correlates of aggression, other research has examined cognitive processes that may predispose individuals to aggressive acts. Recent findings indicate that children who frequently exhibit affective aggression have difficulty understanding the needs, beliefs, and desires of others and, consequently, make attributional errors when evaluating the motives and intents of others (Arsenio, 2006). In contrast, children who exhibit predatory aggression do not typically make such errors, but are nevertheless prone to violent behavior. Therefore, "although they are less likely to engage in 'misfired' aggression, their lack of emotional responsiveness to victims makes it easier for them to use aggression instrumentally and to feel emotionally positive about the resulting physical and psychological gains" (Arsenio, 2006, p. 113). Aileen Wuornos appeared to engage in instances of "misfired" aggression that resulted in bar fights and the like, but these instances of aggression were often committed by a very intoxicated Aileen. However, when examining carefully the available evidence surrounding her homicides, it becomes apparent that they were carried out in a calculated fashion, without empathy during or after the attacks for the victims, and with positive feelings about the monetary gain and the omnipotent power she felt over those men (Shipley & Arrigo, 2004). The aforementioned findings regarding cognitive processes that can potentially predispose individuals to aggressive acts have important implications for treatment and prevention efforts, and findings such as these have lent support to one of the preeminent theories of aggression, the social information processing (SIP) theory.

According to the SIP theory, information regarding social situations is processed in six steps: (1) the person attends to and organizes information about the cue via encoding; (2) the person ascribes attributions of intent and causality to the stimulus via interpretation of the cues; (3) the person addresses his or her interests in the situation at hand via clarification of goals; (4) the person identifies possible ways of responding to the cue, either by constructing new ones or by drawing on memories of past similar situations—a process known as response access or construction; (5) the responder evaluates and compares these response options by making judgments of response efficacy, response valuation, and outcome expectancy—a process called response evaluation and decision; and finally, (6) the individual selects a way of responding and behaviorally enacts it (Crick & Dodge, 1994). It has been proposed that the first two steps are related to affective aggression; while the latter four steps, which are more complicated, are related to predatory aggression (Fontaine,

2007, 2008), and such hypotheses are supported by literature examining the cognitive processes of individuals who exhibit both types of aggression (see Fontaine, 2008, for review). For example, when Aileen assaulted the owner of a bar who had closed her pool table due to her aggressive and disruptive behavior, she likely made cognitive misappraisals (e.g., she may have believed that she was being physically threatened when she was not, etc.), which led to disproportionate and inappropriate emotions, and, ultimately, to affective violence. Her murders, on the other hand, were the result of her pursuit of her own goals (e.g., stealing from the victims, revenge motives) to the detriment of others (as seen in step 3 of SIP), memories of her previous abuse (as in step 4), misappraisal of the likely outcome of the situation if she killed the victims (step 5), and, finally, lethal violence (step 6).

Treatment Implications

Studies have indicated that affective and predatory aggression have distinct underlying causal factors; therefore, researchers have recommended that distinct treatment approaches are warranted (Peters, 2010), and many challenges belie the effective treatment of such behavior. Much controversy exists in the literature regarding prognosis for each type of violent offender. Some researchers have suggested that, due to the underlying neurological mechanisms that are correlated with affective aggression, this type of aggression is less amenable to treatment; while others have suggested that the lack of moral judgment and capacity for empathy, which often characterizes predatory aggression, presents a greater treatment challenge (Fontaine, 2008). Such controversy is further complicated by the higher intercorrelations between the two types of violence, and, as is exemplified by Aileen's violent acts, very few individuals exhibit only one type of aggression (Fontaine, 2007).

The very different treatment courses typically undertaken with individuals engaging in each type of aggression make the treatment implications for someone who exhibits both patterns very difficult. Further, at least a subset of psychopathic predatory aggressors may be undeterred by punishment and may also be less likely candidates for successful rehabilitation (Fontaine, 2007; Shipley & Arrigo, 2004, 2011), as some of these individuals become more effective and prolific aggressors with treatment (Chakhssi, de Ruiter, & Bernstein, 2010; Harris, Rice, & Cormier, 1994; Rice, 1997), which further complicates the development and implementation of effective treatment efforts. In light of these findings, it is recommended that cognitive behavioral treatments that might otherwise include an empathy development component not include such a module when applied to psychopaths, but rather focus on the development of appropriate attributional styles (e.g., teaching offenders to accept sole responsibility for their actions rather than blaming victims), as well as expanding the behavioral repertoire of these individuals to include more prosocial methods (Jeglic et al., 2011).

One model of treatment, which has been applied with some success, is the risk-need-responsivity (RNR) model (Andrews, Bonta, & Hoge, 1990). According to this model, correctional interventions must be structured on three core principles: risk, need, and responsivity. The risk prong refers to the idea that offender treatments must be dynamic, and become increasingly more intense as the offender's risk to the community increases. According to the needs principle, the offender's criminogenic needs and dynamic risk factors; and according to the responsivity principle, therapies must match an offender's learning style, motivation level, and cultural background (Andrews & Bonta, 1998; Ward, Vess, & Collie, 2006). Further, it has been noted that for violent offenders, the effectiveness of any treatment program must be evaluated in terms of rates of violent recidivism post treatment (Jeglic et al., 2011). The effectiveness of treatment programs based on this model has been demonstrated in both community and residential programs (Andrews & Bonta, 2006). Research evaluating the effectiveness of treatments based on this model has indicated that interventions that incorporate cognitive-behavioral and social learning techniques embedded in a relapse prevention framework were effective in reducing the rates of high-risk offender recidivism at two year follow-up (Di Placido, Simon, Witte, Gu, & Wong, 2005; Fylan & Clarke, 2006; Wong, Gordon, & Gu, 2007); such findings have also been replicated with violent sex offenders (Hanson, 2000; Hanson, Bourgon, Helmus, & Hodgson, 2009; Nicholaichuk, Gordon, Deqiang, & Wong, 2000; Scalora & Garbin, 2003). Specifically, treated offenders demonstrated a significant reduction in serious institutional infractions and a decrease in commission of serious violent offenses after release, and modest gains were found even for offenders with high levels of psychopathy. Although treatment did not significantly reduce their overall rates of recidivism or the frequency of reoffense in psychopathic offenders, the severity of violent reoffenses was significantly reduced.

Although treatment of these issues is rife with challenges, and historical data have been somewhat discouraging, particularly with regard to the treatment of psychopathic violent offenders, limited current research is elucidating treatment models that may be effective with his notoriously challenging population. Considerable caution is still warranted, as evidence remains that some offenders will be made worse by treatment. While some suggest targeted approaches as described above, others stress environmental management (when in an institutional setting) and against traditional forms of treatment being effective. The treatment provider not only must determine not only if there is any potential benefit of the treatment, but also has to weigh any potential harm to include the likelihood of others in a group therapy setting being manipulated or exploited by the psychopathic individual as a result of the information shared.

Criticisms of Predatory/Affective Model

Several criticisms of the predatory/affective model have been levied by researchers. For example, some have noted that the distinction between predatory and affective aggression is not applicable to the American justice system, as: (1) there is an overall movement away from discerning levels of violence, including homicide, as many jurisdictions are considering doing away with the classifications associated with homicide (e.g., first/second-degree murder, manslaughter, etc.), and (2) unlike in psychology, motive is not typically a factor in distinguishing predatory and affective violence within legal settings (Bushman & Anderson, 2001). Additionally, the high correlations between the two forms of violence within and between individuals have led to criticism that the constructs are not truly distinct (Polman, Orobio de Castro, Koops, van Boxtel, & Merk, 2007). It has also been noted that the model may be more applicable to children than to adults, who are more often the focus of treatment and assessment related to violent behavior (Nelson, Mitchell, & Yang, 2008). Finally, recent neurological data suggest that the relationship between automatic and conscious aspects of decision making is more interactive than dichotomous, lending support to criticisms of the model who maintain that the two types of aggression are more closely linked than the model implies (Siegel & Victoroff, 2009).

Forensic Psychology and Policy Implications

The research and findings discussed herein warrant several recommendations regarding public policy; however, the proper application of pertinent findings within our justice and mental health systems is often contentious. Fontaine (2007) offers disagreement with other theorists who have posited that those who engage in affective aggression are more impulsive, crueler, more ferocious, and more dangerous and should be punished more severely, stating that such views are inconsistent with the principles of diminished capacity and penal proportionality. Thus, Fontaine (2007) recommends the retention of the murder/manslaughter distinctions, as the components of these two crimes have implications for the culpability and future dangerousness of the respective offenders. Such distinctions and how they are viewed by society are reflected in the severity of punishments given to Aileen Wuornos—her acts of affective aggression were sometimes only punished with a monetary fine, while she received the ultimate penalty for her lethal and predatory acts of violence.

Fontaine (2007) goes on to acknowledge contemporary data suggesting that *at least* a subset of psychopaths who engage in predatory aggression do not respond well to treatment, and are not effectively deterred by the threat or application of punishment. Such findings, the author argues, have important implications for improving the treatment of affective versus predatory violent offenders. For example, Fontaine (2007) notes that separate housing for affective and predatory offenders with increased security for the latter may be indicated; although he acknowledges that any potential benefits from such intervention will likely not be maintained once the external contingencies of a maximum-security environment are removed. Siegel and Douard (2011) have argued that more thorough efforts should be made to evaluate the behavior of a violent offender in order to determine the degree of culpability for their actions, and whether or not they were capable of "consciously deciding not to perform an inappropriate act" (p. 28).

Alternatively, Green and Cohen (2004) have offered what constitutes perhaps one of the most extreme and controversial positions on the issue of free will, determinism, and their relationship to violent and aggressive behavior. They argued that, in light of the findings delineating neurological and physiological abnormalities in those who engage in predatory and affective aggression, the current emphasis in our justice system on levels of culpability and responsibility needs to be abandoned altogether. In other words, if violent behavior can be linked to neuroanatomical or physiological defects over which an aggressor has little or no control, the rehabilitative and retributive purposes of punishment (those more closely associated with culpability and responsibility) should not be considered, though society's need for revenge, deterrence, and incapacitation could still be addressed and considered when determining sentencing (Green & Cohen, 2004). Thus, the proper application of current research findings to and within our criminal justice system remains a controversial issue, even among experts. Whatever the appropriate application of the pertinent research, it is important that they be disseminated to triers of fact in ways that are understandable to a layperson so that decisions regarding culpability and punishment may be made in light of the most current and reliable research findings (Siegel & Victoroff, 2009).

With regard to treatment of violent offenders, some authors have posited that treatment is distinct from "all other forms of monitoring" in that it "prevents recidivism by making the offenders responsible for their own actions, providing them with the tools to restrain themselves from committing further crimes" (Jeglic et al., 2011, p. 59), emphasizing the importance of effective treatment efforts in protecting society and rehabilitating offenders. In a similar vein, other authors have noted that cognitive-behavioral techniques, which are the most promising interventions for aggression, need to be targeted specifically at children and adolescents most at risk for future violent behavior, and suggest that emerging biophysiological data could assist in early identification of these individuals even prior to their engagement in violent behavior (Peters, 2010). Specifically, given that individuals prone to aggression may make cognitive errors in appraising risk and threats, cognitive restructuring techniques may be particularly useful (Fontaine, 2008). Further, given findings that these errors are often the result of rapid processing of information without consideration of other alternatives, treatment programs may also benefit from components that assist offenders in increasing the amount of time they allow themselves to process perceived threats, slights, or insults (Fontaine, 2008), and to assist them in altering underlying deficits in social reasoning (Arsenio, 2006). Such efforts will require an interdisciplinary and comprehensive assessment and treatment approach. Moreover, moral, ethical, and legal conflicts that could arise from the development of such information must be handled judiciously and with respect for the civil liberties of those who have not engaged in violent behavior but may be at high risk for such behavior in the future (Peters, 2010).

Another area of recent controversy has surrounded findings that psychopathic patients either deteriorate or remain unchanged when provided with traditional treatments aimed at reducing their violence, and such treatment should therefore be withheld (D'Silva, Duggan, & McCarthy, 2004; Olver & Wong, 2009; Salekin, 2002; Skeem, 2008; Skeem, Monahan, & Mulvey, 2002). However, Chakhssi, de Ruiter, and Bernstein (2010) have more recently found that such patients represent a minority of psychopathic patients and have subsequently recommended that efforts be made to further elucidate which psychopathic patients are most likely to benefit from treatment so that "treatment decisions can be made on an empirically supported and cost-effective basis" (p. 678), and have noted that "at this time, the blanket decision to withhold treatment from psychopathic patients in general does not seems to be supported by research findings" (p. 678).

With regard to violent risk assessment, it has been noted by Vitacco and colleagues (2009) that psychopathy is related to future aggression in inpatient settings, and that both static and dynamic factors should be utilized when attempting to predict inpatient aggression. These authors indicate that the presence of psychopathic traits may increase a person's basic propensity to use aggression instrumentally, but that propensity may be activated by other dynamic factors, as in the case of Aileen Wuornos (e.g., perception of threat, substance abuse). Such factors may assist mental health professionals in identifying periods during which risk for violence may be particularly high in a population that is at chronically high risk for violence.

Suggestions for Future Research

Several areas warrant the ongoing investigation of predatory and affective aggression. Specifically, future efforts should include longitudinal studies of predatory and affective aggression in order to determine if there are any significant changes over time in how an individual manifests aggression. According to Fontaine (2007), although it has been determined that aggression in general is a stable phenomenon, the stability of each of these types of aggression over time is less clear. Additionally, further clarification is needed regarding the complex nature of the relationships among personality features, types of aggression and violence, and the strength of the relationship between history of animal cruelty and interpersonal violence inflicted on humans (Gupta, 2008). Future studies should investigate gender differences in exposure to serious traumatic experiences and the relationship to psychopathy. Aileen Wuornos's case demonstrates the devastating impact that a combination of biological and environmental factors can have on the development of lethal aggression. These studies may reveal important information regarding factors that may reduce the likelihood of the development of psychopathy, despite exposure to historical factors associated with such a personality style (Weizmann-Henelius et al., 2010). The applicability of this model to various cultural groups (e.g., gender, race, age, countries of origin, etc.) is an area deserving of further elucidation. In addition, future research should examine the relationships between psychopathy and other personality factors (e.g., neuroticism, antagonism) and ecological determinants as risk factors for aggression and violence (Reidy et al., 2007). Moreover, in order to assist in early detection and intervention efforts, future researchers should examine the relationship between attachment, temperamental fearlessness, and callousness as well as the relationship these variables may have to instrumental or predatory aggression (Arsenio, 2006).

With regard to the prediction of inpatient aggression, continued research into the development of appropriate assessment and intervention techniques designed for an inpatient population is needed. Specifically, the construction and validation of specialized instruments that could provide normative data regarding rates of predatory and affective aggression among various populations within an inpatient setting (e.g., psychopaths, psychotic patients, etc.) would be beneficial (Vitacco et al., 2009). Finally, in addition to the distinctions made by the predatory/affective model, future research should further divide these types of aggression into physical, verbal, and relational aggression (Fanti et al., 2009), and examine the relationship of various psychological factors (e.g., parenting style, cognitive errors) to these types of aggression (Nelson et al., 2008).

References

American Psychiatric Association (2000). *Diagnostic and statistical manual of mental disorders* (4th ed., rev.), Washington, DC: Author.

Andrews, D. A., & Bonta, J. (1998). *The psychology of criminal conduct* (2nd ed.). Cincinnati, OH: Anderson.

Andrews, D. A., & Bonta, J. (2006). *The psychology of criminal conduct* (4th ed.). Newark, NJ: LexisNexis.

Andrews, D. A., Bonta, J., & Hoge, R. (1990). Classification for effective rehabilitation: Rediscovering psychology. *Criminal Justice and Behavior, 17*(1), 19–52.

Arrigo, B. A., & Shipley, S. (2001). The confusion over psychopathy (I): Historical considerations. *International Journal of Offender Therapy and Comparative Criminology, 45*(3), 325–344.

Arsenio, W. F. (2006). Happy victimization: Emotion dysregulation in the context of instrumental, proactive Aggression. In D. Snyder, J. Simpson, & J. Hughes (Eds.), *Emotion regulation in families: Pathways to dysfunction and health* (pp. 101–121). Washington, DC: American Psychological Association.

Ayduk, O., Downey, G., & Testa, A. (1999). Does rejection elicit hostility in rejection sensitive women? *Social Cognition, 17*, 245–271.

Baumeister, R. F., & Campbell, W. K. (1999). The intrinsic appeal of evil: Sadism, sensational thrills, and threatened egotism. *Personality and Social Psychology Review, 3*, 210–221.

Blair, R. J. (2001). Neurocognitive models of aggression, the antisocial personality disorders, and psychopathy. *Journal of Neurology, Neurosurgery, and Psychiatry, 71*, 727–731.

Blair, R. J. (2003). Neurobiological bases for psychopathy. *British Journal of Psychiatry, 182*, 5–7.

Blair, R. J. R. (2005). Applying a cognitive neuroscience perspective to the disorder of psychopathy. *Development and Psychopathology, 17*, 865–891.

Bushman, B. J., & Anderson, C. A. (2001). Is it time to pull the plug on the hostile versus instrumental aggression dichotomy? *Psychological Review, 108*, 273–279.

Campbell, M., Adams, P. B., Small, A. M., Kafantaris, V., Silva, R. R., Shell, J., . . . Overall, J. E. (1995). Lithium in hospitalized aggressive children with conduct disorder: A double-blind and placebo-controlled study. *Journal of the American Academy of Child and Adolescent Psychiatry, 34*(4), 445–453.

Chakhssi, F., de Ruiter, C., & Bernstein, D. (2010). Change during forensic treatment in psychopathic versus nonpsychopathic offenders. *Journal of Forensic Psychiatry and Psychology, 21*(5), 660–682.

Cleckley, H. (1976). *The mask of sanity*. St. Louis, MO: Mosby. (Original work published 1941)

Coccaro, E. F., & Kavoussi, R. J. (1997). Fluoxetine and impulsive aggressive behavior in personality-disordered subjects. *Archives of General Psychiatry, 54*, 1081–1088.

Cohen, L. E., & Felson, M. (1979). Social change and crime rate trends: A routine activities approach. *American Sociological Review, 44*, 588–608.

Cornell, D. G., Warren, J., Hawk, G., Stafford, E., Oram, G., & Pine, D. (1996). Psychopathy in instrumental and reactive violent offenders. *Journal of Consulting and Clinical Psychology, 64*, 783–790.

Court TV (1999). *Damsel of death*. London: BCA.

Crick, N. R., & Dodge, K. A. (1994). A review and reformulation of social information processing mechanisms in children's social adjustment. *Psychological Bulletin, 115*, 74–101.

Crick, N. R., & Dodge, K. A. (1996). Social information-processing mechanisms in reactive and proactive aggression. *Child Development, 67*(3), 993–1002.

Day, D. M., Bream, L. A., & Pal, A. (1992). Proactive and reactive aggression: An analysis of subtypes based on teacher perceptions. *Journal of Clinical Child Psychology, 21*(3), 210–217.

Di Placido, C., Simon, T., Witte, T., Gu, D., & Wong, S. C. P. (2006). Treatment of gang members can reduce recidivism and institutional misconduct. *Law and Human Behavior, 30*(1), 93–114.

Downey, G., Feldman, S., & Ayduk, O. (2000). Rejection sensitivity and male violence in romantic relationships. *Personal Relationships, 7*, 45–61.

Doyle, M., & Dolan, M. (2006a). Evaluating the validity of anger regulation problems, interpersonal style, and disturbed mental state for predicting inpatient violence. *Behavioral Sciences and the Law, 24*, 783–798.

Doyle, M., & Dolan, M. (2006b). Predicting community violence from patients discharged from mental health services. *British Journal of Psychiatry, 189*, 520–526.

D'Silva, K., Duggan, C., & McCarthy, L. (2004). Does treatment really make psychopaths worse? A review of the evidence. *Journal of Personality Disorders, 18*, 163–177.

Edens, J. F., Marcus, D., Lilienfeld, S. O., & Poythress, N. G. (2006). Psychopathic, not psychopath: Taxometric evidence for the dimensional structure of psychopathy. *Journal of Abnormal Psychology, 115*, 131–144.

Edens, J. F., Skeem, J. L., & Douglas, K. S. (2006). Incremental validity analyses of the Violence Risk Appraisal Guide and the Psychopathy Screening Checklist: Screening Version in a civil psychiatric sample. *Assessment, 13*(3), 368–374.

Eichelman, B. (1987). Neurochemical and psychopharmacological aspects of aggressive behavior. In H. Y. Meltzer (Ed.), *Psychopharmacology: The third generation of progress* (pp. 697–704). New York: Raven.

Enebrink, P., Andershed, H., & Langstrom, N. (2005). Callous-unemotional traits are associated with clinical severity in referred boys with conduct problems. *Nordic Journal of Psychiatry, 59*, 431–440.

Fanti, K. A., Frick, P. J., & Georgiou, S. (2009). Linking callous-unemotional traits to instrumental and non-instrumental forms of aggression. *Journal of Psychopathology and Behavior Assessment, 31*, 285–298.

Fontaine, R. G. (2007). Disentangling the psychology and law of instrumental and reactive subtypes of aggression. *Psychology, Public Policy, and Law, 13*(2), 143–165.

Fontaine, R. G. (2008). Reactive cognition, reactive emotion: Toward a more psychologically-informed understanding of reactive homicide. *Psychology, Public Policy, and Law, 14*(4), 243–261.

Frick, P. J., Cornell, A. H., Barry, C. T., Bodin, S. D., & Dane, H. E. (2003). Callous-unemotional traits and conduct problems in the prediction of conduct problem severity, aggression, and self-report of delinquency. *Journal of Abnormal Child Psychology, 31*(4), 457–470.

Fylan, F., & Clarke, J. (2006). *Violence reduction strategy*. York, UK: Her Majesty's Prison Full Sutton.

Green, J., & Cohen, J. (2004). For the law, neuroscience changes nothing and everything. *Philosophical Transactions of the Royal Society of London, B*, 1775–1785.

Guay, J. P., Ruscio, J., Knight, R. A., & Hare, R. D. (2007). A taxometric analysis of the latent structure of psychopathy: Evidence of dimensionality. *Journal of Abnormal Psychology, 116*, 101–116.

Gupta, M. (2008). Functional links between intimate partner violence and animal abuse: Personality features and representations of aggression. *Society and Animals, 16*, 233–242.

Haller, J., & Kruk, M. R. (2006). Normal and abnormal aggression: Human disorders and novel laboratory models. *Neuroscience and Biobehavioral Reviews, 30*, 292–303.

Hanson, R. K. (2000). What is so special about relapse prevention? In D. R. Laws, S. M. Hudson, & T. Ward (Eds.), *Remaking relapse prevention with sex offenders* (pp. 27–38). Thousand Oaks, CA: Sage.

Hanson, R. K., Bourgon, G., Helmus, L., & Hodgson, S. (2009). *A meta-analysis of the effectiveness of treatment for sexual offenders: Risk, need, and responsivity*. Corrections research user report no. 2009-01. Ottawa: Public Safety Canada.

Hare, R. D. (1991). *The Hare Psychopathy Checklist–Revised.* Toronto, Ontario, Canada: Multi-Health Systems.

Hare, R.D. (1996). Psychopathy and antisocial personality disorder: A case of diagnostic confusion. *Psychiatric Times, 13*(2), 39–40.

Hare, R. D. (2003). The Hare Psychopathy Checklist–Revised (PCL-R; 2nd ed.). Toronto, Ontario, Canada: Multi-Health Systems.

Hare, R. D., & Neumann, C. S. (2008). Psychopathic traits in a large community sample: Links to violence, alcohol use, and intelligence. *Journal of Consulting and Clinical Psychology, 76*(5), 893–899.

Harris, G. T., Rice, M. E., & Cormier, C. A. (1994). Psychopaths: Is a therapeutic community therapeutic? *Therapeutic Communities, 15*, 283–289.

Harris, G. T., Rice, M. E., & Quinsey, V. L. (1993). Violent recidivism of mentally disordered offenders: The development of a statistical prediction instrument. *Criminal Justice and Behavior, 20*, 315–335.

Hart, S. D., Hare, R. D., & Forth, A. E. (1994). Psychopathy as a risk marker for violence: Development and validation of a screening version of the Revised Psychopathy Checklist. In J. Monahan and H. Steadman (Eds.), *Violence and mental disorder: Developments in risk assessment* (pp. 81–98). Chicago, IL: University of Chicago Press.

Hazelwood, R. & Burgess, A. (1987). Practical Aspects of Rape Investigation: a Multidisciplinary Approach. New York: Elsevier.

Holt, S. E., Meloy, J. R., & Strack, S. (1999). Sadism and psychopathy in violent and sexually violent offenders. *Journal of the American Academy of Psychiatry and the Law, 27*, 23–32.

Hubbard, J. A., Smithmyer, C. M., Ramsden, S. R., Parker, E. H., Flanagan, K. D., Dearing, K. F., . . . Simons, R. F. (2002). Observational, physiological, and self-report measures of children's anger: Relations to reactive versus proactive aggression. *Child Development, 73*, 1101–1118.

Jacobsen, N. S., & Gottman, J. M. (1998). *When men batter women: New insights into ending abusive relationships.* New York: Simon & Schuster.

Jeglic, E. L., Maile, C., & Calkins-Mercado, C. (2011). Treatment of offender populations: Implications for risk management and community reintegration. In G. Lior & S. Hung-En (Eds.), *Rethinking corrections: Rehabilitation, reentry, and reintegration.* Thousand Oaks, CA: Sage Publications.

Kempes, M., Matthys, W., de Vries, H., & van Engeland, H. (2005). Reactive and proactive aggression in children: A review of theory, findings, and the relevance of child and adolescent psychiatry. *European Child and Adolescent Psychiatry, 14*, 11–19.

Kruh, I. P., Frick, P. J., & Clements, C. B. (2005). Historical and personality correlates to the violence patterns of juveniles tried as adults. *Criminal Justice and Behavior, 32*(1), 69–96.

LaBrode, R. T. (2007). Etiology of the psychopathic serial killer: An analysis of antisocial personality disorder, psychopathy, and serial killer personality and crime scene characteristics. *Brief Treatment and Crisis Intervention, 7*(2), 151–160.

Lyons-Ruth, K., & Jacobvitz, D. (1999). Attachment disorganization: unresolved loss, relational, violence, and lapses in behavioral and attentional strategies. In J. Cassidy & P. Shaver (Eds.), *Handbook of attachment: Theory, research, and clinical applications* (pp. 520–534). New York: Guilford Press.

Marcus, D. K., John, S. L. & Edens, J. F. (2004). A Taxometric Analysis of Psychopathic Personality. *Journal of Abnormal Psychology, 113*, 626–635.

Meloy, J. R. (1988). *The psychopathic mind: Origins, dynamics, and treatment*. Northvale, NJ: Jason Aronson.

Meloy, J. R. (2000a). The nature and dynamics of sexual homicide: An integrative review. *Aggression and Violent Behavior, 5*, 1–22.

Meloy, J. R. (2000b). *Violence risk and threat assessment: A practical guide for mental health and criminal justice professionals*. San Diego, CA: Specialized Training Services.

Miller, J. D., & Lynam, D. R. (2003). Psychopathy and the five-factor model of personality: A replication and extension. *Journal of Personality Assessment, 81*, 168–178.

Moffitt, T. E. (2005). The new book of behavioral genetics on developmental psychology: Gene-environment interplay in antisocial behaviors. *Psychological Bulletin, 131*, 533–535.

Murrie, D. C., Marcus, D. K., Douglas, K. S., Lee, Z., Salekin, R. T., & Vincent, G. (2007). Youth with psychopathic features are not a discrete class: A taxometric analysis. *Journal of Child Psychology and Psychiatry, 48*, 714–723.

Nelson, D. A., Mitchell, C., & Yang, C. (2008). Intent attributions and aggression: A study of children and their parents. *Abnormal Child Psychology, 36*, 793–806.

New, A. S., Hazlett, A. E., Buchsbaum, M. S., Goodman, M., Reynolds, D., Mitropoulou, V., . . . Siever, L. J. (2002), Blunted prefrontal cortical 18fluorodeoxyglucose positron emission tomography response to metha-chlorophenylpiperazine in impulsive aggression. *Archives of General Psychiatry, 59*, 621–629.

Newman, J. P. (1998). Psychopathic behavior: An information processing perspective. In D. J. Cook, R. D. Hare, & A. Forth (Eds.), *Psychopathy: Theory, research, and implications for society*. (pp. 81–104). Dordrecht, the Netherlands: Kluwer Academic.

Nicholaichuk, T., Gordon, A., Deqiang, G., & Wong, S. (2000). Outcome of an institutional sexual offender treatment program: A comparison between treated and matched untreated offenders. *Sexual Abuse: A Journal of Research and Treatment, 12*, 139–154.

Nolan, K. A., Volavka, J., Czobor, P., Sheitman, B., Lindenmayer, J., Citrome, L. L., . . . Lieberman, J. A. (2005). Aggression and psychopathology in treatment-resistant inpatients with schizophrenia and schizoaffective disorder. *Journal of Psychiatric Research, 39*, 109–115.

Olver, M. E, & Wong, S. (2009). Therapeutic responses of psychopathic sexual offenders: Treatment attrition, therapeutic change, and long-term recidivism. *Journal of Consulting and Clinical Psychology, 77*, 328–336.

Parrott, D. J., & Zeichner, A. (2006). Effect of psychopathy on physical aggression toward gay men. *Journal of Interpersonal Violence, 21*, 390–410.

Peters, T. O. (2010). Causes and incidents of rape among middle aged and young adult in Lagos State, Nigeria. *Research Journal of Biological Sciences, 5*(10), 670–677.

Pitts, T. B. (1997). Reduced heart rate levels in aggressive children. In A. Raine, P. A. Brennan, D. P. Farrington, & S. A. Mednick (Eds.), *Biosocial bases of violence* (pp. 317–320). New York: Plenum Press.

Polman, H., Orobio de Castro, B., Koops, W. van Boxtel, H. W., & Merk, W. W. (2007). A meta-analysis of the distinction between reactive and proactive aggression in children and adolescents. *Journal of Abnormal Child Psychology, 35*(4), 522–535.

Porter, S., & Woodworth, M. (2006). Psychopathy and aggression. In C. J. Patrick (Ed.), *Handbook of psychopathy* (pp. 481–494). New York: Guilford Press.

Porter, S., Woodworth, M., Earle, J., Drugge, J., & Boer, D. (2003). Characteristics of sexual homicides committed by psychopathic and nonpsychopathic offenders. *Law and Human Behavior, 27*, 459–470.

Raine, R., Moffitt, T. E., Caspi, A., Loeber, R., Stouthamer-Loeber, M., & Lynam, D. (2005). Neurocognitive impairments in boys on the life-course persistent antisocial path. *Journal of Abnormal Psychology, 114*, 38–49, 54.

Reidy, D. E., Zeichner, A., Miller, J. D., & Martinez, M. A. (2007). Psychopathy and aggression: Examining the role of psychopathy factors in predicting laboratory aggression under hostile and instrumental conditions. *Journal of Research in Personality, 41*, 1244–1251.

Reidy, D. E., Zeichner, A., & Seibert, L. A. (2011). Unprovoked aggression: Effects of psychopathic traits and sadism. *Journal of Personality 79*(1), 75–100.

Ressler, N. (2004). Rewards and punishments, goal directed behavior and consciousness. *Neuroscience and Biobehavioral Reviews, 28*, 27–39.

Rice, M. E. (1997). Violent offender research and implications for the criminal justice system. *American Psychologist, 52*, 414–423.

Salekin, R. T. (2002). Psychopathy and therapeutic pessimism: Clinical lore or clinical reality? *Clinical Psychology Review, 22*, 79–112.

Scalora, M. J., & Garbin, C. (2003). A multivariate analysis of sex offender recidivism. *International Journal of Offender Therapy and Comparative Criminology, 47* (3), 309–323.

Shipley, S., & Arrigo, B. A. (2001). The confusion over psychopathy (II): Implications for forensic (correctional) practice. *International Journal of Offender Therapy and Comparative Criminology, 45*(4), 407–420.

Shipley, S. L., & Arrigo, B. A. (2004). *The female homicide offender: Serial murder and the case of Aileen Wuornos*. Upper Saddle River, NJ: Pearson Education, Inc.

Shipley, S. L., & Arrigo, B. A. (2008). Serial killers and serial rapists: Preliminary comparison of violence typologies. In R. N. Kocsis (Ed.), *Serial murder and the psychology of violent crimes*. Totowa, NJ: Humana Press.

Shipley, S. L., & Arrigo, B. A. (2011). Sexual offenses against adults. In P. S. Sturmey & M. McMurran (Eds.). *Forensic case formulation*. West Sussex, UK: John Wiley & Sons.

Siegel, A. (2005). *The neurobiology of aggression and rage*. Boca Raton, FL: CRC Press.

Siegel, A., & Douard, J. (2011). Who's flying the plan: Serotonin levels, aggression, and free will. *International Journal of Law and Psychiatry, 34*, 20–29.

Siegel, A., & Pott, C. B. (1988). Neural substrates of aggression and flight in the cat. *Progressive Neurobiology, 31*, 261–283.

Siegel, A., & Victoroff, J. (2009). Understanding human aggression: New insights from neuroscience. *International Journal of Law and Psychiatry, 32*, 209–215.

Skeem, J. L. (2008, July). *High risk, not hopeless: Recent research on treating individuals with psychopathy*. Paper presented at the annual meeting of the International Association of Forensic Mental Health, Vienna, Austria.

Skeem, J. L., Miller, J. D., Mulvey, E., Tiemann, J., & Monahan, J. (2005). Using a five factor lens to explore the relation between personality traits and violence in psychiatric patients. *Journal of Consulting and Clinical Psychology, 73*, 455–465.

Skeem, J. L., Monahan, J., & Mulvey, E. (2002). Psychopathy, treatment involvement, and subsequent violence among civil psychiatric patients. *Law and Human Behavior, 26*, 577–603.

Skeem, J. L., & Mulvey, E. P. (2001). Psychopathy and community violence among civil psychiatric patients: Results from the MacArthur violence risk assessment study. *Journal of Consulting and Clinical Psychology, 69*, 358–374.

Skilling, T. A., Harris, G. T., Rice, M. E., & Quinsey, V. L. (2002). Identifying persistently antisocial Offenders using the Hare Psychopathy Checklist and DSM antisocial personality disorder criteria. *Psychological Assessment, 14*, 27–38.

Solomon, R. L., & Corbit, J. D. (1974). An opponent-process theory of motivation: I. Temporal dynamics of affect. *Psychological Review, 81*, 119–145.

Stadtland, C., Kleindienst, N., Kroner, C., Eidt, M., & Nedopil, N. (2005). Psychopathic traits and risk of criminal recidivism in offenders with and without mental disorders. *International Journal of Forensic Mental Health, 4*(1), 89–97.

Taylor, J., Iacono, W. G., & McGue, M. (2000). Evidence for a genetic etiology of early-onset delinquency. *Journal of Abnormal Psychology, 109*, 634–643.

Tiihonen, J., Hodgins, S., & Vaurio, O. (2000). Amygdaloid volume loss in psychopathy. *Society for Neuroscience Abstracts*, 2017.

van Honk, J., Harmon-Jones, E., Morgan, B. E., & Schutter, D. J. L. G. (2010). Social explosive minds: The triple imbalance hypothesis of reactive aggression. *Journal of Personality, 78*(1), 67–94.

van Honk, J., Peper, J. S., & Schutter, D. J. L. G. (2005). Testosterone reduces unconscious fear but not consciously experienced anxiety. *Biological Psychiatry, 58*, 218–225.

van Honk, J., & Schutter, D. J. L. G. (2006). Unmasking feigned sanity: A neurobiological model of emotion processing primary psychopathy. *Cognitive Neuropsychiatry, 11*, 285–306.

Vitacco, M. J., Neumann, C. S., Caldwell, M. F., Leistico, A. M., & Van Rybroek, G. J. (2006). Testing factor models of the Psychopathy Checklist: Youth Version and their association with instrumental aggression. *Journal of Personality Assessment, 87*, 74–83.

Vitacco, M. J., Neumann, C. S., & Jackson, R. L. (2005). Testing a four-factor model of psychopathy and its association with ethnicity, gender, intelligence, and violence. *Journal of Consulting and Clinical Psychology, 73*(3), 466–476.

Vitacco, M. J., & Rogers, R. (2001). Predictors of adolescent psychopathy: The role of impulsivity, hyperactivity, and sensation seeking. *Journal of the American Academy of Psychiatry and the Law, 29*, 374–382.

Vitacco, M. J., Van Rybroek, G. J., Rogstad, J. E., Yahr, L. E., Tomony, J. D., & Saewert, E. (2009). Predicting short-term institutional aggression in forensic patients: A multi-trait method for understanding subtypes of aggression. *Law and Human Behavior, 33*, 308–319.

Vitaro, F., Brendgen, M., & Barker, E. D. (2006). Subtypes of aggressive behaviors: A developmental perspective. *International Journal of Behavioral Development, 30*, 12–19.

Vitiello, B., Behar, D., Hunt, J., Stoff, D., & Ricciuti, A. (1990). Subtyping aggression in children and adolescents. *Journal of Neuropsychiatry, 2*(2), 189–192.

Vitiello, B., & Stoff, D. M. (1997). Subtypes of aggression and their relevance to child psychiatry. *Journal of American Academy of Child and Adolescent Psychiatry, 36*, 307–315.

Walsh, Z., & Kosson, D. S. (2008). Psychopathy and violence: The importance of factor level interactions. *Psychological Assessment, 20*(2), 114–120.

Ward, T., Vess, J., & Collie, R. M. (2006). Risk management or goods promotion: The relationship between approach and avoidance goals in treatment of sex offenders. *Aggression and Violent Behavior, 11*(4), 378–393.

Warren, J. I., Reboussin, R., Hazelwood, R. R., & Wright, J. A. (1991). Prediction of rapist type and violence from verbal, physical, and sexual scales. *Journal of Interpersonal Violence, 6*(1), 55–67.

Weizmann-Henelius, G., Putkonen, H., Gronroos, M., Lindberg, N., Eronen, M., & Hakkanen-Nyholm, H. (2010). Examination of psychopathy in female homicide offenders—confirmatory factor analysis of the PCL-R. *International Journal of Law and Psychiatry, 33*(3), 177–183.

Wong, S. C. P., Gordon, A., & Gu, D. (2007). Assessment and treatment of violence-prone forensic clients: An integrated approach. *British Journal of Psychiatry, 190*(49), s66–s74.

Woodworth, M., & Porter, S. (2002). In cold blood: Characteristics of criminal homicides as a function of psychopathy. *Journal of Abnormal Psychology, 111*, 436–445.

CHAPTER TEN

Psychological Theories and Research on Female Criminal Behavior

Elaine Gunnison

Throughout the nineteenth and twentieth centuries, the primary focus of theorists and researchers was on explaining male offending behavior (Belknap, 2007; Chesney-Lind, 1989). In fact, female offenders are sometimes referred to as the forgotten or "invisible" offenders (Belknap, 2007; Chesney-Lind, 1989). Belknap (2007) contends that one likely reason females were overlooked is due to androcentric bias; many of the early theorists examining offending were male, and this led them to focus on male offending. According to Belknap (2007), another reason attention was not placed on the examination of female offending is due to their smaller amount of offending when compared to males. Since males commit more crimes, some researchers focused their attention on understanding and assisting this group first. Those criminologists who attempted to explain female criminal behavior attributed it to biological or social factors that were outside the control of an individual (Freud, 1923; Lombroso & Ferrero, 1895; Thomas, 1923; Pollak, 1950). From the 1950s to the 1970s, female offending, once again, did not receive much focus from theorists and researchers. However, the feminist movement in the 1970s brought more attention to the examination of issues impacting females and resulted in an explosion of research into female offending (Adler, 1975; Simon, 1975).

This chapter will present research regarding what is known about female criminal behavior, including the prevalence of female offending and the types of crimes women commit. Additionally, this chapter will highlight the theoretical precursors to several psychological theories that can explain female criminal behavior. Specifically, psychoanalytic theory, behavioral theory, social learning theory, cognitive theory, personality theory, and evolutionary theory will be discussed, and research as to how these theories can explain female criminal behavior will be presented. Finally, the chapter will explore alternative explanations or catalysts for female offending behavior.

Research on Female Offending

While early theorists focused solely on explaining male offending behavior, today this is not the case (Belknap, 2007; Chesney-Lind, 1989). There is a great breadth of knowledge regarding female offending that has burgeoned since the 1970s. The following section presents the current knowledge of female offending, including a discussion of the prevalence of female offending as well as factors that might contribute to their offending rates.

Prevalence of Female Offending

In terms of the amount of crime, and types of crimes, that females commit, there are some distinct differences between female and male offending groups. When examining official statistics, males get arrested for more crimes than their female counterparts (Federal Bureau of Investigation, 2009). Specifically, females were arrested for approximately 25% of Index I crimes (e.g., murder, rape, robbery, burglary, sexual assault, larceny-theft, arson, and motor vehicle theft) with males being arrested for approximately 75% of index crimes. Additionally, females are more likely to commit property crimes as opposed to violent crimes. In 2009, females represented only 19% of those arrested for violent crimes but 38% of those arrested for property crimes. Chesney-Lind and Pasko (2004, p. 95) state that "women's contribution to serious crimes of violence ... is minor." Pollock (2002, p. 43) adds: "despite a popular belief that women are becoming more violent, women continue to be underrepresented in violent crime rates." Further, Chesney-Lind and Pasko (2004) contend that media attention to violent female criminal activity has contributed, in part, to the perception that trends of violence for this group are burgeoning.

For the Index I crimes, females are more likely to be arrested for the crimes of larceny-theft, robbery, and burglary. Several researchers have discovered that a large portion of women arrested for larceny-theft crimes had committed shoplifting (Cameron, 1953; Chesney-Lind & Pasko, 2004; Pollock, 2002; Steffensmeier, 1980). Drug abuse violations also account for a significant portion of arrests for women (Chesney-Lind & Pasko, 2004). It appears that drug use is strongly correlated with their criminality more so than for males (Pollock, 2002). With the "war on drugs" campaign in the 1980s, an increasing number of women, particularly women of color, found themselves arrested for drug offenses. Bush-Baskette (2000) states that from 1986 to 1991, the incarceration of African American females increased by 828%. In fact, Bush-Baskette (2000) notes that the "war on drugs" movement is often referred to as the "war on women." Pollock (2002) adds that there has been an increase of women sentenced to prison for the commission of drug crimes and who also acknowledge having drug problems. For female offenders, drug use may be a method of numbing past traumatic experiences such as childhood physical and/or sexual abuse, as a means to escape current problems (e.g., poverty, violence), or to cope with the illegal activity they may be a part of such as prostitution (Belknap, 2007; Chesney-Lind & Pasko, 2004; Pollock, 2002). For female offenders involved in the drug selling business, more often than not, females are not the sellers of drugs but rather the "mules" or carrier of drugs for a boyfriend or spouse (Acoca & Raeder, 1999).

Researchers have also discovered that females self-report less criminal involvement than males and are more likely to self-report criminal behavior that is nonviolent (Belknap, 2007; Chesney-Lind, 1989). Steffensmeier and Haynie (2000) state that males offend at a rate of approximately 5–10 times higher than females. This finding was supported regardless of whether the researchers were inspecting official or self-report data. Interestingly, while women are arrested more often for shoplifting, some researchers have found that women self-report similar levels of involvement in this crime as their male counterparts (Chesney-Lind & Shelden, 2004). Moreover, the *Uniform Crime Reports* (2009) states that arrest trends for adult females has increased (i.e., 11.4%) since 2000; however, the arrest trends for juvenile females has decreased (i.e., 13.1%) since 2000.

When race is examined, the *Uniform Crime Reports* (2009) indicate that 69.1% of those arrested were white, 28.3% were black, and the remaining 2.6% were other races (i.e., American Indian/Alaskan Native, or Asian/Pacific Islander). It is important to note that while Caucasian offenders were arrested more, there were disproportionate numbers of African

Americans arrested given their population numbers in the United States. According to the U.S. Census Bureau (2007), African Americans represent approximately 13% of the total U.S. population. Thus, with 28.3% of all arrests being attributed to African Americans in 2009, their arrest rate is not proportionate with their population numbers. However, findings from many self-report criminal surveys do not support the official statistics (Chambliss & Nagasawa, 1969; Gould, 1969; Hirschi, 1969; Tracy, 1987). Results of self-report criminal surveys reveal that Caucasians and African Americans report similar levels of involvement in criminality regardless of gender (Chambliss & Nagasawa, 1969; Gould, 1969; Hirschi, 1969; Tracy, 1987).

Finally, in regards to age, the majority of those arrested in 2009 were those over the age of eighteen (Federal Bureau of Investigation, 2009). However, researchers have long identified an age-crime curve, where those who commit crimes are more likely to be between the ages of 16 and 24 (Hirschi & Gottfredson, 1983). The relationship between age and crime is consistent for both genders.

Overall, females participate in lower levels of criminal involvement than males. Belknap (2007, p. 134) states, "It appears that regarding most offenses, especially serious and violent crimes, it is still a 'man's world.' " However, females are not incapable of committing violent offenses. According to Belknap (2007), approximately 10% to 20% of all homicides committed in the United States are done so by women. Most often, when females do commit a violent crime, it is usually directed at a relative or intimate, such as a child or spouse, and the female acts alone in the commission of the crime (Browne & Williams, 1989; Gauthier & Bankston, 1997; Gauthier, Chaudoir, & Forsyth, 2003). Thus, much of the violent crime perpetrated by females is directed at males rather than females (Belknap, 2007). Belknap (2007) reports, in a gender comparison of homicide rates in the United States from 1976 to 2002, that only 2.4% of homicides during this time period were committed by a female perpetrator with a female victim, while 9.9% of homicides during this same time period were committed by a female perpetrator with a male victim. One explanation for this violence perpetrated by females against males may occur after repeated sexual and/or physical abuse experiences at the hands of a male intimate or spouse (Pollock & Davis, 2005). When females do engage in violent crimes with another person, it is typically a male intimate such as a boyfriend or spouse (Pettiway, 1987). Conversely, as females are more likely to perpetrate a crime against someone they are acquainted with, females are also more likely to be victimized by someone they know. In 2009, the Bureau of Justice Statistics reported that 68% of all violent victimizations experienced by females were from a nonstranger (intimate partner, other relative, friend/acquaintance) versus 45% for males (Truman & Rand, 2010).

Additionally, females are far more likely to commit property offenses (Belknap, 2007; Chesney-Lind & Pasko, 2004; Pollock, 2002). For many female offenders who engage in property crimes, if a co-offender is included, that co-offender is more likely to be female than male (Pettiway, 1987). It should be noted that some researchers have found that females often engage in violence and other property crimes with other females (see Alarid, Marquart, Burton, Cullen, & Cuvelier, 1996; Koons-Witt & Schram, 2003; Sommers & Baskin, 1993). Moreover, it is not uncommon for women to be under the influence of drugs and/or alcohol during the commission of a crime (Belknap, 2007; Chesney-Lind & Pasko, 2004; Pollock, 2002). The following sections present the theoretical precursors that sought to explain female offending behavior as well as several psychological theories that explain criminal offending behaviors.

Theoretical Precursors

At the end of the nineteenth century to the mid-twentieth century, female offending behavior was being examined by theorists. The early theorists' ideas about female offending were consistent with the positivist school of crime, where crime was thought to be due to some individual difference (i.e., biologically determined) as opposed to a rational choice. Lombroso and Ferrero (1895) stated that the explanation for both male and female offending is due to atavistic traits, or denigration in evolutional human development. For instance, criminals exhibited traits such as high cheekbones, long arms, and excessive hair (Lombroso, 1911). Essentially, involvement in criminality was due to their biology—that is, these criminals were born this way. In a departure from a biological explanation for female offending, Thomas (1923) claimed that females committed crime for the thrill, or excitement, and the yearning for new experiences. According to Thomas, due to societal expectations of monogamy, females have pent-up sexual energy, and this sexual tension is released in the commission of criminal acts. In 1950, Pollak explained female offending as being attributed to a mix of biological, psychological, and sociological factors. Specifically, he points to the role of biology (e.g., menstruation, pregnancy) as a contributor to the development of female offending due to the psychological disturbances that they produce. These psychological disturbances spawn females into a cycle of offending or weaken their moral inhibitions toward engaging in criminal behavior. These beliefs regarding female offending shaped early criminal justice responses. Since female offenders were viewed as irrational and could not be held to full accountability for their crimes due to their biology, some questioned what punishment, if any, they should receive for committing crime (Allen, 1987; Belknap, 2007). Today, the view of biology in explaining female (or male) offending has shifted. Raine (2008, p. 244) explains that "responsible researchers no longer claim that biology alone causes behavior problems, for they recognize that behavior results from interactions between nature and nurture, biology and environment. Similarly, responsible biocriminologists today reject biological determininism." Despite the new perspectives on the role of biology as it relates to criminality, each of the abovementioned theorists laid the initial foundation for psychological theories to explain behavior—including female offending behavior.

Psychological Theories of Offending

There are a multitude of psychological theories that can explain female criminality. The following sections present an overview of several psychological theories, including: psychoanalytic theory; behavioral theory; social learning theory; cognitive theory; and personality theory. Besides providing a description of these theories, the empirical status of theory will also be presented. Whenever possible, research as to how the theory explains female offending will be highlighted. Finally, the chapter will provide a brief discussion regarding how this theory may or may not be an effective tool to utilize as a rehabilitative therapy for transforming criminal offending behaviors.

Psychoanalytic Theory

Departing from biological explanations for crime, Freud attributed behavior to unconscious desires in his psychoanalytic theory. In his earliest writings, Freud (1916) stated that individuals engage in criminality out of sense of guilt stemming from the Oedipus complex, which is the unconscious desire of a man to kill his father and sleep with his mother. Subsequent psychoanalytic theorists such as Aichorn (1925) and Glover (1960) attributed criminal behavior to unconscious feelings of guilt over psychosexual conflict or the need for punishment. Freud (1933), like Thomas, viewed female offending as being linked to female sexuality. He asserted that females have a masculinity complex due to penis envy. Those females who cannot resolve their penis envy overidentify with the male identity and will commit crimes.

As Freud further refined his psychoanalytic theory, he later argued that there were three components to the personality of an individual: the Id, the Ego, and the Superego. The Id is the most primitive part of the personality and operates according to the pleasure principle whereby it demands instant gratification for all its urges (e.g., food, sex). On the other hand, the Superego is the conscience, where social norms and moral are internalized. The Ego operates according to the reality principle, where it balances the urges of the Id and the morals of the Superego and is considered the decision-making component of the personality. According to psychoanalytic theory, criminal behavior could be understood by the underdevelopment or weakness of the Superego, the failure of the Ego, and/or expressions of an underlying mental illness (see Redl & Wineman, 1951; Schoenfeld, 1971). Utilizing Freud's theoretical perspective, females who commit crimes are plagued by a weak conscience or a mental illness that inhibits the functioning of their Superego or Ego.

Given the difficulties inherent in attempting to measure the three components of personality by researchers, the empirical validity of this theory in explaining offending behavior is limited (Akers & Sellers, 2007). Additionally, the use of psychoanalytic therapies for offender populations has been found to be unsuitable (Andrews et al., 1990; Lipsey, 1992).

Behavioral Theory

According to behavioral theorists, behavior is learned. The two primary behavioral theories are *classical* and *operant conditioning*. Pavlov (1927) first described classical conditioning and explained that behavior is a response to a stimulus. In order to change behavior (female or male), Pavlov stated that there needed to be a repeated pairing and removal of a stimulus. For example, to change an alcoholic's desire for alcohol, the treatment provider would continuously pair the image of alcohol (conditioned stimulus) with nausea (conditioned response). After repeated pairings of these images together, eventually, the alcoholic would associate nausea, or feel nauseous, when looking, thinking about, or smelling alcohol. The process of linking an image to an undesirable response is referred to as aversion therapy.

Aversion therapy has been used with offenders, primarily male, to decrease their criminal (e.g., pedophilia) or deviant behaviors (i.e., gambling, homosexuality, transvestites, fetishists) (Barker & Miller, 1968; Blakemore et al., 1963; Cooke, 1978; Glynn & Harper, 1961; James, 1962; Maletzky, 1990; Quinsey, Bergersen, & Steinman, 1976; Raymond, 1956). Many of the early uses of aversion therapy were targeted at changing the sexual orientation of homosexuals and are often referred to as conversion therapy (James, 1978). Eventually, later uses of aversion therapy were utilized on sex offenders (Brodsky, 1980; Cooke, 1978; Maletzky, 1990). Maletzky (1990), for example, uses classical conditioning to treat exhibitionists. After treatment, he reported that 87% of his clients extinguished overt exhibitionist behaviors. While Maletzky (1990) reported success, other researchers have found that aversion therapy did not produce permanent changes in sexual behaviors for sex offenders (see Quinsey & Earls, 1990; Quinsey & Marshall, 1983).

In the 1930s, Skinner proposed operant conditioning. In operant conditioning, the presence of a stimulus and response is apparent. If a reinforcer, positive or negative, can immediately follow the response, then behavior can be modified. Essentially, operant conditioning is a form of learning whereby responses to a stimulus eventually can be constrained by their consequences. In the criminal justice system, punishments (e.g., fines, jail/prison sentences, probation, restitution) are utilized to decrease criminal behaviors. Female offenders are more likely to commit property offenses such as shoplifting (Belknap, 2007). Using Skinner's theoretical perspective, the more often females are caught and punished by the criminal justice system for shoplifting offenses, the more likely they will cease committing such crimes. It should be noted, however, that some researchers have pointed out that the implementation of punishments in the criminal justice system occurs long after the criminal behavior is exhibited, which may result in a substantial decrease in the effectiveness of the punishment given the significant lapse in time between the behavior and the consequence (Spiegler & Guevremont, 1993).

To modify criminal behavior utilizing operant conditioning, a therapist would want to reinforce, or reward, positive prosocial behaviors. For example, Patterson and colleagues, at the Oregon Social Learning Center, have implemented the use of operant conditioning in families of preadolescent antisocial boys (Bank, Patterson, & Reid, 1987; Patterson, 1982; Patterson & Gullion, 1976). In this therapy, parents are trained to monitor the behavior and then implement positive reinforcements in their sons. Several studies have reported that this therapy is successful at reducing aversive behaviors in juveniles, and that the juveniles exhibit lower levels of institutional confinement post-therapy (Marlowe, Reid, Patterson, & Weinrott, 1986; Patterson, Chamberlain, & Reid, 1982; Patterson & Fleischman, 1979; Ross & McKay, 1976; Walter & Gilmore, 1973; Weinrott, Bauske, & Patterson, 1979). Ross and McKay (1976), in a study of institutionalized delinquent girls in Ontario, Canada, found that some behavioral modification techniques were effective at reducing recidivism rates of the girls post-release. In another study, Ross and Palmer (1976) found that behavioral therapy techniques were effective at increasing verbal expressions for adolescent girls.

Phillips, Phillips, Fixsen, and Wolf (1973) reported on the success of a residential treatment program for male juvenile offenders, known as the Achievement Place, which utilized operant conditioning to modify the behavior of the residents. Early evaluations of this program indicated that recidivism rates were lower for the Achievement Place residents when compared to incarcerated youth or youth on probation (Kirigin, Wolf, Braukmann, Fixsen, & Phillips, 1979; Phillips et al., 1973). However, subsequent evaluations cast doubt on whether this program can be successful in reducing recidivism (Fonagy, Target, Cottrell, Phillips, & Kurtz, 2002; Kirigin, Braukmann, Atwater, & Wolf, 1982; Quay, 1986). Kirigin et al. (1982) conducted an outcome study evaluation of the Achievement Place and subsequent evaluations of the program by others and found that some significant differences in offending emerged during treatment for males and females in the Achievement Place program as compared to other community based treatment programs for juveniles—although these differences in offending, for both groups, were not significant after a one-year follow-up.

In sum, behavior modification has been used in a variety of settings to curb deviant responses, such as aggression in juveniles (Varley, 1984), in the treatment of sex offenders (Smith, Hayler, & Padalino, 1998), and for female offenders (Ross & McKay, 1976). However, for psychopathic personalities, operant conditioning does not appear to be successful (Ross & Doody, 1973). In using either approach for the modification of offending behavior, Schwitzgebel (1972) cautions that constitutional issues, such as the protection of cruel and unusual punishments and the right to privacy, must be considered. In fact, Roddy (1979) calls for behavioral therapy to be banned for use with juveniles, adult prisoners, and those who are mentally ill due to constitutional concerns.

Observational/Social Learning Theory

Extending on classical and operant conditioning theories, Bandura (1977) asserts that behavior can be learned from others through observation and modeling. The idea that behavior could be learned through imitation stemmed from his classic study of children in his "BoBo doll" experiment (Bandura, 1961, 1963). In several experiments, children were exposed to a role model hitting a BoBo doll aggressively, either in person or via videotape. After viewing the role model act aggressively, either in person or on video, the children were more likely to replicate the aggressive behavior. In order for observational learning to take place, Bandura (1977) asserts that one must: (1) pay attention to another person's behavior; (2) retain the observed behavior in his or her memory; (3) have the ability to reproduce the behavior; and (4) have the motivation to reproduce the behavior.

Many researchers have found that those who engage in crime and delinquency often model the behaviors of parents or antisocial peers (Akers, Marvin, Krohn, Lanza-Kaduce, & Radosevich, 1979; Elliott, Huizinga, & Ageton, 1985; Patterson, 1982; Sutherland, 1947). Additionally, the social learning of behaviors has been linked to a wide range of criminal and deviant actions including battering, computer crime, drunk driving, gang membership, and sexual abuse (Adams, 2009; Bellair & McNulty, 2009; Burton, 2008; Morris & Blackburn, 2009; Wareham, Boots, & Chavez, 2009; Winfree, Giever, & Maupin, 2007) and has been well supported in the literature (Brezina & Piquero, 2000; Kandel, 1974; Lauritsen, 1993; Patterson & Dishion, 1985; Warr, 1993; Warr & Stafford, 1991). Peer associations have been linked to substance abuse, serious and nonserious offenses for females (Jensen, 2003; Neff & Waite, 2007). Heimer and DeCoster (1999) report that cultural and structural factors influence how delinquent girls learn definitions favorable to the commission of violent acts. Thus, it appears that while females may have access to delinquent associations as their male counterparts do, these associations may exhibit less of an influence on their behavior when compared to other factors (i.e., bonds to family, views of their gender role). Erickson, Crosnoe, and Dombusch (2000), in their examination of adolescent deviance, found that males were more influenced by the behavior of their peers than females were. The differences in the influences of peers on males and females may partially explain the incident rates of offending for each group.

Many treatment programs in criminal justice have successfully utilized social learning interventions therapy within the correctional setting (Akers & Jensen, 2007; Gendreau & Ross, 1983). Since many offenders are deficient in social skills (Hains & Herrman, 1989), Goldstein et al. (1986) developed a structured learning therapy based on social learning principles for juvenile offenders. In this therapy, staff model and role play positive social skills, and the youth practice the skills in various settings. Results from evaluations of this structured learning, or social skills, training program indicate that participants of the program exhibited lower levels of aggression when compared to juveniles not enrolled in the program (Goldstein et al., 1986). Other studies have found that juveniles who participate in the program exhibit a greater level of assertiveness upon program completion when compared to juveniles not participating in the program (Pentz, 1980). More recent evaluations have revealed that social skill training can be useful for adult offenders (Leukefeld, McDonald, & Staton, 2003; Schippers, Marker, & De Fuentes-Merillas, 2001). Ross, Currie, & Krug-McKay (1980) state that a social learning treatment model should guide correctional interventions for female offenders, and research has found that social skills training can be an effective intervention for female juveniles (Blake, Amaro, Schwartz, & Flinchbaugh, 2001). Additionally, based on a meta-analytic review, Dowden & Andrews (1999) report that treatment programs that will have the greatest influence on female offenders are those that utilize social learning and behavioral principles.

Cognitive Theory

Recognizing the importance of cognition in the learning process, Bandura (1986) systematizes his social learning theory into social cognitive theory. Bandura (1986) recognizes that cognition can influence: (1) individual behavior; and (2) how individuals interact and learn from one another. A major component of his theory is self-efficacy. According to Bandura (1995, p. 2), "self-efficacy is the belief in one's capabilities to organize and execute the courses of action required to manage prospective situations." Thus, if offenders believe they are unable to make decisions to remove themselves from a life of crime, they are less likely to make the decision to cease from the commission of crimes. Covington (1998) reports that female offenders often have lower levels of self-efficacy. Researchers have found that reductions in self-efficacy have been linked to females as a contributing factor to the involvement in criminality (Salisbury & Van Voorhis, 2009). For instance, if female offenders have poor coping skills, it could lead to decreased self-efficacy and result in future criminal behavior (Pellisier & Jones, 2006). In the context of reentry for female offenders following a period of incarceration, if females have poor coping skills during their stressful reintegration, it will likely decrease their self-efficacy and contribute to their likelihood of reoffending.

Since offenders often exhibit "thinking errors" (see Yochelson & Samenow, 1976), or suffer from deficiencies in cognitive skills, cognitive therapy has been a tool used in the correctional system to improve these skills (Ross & Fabiano, 1985). In cognitive therapy treatment programs, cognitive restructuring and/or cognitive skill enhancement is utilized

(Van Voorhis, Braswell, & Lester, 1997). Cognitive therapy provides a foundation for female offenders to learn new coping skills, thereby increasing their self-efficacy. Many researchers evaluating cognitive intervention programs have found that these interventions are effective for both juveniles and adults (Andrews et al., 1990; Antonwicz & Ross, 1994; Garrett, 1985; Hollin, McGuire, & Hounsome, 2008; Izzo & Ross, 1990; Lipsey, 1992; Moore, Harrison, & Young, 2008; Roberts-Lewis, Parker, & Welch, 2009). For example, Moore et al. (2008) who examined recidivism rates of 63 subjects following a court-mandated cognitive treatment program for drunk driving, found that those who participated in the treatment had lower recidivism rates. Specifically, the recidivism rates were only 13% for the treatment group after a 21-month follow-up. For female offenders, a therapeutic approach emphasizing cognitive processes may promote desistance for this group (Giordano, Cernkovich, & Rudolph, 2002). Additionally, some researchers have found that a combined cognitive-behavioral intervention appears to be promising at reducing recidivism (Pearson, Lipton, & Cleland, 2002; Roberts-Lewis et al., 2009; Wilson, Bouffard, & MacKenzie, 2005). Roberts-Lewis and colleagues (2009) report that cognitive-behavioral treatment is a promising intervention for changing behaviors of female juvenile offenders.

Personality Theory

Several psychologists have proposed personality theories to help explain the behavior of individuals. Gordon Allport (1937) is considered to be the founder of personality theory and offered the first non-Freudian model of personality (Campbell, 2008; Winter, 1997). After reviewing descriptions of over 4,500 personality traits in a dictionary, Allport classified these traits into three levels (Weiten, 1992). The first trait, or dominant trait, is referred to as a cardinal trait, as it "characterizes nearly all of a person's behavior" (Weiten, 1992, p. 424). An example of a cardinal trait would be Mother Teresa, who was very caring and altruistic, and her altruism would be an example of a cardinal trait (Weiten, 1992). For some offenders, committing crime is all they do on a regular basis; thus, for these individuals, being criminal is their cardinal trait. Allport refers to the second level of traits as central traits. These traits are a prominent part of one's personality, and each person has 5–10 central traits (Weiten, 1992). For instance, central traits for one individual could be intelligence, motivation, assertiveness, and drive. However, another person's central traits could be much different (e.g., unintelligent, lazy, etc.). The third trait of Allport's hierarchy is a secondary trait referring to personality traits that arise in one situation for an individual but not in other life situations (Weiten, 1992). An individual, for example, may be a loving and caring individual to friends and family; however, in the commission of a crime, the same person would not hesitate to hurt someone.

Subsequent personality theorists further refined personality theory, and others linked the origins of personality traits to biology. For example, in 1940, Sheldon classified three types of physiques (i.e., endomorph, mesomorph, ectomorph) and linked these physiques to specific personality traits (Weiten, 1992). Sheldon linked offending to the mesomorph (muscular) physique, which was more likely to be male. In 1950, Cattell further refined Allport's personality traits and, utilizing sophisticated statistical analyses, stated that an individual's personality can be attributed to 16 personality traits (Weiten, 1992). Unlike Allport, Cattell (1982) believed that personality could be inherited. Additional researchers have found support for the idea that personality can be inherited (Plomin, Chipuer, & Loehlin, 1990; Rushton, Fulker, Neale, Nias, & Eysenck, 1986). Cattell developed a 16 Personality Factors questionnaire to determine whether individuals exhibited low or high levels on a range of the traits (e.g., warmth, sensitivity, reasoning). Sandhu and Irving (1974), in an investigation of male and female probationers using Cattell's 16 Personality Factors profile, revealed that female probationers were more likely to be aggressive, assertive, stubborn, and competitive than their male counterparts.

Eysenck, in 1960, further systematizes personality theory and also states that the personality may be tied to one's genes (Weiten, 1992). Eysenck was the first theorist to specifically link personality to criminal offending (Rawlings & Dawe, 2008). Unlike Cattell, Eysenck proposed that there were three main personality traits: extroversion (i.e., sociable, active); neuroticism (i.e., anxious, depressed); and psychotism (i.e., aggressive, antisocial). According to Eysenck (1964), those who commit crimes do not possess a strong conscience and have not been conditioned to abstain from crime due to biological factors (e.g., low cortical arousal, anxiety). In the context of his theory, those individuals who commit crimes would be those who were psychotic or neurotic. To assess which personality dimension individuals had, Eysenck developed the Eysenck Personality Questionnaire (EPQ) to tap these traits (Eysenck & Eysenck, 1975). Eysenck (1964) proposed that those who were criminal would score higher on psychoticism, neuroticism, and extroversion of his EPQ assessment.

Barack and Widom (1978) applied the EPQ to 60 criminal women and found that the female offenders were more likely to score higher on the neurotic and extroversion scales. In 1979, Bartol and Holanchock utilized the EPQ to examine the validity of Eysenck's theory with 398 offenders who had committed a range of offenses from violent to nonviolent. The researchers did not find support for Eysenck's theory and, in particular, found that, in their sample, Eysenck's theory did appear to explain criminal behavior of the African American or Hispanic prisoners. Farrington, Biron, and LeBlanc (1982) reviewed 16 studies that measured the relationship between each of the personality traits and criminal convictions (i.e., self-report and official offending) using the EPQ. The researchers found that offenders were more likely to score higher on the psychotic personality trait. Subsequent researchers have found a relationship between psychoticism and criminality (van Dam, Janssens, & De Bruyn, 2005; Furnham & Thompson, 1991; Heaven, Newbury, & Wilson, 2004; Romero, Luengo, & Sobral, 2001; Walker & Gudjonsson, 2006). However, van Dam and colleagues (2007), in their examination of 126 incarcerated adolescent male delinquents, found that, for their sample, only a small number of offenders scored high on all Eysenck's personality dimensions. In addition, the researchers found that Eysenck's personality dimensions were unable to differentiate between male recidivists and male non-recidivists.

In 1966, Kernberg proposed a theory of borderline personality organization. According to Kernberg (1966), personality is organized along a continuum ranging from psychotic (out of touch with reality) to borderline (moderately in touch with reality) to neurotic (in touch with reality). Those individuals who are most susceptible to engaging in crime are those who exhibit a borderline personality. Several researchers have noted that individuals with a borderline personality were more likely to engage in violent behavior such as murder or intimate partner violence (De Barros and de Pádua, 2008; Raine, 1993; Stone, 1998; Stuart, Moore, & Gordon, 2006). Stone (1998) states that females with a borderline personality disorder are less likely to commit murder than their male counterparts. He explains that females with borderline personality disorder "seldom commit murder, probably because women are much less likely to be antisocial or psychopathic than are men" (Stone, 1998, p. 41). Many female offenders suffer from borderline personality disorder and often exhibit higher rates of the disorder compared to males (Jordan, Schlenger, Fairbank, & Caddell, 1986; Sansone & Sansone, 2009). Both antisocial personalities and psychopathy have been linked to criminal behavior.

The *Diagnostic and Statistical Manual of Mental Disorders* (DSM-IV) describes antisocial personality disorder (ASPD) as the disregard for the rights of others which begins early in the life of an individual and persists into adulthood (American Psychiatric Association, 2000). Many researchers have found a link between ASPD and criminal behavior (e.g., violent and nonviolent and substance abuse) (Coid, 1993, 1998; Dolan & Coid, 1993; Eronen, Angermeyer, & Schulze, 1998; Farrington, 1995, 2000; Fridell, Hesse, Jaeger, & Kuhlhorn, 2008; Geberth & Turco, 1997; Hodgins & Cote, 1993; Hubbard & Pratt, 2002; McElroy et al., 1999). Moreover, this association has been found not only for offenders in the United States, but for offenders in other countries such as Korea, Canada, and Sweden (Fridell et al., 2008; Hodgins & Cote, 1993; Kim & Kim, 2005). Additionally, researchers have discovered a connection between ASPD and institutional violence for female inmates (South, Chauhan, & Bale, 2002; Warren, Hurt, & Loper, 2002).

Hodgins and Cote (1993), who examined male inmates in Canada, found that those in their sample with ASPD exhibited an early onset into criminal offending and had more criminal convictions than those without an ASPD diagnosis. McElroy and colleagues (1999) report that, in their sample of 36 male sex offenders, 72% exhibited antisocial personality disorders. In a meta-analytic review of predictors of delinquency for girls, Hubbard and Pratt (2002) report that antisocial personality is a risk factor. More recently, in 2008, Fridell and colleagues (2008, p. 808), who examined approximately 1,000 substance abuse offenders, found that those offenders who had been diagnosed with an antisocial personality disorder "were more likely to be criminally active during an average follow-up period of two decades." Thus, the connection between ASPD and criminal offending has been found for both males and females as well as cross-culturally.

The study of psychopathy has been underway for almost 100 years, with the first discussions of the construct surfacing in the United States between 1915 and 1925 (Rafter, 1997). Moreover, psychopathy has been linked to criminality behavior. Helfgott (2008, p. 65) explains that "psychopathy and antisocial personality disorder are overlapping, but distinct clinical constructs." Additionally, Helfgott (2008, p. 65) further states that, "understanding psychopathy as a clinical entity distinct from A[S]PD is particularly important in differentiating between criminal behavior rooted in psychopathology from criminal behavior committed by individuals who do not possess a personality disorder or other type of mental illness." The distinction that Helfgott (2008) makes between ASPD and psychopathy is useful, as many earlier researchers blurred the lines when discussing these constructs and often used them interchangeably (Rabin, 1986).

In 1976, Cleckley presented 16 characteristics of a psychopath, which included the following: superficial charm, lack of remorse and shame, untruthfulness and insincerity, unreliability, absence of delusions and other irrational thinking, and absence of nervousness or psychoneurotic manifestations. Subsequent researchers have further refined Checkley's checklist (see Hare, 1991). One of the standard tools for assessing psychopathy is Hare's (1991, 2003) Psychopathy Checklist–Revised (PCL-R). The PCL-R is a 20-item checklist that taps the characteristics of a psychopath, including impulsivity, pathological lying, lack of empathy, lack of realistic long-term goals, promiscuous sexual behavior, and poor behavioral control. While some researchers have questioned the ability of the PCL-R to predict recidivism (see Gendreau, Goggin, & Smith, 2002), numerous researchers have found the PCL-R has been found to be predictive of recidivism (Beggs & Grace, 2008; Harris, Rice, & Cormier, 1991; Hart, Kropp, & Hare, 1988; Hemphill & Hare, 2004; Salekin, Rogers, & Sewell, 1996; Walters, 2003).

Offenders who have been classified as a psychopath using Hare's PCL-R have been found by researchers to be both male and female, are not specific to one ethnicity, come from various socioeconomic backgrounds, and engage in various criminal behaviors including child molestation, violence, domestic violence, theft, and serial murder (Beggs & Grace, 2008; Cale & Lilienfeld, 2002; Skeem, Edens, & Camp, 2004; Sullivan, Abramowitz, & Lopez, 2006; Swogger, Walsh, & Kosson, 2007; Vaughn, Newhill, DeLisi, Beaver, & Howard, 2008; Walsh & Kosson, 2007). While psychopathy has been found to be present for both males and females, it should be noted that some researchers have found females to score lower than males on the PCL-R (Hare, 1991; Helfgott, 2008; Jackson, Rogers, Neumann, & Lambert, 2002; Salekin et al., 1997) or that the PCL-R is more predictive of recidivism for males rather than females (Salekin, Rogers, Ustad, & Sewell, 1998). Additionally, researchers have reported that the prevalence rate of psychopathy for female offenders is lower than the rate for men (i.e., 15% for females versus 30% for males (Robins, 1966; Salekin et al., 1997). Besides the difference in prevalence rates, female psychopaths also differ from male psychopaths in that they are less aggressive and violent, recidivate less, lack a grandiose self-concept and detachment, and do not desire domination (Crick & Gropeter, 1995; Cunliffe & Gacono, 2005; Mulder, Wells, Joyce, & Bushnell, 1994; Salekin et al., 1998). Further, researchers have asserted that offenders classified as a psychopath exhibit early onset and continuity in offending (McCrory, Hickey, & Farmer, 2008; Vaughn & DeLisi, 2008; Vaughn, Howard, & DeLisi, 2008). For instance, Vaughn and DeLisi (2008) found that offenders with psychopathic traits in their study were more likely to be classified as career criminals than offenders without such traits. More recently, discussion in the field has emerged regarding female psychopathy as being a manifestation of histrionic personality disorder (Cunliffe & Gacano, 2005; Helfgott, 2008).

Given the versatility in their offending patterns, and given that psychopathic traits can begin in early childhood and continue to be exhibited through adulthood, psychopaths are a difficult group to change in a treatment setting (Patrick, 2006). Van Voorhis (1997, p. 103) states that "psychopaths are extremely difficult to change in treatment and counseling settings." In addition, Van Voorhis (1997) adds that there is no agreement in the field as to *how* difficult this group is to change or how best to rehabilitate psychopaths. While some researchers have labeled psychopaths as untreatable or described them as disruptive during treatment (see Loving, 2002; Rice, Harris, & Cormier, 1992), other researchers have found that treatment can have some success for this group (Skeem, Monahan, & Mulvey, 2002). A study by Caldwell, Skeem, and Salekin (2006) found, in their evaluation study of juvenile treatment programs, that juvenile psychopathic offenders who participated in some form of treatment exhibited lower recidivism rates following treatment.

Evolutionary Psychological Theories

Evolutionary psychological theories emerged in the 1990s and posit that biology may play a role in criminal behavior (Belknap, 2007). Helfgott (2008, p. 51) defines evolutionary psychology as "a branch of psychology that uses a Darwinian framework to explain human behavior in terms of processes of natural selection and adaptation." Theorists utilizing an evolutionary framework would argue that criminal behavior is merely an adaptation to the continued innate drive to reproduce to foster offspring and ensure the continuation of genetic material. These theories have been utilized to explain criminal (e.g., rape, domestic violence, child abuse) and deviant behaviors (e.g., infidelity) (Belknap, 2007). The majority of the discussion around these theories has centered on explaining the crime of rape. Since sex is an innate drive, evolutionary theories would view rape as "normal"—that males are engaging in rape as an adaptive response (Ellis, 1993; Helfgott, 2008). After all, the innate male sex drive yearns to inseminate women—as many as possible. However, females innately resist male sexual advances and only select the male most worthy to have intercourse with as the male can be a good provider to her future children. In this context, all males would be viewed as potential offenders and women as the likely victims (Belknap, 2007). Since, in reality, not all men are rapists, evolutionary theorists would argue that the reason why one male may rape while another may not is due to environmental influences on genes (Ellis & Walsh, 1997). As Ellis and Walsh (1997, p. 231) point out, "it is important to emphasize that the concept of genetic influence is not equivalent to genetic determinism and that genetic influence does not mean that a behavior pattern is unlearned." One of the more recent controversial evolutionary theories was put forth by Thornhill and Palmer in 2000. Following in the footsteps of previous evolutionary psychologists (see Ellis, 1993, Ellis & Walsh, 1997), Thornhill and Palmer (2000) again propose that rape is an adaptation. In their view, rape has evolved to increase the reproductive success for men who are unable to engage in a consensual sexual relationship. The assertions made by Thornhill and Palmer (2000) were met with much criticism, due to an absence of the utilization of scientific findings to back up their claims and to presentation of information as factual when it was rather speculation (Belknap, 2007; Coyne & Berry, 2000; Ward & Siegert, 2002).

In the context of explaining female offending, evolutionary theorists would argue that property and violent offending in women can be explained by resource scarcity (Campbell, Muncer, & Bibel, 2001). For instance, females who commit property crimes do so to provide for themselves or their offspring. For those females committing violent crimes, they engage in this behavior due to competition for strong male providers. As Campbell et al. (2001, p. 488) explain, "where such men [those with resources] are in relatively short supply, female competition manifests itself in direct intra-female aggression." Thus, women who commit property or violent crimes have evolved to over time to ensure the survival of their genetic makeup. Additionally, Campbell and colleagues (2001) further explain that, due to evolutionary pressure, women have a lower threshold for fear, which is why they are more likely to engage in property as opposed to violent crimes. Since evolutionary psychology is an emerging perspective with often controversial tenets, more research is needed to critically examine its future utility in explaining female offending.

In sum, there are a multitude of psychological theories that seek to explain criminal offending behavior. Other theories outside of psychology, from a sociological perspective, attribute female offending behavior to rational choice, peers, strain, or opportunity (Cohen & Felson, 1979; Cornish & Clarke, 1986; Merton, 1938; Sutherland, 1947). Additionally, feminist theories of crime have described masculinity, liberation, the cycle of violence, and power/control in the socialization of females to explain female offending (Hagan, Gillis, & Simpson, 1985; Messerschmidt, 1993; Simon, 1975; Widom, 1989). The next sections present the current research on female offending, which offers further insight into their behavior.

Pathways to Offending

Psychological theories have offered great insight into the understanding and treatment of female offending. Researchers in the psychological field and in other related disciplines, such as sociology and criminal justice, have continued to explore the nature of female offending. Numerous researchers have contended that the pathways to offending for females are distinct and, thus, are different from male pathways into offending (Belknap, 2007; Chesney-Lind & Shelden, 2004; Daly, 1992). From the extant literature, it is clear that prior sexual abuse and physical abuse are catalysts for the onset of offending patterns as well as the persistence in offending patterns for females (Belknap, 2007; Chesney-Lind & Pasko, 2004; Gunnison & McCartan, 2005).

Sexual Abuse

Since the departure from examining biology as the sole attribution to female criminality (see Lombroso, 1911), researchers have been able to identify multiple risk factors for their offending patterns. Sexual abuse figures prominently within the life histories of female offenders. Research into offending has indicated that women in prison have a higher level of sexual victimization than the general population (Belknap, 2007; Siegel & Williams, 2003). In fact, research indicates that the level of victimization may be 2–3 times higher for female offenders (Harlow, 1999). Research has consistently supported prior sexual abuse as a moderate to strong predictor of female offending (Belknap, 2007; Siegel & Williams, 2003). The research further suggests that sexual abuse increases a female's chances for engaging in delinquent and criminal behavior.

Sexual abuse in women has been related to running away (Belknap, Holsinger, & Dunn, 1997), instigation of a criminal career (Chesney-Lind, 1989), prostitution (Simons & Whitbeck, 1991), drug use (Kilpatrick et al., 2000), and aggression (Baskin & Sommers, 1998). Oftentimes, the offenders are sexually victimized by a male family member (i.e., father, stepfather, uncle, or brother) and, thus, the females run away from home and turn to the streets for survival. In order to survive, females will turn to prostitution to gain income. Given their involvement in prostitution, females will often use drugs and/or alcohol in tandem as a way to numb previous abuse and to numb their feelings about being involved in prostitution. If females are not involved in prostitution, they may become involved in the drug trade as a method to gain income. Their entry into the drug trade often leads to drug addiction or further addiction—if they were not involved in the drug trade previously. For instance, Covington and Kohen (1984), in an examination of addicted and nonaddicted women, found that 74% of addicted women reported prior sexual abuse as compared to 50% of the nonaddicted women.

Additionally, numerous researchers have explored female offending and have linked prior sexual abuse to the onset and persistence of criminal offending patterns (Bailey & McCloskey, 2005; Belknap, 2007; Chesney-Lind & Pasko, 2004; Comack, 2005; Gilfus, 1992; Goodkind et al., 2006; Gunnison & McCartan, 2005; Widom, 1989). While sexual abuse has been a consistent predictor of female offending, it has not been a constant predictor of female offending. In other words, not every female offender has experienced prior sexual abuse (see Siegel & Williams, 2003).

Without question, sexual abuse can have a detrimental impact on both males and females (McGuigan & Middlemiss, 2005; Reinemann, Stark, & Swearer, 2003; Romano & De Luca, 2000). For example, Romano and De Luca (2000), who examined the empirical literature on the impact of sexual abuse for males and compared it to the research literature on females, found that regardless of gender, childhood sexual abuse can negatively impact their lives. The researchers did note that females who experienced childhood sexual abuse tended to display more internalizing problems (e.g., depression or anxiety) as a result of their victimization. Women who have experienced physical or sexual abuse are at a higher risk for either chronic or recurrent depression (Andrews, 1995). Other research suggests that depression may even act as a buffer against criminal involvement. That is, females may exhibit passive behavioral problems such as depression rather than the aggressive behavioral problems evidenced in males (Karstedt, 2000). Similar results were found by Reinemann et al. (2003) who interviewed 57 adolescents who were receiving mental health services in a residential treatment center. They found that females who had experienced sexual abuse reported greater levels of depression compared to their male counterparts. More recently, McGuigan and Middlemiss (2005) found that childhood sexual abuse can have a cumulative impact on depression experienced as an adult for women.

Other responses to childhood sexual abuse that females exhibit are substance abuse (internalized pain) and criminal involvement (externalized pain). Several researchers have linked prior sexual abuse to the use of drugs and/or alcohol for females (Bailey & McCloskey, 2005; Belknap, 2007; Chesney-Lind & Pasko, 2004; Comack, 2005; Gilfus, 1992; Goodkind et al., 2006; Kilpatrick et al., 2000; Luster & Small, 1997; Miller & Downs, 1993; Saunders, Kilpatrick, Hanson, Resnick, & Walker, 1999; Widom, 1989). Bailey and McCloskey (2005) examined the link between childhood sexual abuse and later substance abuse (i.e., alcohol and drug use) and found that there is indeed a relationship between the variables. The researchers found that the relationship between childhood sexual abuse and substance abuse held even when they controlled for other factors such as family, alcohol/drug patterns, and early deviant behavior. Because much of the sexual abuse that women experience in childhood has been perpetrated by family members, young girls find it necessary to run away from home (i.e., where the perpetrator[s] reside) and turn to a life of crime on the streets as a means of survival (Belknap, 2007; Bloom, Owen, Rosenbaum, & Deschenes, 2003; Chesney-Lind & Pasko, 2004). Given this reality, it is not surprising that childhood sexual abuse is a pathway for female onset into criminal offending patterns.

Physical Abuse

Physical abuse experienced by females has been linked to the onset of involvement in criminal activity (Acoca, 1998; Belknap et al., 1997; Chesney-Lind & Shelden, 2004). Acoca (1998), who gathered both quantitative and qualitative data on abuse histories of young female offenders, reports that physical abuse was related to the onset of drug abuse and gang membership for young females. In a 1995 study of incarcerated female sexual offenders, Kaplan and Green report that female sexual offenders had higher rates of childhood sexual and physical victimization when compared to female nonsexual offenders. Additionally, Gaarder and Belknap (2002) report that, for female juveniles in their study who had their cases transferred to adult courts, physical abuse (among other factors) at home was experienced by many. Lansford and colleagues (2002) found that early physical abuse was related to aggression at age 16 more so for girls than boys. However, Fagan (2005) found few gender differences between early physical abuse and frequency of offending in adulthood. In 2007, Lansford and colleagues, in a prospective longitudinal study of 574 children, examined the relationship between early physical abuse and later violent offending. The researchers found that males and females who were physically abused at an early age were more at risk as juveniles to be arrested for both violent and nonviolent offenses. Further, the researchers also found that the impact of early physical abuse on females and other life experiences was more pronounced for this group than for their male counterparts. Specifically, "females who had been physically abused were approximately 3 times more likely to have been fired and to have been a teen parent" (Lansford et al., 2007, p. 241). More recently, Teague, Mazerolle, and Legosz (2008), who examined male and female offenders in Queensland,

Australia, found that offenders in their sample who were physically abused engaged in more violent and property crimes than offenders who had not experienced such abuse. Clearly, similar to sexual abuse, the experience of physical abuse by females has a profound and enduring impact on their offending trajectories and may impact their lives in differing ways than male offenders who have experienced such abuse.

In sum, the historical neglect in examining the root causes of female criminality has ended. Several psychological theories have been presented that can provide insight as to how criminality in females may develop (e.g., unconscious unfulfilled desires) or how it is shaped by the external environment (e.g., observational learning). Over the last 90 years, psychological theories have played a large role in shaping the understanding of female offending. While psychological theories can explain female offending, relying on one psychological theory to explain female criminality would serve as a disservice to this group. It is clear from the extant literature that no *one* theory can explain criminality for females effectively given the complexities (i.e., prior sexual abuse, prior physical abuse, drug use) in their onset and persistence in criminal offending. Thus, researchers may obtain a more conceptually complete understanding of female offending by examining factors from a multitude of disciplines such as biology, psychology, sociology, and research by feminist scholars (see Moffitt, 1993; Sampson & Laub, 1993). It is clear that an integrative theoretical focus is needed to best understand female offending. Additionally, discussion was provided to explain how these psychological theories might be useful in rehabilitating female offenders. Unlike claims by some researchers that rehabilitation does not work (see Martinson, 1974), it is clear that rehabilitation for female offenders can be successful (Cullen & Gilbert, 1982; Gendreau, 1996). If treatment providers design their treatment program for female offenders on the specific fundamentals of a psychological theory and recognize other roots causes of female offending, it is clear that rehabilitation efforts can be successful with proper service delivery. For any offender, male or female, treatment must address the criminogenic needs and risk factors for this group (Van Voorhis et al., 1997).

References

Acoca, L. (1998). Outside/inside: The violation of American girls at home, on the streets, and in the juvenile justice system. *Crime and Delinquency*, *44*(4), 561–589.

Acoca, L., & Raeder, M. S. (1999). Severing family ties: The plight of nonviolent female offenders and their children. *Stanford Law and Policy Review, 11*(1), 133–151.

Adams, D. (2009). Predisposing childhood factors for men who kill their intimate partners. *Victims & Offenders, 4*(3), 215–229.

Adler, F. (1975). *Sisters in crime: The rise of the new female criminal*. New York: McGraw-Hill.

Aichorn, A. (1925). *Wayward youth*. New York: Viking Press.

Akers, R. L., & Jensen, G. F. (2007). *Social learning theory and the explanation of crime: A guide for the new century. Advances in criminological theory: Vol. 11*. New Brunswick, NJ: Transaction Publishers.

Akers, R. L., Marvin, D., Krohn, M., Lanza-Kaduce, L., & Radosevich, M. (1979). Social learning and deviant behavior: A specific test of a general theory. *American Sociological Review, 44*, 636–655.

Akers, R. L., & Sellers, C. C. (2007). *Criminological theories: Introduction, evaluation, and application*. Los Angeles, CA: Roxbury.

Alarid, L. F., Marquart, J. W., Burton, V. S., Cullen, F. T., & Cuvelier, S. J. (1996). Women's roles in serious offenses: A study of adult felons. *Justice Quarterly, 13*, 431–454.

Allen, H. (1987). *Justice unbalanced gender: Psychiatry and judicial decisions*. Milton Keynes: Open University Press.

Allport, G. W. (1937). *Personality: A psychological interpretation*. New York: Holt.

American Psychiatric Association. (2000). *Diagnostic and statistical manual of mental disorders* (4th ed., text rev. [DSM-IV-TR]). Washington, DC: Author.

Andrews, B. (1995). Bodily shame as a mediator between abusive experiences and depression. *Journal of Abnormal Psychology, 104*, 277–285.

Andrews, D. A., Zinger, I., Hoge, R. D., Bonta, J., Gendreau, P., & Cullen, F. T. (1990). Does correctional treatment work? A clinically relevant and psychologically informed meta-analysis. *Criminology, 28*(3), 369–404.

Antonwicz, D. H., & Ross, R. R. (1994). Essential components of successful rehabilitation programs of offenders. *International Journal of Offender Therapy and Comparative Criminology, 38*, 97–104.

Bailey, J. A., & McCloskey, L. A. (2005). Pathways to adolescent substance use among sexually abused girls. *Journal of Abnormal Child Psychology, 33*, 39–53.

Bandura, A. (1961). Psychotherapy as a learning process. *Psychological Bulletin, 58*, 143–159.

Bandura, A. (1963). The role of imitation in personality. *Journal of Nursery Education, 18*(3), 207–215.

Bandura, A. (1977). *Social learning theory*. New York: General Learning Press.

Bandura, A. (1986). *Social foundations of thought and action: A social cognitive theory*. Englewood Cliffs, NJ: Prentice Hall.

Bandura, A. (1995). *Self-efficacy in changing societies*. New York: Cambridge University Press.

Bank, L., Patterson, G. R., & Reid, J. B. (1987). Delinquency prevention through training parents in family management. *Behavioral Analyst, 10*(1), 75–82.

Barack, L. I., & Widom, C. S. (1978). Eysenck's theory of criminality applied to women awaiting trial. *British Journal of Psychiatry, 133*, 452–456.

Barker, J. C., & Miller, M. (1968). Aversion therapy for compulsive gambling. *Journal of Nervous and Mental Disease, 146*, 285–302.

Bartol, C. R., & Holanchock, H. A. (1979). Eysenck's theory of criminality: A test on an American prisoner population. *Criminal Justice and Behavior, 6* (3), 245–249.

Baskin, D. R., & Sommers, I. (1998). *Casualties of community disorder: Women's careers in violent crime*. Boulder, CO: Westview Press.

Beggs, S. M., & Grace, R. C. (2008). Psychopathy, intelligence, and recidivism in child molesters: Evidence of an interaction effect. *Criminal Justice and Behavior, 35*(6), 683–695.

Belknap, J. (2007). *The invisible woman: Gender, crime, and justice*. Belmont, CA: Thomson, Wadsworth.

Belknap, J., Holsinger, K., & Dunn, M. (1997). Understanding incarcerated girls: The results of a focus group study. *Prison Journal, 77*(4), 381–404.

Bellair, P. E., & McNulty, T. L. (2009). Gang membership, drug selling, and violence in neighborhood context. *Justice Quarterly, 26*(4), 645–669.

Blake, S. M., Amaro, H., Schwartz, P. M., & Flinchbaugh, L. J. (2001). A review of substance abuse prevention interventions for young adolescent girls. *Journal of Early Adolescence, 21*(3), 294–324.

Blakemore, C. B., Thorpe, J. G., Barker, J. C., Conway, C. G., & Lavin, N. I. (1963). Application of faradic aversion conditioning in a case of transvestism. *Behaviour Research and Therapy, 1*, 26–35.

Bloom, B., Owen, B., Rosenbaum, J., & Deschenes, E. P. (2003). Focusing on girls and young women: A gendered perspective on female delinquency. *Women and Criminal Justice, 14*, 117–136.

Brezina, T., & Piquero, A. R. (2003). Exploring the relationship between social and non-social reinforcement in the context of social learning theory. In R. L. Akers & G. F. Jensen (Eds.), *Social learning theory and the explanation of crime: A guide for the new century. Advances in criminological theory: Vol. 11* (pp. 265–288). New Brunswick, NJ: Transaction Publishers.

Brodsky, S. L. (1980). Understanding and treating sexual offenders. *Howard Journal, 19*(2), 102–115.

Browne, A., & Williams, K. R. (1989). Exploring the effect of resource availability and the likelihood of female-perpetrated homicides. *Law and Society Review, 23*, 63–73.

Bush-Baskette, S. R. (2000). The war on drugs and the incarceration of mothers. *Journal of Drug Issues, 30*(4), 919–928.

Burton, D. L. (2008). An exploratory evaluation of the contribution of personality and childhood sexual victimization to the development of sexually abusive behavior. *Sexual Abuse: A Journal of Research and Treatment, 20*(1), 102–115.

Caldwell, M., Skeem, J., & Salekin, R. (2006). Treatment response of adolescent offenders with psychopathy features: A 2-year follow-up. *Criminal Justice and Behavior, 33*(5), 571–596.

Cale, E. M., & Lilienfeld, S. O. (2002). Sex differences in psychopathy and antisocial personality: A review and integration. *Clinical Psychology Review, 22*, 1179–1207.

Cameron, M. B. (1953). *Department store shoplifting* (Unpublished doctoral dissertation, Indiana University, Bloomington, IN).

Campbell, J. B. (2008). Modern personality theories: What have we gained? What have we lost? In G. Boyle, G. Matthews, & D. H. Saklofske (Eds.), *The sage handbook of personality theory and assessment* (Vol. 1, pp. 190–212). Los Angeles, CA: Sage.

Campbell, A., Muncer, S., & Bibel, D. (2001). Women and crime: An evolutionary approach. *Aggression and Violent Behavior, 6*(5), 481–497.

Cattell, R. B. (1982). *The inheritance of personality and ability: Research methods and findings*. New York: Academic Press.

Chambliss, W. J., & Nagasawa, R. H. (1969). On the validity of official statistics: A comparative study of white, black and Japanese high-school boys. *Journal of Research in Crime and Delinquency*, 71–77.

Chesney-Lind, M. (1989). Girl's crime and woman's place: Toward a feminist model of female delinquency. *Crime and Delinquency, 35*(1), 8–10.

Chesney-Lind, M., & Pasko, L. (2004). *The female offender: Girls, women, and crime*. Thousand Oaks, CA: Sage.

Chesney-Lind, M., & Shelden, R. (2004). *Girls, delinquency, and juvenile justice*. Belmont, CA: Thomson Wadsworth.

Cleckley, H. (1976). *The mask of sanity* (5th ed.). Augusta, GA: E. S. Cleckley.

Cohen, L. E., & Felson, M. (1979). Social change and crime rate trends: A routine activity approach. *American Sociological Review, 44*, 588–605.

Coid, J. W. (1993). Current concepts and classifications of psychopathic disorder. In P. Tyler & G. Stein (Eds.), *Personality disorder reviewed* (pp. 113–164). London: Gaskell.

Coid, J. W. (1998). Axis II disorders and motivation for serious criminal behavior. In A. E. Skodol (Ed.), *Psychopathology and violent crime* (pp. 53–97). Washington, DC: American Psychiatric Press.

Comack, E. (2005). Coping, resisting, and surviving: Connecting women's law violations to their histories of abuse. In L. Alaraid & P. Cromwell (Eds.), *In her own words: Women offenders' views on crime and victimization* (pp. 33–43). Los Angeles, CA: Roxbury.

Cooke, G. (1978). The behavioral treatment of the rapist. *Prison Journal Philadelphia, 58*(1), 47–52.

Cornish, D., & Clarke, R. (1986). *The reasoning criminal*. New York: Springer-Verlag.

Covington, S. (1998). The relational theory of women's psychological development: Implications for the criminal justice system. In R. T. Zaplin (Ed.), *Female offenders: Critical perspectives and effective interventions* (pp. 113–128). Gaithersburg, MD: Aspen.

Covington, S., & Kohen, J. (1984). Women, alcohol, and sexuality. *Advances in Alcohol and Substance Abuse, 4*(1), 41–56.

Coyne, J. A., & Berry, A. (2000). Rape as an adaptation: Is this contentious hypothesis advocacy, not science? *Nature, 404*, 121–122.

Crick, N. R., & Gropeter, J. K. (1995). Relational aggression, gender, and social-psychological adjustment. *Child Development, 66*, 710–722.

Cullen, F. T., & Gilbert, K. E. (1982). *Reaffirming rehabilitation*. Cincinnati, OH: Anderson.

Cunliffe, T., & Gacono, C. B. (2005). A Rorschach investigation of incarcerated female offenders with antisocial personality disorder. *International Journal of Offender Therapy and Comparative Criminology, 49*(5), 530–546.

Daly, K. (1992). Women's pathways to felony court: Feminist theories of lawbreaking and problems of representation. *Southern California Review of Law and Women's Studies*, 2, 11–52.

De Barros, D. M., & de Pádua, S. A. (2008). Association between personality disorder and violent behavior pattern. *Forensic Science International, 179*(1), 19–22.

Dolan, B., & Coid, J. W. (1993). *Psychopathic and antisocial personality disorder: Treatment and research issues*. London: Gaskell.

Dowden, C., & Andrews, D. A. (1999). What works for female offenders? A meta-analytic Review. *Crime and Delinquency, 45*(5), 438–452.

Elliott, D. S., Huizinga, D., & Ageton, S. (1985). *Explaining delinquency and drug use*. Beverly Hills, CA: Sage.

Ellis, L. (1993). Rape as a biosocial phenomenon. In G. H. Hall, R. Hirschman, J. Graham, & M. Zragoza (Eds.), *Sexual aggression: Issues in etiology, assessment, and treatment* (pp. 17–41). Washington, DC: Taylor and Francis.

Ellis, L., & Walsh, A. (1997). Gene-based evolutionary theories in criminology. *Criminology, 35*, 229–276.

Erickson, K. G., Crosnoe, R., & Dombusch, S. M. (2000). A social process model of adolescent deviance: Combining social control and differential association perspectives. *Journal of Youth and Adolescence, 29*(4), 395–425.

Eronen, M., Angermeyer, M. C., & Schulze, B. (1998). The psychiatric epidemiology of violent behaviour. *Social Psychiatry and Psychiatric Epidemiology, 33*, 13–23.

Eysenck, H. J. (1960). Eysenck levels of personality, constitutional factors, and social influences: An experimental approach. *International Journal of Social Psychiatry, 6*, 12–24.

Eysenck, H. J. (1964). *Crime and personality*. London: Routledge & Kegan Paul.

Eysenck, H. J., & Eysenck, S. B. G. (1975). *Manual of the Eysenck personality questionnaire*. London: Hodder and Stoughton.

Fagan, A. A. (2005). The relationship between adolescent physical abuse and criminal offending: Support for an enduring and generalized cycle of violence. *Journal of Family Violence, 20*, 279–290.

Farrington, D. P. (1995). The development of offending and antisocial behavior from childhood: Key findings from the Cambridge study in delinquent development. *Journal of Child Psychology and Psychiatry, 360*, 929–964.

Farrington, D. P. (2000). Psychosocial predictors of adult antisocial personality disorder and adult convictions. *Behavioral Science and the Law, 18*(5), 605–622.

Farrington, D. P., Biron, L., & LeBlanc, M. (1982) Personality and delinquency in London and Montreal. In J. Gunn & D. P. Farrington (Eds.), *Abnormal offenders, delinquency and the criminal justice system* (pp. 153–201). Chichester, England: Wiley.

Federal Bureau of Investigation. (2009). *Uniform crime report*. Washington, DC.

Fonagy, P., Target, M., Cottrell, D., Phillips, J., & Kurtz, Z. (2002). *What works for whom? A critical review of treatments for children and adolescents*. New York: Guilford Press.

Fridell, M., Hesse, M., & Jaeger, M. M., & Kuhlhorn, E. (2008). Antisocial personality disorder as a predictor of criminal behaviour in a longitudinal study of a cohort of abusers of several classes of drugs: Relation to type of substance and type of crime. *Addictive Behaviors, 33*(6), 799–811.

Freud, S. (1916). Introductory lectures on psychoanalysis. In J. Strachey (Ed.), *Standard edition of the complete psychological works of Sigmund Freud* (Vol. 16). London: Hogarth Press.

Freud, S. (1923). Ego and id. In J. Strachey (Ed.), *Standard edition of the complete psychological works of Sigmund Freud*. London: Hogarth Press.

Freud, S. (1933). *New introductory lectures on psychoanalysis*. New York: W. W. Norton.

Furnham, A., & Thompson, J. (1991). Personality and self-reported delinquency. *Personality and Individual Differences, 12*(6), 585–593.

Gaarder, E., & Belknap, J. (2002). Tenuous borders: Girls transferred to adult court. *Criminology, 40*(3), 481–518.

Garrett, C. J. (1985). Effects of residential treatment of adjudicated delinquents. metaanalysis. *Journal of Research in Crime and Delinquency*, 22, 287–308.

Gauthier, D. K., & Bankston, W. B. (1997). Gender equality and the sex ratio of intimate killing. *Criminology, 35*, 577–600.

Gauthier, D. K., Chaudoir, N. K., & Forsyth, C. J. (2003). A sociological analysis of maternal infanticide in the United States, 1984–1996. *Deviant Behavior, 24* (4), 393–404.

Geberth, V. J., & Turco, R. N. (1997). Antisocial personality disorder, sexual sadism, malignant narcissism, and serial murder. *Journal of Forensic Sciences, 42* (1), 49–60.

Gendreau, P. (1996). The principles of effective intervention with offenders. In F. X. Harland, (Ed.), *Choosing correctional options that work: Defining the demand and evaluating the supply* (pp. 117–130). Thousand Oaks, CA: Sage.

Gendreau, P., Goggin, C., & Smith, P. (2002). Is the PCL-R really the "unparalleled" measure of offender risk? A lesson in knowledge cumulation. *Criminal Justice and Behavior, 29*, 397–426.

Gendreau, P., & Ross, R. R. (1983). Correctional treatment: Some recommendations for effective intervention. *Juvenile and Family Court Journal, 34*(4), 31–39.

Gilfus, M. E. (1992). From victims to survivors to offenders: Women's routes of entry and immersion into street crime. *Women and Criminal Justice*, *4*, 63–89.

Giordano, P. C., Cernkovich, S. A., & Rudolph, J. L. (2002). Gender, crime, and desistance: Toward a theory of cognitive transformation. *American Journal of Sociology, 107*(4), 990–1064.

Glover, E. (1960). *Roots of crime*. New York: International Universities Press.

Glynn, J. D., & Harper, P. (1961). Behaviour therapy in transvestism. *Lancet, 1*, 619.

Goldstein, A. P., Coultry, T., Glick, B., Gold, D., Reiner, S., & Zimmerman, D. (1986). Aggression replacement training: A comprehensive intervention for the acting out delinquent. *Journal of Correctional Education, 37*(3), 120–126.

Goodkind, S., Ng, I., & Sarri, R. C., (2006). The impact of sexual abuse in the lives of young women involved or at risk of involvement with the juvenile justice system. *Violence Against Women, 12(5)*, 456–477.

Gould, L. C. (1969). Who defines delinquency: A comparison of self-reported and officially reported indices of delinquency for three racial groups. *Social Problems*, 325–336.

Gunnison, E., & McCartan, L. M. (2005). Female persisters in criminal offending: A theoretical examination of predictors. *Women and Criminal Justice, 16*, 43–65.

Hains, A. A., & Herrman, L. P. (1989). Brief report: Social cognitive skills and behavioral adjustment of delinquent adolescents in treatment. *Journal of Adolescence, 12*, 323–328.

Hagan, J., Gillis, A. R., & Simpson, J. (1985). The class structure of gender and delinquency: Toward a power-control theory of common delinquent behavior. *American Journal of Sociology, 90*(6), 1151–1178.

Hare, R. D. (1991). *The psychopathy checklist-revisited*. North Tonawanda, NY: Multi-Health Systems.

Hare, R. D. (2003). *Manual for the psychopathy checklist-revised*. Toronto, Ontario, Canada: Multi-Health Systems.

Harlow, C. W. (1999). *Prior abuse reported by inmates and probationers*. Washington, DC: U.S. Department of Justice, Office of Justice Programs, Bureau of Justice Statistics.

Harris, G., Rice, M., & Cormier, C. (1991). Psychopathy and violent recidivism. *Law and Human Behavior, 15*, 625–637.

Hart, S., Kropp, P., & Hare, R. (1988). Performance of male psychopaths following conditional release from prison. *Journal of Consulting and Clinical Psychology, 56*, 227–232.

Heaven, P., Newbury, K., and Wilson. V. (2004). The Eysenck psychoticism dimension and delinquent behaviors among non-criminals: Changes across the lifespan? *Personality and Individual Differences, 36*(8), 1817–1825.

Heimer, K., & DeCoster, S. (1999). The gendering of violent delinquency. *Criminology, 37*(2), 277–317.

Helfgott, J. B. (2008). *Criminal behavior: Theories, typologies, and criminal justice.* Los Angeles, CA: Sage.

Hemphill, J. F., & Hare, R. D. (2004). Some misconceptions about the Hare PCL-R and risk assessment: A reply to Gendreau, Goggin, and Smith. *Criminal Justice and Behavior, 31*(3), 203–243.

Hirschi, T. (1969). *Causes of delinquency.* Berkeley, CA: University of California Press.

Hirschi, T., & Gottfredson, M. R. (1983). Age and the explanation of crime. *American Journal of Sociology, 89*, 552–584.

Hodgins, S., & Cote, G. (1993). The criminality of mentally disordered offenders. *Criminal Justice and Behavior, 20*, 115–129.

Hollin, C. R., McGuire, J., & Hounsome, J. C. (2008). Cognitive skills behavior programs for offenders in the community: A reconviction analysis. *Criminal Justice and Behavior, 35*(3), 269–283.

Hubbard, D. J., & Pratt, T. C. (2002). A meta-analysis of the predictors of delinquency among girls. *Journal of Offender Rehabilitation, 34*(3), 1–13.

Izzo, R. L., & Ross, R. R. (1990). Meta-analysis of rehabilitation programs for juvenile delinquents. *Criminal Justice and Behavior, 17*, 134–142.

Jackson, R. L., Rogers, R., Neumann, C. S., & Lambert, P. L. (2002). Psychopathy in female offenders: An investigation of its underlying dimensions. *Criminal Justice and Behavior, 29*, 692–704.

James, B. (1962). A case of homosexuality treated by aversion therapy. *British Medical Journal, 1*, 768–770.

James, S. (1978). Treatment of homosexuality II. Superiority of desensitization/arousal as compared with anticipatory avoidance conditioning: Results of a controlled trial. *Behavior Therapy, 9*, 28–36.

Jensen, G. F. (2003). Gender variation in delinquency: Self-image, beliefs and peers as mediating mechanisms. In R. L. Akers & G. F. Jensen (Eds.), *Social learning theory and the explanation of crime: A guide for the new century. Advances in criminological theory: Vol. 11* (pp. 151–177). New Brunswick, NJ: Transaction.

Jordan, B. K., Schlenger, W. E., Fairbank, J. A., & Caddell, J. M. (1996). Prevalence of psychiatric disorders among incarcerated women part II. Convicted felons entering prison. *Archives of General Psychiatry, 53*(6), 513–519.

Kandel, D. B. (1974). Interpersonal influences on adolescent illegal drug use. In E. Josephson & E. E. Carrol (Eds.), *Drug use: Epidemiological and sociological approaches* (pp. 207–240). New York: Wiley.

Kaplan, M. S., & Green, A. (1995). Incarcerated female sexual offenders: A comparison of sexual histories with eleven female nonsexual offenders. *Sexual Abuse: A Journal of Research and Treatment, 7*(4), 287–300.

Karstedt, S. (2000). Emancipation, crime and problem behavior of women: A perspective from Germany. *Gender Issues*, 21–58.

Kernberg, O. (1966). Structural derivatives of object relationships. *International Journal of Psychoanalysis, 47*, 236–253.

Kilpatrick, D. G., Acierno, R., Saunders, B. E., Resnick, H. S., Best, C. L., & Schnurr, P. (2000). Risk factors for adolescent substance abuse and dependence: Data from a national sample. *Journal of Consulting and Clinical Psychology, 68*, 19–30.

Kim, H., & Kim, H. (2005). Gender differences in delinquent behavior among Korean adolescents. *Child Psychiatry and Human Development, 35*(4), 325–345.

Kirigin, K. A., Wolf, M. M., Braukmann, C. J., Fixsen, D. L., & Phillips, E. L. (1979). Achievement Place: A preliminary outcome evaluation. In J. S. Stumphauzer (Ed.), *Progress in behavior therapy with delinquents*. Springfield, IL: Charles C. Thomas.

Kirigin, K. A., Braukmann, C. J., Atwater, J. D., & Wolf, M. M. (1982). An evaluation of teaching-family (Achievement Place) group homes for juvenile offenders. *Journal of Applied Behavior Analysis, 15*, 1–6.

Koons-Witt, B. A., & Schram, P. J. (2003). The prevalence and nature of violent offending by females. *Journal of Criminal Justice, 31*(4), 361–371.

Lansford, J. E., Dodge, K. A., Pettit, G. S., Bates, J. E., Crozier, J., & Kaplow, J. (2002). A 12- year prospective study of the long-term effects of early child physical maltreatment on psychological, behavioral, and academic problems in adolescence. *Archives of Pediatrics and Adolescent Medicine, 156*, 824–830.

Lansford, J. E., Miller-Johnson, S., Berlin, L. J., Dodge, K. A., Bates, J. E., & Petit, G. S. (2007). Early physical abuse and later violent delinquency: A prospective longitudinal study. *Child Maltreatment, 12*(3), 233–245.

Lauritsen, J. L. (1993). Sibling resemblance in juvenile delinquency: Findings from the National Youth Survey. *Criminology, 31*, 387–409.

Leukefeld, C., McDonald, H. S., & Staton, M. (2003). An employment intervention for drug- abusing offenders. *Federal Probation, 67*(2), 27–31.

Lipsey, M. W. (1992). Juvenile delinquency treatment: A meta-analytic inquiry into the variability of effects. In T. C. Cook, H. Cooper, D. S. Cordray, H. Hartmann, L. V. Hedges, R. L. Light, T. A. Louis, & F. M. Mosteller (Eds.), *Meta-analysis for explanation* (pp. 83–127). New York: Russell Sage.

Lombroso, C. (1911). *Criminal man*. New York: Knickerbocker Press.

Lombroso, C., & Ferrero, W. (1895). *The female offender*. New York: D. Appleton.

Loving, J. L. (2002). Treatment planning with the psychopathy checklist–revised. *International Journal of Offender Therapy and Comparative Criminology, 46*, 281–293.

Luster, T., & Small, S. A. (1997) Sexual abuse history and problems in adolescence: Exploring effects of moderating variables. *Journal of Marriage and the Family, 59*, 131–142.

Maletzky, B. (1990). *Treating the sexual offender*. Newbury Park, CA: Sage.

Marlowe, J. H., Reid, J. B., Patterson, G. R., & Weinrott, M. (1986). *Treating adolescent multiple offenders: A comparison and follow-up of parent training for families of chronic delinquents*. Unpublished manuscript, Social Learning Center, Eugene, OR.

Martinson, R. (1974). What works?—Questions and answers about prison reform. *Public Interest, 35*, 22–54.

McCrory, E., Hickey, N., & Farmer, E. (2008). Early-onset sexually harmful behaviour in childhood: A market for life-course persistent antisocial behaviour. *Journal of Forensic Psychiatry and Psychology, 19*(3), 382–395.

McElroy, S. L., Soutullo, C. A., Taylor, P., Nelson, E. B., Beckman, D. A., Brusman, L. A., ... Keck, P. E. (1999). Psychiatric features of 36 men convicted of sexual offenses. *Clinical Psychiatry, 60*(6), 414–420.

McGuigan, W. M., & Middlemiss, W. (2005). Sexual abuse in childhood and interpersonal violence in adulthood: A cumulative impact on depressive symptoms in women. *Journal of Interpersonal Violence, 20*, 1271–1287.

Merton, R. K. (1938). Social structure and anomie. *American Sociological Review, 3*, 672–682.

Messerschmidt, J. W. (1993). *Masculinities and crime*. Lanham, MD: Rowman & Littlefield.

Miller, B. A., & Downs, W. R. (1993). The impact of family violence on the use of alcohol by women. *Alcohol Health and Research World, 17*, 137–142.

Moffitt, T. E. (1993). Adolescence-limited and life-course-persistent antisocial behavior: A developmental taxonomy. *Psychological Review, 100*(4), 674–701.

Moore, K. A., Harrison, M., & Young, M. S. (2008). A cognitive therapy treatment program for repeat DUI offenders. *Journal of Criminal Justice, 36*(6), 539–545.

Morris, R. G., & Blackburn, A. G. (2009). Cracking the code: An empirical exploration of social learning theory and computer crime *Journal of Crime and Justice, 32*(1), 1–34.

Mulder, R. T., Wells, J. E., Joyce, P. R., & Bushnell, J. A. (1994). Antisocial women. *Journal of Personality Disorders, 8*, 279–287.

Neff, J. L., & Waite, D. E. (2007). Male versus female substance abuse patterns among incarcerated juvenile offenders: Comparing strain and social learning variables. *Justice Quarterly, 24*(1), 106–132.

Patrick, C. J. (2006). *Handbook of psychopathy*. New York: Guilford Press.

Patterson, G. R. (1982). *Coercive family process*. Eugene, OR: Castalia Publishing Co.

Patterson, G. R., Chamberlain, P., & Reid, J. B. (1982). A comparative evaluation of parent training procedures. *Behavior Therapy, 13*, 638–650.

Patterson, G. R., & Dishion, T. J. (1985). Contributions of families and peers to delinquency. *Criminology, 23*, 63–79.

Patterson, G. R., & Fleischman, M. J. (1979). Maintenance of treatment effects: Some considerations concerning family systems and follow up data. *Behavior Therapy, 10*, 168–185.

Patterson, G. R., & Gullion, M. E. (1976). *Living with children: New methods for parents and teachers*. Champaign, IL: Research Press.

Pavlov, I. P. (1927). *Conditioned reflexes: An investigation of the physiological activity of the cerebral cortex*. London: Oxford University Press.

Pearson, F. S., Lipton, D. S., & Cleland, C. M. (2002). The effect of behavioral/cognitive- behavioral on recidivism. *Crime and Delinquency, 48*(3), 476–496.

Pellisier, B., & Jones, N. (2006). Differences in motivation, coping style, and self-efficacy among incarcerated male and female drug users. *Journal of Substance Abuse Treatment, 30*, 113–120.

Pentz, M. A. W. (1980). Assertion training and trainer effects on unassertive and aggressive adolescents. *Journal of Counseling Psychology, 27*(1), 76–83.

Pettiway, L. (1987). Participation in crime partnerships by female drug users. *Criminology, 25*, 741–767.

Phillips, E. L., Phillips, E. A., Fixsen, E. L., & Wolf, M. M. (1973, June). Behavior shaping works for delinquents. *Psychology Today*, 65–72.

Phillips, E. L., Phillips, E. A., Fixsen, D. L., & Wolf, M. M. (1974). *The teaching family handbook*. Lawrence, KS: University of Kansas, Department of Human Development Family Life.

Phillips, E. L., Phillips, E. A., Wolf, M. M., & Fixsen, D. L. (1973). Achievement Place: Development of the elected manager system. *Journal of Applied Behavior Analysis*, 6(4), 541–561.

Plomin, R., Chipuer, H. M., & Loehlin, J. C. (1990). Behavior genetics and personality. In L. A. Pervin (Ed.), *Handbook of personality theory and research* (pp. 225–243). New York: Guilford.

Pollak, O. (1950). *The criminality of women*. Philadelphia: University of Pennsylvania Press.

Pollock, J. M. (2002). *Women, prison, and crime*. Belmont, CA: Wadsworth.

Pollock, J. M., & Davis, S. M. (2005). The continuing myth of the violent female offender. *Criminal Justice Review, 30*(1), 5–29.

Quay, H. C. (1986). Residential treatment. In H. Quay & J. S. Werry (Eds.), *Psychological disorders of childhood* (pp. 558–580). New York, NY: John Wiley & Sons.

Quinsey, V. L., Bergersen, S. G., & Steinman, C. M. (1976). Changes in physiological and verbal responses of child molesters during aversion therapy. *Canadian Journal of Behavioural Sciences, 8*, 202–212.

Quinsey, V. L., & Earls, C. M. (1990). The modification of sexual preferences. In W. L. Marshall, D. R. Laws, & H. E. Barbaree (Eds.), *Handbook of sexual assault: Issues, theories, and treatment of the offender* (pp. 279–295). New York: Plenum.

Quinsey, V. L., & Marshall, W. L. (1983). Procedures for reducing inappropriate sexual arousal: An evaluation review. In J. G. Greer & I. R. Stuart (Eds.), *The sexual aggressor: Current perspectives on treatment* (pp. 267–289). New York: Van Nostrand Reinhold.

Rabin, A. I. (1986). The antisocial personality-psychopathy and sociopathy. In H. Toch (Ed.), *Psychology of crime and criminal justice* (pp. 322–346). Prospective Heights, IL: Waveland Press.

Raine, A. (1993). Features of borderline personality and violence. *Journal of Clinical Psychology, 49*(2), 277–281.

Raine, N. (2008). *The criminal brain: Understanding biological theories of crime*. New York: New York University Press.

Rafter, N. H. (1997). Psychopathy and the evolution of criminological knowledge. *Theoretical Criminology, 1*(2), 235–259.

Raymond, M. (1956). Case of fetishism treated by aversion therapy. *British Medical Journal, 2*, 854–856.

Rawlings, D., & Dawe, S. (2008). Psychoticism and impulsivity. In G. Boyle, G. Matthews, & D. H. Saklofske (Eds.), *The Sage handbook of personality theory and assessment* (Vol. 1, pp. 357–378). Los Angeles, CA: Sage.

Redl, F., & Wineman, D. (1951). *Children who hate*. Glencoe, IL: Free Press.

Reinemann, D. H., Stark, K. D., & Swearer, S. M. (2003). Family factors that differentiate sexually abused and nonabused adolescent psychiatric inpatients. *Journal of Interpersonal Violence, 18*, 471–489.

Rice, M. E., Harris, G. T., & Cormier, C. A. (1992). An evaluation of a maximum-security therapeutic-community for psychopaths and other mentally disordered offenders. *Law and Human Behavior, 16*, 399–412.

Roberts-Lewis, A. C., Parker, S., & Welch, C. (2009). Evaluating the cognitive and behavioral outcomes of incarcerated adolescent females receiving substance abuse treatment: A pilot study. *Journal of Child and Adolescent Substance Abuse, 18*(2), 151–171.

Robins, L. N. (1966). *Deviant children grow up*. Baltimore, MD: Williams & Wilkins.

Roddy, J. (1979). Juvenile aversion therapy: Counter-clockwork constitutional violations. *Juvenile and Family Court Journal, 30*(4), 17–38.

Romano, E., & De Luca, R. V. (2000). Male sexual abuse: A review of effects, abuse characteristics, and links with later psychological functioning. *Aggression and Violent Behavior, 6*, 55–78.

Romero, E., Luengo, M. A., & Sobral, J. (2001). Personality and antisocial behavior: Study of temperamental dimensions. *Personality and Individual Differences, 6*(1), 329–348.

Ross, R. R., Currie, C., & Krug-McKay, B. (1980). *The female offender: Treatment and training*. Ottawa: Ontario Ministry of Correctional Services.

Ross, R. R., & Doody, K. F. (1973). Persistence in the psychopathic personality. *Canadian Journal of Criminology and Corrections, 15*(3), 292–305.

Ross, R. R., & Fabiano, E. A. (1985). *Time to think: A cognitive model of delinquency prevention and offender rehabilitation*. Johnson City, TN: Institute of Social Sciences and Arts.

Ross, R. R., & McKay, B. H. (1976). A study of institutional treatment programs. *International Journal of Offender Therapy and Comparative Criminology, 20*(2), 165–173.

Ross, R. R., & Palmer, W. Modification of emotional expressiveness in adolescent offenders. *Crime and Justice, 4*(2–3), 125–133.

Rushton, J. P., Fulker, D. W., Neale, M. C., Nias, D. K. B., & Eysenck, H. J. (1986). Altruism and aggression: The heritability of individual differences. *Journal of Personality and Social Psychology, 50*, 1192–1198.

Sansone, R. A., & Sansone, L. A. (2009). Borderline personality and criminality. *Psychiatry, 6*(10), 16–20.

Salekin, R. T., Rogers, R., & Sewell, K. W. (1996). A review and meta-analysis of the psychopathy checklist and psychopathy checklist–revised: Predictive validity of dangerousness. *Clinical Psychology: Science and Practice*, *3*, 203–215.

Salekin, R. T., Rogers, R., & Sewell, K. W. (1997). Construct validity of psychopathy in a female offender sample: A multitrait-multimethod evaluation. *Journal of Abnormal Psychology, 106*, 576–585.

Salekin, R. T., Rogers, R., Ustad, K. L., & Sewell, K. W. (1998). Psychopathy and recidivism among female inmates. *Law and Human Behavior, 22*(1), 109–128.

Salisbury, E. J., & Van Voorhis, P. (2009). Gendered pathways: A quantitative investigation of women probationers' paths to incarceration. *Criminal Justice and Behaviors, 36*(6), 541–566.

Sampson, R. J., & Laub, J. H. (1993). *Crime in the making: Pathways and turning points through life*. Cambridge, MA: Harvard University Press.

Sandhu, H. S., & Irving, L. H. (1974). Female offenders and martial disorganization: An aggressive and retreatist reaction. *International Journal of Criminology and Penology, 2*(1), 35–42.

Saunders, B. E., Kilpatrick, D. G., Hanson, R. F., Resnick, H. S., & Walker, M. E. (1999). Prevalence, case characteristics, and long-term psychological correlates of child rape among women: A national survey. *Child Maltreatment, 4*, 187–200.

Schippers, G. M., Marker, N., & De Fuentes-Merillas, L. (2001). Social skills training, prosocial behavior, and aggressiveness in adult incarcerated offenders. *International Journal of Offender Therapy and Comparative Criminology, 45* (2), 244–251.

Schoenfeld, C. G. (1971). A psychoanalytic theory of juvenile delinquency. *Crime and Delinquency, 17*(4), 469–480.

Schwitzgebel, R. K. (1972). Limitation on the coercive treatment of offenders. *Criminal Law Bulletin, 8*(4), 267–320.

Sheldon, W. H. (1940). *The varieties of human physique: An introduction to constitutional psychology*. New York: Harper.

Siegel, J. A., & Williams, L. M. (2003). The relationship between childhood sexual abuse and female delinquency and crime: A prospective study. *Journal of Research in Crime and Delinquency, 40*(1), 71–94.

Simon, R. (1975). *Women and crime*. Lexington, MA: D. C. Heath.

Simons, R. L., & Whitbeck, L. B. (1991). Sexual abuse as a precursor to prostitution and victimization among adolescent and homeless women. *Journal of Family Issues, 12*, 361–379.

Skeem, J. L., Edens, J. F., & Camp, J. (2004). Are there ethnic differences in levels of psychopathy? A meta-analysis. *Law and Human Behavior, 28*(5), 505–527.

Skeem, J. L., Monahan, J., & Mulvey, E. P. (2002). Psychopathy, treatment involvement, and subsequent violence among civil psychiatric patients. *Law and Human Behavior*, *26*, 577–603.

Skinner, B. F. (1938). *The behavior of organisms: An experimental analysis*. New York: Appleton-Century-Crofts.

Skinner, B. F. (1953). *Science and human behavior*. New York: Macmillan.

Smith, C. J., Hayler, B., & Padalino, N. (1998). *An interim report on the Illinois Department of Corrections' juvenile sex offender treatment program*. Chicago, IL: Illinois Criminal Justice Information Authority.

Sommers, I., & Baskin, D. R. (1993). The situational context of violent female offending. *Journal of Research in Crime and Delinquency, 30*(2), 136–162.

South, S. C., Chauhan, P., & Bale, R. (2002). Personality disorders and violence among female prison inmates. *Journal of the American Academy of Psychiatry and the Law, 30*(4), 502–512.

Spiegler, M. D., & Guevremont, D. C. (1993). *Contemporary behavior therapy*. Monterey, CA: Brooks/Cole.

Steffensmeier, D. J. (1980). Sex differences in patterns of adult crime, 1967–1977. *Social Forces, 58*, 1080–1108.

Steffensmeier, D. J., & Allan, E. (1995). Criminal behavior: Gender and age. In J. Sheley (Ed.), *Criminology: A contemporary handbook* (pp. 83–114). Florence, KY: Wadsworth.

Steffensmeier, D. J., & Haynie, E. (2000). Gender, structural disadvantage, and urban crime. *Criminology, 38*, 403–438.

Stone, M. H. (1998). The personalities of murderers: The importance of psychopathy and sadism. In A. E. Skodol (Ed.), *Psychopathology and violent crime* (pp. 29–52). Washington, DC: American Psychiatric Press.

Stuart, G. L., Moore, T. M., & Gordon, K. C. (2006). Psychopathology in women arrested for domestic violence. *Journal of Interpersonal Violence, 21*(3), 376–389.

Sullivan, E. A., Abramowitz, C. S., & Lopez, M. (2006). Reliability and construct validity of the psychopathy checklist–revised for Latino. *Psychological Assessment, 18*(4), 382–392.

Sutherland, E. (1947). *Principles of criminology*. Philadelphia: J. B. Lippincott.

Swogger, M. T., Walsh, Z., & Kosson, D. S. (2007). Domestic violence and psychopathic traits: Distinguishing the antisocial batterer from the other antisocial offenders. *Aggressive Behavior, 33*(3), 253–260.

Teague, R., Mazerolle, P., & Legosz, M. (2008). Linking childhood exposure to physical abuse and adult offending: Examining mediating factors and gendered relationships. *Justice Quarterly, 25*(2), 313–348.

Thomas, W. I. (1923). *The unadjusted girl*. Boston, MA: Little, Brown.

Thornhill, R., & Palmer, C. T. (2000). *A natural history of rape: Biological bases of sexual coercion*. Cambridge, MA: MIT Press.

Tracy, P. E. (1987). Race and class differences in official and self-reported delinquency. In M. E. Wolfgang, T. Thornberry, & R. Figilio (Eds.), *From boy to man, from delinquency to crime* (pp. 87–121). Chicago, IL: University of Chicago Press.

Truman, J. L., & Rand, M. R. (2010). *Criminal victimization, 2009*. Washington, DC: U.S. Department of Justice, Office of Justice Programs, Bureau of Justice Statistics

Van Dam, C., De Bruyn, E. E., & Janssens, J. M. (2007). Personality, delinquency, and criminal recidivism. *Adolescence, 42*(168), 763–777.

Van Dam, C., Janssens, J. M., & De Bruyn, E. E. (2005). PEN, big 5, juvenile delinquency and criminal recidivism. *Personality and Individual Differences, 39* (1), 7–19.

Van Voorhis, P. (1997). An overview of offender classification systems. In P. Van Voorhis, M. Braswell & D. Lester, *Correctional counseling and rehabilitation* (pp. 81–105). Cincinnati, OH: Anderson.

Van Voorhis, P., Braswell, M., & Lester, D. (1997) *Correctional counseling and rehabilitation*. Cincinnati, OH: Anderson.

Varley, W. H. (1984). Behavior modification approaches to the aggressive adolescent. In C. R. Keith (Ed.), *Aggressive adolescent: Clinical perspectives* (pp. 268–298). New York: Free Press.

Vaughn, M. G., & DeLisi, M. (2008). Were Wolfgang's chronic offenders psychopaths? On the convergent validity between psychopathy and career criminality. *Journal of Criminal Justice, 36*(1), 33–42.

Vaughn, M. G., Howard, M. O., & DeLisi, M. (2008). Psychopathic personality traits and delinquent careers: An empirical examination. *International Journal of Law and Psychiatry, 31*(5), 407–416.

Vaughn, M. G., Newhill, C. E., DeLisi, M., Beaver, K. M., & Howard, M. O. (2008). An investigation of psychopathic features among delinquent girls: Violence, theft, and drug abuse. *Youth Violence and Juvenile Justice, 6*(3), 240–255.

Walker, J. S., & Gudjonsson, G. H. (2006). The Maudsley Violence Questionnaire: Relationship to personality and self-reported offending. *Personality and Individual Differences, 12*(5), 473–480.

Walsh, Z., & Kosson, D. S. (2007). Psychopathy and violent crime: A prospective study of the influence of socioeconomic status and ethnicity. *Law and Human Behavior, 31*(2), 209–229.

Walters, G. D. (2003). Predicting institutional adjustment and recidivism with the psychopathy checklist factor scores: A meta-analysis. *Law and Human Behavior, 27*, 541–558.

Walter, H. I., & Gilmore, S. K. (1973). Placebo versus social learning effects in parent training procedures designed to alter the behaviors of aggressive boys. *Behavior Therapy, 4*, 361–377.

Ward, T., & Siegert, R. (2002). Rape and evolutionary psychology: A critique of Thornhill and Palmer's theory. *Aggression and Violent Behavior, 7*, 145–168.

Wareham, J., Boots, D. P., & Chavez, J. M. (2009). Social learning and intimate violence among men participating in a family violence intervention program. *Journal of Crime and Justice, 32*(1), 93–124.

Warr, M. (1993). Age, peers, and delinquency. *Criminology, 31*, 17–40.

Warr, M., & Stafford, M. (1991). The influence of delinquent peers: What they think or what they do? *Criminology, 4*, 851–866.

Warren, J., Hurt, S., & Loper, A. B. (2002). Psychiatric symptoms, history of victimization, and violent behavior among incarcerated female felons: An

American perspective. *International Journal of Law and Psychiatry, 25*(2), 129–149.

Weinrott, M., Bauske, B., & Patterson, G. R. (1979). Systematic replication of a social learning approach to parent training. In S. L. Bates, P. O. Sjoden, & W. S. Dockens III (Eds.), *Trends in behavior therapy* (pp. 331–351). New York: Academic Press.

Weiten, W. (1992). *Psychology: Themes and variations*. Pacific Grove, CA: Brooks/Cole.

Widom, C. S. (1989). The cycle of violence. *Science, 244*, 160–166.

Wilson, D. B., Bouffard, L. A., & MacKenzie, D. L. (2005). A quantitative review of structured, group-oriented, cognitive-behavioral programs for offenders. *Criminal Justice and Behavior, 32*(2), 172–204.

Winfree, L. T., Giever, D. M., & Maupin, J. R. (2007). Drunk driving and the prediction of analogous behavior: A longitudinal test of social learning and self-control theories. *Victims and Offenders, 2*(4), 327–349.

Winter, D. G. (1997). Allport's life and Allport's psychology. *Journal of Personality, 65*(3), 723–731.

Yochelson, S., & Samenow, S. (1976). *The criminal personality*. New York: J. Aronson.

CHAPTER ELEVEN

The Phenomenology of Addiction and the Artifact of Criminal Behavior

David Polizzi

Introduction

The relationship between drug use and criminality has become a well-established fact over the last four decades in American society (Bewley-Taylor, Hallam, & Allen, 2009; Caulkins & Chandler, 2006; Hagedorn, 2006; Mosher & Akins, 2007; Zilney, 2011). Recreational drug use, an artifact of the counterculture movement of the mid-to-late 1960s, witnessed patterns of escalating substance use and abuse, which continued unabated into the early 1970s and beyond. These spiraling increases in the use of recreational drugs caused some to identify the problem of drug use and its concomitant relationship with increases in drug-related criminal activity, a national epidemic that needed to be addressed and resolved. During his first term in office, then president Richard Nixon made his now-famous announcement in a special message to Congress on Drug Abuse Prevention and Control on June 18, 1971, during which he declared a war on drugs. Central to Nixon's "war strategy" was the establishment of what he identified as federally supported local rehabilitation efforts, along with increased law enforcement involvement that would effectively address both sides of the illegal drug problem. In that same speech, Nixon (1971) made the following observation:

> Not very long ago, it was possible for Americans to persuade themselves, with some justification, that narcotic addiction was a class problem. Whether or not this was an accurate picture is irrelevant today, because now the problem is universal. But despite the increasing consciousness of the problem, we have made little headway understanding what is involved in drug abuse or how to deal with it.

Nixon's observation was seemingly lost on those who would later follow him to the White House.

Subsequent presidential administrations have seemed more in favor of focusing their strategic emphasis on law enforcement–guided solutions to the drug problem in the United States, while at the same time appearing much less enthusiastic in implementing serious treatment-focused initiatives. The "war on drugs," and the strategies this policy has pursued, sought to eradicate the illegal sale and use of drugs through the enactment of stiffer penalties for drug-related offenses in the belief that such governmental action would effectively deter subsequent involvement in the "drug lifestyle" (Bewley-Taylor, Hallam & Allen, 2009; Husak, 2009; Joh, 2009). It was believed that the "drug problem" could be corrected if state and federal congressional authorities would simply exhibit the appropriate legislative resolve to get serious about this issue.

Rather than view drug use as a public health concern, the "war on drugs" has ultimately sought to downplay those rehabilitative aspects of drug use initially identified as a necessary part of this strategy (Husak, 2009; Joh, 2009). It could be legitimately argued that even the recent introduction of Drugs Courts and other types of rehabilitative initiatives, ostensibly seen as an alternative to incarceration, remain overly influenced by criminal justice attitudes, which are reflected in the highly coercive application of these so-called clinical practices (Blackburn, 2002; McMurran, 2002; Young, 2002). Though certain studies have focused upon the degree to which coercive treatment practices for mandated offender populations influence treatment retention, such studies seem to confuse the concept of treatment retention with successful treatment outcomes. Because there is indeed a secondary gain for a mandated client to remain in treatment, the focus on treatment retention seems to miss the rather obvious dynamic in play within these types of clinical encounters or referrals. The demand for mandated treatment involvement is often experienced by the individual as merely another part of the sentencing process and therefore is simply viewed as another aspect of his or her punishment (Polizzi, 2009; 2010a). As such, this "war strategy" has come to understand the issue of drug use as a criminal justice problem in need of a rigorous criminal justice response.

From the early 1980s to the present, this criminal justice strategy has witnessed a dramatic increase in rates of conviction and incarceration for all types of arrests related to the possession or sale of illegal drugs (Bewley-Taylor, Hallam, & Allen, 2009; Mauer & King, 2007). Though it is also true that starting in the early 1990s, a greater emphasis was placed on treatment-oriented strategies for drug abuse, the main focus of the war on drugs remains one that is predominately concerned with a criminal justice solution to this issue (Bewley-Taylor, Hallam, & Allen, 2009; Mauer & King, 2007; Mumola & Karberg, 2006). An example of this observation is witnessed in the 2004 finding that reveals drug abuse violations as the largest category of arrest that year in the United States (Mosher & Akins, 2007). In fact, increases in drug-related criminal behavior of all types continue to be witnessed regardless of the adjudicative attempts to quell its seemingly unabated growth, calling into legitimate question the effectiveness of this strategy (Caulkins & Chandler, 2006; Husak, 2009). A recent Bureau of Justice Statistics *Bulletin* published by the U.S. Department of Justice, titled "Prisoners in 2008," provides compelling statistical evidence supporting the above observation. The *Bulletin* reports an impressive 56% decline in African American rates of incarceration from 2000 to 2006, over half of which resulted from fewer convictions for drug-related crimes. However, over the same six-year period, increases in drug-related offenses for Caucasian and Hispanic defendants rose at approximately the same rate, thereby nullifying any actual decreases in rates of incarceration for drug-related offenses over this period (Sabol, West, & Cooper, 2009).

Perhaps the most glaring omission of the "war on drugs" is the continued inability of those who support the rigorous implementation of this strategy to recognize that the adjudication and criminalization of addiction will have little to no deterrent effect on the continued use of illegal substances (Bewley-Taylor, Hallam, & Allen, 2009; Husak, 2009; Joh, 2009). The experience or phenomenology of the addictive process is simply far too complex and psychologically specific to the individual user to be adequately contained by the potential threat of incarceration (Bewley-Taylor, Hallam, & Allen, 2009; Stephens, 1991; Zilney, 2009). Analogously, this same "logic" also appears wanting when applied to those individuals who continue to use and abuse alcohol or cigarettes with full knowledge of the potentially debilitating or fatal consequences of this behavior, with little or no deterrent effect. In fact, it could easily be argued that for certain users, there is simply no deterrent influence that would be strong enough to discourage future substance use. I recall a "twenty something" patient, who was seeking to enter treatment for alcohol abuse. He came to the intake session clearly intoxicated and reeking of alcohol. During the history-gathering segment of the intake, he also revealed that he had recently received a liver transplant due to a prior history of alcoholism. Three months after receiving his new liver, he reported a strange epiphany: "I realized that I could drink again." Ironically enough, this individual also reported that his brother was able to stop using alcohol after witnessing the way in which the client's drinking behavior had become so detrimental to his health that a liver transplant was essential in saving his life due to the chronic and potentially fatal effects from the long-term use of alcohol. Similar clinical examples exist that help to illustrate the powerful phenomenological dynamic at play within the experience of addiction.

During an intake interview, a former client described an experience of heroin overdose that nearly claimed his life. The individual reported that he was working as an orderly in a local hospital and decided that he would take a break from work "to shoot some dope" in a hospital restroom. Overestimating either the strength of the heroin or the amount taken at the time of this experience, he "fell out" or overdosed; unconscious, he fell against the wall and hit the emergency call button next to the commode, alerting hospital staff. Though he was immediately terminated from his job after he was pharmacologically revived, he returned home and used again! When asked about this rather perplexing decision, he quickly replied, "Don't worry, Dave, I only used half as much." It is important to note that the deterrent effect of this experience is not necessarily reflected in the intrinsic existential risks of heroin use, but in the desire not to use too much heroin so as to risk the possibility of not being able to "enjoy the high." Another related and initially counterintuitive example of this process can be witnessed by the way in which heroin addicts respond to the death of an associate or fellow drug user.

It is not uncommon for those working clinically with opiate-addicted clients to hear stories related to the way in which other addicted individuals experienced the death of a fellow drug user. One would perhaps assume that such an event would provide "a wake-up call," a time for reflection for those drug users closest to the individual, who lost their lives to drugs and rethink their own situations (Leonard, 1989; Schoen, 2009; Stolorow, 2011). Unfortunately, such an episode normally evokes the exact opposite response. Not only do these individuals continue to seek out and use drugs, but they will actually attempt to locate the very same heroin that killed their friend or associate based on the simple reasoning that "if it was good enough to kill John, it must be the bomb." Within this context, what becomes most important is not the death of an associate, but the pursuit of a memorable high. When the possibility of death is not a deterrent, and in fact, to some degree "unconsciously sought out," where does this leave us, and where do we begin (Leonard, 1989; Schoen, 2009; Stolorow, 2011)?

Though it is certainly true that the use of alcohol or other powerful illegal substances brings with them the potential for incarceration, chronic physiological and psychological problems, or even death, these factors do not appear to be central to the experience or phenomenology of illegal drug use and its concomitant relationship with criminal behavior (Leonard, 1989; Schoen, 2009). The phenomenology of addiction evokes a specific intentional relationship to world (Husserl, 1962; Smith, 2006), a specific type of being-in-the-world (Heidegger, 1996), a specific type of embodied subjectivity (Merleau-Ponty, 1996) or a different existence (van den Berg, 1972) that evokes a very unique relationship between user and substance (Schoen, 2009). For the heroin user, existence is both anesthetized and nullified, while for the alcoholic, the emptiness of existence is given its fill. Cocaine provides energy for one's day-to-day experience, and hallucinogens offer a doorway into a more livable reality. In each of these examples, existence is "normalized" through the continued use of these substances, and daily lived-experience is rendered more "tolerable."

As such, substance use emerges as a type of response to the suffering encountered within one's lived-experience that seemingly cannot be assuaged be any other means (Flores, 2004). Regardless of one's drugs of choice, substance use becomes the point from which the world is engaged and made meaningful (Chen, 2010; Peele, 1985; Leonard, 1989; Schoen, 2009). Within this context, the potential consequences of continued drug use, albeit incarceration or even death or some other type of physical or psychological impairment, are lessened in significance relative to what the experience of the drug appears to provide to existence. It is not until life becomes unlivable from the point of view of the subjective lived-experience of the user that lasting change finally becomes possible. However, what constitutes the "unlivable" will be unique to the lived-experience of each substance-abusing individual (Chen, 2010; Gray, 2004).

The purpose of this chapter, therefore, will attempt to provide a description of addiction that precedes the emergence of criminal behavior and, in fact, helps to give this experience its specific meaning. By contextualizing drug use in this way, the subsequent involvement with the criminal justice system may come to be viewed as an artifact of the phenomenology of addiction, but not the central meaning of this experience. Incarceration represents a possible horizon (Gurwitsch, 1964; Husserl, 1962) for the individual who continues to use illegal substances or alcohol, but will oftentimes prove insufficient in providing the necessary motivation to discontinue use (Cartier, Farabee, & Prendergast, 2006; Gideon, 2010; Sallmann, 2010; Young, 2002).

Toward a Phenomenology of Addiction

The traditional study of addiction is generally constructed and conceptualized from the perspective of a biological or neurological disease or from the perspective of rational choice or free will (Gray, 2004; Miller, 2010). The disease or medical model approach to addiction presumes the presence of an underlying biological or neurological dysfunction, which in turn manufactures the condition of addiction once the substance has been introduced into the physical body. The rational choice perspective seeks to reject the deterministic proclivities of the disease model theory of addiction by focusing upon the cognitive processes that lead to subsequent drug use. The drug user, therefore, consciously and rationally makes the choice to use drugs and, by implication, rationally chooses to remain addicted (Fingarette, 1988; Gideon, 2010; Peele, 1985).

As such, the rational choice explanation for substance use and addiction most closely reflects those attitudes related to the criminal justice belief that stiffer sanctions for drug use will have a measureable and rationally recognized deterrent effect on subsequent involvement with illegal drugs. Though criminal justice attitudes do not dismiss the disease model concept for drug use and addiction, it is often conflated into a frame of reference that privileges rational choice over any other competing factor by which to understand the addictive process; this attitude can also be witnessed in criminal justice treatment programs that also seem almost exclusively focused on the notion that addiction reflects an "error in thinking" or a set of "irrational beliefs" (Miller, 2010).

As stated above, neither of these traditional explanations for addiction sufficiently address the overall experience of this phenomena or the specific meaning the user gives to this process (Flores, 2004; Maruna, 2001; Measham, 2004; Pavlich, 2009). Too often, explanations for addiction tend to ignore the ways in which individuals take up substance use as a response to the existentially difficult or even traumatic episodes emerging from the day-to-day realities in one's life.

The Phenomenology of Addiction and Embodied Experience

As was briefly discussed above, the addictive process has been traditionally conceptualized as either a disease, evoking a type of biological etiology, or as a type of cognitive disorder focused on errors in thinking. Though a phenomenology of addiction would reject such reductive conceptualizations of this process, some commonalities do exist, albeit from a very different point of philosophical departure. From this perspective, the phenomenology of addiction evokes two areas of inquiry. The first relates to the actual physiological experience of addiction: What does this embodied interaction with the substance provide to the user? Secondly, how does the experience of addiction—or, stated within the language of Heidegger, how does being-in-the-world-as-addict—construct and define the existence of the user? Both of these questions will be explored in turn.

It is necessary to note to that this "dualistic description" of the phenomenology of addiction in no way intends, intentionally or otherwise, to evoke a structuralist or Cartesian understanding of this phenomenon. Embodied subjectivity or being-in-the-world-as addict reflects the same phenomenological continuity that recognizes existence as being-in-the-world-with-others-alongside-things. As such, this reflection on the phenomenology of addiction attempts to recognize the way in which substance use or addiction embodies a specific mode of being-in-the-world (Aho & Aho, 2009; Fuller, 1990; Heidegger, 1996; Leder, 1990; Merleau-Ponty, 1996).

Perhaps most powerfully present within the phenomenology of addiction is the way in which the actual embodied experience of this relationship to one's drug of choice is perceived by the user. Prior to any specific cognitive reflection, the experience of addiction is the experience of the body as intoxicated or in some way "altered" as this relates to the "conscious" perspective of the user. As the chemical influence of the substance begins to be experienced within the body, the body itself is "transformed." Over time, this experience of the body, during episodes of drug use, takes on a degree of normalcy relative to one's engagement to the world and becomes the primary focal point of lived-experience. Merleau-Ponty (1996) states: "I experience my own body as the power of adopting certain forms of behaviour and a certain world, and I am given to myself merely as a certain hold upon the world" (pp. 353–354).

Within this context, the experience of addiction is an attempt to employ a certain hold on the world that is ungraspable without the presence of the substance. The experience of the body, absent that presence, is experienced as unnatural, abnormal, as dysfunctional, as weak, and as vulnerable to further victimization. I have heard many heroin addicts tell me that they feel normal when high and are much better able to engage in the normal tasks of everyday existence; life for them seems to become more "tolerable" during episodes of intoxication. Female victims of sexual abuse describe feelings of euphoria, power, and sexual mastery when using crack cocaine that are simply not present or embodied when not intoxicated; it is therefore not surprising that a correlative relationship seems to exist between victims of sexual abuse, for example, and cocaine addiction. These observations are far more complex than the mere function of the pharmacological effects that the substance provides its user. The embodied experience of the substance appears to "transform" my bodily relationship to the world that allows for a different type of interaction to ensue; a similar type of transformation can be witnessed in the outbreak of disease within the body or within the experience of pain.

Leder (1990) in his important phenomenological text *The Absent Body*, explores the phenomenology of pain and disease from the perspective of embodied existence. Leder (1990) states that in its most mundane or everyday mode of presencing, the body is "invisible" or "disappears" from conscious perception and control. What is implied in this conceptualization of the body is that the physicality of the body recedes into experience and "disappears" into the background—or, as Leder (1990) states, "the body simply 'moves off to one side'; at any time, parts of the surface body are left unused or rendered subsidiary, placed in a background disappearance" (p. 69).

For example, when playing my guitar, my body disappears and my attention is now focused on the notes or chords being played. If I am playing particularly well that day (well of course, being a relative description), the placement of my fingers is more or less automatic; there is no concern about voicing the chord properly. The structure of the chord disappears into my fingers and my fingers into the strings and neck of the guitar. There is a habituated sense of bodily knowing that simply allows my fingers to move from Amin7 to D9th to Bmin7 to E7, etc., without much thought or concern. However, when I attempt to play something new, or if I have not played for some time due to teaching or writing deadlines, my body suddenly reappears. My fingers are dumb to this new possibility, or they hurt due to my lack of regular practice, or the guitar loses its familiarity. Leder (1990) has described this feature of bodily visibility as the body in dys-appearance: "I have used the term 'dys-appearance' to refer to this thematization of the body which accompanies dysfunction and problematic states. Dys-appearance is a mode, though by no means the only one, through which the body appears to explicit awareness" (p. 86).

The body in dys-appearance represents a mode of bodily presencing that is perceived as a problem. What was formerly background now announces its presence and demands our attention. With the onset of sudden or unexpected pain, the body becomes the focal point of my experience and demands that I now attend to this disruption within my normal mode of embodied experience. It becomes what Leder (1990) has described as the body's affective call. As such, my normal intentional relationship with my world is disrupted and my previous projects called into question.

The onset of disease or sudden pain disrupts experience, transforming both bodily possibilities and one's relationship to the world. In fact, the very contours of one's grasp upon the world change and reemerge in very different ways. "It is preciously because the normal and healthy body largely disappears that direct experience of the body is skewed toward times of dysfunction" (Leder, 1990, p. 86). If I suddenly find myself injured, with a sprained ankle or herniated disk, the world becomes a much more formidable space to negotiate. What was once background now becomes focal and articulates a very different set of embodied possibilities (Leder, 1990; Merleau-Ponty, 1996). What was previously second nature now becomes a struggle or even an impossible project to embody. The very presence of this new mode of embodiment demands that I reexamine my relationship to this former world and proceed with caution (Leder, 1990; Merleau-Ponty, 1996).

Even in those instances where catastrophic injury evokes an individual heroic response, the world is still transformed based upon the new limitations placed upon embodied existence (Aho & Aho, 2009; Leder, 1990; Merleau-Ponty, 1996). The loss of a limb or the sudden loss of mobility in one's legs creates the world anew and alters my existence. Though I may refuse to succumb completely to the new reality evoked by sudden illness or serious injury, the way in which I am able to take up my world and its projects is no longer the same. Some of these very same limitations that confront lived-experience are also present when the very visibility of the body itself, presenced as a cultural object, is viewed in a mode of social dys-appearance (Merleau-Ponty, 1996).

Unlike the modes of bodily dys-appearance encountered within the context of chronic or sudden pain or within the context of illness or disease, social dys-appearance is focused upon the very image of the body itself as constructed within social existence. Du Bois (1903) in his classic text, *The Souls of Black Folk*, explores the meaning and social construction of African American experience within the context of antiblack racism, which views the presence of blackness as a problem. For Du Bois, black experience is constructed from the general meaning provided to the black body from the perspective of white racism (Du Bois, 1903; Gordon, 1995a, 1995b; Polizzi, 2003, 2007, 2011; Yancy, 2008). In describing this presencing of social dys-appearance, Leder (1990) observes that "one incorporates an alien gaze, away, apart, asunder, from one's own, which provokes an explicit thematization of the body" (p. 99).

Such an explicit thematization of embodied existence disrupts my very ability to be and threatens to nullify the legitimacy of my projects. My body is no longer my own, and becomes what Yancy (2008) has described as a site of contestation. Within this context, social dys-appearance constructs the visibility of blackness as problematic, which in turn comes to be viewed as an "illness" or dis-ease within the larger social body (Polizzi, 2010b). Addiction, another manifestation of illness within the social body, can be seen as a specific presencing of the body in dys-appearance. However, the initial introduction of alcohol or drugs into the body is often intended as a response to an existing mode of embodiment that is experienced by the individual as problematic or, in some, attributed to the presence of some type of physical or psychological pain.

Take, for example, the individual who feels the need to be slightly intoxicated before approaching a potential love interest or sexual partner. Prior to the first drink, the individual is uncertain of his or her chances, uncertain if he or she is attractive enough, fit enough, or sexy enough to gain the eye of the one he or she would like to meet. Such individuals are uncomfortable in their own skin and are momentarily overwhelmed by the perceived inadequacies of their bodies as legitimate objects of the other's desire. However, all of these perceptions are suddenly chased away with the introduction of alcohol or other substances.

What was previously experienced as a lack or inadequacy is now covered over by an emerging sense of embodied "confidence." The body in dys-appearance gives way to this contradictory emerging sense of social presence and is moved aside. The body in dys-appearance recedes and becomes what Leder (1990) describes as a "bodily I-can" (p. 31). However, this new sense of embodied power remains manufactured and often experienced as alien, foreign, or perhaps even dangerous or shameful in the absence of alcohol or other substances (Schoen, 2009). This "splitting" of embodied potentiality creates a fissure within lived-experience that is oftentimes encountered as a distorted aberration of embodied possibility. The phenomenology of addiction is merely an extreme articulation of this process.

Though there is a wide continuum that describes and separates the use of alcohol or other drugs, a range that moves from casual use to full-blown addiction, the relationship, or intentionally to the substance is generally the same: the physiological and psychological experience of the drug provides for the user the ability to access a type of lived-experience that is perceived not to be present or in the same way accessible in the absence of the drug. Addiction, the extreme manifestation of this example, often employs the drug of choice as a strategy by which to "soften" those aspects of lived-experience that are simply too difficult to confront. Within this context, the presence of physical or psychological suffering related to disease, serious injury, or types of emotional or sexual traumas evoke a degree of bodily dys-appearance that is more or less constant, and tends to disrupt experience, by disallowing the body to recede or disappear.

The experience of addiction, with its ability to transform the mode of bodily appearing, allows for this dys-functional body to be pushed aside and to recede momentarily into the background. The problem, of course, is that once the pharmacological effects of the substance wear off, the body is returned to a mode of dys-appearance, which may in fact be strengthened by the circumstances experienced while intoxicated. Add to this fact that any prior "rational" construction of the drug as potential "remedy" must now include all those aspects of intoxicated embodiment that may, ironically enough, help to strengthen the perception of the body in dys-appearance when sober. As such, the continued reintroduction of drugs or alcohol provides for the user some degree of relief from the experience of bodily dys-appearance regardless of the specific ways in which this manifestation of the body is or has been evoked.

For example, it is not uncommon to witness clinically the co-occurring presence of addiction existing alongside histories of chronic mental illness, or sexual abuse. Often times, the individual will resort to the use of drugs to "self-medicate" those feelings or modes of embodiment that relate to that history, which remain powerfully manifest in one's current experience. The drug of choice becomes the "medicine" or "remedy" by which this experience of bodily dys-appearance is "treated." Taken from this context, the drug of choice can be viewed by what Plato identified as the Pharmakon.

Addiction and the Phenomenology of the Pharmakon

"In classical Greek, a Pharmakon is a drug, and as such it may be taken to mean either a remedy or a poison, either the cure of illness or its cause" (Kamuf, 1991, p. 112). The drug of choice in active addiction evokes both of these potentialities. As remedy, the drug of choice becomes the "strategy" by which the user treats the condition of embodied dys-appearance. The "medicinal" qualities that the drug provides address those aspects of existence that are viewed as more tolerable from the perspective of intoxicated experience. The lingering or untreated effects of sexual or physical abuse, the trauma experienced by emotional, political, social, and psychological marginalization, all become transformed and are either pushed aside or reconfigured within the context provided by the drug. When a client states that "I feel normal when I'm high," that client is describing a current mode of embodiment that has been numbed to the pain of his or her existence. When a client states that "Shooting drugs is the only thing I do well," the client is admitting to his or her own perceived inability to take up their normal projects in a competent way.

However, this remedy does not merely cover over the symptoms of one's "illness," but re-creates the very foundation of one's world. Once "appropriately medicated," the possibilities for existence appear seemingly transformed, and the world becomes, perhaps for the very first time, a "bodily I-can" (Leder, 1990, p. 31). Whether this possibility embodies a more emboldened grasp on the world or provides the doorway by which to withdraw from the mundane grind of one's marginalized existence, the world, and my place in it, no longer remains the same. The presence of this remedy provides me a new vantage point from which to engage my world as long as I continue to prove my fidelity to its curative possibilities; but the drug of choice, which remains forever faithful to the total nature of the Pharmakon, soon informs the user of the way in which remedy is also poison (Derrida, 1991).

Over time, the medicinal qualities of the drug of choice begin to make their own demands upon the user that exist parallel to those rationales, which helped to initiate the use of alcohol or drugs in the first place. As the addictive process unfolds and takes greater hold of the experience of the user, the negative meaning of the Pharmakon comes into clearer focus. Once addicted, the user's relationship to his or her drug of choice now requires that very specific attention be given to the drug itself. No longer used exclusively as the remedy for one's existential suffering, the body, in its demand for the substance, once again appears, but this time within a mode of bodily dys-appearance. The onset of physiological or psychological symptoms within the body, related to the absence of the drug, powerfully articulates the negative qualities of the Pharmakon. However, it must be remembered that the remedial characteristics of the substance still remain, as this relates to the initial "existential condition" of the individual, and may in turn help to neutralize the significance of the newly experienced negative effects of the Pharmakon.

As the "diseased qualities" of the drug of choice or "remedy" begin to emerge, one would perhaps logically conclude that this is the point of departure from which the recovery from addiction begins. Though this is indeed sometimes the case, unfortunately, more often than not, what actually occurs is the continued use of the substance, and such a result should not be surprising. The sudden presence or anticipation of the negative consequences related to the cessation of drug use is oftentimes known in advance and, in spite of this knowledge, may not always have the presumed deterrent effect on the user.

During the 1970s and 1980s, when 28-day treatment stays were still available, heroin users would seek out these inpatient facilities with the purpose of taking a "vacation" from the drug—or at least, this was the experience reported by a number of my clients with a long history of opiate dependence. It is important to note that these inpatient experiences were not at all related to the desire to stop using drugs. In fact, they were fundamentally focused on the intention of making the expense of heroin use more manageable. The inpatient experience allowed the heroin user to be "detoxed" from the drug without having to endure the unpleasant process of heroin withdrawal. Upon their discharged from the facility, they could resume their prior relationship to the substance, given that they were no longer physically addicted, and could more easily manage their habit because they would need much less of the drug to get high.

It will be recalled that I began this chapter with a few clinical accounts of individuals who experienced a variety of adverse consequences related to their drug of choice, but in spite of these "obvious shortcomings," they continued to use. In fact, regardless of the specific consequence brought on by the use of drugs or alcohol, what remained most important to these individuals was the phenomenological benefit they appeared to receive from the experience of drug use. Even in the throes of full-blown addiction and in the presence of all of the concomitant psychological and physiological difficulties that accompany such behavior, the drug of choice still remained central to lived-experience; stated another way, the drug of choice continued to provide a remedy for embodied existence that made being-in-the-world possible for the user (Fuller, 1990). In such cases, human existence becomes primarily defined by this relationship and becomes the point of departure from which the individual takes up their world. Heidegger (1996), in his classic text *Being and Time*, describes this point of departure for human existence as Dasein, or being-in-the-world.

Being-in-the-World-as-Addict

Dasein, or being-in-the-world, is literally translated from the German as a being-there. "It is the term that Heidegger gives to human being in order to disclose itself" (Fuller, 1990, p. 51). This disclosing of human being always finds itself in need of a world, which is inseparable from the ontological reality of its existence. From this context, Dasein is the point of departure from which the meaning of being and the presencing of the world is taken up and "structured" into a fluid unified whole, becoming what Spinelli (2005) has described as the finite openness of human existence. For Heidegger, there is no separation between the meaning of human being and its grounding in the world. These two concepts reflect for Heidegger the inseparable and co-constituting nature of Dasein's interaction with world, which makes it possible for the meaning of human being to be disclosed.

The disclosure of the meaning of being is not only predicated upon the existence of a world, but upon the way in which that world becomes accessible to human existence. The ontological character of Dasein presupposes a specific vantage point from which the world becomes meaningful; however, this point of entry already finds itself within a specific social context, defined by a specific set of preexisting social meanings, which, as a result, helps to limit and restrict the potentialities for being-in-the-world. "As such, my existence is always situated in a structure, or a set of 'thrown' conditions, whose presence I neither chose nor can truly control" (Spinelli, 2005, p. 113). For example, the individual who finds him- or herself struggling with the realities of addiction, sexism, racism, or religious intolerance must establish a style of interaction that addresses these ontic or socially constructed meanings of their own existence, as they attempt to take up the various projects in their world.

The thrown quality of human existence may indeed place various limitations upon the possibility for being, but it is never able to determine completely the way in which I choose to make the thrownness of my experience meaningful and therefore, my own. Obviously, the existential reality of my own human mortality demands that I make choices and pursue my life's projects in the shadow of this inescapable eventuality (Carel, 2007; Heidegger, 1987, 1996). My choices emerge against the backdrop of this existential requirement, but are not rendered meaningless unless I choose to define my existence in such a way (Heidegger, 1996; Stolorow, 2011).

At its most mundane, the thrownness of being-in-the-world finds itself situated within a variety of social contexts that bring with them a demanded fidelity to what "they" say (Heidegger, 1996; Zimmerman, 1981). Though certain limitations or restrictions placed upon the thrown quality of existence are at times inescapable, these restrictions do not necessarily present a serious challenge to my ability to take up my world. However, as stated above, being-in-the-world may also need to confront thrown realities that fundamentality disrupt not only the possibilities for being-in-the world, but the very meaning for that existence. Within this context, being-in-the-world is denied the ability to be as others are allowed to be, and its ability to take up its projects is placed into question. So constructed, being-in-the-world becomes overburdened by the demands of this meaning-generating process and therefore loses the ability to be the sole author of its own existence; but this ability to choose is never completely silenced.

Take for example the powerful cultural figure of Malcolm X. Though his existence was continually defined by the process of antiblack racism, he was still able to effectively resist the annihilating implications of racist discourse. Though his stance did not end the thrown reality of racism in the United States, his example did provide another possibility by which black-being-in-the-world could resist these objectifying definitions for blackness and black potentiality (Polizzi, 2003). However, not all strategies of subversion are created equal and may bring about a plethora of unintended implications that overwhelm and restrict the ability to be. The phenomenon of addiction is such a process.

Perhaps most fundamental to the "structure of addiction" is the way in which this mode of being-in-the-world configures not only the possibilities for human experience, but also the way in which the world becomes meaningful for the individual so engaged. Initially, one's drug of choice becomes the point from which the world is experienced and made one's own. The unique experience that the drug provides to the user helps to construct the very world that the individual will inhabit. From this vantage point, the contours of the world begin to reflect the specific limits of the project of addiction, while at the same time allowing human existence the ability to be.

Over time, however, this project begins to redirect the possibilities of existence and, as a result, collapses the focus of being solely onto the drug itself. In a sense, the drug becomes the world for the user and can be viewed as an alternative type of thrownness. Within this context, the world emerges as that point from which the demands of addiction are pursued and ultimately gratified. Generally speaking, the individual involved in regular drug or alcohol use employs the substance in such a way so as to "soften" the realities of one's thrown existence. One may retreat to alcohol or drugs to relieve the experience of stress or boredom related to the demands of routine existence, or as a release from a tragically marginalized life that is too difficult to confront with a clear eye. As this use of drugs or alcohol moves toward the path of addiction, an alternative thrownness begins to emerge.

Once addicted, the drug becomes the sole focus of being. Whatever the substance had previously provided the individual now gives way to the singular project demanded by the drug itself. In the most extreme cases of addiction, being-in-the-world is configured by this demand and all other possibilities for a future are either rejected or ignored. The configuration of normal human experience designated by moments of labor and play becomes reconceptualized within the process of addiction, whereby the experience of "labor" may be viewed as the effort one makes to obtain the drug, while "play" comes to represent those moments of intoxication (van Kaam, 1965). However, during those episodes when one is lost in "play" of addiction, the need to once again "labor" for the drug is never really far from the user's mind. As such, the central focus is simply obtaining more of the drug, regardless of the means required to do so.

Crime as a Mode of Being-in-the-World-as-Addict

The demands placed upon being-in-the-world by the phenomenology of addiction inevitability leads to some manner of involvement with the criminal justice system for many of those who struggle with this very complex condition. It is important, however, not to lose sight of the fact that the criminal activity involved in the procurement of one's drug of choice remains a ready-to-hand artifact of the addictive process, and not a causal or explanatory definition of this phenomenon. Such criminal activity as prostitution, theft, robbery, and forgery all are directly related to the use of alcohol or other controlled substances and are often viewed by the user as a necessary means to a desired end: the ability to continue being-in-the-world-as-addict (Sallmann, 2010). Even when the consequences of such activity or experience becomes unmistakably apparent to the user—such as arrest and incarceration, or some degree of chronic medical or psychological impairment or condition—the use of the drug oftentimes continues unabated. A clinical example may be helpful in illuminating this point.

During a clinical intake, a former client was asked to describe his perception of the relationship between his use of heroin and his involvement with the criminal justice system. His response was immediate and not at all surprising: "It was directly related to my heroin use," he stated rather emphatically. He went on to describe a cycle of parole and reincarceration due to his continued use of heroin that had gone on for nearly 15 years. He stated that he was initially sentenced to serve two to seven years for heroin possession, and he would eligible for parole after serving two years of that sentence. He reported that on five different occasions, he was granted parole and allowed to return home. During each of these parole episodes, he was able to remain drug-free for a short period of time, but was soon returned to the penitentiary after submitting a positive urine screen for opiate use. At the time of his fifth parole violation, approximately 13 years after his initial conviction, he was returned to the penitentiary with 18 months left to serve on his original sentence. At that time, he was told by penitentiary authorities that he would not be paroled again and would simply be allowed to "max out" his sentence. He had already served nearly double his original maximum sentence, and the penitentiary authorities wanted to stop this seemingly endless cycle of parole, followed by the subsequent return to the penitentiary.

What becomes most glaringly obvious in this case, is the degree to which the continued use of heroin remained the central project of this man's existence. Regardless of the number of times he was placed on parole and abruptly returned to the penitentiary; regardless of the fact that every time he was returned to the penitentiary, he lost all of his accrued time on parole; and regardless of the fact that during this period, he was never arrested for a new crime, his fidelity to heroin remained unshaken. In fact, our therapeutic work together occurred during the period of his life that immediately followed his involvement in the criminal justice system. Though he was no longer on parole, he was fearful that perhaps he would return to heroin use, and made the decision to participate in treatment. He did state that if he had not been required to complete the final phase of his sentence in the penitentiary, he would either be still incarcerated or dead. His being-in-the-world-as-addict helped to thematize a very limited engagement with the world that reflects what Heidegger (1987) has described as a "privation of being-with-one another;" one that is uninterested in sharing a being-with-others in the same way (p. 112).

Though there are many reasons for this man's desire to stop using heroin, most of these reasons were not related to the fear of incarceration. He was now over 50 years of age and suffering from hepatitis C due to his history of heroin dependence; his relationship with his wife, children, and grandchildren had greatly suffered from his addictive history, and he wanted very much to have the opportunity to correct what he described as those very painful moments in his life. Perhaps most importantly, his use of heroin had lost the overwhelming significance that it once had, and now he wanted to be able to pursue those projects and relationships still available that he was unable or unwilling to pursue while still addicted.

Such a transformation of being-in-the-world also calls forth a different type of being-with that is inconsistent with the addictive mode of existence and its concomitant involvement in criminal activity. As one's intentional engagement with the world changes, so too does the meaning of that world, and with it, the meaning of those that Dasein will encounter in this new mode of being-with. Heidegger (1996) describes this mode of being-with in the following way: " 'The others' does not mean everybody else but me—those from whom the I distinguishes itself. They are, rather, those from whom one is, too" (p. 111). As one attempts to expand and reconfigure the possibilities for being-in-the-world, our being-with-others is transformed as well. The importance of those relationships not involved in the "privation" of being-with that is exclusively characterized by the use of drugs allows this mode of being-with to be freed from this limited hold on the world.

However, for those who remain defined by the mode of being-with that is present in being-in-the-world-as-addict-and-criminal, these encounters with others still take on a familiar and shared meaning. From this perspective, my involvement with others takes on a mode of being-with that exists as an "in-between" interaction or mode of engagement that is defined by both moments of a shared being-with and moments of privation. As a shared being-with, addiction, and the criminal behavior that the phenomenology of this experience is likely to embrace, reveals itself through the way in which I encounter others. It is through this shared engagement with the world that I recognize those who are most like me.

At the same time, however, this shared being-in-the-world-as-addict-and-criminal also gives away to a type of being-with that is characterized by modes of privation. Within this context, the normal mode of a shared being-with recedes and reflects my lack of disinterest in others. This distancing from others is not an objective lack of physical presence, but a withdrawing from a certain type of engagement with world, which is specific to this mode of being-with-others (Heidegger, 1987, 1996). Within the actual experience of drug use, or prostitution or other types of criminal activity, being-with loses its shared quality and recedes into a disinterested type of relating.

When characterized by the phenomenology of addiction, all of these moments of being-with become the vantage point from which this type of being-in-the-world discloses the meaning of its presence. While intoxicated, one's relationship to the world is characterized by the experience that the drug provides. Though others may be present, I lose myself in the embrace of the substance. In the act of prostitution, my body is no longer my own, and I wander off until ownership may be reclaimed. In the other acts of violence, the individual before me no longer reflects a shared openness to the world and is transformed into an object of my specific concern. Addiction, then, becomes the way in which the user finds his or her place in the world; while the specific characteristics of being-with provide the contours and hues of that existence. Though criminality may greatly come to reflect the specific way in which this type of being-in-the-world discloses its existence, it represents only one possible configuration for being-in-the-world-as-addict.

Conclusion

As was observed in the opening paragraph of this chapter, the relationship between the use of drugs and one's subsequent involvement in the criminal justice system has become a well-established cultural fact. However, what this chapter has attempted to argue, or at least explore, is that though this relationship exists, an exclusively causal understanding of this phenomenon misses all of the complex nuances that are present within its phenomenology. Such causally driven assumptions related to the problem of addiction have resulted in a plethora of law enforcement strategies focused on deterrence, thereby missing the fundamental structure of the addictive process. Such strategies are destined to be ineffective and costly, given that criminality is merely an artifact of the structure of addiction and not its most essential grounding feature. One may indeed incarcerate addiction, but such strategies will do little to eradicate its presence.

Being-in-the-world-as-addict reflects not only a specific type of embodied existence, but a very specific configuration of one's relationship to the world and to others. Even if drug use was to be suddenly decriminalized, addiction would still remain because the phenomenological roots of this type of being would be untouched by such an eventuality; the possibility of incarceration has little meaningful relationship with those aspects of lived-experience that lead one to the addictive use of drugs or alcohol in the first place. It may be recalled that the introduction of methadone, a synthetic variant of heroin, was used ostensibly to address the consequences or social risks presented by chronic heroin addiction, with the anticipated ancillary benefit of reducing rates of drug-related offenses. The end result of this strategy did witness decreases in these types of drug-related crimes, but the individual remained addicted and often experienced a much more difficult path to recovery. Within this context, the Pharmakon once again stands at the ready to either relieve the sufferings of existence or to be held accountable for the presence of the emerging dis-ease of the social body.

References

Aho, J., & Aho, K. (2009). *Body matters: A phenomenology of sickness, disease, and illness*. Lanham, MD: Lexington Books.

Bewley-Taylor, D., Hallam, C., & Allen, R. (2009). *The incarceration of drug offenders: An overview* (Report 16). Retrieved from the Beckley Foundation Drug Policy Programme website: http://www.beckleyfoundation.org/pdf/BF_Report_16.pdf.

Blackburn, R. (2002). Ethical issues in motivating offenders to change. In M. McMurran (Ed.), *Motivating offenders to change: A guide to enhancing engagement in therapy* (pp. 139–156). West Sussex, UK: John Wiley & Sons.

Carel, H. (2007). Temporal finitude and finitude of possibility: The double meaning of death in *Being and time. International Journal of Philosophical Studies, 15* (4), 541–556.

Cartier, J., Farabee, D., & Prendergast, M. L. (2006). Methamphetamine use, self-reported violent crime, and recidivism among offenders in California who abuse substances. *Journal of Interpersonal Violence, 21*(4), 435–445.

Caulkins, J. P., & Chandler, S. (2006). Long-run trends in incarceration of drug offenders in the United States. *Crime and Delinquency*, *52*(4), 619–641.

Chen, G. (2010). The meaning of suffering in drug addiction and recovery from the perspective of existentialism, Buddhism and the 12-step program. *Journal of Psychoactive Drugs, 42*(3), 363–375.

Derrida, J. (1991). *A Derrida reader: Between the blinds* (P. Kamuf, Ed.). New York, NY: Columbia University Press.

Du Bois, W. E. B. *The souls of black folk: Essays and sketches*. Chicago, IL: A. C. McClurg & Co.

Fingarette, H. (1988). *Heavy drinking: The myth of alcoholism as a disease*. Berkeley, CA: University of California Press.

Flores, P. J. (2004). *Addiction as an attachment disorder*. Lanham, MD: Jason Aronson.

Fuller, A. R. (1990). *Insight into value: An exploration of the premises of a phenomenological psychology*. Albany, NY: State University of New York Press.

Gideon, L. (2010). Drug offenders' perceptions of motivation: The role of motivation in rehabilitation and reintegration. *International Journal of Offender Therapy and Comparative Criminology, 54*(4), 597–610.

Gordon, L. (1995a). *Bad faith and anti-black racism*. Atlantic Highlands, NJ: Humanities Press.

Gordon, L. (1995b). *Fanon and the crisis of European man: An essay on philosophy and the human sciences*. New York, NY: Routledge

Gray, M. T. (2004). Philosophical inquiry in nursing: An argument for radical empiricism as a philosophical framework for the phenomenology of addiction. *Qualitative Health Research, 14*(8), 1151–1164.

Gurwitsch, A. (1964). *The field of consciousness*. Pittsburgh, PA: Duquesne University Press.

Hagedorn, W. B. (2006, April). Current trends and future directions in addictions and offender counseling: Finding balance and trusting the process. *Journal of Addictions and Offender Counseling*, 26, 66–72.

Heidegger, M. (1987). *Zollikon seminars: Protocols, conversations, letters*. (M. Boss, Ed.; F. Mayr & R. Askay, Trans.). Evanston, IL: Northwestern University Press.

Heidegger, M. (1996). *Being and time* (J. Stambaugh, Trans.). Albany, NY: State University of New York Press.

Husak, D. (2009). Predicting the future: A bad reason to criminalize drug use. *Utah Law Review, 2009*(1), 105–115.

Husserl, E. (1962). *Ideas: General introduction to pure phenomenology*. New York, NY: Collier Books.

Joh, E. E. (2009). Imagining the addict: Evaluating social and legal responses to addiction. *Utah Law Review, 2009*(1), 175–194.

Kamuf, P. (1991). From "Plato's pharmacy" in *Dissemination*. In P. Kamuf (Ed.), *A Derrida reader: Between the blinds* (pp. 112–113). New York, NY: Columbia University Press.

Leder, D. (1990). *The absent body*. Chicago, IL and London, UK: University of Chicago Press.

Leonard, L. (1989). *Witness to the fire: Creativity and the veil of addiction*. Boston, MA: Shambhala.

Mauer, M., & King, R. (2007, September). *A 25-year quagmire: The war on drugs and its impact on American society*. Washington, DC: The Sentencing Project.

Maruna, S. (2001). *Making Good: How Ex-Convicts Reform and Rebuild Their Lives*, American Psychological Association, Washington.

Mateyoke-Scrivner, A., Webster, J. M., Hiller, M. L., Staton, M., & Leukefeld, C. (2003). Criminal history, physical and mental health, substance abuse, and services use among incarcerated substance abusers. *Journal of Contemporary Criminal Justice, 19*(1), 82–97.

McMurran, M. (2002). Motivation to change: selection criterion or treatment need? In M. McMurran (Ed.), *Motivating offenders to change: A guide to enhancing engagement in therapy* (pp. 3–14). West Sussex, UK: John Wiley & Sons.

Measham, F. (2004). Drug and alcohol research: The case for cultural criminology. In J. Ferrell, K. Hayward, W. Morrison, & M. Presdee (Eds.), *Cultural criminology unleashed* (pp. 206–218). London, UK: Glasshouse Press.

Merleau-Ponty, M. (1996). *Phenomenology of perception* (C. Smith, Trans.). London, UK: Routledge.

Miller, G. (2010). *Learning the language of addiction counseling* (3rd ed.). Hoboken, NJ: John Wiley & Sons.

Mosher, C. J., & Akins, S. (2007). *Drugs and drug policy: The control of consciousness alteration*. Thousand Oaks, CA: Sage Publications.

Mumola, C. J., & Karberg, J. C. (2006). *Drug use and dependence, state and federal prisoners, 2004*. Bureau of Justice Statistics: Special Report, October: NCJ 213530

Nixon, R. (1971). *Special message to Congress on drug abuse prevention and control*. Retrieved from the American Presidency Project website: http://www.presidency.ucsb.edu.

Pavlich, G. (2009). Being accused, becoming criminal. In R. Lippens and D. Crewe (Eds.), *Existentialist criminology* (pp. 51–69). London, UK, & New York, NY: Routledge-Cavendish.

Peele, S. (1985). *The meaning of addiction: Compulsive experience and its interpretation*. Lanham, MD: Lexington Books.

Polizzi, D. (2003). *The experience of antiblack racism: A phenomenological-hermeneutic of the Autobiography of Malcolm X*. Available from UMI Dissertation Services (UMI No. 3069293).

Polizzi, D. (2007). The social construction of race and crime: The image of the black offender. *International Journal of Restorative Justice, 3*(1), 6–20.

Polizzi, D. (2009). Developing therapeutic trust with court-ordered clients. In D. Polizzi & M. Braswell (Eds.), *Transforming corrections: Humanistic approaches to corrections and offender treatment* (pp. 213–227). Durham, NC: Carolina Academic Press.

Polizzi, D. (2010a). Doing therapeutic work in forensic settings. In D. Polizzi & M. Draper (Eds.), *Surviving your clinical placement: Reflections, suggestions and unsolicited advice* (pp. 13–29). Durham, NC: Carolina Academic Press.

Polizzi, D. (2010b). The social construction of crime as disease: Epidemiological criminology from a phenomenological perspective. In D. Polizzi (Chair), Theory on the Margins. Paper presented at the American Society of Criminology annual meeting, November 2010, San Francisco, CA.

Polizzi, D. (2011). Heidegger, restorative justice and desistance: A phenomenological perspective. In R. Lippens & J. Hardie-Bick (Eds.). *Existential predicaments, crime and governance*. Palgrave Macmillan.

Sabol, W. J., West, H., C., Cooper, M. (2010). Prisoners in 2008. *Bureau of Justice Statistics Bulletin*, December: NCJ228417 (Revised June 30, 2010).

Sallmann, J. (2010). Living with stigma: Women's experiences of prostitution and substance use. *Affilia, 25*(2), 146–159.

Schoen, D. (2009). *The war of the gods in addiction: C. G. Jung, Alcoholics Anonymous, and archetypal evil*. New Orleans, LA: Spring Journal Books.

Smith, D. W. (2006). *Husserl*. London, UK: Routledge.

Spinelli, E. (2005). *The interpreted world: An introduction to phenomenological psychology*. London, UK, & Thousand Oaks, CA: Sage Publications.

Stephens, R. (1991). *The street addict role: A theory of heroin addiction*. Albany, NY: State University of New York Press.

Stolorow, R. D. (2011). *World, affectivity, trauma: Heidegger and post-Cartesian psychoanalysis*. New York, NY, & London, UK: Routledge.

van den Berg, J. H. (1972). *A different existence*. Pittsburgh, PA: Duquesne University Press.

van Kaam, A. (1965). The addictive personality. *Humanitas, 1*(2), 236–246.

Yancy, G. (2008). *Black bodies, white gazes: The continuing significance of white*. Lanham, MD: Rowman & Littlefield.

Young, D. (2002). Impacts of perceived legal pressure on retention in drug treatment. *Criminal Justice and Behavior, 29*(1), 27–55.

Zilney, L. A. (2011). *Drugs: Policy, social costs, crime, and justice*. Boston: Prentice Hall.

CHAPTER TWELVE

Criminality and Co-Occurring Psychiatric and Substance Use Disorders

Arthur J. Lurigio and Thomas Lyons

Mental illnesses are classified on Axis I (clinical syndromes) and Axis II (personality disorders) of the *Diagnostic and Statistical Manual of Mental Disorders, Text Revision* (DSM-IV-TR) of the American Psychiatric Association, which is the widely used nomenclature for serious psychiatric disorders (SPDs) (nonaddictive) and substance use disorders (SUDs) (American Psychiatric Association, 2000). Many studies show that people with SPDs also have high rates of SUDs and vice versa (Kessler, 2004; Mueser, Drake, & Wallach, 1998). A diagnosis of two or more psychiatric disorders—including SPDs and SUDs—made simultaneously or sequentially in the same person, are referred to as comorbid or co-occurring disorders (National Institute on Drug Abuse [NIDA], 2010). (For a comprehensive review of the literature on comorbid disorders, see Mueser, Noordsy, Drake, & Fox, 2003.)

The current chapter discusses the prevalence, causes, and treatment of interactive, co-occurring disorders, particularly among people with criminal justice system involvement, who are diagnosed with such illnesses (on Axis I of DSM-IV-TR) at a higher rate than people with no criminal justice system involvement. The former are also more likely than the latter to be diagnosed with antisocial personality disorder (on Axis II of DSM-IV-TR) (Hills, 2000; Osher, 2006). In this chapter, comorbidity is defined as two or more co-occurring mental illnesses, including at least one SPD and at least one SUD. A diagnosis of antisocial personality disorder can aggravate the symptoms of each type of disorder as well as their co-occurrences (NIDA, 2010). The current chapter also presents the results of a qualitative, longitudinal study of the psychological problems and treatment experiences of jail detainees with SUDs. The findings described in the chapter focus on detainees' access to drug and mental health treatment following their release from jail. Finally, the chapter briefly explores the special treatment needs of women offenders with comorbid disorders.

Prevalence of Co-Occurring Disorders

People with SPDs (major depression, bipolar disorder, and schizophrenia) are commonly afflicted with clinically significant SUDs (NIDA, 2010). Between 7 million and 10 million adults in the United States experience co-occurring SUDs and SPDs annually (Substance Abuse and Mental Health Services Administration [SAMHSA], 2002). Estimates of the percentage of people with lifetime SUDs and comorbid SPDs vary from 20% to 65%. This variation results from the different sampling procedures, definitions of disorders, and assessment tools used in various investigations of comorbidity (Mueser et al., 2003). Interviews with more than 20,000 randomly selected adults in the Epidemiological Catchment Area Study (ECAS) found that nearly half of those diagnosed with schizophrenia (48%) and more than half of those diagnosed with bipolar disorder (56%) had one or more SUDs (Kessler et al., 1994). Overall, the ECAS reported a comorbidity rate of approximately 60% for all substance use and psychiatric disorders (Chiles, Von Cleve, Jemelka, & Turpin, 1990).

Comorbidity rates for major psychiatric disorders are high for untreated drug-dependent persons, higher for persons in drug treatment programs, and higher yet for people with SUDs in the criminal justice system, including prison inmates and jail detainees (Lurigio & Swartz, 2000). For example, 56% of the detainees in the Cook County (Chicago) Department of Corrections (CCDOC) who met the diagnostic criteria for schizophrenia also met the diagnostic criteria for an SUD (Abram & Teplin, 1991). In a study of pretrial detainees in the CCDOC's Day Reporting Center, which examined the prevalence of co-occurring SPDs and SUDs, more than half of the detainees had one or more lifetime psychiatric disorders (Swartz & Lurigio, 1999). The lifetime prevalence rates of SPDs in the sample were higher than those reported in studies of the general population. Furthermore, detainees with a lifetime SPD (and antisocial personality disorder) were highly likely to be comorbid for a current SUD. Specifically, nearly 9 of 10 detainees (89%) with a lifetime SPD (and antisocial personality disorder) met the diagnostic criteria for a current SUD. Similarly, the majority of those with a lifetime SUD (63%) met the diagnostic criteria for a current SPD.

Many offenders with SPDs had other Axis I disorders—for example, post-traumatic stress disorder (Swartz & Lurigio, 1999), which is consistent with findings from the ECAS. In short, constellations of problems (multiple morbidities) were concentrated among detainees with the most severe psychiatric and substance use disorders (cf., Regier et al., 1990).

A study of comorbidity rates among adult probationers in Illinois found that 55% of those with SPDs were dependent on one or more drugs (Lurigio et al., 2003). The rate of polysubstance abuse among probationers with an SPD was nearly three times higher than the rate of polysubstance abuse among probationers who had no SPD. Another study found that 80% of probationers mandated to substance abuse treatment had a comorbid psychiatric disorder (National GAINS Center, 2004). These results as well as numerous findings from other studies suggest that co-occurring SPDs and SUDs are highly common in correctional populations. "[In] criminal justice settings, to be a person with a 'co-occurring disorder' turns out to be more the rule than the exception" (Hills, 2000, p. 35). Nonetheless, such disorders are usually untreated or inadequately treated in jails and prisons (Lurigio, 2004; Osher, 2006).

Causes and Consequences of Co-Occurring Disorders

Shared Genetic Vulnerability: Common Factor Model

Much research has been conducted to determine why SUDs and SPDs co-occur (NIDA, 2010). Investigations have identified genetic and environmental precursors to co-occurring disorders. For example, family and twin studies suggest an inherited susceptibility to SPDs and SUDs. Stress or trauma also can predispose people to both types of illness by altering brain chemistry and function (NIDA, 2010). People diagnosed with antisocial personality disorder and its childhood precursor, conduct disorder, are also likely to be diagnosed with an SUD or an SPD as well as the co-occurrence of those disorders (Compton, Conway, Stinson, Colliver, & Grant, 2005). Among people with an SPD, the presence of antisocial personality disorder is related to the early use of drugs or alcohol and the emergence of severe drug or alcohol use problems in adulthood (Mueser, Drake, & Wallach, 1998).

Cognitive, social, and environmental risk factors are correlated with SPDs and SUDs and contribute to their co-occurrence. These include poverty, poor interpersonal and decision-making skills, social isolation, lack of adult responsibilities, few structured daily activities, and school and vocational failure. The purchasing and sharing of illicit drugs provides people with co-occurring disorders (PCDs) with a purpose in their lives and opportunities for social contact, which motivates them to continue using drugs (Mueser et al., 2003). Hence, complicated causal pathways and confluences of life experiences can lead to comorbidity, including "poverty, [lack of] education, deprivation, stress, unemployment, [impoverished] living conditions, and early trauma" (Mueser & Drake, 2007, p. 65).

Self-Medication

Conventional and clinical wisdom suggests that people with SPDs select specific psycho-pharmacological agents that can relieve the symptoms of mental illness; that is, they self-medicate. For example, people with depressive disorders choose drugs with stimulant effects, such as cocaine or amphetamines. Or people with anxiety disorders choose drugs with sedative effects, such as heroin or alcohol. No studies have suggested a precise match between drug choices and psychiatric symptoms (Mueser et al., 2003). Therefore PCDs ingest a variety of substances to relieve the depression and anxiety that accompanies boredom, loneliness, or the side effects of psychiatric medications. They rarely report that they use specific substances to alleviate the distress and dysfunction associated with specific disorders. "Most offenders with co-occurring disorders use substances for the same reason that their non–mentally ill counterparts do—to be social, fight boredom, or achieve a 'high' " (Hills, 2000, p. 6).

Brain Sensitivity

People with SPDs appear to be hypersensitive to the effects of drugs and alcohol. Small amounts of drugs and alcohol impair the performance of people with SPDs on a variety of cognitive and motor tasks. Furthermore, the use of even small quantities of drugs and alcohol can increase the likelihood of abuse and dependence disorders as well as other negative consequences for people with SPDs (Drake & Wallach, 1993). Drug and alcohol use can precipitate the symptoms of SPDs among people at risk for such illnesses. In general, changes in brain chemistry and function associated with SPDs "may increase the vulnerability to abusing substances by enhancing their positive effects, reducing awareness of the negative effects, or alleviating the unpleasant effects associated with the mental disorder or the medication used to treat it" (NIDA, 2010, p. 5).

No data suggest that substance use causes SPDs. Rather, the use of drugs and alcohol can exacerbate or hasten the occurrence of mental illness in people who are vulnerable to such disorders (Goodwin & Jamison, 1990), "worsening symptoms, precipitating relapses, impairing functioning, and contributing to health problems in serious mental illness" (Mueser & Drake, 2007, p. 66). Thus, among those who already have an SPD, substance use can accelerate psychiatric relapses. Recent research also suggests that the heavy use of cannabis can trigger the symptoms of schizophrenia among users predisposed to the disease (NIDA, 2010).

Adverse Consequences of Comorbidity

PCDs are susceptible to a much wider range of adverse medical, legal, and social consequences than those who have only one disorder or the other (Mueser & Drake, 2007). For example, PCDs have higher rates of morbidity, suicide, psychoses, unemployment, homelessness, arrest, and incarceration than people with a single disorder only (Mueser et al., 2003). In addition, people with no comorbid disorders, compared with PCDs, experience lower rates of infectious diseases (for example, HIV and Hepatitis B and C) or premature death. They are also less likely than PCDs to be hospitalized or to seek emergency room care for psychiatric or other medical crises (Cournos & McKinnon, 1997; Woody, Metzger, Navaline, McLellan, & O'Brien, 1997).

People with an SPD or an SUD only are significantly less likely than PCDs to ignore medication regimes, to commit violent acts or suicide, and to experience psychotic symptoms, family problems, or recurring episodes of SUDs or SPDs (Hills, 2004; Mueser, Drake, & Noordsy, 1998). Moreover, PCDs' symptoms are "more persistent, severe, and resistant to treatment compared with patients who have either disorder alone" (NIDA, 2010, p. 7). In addition, incarcerated PCDs are significantly more likely to return to custody within one year, compared with released inmates who have an SUD only. PCDs are also significantly more likely to return to prison sooner after release than those with an SUD only (Messina, Burdon, Hagopian, & Prendergast, 2004). Compared with offenders who have an SUD or an SPD only, those with co-occurring disorders are more likely to exhibit several cognitive and behavioral impairments, including (Bellack, Bennett, & Gearon, 2007):

- Short attention spans and a limited ability to concentrate
- Difficulty coping with stressful situations

- Lack of social skills
- Poor judgment and compliance with directives and plans (e.g., nonadherence to medications)
- Inability to appreciate the consequences of their behavior (e.g., violations of rules of supervision)
- Limitations in recognizing and incorporating the rules for participating in treatment and criminal justice programs
- Low motivation to engage in treatment

Treatment of Co-Occurring Disorders

Basic Treatment Considerations and Access

PCDs are generally more difficult to diagnose and treat, require more specialized and intensive treatment, and have poorer prognoses and treatment outcomes than those with an SPD or an SUD only (Abram & Teplin, 1991; El-Mallakh, 1998; Osher & Drake, 1996; Ries & Comtois, 1997; Sacks, Sacks, DeLeon, Bernhardt, & Graham, 1997; Woody et al., 1997). The diagnosis, clinical course, and treatment of co-occurring disorders are complicated by the varying nature and intensity of such disorders, especially among people in incarcerative settings, who have limited treatment options and must endure the stressful, pernicious, and oppressive effects of imprisonment, which can exacerbate the symptoms of SPDs (Hills, 2000).

> Adding to the difficult task of diagnosis and treatment planning for [persons with comorbid disorders] is the awareness that [those] disorders vary in the degree to which they are disabling. One disorder may be more severe during a given period of time, they may both be continuous and chronic, or they may both be more intermittent and episodic . . . This instability in presentation poses a challenge to placement evaluators who feel the press of burgeoning inmate populations and are typically left with the decision to track an offender into either mental health or substance abuse services. (Hills, 2000, p. 3)

> Unfortunately, for people with co-occurring disorders, the decision to seek professionalhelp can be frustrating and confusing whether they enter the mental health or the substance abuse treatment systems. The mental health system traditionally has tended to exclude persons who also abuse substances, maintaining that the primary work of providers is with mental illness and not with substance abuse. Substance abuse programs often have excluded from treatment persons with mental illness who were taking prescribed medications by requiring individuals entering treatment to demonstrate their motivation by being "clean" of all drugs—including prescribed medications. (SAMHSA, 2003, p. 5)

As noted above, accessing treatment can be quite difficult for PCDs (NIDA, 2010). For example, a low percentage of PCDs report being treated for both their psychiatric and substance use disorders (19%); nearly 30% receive no treatment for either disorder (National Comorbidity Survey, Kessler et al., 1997). In a national study, substance abuse treatment was a sentencing condition for only 41% of the country's adult probationers. Even more dramatic, mandated psychiatric treatment was a sentencing condition of probation for only 7% of adult probationers (Bureau of Justice Statistics, 1997).

Furthermore, relatively few community-based drug treatment programs accept offenders as clients or provide their clients in general with effective services for comorbid disorders (Lurigio, 2004). In California, 26% of the state's drug treatment programs were designed to treat PCDs; the others were designed to treat patients with SUDs only (Messina et al., 2004). Boot camp programs in jail and therapeutic community programs in prisons customarily prohibit PCDs from participating in services (Hills, 2000). In short, PCDs "are often barred from service and shuffled between providers, seldom receiving comprehensive screening and assessment, let alone an effective package of integrated services" (Osher, 2006, p. 1).

Types of Treatment Models

Sequential or Parallel Models

Treatment programs for people with SPDs or SUDs have historically been administered through separate systems with different eligibility criteria for client services and different training, education, and certification requirements for service providers. PCDs are usually placed in sequential treatment programs in which they are expected to be free of one disorder before being treated for the other. PCDs might also obtain parallel treatment. In these regimens, different practitioners who work in different agencies or clinics provide PCDs with both mental health and substance abuse treatments concomitantly (Hills, 2000; Mueser et al., 2003).

The consequences of sequential and parallel treatments for PCDs include fragmented and ineffective care. PCDs who receive such services must find their own separate ways through the mental health and substance abuse treatment systems. These systems often communicate to their clients different sets of treatment philosophies and goals as well as disparate strategies for recovery. For example, the mainstay of care for people with SPDs (i.e., psychiatric medications) is often prohibited by many drug treatment programs that serve PCDs (Mueser, Drake, & Noordsy, 1998). In addition, sequential programs in prison treat either mental health or substance use problems while failing to deal with the complex, interwoven clinical needs of PCDs. In general, sequential and parallel treatments provide inadequate recovery resources for incarcerees with comorbid disorders (Chandler, Peters, Field, & Juliano-Bult, 2004).

Integrated Models

Integrated treatments for PCDs consider both SPDs and SUDs as "primary" conditions, deliver simultaneous care for co-occurring disorders, and adopt consistent and congruent philosophies and treatment plans for both conditions (El-Mallakh, 1998; Mueser, Drake, & Miles, 1997; SAMHSA, 2003). The essential ingredients of integrated treatments for PCDs include assertive outreach strategies; case management models; comprehensive services (e.g., housing, vocational, and psychiatric rehabilitation); and shared decision-making among staff, clients, and clients' families. They also include treatment engagement and relapse prevention efforts; long-term service options; cross-training for program staff with different backgrounds; self-help groups; and medications for the treatment of SPDs and SUDs (Edens, Peters, & Hills, 1997; Hills, 2000; Mueser et al., 2003).

Integrated treatment for PCDs is more effective than sequential or parallel treatment. Specifically, PCDs in integrated treatment programs have sustained remission rates from substance use that are two to four times higher than those of PCDs in nonintegrated treatment programs. Other benefits of integrated treatment for PCDs consist of longer retention in treatment, lower rates of victimization, and less time in the hospital (SAMHSA, 2002). In integrative treatment models, "caregivers take responsibility for combining interventions into one coherent package" (Drake et al., 2001, p. 474). A review of more than 30 studies of integrated treatment for PCDs concluded that "integrated treatment, especially when delivered for 18 months or longer, resulted in significant reductions of substance abuse and, in some cases, in substantial rates of remission, as well as in reductions in hospital use and/or improvements in other outcomes" (Drake, Mercer-McFadden, Mueser, McHugo, & Bond, 1998, p. 214).

PCDs are very likely to drop out of treatment, owing to their low motivation, cognitive impairment, and disorganized lives. Therefore, integrated programs in the community must be highly accessible and proactive, reaching out to engage clients in services instead of expecting them to locate providers on their own. Comprehensive programs encompass all aspects of clients' lives and are aimed at improving their capacities to achieve independent and fulfilling lives through employment and stable housing (Mueser et al., 2003).

When PCDs and their families participate in the development and modification of treatment plans, clients are more likely to accept and adhere to such plans. Moreover, clients must be motivated to change, engaged in services, and helped to achieve abstinence through systematic or stage-wise approaches to treatment. Impending reoccurrences in their psychiatric conditions and addictions must be interrupted through the application of relapse prevention strategies. The use of prescription medications for SPDs and SUDs can be pivotal in reducing and managing the symptoms of both types of disorders. The symptoms of co-occurring SPDs and SUDs inexorably become more severe and chronic without treatment or with nonintegrated treatment. Integrated programs view client sobriety as a long-term process because PCDs typically need a lot of time to recover (Mueser et al., 2003). In summary, the basic principles of effective treatment for co-occurring disorders within correctional populations are summarized as follows (Hills, 2000):

- Services for PCDs must focus on the integration of treatment programming.
- Both SPDs and SUDs should be treated as "primary."
- Individualized programming should address symptom severity and skill deficits.
- Psychopharmacological interventions should be utilized when appropriate.
- Phases of intervention must be tailored to the setting.
- The treatment continuum must extend into the community.
- Support and self-help groups are critical to successful reintegration into the community.

Criminal Justice-Based Treatment

Overview

Beginning with the passage of the Anti-Drug Abuse Act of 1988, the war on drugs in the United States led to unprecedented numbers of drug-abusing and dependent offenders swelling this country's probation, jail, and prison populations. In response to the growing numbers of these offenders, numerous drug treatment programs have been implemented and evaluated in correctional settings (Lurigio & Swartz, 2000). As suggested earlier in this chapter, drug-abusing and dependent offenders have very high rates of co-occurring disorders. Nonetheless, corrections-based drug treatment programs have been slow to recognize the special needs of offenders with co-occurring disorders (Kessler et al., 1994; Osher, 2006). The lack of specific programs for offenders with comorbidity fueled high rates of rearrests, reincarcerations, and violent behavior within this population (Lurigio & Swartz, 2000).

In criminal justice settings, drug treatment practitioners are cognizant of the existence of comorbid disorders among offenders but mostly in the context of other problems—for example, family conflicts, vocational and educational deficits, and medical conditions (e.g., Barthwell et al., 1995; Peters, 1993; Sacks et al., 1997; Wexler, 1995). Comorbid disorders are independent clinical entities that warrant specific interventions—a conceptualization rarely acknowledged before the 1990s (El-Mallakh, 1998; Mueser, Drake, & Miles, 1997). In other words, the treatment of drug or alcohol problems in criminal justice settings has taken precedence over the treatment of comorbid disorders (SAMHSA, 2003).

Programs for PCDs are limited in prison because of space constraints; competing demands for scanty programmatic resources; and lack of inmate time due to work assignments, cell searches, meals, and early releases to relieve overcrowding. In jails, such programming is disrupted by court appearances and unpredictable lengths of stay (Hills, 2000).

Prison Programs for PCDs

A study of treatment programs for prison inmates with co-occurring disorders found that the most common psychiatric diagnoses among incarcerees were major depression, bipolar disorders, and anxiety disorders, especially post-traumatic stress disorder. A notable proportion of inmates were also diagnosed with schizophrenia. In addition, the study found that 38% of the inmates involved in the research had a co-occurring disorder, 26% had a primary SPD, and 74% had a primary SUD (Peters, LeVasseur, & Chandler, 2004).

Inmates in specialized prisons were more likely to be diagnosed and treated for mental illness and addiction than those in nonspecialized prisons. Therefore, the reported prevalence of PSDs, SUDs, and their co-occurrences were all probably much higher in specialized correctional facilities than in nonspecialized correctional facilities. In specialized prisons, 24% of the inmates were receiving substance abuse treatment, 15% mental health treatment, and 33% psychiatric medications, which also were all likely higher than the percentage of inmates receiving such treatments in nonspecialized prisons (Peters et al., 2004). Among prison-based treatment programs, the demand for care greatly exceeded the availability. Nearly every treatment program for inmates with comorbidity had a waiting list. Furthermore, by the time the inmates were properly identified and diagnosed, many had already served the bulk of their sentences and therefore were ineligible for admission into such programs (Peters et al., 2004).

Prisoners' incentives for entering treatment programs included the possibility of early release, desirable work assignments, safer housing, and other special privileges. On the other hand, clients reported less recreational time because of the rigorous requirements of the programs. Those enrolled in treatment also reported that they were harassed by other inmates and staff because of the stigmatization associated with serious mental illness (Peters et al., 2004). Despite the possible negative repercussions of receiving treatment for co-occurring disorders, large numbers of inmates sought entry into such programs (Peters et al., 2004).

The combination of prison-based treatment and aftercare services is critical to the long-term recovery of inmates with SUDs, SPDs, and their co-occurrence (Osher, 2006). Those with comorbid disorders are less likely to recidivate if they receive treatment while incarcerated. The rate of recidivism drops even further for formerly incarcerated persons who also obtain treatment after release from prison (Messina et al., 2004). Although decreases in recidivism are partially attributable to the effects of drug treatment, aftercare programs can produce more favorable outcomes by helping offenders transition back to the community through the provision of reentry services (Peters et al., 2004).

The need for programs to treat PCDs in correctional settings is well established (Lurigio, 2004; Osher, 2006). Nonetheless, efforts to fill that need have faced several obstacles. For example, many prison systems simply lack the funding necessary to offer integrated treatment. PCDs receive inadequate treatment in correctional settings also because of fundamental differences in the philosophies and goals of the criminal justice and treatment systems. The goals of the former are to protect the public and punish offenders; the goals of the latter are to alleviate symptoms and support recovery (Chandler et al., 2004). Although participation in treatment enhances public safety by decreasing recidivism (Messina et al., 2004), this benefit is rarely appreciated by prison staff (Chandler et al., 2004). In addition, treatments commonly employ positive reinforcement and encouragement, which is antithetical to the philosophy of punishment and retribution. Whereas treatment for SUDs is often legally mandated for convicted offenders, treatment for SPDs is infrequently ordered and mostly unavailable. Indeed, mental health programs are usually the first to be cut during periods of financial retrenchment (Chandler et al., 2004).

Treatment programs for inmates with co-occurring disorders have made numerous modifications to achieve better success (Peters et al., 2004), including the development of highly structured routines; the provision of stage-wise treatment interventions that focus on motivation and engagement issues; and the coordination of prison-based health services in the areas of psychiatry, psychology, and addiction. Other adaptations of prison programs for inmates with comorbidity have involved cross-training for treatment professionals, program administrations, case managers, and security staff; regular updates on clients' progress in obtaining treatment, housing, work, education, and family support; and prerelease and reentry services (Mueser, Drake, & Bond, 1997).

A Qualitative Study of Detainees with Comorbidity

In a longitudinal study of the health care needs of people with SUDs, researchers interviewed 360 detainees in a large urban jail. The interview questions focused on detainees' medical problems as well as their participation in mental health and substance abuse treatment services (Lyons, Lurigio, & Goldstein, n.d.). After being screened by case managers, detainees deemed eligible for diversion from prison were placed into a jail-based substance abuse treatment unit. All had been convicted of nonviolent offenses and diagnosed with substance use disorders. The sample included 290 men and 70 women. At baseline, 59% had used heroin and 57% had used cocaine in the 12 months prior to detention. Nearly one-third of the sample reported mental health problems in the past year, such as depression, schizophrenia, bipolar disorder, suicidal ideation, and anxiety. Among those with self-reported psychiatric distress, 86% had used cocaine or opiates in the past year.

During a two-year follow-up period, 61% of the original detainees were located and reinterviewed in jail, prison, or the community. The written notes of the interviews were coded and analyzed for common themes (Lyons et al., n.d.). Most of the follow-up sample (73%) reported that they had received substance abuse treatment during the follow-up interval: 49% were treated in jail, 12% in prison, and 44% in the community. (Interviewees could have been treated in more than one setting; hence, the combined percentages exceed 100%.) Approximately one-fifth (21%) had received mental health services. Within this subsample, approximately one-third each had received psychiatric care in jail, prison, or the community. Among detainees who self-reported psychiatric problems at baseline, 43% had received mental health services during the follow-up interval.

Open-ended questions examined respondents' perceptions of the quality of mental health treatment as well as its coordination (or lack thereof) with substance abuse treatment. Although respondents frequently reported favorable experiences with community-based mental health providers, many complained that the providers spent too little time with them and other patients, reflecting a general problem of access to mental health care, especially in jail and prison. One interviewee stated, "You have to be really 'out there' to get [treatment] and sometimes rather than treatment they'll just take your clothes off and put you in the quiet room." An interviewee reported that he "saw someone slit his wrists and the staff did little about it. Another older guy kept taking off all his clothes, and it had to happen three times to attract healthcare staff's attention."

An interviewee in prison indicated that "manic depression [was] the main reason for [his] coming into [the] facility" but he "[had] yet to see a psychiatrist in prison." This interviewee also stated that he had a standing order for Paxil, which he had been prescribed despite never seeing a psychiatrist. One respondent reported that "they stopped giving psychotropic medications to anyone [at her prison]. They didn't even talk to anyone about it or try to ease people off it. They just stopped giving [medication]." The interviewee also believed that she was "fortunate" because she knew "she was leaving for home soon and that kept [her] sane." While the sudden discontinuation of medication could not be independently verified, other respondents stated that they were unable to obtain psychiatric medication even when they explicitly asked for such treatment: "They said I didn't need it" was a typical response.

Overall, respondents rated community-based treatment services much more favorably than they rated jail- or prison-based treatment services. In addition, recipients of community-based treatment services were more likely to note that such services had focused on both their mental illness and addiction; services received in jail and prison were less likely to be comprehensive or integrated. One respondent reported that his community-based provider had stated that "anyone coming out of drug addiction should see a therapist," while another reported that the therapists she went to "all emphasized spirituality" and that "spirituality is the key to overcoming drug addiction." However, a few interviewees were also critical of community-based providers. For example, one stated that "The doctor didn't really believe what I was saying about hallucinations."

Many respondents with SPDs refused to seek mental health treatment or decided that it was unnecessary. An interviewee with depression stated that "I haven't got to [the] stage where I can't deal with it myself." The same participant also made no attempt to seek substance abuse treatment. "I didn't want the other guys in the penitentiary to know. You don't put it out there, even if [treatment] is a good thing." Another respondent simply stated, "I don't like to take medicine." An interviewee who was attending Alcoholics Anonymous (AA) meetings in the community stated that she was never medically treated for depression, but that attendance at meetings and her sponsor's support helped her manage her illness. The respondent was unclear about whether she had tried to access mental health services. In a few cases, respondents reported that they refused treatment because they were dubious about its quality. A respondent was prescribed Prozac in prison "but [the doctors] did not explain to [him] what it was for so [he] refused to use it." Several interviewees suggested that inmates with SPDs were overmedicated but offered few other mental health services, stating that "[prison psychiatrists] just want to give you more meds."

As discussed in this chapter, clinical services for SUDs and SPDs are poorly coordinated in jails and prisons. According to interviewees, providers in the fields of mental health and substance abuse treatment often disagreed about the use of psychiatric medication. After being placed in the drug treatment division of a jail, one participant was told he could no longer take his medication (an antidepressant). His counselor stated that he thought the client's symptoms of depression were "drug-related" and would remit with substance abuse treatment. At the time of the interview, the provider prohibited clients from using psychotropic medication. The respondents themselves sometimes rejected psychotropic medications because they believed that these types of medications interfered with their participation in substance abuse treatment or other programs. One informant interviewed in a jail said that he was "depressed, but would not report this to a psychiatrist because [he was] afraid of being kicked off the drug treatment [unit] of the jail." Another avoided psychiatric medication while in prison because he had been denied entry into a work-release program when he was taking it. He explained that "an inmate once went crazy and beat up a counselor because of meds. Since then, no one is allowed in work release while on meds."

The data collected in the qualitative study were based on self-reports, which can be biased and inaccurate. Thus, respondents' frustrations might have arisen from clinical recommendations that they misunderstood or refused despite the potential benefits of such treatments. Nonetheless, these data are consistent with the findings of other studies described in this chapter, which show overall that mental health treatment is scarce in jails and prisons, failing to meet the need for such services, and poorly coordinated with substance abuse treatment.

Women with Co-Occurring Disorders

Since the 1980s, increasing numbers of women have been processed through the criminal justice system at every step in the process (Hills, 2004). In correctional populations, women are significantly more likely than men to be diagnosed with depression and other serious mental health problems. In one study of women offenders, 86% had one or more SUDs

(Sacks, 2004). A large percentage of these women also have co-occurring SPDs (SAMHSA, 2003). For example, a study of women detainees found that 72% met the diagnostic criteria for a comorbid SPD and SUD (Abram, Teplin, & McClelland, 2003). Hence, responding to the treatment needs of female offenders with co-occurring disorders is imperative (Sacks, 2004).

Women are largely ignored in discussions of treatment for offenders with co-occurring disorders. Furthermore, relatively few integrated treatment programs address the problems of women with comorbidity either in the community or the criminal justice system. Gender- and trauma-sensitive treatments are crucial to the success of treating female inmates with SUDs, SPDs, or their co-occurrence (Hills, 2004). Integrated treatment programs for women must address their histories of physical, emotional, and sexual abuse as well as parenting and family reunification issues (Sacks, 2004). "Many come to the attention of social service systems never having had adequate medical care, during pregnancies or otherwise, and they present with a myriad of medical problems that need attention" (Hills, 2004, p. 6) For women inmates with co-occurring disorders, re-entry services are an integral component of treatment, helping sustain their progress after release. The benefits of prison-based treatment diminish unless they are accompanied by post-release services. Thus, the continuation of treatment for female inmates during the post-release period is critical for maintaining their health and sobriety (SAMHSA, 2003).

Summary

Co-occurring SUDs and SPDs are common in the mental health, substance abuse treatment, and criminal justice systems. Comorbidity presents significant challenges to service providers and places a tremendous drain on treatment resources. PCDs suffer from a wide range of health problems and are unlikely to recover without long-term care. Co-occurring disorders are largely ignored in prison settings, which can lead to higher rates of relapse, recidivism, and reincarceration (Peters & Petrilla, 2004). Comorbid SPDs and SUDs among offenders are associated with elevated rates of recidivism, violence, and infectious diseases. Integrated treatment programs are effective at helping PCDs achieve satisfying and productive lives (Lurigio, 2004).

While the nation's correctional population continues to top the seven million mark (Glaze, 2010), integrated programs are needed more urgently than ever to treat co-occurring disorders among jail detainees and prison inmates. Despite high rates of psychiatric comorbidity, practitioners in criminal justice and community settings have focused on SUDs, paying relatively less attention to comorbid disorders (Edens et al., 1997; Sacks et al., 1997). The availability of integrated programs has not yet meet the demand for such care, and existing programs are frequently underfunded, difficult to access, or poorly designed (Chandler et al., 2004).

References

Abram, K. M., & Teplin, L. A. (1991). Co-occurring disorders among mentally ill detainees. *American Psychologist, 46*, 1036–1045.

Abram, K. M., Teplin, L. A., & McClelland, G. M. (2003). Comorbidity of severe psychiatric disorders and substance use disorders among women in jail. *American Journal of Psychiatry, 160*, 1007–1010.

American Psychiatric Association. (2000). *Diagnostic and statistical manual of mental disorders* (4th ed., text rev. [DSM-IV-TR]). Washington, DC: Author.

Barthwell, A. G., Bokos, J., Bailey, M., Nisenbaum, J., Devereux, J., & Senay, E. C. (1995). A continuum of care for substance abusers in the criminal justice system. *Journal of Psychoactive Drugs, 27*, 39–47.

Bellack, A. S., Bennett, M. E., & Gearon, J. S. (2007). *Behavioral treatment for substance abuse in people with serious and persistent mental illness: A handbook for mental health professionals*. New York, NY: Routledge.

Bureau of Justice Statistics. (1997). *Correctional populations in the United States, 1997*. Washington, DC: Author.

Chandler, R., Peters, R., Field, G., & Juliano-Bult, D. (2004). Challenges in implementing evidence-based treatment practices for co-occurring disorders in the criminal justice system. *Behavioral Sciences and the Law, 22*, 431–448.

Chiles, J. A., Von Cleve, E., Jemelka, R. P., & Trupin, E. W. (1990). Substance abuse and psychiatric disorders in prison inmates. *Hospital and Community Psychiatry, 41*, 1132–1134.

Compton, W. M., Conway, K. P., Stinson, F. S., Colliver, J. D., & Grant, B. F. (2006). Prevalence, correlates, and comorbidity of DSM-IV antisocial personality syndromes and alcohol and specific drug use disorders in the United States: Results from the National Epidemiological Survey on Alcohol and Related Conditions. *Journal of Clinical Psychiatry, 66*, 677–685.

Cournos, F., & McKinnon, K. (1997). HIV seroprevalence among people with severe mental illness in the United States: A critical review. *Clinical Psychology Review, 17*, 259–269.

Drake, R. E., Mercer-McFadden, C., Mueser, K. T., McHugo, G. J., & Bond, G. R. (1998). A review of integrated mental health and substance abuse treatment for patients with dual disorders. *Schizophrenia Bulletin, 24*, 589–608.

Drake, R. E., Essock, S., Shaner, A., Carey, K. B., Minkoff, K., Lynde, L., . . . Rickards, L. (2001). Implementing dual diagnosis services for clients with severe mental illness. *Psychiatric Services, 4*, 469–476.

Drake, R. E., & Wallach, M. A. (1993). Moderate drinking among people with severe mental illness. *Hospital and Community Psychiatry, 44*, 780–782.

Edens, J. J., Peters, R. H., & Hills, H. A. (1997). Treating prison inmates with co-occurring disorders: An integrative approach of existing programs. *Behavioral Science and Law, 15*, 439–457.

El-Mallakh, P. (1988). Treatment models for clients with co-occurring addictive and mental disorders. *Archives of General Psychiatry, 53*, 497–501.

Glaze, J. (2010). *Correctional populations in the United States, 2009*. Washington, DC: Bureau of Justice Statistics.

Goodwin, F. W., & Jamison, K. R. (1990). *Manic-depressive illness*. New York: Oxford University Press.

Hills, H. A. (2000). *Creating effective treatment programs for persons with co-occurring disorders in the justice system*. Delmar, NY: The National GAINS Center.

Hills, H. A. (2004). *The special needs of women with co-occurring disorders diverted from the criminal justice system*. Delmar, NY: The National GAINS Center.

Kessler, R. C. (2004). The epidemiology of dual diagnosis. *Biological Psychiatry, 56*, 730–737.

Kessler, R. C., Crum, R. M., Warner, L. A., Nelson, C. B., Schulenberg, J., & Anthony, J. C. (1997). Lifetime co-occurrence of DSM-III-R alcohol abuse and dependence with other psychiatric disorders in the National Comorbidity Survey. *Archives of General Psychiatry, 54*, 313–321.

Kessler, R. C., McGonagle, K. A., Zhao, S., Nelson, C. B., Hughes, M., Eshleman, S., . . . Kendler, K. S. (1994). Lifetime and 12-month prevalence of DSM-III-R psychiatric disorders among persons aged 15–54 in the United States: Results from the National Comorbidity Survey. *Archives of General Psychiatry, 53*, 8–19.

Lurigio. A. J. (2004). The mentally ill offender initiative. *Executive Exchange, 20*, 2–9.

Lurigio, A. J., Cho, Y. I., Swartz, J. A., Johnson, T. P., Graf, I., & Pickup, L. (2003). Standardized assessment of substance-related, other psychiatric, and comorbid disorders among probationers. *International Journal of Offender Therapy and Comparative Criminology, 47*, 630–652.

Lurigio, A. I., & Swartz, I. A. (2000). "Changing the Contours of the Criminal Justice System to Meet the Needs of Persons with Serious Mental Illness." In J. Horney (Ed.), *Policies, Processes, and Decisions of the Criminal Justice System* (pp. 45–108). Washington, D.C.: U.S. Department of Justice, National Institute of Justice.

Lyons, T., Lurigio A. J., & Goldstein P. J. (n.d.). *Mental health and substance abuse treatment: Inmate and former inmate perspectives*. Unpublished manuscript.

Messina, N., Burdon, W., Hagopian, G., & Prendergast, M. (2004). One year returns to custody rates among co-disordered offenders. *Behavioral Sciences and the Law, 22*, 503–518.

Mueser, K. T., & Drake, R. E. (2007). Comorbidity: What have we learned and where are we going? *Clinical Psychology; Science and Practice, 14*, 64–69.

Mueser, K. T., Drake, R. E., & Bond, G. R. (1997). Recent advances in psychiatric rehabilitation for patients with severe mental illness. *Harvard Review of Psychiatric, 5*, 123–137.

Mueser, K. T., Drake, R. E., & Miles, K. M. (1997). The course and treatment of substance use disorders in persons with severe mental illness. In L. S. Onken, J. D. Blaine, S. Genser, & A. M. Horton (Eds.), *Treatment of drug-dependent individuals with comorbid mental disorders* (pp. 236–251). Washington, DC: U.S. Department of Health and Human Services.

Mueser, K. T., Drake, R. E., & Noordsy, D. L. (1998). Integrated mental health and substance abuse treatment for severe psychiatric disorders. *Journal of Practical Psychiatry and Behavioral Health, 8*, 129–139.

Mueser, K. T., Drake, R. E., & Wallach, M. A. (1998). Dual diagnosis: A review of etiological theories. *Addictive Behaviors, 23*, 717–734.

Mueser, K. T., Noordsy, D. L., Drake, R. E., & Fox, L. (2003). *Integrated treatment for dual disorders: A guide to effective practice*. New York: Guilford Press.

National GAINS Center for People with Co-Occurring Disorders in the Justice System. (2004). *The prevalence of co-occurring mental illness and substance use disorders in jails*. Fact Sheet Series. Delmar, NY: Author.

National Institute on Drug Abuse (NIDA). (2010). *Comorbidity: Addiction and other mental illnesses. Research report series*. Washington, DC: Author.

Osher, F. C. (2006). *Integrating mental health and substance abuse services for justice-involved persons with co-occurring disorders*. Delmar, NY: National GAINS Center.

Osher, F. C., & Drake, R. E. (1996). Reversing a history of unmet needs: Approaches to care for persons with co-occurring addictive and mental disorders. *American Journal of Orthopsychiatry, 66*, 4–11.

Peters, R. H. (1993). Drug treatment in jails and detention settings. In J. A. Inciardi (Ed.), *Drug treatment and criminal justice* (pp. 44–80). Beverly Hills, CA: Sage.

Peters, R. H., LeVasseur, M., & Chandler, R. (2004). Correctional treatment for co-occurring disorders: Results of a national survey. *Behavioral Sciences and the Law, 22*, 563–584.

Peters, R. H., & Petrila, J. (2004). Introduction the issues: Co-occurring disorders in the criminal justice system. *Behavioral Sciences and the Law, 22*, 427–429.

Regier, D. A., Farmer, M. E., Rae, D. S., Locke, B. Z., Locke, S. J., Keith, S. J. . . . Goodwin, F. K. (1990). Comorbidity of mental disorders with alcohol and other drug abuse: Results from the epidemiological Catchment Area (ECA) Study. *Journal of the American Medical Association, 264*, 2511–2518.

Ries, R. K., & Comtois, K. A. (1997). Illness severity and treatment services for dually diagnosed severely mentally ill outpatients. *Schizophrenia Bulletin, 23*, 239–246.

Sacks, J. (2004). Women with co-occurring substance use and mental disorders (COD) in the criminal justice system: A research review. *Behavioral Sciences and the Law, 22*, 449–466.

Sacks, S., Sacks, J., DeLeon, G., Bernhardt, A. I., & Graham, G. L. (1997). Modified therapeutic community for mentally ill chemical abusers: Background, influences, program description, and preliminary findings. *Journal of Substance Use and Misuse, 32*, 1217–1259.

Substance Abuse and Mental Health Services Administration (SAMHSA). (2002). *Report to Congress on the prevention and treatment of co-occurring substance abuse disorders and mental disorders*. Rockville, MD: U.S. Department of Health and Human Services.

Substance Abuse and Mental Health Services Administration (SAMHSA). (2003). *Co-occurring disorders: Integrated dual disorders treatment, implementation resource kit*. Rockville, MD: U.S. Department of Health and Human Services.

Swartz, J. A., & Lurigio, A. J. (1999). Psychiatric illness and comorbidity among adult male detainees in drug treatment. *Psychiatric Services, 50*, 1628–1630.

U.S. Department of Health and Human Services. (1999). *Mental health: A report of the Surgeon General*. Washington, DC: U.S. Department of Health and Human Services.

Wexler, H. K. (1995). The success of therapeutic communities for substance abusers in American prisons. *Journal of Psychoactive Drugs, 27*, 57–66.

Woody, G. E., Metzger, D., Navaline, H., McLellan, T., & O'Brien, C. P. (1997). Psychiatric symptoms, risky behavior, and HIV infection. In L. S. Onken, J. D. Blaine, S. Genser, & A. M. Horton (Eds.), *Treatment of drug-dependent individuals with comorbid mental disorders* (pp. 117–131). Washington, DC: U.S. Department of Health and Human Services.

About the Editor and Contributors

The Editor

Jacqueline B. Helfgott is Professor and Chair of the Criminal Justice Department at Seattle University. She has a PhD and MA in Administration of Justice with a graduate minor in psychology from Pennsylvania State University and a BA from the University of Washington in Psychology and Society & Justice. Her research interests include criminal behavior, psychopathy, corrections and offender reentry, and victim impact in criminal justice decision-making. She is author of *Criminal Behavior: Theories, Typologies, and Criminal Justice* (Sage Publications, 2008). Her work has been published in journals including *Journal of Police and Criminal Psychology*, *Journal of Forensic Psychology Practice, International Journal of Offender Therapy and Comparative Criminology, Criminal Justice and Behavior, International Review of Victimology*, and the *Encyclopedia of Prisons and Correctional Facilities* and the *Encyclopedia of Street Crime in America.* She has been involved in research and service in correctional settings since 1987. From 1997 to 2000, she was principal investigator on a project funded by the Soros Open Society Institute's Center on Crime, Communities and Culture that involved development, implementation, and evaluation of *Citizens, Victims, and Offenders Restoring Justice* (*CVORJ*), a prison-based encounter program at the Washington State Reformatory. Her current/forthcoming work includes *No Remorse: Psychopathy and Criminal Justice* (Sage Publications) and coauthor of *Success on the Streets: Creating Opportunities for Offender Reentry* (Lynne Rienner Publishers) and applied research evaluating the Seattle Police Crisis Intervention Team/Mental Health Practitioner Pilot Project. She has served on the Advisory Board for the Washington State Department of Social and Health Services Special

Commitment Center at McNeil Island that houses civilly committed sexually violent predators and currently serves on the Board of Directors for Interaction Transition (a nonprofit, ex-offender transition agency) and the Virginia Mason Separation and Loss (support services for family members following violent death).

The Contributors

Jeffrey Burl is a student in the PhD program in clinical psychology at Drexel University, and he is currently completing his predoctoral clinical internship at the University of North Carolina at Chapel Hill. His research interests include forensic assessment and treatment.

Mark Cohan is an Assistant Professor of Sociology at Seattle University. His areas of expertise include social psychology, with a particular focus on the social production of individual and group identity, and gender and sexuality, where he has examined the narratives of sexual decision-making among adolescent heterosexual males. Currently, Dr. Cohan is involved in an ethnographic study of the steampunk subculture, studying—among other things—how participants invoke notions of authenticity to manage the rather flexible boundaries of the subculture.

Kathleen E. Cook is an Associate Professor in the Psychology Department at Seattle University. Dr. Cook received her doctorate in Social and Personality Psychology from the University of Washington in 2002. Her area of expertise is social psychology, broadly defined. Her emphases in cognitive psychology and quantitative methods point to her specialty in experimental social cognition. Dr. Cook's areas of research application include classroom learning, health perceptions, and jury decision-making.

David Dematteo is an Assistant Professor of psychology at Drexel University and Co-Director of Drexel's JD/PhD Program in Law and Psychology. His research interests include drug-involved offenders, psychopathy, forensic mental health assessment, and diversion from standard prosecution.

Yu Gao is currently an Assistant Professor in the Department of Psychology at Brooklyn College and the Graduate Center of the City University of New York. Her overarching research focus has been the identification of biosocial markers for criminal, delinquent, aggressive, antisocial, and psychopathic behavior in children, adolescents, and adults using noninvasive and easily accessible psychophysiological approaches (e.g., electrodermal and cardiovascular activity, event-related potentials), and advanced statistical methods (e.g., latent growth curve and multilevel modeling). Her approach to this research mission has been to attempt to integrate multiple methodologies within the field of psychology (including developmental, clinical, social, and cognitive neuroscience perspectives) to gain a more comprehensive cross-area perspective on a complex social problem.

Andrea L. Glenn is a Postdoctoral Research Fellow in the Department of Child and Adolescent Psychiatry at the Institute of Mental Health in Singapore. She received her PhD in psychology from the University of Pennsylvania. Her research focuses on understanding the biological factors that contribute to antisocial behavior and psychopathic personality traits, and developing interventions that take biological factors into consideration.

Elaine Gunnison is an Associate Professor and Graduate Director in the Criminal Justice Department at Seattle University. She received her PhD in Criminal Justice from the University of Cincinnati in 2001 with a specialization in life-course criminology, female offending, and corrections. Her research interests include understanding female offending patterns such as desistance and persistence, the applicability of criminological theory to females, and offender reentry. Her research has been published in *Crime and Delinquency*; *Criminal Justice Studies: A Critical Journal of Crime, Law, and Society*; *Federal Probation, The Journal of Criminal Justice*; *The Journal of International and Comparative Criminal Justice*; *The Journal of Crime and Justice*; *Women and Criminal Justice*; *The Journal of Police and Criminal Psychology*; *The Journal of Interpersonal Violence*; *The Western Criminology Review*; *Academic Exchange Quarterly*; and the *Encyclopedia of Gender and Society*; the *Encyclopedia of Criminological Theory*, as well as the *Multimedia Encyclopedia of Women in Today's World* (forthcoming). She is co-author of *Success on the Street: Creating Opportunities for Offender Reentry* forthcoming in 2013 with Lynne Rienner. In November 2007 issue of the *Journal of Criminal Justice Education*, she was listed as 1 of 20 top female scholars in Criminology/Criminal Justice coming out of PhD programs in Criminology/Criminal Justice in the years 1996-2006. She is a member of the Seattle Work Release Advisory Board (SWAB) that seeks to assists offenders in successful reentry into their communities.

Shayne Jones is an Associate Professor of criminology at the University of South Florida. He received his PhD at the University of Kentucky, and completed postdoctoral training at the University of Pittsburgh. His research focuses on the relationship between personality and antisocial behavior, as well as the factors that mediate and moderate this relationship. He also researches factors that influence legal judgments and evaluations, including jury and judicial decision-making.

Daniel A. Krauss is a Professor of psychology at Claremont McKenna College. His research explores the intersection of psychology and the legal system.

Max M. Loomans, psychiatrist, MD, studied medicine at the Erasmus University in Rotterdam. He is currently a PhD candidate in psychiatric residency in the forensic psychiatric center de Kijvelanden where he has worked since 2006 conducting his doctoral research on the affective startle modulation in personality disordered offenders." This research is a combined project of the Department of Psychiatry of the Erasmus Medical Center and Forensic Psychiatric Center de Kijvelanden. The research aim is to differentiate different subgroups in the antisocial spectrum based on their emotional functioning. This involves psychofysiological, psychodiagnostical, and risk assessment parameters, with which concepts as "psychopathy" and the antisocial personality disorder are further examined. Currently he is working as a psychiatry resident at the Erasmus Medical Center. He is member of the editorial board of Psychiatrienet.nl.

Arthur J. Lurigio, a psychologist, is Associate Dean for Faculty in the College of Arts and Sciences, and Professor of Criminal Justice/Criminology and of Psychology at Loyola University Chicago, where he is also a member of the Graduate Faculty and Director of the Center for the Advancement of Research, Training, and Education (CARTE). In 2003, Dr. Lurigio was named a faculty scholar, one of the highest honors bestowed on senior faculty at Loyola University Chicago. Dr. Lurigio's research is focused primarily in the areas of offender drug abuse and dependence, drug treatment services, mental disorders and crime, co-occurring disorders, AIDS prevention, community corrections, police-community relations, criminal victimization, and victim services. In recognition of the overall contributions of his research to practices in the fields of psychology and criminal justice, Dr. Lurigio was conferred the University of Cincinnati Award in 1996; the Hans W. Mattick Award in

2003; the Champion for Recovery: Excellence in Research Award in 2009; the University of Illinois: Distinguished Contributions to Criminal Justice Research and Practice Award in 2010; and the American Psychological Association's Distinguished Career Award in 2010.

Thomas Lyons is Director of the HIV/AIDS Research and Policy Institute and assistant professor at Chicago State University. Dr. Lyons holds a PhD in anthropology from the University of Chicago and did postdoctoral work in medical anthropology at the George Washington University. His interests are in HIV prevention among drug users, including drug-using men who have sex with men, and persons involved in the criminal justice system. He served as a researcher and evaluator for Treatment Alternatives for Safer Communities (TASC), a social service agency in Illinois that provides case management for justice system involved drug users. Dr. Lyons is also a fellow of the Great Cities Institute, University of Illinois at Chicago, where he and Dr. Arthur Lurigio worked together on a longitudinal study of the health care needs of prisoners with co-occurring disorders, described in their chapter in this handbook.

Geoffrey Marczyk is currently in private practice in Newtown Square, Pennsylvania. His research interests include forensic psychology, organizational behavior, and leadership development.

J. Reid Meloy is a diplomate in forensic psychology of the American Board of Professional Psychology, and consults on criminal and civil cases throughout the U.S. and Europe. He is a clinical professor of psychiatry at UC San Diego, School of Medicine, and a faculty member of the San Diego Psychoanalytic Institute. He is a fellow of the American Academy of Forensic Sciences and is past president of the American Academy of Forensic Psychology. He has received a number of awards from various professional organizations and is chairman of Forensis, Inc., and Forensis Europa, Inc., two nonprofit, public benefit corporations devoted to forensic psychiatric and psychological research (www.forensis.org). Dr. Meloy has authored or co-authored over two hundred papers published in peer-reviewed psychiatric and psychological journals, and has authored, co-authored or edited ten books. His first book, *The Psychopathic Mind* (Aronson, 1988), was an integration of the biological and psychodynamic understanding of psychopathy, His most recent edited book, *Stalking, Threatening and Attacking Public Figures* (Oxford University Press, 2008), led to a commissioned study for the National Academy of Sciences on threats toward public figures published in March, 2011 (www.nap.edu).

Dr. Stephen White and he created the WAVR-21 (Specialized Training Services, 2007), the first scientifically based structured professional judgment instrument for workplace targeted violence assessment. His forthcoming edited book with Dr. Jens Hoffman, *The International Handbook of Threat Assessment*, will be published by Oxford University Press in 2013. Dr. Meloy is also a consultant to the counterintelligence division of the FBI and intermittently teaches at the Behavioral Analysis Units in Quantico. He is a member of the Fixated Research Group for the United Kingdom's Home Office concerning threats to the Royal Family and British political figures, and also teaches for the Netherlands National Police. He has been a technical consultant to the television program CSI since its inception in 2001.

Benjamin R. Nordstrom received his medical degree from Dartmouth and his PhD in criminology from the University of Pennsylvania. He received his training in psychiatry and addiction psychiatry at Columbia University. He is currently an assistant professor of psychiatry at Dartmouth Medical School and the Director of Addiction Services at Dartmouth-Hitchcock Medical Center.

Melissa Peskin is a doctoral candidate in clinical psychology at the University of Pennsylvania. She received a master of arts in clinical psychology from the University of Pennsylvania in 2007 and a master of science in psychology from Trinity College, Dublin, in 2004. Her research interests include understanding how chronic stress alters neurobiological functioning in children and adults, and how trauma, maltreatment, and abuse affect the neuroendocrine system.

David Polizzi is an Associate Professor of criminology and criminal justice at Indiana State University. He has published numerous peer reviewed articles, book chapters, scholarly essays and is coeditor of *Transforming Corrections: Humanistic Approaches to Corrections and Offender Treatment* and *Surviving Your Clinical Placement: Reflections, Suggestions and Unsolicited Advice* published by Carolina Academic Press. He is also the founder and current editor-in-chief for the e-publication, the *Journal of Theoretical and Philosophical Criminology*, which can be accessed at jtpcrim.org. Prior to his appointment at Indiana State, he worked as a forensic psychotherapist with clinical populations both within the penitentiary setting as well as in the community for nearly twenty years.

Nahanni Pollard received her PhD from the School of Criminology at Simon Fraser University in 2011. Her research background focuses on criminal justice system analysis, sentencing practices, police studies, simulation modeling and spatial analysis of crime patterns. Her BA and MA are both from Simon Fraser University, where she was involved in research with the Institute for Canadian Urban Research Studies (ICURS) and the IRMACS Complex Modelling Group. Her work has been presented at numerous conferences and has been published in the *Security Journal* and the *Law Enforcement Executive Forum*. She has coauthored book chapters discussing Non-Returnable Arrest Warrants (Routledge, Taylor & Francis), and Simulation of the Criminal Justice System for Policy Analysis (Information Science Reference), in addition to a solo work on Conditional Sentencing Decisions in 2009. Dr. Pollard has worked extensively with law enforcement agencies including the Royal Canadian Mounted Police and the Vancouver Police Department, culminating in numerous research reports and white papers on policing in Canada. She has also worked as a Crime Analyst and later the Policy Advisor for the Vancouver Police Department, and continues to be involved in research initiatives for local police agencies. She currently is a faculty member in the Criminology Department at Douglas College in New Westminster, British Columbia, Canada.

Adrian Raine is University Professor and the Richard Perry Professor of Criminology, Psychiatry, and Psychology at the University of Pennsylvania. Following two years as an airline accountant with British Airways, he received his bachelor's degree in experimental psychology from Oxford University in 1977, and his DPhil in psychology from York University, England, in 1982. After spending four years in two top-security prisons in England where he worked as a prison psychologist, he was appointed as Lecturer in Behavioral Sciences in the Department of Psychiatry, Nottingham University, in 1984. In 1986, he became Director of the Mauritius Child Health project, a longitudinal study of child mental health that today constitutes one of his key research projects. He immigrated to the United States in 1987 to take up a position as assistant professor of psychology at the University of Southern California. He was promoted to associate professor with tenure in 1990 and to full professor of psychology in 1994. In 1999, he was the recipient of an endowed chair, the Robert G. Wright Professorship of Psychology, at USC. He has published five books and 285 journal articles and book chapters, and has been the principal investigator on 17 extramural research grants and main mentor on 11 NIH pre- and postdoctoral awards. He has given 285 invited presentations in 25 countries. For the past 34 years, Dr. Raine's interdisciplinary research has focused on the biosocial bases of antisocial and violent behavior in both children and adults and prevention implications. His other research interests include: nutrition; white-collar crime; neuroethics; neurolaw; alcoholism; schizotypal personality; positive psychology; brain imaging; psychophysiology; neurochemistry; neuropsychology; environmental toxins; behavioral and molecular genetics.

Anna S. Rudo-Hutt is a candidate in clinical psychology at the University of Pennsylvania. Her research interests include the biopsychosocial bases of externalizing disorders and the similarities and differences between the physiological correlates of various forms of psychopathology. Ms. Rudo-Hutt's work thus far has focused on the psychophysiological and hormonal correlates of adolescent delinquency and child conduct disorder.

Jennifer L. Russell received her PhD in clinical psychology from the University of Tulsa in 2009. She completed her predoctoral internship at the Oklahoma Forensic Center, and a postdoctoral fellowship in forensic psychology at Lubbock Regional Mental Health and Mental Retardation Center. She has served as adjunct faculty at Texas Tech University, where she taught undergraduate forensic psychology courses. She is currently the Chief Psychologist of the Competency Program at North Texas State Hospital. Her research and clinical interests include assessment of adjudicative competence, assessment of malingering, assessment of sanity, violence risk assessment, and treatment of offenders with severe mental illness.

Stanton E. Samenow is a clinical psychologist in Alexandria, Virginia. He specializes in criminal and child custody/visitation matters that come before the court. Dr. Samenow is also a lecturer, and consultant in these areas. Appointed by President Reagan, he served on three White House Task Forces on crime. With Dr. Samuel Yochelson, he coauthored the three volume series titled *The Criminal Personality*. This work reports the results of their work at St. Elizabeths Hospital in Washington, D.C.—the longest in-depth clinical research study that has been conducted in North America. Dr. Samenow is the author of numerous professional articles and books, including *Inside the Criminal Mind* and *The Myth of the Out of Character Crime*.

Robert A. Schug is an Assistant Professor of criminal justice and forensic psychology at California State University, Long Beach. His area of specialization is the biology and psychology of the criminal mind. His research interests are predominantly focused upon understanding the relationship between extreme forms of psychopathology and antisocial, criminal, and violent behavior from a bio-psycho-social perspective—with the application of advanced neuroscience techniques from areas such as neuropsychology, psycho-physiology, and brain imaging.

Stacey L. Shipley obtained her doctorate in clinical/forensic psychology from California School of Professional Psychology in Fresno, California. She is the Director of Psychology at North Texas State Hospital, the only maximum-security forensic hospital in Texas. She specializes in the areas of forensic and clinical assessment, violence risk assessment, and evaluating and treating maternal filicide offenders and offenders with severe mental illness. She serves as a consulting expert witness and conducts assessments of competency to stand trial and sanity. She is trained in the investigation and evaluation of violent crimes and offenders, serial crimes, linkage analysis, and threat communications. She has published in the areas of psychopathy, homicide, women and crime, maternal filicide, forensic case formulation for sexual offenders, and serial murder and serial rape typologies. Dr. Shipley is the first author of *Introduction to Forensic Psychology: Court, Law Enforcement, and Correctional Practices* (3rd ed.; in press) with Elsevier/Academic Press.

Joke H. M. Tulen is an Associate Professor of psychophysiology and head of the Research and Education Unit at the Department of Psychiatry of the Erasmus Medical Center in Rotterdam, The Netherlands. Her research focuses on emotional disturbances (its cognitive, affective, somatic, and motoric components) in psychiatric disorders. By means of psychophysiological parameters, emotional disturbances are studied in relation to clinical symptoms and illness severity. In addition, the effects of pharmacological challenge tests and treatments are evaluated in relation to these parameters to determine if the psychophysiological measurements provide relevant effect parameters related to efficacy of treatment.

Hjalmar J. C. van Marle, psychiatrist, MD, and PhD, is Professor in forensic psychiatry at the Faculty of Medicine as well as the Faculty of Law, Erasmus University Rotterdam. Furthermore, from 2002 he is working as a forensic psychiatrist—psychotherapist at the forensic out-patient clinic "De Dok" in Rotterdam, and he is registered as an expert witness at the Courts of Justice. Formerly he was working as a psychiatrist, chief of staff and medical superintendant, respectively, of the maximum security hospital Dr. S. van Mesdagkliniek in Groningen (1979/1982/1984–1990), and of the forensic observation centre the Pieter Baan Centrum in Utrecht (1990–1996). From 1996 to 2003, he was appointed as a psychiatric advisor of the Ministery of Justice, as well as of the Prof. W. P. J. Pompekliniek in Nijmegen. From 1991 to 2003 he was professor in forensic psychiatry at the University of Nijmegen. From 1992 to 2002 he was also working as a psychotherapist at the Dr. H. van der Hoeven tbs-hospital in Utrecht. From 2002 to 2009 he was Chairman of the Research Program of the Forensic Psychiatric Centre of Expertise in Utrecht; until now the chair of the International Scientific Committee of this Centre. His research concerns aggression and psychopathy in schizophrenic patients, cognitive distorsions in child molesters and neuropsychological functioning in mentally disordered offenders. He is member of the editorial board of International Journal of Offender Therapy and Comparative Criminology, Forensische Psychiatrie und Psychologie, the International Journal of Forensic Health, the (Dutch) Journal of Psychiatry and Psychiatrienet.nl.

Yaling Yang received her doctoral degree in psychology from the University of Southern California. She received her postdoctoral training in neurology and psychiatry at the University of California, Los Angeles. She is currently a Research Scholar in the Laboratory of Neuro Imaging in the Department of Neurology at the University of California, Los Angeles.

Index

Note: page numbers followed by t refer to Tables

ABPP. *See* American Board of Professional Psychology (ABPP)
The Absent Body (Leder), 306
Achievement Place, 269
ADHD. *See* Attention-Deficit Hyperactivity Disorder (ADHD)
Adolescent-Limited and Life-Course Persistent Theory of Antisocial Behavior (Moffitt), 27
Adolescent-limited offenders, 72–74
Affective aggression: criticisms of theory, 248; culture and, 241; etiological theories of, 241–46; future research, 251–52; policy implications, 248–51; predatory aggression versus, 230–34, 234–35; research findings, 239–41; sadism and, 237–39; treatment implications, 246–48
Age, 264
Age-Graded Theory of Informal Social Control, 71, 76–78
Agreeableness, 195–97
Aichhorn, August, 120
Ainsworth, Mary, 68
ALF. *See* Animal Liberation Front (ALF)
Allport, Gordon, 272–73
American Board of Professional Psychology (ABPP), 53
Amygdala, 98, 102–3, 130, 133–34
Anger-excitation rapists, 238–39
Anger-retaliatory rapists, 238–39
Angular gyrus, 134
Animal Liberation Front (ALF), 4
Anonymity, 175
Anterior cingulate cortex, 100–101
Anti-Drug Abuse Act of 1988, 329
Antisocial behavior: behavioral inhibition and activation systems, 192–94; Five-Factor Model of personality and, 191–92, 195–99, 199–200; impulsivity and, 190–92; inhibitory traits and, 190; self-control and, 200–201, 202; sensation seeking and, 194–95
Antisocial personality disorder (ASPD): central autonomic network and, 92–94; co-occurring psychiatric and substance use disorders and, 321–23; gender differences, 274–75; information-processing/cognitive deficits in, 17–18; integrated view of, 104–6; neuroanatomical deficiencies and, 98–103; psychopathy and, 15–16, 90–91; psychophysiological deficiencies and, 94–98; somatic marker hypothesis, 91–92; startle reflex and, 96–98; violence inhibition system, 92–93
Antisocial Potential (AP), 75
Applied criminology, 31, 33–34
ASPD. *See* Antisocial personality disorder (ASPD)
Attachment, 177–78

Attachment theory, 68–69, 120
Attention-Deficit Hyperactivity Disorder (ADHD), 70
Attributions, 172–73, 245
Authoritarian personality, 182
Aversion therapy, 267–68

Bandura, Albert, 21, 122, 169–70, 184, 269, 271
BAS. *See* Behavioral activation system (BAS)
Behavioral activation system (BAS), 192–94
Behavioral inhibition system (BIS), 192–94
Behavioral theories of criminal behavior, 19–22, 121–22, 267–69
Behavior modification, 269
Being and Time (Heidegger), 311
Belief, 178
Big Five Model of personality, 195–96
Biological perspective, 24t, 265–66
Biosocial interactions, 138
Birth complications, 125–26
BIS. *See* Behavioral inhibition system (BIS)
Board certification, 53
Borderline personality disorder, 274
Borderline personality organization (BPO), 13–15, 274
Boredom susceptibility (BS), 194–95
Bowlby, John, 68
BPO theory, 13–15
Brain damage/abnormalities, 127–31, 242–43
Broken Windows Theory, 175
Bundy, Ted, 4

Callousness, 236, 241
Cambridge Study in Delinquent Development, 75
CAN. *See* Central autonomic network (CAN)
Cardinal traits, 272
Caspi, Avshalom, 71
Catalano, Richard, 79
Cavum septum pellucidum (CSP), 129–30
CD. *See* Conduct Disorder (CD)
Central autonomic network (CAN), 92–94
Central traits, 272
Cesarean kidnapping, 33
Chapman, David, 4
Classical conditioning, 19–20, 166, 267–68
Classical criminology, 22–23
Cleckley, Hervey, 5, 13, 90
Coe, Kevin, 32–33
Coercion Theory, 74–75
Coercive Control and Social Support Theory, 179
Cognitive Antisocial Potential model, 75
Cognitive deficits, 18–19
Cognitive Neoassociation model of aggression, 172–75
Cognitive theories of criminal behavior, 17–19, 66–69, 271–72
Columbine school shootings, 4
Commitment, 178
Comorbidity. *See* Co-occurring psychiatric and substance use disorders
Competition, 182
Conduct Disorder (CD), 70
Confirmation bias, 174
Conformity, 176–81
Conscientiousness, 195–97
Containment Theory (Reckless), 177
Continuing education (CE), 52–53
Control-Balance Theory, 179
Co-occurring psychiatric and substance use disorders: adverse consequences of, 325–26; basic treatment and access, 326–27; brain sensitivity and, 324–25; criminal justice–based treatment, 329–34; defined, 321–22; integrated treatment models, 328–29; prevalence of, 322–23; self-medication and, 324; sequential or parallel treatment models, 327–28; shared genetic vulnerability and, 323–24; women with, 334–35
Corpus callosum, 101–2
CPTED. *See* Crime Prevention through Environmental Design (CPTED)
Crime Classification Manual (Douglas et al.), 5
Crime in the Making (Sampson & Laub), 27
The Crime of Punishment (Menninger), 6
Crime Prevention through Environmental Design (CPTED), 4
Criminal behavior: antisocial personality disorder and, 15–16; behavioral theories, 19–22; cognitive theories of, 17–19; continuum of, 10–11; interdisciplinary

perspectives, 22–28; Kernberg's Theory of Borderline Personality Organization and, 13–15; psychodynamic theory and, 12–13; reasons for, 9–10
Criminality of everyday life, 4
Criminal justice, 29–31
Criminal justice–based treatment, 329–34
Criminal Personality (Yochelson & Samenow), 6, 211–12
Criminal personality theory, 17
Criminal psychology: antisocial personality disorder and psychopathy, 15–16; behavioral theories, 19–22; cognitive and information processing theories, 16–19; evidence-based practice, 29–31; future challenges, 31–32; historical perspectives, 5–7; interdisciplinary perspectives, 22–28; Kernberg's theory of borderline personality organization and, 13–15; psychodynamic theories of, 12–13; successes and challenges, 28–29
CSP. *See* Cavum septum pellucidum (CSP)
Cullen, Frank, 6
Cultural perspective, 24t
Culture, 241
Culture of control, 4
Curricula, 55–58

Dahmer, Jeffrey, 4
Darras, Benjamin, 4
Dasein, 311–14
Dehumanization, 176
Deindividuation, 176
Denial, 13–15
Depression, 280
Desistance, 77–78, 81–84
Devaluation, 13–15
Developmental and Life-Course theories, 26–28
Developmental approaches: Age-Graded Theory of Informal Social Control, 76–78; Coercion Theory, 74–75; Cognitive Antisocial Potential model, 75; cognitive theories, 66–69; desistance and, 81–84; developmental psychology and, 64–65; dual taxonomy, 71–74; evolution of, 70–71; General Theory of Crime, 80–81; Integrated Cognitive Antisocial Potential Model, 75; Interaction Theory, 78–79; latent trait view, 79–80; life-course/state-dependence theories, 76; psychoanalytic theories, 65–66; Social Development Model, 79; State-Dependence Theory, 76–79; three-pathway model, 75–76; traits and risk factors, 69–70
Developmental psychology, 64–65
Diagnostic and Statistical Manual for Mental Disorders, 5, 321
Differential association theory, 167–68
Diffusion tensor imaging (DTI), 129–30
Disinhibition (DIS), 194–95
Douglas, John, 5
Downs, Diane, 33
Drug use/abuse/addiction: addiction as a remedy, 309–11; being-in-the-world-as-addict, 311–14; co-occurring psychiatric and substance use disorders and, 323–24; crime as artifact of, 314–16; criminal personality and, 217–19; female criminal behavior and, 279–80; gender differences, 263; law enforcement overview, 299–304; phenomenology of addiction, 304–9. *See also* Substance use disorders
DTI. *See* Diffusion tensor imaging (DTI)
dual taxonomy approach, 71–74
Dunedin Multidisciplinary Health and Human Development Study, 71–74
Dys-appearance, 306–9
Dysfunctional impulsivity, 191

Early onset, 73, 74–75
Earth Liberation Front (ELF), 4
ECAS. *See* Epidemiological Catchment Area Study (ECAS)
Edmondson, Sarah, 4
Education and training, forensic psychology: basic competencies and training models, 54–58; credentialing, 53; graduate level, 48–52; opportunities, 47–48; postdoctoral and continuing education, 52–53; undergraduate, 48–49
EEG. *See* Electroencephalogram (EEG) data
Ego, 12, 65–66, 267
Electroencephalogram (EEG) data, 141–42

Electrophysiological studies, 139–41
ELF. *See* Earth Liberation Front (ELF)
Embodied experience, 304–9
Epidemiological Catchment Area Study (ECAS), 322
EPQ. *See* Eysenck Personality Questionnaire (EPQ)
ERP. *See* Event-related potentials (ERP)
Event-related potentials (ERP), 142–43
Evidence-based practice, 29–31
Evolutionary psychological theories, 277–78
Excitation transfer theory, 170–71
Executive functioning (EF), 136–38
Expectancy theory, 20–21
Experience seeking (ES), 194–95
Extraversion, 195–97
Eye blink startle reflex, 96–98
Eysenck Personality Questionnaire (EPQ), 273–74

FBI Behavioral Sciences Unit, 5
Fear conditioning, 141
Female criminal behavior: behavioral theory and, 267–69; biology and, 265–66; cognitive theory and, 271–72; co-occurring psychiatric and substance use disorders and, 334–35; evolutionary psychological theory and, 277–78; personality theory and, 272–77; physical abuse and, 281–82; prevalence of, 262–65; psychodynamic theory and, 266–67; sexual abuse and, 279–81; social learning theory and, 269–71
FFM. *See* Five-Factor Model (FFM)
Five-Factor Model (FFM), 191–92, 195–97, 199–200
fMRI. *See* Functional magnetic resonance imaging (fMRI)
Forensic assessment tools, 6
Forensic psychologists: education and training (*see* Education and training, forensic psychologists); role of, 44–47
Forensic psychology: definitional and interdisciplinary issues, 7–8, 45–47; recognition and growth of, 43–44
Freud, Sigmund, 12, 65–66, 117–19, 266–67
Frontal EEG asymmetry, 142
Frustration-aggression hypothesis, 171–72
Functional imaging, 131–34
Functional impulsivity, 191
Functional magnetic resonance imaging (fMRI), 132
Fundamental attribution error, 173

Gacy, John Wayne, 4
Gendreau, Paul, 6
General Theory of Crime, 25–26, 80–81
Genetic influences: co-occurring psychiatric and substance use disorders and, 323–24; gene-environment transactions, 198–99; neurocriminology and, 122–24; personality and, 273
Gilligan, Carol, 67–68
Glueck, Eleanor, 69–70
Glueck, Sheldon, 69–70
Gottfredson, Michael, 25–26, 71, 74, 79–81, 82, 179
Grand Theft Auto case, 4

Handbook of Sexual Assault (Marshall, Laws, & Barbaree), 6
Hardtime (Johnson), 6
Hare, Robert, 6, 16, 235, 276
Harris, Thomas, 5
Hawkins, J. David, 79
Hazelton, Roy, 5
Hearst, Patty, 3
Heart rate, 94–95, 139–41, 243
Heart rate variability (HRV), 92
Hinckley, John, 3–4
Hippocampus, 103, 130
Hirschi, Travis, 25–26, 71, 79–81, 82, 177–79
Historical, Clinical, Risk-20 (HCR-20) (Webster et al.), 6
Homicides, 230–31, 264
Hostile attribution bias, 173
Human predatory violence, 30

Id, 12, 65–66, 267
Impulsivity, 190–92
Index I crimes, 262–63
Inhibitory traits, 190

Instrumental aggression. *See* Predatory aggression
Insula, 101
Integrated Cognitive Antisocial Potential Model, 75
Integrated treatment models, 328–29
Interaction theories, 79
Interaction Theory (Thornberry), 78–79
Interdisciplinary criminology, 27–28, 31
Involvement, 178
IQ scores, 134–36

Jenkins v. United States (1962), 45
Johnson, Robert, 6
Just World Hypothesis, 182–83

Kernberg's Theory of Borderline Personality Organization (BPO), 13–15
Klaas, Polly, 4
Knox, Amanda, 4
Kohlberg, Lawrence, 67–69
Kohut, Heinz, 119

Labeling theory, 179–81
Latent trait view, 79–80
Latessa, Ed, 6
Laub, John, 71
Learning theory, 20–22, 165–70
Lennon, John, 4
Level of Service Inventory–Revised (LSI-R) (Andrews & Bonta), 6
Life-course persisters, 72–74
Life-Course theories, 25–27, 76
Lindbergh kidnapping, 3
Lindner, Robert, 5
Lying, 212–13

MacKenzie, Doris, 6
Malcolm X, 313
Malignant narcissism/emotional detachment, 235, 237
Malnutrition, 126–27
Manie sans delire, 90
Manson family murders, 3
MAOA (monoamine oxidase A), 124
The Mask of Sanity (Cleckley), 5, 13, 90
Medial hypothalamus, 242
Media violence, 21–22, 33, 175, 184
Meiwes, Armin, 4
Mens rea (guilty mind), 15
Men Who Rape, 6
Mini-theory of crime of human predatory violence, 30
Minor physical anomalies (MPAs), 124–27
Modeling theories, 21
Moffitt, Terrie, 27, 71–74, 81, 82, 134
Monoamine oxidase A (MAOA), 124
Moore, Devin, 4
Moral stages of development, 67–69
MPAs. *See* Minor physical anomalies (MPAs)

NAS. *See* Non-specific arousal system (NAS)
Natural Born Killer case, 4
Negative reinforcement, 19–20, 167t
Neurocriminology: behavioral models of crime and, 121–22; biosocial interactions and, 138; brain damage and, 127–31; early health risks and, 124–27; electrophysiological studies, 139–41; event-related potentials and, 142–43; executive functioning and, 136–38; fear conditioning and, 141; frontal EEG asymmetry, 142; functional imaging and, 131–34; genetics and, 122–24; intelligence and, 134–36; neuropsychology and, 134; psychoanalytic models of crime and, 117–21; slow-wave EEG and underarousal, 141–42
Neuropsychology, 134
Neuroticism, 195–97
Neurotransmitters, 243
Neutralization techniques, 18
Nicotine exposure, 124–25
Nixon, Richard, 299–300
Non-specific arousal system (NAS), 193
Normal criminals, 121

Oedipus complex, 118–19, 266
Offensive aggression. *See* Predatory aggression
Olsen, Jack, 5, 32
Omnipotence, 13–15
On the Witness Stand, 43
Openness to experience, 195–97

Operant conditioning, 19–20, 166–67, 268–69
Opponent-process theory, 244–45
Orbital/ventrolateral frontal cortex (FC), 98–100

Parallel treatment models, 327–28
Parenting: negative emotionality and constraint and, 198; neuropsychological functioning and, 138; self-control and, 201; social learning and, 170
Pavlovian conditioning, 19–20, 166
PCDs. *See* People with co-occurring disorders (PCDs)
Penis envy, 266
People with co-occurring disorders (PCDs): adverse consequences to, 325–26; integrated treatments for, 328–29; prison programs for, 330–32; qualitative study of detainees, 332–34; risk factors, 324; self-medication, 324; sequential and parallel treatments for, 327–28; treatment and access considerations, 326–27. *See also* Co-occurring psychiatric and substance use disorders
Perseverance, 191
Personality: Allport's trait theory, 272–73; authoritarian, 182; behavior inhibition and activation systems and, 192–94; Big Five Model of, 195–96; of criminals per Yochelson and Samenow study, 209–24; defined, 189; Eysenck Personality Questionnaire (EPQ), 273–74; Five-Factor Model of, 191–92, 195–99, 199–200; genetics and, 273; impulsivity, 190–92; inhibitory traits and, 190; psychopathy and, 199–200; self-control and, 200–201, 202; sensation seeking and, 194–95; structural models of, 195–99
PET. *See* Positron emission tomography (PET)
Pharmakon, 309–11
Phenomenological perspective, 24t
Physical abuse, 281–82
Physiological arousal, 171, 174–75
Piaget, Jean, 66–67
Pinel, Philippe, 90
Policy implications, 248–51
Population heterogeneity perspective, 71
Positive reinforcement, 19–20, 167t
Positivist criminology, 22–23, 265–66
Positron emission tomography (PET), 131
Posterior cingulate, 134
Practitioner-scientists, 55
Predatory aggression: versus affective aggression, 230–34, 234–35; criticisms of theory, 248; culture and, 241; etiological theories of, 241–46; future research, 251–52; policy implications, 248–51; psychopathy and, 235–37; sadism and, 237–39; treatment implications, 246–48
Prefrontal cortex, 99–100, 129, 131–33
Prejudice, 181–83
Premeditation, 191, 192
Prenatal smoking exposure, 124–25
Primitive idealization, 13–15
Prison programs, 330–32
Proactive aggression. *See* Predatory aggression
Program for the Investigation of Criminal Behavior, 209
Projection, 182
Projective identification, 13–15
Property crimes, 265, 278
Prostitution, 279–80
Psychoanalytic theories, 65–66, 117–21, 266–67
Psychodynamic theories of criminal psychology, 12–13, 65–66
Psychological criminology, 8–9, 24t
The Psychology of Criminal Conduct (Andrews & Bonta), 6
Psychology of Criminal Conduct (Blackburn), 6
The Psychopath: An Essay on the Criminal Mind (McCord & McCord), 5
Psychopathia Sexualis (Krafft-Ebing), 5
The Psychopathic Mind (Meloy), 6, 234
The Psychopathology of Crime (Raine), 6
Psychopathy: antisocial personality disorder and, 15–16, 90–91; behavior inhibition and activation systems and, 193; gender and, 275–77; historical perspectives, 34; neuroanatomical

deficiencies and, 98–103; personality and, 199–200; predatory aggression and, 235–37; psychophysiological deficiencies and, 94–98; research in, 29–30; sadism and, 237–39; startle reflex and, 96–98; Weak Superego theory and, 13
Psychopathy Checklist–Revised (PCL-R), 6, 16, 29–30, 90, 199–200, 276

Race, 263–64
Rader, Dennis, 4
Rape/rapists, 238–39, 277–78
Reagan, Ronald, 4
Realistic Conflict Theory, 182
Rebel without a Cause (Lindner), 5
Research, 32
Ressler, Robert, 5
Ridgway, Gary, 4
Risk-need-responsivity (RNR) model, 247
RNR. *See* Risk-need-responsivity (RNR) model
Routine activity perspective, 24t, 242
Rule, Ann, 5, 33
Runaways, 279–80

Sadism, 237–39
Sampson, Robert, 71
Scapegoating, 181–82
Schemas, 173–74
Science-practitioners, 54–55
SCL. *See* Skin conductance level (SCL)
Secondary traits, 272–73
Self-control, 179, 200–201, 202
Self-efficacy, 271
Self-medication, 324
Self-serving bias, 173
Semantic dementia, 17
Sensation seeking, 191, 192, 194–95
Sequential treatment models, 327–28
Serious psychiatric disorders (SPDs), 321–22. *See also* Co-occurring psychiatric and substance use disorders
Severe Personality Disorders (Kernberg), 6
Sex Offender Risk Appraisal Guide (SORAG) (Quinsey et al.), 6
Sexual abuse, 279–81
Sexual Homicide: Patterns and Motives (Ressler, Burgess, & Douglas), 5
Silence of the Lambs, 5
SIP. *See* Social information processing (SIP) theory
Skin conductance level (SCL), 95–96, 139, 243
Skinner, B. F., 19, 268
Slow-wave EEG, 141–42
Small Sacrifices (Rule), 5, 33
Smart, Elizabeth, 4
sMRI. *See* Structural magnetic resonance imaging (sMRI)
Social bonding theory, 177–79
Social cognitive theory, 271–72
Social control theory, 177
Social Development Model, 79
Social deviance, 235, 237
Social Identity Theory, 182
Social information processing (SIP) theory, 245–46
Social learning theory, 21, 122, 167–70, 184, 269–71
Social psychological theories of crime, 165–70
Sociological criminology, 8–9, 24t
Somatic marker hypothesis, 91–92
Son: A Psychopath and His Victims (Olsen), 5, 32–33
The Souls of Black Folk (Du Bois), 307
SPDs. *See* Serious psychiatric disorders (SPDs)
Splitting, 13–14
Stanford Prison Experiment, 176
Startle reflex, 96–98
State-dependence theories, 76–79
Static 99 (Hanson & Thornton), 6
St. Elizabeths Hospital, 209
Stereotypes, 32
Stinnett, Bobbie Jo, 4
Structural magnetic resonance imaging (sMRI), 129
Structural models of personality, 195–99
Substance use disorders (SUDs), 321–22. *See also* Co-occurring psychiatric and substance use disorders
Superego, 12, 65–66, 267

Tajfel, Henri, 182
TBH. *See* Triple Balance Hypothesis (TBH)
TBIs. *See* Traumatic brain injuries (TBIs)
Techniques of Neutralization (Sykes & Matza), 177
Technology, 31
Television programs, 4–5
Temporal lobe, 100
Theories of Internal and External Controls (Nye), 177
Thinking errors, 212–22, 271–72, 304
Thornberry, Terrence, 76, 78–79
Three-factor model, 197–98
Three-pathway model, 75–76
Thrill and adventure seeking (TAS), 194–95
TIH. *See* Triple Imbalance Hypothesis (TIH)
Traumatic brain injuries (TBIs), 127–28
Treatment: of co-occurring psychiatric and substance use disorders, 326–27; criminal justice–based treatment, 329–34; integrated models, 328–29; of predatory and affective aggression, 246–51; sequential or parallel models, 327–28; as a vacation from drugs, 311
Triple Balance Hypothesis (TBH), 243
Triple Imbalance Hypothesis (TIH), 243–44
Turner, Susan, 6

Ultimate attribution error, 173
Unconscious processes, 118
Underarousal, 139–41
UPSS model of impulsivity, 191–92
Urgency, 191
Urgency, premeditation, perseverance, and sensation seeking (UPPS model), 191

Van Voorhis, Patricia, 6
VIM. *See* Violence Inhibition Mechanism (VIM)
Violence Inhibition Mechanism (VIM), 17–18
Violence inhibition system, 92–93
Violence Risk Appraisal Guide (VRAG) (Quinsey et al.), 6
Violent behaviors, 241–46. *See also* Affective aggression; Predatory aggression
Violent offenders, 229–30, 246–51
Violent Offenders: Appraising and Managing Risk (Quinsey et al.), 6
Virginia Tech school shootings, 4

War on drugs, 263, 299–301
Weak Superego theory, 12–13
Women. *See* Female criminal behavior
Wuornos, Aileen, 4, 231–34, 235, 245, 246, 249

Yochelson, Samuel, 209–14, 220–22, 224

Criminal Psychology

Criminal Psychology

Volume 2: Typologies, Mental Disorders, and Profiles

Jacqueline B. Helfgott, PhD, Editor

Foreword by J. Reid Meloy

PRAEGER

AN IMPRINT OF ABC-CLIO, LLC
Santa Barbara, California • Denver, Colorado • Oxford, England

Library of Congress Cataloging-in-Publication Data

Criminal psychology / Jacqueline B. Helfgott, PhD, editor ; foreword by J. Reid Meloy.
volumes ; cm
Includes bibliographical references and index.
ISBN 978–0–313–39607–6 (hbk. : alk. paper) — ISBN 978–0–313–39608–3 (ebk.)
1. Criminal psychology. I. Helfgott, Jacqueline B.
HV6080.C7335 2013
364.3—dc23 2012051076

ISBN: 978–0–313–39607–6
EISBN: 978–0–313–39608–3

17 16 15 14 3 4 5

This book is also available on the World Wide Web as an eBook.
Visit www.abc-clio.com for details.

Praeger
An Imprint of ABC-CLIO, LLC

ABC-CLIO, LLC
130 Cremona Drive, P.O. Box 1911
Santa Barbara, California 93116-1911

This book is printed on acid-free paper ∞

Manufactured in the United States of America

For my parents, Esther & Oscar

Contents

Foreword by J. Reid Meloy — xi

Preface by Jacqueline B. Helfgott — xv

SECTION I: TYPOLOGIES AND PROFILES

Chapter One: Criminal Typologies — 3
Jacqueline B. Helfgott

Chapter Two: An Introduction to Criminal Profiling — 43
Richard N. Kocsis

Chapter Three: Mental Illness and Violence: A Misunderstood Relationship — 63
Stacey L. Shipley and Michele L. Borynski

SECTION II: CRIME TYPES

Chapter Four: Prevalence, Risk Factors, and Forms of Violent Offending — 99
Astrid Rossegger, Andreas Mokros, Juliane Gerth, and Jérôme Endrass

Chapter Five: Sexual Deviance, Fantasy Development, and Sex Crime — 127
Henry Richards

Chapter Six: Toward a General Theory of Profit-Driven Crime — 163
R. Thomas Naylor

Chapter Seven: The Psychological Dynamics of Political Crime — 199
Jeffrey Ian Ross

Chapter Eight: Emotional Correlates of Radicalization and Terrorism 215
Stephen K. Rice and Robert Agnew

Chapter Nine: Cybercrime: High-Tech Crime in the Information Age 227
Alex Kigerl

Chapter Ten: Pathways to Copycat Crime 251
Ray Surette

SECTION III: PSYCHOPATHY

Chapter Eleven: Conceptualizing Psychopathy: Criminal and Noncriminal Variants 277
Christopher J. Patrick

Chapter Twelve: Forensic Assessment of Psychopathy 311
Noah C. Venables and Jason R. Hall

Chapter Thirteen: Guidelines for the Evaluation and Interpretation of Psychopathy Research Findings 341
Carl B. Gacono

Chapter Fourteen: Psychopathic Aggression: Will or Determinism? 355
George B. Palermo

Chapter Fifteen: Career Criminality, Childhood Experiences, and Adult Personality among Forensic Patients in the Netherlands 381
Stefan Bogaerts, Marinus Spreen, Zsuzsanna Horváth, Machiel S. Polak, and Maaike Cima

Chapter Sixteen: A Proposed Sexual Homicide Category: The Psychopathic–Sexually Sadistic Offender 403
Shayne Jones, Heng Choon (Oliver) Chan, Wade C. Myers, and Kathleen M. Heide

Chapter Seventeen: Are Male and Female Psychopaths Equivalent? A Rorschach Study 423
Ted Cunliffe, Carl B. Gacono, J. Reid Meloy, and Enna Taylor

Chapter Eighteen: Psychopathy, Borderline Personality Disorder, and Domestic Violence: An Empirical Review 461
Ted Cunliffe, Elizabeth A. Johnson, and Donna E. Weiss

Chapter Nineteen: A Rorschach Understanding of Antisocial and Psychopathic Personalities 487
Carl B. Gacono and J. Reid Meloy

Chapter Twenty: The Popular Conception of the Psychopath: Implications for Criminal Justice Practice 515
Jacqueline B. Helfgott

About the Editor and Contributors 547

Index 559

Foreword

J. Reid Meloy

Ever since the eighteenth and nineteenth centuries—when Franz Gall and Cesare Lombroso, in phrenological leaps of faith, studied the shape of criminal skulls, and Ernst Kretschmer and William Sheldon, in morphological moments of insight, kindled an interest in the physical habitus of the criminal's body—philosophers, biologists, theologians, and psychologists have attempted to discern the criminal's mind. Introducing the unconscious world of psychodynamics shortly thereafter—and challenging a pure biological determinism—Sigmund Freud wrote at the beginning of the twentieth century:

> Two traits are essential in a criminal: a boundless egoism and a strong destructive urge. Common to both of these, and a necessary condition for their expression, is the absence of love, the lack of an emotional appreciation of (human) objects. (Standard Edition, Vol. XXI, p. 178)

None of these pioneers would have imagined the enormity and complexity of criminal psychology at the dawn of the twenty-first century. Jacqueline Helfgott did, and undertook what others might perceive as a Sisyphean task for which she was clearly capable: assemble a multivolume understanding of criminal psychology based upon contemporary theory and empirical research, with the breadth and depth it both required and deserved. She has achieved this remarkable goal with the help of over 100 very accomplished, and in some cases internationally known, contributors.

Dr. Helfgott is a professor and chair of the Criminal Justice Department at Seattle University. We first met in 1989 when she was a young doctoral student at Pennsylvania State University, and had taken an interest in some of our early writing on conscious cognitive processes and psychopathy. She readily understood that there are both unconscious psychodynamics and neurobiological processes that may shape the criminal's conscious thinking—a perspective often lost in some psychology professionals' treatment of choice for criminals, such as a heavy reliance on just cognitive behavioral therapy. To avoid the fundamental attribution error, our tendency to overweight the contribution of personality to motivation and underweight the contribution of the environment, she also paid close attention to both criminology and social psychology. But to really leave a footprint in her profession, she embraced the dynamic interplay between theory and research. Without theory, empirical research is just counting; and without empirical research, theory is just speculation. Or as the British astrophysicist Arthur Eddington once wrote, "No experiment should be believed until it has been confirmed by theory." Dr. Helfgott's early work resulted in two important papers (Helfgott, 1997, 2004) which empirically tested the theory of the relationship between conscious cognitive processes and unconscious psychodynamics in psychopaths, and also applied such findings to the field of forensic psychology practice.

She continues to recognize the importance of engaging both the ivory tower and the street. She has managed the authors and guided in the production of these scholarly volumes; and at the same time, she continues her work on other applied research projects, advisory boards, and various boards of directors concerning treatment of both perpetrators and victims of crime in the Seattle and surrounding Washington State.

When I open a professional or technical book for the first time, I conduct a test that consists of three parts. First, I read something from the book I know a lot about to see how accurate and well referenced it is. Second, I then read something I know nothing about to see if I will learn something new. Finally, I check to see if the writing style delivers the content in a pleasurable manner, or if it is an impediment to learning. In other words, do I have to struggle with poor grammatical choices, moments of illogic, occasional meandering thinking, and awkward syntax to glean something useful from the text? Are there any sentences that approach, for instance, the most elegant and poetic understanding of transference ever written: "So we beat on, boats against the current, borne back ceaselessly into the past"? Probably not, but textbooks should not drive us away, longing for the novels of F. Scott Fitzgerald.

I remember once hearing a well-known forensic psychiatrist testify in a criminal case. His testimony followed a psychiatrist for the defense who had talked in detail about the defendant's propensity to sexually assault his victims only late at night, and his habit of sleeping, instead, throughout the day. He went on with great erudition, his technical use of terms, such as the circadian rhythm sleep disorder of this defendant, superseded only by his boring delivery. When the opposing psychiatrist took the stand and was asked the same question, he responded, "the defendant is a nocturnal predator." Clarity of thought; luminescence in the mind of the listener.

Criminal Psychology, if measured by my admittedly simple yardstick, is a resounding success. The readers of this four-volume set, whether graduate student or seasoned professional, practitioner or academic, will be assured of their existing knowledge, learn much that is new, creative, and scientifically sound, and find it a pleasure to deepen their own thinking.

References

Helfgott, J. (1997). The unconscious defensive process/conscious cognitive style relationship in psychopaths. *Criminal Justice and Behavior, 24*, 278–293.

Helfgott, J. (2004). Primitive defenses in the language of the psychopath: Considerations for forensic practice. *Journal of Forensic Psychology Practice, 4*, 1–29.

J. Reid Meloy is a clinical professor of psychiatry at UC San Diego School of Medicine, and a faculty member of the San Diego Psychoanalytic Institute.

Preface

Jacqueline B. Helfgott

My interest in criminal psychology began sometime around the late 1970s/ early 1980s. I'm not sure if I can identify exactly what led me to willingly want to spend the majority of my adult life and most of my waking hours reading, writing, thinking about crime, violence, and psychopathy, and conducting research and programs inside prisons and other criminal justice contexts. When I think back, I guess it was probably a mix of popular culture and personal experiences that made me so interested in the intersection of psychology and criminology/criminal justice. I grew up in the Northwest with a single mother in graduate school, a social activist grandmother, and two younger brothers. I watched a good amount of TV (mostly *I Dream of Jeannie* and *The Brady Bunch*, and shows my brothers wanted to watch such as *Speed Racer*), but not a lot of crime shows. The crime shows on TV at the time were nothing like they are today. Most of the pop cultural crime and violence I was exposed to growing up was on Saturday morning superhero cartoons such as *Wonder Woman* and *Batman*, *ABC After-School Specials*, or shows such as *Charlie's Angels*, *The Six Million Dollar Man*, and *The Bionic Woman* and in the *Hardy Boys* and *Nancy Drew* books. It was well before the era of the serial murder film, and the most memorable depiction of film violence I was allowed to see as a kid was Sissy Spacek's character in *Carrie* when she unleashed her torment on her classmates at the prom after being publicly doused with pig's blood.

One of my earliest memories of being aware of real-life crime was at the breakfast table sometime in the 1970s while eating cereal with my brothers. The little kid on the back of the milk carton was missing, and there had been a lot of stuff in the news around that time about missing children. A couple of years later, my youngest brother's five-year-old friend was found dead, hung in his mother's closet, murdered by a man who was renting a room from his mom. I knew people growing up who shoplifted, used drugs, did time in juvenile detention, and dropped out of school. At my high school graduation, when everyone threw up their hats to hug their friends, I looked around and realized that everyone I knew had dropped out. I wondered why I continued on to college while all of my close friends from that time did not, and a few of them even ended up spending time in jail or prison. I attributed my own trajectory of academic success and crime desistance to the fact that I grew up seeing my mom studying and reading all the time and my grandma fighting for this or that social cause. But I wondered if it could be that simple.

At the time I graduated from high school, my old high school boyfriend came home to find his mother stabbed to death multiple times—the guy who did it was a drug dealer she knew who was caught shortly after. A couple of years later, I bumped into a neighbor friend who lived across the street, who told me that his younger sister was missing and was determined by police to be a victim of the Green River killer. Some years after that, an 83-year-old woman I knew was attacked with lawn sheers and butcher knives by her schizophrenic son who had gone off his meds. He attacked her for hours, stabbed her in the head, and cut her throat from ear to ear. I helped clean the mess that remained after the police and medics left. She survived the attack, and her son was sent to Western State Hospital upon a "Not Guilty by Reason of Insanity" verdict. He was released to his mother's—his victim's—care five years later. These and other incidents and experiences have made criminal behavior and its response in both the mental health and criminal justice systems very real for me.

I decided to study criminal justice and psychology in college after starting out as an art major and deciding that I would not be able to draw under pressure and that it would probably be more realistic to do something else for a living. I waited tables through college and got to know police officers who came into the restaurants where I worked and who took me on ride-alongs. I completed an internship in community corrections working with an officer in charge of a sex-offender caseload and read case files filled with accounts of bizarre acts of sexual deviancy. I went on tours of prisons and halfway houses and on work releases. I took courses from inspirational faculty, many of whom were leading-edge scholars at the forefront of forensic psychology and criminology, some of the most prominent scholars in the field—cognitive psychologist Elizabeth Loftus, now one of the most cited psychologists in history; Dale Smith, a psychologist who had published work with Hans Toch on inmate adjustment;

and criminology and criminal justice with George Bridges, whose lecture style of story after story made academic criminology seem like one of the most important callings. I took a tour of the Washington State Penitentiary in Walla Walla, where I saw Kevin Coe, the subject of Jack Olsen's book *Son: A Psychopath and His Victims*, soon after he was convicted, standing only feet away from me. I conducted a study on psychologists' views on psychopathy and had the opportunity to interview Seattle-area psychologists who worked in the intersection of criminal justice and mental health, including psychologists who later would go on to evaluate infamous serial killers such as Wesley Dodd. My personal experiences learning about crime from people I knew who were victims or offenders were shaped and explained in a new way through learning from practitioners in the field and academic research.

In my senior year of college in the late 1980s, while finishing up my undergraduate degrees in psychology and society and justice, I read books that to this day I have not been able to get out of my head—Wambaugh's (1987) *The Onion Field*; Olsen's (1983) *Son: A Psychopath and His Victims*; Rule's (1987) *Small Sacrifices*; Cleckley's (1941) *The Mask of Sanity*; Lindner's (1945) *Rebel without a Cause*; McCoy's (1981) *Concrete Mama: Prison Profiles from Walla Walla*; Hare's (1970) *Psychopathy: Theory and Research*; Yochelson and Samenow's (1977) *The Criminal Personality, Volumes 1–3*; Goffman's (1963) *Stigma*; Meloy's (1988) *The Psychopathic Mind*; and Johnson's (1987) *Hard Time: Understanding and Reforming the Prison*. These and other works I read at the time created great intrigue for me, raising question after question at the nexus of psychology and criminology/criminal justice—*What makes a person a law-abiding citizen versus a home invasion robber or a rapist or a murderer? How do police and corrections officers mentally process their jobs and their interactions with offenders? How do the mental health and criminal justice systems work together to respond to criminal behavior? How do victims of crime move on in the aftermath of criminal behavior? What makes a person incapable of feeling and able to hurt other people without feeling any guilt or concern for their welfare? What kinds of things go on in people's minds when they steal, vandalize, kidnap, rape, and murder? How do prison inmates adjust to long-term confinement? Where do fantasies about hurting other people come from in the first place? What is a psychopath, and how do you tell who is and who is not one? If psychopaths and other persistent offenders are so impervious to treatment, what should be done with them? How were psychologists so certain they could tell the difference between a criminal psychopath and a criminal who was just down on his luck? What mental mechanisms are at work when people commit minor crimes like shoplifting and major crimes like child abduction and serial murder? Once a person develops a deviant or criminal identity, what hope is there that the person can change to be a law-abiding citizen?*

In the late 1980s, there were few quick or definitive answers to most of these questions. Forensic psychology did not yet exist in the form of formal academic programs (beyond a few joint psychology and law programs). Computers were just becoming accessible on college campuses, and there was no Internet or Google. I typed my graduate school applications on a typewriter and picked schools I thought sounded good in places I thought I might like to go. I had read Bob Hare's book *Psychopathy*, but as a naïve undergraduate who was working three waitress jobs while going to school full time, it somehow eluded me (until a couple of years later when across the country in graduate school) that he was only 150 miles away at the University of British Columbia. I recall calling and speaking with Stanton Samenow on the phone as I prepared my graduate applications. I don't remember what I asked him or what we discussed, but he was nice enough to speak to a know-nothing college student just starting out. I had no idea where to apply to graduate school. All I knew was that I wanted to study psychopaths and the intersection of criminal justice and psychology. I applied to programs in psychology and criminal justice and landed at Penn State. I had applied to the Psychology Department there but had written a cover letter about wanting to study psychopathy and the intersection of mental health and criminal justice. The Psychology Department called and asked if I minded if they sent my file to the Administration of Justice Department. I got a call the next day with an enthusiastic offer of a research and teaching assistantship in administration of justice with a graduate minor in psychology that would allow me to pursue my research interests, which I gladly accepted.

I did my master's thesis and dissertation in the early 1990s on the unconscious defensive process/conscious cognitive style relationship in psychopaths. When I got to graduate school and started doing research for my master's thesis, I came across Gacono and Meloy's (1988) article, "The Relationship between Conscious Cognitive Style and Unconscious Defensive Process in the Psychopath," published in *Criminal Justice and Behavior*. I still remember the day I got my hands on the article and sat in the library reading it. I was so enthralled that soon after, I began the process of pulling together my thesis and dissertation committee and developing a study to empirically test the hypothetical rape scenario and levels hypothesis on the UDP/CCS relationship in psychopaths proposed in the article. My dissertation committee consisted of two psychologists (Lynne Goodstein, who had done work on inmate adjustment and long-term imprisonment, and Juris Draguns, whose research focused on cross-cultural psychology and personality), a lawyer (Daniel Katkin), and a former probation officer turned professor (William Parsonage). I took courses with Philip Jenkins (who some years later went on to write highly influential work on moral panic theory), Fran Bernat (now the editor of *Women and Criminal Justice*), and was fortunate to have assistance from Bob Hare, Carl Gacono, and Reid Meloy during the process of completing my dissertation. I received training in administering the PCL-R through the old-school method, which involved receiving large cardboard boxes in the mail from Bob Hare and colleagues containing videotapes and files that I was to review, score, and mail back for interrater reliability scores. Juris Draguns taught me how to administer the Rorschach. In my graduate school years, Faith Lutze, who went on to do important work in corrections and offender reentry, and Bruce Arrigo (now editor of the *Journal of Forensic Psychology Practice*), who has made prolific and key contributions in forensic psychology, were classmates; and I had the opportunity to meet other scholars whose work I admired at conferences, such as Adrian Raine, Robert Johnson, Kathleen Heide, and many others. Later, as a newly minted assistant professor, I invited my favorite true crime authors Jack Olsen and Ann Rule to campus to speak and had the opportunity to get to know them as well, especially Jack Olsen, who I consider the greatest true crime writer of all time.

Since those early years that shaped my academic career, I have had the opportunity to engage in research in law enforcement and corrections that has further shaped my perspective and academic pursuits. I have spent a good part of my career teaching courses and conducting research at the intersection of psychology and criminal justice. I have also been fortunate to be able to combine some of my other interests into my work. I have coordinated art and other programs in prisons for most of my career, which has allowed me to spend great amounts of time working directly with people who have committed crimes and who have served long sentences, both in and out of confinement. I have been involved in applied research that has kept me constantly aware of the real issues confronting practitioners and the responsibility academics have to make theory and research accessible to practice. I have worked with truly amazing students, from whom I have learned and who have helped me to expand my views and the questions I ask. Through some of these experiences, I have had been able to learn about the psychology of crime and criminal justice in ways that more formal research endeavors have not allowed. It has always been a bit surprising to me how much more I have learned about crime while painting a mural with a group of Lifers or riding around town with police officers than by analyzing data from psychometric tests and self-reports.

I sometimes find myself envious of the opportunities my students have today for the great many academic programs in forensic psychology. In the 1980s, the field of forensic psychology did not yet exist in the form of established academic programs, scholarly journals, or professional organizations. The academic discipline of criminal justice/criminology was only a generation old, if that. Library research on topics such as "psychopaths," "criminal psychology," or "criminal profiling" at that time resulted in a confusing absence of consensus and muddled terminology that had the potential to generate more frustration than new ideas or frameworks for empirical research. Today, there are a range of opportunities to study the intersection of psychology and crime, with many academic programs in forensic psychology and criminology/criminal justice, and there is disciplinary integration that did not exist 20 years ago.

However, I feel fortunate to have learned from, worked with, and/or gone to school with some of the brightest minds in the field responsible for shaping the study of criminal and forensic psychology today. Many of these scholars have contributed their work to this reference set. The study of criminal psychology and criminal behavior has come incredibly far in a very short time. Theory and anecdote have been tested by empirical research; forensic assessment tools have been developed, standardized, and validated; and much of the important theoretical and empirical work that has been done in the intersection of psychology and criminology/criminal justice is now making its way into practice in law enforcement agencies, courts, prisons and halfway houses, juvenile detention facilities, schools, victim services, and communities.

The volumes and chapters included in *Criminal Psychology, Volumes 1–4* reflect the state of the science of criminal psychology and criminal behavior written by the best and brightest minds in the academic criminology and forensic psychology, practitioners at the front end of the criminal justice and forensic settings, and scholars engaged in creative cutting-edge work. The work is organized into four volumes: Volume 1: Theory and Research; Volume 2: Typologies, Mental Disorders, and Profiles; Volume 3: Implications for Forensic Assessment, Policing, and the Courts; and Volume 4: Implications for Juvenile Justice, Corrections, and Reentry. Volume 1 offers an overview of theory, research, and key findings on criminal psychology and criminal behavior. Volume 2 addresses the utility of criminal typologies and profiles, presents research on specific crime types and psychopathy. The chapters included in Volumes 3 and 4 illustrate how theory and research on criminal psychology enter the criminal justice system in forensic assessment and prediction of dangerousness, law enforcement, criminal law, the courts, and sentencing, juvenile justice, institutional and community corrections, and offender reentry. I am proud of this mix of key and prominent researchers and theorists, whose work is the brick and mortar of today's criminal psychology joined by scholars just starting out in the field and practitioners who have a front-line vantage point. I am grateful to their willingness to contribute their work in this comprehensive, timely, and important collection on criminal psychology and criminal behavior. We have seen an unprecedented amount of attention to criminal psychology in the last 20 years, in all realms—academic, popular culture, and real-world practice. I hope the work contained in this set raises new questions and helps set the stage for what promises to be an era of greater refinement of theory, research, and practice that will provide answers that will help whittle away at the complex underpinnings and sometime tragic effects of criminal behavior.

A project like this is an enormous undertaking that requires the collaboration of many people. I am grateful to the many authors who have contributed their work and would like to thank each one of them individually. There are a number of people who deserve special acknowledgment. First and foremost, my research assistant Teneshia Thurman, who corresponded with over 100 authors, edited 61 chapters, and assisted with all aspects of the project. Teneshia's contributions to this project were enormous and invaluable and required extraordinary patience and attention. I could not have completed the project without her. I would also like to thank Praeger/ABC-CLIO senior editor Debbie Carvalko for her assistance with the project and her advice, contributions, and good humor at key points in the process, and Praeger/ABC-CLIO acquisitions editor Alicia Merritt for inviting me to serve as editor for this set. Special thanks to the energetic and supportive faculty and students I work with in the Criminal Justice Department at Seattle University; to George Palermo (editor of the *International Journal of Offender Therapy and Comparative Criminology*), Carl Gacono and Kathleen Heide, who, in addition to contributing their own work, were instrumental in linking me to other authors; and to Reid Meloy for both contributing work and for writing the foreword. I don't think a single student has completed one of my courses during the course of my career who hasn't heard me say that I think Reid Meloy is the most brilliant theorist that has ever written in the field of criminal psychology. To have him write the foreword for this set is an incredible honor, and I can't think of a more perfect way to introduce to the subject of criminal psychology and the work and authors contained in this collection.

Finally, I would like to thank my family and friends who provided a huge amount of support in the three years it took to complete this project, especially: my daughter Zalia, who saves me from embarrassing myself on a daily basis and has spent many more hours than I would have liked talking to me behind a computer screen; my brothers Ian and Scott; and my parents Esther Helfgott and Oscar Feit, to whom this work is dedicated. My mom is a never-ending source of inspiration. She is my flagger at the fork at the end of the road and the reason I took the right turn instead of the wrong one. My dad died during the course of this project. Even after he had a heart attack and was struggling to recuperate, he was always trying to send me on my way, saying, "Go write your books . . ." He died sitting in his living room chair. When we cleaned out his apartment, there were three books in the little cabinet right next to his chair—a Bible, my dissertation, and the *Criminal Behavior* textbook I wrote a few years ago (Helfgott, 2008). I think he would have enjoyed reading this.

References

Cleckley, H. (1941, 1976, 1988). *The mask of sanity*. St. Louis, MO: Mosby.

Goffman, E. (1963). *Stigma: Notes on the management of spoiled identity*. Englewood Cliffs, NJ: Prentice-Hall.

Hare, R. D. (1970). *Psychopathy: Theory and research*. New York/London: John Wiley & Sons.

Helfgott, J. B. (2008). *Criminal behavior: Theories, typologies, and criminal justice*. Thousand Oaks, CA: Sage.

Johnson, R. (1987). *Hard time: Understanding and reforming the prison*. Belmont, CA: Brooks/Cole.

Lindner, R. M. (1945). *Rebel without a cause*. London: Research Books.

McCoy, J. (1981). *Concrete mama: Prison profiles from Walla Walla*. Columbia, MO: University of Missouri Press.

Meloy, J. R. (1988). *The psychopathic mind: Origins, dynamics, and treatment*. New Jersey/London: Jason Aronson.

Olsen, J. (1983). *Son: A psychopath and his victims*. New York: Macmillan Press.

Rule, A. (1987). *Small sacrifices: A true story of passion and murder*. New York: New American Library.

Wambaugh, J. (1987). *The onion field*. New York: Dell.

Yochelson, S., & Samenow, S. E. (1977). *The criminal personality: Volumes 1–3*. New York: Jason Aronson.

SECTION I

Typologies and Profiles

CHAPTER ONE

Criminal Typologies

Jacqueline B. Helfgott

Introduction

Crime scholars have long searched for a general theory to explain crime (Agnew, 2005; Gottfredson & Hirschi, 1990). However, in recent years, there has been increased attention to the nuances and themes of individual criminal events (Helfgott, 2008; West, 2000), situational and environmental contexts (Brantingham & Brantingham, 1991; Crowe & Zahm, 2004; Felson, 2002, 2006; Kelling & Cole, 1996), the changing nature of crime across the life course (Laub & Sampson, 2006; Moffit, 1993), persistence and desistance in crime for different populations at different times (Cullen & Agnew, 2006; Piquero & Mazerolle, 2001) and crime types (Clinard, Quinney, & Wildeman, 1994; Dabney, 2004; Miethe, McCorkle, & Listwan, 2006) with the idea that we need different explanations for different types of offenses in different circumstances (Andrews & Bonta, 2010). We cannot expect that a single theory will explain the school shooter, the Ponzi schemer, the carjacker, the suicide bomber, the sexual predator, the drug trafficker, the cyberbully, and so on. In short, one theory or theoretical perspective or approach cannot explain all criminal behavior for all people in all situations.

However, "Specificity in the extreme is incompatible with the scientific objective of general understandings of human psychology. Finding uniformity under diverse conditions is a positive in science" (Andrews & Bonta, 2010, p. 3). It is an everyday human activity to cognitively organize the stimuli that surrounds us into categories. To comprehend the world, we do the following:

> [We] reduce the infinite variety of life to categories. We construct images or concepts in our attempt to "know" the world around us. These constructs are a reduction of our experiences, a reduction that treats occurrences as if they were similar, recurrent and general. Phenomena thus become comparable, and comparison is the beginning of scientific and philosophical reflection. (Clinard et al., 1994, p. 1)

Cognitive psychologists tell us that human beings naturally process information in manageable chunks (Bourne, Dominowski, Loftus, & Healy, 1986). To make information meaningful, we organize the stimuli around us into categories or units of information by identifying, organizing, and integrating elements that share common characteristics. This process is an essential component of perception and cognition, and it is mirrored in scientific classification (Knight & Prentky, 1990, p. 23).

Scientists do the same thing that the rest of us do on a more systematic and complex level. "Advances in any science depend on descriptive analytic schemes which identify similarities and differences between the entities comprising the universe of interest" (Blackburn, 1993, p. 61). Originating with the Linnaean Classification of plants, researchers in the physical and social sciences engage in typology construction for the purpose of understanding the nature of the phenomena they study. Biologists classify plants, zoologists classify animals, astronomers classify planets, chemists classify chemicals, pathologists classify diseases, anthropologists classify cultures, psychologists classify mental disorders, and criminologists and criminal behavior scholars classify crimes and criminals.

Typologies of crime and criminal behavior are theoretical frameworks that can be practically applied to organize, classify, and make sense of the wide range of behaviors that violate the law. Typologies are theories made manageable (Helfgott, 2008) that are theoretically, clinically, or empirically constructed by generating a list of crime types that are based on a particular theoretical framework. Criminal typologies are theoretical frameworks that can be practically applied to organize, classify, and make sense of the wide range of behaviors that violate the law (Dabney, 2004). Complex theories have to be simplified so that they can be applied in everyday policy and practice, and typologies provide information with which to make decisions, policies, practices, and laws. In hospitals, doctors diagnose and classify diseases in order to treat patients. In schools, students are tested and grouped in terms of "average" or "accelerated" to place them into appropriate educational programs. In mental health settings, individuals are diagnosed with mental disorders such as "bipolar disorder" or "anxiety disorder" to determine appropriate treatment. In the criminal justice system, offenders are classified into types such as "violent" or "sex" or "property" offender to make determinations regarding a range of criminal justice responses.

Typologies help reduce phenomena to more systematic observation and help to formulate hypotheses and guide research. For example, research suggests that violent and nonviolent criminal behavior may be different phenomena and that individuals who commit violent offenses differ in behavior from those who do not with respect to two important factors that distinguish violent offenders—childhood conduct problems and negative emotionality, traits similar to those associated with psychopathy. This and other research (Cornell et al., 1996) supports the strong empirical link between level of psychopathy and violent crime. Thus, from a continuum/dimensional perspective, it can be said that violent crime is a function of psychopathy level—the greater the number of psychopathic and antisocial traits and characteristics, the greater the probability of committing, and specializing in, violent crime that differentiates nonviolent crime.

The Situational Specificity of Criminal Behavior

Understanding the characteristics of a particular criminal type is the "keystone of theory building and the cornerstone of intervention" (Knight & Prentky, 1990, p. 23) that provides foundation for research on a particular subpopulation and is an essential prerequisite for determining response. Types both emerge from theory and are instrumental in the expansion and reformation of theory. Typologies guide research by formulating hypotheses based on the characteristics of specific types, giving characteristics an empirical interpretation, and incorporating a special case into a more comprehensive theory (Clinard et al., 1994).

Understanding and responding to criminal behavior requires focused attention and research into the nuances of different types and subtypes of crime and to the relationship between individual personality traits and situational contexts. In her 2005 Presidential Address to the American Society of Criminology, Julie Horney, a behavioral psychologist, urged criminologists to be cautious about using simple models that do not reflect reality and argued that advances in interdisciplinary criminology would be greatly enhanced by focus on the situational specificity of behavior.

In response to the centrality and prominence of general theories of crime in the criminological literature that locate the source of criminal behavior in traits such as self-control (e.g., Gottfredson & Hirschi, 1990), she proposed the development of an alternative psychology of criminal behavior that acknowledges individual-environment interaction and the power of situations as impetus for criminal behavior. Most importantly, she argued that the study of criminal behavior needs details that better capture the complexity of human behavior:

> [I]t is worth noting that some people who overuse alcohol do so only in the evenings and never during the workday, some only in social situations but never when alone, and some only when they go out of town to conferences. And lest we think that those who have been involved in crime must be those who lack self control in every arena, it is important to observe that many who have committed serious offenses have also held steady jobs, getting themselves to work on time every day, and many have supported families. Many whose supposed lack of control has led to legal sanctions possess much more self control than I when it comes to diet and exercise. Many drug dealers don't use drugs because they know the negative consequences the drugs would have for them. The dependence of our behavior on particular situations frequently makes us all appear to be walking contradictions. Yet, if we accept situational specificity of behavior as a natural product of learning that is shaped by context, the supposed contradictions in self-control can be seen instead as examples of stimulus control that reflect complex learning environments. (Horney, 2006, p. 8)

This notion of relevance of individual-situation interaction in the study of criminal behavior calls for situational data in longitudinal studies that would allow researchers to examine change across different types of situations.

Criminal Types

Equally important is specificity with respect to crime types. Typologies inform real-world criminal justice policy and practice and influence popular understanding of complex concepts. For theory to be applied, it has to be meaningful and understandable to a wide range of people, including citizens, policymakers, attorneys, judges, law enforcement officers, correctional staff, and administrators. When the criminal justice system utilizes theory in policy and practice, official classification, terminology, and concepts inform the public about how offenders should be viewed, treated, and dealt with (Garland, 1990, p. 257).

Crime prevention policy is dependent upon knowledge about situational and opportunity factors that increase and decrease the likelihood for an offense to occur (Miethe et al., 2006). Police strategy is informed by theories about offender motivation and offense patterns in investigations and profiling (Annon, 1995; Cook & Hinman, 1999; Daéid, 1997; Davis, 1999; Egger, 1999; Godwin, 1998; Holmes & Holmes, 2001; Homant & Kennedy, 1998; O'Toole, 1999; Pinzotto & Finkel, 1990; Wilson, Lincoln, & Kocsis, 1997). Juries and attorneys rely on expert testimony involving social science research on the nature and types of criminal behavior in reaching adjudication and sentencing decisions (Beck, 1998; Faigman, 1999; Hyman, 2004) and in the forensic assessment of risk (Douglas, Vincent, & Edens, 2006; Harcourt, 2007; Quinsey, Harris, Rice, & Cormier, 1998). Effective correctional management and treatment is developed based on theory and knowledge about the needs and risk levels of different types of offenders in correctional populations (Andrews & Bonta, 2010). Victim services can be enhanced and improved with attention to offender typologies and theory and research on victim-offender dynamics, and to the ways in which offense characteristics influence victim impact and recovery in the aftermath of crime (Bowie, Silverman, Kalick, & Edbril, 1990). Determination of when and in what situation juvenile offenders should be adjudicated as adults is guided by theory and research in developmental psychology and life-course criminology. At all stages of the criminal justice system—from arrest to release, from crime prevention strategy to victim services—theory and research play a primary role in the administration of justice.

Crime can be conceptualized into six broad types or categories—*violent, sex, economic, public order, political, cyber, and copycat crime* (Helfgott, 2008). Each crime type is characterized by distinguishing features and subtypes that provide information regarding the specificity of the offense behavior.

A number of authors have offered comprehensive criminal typologies (see Dabney, 2004; Hagan, 2009; Helfgott, 2008; Miethe et al., 2006) that provide a detailed review of the distinguishing features of different crime types and subtypes and the implications for criminal justice practice. Theory and research on the different types of criminal behavior, the nature and nuances of the different types of crimes, and the individual-environment interactions that shape criminal behavior make it an important piece in evidence-based criminal justice practice. Every criminal event is unique, and there are differences and similarities across crime categories. Understanding the features that characterize criminal behavior and crime types is a critical piece in preventing and responding to crime.

Table 1.1 Crime Types

Crime Types	Features	Subtypes
Violent Crime	-Behaviors that violate the law that result in physical harm -Motivated by affective or predatory aggression -Negative emotionality and ability to suspend emotion and attachment at time of offense -Intrinsic personal meaning/autotelic aspects to violence -Relatively difficult to cognitively neutralize	-Homicide -Assault -Robbery
Sex Crime	-Behaviors that violate the law that result in sexual harm -Sexually motivated -Manifestation of fantasy -Heterogeneous with respect to victim, method, developmental pathway, nature of offense -Relatively difficult to cognitively neutralize	-Sexual Homicide -Rape -Child Molestation
Economic Crime	-Behaviors that violate the law resulting in harm of financial loss -Instrumental motivation to obtain financial reward -Relatively easy to cognitively neutralize – simplistic or "normal" neutralizations supported by cultural norms and values -Modus operandi involves some level of planning, purpose, and risk assessment	-Predatory Economic Crime -Market-Based Economic Crime -Commercial Economic Crime
Public Order Crime	-Behaviors that are prohibited by law because they are perceived by the larger society to violate moral sentiment and harm or threaten social order -No clearly identifiable victim -Largely rooted in social problems—addiction, opportunity, poverty, mental illness, and despair	-Sex-Related Offenses -Substance Abuse-Related Offenses -Gambling -Other Public Order Offenses

Table 1.1 (Continued)

Crime Types	Features	Subtypes
Political Crime	-Behaviors that violate the law that are ideologically motivated -Willingness to take action that violates law to further an ideological objective -Relatively easy to cognitively neutralize	-Oppositional Crime -State Crime
Cybercrime	-Behaviors that violate the law involving computers or other technological device motivated by illicit purposes -Relatively easy to cognitively neutralize	-Computer as Target -Computer as Instrument or Incidental
Copycat Crime	-Behaviors that violate the law inspired by another crime that has been publicized in the news media or fictionally or artistically represented in which the offender incorporates aspects of the original offense -Exist on a continuum from minor to major influence -May be easy or difficult to cognitively neutralize depending on the type of offense	-Minor Influence—Ideas from fictional or media representation incorporated in new offense -Major Influence—Mimicry of offense with loss of boundary between fantasy and reality

Source: Helfgott (2008).

Mental Disorders and Criminal Behavior

Mental illness is one of many factors that may play a role in some incidents and types of criminal behavior. Criminal behavior ranges on a continuum from "normal," involving poor judgment and bad decisions within situational contexts; to "everyday problems in living," involving addiction, minor medical or mental health conditions, poverty, and deprivation; to "pathological," involving severe medical or mental health conditions and psychopathology and long-term development of deviant identity (Helfgott, 2008). Jared Loughner, who shot and killed six people outside of an Arizona grocery store, including U.S. District Court judge John Roll, and wounded 14 others, including Congresswoman Gabrielle Giffords, was said to have escalated into mental illness quickly in the days prior to the shooting. Cho Seung-Hui, the Virginia Tech gunman who killed 32 students and faculty members in April 2007 before killing himself, had a history of mental illness and had expressed suicidal thoughts. Andrea Yates, who murdered her five young children in Texas in 2001, had suffered from depression and psychosis and had been treated for psychiatric problems prior to the murders. John Hinckley, who attempted to assassinate Ronald Reagan in 1981, had a history of depression and was determined not guilty by reason of insanity after his defense attorneys successfully argued that his fixation with the film *Taxi Driver* and loss of touch with the distinction between reality and fantasy indicated that he suffered from psychosis. Beyond these extreme cases involving individuals with severe psychopathology who engaged in violent offenses, there are an enormous number of public order offenses such as loitering, vagrancy, illegal drug use, public drunkenness, etc., that are largely rooted in mental illness.

Mental disorder and criminal behavior are distinct concepts that sometimes overlap. The concept of "mental disorder" is problematic for a number of reasons. The term implies a distinction between mental and physical disorder that ignores the connection between the mental and physical, and the term is defined in different ways by different people—some limit the term to the major clinical disorders such as schizophrenia and mood disorders, others include the personality disorders, and still others use the term as a wastebasket category for all forms of mental abnormality whether or not the condition is clinically diagnosable. "No definition adequately specifies precise boundaries for the concept of 'mental disorder' " (APA, 2000, p. xxx). Thus when people speak of "mental disorder" this term encompasses an enormous range of human behavioral symptoms and conditions ranging from everyday problems in living to severe psychopathological disturbances.

Compounding understanding of the relationship between mental illness and crime are the conflicting goals of the mental health and criminal justice systems. According to Blackburn (1993, p. 246), concerns about "the 'psychiatrisation' of crime . . . have been paralleled by concerns over the 'criminalisation' of mental disorder." Furthermore, there have been difficulties in coming up with a consensus on the definition of "mental disorder" and "mental illness" as a clinical or scientific concept. Mental disorder and crime are conceptually distinct; however, psychiatric illness and mental disorders are often implicated as influences in criminal behavior. In the case of personality disorders, specifically antisocial personality disorder and psychopathy, a strong empirical relationship has been established between these disorders and violent criminal behavior (Douglas et al., 2006; Hare, 1998, 2003; Hare & Neumann, 2010; Porter & Porter, 2007), and Andrews & Bonta (2012) suggest, "the days of ignoring the evidence on personality [in criminological theory] are now gone" (p. 201). While most people who are mentally ill do not commit crimes, and many serious mental illnesses render a person unable to form *mens rea* (criminal intent), which prohibits legal sanctions in the criminal justice system, there is research to suggest that certain risk factors, some of which may be associated with specific mental disorders, are associated with criminal behavior and that, on an individual level, mental disorder may play a role in conjunction with other influences as a contributing factor to explain criminal behavior (Andrews & Bonta, 2012; Blackburn, 1993; Hodgins, 1993; Monahan et al., 2001).

Social and behavioral scientists have addressed the relationship between emotional attachment, cognition, and behavior in offenders. Sociologists and psychologists have historically used different terms to explain similar or related phenomena. For example, in sociological terms, crime is associated with weak or broken social bonds (Hirschi, 1969), defensive techniques (Sykes & Matza, 1957), and linguistic accounts that justify and excuse behavior (Gabor, 1994; Scully & Marolla, 1984). Direct parallels can be drawn between Hirschi's (1969) social bond theory and Meloy's (1992) theory of violent attachments; between Sykes & Matza's (1957) techniques of neutralization and Kernberg's (1987) primitive borderline defenses; and between Scully and Marolla's (1984) findings on the vocabulary of rapists, Gabor's (1994) study of crime by the public, and Reiber and Vetter's (1995) research on the deceptive aberration of language in the psychopath. The similarities across disciplines in the explanations of antisocial behavior reflect an important theoretical link that is necessary to examine the congruence between the psychopathy as a categorical versus a dimensional concept. These links are beginning to be made in more interdisciplinary theories and empirical research in recent years in the work and development of work of Akers (1991), Moffit (1993), Tittle (1995) Farrington (2003), Agnew (2006), and others. There is still much work to be done to integrate theories, but Andrews & Bonta (2010) suggest that "the days of ignoring the evidence on personality [in mainstream criminological theory and research] are now gone (p. 201).

To understand the role of mental disorder and crime, it is important to recognize the overlaps between the concepts of mental illness and criminal behavior and to have an understanding of both typologies of mental disorders and criminal behaviors. What are mental disorders? How are they classified? What are the traits and symptoms associated with the different types of mental disorders across the spectrum of human psychopathology? Are symptoms of particular mental disorders risk factors for some but not other types of crime? How do risk factors associated with specific types of mental disorders interact with other types of risk factors (e.g., biological, sociological, phenomenological, situational/opportunity, cultural)? A strong foundation in psychopathology and the classification of mental disorders is an important foundation for understanding (and constructing) typologies of criminal behavior.

The Diagnostic and Statistical Manual of Mental Disorders

The typology approach to understanding human behavior is best typified by the *Diagnostic and Statistical Manual of Mental Disorders* (DSM)—the current edition being the DSM, 4th Edition Text Revision (DSM-IV-TR). The DSM-IV-TR is a categorical system for classification of mental disorders published by the American Psychiatric Association, for the purpose of communication, diagnoses, education, research, and treatment that divides mental disorders into types based on sets of criteria with defining features. The categorical approach used in the DSM-IV-TR is based on the "traditional method of organizing and transmitting information in everyday life" and the fundamental approach used in medical diagnosis (APA, 2000, p. xxxi). Disorders in the DSM-IV-TR are viewed as a "clinically significant behavioral or psychological syndrome or pattern that occurs in an individual and is associated with present distress ... or disability ... or with a significantly increased risk of suffering death, pain, disability, or an important loss of freedom" (APA, 2000, p. xxxi). The authors of the DSM-IV-TR acknowledge the limitations of the categorical model (heterogeneity of diagnostic classes, lack of clear boundaries between types), and state that there is no assumption of complete homogeneity with the view that the categorical model is superior to the dimensional perspective in clinical practice and in stimulating research.

Historically, the initial impetus for developing a classification of mental disorders was the need to collect statistical information. The first attempt to collect data about mental illness in the United States began with one category in 1840 ("idiocy/insanity") and expanded by 1880 to seven categories (dementia, dipsomania, epilepsy, mania, melancholia, monomania, and paresis). In 1952, the first edition of the DSM was published based on the International Classification of Diseases, Sixth Edition (ICD-6), published by the World Health Organization (WHO). To date, six editions of the DSM have been published (DSM-I, DSM-II, DSM-III, DSM-III-R, DSM-IV, and DSM-IV-TR). The DSM classifications are empirically based and developed through a three-stage empirical process that included comprehensive literature reviews, reanalysis of already-collected data sets, and issue-focused clinical field trials.

The DSM is organized around a multiaxial system that involves assessment on several axes. Each axis represents a different domain of information that may help a clinician create a treatment plan and predict treatment outcome. The DSM-IV-TR consists of five axes:

Axis 1: Clinical Disorders, Other Conditions That May Be a Focus of Clinical Attention
Axis II: Personality Disorders, Mental Retardation
Axis III: General Medical Conditions
Axis IV: Psychosocial and Environmental Problems
Axis V: Global Assessment of Functioning (APA, 2000, p. 27)

The distinction between Axis I and Axis II in the DSM reflects the recognition that there is a distinction between mental illness and personality disorder, and that the two are not mutually exclusive and frequently coexist (Blackburn, 1993). Clinical disorders include schizophrenia, substance-related disorders, mood disorders, anxiety disorders, dissociative disorders, sexual and gender identity disorders, eating disorders, sleep disorders, adjustment disorders, and disorders first diagnosed in infancy, childhood, or adolescence such as learning disorders, conduct disorder, and attention deficit/hyperactivity disorder. Personality disorders are divided up into subcategories—Cluster A, Cluster B, and Cluster C. Individuals with Cluster A disorders (paranoid, schizoid, and schizotypal) appear odd or eccentric. Individuals diagnosed with Cluster B disorders (antisocial, borderline, histrionic, narcissistic) appear dramatic, emotional, or erratic. Individuals with Cluster C disorders (avoidant, dependent, obsessive-compulsive) appear fearful or anxious (one way to think of the clusters is that Cluster A individuals act odd, Cluster B individuals act out, and Cluster C individuals act afraid).

A number of Axis I disorders have been associated with criminal behavior, including substance use disorders, sexual disorders, childhood disorders such as conduct disorder, attention deficit/hyperactivity disorder, and oppositional defiant disorder. Impulse control disorders such as intermittent explosive disorder, kleptomania, pyromania, and pathological gambling are disorders that clearly overlap with criminal behavior; however, Blackburn (1993) argues:

> [T]he validity of impulse control disorders as a distinct class is questionable on conceptual grounds. An "impulse" is a circular inference of cause from the behaviour it supposedly impels, and "failure to resist and impulse" is similarly inferred from the observation that an act has been performed. (p. 74)

This (and antisocial personality disorder) is an example of what Blackburn calls the psychiatrization of crime, whereby the domain of social deviance (behavior) is confounded with personal deviance (underlying traits). Axis II disorders, in particular the Axis II, Cluster B disorders—antisocial personality disorder, borderline personality disorder, histrionic personality disorder, and narcissistic personality disorder—have also been linked to criminal behavior. A number of researchers have noted that psychopathy may be more appropriately constructed as a higher-order category comprising criteria from all four Axis II, Cluster B disorders (Blackburn, 1993; Wulach, 1988).

The Relationship between Mental Disorder and Crime

The relationship between mental disorder and crime has long been examined with conflicting findings. Research in the early 1900s found that the criminality rate of the mentally ill was the same as or lower than that of the general population. Later studies in the 1970s found a higher rate of criminal behavior among the mentally ill as compared to the general population. The deinstitutionalization of the mentally ill in the 1960s led to an increase in the percentage of offenders in correctional settings diagnosed as mentally ill. More recent research has found that there is a relationship between certain mental illnesses such as substance abuse disorders, but that major mental illnesses such as schizophrenia and affective disorders show marginal relationship to criminal behavior (Modestin & Ammann, 1995). However, Belfrage (1998) found an overrepresentation of criminality in a sample of mental patients diagnosed with schizophrenia, affective psychosis, or paranoia who were discharged from mental hospitals in Stockholm, Sweden, in the 1980s and followed up 10 years later.

Other research has examined the relationship between specific Axis I (e.g., schizophrenia, substance use disorders) and Axis II or other personality disorders (e.g., antisocial personality disorder, borderline disorder, psychopathy), and some studies have looked at the relationship between Axis I and Axis II disorders and different crime types. For example, Tengström et al. (2004) found that psychopathic traits, not substance abuse are associated with criminal offending and that there was no difference between non-schizophrenics and schizophrenics who scored high on psychopathy between those with and without substance use disorders. An interesting study by Stuart, Moore, Gordon, Ramsey, and Kahler (2006) reported results on the prevalence of psychopathology among 103 women arrested for domestic violence in Rhode Island. The study found that the women arrested for domestic violence had high rates of post-traumatic stress disorder depression, generalized anxiety disorder, panic disorder, substance use disorders (Axis I disorders) and borderline personality disorder, and antisocial personality disorder (Axis II, Cluster B disorders).

The MacArthur Study of Mental Disorder and Violence has been described as the best-designed study ever done on violence risk assessment, involving over 1,000 psychiatric patients. The study examined the relationship between 134 potential risk factors (identified from theory and research on violence and mental disorder and clinical experience) and subsequent violence in a large sample of people diagnosed with mental disorders, Monahan et al. (2001) concluded:

> A historical view of the study of violence by persons with mental illness reveals a determined quest for the single variable (or sometimes a small set of variables) that will determine whether a person will act aggressively toward others. Once in hand, knowledge of this variable would lead inexorably to strategies for prediction or control . . . Among the causative factors postulated at one point or another have been electrical discharges in the temporal lobe; physical abuse in childhood; a vulnerability to shame; overcontrol of violent impulses or its opposite; the failure to inhibit their expression; and most recently, for the people with mental illness in particular, the presence of one or another set of psychotic symptoms. . . .
>
> Of the scores of variables whose relationship with violence we studied in this project, many (indeed most) had some significant association with future violence. None of these relationships was sufficiently strong, however, for it to be fairly said that a given variable constituted the cause of violence, even for a subgroup of patients. Nor . . . does any single concatenation of variables account for violence as a unitary phenomenon. Our data are most

> consistent with the view that the propensity for violence is the result of the accumulation of risk factors, no one of which is either necessary or sufficient for a person to behave aggressively toward others. People will be violent by virtue of the presence or absence of different sets of risk factors. There is no single path in a person's life that leads to an act of violence. (p. 142)

While the MacArthur Study focused specifically on actuarial prediction of violence in a psychiatric population, it is clear from this and other research (e.g., Andrews & Bonta, 2012) that it is not the mental disorder itself that is linked to crime, but the behavioral symptoms and traits that make up the disorder that are, in conjunction with other factors, risk factors for criminal behavior. It is also important to keep in mind that certain risk factors associated with certain disorders may converge in such a way with other factors to produce certain types of criminal behaviors but not others.

Using Typologies in Criminal Justice and Forensic Practice

Criminal typologies are necessary to understand, identify, and respond to crime. In the criminal justice system, knowing how a rapist differs from a pedophile, whether an individual with a history of residential burglary is likely to escalate to armed robbery, or determining whether a violent offender is too dangerous to release, requires knowledge of the distinct nature, extent, features, and dynamics of types and subtypes of crimes as well as how offenses and offenders differ across crime categories. The criminal justice system cannot respond to crime with a "one size fits all" approach. Sanctions, management strategies, treatment approaches, and public safety policies and practices are highly dependent on differentiation of types of crimes and criminals.

Criminal Typologies: Theory and Purpose

Typologies differ with respect to theoretical foundation and purpose. Typologies of crime and criminals have emerged from legalistic, sociological, psychological, biological, or multiple (interdisciplinary) perspectives. Typologies can be offender-based, victim-based, situation-context-based, or organized around multiple traits. Typologies differ with respect to level of theoretical sophistication and complexity and the purpose for which they are constructed and applied. There are three main purposes of typologies of crime and criminals:

1) *Management*: Classification in correctional settings, prediction of dangerousness and implementation of measures to enhance public safety.

2) *Treatment*: Determining the appropriate treatment and rehabilitative programming to target particular needs of types and subtypes of offenders.
3) *Understanding*: Knowledge of nature and dynamics of specific types and subtypes of offenders at a level of specificity not possible with general theories of crime (Blackburn, 1993).

Typologies are also used for other purposes, such as law enforcement investigations (referred to as "criminal profiling" or "offender profiling"), in conjunction with victim typologies to determine the best way to assist victims, and for crime prevention.

The question "*What type of person are we dealing with?*" is of central importance at every stage in the criminal justice process. In law enforcement, decisions have to be made regarding investigative strategy, interviewing and interrogation of suspects, hostage negotiations, and officer safety. These decisions are dependent upon the type of suspect officers are dealing with. At the law enforcement stage of the process, "who, what, and why" are crucial to criminal profiling and the investigative process (Douglas, Burgess, Burgess, & Ressler, 1997). At pretrial, adjudication, and sentencing decisions have to be made about charges, mitigating and aggravating circumstances, type of defense (e.g., insanity), and sentence severity. At the courts/sentencing stage, the "what and why" continue to be important. In corrections and reentry, the focus is "What now?" with treatment, management, release decisions, community supervision, and public safety decisions dependent upon the type of offender under consideration. Knowledge of the differences and similarities within and between different types of offenders can also yield information that can be used to develop crime prevention strategies (Miethe & McCorkle, 2001) and appropriate treatment and outreach programs for victims (Silverman, Kalick, Bowie, & Edbril, 1988; see also Figure 1.1, "The Use of Typologies in the Criminal Justice System").

Examples of Different "Types" of Typologies

Biological

Biological typologies are rooted in biological theories and organized around features such as genetics, evolutionary development, and body type. One of the earliest typologies was developed by Cesare Lombroso, often referred to as the "father of positivist criminology." Lombroso, an Italian physician, is best known for his work *L'Uomo delinquente* (*The Criminal Man*), published in 1876, in which he offered a typology of criminals based on evolutionary development and physical traits. Lombroso

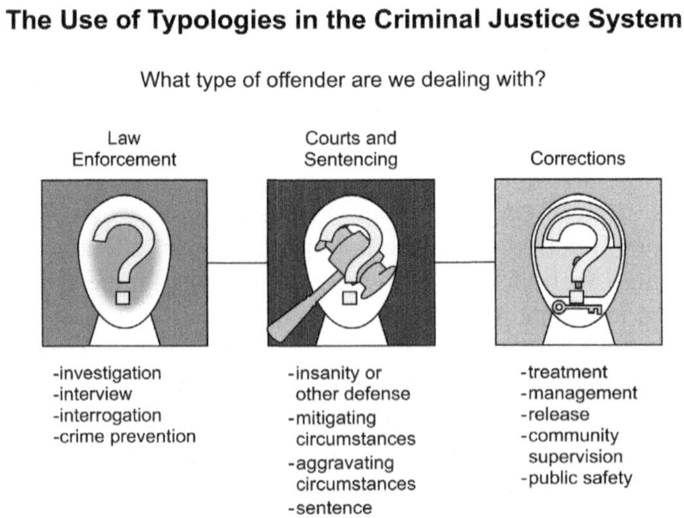

Figure 1.1 The Use of Typologies in the Criminal Justice System. (Helfgott (2008))

contended that there are different types of criminals who differ (by type and degree) in terms of genetic evolution, physical traits, and criminal propensities along a graduated scale from "born criminal" to "normal individual." According to Lombroso, there are "born criminals," "criminaloids," "occasional" and "habitual" offenders, and so on (Lombroso, 2003).

William Sheldon's body type theory is another example of a biological typology. Sheldon constructed a physical and mental typology based on embryology and the physiology of development comprised of three body types—the *endomorph*, *mesomorph*, and *ectomorph*. According to Sheldon, the endomorph is characterized by roundness, short limbs, velvety skin, and tendency to put on fat. In terms of temperament, the endomorph is *viscerotonic*—a comfortable, generally relaxed, extroverted "softie." The mesomorph is characterized by predominance of muscles and bone, large trunk, heavy chest, and large hands and wrists. The mesomorph is *somotonic*—active, dynamic, assertive, and aggressive. The ectomorph is characterized by predominance of skin and limbs and is lean, fragile, and delicate with a small face, fine hair, and sharp nose. The ectomorph is *cerebrotonic*—introverted, sensitive to noise and distractions, socially anxious, inclined to express physical complaints, and troubled by allergies and skin problems. Sheldon's studies and later research by the Gluecks (1956) revealed that mesomorphs were more likely to possess traits associated with aggression, delinquency, and crime (Vold, Bernard, & Snipes, 2002).

The r/K selection theory is also an example of a biological typology. The r/K theory is an evolutionary theory that explains different evolutionary survival strategies. Based on this theory, r-selected types produce a large number of crime-prone offspring, each of whom is unlikely to survive to adulthood. K-selected types produce fewer offspring and invest heavily in each of them, each of whom are likely to survive to adulthood and not likely to be crime-prone (Ellis, 2001).

Legalistic

Legalistic typologies are organized around violations of the criminal law. Legalistic typologies are the oldest and most frequently used forms of classifying crimes and criminals (Clinard et al., 1994). An example of a simple legalistic typology is the distinction made in the criminal law between "misdemeanors" and "felonies." The primary organizing feature for the misdemeanor-felony typology is seriousness of offense, with felonies involving imprisonment of more than one year. A more complex example of a legalistic typology is the FBI's *Uniform Crime Reports*, which classifies offenses based on Part I or Part II offenses in terms of severity of offense, but is more complex because it breaks down each type into multiple subtypes. Another common legalistic typology is the grouping of crime in terms of "crimes against the person," "crimes against property," and "crimes against public order." The organizing principle behind this typology is type of victimization (Miethe & McCorkle, 2001).

The FBI's *Uniform Crime Reports* (UCR) is the most widely accepted legalistic typology. The UCR classifies crimes in terms of *Part I* and *Part II* Offenses. Part I offenses include the following crime categories:

- Murder and nonnegligent manslaughter
- Forcible rape
- Robbery
- Aggravated assault
- Burglary
- Larceny/theft
- Motor-vehicle theft
- Arson

Part II of the UCR includes less serious crimes such as drug offenses, sex crimes and assaults (that do not involve Part I offenses), fraud, embezzlement, vandalism, disorderly conduct, possession of stolen property, commercialized vice, weapons violations, forgery and counterfeiting, gambling, driving under the influence, liquor law violations, vagrancy, and traffic violations. The UCR

Part I make up what is referred to as the *crime index*. The crime index is the average of all Part I offenses. The crime index provides a measure of crime often reported in the form of the crime rate (*x* number of offenses per 100,000 people) that can be compared over time and across geographical location.

Sociological

Sociological typologies are based on sociological theory and organized around social and cultural interactions and social context. Sociological typologies classify offenders and/or offenses based on features such as place of crime, relationship to victim, the activities involved in the crime, etc. Early sociological typologies developed in the nineteenth century distinguished between "professional criminals" (who made a living through crime), "accidental criminals" (who stumbled into crime), and "habitual criminals" (who engage in crime for diverse, more inherent reasons). Other sociological typologies include those that are based on organizational sophistication of the offender and a combination of background (e.g., social class, family background, peer associations, etc.) and definitional factors (e.g., nature of offense, offender self-concept and attitude toward social control agencies, etc.). An example of a sociological typology is Gibbon's role-career model in which he identified 20 offender types based on background and definitional factors, including "amateur shoplifters," "violent sex offenders," "psychopathic assaultists," "white-collar criminals," "automobile thieves-joyriders," "semiprofessional property criminals," "professional thieves," "naïve check forgers," and "incest offenders," among others (Clinard et al., 1994).

Sociological typologies of offenders have been used to describe prisoner adaptation. For example, Irwin (1980) described three types of inmates and prison adaptive modes: "doing time" (prisoners who avoided trouble and got out as soon as possible), "jailing" (immersion in the prison world), and "gleaners" (inmates attached to the formal institutional rules who tried to improve themselves by using available prison resources). Other sociological typologies applied to prisoners are organized around the prison hierarchy. For example "right guys" are at the top of the hierarchy because they adhere to the convict code; "politicians," "characters," and "prison toughs" are considered upper middle class, "square johns" the middle class, and "prison queens," "rapos," and "punks" the lower class (Silverman, 2001). These sociological typologies are organized around status, behaviors, and interactions between inmates.

Sociological typologies can also be based on situation and context. Hickey (2009) offers a "mobility typology" of serial murderers. This typology classifies serial murderers in terms of their mobility in the commission of crime. "Traveling" serial killers are those who travel from place to place, such as Ted Bundy, Henry Lee Lucas, and Otis Toole. "Local" killers commit their crimes in their own neighborhoods and communities, such as the Seattle area Green River Killer Gary Ridgway. "Place-specific" killers murder in their own homes or places of employment, such as Jeffrey Dahmer who murdered in his own home or Christine Falling who murdered children she babysat. Other typologies are organized around the offender-victim relationship. For example researchers have studied the differences between "stranger," acquaintance," "date," and "partner" rape (Cowan, 2000), and offenders' method of "confidence" versus "blitz" attack (Silverman et al., 1988).

The purposes of sociological typologies are theoretical understanding and social policy development. Knowing the social and situational-contextual factors that distinguish particular categories of crimes and criminals is crucial to theoretical understanding and policy and practice. For example, studies involving rapist typologies have found that victims of "confidence" attacks need different services from victims of "blitz" attacks because victims of "confidence" rapes engage in a greater degree of self-blame that needs to be addressed through aftercare services. Knowledge about the different types of serial killers provides insight that may aid law enforcement investigations. And understanding the types of prisoners that emerge through interactions in the prison subculture is important for informal and formal correctional management strategies.

Psychological

Psychological typologies are based on psychological theories and are organized around personality or some other individual psychological feature (e.g., mental illness, intelligence, cognition, psychodynamic development, motivation). Examples of psychological typologies include the *Diagnostic and Statistical Manual of Mental Disorders*, the *Crime Classification Manual* developed by the FBI's National Center for the Analysis of Violent Crime, the distinction between "psychopathy" and other types of personality disorders and conditions, and the Massachusetts Treatment Center rapist and child molester typologies.

The purposes of psychological typologies are theoretical understanding and correctional management and treatment. Sometimes psychological theories are also used by law enforcement to better understand the nature and dynamics of offenders for investigative, hostage negotiation, or public safety purposes. Crime is a behavioral symptom that can be the product of a broad range of underlying conditions. For treatment programs to be successful in correctional populations, they must target the risks, needs, and responsivity of particular types of offenders (Andrews & Bonta, 2003; Dowden & Andrews, 2000). Furthermore, correctional management often depends on and can be enhanced by identification of offender types theoretically rooted in psychological theories.

A classic example of a psychological typology can be found in Hervey Cleckley's (1941) *The Mask of Sanity*. *The Mask of Sanity* brought attention to the phenomenon of psychopathy, in particular to the notion of noncriminal psychopaths. Cleckley's work describes what is known in the literature as the classic conception of psychopathy. Cleckley proposed the notion of psychopathy as a taxon characterized by 16 distinct characteristics:

- Superficial charm and good intelligence
- Absence of delusions
- Absence of nervousness
- Unreliability
- Untruthfulness and insincerity
- Lack of remorse and shame
- Inadequately motivated antisocial behavior
- Failure to learn from experience and poor judgment
- Pathologic egocentricity and incapacity for love
- Lack of affect
- Loss of insight
- Unresponsiveness to interpersonal relations
- Fantastic and uninviting behavior (with and without alcohol)
- Suicide rarely carried out
- Impersonal, trivial, poorly integrated sex life
- Failure to follow any life plan (Cleckley, 1982, p. 204)

Cleckley contended that the "primary" or "true" psychopath can be distinguished from all other psychological conditions by the "defect in affect" or the ability to feel. He contrasted psychopaths with other types and conditions, including "psychotics," "psychoneurotics," "mental defectives," "sexual deviants," "ordinary criminals," "geniuses," and "hedonists." Cleckley's work has been the foundation for much of the contemporary research on psychopathy (discussed in detail in Chapter 4), distinguishing the condition as a unique clinical entity (or type) with implications for correctional classification, management, treatment, and risk assessment.

Lykken (1995) offers a classification of criminal types rooted in psychological theory. He proposes that there are three types of offenders: "normal offenders," "psychotic offenders," and "antisocial personalities." Lykken's criminal types are organized with respect to the level of pathological disturbance present. "Normal" offenders are not psychopathologically disordered. Their crimes include normal people reacting atypically to provocative situations (e.g., passion murder), innocent people who have been wrongly convicted, and "career" or white-collar criminals who commit crime because of life circumstance and opportunity. "Psychotic" offenders are out of touch with reality and, although most are not violent, may commit crime when they fail to take their medication. "Antisocial personalities" are the largest and most complex type, characterized by a "persisting disposition toward antisocial behavior" (p. 21). Within the "antisocial personalities" category, Lykken distinguishes three subtypes (sociopathic, psychopathic, and character neurosis) with further designation of subtypes of each.

Another example of a psychological/motivational typology is the "Power Assertive," Power Reassurance," "Anger Retaliatory," and "Anger Excitation" rape/sexual homicide typology originally developed by Groth (1979), expanded by Knight and Prentky (1987, 1990), and applied to sexual homicide by Keppel and Walter (1999). This typology is based on offender motivation and behavioral features and is used in law enforcement investigation for purpose of investigation, interview/interrogation, and case linkage (Turvey, 2011). The following are the different types of rape/sexual homicide included in this typology:

Power Assertive (PA): rape planned–murder unplanned, power driven, increasing aggression to control victim

Power Reassurance (PR): rape planned–murder unplanned, power driven, fantasy acted out while seeking reassurance from victim

Anger Retaliatory (AR): rape and murder planned, anger/revenge driven, may select symbolic victim

Anger Excitation (AE): rape and murder planned, anger driven, prolonged torture, exploitation, mutilation that energizes killer's fantasy

The FBI's *Crime Classification Manual* (CCM) was modeled after the *Diagnostic Manual of Mental Disorders* as a catalog of violent crime (Douglas et al., 1997). The CCM can be considered a psychological typology in the sense that it, like the PA, PR, AR, AE typology, is based on motivational features. The CCM classifies violent crime into three categories—Homicide, Arson, and Rape/Sexual Assault—based on motivational features of offenses. Offenses are classified based on victimology, crime scene characteristics, staging/nature of offense, and forensic findings. Information is presented for each offense category, including distinguishing features of each offense.

The FBI is also responsible for the well-known "organized"/"disorganized" typology, which distinguishes between offenders who leave organized, mixed, and disorganized crime scenes and who are said to possess certain features. Based on this typology, whether or not a crime scene is left organized or disorganized tells about the offender's criminal sophistication and personality. The organized offender displays psychopathic characteristics and a need for power and control, and exhibits organized behaviors during the commission of a crime, such as planning and staging, bringing weapons to the scene and hiding evidence, and controlled behavior. In contrast, the disorganized offender is said to display characteristics of psychosis; commits crime out of passion, compulsion, frustration, or anxiety; and engages in reactive violence, using whatever objects are found at the scene as weapons. The organized/disorganized typology was developed by FBI profilers from the National Center for the Analysis of Violent Crime and based on interviews conducted by FBI agents with incarcerated sexual murderers from 1979 to 1983 (Ressler, Burgess, & Douglas, 1992). The typology has been heavily criticized by a number of authors (Alison et al., 2002; Canter et al., 2004; Godwin, 1998) for being too simplistic, encouraging law enforcement officers to engage in (pseudo) psychological diagnosis for which they are untrained (Turvey, 2002); however, the organized/disorganized typology has been one of the most commonly cited in the history of profiling (Woodworth & Porter, 2001) and is a good example of a typology that attempts to make theory manageable for practical application in the criminal justice system.

Multi-Trait

Multi-trait typologies attempt to combine dimensions of crime in a single typology. Rather than just using a single trait or dimension (e.g., biological, legal, social, psychological) around which types are organized, multi-trait typologies incorporate multiple theoretical perspectives and crime dimensions. Clinard, Quinney, and Wildeman's (1994) *Criminal Behavior Systems* and Miethe & McCorkle's (2001) and Miethe, McCorkle, & Listwan's (2006) *Crime Profiles* are examples of multi-trait typologies. The purposes of multi-trait typologies include theoretical understanding and social policy development, crime prevention, and criminal investigation. Multi-trait typologies include multiple dimensions and are theoretically interdisciplinary. While some biological, psychological, and sociological typologies include other factors (e.g., Meloy's sexual homicide typology is grounded in biological and psychological theories), multi-trait typologies attempt to incorporate legalistic, sociological, psychological, and biological dimensions to come up with a general typology of crime.

Clinard and colleagues' (1994) multi-trait typology is organized around five theoretical dimensions:

- Legal aspects of selected offenses
- Criminal career of offender
- Group support of criminal behavior
- Correspondence between criminal and legitimate behavior
- Social reaction and legal processing

The authors construct nine theoretical types of criminal behavior in relation to the five dimensions, explaining each type of criminal behavior in terms of five dimensions. The types of crime are:

1) Violent personal (including homicide, rape, assault)
2) Occasional property (including forgery, shoplifting, theft)
3) Public order (including prostitution, public drunkenness, vagrancy)
4) Conventional (including larceny, burglary, robbery)
5) Political (including conspiracy, political demonstrations)
6) Occupational (including workplace theft, embezzlement)
7) Corporate (including insider trading, false advertising, environmental pollution)
8) Organized (including racketeering, organized criminal activity in legitimate business)
9) Professional (including counterfeiting, forgery, confidence games)

While the purpose of Clinard and colleagues' typology is primarily theoretical, Miethe, McCorkle, & Listwan (2006) incorporate the routine activity theory into their multi-trait typology with direct application for crime prevention. Relying on information from the *Uniform Crime Reports* (UCR), the National Crime Victimization Survey (NCVS), local police data, and interviews with offenders, they offer a typology of crime organized around five dimensions:

- Offenders' criminal careers
- Offender versatility
- Level of crime planning
- Offender motivation
- Target selection factors

The authors respond to each of the dimensions for each of seven crime categories:

1) Murder and aggravated assault
2) Sexual assault

3) Personal and institutional robbery
4) Residential and nonresidential burglary
5) Motor vehicle theft
6) Occupational and organizational crime
7) Public order crime

Miethe and colleagues' (2006) typology is unique in that it offers an "anatomy of dangerous persons, places, and situations" with direct implications for crime prevention and public safety strategies.

Meloy (2000) offers an integrative psychobiological sexual homicide typology that includes biological and psychological features such as DSM classification, level of psychopathy, physiological arousal, type of aggression, early childhood trauma, etc. This typology can be seen as a multi-trait typology because it integrates biological and psychological findings to support a theoretically and empirically based psychobiological typology. The typology distinguishes between two types of sexual homicide offenders—"compulsive" and "catathymic" types (Table 1.2).

The two types of sexual homicide offenders are distinguished by underlying psychopathology (DSM Axis I and II diagnoses, level of psychopathy, attachment pathology), nature of sexual homicide (organized/disorganized), and biological factors (autonomic nervous system) and traumatic reinforcers (childhood trauma). Meloy's typology is one of the more sophisticated typologies because it integrates motivational/psychological and biological features and draws from research in biology, psychology, and law enforcement/criminal profiling.

Table 1.2 Meloy's Sexual Homicide Typology

	Compulsive	Catathymic
Nature of sexual homicide	Organized	Disorganized
Axis I diagnosis	Sexual sadism	Mood disorder
Axis II diagnosis	APD/NPD	Various traits & PDs
Psychopathy	Severe (primary)	Mild-moderate
Attachment pathology	Chronically detached	Attachment hunger
ANS	Hyporeactive	Hyperreactive
Early Trauma	Often absent	Often present

Source: Adapted from Meloy (2000).

Typology Construction

Scientific advancement depends on "descriptive analytic schemes which identify similarities and differences between the entities comprising the universe of interest" (Blackburn, 1993, p. 60). Classifying events or people into types is a necessary function of science, theory development, and professional practice. In the criminal justice system, the classification of crime and criminals has direct implications for the way offenders are identified and dealt with in the criminal justice system. Scientific typology construction is a systematic activity that differs from everyday classifications that tend to be based on stereotypes and observational errors. Informal and unscientific classification of individuals into groups is problematic because there is potential for stigmatization, stereotyping, and the denial of individual uniqueness.

Some typologies are rooted in stereotypes, not science. For example, racial profiling in law enforcement involves classifying people into types using race as the organizing characteristic and making predictions about how people behave based on the category to which they belong. Racial profiling is based on stereotype and stigma, not science. There is little in the way of theory or empirical research that links particular racial groups to specific types of offenses. Without an empirically established link between race/ethnicity and criminal behavior, the practice of racial profiling by law enforcement threatens the civil rights of citizens who are targeted by police for nothing more than the color of their skin. However, scientifically based typologies that attempt to avoid stereotypes and everyday errors in reasoning are necessary for communication, program development, policy, prediction, and decision making.

Classifications are rarely truly homogeneous (the same), and most are based on relative homogeneity and the identification of a set of defining criteria that all members of the group share. In the real world, there is no such thing as a homogeneous category or type in which all members are the same and do not possess features of any other group. For example, all blue-eyed people are not the same, nor are they completely different from green- or brown-eyed people. A typology based on eye color would yield groups of people who are similar with respect to the color of their eyes, but the group would be heterogeneous (different) with respect to hair color, body type, personality style, economic status, education, and other factors. With respect to purpose, a typology based on eye color would be useful only to the extent that the categories "blue-eyed," "brown-eyed," "green-eyed," "hazel-eyed" are meaningfully heterogeneous. If eye color were predictive of a particular behavior or associated with amenability to a particular approach or treatment, then the typology would be useful, perhaps for suitability for particular contact lenses or a type of eye surgery.

In the social sciences, in particular criminology and psychology, "the systematic study of behavior is based on an ordering of the diversified world of discrete phenomena" (Clinard et al., 1994, p. 1). To make sense of the range of human behaviors and conditions, individuals are grouped into types based on shared characteristics (e.g., personality type). Human types may be more appropriately viewed along a continuum or dimension rather than as a discrete category or taxon. In other words, most people are a little of this and a little of that—for example, a little narcissistic or a little obsessive-compulsive, etc. This is a dimensional view of personality. A taxon is an either/or classification. Pregnancy is an example of a taxon—a person is either pregnant or not. A categorical classification or taxonomy of personality would hold that a person is either narcissistic or not, obsessive-compulsive or not.

Categories or types that are not inherently taxonomic (where there are no clear boundaries) are often formed by empirically grouping those who share features on several dimensions using statistical methods such as cluster analysis. "This preserves naturally occurring interactions between attributes, and yields polythetic categories defined by continuous rather than dichotomous criteria . . . categorical classification in psychiatry frequently imposes artificial boundaries between normality and abnormality" (Blackburn, 1993, p. 61). For example, while you cannot be a little bit pregnant, you can be a little bit psychopathic. Dividing people up into "pregnant" or "not pregnant" is a relatively easy task requiring a pregnancy test, whereas dividing people up into "psychopathic" or "nonpsychopathic" types is not so simple and requires assessing particular clusters of traits and behaviors (e.g., scoring on the *Psychopathy Checklist–Revised* [*PCL-R*]) (Hare, 1991, 2003), where level of psychopathy can be measured on a 0–40 point scale and a score of 30+ is indicative of primary psychopathy, a condition that many researchers suggest is categorically distinct and should be considered a taxon. Does this mean that someone who receives a score of 30 is a psychopath and someone who receives a score of 29 is not? This is a difficult (theoretical, philosophical, and empirical) question that illustrates the artificial boundaries that separate most psychological (and criminological) "types."

Typologies are constructed in two general ways. First, ideal types are inductively constructed based on a subjective clinical impression. For example, if a psychologist were to form the impression that particular personality types exist based on observations in clinical practice or a theorist were to construct a type based on attributes of central concern to a particular theory or to pragmatically combine variables of immediate interest (Blackburn, 1993). This is sometimes referred to as "armchair" theorizing. The ideal type can never be found in reality and "may be conceived as a distortion of the concrete" (Clinard et al., 1994, p. 11). Second, empirical types are deductively constructed describing patterns that exist in the real world through multivariate statistical methods (Blackburn, 1993; Clinard et al., 1994). For example, hierarchical cluster analysis is used to specify clusters of cases based on their similarity across a number of variables. This allows examination of each cluster to reveal salient features (Silverman et al., 1988), yielding a distinct empirical type. However, the distinction between ideal and empirical typologies is somewhat arbitrary. Ideal types are not completely the result of induction, nor are empirical types solely formed through deduction. "To conceive of types as developing from either source is to ignore the metaphysical problem of the nature of reality and our grasp of it. We construct that which gives meaning to our lives and to the problems of living that are posed by our need to survive" (Clinard et al., 1994, p. 11).

Knight and Prentky Typology of Sexual Offenders: An Example

Knight and Prentky's (1990) typology for classifying sex offenders illustrates the use of both the inductive and deductive approach to typology construction. The authors identified ideal typologies of sex offenders, empirically testing them through using statistical methods. Most sex offender typologies are speculative models of ideal types that have been constructed from the "armchair" with little evidence of reliability or validity. Knight and Prentky employed both deductive and inductive research strategies simultaneously to construct an empirical typological model classifying sexual offenders. The model is one of the most sophisticated and complex typologies of sex offenders developed to date, used in criminal justice decision-making in treatment and management of sex offenders (Fisher & Mair, 1998). The construction of the model is reviewed here to illustrate how complex typologies are constructed.

Knight and Prentky (1990) sought to determine the validity and reliability of test existing (speculative) sex offender typologies:

> Identification of a preliminary target for such a critical assessment required a thorough evaluation of the current status of the theory and research on sexual offenders. In a relatively undeveloped area like the study of sexual aggression, where data on the validation of typological systems were

> virtually nonexistent, we had to use other factors to guide our choice of a preliminary model. We compared the available typologies of sex offenders to determine whether specific types of offenders were described across a number of systems (see Knight et al., 1985). We reasoned that if such types could be identified, they would represent a consensus among clinicians of the most salient subtypes of sexual offenders and thus would provide the best available guesses about taxonomic structure. (p. 25)

The development of the typology involved four stages: theory formulation, implementation, validation, and integration. What follows is a summary of the stages of the construction process of the first version of the Massachusetts Treatment Center Rapist and Child Molester typologies adapted from Knight and Prentky (1990).

Stage 1: Theory Formulation

The authors compared available typologies to determine whether consensus exists regarding specific types of sex offenders. They developed two typologies representative of the types most frequently described in the literature—the Massachusetts Treatment Center: Child Molester Typology 1 (MTC:CM1) and the Massachusetts Treatment Center: Rapist Typology 1 (MTC:R1). They then identified the type-defining dimensions (e.g., amount and nature of aggression, lifestyle impulsivity, etc.) and tested them using cluster analysis to come up with the variables that most differentiate the types.

Stage 2—Implementation

At the next stage, Knight and Prentky clearly defined the types and dimensions and assessed interrater reliability (the degree to which multiple raters agree that specific offenders should be classified as specific types within the typology of interest). They then determined the coverage and degree to which the typology was exhaustive (applicable across the spectrum of offenders) and homogeneous (how cohesive the types are). Upon finding inadequate reliability and coverage for one of the typologies (child molester typology), they had to circle back and make revisions (e.g., omitting variables, adding dimensions) to the typology before moving to the next stage. Finally, less relevant variables were excluded in an effort to include only the most reliable and relevant variables. In other words, variables that multiple raters did not clearly identify and/or that were not found to be mutually exclusive across types were discarded. For example, if "victim selection" was a variable hypothesized to distinguish between types of child molesters, and cluster analysis revealed that different types of child molesters select similar types of victims and raters did not consistently classify offenders into the same types based on this variable, then this would not be a distinguishing variable and would be discarded.

Stage 3—Validation

In the validation stage, the authors looked to the research literature and theory on the developmental roots of sex offending to determine whether the constructed types could be shown to have "distinctive, theoretically coherent developmental roots" (Knight & Prentky, 1990, p. 28). The purpose of linking the typology with theories of the etiology and development of sex offending is to establish construct validity. Construct validity, which involves examining converging lines of evidence to support a particular theory of types, is an important step in the empirical construction of typologies.

Stage 4—Integration

The integrations staged involved responding to the analyses of construct validity to determine which dimensions of the typologies needed modification. Cluster analyses and other statistical methods were used to determine which dimensions carried more or less weight as discriminating factors. For example, in their analysis and validation of the child molester typology, the authors found that two constructs—fixation and regression, which originally represented separate types—were problematic. The fixation type was said to be characterized by "high intensity" (high level of pedophilic interest) and "low social competence," while the regression type was associated with "low intensity" and "high social competence." The fixation-regression types were crossed with an instrumental-expressive aggression distinction to yield eight separate types of child molesters. However, when attempting to classify a group of 68 child molesters using this eight-group typology, the authors found that interrater reliabilities were unacceptably low, certain types were extremely heterogeneous, and there were offenders who fell between the types (e.g., offenders who were highly fixated and had high social competence). As a result, the typology had to be revised to improve and ensure reliability, homogeneity, and validity.

The MTC typologies have continued to be improved and are now in the third version (MTC:R3 and MTC:CM3) (Prentky & Burgess, 2000). Table 1.2 shows the characteristics of the 9 types included in the MRC Rapist typology Version 3 and Figures 1.2 and 1.3 provide visual illustration of the MTC:R3 and MTC:CM3 typologies.

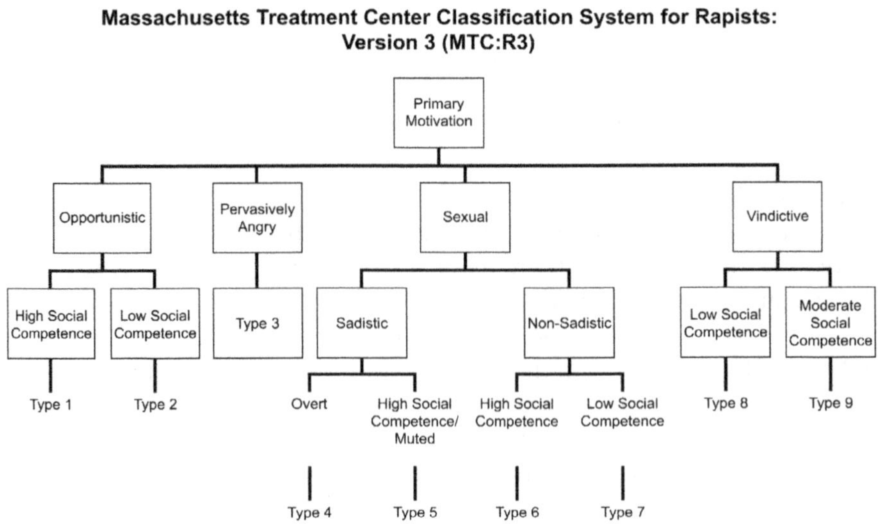

Figure 1.2 Massachusetts Treatment Center Classification System for Rapists: Version 3 (MTC: R3) (Adapted from Prentky & Burgess [2000]. *Forensic management of sexual offenders*. New York: Kluwer/Plenum, p. 62.)

Evaluating Typologies

A criminal typology is only useful to the extent that it describes homogeneous categories of offending, is comprehensive/exhaustive with respect to the stated purpose (i.e., is it a general typology of crime? psychopaths? serial killers? organized criminals? etc.), contains categories that are mutually exclusive that do not overlap, and is complex enough to have explanatory value and simple enough to be applied in criminal justice policy and practice. In evaluating offender typologies, it is important to ask the following questions:

- Is the typology and the categories it includes homogeneous?
- Is the typology and the categories it includes heterogeneous?
- Is the typology and the categories it includes exhaustive?
- Are the categories included in the typology mutually exclusive?
- Is the typology too simple?
- Is the typology too complex?

Homogeneity/Heterogeneity

A typology is homogeneous if it can be said to describe a category of offending consisting of offenders or behaviors that are the same with respect to principal unifying dimension and purpose. For example, we

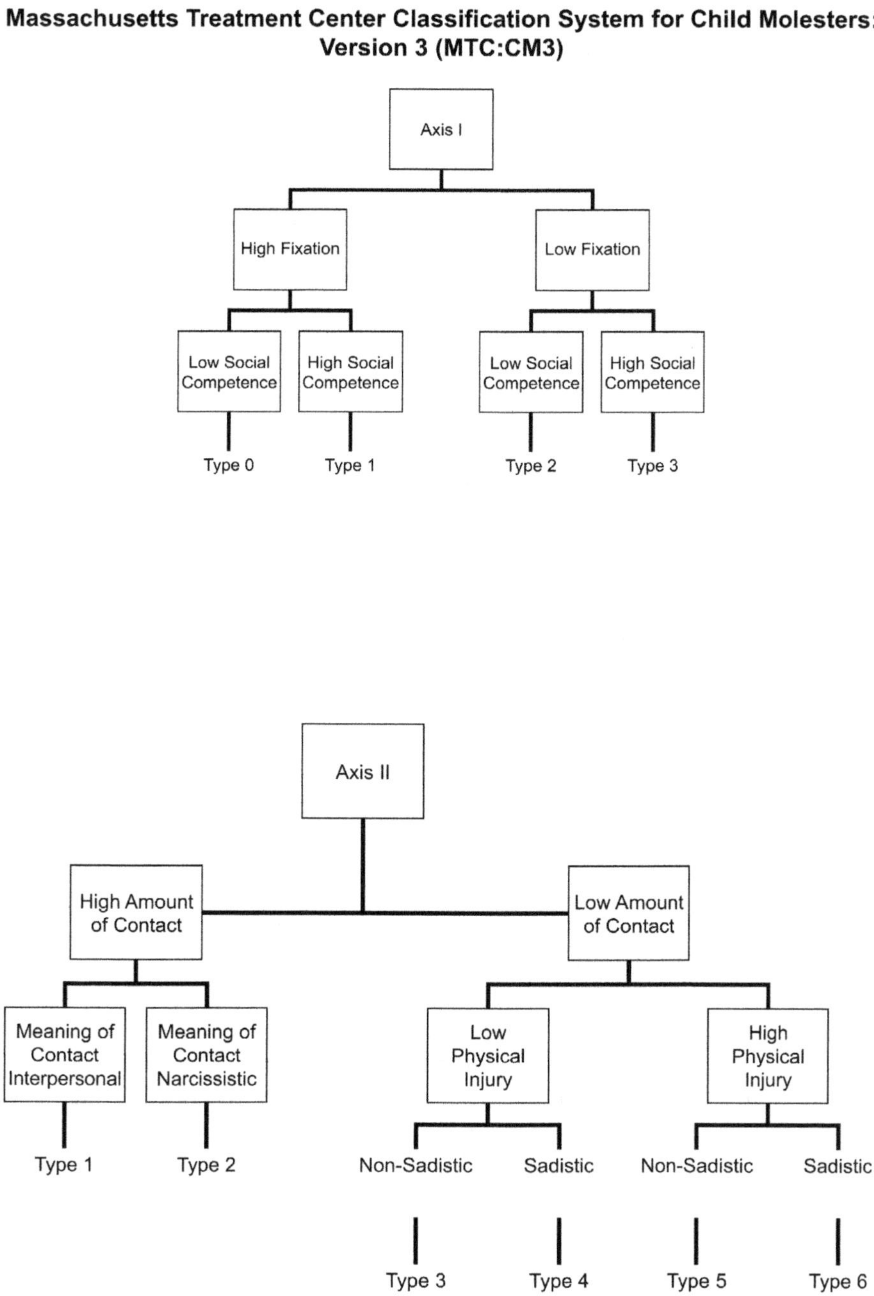

Figure 1.3 Massachusetts Treatment Center Classification System for Child Molesters: Version 3 (MTC: CM3). (Adapted from Prentky & Burgess [2000]. *Forensic management of sexual offenders*. New York: Kluwer/Plenum, p. 62.)

can ask this question about the legalistic *misdemeanor/felony* typology: Are all crimes that fall under the heading of "misdemeanors" the same along the principle unifying dimension? In this case, the organizing principle is severity of offense and sentence. Classification as a felony is based on the seriousness of the offense and punishment of more than one year in prison. But are all felonies the same? Yes and no. The "felony type" is homogeneous with respect to offense severity and punishment. If the purpose of the typology is simply to differentiate for the purpose of legal sanction, then the typology is sufficiently homogeneous with respect to the central organizing principle. However, with respect to other dimensions, the felony category is actually quite heterogeneous. Felony offenses include murder, rape, robbery, assault, drug offenses, arson, sex offenses, embezzlement, fraud, and many other types of offenses. With respect to any purpose beyond legal sanctions, this typology would be much too heterogeneous to be of use. For example, can we say anything about felony offenders that would be helpful in determining correctional management and treatment strategies? Perhaps to some extent, we could say that felony offenders have committed more serious crimes, pose a greater risk, and should be placed in more secure correctional facilities. Or could we? Could we devise an appropriate "treatment" approach for felony versus misdemeanor offenders? Would a treatment program devised for all felony offenders be beneficial for sex offenders, drug offenders, and murderers? Given that these two categories consist of a diverse array of offender types, this legalistic typology would not be of much use for the development of treatment programs.

Exhaustiveness/Exclusiveness

A typology is only useful to the extent that it is exhaustive with respect to the concept it is describing and exclusive in the sense that categories do not overlap. Miethe and McCorkle (2001) state that, "a definitive typology of crimes or criminals is not possible" (p. 14). Criminologists disagree on which dimensions are most important, which definitions of crimes and criminals are socially constructed, and which typologies serve different purposes. Thus, there is no such thing as a "perfect" typology of criminal behavior. Typologies should be assessed with respect to their ability to explain a central concept and the degree to which real-world crimes and criminals exclusively fall into the designated types.

It is probably not possible to come up with a completely exhaustive criminal typology. Such a typology would have to include all possible types of crime. Because definitions of crime change across time and place, typologies of crime are, to some extent, bound by time and culture. For example, most typologies of crime constructed prior to the last decade or so do not include the categories "cybercrime" and "copycat crime." These crime categories have been identified and have gained attention only in recent years and thus were historically not recognized as specific crime types. However, within a typology of crime, it is crucial that each category be exhaustive in terms of including all possible instances of the offense type. For example, until recently, typologies of serial killers did not include women or instrumentally motivated offenders (Hickey, 2009). The FBI definition of serial murder, "three or more separate events in three or more separate locations with an emotional cooling-off period between homicides" (Douglas et al., 1997, p. 21) did not capture many female and instrumental offenders. Thus a crime category must be evaluated in terms of the degree to which it is exhaustive and able to explain all possible expressions of the crime/criminal it proposes to describe.

More importantly, typologies must be assessed in terms of the mutual exclusivity of the categories within it. In other words, a theoretical "type" is only meaningful to the degree that it tells us something about those who can be classified within it. For example, one of the major problems with the *Uniform Crime Reports* is that people who commit more than one crime are classified in terms of the more severe offender. What this means is that a person who commits a rape/murder is classified as a "murderer" in the UCR. This alleviates the problem of mutual exclusivity but distorts the reality of crime in official statistics. In reality, there are many offenders who commit (to use Clinard et al., 1994) public order *and* violent personal *and* occasional property criminal behavior. Theoretically, this is not so much of a problem as long as each category is conceptually distinct. However, conceptual distinction (and mutual exclusivity) between categories is lacking in many existing typologies.

Simplicity/Complexity

If a typology is too simple, it will be criticized for being unsophisticated. If a typology is too complex it will not have real-world application. A balance must be achieved between simplicity and complexity. This is one of the most crucial considerations in typology construction. For example, one of the more heavily criticized typologies in the criminal justice literature is the FBI's "organized/disorganized" typology. However, this typology is probably the most well known and more often applied typologies in research and law enforcement practice. According to Ressler, Burgess, and Douglas (1997), whether or not the crime scene is left organized or disorganized tells something about the offender in terms of criminal sophistication and personality. Organized crime scenes are said to reflect an offender who commits crime out of a need for power and are associated with psychopathy. Disorganized crime scenes are said to reflect an offender who commits crime out of passion, compulsion, frustration, or anxiety and are associated with psychosis. Organized offenders tend to engage in specific behaviors such as premeditation, transporting the victim's body to another location, bringing weapons to the scene, not leaving evidence behind, etc. Disorganized offenders tend to use weapons found at the scene, leave the victim's body and other evidence in full view, seek victims known to them, etc. The organized/disorganized typology has been used for the purpose of case linkage, to provide investigative direction, and to inform interrogation and interview strategies with suspects.

Turvey (2011) argues that the organized/disorganized typology is a false dichotomy developed for law enforcement agencies requesting profiles and criticizes the typology for being too simple, suggesting that it is seductive to those without any education in, or knowledge of, human psychology, and that it is too easy for law enforcement to use without thinking. He suggests that the organized/disorganized classification is an "invitation to be misled" by a "beautiful theory that cannot withstand the scrutiny of critical analysis" designed for training those without a basic knowledge of human psychology (p. 149). According to Turvey (2011), at root of these criticisms are the following problems:

- Most crime scenes will not be one or the other and present on a continuum.
- Only a competent forensic analysis can give insight on how and why a crime scene presents as it does.
- Crime scenes that appear disorganized can be created by nonpsychotic, nonmentally ill offenders.
- Crime scenes that appear organized are not necessarily committed by "psychopaths"
- The dichotomy does not take into account an offender's development over time.
- Ignores distinction between M.O. and signature, focusing only on the physical scene and not on "why" crime occurred as it did.
- Can be misused in court if framed as a clinical assessment.

Thus, the organized/disorganized typology is problematic with respect to a number of factors. The types are not homogeneous constructs (more than one "type" of offender can be "organized" or "disorganized"). The types are not mutually exclusive (a person can be classified as both organized and disorganized). And most importantly, the typology as a whole is too simple, particularly with respect to the association with psychopath and psychosis, which are highly complex constructs. On the other hand, theorists who construct typologies might take a few notes from the FBI profilers who developed the organized/disorganized typology. Criminologists often complain that their research and theories are not practically applied in the criminal justice system. The task at hand is to develop sophisticated typologies that can be simply presented for use in criminal justice policy and practice, and a number of empirically derived typologies have made their way into criminal justice policy and practice that have influenced correctional classification and management, treatment programs, and sex offender classification levels (Helfgott, 2008).

Concluding Comments

Criminal typologies offer a means to merge theory and practice by classifying criminal behaviors with respect to an organizing framework that enables identification of key features of offense behaviors in ways that broad theories do not. Criminal typologies are used at all stages of the criminal justice process in law enforcement, courts, corrections, and the juvenile justice system. Returning to Horney's (2006) call for greater situational specificity in research on criminal behavior, the typology approach provides the necessary details to understand and respond to specific types and subtypes of offense behaviors within the framework of more general theoretical frameworks and with attention to individual-environment interactions, situational context, and the unique nature of specific types and subtypes of crime.

References

Agnew, R. (2005). *Why do criminals offend? A general theory of crime and delinquency*. Los Angeles, CA: Roxbury.

Akers, R. L. (1991). Self control as a general theory of crime. *Journal of Quantitative Criminology, 7*, 201–211.

Alison, L., Bennell, C., Mokros, A., & Ormerod, D. (2002). The personality paradox in offender profiling: A theoretical review of the processes involved in deriving background characteristics from crime scene actions. *Psychology, Public Policy, and the Law, 8*(1), 115–135.

American Psychiatric Association (APA). (2000). *Diagnostic and statistical manual of mental disorders* (4th ed., text rev. [DSM-IV-TR]). Washington, DC: Author.

Andrews, D. A., & Bonta, J. (1995). *Level of Service Inventory–Revised*. North Tonawanda, NY: Multi-Health Systems.

Andrews, D. A., & Bonta, J. (2003). *The psychology of criminal conduct* (3rd ed.). Cincinnati, OH: Anderson Publishing.

Andrews, D. A., & Bonta, J. (2010). *The psychology of criminal conduct* (5th ed.). Cincinnati, OH: Anderson Publishing.

Annon, J. S. (1995). Investigative profiling: A behavioral analysis of the crime scene. *American Journal of Forensic Psychology, 13*(4), 67–75.

Beck, J. C. (1998). Legal and ethical duties of the clinician treating a patient who is liable to be impulsively violent. *Behavioral Sciences and the Law, 16*, 375–389.

Belfrage, H. (1998). A ten-year follow-up of criminality in Stockholm mental patients: New evidence for a relation between mental disorder and crime. *British Journal of Criminology, 38*(1), 145–155.

Blackburn, R. (1993). *The psychology of criminal conduct: Theory, research, and practice*. New York: John Wiley & Sons.

Bowie, S. I., Silverman, D. C., Kalick, S. M., & Edbril, S. D. (1990). Blitz rape and confidence rape: Implications for clinical intervention. *American Journal of Psychotherapy, 44*(2), 180–188.

Bourne, L. E., Dominowski, R. L., Loftus, E. F., & Healy, A. E. (1986). *Cognitive processes*. Englewood Cliffs, NJ: Prentice Hall.

Canter, D., Alison, L. J., Alison, E., & Wentink, N. (2004). The organized/disorganized typology of serial murder: Myth or model? *Psychology, Public Policy, and Law, 10*(3), 293–320.

Cleckley, H. (1941, 1976, 1988). *The mask of sanity*. St. Louis, MO: Mosby, 1976.

Clinard, M. B., Quinney, R., & Wildeman, J. (1994). *Criminal behavior systems: A typology*. Cincinnati, OH: Anderson Publishing.

Cook, P. E., & Hinman, D. L. (1999). Criminal profiling: Science and art. *Journal of Contemporary Criminal Justice, 15*(3), 230–241.

Cornell, D. G., Warren, J., Hawk, G., Stafford, E., Oram, G., & Pine, D. (1996). Psychopathy in instrumental and reactive violent offenders. *Journal of Consulting and Clinical Psychology, 64*(4), 783–790.

Cowan, G. (2000). Beliefs about the causes of four types of rape. *Sex roles, 42*(9–10), 807–823.

Crowe, T., & Zahm, D. (2004). Crime prevention through environmental design. *Land Management, 71*, 22–27.

Dabney, D. A. (2004). *Crime types: A text/reader*. Belmont, CA: Wadsworth.

Daéid, N. N. (1997). Differences in offender profiling in the United States of America and the United Kingdom. *Forensic Science International, 90*, 25–31.

Davis, J. A. (1999). Criminal personality profiling and crime scene assessment: A contemporary investigative tool to assist law enforcement public safety. *Journal of Contemporary Criminal Justice, 15*(3), 291–301.

Douglas, J. E., Burgess, A. W., Burgess, A. G., & Ressler, R. K. (1997). *Crime classification manual*. San Francisco, CA: Jossey-Bass Publishers.

Douglas, K. S., Vincent, G. M., & Edens, J. F. (2006). Risk for criminal recidivism: The role of psychopathy. In C. J. Patrick (Ed.), *The handbook of psychopathy* (pp. 533–554). New York: Guilford Press.

Dowden, C., & Andrews, D. A. (2000). Effective correctional treatment and violet reoffending: A meta-analysis. *Canadian Journal of Criminology and Criminal Justice, 42*(4), 449–467.

Edens, J. F., & Petrila, J. (2006). Legal and ethical issues in the assessment and treatment of psychopathy. In C. J. Patrick (Ed.), *Handbook of psychopathy* (pp. 573–588). New York: Guilford Press.

Egger, S. A. (1999). Psychological profiling: Past, present, and future. *Journal of Contemporary Criminal Justice, 15*(3), 242–261.

Ellis, L. (2001). Sex differences in criminality: An explanation based on the concept of r/K selection. *Mankind Quarterly, 30*(2), 17–37.

Faigman, D. L. (1999). *Legal alchemy: The use and misuse of science and law*. New York: W. H. Freeman.

Farrington, D. P. (2003) Developmental and life-course criminology: Key theoretical and empirical issues. *Criminology, 41*(2), 221–225.

Gabor, T. (1994). *Everybody does it!: Crime by the public*. Toronto, Ontario, Canada: University of Toronto Press.

Garland, D. (1990). *Punishment and modern society: A study in social theory*. Chicago, IL: University of Chicago Press.

Glueck, S., & Glueck, E. T. (1956). *Physique and Delinquency*. New York: Harper & Row.

Godwin, M. (1998). Reliability, Validity, and Utility of Extant Serial Murder Classifications. *The Criminologist*, 22(4), 195–210.

Gottfredson, M. R., & Hirschi, T. (1990). *A general theory of crime*. Palo Alto, CA: Stanford University Press.

Groth, A. N. (1979). *Men who rape: The psychology of the offender*. New York: Plenum.

Harcourt, B. E. (2007). *Against prediction. Profiling, policing, and punishing in an actuarial age*. Chicago: University of Chicago Press.

Hare, R. D. (1998). Psychopaths and their nature: Implications for the mental health and criminal justice systems. In: T. Millon, E. Simonsen, E. Birket-Smith, & R. D. Davis (Eds.), *Psychopathy: Antisocial, criminal, and violent behavior* (pp. 188–212). New York: Guilford Press.

Hare, R. D. (1991, 2003). *Hare Psychopathy Checklist–Revised* (2nd ed.). Toronto, Ontario, Canada: Multi-Health Systems.

Hare, R. D., & Neumann, C.S. (2010). Psychopathy: Assessment and forensic implications. In L. Malatesti & J. McMillan (Eds.) *Responsibility and psychopathy: Interfacing law, psychiatry, and philosophy* (pp. 93–123). Oxford: Oxford University Press.

Helfgott, J. B. (2008). *Criminal behavior: Theories, typologies, and criminal justice*. Thousand Oaks, CA: Sage Publications.

Hickey, E. W. (2009). *Serial murderers and their victims*. Belmont, CA: Wadsworth.

Hirschi, T. (1969). *Causes of delinquency*. Berkeley, CA: University of California Press.

Hodgins, S. (1993). *Mental disorder and crime*. Newbury Park, CA: Sage Publications.

Holmes, S. T., & Holmes, R. M. (2004). *Violence: A contemporary reader*. Upper Saddle River: NJ: Prentice Hall.

Homant, R. J., & Kennedy, D. B. (1998). Psychological aspects of crime scene profiling: Validity research. *Criminal Justice and Behavior, 25*(3), 319–343.

Horney, J. (2006). An alternative psychology of criminal behavior. *Criminology, 44*(1), 1–16.

Hyman, R. (2004). Medea of suburbia: Andrea Yates, maternal infanticide, and the insanity defense. *Women's Studies Quarterly, 32*(3–4), 192–210.

Isidore, C. (2012, March 6). "Stanford found guilty in Ponzi scheme." Retrieved March 6, 2012, from http://money.cnn.com/2012/03/06/news/companies/stanford_guilty/index.htm?iid=HP_LN&hpt=ju_c2.

Keppel, R. D., & Walter, R. (1999). Profiling killers: A revised classification model for understanding sexual murder. *International Journal of Offender Therapy and Comparative Criminology, 43*(4), 417–437.

Knight, R. A., & Prentky, R. A. (1987). The developmental antecedents and adult adaptations of rapist subtypes. *Criminal Justice and Behavior, 14*, 403–426.

Knight, R. A., & Prentky, R. A. (1990). Classifying sexual offenders: The development and corroboration of taxonomic models. In W. L. Marshall, D. R. Laws, & H. E. Barbaree (Eds.), *Handbook of sexual assault: Issues, theories, and treatment of the offender* (pp. 23–52). New York: Plenum.

Kormanik, B. (2012, January 20). "Threat from gangs heightens anxiety in a Brooklyn neighborhood." *The New York Times*. Retrieved from http://www.nytimes.com/2012/01/21/nyregion/brownsville-brooklyn-is-terrorized-by-gangs.html?ref=crimeandcriminals

Laub, J. H., & Sampson, R. J. (2006). *Shared beginnings, divergent lives: Delinquent boys to age 70*. Cambridge, MA: Harvard University Press.

Lombroso, C. (2003). The criminal man. In F. T. Cullen & R. Agnew (Eds.). *Criminological theory: Essential readings* (pp. 23–25). Los Angeles, CA: Roxbury.

Lykken, D. T. (1995). *The antisocial personalities*. Hillsdale, NJ: Lawrence Erlbaum Associates.

Martin, J. (2006, March 31). Absence of motive adds an extra layer of grief. *The Seattle Times*. Retrieved April 4, 2006, from http://seattletimes.nwsource.com/html/localnews/2002901117_nomotive31m.html.

Meloy, J. R. (1992). *Violent attachments*. Northvale, NJ: Jason Aronson.

Meloy, J. R. (2000). The nature and dynamics of sexual homicide: An integrative review. *Aggression and Violent Behavior, 5*, 1–22.

Miethe, T. D., & McCorkle, R. C. (2001). *Crime profiles: The anatomy of dangerous persons, places, and situations* (2nd ed.). Los Angeles, CA: Roxbury Publishing.

Miethe, T. D., McCorkle, R. C., & Listwan, S. J. (2006). *Crime profiles: The anatomy of dangerous persons, places, and situations* (3rd ed.). Los Angeles, CA: Roxbury Publishing.

Modestin, J., & Ammann, R. (1995). Mental disorders and criminal behavior. *British Journal of Psychiatry, 166*, 667–675.

Moffit, T. E. (1993). Adolescent-limited and life-course-persistent antisocial behavior: A developmental taxonomy. *Psychological Review, 100*(4), 674–701.

Monahan, J., Steadman, H. J., Silver, E., Appelbaum, P. S., Robbins, P. C., Mulvey, E. P., . . . Banks, S. (2001). *Rethinking risk assessment: The MacArthur Study of Mental Disorder and Violence*. Oxford: Oxford University Press.

O'Toole, M. E. (1999). Criminal profiling: The FBI uses criminal investigative analysis to solve crimes. *Corrections Today, 61*, 44–46.

Piquero, A., & Mazerolle, R. (Eds.) (2001). *Life-course criminology*. Belmont, CA: Wadsworth.

Prentky, R. A., & Burgess, A. W. (2000). *Forensic management of sexual offenders*. New York: Kluwer/Plenum.

Pinzotto, A. J., & Finkel, N. (1990). Criminal personality profiling: An outcome and process study. *Law and Human Behavior, 14*(3), 215–233.

Porter, S., & Porter, S. (2007). Psychopathy and violent crime. In H. Herve & J. C. Yuille (Eds.), *The psychopath: Theory, research, and practice* (pp. 287–300). Mahwah, NJ: Lawrence Erlbaum.

Quinsey, V. L., Harris, G. T., Rice, M. E., & Cormier, C. A. (1998). *Violent offenders: Appraising and managing risk*. Washington, DC: American Psychological Association.

Reiber R. W., & Vetter, H. J. (1995). The language of the psychopath. In R. W. Reiber (Ed.), *The psychopathology of language and cognition* (pp. 61–87). New York: Plenum Press.

Ressler, R. K., Burgess, A. W., & Douglas, J. E. (1992). *Sexual homicide: Patterns and motives*. New York: Simon & Schuster.

Scully, D., & Marolla J. (1984). Convicted rapists' vocabulary of motives: Excuses and justifications, *Social Problems, 31*, 530–544.

Silverman, D. C., Kalick, S. M., Bowie, S. I., & Edbril, S. D. (1988). Blitz rape and confidence rape: A typology applied to 1,000 consecutive cases. *American Journal of Psychiatry, 145*(11), 1438–1441.

Silverman, I. J. (2001). *Corrections: A comprehensive view*. Belmont, CA: Wadsworth.

Stuart, G. L., Moore, T. M., Gordon, K. C., Ramsey, S. E., & Kahler, C. W. (2006). Psychopathology in women arrested for domestic violence. *Journal of Interpersonal Violence, 21*, 376–389.

Sykes, G. M., & Matza, D. (1957). Techniques of neutralization: A theory of delinquency. *American Sociological Review, 22*, 664–670.

Tengström, A., Hodgins, S., Grann, M., Längström, N., & Kullgren, G. (2004). Schizophrenia and criminal offending: The role of psychopathy and substance use disorders. *Criminal Justice and Behavior, 31*, 367–390.

Tittle, C. R. (1995). *Control balance: Towards a general theory of deviance*. Boulder, CO: Westview Press.

Turvey, B. E. (2011). *Criminal profiling: An introduction to behavioral evidence analysis*. San Diego, CA: Academic Press.

Vold, G. B., Bernard, T. J., & Snipes, J. B. (2002). *Theoretical criminology*. New York: Oxford University Press.

West, A. (2000). Clinical assessment of homicide offenders: The significance of crime scene in offense and offender analysis. *Homicide Studies, 4*(3), 219–233.

Wilson, P., Lincoln, R., & Kocsis, R. (1997). Validity, utility and ethics of profiling for serial violent and sexual offenders. *Psychiatry, Psychology, and the Law, 4*(1), 1–12.

Woodworth, M., & Porter, S. (2001). Historical foundations and current applications of criminal profiling in violent crime investigations. *Expert Evidence, 7*, 241–261.

Wulach, J. S. (1988). The criminal personality as a DSMIII-R antisocial, narcissistic, borderline, and histrionic personality disorder. *International Journal of Offender Counseling and Comparative Criminology, 33*(3), 185–199.

CHAPTER TWO

An Introduction to Criminal Profiling*

Richard N. Kocsis

Criminal profiling can be understood as a psychological technique whereby behaviors evident in a crime or series of related crimes are evaluated typically for the purpose of inferring attributes about the probable offender(s) (Kocsis, 2006). A few examples of such attributes can include, but are not limited to, the age of the offender, their gender, level of education, general appearance, and even aspects of their personality (Rossi, 1982; Vorpagel, 1982). The amalgamation of these characteristics is, in colloquial parlance, referred to as a *criminal profile* and individuals who compile them are often referred to as *profilers* (Douglas, Burgess, Burgess, & Ressler, 2006; Jeffers, 1992; Campbell & DeNevi, 2004). The conversion of a specific task into a vocation is something of a peculiarity given that a universally accepted standard denoting who may engage in constructing a criminal profile does not currently exist (Bekerian & Jackson, 1997; Bumgarner, 2007; Kocsis & Palermo, 2007).

To fully understand what criminal profiling is also requires some explanation of what it is not given the existence of a number of other similarly entitled techniques. One example is DNA profiling which entails the analysis of organic matter typically found at a crime to establish whether

*This chapter is a slightly revised version of the manuscript originally published as: Kocsis, R. N. (2009). Criminal profiling. In R. N. Kocsis (Ed.), *Applied criminal psychology* (pp. 213–233). Springfield, IL: C. C. Thomas.

the genetic code corresponds with that of a person or persons of interest in relation to that crime (Lazer, 2004). Another example is that of racial profiling (a.k.a. actuarial profiling) (Harcourt, 2007) which, as a technique, predominantly involves the conglomeration of demographic characteristics believed to be commonly shared by individuals who engage in a particular form of crime to potentially identify similar future offenders. An illustration of such profiling involves the identification of supposedly typical characteristics of individuals engaged in smuggling narcotics through airports which customs officers may proactively use as a guide to select and search travelers. In contrast, criminal profiling is reactive via the examination of behaviors exhibited at crime scenes. Additionally, the attributes predicted of an offender in a criminal profile are determined by the interpretation of the exhibited behaviors in the particular crime under examination. Consequently, the content of criminal profiles can be quite varied whereas the attributes contained in racial profiles are reflective of a fixed set of aggregated demographics.

Criminal profiling has also developed a number of semantic variations in nomenclature including *offender profiling*, *psychological profiling*, and *criminal personality profiling* to name only a few. The precise basis of such variations in terminology is unclear but their use predominantly appears related to the linguistic preferences of differing regions of the world. Thus, *offender profiling* appears to be commonly used in the United Kingdom and Europe (e.g., Boon, 1995; Canter, 1989; Jackson & Bekerian, 1997) whereas *criminal profiling* seems more common in North America (Hicks & Sale, 2006; Holmes & Holmes, 2002). For convenience however, the technique will continue to be referred to herein as *criminal profiling* or more simply *profiling*.

The basic purpose of criminal profiling is to act as a tool which may assist with lines of inquiry in a criminal investigation (Douglas & Burgess, 1986; Douglas, Ressler, Burgess, & Hartman, 1986; Holmes & Holmes, 2002). A number of differing avenues exist whereby this objective may be achieved. Possibly the most common method is for a profile to serve as a tool for prioritizing the investigation of known suspects. Thus, suspects who possess characteristics matching those of a profile are prioritized for greater scrutiny by investigators in comparison to suspects who do not match the profile (Douglas & Burgess, 1986). In this context it should be noted that the use of criminal profiles are only recommended as a method by which investigative resources, in terms of which leads to pursue first, can be ordered. The degree of congruence that a suspect may have with the predicted attributes of a criminal profile is not advocated as a means by which suspects are to be eliminated from an investigation (Douglas et al., 1986).

The context in terms of what types of crime criminal profiling may be applied to is something of a contested issue. Traditionally, criminal profiling has been recommended as most beneficial to the investigation of intractable crimes (Douglas & Oleshaker, 1995; Fisher, 1993; Ressler & Shachtman, 1992) which are suggestive of some form of psychopathology and/or aberrant psychological drive(s) within the offender(s) (Geberth, 1983; Holmes & Holmes, 2002; Rossi, 1982; Vorpagel, 1982). This is not to suggest that profiling is not potentially applicable to more conventional forms of crime. However, it is in the context of intractable, aberrant, violent crimes where profiling is seen as being of optimal benefit in practical (i.e., operational) terms (Nowikowski, 1995). While some scholars appear to endorse this perspective (e.g., Campbell & DeNevi, 2004; Holmes & Holmes, 2002; Hickey, 2001; Kocsis, 2006) others seem to view profiling as broader in application and potentially extending to a wider variety of offences beyond intractable violent crimes (e.g., Alison, 2005; Canter, 2004b).

Perhaps one of the greatest myths surrounding criminal profiling is the belief that it is a recent innovation. In contrast to popular media depictions, the concept of criminal profiling, that is examining behavioral patterns evident in a crime to glean some impression of the probable offender, has been in use for well over a century. Beyond analogies between criminal profiling and Sir Arthur Conan Doyle's consummate fictional detective Sherlock Holmes (Doyle, 1891) examples of profiling can be found throughout history dating back as far as 1888 and the investigation of the Whitechappel murderer a.k.a. *Jack the Ripper* (Whittington-Egan, 1975). Other instances where criminal profiling has been used (typically via the consultation of a mental health professional) appear throughout history and involve some of the world's most infamous cases. A few such examples include the kidnapping of Charles Lindbergh Jnr. in the 1920s (Shoenfeld, 1936), the evaluation of Adolf Hitler by the US Office of Strategic Services (Langer, 1972), the Mad Bomber of New York and the Boston Strangler in the 1950s and 60s (Brussel, 1968; Frank, 1966). While research and development into dedicated methods for criminal profiling have certainly flourished over approximately the past four decades (Dowden, Bennell, & Bloomfield, 2007), the historical realities indicate that the fundamental concept of profiling, that is, evaluating crime behaviors to infer attributes about the probable offender is in reality very old.

Approaches to Criminal Profiling

Criminal profiling has evolved over time and as a consequence what can be described as differing schools of thought or approaches to the task of constructing a criminal profile have also developed (Kocsis, 2007). In this context, the practice of criminal profiling can be viewed as somewhat analogous to the field of personality theory. In attempting to understand human behavior there is common agreement amongst scholars in the fundamental construct of the mind (Gregory, 2004). However, while there is a general consensus in this basic construct, various rivaling theoretical perspectives (e.g., Psychodynamic, Cognitive Behaviorism, Gestalt) exist which endeavor to explain the operation of the mind (Monte, 1995). Within the topic of criminal profiling there is, akin to the field of personality theory, general agreement with the fundamental notion of evaluating crime behaviors to gain some insight into the probable perpetrator. Also akin to the field of personality theory there are different views concerning the best methods and principles to employ when profiling crimes (Palermo & Kocsis, 2005). Consequently, to explain the process of profiling requires a brief overview of these differing approaches as well as some examination of the clinically orientated origins of criminal profiling and the discrete topic of geographic profiling. It must however be noted that the parameters of the present chapter do not allow for comprehensive coverage of the underlying principles inherent to each of the approaches. As a consequence, the following material is primarily focussed on highlighting some of the key themes and features that typically characterize each approach.

Diagnostic Evaluations: Clinical Perspectives on Profiling Crimes

As previously indicated, the historical origins of criminal profiling largely emanate from the endeavors of various mental health professionals who have been consulted on an intermittent basis to render an evaluation of a crime which may be of some assistance to police investigators. This circumstance in which the task of profiling has occurred has been referred to as *Diagnostic Evaluations* (in acronym, "DE") (Kocsis, 2006). It needs to be clarified that DE are largely an artifact of the practical application of psychiatry/psychology rather than being a coherent research-based approach to profiling *per se*. The term DE is best viewed as a descriptor for the aforementioned circumstance in which a criminal profile is sought from a mental health professional. Consequently, the theoretical basis for DE is the common method by which profiles are constructed. That is, with DE a mental health professional draws upon their disciplinary knowledge typically from psychiatry or psychology to profile the crime. Thus, a profile is produced via an attempt to relate and/or diagnose possible psychopathologies and motivational factors indicative of the behaviors evident in a crime and from this extrapolate some understanding of the probable offender (e.g., Badcock, 1997; Britton, 1997; Boon, 1997; Girod, 2004; Kent, 1999; Palermo, 2004; Proulx, Beauregard, Cusson, & Nicole, 2007; Revitch, & Schlesinger, 1989). It is from this diagnostic-like process of assessing possible psychopathology that the term *Diagnostic Evaluation* was derived (Palermo & Kocsis, 2005).

The legacy and importance of DE should not be underestimated as a number of significant dimensions to the contemporary practice of criminal profiling originate from DE. Foremost amongst them is that all approaches to profiling share a fundamental disciplinary grounding in psychology/psychiatry in attempting to understand human behaviors, motivations and psychopathological factors that may explain exhibited patterns of behavior. Additionally, DE arguably remain one of the most readily accessible means by which a criminal profile may be obtained. That is, investigators to this day may simply elect to consult a mental health professional regarding a particular crime to ascertain whether they can offer some useful insight into the crime and its perpetrator(s) (Kocsis, 2006). Indeed, what have been hailed as some of the most remarkably perspicuous criminal profiles have originated from individuals who could arguably be viewed as proponents of the diagnostic evaluation approach (Palermo & Kocsis, 2005).

Criminal Investigative Analysis

What arguably constitutes the first systematic research-based approach to criminal profiling is the collective work of personnel affiliated with the Behavioral Sciences Unit (in acronym, "BSU") of the Federal Bureau of Investigation's (in acronym, "FBI") training academy (Ressler, Douglas, Groth, & Burgess, 1980; van Zandt, 1994). The BSU approach to criminal profiling has been termed Criminal Investigative Analysis (in acronym, "CIA") (Douglas & Oleshaker, 1995; Hazelwood, Ressler, Depue, & Douglas, 1995). In response to a perceived prevalence of aberrant violent crime and a desire to assist in the investigation of such crimes, agents attached to the BSU began a research program in the late 1970s studying the behavioral patterns manifest in these offences (Ressler, Burgess, & Douglas, 1988). The ultimate purpose of this research being to garner a better understanding of the *modus operandi* and psychological mechanisms driving the perpetrator of these crimes. Integral to these research endeavors however, was an operational agenda for law enforcement to identify features specifically focused on the needs of investigative personnel (Ressler & Shachtman, 1992). Previous research in the area was viewed as predominantly clinical in perspective and thus orientated towards topics which were not considered particularly relevant to the objectives of investigators (e.g., rehabilitation) and thus superfluous in attempting to apprehend the perpetrators of such offences (Ressler, 1985).

The method for constructing a criminal profile using the CIA method is somewhat akin to DE in that it involves a process which can be regarded as similar to the formulation of clinical judgement by a mental health practitioner (Dietz, 1985; Douglas et al., 1986). What differentiates CIA however, is that instead of drawing upon diagnostic criteria for mental disorders, CIA draws upon its own corpus of research concerning crime patterns, related offender characteristics, motivations and avenues for the investigation of offences (e.g., Douglas et al., 2006). The modes of crime which have been studied by the BSU are quite diverse but have predominantly focused upon crimes of interpersonal violence such as sexual assault (Hazelwood, 1995; Hazelwood & Burgess, 1987), arson (Icove & Estepp, 1987) and homicide (Ressler et al., 1988).

Possibly the most renowned piece of research developed in the CIA sphere is the *organized/disorganized* offender typology which was originally derived from the study of sexual murderers and their crime scenes (Ressler, Burgess, Douglas, Hartman, & D'Agostino, 1986). The premise underpinning this dichotomy is that crime scenes are distinguishable and thus interpretable by their degree of behavioral sophistication. Thus, an *organized* crime scene is indicative of a high degree of behavioral sophistication on the part of the offender such as planning and precautionary measures undertaken in respect of the offense. A constellation of distinguishable offender characteristics has been identified as being commonly associated with these organized crime scene behaviors. A few examples of such offender characteristics include a higher standard of education, having a skilled job and possessing a vehicle. In contrast to the patterns indicative of the *organized* category are the features of the *disorganized* category. Thus, a disorganized crime scene is characterized by behaviors that are viewed as being indicative of a low or minimal degree of behavioral sophistication on the part of the offender(s). In this respect, disorganized crimes are described as featuring comparative disarray and are viewed as being perpetrated in a spontaneous/opportunistic manner suggestive of no real planning. Akin to the organized category a constellation of commonly occurring characteristics inherent to offenders who perpetrate crimes in a disorganized fashion have also been identified. Some of these attributes typically include a low standard of education, limited or no employment, and being slovenly in appearance (Ressler et al., 1988).

The construction of a criminal profile involves an assessment of the behaviors exhibited in the crime as compared with the *organized/disorganized* dichotomy. Thus, some interpretation is made as to whether the exhibited behaviors correspond with the behavioral attributes of either the *organized* or *disorganized* category. Once such a determination is made the process of predicting offender characteristics is determined from the corresponding offender characteristics previously developed as indicative of either an organized or disorganized offender (Ressler et al., 1986).

Investigative Psychology

Another research-based approach to profiling is that known as *Investigative Psychology* (in acronym, "IP") which appears to advocate the creation of a disciplinary specialization focused upon psychological principles specifically applicable to the investigation of crime (Canter, 1995, 2000). In this context what may traditionally be viewed as criminal profiling constitutes only one of a range of topics encapsulated by IP. Justification for developing the nomenclature IP is debatable given the prior existence of other analogous specializations. That is, a number of disciplinary fields already exist such as forensic, police and criminal psychology which arguably already embody the topics that appear to form the basis of IP (Arrigo & Shipley, 2005; Aumiller et al., 2008; Bull et al., 2007; Raskin, 1989).

Notwithstanding this, a coherent body of empirical research has developed in IP whereby crime behaviors have been studied for the purpose of gaining some understanding about the attributes of a probable offender which may be used in an investigative capacity. One of the characteristic features of IP research is that it advocates the analysis of crime behaviors independent of the inference of motivations attached to those behaviors. The inference of motivations with behaviors is argued as being a methodological limitation to previous research in the area (Canter & Heritage, 1989). Another common feature of IP research is the use of ideographic methods of analysis and the use of quite specialized statistics such as multidimensional scaling (in acronym, "MDS") (Coxon, 1982).

The findings of IP studies often focus on the identification of discernable themes that characterize particular behavioral styles exhibited in various forms of crime. As a simple example, an analysis of exhibited behaviors in domestic homicides may reveal cogent patterns indicative of either an *instrumental* or *expressive* purpose in the typically enacted behaviors of these crimes (Salfati, 2000). From the identification of these patterns general theorems can then be advanced which characterize and explain the criminal behavior observed. The development of these theorems can in turn inform any predictions concerning the probable offender of similar future crimes. Akin to other approaches to criminal profiling IP's research efforts have examined a range of crime modalities including arson (e.g., Canter & Fritzon, 1998), serial murder (e.g., Godwin, 2000), and sexual assault (e.g., Canter & Heritage, 1989).

Crime Action Profiling

Possibly the most recent research-based approach to criminal profiling is that of *Crime Action Profiling* (in acronym, "CAP"). In many respects CAP is a hybrid of its predecessors and thus akin to CIA, endeavors to focus on issues more pertinent to the operational goals of investigators. Additionally, CAP makes use of similar methods of statistical analysis (i.e., MDS) akin to IP and the initial premise of analyzing crime behaviors independent of inferring motives in an offender.

Where CAP markedly differs from other approaches however, is in the development of models in which crime behaviors are correlated with various offender characteristics and thus operate as mechanisms by which the perpetrators of future crimes may be profiled. The use of CAP models are conceptually similar to the process of reading time from a non-digital wristwatch. The models feature diagrams displaying various crime behaviors as denoted by a range of icons. The crime behaviors exhibited in the offense under consideration are then examined for their correspondence with those in the relevant CAP model. Thereafter, various *arrows* that have been superimposed onto a CAP model serve as guides, dependent upon their proximity to the identified behaviors in the model to attributes about the offender that may be predicted. Thus, through a somewhat mechanized process comparisons can be drawn with displayed behaviors in a crime, and from the interpretation of the CAP model, predictions made about various attributes that may be related to the probable offender.

As a final point the CAP approach adopts a refined perspective in the application of profiling to crimes of an aberrant violent nature. In this respect only three CAP models have thus far been developed. One that is designed for the profiling of sexual murders, another focused upon the profiling of serial rape offences, and a third for the profiling of serial arson offenses. This is not to suggest that the concepts inherent to CAP may not be adaptable to more conventional modes of crime but rather that the key focus is on aberrant violent crimes which profiling is arguably better suited to in terms of assisting criminal investigators beyond standard investigative procedures. The various principles and procedures inherent to the CAP approach to profiling crimes are best summarized in Kocsis (2006).

Geographic Profiling

While not a comprehensive approach to the profiling of crimes, geographic profiling is a discrete topic within the field which is focused upon the geographic relevance of offense locations. The geographic examination of crime is not a recent concept to the discipline of criminology (e.g., Brantingham & Brantingham, 1981; Rengert, & Wasilchick, 1985; Reppetto, 1974). Similarly, the examination of offense localities to garner some insight about a perpetrator is not a recent innovation (Kind, 1987). However, with the surge of interest in the development of criminal profiling, as well as computerized mapping programs known as Geographic Information Systems (in acronym, "GIS"), a reinvigoration of interest in the topic has developed under the label of '*geographic profiling*' (Palermo & Kocsis, 2005). The objective of geographic profiling is the analysis of related crime locations for the purpose of identifying a specific region that may possess some relationship or *nexus* with the perpetrator(s) of the offenses (Rossmo, 1997). The nature of the nexus between the identified geographic region and the offender can manifest itself in a host of differing circumstances including the general location of the offender's residence, workplace or even the residence of a significant other party (e.g., parents, girlfriend). The application of this information to assist in an investigation is not unlike how other information in criminal profiles is used. As a hypothetical example, a geographic profile may identify a region of approximately two square miles containing three distinct suburbs. Investigators can then use this information as a means by which suspects may be prioritized for further investigation. That is, suspects who hold some connection with the identified region, such as their home being situated within any one of the three identified suburbs, can be prioritized for further inquiry over other suspects who do not share such a nexus with the identified region.

Analogous to the general topic of criminal profiling there are a number of rivaling approaches (e.g., Canter, 2004a; Levine, 2000; Rossmo, 2000; Young, 2003) with respect to the calculations and measurements employed in developing geographic profiles each of which possess their own rivaling merits and limitations (Stangeland, 2005; van der Kemp & van Koppen, 2007). In spite of their differences there are however, some fundamental commonalties amongst the approaches. At a basic level all approaches involve the plotting of known offense locations on some form of map. Similarly, all approaches operate on the premise that offense locations possess some form of causality with the offender who is typically not itinerant and thus enjoys some stability in their own lifestyle, location and movement patterns. From these core principles, differing methods have been developed for how offense locations are mapped and used as points of measurement from which the prediction area indicative of a geographic profile is then developed.

The differences amongst these theorems for geographic profiling appear to stem, to some extent, from the disciplinary origins of the differing proponents as well as their reliance on geographic information systems for undertaking certain computations. Thus, the work by Rossmo (2000) predominantly derives from disciplinary principles indicative of geography, whereas the work of Canter (2004a) is more sourced in the disciplinary specialization referred to as *environmental psychology* (Lundrigan & Canter, 2001). The methods advocated by Rossmo (2000) initially emphasized the use of GIS and thus a semi-automated approach for developing geographic profiles. In contrast, Canter's (2004a) work originally used traditional mapping techniques however in subsequent years this has developed to include GIS programs for generating geographic profiles.

The Validity and Utility of Criminal Profiling

Given the renown criminal profiling enjoys in popular media portrayals (Boon, 1995; Herndon, 2007) and true crime literature (Britton, 1997; Canter, 1994; Douglas & Oleshaker, 1995; Hazelwood & Michaud, 2001; McCrary & Ramsland, 2003; Ressler & Shachtman, 1992; Vorpagel & Harrington, 1998) it is difficult to reconcile the paucity of scientifically grounded evidence supporting the technique. This is not to assert that research into the development of criminal profiling has progressed independently of considerations concerning the fundamental validity of the technique. However, only in approximately the past two decades have some concerted attempts been made to test the accuracy (vis-à-vis validity) of profiles via scientifically controlled experiments.

What arguably represents the largest available source of evidence relied upon in support of the merits of criminal profiling are anecdotal accounts (such as those contained in true crime literature) where profiling is used and almost invariably judged to be useful and therefore accurate. Unfortunately, such accounts of profiling successes appear to have given rise to a phenomena whereby the perceived benefits derived from the use of criminal profiles and thereby their continued use have come to be interpreted as a proxy indicator of their accuracy (Poythress et al., 1993). This circumstance has been described as the *operational utilitarian argument* (Kocsis, 2006). The development of this argument is ironically simply a manifestation of the old English proverb "*the proof is in the pudding*." Simply put, if criminal profiles were not deemed accurate and beneficial to police investigators, law enforcement would not continue to use them. As police investigators continue to request profiles, this circumstance is often cited as an indicator that profiles must therefore be accurate (Jeffers, 1992; Poythress et al., 1993).

While the logic of the operational utilitarian argument is intuitively appealing, its rationale is reliant upon the assumption that perceptions concerning profiles are, in fact, reliable. Unfortunately, a number of recent studies have suggested otherwise and have revealed some troubling aspects regarding the perceived merits of criminal profiles. Firstly, a study by Alison, Smith, and Morgan (2003) demonstrated the ambiguity of information contained in profiles. In this particular study participants were asked to gauge the relative merits of two profiles, one of which was genuine, the other which was deliberately contrived to be similar but inaccurate. Alarmingly, in examining the two profiles participants judged both to be equally meritorious indicating that even an incorrect profile could be perceived to possess some merit. Possibly the most confronting research to challenge the operational utilitarian argument however arose from a series of studies which examined the relationship between the belief (i.e., confidence) individuals possess, or were induced to possess in criminal profiling, and their evaluations concerning the merit (i.e., accuracy) of a profile (Kocsis, 2006). These studies found an incremental relationship between belief in profiling and the perceived merits of a criminal profile. Thus, the more an individual believed or was induced to believe in the value of criminal profiling, the more meritorious a criminal profile was perceived to be.

Collectively, these studies provide some evidence that collectively serve to suggest that the perceptions of criminal profiles (such as those from anecdotal accounts) should not be relied upon as a measure of their merit.

Quasi-Experimental Studies on Profiler Accuracy

At a cursory level empirically testing the accuracy of criminal profiles would seem to be a relatively straightforward task of comparing the predictions contained in a criminal profile with the characteristics of the apprehended offender. Unfortunately, developing a suitably robust research methodology wherein such measurements can be objectively undertaken is surprisingly problematic. The difficulties are based partly in the diversity of the information potentially to be found in criminal profiles, and partly in the circumstances (i.e., different modes and complexity of differing crimes) in which a criminal profile is sought. As a consequence, it is questionable how methodologically robust and representative any study may be that endeavors to combine and then measure data imbued with such potential vagaries.

A small number of quasi-experiments have been conducted which simulate the profiling of a crime and thus endeavor to impartially test the abilities of profilers, vis-à-vis, the accuracy of the profiles constructed by them. Through this experimental procedure many of the aforementioned methodological problems surrounding the evaluation of profiles are minimized and/or avoided as participants profile the same crime within roughly the same parameters. A comprehensive discussion of these studies appear in a later chapter of this book series entitled "*Criminal Profiling: Empirical Evidence on Skills and Accuracy.*" However, the overall findings of this research, in summation, provide some tentative support for the capabilities of profilers to accurately predict the characteristics of the unknown offender at a generally superior standard to other compared groups. However, while this research represents promising beginnings in empirically testing the accuracy (i.e., validity) of profiling they must nonetheless be interpreted conservatively, as further replication and exploration will be needed in the future (e.g., Gogan, 2007; Hodges & Jacquin, 2008). In this context, the research thus far should be viewed as merely a tentative start in lending support to the potential of criminal profiling. Unfortunately however, these modest findings appear to have been long surpassed by the apparent reputation and claims of accuracy that profiling already appears to enjoy (Herndon, 2007).

The Utility of Criminal Profiles

In the wake of the paucity of scientific evidence attesting to the validity of criminal profiles one issue that occasionally seems to be overlooked is the utility of profiling in assisting with the resolution of crime (Oleson, 1996). Assuming that a criminal profile can, hypothetically, accurately predict various attributes about an offender does not necessarily imply that knowledge of these attributes will tangibly assist in the investigation and apprehension of the offender and thus effect some meaningful reduction in crime (Farrington, 2007). Ironically, the evidence considering the utility of criminal profiling is, arguably, equally as scant as that examining the accuracy of profiles. A large part of this problem is that identifying and thus quantifying utility is a conceptually difficult task in terms of ascertaining precisely how a profile may have been of some material assistance (Kocsis & Palermo, 2007). While anecdotal examples are readily available where profiles have been used during the course of an investigation and in retrospect the predictions of these profiles viewed as corresponding with the apprehended offender, how exactly these profiles assisted in apprehending the offender is not always clear (Pinizzotto, 1984; Kocsis, 2007). This has led some in the field of profiling to comment that to the best of their knowledge a profile has yet to be directly instrumental in solving a crime (Ressler & Shachtman, 1992).

Nonetheless, an interesting source of information concerning the utility of profiles can be found in the various surveys which have sought to gauge the satisfaction police personnel have derived from the use of criminal profiles during the course of an investigation (e.g., Copson, 1995; Jackson, van Koppen & Herbrink, 1993; Pinizzotto, 1984; Trager & Brewster, 2001). It is important however, to note that these surveys do not measure utility per se, but rather, the perceived usefulness of a profile by police personnel who have used them. The common theme to emerge from these studies is that police personnel generally consider criminal profiles beneficial and of some assistance, but ironically, indications of precisely how the profiles were of assistance is less clear.

Criminal Profiles in the Court Room

While the use of profiling in criminal investigations is well chronicled (e.g., Britton, 1997; Canter, 1994; Douglas & Oleshaker, 1995; Hazelwood, & Michaud, 2001; Ressler & Shachtman, 1992) there have been some comparatively recent attempts to admit into evidence the testimony of profilers in evaluating criminal behaviors. The general view from legal scholars on this issue appear to be one of trepidation (Meyer, 2007; Ormerod, 1999; Risinger & Loop, 2002) which is evidently shared by members of the judiciary around the world when considering the admissibility of such evidence. Judicial comment for example, from the United Kingdom on profiling has opined: "...psychological [i.e., criminal] profiling as an aid to police investigations is one thing, but its use as a means of proof in court is another" (R. v. Guilfoyle, 2001, p. 68). Similar reservations concerning profiling and in particular some of its proponents were expressed in Australia where it was observed that:

> ...courts must exercise constant vigilance to ensure that they are not unwittingly misled. Amongst the many factors which may lead an expert witness into error is a malady which, if encountered in a new car salesperson, might be described as gross product enthusiasm. Some witnesses seem to become so fervid about the potential of their chosen discipline that they lose sight of its limitations and are borne by their enthusiasm into

> making claims that could not be supported by more sober and objective assessment . . . (R. v. Hillier, 2003, p. 10)

Within the United States efforts to have the testimony of profilers admitted into evidence has experienced a somewhat checkered reception as testimony has either been excluded from the outset or, initially admitted, and then subsequently disallowed upon appeal (*Commonwealth v. DeStafano*, 1999; *State v. Fortin* 1999, 2004). The present chapter does not allow for a detailed exposition of the legal reasoning underpinning this circumstance. Suffice to say, without delving too deeply into legal doctrine such as general acceptance (*Frye v. United States*, 1923) or other criteria in the form of the Federal Rules of Evidence (2004), the admission of criminal profiling within the U.S. and abroad appears hampered by its inherently predictive nature. Within most western common law legal systems there is an imperative to assess whether the *probative* value of any posited evidence will outweigh any *prejudicial* impact of that testimony (Davis & Follette, 2002; Kirkpatrick, 1998). Simply put, western common law legal systems chiefly function on the basis of the assessment of directly pertinent factual information evident in the specific case before the court. The obstacle confronting criminal profiling and the testimony that profilers may offer is that they cannot, for example, sufficiently attest to the fact that their predictions relate to the particular person charged and tried for a crime. The testimony derived from profiling can only attest that the characteristics of the *probable* offender match, or do not match, those of the accused. They cannot however, unequivocally claim that due to any correspondence, or lack thereof, the accused is likely guilty or innocent. For this reason the evidence of profilers has in the main thus far been excluded and described as ". . . evidence intended to address guilt by likening a defendant to a profile or stereotype of those likely to commit the crime in question . . ." and as a consequence ". . . has great potential for introducing bias and error" (Davis & Follette, 2002, p. 152).

Perhaps in response to the apparent reluctance of courts in admitting profiling testimony ways of introducing similar alternative testimony has increasingly been explored. These alternative avenues appear to involve testimony that seeks to avoid making inferences about the probable offender but nonetheless provide some form of analysis of the behaviors evident in the specific crime(s). Interestingly, this approach appears to have enjoyed, thus far, some limited success in Canadian jurisdictions in terms of the admission of such testimony (e.g., R. v. Ranger, 2003; R. v. Clark, 2004). However, these alternatives have not gone unnoticed and have also attracted criticism as merely being ". . . a different suit on the same animal" and as "... a distinction without a difference" (Grezlak, 1999, p. 2). As a consequence further examination and testing of the legal merits of this type of testimony in future legal proceedings will invariably be required.

Conclusions

The technique of criminal profiling is indicative of a long-held fascination the human race has had with attempting to understand criminal behaviors and the perpetrators of crime. Although fictional analogies describing profiling can be found in classical literature, historical examples involving the use of some external expert, typically a mental health professional, to examine crimes for the purpose of offering investigators some insight into the probable offender date back to the previous century.

In recent decades, there has been a significant increase of interest in the development of criminal profiling techniques. This heightened interest has, analogous to the field of personality theory, spawned a number of rivaling schools of thought concerning how the prediction (i.e., profiling) of offender characteristics from exhibited crime behaviors may be undertaken. At this time, there does not appear to be any clear indication of the best way to profile crimes, as each approach possesses its inherent strengths and weaknesses. Although some tentative empirical research has emerged to support the capabilities of profilers, this modicum of evidence seems to be eclipsed by the favorable reputation the technique universally appears to enjoy.

In the wake of this apparent popularity, it is perhaps unsurprising that in recent years, an increasing number of attempts to admit, in some capacity, profiles into evidence for legal proceedings have occurred. In the judicial arena at least, however, the scientific merits of criminal profiling appear to have come under far more critical scrutiny than ever before, and in this context has generally been considered unsuitable as a reliable form of evidence in the context of criminal proceedings.

References

Alison, L. (2005). From trait-based profiling to psychological contributions to apprehension methods. In L. Alison (Ed.), *The forensic psychologist's casebook: Psychological profiling and criminal investigation* (pp. 3–22). Devon, UK: Willan Publishing.

Alison, L., Smith, M., & Morgan, K. (2003). Interpreting the accuracy of offender profiles. *Psychology, Crime and Law, 9*, 185–195.

Arrigo, B. A., & Shipley, S. L. (2005). *Introduction to forensic psychology* (2nd ed.). New York: Elsevier Academic Press.

Aumiller, G. S., Corey, D., Brewster, J., Allen, S., Gupton, H., Cuttler, M., & Honig, A. (2008). Defining the field of police psychology: Core domain and proficiencies. *Journal of Police and Criminal Psychology, 22*(2), 65–76.

Badcock, R. (1997). Developmental and clinical issues in relation to offending in the individual. In J. L. Jackson & D. A. Bekerian (Eds.), *Offender profiling: Theory, research and practice* (pp. 9–42). New York: John Wiley & Sons.

Bekerian, D. A., & Jackson, J. L. (1997). Critical issues in offender profiling. In J. L. Jackson, & D. A. Bekerian (Eds.), *Offender profiling: Theory, research and practice* (pp. 209–220). New York: John Wiley & Sons.

Boon, J. C. W. (1995). Offender profiling: Distinguishing the media prurience from the real-life science. *Inter Alia, 1*, 31–35.

Boon, J. C. W. (1997). The contribution of personality theories to psychological profiling. In J. L. Jackson, & D. A. Bekerian (Eds.), *Offender profiling: Theory, research and practice* (pp. 43–60). New York: John Wiley & Sons.

Brantingham, P. L., & Brantingham, P. J. (1981). *Environmental criminology*. Beverly Hills, CA: Sage.

Britton, P. (1997). *The jigsaw man*. London: Bantam Press.

Brussel, J. (1968). *Casebook of a criminal psychiatrist*. New York: Howard Geis.

Bull, R., Cookie, C., Hatcher. R., Woodhams, J., Bilby, C., & Grant, T. (2007). *Criminal psychology: A beginner's guide*. London: Oneworld Publications.

Bumgarner, J. (2007). Criminal profiling and public policy. In R. N. Kocsis (Ed.), *Criminal profiling: International theory, research and practice* (pp. 273–288). Totowa, NJ: Humana Press.

Campbell, J. H., & DeNevi, D. (2004). *Profilers: Leading investigators take you inside the criminal*. New York: Prometheus Books.

Canter, D. (1989). Offender profiles. *The Psychologist, 2*, 12–16.

Canter, D. (1994). *Criminal shadows*. London: HarperCollins.

Canter, D. (1995). Psychology of offender profiling. In R. Bull & D. Carson (Eds.), *Handbook of psychology in legal contexts* (pp. 343–355). Chichester, UK: John Wiley & Sons.

Canter, D. (2000). Offender profiling and criminal differentiation. *Legal and Criminological Psychology, 5*, 23–46.

Canter, D. (2004a). *Mapping murder*. London: HarperCollins.

Canter, D. (2004b). Offender profiling and investigative psychology. *Journal of Investigative Psychology and Offender Profiling, 1*, 1–15.

Canter, D., & Fritzon, K. (1998). Differentiating arsonists: A model of firesetting actions and characteristics. *Legal and Criminological Psychology, 3*, 73–96.

Canter, D., & Heritage, R. (1989). A multivariate model of sexual offence behavior: Developments in "offender profiling"–I. *Journal of Forensic Psychiatry, 1*(2), 185–212.

Commonwealth of Pennsylvania v. DiStefano, No. 96-CR-737 (1999).

Copson, G. (1995). *Coals to Newcastle? Part 1: A study of offender profiling (paper 7)*. London: Police Research Group Special Interest Series, Home Office.

Coxon, A. P. M. (1982). *The user's guide to multidimensional scaling*. London: Heinmann Educational Books.

Davis, D., & Follette, W. C. (2002). Rethinking the probative value of evidence: Base rates, intuitive profiling, and the "*post*-diction" of behavior. *Law and Human Behavior, 26*, 133–158.

Dietz, P. E. (1985). Sex offender profiling by the FBI: A preliminary conceptual model. In M. H. Ben-Aron, S. J. Hucher, & C. D. Webster (Eds.), *Clinical criminology* (pp. 207–219). Toronto, Ontario, Canada: M & M Graphics.

Douglas, J. E., & Burgess, A. W. (1986). Criminal profiling: A viable investigative tool against violent crime. *FBI Law Enforcement Bulletin, 55*(12), 9–13.

Douglas, J. E., Burgess, A. W., Burgess, A. G., & Ressler, R. K. (Eds.). (2006). *Crime classification manual* (2nd ed.). San Francisco, CA: Jossey-Bass.

Douglas, J. E., & Oleshaker, M. (1995). *Mindhunter*. New York: Scribner.

Douglas, J. E., Ressler, R. K., Burgess, A. W., & Hartman, C. R. (1986). Criminal profiles from crime scene analysis. *Behavioral Sciences and the Law, 4*, 401–421.

Dowden, C., Bennell, C., & Bloomfield, S. (2007). Advances in offender profiling: A systematic review of the profiling literature published over the past three decades. *Journal of Police and Criminal Psychology, 22*(1), 44–56.

Doyle, A. C. (1891). *The original illustrated Sherlock Holmes*. Secaucus, NJ: Castle.

Farrington, D. P. (2007). Book review. *International Journal of Offender Therapy and Comparative Criminology, 4*(51), 486–487.

Federal Rules of Evidence. (2004). Washington, DC: U.S. Government Printing Office.

Fisher, A. J. (1993). *Techniques of crime scene investigation* (5th ed.). New York: Elsevier.

Frank, G. (1966). *The Boston strangler*. New York: New American Library.

Frye v. United States, F.1013, D.C. (1923).

Geberth, V. J. (1983). *Practical homicide investigation: Tactics, procedures and forensic techniques*. Boca Raton, FL: CRC Press.

Girod, R. (2004). *Profiling the criminal mind: Behavioral science and criminal investigative analysis*. New York: iUniverse Inc.

Gogan, D. (2007). Investigative experience and profile accuracy: A replication study. In R. N. Kocsis (Ed.), *Criminal profiling: International theory, practice and research* (pp. 383–392). Totowa, NJ: Humana Press.

Gregory, R. L. (Ed.). (2004). *The Oxford companion to the mind*. New York: Oxford University Press.

Grezlak, H. (1999, April 12). Profiling testimony inadmissible in murder trial: Too speculative, prejudicial judge says. *Pennsylvania Law Weekly*, 1–2.

Harcourt, B. (2007). *Against prediction: Profiling, policing and punishing in an actuarial age*. Chicago: University of Chicago Press.

Hazelwood, R., & Michaud, S. G. (2001). *Dark dreams*. New York: St. Martin's Press.

Hazelwood, R. R. (1995). Analyzing the rape and profiling the offender. In R. R. Hazelwood & A. W. Burgess (Eds.), *Practical aspects of rape investigation: A multidisciplinary approach* (2nd ed., pp. 115–126). Boca Raton, FL: CRC Press.

Hazelwood, R. R., & Burgess, A. W. (1987). An introduction to the serial rapist research by the FBI. *FBI Law Enforcement Bulletin, 56*(9), 16–24.

Hazelwood, R. R., Ressler, R. K., Depue, R. L., & Douglas, J. C. (1995). Criminal investigative analysis: An overview. In R. R. Hazelwood & A. W. Burgess (Eds.), *Practical aspects of rape investigation: A multidisciplinary approach* (2nd ed., pp. 115–126). Boca Raton, FL: CRC Press.

Herndon, J. S. (2007). The image of profiling: Media treatment and general impressions. In R. N. Kocsis (Ed.), *Criminal profiling: International theory, practice and research* (pp. 290–303). Totowa, NJ: Humana Press.

Hickey, E. (2001). *Serial murderers and their victims* (3rd ed.). Belmont, CA: Wadsworth.

Hicks, S. J., & Sale, B. D. (2006). *Criminal profiling: Developing an effective science and practice*. Washington, DC: American Psychological Association.

Hodges, E. P., & Jacquin, K. M. (2008). Psychological skills and criminal profile accuracy. In R. N. Kocsis (Ed.), *Serial murder and the psychology of violent crimes* (pp. 259–276), Totowa, NJ: Humana Press.

Holmes, R. M., & Holmes, S. T. (2002). *Profiling violent crimes: An investigative tool* (3rd ed.). Thousand Oaks, CA: Sage.

Icove, D. J., & Estepp, M. H. (1987). Motive-based offender profiles of arson and fire-related crimes. *FBI Law Enforcement Bulletin, 56*(4), 17–23.

Jackson, J. L., & Bekerian, D. A. (1997). *Offender profiling: Theory, research and practice*. New York: John Wiley & Sons.

Jackson, J. L., van Koppen, P. J., & Herbrink, C. M. (1993). *Does the service meet the needs? An evaluation of consumer satisfaction with the specific profile analysis and investigative advice as offered by the scientific research advisory unit of the National Criminal Intelligence Division (CRI)*. The Netherlands, NISCALE Report NSCR 93-05.

Jeffers, H. P. (1992). *Profiles in evil*. London: Warner Brothers.

Kent, J. (1999, September 12). Monsters in the making. *The Sunday Mail Sunday Magazine*, 4–5.

Kind, S. S. (1987). Navigational ideas and the Yorkshire Ripper investigation. *Journal of Navigation, 40*, 385–393.

Kirkpatrick, L. C. (1998). Profile and syndrome evidence: Its use and admissibility in criminal prosecutions. *Security Journal, 11*, 255–257.

Kocsis, R. N. (2006). *Criminal profiling: Principles and practice*. Totowa, NJ: Humana Press.

Kocsis, R. N. (2007). Schools of thought related to criminal profiling. In R. N. Kocsis (Ed.), *Criminal profiling: International theory, practice and research* (pp. 393–404). Totowa, NJ: Humana Press.

Kocsis, R. N., & Palermo, G. B. (2007). Contemporary problems with criminal profiling. In R. N. Kocsis (Ed.), *Criminal profiling: International theory, practice and research* (pp. 335–358). Totowa, NJ: Humana Press.

Langer, W. (1972). *The mind of Adolf Hitler*. New York: New American Library.

Lazer, D. (Ed.). (2004). *DNA and the criminal justice system: The technology of justice*. Boston, MA: MIT Press.

Levine, N. (2000). *Crimestat: A spatial statistics program for the analysis of crime incident locations (version 1.1)*. Washington, DC: National Institute of Justice.

Lundrigan, S., & Canter, D. (2001). A multivariate analysis of serial murderers' disposal site location choice. *Journal of Environmental Psychology, 21*, 423–432.

McCrary, G. O., & Ramsland, K. (2003). *The unknown darkness: Profiling the predators among us*. New York: HarperCollins.

Meyer, C. B. (2007). Criminal profiling as expert evidence. In R. N. Kocsis (Ed.), *Criminal profiling: International theory, research and practice* (pp. 207–248). Totowa, NJ: Humana Press.

Monte, C. (1995). *Beneath the mask: An introduction to personality* (5th ed.). New York: Harcourt Brace.

Nowikowski, F. (1995). Psychological offender profiling: An overview. *The Criminologist, 19*, 255–273.

Oleson, J. C. (1996). Psychological profiling: Does it actually work? *Forensic Update, 46*, 11–14.

Ormerod, D. (1999). Criminal profiling: Trial by judge and jury, not criminal psychologist. In D. V. Canter & L. J. Alison (Eds.), *Profiling in policy and practice* (pp. 207–261). Aldershot, UK: Ashgate.

Palermo, G. B. (2004). *The faces of violence* (2nd ed.). Springfield, IL: C. C. Thomas.

Palermo, G. B., & Kocsis, R. N. (2005). *Offender profiling: An introduction to the sociopsychological analysis of violent crime*. Springfield, IL: C. C. Thomas.

Pinizzotto, A. J. (1984). Forensic psychology: Criminal personality profiling. *Journal of Police Science and Administration, 12*, 32–40.

Poythress, N., Otto, R. K., Darkes, J., & Starr, L. (1993). APA's expert panel into the congressional review of the USS *Iowa* incident. *American Psychologist, 48*, 8–15.

Proulx, J., Beauregard, E., Cusson, M., & Nicole, A. (Ed.). (2007). *Sexual murderers: A comparative analysis and new perspectives*. New York: Wiley.

Raskin, D. C. (Ed.). (1989). *Psychological methods in criminal investigation and evidence*. New York: Springer-Verlang.

Rengert, G. F., & Wasilchick, J. (1985). *Suburban burglary*. Springfield, IL: Charles C. Thomas.

Reppetto, T. A. (1974). *Residential crime*. Cambridge, MA: Ballinger.

Ressler, R. K. (1985). Violent crimes. *FBI Law Enforcement Bulletin*. *54*(8), 1–31.

Ressler, R. K., Burgess, A., & Douglas, J. E. (1988). *Sexual homicide: Patterns and motives*. New York: Lexington Books.

Ressler, R. K., Burgess, A. W., Douglas, J. E., Hartman, C. R., & D'Agostino, R. B. (1986). Sexual killers and their victims: Identifying patterns through crime scene analysis. *Journal of Interpersonal Violence, 1*, 288–308.

Ressler, R. K., Douglas, J. K., Groth, N., & Burgess, A. W. (1980). Offender profiles: A multidisciplinary approach. *FBI Law Enforcement Bulletin, 49*(9), 16–20.

Ressler, R. K., & Shachtman, T. (1992). *Whoever fights monsters*. London: Simon & Schuster.

Revitch, E., & Schlesinger, L. B. (1989). *Sex murder and sex aggression: Phenomenology, psychopathology, psychodynamics and prognosis*. Springfield, IL: Charles C. Thomas.

Risinger, D. M., & Loop, J. L. (2002). Three card monte, monty hall, *modus operandi* and "offender profiling": Some lessons of modern cognitive science for the law of evidence. *Cardoza Law Review, 24*, 193–285.

Rossi, D. (1982). Crime scene behavioral analysis: Another tool for the law enforcement investigator. *Police Chief, 18*, 152–155.

Rossmo, K. (1997). Geographic profiling. In J. L. Jackson & D. A. Bekerian (Eds.), *Offender profiling: Theory, research and practice* (pp. 159–176). New York: John Wiley & Sons.

Rossmo, K. (2000). *Geographic profiling*. Boca Raton: FL: CRC Press.

R. v. Clark, 182 CCC (3d) 1 (Canada, 2004).

R. v. Guilfoyle, 2 Cr. App. Rep. 57. (United Kingdom, 2001).

R. v. Hillier, ACTSC 50, 25 June 2003 (Australia, 2003).

R. v. Ranger, 178 CCC (3d) 375 (Canada, 2003).

Salfati, C. G. (2000). The nature of expressiveness and instrumentality in homicide. *Homicide Studies, 4*(3), 265–293.

Shoenfeld, D. (1936). *The crime and the criminal: A psychiatric study of the Lindbergh case*. New York: Convici-Friede.

Stangeland, P. (2005). Catching a serial rapist: Hits and misses in criminal profiling. *Police Practice and Research, 6*(5), 453–469.

State v. Fortin, 162 N.J. 517, 745 A.2d 509 (1999).

State v. Fortin, 178 N.J. 540; 843 A.2d 974 (2004).

Trager, J., & Brewster, J. (2001). The effectiveness of psychological profiles. *Journal of Police and Criminal Psychology, 16*, 20–28.

van der Kemp, J. J., & van Koppen, P. J. (2007). Fine-tuning geographical profiling. In R. N. Kocsis (Ed.), *Criminal profiling: International theory, practice and research* (pp. 347–364). Totowa, NJ: Humana Press.

van Zandt, C. R. (1994). The real silence of the lambs: The National Center for the Analysis of Violent Crime (NCAVC). *Police Chief, 61*(4), 45–46.

Vorpagel, R. E. (1982). Painting psychological profiles: Charlatanism, coincidence, charisma or new science? *Police Chief, 3*, 156–159.

Vorpagel, R. E., & Harrington, J. (1998). *Profiles in murder*. New York: Plenum.

Whittington-Egan, R. (1975). *A casebook on Jack the Ripper*. London: Wiley.

Young, G. (2003, August). *Mapping mayhem: The geography of crime*. Computeredge.

CHAPTER THREE

Mental Illness and Violence: A Misunderstood Relationship

Stacey L. Shipley and Michele L. Borynski

Introduction

The relationship between mental illness and violence is both controversial and complex. Much research has indicated that individuals with mental illness are at no higher risk of committing violent crimes than individuals without mental illness; in fact, they are more likely to be the victims of violence. Furthermore, Applebaum (2006) noted that "the proportion of violence that they account for is relatively small, suggesting that the well-documented public perception of the mentally ill as dangerous persons is substantially exaggerated" (p. 1319). The pursuit of justice when the perpetrator is mentally ill can be daunting, particularly with violent offenses. The nature of the mental illness and the degree to which it contributed to the crime impacts the criminal justice system's response. First, this chapter will focus on the prevalence of mental disorders, violent crime, and the intersection of mental illness and crime. Although the perception of the link between mental illness and violence is often much greater than it actually is, this relationship does exist and will be described in this chapter. Varying definitions of mental disorders complicate data regarding these issues; for the purposes of this chapter, substance abuse and dependence disorders, and personality disorders, will be considered separately from other types of mental disorders, such as anxiety, depression, and psychosis. With respect to crime, this chapter will focus predominantly upon violence toward others, rather than nonviolent crimes (e.g., property crimes, "white-collar" crimes, etc.) or violence toward self (e.g., suicide) or collective violence (e.g., war, genocide). Next, implications of emerging data on this relationship between mental illness and violent crimes will be addressed. In particular, this chapter will focus upon violence with various forms of psychotic disorders, in comparison to the violence perpetrated by those with antisocial personality disorder and/or those classified as psychopaths. Several vignettes will be provided for illustrative purposes. Lastly, avenues for future research directions will be examined.

Vignette: The Case of Michael

Michael,[1] a 24-year-old Caucasian male, was admitted to a maximum-security psychiatric hospital after killing his father by piercing him through the heart with a sword he had purchased off the Internet a month earlier. The local community was stunned. Although they knew he had not been well since dropping out of college a few years earlier, Michael was regarded as an intelligent, extremely devout Roman Catholic. In fact, his study of the *Catechism of the Catholic Church* made several members of the religious community wonder if he was planning on pursuing a religious life. Even the parish priest had made remarks about Michael being remarkably well versed in Catholic history.

On the day of the offense, Michael's parents planned on taking him to the regional psychiatric hospital. They had become increasingly concerned about his growing bizarre behavior, including talking under his breath, seemingly chanting in Latin, and walking rapidly inside and around the house. Further, he had recently installed a padlock on his bedroom door and refused to remove it. When his father told him to pack an overnight bag for the hospital, Michael became incensed. He went to his room, retrieved the sword, and charged down the hallway where his father was standing. As his father screamed in alarm and terror, Michael stabbed his father through the heart. Michael's mother, standing in the living room, heard the screams, turned and saw Michael remove the sword from his father's body. As she ran out the house, Michael then began pursuing her, but she managed to lock herself inside the car and lean on the horn until a neighbor saw the disturbance and contacted police. When officers arrived at the scene, Michael was pacing around the car, intermittently beating on it with the sword. When officers drew their weapons, he laid down the sword and was arrested without further incident. The officers who transported him to the county jail reported that Michael rocked back and forth in the seat, muttering to himself about someone named "Belial."

When later interviewed at the maximum-security state hospital, Michael was "preoccupied with bizarre delusional thought," stating that he was "the victim of a vast conspiracy" to deprive him of his birthright, which he believed was properties owned by the Catholic Church that would pass to him when he completed his quest to destroy the devil and his minions. Michael reported that he had received a "holy mission" from God to destroy "the root of Evil on Earth," and he realized that the person "posing" as his biological father was the devil incarnate when he saw moles on his father's arm forming a pentagram. When asked why he attempted to kill his mother, as well, Michael reported that he did not realize until he saw his mother's shock and fear that she was in league with his false father and that he only later realized that "the woman saying she is my mother" must be an imposter as well. He reported that it would be "impossible" for the people who were identified as his parents to be his biological parents, as someone destined for a holy mission, such as himself, could not be created out of such "evil beginnings." Michael further reported that there was "no way" he could have a mental illness, rather angrily stating, "You have only to look to my name to see the Truth," making a reference to the Archangel Michael who is often depicted as the commander of the warrior angels in Roman Catholicism. He was, in fact, diagnosed with Schizophrenia, Paranoid Type.

Literature Review

Prevalence of Violent Crime

According to Berkowitz, "Aggression is . . . defined as behavior whose goal is the injury of some person or object," and anger is viewed as "the emotional state resulting from a frustration presumably creating a readiness for aggressive acts" (cited in Frodi, Macaulay, & Thome, 1977, p. 635). "Violent crime, however, constitutes only a small part of the phenomenon of aggression, which covers the intentional infliction of harm more generally" (Blackburn, 1998, p. 158). The case of Michael demonstrates the devastation that can be caused by lethal violence resulting from severe mental illness. While some forms of violence are publicly visible—in large part due to technological advances such satellites and recording devices—most forms of violence, especially interpersonal violence, occur outside of public view. For individuals aged 15 to 44 years old, violence is among the leading causes of death. According to the World Health Organization (WHO; Krug, Dahlberg, Mercy, Zwi, & Lozano, 2002), more than a million people die annually worldwide as a result of self-inflicted (i.e., suicide), collective (e.g., wars, genocide), and interpersonal violence (e.g., child abuse, sexual assault, homicide, etc.). In 2000, nearly a third of the deaths worldwide were due to homicide, with suicide accounting for another half and collective violence accounting for one-fifth.

Of the worldwide homicides, males were predominantly both the victims and the perpetrators (77%). Furthermore, age played a significant role: most homicide victims were males aged 15 to 29 years old, with males aged 30 to 44 years old following in second (Krug et al., 2002). In the United States, rates of homicide are related strongly to race and sex (U.S. Census Bureau, 2012). In 2007, black males had a homicide rate (39.7 per 100,000) over seven times that of white males (5.4 per 100,000). With respect to sex, black females, while having a far lower homicide rate of their male counterparts, had a homicide rate (6.2 per 100,000) over three times higher than white females (1.9 per 100,000) (U.S. Census Bureau, 2012).

Motivations for homicide vary depending on region. In developing countries, high youth homicide rates are reflective of rapid social and economic changes. In countries where the base rate of violence is high, factors including gang violence, alcohol consumption, and weapon availability explain most of the contribution to rates of violence (Farrington & Loeber, 2000; Hawkins et Al., 2000; Krug et al., 2002). For example, although the United States has a high youth homicide rate, the impetus for such assaults tends to be retaliations for prior attacks, revenge motivations, or feeling provoked or angered (Copeland-Linder, Johnson, Haynie, Chung, & Cheng, 2011; Farrington, 1998). The accessibility of guns dramatically increases the lethality of violent acts, with 84% of youth homicides involving guns (Centers for Disease Control and Prevention, 2010). In contrast, violent attacks that result in nonfatal injuries are less likely to involve firearm use and more likely to involve the use of fists, feet, and other types of weapons (e.g., knives, clubs) (Krug et al., 2002). (See Loeber & Farrington, 2011, for an extensive review of youth homicide.)

Victims of crime sustain significant losses, whether through the permanent loss of life or through injuries and more indirect costs related to reporting and testifying (e.g., being unable to go to work) (Hornick, Paetsch, & Bertrand, 2002). When the impact of illicit substance use on costs related to crime is examined, there are significant financial expenses. In 1998, costs of crime related to substance use were estimated at $89 billion—an estimated 69% of all estimated monetary costs to society (Cartwright, 2008). In addition to direct and indirect costs to victims, the cost of crime may impact the larger society through policing, incarceration, and loss of human capital. In the United States, it is estimated that at least half—and potentially as much as 80%—of the health care costs resulting from gun and stabbing injuries are covered through the government, whether through direct funding by public financing or through uncompensated care financing (Waters et al., 2004).

Prevalence of Mental Disorders

Overall Prevalence of Mental Disorders

The prevalence (i.e., the number of new and existing cases of a condition observed at a point in time or during a period of time) of any type of mental illness is remarkably common. Annually in the United States, approximately one-fifth to one-quarter of the population will experience at least one episode of a diagnosable mental illness. Furthermore, while most individuals met criteria for only one disorder, approximately 12% of the U.S. population met criteria for two or more disorders annually (Kessler, Chiu, Demler, & Walters, 2005; Substance Abuse and Mental Health Services Administration, 2010). The numbers are even more staggering when examining the rates of mental illness among adolescents aged 13 to 18. In a recent study, nearly half of the national sample reported symptoms to meet diagnostic criteria for a mental disorder during their lifetimes, and approximately 20% reported symptoms of such severity that it impaired their daily lives (Merikangas et al., 2010).

While the prevalence of a given individual having any type of a mental disorder during his or her lifetime is relatively frequent, individuals who experience more afflictive types of mental illness (e.g., schizophrenia) are much less common respective to the general population (Kessler, Chui et al., 2005). In a given year, approximately one-quarter to one-third of individuals with a diagnosable mental illness (roughly 5% to 8% of the overall adult population) are considered to have a "serious mental illness" (Epstein, Barker, Vorburger, & Murtha, 2004; Substance Abuse and Mental Health Services Administration, 2010), as defined by federal regulations, which typically apply to mental disorders that interfere substantially with some aspect of life activities and ability to function (Center for Mental Health Services, Substance Abuse and Mental Health Services Administration, HHS, 1999). According to the National Survey on Drug Use and Health (NSDUH; Substance Abuse and Mental Health Services Administration, 2011), serious mental illness is defined as:

1. A mental, behavioral, or emotional disorder (excluding developmental and substance use disorders)
2. Diagnosable currently or within the past year
3. Of sufficient duration to meet diagnostic criteria specified within the fourth edition of the *Diagnostic and Statistical Manual of Mental Disorders* (*DSM-IV*)
4. Resulting in serious functional impairment, which substantially interferes with or limits one of more major life activities

It has been noted that the "burden of illness is particularly concentrated among those who experience disability due to serious mental illness"

(National Institute of Mental Health, 2008). Typical diagnoses that fall within this category include schizophrenia, bipolar disorder, severe forms of depression, panic disorder, and obsessive-compulsive disorder.

In 2002 there were 33.2 million adults aged 18 or older with serious mental illness or a substance use disorder. Of these adults, just over 40% (13.4 million) had a mental illness only (no substance use disorder), and roughly 47% (15.7 million) had a substance use disorder but no serious mental illness. For those with both a serious mental illness and a substance use disorder, 12.2% (4.0 million) experienced co-occurring disorders. Approximately 17.5 million U.S. adults—roughly 8.3% of the adult population—were considered to have serious mental illness, either with or without a co-occurring substance abuse disorder. Although geographic region did not appear to impact the rates of serious mental illness, there were notable differences with respect to many demographic characteristics, including age, sex, race, education, employment status, income status, level of social support, marital status, substance abuse/dependence, and status of mental health treatment (Epstein et al., 2004).

On average, adults with serious mental illness tend to be younger, more likely to be female, and identified more as biracial or multiracial than adults without serious mental illness. Rates of serious mental illness tend to decline with age (Epstein et al., 2004; Substance Abuse and Mental Health Services Administration, 2010). In 2009, adults aged 18 to 25 years old had the highest rates of serious mental illness (7.3%), followed by those aged 26 to 49 years old (5.9%) and those aged 50 years or older (2.8%). Approximately 6.4% of women and 3.2% of men have a serious mental illness. Further, with respect to race, those who identified as biracial or multiracial have the highest rates of serious mental illness (9.7%). Among individuals who identify a single race, those most likely to have serious mental illness tend to be Caucasian or Native American/American Indian (5.3% and 5.8%, respectively). Four percent of Hispanics had a serious mental illness, followed by African Americans (just under 4%) and Asian (2%) (Substance Abuse and Mental Health Services Administration, 2010).

Adults with serious mental illness had fewer years of education, were more likely to be unemployed, and had the lowest family income levels as compared to those without serious mental illness. They were more likely to have not completed high school and less likely to have graduated from college, as compared to those without serious mental illness. Individuals with serious mental illness are more likely to be unemployed or not in the labor force than those without serious mental illness (Epstein et al., 2004; Substance Abuse and Mental Health Services

Administration, 2010). Prevalence of serious mental illness increases as the level of family income decreases. At the turn of the millennia, among those earning less than $20,000 annually, 16.3% had serious mental illness compared to the highest income level ($75,000 or more), in which 6.3% had serious mental illness (Epstein et al., 2004).

In 2009, roughly 46% adults with serious mental illness received mental health treatment in the preceding year. Of the 12 million adults who reported an unmet mental health care need (e.g., delay in care, perception of insufficient care), approximately half reported not receiving treatment at all. The most frequently reported barrier to mental health treatment included being unable to afford care (42.5%), beliefs that the problems could be handled without treatment (31.9%), not knowing where to go for services (18.5%), and not having the time for treatment (17.0%) (Substance Abuse and Mental Health Services, 2010). Historically, in comparison to those individuals with serious mental illness that did not receive services, those who received treatment were more likely to be older (more than 26 years of age), female, more educated, and identify as non-Hispanic Caucasian. With older age, the rates of receiving treatment also increased; just under half of adults aged 50 years or older sought treatment, compared to 34.2% of those aged 18 to 25 years old. Women were more likely than men with serious mental illness to receive mental health treatment (52.3% versus 39.5%, respectively). More than half of non-Hispanics or Caucasians with serious mental illness received mental health treatment, whereas fewer than 40% of black non-Hispanics and Hispanics with serious mental illness received mental health treatment (Epstein et al., 2004; Kessler, Chiu, et al., 2005; Wang, Demler, & Kessler, 2002).

Prevalence of Mental Disorders and Relationship to Violent Crime

Public fear of individuals with mental illness is greater than it was 50 years ago. The relationship between mental illness and violence has long been the subject of debate, and perception has been fueled by much misinformation and the impact of the most tragic cases being covered at length in the media. The perception of those with mental illness as uncontrollably violent began facing challenges as data from large-scale epidemiological research began supplanting this position. Some studies suggested that there was virtually no relationship between mental illness and violence. For example, Rice and Harris (1997) contended that, although those with signs of major mental disorder are at a higher risk for both criminal and violent behavior than the general population, there is no substantial evidence that a causal relationship exists between the mental disorder and the violent behavior. In addition, these researchers stated that some individuals with mental disorders are even less likely to commit another violent offense upon release. Furthermore, they noted, "By contrast, diagnoses of personality disorder (especially antisocial personality disorder) and, in most studies, substance abuse, have been found to be strongly related to the commission of criminal and violent acts both among the population at large and among criminal and psychiatric populations" (p. 132). Indeed, excluding diagnoses of substance abuse, individuals without mental illness commit the majority of violent crimes.

Although the dynamics between mental illness and violence carry particular characteristics, many of the strongest predictors of violence among individuals with mental illness also are strong predictors of violence in the general population (Harris & Lurigio, 2007). Bonta, Law, and Hanson (1998), in their meta-analysis of studies published between 1959 and 1995, found that the most important predictors of general and violent criminal recidivism were the same for offenders with mental disorders as for those offenders without mental disorders. For both general criminal recidivism as well as violent recidivism, the strongest predictors were those related to criminal history, including juvenile delinquency, adult criminal history, and violence history. Other factors that were positively related to both general and violent recidivism included: antisocial personality disorder, being male, being single, substance abuse, escape history, and weapon use history. Age, childhood conduct problems, symptoms of psychosis and depression, and recent victimization have been cited as the strongest risk factors for major violence committed by adults, and Elbogen and Johnson (2009) found that these characteristics were more common amongst people with severe mental illness. Among youth, major predictors of youth violence include hyperactivity, impulsivity, attention problems, and poor behavioral controls. In contrast, nervousness and anxiety has a negative relationship with violence toward others (Hawkins et al., 2000).

Yet, assuming there is no impact of mental illness on violent crimes is also a problematic position to take. As noted by Taylor (1995), "An opposite form of denial that was gaining ground—to the effect that people with schizophrenia and other mental illnesses are at no special risk of violence—is equally unlikely to be conducive to helping patients or promoting safety" (p. 163). By the 1990s, growing evidence suggested that neither such extreme position seemed to accurately capture the complex relationship between mental illness and violence. Therefore, an understanding of the complex role of various mental disorders and their relationship to violence is essential.

Anxiety and Mood Disorders and Violence Anxiety disorders are the most frequently occurring type of mental disorder, with approximately 28% of the U.S. population expected to experience a diagnosable anxiety disorder within their lifetime (Kessler, Berglund, et al., 2005). In a recent study, nearly 8% of adolescents aged 13 to 18 reported being severely impaired by a mood disorder, and symptoms of anxiety disorders were found to start at a young age, generally emerging by age six (Merikangas et al., 2010). Anxiety disorders include simple phobias (i.e., an extreme or irrational fear of things or social situations, such as the number 13 or public speaking), generalized anxiety disorder (i.e., chronic feelings of excessive worry without apparent specific cause), post-traumatic stress disorder (i.e., an anxiety disorder associated with serious traumatic events), panic disorder, and obsessive-compulsive disorder. Simple phobias are the most frequently type of anxiety disorder, affecting approximately 8% of the population in a given year (Kessler, Chiu, et al., 2005).

Mood disorders include episodes of major depression (i.e., depressed mood or loss of interest/pleasure in daily activities consistently for at least two weeks), dysthymia (i.e., a chronic mood disorder lasting at least two years), and bipolar disorders (i.e., disorders characterized by the presence of both abnormally elevated and depressed states). Mood disorders are the second-most prevalent class of mental disorders, with a lifetime prevalence occurring in approximately 20% of the U.S. population (Kessler, Berglund, et al., 2005). In a given year, approximately 9.5% of the U.S. population experiences some type of a mood disorder. Mood disorders had the highest percentage (45%) of symptoms classified as serious when compared to other psychiatric disorders (Kessler, Chiu, et al., 2005). In a recent study, nearly 11% of adolescents aged 13 to 18 reported being severely impaired by a mood disorder, and these symptoms typically emerged by age 13 (Merikangas et al., 2010). Major depression is the most frequently occurring type of mood disorder, occurring in roughly 6% of the population annually (Kessler, Chiu, et al., 2005; Substance Abuse and Mental Health Services Administration, 2010).

Serious violence perpetrated by those with anxiety and mood disorders is rare. When it does occur, several studies have implicated the role of mania in violence against others (Breggin, 2003, 2010; Large & Nielssen, 2011; Salloum, Cornelius, Mezzich, & Kirisci, 2002), including verbal aggression by children (Doerfler, Conner, & Toscano, 2011), intimate partner violence (Chang et al., 2011; Rees, et al., 2011), and homicide committed by adults (Schwartz, Wendling, & Guthrie, 2005).

When violence does occur among those with anxiety and/or mood disorders, the victims tend to be family and friends of the mentally ill offender, especially those in close personal relationships (Coid, Yang, Roberts, et al., 2006). Threats of violence involving weapons (with the exception of guns) are more likely among individuals with anxiety disorders than those without mental disorders (Casiano, Belik, Cox, Waldman, & Sareen, 2008). Most of the violence occurs in the home, as was the case with "Michael." Some studies have found high rates of mood disorders among those who commit murder. For example, a recent study of the elderly who murder their physically disabled spouses found that approximately 90% of the offenders were diagnosed with a mental disorder—with major depression accounting for virtually all of the diagnoses (Bourget, Gagné, & Whitehurst, 2010). In another recent study of those admitted to state psychiatric agencies following committing murder, major depression was the most frequently diagnosed mental disorder at 61% of the sample (Matejkowski, Cullen, & Solomon, 2008).

Substance Use Disorders and Violence In 2010, nearly 9% of the U.S. population—an estimated 22.6 million Americans—aged 12 years or older used illicit substances within the last month, and nearly all of these individuals met criteria for a substance dependence disorder based on DSM-IV criteria. Approximately half of Americans reported using alcohol in the previous month, with just under a quarter of the population engaging in at least one binge-drinking episode, which was defined as five more drinks on the same occasion (Substance Abuse and Mental Health Services Administration, 2011). Lifetime prevalence of substance use disorders is just under 15% of the U.S. population (Kessler, Berglund, et al., 2005). When mental disorders co-occur with substance use disorders, the course of the illness is more chronic than mental disorders alone. Additionally, the co-occurrence between a mental disorder and a substance use disorder can create serious complications for treatment (Kessler, Chiu, et al., 2005). Regardless of many demographic and socioeconomic subgroups, among those who had used an illicit substance within the past year, the rates of serious mental illness were over double when compared to those who had not used in the previous year (17.1% versus 6.9%). Although alcohol use per se does not appear to be related to rates of serious mental illness (approximately 8% each for both alcohol users and nonusers), those identified as "heavy" alcohol users were more likely to have serious mental illness than those who were not identified as such.

The co-occurrence of substance use and violence has been well demonstrated (Barrett, Mills, & Teesson, 2011; Casiano et al., 2008; Steadman et al., 1998; Swanson, Borum, Swartz, & Hiday, 1999; Swartz et al.,

1998; Weizmann-Henelius, Putkonen, Naukkarinen, & Eronen, 2009). Those with substance dependence disorders were more likely to engage in violence toward friends, acquaintances, and (to a lesser extent) strangers. Violent events most often occurred in another person's home (Coid, Yang, Roberts, et al., 2006). When guns are present, there is an increased likelihood of threats among individuals with substance disorders (Casiano et al., 2008). Particularly among individuals with psychosis, the use of substances dramatically increases the risk of violence (Addington & Addington, 2006; Spidel, Lecomte, Greaves, Sahlstrom, & Yuille, 2010; Walsh et al., 2001).

Psychosis and Violence Psychotic disorders include schizophrenia (i.e., a disorder characterized by a deterioration of thought processes and emotional responsiveness) and schizoaffective disorders (i.e., recurring episodes of elevated or depressed mood that occur at the same time as or alternately with perceptual distortions). Studies examining the risk of violence from those with psychotic disorders have varied, with some indicating a lowered risk of violence and others reporting higher risks of violence (Spidel et al., 2010; Yee, Large, Kemp, & Nielssen, 2011).

Ultimately, the base rates for violence and psychotic disorders become extremely important in examining the relationship between mental illness and violence. Homicide, even in countries with relatively high violence rates, is an extremely rare occurrence in the range of violent crimes against persons. More recent examinations into the risk of violence toward others indicate that those with psychotic disorders contribute only a very small percentage of violence given the rarity of these conditions. Coid, Yang, Roberts, et al. (2006) estimate that the attributable risk of violence from psychosis is 1.2%. The context of such violence becomes even more important. In countries with relatively high violence rates, homicides committed by the mentally ill contribute only a tiny portion of the overall violence rate. In comparison, in countries where the homicide rate is low, persons with mental illness contribute a much larger proportion of the violence. Coid (2010) further noted, "the base rate effect is still highly important, and psychotic illnesses are relatively uncommon forms of psychiatric morbidity. . . . Taken together, these findings suggest that the base rate of nonlethal violence is relatively high in Britain and that factors other than psychiatric disorder made the highest impact" (pp. 547–548).

Douglas, Guy, and Hart (2009) examined the association between major mental illness (in particular, psychosis) and violence through an extensive meta-analysis of studies—both published research and dissertations—with two goals in mind: "first, to characterize, in general terms, the magnitude of the association between [major mental illness] and violence," and "second, to identify moderating factors—such as study design and issues related to the conceptualization and measurement of psychosis and violence ... that might moderate this association" (p. 683). Douglas et al. (2009) found that "in general, then, psychosis appears to be intermediate in comparison with other putative risk factors. It is comparable to, or larger than, numerous other risk factors, though tends to be smaller than externalizing disorders, such as antisocial personality or psychopathy, or early-onset criminal behavior" (p. 693). In addressing the second goal, one finding from their study was that focusing on the moderator variables (i.e., when the relationship between two variables—such as violence and psychosis, in this case—depends on a third variable). Furthermore, when compared with individuals without mental illness, "psychosis is, in fact, a strong risk factor for violence, increasing the odds of violence three- to four-fold" but that their findings "argue against the practice in research in lumping individuals with psychosis into a single, gross category" (p. 694).

Douglas et al. (2009) found that more disorganized types of psychosis were predictive of violence. For example, it may be that individuals with this type of psychosis experience difficulties in extricating themselves appropriately from tense social situations and respond with violence, rather than being able to successfully defuse misunderstandings. Additionally, positive symptoms (e.g., auditory hallucinations, delusions, disorganized behavior) were more strongly related to violence than were negative symptoms (e.g., flattened affect). Hallucinations, delusions, threat/control-override symptoms (e.g., delusions that make the person in fear for their lives and act or react in the extreme as a result), and symptoms with a paranoid element were all related to violence. As in the case of Michael, who was apparently experiencing a number of positive symptoms, he was compelled to act against the threat to his "holy mission" and "birthright" when his father expressed the intention to have him psychiatrically hospitalized. The relationship of positive symptoms of psychosis and violence has been found elsewhere (Nordstrom, Dahlgren, & Kullgren, 2006; Swanson et al., 2006), including in individuals who commit severe yet nonlethal violence (Yee et al., 2011) and among those who are able to identify the voice in their command hallucinations (Junginger, 1995), suggesting that individuals are more likely to follow through with even very dangerous directives from voices that they trust. In particular, threat/control-override symptoms and their relationship to violence have been the target of much controversy. These symptoms of psychosis or their impaired perception of reality make an individual so paranoid or fearful that they are compelled to act violently to ensure their survival. For example, individuals who experience delusions of food poisoning may well attempt to assault food service workers in inpatient treatment settings. Threat/control-override symptoms have also been associated with severity of violence (Stompe, Ortwein-Swoboda, & Schanda, 2004). That is, individuals with threat/control-override symptoms were much more likely to engage in extreme levels of violence—acts involving endangering the lives of others or actually resulting in another person's death—than more moderate or low levels of violence, such as damaging property at the main purpose or carrying a weapon that was not used. As in the case of Michael, he was compelled to extreme action—piercing his father through the heart—rather than screaming, making threats with no follow-though, or destroying property in the home when his father told him to pack an overnight bag.

Patients with command hallucinations to harm others were twice as likely to be violent than patients without such commands (McNiel, Eisner, & Binder, 2000). Patients with schizophrenia were more likely to be violent if their hallucinations generated negative emotions, including anger, anxiety, and sadness. The violent group also had less successful strategies to cope with their voices than the nonviolent group. In the MacArthur study, there was no relationship between the presence of general hallucinations or command hallucinations (e.g., a voice telling the person to tell the truth) and violence. However, there was a relationship between command hallucinations to commit violence, and actual violence (Green, Schramm, Chiu, McVie, & Hay, 2009; Monahan et al., 2001). For example, although individuals experiencing auditory hallucinations may hear derogatory comments that are unpleasant and upsetting, they do not typically act out violently in response. In contrast, those who experience voices telling them to engage in specific actions—such as "cut her throat"—are more likely to follow through with such orders, perhaps in the mistaken belief that they are powerless to do otherwise or that a worse fate will befall them should they not comply.

A study testing predictors of homicidality in a sample of patients with schizophrenia (Schwartz, Reynolds, Austin, & Petersen, 2003) showed that when the patient with schizophrenia also presented with manic symptoms and substance abuse, it greatly increased their risk for more extreme homicidality. The relationship between psychosis, substance use, and homicide perpetration was recently demonstrated in a study utilizing a national sample of Swedish patients recently discharged from psychiatric care (Fazel, Buxrud, Ruchkin, & Grann, 2010). Furthermore,

Fazel et al. (2010) found that—in addition to psychosis and substance use —prior psychiatric hospitalization for violence, medication noncompliance following discharge, and length of psychiatric history (of at least one year) further assisted in the prediction of homicidality. Coid (2010) noted, "As the first episode of psychosis is relatively short compared to the total duration of the illness, the risk of homicide during a first episode is considerably greater than that of the annual risk among individuals with previously treated psychosis" (p. 547). Other issues regarding psychosis and lethal violence include those cases in which the intended victim does not actually die. As noted by Taylor (1995), "at extremes of violence it is often very much a matter of chance whether the victim dies or not. The 'lucky' offender picks a poor weapon, lacks strength or strikes a rib instead of slipping the knife through an intercostal space, while the 'unlucky' one strikes a victim with an exceptionally thin skull, or for whom the ambulance is delayed" (p. 168). Such circumstances raise the issue that mental health professionals and criminal justice personnel (e.g., judges) should look beyond the surface image of a crime—such as the charge that was ultimately filed—to examine closely the functions of the violent behavior.

For example, consider the case of Heather[2], who was admitted to the maximum-security state hospital after pleading Not Guilty by Reason of Insanity to Injury to a Child to attempting to slash her infant sister with a knife, reporting that command hallucinations instructed her to do so. During the course of an evaluation, it was found that Heather did not stop when she heard her sister's cries—instead, her mother intervened, wrestling Heather to the ground while another family member called for emergency services. By merely examining the admitting offense, one has only a partial picture of the event that could have led to lethal levels of violence without outside intervention.

Amongst individuals with psychotic disorders, paranoia has long been established as playing a critical role in increased risk for violence, and studies have differentiated between paranoid and non-paranoid subgroups (Krakowski, Volavka, & Brizer, 1986; Stompe et al., 2004). Among patients with a paranoid component to their psychosis, understanding the underlying delusion related to their illness is critical (Krakowski, 2005; Krakowski et al., 1986). As noted by Krakowski, Volavka, and Brizer (1986), the "interpersonal element is of great importance: the violence is directed at a specific person, usually a significant individual in the patient's life, who is seen as persecuting or depriving the patient of some basic need" (p. 139). Even amongst geriatric patients, those who present with paranoia are far more likely than those who have psychosis related to dementia to commit serious violence against others who have been incorporated into their delusions. Studies have found that these individuals were more likely to have committed murder, and their acts of violence were typically directed toward family members and friends (Nestor, Haycock, Doiron, Kelly, & Kelly, 1995; Nordstrom et al., 2006).

Individuals with paranoia who have committed homicide have most often done so in either the victim's home, or in their own home as was demonstrated in the case of Michael (Nordstrom et al., 2006). Furthermore, directing rage and anger at the victim through the use of a firearm or a sharp weapon was the most often-cited reason for the murder (Matejkowski et al., 2008). In Michael's case, the actual act of homicidal violence was impulsive, initiated by his fury at his father's intention to have him psychiatrically hospitalized.

Factors leading to violent behavior in hospital settings (e.g., overcrowding, understaffing) may not be as useful to predicting community violence (Serper et al., 2005; Steinert, 2002), and this understanding may be particularly applicable to individuals with high-lethality/low-frequency types of violence (e.g., homicide) prompted by symptoms of mental illness. With respect to violence in the inpatient settings, these individuals tend to function well and do not act out aggressively toward either patients or staff when hospitalized. This reduction in violence may be partially explained by responsiveness to treatment. However, a considerable proportion of the reduction of violent acts may be explained by that the focus of their delusions is often someone on the outside. That is, these individuals do not act out violently because the intended targets are literally not accessible to them. Consider the vignette of Felix below:

> Felix[3] was a patient for many years at a maximum-security state hospital. He was admitted to the hospital as Incompetent to Stand Trial for a murder charge, after he shot and bludgeoned a man he reportedly recognized on a subway that he believed had been raping him; in reality, the victim was a stranger to Felix. In many ways, he was a "model" patient. Having successfully worked through the hospital's privilege system, he had resided at the facility's least restrictive unit for the majority of that time. He had never been in a physical altercation with either staff members or other patients, and it had been some time since he had even broken a relatively minor rule.
>
> Approximately two years prior to the homicide, he first experienced awakening with sensations around his rectum and mouth that he interpreted as having been sexually assaulted during the night. He concluded that a group of individuals, led by the man on the subway, was breaking into his room, anesthetizing him, and raping him. Felix claimed that he

repeatedly saw this man around his residence and was being stalked by him. He changed residences on two occasions and reported break-ins to the police on several occasions, which were not taken seriously, and Felix believed the assaults continued. He purchased a handgun with the intent of either defending himself or shooting the perceived perpetrators. When interviewed many years afterward, Felix continued to express the same delusional beliefs that had apparently been present at the time of the homicide. He reported that he had to "take matters into my own hands, since the police weren't going to handle it." He further reported that, if not for the high fence at the perimeter of the facility, there would be "a lot more rapings and killings going on."

Psychosis and Maternal Filicide One subset of individuals experiencing acutely psychotic symptoms that come to the attention of the criminal justice system is parents, particularly mothers, who kill their children. Filicide is the killing of a child older than one year and is very frequently associated with psychosis in the female perpetrator (Manchester, 2003). Filicide is often associated with mental illness in the parent, as well as suicide. Although filicide is a form of homicide, rates of infanticide are more congruent with suicide rates rather than with murder rates (Putkonen, Weizmann-Henelius, Lindberg, Eronen, & Häkkänen, 2009). According to the American Psychiatric Association's *Diagnostic and Statistical Manual of Mental Disorders*, fourth edition–text revision (DSM-IV-TR; American Psychiatric Association, 2000), the most severe form of postpartum depression—that of postpartum psychosis—often presents with episodes of delusions in which the mother feels that the infant is possessed or the mother has hallucinations that tell her to kill the child.

Perhaps the most well-known case of maternal filicide that stemmed out of postpartum psychosis was that of Andrea Yates. There existed a family history of diagnosed and treated bipolar disorder and major depression. Each time she gave birth, she experienced a postpartum depression, and her mental illness worsened into psychosis. This case exemplifies the most tragic consequences resulting from a history of mental illness exacerbated by undertreated progressive postpartum illness after multiple childbirths (Shipley, 2012):

Ms. Yates drowned all five of her children in June 2001, after her husband Rusty left for work. Ms. Yates' first reported psychotic episode occurred after the birth of her first child Noah in 1994. She did not inform others of her experiences out of delusions that Satan would hear her and harm her children. With her subsequent pregnancies and births, she became more depressed, psychotic, and overwhelmed. As noted by Spinelli (2004), "Mood states of high energy and a hyperreligious focus on Satan and religious doctrine switched to worsening depression, psychosis, and suicide attempts. After her last two children were born, she had a total of four psychiatric hospitalizations. . . . After hospital discharge, a catatonic, psychotic Andrea Yates appeared to her friends and family like a 'caged animal,' staring for hours and scratching bald spots into her head. Discussions about Satan's presence were not uncommon in the Yates home, where a rigid religious belief system dominated the family's life" (p. 1554).

As cited by Oberman (2003), Ms. Yates exemplified the case of a severely mentally ill mother who was left to care for her children with virtually no outside support. In addition to the demands of caring for her five children, she was burdened with active symptoms of depression and psychosis that would have further impaired her ability to meet those needs. Furthermore, she was experiencing additional chronic and acute stressors, which included the death of her father after a long illness, ongoing care of her elderly mother, the birth of her youngest child Mary, and practically non-stop pregnancies and breastfeeding for the previous seven years, since the birth of her first son Noah (Oberman, 2003). Ms. Yates had a long-standing history of mental illness, including four hospitalizations, two attempted suicides, and an outpatient prescription for Haldol, (Gesalman, 2002; Manchester, 2003). Despite this history, each time she was discharged from the hospital, there was no family intervention, and her husband indicated that she was feeling better and had agreed to have more children (Denno, 2003; Spinelli, 2004). Consequently, Ms. Yates would refuse psychoactive medications because of pregnancy or breastfeeding.

At the time of the murders, Ms. Yates was experiencing a severe postpartum psychosis with delusions and hallucinations, but this was not her first episode of mental illness. She had become floridly psychotic as a result of her treating psychiatrist discontinuing the prescribed Haldol, an antipsychotic medication used to help control hallucinations and other symptoms of psychosis. She reported that Satan commanded her to kill her children to save them from the fires and torments of hell. She has delusional beliefs that she was influenced by the devil and that she had irreversibly damaged her children and the only way to protect their innocence and ensure their entrance to heaven, was that she must kill them (Spinelli, 2004). Andrea Yates has reported that she believed she was possessed and was a "Jezebel" and that her poor mothering threatened her children's ability to go to heaven. She saw only two choices: either kill her children while some innocence remained, therefore allowing them entrance in heaven, or continue to damage them and ensure their eternal damnation. In her delusional state, her love for her children and her belief that she was saving them from eternal suffering led her to follow through with drowning all five of her children.

This tragic case brought issues surrounding maternal filicide related to severe mental illness into the national spotlight, particularly the importance of education and opportunities to intervene and prevent the most tragic of outcomes (Shipley, 2012). Most incidents of postpartum depression do not include delusions or hallucinations, but there are suicidal ideation, obsessional thoughts of violence toward the child, and psychomotor agitation. Whereas the postpartum blues are very common (up to 80%); only about 0.2% of childbearing women will experience postpartum psychosis, which typically emerges within two weeks of the childbirth and frequently requires hospitalization (Dobson & Sales, 2000; Manchester, 2003). Postpartum psychosis occurs only in 1 in 500 to 1,000 childbirths, but the risk of reoccurrence is very high (Glover & Kammerer, 2004). Most often, the individual presents with mood lability, rambling speech, disorganized behavior, and hallucinations or delusions. According to Born, Zinga, and Steine (2004, p. 32), symptoms characteristic of this disorder include:

- Delusional beliefs, often related to the baby (e.g., infant death, denial of birth, belief that the infant is possessed or has special powers)
- Hypervigilance about the baby
- Exhilaration and sleeplessness
- Psychomotor hyperkinesias and akinesia affecting expressive and reactive emotions
- Hypersensitivity to neutral comments
- Visual, tactile, olfactory, or auditory hallucinations
- Feelings of being perplexed, confused, or disoriented (organic-like presentation)
- Impaired cognition
- Delirium like symptoms
- Poor appetite
- Stupor
- Waxing and waning course with lucid periods

Studies have shown that homicidal parents have high rates of suicide attempts; that mothers are more likely to commit suicide after the act than fathers; and that suicide attempts by homicidal parents are often highly lethal and successful (Bourget & Gagné, 2002). Bourget and Gagné (2002) identified a psychiatric motive for more than 85% of the mothers in their study and found that the majority of the mothers had prior psychiatric treatment for a depressive or psychotic disorder. Numerous researchers have identified major depression with psychotic features as the most common diagnosis among maternal offenders (Bourget & Gagné, 2002; Bourget,

Grace, & Whitehurst, 2007; Hatters-Friedman & Resnick, 2007; Putkonen et al., 2009).

Historically, Scott (1973) found that psychotic illness accounted for 16% of the diagnoses of women who killed their children. This group included postpartum psychosis, schizoid paranoid psychosis, and depressive psychosis. Their motivations for killing are closely linked to the delusions or command hallucinations. (For an extensive discussion regarding maternal filicide, see Shipley [2012].) The common themes present in the delusions of filicidal mothers include beliefs that the child was defective or possessed by Satan; hallucinatory commands to kill the child; and the idea that the child could be saved from disaster (fates such as being raped, becoming a prostitute, or undergoing torture) only through death. With respect to social and environmental stressors, mothers who committed filicide as a result of mental illness were usually married with the lowest levels of marital stress, were older, attacked older children, and more commonly had multiple victims (Stanton & Simpson, 2002). In addition to experiencing active symptoms of mental illness, mentally ill women who killed their children were also relatively isolated in the caring for the child (Oberman, 2003). In the vast majority of maternal filicide cases, the deaths are the result of depression, psychosis, and impaired reality orientation, rather than motivations that are self-serving, revenge-based, or callous (Sadoff, 1995; Shipley, 2012).

When psychosis is the cause, mothers frequently kill their children based on altruistic beliefs of being merciful or ending real or imagined (delusional) suffering (Shipley, 2012). Mood-congruent delusions or hallucinations may also result in a mother believing that she has irreversibly hurt or damaged her child(ren) in some way (Gold, 2001). Stanton, Simpson, and Wouldes (2000) concluded that impaired reality, disorganized thinking, and the instability of the women's mental states, not abuse or other psychosocial stressors, were the main factors for the mentally ill filicidal mother. "One might postulate that the intensity of the suffering perceived in a delusional state is of such a magnitude as to explain the filicide rationally. However, other features of the illness such as impaired impulse control, affective dysregulation, lack of cognitive flexibility, and unbalanced judgment are likely to contribute" (p. 1459). Command hallucinations and paranoid delusions correlate with a higher risk of violence in general; but delusions and paranoia about the child is a very significant risk factor for maternal filicide. A severe delusional depression, in which the children are a key focus of the delusional system, is a serious red flag (Shipley, 2012). The majority of these women have a major mental illness that they are often trying to manage without treatment and are attempting to appear normal. Furthermore, research has demonstrated that a number of these women kill for motives that they believe are in their child's best interest; therefore, their apparent love and nurturance of their child does not reduce their risk. In fact, the risk may be increased due to the emotional investment in the child if the child becomes the central focus or context of the psychiatric symptoms (Stanton et al., 2000). "Evident devotion to the child and parenting is not likely to be a protective factor" (p. 1459).

Understanding the motivations underlying violence against others is critical. Douglas et al. (2009) argued that all assessments of violence risk should include evaluations of psychosis. First, they found that the presence of psychosis is linked to a higher risk of violence compared to individuals without mental illness, and that some studies have found that nearly half of individuals with major mental illness have a co-occurring substance abuse disorder, which substantially raised the risk of violence. Additionally, they note that while the mere presence of psychosis is "neither necessary nor sufficient of high risk," when the psychosis is "logically linked to the occurrence of future violence should clinicians consider it an important risk factor. Of course, other cofactors may also be present that increase (e.g., substance abuse, psychopathy) or decrease (e.g., social support, stable housing) the individual's risk for violence. As such, violence should never be the sole factor that is considered in determining a person's risk—or lack thereof—for violence" (p. 697). In maternal filicide cases, such as that of Ms. Yates, motivations may be altruistic, with the offender believing that she is acting in her children's best interests even if such actions place the offender at risk of criminal prosecution. However, in other types of offenses spurred on by the most severe personality disorders, the motivations are typically not altruistic but self-serving, particularly amongst individuals who are psychopathic.

The Antisocial Personality Disorder and Psychopathy Continuum and Violence

Violent behavior in criminal offenders with certain types of personality disorders (i.e., persistent, inflexible, and maladaptive patterns of behavior) has been well documented over the last two decades (Blackburn & Coid, 1999; Logan & Blackburn, 2009; Warren, Burnette et al., 2002; Warren, Hurt et al., 2002). Violence among those with personality disorders tends to be a stable characteristic, typically present from a young age (before or around puberty) and is not linked with emotional distress or a specific symptom cluster. Furthermore, it is particularly resistant to change (Coid, Yang, Tyrer, Roberts, & Ullrich, 2006; Huang et al., 2009; Torgersen, Kringlen, & Cramer, 2001).

Worldwide, approximately 6.3% of the population was diagnosed with any personality disorder. Other studies suggest that between 4% and 12% of the adult population is considered to have a formal diagnosis of a personality disorder (Coid, Yang, Tyrer, et al., 2006; Huang et al., 2009; Torgersen et al., 2001). There has been distinction in the literature regarding the relationship between violence and the three clusters of personality disorders. Cluster A (odd, eccentric) personality disorders are characterized by mistrust of others, suspiciousness, and distortions in cognition, and they include paranoid, schizoid, and schizotypal personality disorders. Cluster B (dramatic, emotional, or erratic) personality disorders are characterized by emotion dysregulation, anger, stress reactivity, and aggression; this cluster includes borderline, narcissistic, antisocial, and histrionic personality disorders. Cluster C (anxious, fearful) personality disorders are characterized by rigidity and social inadequacy, and include avoidant, dependent, and obsessive-compulsive personality disorders. Prevalence rates for the three personality clusters fell at 3.6% for Cluster A, 1.5% for Cluster B, and 2.7% for Cluster C (Huang et al., 2009). For example, in a study of the three personality disorder clusters and violence amongst youth, only those with Cluster C personality disorders were not associated with violent crimes. Furthermore, amongst the other personality disorders most significantly related to violence, individuals presenting with narcissistic and paranoid dimensions were at especially high risk of committing violent acts (Johnson et al., 2000).

In contrast to other types of mental illness (e.g., anxiety, mood disorders, psychosis), the presence of particular personality disorders has been linked to increased violence. Antisocial personality disorder (ASPD) is particularly predictive of violence and criminal recidivism. ASPD is "a pervasive pattern of disregard for, and violation of, the rights of others that begins in childhood or early adolescence and continues into adulthood" (American Psychiatric Association, 2000, p. 706). Among prison inmates, the presence of ASPD is especially high, as much as 78% (Rotter, Way, Steinbacher, Sawyer, & Smith, 2002), and this diagnosis is particularly prevalent amongst those convicted of violent offenses (Roberts & Coid, 2009). Reconviction rates for violent offenses—including murder, manslaughter, assault, rape, and robbery—were 3.7 times higher for individuals with ASPD (Hiscoke, Langstrom, Ottosson, & Grann, 2003). Similarly to psychotic disorders, individuals diagnosed with ASPD—and especially those classified as psychopathic—constitute an extremely small percentage of the general population (Lenzenweger, Lane, Loranger, & Kessler, 2007). ASPD has a prevalence of between 3.9% and 5.8% in men and 0.5% and 1.9% in women in the U.S. general population (Compton, Conway, Stinson, Colliver, & Grant, 2005).

In a study of 190 civilly committed and detained sexually violent predators in Washington State, Jackson and Richards (2007) found that personality disorders were frequent, but less than a quarter of the sample was diagnosed with a severe mental illness (e.g., schizophrenia, schizoaffective disorder). Furthermore, the most frequently identified personality disorder was antisocial personality disorder, and this diagnosis constituted over 40% of the study sample. Violence within controlled settings is particularly prevalent among individuals with personality disorders. Within prisons, among offenders convicted of serious violent offenses, individuals with personality disorders—specifically, antisocial personality disorder and narcissism—are more likely to be disruptive (e.g., rule violations) as well as more likely to commit violence within the prison (Coid, 2002). Following discharge from either correctional or psychiatric settings, individuals with antisocial personality disorder are at significantly higher risk of violent reoffending than individuals without this diagnosis (Hiscoke et al., 2003; Johnson et al., 2000; Listwan, Van Voorhis, & Ritchey, 2007; Tardiff, Murzak, Leon, & Portera, 1997).

One subset of individuals diagnosed with antisocial personality disorder (ASPD) that warrants particular attention are those individuals who are further classified as psychopaths (For an extensive review of the historical and treatment considerations regarding psychopathy, see Arrigo & Shipley, 2001, and Shipley & Arrigo, 2001.) Hervey Cleckley's *The Mask of Sanity* (1941) marked the beginning of the modern clinical construct of the psychopath, which has remained relatively stable to the present (Hart & Hare, 1998). Cleckley fashioned his description of the psychopath based on observations of white, middle-class, male patients in an inpatient mental hospital (Dinges et al., 1998). Hart and Hare (1998) summarized the essential features of Cleckley's psychopath:

> Interpersonally, psychopaths are grandiose, arrogant, callous, superficial, and manipulative; affectively, they are short-tempered, unable to form strong emotional bonds with others, and lacking in empathy, guilt or remorse; and behaviorally, they are irresponsible, impulsive, and prone to violate social and legal norms and expectations. (p. 25)

Hare (1980) developed the Hare's Psychopathy Checklist (PCL), followed by a current, revised version, the PCL-R (Hare, 1991, 2003), to operationalize the concept of psychopathy based on the primary features of Cleckley's original criteria. Psychopathic traits—most especially regarding the callous and unemotional traits—have been found to have considerable stability from childhood and adolescence through adulthood (Burke,

Loeber, & Lahey, 2007; Lynam, Caspi, Moffitt, Loeber, & Stouthamer-Loeber, 2007; Muñoz & Frick, 2007; Obradovic, Pardini, Long, & Loeber, 2007). Psychopathy in the general population is extremely rare (Farrington, 2006), and some studies have found that approximately 1% to 2% of the general population is estimated to meet criteria to be classified as psychopathic (Neumann & Hare, 2008).

An extensive body of research indicates that violent recidivism of those classified as psychopathic is substantially higher than for those classified as non-psychopathic (Coid & Ullrich, 2010; Edens, Campbell, & Weir, 2007; Gretton, Hare, & Catchpole, 2004; Harris, Rice, & Cormier, 1991; Serin, Peters, & Barbaree, 1990; Walters, 2003a, 2003b). Similarly to adults, psychopathy among adolescents has been strongly related to both general and violent recidivism (Catchpole & Gretton, 2003). Among individuals convicted for homicide, a Finnish study demonstrated a fairly high prevalence of psychopathy (approximately 30%) among male offenders, although the prevalence of psychopathy in female homicide offenders was much lower (about 10%) (Weizmann-Henelius, Grönroos et al., 2010).

The relationship between ASPD/psychopathy and violence in men is a strong one. However, research on women in this area is scarce. For example, research regarding the relationship between psychopathy and homicide has almost exclusively focused on men, whereas research examining psychopathy in women has focused on crimes other than homicide (in Weizmann-Henelius, Grönroos, et al., 2010). Issues such as gender bias in diagnosing and the lack of research interest in these women due to smaller numbers has contributed to the paucity of information on these women (Shipley & Arrigo, 2004).

Motivations in violence amongst psychopathic individuals differ considerably from those with psychotic disorders. Consider the following quote by an individual classified as a psychopath incarcerated for kidnapping, rape, and extortion (Hare, 1993, p. 33):

> Do I care about other people? That's a tough one. But, yeah, I guess I really do . . . but I don't let my feelings get in the way . . . I mean, I'm as warm and caring as the next guy, but let's face it, everyone's trying to screw you . . . You've got to look out for yourself, park your feelings. Say you need something, or someone messes with you . . . maybe tries to rip you off . . . You take care of it . . . do whatever needs to be done . . . Do I feel bad if I have to hurt someone? Yeah, sometimes. But mostly it's like . . . uh . . . [laughs] . . . how did you feel the last time you squashed a bug?

Implications and Future Research

The intersection between mental illness and violent crimes against others is a complex one. The process of formally assessing violence risk is beyond the scope of this chapter, yet it nevertheless raises the question of appropriate placement for individuals who suffer from mental illness but pose a substantial risk of harm to others in the community. Specific symptoms or a diagnostic category is only the starting point when examining the relationship between mental illness and violence toward others. Particularly critical to a finer analysis is to examine the function of violence; that is, it is critical to investigate the purpose of the intended or completed behavior. In some individuals, violence may be indicative of emotional turmoil and psychotic processes (such as the case of Michael); while in others, violence may be a means to an end, as demonstrated by the psychopathic inmate quoted above. Taylor (1995) noted, "The key to limiting harm to and by a person with schizophrenia is for the clinician to discard the all-or-nothing concept of dangerousness and accept the multiplicity and variety of risks that may arise, their multifactorial basis and the mixed intervention strategies that may thus be necessary to influence the risks. The judgment of risk is best viewed as a continuum, with predictors, counteractions and monitoring taking place with recognized limits of confidence, time scale and circumstances" (p. 172). When evaluating a patient's risk of violence toward others, it is critical to directly investigate the relevant issues pertaining to that individual's risk of violence toward others. Unless specific inquiries are made, conclusions regarding many facets of the individual's risk level may be inadequately addressed—or wholly overlooked. That is, some individuals may present superficially well, particularly when questions posed to them are unrelated to the symptoms that increase their risk of violence toward others. In fact, many individuals who have engaged in lethal forms of violence are friendly, do not engage in frequent acts of aggression, and present as "model" patients in inpatient settings. A targeted and deeply investigative approach is not only desirable, *but essential* for accurately assessing their risk towards others.

In addition to the complexity of violence risk prediction itself, such assessments are under constant assailment from other outside forces. These forces may include political and economic forces to expedite patient movement through inpatient treatment, often taking exception to individuals who remain in higher-security settings despite the absence of overt, aggressive behavior but persisting delusions that led to the original, highly lethal offenses remain undiminished. Public misperceptions about the actual risk of violence attributed to the presence of mental disorders may also play a role. In particularly high-profile cases, considerations of public impressions of length of treatment may—consciously or unconsciously—guide treatment decisions regarding placement. Understanding the impact of local, statewide, and national influences on placement decisions may be particularly useful for those individuals responsible for making those decisions in order to help insulate them against spurious factors that may come into play.

Since the 1960s, the number of available beds for psychiatric inpatient services has declined sharply, from 314 beds per 100,000 persons to 17 beds per 100,000 persons in 2005, a number far below the estimated 50 beds per 100,000 persons that is needed for minimal treatment capacity (Torrey, Kennard, Eslinger, Lamb, & Pavle, 2010). This decline is attributable to various factors, which include newly developed medications that controlled for some of the most serious mental disorders (e.g., schizophrenia), stricter standards with respect to involuntary hospitalization, and changes in funding of mental health care costs—including the substantial underfunding of community mental health services. In the absence of adequate levels of both inpatient and outpatient mental health services, individuals suffering from mental illness have not simply vanished or their needs for treatment dissipated. Instead, they have been relegated to other avenues of social services, such as general hospital emergency rooms functioning as acute psychiatric treatment centers, transferring those in need of longer-term care to nursing homes, and, most frequently, mentally ill individuals are coming into contact with the criminal justice system.

Despite that most crimes are committed by those who are not mentally ill, those with mental illness are more likely to be convicted of crimes than are non-disordered inmates, and more frequently convicted of violent crimes (Hodgins & Cote, 1993; Yee et al., 2011). Prisons and jails are now functioning as acute psychiatric inpatient treatment centers (Lamb, Weinberger, Marsh, & Gross, 2007). In a recent study of individuals with serious mental illness, over half of the sample had recent contact with both the state department of corrections and the state psychiatric hospital system (Jones et al., 2011). With the onset of deinstitutionalization, arrest rates for individuals with mental illness have increased, often leading to the conclusion that "the mentally ill are being overarrested and warehoused in city and county jails" (Markowitz, 2011, p. 37). As correctional staff personnel function to serve the safety and security of the institution—not as trained mental health professionals—individuals with mental illness are often retained without adequate treatment. As Markowitz

(2011, p. 38) noted, "Although many jails and prisons provide mental health services, and several communities have programs to divert mentally ill offenders from jail to treatment . . . the availability of these services and programs is limited relative to the need for them." When appropriate or adequate treatment for those experiencing mental illness is unavailable, neither the patient nor the community are served from these unfortunate circumstances. Serious or lethal violence committed by those with mental disorders is rare, overall, but the life-altering impact on victims, their families, and the mentally ill offender is especially tragic when it could have been prevented through proper treatment.

Notes

1. Alias used to protect the individual's true identity.
2. Alias used to protect the individual's true identity.
3. Alias used to protect the individual's true identity.

References

Addington, D., & Addington, J. (2006). Early intervention in psychosis: Who refers? *Schizophrenia Research, 84*, 176–177.

American Psychiatric Association. (2000). *Diagnostic and statistical manual of mental disorders* (4th ed., text rev.). Washington, DC: Author.

Applebaum, P. S. (2006). Violence and mental disorders: Data and public policy. *American Journal of Psychiatry, 168*, 1319–1321.

Arrigo, B. A., & Shipley, S. L. (2001). The confusion over psychopathy (I): Historical considerations. *International Journal of Offender Therapy and Comparative Criminology, 45*, 325–344.

Barrett, E. L., Mills, K. L., & Teesson, M. (2011). Hurt people who hurt people: Violence amongst individuals with comorbid substance use disorder and post traumatic stress disorder. *Addictive Behaviors, 36*, 721–728.

Blackburn, R. (1998). Criminality and the interpersonal circle in mentally disordered offenders. *Criminal Justice & Behavior, 25*, 155–176.

Blackburn, R., & Coid, J. W. (1999). Empirical clusters of DSM-III personality disorders in violent offenders. *Journal of Personality Disorders, 13*, 18.

Bonta, J., Law, M., & Hanson, K. (1998). The prediction of criminal and violent recidivism among mentally disordered offenders: A meta-analysis. *Psychological Bulletin, 123*, 123–142.

Born, L., Zinga, D., & Steine, M. (2004). Challenges in identifying and diagnosing postpartum disorders. *Primary Psychiatry, 11*, 29–36.

Bourget, D., & Gagné, P. (2002). Maternal filicide in Quebec. *Journal of the American Academy of Psychiatry and the Law, 30*, 345–351.

Bourget, D., Gagné, P., & Whitehurst, L. (2010). Domestic homicide and homicide-suicide: The older offender. *Journal of the American Academy of Psychiatry and the Law, 38*, 305–311.

Bourget, D., Grace, J., & Whitehurst, L. (2007). A review of maternal and paternal filicide. *Journal of the American Academy of Psychiatry and the Law, 35*, 74–82.

Breggin, P. R. (2003). Suicidality, violence and mania caused by selective serotonin reuptake inhibitors (SSRIs): A review and analysis. *International Journal of Risk and Safety in Medicine, 16*, 31–49.

Breggin, P. R. (2010). Antidepressant-induced suicide, violence, and mania: Risks for military personnel. *Ethical Human Psychology and Psychiatry: An International Journal of Critical Inquiry, 12*, 111–121.

Burke, J. D., Loeber, R., & Lahey, B. B. (2007). Adolescent conduct disorder and interpersonal callousness as predictors of psychopathy in young adults. *Journal of Clinical Child and Adolescent Psychology, 36*, 334–346.

Cartwright, W. S. (2008). Economic costs of drug abuse: Financial, cost of illness, and services. *Journal of Substance Abuse Treatment, 34*, 224–233.

Casiano, H., Belik, S. L., Cox, B. J., Waldman, J. C., & Sareen, J. (2008). Mental disorders and threats made by noninstitutionalized people with weapons in the National Comorbidity Survey replication. *Journal of Nervous and Mental Disease, 196*, 437–445.

Catchpole, R. E. H., & Gretton, H. M. (2003). The predictive validity of risk assessment with violent young offenders: A 1-year examination of criminal outcome. *Criminal Justice and Behavior, 30*, 688–708.

Center for Mental Health Services, Substance Abuse and Mental Health Services Administration, HHS. (1999). Estimation methodology for adults with serious mental illness (SMI). *Federal Register, 64*, 33890–33897. Retrieved from http://www.gpo.gov/fdsys/pkg/FR-1999-06-24/html/99-15377.htm.

Centers for Disease Control and Prevention. (2010). Youth violence facts at a glance. Retrieved from http://www.cdc.gov/violenceprevention/pdf/yv-datasheet-a.pdf.

Chang, J. C., Cluss, P. A., Burke, J. G., Hawker, L., Dado, D., Goldstrohm, S., & Scholle, S. H. (2011). Partner violence screening in mental health. *General Hospital Psychiatry, 33*, 58–65.

Cleckley, H. (1941). *The mask of sanity*. St Louis, MO: C. V. Mosby.

Coid, J. W. (2002). Personality disorders in prisoners and their motivation for dangerous and disruptive behaviour. *Criminal Behaviour and Mental Health, 12*, 209–226.

Coid, J. (2010). Epidemiological linkages between mental ill-health and violence: Risk factors and wider consequences. In C. L. Cooper, U. Goswami, & B. J. Sahakian (Eds.), *Mental health and wellbeing*. United Kingdom: Wiley Blackwell.

Coid, J., & Ullrich, S. (2010). Antisocial personality disorder is on a continuum with psychopathy. *Comprehensive Psychiatry, 51*, 426–433.

Coid, C., Yang, M., Roberts, A., Ullrich, S., Moran, P., Bebbington, P., ... Singleton, N. (2006). Violence and psychiatric morbidity in the national household population of Britain: Public health implications. *British Journal of Psychiatry, 189*, 12–19.

Coid, J., Yang, M., Tyrer, P., Roberts, A., & Ullrich, S. (2006). Prevalence and correlates of personality disorder in Great Britain. *British Journal of Psychiatry, 188*, 423–431.

Compton, W. M., Conway, K. P., Stinson, F. S., Colliver, J. D., & Grant, B. F. (2005). Prevalence, correlates, and comorbidity of DSM-IV antisocial personality syndromes and specific drug use disorders in the United States: Results from the National Epidemiologic Survey on Alcohol and Related Conditions. *Journal of Clinical Psychiatry, 66*, 677–685.

Copeland-Linder, N., Johnson, S. B., Haynie, D. L., Chung, S., & Cheng, T. L. (2011). Retaliatory attitudes and violent behaviors among assault-injured youth. *Journal of Adolescent Health*. doi:10.1016/j.jadohealth.2011.04.005.

Denno, D. (2003). Who is Andrea Yates? A short story about insanity. *Duke Journal of Gender Law and Policy, 10*, 61–75.

Dobson, V., & Sales, B. (2000). The science of infanticide and mental illness. *Psychology, Public Policy, and Law, 6*, 1098–1112.

Doerfler, L. A., Connor, D. F., & Toscano, P. F., Jr. (2011). Aggression, ADHD symptoms, and dysphoria in children and adolescents diagnosed with bipolar disorder and ADHD. *Journal of Affective Disorders, 131*, 312–319.

Douglas, K. S., Guy, L. S., & Hart, S. D. (2009). Psychosis as a risk factor for violence to others: A meta-analysis. (2009). *Psychological Bulletin, 135*, 679–706.

Edens, J. F., Campbell, J. S., & Weir, J. M. (2007). Youth psychopathy and criminal recidivism: A meta-analysis of the Psychopathy Checklist measures. *Law and Human Behavior, 31*, 53–75.

Elbogen, E. B., & Johnson, S. C. (2009).The intricate link between violence and mental disorder: Results from the national epidemiological survey on alcohol and related conditions. *Archives of General Psychiatry, 66*, 152–161.

Epstein J., Barker, P., Vorburger, M., & Murtha, C. (2004). *Serious mental illness and its co-occurrence with substance use disorders, 2002 (DHHS Publication No. SMA 04-3905, Analytic Series A-24)*. Rockville, MD: Substance Abuse and Mental Health Services Administration, Office of Applied Studies.

Farrington, D. P. (1998). Predictors, causes, and correlates of male youth violence. In M. Tonry & M. H. Moore (Eds.), *Youth violence* (Vol. 7, pp. 421–475). Chicago: University of Chicago Press.

Farrington, D. P. (2006). Family background and psychopathy. In C. Patrick (Ed.), *Handbook of psychopathy* (pp. 229–250). New York: Guilford Press.

Farrington, D. P., & Loeber R. (2000). Epidemiology of youth violence. *Child and Adolescent Psychiatric Clinics of North America, 9*, 733–748.

Fazel, S., Buxrud, P., Ruchkin, V., & Grann, M. (2010). Homicide in discharged patients with schizophrenia and other psychoses: A national case study. *Schizophrenia Research, 123*, 263–269.

Frodi, A., Macaulay, J., & Thome, P. (1977). Are women always less aggressive than men? A review of the experimental literature. *Psychological Bulletin, 84*, 635–657.

Gesalman, A. B. (2002). Signs of a family feud: The trial of Andrea Yates tests the insanity defense as relatives try to cope with an "unspeakable" crime. *Newsweek*, January 21.

Glover, V., & Kammerer, M. (2004). The biology and pathophysiology of peripartum psychiatric disorders. *Primary Psychiatry, 11*, 37–41.

Gold, L. H. (2001). Clinical and forensic aspects of postpartum disorders. *Journal of the American Academy of Psychiatry and the Law, 29*, 344–347.

Green, B., Schramm, T. M., Chiu, K., McVie, N., & Hay, S. (2009). Violence severity and psychosis. *The International Journal of Forensic Mental Health, 8*, 33–40.

Gretton, H. M., Hare, R. D., & Catchpole, R. E. (2004). Psychopathy and offending from adolescence to adulthood: A ten-year follow-up. *Journal of Clinical and Consulting Psychology, 72*, 636–645.

Hare, R. D. (1980). A research scale for the assessment of psychopathy in criminal populations. *Personality and Individual Differences, 1*, 111–120.

Hare, R. D. (1991). *The Hare Psychopathy Checklist–Revised*. Toronto, Ontario, Canada: Multi-Health Systems.

Hare, R. D. (1993). *Without conscience: The disturbing world of the psychopaths among us*. New York: Guilford Press.

Hare, R. D. (2003). *The Hare Psychopathy Checklist–Revised* (2nd ed.). Toronto, Ontario, Canada: Multi-Health Systems.

Harris, A., & Lurigio, A. J. (2007). Mental illness and violence. A brief review of research and assessment strategies. *Aggression and Violent Behavior, 12*, 542–551.

Harris, G. T., Rice, M. E., & Cormier, C. A. (1991). Psychopathy and violent recidivism. *Law and Human Behavior, 15*, 625–637.

Hart, S. D., & Hare, R. D. (1998). Psychopathy: Assessment and association with criminal conduct. In D. M. Stoff, J. Brieling, & J. Maser (Eds.), *Handbook of antisocial behavior* (pp. 22–35). New York: John Wiley & Sons.

Hatters-Friedman, S., & Resnick, P. J. (2007). Child murder by mothers: Patterns and prevention. *World Psychiatry, 6*, 137–141.

Hawkins, J. D., Herrenkohl, T. I., Farrington, D. P., Brewer, D., Catalano, R. F., Harachi, T. W., & Cothern, L. (2000). Predictors of youth violence. *Juvenile Justice Bulletin, Office of Juvenile Justice and Delinquency Prevention*, 1–11.

Hiscoke, U. L., Langstrom, N., Ottosson, H., & Grann, M. (2003). Self-reported personality traits and disorders (DSM-IV) and risk of criminal recidivism: A prospective study. *Journal of Personality Disorders, 17*, 293–305.

Hodgins, S., & Cote, G. (1993). The criminality of mentally disordered offenders. *Criminal Justice and Behavior, 20*, 115–129.

Hornick, J. P., Paetsch, J. J., & Bertrand, L. D. (2002). *A manual on conducting economic analysis of crime prevention programs*. Ottawa: Canadian National Crime Prevention Centre.

Huang Y, Kotov, R., de Girolamo, G., Preti, A., Angermeyer, M., Benjet, C., . . . Kessler, R. C. (2009). DSM–IV personality disorders in the WHO World Mental Health Surveys. *British Journal of Psychiatry; 195*, 46–53.

Jackson, R. L., & Richards, D. T. (2007). Evaluation for civil commitment of sex offenders: A survey of experts. *Sexual Abuse, 19*, 425–448.

Johnson, J., Cohen, P., Smailes, E., Kasen, S., Oldham, J. M., Skodal, A. E., & Brook, J. S. (2000). Adolescent personality disorders associated with violence and criminal behavior during adolescence and early adulthood. *American Journal of Psychiatry, 157*, 1406–1412.

Jones, N. T., Sheitman, B., Edwards, D., Jr., Carbone, J., Hazelrigg, M., & Barrick, A. L. (2011). Psychiatric and criminal histories of persons referred for pretrial evaluations: Description and policy implications. *Journal of Forensic Psychiatry and Psychology, 22*, 99–109.

Junginger, J. (1995). Command hallucinations and the prediction of dangerousness. *Psychiatric Services, 46*, 911–914.

Kessler, R. C., Berglund, P., Demler, O., Jin, R., Merikangas, K. R., & Walters, E. E. (2005). Lifetime prevalence and age-of-onset distributions of DSM-IV disorders in the National Comorbidity Survey Replication. *Archives of General Psychiatry, 62*, 593–602.

Kessler, R. C., Chiu, W. T., Demler, O., & Walters, E. E. (2005). Prevalence, severity, and comorbidity of 12-month DSM-IV disorders in the National Comorbidity Survey Replication. *Archives of General Psychiatry, 62*, 617–627.

Krakowski, M. (2005). Schizophrenia with aggressive and violent behaviors. *Psychiatric Annals, 35*, 45–49.

Krakowski, M., Volavka, J., & Brizer, D. (1986). Psychopathy and violence: A review of literature. *Comprehensive Psychiatry, 27*, 131–148.

Krug, E. G., Dahlberg, L. L., Mercy, J. A., Zwi, A. B., & Lozano, R. (Eds.). (2002). *World Report on Violence and Health.* Geneva: World Health Organization.

Lamb, H. M., Weinberger, L. E., Marsh, J. S., & Gross, B. H. (2007). Treatment prospects for persons with severe mental illness in an urban county jail. *Psychiatric Services, 58*, 782–786.

Large, M. M., & Nielssen, O. (2011). Violence in first-episode psychosis: A systematic review and meta-analysis. *Schizophrenia Research, 125*, 209–220.

Lenzenweger, M. F., Lane, M. C., Loranger, A. W., & Kessler, R. C. (2007). DSM-IV personality disorders in the National Comorbidity Survey Replication. *Biological Psychiatry, 62*, 553–564.

Listwan, S. J., Van Voorhis, P., & Ritchey, N. P. (2007). Personality, criminal behavior, and risk assessment: Implications for theory and practice. *Criminal Justice and Behavior, 34*, 60–75.

Loeber, R., & Farrington, D. P. (2011). *Young homicide offenders and victims: Risk factors, prediction, and prevention from childhood.* New York: Springer.

Logan, C., & Blackburn, R. (2009). Mental disorder in violent women in secure settings: Potential relevance to risk for future violence. *International Journal of Law and Psychiatry, 32*, 31–38.

Lynam, D. R., Caspi, A., Moffitt, T. E., Loeber, R., & Stouthamer-Loeber, M. (2007). Longitudinal evidence that psychopathy scores in early adolescence predict adult psychopathy. *Journal of Abnormal Psychology, 116*, 155–165.

Manchester, J. (2003). Beyond accommodation: Reconstructing the insanity defense to provide an adequate remedy for postpartum psychotic women. *Journal of Criminal Law and Criminology, 93*, 713–752.

Markowitz, F. E. (2011). Mental illness, crime, and violence: Risk, context, and social control. *Aggression and Violent Behavior, 16*, 36–44.

Matejkowski, J. C., Cullen, S. W., & Solomon, P. L. (2008). Characteristics of persons with severe mental illness who have been incarcerated for murder. *Journal of the American Academy of Psychiatry and the Law, 36*, 74–86.

McNiel, D. E., Eisner, J. P., & Binder, R. L. (2000). The relationship between command hallucinations and violence. *Psychiatric Services, 51*, 1288–1292.

Merikangas, K. R., He, J., Burstein, M., Swanson, S. A., Avenevoli, S., Cui, L., . . . Swendsen, J. (2010). Lifetime prevalence of mental disorders in U.S. adolescents: Results from the National Comorbidity Study-Adolescent Supplement (NCS-A). *Journal of the American Academy of Child and Adolescent Psychiatry, 49*, 980–989.

Monahan, J., Steadman, H., Silver, E., Appelbaum, P., Robbins, P., Mulvey, E., . . . Banks, S. (2001). *Rethinking risk assessment: The MacArthur study of mental disorder and violence*. New York: Oxford University Press.

Muñoz, L. C., & Frick, P. J. (2007). The reliability, stability, and predictive utility of the self-report version of the Antisocial Process Screening Device. *Scandinavian Journal of Psychology, 48*, 299–312.

National Institute of Mental Health. (2008). Prevalence of serious mental illness among U.S. adults by age, sex, and race. Retrieved from http://nimh.nih.gov/statistics/SMI_AASR.shtml.

Nestor, P. G., Haycock, J., Doiron, S., Kelly, J., & Kelly, D. (1995). Lethal violence and psychosis: A clinical profile. *Bulletin of the American Academy of Psychiatry and the Law, 23*, 331–341.

Neumann, C. S., & Hare, R. D. (2008). Psychopathic traits in a large community sample: Links to violence, alcohol use, and intelligence. *Journal of Consulting and Clinical Psychology, 76*, 893–899.

Nordstrom, A., Dahlgren, L., & Kullgren, G. (2006). Victim relations and factors triggering homicides committed by offenders with schizophrenia. *Journal of Forensic Psychiatry and Psychology, 17*, 192–203.

Oberman, M. (2003). Mothers who kill: Cross-cultural patterns in and perspectives on contemporary maternal filicide. *International Journal of Law and Psychiatry, 26*, 493–514.

Obradovic, J., Pardini, D., Long, J. D., & Loeber, R. (2007). Measuring interpersonal callousness in boys from childhood to adolescence: An examination of longitudinal invariance and temporal stability. *Journal of Clinical Child and Adolescent Psychology, 36*, 329–337.

Putkonen, H., Weizmann-Henelius, G., Lindberg, N., Eronen, M., & Häkkänen, H. (2009). Differences between homicide and filicide offenders: Results of a nationwide register-based case-control study. *BioMed Central Psychiatry, 9*, 27. Available at: http://www.biomedcentral.com.

Rees, S., Silove, D., Chey, T., Ivancic, L., Steel, Z., Creamer, M., . . . Forbes, D. (2011). Lifetime prevalence of gender-based violence in women and the relationship with mental disorders and psychosocial function. *Journal of the American Medical Association, 306*, 513–521.

Rice, M. E., & Harris, G. T. (1997). The treatment of mentally disordered offenders. *Psychology, Public Policy, and the Law, 3*, 126–183.

Roberts, A. D., & Coid, J. W. (2009). Personality disorder and offending behaviour: Findings from the national survey of male prisoners in England and Wales. *Journal of Forensic Psychiatry and Psychology, 21*, 221–237.

Rotter, M., Way, B., Steinbacher, M., Sawyer, D., & Smith, H. (2002). Personality disorders in prison: Aren't they all antisocial? *Psychiatric Quarterly, 73*, 337–349.

Sadoff, R. L. (1995). Mothers who kill their children. *Psychiatric Annals, 25*, 601–605.

Salloum, I. M., Cornelius, J. R., Mezzich, J. E., & Kirisci, L. (2002). Impact of concurrent alcohol misuse on symptom presentation of acute mania at initial evaluation. *Bipolar Disorders, 4*, 418–421.

Schwartz, R. C., Reynolds, C. A., Austin, J. F., & Petersen, S. (2003). Homicidality in schizophrenia: A replication study. *American Journal of Orthopsychiatry, 73*, 74–77.

Schwartz, R. C., Wendling, H. M., & Guthrie, H. K. (2005). Examining anxiety as a predictor of homicidality: A pilot study. *Journal of Interpersonal Violence, 20*, 848–854

Scott, F. (1973). Parents who kill their children. *British Journal of Psychiatry, 13*, 120–126.

Serin, R. C., Peters, R. DeV., & Barbaree, H. E. (1990). Predictors of psychopathy and release outcomes in a criminal population. *Psychological Assessment: A Journal of Consulting and Clinical Psychology, 2*, 419–422.

Serper, M. R., Goldberg, B. R., Herman, K. G., Richarme, D., Chou, J., Dill, C. A., & Cancro, R. (2005). Predictors of aggression on the psychiatric inpatient service. *Comprehensive Psychiatry, 46*, 121–127.

Shipley, S. L. (2012). Perpetrators and victims: maternal filicide and mental illness. In R. Muraskin (Ed.), *It's a Crime: Women and Justice* (5th ed.). Upper Saddle River, NJ: Prentice Hall.

Shipley, S. L., & Arrigo, B. A. (2001). The confusion over psychopathy (II): Implications for forensic (correctional) practice. *International Journal of Offender Therapy and Comparative Criminology, 45*, 407–420.

Shipley, S. L., & Arrigo, B. A. (2004). *The female homicide offender: Serial murder and the case of Aileen Wuornos*. Upper Saddle River, NJ: Pearson Education, Inc.

Spidel, A., Lecomte, T., Greaves, C., Sahlstrom, K., & Yuille, J. C. (2010). Early psychosis and aggression: Predictors and prevalence of violent behaviour amongst individuals with early onset psychosis. *International Journal of Law and Psychiatry, 33*, 171–176.

Spinelli, M. G. (2004). Maternal infanticide associated with mental illness: Prevention and the promise of saved lives. *American Journal of Psychiatry, 161*, 1548–1557.

Stanton, J., & Simpson, A. (2002). Filicide: A review. *International Journal of Law and Psychiatry, 25*, 1–4.

Stanton, J., Simpson, A., & Wouldes, T. (2000). A qualitative study of filicide by mentally ill mothers. *Child Abuse and Neglect, 24*, 1451–1460.

Steadman, H. J., Mulvey, E. P., Monahan, J., Robbins, P. C., Appelbaum, P. S., Grisso, T., . . . Silver, E. (1998). Violence by people discharged from acute psychiatric inpatient facilities and by other in the same neighborhoods. *Archives of General Psychiatry, 55*, 393–401.

Steinert, T. (2002). Prediction of inpatient violence. *Acta Psychiatrica Scandinavica, 412*(suppl), 133–141.

Stompe, T., Ortwein-Swoboda, G., & Schanda, H. (2004). Schizophrenia, delusional symptoms, and violence: The threat/control-override concept reexamined. *Schizophrenia Bulletin, 30*, 31–44.

Substance Abuse and Mental Health Services Administration. (2010). Results from the 2009 National Survey on Drug Use and Health: Mental Health Findings (Office of Applied Studies, NSDUH Series H-39, HHS Publication No. SMA 10-4609). Rockville, MD: Author.

Substance Abuse and Mental Health Services Administration. (2011). Results from the 2010 National Survey on Drug Use and Health: Summary of National Findings, NSDUH Series H-41, HHS Publication No. (SMA) 11-4658. Rockville, MD: Author.

Swanson, J., Borum, R., Swartz, M., & Hiday, V. (1999). Violent behavior preceding hospitalization among persons with severe mental illness. *Law and Human Behavior, 23*, 185–204.

Swanson, J. W., Swartz, M. S., Van Dorn, R. A., Elbogen, E. B., Wagner, H. R., Rosenheck, R. A., . . . Lieberman, J. A. (2006). A national study of violent behavior in persons with schizophrenia. *Archives of General Psychiatry, 63*, 490–499.

Swartz, M. S., Swanson, J. W., Hiday, V. A., Borum, R., Wagner, H. R., & Burns, B. J. (1998). Violence and serious mental illness: The effects of substance abuse and non-adherence to medication. *American Journal of Psychiatry, 155*, 226–231.

Tardiff, K., Murzak, P., Leon, A., & Portera, L. (1997). A prospective study of violence by psychiatric patients after hospital discharge. *Psychiatric Services, 48*, 678–681.

Taylor, P. J. (1995). Schizophrenia and the risk of violence. In S. R. Hirsch & D. R. Weinberger (Eds.), *Schizophrenia* (pp. 163–183). Oxford, UK: Blackwell Science.

Torgersen, S, Kringlen, E, & Cramer, V. (2001). The prevalence of personality disorders in a community sample. *Archives of General Psychiatry, 58*, 590–596.

Torrey E. F., Kennard, A. D., Eslinger, D., Lamb, R., & Pavle, L. (2010). *More mentally ill persons are in jails and prisons than hospitals: A survey of the states.* Arlington, VA. Treatment Advocacy Center.

U.S. Census Bureau (2012). Murder victims by age, sex, and race: 2008. Retrieved from http://www.census.gov/compendia/statab/2012/tables/12s0311.pdf.

Walsh, E., Gilvarry, C., Samele, C., Harvey, K., Manley, C., Creed, F., . . . Fahy, T. (2001). Reducing violence in severe mental illness: Randomised controlled trial of intensive case management compared with standard care. *BMJ, 323*, 1093–1096.

Walters, G. D. (2003a). Predicting criminal justice outcomes with the Psychopathy Checklist and Lifestyle Criminality Screening Form: A meta-analytic comparison. *Behavioral Sciences and the Law, 21*, 89–102.

Walters, G. D. (2003b). Predicting institutional adjustment and recidivism with the Psychopathy Checklist factor scores: A meta-analysis. *Law and Human Behavior, 27*, 541–558.

Wang, P. S., Demler, O., & Kessler, R. C. (2002). Adequacy of treatment for serious mental illness in the United States. *American Journal of Public Health, 92*, 92–98.

Warren, J. I., Burnette, M., South, S., Chauhan, P., Bale, R., & Friend, R. (2002). Personality disorder and violence among female prison inmates. *Journal of American Academy of Psychiatry and Law, 30*, 502–509.

Warren, J. I., Hurt, S., Loper, A. B., Bale, R., Friend, R., & Chauhan, P. (2002). Psychiatric symptoms, history of victimization, and violent behavior in incarcerated female felons: An American perspective. *International Journal of Law and Psychiatry, 25*, 129–149.

Waters, H., Hyder, A., Rajkotia, Y., Basu, S., Rehwinkel, J. A., & Butchart, A. (2004). *The economic dimensions of interpersonal violence.* Geneva: Department of Injuries and Violence Prevention, World Health Organization.

Weizmann-Henelius, G., Grönroos, M., Putkonen, H., Eronen, M., Lindberg, N., & Häkkänen-Nyholm, H. (2010). Psychopathy and gender-based differences in childhood psychosocial characteristics in homicide offenders—a nationwide register-based study. *Journal of Forensic Psychiatry and Psychology, 21*, 801–814.

Weizmann-Henelius, G., Putkonen, H., Naukkarinen, H., & Eronen, M. (2009). Intoxication and violent women. *Archives of Women's Mental Health, 12*, 15–25.

Yee, N. Y., Large, M. M., Kemp, R. I., & Nielssen, O. B. (2011). Severe non-lethal violence during psychotic illness. *Australian and New Zealand Journal of Psychiatry, 45*, 466–472.

SECTION II

Crime Types

CHAPTER FOUR

Prevalence, Risk Factors, and Forms of Violent Offending

Astrid Rossegger, Andreas Mokros, Juliane Gerth, and Jérôme Endrass

Introduction

In 2006, the World Health Organization (WHO; World Health Organization, 1996) defined violence as "the intentional use of physical force or power, threatened or actual, against oneself, another person, or against a group or community, that either results in or has a high likelihood of resulting in injury, death, psychological harm, maldevelopment or deprivation." Thus, a wide range of harmful behavior is subsumed under the term "violence," which extends all the way from self-harming or suicidal behavior to physical violence between individuals, and includes, on the far end of the continuum, collective violence such as war or genocide. As we see, the definition by the WHO includes legal forms of violence (use of force), such as suicide or the use of force by the state (police, military), as well as illegal forms of violence such as assault, murder, and war crimes.

In this chapter, we will focus on violent offenses that include any form of violent behavior and use of force that violates the law. There is no international consensus on the definition of violence, nor is there any global consensus regarding which index should be used for obtaining the best estimation of true crime rates. Usually, this notion encompasses the concept of violence in the form of murder, attempted murder, manslaughter, assault, or robbery. Sexual violence is also often subsumed under the heading of "violent offenses," which include rape, sexual assault, and child sexual abuse. Threats, blackmail, and coercion are special forms of violence, insofar as harm (physical or other) is threatened, but not carried out.

There is an abundance of national and international statistics on the prevalence of violence, such as "Eurostat" (Tavares & Thomas, 2010), the *European Sourcebook of Crime and Criminal Justice Statistics* (Aebi et al., 2010), the Bureau of Justice Statistics of the U.S. Department of Justice (Federal Bureau of Investigation, 2008), and the *International Statistics on Crime and Justice* (European Institute for Crime Prevention and Control, 2010). On the basis of police records, these reports provide rates for a wide range of offense types. Prosecution and conviction statistics are also displayed, but are less detailed across different countries and offense categories.

Unsurprisingly, rates decrease and demonstrate a funnel-shaped regression when comparing the numbers of police statistics to prosecution statistics, and finally, to conviction statistics. For example, in 2006, only one out of two offenses that were registered by the police was prosecuted in Austria, leading to a conviction rate of 7%. In Germany only 12% of the offenses recorded by the police were prosecuted, but given the high success rate of the prosecution, the conviction rate was in the end 9%, even slightly higher than in Austria (European Institute for Crime Prevention and Control, 2010).

The question of which type of statistical data could possibly be the best proxy for true crime rates is subject to current scientific discourse: conviction statistics are the most restrictive, as they only cover offenses that finally led to a conviction. The advantage of conviction statistics is that in constitutional states, it can be assumed that persons convicted of a violent crime are actually guilty of having committed that crime. The disadvantage of this statistic is that data may be distorted in one direction only, namely underestimation. Not all offenses are reported, and *if* they are, there is not always enough evidence to be able to convict the offender, especially since for most constitutional states, the caveat "*in dubio pro reo*" applies (Quinsey, Harris, Rice, & Cormier, 2006). Furthermore, it has been shown that an offender's race, gender, and age frequently have an influence upon final sentencing, and, hence, upon conviction rates. For example, rates from prosecution to conviction records decrease more strongly in female offender populations than in male ones (European Institute for Crime Prevention and Control, 2010). On the other hand, police statistics—which include all offenses that have been reported to and registered by the police—might lead to an overestimation of prevalence rates, especially prevalence rates of more severe violent offenses, because police and prosecution tend to bring charges for more severe offenses first, and settle for "less" later on in the judicial process (Ostendorf). For England and Wales, for example, Richards was able to show that approximately 15% of cases registered as homicide (murder, manslaughter, and infanticide) by the police were being reclassified in the course of the judicial process (Richards, 1999). For these reasons, experts argue for the use of prosecution statistics when estimating multivariable models for violent offending (Quinsey et al., 2006). International comparisons can be carried out only if data sources are homogeneous (e.g., police-registered offenses).

Even while utilizing the same basis of reference (here namely, police records), any comparison of the incidence and prevalence rates will be strongly affected by differences in penal law across countries as well as by political and sociocultural factors related to the respective countries studied (European Institute for Crime Prevention and Control, 2010). Differences in the definition of elements of crime, of criminal proceedings, and of reporting of crime may contribute to at least a partial incommensurability of police-record-based statistics: In Europe, countries such as Moldavia, Russia, and Slovakia do not record coerced sexual intercourse as a sexual offense if the victim was married to the perpetrator. In Switzerland, only male-female vaginal penetration is recorded as rape, whereas non-vaginal coerced sexual intercourse is recorded as "sexual coercion"; while in Germany, rape subsumes sexual assault as well. Countries such as Austria, the Netherlands, and Sweden keep "slapping and punching" as part of the definition of a violent assault, while Latvia and the Czech Republic do not record it (Aebi et al., 2010). Aside from the heterogeneity of offense categorization, the age threshold for criminal responsibility varies considerably: In Portugal, minors reach this level when they are 16 years of age; in Switzerland and the United States (under federal law), the threshold is set at 10 years of age, which is remarkably lower than in Portugal. The implications of this threshold are that while in the United States and Switzerland, crimes committed by pubescent boys and girls are likely to be recorded as offenses, in Portugal they will not appear in their national registry. Furthermore, there is a difference in dealing with multiple offenses (e.g., a robbery including the use of an illegal weapon). While Ireland, for example, counts multiple offenses as one offense; in Swedish statistics, they are represented as two or more offenses (Aebi et al., 2010). These peculiarities are reinforced by other factors, such as the tendency to report a violent incident to law enforcement, as well as to victim support and witness protection entities. All these factors have an effect on the prevalence rates of violence, and if there is no possibility to at least partially control for them, any attempt to compare international prevalence rates of violence will be biased and may lead to absurd results, as can be shown in the following example:

According to the *International Statistics on Crime and Justice* report of the European Institute for crime prevention and control (2010), Pakistan was listed as the country with the lowest rate of assault for the year 2006, whereas in the same year, Scotland had the highest figure. Assaults occurred roughly 17,000 times more often in Scotland than in Pakistan, a country confronted with civil war and terrorism. It is very likely that this ratio does not represent the true rates of violence in these countries. This example shows that international comparisons only make sense if there is a basis for commensurability, such as comparable moral values, comparable level of development, democracy, and constitutional legality.

Moreover, the prevalence of violent offenses, based on police statistics, can be compared across different countries only if numbers of incidences are calculated per capita. Typically, prevalence rates are expressed per 100,000 population, and offenses that are commonly categorized as violence offenses are namely homicide, assault, rape, and robbery.

Pointing out trends over time, while stating differences or similarities on that measure, is the most appropriate method, assuming that regulations and legal definitions of offenses remain stable within the same systems over an extended period of time (Aebi et al., 2010). One way to overcome the aforementioned methodological difficulties could be the use of victim surveys. There is evidence that victim surveys lead to a reliable estimate of violence prevalence (Killias, Kuhn, & Aebi, 2011). The limitation of this approach is that there is currently no international consensus as to which instrument should be used, and hence, no data is available yet.

The United States, Japan, England and Wales, Germany, and Switzerland

In the following section, crime trends will be presented for the United States, Japan, England and Wales, Germany, and Switzerland. These countries are estimated to be suitable for an international trend comparison, since it is assumed that political and economic status and standards of civilization are comparable.

Data published by Eurostat in 2010 regarding homicide and violence against others (1997–2008) were used for this comparison (Tavares & Thomas, 2010). It is assumed that the heterogeneity of the definition of homicide is rather limited across developed constitutional countries, and is therefore suitable for the purpose of prevalence rate comparison.

Table 4.1 Trends in Homicidal Violence

	Percental change in homicide rates (reference = 0 in 1997)[a]					
	1998	2000	2002	2004	2006	2008
USA	−7% (16,974)	−15% (15,586)	−11% (16,229)	−11% (16,148)	−6% (17,030)	−11% (16,272)
Japan	+8% (1,388)	+9% (1,391)	+9% (1,396)	+12% (1,419)	+4% (1,309)	— —
England & Wales	+2% (750)	+15% (850)	+37% (1,047)	+19% (868)	+6% (758)	−6% (662)
Germany	−17% (975)	−19% (960)	−23% (914)	−35% (809)	−45% (727)	−55% (656)
Switzerland	−14% (76)	−18% (69)	+7% (86)	0% (79)	−26% (60)	−35% (54)

Notes: Data is retrieved from Eurostat statistics (Tavares & Thomas, 2010). No data available for Japan for the years 2007 and 2008.

"Intentional killing of a person, including murder, manslaughter, euthanasia and infanticide" are all forms of violence that are considered by Eurostat to constitute homicide. Additionally, Eurostat lists the prevalence rates of "violence against a person (such as physical assault)," "robbery," and "sexual offenses (including rape and sexual assault)" (Tavares & Thomas, 2010).

When comparing data for homicide und nonlethal violent offenses (shown in Tables 4.1 and 4.2, it becomes obvious that the two trends develop inversely. While homicide rates generally decrease especially in Germany and Switzerland (-55% and -35%, respectively—calculated on the basis of absolute numbers), the rates of physical, nonlethal violence increased considerably. An exception to this trend is the United States, where a decrease not only in homicidal violence, but also in nonlethal violence has been observed over the past decade (-11% and -16%, respectively—calculated on the basis of absolute numbers). Japan, on the other hand, shows a slight increase in homicide rates as well as nonlethal violence of 4% and 73%, respectively.

There is a lively debate on the reasons for this inverse development. All attempts so far have only offered explanations limited to specific countries (e.g., the decrease of the birth rate or the high incarceration rate in the United States). Factors such as demographic changes can be observed in all of the countries mentioned above and thus cannot be used to explain the different developments (cf. Killias et al., 2011). Studies, which

Table 4.2 Trends in Nonlethal Violence

	Percental change in nonlethal violent rates (reference = 0 in 1997)[a]					
	1998	2000	2002	2004	2006	2008
USA	−6%	−13%	−13%	−18%	−14%	−16%
	(1,533,887)	(1,425,486)	(1,423,677)	(1,360,088)	(1,418,043)	(1,382,082)
Japan	+3%	+55%	+73%	+73%	—	—
	(41,751)	(64,418)	(76,573)	(76,616)	—	—
England & Wales	+75%	+95%	+131%	+148%	+149%	+134%
	(605,797)	(733,387)	(1,014,239)	(1,201,967)	(1,205,065)	(1,034,972)
Germany	0%	0%	+6%	+13%	+15%	+13%
	(181,306)	(187,103)	(197,492)	(211,172)	(215,471)	(210,885)
Switzerland	+7%	+9%	+23%	+50%	+57%	+56%
	(8,015)	(8,152)	(9,265)	(11,917)	(12,784)	(12,560)

Notes: Data is retrieved from Eurostat statistics (Tavares & Thomas, 2010) . No data available for Japan for the years 2006, 2007, and 2008
[a]Numbers in parentheses indicate absolute numbers of cases of nonlethal violence.

concentrate on comparing trends of different offenses within a country, are more informative and useful to understand these developments. Better medical treatment and the decrease of lethality of violence following from that can be used, for example, to explain the seeming paradox of decrease in homicide and concurrent increase in nonlethal violence (Harris, Thomas, Fisher, & Hirsch, 2002).

Offense and Offender Characteristics

In the following section, characteristics of violent offenders in general, as well as characteristics of specific offender subgroups, are discussed.

Motivational Background of Violent Offenses

Half a century ago, Feshbach (1964) suggested the classification of violence in terms of motivation, while distinguishing among instrumental, expressive, and hostile types of aggression. According to Feshbach (1964), the term *instrumental* aggression covers the use of violence as a means to achieve some gain. *Expressive* violence, in contrast, serves as a response to provocation, threat, or fear. *Hostile* aggression, finally, specifically aims toward causing harm. On the basis of the motivational approach put forward by Feshbach (1964), Woodworth & Porter (2002) proposed a dichotomous distinction between instrumental and reactive violence—an approach that proved to be helpful in forensic psychology. Reactive violence matches expressive forms of violence as generally unpremeditated, impulsive responses to threat. Instrumental violence, in contrast, is a combination of instrumental and hostile forms of aggression in which violence is a goal-oriented and intentional causing of damage.

Offense Characteristics

There is one robust characteristic of violent offending that is not affected by different cultural backgrounds, societal factors, or economic development, namely the fact that in the vast majority of severe violence, the perpetrators knew their victims. The U.S. Bureau of Justice published data of more than 33 million nonfatal violent crimes and approximately 80,000 murders that were committed in the United States between 1998 and 2002 (Durose et al., 2005). These data show that in more than half (54%) of all violent crimes (nonfatal and fatal) the victim was known to the offender; and in more than 1 out of 10 violent crimes (11%), violence was committed against a family member (spouse, child, other family member). Data from Europe corroborate the U.S. data: In a representative study of more than 400 violent and sex offenders from Switzerland, 66% of the victims were known to the perpetrator prior to the index offense (Endrass, Rossegger, & Urbaniok, 2007). When analyzing the epidemiological data on homicides, it becomes more evident that severe violence is mostly targeted toward at least somewhat familiar subjects, since only 0.1% of homicidal assaults were directed against complete strangers (Durose et al., 2005).

For perpetrators with major mental health disorders it is even more likely that they knew their victims before the offense: Taylor (1993) showed that when schizophrenic patients display violent behavior, family members, especially mothers, are the most likely targets for violence, which is typically perpetrated in a domestic setting (Estroff, Swanson, Lachicotte, Swartz, & Bolduc, 1998; Steadman et al., 1998).

Only a relatively small proportion of violent incidents are characterized by weapon use. Unsurprisingly, the prevalence of weapon use is higher among fatal violent offenses. The Data from the U.S. Bureau of Justice shows that weapons (guns, knives, sharp and blunt objects) were used in 25% of all nonfatal cases, while 64% of all the fatal offenses involved a firearm (handgun, rifle, shotgun, other), 17% a knife, 6% a blunt object (baseball bat, rock), and in 4% of the cases, by other means (fire/incendiary, narcotics, asphyxiation, other [Durose et al., 2005]). These data from the United States can easily be compared to data from Switzerland—a country with comparable gun legislation. When comparing the data of the OECD countries, there are similarities in weapon use with nonfatal assaults, but substantial differences when compared to fatal violence: According to the Swiss Bureau of Statistics, in 19% of all nonfatal violent offenses registered by the police in Switzerland between 2009 and 2010, a knife or similar weapon was used; in 4% of the cases, a blunt object; in 2% of the cases, a firearm; and in 11% of the cases, other means were used to commit the violent offense. In fatal offenses, 49% of the cases were committed with a knife or a similar weapon, while in only 17% of the cases, a firearm was used; in 17%, physical force; in 3%, blunt objects; and in 12%, other means were employed (Swiss Federal Statistical Office).

Domestic Violence

The prevalence of domestic violence is so high and has such severe consequences that the WHO (2005) commissioned a special report on violence and health, using the data of 35 countries. This study revealed that between 10% and 52% of women were reporting physical violence, and between 10% and 30% reporting sexual violence, from the current or a previous intimate partner. Data from this investigation also indicates that substance abuse plays an important role in violence incidences between intimate partners. In the United States, for example, among all cases of nonfatal intimate partner violence reported to the police between 2001 and 2005, alcohol or drugs were involved 42% of the time (Catalano, 2007). In Northern Ireland there is other evidence supporting the co-occurrence of substance abuse and domestic violence: According to Stevenson, Goodall, and Moore (2008), alcohol was involved in more than half of all cases of domestic violence recorded by the police.

Substance abuse is not only highly prevalent among cases of domestic violence; it is also an important risk factor for recidivism among wife assaulters. Accordingly, substance abuse is addressed in an item of the "DVRAG"—an actuarial risk assessment instrument that was designed to estimate the risk for recurrence of domestic violence (Hilton, Harris, & Rice, 2010).

While substance abuse plays an unequivocally important role in (ex-) partner violence, research has found this form of violence to be characterized by a far more complex interaction of causative and co-occurring factors. Using multivariate analyses, Holtzworth-Munroe and Meehan (2004) developed an empirical typology suggesting that domestically violent batterers form three distinct subtypes: "family only," "borderline/ dysphoric," and "generally violent/antisocial." The authors assumed that the three groups of wife assaulters could be differentiated along dimensions of psychopathology, whether they committed generalized versus partner-specific violence, and the severity and frequency of the partner violence they perpetrated. "Family only" batterers do not display symptoms of severe psychopathology, they committed the least severe partner violence of the three subtypes, and they were unlikely to generalize their violence. Contrary to the "family only" batterers, "Borderline/dysphoric" batterers show symptoms of major mental health disorders and are generally more violent and impulsive. More specifically, they are characterized by depression and anger, are likely to frequently behave violently in a domestic context, and are prone to use violence in various situations. The generally violent/antisocial batterers are characterized by general antisocial features, frequent substance abuse, the most severe partner violence, and the use of violence both against the partner and others. Holtzworth-Munroe and Meehan (2004) also delineated a different etiology for the violence perpetrated by each subtype of wife assaulters and suggested that batterer treatment would be more efficient if it were subtype-specific.

Stalans, Yarnold, Seng, Olson, and Repp (2004) applied this typology to violent offenders in general and found that the strongest predictor of violent recidivism while on probation was whether the offender was a generalized aggressor or not, whereby generalized aggressors were more likely to be arrested for new violent crimes. For generalized aggressors and "family only" batterers, treatment noncompliance was an important risk predictor of violent recidivism (Stalans et al., 2004).

In the domestic violence project of the WHO, only wife and child assault are investigated. Violence committed by female spouses upon their male partners was not surveyed. Though the authors concede that not addressing female to male violence is at least controversial, they elaborate that though the proportion of male victims of domestic violence is inconclusive, male batterers perpetrate the vast majority of severe forms of domestic violence. This is also the principal argument put forward by Hilton et al. (2010), supporting their decision to develop a risk instrument for domestic violence committed by men against their female partners/spouses. It is important to note, however, that there is an ongoing scientific controversy regarding the question of the gender proportion in domestic violence: Whereas in some official statistics, male victims are not even listed, other data claim to document that the rate of domestic violence does not differ between the genders (Archer, 2000; O'Leary, Smith Slep, & O'Leary, 2007).

Female Violent Offenders

According to several authors (Denov, 2001; Weizmann-Henelius, Viemerö, & Eronen, 2003), there is a social taboo associated with female violence, which might result in a certain reluctance to classify women offenders in a particular way. There exists substantial controversy regarding the question of whether gender influences violence. Whereas some authors claim that gender is a very poor predictor of violent behavior (Archer, 2000), others posit that gender is important not only regarding the prevalence and type, but also regarding risk factors of violent offending (Rossegger et al., 2009). Furthermore, there is an ongoing debate as to whether the causes of male offending can be generalized to describe female offending as well (Coid et al., 2003; Hollin & Palmer, 2006). Some researchers argue that gender-neutral theories would suffice to explain both female and male criminality (Loucks & Zamble, 1999; Steffensmeier & Allan, 1996). This is contrasted by the fact that female violent offenders seem to display a different offense pattern as compared to male violent offenders and that the victims of female violent offenders are often people close to them (e.g., parents, husbands, and boyfriends as well as children) as the offense tends to be the result of an interpersonal conflict (Campbell, Muncer, & Bibel, 2001; Eckhardt & Pridemore, 2009; Roe-Sepowitz, 2007; South Richardson & Hammock, 2007; Steffensmeier & Allan, 1996; Weizmann-Henelius et al., 2003; Yourstone, Lindholm, & Kristiansson, 2008). Compared to male offenders, female violent offenders are older when they offend; they are more likely to be married and to have children. Furthermore, female offenders are more likely to have been victims of physical, psychological, and sexual abuse—both in childhood and adolescence. Additionally, women who commit violent offenses are more likely to abuse substances, and to suffer from physical and mental illness (Chesney-Lind & Pasko, 2003; Forsyth, Wooddell, & Evans, 2001; Hollin & Palmer, 2006; Putkonen, Weizmann-Henelius, Lindberg, Rovamo, & Hakkanen, 2008; Rossegger et al., 2009; Steffensmeier & Broidy, 2001; Weizmann-Henelius et al., 2003). Contrary to male offenders, female violent offenders display fewer criminogenic factors: Female offenders are less likely to have prior convictions (Forsyth et al., 2001; Yourstone et al., 2008), are less likely to recidivate than male offenders (Steffensmeier & Broidy, 2001), and have lower rates of psychopathy (see the Hare Psychopathy Checklist–Revised [Hare, 2003]; Loucks & Zamble, 1999; Salekin, Rogers, & Sewell, 1997; Vitale, Smith, Brinkley, & Newman, 2002).

Risk Factors for Violent Offending

The famous experiments on the subject of obedience performed by Milgram (1963) and by Zimbardo and his colleagues (Haney, Banks, & Zimbardo, 1973) proved that anyone's tendency toward violence can be moderated by contextual factors. However, forensic psychological research seems to indicate that when it comes to violent offending, psychological traits—as opposed to situational factors—are of particular importance. This premise can be deduced from the fact that data from both self-report surveys of the general population (Budd, Sharp, & Mayhew, 2005) and from crime registry data in follow-ups of convicts (e.g., Harrendorf, 2007) indicate that, in the United States as well as in Europe, a minority of offenders is responsible for a sizable proportion of violent offenses: In the United States, in a prospective study of the 1958 birth cohort of boys born in Philadelphia, 8% were repeat offenders who were responsible for 68% of the crimes registered in the Uniform Crime Report (Tracy, Wolfgang, & Figlio, 1990). Data from a survey of 11,961 individuals aged 10 to 65 years from England and Wales indicated that among those who admitted to at least one violent offense during the last year (6% of the entire sample), one-fifth of respondents claimed responsibility for the majority of assaults and robberies (Budd et al., 2005).

To find robust risk factors for first-time violent offending, birth cohort studies with long follow-up periods are necessary; this type of research design is extremely time and cost-intensive. However, the biggest problem of longitudinal study samples from the general population is the low base rate of violent offending: Arseneault, Moffitt, Caspi, Taylor, and Silva (2000) studied 961 young adults who constituted 94% of a total-city birth cohort in New Zealand from 1972 to 1973. The prevalence rate of violent offenses (at least one court conviction) was only 4%. A Swiss longitudinal prospective study examined a subsample of a public mental health study of army conscripts (Sieber & Angst, 1981), and found that only 4% had a criminal record for an offense at the age of 19. Among those 4%, 28% have committed a violent offense (Laubacher et al., in press).

Major Mental Health Disorders

As discussed previously, it is a well-replicated finding that individuals suffering from schizophrenia display an increased risk for committing violent acts against others (e.g., Douglas, Guy, & Hart, 2009; Fazel, Gulati, Linsell, Geddes, & Grann, 2009; Hodgins, 2008; Monahan et al., 2001).

Cohort studies suggest that major mental health disorders increase the risk for violent offenses: A Swedish birth cohort study with a 30-year follow-up showed that the odds for violent offenses were four times higher for males with either schizophrenia, major affective disorders, paranoid states, or other psychoses, compared to males without any of these disorders (Hodgins, 1992; Hodgins, Mednick, Brennan, Schulsinger, & Engberg, 1996). Tiihonen, Isohanni, Räsänen, Koiranen, and Moring (1997) found that within the Finnish birth cohort, the prevalence of violent behavior in psychotic men was even higher when controlled for socioeconomic background. These results have been corroborated by various public mental health studies: Findings from a German sample of schizophrenic patients ($N = 1,705$), who were followed up for 7 to 12 years post release (Soyka, Morhart-Klute, & Schöch, 2004), demonstrated that the risk for violence (ranging from verbal threats to homicide) was increased fivefold among the schizophrenic patients compared with the population at large. Similarly, a recent U.S. study of 1,410 patients with schizophrenia found that positive symptoms of schizophrenia were associated with both minor and serious violence, even after controlling for several possible confounds and covariates (Swanson et al., 2006). Another study from the United States examining a population-based sample also found an estimate of a fivefold increase for the risk of assaults among individuals suffering from psychotic symptoms (Mojtabai, 2006). A recent meta-analysis confirmed the close association between major mental illness and violent offending (Douglas et al., 2009; Fazel et al., 2009).

Using data from offender populations, other investigations have supported the hypothesis that major mental health disorders pose a relevant risk factor for violent offending. Among violent offenders, the prevalence of major mental illness is substantially elevated as compared to the general population. Lindqvist and Allebeck (1990) investigated a sample of offenders convicted for homicide, and found that 53% suffered from an Axis I mental health disorder. Using data covering a time span of 25 years, a group of Danish researchers found that almost half of the female homicide offenders were diagnosed with a psychotic disorder (Gottlieb, Gabrielsen, & Kramp, 1987).

It is, however, important to keep in mind that offenders diagnosed with a schizophrenic disorder represent a minor fraction of violent crime in absolute terms (Walsh, Buchanan, & Fahy, 2002). Within the subgroup of schizophrenic patients, characteristics such as being male, lack of acceptance of the illness, and hostility syndrome upon hospital admission (Soyka, Graz, Bottlender, Dirschedl, & Schoech, 2007), as well as delusional perception and paranoid ideation (Mojtabai, 2006; Swanson et al., 2006) are associated with violence risk, whereas negative symptoms constitute a protective factor (Swanson et al., 2006).

Substance Abuse

Extensive research has documented a robust association between substance abuse and interpersonal violence in both men and women (Coid et al., 2006; Grann & Fazel, 2004; Hodgins, 2008; Monahan et al., 2001; Stuart, Moore, Ramsey, & Kahler, 2004). Since many studies have investigated substance abuse and major mental health disorders as predictors for violence within the same sample, a meta-analysis analyzed whether both risk factors contributed independently to the outcome (Fazel et al., 2009). These authors found that substance abuse had played a mediating role in the association of major mental illness and violent offending. The risk in patients with substance use disorders was unaffected by the presence or absence of psychotic symptoms (Fazel et al., 2009). Tiihonen et al. (1997) found that elevated risk for violence was especially correlated with alcohol-induced psychoses as well as with comorbid schizophrenia and substance use disorder.

Adverse Childhood Experiences

Both female and male violent offenders were often found to have a history of adverse childhood domestic constellations (absent and/or criminal parents, neglect), poor socioeconomic backgrounds, and previous psychiatric hospitalization, and were found to be less educated, and under- or unemployed at the time of offense (Loucks & Zamble, 1999; McCorkle, 1995; Steffensmeier & Broidy, 2001; Yourstone et al., 2008). Several studies found that adverse childhood experiences were associated with an increased risk for violent behavior and/or other antisocial behavior (Caspi et al., 2002; Nilsson et al., 2005; Reif et al., 2007). This can be exemplified by viewing the results of a Finnish cohort study, which showed that boys living in non-intact families with low parental education level displayed a higher level of (violent) criminal offenses (Sourander et al., 2006). Both severity and accumulation of adversities were positively correlated with violent behavior (Caspi et al., 2002).

Reoffending among Violent Offenders

Recidivism Rates

Recidivism is generally defined as a return to crime (Bonta, Dauvergne, & Rugge, 2003). As always, when calculating prevalence rates, the definition of the event measured as well as the source of the information is crucial. When assessing prevalence rates of crime recidivism, one needs to decide which indices to use, namely new arrests statistics (often police statistics), new charges or new convictions (criminal records [Bonta et al., 2003; Quinsey et al., 2006]). Similar to the debate on the, right' index, which is used to measure violent crime, the scientific community debates which statistic is the best proxy for, true' recidivism rates. (e.g., Bonta et al., 2003 or Quinsey et al., 2006).

Bonta et al. (2003) showed that recidivism rates are substantially influenced by the source of information. The authors refer to three empirical studies that report re-conviction and re-arrest rates (Beck, 1989; Corbo, 1992; Langan & Levin, 2002). In those three studies, re-arrest rates were substantially higher: 16% (63%, versus 47% [Beck, 1989]), 24% (62% versus 38% [Corbo, 1992]), 21% (68% versus 47% [Langan & Levin, 2002]).

Risk Factors for Recidivism

Risk factors for recidivism among violent offenders differ from risk factors for first-time offenders among the general population. Bonta, Law, and Hanson (1998) identified socio-demographic characteristics as being "young age" and "single and male" as strong predictors for reoffending. Also, employment problems, substance abuse, antisocial personality disorder, and psychopathy have been identified as being related to violent recidivism (Bonta et al., 1998). A psychotic disorder, however, is a relevant risk factor for first-time offending (Douglas et al., 2009; Fazel et al., 2009; Hodgins, 2008; Monahan et al., 2001), but is also a robust protective factor for violent reoffending (Bonta et al., 1998).

The risk of recidivism can be assessed with a variety of risk-assessment instruments, which were specifically designed to evaluate repeated violent offending. Among these tools are two well-validated risk assessment instruments, which were conceptualized specifically for this purpose: the Historical, Clinical, and Risk Management Violence Risk Assessment Scheme (HCR-20 [Webster, Eaves, & Hart, 1997]) and the Violence Risk Appraisal Guide (VRAG; Quinsey et al., 2006). Apart from "general-purpose" risk-assessment instruments such as the HCR-20 and the VRAG, there are instruments that were developed to predict a specific form of violence, such as intimate partner violence (Spousal Assault Risk Assessment Guide—SARA; Kropp, Hart, Webster, & Eaves, 1995) or ODARA (Hilton et al., 2010).

The HCR-20 consists of 10 items relating to historical variables such as mental illness or employment problems, 5 items relating to current clinical status (e.g., mental illness symptoms, lack of insight), and 5 items relating to future risk variables (e.g., noncompliance, poor social network). This instrument was developed, and its items were selected, based upon forensic research findings and the opinions of forensic experts. Items are dichotomous (0/1 score for no/yes) and scoring is clinical and intuitive; there are no precise scoring rules.

The VRAG (Quinsey et al., 2006) belongs to the category of actuarial risk assessment instruments. It consists of 12 weighted items, which have precise scoring rules. The final sum scores can be assigned to one out of nine risk categories for which there are known recidivism rates from the normative sample. The items of the VRAG were selected by a purely statistical process from approximately 50 predictor variables, which, in turn, were chosen on the basis of the forensic literature and clinical data collected from more than 600 violent offenders. These data cover a variety of areas, including socio-demographic variables, childhood maladjustment, adult maladjustment, characteristics of the index offense and psychiatric disorders (personality disorder/schizophrenia). It was found, for example, that intelligence, education, use of weapons or income were not linked to violent recidivism (Quinsey et al., 2006). The categories "young age" and "broken home environment," as well as a criminal history for nonviolent offenses, a personality disorder or substance abuse, school maladjustment, failure on conditional release, and psychopathy, represent risk factors for violent recidivism. On the other hand, the categories "female victim," "severely injured" or "dead victim," "suffering from schizophrenia," and "being married" have been shown to constitute protective factors (Quinsey et al., 2006). The sum score of the Psychopathy Checklist–Revised (PCL-R; Hare, 2003) a clinical rating scale, which has been shown to have moderate- to high-effect sizes in predicting violent reoffending (Hare, Clark, Grann, & Thornton, 2000; Leistico, Salekin, DeCoster, & Rogers, 2008; Mokros, Stadtland, Osterheider, & Nedopil, 2010), contributes to the final score of the VRAG (Quinsey et al., 2006) and the HCR-20 (Webster et al., 1997). In the PCL-R, it is primarily the antisocial component of the scale (Factor 2) that is more closely linked to violent conduct (Walters, Knight, Grann, & Dahle, 2008; Yang, Wong, & Coid, 2010). Compared to non-psychopathic offenders, psychopathic offenders tend to recidivate after release faster, more frequently, and well into their 50s (Porter, Birt, & Boer, 2001). Moreover, psychopathic inmates appear to be more successful in being granted conditional release than non-psychopathic offenders (Porter, ten Brinke, & Wilson, 2009).

Risk Factors for Violent Infractions

Violent infractions during incarceration, however, are manifested in different ways from violence in the community: from potentially harmful acts (such as threats or verbal arguments) to minor assaults (such as slaps in the face or pushing someone), up to major (lethal) attacks. The prevalence of violence in the U.S. penal system is estimated to range from 21% to 36% (Cunningham, Reidy, & Sorensen, 2008; Cunningham, Sorensen, & Reidy, 2005). Numbers in Switzerland (20%–27%) seem to be comparable, with a tendency to be lower. Furthermore, violent infractions in Swiss prisons tend to be less grave; generally they do not lead to injury of the victim, while occurring at the spur of the moment, and are almost exclusively of a reactive nature (Endrass, Laubacher, Urbaniok, & Rossegger, 2008; Endrass, Rossegger, Urbaniok, Laubacher, & Vetter, 2008).

Risk factors for violent infractions during incarceration are only partially congruent with risk factors associated with reoffending. Apparently, intramural behavior is affected by other variables than extramural behavior, which is reflected by the finding that risk-assessment instruments show a poor performance in predicting violent infractions during imprisonment.

The PCL-R, for example, was not found to be useful in predicting inmates' risk of engaging in violent behavior. In merely one single study examining sexual offenders, the checklist was able to reliably distinguish between violent and nonviolent inmates (Edens, Buffington-Vollum, Colwell, Johnson, & Johnson, 2002). Other studies found either very weak (Kroner & Mills, 2001) or no associations at all (Buffington-Vollum, Edens, Johnson, & Johnson, 2002; Edens, Poythress, & Lilienfeld, 1999). Interestingly, there is evidence that the PCL-R is at least moderately correlated with the categories "verbal aggression" and "nonviolent infractions" (AUC = 0.75; Buffington-Vollum et al., 2002; Coid et al., 2003; Edens et al., 1999; Edens et al., 2002). Likewise for the VRAG, only the most moderate of relationships were found for violent infractions during incarceration (Doyle, Dolan, & McGovern, 2002; Kroner & Mills, 2001). None of these studies was conducted in a German-speaking country. However, two current inquiries from Switzerland now replicate those findings: In violent and sexual offenders currently jailed in the Zurich State Penitentiary Pöschwies, the PCL-R as well as the VRAG turned out to be little or not at all predictive for physical violence (Endrass, Rossegger, Frischknecht, Noll, & Urbaniok, 2008; Endrass, Rossegger, Urbaniok, et al., 2008).

A possible explanation for this might be that these instruments primarily assess the risk of instrumental violence—a form of violent behavior only accounting for a minor fraction of violent incidents in prisons (Endrass, Rossegger, Urbaniok, et al., 2008; Porter & Woodworth, 2006, 2007; Woodworth & Porter, 2002).

In summarizing the most robust risk factors associated with violent infractions throughout various studies (Cunningham & Reidy, 2007; Cunningham & Sorensen, 2007; Franklin, Franklin, & Pratt, 2006; Mills & Kroner, 2003), we conclude that "young age" seems to be one of the most important predictors throughout the studies. Additionally, it can be assumed that risk is further increased by characteristics such as "short duration of sentence," "previous breach of rules," and "previous sentences" (Cunningham & Sorensen, 2007). Psychopathology may also contribute to increasing risk (Cunningham & Reidy, 2007; Friedmann, Melnick, Jiang, & Hamilton, 2008; Mills & Kroner, 2003). In addition, marital status and social status have been revealed by the research to be moderately protective (Gendreau, Goggin, & Law, 1997).

Violence across the Life Span

According to the age-invariance theory by Hirschi and Gottfredson (1983), the probability of engaging in criminal activity decreases across the life span irrespective of the domain of criminal conduct. Birth cohort studies conducted in various countries over the last decades corroborate this assumption (Farrington, 1995, 2000; Haapasalo & Hamalainen, 1996; Loeber et al., 2001; Moffitt, 1993; Vermeiren, 2003). Such studies were able to show that a majority of delinquent adolescents only offend once and with an offense of low severity, while a smaller group of delinquent adolescents is responsible for a large number of offenses of different types and severity (Junger-Tas, Terlouw, & Klein, 1994; Moffitt, 1993). Due to such empirical findings, Moffitt (1993) proposed a developmental dual taxonomy, which specifies two different groups of offenders—the "adolescence-limited" and the "life-course-persistent offenders"—who differ in regard to the continuity and severity of their antisocial behavior. According to Moffitt, the antisocial behavior of the first group is limited to middle adolescence, while 5%–6% of all juvenile delinquents—the "life-course-persistent offender group"—usually begin offending in childhood or early adolescence and continue to do so throughout their lives (1993).

The concept of "life-course-persistent offenders" is supported by results of studies on adult violent offenders such as the Berlin Crime study, a German prospective study among prison inmates by Dahle and colleagues (Dahle, 1998). In this study, five offender groups with differing offending patterns over the life span are distinguished.

Thus, it has been a key concern of numerous studies to find predictors for continuity and discontinuity of delinquent behavior in young offenders. Two of the most important characteristics of continuity of delinquent behavior seem to be the number and severity of the offenses committed in youth. In a German study, the Tübinger Young Offenders Study (Mischkowitz, 1993), the number of prior convictions was found to be predictive of the continuation of antisocial behavior, while an early start or severity of delinquency was not. The research of Cottle, Lee, and Heilbrun (2001) also supported the premise that the number and type of prior offenses were predictive of continued delinquency. Among antisocial youth, the subgroup of individuals who show callous-unemotional traits seems to be at particularly high risk of continuing to act aggressively into adulthood (Frick & Viding, 2009; Salekin, 2008). Life-course-persistent or career criminals are characterized by higher levels of psychopathic traits (Vaughn & DeLisi, 2008).

Conclusion

Whether a violent incident will be classified as an offense and thus appear in official statistics depends upon numerous factors. Herein we find the explanation for the heterogeneity of results. Comparing national trends can only be recommended for those countries, which do not differ substantially with regard to criminal justice system, penal code, and methodology utilized in the recording of police statistics. The comparison of crime statistics of the United States, Japan, England, Wales, Germany, and Switzerland indicate similar trends (decrease of homicide, increase of violence against a person).

As heterogeneous as violent offenses may be, robust patterns can be detected in the research findings. In most cases, victim and perpetrator knew each other prior to the offense—this being especially true in cases of homicide and offenses perpetrated by schizophrenic persons in which victims often are family members or relationship partners. Studying offense characteristics has shown that weapons are used only in a minority of cases of violent offending.

Cohort studies are of central importance in the assessment of risk factors for violent offending. Even if not all of the risk factors have been identified, so far it has been possible to determine quite a number of such factors, which seem to have shown to be robust throughout many different studies. Risk factors that have been identified by various studies all over the world are major mental illness, substance abuse, personality disorder/psychopathy, and adverse childhood experiences. Risk factors for violent offending found in samples from the general population differ from the risk factors found in the violent offender population.

The most important risk factors for reoffending include the categories of "young age," "criminal history," and "never married," as well as mental health diagnoses of personality disorders or psychopathy, and "failure on conditional release."

The probability of engaging in criminal activity decreases across the life span. Birth cohort studies were able to show that a majority of delinquent adolescents only offend once, and with an offense of low severity, while a smaller group of delinquent adolescent is responsible for a large number of offenses of different types and severity. A developmental, dual taxonomy was proposed, which specifies two different groups of offenders—the "adolescence-limited" and the "life-course-persistent offenders."

Acknowledgments

We would like to thank Dr. Marilyn Immoos and Arja Laubacher for proofreading.

References

Aebi, M. F., Aubusson de Cavarlay, B., Barclay, G., Gruszczynska, B., Harrendorf, S., Heiskanen, M., . . . Þórisdóttir, R. (2010). *European sourcebook of crime and criminal justice statistics* (p. 285). Den Haag: Boom Juridische Uitgevers.

Archer, J. (2000). Sex differences in aggression between heterosexual partners: A meta-analytic review. *Psychological Bulletin, 126*(5), 651–680. doi:10.1037// 0033-2909.126.5.651.

Arseneault, L., Moffitt, T. E., Caspi, A., Taylor, P. J., & Silva, P. A. (2000). Mental disorders and violence in a total birth cohort: results from the Dunedin Study. *Archives of General Psychiatry, 57*(10), 979–986.

Beck, A. J. (1989). *Recidivism of prisoners releasd in 1983*. Washington DC: U.S. Department of Justice.

Bonta, J., Dauvergne, M., & Rugge, T. (2003). *The reconviction rate of federal offenders*. Public Works and Government Services Canada.

Bonta, J., Law, M., & Hanson, K. (1998). The prediction of criminal and violent recidivism among mentally disordered offenders: A meta-analysis. *Psychological Bulletin, 123*(2), 123–142.

Budd, T., Sharp, C., & Mayhew, P. (2005). *Offending in England and Wales: First results from the 2003 crime and justice survey (Home Office Research Study 275)*. London: Home Office Research, Development and Statistics Directorate.

Buffington-Vollum, J. K., Edens, J. F., Johnson, D. W., & Johnson, J. K. (2002). Psychopathy as a predictor of institutional misbehavior among sex offenders: A prospective replication. *Criminal Justice and Behavior, 29*(5), 497–511.

Campbell, A., Muncer, S., & Bibel, D. (2001). Women and crime: An evolutionary approach. *Aggression and Violent Behavior, 6*(5), 481–497.

Caspi, A., McClay, J., Moffitt, T. E., Mill, J., Martin, J., Craig, I. W., . . . Poulton, R. (2002). Role of genotype in the cycle of violence in maltreated children. *Science, 297*(5582), 851–854. doi:10.1126/science.1072290.

Catalano, S. (2007). Intimate partner violence in the United States (2007/12/19 ed.). Washington, DC: Bureau of Justice Statistics.

Chesney-Lind, M., & Pasko, L. (2003). *The female offender: Girls, women and crime* (2nd ed.). Thousand Oaks, CA: Sage.

Coid, J., Petruckevitch, A., Bebbington, P., Jenkins, R., Brugha, T., Lewis, G., . . . Singleton, N. (2003). Psychiatric morbidity in prisoners and solitary cellular confinement, I: Disciplinary segregation. *Journal of Forensic Psychiatry and Psychology, 14*(2), 298–319.

Coid, J., Yang, M., Roberts, A., Ullrich, S., Moran, P., Bebbington, P., . . . Singleton, N. (2006). Violence and psychiatric morbidity in the national household population of Britain: public health implications. *British Journal of Psychiatry, 189*, 12–19. doi:10.1192/bjp.189.1.12.

Corbo, C. A. (1992). *Release outcome—1984: A follow-up study*. Trenton, NJ: New Jersey Department of Corrections.

Cottle, C., Lee, R. J., & Heilbrun, K. (2001). The prediction of criminal recidivism in juveniles: A meta-analysis. *Criminal Justice and Behavior, 28*(3), 367–394.

Cunningham, M. D., & Reidy, T. J. (2007). Assertions of "future dangerousness" at federal capital sentencing: Rates and correlates of subsequent prison misconduct and violence. *Law and Human Behavior, 32*, 46–63.

Cunningham, M. D., Reidy, T. J., & Sorensen, J. R. (2008). Assertions of "future dangerousness" at federal capital sentencing: Rates and correlates of subsequent prison misconduct and violence. *Law and Human Behavior, 32*(1), 46–63. doi:10.1007/s10979-007-9107-7.

Cunningham, M. D., & Sorensen, J. R. (2007). Capital offenders in Texas prisons: Rates, Correlates and an actuarial analysis of violent misconduct. *Law and Human Behavior, 31*(6), 553–571.

Cunningham, M. D., Sorensen, J. R., & Reidy, T. J. (2005). An actuarial model for assessment of prison violence risk among maximum security inmates. *Assessment, 12*(1), 40–49. doi:10.1177/1073191104272815 [doi].

Dahle, K.-P. (1998). Straffälligkeit im Lebenslängsschnitt [Delinquency across the life-span]. In H.-L. Kröber & K.-P. Dahle (Eds.), *Sexualstraftaten bei Gewaltdelinquenz: Verlauf—Behandlung—Opferschutz [Sexual offenses and violent delinquency: Course—therapy—victim protection]*. Heidelberg, Germany: Kriminalistik-Verlag.

Denov, M. S. (2001). A culture of denial: Exploring professional perspectives on female sex offending. *Canadian Journal of Criminology, 43*(3), 303–329.

Douglas, K. S., Guy, L. S., & Hart, S. D. (2009). Psychosis as a risk factor for violence to others: A meta-analysis. *Psychological Bulletin, 135*(5), 679–706.

Doyle, M., Dolan, M., & McGovern, J. (2002). The validity of North American risk assessment tools in predicting in-patient violent behaviour in England. *Legal and Criminological Psychology, 7*(2), 141–154.

Durose, M. R., Wolf Harlow, C., Langan, P. A., Motivans, M., Rantala, R. R., & Smith, E. L. (2005). Family violence statistics including statistics on strangers and acquaintances (p. 76). Washington, DC: Bureau of Justice Statistics.

Eckhardt, K., & Pridemore, W. A. (2009). Differences in female and male involvement in lethal violence in Russia. *Journal of Criminal Justice, 37*(1), 55–64.

Edens, J. F., Buffington-Vollum, J. K., Colwell, K. W., Johnson, D. W., & Johnson, J. K. (2002). Psychopathy and institutional misbehavior among incarcerated sex offenders: A comparison of the Psychopathy Checklist–Revised and the Personality Assessment Inventory. *International Journal of Forensic Mental Health, 1*(1), 49–58.

Edens, J. F., Poythress, N. G., & Lilienfeld, S. O. (1999). Identifying inmates at risk for disciplinary infractions: a comparison of two measures of psychopathy. *Behavioral Sciences and the Law, 17*(4), 435–443.

Endrass, J., Laubacher, A., Urbaniok, F., & Rossegger, A. (2008). Straf- und Massnahmenvollzug. In T. Widmer & F. Strebel (Eds.), *Studie zur Stellung der muslimischen Bevölkerung im Kanton Zürich*. Zürich: Universität Zürich, Institut für Politikwissenschaft.

Endrass, J., Rossegger, A., Frischknecht, A., Noll, T., & Urbaniok, F. (2008). Using the Violence Risk Appraisal Guide (VRAG) to predict in-prison aggressive behavior in a Swiss offender population. *International Journal of Offender Therapy and Comparative Criminology, 52*(1), 81–89.

Endrass, J., Rossegger, A., & Urbaniok, F. (2007). *Zürcher Forensik-Studie*. Zürich: Psychiatric/Psychological Service.

Endrass, J., Rossegger, A., Urbaniok, F., Laubacher, A., & Vetter, S. (2008). Predicting violent infractions in a Swiss state penitentiary: A replication study of the PCL-R in a population of sex and violent offenders. *BMC Psychiatry, 8*, 74. doi:10.1186/1471-244X-8-74.

Estroff, S. E., Swanson, J. W., Lachicotte, W. S., Swartz, M., & Bolduc, M. (1998). Risk reconsidered: Targets of violence in the social networks of people with serious psychiatric disorders. *Social Psychiatry and Psychiatric Epidemiology, 33*(1), 95–101.

European Institute for Crime Prevention and Control. (2010). *International Statistics on Crime and Justice* (p. 64). United Nations Office on Drugs and Crime (UNODC).

Farrington, D. P. (1995). The twelfth Jack Tizard Memorial Lecture. The development of offending and antisocial behaviour from childhood: key findings from the Cambridge Study in Delinquent Development. *Journal of Child Psychology and Psychiatry, 36*(6), 929–964.

Farrington, D. P. (2000). Psychosocial predictors of adult antisocial personality and adult convictions. *Behavioral Sciences and the Law, 18*(5), 605–622. doi:10.1002/1099-0798(200010).

Fazel, S., Gulati, G., Linsell, L., Geddes, J. R., & Grann, M. (2009). Schizophrenia and violence: Systematic review and meta-analysis. *PLoS Medicine, 6*(8). doi:10.1371/journal.pmed.1000120.

Federal Bureau of Investigation. (2008). *Violent Crime*. U.S. Department of Justice.

Feshbach, S. (1964). The function of aggression and the regulation of aggressive drive. *Psychological Review, 71*, 257–272.

Forsyth, C. J., Wooddell, G., & Evans, R. D. (2001). Predicting symmetry in female/male crime rates. *Journal of Police and Criminal Psychology, 16*(2), 1–9.

Franklin, T. W., Franklin, C. A., & Pratt, T. C. (2006). Examining the empirical relationship between prison crowding and inmate misconduct: A meta-analysis of conflicting research results. *Journal of Criminal Justice, 34*(4), 401–412.

Frick, P. J., & Viding, E. (2009). Antisocial behavior from a developmental psychopathology perspective. *Development and Psychopathology, 21*(4), 1111–1131. doi:10.1017/S0954579409990071.

Friedmann, P. D., Melnick, G., Jiang, L., & Hamilton, Z. (2008). Violent and disruptive behavior among drug-involved prisoners: Relationship with psychiatric symptoms. *Behavioral Sciences and the Law, 26*, 389–401.

Gendreau, P., Goggin, C. E., & Law, M. A. (1997). Predicting prison misconducts. *Criminal Justice and Behavior, 24*(4), 414–431.

Gottlieb, P., Gabrielsen, G., & Kramp, P. (1987). Psychotic homicides in Kopenhagen from 1959 to 1983. *Acta Psychiatrica Scandinavica, 76*, 285–292.

Grann, M., & Fazel, S. (2004). Substance misuse and violent crime: Swedish population study. *British Medical Journal, 328*(7450), 1233–1234. doi:10.1136/bmj.328.7450.1233.

Haapasalo, J., & Hamalainen, T. (1996). Childhood family problems and current psychiatric problems among young violent and property offenders. *Journal of the American Academy of Child and Adolescent Psychiatry, 35*(10), 1394–1401.

Haney, C., Banks, W. C., & Zimbardo, P. G. (1973). Interpersonal dynamics in a simulated prison. *International Journal of Criminology and Penology, 1*, 69–97.

Hare, R. D. (2003). *Hare Psychopathy Checklist–Revised (PCL-R)*. Toronto, Ontario, Canada: Multi-Health Systems.

Hare, R. D., Clark, D., Grann, M., & Thornton, D. (2000). Psychopathy and the predictive validity of the PCL-R: An international perspective. *Behavioral Sciences and the Law, 18*(5), 623–645. doi:10.1002/1099-0798(200010).

Harrendorf, S. (2007). *Rückfälligkeit und kriminelle Karrieren von Gewalttätern: Ergebnisse einer bundesweiten Rückfalluntersuchung [Recidivism and criminal careers of violent offenders: Results of a countrywide study of recidivism]*. Göttingen, Germany: Universitätsverlag.

Harris, A. R., Thomas, S. H., Fisher, G. A., & Hirsch, D. J. (2002). Murder and medicine: The lethality of criminal assault 1960–1999. *Homicide Studies, 6*, 128–166.

Hilton, N. Z., Harris, G. T., & Rice, M. E. (2010). *Risk assessment for domestically violent men*. Washington, DC: American Psychological Association.

Hirschi, T., & Gottfredson, M. (1983). Age and the explanation of crime. *American Journal of Sociology, 89*, 552–584.

Hodgins, S. (1992). Mental disorder, intellectual deficiency, and crime: Evidence from a birth cohort. *Archives of General Psychiatry, 49*(6), 476–483.

Hodgins, S. (2008). Violent behaviour among people with schizophrenia: A framework for investigations of causes, and effective treatment, and prevention. *Philosophical Transactions of the Royal Society of London, Series B: Biological Sciences, 363*(1503), 2505–2518. doi:10.1098/rstb.2008.0034.

Hodgins, S., Mednick, S. A., Brennan, P. A., Schulsinger, F., & Engberg, M. (1996). Mental disorder and crime. Evidence from a Danish birth cohort. *Archives of General Psychiatry, 53*(6), 489–496.

Hollin, C. R., & Palmer, E. J. (2006). Criminogenic need and women offenders: A critique of the literature. *Legal and Criminological Psychology, 11*, 179–195.

Holtzworth-Munroe, A., & Meehan, J. C. (2004). Typologies of men who are maritally violent: Scientific and clinical implications. *Journal of Interpersonal Violence, 19*(12), 1369–1389. doi:10.1177/0886260504269693.

Junger-Tas, J., Terlouw, G. J., & Klein, M. W. (1994). *Delinquent behavior among young people in the Western world: First results of the International Self-Report Delinquency Study*. Amsterdam: Kugler.

Killias, M., Kuhn, A., & Aebi, M. F. (2011). *Grundriss der Kriminologie: Eine europäische Perspektive* (2nd ed.). Bern, Switzerland: Stämpfli Verlag AG.

Kroner, D. G., & Mills, J. F. (2001). The accuracy of five risk appraisal instruments in predicting institutional misconduct and new convictions. *Criminal Justice and Behavior, 28*(4), 471–489.

Kropp, P. R., Hart, S. D., Webster, C. D., & Eaves, D. (1995). *Manual for the Spousal Assault Risk Assessment Guide* (2nd ed.). Vancouver, British Columbia, Canada: British Columbia Institute on Family Violence.

Langan, P. A., & Levin, D. J. (2002). *Recidivism of prisoners released in 1994*. Washington DC: U.S. Department of Justice.

Laubacher, A., Rossegger, A., Endrass, J., Angst, J., Urbaniok, F., & Vetter, S. (in press). Adolescent delinquency and antisocial personality as precursors to adult sex and/or violent re-offending: A prospective study of a representative sample of Swiss men. *International Journal of Offender Therapy and Comparative Criminology*.

Leistico, A. M., Salekin, R. T., DeCoster, J., & Rogers, R. (2008). A large-scale meta-analysis relating the hare measures of psychopathy to antisocial conduct. *Law and Human Behavior, 32*(1), 28–45. doi:10.1007/s10979-007-9096-6.

Lindqvist, P., & Allebeck, P. (1990). Schizophrenia and crime. A longitudinal follow-up of 644 schizophrenics in Stockholm. *The British Journal of Psychiatry, 157*, 345–350.

Loeber, R., Farrington, D. P., Stouthamer-Loeber, M., Moffitt, T. E., Caspi, A., & Lynam, D. (2001). Male mental health problems, psychopathy, and personality traits: Key findings from the first 14 years of the Pittsburgh Youth Study. *Clinical Child and Family Psychology Review, 4*(4), 273–297.

Loucks, A., & Zamble, E. (1999). Predictors in recidivism in serious female offenders: Canada searches for predictors common to both men and women. *Corrections Today, 61*(1), 26–32.

McCorkle, R. C. (1995). Gender, psychopathology, and institutional behavior: A comparison of male and female mentally ill prison inmates. *Journal of Criminal Justice, 23*(1), 53–61.

Milgram, S. (1963). Behavioral study of obedience. *Journal of Abnormal and Social Psychology, 67*, 371–378.

Mills, J. F., & Kroner, D. G. (2003). Antisocial constructs in predicting institutional violence among violent offenders and child molesters. *International Journal of Offender Therapy and Comperative Criminology, 47*(3), 324–334.

Mischkowitz, R. (1993). *Kriminelle Karrieren und ihr Abbruch: Empirische Ergebnisse einer kriminologischen Langzeituntersuchung als Beitrag zur "Age-Crime-Debate."* Bonn, Germany: Forum Verlag Godesberg.

Moffitt, T. E. (1993). Adolescence-limited and life-course-persistent antisocial behavior: a developmental taxonomy. *Psychological Review, 100*(4), 674–701.

Mojtabai, R. (2006). Psychotic-like experiences and interpersonal violence in the general population. *Social Psychiatry and Psychiatric Epidemiology, 41*(3), 183–190. doi:10.1007/s00127-005-0020-4.

Mokros, A., Stadtland, C., Osterheider, M., & Nedopil, N. (2010). Assessment of risk for violent recidivism through multivariate Bayesian classification. *Psychology, Public Policy, and Law, 16*, 418–450.

Monahan, J., Steadman, H. J., Silver, E., Appelbaum, P. S., Clark Robbins, P., Mulvey, E. P., . . . Banks, S. (2001). *Rethinking risk assessment: The MacArthur study of mental disorder and violence*. New York: Oxford University Press.

Nilsson, K. W., Sjoberg, R. L., Damberg, M., Alm, P. O., Ohrvik, J., Leppert, J., . . . Oreland, L. (2005). Role of the serotonin transporter gene and family function in adolescent alcohol consumption. *Alcoholism: Clinical and Experimental Research, 29*(4), 564–570. doi:10.1097/01.ALC.0000159112.98941.B0.

O'Leary, K. D., Smith Slep, A. M., & O'Leary, S. G. (2007). Multivariate models of men's and women's partner aggression. *Journal of Consulting and Clinical Psychology, 75*(5), 752–764. doi:10.1037/0022-006x.75.5.752.

Ostendorf, H. Lagebild der Kriminalität. Retrieved September 28, 2011, from Bundeszentrale für politische Bildung http://www.bpb.de/die_bpb/NR6YMW.html.

Porter, S., Birt, A. R., & Boer, D. P. (2001). Investigation of the criminal and conditional release profiles of Canadian federal offenders as a function of psychopathy and age. *Law and Human Behavior, 25*, 647–661.

Porter, S., ten Brinke, L., & Wilson, K. (2009). Crime profiles and conditional release performance of psychopathic and non-psychopathic sexual offenders. *Legal and Criminological Psychology, 14*, 109–118.

Porter, S., & Woodworth, M. (2006). Psychopathy and aggression. In C. J. Patrick (Ed.), *Handbook of psychopathy* (pp. 481–494). New York: Guilford Press.

Porter, S., & Woodworth, M. (2007). "I'm sorry I did it . . . but he started it": A comparison of the official and self-reported homicide descriptions of psychopaths and non-psychopaths. *Law and Human Behavior, 31*(1), 91–107.

Putkonen, H., Weizmann-Henelius, G., Lindberg, N., Rovamo, T., & Hakkanen, H. (2008). Changes over time in homicides by women: A register-based study comparing female offenders from 1982 to 1992 and 1993 to 2005. *Criminal Behaviour and Mental Health, 18*(5), 268–278. doi:10.1002/cbm.711.

Quinsey, V. L., Harris, G. T., Rice, M. E., & Cormier, C. A. (2006). *Violent offenders: Appraising and managing risk* (2nd ed.). Washington, DC: American Psychological Association.

Reif, A., Rosler, M., Freitag, C. M., Schneider, M., Eujen, A., Kissling, C., . . . Retz, W. (2007). Nature and nurture predispose to violent behavior: Serotonergic genes and adverse childhood environment. *Neuropsychopharmacology, 32*(11), 2375–2383. doi:10.1038/sj.npp.1301359.

Richards, P. (1999). *Homicide statistics*. London: House of Commons Library.

Roe-Sepowitz, D. (2007). Adolescent female murderers: Characteristics and treatment implications. *The American Journal of Orthopsychiatry, 77*(3), 489–496.

Rossegger, A., Wetli, N., Urbaniok, F., Elbert, T., Cortoni, F., & Endrass, J. (2009). Women convicted for violent offenses: Adverse childhood experiences, low level of education and poor mental health. *BMC Psychiatry, 9*, 81. doi:10.1186/1471-244X-9-81.

Salekin, R. T. (2008). Psychopathy and recidivism from mid-adolescence to young adulthood: Cumulating legal problems and limiting life opportunities. *Journal of Abnormal Psychology, 117*(2), 386–395. doi:10.1037/0021-843X-.117.2.386.

Salekin, R. T., Rogers, R., & Sewell, K. W. (1997). Construct validity of psychopathy in a female offender sample: A multitrait-multimethod evaluation. *Journal of Abnormal Psychology, 106*(4), 576–585.

Sieber, M., & Angst, J. (1981). *Drogen-, Alkohol-, und Tabakkonsum. Ein Beitrag zur Epidemiologie und Ätiologie bei jungen Erwachsenen*. Bern, Switzerland: Verlag Hans Huber.

Sourander, A., Elonheimo, H., Niemela, S., Nuutila, A. M., Helenius, H., Sillanmaki, L., . . . Almqvist, F. (2006). Childhood predictors of male criminality: A prospective population-based follow-up study from age 8 to late adolescence. *Journal of the American Academy of Child & Adolescent Psychiatry, 45*(5), 578–586. doi:10.1097/01.chi0000205699.58626.b5.

South Richardson, D., & Hammock, G. S. (2007). Social context of human aggression: Are we paying too much attention to gender? *Aggression and Violent Behavior, 12*, 417–426.

Soyka, M., Graz, C., Bottlender, R., Dirschedl, P., & Schoech, H. (2007). Clinical correlates of later violence and criminal offences in schizophrenia. *Schizophrenia Research, 94*(1–3), 89–98. doi:10.1016/j.schres.2007.03.027.

Soyka, M., Morhart-Klute, V., & Schöch, H. (2004). Delinquency and criminal offenses in former schizophrenic inpatients 7–12 years following discharge. *European Archives of Psychiatry and Clinical Neuroscience, 254*, 289–294.

Stalans, L. J., Yarnold, P. R., Seng, M., Olson, D. E., & Repp, M. (2004). Identifying three types of violent offenders and predicting violent recidivism while on probation: A classification tree analysis. *Law and Human Behavior, 28*(3), 253–271.

Steadman, H. J., Mulvey, E. P., Monahan, J., Robbins, P. C., Appelbaum, P. S., Grisso, T., . . . Silver, E. (1998). Violence by people discharged from acute psychiatric inpatient facilities and by others in the same neighborhoods. *Archives of General Psychiatry, 55*(5), 393–401.

Steffensmeier, D., & Allan, E. (1996). Gender and crime: Toward a gendered theory of female offending. *Annual Review of Sociology, 22*, 459–487.

Steffensmeier, D., & Broidy, L. (2001). Explaining female offending. In C. Renzetti & L. Goodstein (Eds.), *Women, crime, and criminal justice: Original feminist readings* (pp. 111–134). Los Angeles, CA: Roxbury.

Stevenson, T., Goodall, E., & Moore, C. (2008). A retrospective audit of the extent and nature of domestic violence cases identified over a three year period in the two district command units of the police service of Northern Ireland. *Journal of Forensic and Legal Medicine, 15*(7), 430–436. doi:10.1016/j.jflm.2008.02.012.

Stuart, G. L., Moore, T. M., Ramsey, S. E., & Kahler, C. W. (2004). Hazardous drinking and relationship violence perpetration and victimization in women arrested for domestic violence. *Journal of Studies on Alcohol, 65*(1), 46–53.

Swanson, J. W., Swartz, M. S., Van Dorn, R. A., Elbogen, E. B., Wagner, H. R., Rosenheck, R. A., ... Lieberman, J. A. (2006). A national study of violent behavior in persons with schizophrenia. *Archives of General Psychiatry, 63*(5), 490–499. doi:10.1001/archpsyc.63.5.490.

Swiss Federal Statistical Office. Gewalt allgemein. Retrieved August 18, 2011, from http://www.bfs.admin.ch/bfs/portal/de/index/themen/19/03/02/key/02/03.html.

Tavares, C., & Thomas, G. (2010). *Population and social conditions*. Eurostat.

Taylor, P. J. (1993). Schizophrenia and crime: distinctive patterns in association. In S. Hodgins (Ed.), *Mental disorder and crime* (pp. 63–86). Newbury Park, London, New Delhi: Sage Publications.

Tiihonen, J., Isohanni, M., Räsänen, P., Koiranen, M., & Moring, J. (1997). Specific major mental disorders and criminality: A 26-year prospective study of the 1966 Northern Finland birth cohort. *American Journal of Psychiatry, 154*, 840–845.

Tracy, P. E., Wolfgang, M. H., & Figlio, R. M. (1990). *Delinquency careers in two birth cohorts*. New York: Plenum Press.

Vaughn, M. G., & DeLisi, M. (2008). Were Wolfgang's chronic offenders psychopaths? On the convergent validity of psychopathy and career criminality. *Journal of Criminal Justice, 36*, 33–42.

Vermeiren, R. (2003). Psychopathology and delinquency in adolescents: A descriptive and developmental perspective. *Clinical Psychology Review, 23*(2), 277–318.

Vitale, J., Smith, S., Brinkley, B., & Newman, J. (2002). The reliability and validity of the Psychopathy Checklist–Revised in a sample of female offenders. *Criminal Justice and Behaviour, 29*(2), 202–231.

Walsh, E., Buchanan, A., & Fahy, T. (2002). Violence and schizophrenia: Examining the evidence. *British Journal of Psychiatry, 180*, 490–495.

Walters, G. D., Knight, R. A., Grann, M., & Dahle, K. P. (2008). Incremental validity of the Psychopathy Checklist facet scores: Predicting release outcome in six samples. *Journal of Abnormal Psychology, 117*(2), 396–405. doi:10.1037/0021-843X.117.2.396.

Webster, C. D., Eaves, D., & Hart, S. D. (1997). *HCR-20: Assessing risk for violence* (2nd ed.). Vancouver, British Columbia, Canada: Mental Health Law & Policy Institute, Simon Fraser University.

Weizmann-Henelius, G., Viemerö, V., & Eronen, M. (2003). The violent female perpetrator and her victim. *Forensic Science International, 133*(3), 197–203.

Woodworth, M., & Porter, S. (2002). In cold blood: characteristics of criminal homicides as a function of psychopathy. *Journal of Abnormal Psychology, 111* (3), 436–445.

World Health Organization. (1996). WHO global consultation on violence and health. Violence: a public health priority (Vol. document WHO/EHA/SPI .POA.2). Geneva, Switzerland: World Health Organization.

World Health Organization. (2005). WHO multi-country study on women's health and domestic violence against women. Initial results on prevalence, health outcomes and women's responses. Geneva, Switzerland: Author.

Yang, M., Wong, S. C., & Coid, J. (2010). The efficacy of violence prediction: a meta-analytic comparison of nine risk assessment tools. *Psychological Bulletin, 136*(5), 740–767. doi:10.1037/a0020473.

Yourstone, J., Lindholm, T., & Kristiansson, M. (2008). Women who kill: a comparison of the psychosocial background of female and male perpetrators. *International Journal of Law and Psychiatry, 31*(4), 374–383. doi:10.1016/j.ijlp.2008.06.005.

CHAPTER FIVE

Sexual Deviance, Fantasy Development, and Sex Crime

Henry Richards

The Received View of Sexual Fantasy in the Forensic Context: Specious Acknowledgment, Little In-Depth Research

The centrality of sexual fantasies to the sexual abuse field is reflected in an orthodoxy of bromides, many of which enjoy some empirical support. It has long been assumed that violent, predatory sexual recidivists offenders have more frequent and complexly organized sexual fantasies than do opportunistic offenders and nonrecidivists (Deu & Edelmann, 1997; Prentky et al., 1989). Clinical lore holds that the content of offender fantasies foreshadows their offense conduct (Looman, 1995). Some offenders assert that fantasies caused their offenses (MacCulloch, Snowden, Wood, & Mills, 1983). Among men not known to be offenders, aggressive and coercive sexual fantasies are correlated with corresponding sexual behaviors (Knight & Sims-Knight, 2003), holding rape promoting attitudes and beliefs (Zurbriggen & Yost, 2004) and endorsing a willingness to rape if immunity from detection was assured (Greendlinger & Byrne, 1987; Smeaton & Byrne, 1987). Sexual fantasy analysis has been incorporated in serial sex crime profiling schemes (Hazelwood & Warren, 1995) and has played a large role in the phenomenological and theoretical study of sexual homicide offenders as well as sadistic sexual offenders (Gray, Watt, Hassan, & MacCulloch, 2003; M. J. MacCulloch, Snowden, Wood, & Mills, 1983; M. MacCulloch, Gray, & Watt, 2000).

Working with sexual fantasies is almost axiomatic to the practice of sex offender assessment and treatment (Wright, Hatcher, McAnulty, & Burnette, 2006; Zamboni & Crawford, 2002), and sexual fantasies are usually considered as a critical, if not necessary component to the development of deviant sexual preferences and paraphilia. Despite the centrality of sexual fantasy to the assessment and treatment of sex offenders, the empirical research in this area is relatively limited in scope and number of studies. This may be due to the inherently ephemeral and private nature of fantasies, and their myriad variations, all of which limit the face validity of classification schemes that are needed for research purposes.

It could be argued that another reason for the limited research in this area is that for decades, the dominant paradigms of psychology placed little value on fantasy. For example, although psychoanalysis was founded on the study of dreams and fantasies, and is infamous for interpreting almost any psychological event as sexual, traditional psychoanalysis dealt primarily with unconscious fantasies, and those that could be made conscious through psychoanalysis. Consciously manipulated sexual fantasy was viewed as an artifact of internal conflict, a marker of sexual inadequacy, or, if the analyst was the object of the fantasy, as a form therapeutic resistance. Paradoxically (and ignoring the distinction between conscious and unconscious fantasy), some have asserted that Freud's claim that the whole enterprise of personality rests on a currency of unconscious sexual fantasy has been proven to be false, because personality functioning is preserved when sexual fantasies are virtually eliminated (at least as pleasurable, spontaneous, erotic experiences) through the administration of antiandrogens (Friedman & Downey, 2000). Behaviorism provided little incentive to the study of the content of sexual fantasies beyond relegating them to the categories of deviant fantasies and normal fantasies, to be, respectively, extinguished or reinforced during reconditioning of sexual arousal and interest. Early cognitive-behavioral conceptualizations were also skeletal, focusing on belief, affect, and their relationship, and required only marginally more detailed information about the content of sexual fantasies than had the behavioral conditioning approach to treatment.

Sexual fantasy has taken on an important role in cognitive-behavioral understandings and treatments with the advent of an emphasis on attachment, which can serve as a context for understanding sexual fantasies, and the development of cognitive schemas and scripts that relate fantasy to internalized views of self, other, and the sexual situation. In therapy, fantasy can be used to both assess and actively modify these internal guides. Similarly, as the integration therapies has proceeded, including among psychodynamic approaches, thinkers such as Kernberg (Kernberg, 2006) have used fantasy as a key diagnostic tool and as an indicator of the effectiveness of in-session interventions and overall therapeutic approach. One limitation to psychodynamic formulations is that typically the investigations that inform them (typically extended case studies and generalizations across such studies) are also used to justify them.

After decrying the paucity of research and conceptual work in this area of sex offender studies, a counterbalancing development in the form of a series of systematic investigations using a new approach to the area should not go unmentioned. In a series of articles, Dion Gee and coauthors investigated the function (Gee, Ward, & Eccleston, 2003), content (Gee, Devilly, & Ward, 2004), structure (Gee, Ward, Belofastov, & Beech, 2006), and implications for criminal profiling of sex offender sexual fantasy (Gee, Belofastov, & Kocsis, 2007). These contributions, which are mainly theoretical and conceptual, were based on intensive study of the sexual fantasies of 24 adult male sex offenders in Australia using the Grounded Theory method. The Sexual Fantasy Structural Properties Model (SFSPM) and a related coding scheme was the end product of an in-depth exploration of the phenomenology of sexual fantasy in this small sample. At the broadest level, fantasies are classified in SFSPM as either general sexual fantasies, or offense-focused fantasies. The latter consists of two types as nonspecific offense fantasies in which there is no identified victim or specific victim characteristics and/or offense-specific fantasies in which a victim or victim prototype is incorporated in the fantasy (Gee et al., 2004). Rather than considering nonspecific offense fantasies as innocuous, these researchers have suggested: "The recurrent use of nonspecific offence fantasy may provide the offender with a way of desensitizing himself to the offence themes present within the fantasy, a process which increases the likelihood of offending" (Gee et al., 2004, p. 327).

Unfortunately, the reports from SFSPM have been based on a small number of subjects, making generalizations from data collected using it very provisional. This system classifies sexual fantasies into categories that do not include information of erotic body parts or sexual acts featured in the studied memories, which certainly represents a limitation in the scheme; from the practical viewpoint of working with fantasies in assessment and treatment—where body parts and sex acts are the basic currency— or considering fantasies from a psychoanalytic (Kernberg, 2006) or embodied mind (Hanna & Maiese, 2009) point of view.

A study that is similar to the series of investigations described in the preceding paragraphs was conducted by Beech, Swaffer, Multra, and Fisher (2009), in which they intensely studied the fantasies and offense-related cognitions of a small sample (n = 10) of rapists undergoing treatment. They found that as treatment progressed, there was both a reduction of justifications for offending and of the denial of excessive sexual fantasy activity prior to offending.

The Received View of Sexual Fantasy in the Forensic Context

Despite the limited conceptual and methodological toolbox for investigation of sexual fantasies, a paucity of studies, the sex offender practice community has a generally accepted received view of the sexual fantasies in offenders. This shared view can be partially captured in generalizations such as those in the opening paragraphs of this chapter, and other understandings that have implications for how members of the practice community think about and do the work of research, assessment, treatment, and expert testimony. The following few paragraphs attempt to summarize a non-exhaustive set of such generally held views in the form of concise assertions, but these are not meant as *ex cathedra* declarations.

Sexual fantasies are seminal but typically silent milestones of human development. Adults typically recall having their earliest sexual fantasies at approximately ages 11 to 13, with boys having a somewhat earlier onset for sexual fantasy life than girls, but this difference may be due to not including emotional and romantic fantasies in girls as erotic. The frequency of sexual fantasies over the life span, in both males and females, tends to closely follow the body's production of sex-regulatory hormones, but these hormonal changes do not seem to alter content of sexual fantasies over the life span in any systematic way. One implication of this lack of patterned change over time is the possibility that relative stability is one source of adult interest in underage partners. The preservation through memory and fantasy of sexual feelings and experiences toward once-age-appropriate persons, either real or imagined, may decades later continue to prompt feelings and fantasies toward individuals of that age, who are now age inappropriate. However, following theoretical views of pedophilia as a sexual orientation with early onset, pedophilic fantasy may be born at the headwaters of sexual orientation in childhood.

In addition to whatever spontaneous internal sources that may be hypothesized (ranging from phylogenic development of behavior to archetypal predispositions to specific fantasies [see Stevens, 1983]) external sources of sexual fantasy seem to provide the palate and the paints, if not the canvas on which fantasies are drawn. Fairly apparent external influences are communications media, art, erotica of all kinds, and intentional instruction or modeling in sexuality generally, and more specifically in the generation and use of sexual fantasy. Transmission of fantasies by older children or more experienced adolescents may play an important role in the formation of early sexual fantasies. Also not to be overlooked are orienting fantasies—that is, childhood fantasies that function as a component of the development of sexual orientation prior to or during the development of a practical or realistic understanding of sexual matters. These orienting fantasies may differ from erotic fantasies proper, which have a direct, reciprocal relationship with more developed sexual feelings and more mature forms of sexual arousal.

Clearly for most people, adolescence is the era of life in which sexual exploration of all kinds is normative, but especially exploration in fantasy and of fantasies. In this era, core erotic fantasy themes build on orienting fantasies, and both kinds of fantasy are consolidated as internalized guides to sexual experience and expression. The use of pornography to facilitate both fantasy and masturbation is a well-known phenomenon. Sexual obscenity laws are based on the generalization that pornography serves as a link between private internal experience and socially significant behavior.

Like all mental content, sexual fantasy is dependent on underlying physiological structures and neurochemical dynamics. Although these mechanisms are of particular interest for the purposes of this chapter as the basis for antiandrogen pharmacotherapy in paraphilia and sexual offenders, a few general observations on the topic are offered here. The generation of sexual fantasies and arousal to a sexual stimulus appear to be subserved by different mechanisms. Although sexual hormones are usually required at some threshold level for normal development and sexual response, elevation beyond that level may not result in increased sexuality, including fantasies, making studies in males and females with abnormally deficient sex hormone levels more telling of effects below this threshold. In both genders, individuals with hormonal deficits respond normally on exposure to erotic films, but have decreased sexual response to self-generated fantasies and fewer of them, a pattern that is returned to normal in androgen replacement therapy (Bancroft & Wu, 1983; Cooper, Sandhu, Losztyn, & Cernovsky, 1992). Nonetheless, sex offenders with elevated testosterone do not appear to be more frequent or aggressive offenders than their normal-level testosterone counterparts, suggesting that even in pathological conditions, threshold levels of androgens may be more important than elevations beyond the threshold.

Currently prevailing theory depicts one's preferred sexual fantasies as resulting from the interaction of sexual orientation (which is itself multi-determined), early learning (from life experience and teaching), followed by a process of operant conditioning in which fantasies are reinforced as habitual by the pleasure of engaging in the fantasy (unconditional stimulus). Frequent accompaniment of the fantasy with masturbation has a major hand in shaping the nature and frequency of fantasies and thoughts, which in turn shape masturbation and other sexual practices. Sex drive conceptualized as the psychophysical effect of androgens usually provides only a critical threshold factor in this reciprocal process, but in some cases hormonal and neurochemical abnormalities may prove to be a major impetus to the frequency and type of manifested sexual expression. This general model provides the basis for interventions such as masturbatory reconditioning procedures, aversive conditioning procedures, and antiandrogen therapy, all of which target sexual fantasies to a greater or lesser extent, but are more focused on sexual arousal and interest. A broader model that incorporates one's personality, mature beliefs, attachment style, interpersonal repertoire, gender role, romantic, and sexual scripts or schema would be required to optimally guide broader-spectrum treatment approaches, such as sex-offender-specific cognitive behavioral therapy, which may produce greater and more resilient treatment changes than narrowly focused techniques for suppressing deviant sexual arousal and deviant sexual fantasies, urges, or thoughts.

Definitions: Sexual Fantasy, Normal (Nondeviant) and Abnormal (Deviant)

The sex offender field is thoroughly infiltrated with the concept of deviant sexuality, and sexual fantasies have not been immune to this moralistically tainted vestige of our legal tradition, although DSM-IV-TR has dropped this term in favor of paraphilic or simply pathological. Inherent to this nomenclature is an emphasis on social mores, taboos, and prohibitions. Modern psychopathology contrasts normal and abnormal aspects of functioning, states of mind, etc., within a statistical frame of reference (i.e., that which is outside of the norm, unexpected) or that of adaptiveness versus dysfunction vis-à-vis biological and psychosocial needs. In deviance, the underlying frame of reference is normative in the sense of a turning or veering away from socially condoned and expected behaviors; thus it has the same base metaphor that biblical writers used for sin, missing the mark, straying from the path, or twisted from the natural form. Referring to the sexual fantasies of offenders or even of individuals diagnosable with paraphilia as deviant is problematic because they are for the most part identical in content to the fantasies of individuals who have never been diagnosed with a paraphilia or committed a sexual offense. Fantasies that would be typified as deviant if reported by an offender but are nonetheless fairly common in non-offender populations include fantasies that evoke sexual arousal toward children, fantasies involving group sex, and fantasies of using force or one's being forced to engage in sexual activity.

How do the fantasies of individuals who have not been diagnosed with a paraphilia differ from those of individuals who are offenders? If they are for the most part similar, are they embedded in similar cognitive structures and sexual scripts? Does fantasy serve the same function in offender at and non-offenders? How do sexual fantasies develop, or later activated? How stable are fantasies over time and situation? What emotions can be primed or evoked by sexual fantasies beyond erotic arousal? Answering such questions require some preliminary definitions. Not addressing this definitional problem contributes to confusion and imprecision in both treatment formulations and research.

Relying on tacit knowledge of what is meant by deviant sexual fantasy is reasonable if the discussion is limited to individuals who have committed an illegal and nonconsensual sexual act (whether or not apprehended) and further limited to those fantasies in which offenders imagine acts that, actualized, would be crimes. In proposing the use of the term "offen[s]e-focused fantasy," Gee, Devilly, and Ward (2004) succinctly summarized the problem:

> As noted previously by many authors, the concept of deviant sexual fantasy is not only contentious, but can also be misleading. As comparative studies have indicated (e.g., Looman, 1995), there is often little difference between the fantasy content themes of sexual offenders, nonsexual offenders, and community samples, even with respect to deviant themes. In fact, the rate of any males experiencing fantasies of any specific type (deviant or nondeviant) approaches 95% (Leitenberg & Henning, 1995). By moving away from the notion of "deviant fantasy themes" future research may prove more fruitful in drawing distinctions between the fantasy themes evident in community samples, and those more "preparatory" fantasies often seen to accompany sexual offending (see Gee, Ward, & Eccleston, 2003). (Gee et al., 2004, p. 327)

In their comprehensive review of the subject (to be cited frequently in the next section of this chapter on sexual fantasy in the general population), Leitenberg and Henning (1995, p. 470) define sexual fantasy broadly as "almost any mental imagery that is sexually arousing or erotic to the individual. The essential element of a deliberate sexual fantasy is the ability to control in imagination exactly what takes place. Even reminiscences of past events can be altered so that only particularly exciting aspects are recalled or enhanced." (This definition precludes the unconscious fantasies or fantasies that may be transparently sexual but are draped in figurative representations, such as a pleasurable fantasy of bareback horse riding or fantasizing about people admiring one for the size and distinction of a possession such as an oversized gavel used in presiding over an assembly). Conscious control for the purpose of erotic pleasure, and any specific content, is emphasized, and the role of unintentional, spontaneous, or compulsive aspects of fantasy are excluded. Leitenberg and Henning's (1995) definition could be interpreted as excluding as sexual fantasies those involving intrusive, unwonted sexual images (that may or may not be accompanied by unwelcome sexual urges) or fantasies the individual suppresses or otherwise fails to imbue with willing erotic interest or intent. Such experiences would qualify as sexual fantasy only if the individual experiencing them at some point willingly adopts the intrusive image for erotic purposes.

According to the DSM-IV-TR (APA, 2000, p. 457), "Obsessions are persistent ideals, thoughts, impulses, or images that are experienced as intrusive and inappropriate and that cause marked anxiety or distress." Sexual imagery (e.g., a recurrent pornographic image) is used as an example of an obsession in the DSM-IV-TR text discussion of the diagnostic features of obsessive compulsive disorder (OCD). However, many sexual behaviors are excluded as counting as compulsive behaviors, because they are pleasurable, are presumably ego-syntonic, and are avoided because of their consequences rather than some other source of distress. Including sexual imagery as an obsession, and excluding sexual behavior as a compulsion, presents something of a dilemma in diagnosing and treating sex offenders who may have obsessive sexual fantasies, sexually compulsive behavior (i.e., unwanted, uncontrolled masturbation) and paraphilic objects of desire, such as arousal to minors.

These cases of comorbid of sex-related obsessive-compulsive disorder and paraphilia may not be rare in offenders with personality disorders that meet, or approach meeting, criteria for the personality disorders often associated with OCD (i.e., avoidant personality disorder, dependent personality disorder, and obsessive-compulsive personality disorder). Leitenberg and Henning's (1995) definition of sexual fantasy avoids this by making deliberate generation of the fantasy and control over it as inherent qualities of sexual fantasy:

> In short, the term sexual fantasy refers to almost any mental imagery that is sexually arousing or erotic to the individual. The essential element of a deliberate sexual fantasy is the ability to control in imagination exactly what

> takes place. Even reminiscences of past events can be altered so that only particularly exciting aspects are recalled or enhanced. (Leitenberg & Henning, 1995, p. 470)

The aforementioned definition was created for the purpose of describing sexual fantasies as investigated in a large number of studies, primarily with nonclinical, non-offending samples, which may, in part, account for an emphasis of factors sometimes in doubt in offenders (volitional control, pleasurable experience predominating in fantasy, etc.) that may be safely assumed in non-offenders without paraphilias. Gee, Belofastov, and Kocsis (Gee, Belofastov, & Kocsis, 2007) elaborated on this very broad definition of sexual fantasy to create a definition more useful for criminal profiling or in clinical work with offenders. According to these authors, a sexual fantasy is:

> an imaginative process accompanied by withdrawal from the immediate demands of the external world and a narrowing in focus of an individual's internal world. Such processes allow an individual to create an elaborate, emotionally anchored, mental picture that has its origins in daydreaming and involves erotica that creates or intensifies sexual arousal. (Gee et al., 2007, p. 50)

This definition maintains the same emphasis on deliberate control as Leitenberg and Henning's (1995) definition, but less explicitly, and expressed passively in the phrase "allow an individual to create" versus a possible alternative, "make the individual experience." Gee et al.'s (2007) definition appears to make a distinction between daydreams as a precursor to fantasies, and sexual fantasies proper. Since daydreams may be spontaneous, well-structured experiences with imagery and narrative (and sometimes dialogue) and may also be intrusive and unwonted (such as may occur while performing work requiring concentration), this definition may tend to encourage the neglect of such potentially significant phenomena in the context of sexual offending, which also is the case with Leitenberg and Henning's (1995) definition.

Fantasy and Psychiatric Diagnosis

The first sentences of the first two paragraphs of the DSM-IV-TR (APA, 2000) section on Paraphilias are quoted below:

> The essential features of a Paraphilia are recurrent, intense sexually arousing fantasies, sexual urges, or behaviors involving 1) nonhuman objects, 2) the

suffering or humiliation of oneself or one's partner, or 3) children or other nonconsenting persons that occur over a six month periods (Criterion A).

> Paraphilic imagery may be acted out with a nonconsenting partner in a way that may be injurious to the partner (as in Sexual Sadism or Pedophilia). For some individuals paraphilic fantasies or stimuli are obligatory for erotic arousal and are always included in sexual activity. (APA, 2000, p. 566)

Not only do these statements establish the centrality of sexual fantasy to paraphilic behavior, but they assume the potential for paraphilic images to result directly in behavior; that is, they can be acted out as proximate causes of sexual acts, and furthermore, the statements imply that these actions may be harmful and, therefore, often criminal. As with many foundational texts, most of the critical terms in these sentences are not defined, assuming the reader will have a grounded understanding of what constitutes "sexually arousing fantasies" and can distinguish the intense from the tepid varieties, and can distinguish sexual urges from sexual fantasies. Without a further specified model, these sentences imply the existence of imageless sexual urges and intensely arousing fantasies without urges to act. Close deconstructive glossing of any text may uncover paradoxical and counterintuitive assumptions, but in the context of highly contested legal proceedings involving sex offenders, these opening passages in the diagnostic manual are far from trivial and sometimes result in bitterly disputed views, such as the various positions (to even include history of the current wording) taken regarding the "turn" in diagnosis due to the use of "or" rather than "and" in sentence 1, which reflects the different wording of this passage in DSM-IIIR versus DSM-IV. First and Halon (2008) claimed that these changes would have no effect on caseness, meaning that the same cases would be identified with either wording; whereas First and Frances (2008), who were at the table during the changes made for DSM-IV, state that the change to "or" was a mistake and that it has allowed some forensic evaluators to diagnosis paraphilia on behavior alone, such as repeated rape. Whether paraphilia can be diagnosed on fantasy alone has not become as much a focus of contention, although this may change as the effect of sexual behavior over the Internet generates legal cases where this kind of diagnostic question may be critical.

The DSM-IV-TR description of the disease course of the paraphilias also centers largely on sexual fantasies. Although the DSM-IV-TR eschews explanation wherever possible, the relationship between fantasy and paraphilia appears to be closer than fantasy's relationship to disorders such as schizophrenia, delusional disorder, schizotypal personality disorder, and histrionic personality disorder (disorders in which fantasy may play an important role). Fantasy is included in the second criterion of narcissistic personality disorder ("is preoccupied with fantasies of unlimited success, power, brilliance, beauty, or ideal love"; and in the context of this chapter, one is tempted to add sexual prowess to this list. Sexual fantasies due to the presence of a paraphilia are part of the exclusionary criteria for obsessive-compulsive disorder.

Sexual Fantasy in Everyday Life

Understanding sexual fantasy in the general population is important to being able to gauge what might be disproportionate or unusual in individuals who go on to offend, and especially those who do not have the compulsive, repetitive symptoms of paraphilia, which require clinical expertise to diagnose. A comprehensive review of the literature on sexual fantasy was conducted by Leitenberg and Henning (1995), and there has not been an inundation of reviews on the topic since that point in time. Most of the studies reviewed by Leitenberg and Henning (1995) administered either checklists of sexual fantasy content or open-ended questionnaires prompting narrative descriptions. Either format asked anonymous subjects about the occurrence of certain types of fantasies, their frequency, and their preferred fantasies. A few studies asked non-anonymous participants to maintain a sexual fantasy log. Not all studies made the distinction between sexual thoughts and sexual fantasies, a distinction that requires fancy definitional footwork to justify logically, since it implies imageless thought about sex in the abstract, although the existence of sexual imagery without closely associated cognitions may be a more tenable proposition.

Sexual fantasies have been studied in three major contexts: as associated with masturbation, during sexual intercourse, and during nonsexual activity. Not surprisingly, gender is a major determinant of the rate of occurrence of sexual fantasies. Most studies find that men have sexual fantasies more frequently than women both during masturbation and during nonsexual activity. Some studies have found no significant difference between genders on fantasy occurring during sexual intercourse. Studies suggest that having sexual fantasies during masturbation is not universal, although Leitenberg and Henning (1995) summarized a study that found 85.9 % of males reporting their occurrence and 68.8% of women. A measurement artifact arises in studying these gender differences due to the fact that men masturbate more frequently than women and begin doing so at an earlier age. As a result, men may have a higher incidence of sexual fantasy during masturbation based only on these differences. As with most correlates of behavior with sexual fantasy, the direction of causality between the frequency of sexual fantasy and the frequency of masturbation is uncertain. Most studies show that men and women experience sexual fantasies about equally during sexual intercourse. Studies of sexual fantasies during waking hours outside of sexual activity suggest that a majority of both men and women have sexual daydreams with little difference between the genders.

That adults frequently fantasize about sex during sexual intercourse bares further examination. This is consistent with viewing sexual fantasy as having a facilitative, arousal-enhancing function, analogous to adding spices to one's dish "to taste" to enhance the experience. The focus of the fantasies may be more often explicitly genital (perhaps more frequently in males) or the fantasies may add elements of romance, commitment, and emotional content (perhaps more frequently for women). Also, the fantasies may frequently be about other real or imagined partners, either substituting for the current partner, or as a third party in the interaction. The main point here is that ever having such fantasies is the norm. Although fantasies involving infidelity to a committed relationship or that promote jealousy or otherwise overstep bounds of sexual propriety may add to arousal; like other sexual fantasies occurring during intercourse, they are usually considered as deeply personal and not shared with the partner. A recurrent caveat must be added here in regard to many sexual fantasies entertained by non-offenders: these fantasies are rarely intended to be translated into actuality.

Sexual thoughts and daydreams are also ubiquitous and, as mentioned earlier, for most purposes not distinct from sexual fantasy. In a large-sample, well-designed national survey of human sexuality, 54% of men and 19% of women said they thought about sex every day or several times a day (Laumann, Gagnon, Michael, & Michaels, 1994), and about 95% of males and females report that they have experienced sexual fantasies at some point. Although there may be reporting biases due to gender role expectations, these data appear to conform to cultural expectation regarding the frequency of experience related to sexual interest and gender.

Sexual fantasy frequency is highly correlated with other sexual behaviors, and does not appear to be usually a function of sexual frustration or deprivation. It thus appears that sexual fantasies in contexts other than during intercourse typically have an arousal promotion function, rather than serving as substitute discharge of sexual tension. Approximately 25% of the population feels strong guilt about their sexual fantasies. Not surprisingly, these individuals usually have their condemnatory beliefs and attitudes toward sex more generally, and these feelings and beliefs are associated with a lower rate of occurrence of sexual fantasy (Chick & Gold, 1987; Pelletier & Herold, 1988).

Factor analytic studies of sexual fantasies in nonclinical populations yield numerous factors, many of which were enumerated in Leitenberg and Henning (1995), and which can be summarized as consisting of three thematic clusters, which referred to as Conventional, Exploratory, and Coercive for purposes of this chapter. The most common content cluster across studies could be called conventional sexual fantasies. This is a set of conventional, intimate heterosexual fantasies of non-strangers who were past, present, or imaginary lovers. A second content cluster, exploratory fantasies, combines scenes of "nonstandard" or "forbidden" sexual imagery (unusual settings, positions, or practices, or with stranger or controversial partners) with scenarios representing sexual power or irresistibility, the latter to include seduction scenes and simultaneous encounters with multiple sexual partners. The third content cluster is a coercion cluster, which brings together submission-dominance themes, use of physical force, and sadomasochistic imagery. Although the genders differed somewhat in the form of expression and frequency of fantasies among these three clusters, no one cluster was primarily representative of either gender.

As might be expected, the expression of sexual fantasy themes differs by gender. Men frequently imagine themselves as the active, initiating partner who performs sexually toward their partner, and women more often imagine themselves in the complementary role as the receptive person who is acted upon. Men report more explicit and visual imagery, whereas women report more emotional and romantic content. Fantasies of simultaneous sex with more than one partner are more common among men. While both genders have fantasies that affirm their sexual power and irresistibility, submission fantasies of being forced or overpowered, due to one's being irresistible, are more frequently experienced by women. Men more frequently experience dominance fantasies in which their physical power and confident/domineering attitude overpower a woman's reluctance or resistance to engage sexually. As noted by Leitenberg and Henning (1995), these sensory and thematic differences are mirrored in the graphic photographs and drawings marketed primarily to men, and in the eroticized romantic fiction that is written to the tastes of women readers. The content of sexual fantasies in homosexual men and women appears to not differ significantly from their heterosexual peers, except in regard to preference for the gender of one's partner, and the exception for male homosexuals, on average, preferring anal sex fantasies more frequently than do others.

Submission fantasies are common among normal (non-paraphilic, non-offending) women, making accurate information and framing of the reality regarding this type of fantasy of particular importance for the education of sex offenders, adolescent boys who are at risk for developing attitudes supportive of rape. Also, adolescent girls may need to be given an early understanding of the normality of these fantasies and of the gap between how girls often experience submission fantasies and how boys are likely to misunderstand them as wished to be fulfilled in reality. Several studies have shown that having fantasies of being overpowered resulting in a sexual experience (sexual surrender) occurs in women at rates between 30% (Kanin, 1982; Sue, 1979; Talbot, Beech, & Vaughn, 1980) and 50% (Pelletier & Herold, 1988), with 30% being the more representative finding. In one study, Knafo and Jaffe (1984) found that among 21 sexual fantasy options, the fantasy of sexual surrender to an overpowering acquaintance was the most frequently endorsed fantasy occurring during sexual intercourse among female subjects, and the fourth-most commonly occurring fantasy during solitary masturbation. Other studies have shown that about half as many males report having experienced the fantasy of submitting sexually to an overpowering or dominant partner, a rate high enough to classify this fantasy as normal in males as well, although it is possible that the preference given to this fantasy by males who experience it is not as high as the average preference given to it by women.

Key in understanding the implications of these rates of submission fantasies in women is appreciating the wide emotional and psychological gulf between fantasized submission in the real or imaged context of a desired romantic-erotic relationship, and a rape fantasy. In normal submission fantasies insistent force is titrated unwaveringly to the desires of the person directing the fantasy. Usually the force component is perceived as stemming from the woman's desirability and not related to the male partner's anger, vindictiveness, or impersonal lust, and the experience is globally pleasurable. This author is not aware of studies that provide the rate women (or men) experience submission fantasies that do indeed parallel rape, that is, fantasies consisting of intrusive, obsession-like sexual imagery in which the person is the subject of sexual assault accompanied by intense fear, pain, or with other intense negative affect,

As mentioned previously, men have a lower rate of submission fantasies than do women, but have an almost threefold greater rate of occurrence of the fantasy of forcing sex, with an average across studies several studies of 34% of men experiencing this fantasy versus 13% of women. (These rates were derived by inspection of studies summarized in Leitenberg & Henning, 1995, pp. 483–484.) Men may entertain these fantasies while also focusing on the desire and pleasure of their partner (Zurbriggen & Yost, 2004). The high rate of sexual coercion fantasies among men is sobering in the light of studies indicating pervasive acceptance among young men of attitudes that may promote rape. Studies of rape attitudes and beliefs in college males suggest that about 35% of these youth endorse having a proclivity to rape (Greendlinger & Byrne, 1987; Rapaport & Burkhart, 1984; Smeaton & Byrne, 1987), and almost half endorse that they are likely to force a woman to do something sexual against her wishes (Dean & Malamuth, 1997). Unfortunately, strengthening deterrents and implementing wide-net preventive interventions may be of limited effectiveness for men with certain personality characteristics, suggesting that these men should be targeted for specialized intervention and prevention efforts. Research summarized elsewhere in this chapter suggests that whether proclivities toward sexual deviance in fantasy and attitude will be expressed in behavior is a largely a function of the male's standing on facets of the Dark Triad: Narcissism, Machiavellianism, and Psychopathy.

The Role of Sexual Fantasies in Offending

Sexual fantasies have a central role in several theoretical and empirically based models of sexual offending. The Massachusetts Treatment Center Rapist Typology Version 3 (MTC:R3) is perhaps the best empirically grounded rapist typology and is associated with an empirically tested model for understanding the development of offending through different causal routes (Knight & Guay, 2006). Although the MTC:R3 typology itself is of limited utility for the purposes of this chapter, the associated explanatory model is treated here as representative of theory-building regarding the fantasy-behavior nexus in offending. (For brevity of explanation, this chapter uses descriptive titles for the pathways that were not proposed by the MTC: R3 authors.)

The MTC:R3 explanatory model of coercion against women consists of three pathways, referred to here as the Sexualization, Antisocial/ Vindictive, and Sexual Entitlement pathways. The Sexualization pathway begins with the escalation of sexual fantasies that contribute to compulsive sexual behaviors and sexual preoccupation. In the presence of emotional detachment factors such as negative masculinity, poor perspective taking, and impaired empathy (often exacerbated by the lacunae of childhood sexual abuse), sexual fantasies are increasingly dominated by aggressive themes, which are eventually acted upon. This pathway incorporates the triggering effects of negative affect and neuroticism on the use of sexual fantasy as a self-regulation mechanism that reduces or temporarily eliminates intolerable or unpleasant emotions.

The Antisocial/Vindictive pathway prescribes a much less prominent role for fantasy in the development of offending. This pathway frequently has its roots in childhood physical and psychological abuse (but not traumatic sexual abuse), which contribute to the formation of an impulsive, aggressive personality style that in the course of sexual development is expressed in acts of exploitation and aggressive coercion, although such acts are likely to occur in nonsexual domains as well. Individuals who develop an offense pattern along this pathway may have sexually aggressive fantasies, and periods of sexual preoccupation, but these are less frequent and contribute less causally to the entire chain of offending than is the case for the other pathways.

In the Sexual Entitlement pathway, the same emotional detachment factors critical to the Sexualization pathway are involved, but in the absence of the destabilizing and negative affect promoting influence of a history of significant childhood abuse. Psychopathy plays a critical role in the MTC:3R and the associated pathway model. The traits of psychopathy featured in the Sexual Entitlement pathway are essentially those of the Affective/Interpersonal factor, Factor 1, of the Hare Psychopathy Checklist–Revised (PCL-R). What has been referred to here as the Antisocial/Vindictive pathway includes traits that are conceptually similar to the PCL-R Lifestyle/Antisocial Acts factor, PCL-R Factor 2, and has high conceptual overlap with antisocial personality disorder traits, as does PCL-R Factor 2. Among Knight & Guay's (2006) pathways, the Sexualization pathway may have the most obvious and direct connection with sexual obsession and paraphilia (and sexual fantasy), and the Antisocial/Vindictive the least connection. Of course, any given offender may have arrived at his offense pattern through a combination of these pathway influences, as well as influences not specified in the MTC:3R model. The pathways of this model are conceptually similar to those found by Lussier, Leclerc, Cale, and Proulx (2007) in a study of 553 men. They called their three broad dimensions of sexual deviance internalization, externalization, and sexualization, dimensions that appear to overlap significantly with, respectively, what has been referred to as the MTC:3R Sexual Entitlement, Antisocial/Vindictive, and Sexualization pathways. Fantasy figures most prominently in the Sexualization pathway contained in both models.

Having described a model that specifies a crucial role for sexual fantasy in the development of sexual offending, it is useful to consider the ideas and evidence opposed to the centrality of sexual fantasy to offending. Dennis Howitt (2004) has challenged the almost universal assumption of the role of deviant, compulsive fantasy in the origin of sexual offending. He observes that the research on the topic is sparse, and that studies of behavioral interventions aimed specifically at reducing deviant fantasies have yielded, in aggregate, a negative effect size in relation to sexual recidivism (Hall, Shondrick, & Hirschman, 1993). Howitt notes that Langevin, Lang, and Curnoe (1998) reported that the baseline of sexual fantasies of sexual offenders was not particularly high, and that Daleiden, Kaufman, Hilliker, and O'Neil (1998) reported that the relative lack of *nondeviant* fantasies differentiated offenders from non-offenders, whereas the mean count of all fantasies did not.

Another interesting point made by Howitt (2004) is related to the finding that fantasies of dominance and submission are common among normal men and are highly arousing; and fantasies of beating or harming a woman are infrequent but, when they do occur are highly arousing (Smith & Over, 1991). Putting aside possible minimization of the later type of fantasy due to social desirability, the large difference in relative frequency of two highly arousing fantasy types suggests that the sexual fantasies of normal men are not engaged in solely on the basis of the arousal they induce. The attention drawn by Howitt to these facts inspires the following speculations: If a kind of Darwinist natural selection takes place among fantasies competing for survival in the mental habitat of limited time and sexual capacity, the selection process is not based solely on the principle of maximizing arousal in normal men. However, arousal may be the predominant process for replication of fantasies in men who become repeat offenders. This difference could be attributable to factors (in interaction or redundantly) known or assumed to differ from offenders and non-offenders, such as having a relational context of sexuality, internalized mores, and, perhaps of particular importance, higher executive functioning directed at achieving coherence and minimizing dissonance within the entire self-system—for example, exerting effort to minimized dissonance among one's sexual imagery and actions, relationship expectations, and moral values.

Mediators and Moderators of Sexual Fantasy's Effect on Behavior

Consistent with the theory underlying the pathways of the MTC:3R model, the relationship between fantasy and behavior may be largely mediated by personality factors, particularly the so-called Dark Triad of Psychopathy, Machiavellianism, and Narcissism. Williams, Cooper, Howell, Yuille, and Paulhus (2009) found that in a nonclinical, non-correctional sample, men who acted on deviant interests were almost exclusively also high-rate fantasizers, and that their fantasies were consistent with their deviant behaviors. The reverse was not true, with only 38% of high-rate fantasizers acting on their fantasies. Further, personality variables were related to engaging in specific sexual deviance, with neuroticism correlated highly with frotterism and bondage, as measured by the Multidimensional Assessment of Sex and Aggression (MASA; Knight, Prentky, & Cerce, 1994), and psychopathy correlated highly with bondage and sadism. They also found that subclinical levels of the Dark Triad traits were significantly and moderately correlated with aggression-related behavioral deviance such as bondage, sadism, and sexual assault, with psychopathy accounting more variance than the other two traits.

Of particular relevance to the subject of this chapter, they found an interaction effect such that among subjects with higher but still subclinical psychopathy, a significant, positive relationship existed between deviant sexual fantasy and deviant behavior, whereas this relationship did not obtain members of the low-psychopathy contrast group. They found a similar interaction effect for psychopathy on the relationship of pornography and behavior. Their findings suggests that low-psychopathy males may engage in fantasy and pornography use with little increase in deviant behavior, whereas the same levels of fantasy and pornography use will promote additional deviant sexual behavior in their peers whose standing on psychopathy is higher although still in the subclinical range. Additionally, the higher-psychopathy males are more likely to seek out higher levels of fantasy and stimulation, including materials or fantasies with violent themes. The authors' conclusions are eye-opening in their lack of the usual tentativeness of generalizations from research findings, which are often weak or equivocal:

> Our interaction analyses were invaluable in answering the key question raised at the out-set of this article: What determines whether sexually deviant behaviors are predictable from sexually deviant fantasies? To a large extent, the answer seems to be personality. We demonstrated that sexually deviant fantasies translated into sexually deviant behavior only for individuals scoring high in psychopathy. (Williams et al., 2009, p. 215)

Neuroticism also played an important mediating role:

> Fantasies associated with neuroticism are likely to be experienced quite differently from those associated with psychopathy. For neurotic individuals, sexually deviant fantasies may be intrusive and unwanted (i.e., ego-dystonic). In contrast, these fantasies may be appealing and welcomed by

> those scoring high in psychopathy (i.e., ego-syntonic). With respect to bondage, for example, neurotics may envision themselves as the hapless victims of bondage, whereas psychopaths may picture themselves in control ... Our results suggest that although the deviant sexual fantasies of subclinical psychopaths are associated with deviant sexual behaviors, the same cannot be said for the sexually deviant fantasies of neurotics. (Williams et al., 2009, p. 214)

Other personality traits may also moderate the fantasy-behavior causal nexus. Fantasy-proneness is an individual difference that is probably highly correlated with Openness in the Five-Factor Model of personality (McCrae & Costa, 1997). Evidence that individuals high in fantasy-proneness also have more sexual fantasies is equivocal (Lynn & Rhue, 1988), although it is known that these individuals spend considerable time fantasizing and may become enwrapped in their fantasies, which are often particularly vivid.

Sensation seeking, associated with psychopathy in the PCL-R, is another trait that may be significant in mediating fantasy's effects on behavior. Skovran, Huss, and Scalora (2010) found that sexually deviant psychopaths scored significantly higher on sexual-sensation-seeking measures, which included a fantasy component, than non-psychopathic sex offenders. The more psychopathic men also endorsed higher frequencies of exploratory sexual fantasies (trying partner-swapping or group intercourse) and had more diverse and more frequent sexual fantasies than other offenders. However, psychopaths were not exceptional in the frequency of sadomasochistic fantasies in this study, a finding the authors attribute to psychopaths being hypothetically less prone to paraphilia and, therefore, also less prone to paraphilic fantasy.

Sexual Fantasies in Juvenile Sex Offenders

Adolescence is a particularly critical period for sexual development, including fantasy development. Aylwin, Reddon, and Burke, (2005) recruited 87 residents of a sex offender treatment facility. These residents were engaged in a treatment model that taught, among other skills, intervening with deviant fantasies through covert desensitization using nonsexual aversive imagery. Residents maintained a fantasy log over 12 months, noting which fantasies were masturbated to, and which deviant fantasies were intervened with and interrupted or stopped. On average, 20 nondeviant fantasies were recorded weekly by the participants in early weeks of the program; these increased to a peak of 125 in the fifth month of treatment, and declined to stabilize at just under 50 per week in the last two months of treatment.

Over the course of treatment, the proportion of deviant fantasies successfully intervened rose from 15% to 70%, while the proportion of nondeviant fantasies increased. The deviant-to-nondeviant ratio at baseline of 60 to 40 was almost reversed by the end of treatment. This suggests that at the progressively throughout treatment, fewer deviant fantasies required intervention. Also over the course of treatment, an increasingly smaller percentage of fantasies were masturbated to, and the ratio of deviant to nondeviant masturbation instances shifted from deviant events predominating (2.5 times the nondeviant instances) to the reverse, with nondeviant instances predominating at the twice the rate of deviant events. Despite the major limitations of this study (no control group and no linking of fantasy changes to recidivism) the data appear to tell the story anticipated by treatment advocates and, more specifically, those who advocate intensive early intervention in sexually aggressive youth during the critical period of adolescence.

Schizophrenia

A unique study of the aggressive sexual fantasies of male sex offenders diagnosed with schizophrenia was conducted in UK hospitals in the late 1990s (Smith, 1999). Previous literature on this topic asserted that sadistic features were rare in this population, in contrast to estimates of 5% to 10% and as high as 45% of non–mentally ill rapists meeting criteria for sexual sadism. A clinical rating scale was administered by the researcher using the extensive criminal and psychiatric records of 84 patients to determine the presence and type of aggressive sexual fantasy experienced by the offender at the time of the index offense. The definition of sexual fantasy used was "any form of mental imagery that was sexually arousing or erotic to the individual (not necessarily associated with orgasm," and aggressive sexual fantasy required the additional element of "contact sexual activity with a woman specifically without her consent, i.e., sexual assault" (Smith, 1999, p. 541). Aggressive sexual fantasies were categorized as either non-sadistic or sadistic in nature. Non-sadistic fantasy was defined as sexual contact under protest and without consent from the victim, whereas the sadistic fantasy type required one or more of these additional elements: use of excessive force, infliction of physical pain, domination, and humiliation.

The mean age at the time of the index offense was 28 years, and the median length of inpatient hospitalization prior to the study was

50 months. Results indicated that 24% (19) of the men experienced sexually aggressive fantasies at the time of their offenses, and that all of these men had disclosed their fantasies prior to the study. Of these men, 14 had experienced sadistic fantasies when offending (17% of the total sample). A combination of records and self-disclosure indicated that 28% (23) of the subjects had sexually offended before onset of their psychotic illness. Subjects who had experienced index offense-aggressive sexual fantasies were significantly more likely to offend prior to the onset of schizophrenia. Also, from a list of childhood variables (inclusive of sexual abuse, parental violence, and physical aggression and discipline problems), only social isolation and deviant sexual behavior were significantly associated with experiencing aggressive sexual fantasies at the time of the index offense.

Smith (1999) concluded that sexually deviant fantasy may develop independently during childhood and adolescence and prior to the typical onset of male schizophrenia in early adulthood. It was also observed that the records of these subjects supported the view that the intensity of their aggressive fantasies waxed and waned in tandem with the severity of their psychotic symptoms, with some men reporting such fantasies only during periods of active psychosis.

Guiding Fantasies: From Core Fantasies to Scripts, Action-Plans, and Object Relations of Erotic Situations (Lovemaps)

Attention to core fantasies is a common clinical practice across theoretical frameworks used to guide treatment. Core fantasies are viewed as usually of early origin (or shaped by early experience), vivid, highly arousing, and related in content and narrative process to previous enacted or intended sexual conduct. Core fantasies are considered as emblematic of the most motivating sexual interests and desires of the individual, and, therefore, more likely to result in offense behavior than less central sexual fantasies.

Perhaps original to this chapter is the suggestion that because core fantasies become such by virtue of being identified through clinical judgment in the context of case formulation, they should be viewed as transitional constructs that bridge self-reportable experiences to higher order hypothetical constructs. Hypothetical constructs that entail imagery and implicit ideas, and that are effectively psychological structures because of their influence on behavior over time and across situations have become increasingly important to the understanding of many domains of human behavior. These hypothetical constructs include cognitive schema, social and interpersonal scripts, and action plans. In the domain of sexuality we may speak of internalized object relations of erotic situations, or Lovemaps, that is, mental templates of the person's idealized erotic or sex life (Money, 1986), in which core fantasies are integral.

Gee et al. (2007) identifies core sexual fantasies as sexual fantasies "whose material is organized around a small number of basic themes that are laid down early in life and which closely relate to the sexual experiences of childhood and adolescence" (p. 50). They speculate that these core fantasies may have their origins in serendipitous physical contact or play, exposure to a sexualized, emotionally intense environment, or sexual trauma in the form of molestation or sexual abuse. It may be useful to differentiate between offense-specific core fantasies, and core fantasies held by both offenders and non-offenders.

These core fantasies may begin as sexual images that are particularly alluring or stimulating but perhaps also vague and even incongruous, until they are shaped by the imagination and by reward contingencies. Perhaps the selection of elements of core fantasies follows something like Darwinian natural selection, with the criteria of survival of elements being their capacity to enhance arousal and pleasure, as well as their adaptation to a personality; that is, core fantasies would typically take on characteristics representing compromises that facilitate erotic experience while accommodating nonerotic regulatory mechanisms, such as internalized social norms, guilt, or consonance with one's broader self-concept. Core fantasies frequently are the focus of attention during the highest states of arousal, either due to mental imagery alone or in combination with external stimulation. The term guiding fantasy is proposed for core fantasies that motivate offense-related behavior, or facilitate the initiation of such behavior.

Individual core fantasies may influence behavior, but eventually their content and relationship to each other is shaped into an erotically stimulating and potentially satisfying sequence, the guiding fantasy—a narrative which provides an action and experience template for offending, inclusive of preparatory behaviors such as physiological and emotional feed-forward arousal which increases the perceptual salience of sexual and victim-related cues and of situational opportunities for offending. The guiding fantasy motivates action toward offending, and disinhibits internal constraints against offending. Anticipation of desired self-states or avoidance of unwonted self-states, as well as expectations of the complementary or congruent responses of the victim may be considered as part of the guiding fantasy and should be explored when eliciting offender self-reports of fantasies.

Ward and Hudson (2000) describe core fantasies as facilitating enactment of the imagined offense and as becoming increasingly frequent and intense. Meloy (2000) has posited that these fantasies are pleasurable during self-guided recall and masturbation; but with repetition, they become less rewarding, and motivation to act on the fantasies in the external environment increases. Building on this observation, an opponent process relationship is proposed between indulging privately in erotic pleasure from the guiding fantasy (State A) and a tension-fraught action-tendency to realize the fantasy (State B), similar to the mechanism that has been used to explain heroin dependency and other "addictions" (Solomon, 1980). An action tendency (Lang, 1993) is a readiness and proclivity to act that is evoked by the basic emotions, which can be understood alternatively in terms of respondent and operant condition theory, embodied mind theory (Varela, Thompson, & Rosch, 1991), and extended mind theory (Clark & Chalmers, 1998), and has been measured using the Action Tendency Questionnaire (ATQ) (Frijda, Kuipers, & ter Schure, 1989) in the context of exploring sexual arousal as an emotion (Both, Spiering, Everaerd, & Laan, 2004). Unlike habits à la the animal-learning tradition, action-tendencies are knowledge structures, in that they connect and articulate with symbolic and semantic information and structures. These action-tendencies may have an experiential component in sex offenders that is similar to complex readiness-to-act sequences that are experienced by recovering smokers or intravenous drug users, and may consist, in part, as a (State B) proprioceptive component of a core sexual fantasy. Using such concepts, it is imaginable that a model linking fantasy, urges to act, rehearsal behaviors, and offending could be constructed that would be more satisfying than currently available models that stumble or gloss over connections (and distinctions) between these domains.

The idea that offending can be the result of an automatic process triggered by fantasy is incorporated in Ward and Hudson's (2000) conceptualization of implicit planning. Environment and contextual cues associated with the fantasy may bring online (to use the computer metaphor of the automatic, cognitive unconscious mind) sequences of overt and covert behaviors that result in an offense. These contextual factors may be internal to the person (as in moods or intoxication states) or external (such settings such as parks, bars, etc., or exposure to sexually explicit cues via pornography or live sexual entertainment venues). Priming of salience for sexual offense relevant cues may be an early aspect of implicit planning that is strongly related to fantasy. Salience of sexual cues and incipient arousal may contribute to careless or preconscious processing resulting in seeming unimportant decisions (SUDs) of relapse prevention terminology, or behavioral subprograms such as the cognitive drug-use action plans cited by Ward and Hudson (2000).

The idea of a fantasy script (event schema) has taken on particular importance in both treatment for sexual deviancy and for criminal profiling (Kuhn, 1962). A script usually reflects the elaboration of one, or a combination of several core sexual fantasies. A sexual script could be described as the downstream product of a continuous process of condensing, refining, and adding coherence to a pleasurable, self-affirming narrative. Gee et al. (2007) describe the script as a set of rules for predicting, interpreting, responding to, and controlling a set of interpersonal scenes that are meaningful to an individual. These authors cite Hazelwood and Warren (1995) as having identified the key components of a script as specifying the sexual conduct to be engaged in (behavioral component), the type of location or circumstances of the fantasy (situational component), the nature of the relationship between parties in the fantasy (relational component), the age, gender, physical and psychological attributes of the fantasized participants (demographic component), and the way in which the individual guiding the fantasy perceives themself within the fantasy (self-perception).

When activated in the absence of effective intervention, guiding fantasies (whether conceived as core fantasies, as event schema, or as scripts) set the stage for relapse, either gradually or precipitously; but while the mental and logistical furniture is put in place, the offender's conscience is protected by a screen of plausible deniability, that is, the process is largely automatic, and requires little to no deliberation, or conscious sense of choosing to relapse. Higher-order executive functions eventually come online, however, and the relapse process becomes one of conscious choice and conscious planning, including the conscious appraisal of the extent of one's control over sexual impulses through learned interventions or will power.

The fantasies leading a pedophile to plan on enjoying a peaceful summer vacation at a state park without a community chaperone, and to pleasurably imagine himself doing so as he prepares for the trip, such as by daydreaming about fishing or hiking, may not qualify as erotic fantasies *per se*; but there is doubtlessly an erotic action plan lurking somewhere in the background of such superficially benign fantasies. The desired and intended sexual consummation of the fantasy may be banished from consciousness, or only latently present. Thus, it is reasonable to propose treating all mental simulations or rehearsals of the steps leading up to an intended offense *in toto* as erotic fantasies—part of the guiding fantasy—although the immediate purpose of each the imagined actions taken individually is not orgasmic in purpose. This would include action plan-images such as of images of driving to an area habitually used for sexual cruising, or more obviously, collecting items for a rape kit. The witticism that sex is a mixture of friction and fiction may not apply to highly eroticized action sequences, whose meaning is grounded in distal (and at times peripheral) wishes for sexual consummation. These action plans, like a trophy taken in a sexual offense, are to some extent a kind of cognitive-behavioral fetish. An example would be the sensual pleasure an offender might feel in the ritual of washing and polishing the preferred clothing and car used in predatory offenses.

The Inversion of the Normal Sexual Fantasy-Interpersonal Reality Relationship in Compulsive Offenders

Howitt describes a separation of sexual fantasy and sexual reality as typical of normal individuals:

> It is believed that fantasy and reality may occupy very different domains of experience; individuals see fantasy as separate from reality and the two can successfully coexist . . . It is important to add that within the range of sexual fantasies found in non-forensic populations, heterosexual and homosexual, are themes that would be frequently regarded as deviant if revealed by an offender. (Howitt, 2007, p. 184)

Howitt's reiteration of this component of the received view—that sexual fantasies normally serve as a warm-up act to the sexual/romantic relationship, which is the headliner—is a useful departure point for some observations about the relationship of fantasy and reality in compulsive sex offenders. If sexual fantasy serves sexual and relationship reality in a normal individual, conversely, one may reason that this relationship might become turned on its head in some sexual offenders, with sexual reality serving fantasy, which has become (for them) the main event, leaving the relational context underdeveloped, or depleted over time to the advantage of fantasy, which fills the void. The offender's relationships become or remain skeletal or even vestigial structures, like a tailor's mannequin on which the cloth of eroticism is fitted, but always following rigidly a pre-drawn pattern. The fantasy to be fitted onto reality of the offense scene may only focus on isolated eroticized components of self or other, such as a genital focus, or the evocation of a specific emotion or experience of self or the victim. It is likely that the offender will attempt to evoke in the victim complementary experiences to what the offender imagines becoming. For example, the desire to become all-powerful on the part of the perpetrator requires evoking the experience of helplessness or awe on the part of the victim. Vampire, leach, or other parasitic metaphors are communicative of the relationship between fantasy and reality in extreme cases, because these images depict concretely the use of external reality of the other as a radical part object, the supply for feeding the offender's fantasy, their internal fetish. As in those cultural legends, transformation (becoming something, or maintaining an existence that will otherwise crumble into dust) is at stake in the fantasy-reality nexus in the offense. At the most basic level, this process of the offense feeding the fantasy may be simply that the offense provides a sense of accomplishment in having obtained what was fantasized and longed for. This is likely to be followed by buyer's remorse, in that the reality is not exactly what was imagined, and the belief that the fantasized scenario could have been realized if things had gone differently, or could be in the future, may dampen the pleasure of the recall of the offense. This relationship between fantasy and reality exposes sexual compulsion as an impoverished art form: an attempt to concretize the imagined ideal event or object.

It can be said that the reality can serve fantasy only as far as the reality is assimilated by the offender, a capacity that has an upper limit that is usually far short of the full humanity of the victim, due to the offender's distortions of the other as a person, as a part, and of the interaction. This gap (of fantasy and reality) may be evidenced by the absence of sexual climax during the offense, due to the poor management of conflicting emotions, situational contingencies, and the awareness of the dissonance between the fantasy and the reality. Later, after the offense, the revised memory of the offense (with further distortions and embellishments) both reinforces the guiding fantasy and contributes to an upgraded version, analogously to software programs that are continually customized based on how the operator uses them.

In substance addiction, there is a phenomenon often called chasing after the perfect high: longing for and striving to obtain a higher high, which is hoped for on each use of the drug, each new source of supply that is discovered, each new shooting gallery, new works, etc. A similar process may obtain in sexual offending, but perhaps in a more extreme fashion. Once sexual fantasies become the protected and venerable fetish (the concentrated center of feeling and sexual significance), there is no end to its adornment and refinement. The sexual fantasy (and never the sexual reality) has the possibility of becoming a super stimulus.

A neurological conceptualization of esthetics has been proposed by V. S. Ramachandran and William Hirstein (1999), which incorporates the process that in nature (and artistic caricature) can result in a super-stimulus. This process is repetitive, highly selective enhancement of pleasurable and subtraction of unattractive features of an object of beauty, or sexual attraction. The additive side of this process (the exaggeration of the response-producing cue leading to an exaggerated response) is referred to as the peak shift effect. These authors summed up the super-stimulus phenomena simply, by using a famous ethnological example:

> Ethnologists have long known that a seagull chick will beg for food by pecking at its mother's beak. Remarkably, it will peck just as vigorously at a disembodied beak with no mother attached or even a brown stick with a red dot at the end (the gull's beak has a vivid red spot near the tip). The stick with the red dot is an example of a "releasing stimulus" or "trigger feature" since, as far as the chick's visual system is concerned this stimulus is as good as the entire mother bird. What is even more remarkable, though, was Tinbergen's discovery . . . that a very long, thin brown stick, with three red stripes at the end is even more effective in eliciting pecks than the original beak, even though it looks nothing like a beak to a human observer. The gull's form recognition areas are obviously wired-up in such a way that Tinbergen had inadvertently produced a super stimulus, or a caricature in "beak space" (e.g., the neurons in the gull's brain might embody the rule "more red contour the better"). Indeed, if there were an art gallery in the world of the seagull, this "super beak" would qualify as a great work of art—a Picasso. (Ramachandran & Hirstein, 1999, p. 19)

These authors use the same principles to explain the caricature-like bodies of pornographic material, of Chippendale models, shrinking feet in ancient China, and shrinking skirts in the 1960s. More seriously, they apply the model to nude sculptures of the eleventh-century goddess Parvati, interpreting these as the result of the peak shift effect acting on Indian religious art tradition over centuries to render the perfected, idolized image of the body and posture of the "feminine pleasuring body" of that culture and time. That end-product is a sculptural icon is a super-stimuli to be used for spiritual (and erotic) contemplation, and despite its extremes, was a transparent commonplace in eleventh century South Asia.

Sexual Fantasy in Offenders as Perversion of Transcendental Yearning

The previous topic, that of sexual fantasies as potential super-stimuli, serves to transition to the final topic of this chapter, one that is not typically discussed in the context of forensic matters, that is, the topic of the transcendental function of sexual fantasy and its distortion (often through persistent unknowing) in sexual offending. Some degree of appreciation of the potentially restorative and generative influences of the transcendental motive on sexual fantasy is a useful preliminary to recognizing mangled forms of the same motive in fantasies that contribute to sexually dangerous behaviors. For brevity, the transcendental motive refers here to the human desire for self-transcendence that combines self-detachment and self-actualization with a process of climbing out and above the self toward others and the world in expressing values, concern, and action (Frankl, 1966). Put more simply, the self finds expression in less selfish engagement with others (construed as broadly as possible) and the world.

At least one therapeutic approach attends to the transcendental motive in sexuality. Carl Jung and his followers developed the technique of active imagination, as an aide to therapy, and to self-analysis and integration (Stevens, 1983). More specifically, the extended imaginary encounter with the contrasexual projection of aspects of life not realizable in one's gender (the Anima or Animus figure) is an important aspect of Jungian practice. The process of personal transformational change though sexualized fantasy can be illustrated by an historical example that is not limited by the specifics of a technique and not embedded in the context of Jungian psychology. This example is memorialized in the *Divine Comedy*; that is, Dante's encounter with Beatrice as an imagined being. Dante's eroticism is highly sublimated, as are the imaginary encounters encouraged in the practice of Jungian active imagination. These phenomena can be observed in the life and writings of St. Theresa de Avila and representations of her Ecstasy in stone by Bernini; and in the oral, sadomasochistic, homoerotic, spiritually transmogrified paintings and poems of William Blake, in which even the clouds praise God and have buttocks. It might be said that in Western cultural tradition, with the right spiritual preparation and practice, the postponed orgasm permits a luminosity that promotes the unfolding of higher levels of character and consciousness. The urge to transform by contact with a numinous other is perhaps a frequently overlooked contributor to pedophilic and hebophilic offenses. This is all the more so among sex offenders with extreme religiosity, who may experience obsessive images of sacred and profane content, and may harbor sexual fantasies with religious content that they may be particularly reluctant to divulge.

In sexual offending, the offender's anxiety of dissolution of the personality is brought on by the simultaneous experience of an animal and a symbolic existence that we all must manage (Becker, 1962). Being without adequate personal or cultural defenses, the offender experiences this in a heightened way, and the anxiety (dread) all mediated by desperate attempts of self-esteem maintenance, is contained by the person falling into one pole of the human dilemma, the animal, bodily self. This is an effective escape from the human dilemma for a fleeting period, or at least the promise of such an escape. Usually ego inflation and narcissism expressed in manic defenses (although taking the form of the antihero) are prominent with narcissistic rapists, and there is an inchoate hope or delusion of not only managing, but transcending the damning animal/symbolic duality. Nonetheless, the need to shelter a ungrounded, fragmenting, or fragile self through the reparation offered by the (anti)heroic act of simultaneously violating moral, personal, and bodily boundaries can be an important motive for offending.

That deep longings for transformation and heroism is implicated in their offending is rarely confessed to by offenders; and more often than not, this transcendent motive goes unseen in treatment, unless the clinical observers involved in the case are open to the possibility that the universal bent toward transcendence can be expressed not only in concentration on good acts and their symbolic representations, but also in reprehensive and damaging acts and fantasies, and in the mutilation or perversion of the good, either in persons, or in symbols. This is the malignant anality of sadism that uses love (or good) in the service of aggression and expels the remainder as excrement. Fantasies of anal defilement and defilement by excrement are associated with sexual sadism. Other than physical mutilation of the victim or self, these are the most straightforward manifestations of what has identified by Otto Kernberg (1992) as intra-psychic dynamic perversity in order to differentiate it from mere behavioral acts of perversion. In acts of perversion, the underlying fantasy is to use aggression to find and experience love, not to destroy and debase love, as is the driving fantasy in the dynamic of perversity (Kernberg, Nobus, & Downing, 2006; Kernberg, 2012). His approach advocates gauging the difference between these two conditions by means of the transference context in which perverse fantasies are produced. If such fantasies are introduced in a way that contributes to unnecessary garbling, demeaning, or voiding of the helping and health frame of the therapist-patient relationship, then the fantasies represent a form of perversity and are diagnostic of malignant narcissism, a severe form of personality disorder.

The dynamic of perversity in sexual fantasy is illustrated by the "art" and evil antics of Aleister Crowley, infamous Satanist, sadomasochist, pedophile (he journaled sexual abuse of his own children), drug addict, necrophile, and author of *White Stains* (1898), which Crowley claimed to be a rewrite of von Krafft-Ebing's (1894) *Psychopathia Sexualis* in a lyrical form.

Here is part of "Hymn to Pan" (Crowley, 1919), possessing a style that may parody Percy Bysshe Shelley's "Hymn of Pan" and Oscar Wilde's "Hymn to Pan" (suggesting Crowley's perverted need to debase the good). The piece was read at Crowley's funeral:

> The eagle slashes with beak and claw;
> The gods withdraw:
> The great beasts come, Io Pan! I am borne
> To death on the horn
> Of the Unicorn.
> I am Pan! Io Pan! Io Pan Pan! Pan!
> I am thy mate, I am thy man,
> Goat of thy flock, I am gold, I am god,
> Flesh to thy bone, flower to thy rod.
> With hoofs of steel I race on the rocks
> Through solstice stubborn to equinox.
> And I rave; and I rape and I rip and I rend
> Everlasting, world without end. (Crowley, 1919)

Erotomania and pedophilia may be disorders that often lead to offenses that may include features of perversity or perversion, but the range of disorders that may carry this influence is very broad. One case with which this author studied intensely was that of a non-psychotic man who entertained erotic fantasies and wrote journal entries and stories of killing a woman, wearing her skin, eating her to absorb her hormones (in small packets to be frozen to spread out the absorption rate), or surgically swap heads with a female volunteer, because as, Jesus said in John 15:13, "Greater love hath no man than this, that a man lay down his life for his friends." This man had erotic fantasies of cannibalism during consensual oral sex with a female partner. His sharing these fantasies, probably in the hope that they would be supported, resulted in the end of that relationship. This man was drawn to women and to a desire to transform himself into a woman, by both what he saw as the higher spiritual qualities of women, and the erotic appeal of imagining taking their bodies, even being their bodies. This was a sad quest for love that took the snaking path of aggression through garden of fantasy, and out the other side. Similarly, the imagined innocence, softness, freshness, etc., of the child's body for some pedophiles has the same kind of aura of erotic religiosity, and of yearning for positive transformation. Other offenders may be drawn to these traits specifically out of an anticipated pleasure in marring or destroying these qualities, and sexual fantasy imagery is likely to be congruent with these desires, some drawing the offender toward a transformative fire of renewal and rebirth, and others being drawn to kick manure and urinate on the fire in hope that putting it out will end their conundrum.

References

Abelson, R. P. (1981). Psychological status of the script concept. *American Psychologist, 36*(7), 715–729.

American Psychiatric Association. (2000). *Diagnostic and statistical manual of mental disorders* (4th ed., text rev.). Washington, DC: Author.

Aylwin, A. S., Reddon, J. R., & Burke, A. R. (2005). Sexual fantasies of adolescent male sex offenders in residential treatment: A descriptive study. *Archives of Sexual Behavior, 34*(2), 231–239.

Bancroft, J., & Wu, F. C. (1983). Changes in erectile responsiveness during androgen replacement therapy. *Archives of Sexual Behavior, 12*(1), 59–66.

Becker, E. (1962). *The birth and death of meaning: A perspective in psychiatry and anthropology*. New York: Free Press of Glencoe.

Beech, A., Swaffer, T., Multra, V., & Fisher, D. (2009). Evaluating rapists' distorted beliefs and deviant sexual fantasies: A preliminary study. *Journal of Aggression, Conflict and Peace Research, 1*(1), 25–35.

Both, S., Spiering, M., Everaerd, W., & Laan, E. (2004). Sexual behavior and responsiveness to sexual stimuli following laboratory-induced sexual arousal. *The Journal of Sex Research, 41*, 242.

Chick, D., & Gold, S. R. (1987). A review of influences on sexual fantasy: Attitudes, experience, guilt and gender. *Imagination, Cognition and Personality, 7*(1), 61–76.

Clark, A., & Chalmers, D. (1998). The extended mind. *Analysis, 58*, 7–19.

Cooper, A. J., Sandhu, S., Losztyn, S., & Cernovsky, Z. (1992). A double-blind placebo controlled trial of medroxyprogesterone acetate and cyproterone acetate with seven pedophiles. *The Canadian Journal of Psychiatry/La Revue canadienne de psychiatrie, 37*(10), 687–693.

Crowley, A. (1898). *White stains*. Amsterdam, NL: Leonard Smithers.

Crowley, A. (1919). "Hymn to pan." *The Equinox: The Review of Scientific Illuminism, 3*(1).

Daleiden, E. L., Kaufman, K. L., Hilliker, D. R., & O'Neil, J. N. (1998). The sexual histories and fantasies of youthful males: A comparison of sexual offending, nonsexual offending, and nonoffending groups. *Sexual Abuse: Journal of Research and Treatment, 10*, 195–209.

Dean, K. E., & Malamuth, N. M. (1997). Characteristics of men who aggress sexually and of men who imagine aggressing: Risk and moderating variables. *Journal of Personality and Social Psychology, 72*(2), 449–455.

Deu, N., & Edelmann, R. J. (1997). The role of criminal fantasy in predatory and opportunist sex offending. *Journal of Interpersonal Violence, 12*(1), 18–29.

First, M. B., & Frances, A. (2008). Issues for DSM-V: Unintended consequences of small changes: The case of paraphilias. *The American Journal of Psychiatry, 165*(10), 1240–1241.

First, M. B., & Halon, R. L. (2008). Use of DSM paraphilia diagnoses in sexually violent predator commitment cases. *Journal of the American Academy of Psychiatry and the Law, 36*(4), 443–454.

Frankl, V. (1966). Self-transcendence as a human phenomenon. *Journal of Humanistic Psychology, 6*, 97–106.

Friedman, R. C., & Downey, J. I. (2000). Psychoanalysis and sexual fantasies. *Archives of Sexual Behavior, 29*(6), 567–586.

Frijda, N. H., Kuipers, P., & ter Schure, E. (1989), Relations among emotion, appraisal, and emotional action readiness. *Journal of Personality and Social Psychology, 57*, 212–228.

Gee, D., Belofastov, A., & Kocsis, R. N. (2007). Profiling sexual fantasy: Fantasy in sexual offending and the implications for criminal profiling. In *Criminal profiling: International theory, research, and practice* (pp. 49–71). Totowa, NJ: Humana Press.

Gee, D., Ward, T., Belofastov, A., & Beech, A. (2006). The structural properties of sexual fantasies for sexual offenders: A preliminary model. *Journal of Sexual Aggression, 12*(3), 213–226.

Gee, D., Ward, T., & Eccleston, L. (2003). The function of sexual fantasies for sexual offenders: A preliminary model. *Behaviour Change, 20*(1), 44–60.

Gee, D. G., Devilly, G. J., & Ward, T. (2004). The content of sexual fantasies for sexual offenders. *Sexual Abuse: Journal of Research and Treatment, 16*(4), 315–331.

Gray, N. S., Watt, A., Hassan, S., & MacCulloch, M. J. (2003). Behavioral indicators of sadistic sexual murder predict the presence of sadistic sexual fantasy in a normative sample. *Journal of Interpersonal Violence, 18*(9), 1018–1034.

Greendlinger, V., & Byrne, D. (1987). Coercive sexual fantasies of college men as predictors of self-reported likelihood to rape and overt sexual aggression. *Journal of Sex Research, 23*(1), 1–11.

Grubin, D. (1994). Sexual sadism. *Criminal Behaviour and Mental Health, 4*(1), 3–9.

Hall G. C., Shondrick, D. D., & Hirschman R. (1993). The role of sexual arousal in sexually aggressive behavior: A meta-analysis. *Journal of Consulting and Clinical Psychology, 61*, 1091–1095.

Hanna, R., & Maiese, M. (2009). *Embodied minds in action*. New York: Oxford University Press.

Hazelwood, R., & Warren, J. (1995). The serial rapist. In R. Hazelwood & A. Burgess (Eds.), *Practical aspects of rape investigation* (2nd ed., pp. 337–359). Boca Raton, FL: CRC Press.

Howitt, D. (2004). What is the role of fantasy in sex offending? *Criminal Behaviour and Mental Health, 14*(3), 182–188.

Kanin, E. J. (1982). Female rape fantasies: A victimization study. *Victimology, 7*, 114–121.

Kernberg, O. (1992). *Aggression in Personality Disorders and Perversion*. New Haven, CT: Yale University Press.

Kernberg, O. F. (2006). Identity: Recent findings and clinical implications. *The Psychoanalytic Quarterly, 75*(4), 969–1004.

Kernberg, O. F. (2012). *The insurable nature of love and aggression*. Washington, DC: American Psychiatric Press.

Kernberg, O. F., Nobus, D., & Downing, L. (2006). Perversion, perversity, and normality: Diagnostic and therapeutic considerations. In *Perversion: Psychoanalytic perspectives/perspectives on psychoanalysis* (pp. 19–38). London: Karnac Books.

Knafo, D., & Jaffe, Y. (1984). Sexual fantasizing in males and females. *Journal of Research in Personality, 18*, 451–467.

Krafft-Ebing, R. (1894). *Psychopathia sexualis, with especial reference to the antipathic sexual instinct: A medico-forensic study*. New York: Rebman.

Knight, R. A., & Guay, J. P. (2006). The role of psychopathy in sexual coercion against women. In C. P. Patrick (Ed.), *The handbook of psychopathy* (pp. 512–532). New York: Guilford Press.

Knight, R. A., Prentky, R. A., & Cerce, D. D. (1994). The development, reliability, and validity of an inventory for the Multidimensional Assessment of Sex and Aggression. *Criminal Justice and Behavior, 21*, 72–94.

Knight, R. A., & Sims-Knight, J. E. (2003). Developmental antecedents of sexual coercion against women: Testing of alternative hypotheses with structural equation modeling. In R. A. Prentky, E. Janus, & M. Seto (Eds.), *Sexual coercion: Understanding and management*. New York: New York Academy of Sciences.

Lang, P. J. (1993). The motivational organization of emotion: Affect reflex connections. In S. VanGoozen, N. E. Van der Poll, & J. A. Sergeant (Eds.), *The emotions: Essays on emotion theory* (pp. 61–96). Hillsdale, NJ: Lawrence Erlbaum Associates.

Langevin, R., Lang, R. A., & Curnoe, S. (1998). The prevalence of sex offenders with deviant fantasies. *Journal of Interpersonal Violence, 13*, 315–327.

Laumann, E. Q., Gagnon, J. H., Michael, R. T., & Michaels, S. (1994). *The social organization of sexuality: Sexual practices in the United States*. Chicago: University of Chicago Press.

Leitenberg, H., & Henning, K. (1995). Sexual fantasy. *Psychological Bulletin, 117* (3), 469–496.

Looman, J. (1995). Sexual fantasies of child molesters. *Canadian Journal of Behavioural Science/Revue canadienne des sciences du comportement, 27*(3), 321–332.

Lussier, P., Leclerc, B., Cale, J., & Proulx, J. (2007). Developmental pathways of deviance in sexual aggressors. *Criminal Justice and Behavior, 34*(11), 1441–1462.

Lynn, S. J., & Rhue, J. W. (1988). Fantasy proneness: Hypnosis, developmental antecedents and psychopathology. *American Psychologist, 43*, 35–44.

MacCulloch, M., Gray, N., & Watt, A. (2000). Brittain's sadistic murderer syndrome reconsidered: An associative account of the aetiology of sadistic sexual fantasy. *Journal of Forensic Psychiatry, 11*(2), 401–418.

MacCulloch, M. J., Snowden, P. R., Wood, P. J., & Mills, H. E. (1983). Sadistic fantasy, sadistic behaviour and offending. *British Journal of Psychiatry, 143*, 20–29.

McCrae, R. R., & Costa, P. T., Jr. (1997). Conceptions and correlates of openness to experience. In R. Hogan, and J. A. Brigs (Eds.), *Handbook of personality psychology* (pp. 825–847). San Diego, CA: Academic Press.

Meloy, J. M. (2000). The nature and dynamics of sexual homicide: An integrative review. *Aggression and Violent Behavior*, 5, 1–22.

Money, John. (1986). *Lovemaps: Clinical concepts of sexual/erotic health and pathology, paraphilia, and gender transposition in childhood, adolescence, and maturity*. New York: Irvington Publishers.

Pelletier, L. A., & Herold, E. S. (1988). The relationship of age, sex, guilt, and sexual experience with female sexual fantasies. *Journal of Sex Research*, 24, 250–256.

Person, E. S. (1995). *The force of fantasy: Its role, its benefits and what it reveals about our lives*. London: HarperCollins.

Prentky, R. A., Burgess, A. W., Rokous, F., Lee, A., Hartman, C., Ressler, R., & Douglas, J. (1989). The presumptive role of fantasy in serial sexual homicide. *American Journal of Psychiatry, 146*, 887–891.

Ramachandran, V. S., & Hirstein, W. (1999). The science of art: A neurological theory of aesthetic experience. *Journal of Consciousness Studies, 6*, 15–51.

Rapaport, K., & Burkhart, B. R. (1984). Personality and attitudinal characteristics of sexually coercive college males. *Journal of Abnormal Psychology, 93*(2), 216–221.

Skovran, L. C., Huss, M. T., & Scalora, M. J. (2010). Sexual fantasies and sensation seeking among psychopathic sexual offenders. *Psychology, Crime and Law, 16*(7), 617–629.

Smeaton, G., & Byrne, D. (1987). The effects of R-rated violence and erotica, individual differences, and victim characteristics on acquaintance rape proclivity. *Journal of Research in Personality, 21*(2), 171–184.

Smith, A. D. (1999). Aggressive sexual fantasy in men with schizophrenia who commit contact sex offences against women. *Journal of Forensic Psychiatry, 10* (3), 538–552.

Smith, D., & Over, R. (1991). Male sexual fantasy: Multidimensionality in content. *Behavioral Research and Therapy, 29*, 267–275.

Solomon, R. L. (1980). An opponent process theory of acquired motivation. *American Psychologist, 35*, 691–712.

Stevens, A. (1983). *Archetypes: A natural history of the self*. New York: Quill.

Sue, D. (1979). Erotic fantasies of college students during coitus. *Journal of Sex Research, 15*, 299–305.

Talbot, R. M. R., Beech, H. R., & Vaughn, M. (1980). A normative appraisal of erotic fantasies in women. *British Journal of Social and Clinical Psychology, 19*, 81–83.

Timbergen, N. (1954). Curious naturalists. New York: Basic Books.

Varela, F. J., Thompson, E., & Rosch, E. (1991). *The embodied mind: Cognitive science and human experience*. Cambridge, MA: MIT Press.

Ward, T., & Hudson, S. M. (2000). Sexual offenders' implicit planning: A conceptual model. *Sexual Abuse: Journal of Research and Treatment, 12*(3), 189–202.

Williams, K. M., Cooper, B. S., Howell, T. M., Yuille, J. C., & Paulhus, D. L. (2009). Inferring sexually deviant behavior from corresponding fantasies: The role of personality and pornography consumption. *Criminal Justice and Behavior, 36*(2), 198–222.

Wright, L. W., Jr., Hatcher, A. P., McAnulty, R. D., & Burnette, M. M. (2006). Treatment of sex offenders. In *Sex and sexuality, Vol. 3: Sexual deviation and sexual offenses* (pp. 159–177). Westport, CT: Praeger Publishers/Greenwood Publishing Group.

Zamboni, B. D., & Crawford, I. (2002). Using masturbation in sex therapy: Relationships between masturbation, sexual desire, and sexual fantasy. *Journal of Psychology and Human Sexuality, 14*(2–3), 123–141.

Zurbriggen, E. L., & Yost, M. R. (2004). Power, desire, and pleasure in sexual fantasies. *Journal of Sex Research, 41*(3), 288–300.

CHAPTER SIX

Toward a General Theory of Profit-Driven Crime*

R. Thomas Naylor

Everybody loves a good crime story starring tough cops against ruthless malefactors with a supporting cast of stubborn prosecutors who buck political interference and best duplicitous defense lawyers to see that justice is done. Perhaps that taste reflects a need to escape periodically into comforting fantasy in apparently perilous times. Or perhaps it represents the search for moral certainty in a world that seems increasingly fraught with confusion. After all, on the surface, the realm of criminal justice seems one place where principles are clear along with a common agreement that those who transgress generally accepted rules of social conduct need to be called sharply to account.

Alas, once beyond the realm of pop fable and pulp fiction, the reality is rather different. What seems beyond the pale in one era may seem a minor transgression to be laughed off in another (Naylor, 2003). What is a crime today, notably but certainly not exclusively, if it is profit-driven, may even be a blessing tomorrow. Just as today's terrorist becomes tomorrow's

*This paper began with work done for the Canada's federal department of justice early in the millennium that was later reworked into R. T. Naylor "Towards a General Theory of Profit-Driven Crime," *British Journal of Criminology*, 43, 2003. Some of the themes were elaborated upon in "Violence and Illegal Economic Activity: A Deconstruction," Proceedings of a Conference on Illegal Market Violence Sponsored by the Guggenheim Foundation, *Crime, Law and Social Change*, 52(4), March 2009. Those two papers have been amalgamated here with considerable updating and clarification.

freedom fighter, en route in some cases to becoming a distinguished international statesman, perhaps even with a Nobel Prize to their name, so today's economic criminal becomes tomorrow's martyr to free speech or, more often, to "free markets."

But even taking criminal code transgressions more or less at face value, it is not always clear why particular offenses occupy their respective positions on the most unwanted list in either popular or official perceptions. Nor has there been much progress in the long debate over motivation—unless someone is willing to count as "progress" the recent shift away from stressing a complex mix of cultural, social, genetic, and economic influences toward assuming the perpetrator just makes a simple-minded calculus of potential pecuniary benefits versus probable "costs." Even worse, in some ways, debate over the extent and causes of violence in criminal activity, and the appropriate remedies, seem to have been driven less by cool analysis than by sizzling headlines, backed up where possible by Technicolor photos of mutilated bodies.

The problem with understanding the logic of crime, certainly of the economically motivated forms, is not just the legal definition of a particular offense—something specified in criminal codes, then wrangled over by lawyers and judges. Rather, the kind of information the justice system needs to locate, prosecute, and punish perpetrators is very different from what is required to understand the modus operandi of criminal enterprises and, beyond them, criminal markets as a whole. That, in turn, may have considerable bearing how well understood are issues like what drives the criminal offense, how responsibilities within it are broken down by participants, how different types of offenses reinforce each other, the degree of social harm each act represents, and how prone certain rackets are to acts of violence. Not least, it also helps to assess whether a propensity to violence derives from the character of the offender, the nature of the offense, or the societal context—maybe all at once.

Crime and Its Confusions

One thing long confusing debate has been alarmingly sloppy terminology and with it a lack of simple logic in the definition and analysis of offenses. If language is confused, whether by accident or intent, so too will be diagnosis and prescription along with any policy based on them. For example, the frequency with which a term like "economic crime" is used by police, prosecutors, and press alike contrasts starkly with the infrequency with which it is defined. If anyone bothers to try, then the "definition" usually comes down to just a list of the latest business-related scams to concern law enforcement—securities fraud, telemarketing fraud, Internet fraud, payment card fraud, unauthorized use of computers, theft of telecommunications, fraud against governments, tax evasion, and currency counterfeiting. A list like that, taken from police websites, manages among its sins to confound means (telephone pitches and computerized communications) with ends (fraudulent transfers of wealth).

In fact the current terminology is sometimes simply absurd. For example, in most types of today's "economic crimes," the perpetrator might well use a computer at some point, albeit for a variety of purposes—to make off with personal or commercial information, to hack into financial institution accounts, to produce counterfeit documents, to plot with confederates, or to ask their boyfriend or girlfriend to bring over a ham sandwich and some potato salad, no doubt making them coconspirators in the process. There are even administrative divisions of police forces dedicated to "computer assisted crime." But the concept is about as informative as "pen-and-paper assisted crime" would have been a couple of technological generations back. Similarly, scams pulled off over the telephone, routinely lumped into the "telemarketing" class, include things like: fake prize awards requiring prior payment of "fees"; phony promises of credit cards similarly requiring advance fees; offers of free trips or discount travel that never materialize; etc. Calling them "telemarketing fraud" makes as much sense as calling burglary through a second-floor window "ladder fraud."

Nor does the confusion end there. Sometimes the term "commercial crime" is used synonymously with "economic crime"; at other times the term "white-collar crime" is interchangeable with both, even though logically, "economic crime" or "commercial crime" refer to acts, while white-collar crime presumably refers to actors—unless someone somewhere has managed to legislate criminal sanctions against wearing clean shirts. There are even efforts to assimilate the term "organized crime" (itself notoriously resistant to definition) with "economic crime" on the apparent (and false) assumption that it requires an exceptional degree of "organization" to commit "complex" business-related offenses.[1] Tell that to "rogue traders" who brought multibillion-dollar financial houses to their knees, or sometimes to their graves. Even the alternative term, "business crime," is of little help—for it leaves unstated whether the problem is crimes against businesses, crimes by businesses, or simply crimes that use the resources of businesses perhaps without their knowledge to pull off a job.

Indeed the very use of a composite category like "crime" is misleading. Ultimately what is important is not "crime," a metaphysical concept akin to Original Sin, but "crimes," a term that focuses attention onto what makes them different instead of forcing an artificial unity.[2] "Crime" applied to all profit-driven offenses lumps together some actions that involve force or fraud and some that operate via free-market exchange; some of them have victims and some have clients; some occur by stealth at night and some take place in a normal business context by day; some are plotted by men with black eye-patches in smoky dives and some by people in the latest brand-name sportswear on the golf fairway. The only thing they have in common, apart from the motive of money (that may be only a partial explanation) is that they violate statutes prescribing criminal sanctions (themselves increasingly hard to differentiate from civil or regulatory laws) for certain acts.

Cleaning up the terminological obscurantism might also help clarify the economic logic of profit-driven offenses, allowing their relative seriousness to be more accurately judged. It might facilitate breaking the acts down into concrete steps in which various participants perform a host of roles of different degrees of importance while showing different degrees of awareness and involvement; and in that way it could help to clarify the nature of the offenses at each stage. It might help to explain why some criminal acts are more prone to violence than others. Not least, in some cases it might serve to call into question whether particular offenses really ought to be criminal.

Furthermore the more is understood about the real (rather than the mythical) economic "organization" of crimes, the more effective might tools be designed for deterrence and prevention, approaches that have far more to recommend them than the current knee-jerk instinct to clap offenders into one of the crime schools that still go by the quaint name "penitentiaries"—even though it has been many decades, perhaps a couple of centuries, since anyone, including their inmates, really saw them as houses of penance (Naylor, 2004a).

Unholy Trinity

1. Predatory Crimes

Stripped to fundamentals, profit-driven crimes fall into three major categories. The most straightforward consists of *predatory crimes*—everything from purse-snatching to ransom kidnapping to extortion. The essence of these offenses is the involuntary redistribution of wealth (in physical or financial or informational form) from one party to another using force (or its threat), although guile and deception may suffice. They usually occur outside the confines of normal business transactions, although an apparent business may serve as a front. Losses are usually easy to identify.

So, too, are the victims, be they individuals, institutions, or corporations. Not least, the morality is unambiguous. Someone has been wronged by someone else: hence the need for appropriate restitution or compensation to the victim.

This was precisely the form of profit-driven crime with which the law enforcement apparatus historically was designed to deal. The commandment "Thou shalt not covet thy neighbor's ass" made matters crystal clear. Equally clear was that responsibility for solving or resolving such crimes was the exclusive preserve of the criminal justice system, once it took on something like present-day forms. Neither tax authorities nor government regulatory agencies figured in the equation unless in a derivative and subordinate role. In fact, to this day the mind-set of law enforcement remains heavily biased toward a "cops-and-robbers" view that sees economically motivated crimes as essentially predatory phenomena.

However, other forms of profit-driven crimes are quite different in terms of inherent nature and economic impact. In these other categories, the harm is sometimes harder to assess, the identity or even the existence of victims more problematic to determine, and the borderline between the responsibilities of economic regulator, tax authority, and police no longer so clear.

2. Market-Based Crimes

The second category consists of *market-based crimes*. Although there are certainly incidents of contraband goods and services dating back centuries, if not millennia, the most important of what are today regarded as market-based offenses date from decisions particularly in the early part of the twentieth century to criminalize personal vice—the consumption of drugs or alcohol, gambling, prostitution, etc.[3]

Market-based crimes involve production and/or distribution of *new* goods and services that are inherently illegal—as distinct from predatory crimes that involve the misappropriation of existing wealth. Their "organization" takes the form of multilateral exchanges involving producers, distributors, retailers, and money-managers on the supply side, and willing consumers on the demand side. Since they represent voluntary transfers, there is difficulty defining a victim. Rather than misappropriating property by force or fraud, the supplier *earns* income in illegal markets just as surely as someone in legal business, and quite possibly at what might be called "fair market price," whatever that really means in either its legal or illegal manifestations. Although payments in kind sometimes occur, overwhelmingly, the transfers are financial. Since with market-based crimes, there are no definable victims except perhaps some abstract and largely meaningless construct like "society," moral considerations are cloudy and potentially subject to sudden, radical change. And since what is involved is a voluntary market exchange, policy focuses not on restitution to victims, but on finding a way to handle "proceeds," usually by some sort of procedure to forfeit the earnings (net or gross) with or without additional fines and forfeitures of things like "instrumentalities" (another vague and often abused category). These "proceeds" are forfeited, not to victims who do not exist, but to the state or its agencies. And they are forfeited by a process that sometimes creates a substantial list of its own victims. The ultimate irony of market-based crimes is that sometimes the only really definable victims fall afoul not of the crime that gave rise to the funds, but to forfeiture proceedings when they turn into a kind of state-sanctioned predatory crime (Naylor, 2001, 2007b, 2011b).

Market-based crimes are further subdivided into those involving evasion of regulations, taxes, or prohibitions. Regulations in turn can be further subdivided into those that affect terms of sale (e.g., by limits on prices for rationed goods), the range of clients permitted (e.g., by prescriptions for certain drugs), and the total, type, or timing of product on the market (e.g., by quotas).

Whether the restrictions affect price, client allocation, or the flow of supply, in all three subcategories there can emerge a *parallel* market in which *relative contraband* (the commodity is legal, the mode of delivery is not) is available at a higher price than on the legal-but-controlled market. This is the case, for example, with black market steroids or Viagra diverted from the legal pharmaceutical distribution system, and, to some degree, with the illegal trade in wildlife (Naylor, 2004b).

This can produce another complication. Some countries try to make a clear distinction between regulatory and criminal offenses; others treat what they deem the worst forms of regulatory offenses as criminal ones. The boundary is fuzzy. Hence the term "quasi-criminal," itself a symptom of the growing confusion between civil, criminal and regulatory matters.

Taxes, too, subdivide—into indirect taxes that fall on items purchased and direct taxes that fall on income or (increasingly rarely) on wealth. It is the first category (such as sales, value-added, excise, and import taxes) that cause the emergence of a parallel market dealing in *fiscal contraband*. In this case the goods subject to excise, sin, or luxury taxes may be available on that parallel market at a lower price than on the legal one: the difference is largely (though not exclusively) a function of evaded tax. The most obvious cases of markets in fiscal contraband involve tobacco, alcohol, and fuel. In places with a luxury tax, items such as jewelry might also fit.

Prohibitions can also be subdivided into those that explicitly prohibit certain goods and services and those that ban the acquisition of certain goods because of how they were acquired. In the first case, the goods and services are *absolute contraband.* There is no corresponding legal price. Hence the illegal market stands alone. It is a "black" rather than a parallel market. This is clearest in the case of banned recreational drugs, but also with such things as kiddy porn.[4]

There are also certain services that could fall into any of the three subcategories depending on context. Underground gambling, for example, is absolute contraband in areas that ban it completely. It is fiscal contraband where placing bets is permitted only in outlets that pay taxes. It is relative contraband, subject to diversion onto a parallel market, if the law permits only state-owned establishments to encourage citizens to ruin themselves financially in the long run in exchange for an adrenaline rush in the short.

These differences are important, both for the kinds of policy options that might be called for, and for methods of evaluating success or failure of such policies. For example, a policy successful in inhibiting traffic in a regulated good or service will work by restricting the amount that leaks onto the parallel market and thereby increases the spread between legal and illegal prices. A policy successful against the second, a taxed good or service, will increase the supply on the legal market relative to the illegal and therefore reduce the spread. A policy successful against the third, prohibited one, cannot be evaluated by reference to price alone. With no legal source or substitute, price hikes as a result of increased enforcement almost always do more to increase the amount of income spent on the banned item than to reduce the quantity consumed. Nonetheless, all three types fall into the general category of market-based crimes, and are therefore fundamentally different from profit-driven crimes of a predatory nature.

So much for theory. In practice, the contrast is on occasion murkier. Some predatory crimes, for example, require market-based ones to dispose of the merchandise or launder the proceeds. However, the primary act to generate the money is predatory, since it involves an involuntary transfer of existing wealth; using this typology, the market-based crime is a secondary offense. The matter becomes clearer when the acts are put in sequence—first the predatory act to acquire, then the market-based one to dispose of the property, then perhaps a tertiary offense to launder the money.

Similarly, some market-based offenses are committed in an environment punctuated by force or fraud. Sometimes drug dealers settle accounts at gunpoint. But that affects distribution of profit between dealers, not the relations of dealer and customer. Sometimes, dealers secretly adulterate their merchandise before sale or otherwise rip off their customers—but that is similar to the actions of mainstream businesses committing commercial crimes. However, most illegal markets seem competitive, probably more so than most legal ones, and dealers seem anxious to maintain customer loyalty. The norm in market-based offenses seems to be consensual market exchange—at least at the retail level in wealthy market countries, although the situation can be more complex at points of production and at the level of intranational or international trade.

Another complication occurs in defining the institutional form through which market-based crimes occur. A predatory offense occurs in a non-business context. If there is an apparently legitimate business, it is a front, set up purely to defraud, with little or no independent existence. With a commercial offense, a legitimate-looking *and* functional business is almost always the main vehicle. With market-based offenses, the institutional instrument is often confounded with a business firm—there is a huge literature premised on this exaggerated analogy (for a discussion of the shortfalls of the analogy, see Levi & Naylor, 2000). But in reality, since the market-based offense deals with illegal goods and services, it should be seen as occurring via an underground *network* of participants, even if that network is hidden within a legal business structure. The result may be radically different types of networks interacting with legal business structures in radically different ways.

Illegal wildlife, for example, starts with poachers. It is then traded to underground traffickers. Subsequently, the product, alive or dead, as the case may be, is turned over to smugglers who handle the transfer to place of sale. After working through commercial networks, it is eventually sold overtly in legitimate outlets, varying from pet stores to fashion boutiques to traditional pharmaceutical outlets. Guns, however, might start with legal suppliers, licensed dealers, or gun shows, and enter black market chains to be sold covertly on the street.[5] Jewelry, by contrast to both, starts in a legal manufacturing operation (even though the materials may be smuggled) and is traded through regular channels (though often with no paper), to be sold through apparently respectable shops (with the jeweler either making the client a cash deal or selling the item for full price and himself pocketing the tax money; Naylor, 2010).

3. Commercial Crimes

A third category might be called commercial crimes (with a more restricted meaning than usually ascribed to the term by police forces with "commercial crime" divisions). These crimes are committed by apparently legitimate entrepreneurs, investors, and corporations. (Crimes committed *against* them by, for example, an employee embezzling from a purchasing account, fall into the predatory category.)

Commercial crimes involve production or distribution of inherently legal goods and services using illegal methods in a legal (looking) business milieu. They appear to involve voluntary exchanges—the fraudulent, involuntary aspect remains hidden from the view of the victims, who could be workers, suppliers, or the public as a whole. Transfers of money occur using normal bank instruments, albeit probably with falsified accounting entries. There is some notion of unfair market value, vague and difficult to define though that may be. Although the morality is in theory unambiguous, since fraud is involved, actually defining where it occurs, how it takes place, and the sums at play can be a problem—otherwise, the profession of forensic accountancy would not be thriving. And if the offense is proven, it, like a predatory one, calls for restitution or compensation to victims, not forfeiture of "proceeds" to the state—although there may be fines imposed on top.

Commercial crimes can be further subdivided into those involving: fraud against suppliers of inputs used in production; deception against customers of the product; and externalization of costs at the expense of the larger society. The first subdivision might involve bankruptcy frauds in which an entrepreneur places orders, then diverts stock to black market sale before reneging on commercial debts (Levi, 1981/2007). The second might involve fraudulent product guarantees and the like. The third might occur in the form of acts such as illegal dumping of toxic waste. However, all share the fundamental characteristic of dealing in production and sale of inherently legal goods and services in illegal ways.

Commercial crimes are somewhat more complex than the other two categories. For one thing, there may be problems in defining just when an offense occurs. It seems objectively clear when a predatory offense takes place—for example, someone sticks a knife in someone else's ribs and makes off with their wallet, or, going upscale, breaks into their townhouse, lifts their Picasso, and drives off in their BMW. The occurrence of a market-based offense, too, is usually quite clear, although there could be considerable debate over whether it *should* be an offense. But if the act falls into the commercial category, it is often difficult to determine if it is really a crime. Where does sharp business practice end and fraud begin? At what point does a high-pressure sales tactic become a confidence trick? At what point does effective advertising become deliberately deception? It is at least arguable that all advertising involves a con job, since it is always based on manipulation and usually on outright lies. In theory, a telemarketing fraud involves coaxing people into paying for inferior, misrepresented, or nonexistent goods. But the instructions given to salesmen for bona fide companies using telemarketing techniques to sell genuine good-quality products involve such transparent duplicity to make an unwilling potential client say "yes," that it is sometimes hard to see much distinction.

This same ambiguity appears in securities cases that also fall logically into the commercial crime category. If the instance involves falsifying a prospectus with completely fabricated sales figures or seeding an ore sample prior to announcing an issue of junior gold-mine shares, the fraud is apparent. However, that kind of clarity is rare. Most prospectuses are designed to excite rather than inform. If this is a crime, then the paddy wagons should be rolling almost nonstop between the financial districts of the big cities and the local jails. It was for good reason that Mark Twain referred to a gold mine as a hole in the ground with a liar on top (Naylor, 2007a).

Another problem with the commercial crime category is the fact that at the heart of the definition is a presumed absence of fair market value. But "fair market value" is more an ideological than an operational construct. Efforts to establish a clear meaning usually refer to neoclassical concepts of perfect competition that cannot, except under the most unrealistic assumptions, actually lead to a market-clearing general equilibrium. The theory of market behavior that most closely approximates reality is not neoclassical but neo-Schumpeterian. In this view, each firm attempts to introduce into the marketplace an innovation to create a temporary monopoly and, with it, temporary monopoly profits. Over time, others will try to move in to capture those high profits, with the result that competition wipes them out.[6] If this is how markets behave, then "fair market value" is objectively meaningless in the short run, realistically the only time horizon over which criminal transactions—except those done by too-big-to-fail-or-to-be-prosecuted banks—can be presumed to exist.

Crime and Economic Welfare

Thus the three major types of profit-driven crime differ on a number of fundamental economic grounds (displayed in Table 6.1). But if any one characteristic sums up the distinction between the three major forms of profit-driven crime, it is the following: predatory crimes involve the illegal redistribution of existing wealth; market-based crimes involve the illegal earning of new income; commercial crimes involve the illegal redistribution of legally earned income in marketplace transactions.

Table 6.1 Summary: Primary Offenses

Type	Transfer of	Via	Method
Predatory	Wealth	Theft	Force or guile
Market-based	Illegal income	Trafficking	Illegal market exchange
Commercial	Legal income	Commercial deception	Fradulent transaction

This threefold distinction is therefore useful in clarifying another common source of confusion—does criminal activity increase or decrease national wealth? Some insist it is purely negative, entailing losses to legitimate citizens plus the cost of operating the criminal justice and corrections system. Others argue that certain types of crimes, judged strictly in economic terms, constitute a net benefit by generating new incomes to some citizens.[7] The reality is that both sides are right, for they are talking about two quite different things.

To understand this, keep in mind the distinction between wealth and income. In economic terms, wealth refers to a *stock* of assets (physical, financial, even informational) that have been accumulated over time, and is measured by its value at a particular point in time. On the other hand, income refers to a *flow* of purchasing power accruing to an economic entity (firm, worker, renter, etc.) per unit time. The difference can be handily summed up by the fact that a bank account balance represents wealth, while the interest earned each day or month or year (depending on the convention selected) on the accumulated balance represents income. When income flows increase, GDP rises. But there is no direct relationship between wealth and GDP. It is possible to have enormous amounts of accumulated wealth in an economy functioning on its knees—albeit if most of that wealth is held at home in financial form, in practice it will also sink in value, but not necessarily in strict tandem with GDP. This distinction is central to what follows.

Predatory crimes are crimes purely of redistribution of existing wealth. They do not generate new goods and services and therefore do not directly increase total income flows. Therefore, barring indirect consequences like the costs of increased security (that could be argued either way), their net effect on GDP is zero.

Market-based crimes, by contrast, involve the production and distribution of *new goods and services*. Judged in strictly economic terms, they have a positive impact on GDP. Indeed, it is now standard procedure in many countries to try to estimate the value of underground transactions in both legal and illegal goods and services provided they are based on consensual exchanges, and to add that value to national income data to get a better picture of just how "well" their economies are doing. This is, of course, simply further evidence of how ludicrous a measure of "welfare" GDP or per capita GDP really is (Naylor, 2005a, 2005c).

Commercial crimes involve the application of illegal methods to the production and distribution of legal goods and services that would otherwise be produced by someone else using legal methods. Their impact on GDP depends on the subcategory into which they fall.

If the offense involves defrauding a supplier by underpaying or not paying for inputs, it redistributes income, probably leaving GDP unchanged. If the offense involves cheating a customer who overpays for value not received, GDP, adjusted for the quality of goods, probably falls—the customer will have to divert extra income into making up the shortfall in quality or quantity, therefore reducing that available for other expenditures. If the offense involves a firm cutting costs at the expense of a non-transacting party—the environment, for example—the same supply of goods and services becomes available to the market at a lower cost, or a larger supply at the same cost. In both cases, conventionally measured GDP actually increases—though obviously sane environmental accounting should factor out such a spurious increase.

In all cases, when assessing the overall economic effects of criminal acts, it is necessary to distinguish between the immediate impact of the act at the micro level, and the consequences of increased expenditure for policing, prosecution, and correction at the macro level. If an economy is at "full employment"—another highly problematic concept whose actual operational definition is constantly subject to political manipulation—arguably, the diversion of resources into economically "unproductive" activity associated with crime control might be seen as a net loss. But if the economy has unemployed resources, on the strict (and frankly absurd) definition of "unemployed" used in most national income statistics, increased expenditure on police, prosecution, and imprisonment operates just like any other net injection of funds to produce a multiplier effect. One reason the U.S. economy did not stumble in the immediate post–Cold War period was probably that increased expenditure for the prison-industrial complex more than offset (temporary) reductions in what had previously gone to the military-industrial complex.[8]

Secondary Crimes

The existence of these distinctions has further implications in terms of just what secondary criminal acts are normally involved in their commission—secondary in the sense that they are logically derivative from the underlying offense, albeit there is a tendency now to escalate their importance to the ebb and flow of criminal activity beyond that of the basic profit-seeking crime with which they are associated. Take as examples money laundering, tax evasion, corruption, and criminal association. A fifth secondary crime, the use of violence in illicit activity, is sufficiently complex and important to merit a discussion by itself.

1. The Spin on the Wash

With all three types of crimes, it may be necessary for the criminal to, first, hide and, later, launder money to evade detection and enjoy the proceeds. But in the event the perpetrator is caught, the ultimate fate of the money is quite different.

With predatory offenses, there are no "proceeds" in the normal sense, and therefore no presumption of forfeiture. Recovered property from a predatory crime is supposed to be restored to the victim—though it may not be due to complicated court processes or even by the occasional act of informal forfeiture when recovered property, usually in cash or valuable small items, vanishes from the police evidence room.

In market-based offenses, there are illicitly earned proceeds with no victim to whom restitution is legally due. Someone purchasing heroin hardly reacts to the arrest of the supplier by claiming his or her money back. On the other hand, asset forfeiture proceedings are so fouled by definitional clutter that they can end up being in themselves a more serious offense than the actions that generated the money being forfeited. And there is a long list of owners or co-owners whose property gets seized incidentally to the actual crime, not because they actually did anything to aid and abet, but simply because of overambition and/or greed on the part of police or prosecutors.

In commercial offenses, there might be a mixture of both fraudulently obtained property and illicit profits. Logically, they should be treated distinctly; but in this kind of offense, usually the most complex to unscramble, determining which earnings are licit and which are not, and which among the illicit is best counted as illegal profit and which seems more akin to fraudulent transfers, can be a logistical nightmare. But then, what else are forensic accountants for?

2. Rendering unto Caesar?

The major types of profit-driven crimes also differ in their fiscal implications. With predatory offenses in which both the basic act (misappropriation of resources) and the method by which it is carried out (force or deception) are illegal, in principle there are no fiscal implications. Income taxes are levied on net new income flows, not on redistribution of existing wealth. Criminals who commit predatory offenses should repay victims and perhaps incur fines in addition to or instead of prison terms. But logically, they should not be expected to pay taxes on their ill-gotten gains other than any interest or profits gained from reinvesting the proceeds. This absence of fiscal implication exists because the victim, to whom full restitution should be made, would end up being the one who bears the burden of the tax in the form of reduced funds available for compensation or restitution.

With market-based offenses, in which the basic act (the sale of explicitly banned goods or services) is illegal but the method by which it is carried out (voluntary market exchange) is not, the fiscal implications are also unambiguous. Income taxes are legally due on the proceeds of the sale of any good or service, legal or illegal in nature. Failure to render such taxes to the fiscal authorities adds an additional layer of criminality over and above the basic offense. If the commodity sold is one taxed in legal markets, there may be yet another layer of fiscal offense from the failure to pay excise, sales, and value-added taxes. This, of course, does not usually apply in the case of traffic in prohibited goods (although American anti-marijuana laws were originally written as sales tax statutes) or on goods that have been stolen. And with regulated commodities, it may or may not apply, depending on whether the goods were diverted to the black market directly from the supplier or after passing through the formal marketing chain (see Table 6.2).

With commercial offenses, the situation is more complicated. Whether or not the offense has any fiscal implications depends on the type of tax.

If a commodity is subject to import or excise taxes, evasion turns the commodity into fiscal contraband that can be seized and destroyed—it is in effect a market-based offense. However if a commodity is subject, not to import or excise, but only to sales or value-added taxes, evasion of those taxes constitutes a commercial offense. What is involved is the sale of a legal good or service by illegal means. The commodity is not in itself fiscal

Table 6.2 Summary: Secondary Offenses

	Corruption	Money Laundering	Tax Evasion
Predatory	Rare	Rare	Nil
Market-based	Sometimes	Frequent	Frequent
Commercial	Frequent	Sometimes	Sometimes

contraband. No official seizes and destroys a carton of Cheez Whiz because a corner-store owner sold a few bottles for cash without charging sales tax. If the vendor then goes on to evade taxes on the resulting incomes, that is a separate fiscal offense.

Thus, three distinct fiscal offenses are committed. The first, evasion of excise and other special taxes applicable to a particular commodity, converts that commodity into fiscal contraband. Here the fiscal offense and the market-based crime become synonymous. The second, the evasion of sales tax, involves a crime with respect to methods of production or distribution, converting a legal act into a commercial crime. The third, evasion of income tax, involves a secondary offense, applying as it does not to the initiating act but to the financial proceeds. It applies mainly to market-based offenses, although it could also be present in a commercial one as well.

On the other hand, evasion of income taxes per se has *no* direct implications in terms of criminalization of an underlying transaction. Income tax evasion is a completely separate category, properly dealt with in an income tax act, not a criminal code—with, of course, the additional complication that evasion of income taxes represents in most countries a crime per se. A transaction can be perfectly proper in its own right, even if the transactor evades taxes on the income generated. In fact, most income tax evasion occurs with respect to otherwise perfectly legal transactions (see Table 6.3).

Thus, the three types of crime imply three different types of responsibilities for the criminal justice system with respect to the resulting proceeds. With predatory offenses, the role of the justice system is to find and restore to the proper owner misappropriated property, and nothing more. In market-based offenses, that role may consist of both finding and taxing hidden revenues, or of finding and forfeiting illegal profits—it would be illogical to attempt both, although that does not keep justice apparatchiks from trying to do so. In commercial offenses, that role may take all three forms—restoring misappropriated (fraudulently obtained) property, finding and taxing hidden revenues, and/or finding and forfeiting misbegotten profits. In all cases, fines can be used as a form of punishment of the guilty party—they are quite distinct in logic and purpose from restitution or compensation to the victim and either tax collection by or forfeiture to the state.

Table 6.3 Fate of the Proceeds

Predatory	Restitution
Market-based	Taxation or forfeiture
Commercial	Compensation, taxation, or forfeiture

3. Handshakes and Handouts

With the possible exception of drug trafficking, no criminal act has achieved greater notoriety of late than corruption. The struggle against it in the international context is led by transnational corporations worried about the possibility their competitors might steal the edge, particularly if "victim" corporations come from countries where bribes are not tax deductible. Politicians, too, routinely rail against corruption in public, though how many continue to practice it in private is anyone's guess. New governments see the fight against corruption as an excellent means of discrediting a predecessor regime and purging the public service of old regime loyalists, clearing space for patronage appointments of their own supporters. The battle has been recently joined by international lending institutions whose main concern is that leakage of foreign exchange into the offshore retirement accounts of "developing country" officials will threaten the capacity of their countries to repay their foreign debts. Thus, for a variety of reasons, a powerful anticorruption coalition has formed—albeit with corruption defined, implicitly or explicitly, as nothing more than the direct payment of bribes, likely its least insidious and most traceable form.

Despite the fervor, in profit-driven crime, corruption (in the limited sense of cash payment for economic advantage) is not a primary offense. Predatory acts do not involve corruption per se. Nor, strictly speaking, do market-based offenses, to the extent the market exchanges involve fair value and free transfer. However, corruption can occur as a secondary consequence of both when perpetrators attempt to subvert the law enforcement system to cover up their actions. Corruption probably occurs more commonly in certain types of commercial offenses when those seeking commercial advantage use it to bypass normal mechanisms for getting access to contracts or resources. Where corruption is likely most pervasive is in the commission of regulatory offenses that are often distinct from those enumerated in criminal codes. In those cases, it takes a form that is particularly difficult to root out.

It is no mystery why in some countries, economic regulations are so spottily enforced. Regulatory agencies quickly become captive of the industries they supposedly regulate. First, they become dependent on them for the primary information necessary to enforce the rules. Second, between regulator and regulated, there is usually a revolving door through which top personnel routinely come and go. But third, even more important, corporations subject to regulation are almost always heavy political donors. They therefore influence directly, through campaign contributions and lobbying of politicians, and indirectly, through information designed to mold public opinion, both the shape of regulatory legislation and the degree of enthusiasm with which it is enforced. Indeed, one of the major reasons why corporations do not face more criminal sanctions is not because they respect the need for worker safety and environmental integrity so scrupulously, but because of their capacity to shape the regulatory context through a form of legalized influence-peddling.

4. Criminal Association, or Association of Criminals?

On the surface, the three types of offenses also seem to vary according to the dominant nature of the perpetrator. With predatory crime, the popular presumption is that the great majority of offenses are the work of individuals or, at worst, gangs that are regarded, and usually treated under law, as merely aggregations of individuals—albeit there is an increasing fad to attack gangs, too, amorphous and opportunistic though they usually are, as some form of "organized crime."

However, the rise of market-based offenses is associated in the public (and police) mind with the nonsensical category of "organized crime"—as if any crime, short of an opportunistic act of purse snatching, did not require some sort of organization. This involves applying to a group the notion that the whole is larger than the sum of the parts, with the further proviso that it should be so treated in law. Although members of "organized crime" groups are quite capable of episodic predatory actions, what seems to produce a compelling need to "organize" is the fact that market-based offenses require a continuous supply of goods and services and, by virtue of being exposed on an ongoing basis, also require an organized interface with police and politicians to assure protection.

This view seems to justify two legal departures. One is harsher punishments to members of an "organized crime" group than would be received had an individual been charged with the same offense. This, in effect, creates two classes of offenders, differentiated not by what they do, but by who they are (see Table 6.4). The second is to make membership in proscribed organizations an offense per se. At that point, association rather than action becomes the crime.

Table 6.4 Offenses and Offenders: The Stereotypical Distinction

Offense	Offender
Predatory	Individual
Market-based	Group
Commercial	Corporation

Table 6.5 The Criminal Firm: Two Views

Model I	Model II
Large "organizations"	Individuals, small groups
Management hierarchy	Arms-length ad hoc deals
Long-term planning	Opportunistic
Huge profits	Modest profits
Profits concentrated	Profits widely dispersed
Infiltrate legal markets	Most money stays on the street
Legal markets corrupted	Most invested cash behaves legally

If predatory offenses involve gangs defined as merely the sum of their individual members, and market-based ones involve "organized crime groups" with a collective existence that is higher than a mere gang, commercial crimes are frequently associated with the highest form of collective existence in which the whole is not merely greater than, but qualitatively distinct from, the sum of the parts (see Table 6.5). At this point the concept emerges of the "corporate criminal," a reference not just to individual executives or managers, but to the corporate body itself.

The stereotype is correct in one respect—most predatory crimes are the work of individuals or ad hoc groups with no permanence. However, with respect to "organized crime," it is seriously flawed. Debate often confounds two quite distinct things—a criminal association, and an association of criminals. Time after time, too, serious research has shown that, to the extent "organized crime" groups actually exist, they are not economic, but political and social in nature. They form a kind of underground government to adjudicate disputes and allocate property rights. But once the rules are set, each individual member operates alone or in partnership with others, who may or not be members of the group (Naylor, 1997).

In the same vein, criminal markets are based not on hierarchical administrative structures operating on command to monopolize a market, but on loose and ad hoc networks engaged in arms-length commercial transactions. Furthermore, when fact replaces myth, the notion of huge amounts of criminal profit waiting to take over the commanding heights of the legal economy in order to corrupt its functioning also vanishes. Some criminals are rich, but most seem to have modest incomes that they quickly dissipate in fast living; and when they do invest in the legal sector, they are more likely to put their money into a retirement savings plan than to stage a fraudulent bankruptcy.[9]

On the surface, the concept of "corporate crime" fares much better in being assimilated with "commercial crime" than does "market-based" with "organized," with the proviso that "corporate crime" refers to perpetrators and "commercial crime(s)" to the offenses. However, there are seemingly intractable problems with defining a corporate *mens rea*, difficulties in determining whether it makes sense to permit jury trials for corporate offenses, disputes about whether normal protections afforded persons facing prosecution should be extended to corporations and, indeed, a diatribe over whether it is even possible for a corporate crime to exist independently of the actions of managers and executives.[10]

5. Crime and Violence

Perhaps the most worrisome of the five secondary crimes is that of violence in the course of perpetrating an offense. Not only does it differ between the three fundamental forms of profit-driven crime, it is probably subject to even greater confusion than the other four secondary offenses. And no discussion of the role played by violence in contemporary "illegal" economic activity is likely to be constructive if it fails to keep in mind several potential ambiguities.

First, violence is not simply the act or threat of physical harm. Most such acts take the form of psychological or social coercion. Although extending the concept into the psychological and social may seem a stretch, it is only when "softer" forms of violence fail to accomplish the job that more physical methods are likely to be used. Even then, an implicit threat may suffice. After all, why, apart from indulging the sadism that also runs through the ranks of some police and intelligence services, go to the trouble and risk the opprobrium of the waterboard treatment when a couple of tattooed thugs with shaven skulls trying on brass knuckles at the back of the interrogation room will do the trick?

Second, even considering only physical violence conducted on an individual basis for economic ends, there is a clear distinction between intentional violence (i.e., used in actual perpetration of an act of illegal enrichment), incidental violence (that occurs in the course of the action but might not be necessary to it), and accidental violence (such as hitting an innocent bystander with a car in the course of fleeing a pursuing police vehicle). While those individuals caught in the line of fire may not care much about the difference, a society interested in evolving greater understanding of the propensity for violence, as well as the means to alleviate it, needs to pay attention.

Third, even taking the narrow definition that economically motivated violence consists of consciously directed acts or threats of physical harm by individuals for the purpose of illegally accumulating or reallocating income or wealth, it must be determined if violence is the result of something in the act of "illegal" enrichment or a response to efforts to suppress it. While the violence of the state is often a reaction to the violence of the criminal, the reverse is also true. And once an interactive cycle of violence is set in motion, it may be impossible to separate action from reaction, or to say for sure if the reduction in the use of violence on one side will lead to the same on the other.

Fourth, continuing the same line of thought, does illegal activity lead to or in some way encourage violence on either side, or does the prior and/or independent existence of societal violence mean illegal economic activity (or its attempted suppression) is more likely to involve violence? There are certainly instances in any society, no matter how pacific its prevailing ethos, when particular individuals behave in a violent way. But obviously the more tolerant the society is of violence in general, the more accepting it is of interpersonal violence in the conduct of other forms of social interaction, or the more it condones violent role models in, for example, the mass media, the more likely illicit economic activity of any sort will use similar means. Hence, instead of simply looking at the nasty things certain individuals do, it is necessary to keep in mind the broader context in which those incidents occur. If not, any analysis of the problem risks becoming "academic" in the worst sense of the term.

Fifth, following from the fourth, one of the most important structural and contextual factors influencing (not determining) the level of violence, is the nature of the regulatory environment. It can transform a racket that is relatively free of violence into one with an increasing amount of it, even though the essence of the illegal business remains the same. Take, for example, the results of the early-twentieth-century U.S. federal crackdown on the sex trade—the banning of the interstate movement of females for purposes of prostitution, a traffic usually imputed to Chinese traffickers enslaving white women to the demon opium, then the forced closure of traditional red-light districts. Previously most prostitutes operated under the eye of both madams (houses of prostitution being one of the few equal-opportunity enterprises at that time) and police officers who took payoffs for dealing with rowdy or abusive customers.Closure of the red-light areas led to a migration of prostitutes into other areas where they upset the sensibilities of upright citizens, including, no doubt, some of those who had previously frequented the brothels. Streetwalking also increased the women's vulnerability to predators, who now included police intent on shaking them down as well as violent customers whom brothel bullies had formerly kept in check. The result was also to increase the role of pimps who traded their services as "protectors" for a rising cut of the prostitutes' income. They might also, from time to time, decide to raise those incomes further by beating their "girls" and robbing clients who were no longer in a position to complain to the police. In other words, the idiosyncratic tastes of some clients client aside, there was little inherently violent about the sex trade per se—it was the shift in social, geographic, and regulatory context that accounted for an increase in the level.[11]

Sixth, before being able to determine if any simple and credible generalizations about the relationship between violence and illicit economic activity are possible, it is necessary to take explicit account of the nature of the crimes themselves.

With predatory crimes, criminal codes make an important distinction, for example, between robbery, burglary, and fraud. Only the first entails a direct threat of personal violence; the second may involve violence against property with perhaps an implied threat of violence against people in the event of inadvertent interference; and the third implies no direct physical violence at all—except perhaps to intimidate victims after the fact if they tried to regain their property. Yet empirically speaking, the economic losses to victims are probably in inverse relationship to the likelihood of violence: fraud probably generates far more illicit wealth, not just in total but in terms of the average incident, than burglary; and a well-planned burglary by stealth may produce a higher average return than someone pulling a knife on someone else in a dark alley. In other words, contrary to the simple stereotype, it is theoretically possible that the lower the return from a predatory offense, the higher the probability of violence.

With commercial crimes, whether committed against suppliers, competitors, or clients, or against society as a whole in the form of environmental offenses, there may be indirect consequences conducive to violence—a blight of homelessness following a series of institutionalized mortgage frauds, for example. But since the acts employ guile or deception against businesses or people in a business environment, rarely do they involve direct violence (in the narrow sense) against individuals or groups.

That leaves market crimes as possible incubators of violence. Ironically, market-based crimes, the category where it can be most confidently stated that they increase measured economic prosperity by raising GDP, are also the ones most associated in the public mind with large-scale acts of violence. To ascertain if there is any real basis for such a belief, it is necessary to ask at what stage, with what motive, and against what parties is violence in a market-based crime likely to occur.

Violence in Illegal Markets

A market-based crime involves four distinct stages in terms of generating a flow of income that eventually turns into wealth. First comes production (or commercial acquisition) of new goods or services. Second comes selling them to willing clients. Third comes the distribution of resulting income flows among participants on the supply side who include not just producers or wholesale suppliers of the goods or services per se, but also those who provide legal, political, or physical protection or financial services ranging from providing investment capital to laundering the take. Fourth comes the spending or saving or investing of *net* profit by the entrepreneurs involved. Hence the problem is to figure out if violence is part of the process of producing the good or service, of marketing the product, of distributing the income among participants (workers, partners, investors, corrupted regulators, etc.), or of using (and enjoying) the resulting increase in wealth; or if, instead, it is quite aberrant.

Assume in a market-based crime, violence does exist—never forgetting that this is an assumption, not a fact. If it occurs at the level of *production*, it is most likely protective, to guard the production facilities against competitors or regulators. If it occurs at the level of *marketing*, it is probably much the same, but in this case to guard market share from competitors as well as perhaps to ward off predation by potential clients. If it occurs at the level of *distribution of resulting income*, it is perhaps the result of a falling out of participants from which damage to clients, regulators, competitors, or bystanders is purely incidental or accidental. If it occurs at the level of the *redistribution of wealth*, it is more likely initiated by outsiders trying to make off with some of the spoils from one or another participant without doing any of the work. Given the recent anti-money-laundering mania, it is at this stage, too, that regulators are most likely to concentrate their attention. But an aggressive forensic accountant confronting a defensive private banker is unlikely to generate much in the way of violence beyond the two occasionally stabbing at each other with pencils across a mahogany desk.

In strict theory, violence in illicit market activity could take any or all of these forms; but it could just as well take none at all. There is actually nothing in the inherent logic of production, marketing, income distribution, or wealth redistribution in illegal markets that suggests an *inevitability* of or even, in most cases, a strong logical propensity to violence. True, given the fact that illegal markets have no access to the mechanisms of peaceful dispute resolution that are normal for legal ones, there might be a temptation to resort to crude force. But ongoing illegal market activity seems to rely more on trust between peers or extended family members, and the threat of excommunication for future deals, than on hiring a biker with a baseball bat to settle disagreements. Clearly such violence does occur from time to time, a function partly of the nature of the market (is it prone to attack by upstarts or already dominated by existing underground entrepreneurs?) and partly of the nature of the commodity (selling crack cocaine is more likely to be associated with violence than peddling counterfeit Louis Vuitton handbags). Therefore, it is necessary to ask further if there is potentially something in the nature of particular illegal markets rather than illegal markets per se, that is conducive to violence.

An informal taxonomy of 12 major illegal markets below rates violence as likely (L), possible though unlikely (P), or so rare as to be aberrant (A) in each of the four stages—this is purely a theoretical exercise, there is no hard data to back it up.

Neat though such a taxonomy may look, it calls for a number of important clarifications and cautions.

Clarifications and Cautions

First, it is possible that a good or service offered in a market context is derived from a previous predatory crime. Art or antiquities could be stolen at gunpoint, wildlife poached by threatening or killing wildlife-reserve personnel, human organs for resale obtained by threat or force, tobacco hijacked by holding up a truck or warehouse, etc. These are not merely possibilities—each has occurred. But none is essential to the *existence* of the particular illegal markets; and the preceding predatory offense is logically and legally distinct from the market-based one.

Second, there are often class differences across different stages of the supply chain that directly affect the propensity to physical violence. Antiquities trafficking, for example, might involve some violence at the bottom end. Although those raiding archeological sites, or even museums, prefer to work by stealth at night, regulatory pressures can lead to physical clashes. When archeological sites are the target, there is scope for violent settling of accounts between rival gangs. But the article in question then passes through a series of increasingly respectable intermediaries to be ultimately retailed through upscale outlets to the most reputable of citizens (Naylor, 2008b, 2011a). Although other ambitious prosecutors might hope to emulate Rudolph Guiliani, who began his political ascent from district attorney to presidential hopeful by filling newspapers with pictures of Wall Street brokers in handcuffs, crooked art and antiquity dealers are no more likely than dishonest bankers to either physically hold up their clients or resist arrest by violent means. It may be emotionally satisfying to see both types ritually humiliated, but that has little to do with justice and everything to do with political ambition—or, in the case of Wall Street arrests, with conveying to the "small investor"—the potentially disastrous reassurance that financial markets are something other than a crap game rigged in favor of rich insiders.

Third, the only entry in Table 6.6 to earn an L (likely violent) even at the primary production stage, the racket dealing with wildlife trafficking, is the sole one of the 12 that can be said to *require* violence in the provision of the raw material, albeit applied mainly to large mammals, minimally to aquatic species, and never to flora, a category that actually bulks larger in the wildlife trade and has an even greater negative ecological significance. This violence is not intrinsically between people, but between humans and other species. Nonetheless this probably heightens greatly the possibility of interpersonal violence as well. The capital equipment, at least in pursuit of large mammals, may involve high-powered, even military-issue weapons. With the capacity to use those weapons comes a temptation to do so. Strengthening that probability in some countries plagued by poaching, security personnel are equipped and ready to respond in kind—often with orders to shoot to kill. That means the poachers, too, are going to be quick on the draw not just against their animal prey, but against human guardians as well (Naylor, 2004b; 2011a).

Table 6.6 Taxonomy of Illegal Markets and Economic Stages of Market-based Crime

	Economic Stage			
Racket	Production	Marketing	Income Distribution	Wealth Redistribution
"Narcotics"	P	P	P	P
Sex	P	P	P	P
Gambling	A	A	P	P
Alcohol, tobacco, fuel	A	A	A	P
Art & antiquities	P	A	A	A
Wildlife	L	A	A	A
Arms	P	P	A	A
Migrants	A	P	A	P
Intellectual property	A	A	A	A
Organ trafficking	A	A	A	A
Toxic waste	A	A	A	A
Luxury products smuggling	A	A	A	A

Fourth, in addition to the above clarifications that are of a more general sort, there are a number of specific cautions required in interpreting Table 6.6:

(a) The point at which A (aberrant) passes to P (possible) passes to L (likely) is arbitrary. It has to be defined exogenously using criteria that may have nothing to do with the inherent logic of any of the markets. At best any such ranking is ordinal, not cardinal.
(b) Even ordinality can only be verified empirically with sufficient data from sufficient times and places, with all the problems of inconsistencies or inaccuracies in reporting, along with official or media exaggerations, taken into account. That also means what passes for data is based not just on incidents, but incidents reported in (and generally sensationalized by) the media or (an equal source of selection bias) cases pursued by the authorities. These two are not inseparable—the media depend on the police for leads, and the police soak up the publicity, partly because it feeds back to reinforce their recurring requests for higher budgets and more arbitrary powers.
(c) Given the possibility, indeed the high probability, of an ever-changing social context, the same racket run in two different contexts is likely to show a different propensity to generate violence. More than just a caution to keep context always in mind, this feature also makes the results of simply aggregating incidents across time and space even more difficult to interpret.
(d) Even if the above cautions are kept it mind, it remains unclear if the exercise yields anything of *predictive* value. It may illustrate only what has been rather than what might be. Of course, not every exercise in social science needs to have a predictive or prescriptive perspective. It often suffices to be able to understand the past in order to be aware of *possible* scenarios for the future. That may suffice to alert regulators or lawmakers to a range of options, but it gives no serious information about which is preferable—that, in fact, is itself likely to be highly variable depending on time and place.
(e) Even taking that very modest objective, it is necessary to further disaggregate the table, not just according to the stage and nature of the process by which each good or service traded moves through the production-marketing-financing chain, but also according to the type(s) of legal violation(s) each good or service entails.

Table 6.6 involves three distinct types of such legal violations that can be distinguished in any market-based crime: the contravention of prohibitions, regulations and taxes, and sometimes more than one of those at any time. "Narcotics" (defined as all recreational drugs that have been criminalized) are absolute contraband—the very act of handling them in a nonofficially licensed and registered context is illegal per se. However alcohol, tobacco, and fuel offenses involve commodities that are quite legal provided taxes are paid—although tobacco and alcohol may be subject to other regulatory restrictions, too. Most of the rest are inherently legal—even illegal immigrants are illegal because they come without papers, not because they are immigrants per se. Therefore for most rackets, the offense comes not in the delivery of these particular goods and services to buyers, but just in how they are delivered. A category like "arms," though, is so broad that it embraces things that are absolutely prohibited (nuclear materials, for example) and those that are simply regulated (like automatic rifles), while any given black-market arms shipment might involve both.[12]

Violence, then, will probably vary with the type of legal violation. The nature and therefore severity of the violation determines in good measure the nature and severity of the penalties. They in turn affect both the violence of regulators against perpetrators and the response of perpetrators to possible arrest and incarceration. But this is again tantamount to saying that society's reaction to the offense is more important than the offense itself in generating violence.

It is also *possible* that the violence level will rise with the amount of money involved. But the counterargument also has merit. Increased sums are associated with an increase in visibility, in jealousy of competitors, and in a desire on the part of regulators to make an example. However, despite stereotypes, in crime small is beautiful, and silence is golden (Reuter, 1983). So the enterprises in a given business that make the most money probably last the shortest length of time, and ultimately have the smallest impact on the overall supply of goods and services.

In the list of 12 illegal market activities, only two (the drugs and sex trades) stand out as having a possible (but still not all that likely) propensity to violence at *all* stages. Yet even with drugs, the likelihood and degree of violence will depend on (apart from the context that may vary greatly over time) the type of drug, the social profile of both supplier and client, and the amount of money involved. So too with the modern sex trade. For every case of underage peasant girls found chained to beds in a Bangkok brothel, how many instances exist of young women from North American middle-class families "working their way through college," so to speak? No doubt even in North America much of the trade has an implicit air of violence about it, usually directed against clients who fail to pay their bills or prostitutes who hold back on their pimps. But the existence or nonexistence of a predatory pimp, for example, reflects less the nature of the sex trade as a business than it does the nature of the neighborhood in which the trade is plied. This suggests that a search for the determinants of violence requires paying attention not just to the crime, but to the distribution of *legal* income and therefore the alternative economic prospects and social class background of the participants.

Obviously economic desperation and lack of social constraints against attempting to resolve material deprivation by illicit means are prime incentives to violence, and always have been. The stereotype (sometimes exaggerated) of inner-city violence today would be no surprise to anyone who had studied conditions in the sprawling slums of major European or American cities in centuries past, when they were no-go areas for any "respectable" citizen not accompanied by a strong military detachment.[13] The main difference is that today violence in deprived areas probably rises and falls at least partially in inverse relationship to government action on job creation, wealth redistribution, and provision of social services, whereas in the past it was a given over generations. A second difference is that today everyone talks about it, and some people actually care.

If there seems no strong *prima facie* case for expecting much violence in a full dozen of the best-known forms of market-based crime, it is worth asking why perceptions to the contrary seem so prevalent. Apart from the simple propensity of the media to sensationalize, there is also an institutional bias toward seeing today's market-based crime through lenses originally ground in an era when predatory crime, the form in which narrowly defined violence is probably most prevalent and the thing the justice system was originally designed to handle, was the dominant concern. There are also in some cases big political and administrative advantages to distortion and exaggeration.

Consider, for example, the still-current popular and police view of the bootlegging plague that hit the United States in the 1920s. How many of today's media pundits and scriptwriters, not to mention career criminologists and police-academy instructors, were not raised on the image of Eliot Ness and the Untouchables kicking down doors at gunpoint and shouting "Treasury officers, hands up!" before escorting a file of formerly tommy-gun-wielding scofflaws to the waiting paddy wagons? Granted, many at the time, including senior cops, felt that congressmen capable of passing a law prohibiting the production and sale of alcoholic beverages must have been dead drunk at the time; or perhaps they, like those who almost unanimously passed America's appalling Patriot Act, accidentally left their reading glasses at home. But the cops did their duty, nonetheless. Combating violence was one popular rationalization, both for cracking down on bootlegging and, later, for repealing Prohibition. Yet stripping away the layers of hype reveals a somewhat different story.

Prohibition probably did not reduce overall booze consumption in either quantitative or value terms; it just shifted the form and quality, and changed the distribution of the resulting income. What used to go to the government in taxes went to crooked entrepreneurs in profits, part of which was passed on to the police in bribes. Facing this persistence of demand, justice bureaucrats insisted on raising penalties against the trafficking groups, while politicians searched for scapegoats. Since they had trouble admitting that the citizenry at large rejected the legitimacy of a major government initiative, the reassuring alternative explanation was foreign conspiracies, the biggest and baddest of which were the work of violent Italian-led syndicates, in satisfying the nation's booze habit and, incidentally, its allegedly growing appetite for opiates.[14]

The reality was very different. In rural areas and small towns, illicit alcohol was usually homemade for home use or artisanal production for local sale by a class of producer whose heavy weaponry consisted of a shotgun to blast away at scavenging birds that failed to be sufficiently intimidated by scarecrows in the grain fields. This was particularly true after the Great Depression caused farm prices to plummet and left huge stocks of perishable grain, especially corn, with no market unless it was transformed into whiskey. There were other options, too. Those people without access to the kind of raw material most farmers had at their fingertips, and who lived within a reasonable distance of the Mexican or Canadian borders, given the rapid spread of the automobile in the 1920s, could easily smuggle their own supplies of the finished product, as well as accommodating friends and neighbors. Henry Ford (initially an ardent Prohibitionist) was much more important than Al Capone in keeping the nation happily besotted.

Even in cities, most alcohol was homemade or provided by doctors who ran in conjunction with pharmacists a scam prescribing booze for medicinal purposes. The gang presence was mainly in the provision of genuine imported stuff in a few urban centers to an upscale clientele too smart and wealthy to drink local rotgut. Here and only here did much violence occur. Various outfits hijacked each other's loads and torched speakeasies that bought from the competition. Yet most of the time, even in these cases, there was a modus vivendi.

And ultimately the real reason for the repeal of the anti-booze laws was not a high level of violence—how it could be used both to rationalize police crackdowns and justify the end of Prohibition is another question. The real reasons were the collapse of income-tax and customs revenues during the Depression, leading the federal government to restore recreational alcohol that in the old days had been its principal source of excise tax revenue; the fact that big business interests formerly supporting Prohibition to reduce absenteeism and raise labor productivity now faced a huge labor glut that assured the good behavior of those who still had jobs; and the realization by the political elite that cheap booze was one way of alleviating the symptoms of public misery in the Depression and of blunting the appeal of socialist and communist movements. Yet the stereotype of cities riddled by random machine-gun fire persisted in good measure. That was because, in addition to feeding the egos and ambitions of the justice apparatus, it allowed explanations of the principal cause of the problem to be shifted from bad policy to bad people, a stereotype carried over into the modern Drug War.

Given all the qualifications and complications involved in the exercise, perhaps the best answer to the broad question of whether illicit markets are more prone to violence than licit ones is "maybe, but it depends." What it depends on is so highly variable in time and space, and so specific to the conditions of the particular incident, that while a generalization might capture some truth at one geographical and chronological point, its usefulness is likely only ex post. Inability to control the multitude of explanatory factors, to capture correctly the social variables, and to anticipate random disturbances along with systemic shocks means that the *predictive* and/or *prescriptive* power of any such exercise is likely low.

However, one conclusion does seem reasonable. There is little or nothing in the inherent logic of illegal markets to lead to the expectation of violence in their conduct. To the extent violence does occur, the best place to look for its explanation is in the societal and political context. Violent societies produce violent criminals along with violent police forces. And regulatory violence, something that may be intensified by misapprehensions about the level of violence supposedly prevailing in various rackets, could then become self-justifying by sparking a yet higher level of violence in response.

And Justice for All?

Rather than representing a static taxonomy of simple acts, the categorization suggested above tries to comprehend complex and interactive processes, both in the execution of a crime, the motivations of those involved, and the propensity for violence at least in the market-based variety. Therefore, when actually applied, there will be ambiguities, complexities, and complications, not to mention cases that fall through the cracks.

For example, in predatory cases where deception, rather than intimidation, is the primary tool for redistributing wealth, someone gains at another's expense with no pretense to an exchange of value. On the other hand, a commercial crime involving a fraudulent sales pitch implies gaining consent, albeit to unfair or duplicitous terms of exchange. In cases of straight con jobs, where there is no value at all transferred in exchange for the other party's income or wealth, the border becomes so fuzzy that it probably matters little which category is used. Or the judgment may depend on a secondary factor—did the offense take place within and as an extension of a genuine business context, or was the apparent business simply a shell whose sole function was deception?

On the other hand, careful application of the taxonomy often permits the ambiguity to be removed. Loan sharking at first seems like a commercial crime—it involves a legal service, the lending of money, on illegal terms. However, it is often argued that the usurious interest rates are only possible to the extent that intimidation stands behind them, making the repayments smack of extortion, a clearly predatory offense. Yet normally the clients are fully aware of the terms on which the loan is negotiated—rarely can it be argued that someone is forced to borrow from a loan shark, and if that person is so forced, it is usually not the loan shark, but the person to whom the money being borrowed was ultimately owed, that does the forcing. This suggests a clear case of a market-based, regulation-evading crime. Ultimately, in such a case, the matter comes down not to a theoretical issue, but an empirical one. Are most instances of usury accompanied by the threat of force? Do they involve duplicity in getting the client to accept the terms? Or are the negotiations perfectly open, in which case extremely high interest rates might reflect higher risks and "market imperfections," economist jargon for the fact that nothing in life is smooth or free?

Another complication emerges because some offenses may seem to fall into several categories at once. However, this may be due to the fact that they involve a series of subsidiary acts, each of which may have distinct economic characteristics. So it is with currency counterfeiting. When phony money is passed on the wholesale level to complicit underworld parties, perhaps in exchange for real currency at some deep discount or in exchange for drugs, the act seems to fit the market-based category—there is a consensual transaction in an illegal commodity. But when phony money is passed to unwitting retail parties, it would involve a predatory offense.

The same occurs with credit card fraud. Theft of a credit card, or of the number, is a clear case of a predatory offense. Sale of a stolen credit card is a market-based offense. Use of a stolen credit card, or number, is, once again, predatory. However, it is possible to argue that when a merchant does a multiple run-through for the same sale, it is a commercial crime—on the surface, this seems to constitute a twisting of the terms of trade in an otherwise legitimate business transaction. This is another instance in which the frontier between a predatory and a commercial offense gets so blurred that the choice of category becomes arbitrary.

The same also holds true with intellectual property crime. The sale of goods using fake brand names, for instance, or of bootleg videocassettes and software, involves both a predatory component (the misappropriation of intellectual capital, a form of wealth), a market-based one (the sale of illegal goods), and a commercial one (the misrepresentation of the product if it is sold as if it were the genuine article and at the same high price). What is interesting here is the various layers involved. One person or group commits the predatory offense of manufacturing something based on stolen intellectual property; another markets the product through underground channels to, in most cases, fully knowledgeable distributors; the third sells it to an (often) unsuspecting public. While each layer has committed a distinct offense in terms of this typology, they are all essential to each other's existence.

Despite such complications, the typology has interesting implications with respect to definitions of offenses, prioritization of harm, division of responsibility in complex actions, and even whether something should be a crime at all. For a start, it gives much more clarity of meaning than categories like "economic crime" ("business crime," "commercial crime," "white-collar crime," etc.), which are poorly defined, if not indefinable, and often confuse acts with actors. It lays the stress on what makes various crimes different, rather than giving the illusion of a catch-all category of "crime" committed by a readily definable subset of evil beings.

It also shifts attention away from the technological fetishism implied by terms like telemarketing fraud, computer-assisted crime, etc. In fact, it suggests that even terms like "credit card fraud" might be best avoided since what is involved is a series of distinct acts—from theft of a card (predatory) to resale on the black market (market-based) to fraudulent use (commercial). Similarly, with a term such as "intellectual property crime," that, when dissected according to this terminology, consists of acts of theft (of the patent, trademark, or copyright), underground trafficking (when knockoffs are smuggled), and commercial misrepresentation (when they are sold as the real thing), all of which are confusingly lumped together in a common category.

It further serves to bring into relief the reasons why certain types of offenses fail to command much public opprobrium. Indeed, in some cases the very existence of the offense can be a subject of considerable dispute. There is not now, nor in the foreseeable future is there likely to be, a credible lobby, including veteran police officers, to call for the legalization of armed robbery as there is for marijuana and sometimes other banned substances. Similarly, given the difficulty of defining the border between fraud and sharp business practices, although some commercial offenses may be clear enough to be fit objects for criminal prosecution, others will not. Many things now seen as commercial crimes are perhaps better handled as regulatory matters.

The typology, too, sheds light on the question of just who is responsible for particular proscribed acts. This is particularly useful in market-based offenses where there is a truly consensual exchange between supplier of and customer for new goods and services. The point is that a market-based crime, like a tango, takes two—there can be no market unless there is a supply side and a demand side. Why, then, should suppliers be singled out for special treatment? That is the usual approach taken today, and it picks up momentum as more countries move toward decriminalization, if not outright legalization, of certain drugs, for example. But it has no basis in morality and logic. There is no victim in any normal sense—that is why it is common to allege that the real victim is "society," an essentially meaningless phrase. Hence, on the surface, there is nothing to differentiate the supply side from the demand side. But on a deeper view, there actually is. With predatory and commercial offenses, the "supplier," so to speak, takes the initiative against an unwilling victim. On the other hand, an illegal market is always demand driven. The customer is, in that sense, more guilty than the supplier—though the criminal justice system works on precisely the opposite assumption.

In fact, a solid argument can be (and frequently is) made that criminal law has no business attempting to regulate personal moral choices—as distinct from the possible consequences of personal moral choices. By this point of view, the main offense being committed by either party to a consensual but illegal market exchange is purely a fiscal and/or regulatory one. This logic becomes more compelling when it is considered that market-based offenses involve not the involuntary redistribution of existing wealth, but the creation of new goods and services and therefore of new income flows. Thus, the typology suggests that purportedly nasty crimes like trafficking in drugs, that involve fair market exchange, are in a fundamental way actually cleaner than supposedly less harmful ones like telemarketing fraud where unsuspecting people are ripped off. Yet the punishments are meted out in reverse order.

The typology also permits the deconstruction of an act into a series of constituents to better illustrate the chain of responsibility and the flow of command than would stereotypes about "organized crime" that owe more to Hollywood and police hype than to serious research. This is the case, for example, with auto theft. While joyriding involves a purely predatory act, sale of stolen cars might fall more into the predatory or the market-based category depending on the sequence. Sometimes cars are stolen, and the thieves attempt subsequently to sell them—with no prior guarantee of success or of price in the event of success. (Most such cars probably end up in chop shops.) Such an act should likely be seen more as predatory, since the sale was a secondary part of the process both in sequence and in apparent motivation. However, in more sophisticated operations, cars are stolen to order, with payment terms pre-negotiated. In this instance the market-based crime precedes and creates the need for the predatory act. Use of the typology then permits isolation of, not just the linear sequence, which is more or less in the nature of things, but of the driving force (no pun intended) behind a crime like auto theft.[15] While, from the point of view of prosecution, it matters little if the predatory offense precedes and precipitates the market-based one, from the point of view of understanding the modus operandi of the criminal economy, and of devising effective preventive and deterrent policies, it well may.

Finally, the optimist might suggest that such a terminological clarification could provide some guidance to simplifying existing criminal codes that are often a bizarre amalgam of overlapping offenses, some so arcane as to be preposterous. Alas, given the vested interests of lawyers and legislators, and the ad hoc, reactive way in which new offenses are created—all too often in response to a mixture of public hysteria, interest group pressure and political opportunism—that would seem too fond a hope.

Notes

1. In fact, the organizational complexity of even the more serious profit-driven crimes is usually greatly exaggerated in comparison to legitimate business activities. And the popular analogy of profit-driven crimes with business firm activities hides much more than it reveals. See Levi and Naylor (2000).

2. Thanks to Mike Levi for this point.

3. For a critical view of the creation of market-based offenses in the early part of this century, see, among others, Gray (1998) and Thornton (1991).

4. The case of stolen goods is more complex. Traffic in the commodity in general is legal, while traffic in a special subset of the commodity, the ones appropriated through a former predatory crime, is banned—not because of the commodity per se, but because of how the particular subset was acquired. Furthermore, there is a legal reference price. In this case, it is unclear if the result should be classified as a black market in relative contraband or as a parallel market in absolute contraband! Further complicating the situation, in this case the

illegal price is almost always lower than the legal, making the market operate in a way more akin to that for fiscal contraband.

5. On the arms black market, see Naylor (2002/2004), chap. 3, "Loose Cannons: Covert Commerce and Underground Finance in the Modern Arms Trade."

6. This is argued by Schumpeter (1934). Probably because it cannot be converted into simplistic and mechanistic mathematical formulae, it has been largely ignored in mainstream micro theory.

7. Indeed, some argue that much underground economic activity is actually good in so far as it permits the growth of entrepreneurship otherwise stifled by government regulation, and challenges "bad" laws which retard economic development. The most influential version of this doctrine was by de Soto (1989). For a critique, see Thoumi (1995), chapter 2.

8. Over the last decade, the military budget has fallen by about $50 billion, while the crime control budget has risen by about $100 billion. Furthermore, the fact that the United States employs so many people in construction and maintenance of prisons, and jails such a large percentage of its economically active population, may itself account for the fact that its unemployment rate is noticeably lower than that of other wealthy Western countries. An excellent recent treatment of these issues is by Dyer (2000).

9. The pioneering work by Reuter (1983) on bookmakers and loan sharks has been replicated since by many analysts. For instance, Desroches found exactly the same patterns among incarcerated high-level drug dealers in Ontario. Van Duyne confirmed these patterns with his analysis of the results of proceeds-of-crime actions in the Netherlands (Private communication). Of course, most of this work has been on the retail level—one would expect market power and relative size to rise further downstream.

10. There is an enormously contentious literature dealing with the issue of "corporate crime." This debate started with Edwin Sutherland (1949) and was considerably elaborated by Christopher Stone (1975); picked up steam through Marshall Clinard and Peter Yeager (1980); and probably reached its peak with John Braithwaite (1984). Although there has been much literature since, the battle lines were essentially set—between legalists who saw the corporation as unable to commit crimes separate from those of its executives, and those who argued for a distinct and collective corporate responsibility. On the notion of a corporate *mens rea* and the various permutations and combinations suggested, see Mokhiber (1988, pp. 23–24.)

11. On these issues one of the best treatments is by Woodiwiss (2001). See also the excellent survey by Lawrence Friedman (1993).

12. On the illicit arms trade and the frequent role of governments and/or their intelligence agencies, see Naylor (2008a).

13. One of the most graphic works is Ashbury's (1927) classic *The Gangs of New York*. It bears little resemblance to the recent Hollywood thriller of the same name.

14. Harry Anslinger, head of the Federal Bureau of Narcotics, and a former deputy director of the agency in charge of enforcing the alcohol ban, later insisted that the presumed epidemic of booze and drugs was the work of "the Grand Council of the Mafia, with its plan for an international cartel that controlled every phase of criminal activity" (see Anslinger & Oursler, 1962). He claimed that by the 1930s, "the Mafia" had taken over from the Chinese the business of supplying the United States with opiates.

15. This seems to be a problem, for example, with script analysis, which seems to identify a linear sequence of subcomponents of a complex criminal act with causation. However, it is possible that in some instances, the initiative, direction, and alterations in direction of an act comes from persons involved anywhere in the chain of subcomponents, even though ex post understanding the completed act requires a linear and logical sequence.

References

Anslinger, H., & Oursler, W. (1962). *The murderers: The story of the narcotics gangs* New York: Farrar, Straus & Cudahy.

Ashbury, H. (1927). *The gangs of New York*. New York: Knopf.

Braithwaite, J. (1984). *Corporate crime in the pharmaceutical Industry*. London: Routledge.

Clinard, M., & Yeager, P. (1980). *Corporate crime*. New York: Free Press.

de Soto, H. (1989). *The other path: The invisible revolution in the Third World*. New York: Harper and Row.

Dyer, J. (2000). *The perpetual prisoner machine: How America profits from crime* Boulder, CO: Westview Press.

Friedman, L. (1993). *Crime and punishment in American history*, New York: Basic Books.

Gray, M. (1998). *Drug crazy: How we got into this mess and how we can get out*. New York: Random House.

Levi, M. (1981/2007). *The phantom capitalists: The organisation and control of long-firm fraud*. London: Heinemann.

Levi, M., & Naylor, R. T. (2000). *Organised crime, the organisation of crime and the organisation of business*. UK Department of Trade and Industry, Office of Science and Technology, Crime Foresight Initiative.

Mokhiber, R. (1988). *Corporate crime and violence*. San Francisco, CA: Sierra Club.

Naylor, R. T. (1997). Mafias, myths and markets: On the theory and practice of enterprise crime. *Transnational Organized Crime, 3*(3).

Naylor, R. T. (2001). Licensed to loot? A critique of the follow-the-money approach to crime control" *Social Justice, 28*(3).

Naylor, R. T. (2002/2004). *Wages of crime: Black markets, illegal finance and the underworld economy* Ithaca, New York, & Montreal, Quebec, Canada: Cornell University Press & McGill-Queen's University Press.

Naylor, R. T. (2003). Predators, parasites or free-market pioneers? In M. Beare (Ed.), *Critical reflections on transnational organized crime, money laundering and corruption*. Toronto, Ontario, Canada: University of Toronto Press.

Naylor, R. T. (2004a). Mafias, myths and markets. In *Wages of crime: Black markets, illegal finance and the underworld economy* (Chap. 1). Ithaca, NY: Cornell University Press.

Naylor, R. T. (2004b). The underworld of ivory. *Crime, Law and Social Change*, 42.

Naylor, R. T. (2005a). The rise and fall of the underground economy. *Brown Journal of World Affairs*.

Naylor, R. T. (2005b) *Satanic purses: Money, myth and misinformation in the war on terror* Montreal, Quebec, Canada: McGill-Queen's University Press.

Naylor, R. T. (2005c). The underground economy: A ruse by any other name? *Challenge Magazine, 48*(6).

Naylor, R. T. (2007a). The alchemy of fraud: Investment scams in the precious metal-mining business. *Crime, Law and Social Change, 47*(2), 261–295.

Naylor, R. T. (2007b). Criminal profits, terror dollars and nonsense. *Crime and Justice International*.

Naylor, R. T. (2008a). *Patriots and profiteers: Sanctions, embargos and state-sponsored crime* (2nd ed.). Montreal, Quebec, Canada: McGill-Queens University Press.

Naylor, R. T. (2008b). The underworld of art. *Crime, Law and Social Change*, 50(3).

Naylor, R. T. (2010). The underworld of gemstones [Parts I, II, III]. *Crime, Law and Social Change*, 53(2, 3, 4).

Naylor, R. T. (2011a). *Crass struggle: Greed, glitz and gluttony in a wanna-have world*. Montreal, Quebec, Canada: McGill-Queen's University Press.

Naylor, R. T. (2011b). The international anti-money laundering regime: A flawed policy in search of an imaginary purpose. In G. Antonopoulus (Ed.), *Essays in comparative international criminology in honor of Petrus Van Duyne*.

Reuter, P. (1983). *Disorganized crime: The economics of the visible hand*. Boston, MA: MIT Press.

Schumpeter, J. (1934). *The theory of economic development*. Cambridge: Harvard University Press.

Stone, C. (1975). *Where the law ends: The social control of corporate behavior*. New York: Harper & Row

Sutherland, E. (1949). *White collar crime*. New York: Holt, Rinehart and Winston.

Thornton, M. (1991). *The Economics Of Prohibition*. Salt Lake City, UT: University of Utah Press.

Thoumi, F. (1995). *Political Economy & Illegal Drugs in Colombia*. Boulder, CO: Lynne Rienner.

Woodiwiss, M. (2001). *Organized crime and American power*. Toronto, Ontario, Canada: University of Toronto Press.

CHAPTER SEVEN

The Psychological Dynamics of Political Crime*

Jeffrey Ian Ross

Introduction

Political crime is rarely examined when studying the dynamics of crime, justice, and law. Yet, understanding political offenses or illegalities[1] is fundamental to comprehending the workings of a criminal justice system that selectively defines, enforces, and adjudicates who are defined as criminals (Kirchheimer, 1961). As a variety of scholars, jurists, policy makers, legislators, and activists have argued, the law and (by extension) crime qualify as political acts. Hence, interpreting law, crime, and criminals requires a political focus (e.g., Quinney, 1970; Allen, 1974; Chambliss, 1976; Quinney, 1977; Chambliss & Seidman, 1982).[2]

Indeed various criminal acts are explicitly political. For example, sedition and treason are typically viewed by states as political offenses because of their real or alleged threats to public order, homeland or national security.[3] As a result, these behaviors have been codified in law.[4] However, some state reactions to dissent are either criminal or can be considered as such. This is the case when governments occasionally engage in repressive actions during

*Portions of this chapter are adapted and reprinted from: "A model of the psychological causes of oppositional political terrorism" by Jeffrey Ian Ross. *Peace and Conflict: Journal of Peace Psychology*, Vol. 2, Iss. 2.

which law-abiding individuals are placed under surveillance and/or harassed or groups are infiltrated and/or destabilized.

These types of state responses are rarely recognized in domestic criminal law. Both actions, oppositional and state-initiated, are increasingly understood by many scholars and activists as political crimes. Likewise, and according to recent theoretical advances in criminology, sociology, political science, and law, many controversial behaviors are considered politically and socially harmful, yet are not presently classified in legal codes as criminal. Legal definitions of crime are often too narrow, and the law is frequently too slow, and or reflects narrow especially elite interests, to incorporate these kinds of actions. In other words, we cannot impose the kind of neutrality upon the law that might be implicit in the statement, "Equal Justice under the Law."

Thus, an alternative, more contemporary, and inclusive definition and conceptualization of crime is needed. One definition that is gaining increasing legitimacy recognizes that crime is not only a type of deviance that has been codified or has been conceptualized as a violation of a criminal law, but it can be interpreted by the wider body politic as a social harm, moral transgression, and/or civil or human rights violation (e.g., Bohm, 1993; Schwendinger & Schwendinger, 1975).[5]

This "social justice" perspective acknowledges that some behaviors are not traditionally labeled criminal but should be, and that certain activities that do not violate the existing law, yet fall under the previously mentioned characteristics, should be considered crimes. This notion would accommodate not only the actions of individuals and organizations, but also those of states, their employees, and contractors. Thus, political crime is a more far-ranging label than those previously considered.

Obstacles to Understanding and Interpreting Political Crime

As the previous discussion suggests, it is difficult to come to terms with political crime. Several reasons contribute to this state of affairs. In general, there is often a lack of: consensus with respect to a definition, availability of good information, rigorous analysis, and/or interest in political crimes. Undoubtedly, considerable confusion exists about what constitutes a political offense. Experts are often divided over how to define political illegalities, and many seem to purposefully define political crime differently. Moreover, information presented by the mass media (e.g., movies, books) and news media (e.g., newspaper, radio, television) minimizes the ability of the general public to understand political crimes properly (e.g., Barak, 1994; Warr, 1995).

Although this is less the case with oppositional political crimes (e.g., terrorism), the media construction of state crimes (e.g., genocide) often presents them as unavoidable illegalities, the "just deserts" inflicted upon "irrational" dissidents, or the collateral consequences of war. Perhaps more importantly, the identification of crimes by the state is not popular. Many people do not criticize their own political systems' legitimacy because of high levels of nationalism, trust, deference to authority, apathy, or repeated experiences of powerlessness (e.g., Ross, 2000a, chap. 5).

Clarifying the Definition of Political Crime

In sum, political crimes consist of:

> crimes against the state (violations of law for the purpose of modifying or changing social conditions) . . . [and] crimes by the state, both domestic (violations of law and unethical acts by state officials and agencies whose victimization occurs inside [a particular country]) and international (violations of domestic and international law by state officials and agencies whose victimization occurs outside the U.S.). (Beirne & Messerschmitt, 1991, p. 240)

Given this categorization, a domestic political crime could involve a correctional officer violating a prisoner's civil, human, or constitutional rights here in the United States (Ross, 2008). On the other hand, an international political crime could include the destabilization of a foreign government, as the United States was accused of attempting in Allende's Chile in 1970 (Agee, 1975). Alternatively, the 1998 bombing of the U.S. embassies in Kenya and Tanzania, allegedly committed by the al-Qaeda terrorist organization, would also qualify as an international criminal action.

Jurists usually distinguish a crime by referring to the existing criminal code, and if this is insufficient, they examine the context. The latter includes the perpetrators' motives, affiliations, targets/victims, and the effects of the action (e.g., Koistra, 1985; Ross, 2003). Although democratic governments and their employees are bound by specific laws and statutes forbidding them to engage in illegalities (typically embedded in criminal and administrative law), they periodically violate these rules for particular purposes.

Crimes committed by the state are somewhat unique because they include illegalities committed by the government as a whole, by organizational units of the state, and by individual officials who break the law for their own personal or their agency's gain (Ross, 1995/2000, 2000b).

These types of crime differ because the former two categories are organizationally based, whereas the latter is regarded as individual crimes of occupational corruption. Just as some types of white-collar crime are organizationally based (e.g., the Ford Pinto case of violence against consumers; e.g., Cullen, Maakestad, & Cavender, 1987), some specific political state crimes are also considered organizational (e.g., Kauzlarich & Kramer, 1993, 1998). For instance, the Federal Bureau of Investigation's (FBI) ongoing illegal surveillance of American citizens (1925–1972) was an agency-wide operation conducted with the guidance of top FBI officials and involving almost every field office in the United States (Churchill & Vander Wall, 1990; Davis, 1992).

Theories of Political Crime

No widely accepted causal theories of crime, including political crime, exist. Though this hinders our ability to specify an appropriate explanation for political crime, we can examine relevant theories. Merton (1938, 1964, 1966) provided one of the earliest explanations that, in part, touches on political crime. According to his anomic theory of deviance (i.e., strain theory), individuals live in societies that have a considerable amount of "structural dysfunctionalism." This, in turn, leads people to experience an ends/means discrepancy. These processes combined together create stress. In order to minimize the discomfort, individuals have five options, one of which is rebellion (nominally a type of political crime). Merton's anomic theory of deviance, which partially explains political crime, is used by Kelly (1972) and Alexander (1992a, 1992b). Unfortunately, Merton's theory, regardless of who uses it, is too limited for a more encompassing understanding of political crime.

Similarly, Moran (1974) describes "sequential stages which in successive combination might account for the development of a political criminal" (p. 73). The first are what he calls "predisposing conditions or background factors, the conjunction of which forms a pool of potential political criminals. These conditions exist prior to an individual's decision to commit a political crime and by themselves do not account for his behavior" (pp. 73–74). The aforementioned conditions include the concept of strain and "a political problem solving perspective." The latter consists of "situational contingencies which lead to the commission of political crimes by predisposed individuals" (p. 74). Moran advocates a five-stage "developmental model" consisting of the following steps: (a) strain; (b) "political problem solving perspective"; (c) a turning point event; (d) commitment to act; and (e) engaging in the political crime.

Although he recognizes many of the limitations of his idea, the cases upon which Moran builds his model may be too ideographic to legitimately support the kinds of generalizations he made.

An alternative perspective has been offered by Turk (1982). His structural conflict theory posits that although power and inequality are important factors in explaining political crime, the cultural gap between offenders and authorities is the primary factor that leads to the commission of political crime. Turk's theory is interesting, but it is limited in its explanatory power.

Merton's, Moran's, and Turk's theories are useful in describing, and in some cases explaining, various types of political crime, but they are not very helpful in accounting for all types of this phenomenon. The dynamic nature of such activities needs to be more thoroughly explored, and furthermore, the macro- and micro-level processes in political crime should be linked (e.g., Frenkel-Brunswik, 1952).

The Psychological Interpretation

Often, research about political crime has taken a static perspective or maintained that political crime primarily results from either state or oppositional activities. Like many other phenomena in the social and natural sciences, the process of political crime follows an interactive, iterative, or what I call "dynamic" pattern. In short, building on Newtonian physics, nothing in nature is static, and neither is political crime. One of the central hypotheses underlying political crime is grounded in the interaction between anti-systemic crime and state crime (Ross, 2003, chap. 2).

In an effort to illustrate how dynamic political crime can be, we can turn to numerous historical examples whereby state crimes can cause oppositional crimes and vice versa. In other words, political crime does not exist in a vacuum. Rather, as previously mentioned, it is affected by a series of factors that are endemic to the people who commit the crimes, the occupations they hold, the organizations that employ them (or of which they are members), and, more generally, the context in which a particular crime exists. Thus, political crime is a response to a variety of subtle, ongoing, interacting, and changing psychological and structural factors manifested by perpetrators, victims, state agencies, and audiences.[6]

A vast array of theories may shed light on the nature of political crime. Moreover, one must accept the fact that each type of political crime may have a different cause. The relative cause of a particular political crime, therefore, depends on the situational dynamics. One category of theories are "macro" theories because they clarify how environmental factors (including institutions, economics, political systems, and cultures) affect individuals and groups. Among the macro theories are sociological explanations, sometimes called structural explanations. On the other hand, "micro" theories explain phenomena pertinent to people, their differences, their mental states, and their interactions. The micro theories typically explain individual-level behavior and encompass explanations subsumed by psychology.

Psychological theories are rooted in individual-level processes. Differential association theory (e.g., Sutherland, 1947) fits conveniently into this paradigm.[7] Sutherland's theory was first used to explain the process by which adolescent males become deviant and engage in delinquent behavior, including joining gangs. Later he reformulated and expanded his theory to include the illegal actions of the wealthy, whom he labeled white-collar criminals (Sutherland, 1949a, 1949b). His theory, by logical extension, is applicable to political crime and criminals.

Differential association theory purports that crime is learned behavior that one adopts through affiliating and interacting with others. Favorable attitudes as well as logistical information about how to commit crimes are learned from close friends or acquaintances. In addition, one is socialized into having favorable definitions or attitudes about crime. This later process is pertinent to understanding how individuals come to regard crime as a viable course of action.[8]

In particular, Sutherland argued that criminal behavior is learned in a process of symbolic interaction with others, primarily in groups.[9] Although nine statements constitute the theory, it is the sixth that Sutherland claimed as *the* principle of differential association. It argues that a person commits crimes because he or she learned "definitions" (rationalizations and attitudes) favorable to violation of the law in "excess" of the definitions unfavorable to breaking the law (Akers, 1994, p. 93).

Sutherland does not simply argue that association with "bad company" leads to criminality. Rather, he implies that one learns criminal behavior in intimate communication with criminal and noncriminal "patterns" and "definitions." Criminal behavior is explained by one's exposure to others' favorable definitions of crime that are weighed against one's contact with conforming, noncriminal definitions. The process varies according to the "modalities" of association. "That is, if persons are exposed first, more frequently, for a longer time, and with greater intensity to law-violating definitions than to law-abiding definitions, then they are more likely to deviate from the law" (Akers, 1994, p. 93).

Sutherland's theory is as pertinent to political crime and criminals as it is to juvenile delinquency and the vagaries of white-collar crime. It follows that political criminals acquire their behaviors through interactive learning with others. Although there will always be "lone wolves," it stands to reason that political criminals develop a belief (or definitions) that crime offers positive outcomes when those definitions favorable to violation of law exceed those definitions unfavorable to committing crimes. Whether considering oppositional terrorism by nationalist-separatists or human rights abuses by military officers, it is logical to assume that these behaviors are learned and conducted by individuals within various networks where a system of shared norms and values exists.

Sutherland's theory is able to explain people's actions as learned behavior occurring within an environment that formally and informally instructs them that criminal behavior (or at least these types of political actions) is favorable, indeed more desirable than behaviors that do not violate the law. Thus, systematic violations of citizens' rights sanctioned by an organizational program within MI-5 (one of the British National Security Agencies) or the FBI (the American agency tasked with responding to domestic terrorism, and other criminal offenses of a national matter), for example, can in part be explained by this micro-theoretical perspective.

It follows that Sutherland's theory is able to explain the process by which otherwise law-abiding police officers, acting within their bureaucracy, can violate both the law and individuals' human rights, knowing all the while that their actions are illegal and should be kept secret.

Summary

Although many political crimes are committed by groups that are formally or loosely structured, whether oppositional in nature or organized by state organizations, these activities are, in the final analysis, committed by individuals. These people are working within the structural confines of both informal and complex organizations, political systems, political economies, and different cultures. They make decisions and act, while often denying that any wrongdoing has occurred. In sum, political crime is the result of a complex interplay among individuals (I), situations/opportunities (S), organizations (O), and resource adequacy (R). These combined factors have been identified as the ISOR explanation (Ross, 2003, chap. 3).

In general, governmental response to political crime ranges from apathy to policy advocacy to organizational or political change. In general, antisystemic political crimes are met with state resistance or change, whereas state crimes are met with apathy, resistance, or demand for change from the public or its elected representatives. Apathy and resistance are the most disconcerting responses to state crime because they prevent its control and encourage future commission. For example, a state that is the victim of espionage can simply ignore that a threat to national security has taken place. Alternatively, a state can analyze the event or can engage in counterespionage. In this context, the ISOR relationship is not simply a resource mobilization theory or a crime prevention method brought into alignment with environmental design theories.

Even though conflict and differential association theories were developed to further the understanding of nonpolitical crime, they can easily explain political law-breaking and, as a result, help us to understand the dynamics of political crime. Conflict in general, rather than that specifically motivated by economic factors alone, is the most important reason why people engage in political crime. Groups and in-group socialization are equally important and powerful motivators.

A Focus on Psychological Explanations of Oppositional Political Terrorism[10]

By far the greatest amount of scholarly attention to the psychological causes of any type of political crime has been directed towards oppositional political terrorism.[11] In general, five principal factors have been identified. Psychology has different schools, theories, and/or areas of research that offer some insight into the causes of terrorism. Seven psychological theories that explain terrorists' behavior are most prominent in the scholarly literature:

1. Psychoanalytical (Morf, 1970)
2. Learning (Pitcher & Hamblin, 1982)
3. Frustration-aggression (Gurr, 1970)
4. Narcissism-aggression (Pearlstein, 1991)
5. Trait (Russell & Miller, 1983)
6. Developmental (Sayari, 1985)
7. Motivational/rational choice (Crenshaw, 1990)

These theories are partial explanations, as none are in and of themselves sufficient to explain the psychological causes of terrorism. The alternative strategy proposed here *integrates* these approaches.[12]

According to this integrated view (which incorporates both permissive and precipitant causes), childhood and adolescent experiences condition individuals to develop personality traits that predispose them to engage in acts of terrorism. The development of these traits can be explained by biological, psychoanalytic, learning, and frustration- or narcissism-aggression theories. These attributes motivate individuals to commit terrorism alone, form bonds with other people who are predisposed to engage in terrorism, or develop, join, remain in, or lead terrorist organizations. These processes, in turn, shape the cost-benefit calculus of individual terrorists.

The psychological part of the model consists of five etiological factors of terrorism listed in increasing order of importance: *the development of facilitating traits*, *frustration or narcissism-aggression*, *associational drives*, *learning opportunities*, and *cost-benefit calculations*. These processes are present in each individual, but their importance and unique combination varies among terrorists, groups, and contexts.

A considerable scholarly effort has been directed at identifying basic personality traits of terrorists (e.g., Gutmann, 1979), to learn *the development of facilitating traits*. The underlying assumption of this work is that specific characteristics predispose people to individually engage in terrorism, join terrorist organizations, and/or commit this type of political violence on behalf of a group. Although a generalized personality profile of terrorists has been criticized and largely discounted (Crenshaw, 1986, p. 385; Wilkinson, 1977, p. 193), the results from profiling studies (Jager, Schmidtchen, & Süllwold, 1981; Russell & Miller, 1983) have provided investigators some insights on the personality traits of terrorists. A few of the more prominent characteristics are, from least to most reported: fear, hostility, depression, guilt, antiauthoritarianism, a perceived lack of manliness, self-centeredness, extreme extroversion, a need for high risks or stress, and alienation (see Ross, 1994a, pp. 20–24).[13]

Despite being periodically discredited (Friedland, 1992, p. 86), some analysts have argued that terrorism is caused by frustration manifested in aggression—that is, *frustration-aggression* (see Dollard, Doob, Miller, Mowrer, & Sears, 1939; Gurr, 1970).[14] Even though it is recognized that not all frustration experienced by individuals results in aggression (Merton, 1938), under some conditions, a proportion of it does. In the main, frustration may be caused by the accumulation of unresolved grievances. Even though frustration-aggression may cause individuals to lash out at the targets of their frustration on their own, they may also perceive that it would be better to join others who share the same beliefs (Sutherland, 1947).

Some terrorists are individuals who have previously received significant blows to their ego. This psychological injury, it is argued, leads to aggression if an individual encounters an appropriate target. This is what is meant by *narcissism-aggression* (Pearlstein, 1991). Narcissistic injury and rage may be present, but they are generally not sufficient as an explanation, because those experiencing this reaction may engage in something other than an act of terrorism to placate their anger. Instead, many terrorists experience frustration, a need to consolidate or make up for the lack of meaning in their previous careers (such as criminals who turn to terrorism), or want to redress grievances held by others.[15]

Although some terrorist events are committed by individuals acting alone, the majority of violent political acts of this nature are performed by groups through what are called *associational drives* (Oots, 1986). Joining a terrorist group can be a conscious attempt (or unconscious reaction) to affiliate with others who share similar personalities, can provide benefits, and further their individual goals.[16] There is a tendency for some marginal, isolated, and lonely individuals with troubled family backgrounds to be attracted to particular terrorist organizations. For these individuals, belonging to the terrorist group is the first time they feel a sense of belonging (Post, 1984). In fact, Weinberg and Davis (1989) identify a "push/pull dynamic": recruits may experience a "push provided by internal psychological attributes and . . . [a] pull offered by the organizations to which these individuals become attached" (p. 97).

Belonging to a terrorist organization, then, serves a series of purposes: it educates and socializes individual members (Post, 1984, p. 251); legitimizes the collective grievances of individual members; satisfies the need of its members to belong; expresses members' individual traits; and develops a shared identity and commitment to a cause (Hacker, 1976, p. 295). The group "diminishes or eliminates conflicts among the followers through group identification in the service of a cause, [and] cements the group into a coherent whole" (Hacker, 1976, p. 43); it "permits precise role definitions in relation to and in the service of the cause" (p. 43) and protects individual members (p. 295).

Terrorist groups also provide *learning opportunities*. The groups and the commission of terrorism itself satisfy a number of psychological needs of those predisposed to use this form of political behavior. Although terrorists may bring some knowledge and skills to the organization, members of a group are exposed to many varied learning experiences, allowing them to adopt different roles that shape their orientations and behavior.[17] Terrorism is thus a learned behavior that can be explained by general principles of learning theory. Certainly learning in other conflict situations has been identified (Pitcher & Hamblin, 1982), and the two most important learning theories applicable to terrorism are operant conditioning (Skinner, 1938), and social learning/modeling (Bandura, 1973).[18] The first recognizes that in order to get some sort of benefit or achieve a goal or reward, a person continuously modifies his or her behavior in an active fashion through a sequence of steps. The second suggests that individuals learn through a process of observing and/or interacting with others, then modelling or imitating that behavior.

Ultimately, the choice to engage in a terrorist action is a conscious or unconscious *cost-benefit calculation*, sometimes referred to as an expression of political strategy (Crenshaw, 1990), in which expected utility is calculated individually by each terrorist, collectively by the terrorist group, or simply as a result of leadership deliberations.[19] In other words, terrorists do what they do not because they are crazy or suffer from psychological maladjustments, but because they are relatively rational human beings (Corrado, 1981), and examinations of their motivations will show a well-thought-out logic for their behavior (Kaplan, 1978). Most terrorist groups (e.g., Baader-Meinhoff Gang, Shining Path, Tupamaros, etc.) see their actions as cost-effective means to: achieve individual, collective, tangible, or symbolic recognition, attention, or publicity for their cause; disrupt and discredit appropriate targets; create fear and/or hostility in an audience identified as the "enemy"; provoke overreaction by the government and its coercive agencies; create sympathy amongst potential supporters; and increase control, discipline, and morale within the terrorist group (Hacker, 1976). In this light, terrorist choices are rational, based on the purposes and goals of terrorism. It has been argued that the greater the sophistication—as measured in terms of planning, selection of target, and risk involved—the greater the amount of rational choice involved in the process.

In summary, the psychological causes are affected by the structural ones. The organization of society, including the type of political and economic system as well as historical factors, present options that affect the decisions and choices of individuals and organizations to engage in terrorism.

Conclusion

This chapter sought to provide a backdrop for an applicable theory of political crime, and some of the research that has been done on the psychological approaches to understanding oppositional political terrorism. One must recognize that although creating a theory of political crime may be difficult, it is a necessary, though not solely sufficient, step in the process of understanding this phenomenon and establishing better controls or methods of prevention.

Notes

1. I have used the terms *political crimes*, *offenses*, and *illegalities* interchangeably throughout this chapter.

2. Scheingold (1998) continues this tradition. He labels this kind of activity as "political criminology." Unfortunately, this approach unnecessarily confuses traditional political crime with the political ramifications of crime policy.

3. Some, but not all, political crimes can be identified as crimes against the social or public order. Violations of this nature "disturb or invade society's peace and tranquility" (Schmalleger, 2002, p. 431).

4. While *state* means a governmental entity, a nation is typically composed of a group that shares the same language, history, and customs. Thus, it is technically a mistake to confuse a nation with a state or even a country.

5. These alternative definitions began mostly with the scholarship of Sutherland (1949a, 1949b), who encouraged a definition resting on socially injurious behavior. Then, two decades later, Schwendinger and Schwendinger (1970) expanded the scope of crime by calling for a definition resting squarely on human rights violations. For them, a criminal was an individual, organization, state, or social relationship that denied individuals the right to realize their human potential (see also Bohm, 1993). Racism, sexism, and economic exploitation resulting from profit-maximizing social relations also have been treated as crimes, for they violate individuals' basic human rights (e.g., Quinney, 1977). Bohm (1993) has suggested a much more inclusive definition of crime, focusing on human rights violations conducted by the state, which are considered political crimes.

6. Depending on the circumstances, any of these actors can be an audience.

7. In particular, Burgess and Akers (1968) explained the rich meanings and relevance of differential association by extending it through a synthesis with learning and behavior modification theories.

8. After some revision, differential association theory was detailed by Sutherland in nine points or statements, all of which are important for understanding the process by which one learns favorable attitudes for doing crime (Sutherland, 1947, pp. 6–7).

9. Many political crimes (e.g., espionage, treason, sedition, terrorism) are committed by individuals without any group support.

10. This section builds upon Ross (1994, 1999, 2006: pp. 86–90).

11. The author uses Schmid's widely accepted definition of terrorism.

12. Analysts must take into account the difficulty of integrating theories with fundamentally different underlying logics.

13. Many of these traits are connected, in whole or in part, with symptoms identified in the *Diagnostic and Statistical Manual of Mental Disorders* of the American Psychiatric Association.

14. The source of that frustration, whether relative or absolute deprivation, is not as important as how it translates into to frustration-aggression (Gurr, 1970).

15. These hypotheses are laid out in a unidirectional fashion. Perhaps with empirical testing, there might be some bidirectionality in these interactions. In other words, feedback is probably present but should be clearer to see after more research has been done.

16. This process builds upon Sutherland's concept of differential association (Sutherland, 1947) and is similar to the pattern with individuals joining and staying in religious cults (Conway & Seligman, 1995).

17. This point builds upon Burgess and Akers (1968), who applied learning theory and behavior modification to Sutherland's concept of differential association.

18. Crenshaw (1990, pp. 8–11) expresses the same point but does not label it by its psychological terminology.

19. This position is not unanimously held. Post (1990), for example, takes issue with this perspective. Natasha J. Cabrera, personal communication, suggests that it could be that it is not so much that terrorists are rational, but rather that the consequences (death, arrest, etc.) may have little or no value to them.

References

Agee, P. (1975). *Inside the company: CIA diary*. New York: Routledge.

Akers, R. L. (1994). *Criminological theories: Introduction and evaluation*. Los Angeles, CA: Roxbury.

Alexander, D. W. (1992a). *Applying Merton's theory of anomie to political criminality*. Paper presented to the American Society of Criminology annual meeting, New Orleans, LA.

Alexander, D. W. (1992b). *Political crime: An application of Merton's theory of social structure and anomie* (Unpublished master's thesis). Virginia Polytechnic Institute and State University, Blacksburg, VA.

Allen, F. A. (1974). *The crime of politics: Political dimensions of criminal justice*. Cambridge, MA: Harvard University Press.

Bandura, A. (1973). *Aggression: A social learning analysis*. Englewood Cliffs, NJ: Prentice-Hall.

Barak, G. (Ed.). (1994). *Media, process, and the social construction of crime: Studies in newsmaking criminology*. New York: Garland.

Beirne, P., & Messerschmidt, J. (1991). *Criminology*. New York: Harcourt Brace Jovanovich.

Bohm, R. M. (1993). Social relationships that arguably should be criminal although they are not: On the political economy of crime. In K. D. Tunnell (Ed.), *Political crime in contemporary America* (pp. 2–29). New York: Garland.

Burgess, R. L., & Akers, R. L. (1968). Reinforcement theory of criminal behavior. *Social Problems, 14*, 128–147.

Chambliss, W. J. (1976). The state and criminal law. In W. J. Chambliss & M. Mankoff (Eds.), *Whose law, what order?* (pp. 66–106). New York: John Wiley.

Chambliss, W. J., & Seidman, R. (1982). *Law, order, and power* (2nd ed.). Reading, MA: Addison-Wesley.

Churchill, W., & Vander Wall, J. (1990). *The COINTELPRO papers: Documents from the FBI's secret wars against domestic dissent*. Boston: South End.

Conway, F., & Sigelman, J. (1995). *Snapping: America's epidemic of sudden personality change* (2nd ed.). New York: Stillpoint Press.

Corrado, R. R. (1981). A critique of the mental disorder perspective of political terrorism. *International Journal of Law and Psychiatry, 4*, 1–17.

Crenshaw, M. (1986). The psychology of political terrorism. In M. G. Herman (Ed.), *The political psychology of contemporary problems and issues* (pp. 379–413). San Francisco, CA: Jossey-Bass.

Crenshaw, M. (1990). The logic of terrorism: Terrorist behavior as a product of strategic choice. In W. Reich (Ed.), *Origins of terrorism: Psychologies, ideologies, theologies, states of mind* (pp. 7–24). Washington, DC: Woodrow Wilson International Center for Scholars and Cambridge University Press.

Cullen, F., Maakestad, W., & Cavender, G. (1987). *Corporate crime under attack: The Ford Pinto case and beyond*. Cincinnati, OH: Anderson.

Davis, J. K. (1992). *Spying on America: The FBI's Domestic Counterintelligence Program*. New York: Praeger.

Dollard, J., Doob, L. W., Miller, N. E., Mowrer, O. H., & Sears, R. R. (1939). *Frustration and aggression*. New Haven, CT: Yale University Press.

Frenkel-Brunswik, E. (1952). Interaction of psychological and sociological factors in political behavior. *American Political Science Review, 46*(1), 44–65.

Friedland, N. (1992). Becoming a terrorist: Social and individual antecedents. In L. Howard (Ed.), *Terrorism: Roots, impact, responses* (pp. 81–93). New York: Praeger.

Gurr, T. R. (1970). *Why men rebel*. Princeton, NJ: Princeton University Press.

Gutmann, D. (1979). Killers and consumers: The terrorist and his audience. *Social Research 46*, 516–526.

Hacker, F. J. (1976). *Crusaders, criminals, crazies: Terror and terrorism in our time*. New York: W. W. Norton.

Jager, H., Schmidtchen, G., & Süllwold, L. (Eds.). (1981). *Analysen zum terrorismus* (Vol. 2). Opladen: Westdeutscher Verlag.

Kaplan, A. (1978). The psychodynamics of terrorism. *Terrorism: An International Journal 1*, 237–254.

Kauzlarich, D., & Kramer, R. C. (1993). State-corporate crime in the U.S. nuclear weapons production complex. *Journal of Human Justice, 5*, 4–28.

Kauzlarich, D., & Kramer, R. C. (1998). *Crimes of the American nuclear state*. Boston, MA: Northeastern University Press.

Kelly, R. J. (1972). New political crimes and the emergence of revolutionary nationalist ideologies. In F. Adler & G. O. W. Mueller (Eds.), *Politics, crime and the international scene: An inter-American focus* (pp. 23–35). San Juan, Puerto Rico: North-South Center Press.

Kirchheimer, O. (1961). *Political justice: The use of legal procedure for political ends*. Princeton, NJ: Princeton University Press.

Koistra, P. G. (1985, March). What is a political crime? *Criminal Justice Abstracts, 17*, 100–115.

Merton, R. K. (1938). Social structure and anomie. *American Sociological Review, 3*, 672–682.

Merton, R. K. (1964). Anomie, anomia, and social interaction: Contexts of deviant behavior. In M. B. Clinard (Ed.), *Anomie and deviant behavior* (pp. 397–408). New York: Free Press.

Merton, R. K. (1966). Social problems and sociological theory. In R. K. Merton & R. A. Nisbet (Eds.), *Contemporary social problems* (pp. 775–823). New York: Harcourt Brace.

Moran, R. (1974). *Political crime* (Doctoral dissertation). University of Pennsylvania, Philadelphia, PA.

Morf, G. (1970). *Terror in Québéc*. Toronto, Ontario, Canada: Clarke, Irwin and Company, Ltd.

Oots, K. L. (1986). *A political organization approach to transnational terrorism*. Westport, CT: Greenwood Press.

Pearlstein, R. M. (1991). *The mind of a political terrorist*. Wilmington, DE: Scholarly Resources.

Pitcher, B., & Hamblin, R. (1982). Collective learning in ongoing political conflicts. *International Political Science Review, 3*, 71–90.

Post, J. M. (1984). Notes on psychodynamic theory of terrorist behavior. *Terrorism: An International Journal, 7*, 241–256.

Post, J. M. (1990). Terrorist psycho-logic: Terrorist behavior as a product of psychological forces. In W. Reich (Ed.), *Origins of terrorism: Psychologies, ideologies, theologies, states of mind* (pp. 25–42). Washington, DC: Woodrow Wilson International Center for Scholars and Cambridge University Press.

Quinney, R. (1970). *The social reality of crime*. Boston, MA: Little, Brown.

Quinney, R. (1977). *Class, state, and crime*. New York: David McKay.

Ross, J. I. (1994). The psychological causes of oppositional political terrorism: Toward an integration of findings. *International Journal of Group Tensions, 24*, 157–185.

Ross, J. I. (1995/2000). *Controlling state crime* (2nd ed.). New Brunswick, NJ: Transaction Books.

Ross, J. I. (1999). Beyond the conceptualization of terrorism: A psychological-structural model of the causes of this activity. In C. Summers & E. Markusen (Eds.), *Collective violence: Harmful behavior in groups and governments* (pp. 169–194). Lanham, MD: Rowman & Littlefield.

Ross, J. I. (2000a). *Making news of police violence: Comparing Toronto and New York City*. Westport, CT: Praeger.

Ross, J. I. (Ed.). (2000b). *Varieties of state crime and its control*. Monsey, NY: Criminal Justice Press.

Ross, J. I. (2003). *The dynamics of political crime*. Thousand Oaks, CA: Sage Publications.

Ross, J. I. (2008). *Special problems in corrections*. Upper Saddle, NJ: Prentice Hall.

Russell, C. A., & Miller, B. H. (1983). Profile of a terrorist. In L. Z. Freedman & Y. Alexander (Eds.), *Perspectives on terrorism* (pp. 45–60). Wilmington, DE: Scholarly Resources.

Sayari, S. (1985). *Generational change in terrorist movements: The Turkish case*. Santa Monica, CA: Rand Corporation. Report

Scheingold, S. (1998). Constructing the new political criminology: Power, authority, and the post-liberal state. *Law and Social Inquiry, 23*(4), 857–895.

Schmalleger, F. (2002). *Criminal law today*. Upper Saddle River, NJ: Prentice Hall.

Schmid, A. P. (1983). *Political terrorism: A research guide to concepts, theories, data bases and literature*. New Brunswick, NJ: TransAction Books.

Schwendinger, H., & Schwendinger, J. (1975). Defenders of order or guardians of human rights? In I. Taylor, P. Walton, & J. Young (Eds.), *Critical criminology* (pp. 113–146). London: Routledge & Kegan Paul.

Skinner, B. F. (1938). *The behavior of organisms: An experimental analysis*. New York: Appleton-Century-Crofts.

Sutherland, E. H. (1947). *Principles of criminology* (4th ed.). Philadelphia, PA: J. B. Lippincott.

Sutherland, E. H. (1949a). *White collar crime*. New York: Holt, Rinehart and Winston.

Sutherland, E. H. (1949b). The white collar criminal. In V. C. Branham & S. B. Kutash (Eds.), *Encyclopedia of criminology* (pp. 511–515). New York: Philosophical Library.

Turk, A. T. (1982). *Political criminality*. Beverly Hills, CA: Sage.

Warr, M. (1995). Public perceptions of crime and punishment. In J. F. Sheley (Ed.), *Criminology* (2nd ed., pp. 15–31). Belmont, CA: Wadsworth.

Wilkinson, P. (1977). *Terrorism and the liberal state*. New York: John Wiley & Sons.

CHAPTER EIGHT

Emotional Correlates of Radicalization and Terrorism*

Stephen K. Rice and Robert Agnew

Introduction

The 2011 Arab Spring was notable not only for its illustration of the social and political forces in the Middle East and North Africa, but also for shining light on the key role that emotions such as anger, humiliation, disgust, and moral outrage played in Tripoli's Green Square, Manama's Pearl Square, and Cairo's Tahrir Square. Even in the singular case of Mohamed Bouazizi's self-immolation in Tunisia, press accounts depict a well-liked and good man, humiliated. The linguistic framing of "days of rage" was all too obvious.

Further, in contemplating similar events in Algiers, Riyadh, or Amman, one must draw attention to the set of variables that relate to ascribed and temporal characteristics (of birth and of epoch, respectively) and how these characteristics interact with street-level emotions to spark social action. Drawing on complementary work by criminologist Lawrence Sherman, under what conditions are sanctions at the level of the individual (e.g., torture) or the community (e.g., the mistreatment of a respected voice; restrictions on mass communication) perceived as unjust, thereby

---

*Portions of this chapter are reprinted from the *Journal of Criminal Justice*, Vol. 37, Iss. 3, Stephen K. Rice, "Emotions and terrorism research: A case for a social-psychological agenda," pp. 248–255. Copyright © 2009, with permission from Elsevier.

leading to defiant pride? (Sherman, 1993). Perceptions of fairness also tie to frameworks for evaluating the legitimacy of authority, a salient issue in Egypt with regard to the Egyptian Supreme Council of the Armed Forces, Muslim Brotherhood, or Mohamed ElBaradei.

A focus on social psychological processes may also serve the research community well as a predictor of radicalization and terroristic violence. For the purpose of this chapter, radicalization focuses on the "collectively defined, individually felt radical moral obligation to participate in direct action" (Githens-Mazer, 2009), while terrorism can be thought of as the commission of criminal acts, usually violent, that target civilians or violate conventions of war when targeting military personnel and that are committed at least partially for social, political, or religious ends (Agnew, 2010).

Many conservative and right-wing movements in the United States, for example, evince fear, threat, and vulnerability in their rhetoric (Durham, 2007). Within this context, social mobilization can be thought of as an adaptive response to perceived indignities in repressive environments. Furthermore, insomuch as terroristic tactics in Aden and Cyprus during the final years of the British Empire were conceived of to inspire fear (Lewis, 2004), contemporary terror impulses have been conditioned largely by social psychological processes such as humiliated fury, moral outrage, contempt, and hopelessness. Humiliated fury, for example, relates to deprivation that is perceived as illegitimate or unjust, or that of a colonizing act perpetuated by the powerful over the powerless (Lindner, 2001; Scheff, 1997). Egregious negative affect encumbers moderate voices to the extent that humiliation has been characterized as the "nuclear bomb" of emotions (Lindner, 2006).

The goal of this chapter is to illuminate how negative affect should come to hold a more prominent position in the study of radicalization and terrorism; in essence, how emotions complement place (historical and social positioning) in this area of scholarship (Agnew, 2010; Rice, 2009; Tosini, 2010). If psychological structures constitute, in part, what it "means to be human" in the study of violent extremism and sacred values (Atran, 2010), then the time is ripe to assess how negative affect informs more commonplace structural and rational choice considerations (e.g., Dugan, LaFree, and Piquero, 2005; Turk, 2004).

Emotions, Radicalization, and Terror: A Review

In the years surrounding 1990, criminological and criminal justice theory came to highlight affect via defiance, deference, restoration, shame, and strain (Agnew, 1992; Braithwaite, 1989; Sherman, 1993; Tyler,

1990), and this theoretical foundation finds salience through the similarities between crime and terrorism as socially constructed, as male-dominated, and as disruptive to social trust (LaFree & Dugan, 2004). Anger and humiliation have also come to hold positions in segments of the Muslim world through perceived impotence and immobility in the face of state violence (Gerges, 2005); restrictions on personal movement amongst Palestinians in the West Bank, Gaza, and East Jerusalem, for example, condition anger ("The Hamas Conundrum," 2007).

Just as terrorism can be framed as collective violence (Roche, 2004), it too is a form of *cognitive* violence (Rice, 2009). More so than a response to poor education or economic disadvantage, terrorism may too be understood as a byproduct of perceived indignities in repressive environments (Krueger & Maleckova, 2003; Turk, 2004). Individual absolute (and to a lesser degree, relative) deprivation has received attention as a predictor of terrorism, with extant research tending to indicate a weak relationship at best (Araj, 2008; Atran, 2003; De Coning, 2004; Maleckova, 2005; Pape, 2005; Piazza, 2006; Smelser, 2007; Turk, 2004). For example, Krueger and Maleckova (2003) and Maleckova (2005) indicate that poorly educated and poor Palestinians are not more likely to support or engage in terrorism, and in some regions the middle class and educated (including college students) are drawn to terroristic violence (Maleckova, 2005; Post, 2007; Victoroff, 2005). At the macro level, evidence is similarly weak on the relationship between material deprivation and numbers of terrorist acts (Maleckova, 2005; Newman, 2006; Pape, 2005; Piazza, 2006).

Interestingly, a great many works from defense and security analysts cast emotions as peripheral to the root causes of terror campaigns or fail to recognize emotions altogether. To Sirseloudi (2005), political, social, and historical causes relate to the early detection of terror campaigns while feelings of being threatened or humiliation do not hold central positions. Applying rational choice theory to terrorism, economists seek to understand the relationship between a quantity response in an activity such as terrorism and price changes (e.g., defense of targets, attacks against training centers, infiltration, capture of leaders) (Anderton & Carter, 2006). Within criminal justice, Dugan et al.'s (2005) rational choice framework highlights the effect of target hardening and deterrence such as changes to Cuban law and airport metal detectors on airline hijackings.

These orientations stand in stark contrast to what we have come to know about Osama bin Laden's hatred toward the United States. In his excellent work *The Looming Tower: Al-Qaeda and the Road to 9/11*, Lawrence Wright (2006) outlines the intensity of bin Laden's pre-9/11 defiant gestures—gestures that harkened to "war cries" of the Crusades and early struggles of Islam. As Wright explains, "The most frightening aspect of this new threat, however, was the fact that almost no one (e.g., the F.B.I.) took it seriously. . . . Up against the confidence that Americans placed in modernity and technology and their own ideals to protect them from the savage pageant of history, the defiant gestures of bin Laden and his followers seemed absurd and even pathetic" (Wright, 2006, pp. 4–6).

Affect Modeled as Key Predictor

Within such an environment conditioned principally by rational choice and structural considerations (e.g., legal and/or policy change, level of modernization, or social and cultural facilitation) (Ross, 1993), strong emotions such as humiliation, rage and disgust fail to adequately be incorporated into causal models (Rice, 2009). This is unexpected, given that emotions can "mobilize conflict and comprise the essence of solidarity" (Irvine, 1995, p. 392) and that violence can be a problem-solving response for those experiencing personally or vicariously experienced strains (Agnew, 2001, 2002; Brezina, 2000).

Instead, what is required is an emotions-based, collectivity-based model that links discourse related to the historical, social, and political positioning of terrorists to intrapsychic and interpersonal emotional processes. For example, how might an individual-focused sanction such as imprisonment (Zawahiri, 2001) or communal restrictions on necessities (Nassar, 2004) lead to defiance? Through ethnographic investigation, for example, terrorists are found to express themselves via situational affect, claiming historical injustice (Atran, 2003).

One may also find that when faced with egregious injustice, disenfranchised individuals may misdirect anger toward not only the source(s) of injustice but toward groups which are thought to serve them (Sherman, 1993). This process can be seen in al-Qaeda's condemnation of the House of Saud upon the insertion of 500,000 U.S. troops in the kingdom in the early 1990s, a move al-Qaeda depicted as defilement of the holy land of Arabia by non-Muslims (Bergen, 2006).

Further, evoking "elevators," or pathways (McCauley & Moskalenko, 2008; Rice, 2009), a reframing of research orientations may be salient for terror phenomena that suggest movement of actors across a continuum of zealotry. For example, in Sageman's (2008) assessment of al-Qaeda members' personal histories, he finds moral outrage primed by outside influences such as the gross mistreatment or death of a respected voice, while Ross (1999) explicates factors that facilitate nonlinear intensity of involvement (that is, joining, forming, and leading). To Ross (1999), structural inputs create opportunities, but psychological theory explains intensity. Similarly, Turk (2004) models processual measures (e.g., socialization, training) in explaining the development of terroristic self-concept—as one who feels he or she must fight against threats from without. To these models, the *intergroup* is paramount, such as how perceived threats to an ingroup initiate pathways toward radicalization and terrorism (McCauley & Moskalenko, 2008).

Ties to General Strain Theory

Agnew's (1992, 2001) general strain theory provides a medium to also understand how individuals come to see themselves as bearers of the responsibility to fight such threats. General strain theory presumes that personally-felt strains such as little autonomy or status, loss of valued intimates, discrimination, or abuse by authority facilitate negative emotions (anger, most importantly, but also fear, frustration, and malicious envy) and an increased need for corrective action, such as violence.

Drawing on the emotions and injustice literature (e.g., Mikula, 1993; Tedeschi & Felson, 1994), general strain asserts that strong negative emotions disrupt cognitive processes in ways that impede noncriminal coping, reduce one's ability to express grievances, reduce violence's perceived costs, reduce one's likelihood to feel shame or guilt, and energize the individual for action (Agnew, 2001, p. 327). Tying to "elevators," terrorism research may also find complementarity in predictions of a nonlinear effect of cumulative strains on crime (Agnew, 2006a; Mazerolle & Piquero, 1997).

In a general strain theory of terrorism, Agnew (2010) asserts that terrorism is most likely to result from collective strains, or those strains experienced by groups or collectivities (e.g., a religious, political, or territorial group) under circumstances such as strains being high in magnitude with civilians victims, perceived as unjust, and caused by more powerful others—including complicit civilians—with whom members of the strained collectivity have weak ties. With regard to the first category, strains being high in magnitude, Agnew (2010) points to acts that cause a high degree of harm (e.g., death, dispossession, threats to identity); are of frequent, long duration; and are widespread (especially amongst civilians) as being facilitative of radicalization and/or terroristic coping. Such strains frequently feature egregious physical and/or cognitive violence perpetrated against the body, as witnessed by groups such as Basque Homeland and Liberty, Irish Republican Army, Shining Path, Hezbollah, Hamas, and al-Qaeda (Hoffman, 2006; Post, 2007).

Further, strains thought to be caused by powerful others—including "complicit" civilians with whom members of the strained collectivity have weak ties—hold prominence. As Agnew (2010) explains, these "others" tend to differ from the strained collectivity with regard to a salient social dimension such as religion, class, territory, or ideology. They tend to be powerful because of their heightened resources such as military capacity and/or support from others. Finally, members of the strained collectivity have weak emotional and material ties to the source of strain. These weak ties may stem from lack of contact, strong cultural differences (e.g., differences in language, values, beliefs, norms), and/or large differences in wealth, status, or power, which tend to limit positive interaction and mutually beneficial exchange (Black, 2004; Goodwin, 2006; Senechal de la Roche, 1996).

Negative emotions such as anger play a key role in both general strain theory and in the explanation of terrorism. For example, as specified by Agnew (2010), a member of the Tamil Tigers stated that "In the late '90s when I was in school, the Sri Lanka military bombed by village. An elderly woman lost both legs, one person dies and two students were injured. I was angry with the [military] and joined the Tigers one year later" (Post, 2007, p. 92). As such, as opposed to instrumental pursuits such as installing a caliphate or attempting to undermine Western economies, terrorist rhetoric oftentimes aims to convey rage, to exact revenge, and to use such expressives to mobilize followers. As Stern (2004) outlines, Osama bin Laden's desires for spectacular attacks were framed through evocations of injustice (followers "follow strong horses, not weak ones"; p. 7). Further, McCauley (2006) argues that negative identity drives the fear and humiliation that individuals feel when their target of hate is perceived to be winning or strengthening in influence. This negative identity oftentimes stems from a perceived lack of alternatives and visceral rejection of desirable or "proper" roles. In an example cited by Knutson (1981), Croatian Zvaonko Busic takes on the role of terrorist after feeling crushed by his inability to achieve a university education. Similar to how threats to status or prestige can weigh heavily on a would-be criminal offender's mind (Lind & Tyler, 1988), perceived low status can also relate to terroristic violence (Smelser & Mitchell, 2002).

As primary mediator, the centrality of negative emotions to general strain theory evokes Homans's (1974) straightforward proposition about responses to injustice: those treated fairly will experience positive emotions, while those treated poorly are likely to feel anger. Hegtvedt & Markovsky (1995), for example, find that individuals who experience outcomes that are out of alignment with what is expected are likely to experience negative emotions, especially when coupled with a perception that he or she is not responsible for the non-proportionality (a tendency that has received attention with regard to both terrorism and general strain theory vis-à-vis external attribution—or the tendency to attribute one's own adversity onto others) (Crenshaw, 2004). To Agnew (1992), external attribution is modeled as a facilitator of delinquent coping.

Perceived violations of justice rules have also been incorporated as an important moderator within general strain theory modeling (Agnew, 2001). Perceived unfairness or disrespect on the part of sanctioning agents is linked to a lashing out, particularly when the reaction is coupled with unacknowledged shame and defiant pride among those who are poorly bonded to the sanctioning agent or to the community the agent represents (Sherman, 1993). Perceptions of fairness also tie to one's interpretation of frameworks for evaluating authority legitimacy. As Benjamin and Simon (2005) explain, bin Laden anticipated widespread collateral benefits after September 11, 2001—that of a superpower that would lash out and foment rebellion throughout the Muslim world, thereby benefiting his cause through changes in frameworks for evaluating U.S. legitimacy. As has also been seen historically in Northern Ireland, with increased support for the Irish Republican Army coming as a result of perceived indignities by British security forces, counterterrorism may beget more terrorism (LaFree, 2007).

By shifting terms of the dialogue toward a "far enemy," organizations such as al-Qaeda communicate symbolic messages about group membership to jihadists: that they are respected members of a community and that they should feel pride in the group as a whole (e.g., see Sageman's [2008] assertion that "in-group love" facilitates the formation of an "interactive 'echo chamber' encouraging escalation of grievances and beliefs in conspiracy to the point of hatred" [p. 87]). As suggested throughout this chapter, the growing role of multiple identities demarcates psychological space that may be both opportunistic and ephemeral, such as in Abdullah Azzam's, Osama bin Laden's, and Ayman al-Zawahiri's long-standing ties to a network that benefited from U.S. financial support during the Afghan-Soviet war (Gerges, 2006) or in Pakistani president Pervez Musharraf's possible misuse of U.S. coalition support funds for counterterrorism along the Afghan border (Sanger & Rohde, 2007).

Given that a great number of individuals who experience the collective strains outlined above do not, in fact, engage in terrorism, it too is important to consider the factors which *condition* the effect of strains on terrorism. As outlined by Agnew (2010), these conditioners include coping resources, skills, and opportunities; social control; association with close others who support terrorism; and anticipated costs and benefits of terrorist acts.

Coping resources, skills, and opportunities refer to the ability to cope through non-terroristic means such as legal and political skills and extensive financial resources, one's willingness to engage in risky behavior, and degree of organization. Social control refers to variation in the level of control (or even bonds) that a source of strain exercises over a strained collectivity (e.g., Goodwin [2007] points to the close ties between the ANC and whites in the antiapartheid movement as explaining ANC's general avoidance of terrorism against white civilians). Association with close others who support terrorism is just that: dispositions for terrorism that are impacted by others who model and reinforce terrorism, teach beliefs favorable to terrorism, and provide training and support necessary for terrorist activities. Finally, anticipated costs and benefits of terrorist acts refer to costs at least partly determined by the success or failure of previous acts and immediate factors such as the absence of capable guardians and availability of attractive targets (for a complete discussion of conditioners, see Agnew, 2010).

Conclusion

The intersection of criminology and social psychology is well positioned to predict and explain terrorism's psychological space. Both disciplines will benefit from an agenda that explores the impact of strain, procedural and distributive injustice, humiliated fury, disgust, and defiance to complement the more developed structural and rational choice theses in extant scholarship. Further, social markers such as "Muslim" and "Arab" should be disentangled for important perceptual differences within-faith and within-ethnicity, such has been done with black and nonblack Hispanics' perceptions of racial and ethnic profiling (Rice, Reitzel, & Piquero, 2005). In addition, anger, general strain theory's primary mediator, demonstrates itself as a process that exhibits variability across cultures in normative social approval, perceived effects for self, reaction tendencies, and emotional memory (Horton, Rice, Piquero, & Piquero, 2012). To this point, might negative affect be triggered differently across the globe, serving as an input to counterterrorist strategy?

How best to accomplish these goals? Thoits's (1989) call for emotions as predictor variables, not to mention her call for the geographic mapping of affect, provides strong guidance, as does Maltz's (1998) call for "visualizing" violence. Further, scholarship concentrating on personal narrative and affect should hold a central position (Atran, 2008; Sageman, 2008; Rice, Dirks & Exline, 2009). As Atran (2008) asserts with regard to political violence, "approaches based on 'gut feelings,' or on theories that are not systematically built or tested on data from the field, will not prevent the next and future generations of youth from taking a path to political violence, no matter how effective may be law enforcement and military measures in the short term" (Atran, 2008, pp. 1–2). Efforts to map the temporal level between background factors (e.g., personal associations) and situational factors (e.g., the presence of non-hardened targets), what Agnew (2006b) calls "storylines," may also hold promise. In short, "hot," "wet" affect must come to supplement the coldly rational in understanding the major correlates of radicalization and terrorism.

References

Agnew, R. (1992). Foundation for a general strain theory of crime and delinquency. *Criminology, 30*, 47–87.

Agnew, R. (2001). Building on the foundation of general strain theory: Specifying the types of strain most likely to lead to crime and delinquency. *Journal of Research in Crime and Delinquency, 38*, 319–361.

Agnew, R. (2002). Experienced, vicarious, and anticipated strain: An exploratory study on physical victimization and delinquency. *Justice Quarterly, 19*, 603–632.

Agnew, R. (2006a). *Pressured into crime: An overview of general strain theory*. Los Angeles, CA: Roxbury Publishing.

Agnew, R. (2006b). Storylines as a neglected cause of crime. *Journal of Research in Crime and Delinquency, 43*, 119–147.

Agnew, R. (2010). A general strain theory of terrorism. *Theoretical Criminology, 14*, 131–153.

Anderton, C. H., & Carter, J. R. (2006). Applying intermediate microeconomics to terrorism. *Journal of Economic Education, 37*, 442–458.

Araj, B. (2008). Harsh state repression as a cause of suicide bombing: The case of the Palestinian-Israeli conflict. *Studies in Conflict and Terrorism, 31*, 284–303.

Atran, S. (2003). Genesis of suicide terrorism. *Science, 299*, 1534, 1535, 1538.

Atran, S. (2008, March 12). The making of a terrorist: A need for understanding from the field. Testimony before the United States House Appropriations Subcommittee on Homeland Security, Washington, DC. Retrieved from http://sitemaker.umich.edu/satran/files/atran_congress_12march08.pdf.

Atran, S. (2010). *Talking to the enemy: Faith, brotherhood, and the (un)making of terrorists*. New York: Ecco.

Benjamin, D., & Simon, S. (2005). *The next attack: The failure of the war on terror and a strategy for getting it right*. New York: Times Books.

Bergen, P. L. (2006). *The Osama bin Laden I know: An oral history of al Qaeda's leader*. New York: Free Press.

Black, D. (2004). Terrorism as social control. *Sociology of Crime, Law and Deviance, 5*, 9–18.

Braithwaite, J. (1989). *Crime, shame, and reintegration*. Cambridge, UK: Cambridge University Press.

Brezina, T. (2000). Delinquent problem-solving: An interpretive framework for criminological theory and research. *Journal of Research in Crime and Delinquency, 37*, 3–30.

Crenshaw, M. (2004). The psychology of political terrorism. In J. T. Jost & J. Sidanius (Eds.), *Political psychology* (pp. 411–431). New York: Psychology Press.

De Coning, C. (2004). Poverty and terrorism: The root cause debate? *Conflict Trends, 3*, 20–29.

Dugan, L., LaFree, G., & Piquero, A. R. (2005). Testing a rational choice model of airline hijackings. *Criminology, 43*, 1031–1065.

Durham, M. (2007). *White rage: The extreme right and American politics*. New York: Taylor & Francis.

Gerges, F. A. (2005). *The far enemy: Why jihad went global*. New York: Cambridge University Press.

Gerges, F. A. (2006). *Journey of the jihadist: Inside Muslim militancy*. Orlando, FL: Harcourt.

Githens-Mazer, J. (2009, June). Speech to International Terrorism and Intelligence, Washington DC.

Goodwin, J. (2006). A theory of categorical terrorism. *Social Forces, 84*, 2027–2046.

Goodwin, J. (2007). "The struggle made me a nonracialist": Why there was so little terrorism in the antiapartheid struggle. *Mobilization: An International Quarterly Review, 12*, 193–203.

Hegtvedt, K. A., & Markovsky, B. (1995). Justice and injustice. In K. S. Cook, G. A. Fine, & J. S. House (Eds.), *Sociological perspectives on social psychology* (pp. 257–280). Boston, MA: Allyn and Bacon.

Hoffman, B. (2006). *Inside terrorism*. New York: Columbia University Press.

Homans, G. (1974). *Social behavior: Its elementary forms*. New York: Harcourt Brace Jovanovich.

Horton, R., Rice, S. K., Piquero, N. L., & Piquero, A. R. (2012). On the variability of anger cross-culturally: An assessment of general strain theory's primary mediator. *Deviant Behavior, 33*, 1–22.

Irvine, L. (1995). Symbolic interactionism as affect control (review). *Contemporary Sociology, 24*, 392–394.

Knutson, J. N. (1981). Social and psychodynamic pressures toward a negative identity. In Y. Alexander & J. M. Gleason (Eds.), *Behavioral and quantitative perspectives on terrorism* (pp. 105–152). New York: Pergamon.

Krueger, A. B., & Maleckova, J. (2003). Education, poverty and terrorism: Is there a causal connection? *Journal of Economic Perspectives, 17*, 119–144.

LaFree, G. (2007). Expanding criminology's domain: The American Society of Criminology 2006 presidential address. *Criminology, 45*, 1–31.

LaFree, G., & Dugan, L. (2004). How does studying terrorism compare to studying crime? In M. Deflem (Ed.), *Terrorism and counter-terrorism: Criminological perspectives* (pp. 53–74). New York: Elsevier.

Lewis, B. (2004). *The crisis of Islam: Holy war and unholy terror*. New York: Random House.

Lind, E. A., & Tyler, T. R. (1988). *The social psychology of procedural justice*. New York: Harcourt Brace Jovanovich.

Lindner, E. G. (2001). Humiliation as the source of terrorism: A new paradigm. *Peace Research, 33*, 59–68.

Lindner, E. G. (2006). *Making enemies: Humiliation and international conflict*. London: Praeger Security International.

Maleckova, K. (2005) Impoverished terrorists: Stereotype or reality? In T. Bjorgo (Ed.), *Root causes of terrorism* (pp. 33–43). London: Routledge.

Maltz, M. D. (1998). Visualizing homicide: A research note. *Journal of Quantitative Criminology, 14*, 397–410.

Mazerolle, P., & Piquero, A. R. (1997). Violent responses to strain: An examination of conditioning influences. *Violence and Victims, 12*, 323–343.

McCauley, C. (2006). Psychological issues in understanding terrorism and the response to terrorism. In B. Bongar (Ed.), *Psychology of terrorism* (pp. 13–31). New York: Oxford University Press.

McCauley, C., & Moskalenko, S. (2008). Mechanisms of political radicalization: Pathways toward terrorism. *Terrorism and Political Violence, 20*, 415–433.

Mikula, G. (1993). On the experience of injustice. *European Journal of Social Psychology, 4*, 223–244.

Nassar, J. R. (2004). *Globalization and terrorism: The migration of dreams and nightmares*. Lanham, MD: Rowman & Littlefield.

Newman, E. (2006). Exploring the root causes of terrorism. *Studies in Conflict and Terrorism, 29*, 749–772.

Pape, R. A. (2005). *Dying to win: The strategic logic of suicide terrorism*. New York: Random House.

Piazza, J. A. (2006). Rooted in poverty? Terrorism, poor economic development, and social cleavages. *Terrorism and Political Violence, 18*, 159–177.

Post, J. M. (2007). *The mind of the terrorist*. New York: Palgrave Macmillan.

Rice, S. K. (2009). Emotions and terrorism research: A case for a social-psychological agenda. *Journal of Criminal Justice, 37*, 248–255.

Rice, S. K., Dirks, D., & Exline, J. J. (2009). Of guilt, defiance and repentance: Evidence from the Texas death chamber. *Justice Quarterly, 26*, 295–326.

Rice, S. K., Reitzel, J. D., & Piquero, A. R (2005). Shades of brown: Perceptions of racial profiling and the intra-ethnic differential. *Journal of Ethnicity in Criminal Justice, 3*, 47–70.

Roche, R. S. de la (2004). Toward a scientific theory of terrorism. *Sociological Theory, 22*, 1–4.

Ross, J. I. (1993). Structural causes of oppositional political terrorism: Towards a causal model. *Journal of Peace Research, 30*, 317–329.

Ross, J. I. (1999). Beyond the conceptualization of terrorism: A psychological-structural model of the causes of this activity. In C. Summers & E. Markusen (Eds.), *Collective violence: Harmful behavior in groups and government* (pp. 169–192). New York: Rowman & Littlefield.

Sageman, M. (2008). *Leaderless jihad: Terror networks in the twenty-first century*. Philadelphia, PA: University of Pennsylvania Press.

Sanger, D. E., & Rohde, D. (2007, May 20). U.S. pays Pakistan to fight terror, but patrols ebb. *The New York Times*, p. A1.

Scheff, T. (1997). *Emotions, the social bond, and human reality: Part/whole analysis*. Cambridge, UK: Cambridge University Press.

Senechal de la Roche, R. (1996). Collective violence as social control. *Sociological Forum, 11*, 97–128.

Sherman, L. W. (1993). Defiance, deterrence, and irrelevance: A theory of the criminal sanction. *Journal of Research in Crime and Delinquency, 30*, 445–473.

Sirseloudi, M. P. (2005). How to predict the unpredictable: On the early detection of terrorist campaigns. *Defense and Security Analysis, 21*, 369–386.

Smelser, N. J. (2007). *The faces of terrorism: Social and psychological dimensions*. Princeton, NJ: Princeton University Press.

Smelser, N. J., & Mitchell, F. (2002). *Terrorism: Perspectives from the behavioral and social sciences*. Washington, DC: National Academy Press.

Stern, J. (2004). *Terror in the name of God: Why religious militants kill*. New York: HarperCollins.

Tedeschi, J. T., & Felson, R. B. (1994). *Violence, aggression, and coercive actions*. Washington, DC: American Psychological Association.

The Hamas conundrum [Editorial]. (2007, March 26). *New York Times*. Retrieved from http://www.nytimes.com/2007/03/26/opinion/26mon1.html.

Thoits, P. A. (1989). The sociology of emotions. *Annual Review of Sociology, 15*, 317–342.

Tosini, D. (2010). Calculated, passionate, pious extremism: Beyond a rational choice theory of suicide terrorism. *Asian Journal of Social Science, 38*, 394–415.

Turk, A. (2004). Sociology of terrorism. *Annual Review of Sociology, 30*, 271–286.

Tyler, T. R. (1990). *Why people obey the law*. New Haven, CT: Yale University Press.

Victoroff, J. (2005). The mind of the terrorist: A review and critique of psychological approaches. *Journal of Conflict Resolution, 49*, 3–42.

Wright, L. (2006). *The looming tower: Al-Qaeda and the road to 9/11*. New York: Alfred A. Knopf.

Zawahiri, A. (2001, December). Knights under the prophet's banner. Serialized in *Al-Sharq al-Awsat*.

CHAPTER NINE

Cybercrime: High-Tech Crime in the Information Age

Alex Kigerl

Today, as more of our activities and transactions migrate into cyberspace and reside on computer networks, new opportunities for criminal threats present themselves. Changes in our lives, with new structures, tools, and routines, often come with vulnerabilities that potential offenders may exploit. At no time has this been more true than of the current information age, with an entire new space, albeit digital, where humans can interact. Like many novel introductions to society, cyberspace poses new threats to the law, which requires new law enforcement efforts.

Cyberspace is unlike any space in which crimes have occurred in the past. Distance and time have less meaning over the Internet. A single individual can come into contact with literally millions of other participants or resources via electronic transmissions anywhere in the world where there is Internet access. Such transmissions are not as limited by physical space or time, unlike traditional behaviors. A single action in cyberspace can affect thousands of users and cross dozens of jurisdictions. This limitless ability for offender and victim to meet in cyberspace is one of the potential reasons cybercrime is so prevalent (Yar, 2005).

Crimes committed behind a computer terminal are more anonymous and impersonal. Given the right tools to obfuscate one's location, an attacker can be nearly untraceable. Collecting evidence to prove guilt takes much more technical ability and time than that of crimes committed in physical space. The lack of face-to-face encounters during an act in cyberspace also makes such interactions impersonal. Consequently, participants may have fewer inhibitions or compunctions about their conduct on a computer network (Suler, 2004). The perceptions of anonymity and impersonality online may be incentive for criminality for certain individuals who otherwise would not violate the law outside of the network.

This brings up the need to ask what the psychology of the cybercriminal is like, and how the cybercriminal differs from other criminal types. There is evidence that some of the characteristics of the street criminal are also predictors to some extent of cybercriminals: young, male, with a financial incentive to rely on crime rather than legal means to make a living (Goode & Cruise, 2006; Greenburg, 2007; Hinduja, 2003; Kigerl, 2010, 2011). Some of the personality traits explaining cybercrime may also be the same for all other crimes, both street crime and white-collar crime. Namely, offenders are often less risk-averse and have lower levels of self-control, despite cyberspace appearing to be a low-risk environment to begin with (Goles et al., 2007; Higgins, Fell, & Wilson, 2007; Mon, 2002).

However, cyberspace and the skills required to navigate it provide a different environment from that of the physical world, and thus the psychological type drawn to deviance online may be different from the personality drawn to more traditional forms of misconduct. For example, those with hacking experience self-report having a more rational thinking style and also score higher on the Autism-Spectrum Quotient Scale, suggesting they have poorer social skills but greater attention to detail (Bachmann, 2010; Schell & Melnychuk, 2011). Additionally, college students who have attempted unethical behavior in cyberspace (stealing passwords, piracy) are found to be more introverted and, contrary to expectations, are no more likely to desire anonymity over the Internet than other students (Hinduja, 2007; Rogers, Seigfried, & Tidke, 2006).

Yet it is not easy to generalize about those who commit cyberattacks, even within a single country. Any given cyberattack can have originated from anywhere in the world, and often many of them originate outside of the nation being targeted (Fossi et al., 2010). The incentives for engaging in cybercrime in one country may be different than that of others.

One thing that is certain is that there is often a place for just about anyone in the cybercrime community. Regardless of technical skill or income, there are often ways to profit from cybercrime. Those without technical skills but with money to invest can hire cybercriminals, rent out a botnet, purchase a phishing server, and basically pay for services from other criminals to make money (Brody, Mulig, & Kimball, 2007). Those without money or technical skills can still afford to buy stolen credit cards or other credential goods to do with as they please (Ben-Itzhak, 2009; Giles, 2009).

It is not easy to study the cybercriminal, as such individuals are often safely concealed behind many nodes in a complex network and hidden from view. Most research focuses on the cyberattacks of the offender, which easily breach the layers of hardware over digital space and enter our homes and offices. Yet with what evidence we have, a partial picture can be painted of the profile of these offenders. Cyberspace has created new opportunities for deviance, which may draw certain individuals to it. These new opportunities and the offenders that come with them therefore require new efforts in understanding the behavior of committing crimes in cyberspace.

Crimes in Cyberspace

Cybercrime is no longer just lone hackers trespassing on private networks for fun. Today, cybercrime is often organized and profit-driven. There are multiple online communities for those involved in computer crimes to associate and collaborate with (Giles, 2009; Holt & Lampke, 2010). Cybercrime today is a successful and market-driven business model, well organized and with a hierarchical and industrious division of labor (Ben-Itzhak, 2009; Wierdrick-Kozlowski & Stinchcombe, 2008).

Often a single criminal act, whether perpetrated by an individual, group, or community, can be associated with a wide variety of types of crime. Generally, cybercrime is any criminal action that is facilitated or committed using a computer, network, or hardware device (Gordon & Ford, 2006). Such crimes can be perpetrated in a number of varying ways and come with a range of motivations for each individual cybercriminal. Cybercrimes can use computers as ancillary tools in assistance of older forms of crime (fraud), or can be crimes that are just as new as the Internet (malware). Cybercrimes can exploit technical vulnerabilities (absence of antivirus) or social vulnerabilities (clicking malicious links). Motivations for each offense can range from curiosity (network intrusion, hacking), to fame (among cybercrime communities), monetary gain, revenge (e.g., company insiders who were fired), political activism (cyberterrorism), or even as part of "legal" work (such as government cyberwarfare against other nations) (Rogers, 2006).

Some crimes committed in cyberspace were crimes even before the introduction of the Internet; criminals just find new ways to commit them utilizing technology. Called computer-assisted crimes, these include fraud, theft, money laundering, harassment, and obscene content (child pornography), all of which can be committed with or without a computer. The Internet has created an entirely different environment that makes some crimes novel in light of history. Called computer-focused crimes, these are legal violations that depend on technology to exist, and are just as new as the Internet itself. These include computer trespass, malware distribution, and website defacement (Furnell, 2002).

Cybercrimes can also be either technical or social. More technically oriented cybercriminals will work by exploiting technical vulnerabilities to gain access to computer resources. They may utilize viruses, rootkits, keystroke loggers, and other malicious software and tools to steal credential information or interfere with network activity (Gordon & Ford, 2006).

The more technical crimes always rely on tools and software in order to be carried out. A cybercriminal can have all of the knowledge of technical vulnerabilities and hacking in the world, but all of those skills are useless without the proper tools. Some of the tools used by offenders are often commonplace, such as web browsers, e-mail, and online chat. These applications are usually not used to commit any kind of criminal act. Other tools, however, have an almost exclusively malicious purpose, called crimeware (Gordon & Ford, 2006). Crimeware includes viruses, worms, trojans, spyware, exploit kits, and botnets, among many other examples.

One of the more popular crimeware applications is the botnet, which is a group of infected computers (called zombies) that can all be controlled remotely by a single botmaster. The botmaster can have many thousands of zombies at his or her command. The botnet is important because a multitude of crimes are often committed with it, not to mention it can overlap with many other malicious software types. For example, a botnet can simultaneously have the functionality of a virus that infects other files, or a worm that propagates itself. A botnet can be spyware, a rootkit, and a spambot, all rolled into one (Schiller et al., 2007). It has been estimated that as many as 15% to 25% of computers have a botnet client running on them (Weber, 2007).

Two of the most common reasons to own a botnet are to attack servers and to send spam. When a botnet attacks a server (which may or may not host a website), each bot in the botnet floods that server with communications requests, called a distributed denial of service attack (DDoS) (Schiller et al., 2007). This can be done to take websites offline, but it can also be used for more destructive ends, such as attacking the critical infrastructure of an entire country (Clarke & Knake, 2010). Banks, utilities companies, industry, and government all rely on and communicate via networks of servers, many of which are subject to attack over the Internet. These vulnerabilities can allow a foreign country to attack another, bringing much of their infrastructure offline, in what is termed cyberwarfare (Clarke & Knake, 2010).

The most profitable use for a botnet, however, is to send spam. Approximately 80% of spam is sent from botnets (IronPort Systems, 2006). Spam introduces a more social means for exploiting vulnerabilities. Oftentimes the weakest link in a system is not any technical vulnerability, but rather the victims themselves. Why bother spending time attempting to crack encrypted channels, scan hosts for vulnerable ports, or inject malicious code into a website, when it is usually easier to socially engineer the victim into unwittingly giving up the information the offender desires?

Of course, in order to socially engineer anyone, the criminal needs to communicate with a target, often with as many as possible. Spam is the best means to do this. Spam is the sending of unsolicited bulk commercial electronic messages (CAN SPAM Act, 2005). Much of spam is carried out by e-mail, but it is not limited to this form of communication. Any electronic communication can be spammed (chat, phone, text message, comment, and fax spam can occur, to name a few). An estimated 60% of all traffic on the Internet is actually spam (Ananthaswamy, 2009).

Spam is often used to sell a product, steal information, or spread malware (Schiller et al., 2007). When spam appears to be selling a product, or spamvertising, it may be just as fraudulent as any other form of spam. Buying a spamvertised product with a credit card can just end up with the spammer emptying the buyer's bank account, rather than actually mailing the purchased item (Saltzman, 2009).

More obvious forms of fraudulent spam include phishing and advance fee fraud. Phishing is an attempt to deceive the recipient into handing over to the phisher credential goods, such as credit card information or website logins, which can often be converted into cash (Brody, Mulig, & Kimball, 2007). An example may be an e-mail linking the target to a website that appears to be the recipient's own bank requesting that the user enter his or her password, when in fact the website is owned by the phisher. Advance fee fraud, on the other hand, is an attempt to defraud the recipient into wiring the fraudster money directly (Tive, 2006). This is usually done by a confidence scam, in which the victim is made to believe they can receive a large sum of money, if only they wire an "advance fee" first. Phishing can be more deceptive and harder to spot, but advance fee fraud has the advantage of receiving funds immediately.

Many of these different cybercrime types and strategies often go well together. Much of them in fact depend on one another. To steal credit cards, one needs a phishing site as well as a phishing server. To direct traffic to a fraudulent site, spam has to be sent that links to it. And in order to send spam, a botnet will likely be required, not to mention a mailing list of recipients containing many tens of thousands of e-mail addresses.

Not all cybercriminals can do this by themselves, and so multiple cybercrime communities and gangs have emerged. This allows for a well-organized business model, complete with a division of labor and its own market forces (Ben-Itzhak, 2009). An aspiring offender can hire a spammer to send spam to direct traffic to a business (illegitimate or otherwise). The offender can also rent a botnet from a botmaster and purchase a spam list online to send spam on his or her own. The cybercriminal can also rent what is called bulletproof hosting, which is a server hosted in countries that are unlikely to cooperate with law enforcement and are thus difficult to take down (Brody, Mulig, & Kimball, 2007). The offender can then upload a phishing website to the server that was purchased elsewhere to steal credit card information, and then hire someone who specializes in converting the credential goods into cash and laundering the money (Goodin, 2007; Holt & Lampke, 2010).

These market forces have created opportunities to profit from cybercrime, but also opportunities to make money off of cybercriminals legally. Known as "crimeware as a service," malware writers can make a living simply selling malware to customers. Customers may use the crimeware illegally, but the malware writer is doing nothing illegal (Wierdrick-Kozlowski & Stinchcombe, 2008).

In addition to crimeware and services, credential goods are also a highly sought and traded item. Credential goods can be any identifying information that can be converted into cash or used to facilitate cybercrime. It can include credit cards, bank accounts, eBay and PayPal logins, e-mail accounts, and just about anything that requires authorization to access. Some offenders can accumulate so many stolen credentials (tens of thousands) that they must be sold online, as they cannot use them all themselves. Many websites exist where visitors can buy and sell these credentials, called carding forums (Holt & Lampke, 2010).

These online communities have supply and demand, market competition, and buyer reviews and ratings similar to any legitimate online store. Buyers can leave feedback and ratings on the quality of the goods traded, so that sellers can achieve verified or trusted member status. Sellers may have to lower their prices depending on what other members are selling. Credentials vary as do their prices. Credit cards from the United States may be sold for as little as one dollar, whereas credit cards from other countries, being harder to come by, may go for more (Holt & Lampke, 2010).

There are multiple ways to commit crimes in cyberspace. Use of both social and technical skills can be applied to defraud victims of their data or money. But cybercrime's potency often lies in its utilization of community. Each type of crime, type of technology, and type of offender can fit well in the division of labor involved in cybercrime. Cybercrime is not unlike many other businesses.

The Profile of a Cybercriminal

Cybercrime today may be similar to what might be expected from a business or group of entrepreneurs. Cybercrime has even been compared to organized crime (Williams, 2001). Yet there are too many striking differences from legitimate and illegitimate businesses to leave it there. Cybercriminals may have online communities, but their social interactions are almost always behind a computer screen, with people from around the world that the offender will likely never meet in person.

So what is the psychology of cybercrime, and what kind of person is drawn to such illegal acts? It has been speculated that they should likely have a certain set of characteristics. Among them might include (1) at least some technical knowledge, (2) disregard for the law or rationalizations why certain laws are invalid, (3) low risk aversion and perhaps a thrill factor, (4) the enjoyment of controlling or outsmarting others, and (5) a motive, such as money, thrill, or political animosity (Shinder, 2010).

Really understanding what differentiates a cybercriminal from a law-abiding citizen is difficult, as such offenders are not easy to sample. However, parallels can be drawn between an individual who commits computer crimes and other offenders. Technically, cybercrime is a form of white-collar crime, and certainly there are some similarities.

White-collar crime can be defined by the type of offender committing a criminal act, or as a type of offense committed. The offender-related definition suggests that the occupational status of the offender determines if the crime is a white-collar crime. For instance, Medicaid fraud is a white-collar crime only if a doctor commits it, rather than a clerical worker. The offense-based definition would not make this distinction. An offense-based interpretation would suggest that any criminal act that requires fraud, forgery, or deception would be classified as white-collar crime (Daly, 1989). Much of cybercrime would be offense-based white-collar crime, as deception and concealment are necessary to carry out most profit-motivated cybercrimes. Except in the case of corporate espionage (McQuade, 2009), corporate insiders hacking their own companies (Schell & Melnychuk, 2011) or cyberwarfare (Clarke & Knake, 2010), it is unlikely that serious cybercriminals hold high status occupations, as most of their income should originate exclusively from their criminal activities.

In any event, there is likely a common personality associated with most all types of criminal offenders, whether street criminals, white-collar criminals, or cybercriminals. A proposed personality archetype of the criminal would be one characterized by a tendency for risk taking, impulsivity, and low self-control (Gottfredson & Hirschi, 1990). Low self-control has been operationalized to consist of six dimensions of personality. These dimensions include impulsivity, preference for simple tasks (desiring easier activities), risk seeking, preference for physical activities over mental ones, self-centeredness (lower sympathy for others), and temper-control problems (quick to anger, etc.) (Grasmick, Tittle, Bursik, & Arneklev, 1993). Historically self-control theory has been applied to street crime, of which there is support (Pratt & Cullen, 2000). But self-control can be applied to many crime types, considering that all crime involves some sort of risk to the offender; something to which the offender should be less averse.

In the case of white-collar criminals, there appears to be a pattern of low self-control among high-status offenders when compared to those of similar status who choose not to offend. Bickle, Schlegel, Fassbender, and Klein (2006) sampled 150 active corporate managers and 76 white-collar criminals who formerly held such positions. Survey results revealed that the white-collar offenders were more likely to be male, hedonistic, narcissistic, and have low self-control.

Another study conducted interviews with 8 managers and 10 employees each for two different corporations in Taiwan. One corporation was known for repeated health and safety violations, contaminating nearby rivers and soil. The other corporation was a comparison with no known criminal activity. Managers from the more criminally inclined corporation were found to pursue more short-term gratification and were less avoidant of negative consequences of their acts. In other words, they had less self-control (Mon, 2002).

White-collar crime still has some differences from street crime. A review of 4,448 sentencing records found that those who had committed a white-collar offense (mail fraud, tax evasion, forgery) were more likely to specialize in white-collar crime among four offense categories (violence, theft, white-collar crimes, and public order/minor offenses). Those convicted for any of the other crime categories were less likely to specialize and instead were just as likely to commit one of the other four types. White-collar offenders also had fewer problems with the law from their past, although still more problems than the general public (Benson & Moore, 1992).

Risk taking and specialization in crime types are probably some characteristics that white-collar offenders and cybercriminals share in common. Considering that committing cybercrime often requires a certain skill set, it is unlikely that they would be as versatile as street criminals, and therefore likely are specialists to some extent. Not only is it likely that cybercriminals specialize in cybercrime in general, but it seems that they may specialize within the different types of cybercrimes as well. Cybercriminals are known to have a division of labor and to rely on certain skill sets, resulting in specialization in certain crimes such as sending spam, hosting botnets, laundering money, or trafficking in stolen credit cards (Ben-Itzhak, 2009).

Research done directly on certain types of cybercriminals confirms the findings of what predicts white-collar crime offending. While more serious offenders are difficult to sample, participants in lesser forms of crimes in cyberspace, such as digital piracy, are much easier to come by. Piracy is important to understand when considering cybercrime as a whole. Many carding forums where stolen credit cards are traded are also places to illicitly trade copyrighted material. Some botnets even use the P2P protocol (file sharing) to communicate with their botmaster, and often uploading a file via P2P is one of the best ways to spread malware (Schiller et al., 2007).

Research has investigated whether digital pirates bear any psychological differences from the general public. It has been suggested that because criminals engage in behaviors that are at odds with the mores of mainstream society, offenders will find rationalizations that allow them to temporarily put these norms on hold to permit perpetrating the crimes they commit. This is called neutralization and consists of multiple psychological techniques to avoid guilt, such as denying responsibility, arguing that the crime injures no one, and blaming the victim (Hinduja, 2007).

There appears to be some support for techniques of neutralization as applied to software piracy. A survey of 433 college students measured their software-sharing activities and nine different dimensions of neutralization (e.g., denial of responsibility, denial of injury) associated with their beliefs about piracy. Only four of the nine dimensions were associated with piracy, however, and explained only a small amount of the variation in pirating behavior (Hinduja, 2007).

A second study also found only limited support for neutralization among pirates. Three types of file-sharing behaviors were recorded among 585 students: music, video, or software piracy during the previous year, or willingness to do so in the future. Neutralization techniques were found to predict having engaged in all three forms of piracy in the past to some extent, but only predicted the willingness to engage in piracy of music in the future (Morris & Higgins, 2009). Neutralization may be only slightly related to piracy because file sharing is not necessarily as stigmatized by society as other crimes, considering that 60.2% of the college sample was found to have participated in this form of crime (Morris & Higgins, 2009). A stronger relationship may be found among more serious cybercriminals.

One survey of 455 college students attempted to look at other predictors of piracy. The survey was taken either in a classroom or at home online. The more a respondent saw him- or herself as a risk taker, the more favorable attitudes they had toward software piracy, consistent with low self-control. Also of interest was the fact that knowledge of file-sharing laws decreased favorable attitudes in the classroom setting, but not when the survey was taken at home (Goles et al., 2007). This suggests that individuals are less inhibited when online compared to face-to-face interactions. The secrecy of cybercrime could easily be a part of its appeal.

Despite this, it has also been determined that software pirates do not appear to desire anonymity online more than their non-pirating peers. A survey of 507 college students from 30 different classes found that those who regularly pirate software do not value the anonymous nature of the Internet more than those who do not illegally download software. While the anonymity of the Internet may nudge someone toward illegal behavior, the people so nudged may not seek it out deliberately. Risk takers, such as pirates, may also not desire anonymity any more than their peers (Hinduja, 2007).

Another study of 338 college students found similar results. Self-report measures found that those who agreed with statements indicating low self-control, as well as those that had peers who pirated copyrighted material, were more likely to illegally download movies (Higgins, Fell, & Wilson, 2007). The peer influences finding is important here, considering that peer influences are strong predictors of street crime (Akers, Krohn, Lanza-Kaduce, & Radosevich, 1979). In spite of this, it may not be as important a factor in more serious types of cybercrime offending, simply because it is harder to come by serious cybercriminals in real life. Although there are many online communities for serious offenders, these are often business relationships. It is more likely that technical skills and a motivation to offend precede seeking out criminal groups online.

There is evidence that technical skills are related to piracy to some extent. A survey of 433 college students found that those scoring higher on a measure of Internet proficiency (e.g., using online auctions, building a web page) were more likely to pirate software online. The pirates were also more likely to be male (Hinduja, 2003). It makes sense that technically skilled users have better ability and thus incentive to participate in cybercrime.

Related to piracy, other research has focused on those who make college students' software piracy possible: software crackers. Software cracking is the removal of protections from software that are designed to make illegal distribution more difficult, such as removing expiration dates from trial software versions. Interviews with 24 software crackers solicited from related forums found that most were male and were younger (in their 20s), similar to street crime. Only a quarter had met with members of their community in real life (Goode & Cruise, 2006), suggesting that real-life peer influences might not play as strong a role as that of street crime.

The research so far hints that younger males may be more likely to be involved in cybercrime, similar to street crime. One study focusing on just this question downloaded all 18,675 profiles from a large carding forum. Forums always have profiles for each registered user, where personal details such as age and gender can be optionally filled in. Only 2,232 profiles listed gender (the rest left that field blank), but of those, 94% were male. Of the 77 profiles that included age, the median age was 21 (Kigerl, 2011).

Other research focusing on hackers (whether involved in illegal activities or not) has confirmed the seeming overrepresentation of males among these groups, although the effect of age is much less clear. A sample of 200 hackers at a Hackers on Planet Earth (HOPE) conference in New York City and a DefCon 8 hack conference in Las Vegas were surveyed. Only 9% of the sample consisted of women, with a mean age of 25. Contrary to existing myths, the hacker sample was not found to score higher on measures of depression, anger, anxiety, or OCD symptoms. They did, however, score higher than average on a scale of creativity. However, most said they hack for white hat (ethical) reasons, and therefore cannot be considered cybercriminals (Schell, Dodge, & Moutsatsos, 2002).

Another sample of 136 hackers from multiple hacking conventions attempted to address whether they score higher on measures of autism. Only 2.2% of the sample reported having hacking offenses such as cracking passwords and changing grades, so these findings may not be generalizable to cybercriminals, either. The Autism-Spectrum Quotient (AQ) was administered to the sample, which attempted to measure dimensions of autism such as low social and communication skills, high attention to detail, and preference for routine. Previously, those with computer science degrees have been found to score high on this scale (Baron-Cohen, Wheelwright, Skinner, Martin, & Clubley, 2001). The present hacker sample also scored above average on this scale, especially the men (Schell & Melnychuck, 2011).

It has been assumed that cybercriminals and hackers are more introverted. Rogers, Smoak, and Liu (2006) attempted to investigate this assumption. A sample was drawn from a Canadian college in a liberal arts department. "Cybercrime" was measured by whether participants had ever used another's password without authorization, used or wrote a virus, or obtained someone else's credit card information without authorization, among other behaviors excluding piracy (because it is too common). The five-factor personality scale was administered. Contrary to popular assumptions, deviant computer users actually scored higher on extroversion, although the remaining four personality scales were insignificant. Interestingly, this study was replicated by Rogers, Seigfried, and Tidke (2006) using a sample of college students from an IT department in the United States and found opposite results. The results suggested that computer deviants were less extroverted. Neither study controlled for technical skills, so it may be that personality interacts with technical background in certain ways when predicting cybercrime activity.

Another study of hacking convention participants acquired 124 subjects from the Washington, D.C., ShmooCon 2008 convention. Only participants who admitted to having attempted a computer intrusion were selected, such as malware distribution and social engineering, so there were potentially more "unethical" hackers in the sample. It was found that the participants preferred a more rational thinking style than the general public, and were also more confident in their ability to make decisions. The respondents also scored higher on measures of risk taking, which had an even stronger effect size than rational thinking variable. Additionally, within the sample, risk takers who reported being more rational had claimed to have carried out more hacking attempts. That risk takers were found to have made more hacking attempts is consistent with self-control theory. Of the existing hacking attempts reported, more of those attempts were actually successful the higher the respondent scored on rationality. On the flip side, risk taking was inversely related to successful hacking attempts. Interestingly, age was not related to hacking success. Lastly, those subjects who were unemployed reported more hacking attempts (Bachmann, 2010).

Economic circumstances motivating cybercrime, such as unemployment, may have some similarities with street crime as well. Unemployment is well known to be a factor in street crime (Raphael & Winter-Ebmer, 2001). It has also been suggested that countries with fewer IT jobs per capita have more cybercriminals (Greenberg, 2007, 2008). If someone has a computer science degree and cannot find legitimate work in the IT industry, then cybercrime can sound very appealing.

One study found a link between unemployment and whether a given nation sent a high volume of e-mail spam. One hundred and fourteen countries were selected, and their spam output in 2008 was measured. Countries with low unemployment rates actually sent more spam. Countries with many Internet users also sent more spam. However, there was an interaction between these two variables such that the effect of Internet users on spam was strongest in nations with high unemployment rates (Kigerl, 2010).

So cybercriminals may be characterized as having more incentives to offend. If legal employment is difficult to come by, cybercrime is a viable alternative, as there is much money to be made by participating in it (Brody, Mulig, & Kimball, 2007; Dyrud, 2005; Kanish et al., 2008).

In many ways the characteristics of cybercriminals may be similar to both street crime and white-collar crime: male with a tendency to take risks. In other ways, cybercriminals may be similar only to street criminals, in that there may be more economic hardship to nudge them toward illicit activities, evidenced by unemployment being associated with higher spam rates (Kigerl, 2010) and hacking attempts (Bachmann, 2010). However, cybercrime may share more in common with white-collar crime, requiring more technical skills, group dynamics and organization, and specialization in offending strategies. There also may be some personality characteristics of cybercriminals not found in other criminal types, such as poorer social skills and introversion, preference for routine, rational thinking styles, and close attention to detail.

Theories of Cybercriminal Behavior

While the profile of a cybercriminal paints a picture of what such offenders are like, these traits are neither necessary nor sufficient in predicting the occurrence of cybercrime. A cybercriminal does not have to be male, impulsive, or even technically skilled to commit an offense in cyberspace. A more comprehensive theory is called for.

Early discussions about predicting an offense in cyberspace focused on whether a new theory was required, considering the historical novelty of cyberspace itself. Cyberspace is an environment quite unlike physical reality, where traditional laws and understandings about the physical world do not apply. Therefore, debate focused on whether a different theory customized to cyberspace was needed to predict criminal behavior.

A contrast can be made between physical space and digital space. In cyberspace, physically defined locations lose their importance. Whether a website is hosted in the next room or across the world is less meaningful, as both websites can be opened simultaneously without costing much in time. This stretches out social relations across space as well, as online communities can be composed of members from all over the world. Each community is not as isolated by the constraints of physical distance from other communities. Although the regular visitors of an online community may be socially isolated from other communities by choice alone, there are no real barriers to joining many different membership communities. Anonymity in cyberspace also means that fewer participants' identities are certain, as they can assume a new pseudonym and claim to be just about anyone. The Internet allows for the multiplication of exchanges of goods, ideas, and persons from around the world. Ideas and information can propagate much faster over decentralized networks (Adams, 1998). The differences of this new space prompted suggestions that a new theory was required (Capeller, 2001; Snyder, 2001).

Routine Activity Theory

An existing theory of criminal behavior, routine activity theory (RAT), has been put forth as appropriate, rather than developing an entirely new theory specialized to the Internet (Pease, 2001). Routine activity theory can be powerfully descriptive of deviance on the Internet because it focuses on three different conditions being true and meeting in space that allow a crime to occur. Considering the lessened restrictions of time and space over a global network, these three conditions have a magnified ability to intersect in cyberspace.

The three conditions of RAT that must co-occur and meet in space are: (1) there is a motivated offender present, one willing to commit a crime; (2) a suitable target exists that the motivated offender desires to act on in the commission of a crime, such as something to steal; and (3) the absence of a capable guardian that might prevent the crime from occurring, such as a police officer (Cohen & Felson, 1979). An equation can be formulated that summarizes these conditions: offender + target − guardian = crime.

The motivated offender condition is crime from the offender's point of view. The offender will only act if he or she thinks the target is suitable and a guardian is absent (Akers & Sellers, 2004). The target is suitable if the offender values something about it and the target is visible and accessible to the offender—that is, the two meet in space (Felson & Clarke, 1998). A capable guardian can be just about anything. It can be a security guard, a lock, fences, alarms, or even a suitable target willing to defend itself (Cohen & Felson, 1979).

RAT and Cybercrime

Actions in the new environment of the Internet can be appropriately explained to some extent by RAT. With approximately two billion Internet users worldwide in 2010 (Internet World Stats, 2010), and the fact that few of these users have any real barriers to meeting in cyberspace, there is great potential for motivated offenders to find suitable targets over the Internet. People's actions are less restrained on the Internet, because there is more confidence associated with the anonymity and impersonal nature of cyberspace. This has been termed the online disinhibition effect (Suler, 2004) and applies to both offenders and targets. Being less risk-averse can incline someone toward crime, but it can also predispose one to being a victim (Schreck, Stewart, & Fisher, 2006). Targets that take risky actions online—that click malicious links, download malicious files, and do not update and patch their software—are going to be most suitable. A capable guardian could be security software, such as antivirus software, a firewall, or a spam filter. But given the ability to reach a massive audience online, the motivated offender can easily find an out-of-date antivirus or an insecure port in a firewall, and maybe get a few messages through a spam filter; not to mention find a victim that has none of these protections at all. Routine activity theory is all about these three conditions meeting in space. And it is much easier for two individuals that meet these conditions to find each other in cyberspace.

Research has tested whether any of the conditions of RAT are predictive of cybercrime victimization. One survey of 172 college students attempted to look at the predictors of the number of malware infections and the number of hours and dollars lost from such victimizations. The presence of capable guardians was measured by whether participants used antivirus, antispyware, and firewalls. The suitability of each target (student) was indicated by the amount of time spent online both at home and at work. Both the suitability of a given target and the absence of the measured capable guardians were predictive of subsequent malware victimization (Choi, 2008).

Other research has found only limited support for the predictive power of certain routine activities and malware victimization. Another survey, with 788 subjects, used data loss due to malware infection as an outcome variable. Most legitimate online activity (e.g., chat, e-mail) was unrelated to victimization. More risky behavior online, such as media piracy and unauthorized access to the internet (stealing Wi-Fi), was related to malware infection. After controlling for spurious factors, however, only media piracy and whether friends downloaded pornography from the Internet were predictive of victimization. Piracy being one of the best ways to spread malware, it makes sense that it is predictive of infection. Measures of guardianship, such as the use of antivirus, computer skills, and regularly updating software, were not related to victimization (Bossler & Holt, 2007). These variables may be guardians, but apparently they are not always capable.

Malware infection is only one way to fall victim to cybercrime. Hutchings and Hayes (2009) looked at phishing attacks and victimization. One hundred and four participants were randomly selected from a telephone directory and interviewed. More time spent using a computer and experience with online banking resulted in being the recipient of more phishing attacks. Internet use was not related to phishing attacks after controlling for the use of online banking. Naturally, more time spent using a computer would make one more susceptible, and therefore more suitable, for being targeted for a phishing scam. It is also plausible that a phishing e-mail masquerading as the target's bank would be better directed at online banking users. Therefore, banking users are more suitable for these kinds of phishing scams.

Similar to some findings of antivirus software use, the use of a spam filter did not decrease the chances of receiving a phishing attack. It may be questioned whether users know enough about their e-mail client to self-report whether they use filters or not. Unfortunately, only one respondent reported actually being a victim of a phishing attack (giving up credential information), which is not enough data to be able to predict victimization (Hutchings & Hayes, 2009).

Additional research on being the target of online fraud looked exclusively at suitable targets. Internet fraud was the dependent variable, which could be a phishing scam, advance fee fraud, or other forms of online fraud. A phone survey of 922 randomly sampled subjects found that those who were younger, more educated, and male and had higher incomes spent more time online and made more website purchases. Thus, they were more likely to be suitable targets (Pratt, Holtfreter & Reisig, 2010). It is worth noting that those with higher education and income often perceive there to be fewer risks online, and therefore use the Internet more (Reisig, Pratt & Holtfreter, 2009). Risk takers make better offenders, but they also make better targets for offenders. Both hours spent online and the number of website purchases predicted being the target of Internet fraud, controlling for the personal characteristics mentioned. The impact these personal characteristics (e.g., age, income) have on being the target of cyberattacks were fully mediated by time spent online and the number of website purchases (Pratt, Holtfreter & Reisig, 2010).

Time spent online and therefore the chance to expose a potential target to a cyberattack is also associated with less technical cybercrimes. The number of hours spent in chat rooms and using instant messaging is associated with an increased chance of being the recipient of cyberbullying. Piracy, stealing others' data, and attempting to guess others' passwords were also related to cyberbullying victimization (Holt & Bossler, 2009).

Indicators of the frequent use of the Internet and Internet services appear to measure suitable targets well. Naturally, the type of target that an offender will meet in cyberspace will likely be one that is in cyberspace often. What exists as a promising capable guardian to protect these targets is not as clear, as technological protections do not always seem to be successful at preventing attack and victimization.

It could be that those without antivirus (AV) never realize they are infected with malware, and therefore cannot self-report being a victim. What service will report to them that they are victims? It is also not that difficult to bypass AV, as much malware encrypts itself and makes detection more difficult (Schiller et al., 2007). Many crimeware applications, called "crypters," can be cheaply purchased online that can make a new malware threat fully undetectable to any AV program. Keeping software up to date is not a bulletproof solution, either. It is easy to exploit a system, for a perpetrator only has to find a single vulnerability. But to truly protect a computer or network, the defender must patch every vulnerability, most of which are not even known.

RAT and the Psychology of Cybercrime

The conditions of RAT suggest a crime can occur when an offender is motivated enough in the presence of a suitable target. These predictors have a human element to them that makes them relevant to psychology. What distinguishes between a motivated versus an unmotivated offender in cyberspace? Most likely much of the personality- and trait-related differences among individuals considered to have cybercriminal tendencies discussed in the previous section are potential predictors of being a motivated offender.

Motivated offenders may be bigger risk takers, as appears to be the case of digital pirates (Goles et al., 2007; Higgins, Fell, & Wilson, 2007) and hackers (Bachmann, 2010). They may be either extroverted or introverted, depending on their level of IT experience and skill when it comes to software pirates (Rogers, Seigfried, & Tidke, 2006; Rogers, Smoak, & Liu, 2006). Motivated offenders may adopt a more rational and logical thinking style, as evidenced by hackers' (whether malicious or not) self-reports (Bachmann, 2010). Lastly, those with hacking experience appear to have a greater preference for solitary activities and other features characteristic of high scorers on the Autism Quotient (Schell & Melnychuk, 2011).

Psychology can also play a role in suitable targets, which are not necessarily inanimate objects or computer systems. There is a psychological element to many cybercrimes that exploit other people's decision making, such as that relying on social engineering. Also, in the case of protecting oneself from cybercrimes, the victim may also be in charge of capable guardianship; that being to install antivirus and other protections. The type of person who is suitable, or who does not ensure there are capable guardians in place, may differ from targets who do not meet these characteristics.

Some of the predictors of motivated offenders ought to also be true of suitable targets, especially levels of self-control and tendencies to take risks. Prior research has linked low self-control to both routine activities (Holtfreter, Reisig, & Pratt, 2008) and street crime and fraud victimization (Holtfreter, Reisig, Piquero, & Piquero, 2010; Schreck, Stewart, & Fisher, 2006). This is likely also true for cybercrime victimizations. Individuals who taker greater risks online and have fewer protections in place, such as antivirus, naturally are more susceptible to malware victimization (Choi, 2008), and also spend more time online (Reisig, Pratt, & Holtfreter, 2009). Interestingly, however, there may not be a relationship between the technical sophistication of the target and subsequent malware victimization (Bossler & Holt, 2007).

Routine activity theory is fairly well supported by observations. The theory fits well with the emerging reality of cyberspace. RAT describes multiple conditions that can meet in cyberspace; but those constituent parts individually can also be described by psychology, namely the psychology of motivated offenders and their victims. RAT suggests what the risks might be for falling prey to cybercrime. However, understanding the risks does not always ensure we understand the solutions to a given problem. Even if every Internet user in the world used up-to-date antivirus and spam filters, this would unlikely be enough. A cybercriminal needs only a few victims out of many thousands or millions targeted to be successful. Given the easy multiplication of an attack vector over digital space distributed over countless targets, it will continue to be a significant struggle to deter cybercriminals.

Conclusion

The presence of cyberspace has created new opportunities for criminal behavior. The nature of cyberspace and the Internet changes our prior understanding of the physics of criminal actions. The weakened relevance of time, distance, and quantity creates a greater ability for motivated offenders and potential victims to meet in space and propagate such offenses over vast distances. The environment of cyberspace provides a novel way for these conditions which cause crime to occur.

However, the psychology of would-be offenders, and even their victims, also play a role; not just the environment of a digital network. The type of person attracted to crimes in cyberspace may be similar to criminals in general in certain ways (e.g., male, risk takers) (Higgins, Fell, & Wilson, 2007). Yet there may be some personality characteristics and thinking styles unique to cybercriminals, such as lessened social interest, attention to detail, and self-reported rationality and logical cognitive styles (Bachmann, 2010; Schell & Melnychuk, 2011).

A person such as this, someone with greater interest in things than people and with a desire to understand complex technical systems, may be attracted to the environment in cyberspace. Couple this with a tendency to take risks and act out on one's impulses, and there can be an increased chance that a crime will be carried out over the networks they navigate. Their victims may similarly be risk takers, only in a different way. Instead of taking risks by breaking the law, victims may take risks such as ignoring the option to install the proper protections on their systems, or failing to carefully consider the dangers of each potentially fraudulent scheme that targets them (Choi, 2008; Holtfreter et al., 2010).

Cybercrime also has some parallels with white-collar crime, such as the potential for more technical skills and offense specialization (Benson & Moore, 1992; Ben-Itzhak, 2009). Technically, cybercrime may even be defined as white-collar crime (Croal, 1992). However, the majority of cybercrimes reside in cyberspace, not in an office building. Cyberspace is one of the best places to commit a crime, considering the anonymity and impersonal nature of such an environment. The ability to propagate a cyberattack across thousands of hosts and, through multiple jurisdictions, also makes law enforcement much more difficult.

The reality that cyberspace does not have the same borders we are familiar with can confuse legal responses to crimes committed in this space. Many attacks in one country do not originate from that same country (Balkin et al., 2007). That is why international laws and cooperation are necessary. Most solutions to cybercrime focus on technical prevention rather than legal punishment. Similar to using a padlock to prevent burglary, most efforts are geared toward reducing the success rate of cyberattacks (e.g., spam filters, antivirus). This will only make cybercrime slightly less profitable; so legal punishment is also called for.

It is difficult to study cybercriminals, because they are a rarity among prison populations and are therefore not easy to sample or follow up on. As more time is given to observe the impact of law enforcement on cybercriminals, perhaps a better idea of how to control them might emerge. Incapacitation and deterrence of street criminals has been met with only limited success (Baily, 1998; Visher, 1987), but the fewer number of cybercriminals and their tendencies for rational thinking styles might make them different in some ways. Future research should further seek to determine the impact law enforcement is capable of having on existing cyber offenders, and whether their characteristic thinking styles play a role.

Cybercrime is a business, and is part of a shadow economy of which most Internet users are not aware. The criminal participants of this business share some commonalities with other offender types, but they are also in a class of their own. Fighting cybercrime will require more than just an understanding of the technical aspects of each cyberattack; it will also require an understanding of the psychology of the cybercriminals themselves.

References

Adams, P. (1998). *Network Topologies and Virtual Place*. Annals of the American Geographers Number 1, March 1998, pp 88–106.

Akers, R. L., & Sellers, C. S. (2004). *Criminological theories: Introduction, evaluation, and application* (4th ed., p. 33). Los Angeles, CA: Roxbury.

Akers, R. L., Krohn, M. D., Lanza-Kaduce, L., & Radosevich, M. (1979). Social learning and deviant behavior: A specific test of general theory. *American Sociological Review, 44*, 636–655.

Ananthaswamy, A. (2009, August 15). Defeat worms, send them to quarantine: The best way to stop highly virulent worms wreaking havoc on the internet is to give it an immune system. *New Scientist*, 16–17.

Bachmann, M. (2010). The risk propensity and rationality of computer hackers. *International Journal of Cyber Criminology, 4*(1–2), 643–656.

Baily, W. (1998). Deterrence, brutalization and the death penalty. *Criminology, 36* (4), 711–733.

Balkin, J. M., Grimmelmann, J., Katz, E., Kozlovski, N., Wagman, S., & Zarsky, T. (2007). Chapter 10: The Council of Europe's Convention on Cybercrime. In *Cybercrime: Digital cops in a networked environment*. New York: New York University Press.

Baron-Cohen, S., Wheelwright, S., Skinner, R., Martin, J., & Clubley, E. (2001). The autism-spectrum quotient (AQ): Evidence from Asperger syndrome/ high-functioning autism, males and females, scientists and mathematicians. *Journal of Autism and Developmental Disorders, 31*(1), 5–17.

Ben-Itzhak, Y. (2009). Organized cybercrime and payment cards. *Card Technology Today, 21*(2), 10–11.

Benson, M. L., & Moore, E. (1992). Are white-collar and common offenders the same? An empirical and theoretical critique of a recently proposed general theory of crime. *Journal of Research in Crime and Delinquency, 29*(3), 251–272.

Bickle, G., Schlegel, A., Fassbender, P., & Klein, U. (2006). Some personality correlates of business white-collar crime. *Applied Psychology: An International Review, 55*(2), 220–233.

Bossler, A. M., & Holt, T. J. (2007, November 14). Examining the utility of routine activities theory for cybercrime. Paper presented at the annual meeting of the American Society of Criminology, Atlanta Marriott Marquis, Atlanta, GA.

Brody, R. G., Mulig, E., & Kimball, V. (2007). Phishing, pharming and identity theft. *Academy of Accounting and Financial Studies Journal, 11*, 43–56.

CAN SPAM Act: Controlling the Assault of Non-Solicited Pornography and Marketing Act of 2003, 15 U.S.C. Sec. 7701 (2005).

Capeller, W. (2001). Not such a neat net: Some comments on virtual criminality. *Social Legal Studies, 10*, 229–242.

Choi, K. S. (2008). Computer crime victimization and integrated theory: An empirical assessment. *International Journal of Cyber Criminology,* 2(1), 308–333.

Clarke, R. A., & Knake, R. (2010). *Cyber war: The next threat to national security and what to do about it*. New York: HarperCollins.

Cohen, L. E., & Felson, M. (1979). Social change and crime rate trends: A routine activity approach. *American Sociological Review*, 44(4), 588–608.

Croal, H. (1992). *White Collar Crime*. Open University Press.

Daly, K. (1989). Gender and varieties of white-collar crime. *Criminology, 27*(4), 769–794.

Dyrud, M. (2005). "I brought you a good news": An analysis of Nigerian 419 letters. Proceedings of the 2005 Association for Business Communication Annual Convention.

Felson, M., & Clarke, R. V. (1998). Opportunity makes the thief: Practical theory for crime prevention. *Policing and Reducing Crime Unit: Research, Development and Statistics Directorate, 98*, 1–36.

Fossi, M., Turner, D., Johnson, E., Mack, T., Adams, T., Blackbird, J., . . . Wueest, C. (2010, April). *Symantec global internet security threat report*. Symantec, 15.

Furnell, S. (2002). *Perceptions of cybercrime. Cybercrime: Vandalizing the information society*. London: Addison-Wesley.

Giles, J. (2009, May 23).Your life, sold for $15. *New Scientist*, 36–39.

Goles, T., Jayatilaka, B., George, B., Parsons, L., Chambers, V., Taylor, D., & Brune, R. (2007). Softlifting: Exploring determinants of attitude. *Journal of Business Ethics, 77*, 481–499.

Goode, S., & Cruise, S. (2006). What motivates software crackers? *Journal of Business Ethics*, 65, 173–201.

Goodin, D. (2007). Ukrainian eBay scam turns Down syndrome man into cash machine: How a mule made an ass of me. *The Register*. Retrieved March 9, 2011 from http://www.theregister.co.uk/2007/11/08/ebay_victims_track_their_mules/.

Gordon, S., & Ford, R. (2006). On the definition and classification of cybercrime. *Journal of Computational Virology*, 2, 13–20.

Gottfredson, M. R., & Hirschi, T. (1990). A general theory of crime. Stanford, CA: Stanford University Press.

Grasmick, H. G., Tittle, C. R., Bursik, R. J., Jr., & Arneklev, B. J. (1993). Testing the core empirical implications of Gottfredson and Hirschi's general theory of crime. *Journal of Research in Crime and Delinquency, 30*, 5–29.

Greenberg, A. (2007, July 16). The top countries for cybercrime: China takes over the U.S. in hosting web pages that install malicious programs. *MSNBC*. Retrieved September 16, 2010, from http://www.msnbc.msn.com/id/19789995/.

Greenberg, A. (November 19, 2008). Economic bust, cybercrime boom. *Forbes.com*. Retrieved February 13, 2011, from http://www.forbes.com/2008/11/18/cybercrime-boom-fraud-tech-security-cx_ag_1119crime.html.

Higgins, G. E., Fell, B. D., & Wilson, A. L. (2007). Low self-control and social learning in understanding students' intentions to pirate movies in the United States. *Social Science Computer Review, 25*(3), 339–357.

Hinduja, S. (2003). Trends and patterns among online software pirates. *Ethics and Information Technology, 5*, 49–61.

Hinduja, S. (2007). Neutralization theory and online software piracy: An empirical analysis. *Ethics of Information Technology, 9*, 187–204.

Hinduja, S. (2008). Deindividuation and internet software piracy. *CyberPsychology and Behavior, 11*(4), 391–398.

Holt, T. J., & Bossler, A. M. (2009). Examining the applicability of lifestyle-routine activities theory for cybercrime victimization. *Deviant Behavior, 30*(1), 1–25.

Holt, T. J., & Lampke, E. (2010). Exploring stolen data markets online: Products and market forces. *Criminal Justice Studies, 23*(1), 33–50.

Holtfreter, K., Reisig, M. D., & Pratt, T. C. (2008). Low self-control, routine activities, and fraud victimization. *Criminology, 46*, 189–220.

Holtfreter, K., Reisig, M. D., Piquero, N. L., & Piquero, A. R. (2010). Low self-control and fraud: Offending, victimization, and their overlap. *Criminal Justice and Behavior, 37*, 188–203.

Hutchings, A., & Hayes, H. (2009). Routine activity theory and phishing victimization: Who got caught in the "net"? *Current Issues in Criminal Justice, 20*(3), 432–451.

Internet World Stats (2010, June 30, 2010). World internet users and population stats. Retrieved March 18, 2011, from: http://www.internetworldstats.com/stats.htm.

IronPort Systems. (2006, June). Spammers continue innovation: IronPort study shows image-based spam, hit and run, and increased volumes latest threat to your inbox. Retrieved March 8, 2011, from http://www.marketwire.com/press-release/spammers-continue-innovation-ironport-study-shows-image-based-spam-hit-run-increased-682259.htm.

Kanish, C., Kreibich, C., Levchenko, K., Enright, B., Voelker, G. M., Paxson, V., & Savage, S. (2008). Spamalytics: An empirical analysis of spam marketing conversion. *Communications of the ACM*.

Kigerl, A. (2010). *Routine activity theory and the determinants of high cybercrime countries* (Unpublished manuscript).

Kigerl, A. (2011). *Profiling cybercriminals: The demographics of carding forum members* (Unpublished manuscript).

McQuade, S. C. (2009). Corporate espionage. In S. C. McQuade (Ed.), Encyclopedia of Cybercrime. Westport, CT: Greenwood Publishing Group.

Mon, W. (2002). Causal factors of corporate crime in Taiwan: Qualitative and quantitative findings. *International Journal of Offender Therapy and Comparative Criminology, 46*(2), 183–205.

Morris, R. G., & Higgins, G. E. (June 2009). Neutralization potential and self-reported digital piracy: A multitheoretical exploration among college undergraduates. *Criminal Justice Review, 34*(2), 173–195.

Pease, K. (2001). Crime futures and foresight: Challenging criminal behavior in the information age. In D. Wall (ed.) *Crime and the Internet*. London: Routledge.

Pratt, T. C., & Cullen, F. T. (2000). The empirical status of Gottfredson and Hirschi's general theory of crime: A meta-analysis. *Criminology*, 38(3), 931–964.

Pratt, T. C., Holtfreter, K., & Reisig, M. D. (2010). Routine online activity and internet fraud targeting: Extending the generality of routine activity theory. *Journal of Research in Crime and Delinquency, 47*, 267–296.

Raphael, S., & Winter-Ebmer, R. (2001, April). Identifying the effect of unemployment on crime. *Journal of Law and Economics, 44*(1), 259–283.

Reisig, M. D., Pratt, T. C., & Holtfreter, K. (2009, January 6). Perceived risk of internet theft victimization: Examining the effects of social vulnerability and financial impulsivity. *Criminal Justice and Behavior, 36*, 369–384.

Rogers, M. K. (2006). A two-dimensional circumplex approach to the development of a hacker taxonomy. *Digital Investigation, 3*(2), 97–102.

Rogers, M. K., Seigfried, K., & Tidke, K. (2006). Self-reported computer criminal behavior: A psychological analysis. *Digital Investigation, 3*, 116–120.

Rogers, M. K., Smoak, N., & Liu, J. (2006). Self-reported criminal computer behavior: A big-5, moral choice and manipulative exploitive behavior analysis. *Deviant Behavior, 27*, 1–24.

Saltzman, M. (2009, March 20). What happens when you buy "spam"? *Sympatico Sync*. Retrieved March 16, 2011, from: http://sync.sympatico.ca/How-To/ContentPosting_MS?newsitemid=34c50777-f4eb-4751-bb9f-82c9a6f07ab4&feedname=MARC-SALTZMAN.

Schell, B. H., & Melnychuk, J. (2011). Chapter 8: Female and male hacker conferences attendees: Their autism-spectrum quotient (AQ) scores and self-reported adulthood experiences. In T. J. Holt & B. H. Schell (Eds.), *Corporate hacking and technology-driven crime: Social dynamics and implications* (pp. 144–169). Hershey, PA: IGI Global.

Schell, B. H., Dodge, J. L., & Moutsatsos, S. S. (2002). *The hacking of America: Who's doing it, why, and how*. Westport, CT: Quorum Books.

Schiller, C. A., Binkley, J., Harley, D., Evron, G., Bradley, T., Willems, C., & Cross, M. (2007). *Botnets: The killer web app*. Walthan, MA: Syngress Publishing.

Schreck, C. J., Stewart, E. A., & Fisher, B. S. (2006). Self-control, victimization, and their influence on risky lifestyles: A longitudinal analysis using panel data. *Journal of Quantitative Criminology, 22*, 319–340.

Shinder, D. (July 19, 2010). Profiling and categorizing cybercriminals. *Tech Republic*. Retrieved March 16, 2010, from: http://www.techrepublic.com/blog/security/profiling-and-categorizing-cybercriminals/4069.

Snyder, F. (2001). Sites of criminality and sites of governance. *Social and Legal Studies, 10*, 251–256.

Suler, J. (2004). The online disinhibition effect. *Cyberpsychology Behavior, 7*, 321–326.

Tive, C. (2006). *419 scam: Exploits for the Nigerian con man*. Lincoln, NE: iUniverse.

Visher, C. A. (1987). Incapacitation and crime control: Does a "lock 'em up" strategy reduce crime? *Justice Quarterly, 4*(4), 513–543.

Weber, T. (2007). Criminals may overwhelm the web. *BBC News*. Retrieved February 6, 2011, from: http://news.bbc.co.uk/2/hi/business/6298641.stm.

Wierdrick-Kozlowski, J., & Stinchcombe, N. (2008). Finjan identifies the latest cybercrime business model—crimeware as a service. *Software World, 39*(3), 16.

Williams, P. (2001, August). Organized crime and cybercrime: Synergies, trends, and responses. *Computer Crime Research Center*. Retrieved January 26, 2011, from http://www.crime-research.org/library/Cybercrime.htm.

Yar, M. (2005). The novelty of "cybercrime": An assessment in light of routine activity theory. *European Journal of Criminology, 2*(4), 407–427.

CHAPTER TEN

Pathways to Copycat Crime

Ray Surette

Introduction

A behavioral process that is widely accepted is the ability of the media to generate copycat crime. As media technology has evolved so that a mediated experience has come to approach that of a real-world experience, concerns with emulation of media-modeled behaviors have grown (Helfgott, 2008). Waves of fads and fashions have established the fact that people lift behavior models from the media, and this connection has been extrapolated to include the mimicking of media-portrayed criminal acts (Miller, 2000). Recent research suggests that copycat crime is a common part of many offender criminal histories, with approximately one of four reporting a copycat attempt (Surette, 2012). Despite concern, there has been little theoretical work on copycat crime dynamics. In partial response, this chapter offers an individual-level, multipath, hypothesized copycat crime model derived from prior relevant research on media, crime, and imitation.

What is unique about copycat crime is that any type of crime from homicide to minor civil disobedience can be a copycat offense. At its simplest, copycat crime is any crime whose occurrence or form is influenced by prior media content. For a crime to be a copycat crime, however, it must be inspired by an earlier, media-publicized or portrayed crime; that is, there must be a pair of crimes linked through the media.[1] The perpetrator of a copycat crime must have been exposed to a media "generator crime" and must have incorporated elements of that crime into his or her crime. In broad terms, copycat crime results from the interaction of factors from three sources: media content, persons at risk to be copycats, and the immediate and wider social and cultural setting in which the media content is consumed.[2] In this chapter, the setting and media content factors will not be discussed. Instead, the psychological pathways that individuals travel between exposure to a generator copycat crime portrayed in the media and a copycat crime attempt in the real world will be illustrated. Despite wide types of crimes being able to be copycat crimes, it is hypothesized that copycat offenders will follow common paths to their varied copycat offenses. The research question addressed is: Given exposure to a criminogenic generator crime, what psychological steps are likely traveled for a copycat crime attempt to result? Adapting concepts from Bandura's (1973) observational learning, Akers's (1998) social learning, Sutherland's (1947) differential association, Anderson, Gentile, and Buckley's (2007) general aggression model, Rogers's (2003) social diffusion of innovations, and a set of communication-based social cognition models, a three-path, individual-level copycat crime model is offered.

Three Paths to Copycat Crime

As diagrammed in Figure 10.1, three distinct paths to copycat crime are postulated. All three paths are grounded in social learning and cognitive theories and reflect media effects and communication research. The first two paths have been extensively researched in the cognitive communication field and have been applied to consumer use of news and infotainment media content. As configured, the model focuses on the cognitive psychological steps speculated to occur between exposure to a copycat-generation crime and copycat attempts, and conceptually originates in Anderson and his colleagues' General Aggression Model and Bandura's social learning model. Discussed in order of least to most traversed, path 1 (central systematic processing, where all relevant and available information is collected and assessed before making a decision) and path 2 (heuristic peripheral, where decisions are made based on incomplete information) largely reflect communication concepts, while path 3 (narrative persuasion) reflects recent entertainment education theory[3] and research on the impact of media-communicated stories.[4] The first two paths are determined by the cognitive motivation (the willingness to invest time gathering and evaluating information) of a copycat offender. When cognitive motivation is high, the first path, *central systematic*, is followed as long as the individual has the capability to understand the information gathered. Instrumental copycat crimes such as the mimicked bank robbery from the film *Set It Off* provide examples

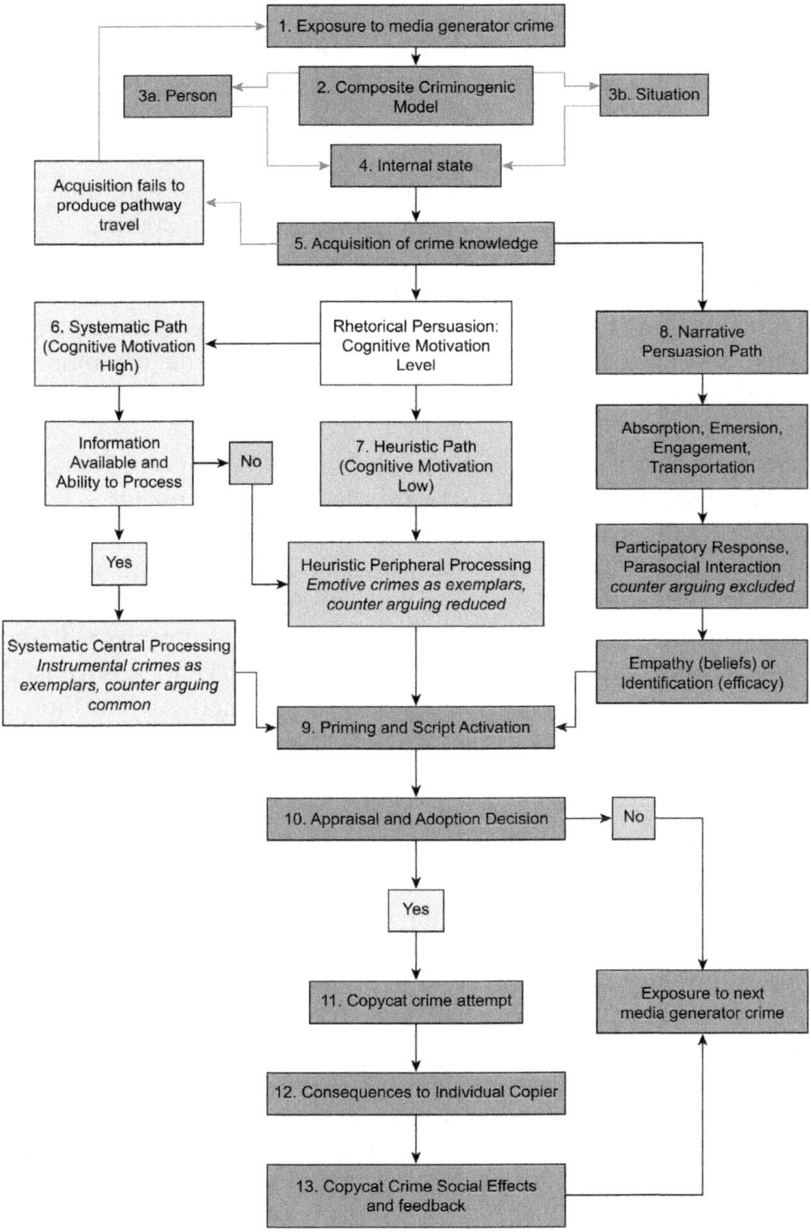

Figure 10.1 A Multi-Path Copycat Crime Model.

of copycat offenders following a systematic central processing path to a copycat crime. The second path, *heuristic peripheral*, is followed when cognitive motivation, or the ability to process available information, is low and its copycat exemplars are spontaneous emotive crimes, such as unplanned opportunity assaults or rapes and some hate crime clusters. In the heuristic process, only a subset of relevant information is retrieved, and that which is retrieved is the most accessible from memory (Shrum, 2002, p. 79). The third path denotes the psychological involvement people experience when using the media as entertainment and escapism. In this path, factual information is not the goal; being told an interesting story is. After diverging through the three possible paths, the model reconverges within the communication research concepts of priming and scripts and continues through its final steps.

Conceptually, the model can be divided into three sections. The top portion of the model, from exposure to a media generator crime to acquisition of crime knowledge (step 1 to step 5), is felt to be a common experience for most media consumers in that many persons are expected to learn criminally instructive information, particularly from repeated media exposures (Bandura, 2004). Thus, repeated playing of certain video games will impart the basic knowledge of how to be a sniper to many teenagers. That is, they will acquire the instructions and know the steps necessary to hunt and shoot other humans from a distance. However, very few will transverse the middle portion of the model (step 6, 7, or 8 to step 9) and follow one of the three copycat paths down to an "appraisal and adoption decision," at which committing a copycat crime is seriously considered. It is speculated that most individuals who reach this point in the model will decide not to consider a copycat crime and will exit. The bottom portion of the model (step 10 to step 13) is thus the least traveled road for at-risk copycat offenders, for these individuals come to a positive appraisal of copying generator crimes and decide to adopt and implement the crimes modeled. These actual copycat crime attempts are hypothesized to be rare as a proportion of all crime, but not rare in terms of criminal life histories. That is, most of the crimes committed by offenders will not be copycat crimes, but many offenders (about one of four) will have attempted copycat crime in their lifetimes (Surette, 2012). The model is both a map of possible individual-level pathways to copycat crime and a diagram of a filtering process of potential copycat offenders in which only those with a unique combination of factors make it to actually attempting a copycat crime. The separate steps of the model and the theoretical concepts and premises incorporated at each step are discussed in turn.

Step 1: Exposure to a Media Generator Crime

Exposure to media generator crimes is common, and many if not most persons in a media-saturated society are exposed to a large number of possible generator crimes on a regular basis. Thus, while a number of characteristics have been forwarded as increasing the probability of a media-rendered crime to generate copycats, it is speculated that individual-level psychological and social environment factors will more determine who and how many will undertake the copycat crime paths. Regarding generator crime characteristics, criminogenic content can be defined as content that positively portrays or encourages crime. A significant potential effect of criminogenic content is the disconnection of the negative psychological and moral aspects of committing a crime for the media consumer. Distilling the research on media effects, the most criminogenic content is hypothesized as content where innovative and successful crimes are justified, are explicitly rewarded, go unpunished, are stripped of negative consequences, involve guns, are realistic or humorous, and contain criminal models who commit crimes with positive prosocial motives, who are heroic, and who are demographically similar to the consumer (Bandura, 1973, p. 207; Bandura, 2001, pp. 277–278; Fisch, 2002, p. 416; Haridakis, 2002, p. 333; Wilson, Colvin, & Smith, 2002, p. 37). Such content combined with consumer multiple viewings, emotional reaction to the content, and the opportunity for real-world rehearsal will maximize content-related copycat effects (Bandura 1973, pp. 78, 207). Although U.S. crime and justice media content has been repeatedly identified as providing all of these elements, not all criminogenic content will generate copycat crime due to the necessity of multiple individual and setting factors interacting.

Step 2: Composite Criminogenic Model

At-risk copycat offenders take elements from multiple crime models to create a composite behavior model to mimic. Crime models can be tapped from family, community, and media, with copiers mixing elements from all three sources.

Steps 3a, 3b, and 4: Person, Situation, and Internal State

Derived from a general learning model (GLM) forwarded by Buckley and Anderson (2006, pp. 369–370), these steps incorporate factors that individuals bring to an exposure to a media generator crime. Step 3a involves the personality characteristics of a potential copycat offender. Beliefs, goals, tendencies, and experiences that define individuals as unique interact at this step with media exposure. In step 3b factors associated with the situation in which media exposure occurs come into play. The type of media, characteristics of the setting in which exposure happens, and criminal encouragement from other people present while exposure to the criminogenic media content occurs play a role. The person and situation factors combine to produce a "present internal state" in step 4. Because characteristics of the person and the situation can differ from day to day and exposure to exposure, the "present internal state" of any individual can vary from one exposure to the next. The "present internal state" is described as a "learning encounter" by Buckley and Anderson's [2006] and determines how the media provided knowledge affects the individual. Criminogenic media are hypothesized to have three effects on an individual's present internal state. First, an increase in general criminal schema is hypothesized to result from increased criminal thoughts, criminal affect and arousal, and increased criminal interpretations of events. Second, the increased likelihood of criminal self-schemata being adopted is hypothesized to result from automatic self-associations with criminal traits and actions. Third, increased crime-related cognition is hypothesized from increased automatic recognition of and linkage of crime associated words. At the conclusion of step 4, if the internal state of the individual fails to reach a necessary psychological pro-crime threshold level, the model is exited until another exposure to a media generator crime. It is postulated that most media consumers exit at this point. Discussed in detail later, two factors related to the step 3a, "Person", are forwarded as crucial for the completion of a copycat crime process. First, a person's self-perception of their criminal efficacy (see Bandura, 2004) and second, their real-world criminal history are felt to play major roles in whether an individual exits or continues onward through the model.

Step 5: Acquisition of Crime Knowledge

At this step the individual has learned the behavioral steps to commit an observed crime and, as stated, many will reach this step. Observational learning is a pervasive learning process, and research has established that the mass media can function as a primary learning group for individuals, especially those who are socially isolated and are heavy media consumers (Bandura, 1973). Attention to the behavior model, retention (symbolic coding and mental rehearsal) of the modeled behavioral steps, processing the capability to physically imitate the behavior, and an expectation of reinforcement for displaying the behavior have been established as important for observational learning (Bandura, 1973). For media-generated copycat crimes, mass communication theory provides the concept of "exemplars," which are speculated to play an important role in copycat crime (Petty, Priester, & Brinol 2002). Generator crimes that are exciting and raise strong emotions are hypothesized to be more likely to result in criminogenic knowledge acquisition than their counterparts (Bandura, 1973).

Steps 6, 7, and 8: Three Copycat Pathways

Following crime knowledge acquisition, the model diverges into three possible pathways determined by the consumer's underlying goal for interacting with the media. Discussed in order from least traveled to most traveled, the paths diverge depending upon whether the consumer is interacting with the media as a source of entertainment or as a source of instruction. The two instruction motivation paths are associated with "rhetorical persuasion," in which an individual must make a real-world decision and looks to the media for helpful decision-making instructions. As diagrammed, paths 1 and 2 first differentiate based upon the cognitive motivation level of an individual and imply different sorts of copycat crime. The first path is related to thoughtful planned "instrumental" crimes ("Here are instructions on how to successfully commit this crime"); the second path involves less rational, emotive copycat crimes ("They are rioting on television and no one's getting arrested! It looks exciting! Let's do the same here"). In the third path, no real-world decision is pending, and instruction is not a goal. In this path, narrative persuasion operates, and deep psychological involvement with media content and storyline develops. This path describes how most people use and interact with most media, seeking entertainment, not explicit instructions.

Path 1: Systematic Central Processing—Motivation to Cognitively Process Information High

This first path is based on the theory of reasoned action, which assumes that people consider the implications of their actions (Petty et al., 2002). In a central route to persuasion, a person is actively involved in evaluating information, scrutinizes all relevant information, and extensively applies prior knowledge (Petty et al., 2002). The central systematic path depends on a copier's ability to cognitively process information and the concept of "counter-arguing." Counter-arguing entails the questioning and scrutiny expended to evaluate media-supplied information and is crucial for the central systematic path. People who have difficulty distinguishing fact from fiction (who have trouble counter-arguing and evaluating the validity of media-provided information) have difficulty traveling this path (Shrum, 2002). An individual's capability to cognitively process media-supplied information can also be reduced by the presence of distractions and time pressure. If extensive information is not available or the ability to process that information is not present, the individual (and model) shifts to path 2. Due to the extensive search and evaluation of the information provided, when followed, the systematic central processing path takes comparatively longer to transverse and fits most logically with instrumental planned copycat crimes.

Developed in communication research to explore how the media related to attitude change, when applied to copycat crime, the central systematic path is determined by how much thought and reflection is expended on the decision to copy. More cognitively demanding, systematic central processing is followed when it is possible to determine the validity of information (Shrum, 2002) and when an individual is motivated to expend the effort to systematically access and consider a lot of information before making a copycat crime decision. In this path, media consumer counter-arguing with the information provided in the media content occurs. Hence, the realistic chances of successfully copying a generator crime would be considered. The at-risk copycat would conduct an extensive search of all relevant information, evaluate the information, and weigh counterarguments that question the validity of the media-provided information in this path. In sum, when the motivation to elaborate on media-supplied information is high, such as when the consequences of a failed crime attempt are seen as serious, path 1 would be followed (Petty et al., 2002).

Path 2: Heuristic Peripheral Processing—Motivation to Cognitively Process Low

When the potential copycat offender is not motivated to closely search the media for crime information than the second path, heuristic peripheral cognitive processing is employed. In this path, only readily available information is accessed and used (Shrum, 2002). The second path is therefore taken when motivation to develop a reasoned action is not significant and behavior is spontaneous. In this path, behavior can result from a relatively automatic process that requires little conscious thought. Path 2 is more common than path 1 because a heuristic sufficiency principle operates for most people (Shrum, 2002). That is, most decision making involves a limited assessment process in which only some information is retrieved until a sufficient, usually not a substantial amount, is felt to be on hand to make a decision. Specifically, the information that is commonly utilized for decision making is that which is most accessible from memory. In this second path, decisions are indirect, more passive, and less articulated (Petty et al., 2002). The easiest information to retrieve is what will be used with information that has been accessed frequently and recently, and is vivid (emotional and image provoking), being most likely to be utilized (Shrum, 2002). Similar to priming, as the accessibility of a set of information increases, so does that of closely related constructs. The activation of a particular construct such as aggression or anger can similarly activate behaviors that are closely related to these constructs, such as crime or violence (Shrum, 2002).

Heavy contemporary media consumption thus enhances path 2 by making criminogenic information easy to access, higher in frequency, more recent in exposure, and more vivid in nature. Media reliance encourages heuristic peripheral processing and discourages systematic processing. Lastly, due to the speed and shallowness of the cognitive effort involved in this path, navigating this path is hypothesized as rapid and most logically spawns emotional and spontaneous copycat crimes.

Path 3: Narrative Persuasion

The most common copycat crime path, which precedes the two cognitive motivation paths, is *narrative persuasion*. This path is entered at the acquisition stage when media information is simply absorbed, not assessed. Interaction with media-supplied narratives is felt to be qualitatively different from the processing and assessment of the validity of informational media. As most media consumed is narrative or story-based, neither of the cognitive processing paths captures the phenomenological experience of reading, hearing, or viewing a work of fiction. Variously termed concepts of "transportation," "engagement," or "absorption" have been used to describe this different type of media impact. The narrative persuasion path is derived from research on the ability of media narratives to influence attitudes and behaviors and from entertainment-education research on the utility of using entertainment media to invoke social change. As most people utilize the media as a source of entertainment, this path is speculated as the one most involved in copycat crime via media-supplied narratives (Strange, 2002). The majority of copycat offenders, even those who eventually travel paths 1 or 2, will first travel the narrative persuasion path.

The psychological dynamics of narrative persuasion start with the premise that narrative content will have more impact with more consumer engagement. Engagement, in turn, will be greatest when viewer goals are met, thereby leading to increased involvement with the content. If the consumer goal is a vicarious relationship, increased identification with the criminogenic model will lead to increased engagement. If the goal is arousal and diversion and there is interest in the narrative genre (the consumer likes the story type—i.e., enjoys crime stories) or if quality of the presentation is high (well-crafted or realistic special effects, for example), increased engagement will result (Slater & Rouner, 2002). Concluding the narrative persuasion process, increased consumer engagement results in their transportation. This path's dynamics suggest that consumer demographic similarity to characters in a narrative is likely to be less important than how emotionally involved one becomes with those characters as a consequence of transportation. An empathetic response to the characters by the consumer is felt to have greater impact than consumer identification with the characters as simply similar to themselves (Slater & Rouner, 2002). Narrative persuasion further allows initially unsympathetic consumers to be addressed through the use of emphatic transitional characters, who initially espouse counter-attitudinal beliefs but model the process of attitude and behavior change (Slater & Rouner, 2002). Thus, a consumer initially unlikely to copy a particular crime would be persuaded to do so by observing an emphatic model, who is shown as also initially unwilling to commit the crime but who eventually undergoes a transformation in which the crime is seen by the character in a positive light.

In gist, when engagement with criminogenic content is high, transformation or absorption results, and the consumer is transported to a world where criminal behavior is justified, rewarded, or unlikely to be punished. In high transportation, the individual can also be distanced temporarily from current and previous beliefs and experiences (Green & Brock, 2000). Transportation is therefore a convergent mental process, a focusing of attention that may occur in response to either fictional or nonfictional narratives (Green & Brock, 2000). Even when the narrative is clearly labeled as fiction, real-world beliefs are affected by the magnitude of transportation. Once a reader is rolling along inside a compelling narrative, the beliefs implied in the story can be adopted regardless of whether they correspond with reality (Green & Brock, 2000).

Due to the large quantity of crime-related narratives in the media, media content in general can be thought of as a haphazard entertainment-education effort. Heightening the media's narrative persuasive effect, the higher the level of engagement with the narrative, the less counter-arguing with the content's informational messages will occur (Brock, Strange, & Green, 2002).[5] The narrative persuasion path provides a mechanism to influence individuals who would be resistant to following the cognitive persuasion paths (Green, Garst, Brock, & Chung, 2006). Rather, in the narrative persuasion path, media consumers are "side-participants" in the story line—prepared to play an active role when given the opportunity (Polichak & Gerrig, 2002). In the end, narrative persuasion thereby provides a mechanism for overcoming resistance to imitating criminal behavior by decoupling the thoughtful consideration of the likely negative sanctions and social reaction to copying (Slater & Rouner, 2002).

While narrative persuasion can provide a path that alone can result in copycat crime, it is speculated that it is not uncommon for copycat offenders to complete this path and then revert in the model to either path 1 or 2 depending upon their criminal capabilities and motivations. Thus, both spontaneous and instrumental copycat crimes can result from narrative persuasion. Irrespective, high levels of consumer transformation when combined with empathy (and, to a lesser degree, identification with a criminal model), and rhetorical persuasion, all lead a potential copycat offender to adopt pro-crime definitions and to be primed for criminal emulation.

Step 9: Priming and Script Activation

Applied to the media, priming refers to the effects of the content of the media on people's later behavior and judgments. When primed, the probability of imitation is increased. From the theory of differential association, criminal definitions also come into play at this step. Criminal definitions refer to pro- and anticrime beliefs and whether media provided crime exemplars are discounted or not (Petty et al., 2002). In the elaboration likelihood model of communication, definitions are conceived as "favorable and unfavorable thoughts" toward information that lead to favorable and unfavorable definitions. The media is today recognized as playing a significant role in what types of definitions individuals are exposed to and eventually adopt. A basic copycat crime model dynamic is that traversing the paths results in more criminal definitions an individual holds, which increases the likelihood that a copycat crime will be primed. Priming also provides a psychological concept to explain inexact imitation in which the imitated behavior is related to but not identical to the observed behavior. Priming can be understood within this essay as providing a set of ideas and beliefs that construct a particular social reality—the perception that the nature of the world is such that a particular type of crime is appropriate, justified, and likely to be successful. Once primed, an individual is more likely to copy a media-modeled crime, particularly if being primed cues up preestablished criminal scripts.

Anderson and his colleagues (2007) describe this cognitive process as the activation of related memory nodes (single constructs such as "gun" or "crime") or of complex knowledge structures (constellations of related constructs or full behavior scripts).[6] Activation is not necessarily conscious, and partial activation can influence other cognitive and emotional processes, decisions, and behavior. In this way, priming of criminogenic ideas is equivalent to partial activation of previously held knowledge nodes (Anderson, Gentile, & Buckley, 2007). When total activation occurs, the copycat-related knowledge structure is activated and a copycat crime script is accessible. Considering copycat crime as a unique subset of Anderson and colleagues' general aggression model (aggression is not necessary for a copycat crime), a generator crime can be conceived as eventually activating associated scripts that include related "commit the generator crime" knowledge structures. Within Buckley and Anderson's (2006) more generic general learning model (GLM), each exposure to a media generator crime would be considered another learning trial. Each generator crime exposure primes criminogenic knowledge structures and constitutes additional learning trials that instruct at-risk copycat consumers. When a generator crime results in a copycat crime being primed or a copycat script being activated, the at-risk copycat offender must make an appraisal decision.

Step 10: Appraisal and Adoption Decision

At this point in the model, a potential at-risk copycat offender must decide whether to implement his or her copycat script. For copycat crime implementation, the most important attitude changes are related to efficacy about whether the modeled crime is doable and a good idea. When the behavior requires new skills and self-perceptions of confidence do not exist (self-efficacy in Bandura's terminology) new pro-crime attitudes will not alone lead to copycat behavior (Petty et al., 2002). Therefore, efficacy, or the belief that you can successfully complete a task, has special relevance for copycat crime (Bandura, 1995). High self-efficacy belief regarding crime leads to an increased motivation to copy by raising an individual's criminal goals, the effort they are willing to expend, their perseverance in the face of difficulties, and their resilience to failures regarding copying a crime. On the other hand, low self-efficacy regarding difficult law-abiding tasks, such as the ability to gain or hold a job, should also translate into more simple copycat crimes by individuals who shy away from difficult tasks. Conversely, high self-efficacy beliefs should translate into more difficult copycat crimes by individuals who see such crime as challenges rather than as threats (Bandura & Walters, 1963).

Criminal history thus plays a role in varied ways in copycat crime. A criminal history should usually come into play via the creation of a Skinnerian pattern of rewards and punishments for copying the behavior of others, criminal and otherwise; and past criminal experience should also increase perceptions of self-efficacy and subsequent beliefs in the likely success of copying crime. Therefore, a prior criminal history is hypothesized as related to high self-efficacy regarding crime and increased copycat crime likelihood (Bandura, 1995). Prior knowledge of content (a criminal history), interest in the content (a decision to commit a crime already in place) and the usefulness of information (the amount of criminogenic content) all increase the likelihood of a decision to implement a copycat crime (Fisch, 2002); and established offenders who see media-modeled crimes as good means of obtaining material goods or social prestige will copy if given the opportunity (Rogers, 2003). The uses-and-gratifications perspective from communication theory further predicts that offenders dedicated to committing a crime will be more at risk for copycat effects as criminogenic media gratifies and fills a need for them (Rubin, 2002). In addition, individuals who enjoy seeing laws broken or seeing those in authority defied should experience increased enjoyment from criminogenic media and increased likelihood to copy that media (Bryant & Miron, 2002).

In gist, some individuals reach this step with personal and criminal histories that tilt them toward attempting a copycat crime. Others are predisposed to reject the idea. If the appraisal is negative and the decision is not to adopt the copycat crime script, the individual exits the model until exposure to another generator crime (Rogers, 2003). If the decision is to implement, a copycat crime attempt results.

Step 11: Copycat Crime Attempt

The attempt step determines how much copycat crime a society generates. For an actual copycat crime attempt to occur, the at-risk copycat crime offender must, first, have the ability to physically copy the modeled crime and, second, be in a setting with opportunities to implement the specific crime. As the linchpin between the desire to copy a crime and the consequences to copying individuals, performance of the actual copycat crime is the key step in the model and helps determine the spread and persistence of copycat behavior in societies. If the at-risk offender does not attempt a crime, the social effects are limited to individual psychological ones and are socially invisible. Besides the number of opportunities a society offers to copy different types of crime, the copycat attempt rate can be influenced by faulty reasoning on the part of the copiers. Humans have a self-reflective capability to observe and correct errors; however, cognitive errors can produce faulty processing and result in copying attempts that are not in an individual's best interests (Bandura, 2001). Bandura (2001) lists three common errors: faulty success estimation by comparison with distorted media versions of social reality (women in pornography appear to enjoy sexual aggression, so a copycat rape would be accepted); group-based verifications that foster bizarre views of reality when the reference group is encapsulated from outside social ties and influences (fringe web-based communities that encourage violent acts); and faulty deductive reasoning based on erroneous information (criminals frequently get away with crime in the movies). Media content can foster all three errors.

Step 12: Consequences to Individual Copiers

The penultimate step in the model addresses what happens to a copier in the real-world following a copycat crime attempt—rewards or punishments? In that social learning theory assigns greater weight to similarity of probable consequences than to similarity of personal attributes in predicting copying, outcomes outweigh copier similarity in predicting individual future copycat behavior (Bandura, 1973). This is important because it suggests that individual copycat offender characteristics will be less important than setting and environmental factors in determining whether copycat crimes occur or not. A distinct copycat offender personality may not exist or, if it does, may not be very important for how much copycat crime a society experiences. Alternatively, the proportion of at-risk copycat offenders in a population may be similar across cultures, but copycat rates will vary culturally based on varied opportunities to implement copycat scripts and variations in the social consequences of prior copycat crime attempts.

An important consideration related to consequences is the deterrent effect of media-portrayed punishment. The portrayal of final punishment for crime—the final-scene capture or the killing of the villain, for example—has long been assumed to mitigate the criminogenic effects of prior successful crime portraits (Hays, 1932). There is reason to believe that the assumption of corrective punishment is not an effective counterbalance, however. Punishment in the context of copycat crime needs to be considered in two ways: first, as the punishment levied on the media criminal model (the punishment observed in the media content); and second, as the estimation of the likelihood of punishment that a potential copycat copier extracts (the actual punishment the copier experiences).

The crucial issue regarding the first role involves the ability of the portrayal of punishment to deter copying. Working against deterrence, punishment portrayed in some ways is an ineffective deterrent. For example, an incentive to imitate that is independent of the exposure to modeled punishment will increase imitation (Bandura, 1973). For example, a media message common to some music-video plotlines portray the police negatively and as social oppressors. Thus, consumers may side with and emulate punished criminal models when they are portrayed heroically (Brown & Cody, 1991; Vidmar & Rokeach, 1974). This leads to the second consideration of content-portrayed punishment: its effect on the expectation of punishment from copying the modeled crime. As it is the expectation of results that most strongly determine copying, the effect of the observation of media-portrayed punishment on the expectation of real-world punishment is crucial for copycat crime. A factor that interacts with the media portrayal of punishment and consumer expectation of punishment is consumer mood. Good mood while viewing raises the belief that positive consequences of action are more likely; bad mood increases belief in negative consequences (Petty et al., 2002). Therefore, a positive mood in the media consumer would reduce the deterrent effect of observing model punishment. Action media, which generally induces a positive mood in male viewers, should by extension reduce the deterrent effect of observed punishment.

Regarding actual experienced punishment, if individuals have learned that imitation is rewarding, the degree to which observers have been previously rewarded or punished for compliant versus criminal behavior influences the extent to which criminogenic imitation will occur (Bandura & Walters, 1963). As copycat crime can be both rewarding (fame, glory, publicity) or punishing (failure, capture, prison, death) the relative perception of the ratio of rewards and punishments simultaneously influences an individual's copycat crime propensity. Applying Skinnerian conditioning tenets, inconsistent patterns of punishment and rewards or random reward patterns for copying crimes generate copycat crime behavior that will be the hardest to eliminate. As Bandura (1973) states: "children who learned that the benefits of crime are obtained at the risk of some negative outcomes are not easily discouraged by nonreward or censure" (p. 224). Sporadic punishment or frequent neutral results will not counteract the copy-sustaining effects of periodic random rewards.

In sum, punishments portrayed in media content will not necessarily dissuade copying. Depicted punishments can be seen as informative regarding ways of avoiding similar mistakes, and potential copycats may subsequently act on the belief that with slight modification of tactics, they can gain the benefits of crime without suffering the costs. Affixing a punishment to the end of a succession of successful crimes or to near-successful ones should not be expected to remove criminogenic learning effects (Bandura, 1973). Due to a common error in overestimating their odds of success, habitual offenders will likely alter their crime techniques based on the criminogenic content, confident that they have reduced their risk of failure (Bandura, 1973, citing Claster, 1967). A reasonable hypothesis is that criminogenic content that shows a string of successful crimes or crimes that failed due to perceived correctable mistakes made by a media-portrayed criminal model means that even seeing ultimate punishment will not substantially counteract media criminogenic copycat effects.

Step 13: Social Effects and Feedback

The final step in the model looks at the effects of the copied behavior on the environment of the copiers. Does the performance of copycat crimes work to counteract, attenuate, or augment future subsequent copying? If copycat offenders are caught and punished, if social approbation follows, if media criminogenic content is reduced, and if society changes as a result of a wave of copycat crime, a supportive social environment for copycat crime would be altered to be less supportive. If opposite results follow, a more supportive social environment for copycat crime would occur, and one would expect a downstream increase in the society's copycat crime rate. Important social effects occur at the broader cultural level where media content is determined and at the family and neighborhood levels.

Copycat cultures involve the large-scale environments and cultural characteristics that copycat offenders occupy. Prior research suggests that characteristics in these realms are more important in the generation of copycat crime than individual and media content characteristics and may be more useful for identifying at-risk media consumers. Paraphrasing Bandura (1973): "social conditions that increase the permissibility and functional value of [crime] easily override the effects of personal dispositions. For this reason, it is primarily types of social inducements rather than types of people that should be examined in predicting who will put into practice what has been learned from [the media]" (p. 269). In sum, social learning theory assigns greater weight to similarity of probable consequences than to similarity of personal attributes in predicting modeling. People in similar settings will behave similarly more than similar people in different settings will. This acknowledgment does not, however, relieve the media of a significant causative role. While media are not seen as the dominant cause of copycat crime, they supply criminal role models and crime portraits that create a supportive social atmosphere in which the predisposed few emulate the crimes they see, hear, and read about (Bandura, 1973). In gist, the more forcefully crime is portrayed as rewarding, justified, or unchallenged, the more copycat crime will be generated, and the more a pervasive crime culture and a history of crime media will exacerbate copycat effects (Akers, 1998).

It is at the family and neighborhood environment levels that the final determinants of copycat crime operate. In these realms, the potential copycat offenders estimate the likelihood of reward versus punishment and the expected social reaction to a copycat offense. Magnifying this environmental mix, the presence of criminogenic parents should produce more copycat offspring (Mazur, 2006; Bandura & Walters, 1963). Criminogenic parents can either be offenders themselves or verbally support criminogenic values. Even if they preach law abiding and punish law breaking, if they are offenders, they provide strong criminogenic models that supplement the media-provided ones. The media's criminogenic effects will be further enhanced by racial strife, income disparities, and detrimental social conditions and contribute to an increased number of people at risk for criminogenic media influences (Fisher, 1980). A criminogenic media also supports criminogenic cultures, neighborhood structures, and family environments, which in turn increase the capability of the media to teach crime (Akers, 1998). In gist, the hypothesized relationship is that social disorganization plus criminogenic media content equals increased copycat crime rates (Akers, 1998).

Who Follows the Paths?

Concerning the question of who follows the paths, a constellation of five umbrella concepts have emerged as hypothesized flags for at-risk copycat individuals. Immersion in crime-related content appears significant, as well as a set of psychological traits. In addition, a personal belief in criminal efficacy and an individual's personal history of inconsistent punishment for crime are hypothesized as important. Lastly, a number of family, community, and cultural environment factors have been linked to copycat crime behaviors.

Thus, media use that reflects a concentration on a single media source to the exclusion of other media and interpersonal contacts has been forwarded as a copycat crime flag (Akers, 1998; Rogers, 2003). In particular, offenders who immerse themselves in a criminogenic niche media (for example, watching criminogenic excerpts from a single video repeatedly) and are weakly networked into law-abiding groups and strongly networked into deviant groups are seen to be at greater risk (Meloy & Mohandie, 2001; Rogers, 2003). The likelihood of media immersion increases as peers and family decrease in importance (Akers, 1998), and by extension, individuals who are deeply immersed in popular culture and media dependent should also show an increased copycat propensity (Rogers, 2003). Weak social bonding also plays a role, and individuals with less to lose from failed criminality are speculated to more often choose copycat crime as these individuals will rely more on media for positive social reinforcement (Akers, 1998). Immersion is also associated with identification with media offenders. Because media-immersed consumers are not necessarily heavy consumers in terms of total hours but appear to form para-social relationships with media personalities, media-immersed individuals who imagine themselves as the media criminals should be more likely to copy their offenses (Mazur, 2006, p. 297, citing Dowrick & Raeburn, 1995). Finally, even without media immersion, social isolation increases copycat crime risk due to the media increasing in importance as information sources (Akers, 1998).

Regarding other individual traits, the decision to copy a crime is weighed not only against the expected outcome of the crime, but also against expected outcomes of alternate law-abiding behaviors. So copycat crime should be more attractive to those who do not see law-abiding behavior as likely to be rewarded (Akers, 1998; Bandura, 1973; Rogers, 2003). In addition, persons who see media personalities as opinion leaders and as friends are postulated as more likely copycat crime candidates (Mundorf & Laird, 2002; Rogers, 2003). Other copycat flags are found in individual media preferences and usage motives. Individuals who prefer crime content and who consume high amounts of media content combined with viewing motives of information seeking or learning are hypothesized as more at risk to be copycats (Akers, 1998; Haridakis, 2002). Additional personality traits that have been flagged include low self-control (Akers, 1998), high criminal innovativeness (Rogers, 2003), and behavior disinhibition tendencies (Haridakis, 2002). Regarding consumer intelligence, the hypotheses regarding copycat crime are mixed, and the role of intelligence levels in copycat crime is likely interactive with other factors.[7]

Regarding the type of copycat crime that generates much public interest and concern, rare bizarre violence by individuals without known violent histories, four characteristics plus media immersion have been noted as predictive. Serious violent copycat criminals are felt to be distinguishable from non-copycat criminals by the presence of fixated immersion in violent media (Meloy & Mohandie, 2001; Myers, Eggleston, & Smoak,

2003). Repetitive viewing, in which the copier watches media content multiple times prior to offending and displays self-editing of content by repetitively watching only the copied sequences (sometimes using freeze-framing to slow down the violent content), delineate the extreme violent media–copycat crime relationship. Additionally, characteristics of delusion, with a history of high interest in guns and law enforcement encounters, and the traits of idleness, isolation, and deterioration in socioeconomic functions accompanied by perceptions of persecution and resentment, have been forwarded as predictors of a propensity to copy violent models (Bandura, 1973).

In addition, a perception of one's criminal efficacy is a key to copycat crime risk, and a past criminal history is thought to increase an individual's perception of their criminal efficacy. When coupled with an inconsistent history of sporadic punishment for criminality and the presence of family and neighborhood crime models, copycat crime risk is further increased. Lastly, when media-immersed established offenders live in a culture that encourages copycat crime, a copycat effect is expected to be maximized. Defined as cultures with pervasive crime and crime media, social conditions that increase the permissibility of crime and increase the functional value of crime so that crime is often rewarded, justified, or unchallenged, the United States has many features of a copycat crime culture.

Conclusion

In total, the hypothesized dynamics of copycat crime are that copiers mix and match from multiple models of crime and, depending upon their criminal reward history, their culture, and their media interaction, follow or exit copycat crime paths. It is expected that media influence decreases after the first copycat crime by an individual offender as their real-world environment clicks in to reward or punish copying (Akers, 1998). Unless media attention was the goal and result, what happens to the copycat offender in their world determines subsequent imitation. Whether copycat crime paths are followed by a particular individual depends on the interaction of the content of a particular media product (the characterizations of crime and punishment in the generator crime), the individual's predispositions toward crime (personal criminal history, family, and environmental factors), and the media's social context (preexisting cultural norms, crime opportunities, and pervasiveness and credibility of the media). A criminogenic copycat effect ultimately depends on the combined influences of social context, media content, and consumer characteristics. While a number of at-risk factors have been forwarded, neither their relative importance nor how predictive they are for copycat offending is known. Pending future research, at this point the assumption is that the more factors present, the more predisposed an individual is to embark on a copycat crime pathway.

Notes

1. Copycat crime has been described as a subtype of a broader class of technology-related crimes that emerged in the late twentieth century, including computer scams, cyberstalking, and hacking (Helfgott, 2008, p. 377).

2. Helfgott (2008, pp. 386–387) conceptually expands these three areas to five that interact to produce an individual-level copycat crime response. She includes individual criminogenic factors reacted to psychological development and social history; an individual's relationship to media regarding trust, identification, and level of interaction; factors such as the cultural value of fame, crime, violence, and legitimacy of media that affect the perceived importance of media to an individual; demographic factors including age, gender, and race; and content characteristics reflecting how crime and criminality are portrayed in the media.

3. Defined, *entertainment education* is the process of designing and implementing a media message to both entertain and educate in order to increase audience members' knowledge about an issue, create favorable attitudes, and change behavior. Entertainment education has been employed using soap operas, rock music, feature films, talk shows, cartoons, comics, and theater as formats (Singhal & Rogers, 1999).

4. Media narratives are the ubiquitous stories we consume every day in the news, books, films, plays, video games, and so forth (Brock, Strange & Green, 2002). By psychological mechanisms described as "pleasurable absorption," "transportation," and "immersion," narratives can evoke "participatory responses" and "parasocial interaction" with story characters in consumers in which reactions to content are made as if someone was really experiencing the portrayed events (Allbritton & Gerrig, 1991; Gerrig, 1993; Sood, Menard & Witte, 2004, p. 129).

5. Narrative persuasion via new media interactive technologies should be enhanced as they share a common goal of the transformation of experience via media use (Biocca, 2002, p. 98).

6. Knowledge structures are a key "general aggression model" concept, and in this social cognitive approach, personality is conceived as the sum of a person's knowledge structures. They influence perception at multiple levels from basic visual to complex behavioral sequences; guide interpretations and behavioral responses; and contain affective states, behavioral programs, and beliefs. Through high usage or practice, a particular script can become automated and active easily, quickly, and without awareness (Anderson, Gentile, & Buckley, 2007).

7. People of moderate intelligence should be easier to persuade than people of low or high intelligence, as this maximizes both reception to media-based messages and yielding to the content of those messages. High intelligence helps reception processes but leads to resistance to yielding. Low intelligence helps yielding processes but lowers information reception (Petty et al., 2002, p. 162).

References

Akers, R. L. (1998). *Social learning and social structure: A general theory of crime and deviance*. Boston, MA: Northeastern University Press.

Allbritton, D., & Gerrig, R. (1991). Participatory responses in prose understanding. *Journal of Memory and Language, 30*, 603–626.

Anderson, C., Gentile, D., & Buckley, K. (2007). *Violent video game effects on children and adolescents: Theory, research, and public policy*. New York: Oxford University Press.

Bandura, A. (1973). *Aggression: A social learning analysis*. Englewood Cliffs, NJ: Prentice-Hall.

Bandura, A. (1995). *Self-efficacy in changing societies*. Cambridge: Cambridge University Press.

Bandura, A. (2001). Social cognitive theory of mass communication. *Media Psychology, 3*(3), 265–299.

Bandura, A. (2004). Social cognitive theory for personal and social change by enabling media. In A. Singhal, M. Cody, E. Rogers, & M. Sabido (Eds.), *Entertainment-education and social change* (pp. 75–96). Mahwah, NJ: Lawrence Erlbaum Associates.

Bandura, A., & R. Walters. (1963). *Social learning and personality development*. New York: Holt, Rinehart, and Winston.

Biocca, F. (2002). The evolution of interactive media. In M. Green, J. Strange, & T. Brock (Eds.), *Narrative impact* (pp. 97–130). Mahwah, NJ: Lawrence Erlbaum Associates.

Brock, T., Strange, J., & Green, M. (2002). Power beyond reckoning: An introduction to narrative impact. In M. Green, J. Strange, & T. Brock (Eds.), *Narrative impact* (pp. 1–15). Mahwah, NJ: Lawrence Erlbaum Associates.

Brown, W., & Cody, M. (1991). Effects of a prosocial television soap opera in promoting women's status. *Human Communication Research, 18*, 114–142.

Bryant, J., & Miron, D. (2002). Entertainment as media effect. In J. Bryant & D. Zillmann (Eds.), *Media effects: Advance in theory and research* (pp. 549–582). Mahwah, NJ: Lawrence Erlbaum Associates.

Buckley, K., & Anderson, C. (2006). A theoretical model of the effects and consequences of playing video games. In P. Vorderer & J. Bryant (Eds.), *Playing video games—motives, responses, and consequences* (pp. 363–378). Mahwah, NJ: Lawrence Erlbaum Associates.

Claster, D. S. 1967. Comparison of risk perception between delinquents and nondelinquents. *Journal of Criminal Law, Criminology and Police Science, 58*, 80–86.

Dowrick, J., & Raeburn, J. (1995). Self-modeling: Rapid skill training for children with physical disabilities. *Journal of Developmental and Physical Disabilities, 7*, 25–37.

Fisch, S. (2002). Vast wasteland or vast opportunity? Effects of educational television on children's academic knowledge, skills, and attitudes. In J. Bryant & D. Zillmann (Eds.), *Media effects: Advance in theory and research* (pp. 397–426). Mahwah, NJ: Lawrence Erlbaum Associates.

Fisher, C. (1980). The spread of violent crime from city to countryside, 1955 to 1975. *Rural Sociology, 45*(3), 416–434.

Gerrig, R. (1993). *Experiencing narrative worlds*. New Haven, CT: Yale University Press.

Green, M., & Brock, T. (2000). The role of transportation in the persuasiveness of public narratives. *Journal of Personality and Social Psychology, 79*, 701–721.

Green, M., Garst, J., Brock, T., & Chung, S. (2006). Fact versus fiction labeling: Persuasion parity despite heightened scrutiny of fact. *Media Psychology, 8*, 267–285.

Haridakis, P. (2002). Viewer characteristics, exposure to television violence, and aggression. *Media Psychology, 4*(4), 323–352.

Hays, W. H. (1932). President's report to the Motion Picture Producers and Distributors' Association. Washington, DC: U.S. Government Printing Office.

Helfgott, J. (2008). *Criminal behavior: Theories, typologies, and criminal justice*. Thousand Oaks, CA: Sage.

Mazur, J. M. (2006). *Learning and behavior*. Upper Saddle River, NJ: Pearson/ Prentice Hall.

Meloy, J. R., & Mohandie, K. (2001). Investigating the role of screen violence in specific homicide cases. *Journal of Forensic Science, 46*(5), 1113–1118.

Miller, D. L. (2000). *Introduction to collective behavior and collective action* (2nd ed.). Prospect Heights, IL: Waveland Press.

Mundorf, N., & Laird, K. (2002). Social and psychological effects of information technologies and other interactive media. In J. Bryant & D. Zillmann (Eds.), *Media effects: Advance in theory and research* (pp. 583–602). Mahwah, NJ: Lawrence Erlbaum Associates.

Myers, W., Eggleston, C., & Smoak, P. (2003). A media violence–inspired juvenile sexual homicide offender 13 years later. *Journal of Forensic Science, 48*(6), 1–6.

Petty, R., Priester, J., & Brinol, P. (2002). Mass media attitude change: Implications of the elaboration likelihood model of persuasion. In J. Bryant & D. Zillmann (Eds.), *Media effects: Advance in theory and research* (pp. 155–198). Mahwah, NJ: Lawrence Erlbaum Associates.

Polichak, J., & Gerrig, R. 2002. "Get up and win!" Participatory responses to Narrative. In M. Green, J. Strange, & T. Brock (Eds.), *Narrative impact* (pp. 71–95). Mahwah, NJ: Lawrence Erlbaum Associates.

Rogers, E. (2003). *Diffusion of innovations*. New York: Free Press.

Rubin, A. (2002). The uses-and-gratifications perspective of media effects. In J. Bryant & D. Zillmann (Eds.), *Media effects: Advance in theory and research* (pp. 525–548). Mahwah, NJ: Lawrence Erlbaum Associates.

Shrum, L. J. (2002). Media consumption and perceptions of social reality: Effects and underlying processes. In J. Bryant & D. Zillmann (Eds.), *Media effects: Advance in theory and research* (pp. 69–95). Mahwah, NJ: Lawrence Erlbaum Associates.

Singhal, A., & Rogers, E. (1999). *Entertainment-education: A communication strategy for social change*. Mahwah, NJ: Lawrence Erlbaum Associates.

Slater, M., & Rouner, D. (2002). Entertainment education and the persuasive impact of narratives. In M. Green, J. Strange, & T. Brock (Eds.), *Narrative impact* (pp. 157–181). Mahwah, NJ: Lawrence Erlbaum Associates.

Sood, S., Menard, T., & Witte, K. (2004). The theory behind entertainment-education. In A. Singhal, M. Cody, E. Rogers, & M. Sabido (Eds.), *Entertainment-education and social change* (pp. 117–149). Mahwah, NJ: Lawrence Erlbaum Associates.

Strange, J. (2002). How fictional tales wag real-world beliefs. In. M. Green, J. Strange, & T. Brock (Eds.), *Narrative impact* (pp. 263–286). Mahwah, NJ: Lawrence Erlbaum Associates.

Surette, R. (2012). *The prevalence of copycat crime: A research note*. Unpublished manuscript. Orlando, FL: University of Central Florida.

Sutherland, E. (1947). *Principles of criminology* (4th ed.). New York: Harper & Row.

Vidmar, N., & Rokeach, M. (1974). Archie Bunker's bigotry: A study in selective perception and exposure. *Journal of Communication, 24*(1), 36–47.

Wilson, B., Colvin, C., & Smith, S. (2002, March). Engaging in violence on American television: A comparison of child, teen, and adult perpetrators. *Journal of Communication*, 36–60.

SECTION III

Psychopathy

CHAPTER ELEVEN

Conceptualizing Psychopathy: Criminal and Noncriminal Variants

Christopher J. Patrick

The concept of psychopathy is essential to an understanding of criminal behavior because psychopathic individuals account for a disproportionate amount of crime in society (Hare, 2003; Skeem, Polaschek, Patrick, & Lilienfeld, 2011) and because psychopathy provides such a compelling illustration of the importance of individual difference factors ("criminogenic traits"; Herrnstein, 1983) in the occurrence of crime. At the same time, confusion and debate persist regarding the meaning and appropriate use of the term "psychopathic" (Skeem et al., 2011), and there has been a resurgence of interest in recent years in the idea that psychopathy can occur in noncriminal, or even "successful" (Hall & Benning, 2006), forms. The goal of the current chapter is to review differing ways in which psychopathy has been conceptualized and measured in criminal and noncriminal samples, to identify points of disagreement that have persisted over the years, and to suggest how these points of disagreement might be addressed and perhaps resolved through an integrative model of psychopathy that has recently been proposed.

The chapter begins with an overview of historic conceptions of psychopathy. The next section covers contemporary approaches to conceptualization and assessment of psychopathy, and the related diagnostic concept of antisocial personality disorder, in criminal offenders. This is followed by a section on conceptualization and assessment of psychopathy in noncriminal samples. The fourth section of the chapter identifies persisting points of disagreement regarding how psychopathy should be defined and measured. The fifth section provides a summary of a new theoretic perspective on psychopathy, the Triarchic Model (Patrick, Fowles, & Krueger, 2009), that was formulated to integrate differing historic and contemporary conceptions. The final section discusses how persisting points of contention in the field might be reconciled in terms of the Triarchic Model.

Historic Conceptions of Psychopathy

Early 1800s to Early 1900s

French physician Philippe Pinel (1806/1962) is generally considered to have provided the first published account of the condition that came to be known as psychopathy. Pinel used the term *manie sans delire* ("insanity without delirium") to describe cases of individuals who engaged repeatedly in impulsively violent acts while otherwise appearing sound in mind. Other early accounts of psychopathy (e.g., Partridge, 1928a, 1928b; Prichard, 1835) likewise emphasized reckless, explosive behavioral acts, frequently accompanied by drug or alcohol problems and sometimes by suicidal acts. As discussed further below, these tendencies reflect the disinhibitory (Gorenstein & Newman, 1980) or externalizing (Krueger et al., 2002; Patrick, Hicks, Krueger, & Lang, 2005) component of psychopathy included in modern conceptions of the disorder. In contrast, a different set of characteristics emphasized by early writers (highlighted later by Cleckley, 1941/1976; see next section) consisted of confidence, social assertiveness, persuasiveness and charm, attention seeking, and shallow emotions (see, e.g., Kraepelin's [1904] "swindler" psychopathic subtype, and Schneider's [1950] "self-seeking" subtype). Separate from this, a third emphasis in early historic accounts of psychopathy consisted of tendencies involving emotional coldness, brutality, and predatory exploitation of others (cf. Schneider's [1950] "active affectionless" subtype; see also: Pinel, 1806/1962; Rush, 1812).

The first use of the term "psychopathic" was by German psychiatrist J. L. Koch (1891), who applied the label to a broad array of chronic disorders—including neurotic conditions and some forms of mental retardation along with "character disorders" of differing types—that he considered to arise from organic (physical, brain-based) causes. Subsequently, Kraepelin (1904, 1915) used the term more narrowly, in reference to non-neurotic "pathological personality" conditions (or character disorders). An alternative term, "sociopathic," was introduced by Birnbaum (1909) to encourage a shift from the notion of constitutional etiology toward a more social-environmental perspective on causality.

The term sociopathic was popularized in the United States by psychiatrist Adolf Meyer, and the first edition of the *Diagnostic and Statistical Manual of Mental Disorders* (DSM-I; American Psychiatric Association [APA], 1952) included a category of "sociopathic personality disturbance" encompassing a range of problems including delinquent behavior, addictive disorders, and sexual deviations. One disorder specified in this category was "sociopathic personality disturbance: antisocial reaction," involving prominent aggressive tendencies and chronic law breaking.

Cleckley, Lykken, and DSM-II: Psychopathy as Masked Psychological Disturbance

Modern conceptions of psychopathy are traceable to American psychiatrist Hervey Cleckley's classic text, *The Mask of Sanity* (1941/1976). Drawing on his experiences with psychopathic patients at Georgia's University Hospital in Augusta, Cleckley characterized psychopathy as a deep-rooted emotional pathology masked by an outward appearance of good mental health. In contrast with other psychiatric inpatients who present as overtly distressed or disturbed, psychopaths appear on first impression to be sociable, self-assured, and psychologically well adjusted; however, their pathology is clearly revealed by their actions and attitudes across time. To establish a formal procedure for diagnosis, Cleckley specified 16 specific criteria for the disorder, including: (1) indicators of behavioral deviancy, such as irresponsibility, recklessness, absence of planning, failure to learn by experience, sexual promiscuity, and impulsive antisocial behavior; (2) deficits in emotional reactivity and social relations, including shallow affect, absence of remorse or shame, incapacity for love, disloyalty, deceitfulness, and deficient insight; and (3) indicators of psychological stability and social efficacy (charm and good intelligence, lack of psychotic symptoms, absence of anxiety or neurotic problems, immunity to suicide). Cleckley did not describe psychopathic patients as characteristically violent, or deliberately cruel. Instead, he considered the harm they caused others to be a by-product of their shallow, irresponsible natures.

Cleckley's conception served as the foundation for the first documented experimental investigation of psychopathy, by David Lykken (1957). In this pathbreaking study, Lykken identified subgroups of primary ("Cleckley") and secondary ("neurotic") psychopaths and evaluated them in various ways (i.e., on questionnaire measures of neuroticism and fear, behavioral responding in a passive avoidance learning task, and physiological reactivity in an aversive conditioning procedure) in relation to one another and to healthy controls. This work demonstrated differences in fear responding in primary psychopathic participants compared to the other groups across differing domains of measurement and formed the basis for Lykken's low fear hypothesis of primary psychopathy (Lykken, 1978, 1995; see also Patrick, 1994, 2007; Fowles & Dindo, 2006, 2009). This study served as a point of reference for Robert Hare's influential research in the 1960s and 1970s on autonomic responding in psychopathic criminals defined according to Cleckley's criteria (cf. Hare, 1978), as well as inspiring key follow-up studies by others (e.g., Newman, Widom, & Nathan, 1985; Schmauk, 1970; Waid, 1976).

Cleckley's conception of psychopathy also served as a key referent for the diagnosis in the second edition of the DSM (DSM-II; APA, 1968). While labeled "antisocial personality" as opposed to psychopathy, the diagnostic criteria for the disorder in DSM-II focused on tendencies toward irresponsibility, selfishness, disloyalty, and absence of remorse or shame as emphasized by Cleckley. However, a key shortcoming of the DSM-II (carried over from DSM-I) was that diagnoses were made on the basis of perceived resemblance to narrative prototypes, rather than on the basis of specific, behaviorally based criteria. Because of this, the interrater reliability of diagnoses based on the DSM-II was generally poor.

Contemporary Conceptions: I. Criminal Psychopathy

McCord and McCord, Robins, & DSM-III/IV: Psychopathy as Severe, Persistent Criminal Deviance

In contrast with Cleckley's characterization, other influential writers of his time concerned with psychopathy in criminal as opposed to psychiatric samples emphasized callousness, exploitativeness, and viciousness in their accounts of the disorder. For example, McCord and McCord (1964) highlighted symptoms of emotional coldness, social detachment, and dangerousness, along with behavioral disinhibition. Like Cleckley, McCord and McCord described psychopaths as deficient in anxiety and emotional responsiveness, but they viewed these impairments as arising from severe social disconnectedness ("lovelessness" and "guiltlessness") rather than from a core underlying deficit in affective capacity. Also in contrast with Cleckley, these authors considered aggressive tendencies to be more central to psychopathy. Specifically, they described psychopathic individuals as reacting characteristically to provocative or threatening situations with rage rather than fear, due to impaired social concern and an affiliated weakness in inhibitions against aggression.

In a similar vein, Robins (1966, 1978) emphasized early and persistent aggressive antisocial behavior in her empirically based description of maladjusted youth who develop into adult "sociopaths." The work of Robins provided for identification of objective behavioral referents that could improve diagnostic reliability, and served as the foundation for the diagnosis of antisocial personality disorder (ASPD) represented in the third and fourth editions of the DSM (DSM-III, DSM-IV; APA, 1980, 2000). The DSM-III criteria for ASPD included aggression, destructiveness, and other forms of delinquency during childhood, along with tendencies toward reckless irresponsibility, impulsivity, deception, aggressiveness, and illegal conduct in adulthood. Although highly reliable, the DSM-III diagnosis of ASPD drew criticism from psychopathy experts (e.g., Frances, 1980; Hare, 1983) because it omitted central features such as superficial charm, deficient anxiety, lack of remorse or empathy, and general poverty of affect emphasized by Cleckley. Some effort was made to address this in the revised third edition of the DSM (DSM-IIIR; APA, 1987) by adding a "lacks remorse" item to the adult criteria for the disorder, but this change was generally viewed as insufficient. Nonetheless, despite continued criticisms of the DSM-IIIR operationalization, and field trials (Widiger et al., 1996) conducted specifically to evaluate an alternative consisting of a streamlined version of Hare's (1991) diagnostic inventory for psychopathy (see the next section), the criteria for ASPD in the current fourth edition of the DSM (DSM-IV; APA, 2000) remain largely the same as those in DSM-IIIR.

Notably, the proposed system for characterization of personality pathology in the upcoming fifth edition of the DSM (DSM-5; APA, 2012) includes provisions to address, at least in part, this perceived shortcoming. Specifically, a new conception of ASPD has been proposed that encompasses trait constructs from two distinct domains, labeled "antagonism" and "disinhibition." Paralleling this, a specifier has been proposed for the diagnosis of child conduct disorder in the DSM-5, in order to distinguish between psychopathic ("callous-unemotional") and non-psychopathic (not "callous-unemotional") variants of conduct disorder. Although it remains unclear at the present time whether these proposed changes will in fact be adopted for the DSM-5, they do provide intriguing alternatives to existing versions of these diagnoses represented in DSM-IV.

Psychopathy in Criminal Offenders and Conduct Disorder Youth: The Psychopathy Checklist–Revised and Its Descendants

To address criticisms of the global rating approach to diagnosis (cf. Lykken, 1957) used in his research up through the late 1970s, Hare (1980) developed a criterion-based interview protocol, the Psychopathy Checklist–Revised (PCL-R), for assessing psychopathy in criminal offender samples. The PCL-R's 20 items refer extensively to criminal acts/attitudes and capture the maladaptive (affective-interpersonal, behavioral deviancy) features identified by Cleckley, but provide limited coverage of the positive adjustment features. In particular, absence of nervousness and neurotic (anxious, depressive) symptomatology are not part of the PCL-R definition. High overall scores on the PCL-R show positive associations with measures of impulsivity and aggression, Machiavellianism, and persistent violent offending, and negative relations with measures of empathy and affiliation. This pattern of external correlates is more in line with the cruel-disinhibited conception of criminal psychopathy advanced by Cleckley's contemporaries than with Cleckley's own portrayal of psychopathy as a masked disturbance blending behavioral dyscontrol with emotional stability and social efficacy.

Despite being developed to measure psychopathy as a unitary disorder, the PCL-R has been shown to contain distinguishable item subsets, or factors (Harpur, Hare, & Hakstian 1989; Hare et al., 1990). Factor 1 of the PCL-R is an affective-interpersonal factor (divisible into affective and interpersonal facets; cf. Cooke & Michie, 2001; Hare, 2003), and Factor 2 is an antisocial deviance factor (divisible into impulsive-irresponsible and antisocial behavior facets; cf. Hare, 2003). As a function of the unitary-disorder assumption that guided its development, the two factors of the PCL-R, and their lower-order facets, are moderately intercorrelated. Factor 1 is associated with pathological tendencies including low empathy, high narcissism, and perpetration of instrumental aggression (Hare, 2003). After controlling for its overlap with Factor 2, PCL-R Factor 1 also shows positive and negative relations, respectively, with measures of social dominance (e.g., Verona, Patrick, & Joiner, 2001) and indices of negative affectivity (i.e., scale measures of fear, distress, depression; Hicks & Patrick, 2006). In contrast, Factor 2 is associated more exclusively with maladaptive tendencies, including impulsivity, general sensation seeking, early and persistent antisocial deviance, aggressiveness (reactive aggression, in particular), and alcohol and drug problems.

A number of different inventories are available for assessing psychopathy in child and adolescent participants. The major ones currently in use consist of youth-adapted versions (or "downward extensions"; Salekin, 2006) of Hare's PCL-R. These include the youth version of the PCL-R (PCL:YV; Forth, Kosson, & Hare, 2003), the Antisocial Process Screening Device (APSD; Frick & Hare, 2001), and the Child Psychopathy Scale (CPS; Lynam, 1997; Lynam et al., 2005). Like the PCL-R, these instruments index an antisocial-aggressive variant of psychopathy more akin to McCord and McCord's characterization than Cleckley's. For example, the APSD, designed for use with clinic-referred children (ages 6–13) exhibiting behavioral problems, comprises 20 items rated either by parents or teachers. The items of the APSD capture two distinguishable factors. The first is a Callous-Unemotional (CU) factor that reflects callousness toward others and emotional insensitivity, and the second is an Impulsive/Conduct Problems (I/CP) factor that reflects impulsive tendencies, reckless/delinquent behavior, and inflated self-importance. Some research (e.g., Frick, Boden, & Barry, 2000) has suggested separable impulsive and narcissistic components to the I/CP factor. High I/CP children who score low on the CU factor show reduced intellectual ability, elevated anxiety and negative emotional reactivity, and proneness to angry-reactive (but not proactive-premeditated) aggression (Frick & Marsee, 2006). By contrast, children high in both CU and I/CP tendencies appear intellectually normal and low in anxiety and neuroticism. They are less reactive to distressing stimuli, learn less readily from punishment, and tend to be attracted to activities entailing novelty and risk. High CU+I/CP children also show high levels of both proactive and reactive aggression and exhibit more persistent violent behavior across time.

Contemporary Conceptions: II. Noncriminal Psychopathy

The most widely used approach to assessing psychopathy in noncriminal samples has consisted of self-report inventories. Traditional inventories of this kind (e.g., MMPI Psychopathic Deviate scale, CPI Socialization scale, MCMI Antisocial scale) have emphasized measurement of the antisocial deviancy (Factor 2) component of psychopathy. Newer measures including the Psychopathic Personality Inventory (PPI; Lilienfeld & Andrews, 1996; Lilienfeld & Widows, 2005), Levenson Self-Report Psychopathy Scale (LSRP; Levenson, Kiehl, & Fitzpatrick, 1995), Hare Self-Report Psychopathy Scale (HSRP; Paulhus, Hemphill, & Hare, in press; Williams, Paulhus, & Hare, 2007), Youth Psychopathic Traits Inventory (YPI; Andershed, Kerr, Stattin, & Levander, 2002), and Elemental Psychopathy Assessment (EPA; Lynam et al., 2011) include coverage of affective-interpersonal (Factor 1) features of psychopathy along with antisocial deviance features.

The LSRP, HSRP, and YPI were all patterned after the PCL-R, targeting factors/facets identified in differing structural models of the PCL-R. The LSRP was designed to index "primary" versus "secondary" variants of psychopathy reflected in the two factors of the original PCL/PCL-R factor model (Hare et al., 1990; Harpur et al., 1989), the YPI was designed to capture facets of psychopathy represented in Cooke and Michie's (2001) alternative three-factor model of the PCL-R, and the latest version of the HSRP was developed to index psychopathy facets associated with the four-factor PCL-R model (Hare, 2003). In contrast with this approach, Lynam and colleagues (2011), building on earlier work identifying traits of the Five-Factor Model of personality (FFM) that appear characteristic of psychopathy (e.g., Lynam & Widiger, 2007; Miller, Lynam, Widiger, & Leukefeld, 2001), developed the EPA to assess maladaptive variants of the set of FFM traits that have been shown to relate most to psychopathy. The EPA is quite new, and therefore criterion-related validity evidence for this measure has just begun to appear in the literature (Miller et al., 2011).

Also in contrast with self-report measures patterned after the PCL-R, the PPI was developed to comprehensively index trait dispositions embodied in Cleckley's account of psychopathy from a personality-based descriptive standpoint. Over the past decade, the PPI has become the most commonly used self-report measure of psychopathy in research studies. Its original version (cf. Lilienfeld & Andrews, 1996) consisted of 181 items; the published revised version (PPI-R; Lilienfeld & Widows, 2005) comprises 154 items. The items of the PPI are organized into eight unidimensional subscales, each tapping a relevant dispositional construct. Unlike the PCL-R, the PPI includes specific scales tapping lack of anxiousness (Stress Immunity) and deficient fear (Fearlessness), along with scales indexing dominance (Social Potency), impulsivity (Carefree Nonplanfulness), oppositionality (Rebellious Nonconformity), alienation (Blame Externalization), aggressive exploitativeness (Machiavellian Egocentricity), and lack of empathic concern (Coldheartedness). Exploratory factor analyses of the subscales of the PPI (e.g., Benning, Patrick, Hicks, Blonigen, & Krueger, 2003; Ross, Benning, Patrick, Thompson, & Thurston, 2009) have revealed two higher-order factors. The first (PPI-I) is defined by the Social Potency, Stress Immunity, and Fearlessness subscales, the second (PPI-II) by the Carefree Nonplanfulness, Rebellious Nonconformity, Blame Externalization, and Machiavellian Egocentrity scales; Benning, Patrick, Blonigen, Hicks, & Iacono (2005) labeled these two higher-order factors *Fearless Dominance* and *Impulsive Antisociality*, respectively. The eighth PPI subscale, Coldheartedness, does not load on either of these factors, indicating that it taps something distinct. Notably, scores on PPI-I are associated with emotional stability and social efficacy (e.g., higher well-being; higher interpersonal assertiveness; lower anxiousness and depression) as well as with elevated scores on measures of narcissism and thrill seeking, and reduced emotional empathy (Benning et al., 2005; Blonigen, Hicks, Krueger, Patrick, & Iacono, 2005; Douglas et al., 2008; Patrick, Edens, Poythress, Lilienfeld, & Benning, 2006; Ross et al., 2009). In contrast, scores on PPI-II are more uniformly indicative of deviancy—including impulsivity and aggressiveness, child and adult antisocial behavior, substance problems, high negative affect, and suicidal ideation.

In contrast with the interrelated factors of the PCL-R, the two-higher order factors of the PPI are uncorrelated (Benning et al., 2003). Despite their lack of overlap and the fact that PPI-I appears to index aspects of psychological adjustment along with affective-interpersonal deviancy, recent work by Ross et al. (2009) demonstrates that the two PPI factors correlate to a comparably robust degree with scores on a personality-based index reflecting the resemblance of individuals' Five-Factor Model (FFM) profiles to an expert-generated psychopathy prototype (Miller et al., 2001). This finding indicates that PPI-I and II capture differing elements of the prototypic psychopathy profile defined in FFM trait terms. Specifically, Ross et al. found that scores on PPI-I were associated with low neuroticism (N) and agreeableness (A) and high extraversion (E) and openness (O), whereas scores on PPI-II were associated with *high* N and low conscientiousness (C), along with low A. Notably, Ross et al. found that the coldheartedness subscale of the PPI (which, as mentioned, captures variance distinct from PPI-I and II) also evidenced a robust positive relationship with FFM prototype scores, with the basis of the relationship being low N, low E, low A, and low O.

The fact that uncorrelated but complementary dimensions emerged from an effort to index Cleckley's conception of psychopathy in trait-descriptive terms when structural unitarity of indicators was not imposed as a requirement (as with the PCL-R, and inventories patterned after it) has interesting implications for ideas about the essential nature of psychopathy. It suggests that psychopathy, at least as described by Cleckley, reflects a configuration or blending of disparate dispositions, possibly arising from separate underlying etiologies (cf. Fowles & Dindo, 2006, 2009; Patrick, 1997, 2007; Patrick & Bernat, 2009; Patrick et al., 2009)—as opposed to a unitary dispositional entity undergirded by a single, coherent etiology. At the same time, it remains possible that the callous-aggressive conceptualization of psychopathy emphasized by specialists in criminality and delinquency may reflect a more unitary entity. Nonetheless, even instruments such as the PCL-R and its derivatives that have sought to index criminal psychopathy as a unitary entity display evidence of multidimensionality—in the form of distinct, albeit correlated factors. These factors exhibit diverging relations with many different criterion variables across domains of self-report, behavioral response, and physiological reactivity—with evidence of suppressor effects emerging in relations with some criteria such as anxiety and negative affectivity (e.g., Frick, Lilienfeld, Ellis, Loney, & Silverthorn, 1999; Hicks & Patrick, 2006), mood and anxiety (internalizing) disorder symptoms (e.g., Blonigen et al., 2010; Hicks & Patrick, 2006), and suicidal behavior (Douglas et al., 2008; Verona, Hicks, & Patrick, 2005). The emergence of suppressor effects presents an especially strong challenge to unitary perspectives on psychopathy because effects of this sort normally signify the presence of highly distinctive underlying constructs embedded within a common measurement instrument (cf. Paulhus, Robins, Trzesniewski, & Tracy, 2004)

Ongoing Points of Contention in Conceptualizing Psychopathy

It should be clear from the foregoing historic overview that scholars in the field have grappled with issues of definition since psychopathy was first identified as a distinguishable psychiatric condition. In particular, questions regarding the scope and appropriate boundaries of the construct continue to spark debate and controversy. As a point of reference for sections that follow, we briefly consider here some of the most crucial unresolved issues of this kind that continue to be debated in the field.

1. Should the Diagnostic Criteria for Psychopathy Be Limited to Maladaptive Features, or Are Indicators of Positive Adjustment Also Relevant?

Cleckley (1941/1976) characterized psychopathy as an inherently paradoxical condition in which severe behavioral maladjustment and salient indications of psychological stability occur hand in hand: "The surface of the psychopath ... shows up as equal to or better than normal and gives no hint at all of a disorder within. Nothing about him suggests oddness, inadequacy, or moral frailty ... Yet he has a disorder that often manifests itself in conduct far more seriously abnormal than that of the schizophrenic" (p. 383). As noted earlier, his 16 diagnostic criteria for the disorder included specific indicators of positive adjustment. In contrast, the current diagnostic criteria for ASPD (APA, 2000) focus exclusively on behaviors indicative of deviancy beginning early in life (before the age of 15) and continuing into adulthood. Similarly, despite being developed with Cleckley's conceptualization as a referent, Hare's (1991, 2003) PCL-R is heavily oriented toward criminal deviancy and includes no items that are purely indicative of adjustment (Patrick, 2006).

The question of whether psychological/emotional stability is central to psychopathy is crucial from a case management standpoint because individuals exhibiting antisocial personality as defined by DSM criteria typically display other problems of clinical concern including heightened rates of anxiety- and mood-related (aka "neurotic" or internalizing) psychopathology (Achenbach & Edelbrock, 1978; Krueger, 1999b; Vaidyanathan, Patrick, & Iacono, 2011) along with increased suicidal behavior (Verona & Patrick, 2000; Verona, Sachs-Ericsson, & Joiner, 2004) and substance dependence (Krueger, 1999b; Sher & Trull, 1994). In contrast with this picture for APSD, Cleckley characterized psychopathic individuals as relatively immune to neurotic forms of psychopathology (cf. point 3, below) and suicide, and he did not consider psychopaths to be particularly susceptible to alcohol or drug addiction (although he did note that individuals with the disorder tended to act in highly erratic ways when intoxicated—as though alcohol operated as fuel for the "fire" of their underlying pathology). As discussed in subsequent sections, emerging evidence indicates that a reconciliation of these contrasting clinical pictures lies in the fact that distinguishable facets of psychopathy exhibit contrasting associations with problems of these differing types.

2. Is Aggression a Central Feature of Psychopathy?

Specific proclivities toward aggression or violence were not a part of Cleckley's (1941/1976) diagnostic criteria for psychopathy. In fact, Cleckley expressly discounted violent behavior as a defining feature of the disorder: "I am aware of the fact that many persons showing the characteristics of those here described do commit major crimes and sometimes crimes of maximal violence. There are so many, however, who do not, that such tendencies should be regarded as the exception rather than as the rule, perhaps, as a pathologic trait independent, to a considerable degree, of the other manifestations which we regard as fundamental" (p. 262).

In contrast, contemporaries of Cleckley who focused on psychopathy as a distinct variant of criminal deviance highlighted hostility, aggression, and cruelty as characteristic features. Reflecting this emphasis, Hare's PCL-R includes a criterion dealing with hot-temperedness and aggression ("poor behavioral controls") along with other items ("callous/lack of empathy," "early behavior problems," "juvenile delinquency," "criminal versatility") that are scored in part on the basis of cruelty and violent offense behavior, and overall scores on the PCL-R show robust associations with traits involving antagonism and aggression (Lynam & Derefinko, 2006) and are reliably predictive of aggressive acts and violent recidivism (Douglas, Vincent, & Edens, 2006). Youth-oriented inventories modeled after the PCL-R (i.e., PCL:YV, APSD, CPS) likewise exhibit robust associations with aggressive traits and behaviors (Salekin, 2006).

3. Is Deficient Anxiety Fundamental to Psychopathy?

Cleckley listed "absence of 'nervousness' or psychoneurotic manifestations" as a defining feature of the disorder: "It is highly typical for [psychopathic individuals] not only to escape the abnormal anxiety and tension fundamentally characteristic of [neurotic patients] but also to show a relative immunity from such anxiety and worry as might be judged normal or appropriate in disturbing situations" (p. 340). It was this distinctive element of the disorder that served as inspiration for Lykken's (1957, 1995) low fear hypothesis of primary psychopathy. In contrast with Cleckley, contemporary diagnostic protocols for assessing psychopathy in adult offenders (PCL-R) or youth with conduct problems (PCL:YV, APSD, CPS) do not include items pertaining to lack of anxiety, and overall scores on these instruments tend to show positive rather than negative relations with measures of trait anxiousness and with anxiety and depressive ("internalizing"; Achenbach & Edelbrock, 1978; Krueger, 1999b) symptomatology (e.g., Hare, 2003; Lynam & Derefinko, 2006; Salekin, 2006).

4. Is Criminal Deviance a Core Element of Psychopathy, or a Secondary Manifestation?

The question of whether persistent law breaking comprises an essential feature of psychopathy has been a topic of recent debate in the literature (see review by Skeem & Cooke, 2010a, and accompanying commentaries by Hare & Neumann, 2010, and Skeem & Cooke, 2010b). Points of contention include whether the PCL-R and affiliated instruments overemphasize maladaptive delinquent acts as a basis for diagnosing psychopathy, the notion that underlying trait dispositions need to be distinguished from behavioral sequelae in assigning diagnoses, the idea that an underlying psychopathic disposition can be expressed in ways other than persistent criminal deviance, and, relatedly, the perspective that alternatives to PCL-R-based instruments are needed to identify psychopathic individuals who are successful as opposed to maladaptively antisocial.

Regarding criminal deviance in psychopathy, Cleckley identified persistent antisocial behavior as a diagnostic criterion for the disorder, but with the qualifier "inadequately motivated." By this he meant that the antisocial acts of psychopathic individuals, in contrast with those of most common criminals, exhibit a peculiar aimless quality that also characterizes their behavior and decision making in various spheres of life: "The criminal usually works consistently and with what abilities are at his command toward obtaining his own ends. . . . The psychopath very seldom takes much advantage of what he gains and almost never works consistently in crime or in anything else to achieve a permanent position of power or wealth or security" (p. 261). This element of whimsicality is likewise evident in the narrative descriptions of several other of Cleckley's criteria, including "unreliability," "untruthfulness and insincerity," "poor judgment and failure to learn by experience," "general poverty in major affective reactions," "unresponsiveness in general interpersonal relations," "fantastic and uninviting behavior with drink and sometimes without," and "sex life impersonal, trivial, and poorly integrated."

5. Are There Different Subtypes of Psychopaths?

Cleckley was concerned mainly with clarifying and circumscribing the concept of psychopathy as an antidote to historic developments that had operated to broaden and obscure it, and thus he devoted limited attention to the possibility of distinctive subtypes. However, the idea that variants of psychopathy exist, distinguishable in terms of overt symptomatology and underlying etiologic mechanisms, dates back to at least the time of the first (1941) edition of Cleckley's *The Mask of Sanity* (see Karpman, 1941) and was featured prominently in the earliest experimental study of the disorder (Lykken, 1957). Nonetheless, to date only a handful of empirical studies have undertaken to test for the presence of subtypes of psychopaths defined according to contemporary diagnostic inventories such as the PCL-R, and certain crucial questions remain unresolved. How many subtypes are there? What measurable characteristics and quantitative methods are most appropriate for identifying them? Is there a "true" ("primary") psychopathy subtype, representing a distinctive phenotypic entity with a discrete underlying etiology? If so, should other variants of the disorder be regarded as "secondary" or "pseudo" psychopathy subtypes? Clearly, effective answers to questions of this sort are crucial to a comprehensive understanding of the psychopathy construct.

6. Do "Successful" Psychopaths Exist?

To some, the term "successful psychopathy" is a misnomer because psychopaths are by definition maladjusted (cf. point 1, above). To others, attributes conducive to success are inherent in the underlying disposition that gives rise to psychopathy. For example, based on the concept of temperamental fearlessness as the basis for primary psychopathy, Lykken (1995) postulated that "the hero and the psychopath may be twigs on the same genetic branch"—with the caveat that successful outcomes were dependent on highly effective socialization. Along similar lines, Cleckley (1941/1976) maintained that some individuals possessing the core dispositional substrate for psychopathy (which he believed to involve a deep-rooted affective impairment) manage to rise to positions of responsibility or leadership in society, such as legal, medical, psychiatric, or military positions, despite exhibiting disturbances at some level in behavior and social relations. Cleckley referred to cases of this type as "incomplete manifestations" of the disorder specifically because they lacked the level of debilitation observed in clinical cases.

Until quite recently, surprisingly little empirical research was conducted to address this intriguing question; for many years, a study by Widom (1977) comprised the only published work on the topic. However, during the past decade or so, additional published studies have appeared (e.g., Ishikawa, Raine, Lencz, Bihrle, & Lacasse, 2001; Mullins-Sweatt, Glover, Derefinko, Miller, & Widiger, 2010; Raine et al., 2004), promoting a resurgence of interest in the phenomenon of successful psychopathy. However, certain key issues need to be addressed before significant progress can be made in this area. Chief among these is the question of how successful psychopathy should be defined and identified. To date, the main approach that has been taken is to recruit and study individuals who exhibit many of the features of psychopathy encompassed by contemporary assessment devices (in particular, the PCL-R) but who have evaded detection by the law. However, individuals identified in this way are typically maladjusted in many respects and unaccomplished professionally and socially. This disjunction points to a need for alternative ways of conceptualizing and operationalizing the phenomenon of successful psychopathy (Hall & Benning, 2006).

Reconciling Contrasting Conceptualizations and Controversies: The Triarchic Model of Psychopathy

The Triarchic Model of psychopathy (Patrick et al., 2009) was formulated to address persisting controversies and unresolved issues in the field. The essence of the model is that various competing perspectives and apparent contradictions in the literature can be reconciled by conceiving of psychopathy as encompassing three distinct but intersecting phenotypic components: disinhibition, boldness, and meanness. The labels for these component constructs were selected as readily interpretable summary descriptors. The Triarchic Model differs from other contemporary factor- or facet-oriented models of psychopathy (e.g., Cooke & Michie, 2001; Hare & Neumann, 2006; Frick, O'Brien, Wooton, & McBurnett, 1994; Frick et al., 2000) in certain notable ways. It is a construct-based model not tied to any existing assessment instrument. Existing psychopathy inventories can be viewed as indexing the Triarchic constructs to varying degrees and in differing ways. Further, in contrast with factor- or facet-oriented models embodied in specific inventories, the three components of the Triarchic Model are not regarded as elements or indicators of a unitary higher-order psychopathy construct. Instead, the Triarchic constructs are seen as building blocks for alternative conceptualizations or variants of psychopathy (psychiatric and criminologic, primary and secondary, successful and unsuccessful, aggressive and nonaggressive, anxious and non-anxious, etc.) described by historic and contemporary writers.

The Triarchic conceptualization emerged from efforts to summarize and integrate historic and contemporary conceptualizations of psychopathy in terms of prominent recurring themes (Patrick, 2010a; Patrick et al., 2009). Concepts and findings from the broader personality, psychopathology, and neurobiological literatures also served as points of reference for the model. As such, the Triarchic Model can be considered a meta-conceptualization (i.e., an organizing descriptive framework for reconciling various existing conceptualizations and integrating findings across them) rather than a new theory of psychopathy or a replacement for existing conceptualizations. A basic tenet of the model is that its three constituent constructs, while all of relevance to the phenomenon of psychopathy, *are distinguishable phenotypicallly and can be conceptualized, assessed, and investigated separately*. The following subsections describe each of these constructs in turn.

Disinhibition

This term as used here denotes a general proneness toward problems of impulse control, reflecting poor planfulness, a focus on immediate over delayed gratification, difficulty in controlling emotions and urges, and a lack of behavioral restraint. Related constructs in the literature include weak inhibitory control (Kochanska, Murray, & Coy, 1997), disinhibitory psychopathology (Gorenstein & Newman, 1980; Sher & Trull, 1994), and externalizing (Achenbach & Edelbrock, 1978; Krueger et al., 2002). With respect to personality traits, disinhibition represents the intersection of impulsivity and negative emotionality (Krueger, 1999a; Sher & Trull,

1994). It is manifested behaviorally by impulsive action leading to adverse consequences, irresponsibility, impatience, distrust and alienation, aggressive behavior (reactive or angry aggression, in particular), repeated illicit and rule-breaking actions, and proneness to abuse alcohol and other drugs (Krueger, Markon, Patrick, Benning, & Kramer, 2007).

Historically, descriptions of psychopathy have placed emphasis on this disinhibitory (externalizing) facet to varying degrees, and to a considerable degree, disagreements about how psychopathy should be defined and what problematic tendencies it encompasses are traceable to this facet. Empirically, the construct of externalizing encompasses a diverse array of problem behaviors including conduct problems in childhood, antisocial behavior in later adolescence and adulthood, reactive aggression, and substance-related problems of differing types (Krueger et al., 2002, 2007; Young, Stallings, Corley, Krauter, & Hewitt, 2000). As mentioned earlier, certain historic writers (e.g., Prichard, 1835) defined psychopathy broadly to include alcohol and drug addiction and other non-normative behaviors (e.g., differing forms of sexual deviancy) that can be viewed as expressions of externalizing proneness; other writers (e.g., Arieti, 1963, 1967; Partridge, 1928a, 1928b) described psychopathy in terms that appear more characteristic of externalizing individuals; and others (e.g., Craft, 1966; Kraepelin, 1915) described subtypes of psychopaths who would more aptly be characterized as high externalizers. The traditional notion of the "symptomatic" or secondary psychopath (Karpman, 1941; Lykken, 1957) appears consistent with the clinical presentation of the high disinhibited-externalizing individual. Research over the past 10 years or so has shown that variance distinctly associated with the PCL-R's antisocial deviance factor (Factor 2) reflects externalizing proneness to a large extent (Patrick et al., 2005), as does the impulsive antisocial factor of the PPI (PPI-II; Blonigen et al., 2005). Judging from its documented external correlates, the I/CP factor of the APSD (Frick & Hare, 2001) also appears to reflect proneness to externalizing (i.e., disinhibition).

However, in general, investigators in the psychopathy area would not consider externalizing to be the same as psychopathy. In particular, as a whole, individuals with externalizing problems show high rather than low levels of negative affectivity (Krueger, 1999a). Externalizing proneness is also associated with (1) higher rather than lower occurrence of anxiety and depressive (i.e., internalizing) problems in childhood and adulthood (Achenbach & Edelbrock, 1978; Krueger, 1999b), and (2) higher rather than lower tendencies toward suicidal behavior (Verona & Patrick, 2000; Verona et al., 2004). In contrast with the excessive, dysregulated emotion that is characteristic of externalizing proneness, psychopathy is marked by salient "emotional detachment"—that is, affective insensitivity and lack of connectedness with other people (Cleckley, 1941/1976; Lykken, 1995; McCord & McCord, 1964; Patrick, 1994; Patrick, Bradley, & Lang, 1993). The Triarchic Model proposes that this distinguishing feature of psychopathy reflects the presence of boldness or meanness, or both. Stated somewhat differently, it is when disinhibitory or externalizing tendencies occur in combination with high levels of dispositional boldness and/or meanness that a diagnosis of psychopathy would be regarded as applicable.

Boldness

The term "bold" describes a behavioral style involving calmness and poise in situations entailing danger or pressure, a capacity to recover rapidly from stressful experiences, social assertiveness and self-assurance, and high tolerance (if not preference) for uncertainty and risk. Related terms in the literature include fearless temperament (Kochanska, 1997; Lykken, 1995), fearless dominance (Benning et al., 2005), hardiness (Kobasa, 1979), and resiliency (Block & Block, 1980). In terms of personality dispositions, boldness reflects the confluence of stress immunity, thrill-adventure seeking, and dominance (Benning et al., 2003, 2005; Kramer, Patrick, Krueger, & Gasperi, 2012). Its observable expressions include social assertiveness, persuasiveness, imperturbability, venturesomeness, and courage.

As conceptualized in the Triarchic Model, boldness is not identical to "fearlessness." According to the model, fearlessness is viewed as an underlying genotypic (constitutionally based) disposition, involving diminished sensitivity of the brain's defense-mobilization system to signals of danger or punishment (Fowles & Dindo, 2006; Kramer et al., 2012; Patrick, Durbin, & Moser, 2012). From this perspective, boldness represents one way in which underlying genotypic fearlessness can be manifested phenotypically. However, as discussed next below, genotypic fearlessness may also contribute to phenotypic meanness.

Cleckley's conception of psychopathy emphasized boldness together with disinhibition (externalizing proneness). Boldness was evident in his case histories and his diagnostic criteria, which included social charm, absence of anxiety or neurotic symptoms, lack of affective responsiveness, insensitivity to punishment ("failure to learn by experience"), and disinclination toward suicide. Other historic writers whose accounts of psychopathy focused on individuals in psychiatric rather than offender samples (e.g., Kraepelin, Schneider) also described bold-externalizing variants.

Unresponsiveness to punishment and lack of fear were also emphasized in early psychophysiological work on psychopathy by Robert Hare (cf. Hare, 1978) and in influential theories by Don Fowles (1980) and David Lykken (1995).

Lilienfeld's self-report PPI, which was designed to index traits reflected in Cleckley's conception of psychopathy, includes a broad factor (PPI-I) that directly reflects boldness. The PPI subscales that serve as indicators of this factor are Social Potency, Stress Immunity, and (to a lesser extent) Fearlessness.[1] Notably, scores on PPI-I are orthogonal to (uncorrelated with) impulsive-antisocial tendencies as indexed by PPI-II. Accordingly, boldness as indexed by PPI-I can be viewed as indexing a more adaptive expression of dispositional fearlessness—distinct from aggressive externalizing deviance—that is likely to be of importance for conceptualizing psychopathy in nonviolent, noncriminal samples (cf. Lykken, 1995). Boldness also appears to be tapped somewhat by Factor 1 of the PCL-R (Benning et al., 2005), in particular, by Interpersonal facet items of charm/glibness and grandiose sense of self-worth (Patrick, Hicks, Nichol, & Krueger, 2007). However, the Interpersonal facet of the PCL-R indexes boldness less directly and distinctively than PPI-I, given its overlap with the PCL-R's Affective, Lifestyle, and Antisocial facets.

Meanness

The term "mean" describes a constellation of tendencies including deficient empathy, inability to form close personal relations, rebelliousness, exploitativeness, and empowerment through cruelty and destructiveness. Terms related to meanness include callousness (Frick et al., 1994), antagonism (Lynam & Derefinko, 2006), and coldheartedness (Lilienfeld & Widows, 2005). In terms of interpersonal trait dimensions (Leary, 1957; Wiggins, 1982), meanness entails high dominance in conjunction with low nurturance/affiliation (Blackburn, 2006; Harpur et al., 1989). Relevant to this, Saucier (1992) documented a construct similar to meanness (represented by adjective descriptors such as unemotional, insensitive, and tough) involving the intersection of low affiliation, high dominance, and low neuroticism (i.e., high emotional stability). From this perspective, meanness can be viewed as disaffiliated agency—a style in which goals and resources are actively pursued without regard for and at the expense of others (e.g., akin to Schneider's [1950] "active affectionless" variant of psychopathy). Unlike social withdrawal, which entails passive disengagement from others (cf. "moving away from people"; Horney, 1945), meanness involves active confrontation and exploitativeness ("moving against people"; Horney, 1945). Affiliated behavioral expressions include disdain toward others, defiance of authority, lack of close relationships with other people, arrogance, aggressive competitiveness, cruelty toward people and animals, proactive (predatory or instrumental) aggression, exploitation of others for personal gain, and engagement in destructive acts for excitement.

Meanness is of central relevance to historic descriptions of psychopathy focusing on individuals in criminal and delinquent samples (McCord & McCord, 1964; Quay, 1964, 1986). The Affective facet of the PCL-R consists of items that capture McCord and McCord's lovelessness (item 7, "shallow affect," and item 8, "callous/lack of empathy") and guiltlessness (item 6, "lack of remorse or guilt," and item 16, "failure to accept responsibility for own actions"). The PCL-R's Interpersonal items also include elements of meanness: item 1 ("glibness and superficial charm") includes reference to excessive slickness and toughness; item 2 ("grandiose sense of self-worth") entails arrogance and a sense of superiority over others; item 4 ("pathological lying") entails deceptiveness in social interactions and enjoyment in deceiving others; and item 5 ("conning/manipulative") entails active exploitation for gain without consideration of effects on victims. The best-established inventories for assessing psychopathy in children and adolescents (PCL:YV, CPS, and APSD) were patterned after the PCL-R, and thus also emphasize meanness (callousness and exploitativeness, along with emotional detachment and social disconnectedness) in their affective-interpersonal items.

An important question is whether tendencies toward meanness can be measured separately from criminal or antisocial tendencies. With regard to the PCL-R, a structural modeling analysis revealed that the majority of its items are primarily indicators of a broad factor that reflects *aggressive* externalizing deviancy (Patrick et al., 2007). PCL-R items reflecting aggressive criminal deviance (i.e., items comprising the PCL-R's Antisocial facet: early behavioral problems, poor behavioral controls, criminal versatility, and juvenile delinquency) serve as the strongest and purest indicators of this general factor. Additionally, most items of the PCL-R's Affective and Interpersonal facets also load prominently on this general factor. The strong saturation of most items of the PCL-R with aggressive externalizing deviancy can be attributed to the fact that the scoring criteria for most items include reference to antisocial or criminal behavior.

However, recent research on the structure of problems and traits in the domain of externalizing demonstrates that the meanness facet of psychopathy can be separated from its disinhibitory (externalizing) facet. Based on analyses of self-report data collected from incarcerated as well as non-incarcerated men and women, Krueger et al. (2007) developed a set of 23 unidimensional construct scales to comprehensively index the domain of externalizing problems and traits. The best-fitting structural model of these 23 scales was a bifactor model that included a superordinate externalizing (disinhibition) factor on which all subscales loaded, along with two subordinate factors that accounted for residual variance in particular subscales. Within the model, the two subfactors were parameterized to be independent from one another and from the overarching externalizing factor. The strongest and most selective indicators of the general externalizing factor were scales tapping problematic impulsivity and irresponsibility. One of the two subfactors was defined by residual variance in scales indexing lack of empathy, aggression (in particular, proactive/relational and destructive forms), rebelliousness, excitement seeking, and dishonesty. The other subfactor was defined by residual variance in scales tapping use of or problems with alcohol and other drugs.

The findings of this research indicate that, separately from general disinhibition, a disposition entailing low empathy and excitement-seeking tendencies contributes to aggressive behavior—in particular, aggression involving predatory coercion and abuse of others. Other variables that served to define this callous-aggression subfactor included rebelliousness and dishonesty. In turn, these indicators clearly parallel the item content and observed correlates of the APSD's callous-unemotional (CU) factor. In particular, the items of this factor pertain to shallow affect and insincerity, lack of guilt, lack of concern for the feelings of others, disregard for responsibilities (schoolwork), and lying/manipulativeness (Frick et al., 1994). In addition, children or adolescents with conduct disorder who are high on the APSD CU factor show elevated rates of proactive aggression as well as reactive aggression, and enhanced thrill-seeking tendencies in comparison to those low on the CU factor (Frick & Dickens, 2006; Frick & White, 2008). High scores on this factor also predict lack of reactivity to affectively distressing or threatening stimuli, high tolerance for novelty and risk, and low scores on measures of neuroticism and anxiety, (Blair, 2006; Frick & Dickens, 2006; Frick & White, 2008; Marsh et al., 2008). However, if it is the case that meanness reflects underlying fearlessness, it entails a more harmful, maladaptive expression of low fear in comparison with boldness.

Operationalizing Boldness, Meanness, and Disinhibition: The Triarchic Psychopathy Measure

The Triarchic Psychopathy Measure (TriPM; Patrick, 2010b) was developed to index the disinhibition, meanness, and boldness components of psychopathy as distinctive constructs. The inventory contains 58 items that yield scores on three subscales corresponding to the constructs of the Triarchic Model.

The items for the TriPM Disinhibition and Meanness scales (20 and 19 items, respectively) are derived from the Externalizing Spectrum Inventory (ESI; Krueger et al., 2007). The ESI was developed to comprehensively assess problem behaviors and traits within the domain of externalizing (disinhibitory) psychopathology as represented in DSM-IV and the broader literature on disorders of this kind. It includes 415 items organized into 23 subscales that index constructs involving impulsivity and stimulation seeking, aggression of various types, alienation and externalization of blame, theft and dishonesty, and substance use and abuse. Confirmatory factor analyses of these 23 scales demonstrated an overarching "externalizing" factor on which all subscales loaded substantially (.45 or higher), together with subsidiary "callous aggression" and "substance abuse" subfactors that accounted for residual variance in some subscales.

Scores on the overarching externalizing factor of the ESI reflect general proneness to disinhibition in varying forms; in criminal offender participants (Venables & Patrick, 2012), higher scores on this broad factor are associated with lower dispositional restraint and higher negative affectivity, increased nonaggressive child and adult symptoms of DSM-IV ASPD, higher rates of drug and alcohol dependence, and higher scores on Factor 2, but not Factor 1, of the PCL-R (in particular, the impulsive-irresponsible lifestyle facet). The TriPM Disinhibition scale consists of items from the following ESI subscales, which exhibit the highest and purest loadings on the broad ESI externalizing factor: Irresponsibility, Problematic Impulsivity, Theft, Alienation, Boredom Proneness, Impatient Urgency, Fraudulence, Dependability (-), and Planful Control (-). Scores on the TriPM Disinhibition scale correlate very highly ($r > .9$) with scores on the broad externalizing factor of the full 415-item ESI.

The callous aggression subfactor of the ESI reflects tendencies toward emotional insensitivity and proactive/predatory aggression, distinct from hostility and reactive-aggressive tendencies associated with general externalizing (disinhibition); ESI scales with appreciable loadings on the callous aggression subfactor include Empathy (-), Relational Aggression, Destructive Aggression, Physical Aggression, Excitement Seeking, and Honesty (-). In criminal offender participants (Venables & Patrick, 2012), higher scores on this subfactor are associated with heightened dispositional dominance and aggressiveness, high narcissism, elevations on aggressive child and adult symptoms of ASPD, and higher scores on both Factor 1 (affective and interpersonal facets) and Factor 2 of the PCL-R (antisocial behavior facet). The TriPM Meanness scale was formed by selecting items from these scales that operate more predominantly as indicators of the callous aggression subfactor, and less so as indicators of the general externalizing (disinhibition) factor. In particular, Empathy (-) and Relational Aggression subscales as a whole load more strongly on the callous aggression subfactor than on the general externalizing factor, and thus items from these two scales are represented most strongly in the TriPM Meanness scale. Scores on the TriPM Meanness scale, after controlling for moderate overlap ($r \sim .5$) with scores on the TriPM Disinhibition scale, correlate very highly ($r > .8$) with scores on the callous aggression subfactor of the full 415-item ESI.

The source of items for the TriPM (19-item) Boldness scale is a new inventory (Patrick, Kramer, Vaidyanathan, Benning, & Hicks, 2012) developed to extend and refine measurement of the "fearless dominance" construct indexed by scores on Factor 1 of the PPI. As noted earlier in the section on noncriminal psychopathy that focused on self-report measures, this factor of the PPI is important to assess because it: (1) captures the imperturbality and social efficacy features of psychopathy highlighted by Cleckley; (2) shows convergent validity in relation to measures of narcissism, thrill-seeking, and (lack of) empathy; and (3) captures unique variance in Factor 1 of the PCL-R—in particular, its Interpersonal facet (Benning et al., 2005). The Boldness Inventory contains nine subscales consisting of items that index boldness in the realms of interpersonal behavior (Persuasiveness, Social Assurance, and Dominance subscales), emotional experience (Resiliency, Self-Assurance, and Optimism subscales), and venturesomeness (Courage, Intrepidness, and Tolerance for Uncertainty subscales). The TriPM Boldness scale includes representation of items from each of these nine subscales. Scores on the TriPM Boldness scale correlate very highly (~ .8) with scores on PPI-I computed from the Social Potency, Stress Immunity, and Fearlessness subscales of the PPI (Patrick, 2010b). By contrast, the TriPM Boldness scale correlates minimally with the TriPM Disinhibition scale and only modestly ($r \sim .2$) with the TriPM Meanness scale.

Like the self-report-based EPA measure Lynam et al. (2011) described earlier, the TriPM is relatively new and data concerning its criterion-related validity have emerged only recently (Patrick, 2010b; Phillips, Sellbom, Ben-Porath, & Patrick, 2012; Venables & Patrick, 2012). A number of foreign-language translations of the inventory are in use (including Dutch, Finnish, German, Portuguese, and Spanish), so it is anticipated that validity data will accumulate rapidly over time. Hand in hand with this, it will useful to evaluate whether alternative scales measures of the Triarchic constructs (boldness, meanness, disinhibition) can be derived from other existing psychopathy inventories such as the PPI, YPI, or EPA. As discussed in the final section below, research examining the common and distinctive correlates of these three components of psychopathy should help to address and perhaps resolve continuing points of disagreement in the field.

The Triarchic Model as a Framework for Addressing Historic Points of Contention

In this section, I revisit aforementioned points of contention in the conceptualization of psychopathy and discuss how these points might be addressed from the standpoint of the Triarchic Model.

1. Should the Diagnostic Criteria for Psychopathy Be Limited to Maladaptive Features, or Are Indicators of Positive Adjustment Also Relevant?

The Triarchic Model defines psychopathy in terms of salient disinhibition accompanied by emotional detachment in the form of boldness or meanness, or both. The boldness component in particular has both adaptive and maladaptive aspects to it—social poise, emotional stability, and venturesomeness on one hand, and narcissism, emotional insensitivity, and risk-taking on the other. From the standpoint of the model, a more purely maladaptive variant of psychopathy does exist—i.e., a "mean-disinhibited" (aka "antagonistic-unconscientious" [Lynam & Derefinko, 2006] or callous-unemotional conduct disorder type [Frick & Marsee, 2006]), but to capture the "bold-disinhibited" type described by Cleckley (1941/1976), some consideration of adaptive as well as maladaptive features is necessary.

2. Is Aggression a Central Feature of Psychopathy?

In the Triarchic Model, tendencies toward aggression are represented in the disinhibition and meanness constructs. Disinhibition encompasses tendencies toward mistrust and hostility, and more reactive (angry, impulsive) forms of aggression. Meanness encompasses tendencies toward callousness and exploitativeness, and more proactive (instrumental, strategic) forms of aggression. A "mean-disinhibited" type of psychopath certainly exists, in which aggressive behavior of differing types is salient (Frick & Marsee, 2006; Porter & Woodworth, 2006), but aggression is not characteristic of the "bold-disinhibited" psychopath described by Cleckley (1941/1976).

3. Is Deficient Anxiety Fundamental to Psychopathy?

The three phenotypic components of the Triarchic Model, when assessed separately from one another, exhibit differential relations with trait anxiety: Boldness is correlated negatively with anxiety (Benning et al., 2005; Patrick et al., 2006), whereas Disinhibition is correlated positively with anxiety and Meannness is correlated negligibly with anxiety (Venables & Patrick, 2012). Cluster analytic studies of criminal offenders scoring high on the PCL-R have consistently demonstrated one subtype characterized by low anxiousness and average levels of dispositional impulsivity and aggression, and another by high anxiousness together with very high levels of impulsivity and aggressiveness (Hicks, Markon, Patrick, Krueger, & Newman, 2004; Skeem, Johansson, Andershed, Kerr, & Louden, 2007). Thus, low anxiousness is fundamental to one variant of criminal psychopathy (the bold-disinhibited, or "primary" type) but not to another variant (the "disinhibited-mean," "aggressive-externalizing," or "secondary" type). There may be other variants of criminal or antisocial psychopathy (e.g., predominantly mean, or callous-unemotional type [Frick & Marsee, 2006]) that entail average as opposed to low or high levels of anxiousness.

4. Is Criminal Deviance a Core Element of Psychopathy, or a Secondary Manifestation?

Recent research with criminal offenders indicates that tendencies toward boldness, meanness, and disinhibition are each associated independently with a higher occurrence of criminal behaviors—in adult males, at least (Patrick, 2010b; Venables & Patrick, 2012). One perspective on these observed associations is that criminal behaviors are a "downstream" expression of more basic trait dispositions, and should thus be viewed as consequences of psychopathic propensities rather than as defining features (Cooke, Michie, Hart, & Clark, 2004). Another perspective is that antisocial behaviors should be regarded as effective indicators of a higher-order construct of psychopathy because they cohere with other, putatively trait-like indicators (Hare & Neumann, 2010). From the standpoint of the Triarchic Model, antisocial behavior per se (i.e., considered generically) is the complex product of differing "criminogenic" trait dispositions, and thus is not selectively indicative of boldness, meanness, or disinhibition. However, it is conceivable that antisocial behavior could be subclassified in certain ways (e.g., on the basis of motives or spontaneity) that might provide for more effective mapping onto these Triarchic constructs.

5. Are There Different Subtypes of Psychopaths?

From the perspective of the Triarchic Model, alternative variants of psychopathy are defined by differing configurations of boldness, meanness, and disinhibition. Accordingly, from a research standpoint, designations such as "bold-disinhibited" and "mean-disinhibited" may ultimately prove more meaningful than designations like "primary" versus "secondary," or "low anxious" versus "high anxious." A question that arises in this context is whether certain individuals who are high in boldness and/or meanness but low in disinhibition might qualify for a diagnosis of psychopathy. For example, should a high-bold/high-mean individual (e.g., a ruthless corporate executive, such as that portrayed by actor Michael Douglas in the film *Wall Street*; Pressman & Stone, 1987)—or an extremely mean but neither bold nor clearly disinhibited individual, such as Russian serial murder Andrei Chikatilo (Cullen, 1993)—be considered psychopathic? Questions of this type will need to be addressed through extensions of existing theories in conjunction with further systematic research.

6. Do "Successful" Psychopaths Exist?

As suggested by Hall and Benning (2006), successful psychopathy may reflect a preponderance of certain etiologic influences (reflected particular symptomatic features) over others. Drawing on findings regarding the differential correlates of the two factors of the PCL-R and the PPI and theories positing distinct etiologic underpinnings to differing features of psychopathy (Patrick & Lang, 1999; Patrick & Bernat, 2009; Fowles & Dindo, 2006, 2009), these authors suggested that affective-interpersonal features reflecting a fearless temperament (considered by Lykken [1995] to the core substrate for psychopathy) may be conducive to success when unaccompanied by dispositional weaknesses in inhibitory control capacity. For example, individuals high in boldness but low in disinhibition might be expected to achieve higher success in occupations calling for leadership and/or courage because their psychopathic tendencies entail social efficacy, emotional resilience, and venturesomeness. In an intriguing test of this hypothesis, Lilienfeld, Waldman, Landfield, Rubenzer, and Faschingbauer (in press) used personality trait ratings of former U.S. presidents generated by expert historians to estimate scores on the two factors of the PPI (cf. Ross et al., 2009). They found that higher estimated levels of fearless dominance predicted higher ratings of presidential performance, persuasiveness, leadership, and crisis management ability, along with higher scores on objective indicators of performance such as initiation of new legislation and social programs. By contrast, higher estimated levels of impulsive antisociality predicted objective indicators of a negative nature such as documented abuses of power and impeachment resolutions. Further research along these lines should provide valuable new insights into dispositional tendencies underlying psychopathy and the differing ways in which psychopathic tendencies can be expressed.

Acknowledgment

Preparation of this chapter was supported by grants MH072850 and MH089727 from the National Institute of Mental Health.

Note

1. The PPI Fearlessness subscale cross-loads on PPI-II. This appears to be the case because the items of this subscale reflect not just tendencies toward thrill-seeking and tolerance of danger, but also boredom susceptibility and weak restraint; the thrill-seeking component of PPI Fearlessness in particular accounts for its relationship with PPI-I, whereas the boredom/weak restraint component accounts for its association with PPI-II (cf. Benning et al., 2005a).

References

Achenbach, T. M., & Edelbrock, C. S. (1978). The classification of child psychopathology: A review and analysis of empirical efforts. *Psychological Bulletin, 85*, 1275–1301.

American Psychiatric Association (APA). (1952). *Diagnostic and statistical manual of mental disorders*. Washington, DC: Author.

American Psychiatric Association (APA). (1968). *Diagnostic and statistical manual of mental disorders* (2nd ed.). Washington, DC: Author.

American Psychiatric Association (APA). (1980). *Diagnostic and statistical manual of mental disorders* (3rd ed.). Washington, DC: Author.

American Psychiatric Association (APA). (1987). *Diagnostic and statistical manual of mental disorders* (3rd ed., rev.). Washington, DC: Author.

American Psychiatric Association (APA). (2000). *Diagnostic and statistical manual of mental disorders* (4th ed., text rev.). Washington, DC: Author.

American Psychiatric Association (APA). (2012). *DSM-V Development*. Retrieved February 7, 2012, from http://www.dsm5.org/about/Pages/DSMVOverview.aspx.

Andershed, H., Kerr, M., Stattin, H., & Levander, S. (2002). Psychopathic traits in non-referred youths: A new assessment tool. In E. Blau & L. Sheridan (Eds.), *Psychopaths: Current international perspectives* (pp. 131–158). Amsterdam: Elsevier.

Arieti, S. (1963). Psychopathic personality: Some views on its psychopathology and psychodynamics. *Comprehensive Psychiatry, 4*, 301–312.

Arieti, S. (1967). *The intrapsychic self: Feeling, cognition, and creativity in health and mental illness*. New York: Basic Books.

Benning, S. D., Patrick, C. J., Blonigen, D. M., Hicks, B. M., & Iacono, W. G. (2005). Estimating facets of psychopathy from normal personality traits: A step toward community-epidemiological investigations. *Assessment, 12*, 3–18.

Benning, S. D., Patrick, C. J., Hicks, B. M., Blonigen, D. M., & Krueger, R. F. (2003). Factor structure of the Psychopathic Personality Inventory: Validity and implications for clinical assessment. *Psychological Assessment, 15*, 340–350.

Birnbaum, K. (1909). *Die psychopathischen Verbrecker*. Leipzig, Germany: Thieme.

Blackburn, R. (2006). Other theoretical models of psychopathy. In C. J. Patrick (Ed.), *Handbook of psychopathy* (pp. 35–57). New York: Guilford Press.

Blair, R. J. R. (2006). Subcortical brain systems in psychopathy: The amygdala and associated structures. In C. J. Patrick (Ed.), *Handbook of psychopathy* (pp. 296–312). New York: Guilford Press.

Block, J. H., & Block, J. (1980). The role of ego-control and ego resiliency in the organization of behavior. In W. A. Collins (Ed.), *Development of cognition, affect, and social relations: The Minnesota symposium on child psychology* (Vol. 13, pp. 39–101). Hillsdale, NJ: Lawrence Erlbaum Associates.

Blonigen, D. M., Hicks, B., Krueger, R., Patrick, C. J., & Iacono, W. (2005). Psychopathic personality traits: Heritability and genetic overlap with internalizing and externalizing pathology. *Psychological Medicine, 35*, 637–648.

Blonigen, D. M., Patrick, C. J., Douglas, K. S., Poythress, N. G., Skeem, J. L., Lilienfeld, S. O., ... Krueger, R. F. (2010). Multimethod assessment of psychopathy in relation to factors of internalizing and externalizing from the Personality Assessment Inventory: The impact of method variance and suppressor effects. *Psychological Assessment, 22*, 96–107.

Cleckley, H. (1976). *The mask of sanity* (5th ed.). St. Louis, MO: Mosby. (Originally published 1941)

Cooke, D. J., & Michie, C. (2001). Refining the construct of psychopathy: Towards a hierarchical model. *Psychological Assessment, 13*, 171–188.

Cooke, D. J., Michie, C., Hart, S. D., & Clark, D. A. (2004). Reconstructing psychopathy: Clarifying the significance of antisocial and socially deviant behavior in the diagnosis of psychopathic personality disorder. *Journal of Personality Disorders, 18*, 337–357.

Craft, M. (1966). *Psychopathic disorders and their assessment*. New York: Pergamon Press.

Cullen, R. (1993). *The killer department*. Birmingham, UK: Orion Media.

Douglas, K. S., Lilienfeld, S. O., Skeem, J. L., Poythress, N. G., Edens, J. F., & Patrick, C. J. (2008). Relation of antisocial and psychopathic traits to suicide-related behavior among offenders. *Law and Human Behavior, 32*, 511–525.

Douglas, K. S., Vincent, G. M., & Edens, J. F. (2006). Risk for criminal recidivism: The role of psychopathy. In C. J. Patrick (Ed.), *Handbook of psychopathy* (pp. 533–554). New York: Guilford Press.

Forth, A. E., Kosson, D. S., & Hare, R. D. (2003). *The Psychopathy Checklist: Youth Version*. Toronto, Ontario, Canada: Multi-Health Systems.

Fowles, D. C. (1980). The three arousal model: Implications of Gray's two-factor learning theory for heart rate, electrodermal activity, and psychopathy. *Psychophysiology, 17*, 87–104.

Fowles, D. C., & Dindo, L. (2006). A dual-deficit model of psychopathy. In C. J. Patrick (Ed.), *Handbook of psychopathy* (pp. 14–34). New York: Guilford Press.

Fowles, D. C., & Dindo, L. (2009). Temperament and psychopathy: A dual-pathway model. *Current Directions in Psychological Science, 18*, 179–183. doi:10.1111/j.1467-8721.2009.01632.x.

Frances, A. J. (1980). The DSM-III personality disorders section: A commentary. *American Journal of Psychiatry, 137*, 1050–1054.

Frick, P. J., Boden, D. S., & Barry, C. T. (2000). Psychopathic traits and conduct problems in community and clinic-referred samples of children: Further development of the Psychopathy Screening Device. *Psychological Assessment, 12*, 382–393.

Frick, P. J., & Dickens, C. (2006). Current perspectives on conduct disorder. *Current Psychiatry Reports, 8*, 59–72.

Frick, P. J., & Hare, R. D. (2001). *The antisocial process screening device (APSD)*. Toronto, Ontario, Canada: Multi-Health Systems.

Frick, P. J., Lilienfeld, S. O., Ellis, M., Loney, B., & Silverthorn, P. (1999). The association between anxiety and psychopathy dimensions in children. *Journal of Abnormal Child Psychology, 27*, 383–392.

Frick, P. J., & Marsee, M. A. (2006). Psychopathy and developmental pathways to antisocial behavior in youth. In C. J. Patrick (Ed.), *Handbook of psychopathy* (pp. 353–374). New York: Guilford Press.

Frick, P. J., O'Brien, B. S., Wooton, J. M., & McBurnett, K. (1994). Psychopathy and conduct problems in children. *Journal of Abnormal Psychology, 103*, 700–707.

Frick, P. J., & White, S. F. (2008). The importance of callous-unemotional traits for developmental models of aggressive and antisocial behavior. *Journal of Child Psychology and Psychiatry, 49*, 359–375.

Gorenstein, E. E., & Newman, J. P. (1980). Disinhibitory psychopathology: A new perspective and a model for research. *Psychological Review, 87*, 301–315.

Hall, J. R., & Benning, S. D. (2006) The "successful" psychopath: Adaptive and subclinical manifestations of psychopathy in the general population. In C. J. Patrick (Ed.), *Handbook of psychopathy* (pp. 459–478). New York: Guilford Press.

Hare, R. D. (1978). Electrodermal and cardiovascular correlates of psychopathy. In R. D. Hare & D. Schalling (Eds.), *Psychopathic behavior: Approaches to research* (pp. 107–143). Chichester, UK: Wiley.

Hare, R. D. (1980). A research scale for the assessment of psychopathy in criminal populations. *Personality and Individual Differences, 1*, 111–119.

Hare, R. D. (1983). Diagnosis of antisocial personality disorder in two prison populations. *American Journal of Psychiatry, 140*, 887–890.

Hare, R. D. (1991). *The Hare Psychopathy Checklist–Revised*. Toronto, Ontario, Canada: Multi-Health Systems.

Hare, R. D. (2003). *The Hare Psychopathy Checklist–Revised* (2nd ed.). Toronto, Ontario, Canada: Multi-Health Systems.

Hare, R. D., Harpur, T. J., Hakstian, A. R., Forth, A. E., Hart, S. D., & Newman, J. P. (1990). The Revised Psychopathy Checklist: Reliability and factor structure. *Psychological Assessment, 2*, 338–341.

Hare, R. D., & Neumann, C. N. (2006). The PCL-R assessment of psychopathy: Development, structural properties, and new directions. In C. J. Patrick (Ed.), *Handbook of psychopathy* (pp. 58–88). New York: Guilford Press.

Hare, R. D., & Neumann, C. S. (2010). The role of antisociality in the psychopathy construct: Comment on Skeem and Cooke (2010). *Psychological Assessment, 22*, 446–454.

Harpur, T. J., Hare, R. D., & Hakstian, R. (1989). A two-factor conceptualization of psychopathy: Construct validity and implications for assessment. *Psychological Assessment: A Journal of Consulting and Clinical Psychology, 1*, 6–17.

Herrnstein, R. J. (1983). Some criminogenic traits of offenders. In J. Q. Wilson (Ed.), *Crime and public policy* (pp. 31–46). San Francisco, CA: Institute for Contemporary Studies.

Hicks, B. M., Markon, K. E., Patrick, C. J., Krueger, R. F., & Newman, J. P. (2004). Identifying psychopathy subtypes on the basis of personality structure. *Psychological Assessment, 16*, 276–288.

Hicks, B. M., & Patrick, C. J. (2006). Psychopathy and negative affectivity: Analyses of suppressor effects reveal distinct relations with trait anxiety, depression, fearfulness, and anger-hostility. *Journal of Abnormal Psychology, 115*, 276–287.

Horney, K. (1945). *Our inner conflicts*. New York: W. W. Norton & Co.

Ishikawa, S. S., Raine, A., Lencz, T., Bihrle, S., & Lacasse, L. (2001). Autonomic stress reactivity and executive functions in successful and unsuccessful criminal psychopaths from the community. *Journal of Abnormal Psychology, 110*, 423–432.

Karpman, B. (1941). On the need of separating psychopathy into two distinct clinical types: The symptomatic and the idiopathic. *Journal of Criminal Psychopathology, 3*, 112–137.

Kobasa, C. S. (1979). Stressful life events, personality, and health: An inquiry into hardiness. *Journal of Personality and Social Psychology, 37*, 1–11.

Koch, J. L. A. (1891) *Die psychopathischen Minderwertigkeiten*. Dorn: Ravensburg.

Kochanska, G. K. (1997). Multiple pathways to conscience for children with different temperaments: From toddlerhood to age 5. *Developmental Psychology, 33*, 228–240.

Kochanska, G., Murray, K., & Coy, K. C. (1997). Inhibitory control as a contributor to conscience in childhood: From toddler to early school age. *Child Development, 68*, 263–267.

Kraepelin, E. (1904, 1915). *Psychiatrie: Ein lehrbuch* (7th ed., 1904; 8th ed., 1915). Leipzig, Germany: Barth.

Kramer, M. D., Patrick, C. J., Krueger, R. F., & Gasperi, M. (2012). Delineating physiological defensive reactivity in the domain of self-report: Phenotypic and etiologic structure of dispositional fear. *Psychological Medicine, 42*, 1305–1320.

Krueger, R. F. (1999a). Personality traits in late adolescence predict mental disorders in early adulthood: A prospective-epidemiological study. *Journal of Personality, 67*, 39–65.

Krueger, R. F. (1999b). The structure of common mental disorders. *Archives of General Psychiatry, 56*, 921–926.

Krueger, R. F., Hicks, B., Patrick, C. J., Carlson, S., Iacono, W. G., & McGue, M. (2002). Etiologic connections among substance dependence, antisocial behavior, and personality: Modeling the externalizing spectrum. *Journal of Abnormal Psychology, 111*, 411–424.

Krueger, R. F., Markon, K. E., Patrick, C. J., Benning, S. D., & Kramer, M. (2007). Linking antisocial behavior, substance use, and personality: An integrative quantitative model of the adult externalizing spectrum. *Journal of Abnormal Psychology, 116*, 645–666.

Leary, T. (1957). *Interpersonal diagnosis of personality*. New York: Ronald Press.

Levenson, M. R., Kiehl, K. A., & Fitzpatrick, C. M. (1995). Assessing psychopathic attributes in a non institutionalized population. *Journal of Personality and Social Psychology, 68*, 151–158.

Lilienfeld, S. O., & Andrews, B. P. (1996). Development and preliminary validation of a self report measure of psychopathic personality traits in noncriminal populations. *Journal of Personality Assessment, 66*, 488–524. doi:10.1207/s15327752jpa6603_3.

Lilienfeld, S. O., Waldman, I. D., Landfield, K., Rubenzer, S., & Faschingbauer, T. R. (2012). Psychopathic personality traits among U.S. presidents: Implications for job performance and leadership. *Journal of Personality and Social Psychology*.

Lilienfeld, S. O., & Widows, M. R. (2005). *Psychopathic Personality Inventory–Revised (PPI-R) professional manual*. Odessa, FL: Psychological Assessment Resources.

Lykken, D. T. (1957). A study of anxiety in the sociopathic personality. *Journal of Abnormal and Clinical Psychology, 55*, 6–10.

Lykken, D. T. (1978). The psychopath and the lie detector. *Psychophysiology, 15*, 137–142.

Lykken, D. T. (1995). *The antisocial personalities*. Hillsdale, NJ: Lawrence Erlbaum Associates.

Lynam, D. R. (1997). Pursuing the psychopath: Capturing the fledgling psychopath in a nomological net. *Journal of Abnormal Psychology, 106*, 425–438.

Lynam, D. R., Caspi, A., Moffitt, T. E., Raine, A., Loeber, R., & Stouthamer-Loeber, M. (2005). Adolescent psychopathy and the Big Five: Results from two samples. *Journal of Abnormal Child Psychology, 33*, 431–444.

Lynam, D. R., & Derefinko, K. J. (2006). Psychopathy and personality. In C. J. Patrick (Ed.), *Handbook of psychopathy* (pp. 133–155). New York: Guilford Press.

Lynam, D. R., Gaughan, E. T., Miller, J. D., Miller, D. J., Mullins-Sweatt, S., & Widiger, T. A. (2011). Assessing the basic traits associated with psychopathy: Development and validation of the Elemental Psychopathy Assessment. *Psychological Assessment, 18*, 106–114.

Lynam, D. R., & Widiger, T. A. (2007). Using a general model of personality to identify the basic elements of psychopathy. *Journal of Personality Disorders, 21*, 160–178.

Marsh, A. A., Finger, E. C., Mitchell, D. G., Reid, M. E., Sims, C., Kosson, D. S., . . . Blair, R. J. R. (2008). Reduced amygdala response to fearful expressions in children and adolescents with callous-unemotional traits and disruptive behavior disorders. *American Journal of Psychiatry, 165*, 712–720.

McCord, W., & McCord, J. (1964). *The psychopath: An essay on the criminal mind.* Princeton, NJ: Van Nostrand.

Miller, J. D., Gaughan, E. T., Maples, J., Gentile, B., Lynam, D. R., & Widiger, T. A. (2011). Examining the construct validity of the elemental psychopathy assessment. *Assessment, 18*, 106–114.

Miller, J. D., Lynam, D. R., Widiger, T. A., & Leukefeld, C. (2001). Personality disorders as extreme variants of common personality dimensions: Can the Five-Factor Model adequately represent psychopathy? *Journal of Personality, 69*, 253–276.

Mullins-Sweatt, S. N., Glover, D. G., Derefinko, K. J., Miller, J. D., & Widiger, T. A. (2010). The successful psychopath. *Journal of Research in Personality, 44*, 554–558.

Newman, J. P., Widom, C. S., & Nathan, S. (1985). Passive-avoidance in syndromes of disinhibition: Psychopathy and extraversion. *Journal of Personality and Social Psychology, 48*, 1316–1327.

Partridge, G. E. (1928a). Psychopathic personalities among boys in a training school for delinquents. *American Journal of Psychiatry, 8*, 159–186.

Partridge, G. E. (1928b). A study of 50 cases of psychopathic personality. *American Journal of Psychiatry, 7*, 953–973.

Patrick, C. J. (1994). Emotion and psychopathy: Startling new insights. *Psychophysiology, 31*, 319–330.

Patrick, C. J. (1997). Deconstructing psychopathy. *Psychological Inquiry, 8*, 244–251.

Patrick, C. J. (2006). Back to the future: Cleckley as a guide to the next generation of psychopathy research. In C. J. Patrick (Ed.), *Handbook of psychopathy* (pp. 605–617). New York: Guilford Press.

Patrick, C. J. (2007). Getting to the heart of psychopathy. In H. F. Hervé and J. C. Yuille (Eds.), *Psychopathy: Theory, research, and social implications* (pp. 207–252). Hillsdale, NJ: Erlbaum.

Patrick, C. J. (2010a). Conceptualizing psychopathic personality: Disinhibited, bold, or just plain mean? In R. J. Salekin & D. R. Lynam (Eds.), *Handbook of child and adolescent psychopathy* (pp. 15–48). New York: Guilford Press.

Patrick, C. J. (2010b). *Operationalizing the Triarchic conceptualization of psychopathy: Preliminary description of brief scales for assessment of boldness, meanness, and disinhibition*. Unpublished test manual, Florida State University, Tallahassee, FL. Test is available online at https://www.phenxtoolkit.org/index.php?pageLink=browse.protocoldetails&id=121601.

Patrick, C. J., & Bernat, E. M. (2009). Neurobiology of psychopathy: A two-process theory. In G. G. Berntson & J. T. Cacioppo (Eds.), *Handbook of neuroscience for the behavioral sciences* (pp. 1110–1131). New York: John Wiley & Sons.

Patrick, C. J., Bradley, M. M., & Lang, P. J. (1993). Emotion in the criminal psychopath: Startle reflex modulation. *Journal of Abnormal Psychology, 102*, 82–92.

Patrick, C. J., Durbin, C. E., & Moser, J. S. (2012). Conceptualizing proneness to antisocial deviance in neurobehavioral terms. *Development and Psychopathology, 24*, 1047–1071.

Patrick, C. J., Edens, J. F., Poythress, N., Lilienfeld, S. O., & Benning, S. D. (2006). Construct validity of the PPI two-factor model with offenders. *Psychological Assessment, 18*, 204–208.

Patrick, C. J., Fowles, D. C., & Krueger, R. F. (2009). Triarchic conceptualization of psychopathy: Developmental origins of disinhibition, boldness, and meanness. *Development and Psychopathology, 21*, 913–938.

Patrick, C. J., Hicks, B. M., Krueger, R. F., & Lang, A. R. (2005). Relations between psychopathy facets and externalizing in a criminal offender sample. *Journal of Personality Disorders, 19*, 339–356.

Patrick, C. J., Hicks, B. M., Nichol, P. E., & Krueger, R. F. (2007). A bifactor approach to modeling the structure of the Psychopathy Checklist-Revised. *Journal of Personality Disorders, 21*, 118–141.

Patrick, C. J., Kramer, M. D., Vaidyanathan, U., Benning, S. D., & Hicks, B. M. (2012). *Refining measurement of the fearless dominance component of psychopathy: Development and preliminary validation of the Boldness Inventory*. Manuscript submitted for publication.

Patrick, C. J., & Lang, A. R. (1999). Psychopathic traits and intoxicated states: Affective concomitants and conceptual links. In M. E. Dawson, A. M. Schell, & A. H. Boehmelt (Eds.), *Startle modification: Implications for clinical science, cognitive science, and neuroscience* (pp. 209–230). New York: Cambridge University Press.

Paulhus, D. L., Hemphill, J. F., & Hare, R. D. (in press). *Manual for the Self-Report Psychopathy scale*. Toronto, Ontario, Canada: Multi-Health Systems.

Paulhus, D. L., Robins, R. W., Trzesniewski, K. H., & Tracy, J. L. (2004). Two replicable suppressor situations in personality research. *Multivariate Behavioral Research, 39*, 303–328.

Phillips, T. R., Sellbom, M., Ben-Porath, Y., & Patrick, C. J. (2012). *Further development and construct validation of MMPI-2-RF indices of global psychopathy, fearless-dominance, and impulsive-antisociality in a sample of incarcerated women.* Manuscript submitted for publication.

Pinel, P. (1962). *A treatise on insanity* (D. Davis, Trans.). New York: Hafner. (Original work published 1806)

Porter, S., & Woodworth, M. (2006). Psychopathy and aggression. In C. J. Patrick (Ed.), *Handbook of psychopathy* (pp. 481–494). New York: Guilford Press.

Pressman, E. R. (Producer), & Stone, O. (Director). (1987). *Wall Street* [Motion picture]. United States: 20th Century Fox.

Prichard, J. C. (1835) *A treatise on insanity and other disorders affecting the mind.* London: Sherwood, Gilbert & Piper.

Quay, H. C. (1964). Dimensions of personality in delinquent boys as inferred from the factor analysis of case history data. *Child Development, 35*, 479–484.

Quay, H. C. (1986). Classification. In H. C. Quay & J. S. Werry (Eds.), *Psychopathological disorders of childhood* (3rd ed., pp. 1–42). New York: Wiley.

Raine, A., Ishikawa, S. S., Arce, E., Lencz, T., Knuth, K. H., Bihrle, S., . . . Colletti, P. (2004). Hippocampal structural asymmetry in unsuccessful psychopaths. *Biological Psychiatry, 55*, 185–191.

Robins, L. N. (1966). *Deviant children grown up*. Baltimore, MD: Williams & Wilkins.

Robins, L. N. (1978). Sturdy predictors of adult antisocial behaviour: Replications from longitudinal studies. *Psychological Medicine, 8*, 611–622.

Ross, S. R., Benning, S. D., Patrick, C. J., Thompson, A., & Thurston, A. (2009). Factors of the Psychopathic Personality Inventory: Criterion-related validity and relationship to the BIS/BAS and Five-Factor models of personality. *Assessment, 16*, 71–87.

Saucier, G. (1992). Benchmarks: Integrating affective and interpersonal circles with the Big-Five personality factors. *Journal of Personality and Social Psychology, 62*, 1025–1035.

Salekin, R. T. (2006). Psychopathy in children and adults: Key issues in conceptualization and assessment. In C. J. Patrick (Ed.), *Handbook of psychopathy* (pp. 389–414). New York: Guilford Press.

Schmauk, F. J. (1970). Punishment, arousal, and avoidance learning in sociopaths. *Journal of Abnormal Psychology, 76*, 325–335.

Schneider, K. (1950). *Psychopathic personalities* (9th ed., M. Hamilton, Trans., 1958). Springfield, IL: Charles C. Thomas.

Sher, K. J., & Trull, T. (1994). Personality and disinhibitory psychopathology: Alcoholism and antisocial personality disorder. *Journal of Abnormal Psychology, 103*, 92–102.

Skeem, J. L., & Cooke, D. J. (2010a). Is criminal behavior a central component of psychopathy? Conceptual directions for resolving the debate. *Psychological Assessment, 22*, 433–445.

Skeem, J. L., & Cooke, D. J. (2010b). One measure does not a construct make: Toward reinvigorating psychopathy research. Reply to Hare & Neumann (2010). *Psychological Assessment, 22*, 455–457.

Skeem, J. L., Johansson, P., Andershed, H., Kerr, M., & Louden, J. E. (2007). Two subtypes of psychopathic violent offenders that parallel primary and secondary variants. *Journal of Abnormal Psychology, 116*, 395–409.

Skeem, J. L., Polaschek, D., Patrick, C. J., & Lilienfeld, S. O. (2011). Psychopathic personality: Bridging the gap between empirical evidence and public policy. *Psychological Science in the Public Interest, 12*, 95–162.

Vaidyanathan, U., Patrick, C. J., & Iacono, W. G. (2011). Patterns of comordibity among common mental disorders: A person-centered approach. *Comprehensive Psychiatry, 52*, 527–535.

Venables, N. C., & Patrick, C. J. (2012). Validity of the Externalizing Spectrum Inventory in a criminal offender sample: Relations with disinhibitory psychopathology, personality, and psychopathic features. *Psychological Assessment, 24*, 88–100.

Verona, E., Hicks, B. M., & Patrick, C. J. (2005). Psychopathy and suicidal behavior in female offenders: Mediating influences of temperament and abuse history. *Journal of Consulting and Clinical Psychology, 73*, 1065–1073.

Verona, E., & Patrick, C. J. (2000). Suicide risk in externalizing syndromes: Temperamental and neurobiological underpinnings. In T. E. Joiner (Ed.), *Suicide science: Expanding the boundaries* (pp. 137–173). Boston: Kluwer Academic Publishers.

Verona, E., Patrick, C. J., & Joiner, T. E. (2001). Psychopathy, antisocial personality, and suicide risk. *Journal of Abnormal Psychology, 110*, 462–470.

Verona, E., Sachs-Ericsson, N., & Joiner, T. E. (2004). Suicide attempts associated with externalizing psychopathology in an epidemiological sample. *American Journal of Psychiatry, 161*, 444–451.

Waid, W. M. (1976). Skin conductance response to both signalled and unsignalled noxious stimulation predicts level of socialization. *Journal of Personality and Social Psychology, 34*, 923–929.

Widom, C. S. (1977). A methodology for studying noninstitutionalized psychopaths. *Journal of Consulting and Clinical Psychology, 45*, 674–683.

Widiger, T. A., Cadoret, R., Hare, R., Robins, L., Rutherford, M., Zanarini, M., . . . Frances, A. (1996). DSM-IV antisocial personality disorder field trial. *Journal of Abnormal Psychology, 105*, 3–16.

Wiggins, J. S. (1982). Circumplex models of interpersonal behavior in clinical psychology. In P. C. Kendall & J. N. Butcher (Eds.), *Handbook of research methods in clinical psychology* (pp. 183–221). New York: Wiley.

Williams, K. M., Paulhus, D. L., & Hare, R. D. (2007). Capturing the four-factor structure of psychopathy in college students via self-report. *Journal of Personality Assessment, 88*, 205–219.

Young, S. E., Stallings, M. C., Corley, R. P., Krauter, K. S., & Hewitt, J. K. (2000). Genetic and environmental influences on behavioral disinhibition. *American Journal of Medical Genetics (Neuropsychiatric Genetics), 96*, 684–695.

CHAPTER TWELVE

Forensic Assessment of Psychopathy

Noah C. Venables and Jason R. Hall

The utility of the psychopathy construct—and specific assessment instruments such as Hare's Psychopathy Checklist–Revised (PCL-R; Hare, 1991, 2003)—in the prediction of crime and violence remains one of the most intensely researched issues in the psychopathy field. This topic is of heightened importance when forensic evaluations of risk inform judicial decisions that will weigh individuals' civil liberties versus creating societal safeguards against those determined to pose a significant risk to others. The decision as to whether or not to release an individual back into the community, or to devote more resources toward managing an individual within an institution, places considerable pressure on those in forensic, clinical, and criminal justice settings to accurately determine risk and make judgments regarding whether perceived costs (e.g., financial, restrictions on civil liberties) outweigh the perceived benefit of increased community safety. As discussed elsewhere in this series, there are general debates as to the accuracy in predicting risk for future crime and violence; however, as discussed in the current chapter, there are specific debates regarding the utility of the psychopathy construct and assessment tools such as the PCL-R in the prediction of dangerousness, violence risk, recidivism, and decision making regarding sentencing and institutional placement.

In this chapter, we review the use of the psychopathy construct, and in particular, the use of the PCL-R in the context of forensic risk assessment.

Toward this end, we begin by discussing the theoretical roots of psychopathy and how differing theoretical orientations have shaped our current understanding of this multifaceted construct. We next discuss the evolution of assessment instruments designed to measure psychopathy, including the development of Hare's PCL-R and its impact in the field of psychopathy research, and the use of self-report instruments such as the Psychopathic Personality Inventory (PPI; Lilienfeld & Andrews, 1996; Lilienfeld & Widows, 2005). We then survey the existing literature regarding the predictive validity of the PCL-R and PPI in relation to future antisocial behavior, including general and violent recidivism and institutional misconduct. We then conclude with recommendations for future research on the forensic assessment of psychopathy.

Historical Accounts of Psychopathy

Before we begin to discuss contemporary assessment instruments, we find it appropriate to first briefly describe the historical perspectives of psychopathy that have influenced a field devoted to the assessment of problematic traits and behaviors that define the syndrome. Early accounts of the psychopathy syndrome placed clear emphasis on violent, aggressive, exploitative, and antisocial behaviors, presumably owing to the salience of such behaviors in individuals who otherwise appear relatively normal and rational. Themes such as explosive, irresponsible, reckless, and impulsive behaviors received much emphasis in the description of psychopathy (Partridge, 1928a, 1928b; Pinel, 1962; Prichard, 1835). These features are largely what would now be considered to be the disinhibitory (Gorenstein & Newman, 1980) or externalizing (Krueger et al., 2002; Patrick, Hicks, Krueger, & Lang, 2005) features of psychopathy included in modern conceptualizations of the syndrome. Partridge (1928a, 1928b) described "sociopathic" individuals as being emotionally labile, often suffering from feelings of inadequacy or inferiority, alienated, and as being impulsively aggressive (rather than aggressing for instrumental—goal and resource seeking—reasons). Disinhibitory/externalizing features that include dysregulated emotionality (negative affect in particular) and impulsive forms of violence and aggression are characteristic of high externalizing individuals (cf. Patrick & Bernat, 2009; Venables & Patrick, 2012) and, as discussed in greater detail below, represents one main facet of the current conceptualization of psychopathy.

Another set of features that were described in early accounts of psychopathy that clearly differ—and perhaps are at odds with—the externalizing/disinhibitory features described above portrays the psychopath as exhibiting social poise and charm, confidence, interpersonal dominance and efficacy, persuasiveness, and exhibiting a notable absence of emotionality. Kraepelin (1904) described a group he labeled as "swindlers," whom he characterized as charming and glib, but who clearly lacked meaningful attachment and loyalty to others. The individuals described by Kraepelin (1904) often engaged in defrauding others and were con artists who amassed large amounts of debt that went unpaid. Schneider (1934) characterized "self-seeking" psychopaths as exhibiting similar superficial interpersonal features, in addition to egocentricity, demanding the attention of others, and deficient or abnormal emotionality in their interactions with others. These interpersonal features describe psychopathic individuals whose pathological deceit and fraudulent behaviors, coupled with deficient emotionality, are characteristic of their interactions with others. Indeed, this set of features would receive prominent attention in Cleckley's (1941/1976) conceptualization of the psychopath.

Cleckley's classic monograph *The Mask of Sanity* was first published in 1941 and has served as the foundation for modern conceptualization and measurement of psychopathy. Hervey Cleckley was a psychiatrist in an inpatient psychiatric facility where he took note of a group of patients who appeared quite different than the typical patient suffering from severe psychopathology. Central to Cleckley's description of psychopathic individuals was the outward appearance of robust mental health that masked a deep characterological disturbance. In contrast to patients observed to be irrational, disturbed, agitated, and withdrawn, psychopathic patients presented as confident, affable, and psychologically well-adjusted at first blush. It was only through continued observation across a variety of settings before the masked disturbance of the psychopathic individual was unveiled, including affective and interpersonal shallowness and irresponsible and unreliable behaviors. Cleckley's account of psychopathy in *The Mask of Sanity* was largely based on several illustrative case examples, from which he formulated a list of 16 criterion-based items as the initial basis for the systematic assessment of psychopathy. As illustrated by Patrick (2006), the 16 items can be grouped into three main conceptual categories (see Table 12.1): (1) positive adjustment features including superficial charm and "good" intelligence, absence of delusional and grossly irrational thinking, absence of nervousness, and suicide rarely carried out; (2) behavioral deviance items including "unreliability," sexual deviancy and promiscuity, impulsive and antisocial behavior, failure to learn from experience, devoid of any coherent life plan, and enhanced recklessness under states of intoxication; and (3) indicators of deficient emotionality and shallow interpersonal style such as lack of remorse or shame, poverty

Table 12.1 Cleckley's (1941/1976) 16 Diagnostic Criteria for Psychopathy Grouped According to Conceptual Categories

Conceptual Category	Criterion/Symptom Label
Positive Adjustment Features	1. Superficial charm and good "intelligence"
	2. Absence of delusions and other signs of irrational thinking
	3. Absence of "nervousness" or psychoneurotic manifestations
	14. Suicide rarely carried out
Persistent Behavioral Deviance	7. Inadequately motivated antisocial behavior
	8. Poor judgment and failure to learn by experience
	4. Unreliability
	13. Fantastic and uninviting behavior with drink and sometimes without
	15. Sex life impersonal, trivial, and poorly integrated
	16. Failure to follow a life plan
Affective-Interpersonal Deficits	5. Untruthfulness and insincerity
	6. Lack of remorse or shame
	9. Pathological egocentricity and incapacity for love
	10. General poverty in major affective reactions
	11. Specific loss of insight
	12. Unresponsiveness in general interpersonal relations

Source: Patrick (2006).

in emotional reactivity, egocentricity and incapacity for love, untruthfulness and insincerity, absence of loyalty and interpersonal unresponsiveness, and deficient insight.

It is notable that Cleckley (1941/1976) did not describe psychopaths as being particularly aggressive, violent, or cruel toward others. Rather, he surmised that the lack of emotional reactivity (including angry/hostile reactivity) might in fact serve as a protective buffer against outburst of anger and violence. Cleckley's contribution to the field of psychopathy assessment is in his focus on personality characteristics and features beyond antisocial and deviant behaviors. As such, he described the possibility for "successful" psychopaths, that is, individuals who appear to possess many of the core emotional and interpersonal features of the syndrome, but go on to have successful careers as doctors, lawyers, scholars, politicians, and businessmen (cf. Hall & Benning, 2006; Lykken, 1995). As such, Cleckley placed a clear emphasis on psychopathy developing from a core lack of emotionality, akin to semantic aphasia in the domain of language processing, where an individual may understand a subset of words or phrases but fail to see the broader significance or whole picture. Similarly, psychopathy is the likely result of a deficit in emotional processing, whereas overt problematic behaviors are symptomatic expressions of this core deficit.

However, not all writers on the topic of psychopathy in the mid-twentieth century were in agreement on the conceptualization of the syndrome. For example, McCord and McCord's (1964) *The Psychopath: An Essay on the Criminal Mind* placed an emphasis on disinhibited, cruel, and exploitative behaviors in addition to emotional coldness and social detachment. The McCords and Cleckley were in agreement that psychopaths were devoid of anxiousness and exhibited affective impairments; however, the McCords viewed the emotional disturbances as reflecting a deep social disconnectedness ("lovelessness" and "guiltlessness") rather than a global poverty of affect. Psychopaths were described as responding to threatening situations out of fury and anger rather than fear due to the lack of social connectedness and inhibitions against aggression. Whereas Cleckley described psychopaths as being neither "deeply vicious" nor "explosive," the McCords placed clear emphasis on criminal psychopaths as being vicious, emotionally cold, and predatory in nature. Robins (1966, 1978) also placed an emphasis on early developing and persistent impulsive and aggressive behaviors in her account of disturbed youths who later became "sociopathic" adults. The developmental account and emphasis on impulsive-aggressive behaviors posited by Robins served as the framework for the modern psychiatry conceptualization of antisocial personality disorder (ASPD) included in the third and fourth editions of the *Diagnostic and Statistical Manual of Mental Disorders* (DSM-III, DSM-IV; American Psychiatric Association, 1980, 2000), which places emphasis on aggressive, destructive, and rule-breaking behaviors in childhood and illegal, deceitful, impulsive, reckless, and irresponsible behaviors in adulthood.

It is important to note that, while Cleckley's (1941/1976) views were influenced by his work in inpatient psychiatric facilities, the McCords' (1964) account was based on their experiences with psychopathic adult criminal offenders, and Robins's (1966, 1978) view was influenced by her work with troubled youth. Cleckley's emphasis on the emotional and interpersonal features may in part have been influenced by his observations of patients who were largely of higher rather than lower socioeconomic status, who may have possessed the familial support and financial resources that served to help avoid the legal consequences of their actions. In contrast, others such as the McCords and Robins described a subgroup of youth and adults who engaged in persistent antisocial behavior, but were distinguishable through their severity, persistence, and lack of morality. These antisocial individuals were remarkable in their aggressiveness, affective coldness, and indifference for the rights, feelings, and welfare of others as inferred through predatory exploitation of their victims. Such individuals often came from impoverished and abusive backgrounds, and whose serious and persistent antisocial behaviors were grounds for repeated penalties imposed by the criminal justice system. As such, McCord and McCord (1964) posited that abuse and neglect were significant risk factors in the development of criminal psychopathy, which contrasts with Cleckley's etiological account of psychopathy stemming from traits involving deficient emotionality (see Lykken, 1995, for a contemporary description of temperamental versus environmental influences on antisocial behavior).

In summary, differing conceptualizations of psychopathy have contributed multiple perspectives of the syndrome, which have served as the foundation from which contemporary conceptualizations and approaches to assessment have emerged. Cleckley (1941/1976) described psychopathy as a paradoxical syndrome in which surface-level positive adjustment features (e.g., charm, intelligence, and a lack of nervousness or psychopathology) provides a façade that masks the psychopaths' irresponsible and impulsive behaviors that stem from deficient emotionality and a shallow interpersonal style. As discussed further below, contemporary clinical diagnostic instruments that operationalize psychopathy as a unitary condition (rather than multifaceted) appear to index the syndrome with less accordance with Cleckley's conceptualization than do instruments that explicitly operationalize psychopathy as a multifaceted constellation of traits and behaviors (cf. Patrick, Fowles, & Krueger, 2009). Also influential in shaping modern psychopathy assessment were Cleckley's contemporaries, who wrote on the topic based on their research and experience in working with criminal offenders and described psychopaths as emotionless predators. Whereas Cleckley described individuals who were affable and seemingly well intended but also ineffectual, irresponsible, and untrustworthy, McCord and McCord (1964) portrayed psychopaths as cold and exploitative in their interactions with others. As discussed further below, contemporary assessment and diagnostic instruments more so reflect this latter conceptualization, though despite indexing psychopathy as a unitary construct, nonetheless appear to tap separable affective-interpersonal and antisocial-behavioral deviance features.

Clinical Diagnostic Assessment: Hare's Psychopathy Checklist

The dominant contemporary diagnostic tool for the assessment of psychopathy in adult forensic settings is Hare's Psychopathy Checklist–Revised (PCL-R; Hare, 2003). Hare's initial efforts toward a reliable and empirically validated clinical diagnostic instrument for the assessment of psychopathy consisted of a global ratings system that was based on Cleckley's (1976) description, in which a diagnostic rating from 1 to 7 was assigned to indicate an individual's likeness to a prototypical psychopath (1 = clearly non-psychopathic, 7 = definitely psychopathic). However, these ratings required considerable experience and knowledge of Cleckley's conceptualization and were not easy to disseminate to other researchers or clinicians (Hare, 1980). The original PCL consisted of 22 items that were chosen from a larger item pool on the basis of how effectively as a set they discriminated between high and low scores on the global ratings system. Each item of the PCL is coded on a three-point scale (0, 1, 2) according to the extent to which an individual appears to meet the item criteria. Sources of information include a semi-structured clinical interview and review of case history information contained within institutional files. The standard interview covers a range of topics including education, employment history, family and home life background, relationships and children, and drug and alcohol use. The subsequent revised version (PCL-R; Hare, 1991) dropped two items ("previous diagnosis of psychopathy or similar" and "antisocial behavior not due to alcohol intoxication") and the scoring criteria for the 20 remaining items changed slightly (see Table 12.2 for a list of PCL-R items). The items and scoring criteria remained the same in the most recent edition of the PCL-R (2nd ed.; Hare, 2003) as they were in the first (Hare, 1991). The PCL-R manual provides a description of each item and information to be used in making decisions on rating individuals. Scores on the 20 items can be summed to yield a global/total psychopathy score, and score cutoffs (Hare, 2003) are used to designate an individual as psychopathic (PCL-R total score $\geq$ 30), non-psychopathic ($\leq$ 20), or intermediate (total scores between 20 and 30). Total psychopathy scores of the PCL-R are quite reliable, with interrater reliability coefficients often > .8 (Hare, 2003).

The popularity of the PCL-R has led to the development of similar instruments for use in settings other than adult forensic/correctional populations. A shortened version, the Psychopathy Checklist: Screening Version (PCL:SV; Hart, Cox, & Hare, 1995), was initially developed as a time-saving screening instrument for use in forensic/criminal settings, but also for use with civil psychiatric patients, with community samples, and in personnel selection. The procedures for rating the PCL:SV are quite similar to those for the PCL-R. In addition, scores on the PCL:SV are strongly correlated with PCL-R scores (weighted $r \sim .8$; Hart et al., 1995). Whereas a score of 30 out of 40 on the PCL-R is the recommended cutoff score for a catergorical diagnosis of psychopathy (Hare, 2003), the

Table 12.2 Items, Facets, and Factors of the Psychopathy Checklist–Revised (PCL-R)

Factor 1: Affective-Interpersonal		Factor 2: Impulsive-Antisocial	
Interpersonal Facet	Affective Facet	Lifestyle Facet	Antisocial Facet
Glibness/ superficial charm	Lack of remorse or guilt	Need for stimulation/ proneness to boredom	Poor behavioral controls
Grandiose sense of self-worth	Shallow affect	Parasitic lifestyle	Early behavioral problems
Pathological lying	Callousness/ lacks empathy	Lack of realistic long-term goals	Juvenile delinquency
Conning/ manipulativeness	Failure to accept responsibility for own action	Impulsivity Irresponsibility	Revocation of conditional release Criminal versatility

Note: Two items from the PCL-R are not included in this factor structure: Promiscuous sexual behavior; Many short-term marital relationships.
Source: Hare (2003).

corresponding cutoff for the PCL:SV is 18 (Hart et al., 1995). The factor structure of the PCL:SV mirrors that of the PCL-R (discussed below), and evidence suggests that the pattern of external correlates is highly similar between the two measures (Hart et al., 1995; Hare & Neumann, 2006).

Two other derivatives of the PCL-R have been developed for use with psychopathic and antisocial youth: the Psychopathy Checklist Youth Version (PCL:YV; Forth, Kosson, & Hare, 1997, 2003) and the Antisocial Process Screening Device (APSD; Frick & Hare, 2001; Frick, O'Brien, Wooton, & McBurnett, 1994). Both the PCL:YV and APSD are 20-item measures adapted from the PCL-R to provide a "downward" extension of the psychopathy construct for the measurement of relevant traits and behaviors in adolescents. The specific items and scoring criteria were adapted to reflect more developmentally appropriate content for use with adolescents (e.g., "many short term marital relationships" was removed) and to better index adolescents' peer groups, family, and academic-related experiences (e.g., the scoring of the "irresponsibility" item evaluates concern for school work). It is assumed that PCL-R/SV psychopathy is largely the same construct in adolescents and adults (the use of the PCL: YV is recommended for ages 12–18 years old; Hart et al., 1995).

The procedures for administering the PCL:YV and APSD differ. The procedures for administering the PCL:YV largely parallel those used for the PCL-R. That is, it is intended for use by highly trained raters who utilize information obtained in a semi-structured interview with the youth and a review of criminal or other available institutional records. In contrast, either parents or teachers can complete the APSD as a ratings scale (for 6- to 13-year-olds), or self-report information can be provided by adolescents' aged 13–18 years old. Specific scales emphasize emotional deficits (callous-unemotional traits), interpersonal dominance and narcissism, impulsive/irresponsible behaviors, and (for the PCL:YV) criminality and antisocial behaviors (e.g., Fite, Greening, Stoppelbein, & Fabiano, 2009; Salekin, 2006; Salekin, Brannen, Zalot, Leistico, & Neumann, 2006).

PCL-R Factor Structure and External Correlates

Factor analytic work on the structure of the PCL-R has provided evidence suggesting two (Harpur, Hare, & Hakstian, 1989), or alternatively, three (Cooke & Michie, 2001) or four (Hare, 2003; Hare & Neumann, 2006), moderately correlated but distinguishable item subsets or "factors" underlying PCL-R scores. Although there is accumulating evidence for the discriminant validity of PCL-R scores based on three (Hall, Benning, & Patrick, 2004) and four (Kennealy, Hicks, & Patrick, 2007; Hare & Neumann, 2006) factor models, most research to date examining the validity of separable psychopathy dimensions has focused on the two-factor model (Hare, 1991; Harpur et al., 1989). Table 12.2 provides the items labels along with factors/facets each item most strongly loads onto (as discussed below). PCL-R Factor 1 represents the core affective-interpersonal features of psychopathy in terms of items such as callousness/lack of empathy, deficient depth and breadth of emotional experience, failure to accept responsibility for actions, glibness and superficial charm, grandiosity, pathological lying, and conning/manipulativeness. Factor 2 indexes behavioral deviancy and impulsive-antisocial tendencies through PCL-R items that focus on chronic impulsive and irresponsive behavior, stimulation seeking, poor behavioral controls, failure to establish a life plan, and antisocial behavior beginning in childhood and continuing into adulthood. PCL-R factor scores typically exhibit moderate correlations ($r \sim .5$; Hare, 2003). The items of the PCL-R are viewed as having a hierarchical organization (Hare & Neumann, 2006), in which items comprising its affective-interpersonal (Factor 1) and antisocial deviance (Factor 2) components can be further subdivided into facets reflecting social guile and manipulativeness (Interpersonal facet), callous-unemotionality (Affective facet), impulsive-irresponsible tendencies (Lifestyle facet), and antisocial behaviors in childhood through adulthood (Antisocial facet). A similar factor structure has been found in the PCL:YV (for reviews, see Kotler & McMahon, 2010; Salekin, 2006).

In support of the notion that the affective-interpersonal features of psychopathy demarcate a condition distinct from other impulse-related (externalizing) disorders, the two broad factors of the PCL-R show differing relations with a broad range of criterion variables—particularly after controlling for their shared variance, which can be viewed as indexing callous-aggressiveness (Patrick et al., 2009; Venables & Patrick, 2012) or antagonism (Lynam & Derefinko, 2006). In particular, variance specific to Factor 1 shows positive relations with trait measures of social dominance (Harpur et al., 1989; Verona, Patrick, & Joiner, 2001) and negative associations with measures of anxiety or fearfulness (Hicks & Patrick, 2006; Kennealy et al., 2007). By contrast, variance specific to Factor 2 shows *positive* relations with measures of anxiety and distress-proneness (Hicks & Patrick, 2006), as well as with measures of anger and hostility (Hicks & Patrick, 2006), impulsivity (Kennealy et al., 2007; Verona et al., 2001), substance abuse (Patrick et al., 2005; Reardon, Lang, & Patrick, 2002; Kennealy et al., 2007), and suicidality (Douglas et al., 2008; Verona et al., 2001; Verona, Hicks, & Patrick, 2005).

Not surprisingly, given the contrasting (in some cases opposing; e.g., Hicks & Patrick, 2006; Verona et al., 2005) external correlates of the two PCL-R factors, individuals scoring high on the PCL-R do not comprise a homogeneous group in terms of trait characteristics as indexed by measures other than the PCL-R. For example, a study by Hicks, Markon, Patrick, Krueger, and Newman (2004) that used model-based cluster analysis to classify the personality profiles of male offenders with high overall PCL-R scores ($\geq$ 30) identified two subgroups with markedly different profiles: (1) an "aggressive" subgroup with high scores on negative emotional traits (including anxiousness, alienation, and aggression) and low scores on traits reflecting planfulness and restraint; and (2) a "stable" subgroup low in anxiousness and high on traits reflecting agency (well-being, social dominance, and achievement). A subsequent study (Hicks, Vaidyanathan, & Patrick, 2010) that classified personality profiles of female offenders with high overall PCL-R scores (> 25)[1] yielded findings consistent with this: Two subgroups were identified, distinguished by low versus high negative emotional traits and high versus low impulsiveness. Consistent with this, a study by Skeem, Johansson, Andershed, Kerr, and Eno Louden (2007) that classified high PCL-R ($\geq$ 29) male offenders using scores of the PCL-R three-factor model (Cooke & Michie, 2001) and a measure of trait anxiety identified distinctive "primary" and "secondary" psychopathy subgroups differentiated most strongly by low versus high anxiousness. In turn, these findings dovetail with studies by Newman and colleagues (e.g., Lorenz & Newman, 2002) reporting markedly different patterns of performance on laboratory tasks for low- versus high-anxious subgroups of high-PCL-R offenders. The clear implication of these findings is that the PCL-R criteria for psychopathy does not capture a homogenous diagnostic condition; individuals identified as psychopathic by the PCL-R comprise at least two markedly different subgroups—one characterized by high anxiousness in particular, possibly in conjunction with heightened trait aggression and impulsivity; and another by low anxiousness and perhaps elevated levels of dominance and efficacy. This point is important to bear in mind when interpreting results from studies that have evaluated the utility of the PCL-R that rely upon total scores to define extreme groups.

Self-Report Assessment: The Psychopathic Personality Inventory

A counterpart to the PCL-R for assessing psychopathy in community as well as offender samples on the basis of self-report is the Psychopathic Personality Inventory (PPI; Lilienfeld & Andrews, 1996). The PPI was initially developed to provide an efficient questionnaire-based self-report instrument to index psychopathy consistent with Cleckley's (1941/1976) conceptualization. The 187-item PPI, which is now available in a shorted 154-item revised form (PPI-R; Lilienfeld & Widows, 2005), contains eight unidimensional subscales (Machiavellian Egocentricity, Social Potency [renamed to Social Influence in PPI-R], Fearlessness, Impulsive Nonconformity [Rebellious Nonconformity in PPI-R], Alienation [Blame Externalization in PPI-R], Carefree Nonplanfulness, Stress Immunity, and Coldheartedness). Notably, the PPI/PPI-R does not directly contain items pertaining to criminality or antisocial behaviors, nor was the instrument developed with any preconceived notions as to the higher-order structure of the inventory, and in turn, the psychopathy construct. Factor analytic work on the structure of the PPI (e.g., Benning, Patrick, Hicks, Blonigen, & Krueger, 2003; Ross, Benning, Patrick, Thompson, & Thurston, 2009) has suggested that seven of the eight PPI subscales reflect two higher-order factors: PPI-I (*Fearless Dominance*; Benning, Patrick, Blonigen, Hicks, & Iacono, 2005a) and PPI-II (*Impulsive Antisociality*; Benning et al., 2005a; also referred to as *Self-Centered Impulsivity*; Lilienfeld & Widows, 2005). Whereas the PCL-R factors exhibit a moderate correlation, the PPI-I and PPI-II largely emerge as uncorrelated (for a review see Marcus, Fulton, & Edens, in press). Coldheartedness, the remaining PPI subscale, emerges as largely independent of the PPI higher-order factors.

As with the PCL-R, a growing body of evidence has accumulated for distinctive affective-interpersonal and impulsive-antisocial deviancy factors to the PPI that, although not equivalent to the interview-based PCL-R factors (Blonigen et al., 2010), do show similar patterns of relations with external criterion variables (Benning, Patrick, Salekin, & Leistico, 2005b; Blonigen et al., 2010; Poythress et al., 2010). Scores on PPI-I are associated with emotional resiliency/stability (e.g., lower anxiousness and depression) and social poise (e.g., well-being, assertiveness), increased narcissistic tendencies and thrill-seeking behaviors, and deficient empathy. As with Factor 2 of the PCL-R, scores on PPI-II are more indicative of maladaptive traits and behaviors that are largely consistent with externalizing psychopathology (cf. Venables & Patrick, 2012)—including child and adult antisocial behaviors, problematic substance use, impulsivity and aggressiveness, negative emotionality, and suicidal ideation (Benning et al., 2005a; Benning et al., 2005b; Blonigen, Hicks, Krueger, Patrick, & Iacono, 2005; Douglas et al., 2008; Marcus et al., in press; Patrick, Edens, Poythress, Lilienfeld, & Benning, 2006; Ross et al., 2009).

The foregoing review of historical perspectives and contemporary assessment instruments strongly suggests that psychopathy is not a unitary syndrome. Despite being designed to assess psychopathy as a unitary construct, the affective-interpersonal and impulsive-antisocial factors of the PCL-R consistently show diverging patterns of associations with external criteria in the domains of personality and psychopathology (as presently reviewed), but also in the domain of neurobiology (see Patrick & Bernat, 2009, for a review). The heterogeneity of psychopathy is important to bear in mind in the following section, in which we discuss the utility of the psychopathy construct and specific assessment instruments such as the PCL-R and PPI/PPI-R in the context of forensic risk assessment. There are several important questions we seek to address in subsequent sections: What is important about psychopathy in the prediction of risk or dangerousness—i.e., affective-interpersonal traits or impulsive-antisocial features? Do the two main factors of psychopathy interact to predict dangerousness or risk in a multiplicative fashion above and beyond either dimension alone? Does psychopathy provide incremental validity over purpose-built risk assessment tools in forensic applications? As we discuss below, the utility of psychopathy in the domain of forensic assessments determining risk and dangerousness largely hinges on the answers to these important questions.

Psychopathy and Prediction of Recidivism and Violence

In the three decades since its initial development, the PCL (and its variants) have increasingly been utilized in a variety of legal contexts, both criminal and civil, to aid in the prediction of future risk for crime and violence. In fact, recent surveys of forensic practitioners in the United States have revealed that the PCL-R is among the most commonly used clinical instruments for assessing future risk (Lally, 2003)—for instance, in cases regarding commitment pursuant to sexual predator laws, civil commitment, parole determinations, institutional placement, death penalty sentencing, sentence enhancement/mitigation, and transfer from juvenile to adult courts (Walsh & Walsh, 2006; Zinger & Forth, 1998). Furthermore, courts in the United States have generally found PCL assessments of psychopathy to meet both *Frye* and *Daubert* standards for admission as scientific evidence, particularly in cases involving Caucasian male defendants—although the PCL has been challenged on the grounds that the measure has not been sufficiently validated as a predictor of future dangerousness in other ethnic groups, or among female offenders (Walsh & Walsh, 2006).

The link between psychopathy (particularly as measured by the PCL family of instruments) and antisocial behavior has been firmly established by a substantial volume of research (for a review, see Leistico, Salekin, DeCoster, & Rogers, 2008)—although the issue of whether crime represents a corollary of psychopathic personality features versus a core component of the syndrome remains a matter of vigorous debate (Hare & Neumann, 2010; Skeem & Cooke, 2010). As argued by Hare and Neumann (2009), the association between psychopathy and antisocial behavior is a logical one:

> [M]any of the characteristics important for inhibiting antisocial and violent behavior—empathy, close emotional bonds, fear of punishment, guilt—are lacking or seriously deficient in psychopathic people. Moreover, their egocentricity, grandiosity, sense of entitlement, impulsivity, general lack of behavioural inhibitions, and need for power and control constitute what may be described as a prescription for the commission of antisocial acts. (p. 796)

In light of such assumptions, a critical question that has driven a great deal of research in this area is whether measures of psychopathy can in fact adequately *predict* future misconduct—particularly general and violent crime, institutional behavior problems, and sexual offending. This topic has been the subject of numerous empirical studies, several literature reviews (Douglas, Vincent, & Edens, 2006; Hare & Neumann, 2008, 2009; Hart, 1998; Hemphill & Hart, 2003; Skeem, Polaschek, Patrick, & Lilienfeld, 2011), as well as multiple meta-analytic investigations (Campbell, French, & Gendreau, 2009; Edens & Campbell, 2007; Edens, Campbell, & Weir, 2007; Gendreau, Goggin, & Smith, 2002; Guy, Edens, Anthony, & Douglas, 2005; Hemphill, Hare, & Wong, 1998; Kennealy, Skeem, Walters, & Camp, 2010; Leistico et al., 2008; Salekin, Rogers, & Sewell, 1996; Singh, Grann, & Fazel, 2011; Walters, 2003a, 2003b; Walters, Knight, Grann, & Dahl, 2008; Yang, Wong, & Coid, 2010). Given the sheer volume of research in this area, an exhaustive review of this literature would be well beyond the scope of this chapter; rather, our intent is to focus on the results of meta-analytic research in order to highlight consistent trends regarding (1) relative contributions of the two psychopathy factors to prediction of future misconduct, and (2) incremental validity of psychopathy scales vis-à-vis purpose-built risk assessment tools.

Psychopathy Factors and Recidivism

Meta-analytic studies examining the question of whether psychopathy assessments can accurately predict recidivism have focused almost exclusively on the PCL family of measures (i.e., the PCL, PCL-R, PCL:SV, and PCL:YV—referred to collectively in this section by the generic term "PCL" when multiple versions are referenced, e.g., meta-analyses that include the PCL, PCL-R, and/or PCL:SV). Early meta-analytic research in this area (e.g., Salekin et al., 1996), which reported effect sizes in the moderate to large range (Cohen's $d = .79$) for total PCL scores in the prediction of violence, has often been criticized for including both prospective and retrospective outcome measures (see Gendreau et al., 2002), thus inflating psychopathy-recidivism relationships due to criterion contamination and thereby overstating the predictive validity of the PCL. Subsequent meta-analyses, which focused instead on studies that used prospective outcome measures, have consistently revealed a small-to-moderate, but significant relationship between PCL total scores and future misconduct, including institutional behavior problems as well as general and violent recidivism. This effect is evident for both male (Hart, Kropp, & Hare, 1988; Serin, Peters, & Barbaree, 1990) and female (Richards, Casey, & Lucente, 2003; Salekin, Rogers, Ustad, & Sewell, 1998) offenders, juvenile offenders (Gretton, McBride, Hare, O'Shaugnessy, & Kumka, 2001), forensic psychiatric inpatients (Gustafson et al., 1998; Harris, Rice, & Cormier, 1991), community samples (Neumann & Hare, 2008), and offenders with serious mental disorders (Dolan & Davies, 2006; Tengstrom, Grann, Langstrom, & Kullgren, 2000) and intellectual disabilities (Gray, Fitzgerald, Taylor, MacCulloch, & Snowden, 2007); the effect also generalizes well to European samples (Hare, Clark, Grann, & Thornton, 2000). As reviewed by Leistico and colleagues (2008), predictive validity of PCL scores have generally been stronger: (1) in samples of Caucasian offenders (compared to offenders of other ethnic groups); (2) among males (compared to females); (3) when longer follow-up intervals are used; and (4) in studies conducted outside the United States. Of note, the PCL does exhibit adequate predictive validity for general and violent recidivism among sexual offenders, but is less useful in the prediction of sexual reoffending *per se* (Barbaree, Seto, Langton, & Peacock, 2001)—although some studies have indicated that the interaction of PCL scores with measures of deviant sexual arousal (e.g., phallometric testing) greatly improve the prediction of sexual violence (Harris et al., 2003; Rice & Harris, 1997).

Thus, it is clear that the PCL measures demonstrate some degree of predictive validity with regard to future antisocial behavior. However, as reviewed above, PCL psychopathy comprises two correlated but distinct factors (see Table 12.2): one reflecting notable interpersonal-affective features that distinguish psychopathy from general antisocial conduct (and the much more common diagnosis of antisocial personality disorder), such as superficial charm, narcissism, conning/deceptiveness, lack of empathy or remorse, and shallow emotions (Factor 1); and the other factor consisting of features reflecting a chronically antisocial and disorganized lifestyle, including impulsivity, irresponsibility, parasitic reliance on others, lack of a life plan, poor behavioral controls, and an early-onset, persistent pattern of rule violation/crime (Factor 2). To what extent do these two distinct components of psychopathy relate to prediction of future antisocial behavior? This question gets at the heart of whether assessment of the distinguishing personality features of psychopathy aids in the prediction of criminal behavior above and beyond assessment of more general antisocial tendencies. Hare and colleagues (Hare, 2003; Hare & Neumann, 2008, 2009) have consistently argued that assessment of Factor 1 traits yields unique information relevant to judgments regarding risk for future misconduct. In particular, it has been argued that Factor 1 is predictive of higher levels of instrumental or "cold-blooded" (i.e., goal-oriented) violence, as opposed to highly emotional, reactive forms of violence (i.e., in response to perceived provocation), and that the crimes of psychopathic individuals tend to be more brutal or violent in nature.

Several meta-analyses have evaluated the predictive validity of the two PCL factors separately, and these studies have consistently indicated that

Factor 2—which assesses general antisocial features that are not specific to psychopathy—is more strongly related to future antisocial conduct than Factor 1 (Edens & Campbell, 2007; Edens et al., 2007; Gendreau et al., 2002; Guy et al., 2005; Hemphill et al., 1998; Kennealy et al, 2010; Leistico et al., 2008; Walters, 2003b; Walters et al., 2008; Yang et al., 2010). The relative superiority of Factor 2 for prediction of antisocial behavior holds true across various outcome measures, including general and violent recidivism and institutional misconduct. Although to date no meta-analyses have evaluated the relative predictive validity of the two PPI factors, several individual studies using retrospective measures of antisocial behavior have found a pattern of results that largely parallels findings from studies using the PCL (Edens & McDermott, 2010; Patrick et al., 2006; Poythress et al., 2010; Uzieblo, Verschuere, Van den Bussche, & Crombez, 2009; Vaughn, Howard, & DeLisi, 2008)—although far fewer studies utilizing the PPI have used prospective outcome measures. In two studies that did use prospective measures of antisocial behavior, Edens and colleagues (Edens, Poythress, Lilienfeld, & Patrick, 2008; Edens, Poythress, Lilienfeld, Patrick, & Test, 2008) found that PPI-II (Impulsive Antisociality/ Self-Centered Impulsivity) exhibits substantially stronger correlations (compared to PPI-I Fearless Dominance) with aggressive institutional infractions. The latter of these two studies also found PPI-II to be significantly related to total, aggressive, and nonaggressive infractions, whereas PPI-I was essentially unrelated to institutional misconduct. However, the former study did find PPI-I to be associated with total disciplinary charges, and nonaggressive infractions in particular.

Although the studies reviewed above may shed light on the relative strength of the associations between the two psychopathy factors and future antisocial behavior, another key issue to consider when evaluating the predictive validity of psychopathy scales is whether they exhibit additive or interactive effects—that is, when the two factors are considered jointly, is prediction of recidivism or violence substantially enhanced? Hare and Neumann (2009) have argued that the two PCL factors interact in a manner that is potentially informative regarding risk for violence, noting, "Simple comparisons of the predictive validity of the PCL factors should be tempered by consideration of the interactive effects of these factors" (p. 794). In support of this argument, Hare and Neumann cite evidence from two empirical studies that have reported a significant interaction between the two factors in prediction of violence (Harpur & Hare, 1991; Walsh & Kosson, 2008), concluding that, "high scores on both psychopathy factors are what represents a case of psychopathy and that the combination of these two factors is what puts people at heightened risk for violence" (p. 794). In contrast, Skeem and Mulvey (2001)—using a different index of violence from the same sample used by Walsh and Kosson (2008)—failed to find a significant Factor 1–by–Factor 2 interaction effect for violence prediction. In a recent meta-analysis, Kennealy and colleagues (2010) directly tested the hypotheses that: (1) the two factors of the PCL combine additively (i.e., both contribute uniquely after controlling for the other) to predict violence; and (2) that the two PCL factors interact to effectively multiply risk for violence at high levels of both trait scales. Consistent with prior research, this study found much stronger unique predictive validity for Factor 2 (Cohen's d = .40) than for Factor 1 (Cohen's d = .11), suggesting that the interpersonal-affective features of psychopathy contribute only modestly to prediction of violence, once antisocial deviance features are accounted for. Moreover, Kennealy et al. found no evidence of an interaction effect, indicating that joint elevation on both factors does not increase risk for violence multiplicatively beyond the additive effects of the two factors. Indeed, Kennealy et al. reported that Factor 2 alone would predict future violence more accurately than Factor 1 alone or the Factor 1–by–Factor 2 interaction in the vast majority of studies evaluated (81% and 96%, respectively).

To summarize, the balance of evidence regarding the predictive validity of the two psychopathy factors indicates that: (1) total psychopathy scores exhibit moderate correlations with future antisocial behavior, including general and violent recidivism and institutional behavior problems; (2) the antisocial deviance factor of psychopathy (whether measured via the PCL or PPI) exhibits markedly higher correlations with future antisocial behavior, relative to the distinctive interpersonal-affective features that are more unique to the psychopathy construct (although more research is needed to further evaluate the predictive validity of the PPI using prospective outcome measures); (3) after controlling for antisocial deviance features, the interpersonal-affective features of psychopathy contribute (at best) modestly to the prediction of violence; and (4) the two factors of the PCL do not interact to predict violence. Clearly, the antisocial deviance features of psychopathy are superior predictors of future antisocial behavior in comparison to the interpersonal-affective features, whether measured via the PCL or PPI (although comparatively few studies have assessed the predictive validity of the PPI). One plausible explanation for this finding is that the items of PCL Factor 2 in particular are largely indicative of externalizing proneness, which in turn predicts violence and crime. Consistent with this, high scores on Factor 2 are associated with greater problems with alcohol and drugs and elevated levels of disinhibitory personality traits (Hare, 2003), and recent work confirms a strong association between PCL-R Factor 2 and a latent factor accounting for the comorbidity among common externalizing disorders (i.e., antisocial personality disorder and alcohol/substance use disorders; Patrick et al., 2005). However, an alternative possibility has to do with predictor/criterion overlap. That is, scores on Factor 2 of the PCL-R in part reflect the occurrence of criminal behavior in childhood as well as adulthood (e.g., through items dealing with early behavior problems, poor behavioral controls, and delinquency). This raises questions as to whether the part of Factor 2 that reflects past criminality and violence may be the key ingredient accounting for the ability of scores on the PCL-R to prospectively predict violence—i.e., past behavior predicting future behavior. A related inquiry is whether PCL-R-based diagnosis of psychopathy—which entails specialized training, a lengthy clinical interview, and detailed file review—offers incremental validity above and beyond purpose-built risk assessment measures. This latter question is addressed in the following section.

Psychopathy and Contemporary Approaches to Risk Assessment

Contemporary purpose-built risk assessment instruments such as the Violence Risk Appraisal Guide (VRAG; Quinsey, Harris, Rice, & Cormier, 1998), the Historical Clinical Risk Management-20 (HCR-20; Webster, Douglas, Eaves, & Hart, 1997), the Sexual Violence Risk-20 (SVR-20; Boer, Hart, Kropp, & Webster, 1997), and the Level of Service Inventory–Revised (LSI-R; Andrews & Bonta, 1995) have demonstrated that a standardized risk assessment approach—whether based on actuarial or structured clinical assessment—can significantly improve upon unstructured clinical judgment in the prediction of crime and violence (Skeem & Monahan, 2011). The PCL-R demonstrates fairly high correlations (with coefficients in the .6–.8 range) with multiple risk assessment measures, and PCL-R scores are in fact incorporated in the scoring of several measures, including both actuarial (e.g., the VRAG) and structured clinical instruments (e.g., the HCR-20 and SVR-20). Although the PCL measures exhibit a high degree of convergent validity with various risk assessment instruments, to what extent do they demonstrate incremental validity vis-à-vis contemporary risk assessment measures? In other words, do PCL-based assessments of psychopathy predict antisocial behaviors above and beyond purpose-built risk assessment instruments? As noted by Hare (2003), the purpose of the PCL measures is to assess and diagnose a personality disorder, not to predict crime or violence. Hare and Newman (2009) wrote, "the PCL-R and its derivatives reflect relatively static risk factors and are properly used as supplements to more general risk evaluation" (p. 797). Nonetheless, the immense popularity of the PCL measures in forensic risk assessment, which even surpasses tools developed expressly for the purpose of evaluating risk for future misconduct, necessitates a critical evaluation of the PCL's incremental validity in comparison to risk assessment measures.

Several meta-analyses have addressed this question by comparing the predictive validity of risk assessment measures side-by-side with the PCL-R. Gendreau et al. (2002), for instance, compared the PCL to the LSI-R, and found that the latter outperformed the PCL in prediction of general recidivism and (to a markedly lesser extent) violent recidivism. However, this study has since been criticized for inclusion of multiple unpublished findings of varying methodological quality, and for exclusion of several PCL studies with relevant data (Hemphill & Hare, 2004). Nevertheless, this finding generated considerable interest in light of the fact that the LSI-R is much quicker to administer and requires less training than the PCL-R, and is therefore more economical to administer. Similarly, Walters (2003a) found that the Lifestyle Criminality Screening Form (a brief instrument coded from institutional file data that requires no interview) performed as well as the PCL-R in the prediction of institutional behavior problems and general recidivism. In a meta-analytic comparison of multiple risk assessment measures that included both the PCL-R and the LSI-R, as well as the HCR-20 and VRAG, Campbell et al. (2009) found that all of the measures predicted violent recidivism equally well, although there was greater variability in prediction of violent institutional misconduct, and the predictive validity of the PCL varied considerably depending on the version of the instrument used (with a marked advantage for the PCL:SV over the PCL/PCL-R). Yang et al. (2010) compared nine risk assessment measures (including the PCL-R) on predictive validity for violence using multilevel regression across 28 studies, and found that all measures and their subscales predicted violence equally well, with the exception of PCL-R Factor 1, which did not exceed chance levels of prediction. Finally, in perhaps the most comprehensive meta-analytic comparison of risk assessment measures to date, Singh et al. (2011) compared predictive validities of 9 different risk assessment tools from 68 studies, comprising a total combined sample size of 25,980 participants across 88 independent samples in 13 countries. These authors reported that risk assessment tools designed specifically for evaluation of violence risk exhibited the highest predictive validity, whereas the PCL-R was among the poorest predictors. It should be noted, however, that this study did not examine predictive validity of the PCL-R factors separately, and that outcome measures (i.e., general versus violent recidivism, sexual offending, institutional behavior problems) were also not examined separately.

Taken as a whole, the studies reviewed above suggest that the predictive validity of PCL-R psychopathy is roughly on par with contemporary risk assessment instruments, although the PCL-R is outperformed in some instances by instruments designed specifically to predict violence. Considering that the PCL-R is designed to assess a personality construct, and was not intended as a risk assessment instrument *per se*, this finding speaks to the impressive overall construct validity of the PCL-R. However, direct tests of incremental validity—i.e., evaluating the predictive validity of one measure after statistically controlling for another via multivariate analysis—have tended to more strongly favor purpose-built risk assessment tools (Douglas, Ogloff, & Hart, 2003; Douglas, Ogloff, Nicholls, & Grant, 1999; Douglas, Yeomans, & Boer, 2005). In light of the fact that the PCL-R is among the most resource-intensive measures in forensic practice—both in terms of administration time and required training—these findings call into question whether routine assessment of psychopathy as the preferred index of violence risk is truly justified, given the range of more efficient alternatives. Furthermore, as noted by Skeem and colleagues (2011), many of the newer dynamic risk assessment measures include features that may be of greater practical use to clinicians, such as:

> [I]dentifying treatment targets, measuring treatment change, identifying acute changes in risk that can be used for day-to-day offender management, and assessment of specific types of violence risk. Commonly these instruments have also been validated so that probabilities of offending over fixed time periods can be inferred from specific ranges of scores. (p. 128)

Summary and Future Directions

Psychopathy is among the most widely researched personality disorders, and is perhaps the clinical construct of greatest interest to practitioners of forensic psychology and psychiatry. The frequency with which diagnoses of psychopathy are at issue in both civil and legal proceedings regarding prediction of future dangerousness has been steadily on the rise over the past three decades. In light of these developments, it is hardly surprising that one of the most active areas of research in the psychopathy field is the issue of whether psychopathy can adequately predict future antisocial behavior. The verdict, according to the extant literature reviewed here, appears to be a qualified "yes." Numerous empirical studies and well over a dozen meta-analyses have revealed a consistent trend for psychopathy (as measured by total scores on Hare's PCL and its derivatives, the PCL-R, PCL:SV, and PCL-YV) to predict a host of antisocial outcomes, including general and violent recidivism and institutional misconduct. Furthermore, this finding has been obtained across a variety of medico-legal settings and populations, including incarcerated offenders, sex offenders, forensic hospital inpatients, civil psychiatric inpatients, and community samples—albeit with some caveats owing to decreased predictive validity among female and minority offenders.

However, as we have discussed, psychopathy is a multifaceted construct, a notion rooted in historical conceptualizations of the disorder and supported by contemporary empirical research. Both the PCL-R and the self-report PPI reflect the multifaceted nature of psychopathy: both measures are underpinned by a latent two-factor structure, comprising (1) the distinctive interpersonal-affective features of psychopathy that distinguish it from other externalizing disorders, and (2) an antisocial deviance factor consisting of traits that are more generic to criminal offending and disinhibitory psychopathology more broadly. Several meta-analyses have now concluded that the PCL-R's predictive validity derives much more strongly from its assessment of the antisocial deviance features of psychopathy. Despite the intuitive appeal of certain personality features of psychopathy as predictors of violence, empirical research has largely negated this notion; the interpersonal-affective features that are unique to psychopathy contribute only modestly to prediction of antisocial behavior once Factor 2 is accounted for, and the two factors do not interact to predict violence.

Studies that have compared the predictive validity of the PCL-R against purpose-built risk assessment instruments have generally found PCL-R scores (particularly Factor 2) to be roughly equivalent to other measures that may be more economical to administer (in terms of required training and labor needed for administration); furthermore, PCL-R psychopathy (particularly Factor 1) is of questionable incremental validity relative to other risk assessment measures when evaluated in a multivariate framework. Taken together, these findings have clear implications for choice of assessment instrument in the context of forensic risk evaluation. In accord with recommendations by Hare (2003), we would argue that the PCL-R is not appropriate for use as a stand-alone risk assessment tool, and was never intended to be. Rather, the PCL-R is best utilized as a complement to other risk assessment indices that have been designed to predict specific outcomes, and can potentially yield valuable practical information for clinicians regarding treatment and management of antisocial behavior.

In closing, this review has highlighted several areas in which additional research is necessary. First, research on the predictive validity of the PCL-R in female offenders and in minority populations has generally yielded inconsistent and diminished effects when compared to findings for male Caucasian offenders, yet the reasons for these discrepancies remain unclear. Future research in this area that utilizes concurrent assessments of potential moderating variables (e.g., personality dimensions, history of trauma/abuse) would help to clarify issues regarding the generalizability of the PCL-R as it relates to violence and recidivism. Second, although evidence supporting the construct validity of the PPI has been steadily accumulating in recent years, very few studies have used prospective designs to evaluate its predictive validity with regard to future antisocial behavior. Given that one of the drawbacks of using the PCL-R is its lengthy administration time and training requirements, increased utilization of self-report personality-based psychopathy screenings may be utilized (notwithstanding issues of self-report psychopathy assessments; cf. Lilienfeld & Fowler, 2006). However, the predictive validity of the PPI will have to be more firmly established across settings and populations before more widespread adoption. Third, although numerous studies (and several meta-analyses) have compared predictive validity effect sizes for the PCL measures versus purpose-built risk assessment measures, relatively few have conducted direct tests of incremental validity, wherein the predictive effect of one measure is evaluated after statistically controlling for the other using multivariate analysis. Additional studies of this type would permit stronger inferences to be drawn regarding the incremental validity of the PCL-R in comparison to other risk assessment approaches.

Note

1. The use of a lower cutoff level in this study was based on prior research supporting a lower PCL-R total score threshold for a diagnosis of psychopathy in female offenders (e.g., Kennealy et al., 2007).

References

American Psychiatric Association. (1980). *Diagnostic and statistical manual of mental disorders* (3rd ed.). Washington, DC: Author.

American Psychiatric Association. (2000). *Diagnostic and statistical manual of mental disorders* (4th ed., text rev.). Washington, DC: Author.

Andrews, D. A., & Bonta, J. (1995). *The Level of Service Inventory-Revised* (LSI-R). Toronto, Ontario, Canada: Multi-Health Systems.

Barbaree, H. E., Seto, M. C., Langton, C. M., & Peacock, E. J. (2001). Evaluating the predictive accuracy of six risk assessment instruments for adult sex offenders. *Criminal Justice and Behavior, 28*, 490–521. doi:10.1177/009385480102800406

Benning, S. D., Patrick, C. J., Blonigen, D. M., Hicks, B. M., & Iacono, W. G. (2005a). Estimating facets of psychopathy from normal personality traits: A step toward community-epidemiological investigations. *Assessment, 12*, 3–18.

Benning, S. D., Patrick, C. J., Hicks, B. M., Blonigen, D. M., & Krueger, R. F. (2003). Factor structure of the Psychopathic Personality Inventory: Validity and implications for clinical assessment. *Psychological Assessment, 15*, 340–350.

Benning, S. D., Patrick, C. J., Salekin, R. T., & Leistico, A. R. (2005b). Convergent and discriminant validity of psychopathy factors assessed via self-report: A comparison of three instruments. *Assessment, 12*, 270–289.

Blonigen, D. M., Hicks, B., Krueger, R., Patrick, C. J., & Iacono, W. (2005). Psychopathic personality traits: Heritability and genetic overlap with internalizing and externalizing pathology. *Psychological Medicine, 35*, 637–648.

Blonigen, D. M., Patrick, C. J., Douglas, K. S., Poythress, N. G., Skeem, J. L., Lilienfeld, S. O., ... Krueger, R. F. (2010). Multimethod assessment of psychopathy in relation to factors of internalizing and externalizing from the Personality Assessment Inventory: The impact of method variance and suppressor effects. *Psychological Assessment, 22*, 96–107.

Boer, D., Hart, S., Kropp, P., & Webster, C. (1997). *The Sexual Violence Risk 20 (SVR-20)*. Vancouver, British Columbia, Canada: Mental Health, Law, & Policy Institute, Simon Fraser University.

Campbell, M. A., French, S., & Gendreau, P. (2009). The prediction of violence in adult offenders: A meta-analytic comparison of instruments and methods of assessment. *Criminal Justice and Behavior, 36*, 567–590. doi:10.1177/009385480102800406.

Cleckley, H. (1976). *The mask of sanity* (5th ed.). St. Louis, MO: Mosby. (Original work published 1941)

Cooke, D. J., & Michie, C. (2001). Refining the construct of psychopathy: Towards a hierarchical model. *Psychological Assessment, 13*, 171–188.

Dolan, M., & Davies, G. (2006). Psychopathy and institutional outcome in patients with schizophrenia in forensic settings in the UK. *Schizophrenia Research, 81*, 277–281.

Douglas, K. S., Lilienfeld, S. O., Skeem, J. L., Poythress, N. G., Edens, J. F., & Patrick, C. J. (2008). Relation of antisocial and psychopathic traits to suicide-related behavior among offenders. *Law and Human Behavior, 32*, 511–525.

Douglas, K. S., Ogloff, J. R. P., & Hart, S. D. (2003). Evaluation of a model of violence risk assessment among forensic psychiatric patients. *Psychiatric Services, 54*, 1372–1379.

Douglas, K. S., Ogloff, J. R. P., Nicholls, T. L., & Grant, I. (1999). Assessing risk for violence among psychiatric patients: The HCR-20 violence risk assessment scheme and the Psychopathy Checklist: Screening Version. *Journal of Consulting and Clinical Psychology, 67*, 917–930.

Douglas, K. S., Vincent, G. M., & Edens, J. F. (2006). Risk for criminal recidivism: The role of psychopathy. In C. J. Patrick (Ed.), *The handbook of psychopathy*. New York: Guilford Press.

Douglas, K. S., Yeomans, M., & Boer, D. P. (2005). Comparative validity analysis of multiple measures of violence risk in a general population sample of criminal offenders. *Criminal Justice and Behavior, 32*, 479–510.

Edens, J. F., & Campbell, J. S. (2007). Identifying youths at risk for institutional misconduct: A meta-analytic investigation of the Psychopathy Checklist measures. *Psychological Services, 4*, 13–27. doi:10.1037/1541-1559.4.1.13.

Edens, J. F., Campbell, J. S., & Weir, J. M. (2007). Youth psychopathy and criminal recidivism: A meta-analysis of the Psychopathy Checklist measures. *Law and Human Behavior, 31*, 53–75. doi:10.1007/s10979-006-9019-y.

Edens, J. F., & McDermott, B. E. (2010). Examining the construct validity of the Psychopathic Personality Inventory–Revised: Preferential correlates of fearless dominance and self-centered impulsivity. *Psychological Assessment, 22*, 32–42. doi:10.1037/a0018220.

Edens, J. F., Poythress, N. G., Lilienfeld, S. O., & Patrick, C. J. (2008). A prospective comparison of two measures of psychopathy in the prediction of institutional misconduct. *Behavioral Sciences and the Law, 26*, 529–541. doi:10.1002/bsl.823.

Edens, J. F., Poythress, N. G., Lilienfeld, S. O., Patrick, C. J., & Test, A. (2008). Further evidence of the divergent correlates of the Psychopathic Personality Inventory factors: Prediction of institutional misconduct among male prisoners. *Psychological Assessment, 20*, 86–91. doi:10.1037/1040-3590.20.1.86.

Fite, P. J., Greening, L., Stoppelbein, L., & Fabiano, G. A. (2009). Confirmatory factor analysis of the Antisocial Process Screening Device with a clinical inpatient population. *Assessment, 16*, 103–114.

Forth, A., Kosson, D. S., & Hare, R. D. (1997). *The Hare Psychopathy Checklist: Youth Version*. Toronto, Ontario, Canada: Multi-Health Systems.

Forth, A. E., Kosson, D. S., & Hare, R. D. (2003). *The Psychopathy Checklist: Youth Version*. Toronto, Ontario, Canada: Multi-Health Systems.

Frick, P. J., & Hare, R. D. (2001). *The antisocial process screening device (APSD)*. Toronto, Ontario, Canada: Multi-Health Systems.

Frick, P. J., O'Brien, B. S., Wooton, J. M., & McBurnett, K. (1994). Psychopathy and conduct problems in children. *Journal of Abnormal Psychology, 103*, 700–707.

Gendreau, P., Goggin, C., & Smith, P. (2002). Is the PCL-R really the "unparalleled" measure of offender risk? A lesson in knowledge accumulation. *Criminal Justice and Behavior, 29*, 397–426.

Gorenstein, E. E., & Newman, J. P. (1980). Disinhibitory psychopathology: A new perspective and a model for research. *Psychological Review, 87*, 301–315.

Gray, N. S., Fitzgerald, S., Taylor, J., MacCulloch, M. J., & Snowden, R. J. (2007). Predicting future reconviction in offenders with intellectual disabilities: The predictive efficacy of VRAG, PCL-SV, and the HCR-20. *Psychological Assessment, 19*, 474–479.

Gretton, H. M., McBride, M., Hare, R. D., O'Shaughnessy, R., & Kumka, G. (2001). Psychopathy and recidivism in adolescent sex offenders. *Criminal Justice and Behavior, 28*, 427–449.

Gustafson, D., Hare, R. D., Hart, S. D., Heilbrun, K., Nunez, C., & White, A. J. (1998). Inpatient and postdischarge aggression in mentally disordered offenders: The role of psychopathy. *Journal of Interpersonal Violence, 13*, 514–527.

Guy, L. S., Edens, J. F., Anthony, C., & Douglas, K. S. (2005). Does psychopathy predict institutional misconduct among adults? A meta-analytic investigation. *Journal of Consulting and Clinical Psychology, 73*, 1056–1064. doi:10.1037/0022-006X.73.6.1056.

Hall, J. R., & Benning, S. D. (2006). The "successful" psychopath: Adaptive and subclinical manifestations of psychopathy in the general population. In C. J. Patrick (Ed.), *Handbook of Psychopathy* (pp. 459–478). New York: Guilford Press.

Hall, J. R., Benning, S. D., & Patrick, C. J. (2004). Criterion-related validity of the three-factor model of psychopathy: Personality, behavior, and adaptive functioning. *Assessment, 11*, 4–16.

Hare, R. D. (1980). A research scale for the assessment of psychopathy in criminal populations. *Personality and Individual Differences, 1*, 111–119.

Hare, R. D. (1991). *The Hare Psychopathy Checklist–Revised.* Toronto, Ontario, Canada: Multi-Health Systems.

Hare, R. D. (2003). *The Hare Psychopathy Checklist–Revised* (2nd ed.). Toronto, Ontario, Canada: Multi-Health Systems.

Hare, R. D., Clark, D., Grann, M., & Thornton, D. (2000). Psychopathy and the predictive validity of the PCL-R: An international perspective. *Behavioral Sciences and the Law, 18*, 623–645.

Hare, R. D., & Neumann, C. S. (2006). The PCL-R assessment of psychopathy: Development, structural properties, and new directions. In C. J. Patrick (Ed.), *Handbook of psychopathy* (pp. 58–88). New York: Guilford Press.

Hare, R. D., & Neumann, C. S. (2008). Psychopathy as a clinical and empirical construct. *Annual Review of Clinical Psychology, 4*, 217–246.

Hare, R. D., & Neumann, C. S. (2009). Psychopathy: Assessment and forensic implications. *The Canadian Review of Psychiatry, 54*, 791–802.

Hare, R. D., & Neumann, C. S. (2010). The role of antisociality in the psychopathy construct: Comment on Skeem and Cooke (2010). *Psychological Assessment, 22*, 446–454. doi:10.1037/a0013635.

Harpur, T. J., & Hare, R. D. (1991). *Psychopathy and violent behavior: Two factors are better than one.* Paper presented at the 99th Annual Convention of the American Psychological Association, San Francisco, CA.

Harpur, T. J., Hare, R. D., & Hakstian, R. (1989). A two-factor conceptualization of psychopathy: Construct validity and implications for assessment. *Psychological Assessment: A Journal of Consulting and Clinical Psychology, 1*, 6–17.

Harris, G. T., Rice, M. E., & Cormier, C. A. (1991). Psychopathy and violent recidivism. *Law and Human Behavior, 15*, 625–637.

Harris, G. T., Rice, M. E., Quinsey, V. L., Lalumiere, M. L., Boer, D., & Lang, C. (2003). A multisite comparison of actuarial risk instruments for sex offenders. *Psychological Assessment, 15*, 413–425.

Hart, S. D. (1998). The role of psychopathy in assessing risk for violence: Conceptual and methodological issues. *Legal and Criminological Psychology, 3*, 121–137.

Hart, S., Cox, D., & Hare, R. D. (1995). *Manual for the Psychopathy Checklist: Screening Version (PCL:SV)*. Toronto, Ontario, Canada: Multi-Health Systems.

Hart, S. D., Kropp, P. R., & Hare, R. D. (1988). Performance of psychopaths following conditional release from prison. *Journal of Consulting and Clinical Psychology, 56*, 227–232.

Hemphill, J. F., & Hare, R. D. (2004). Some misconceptions about the Hare PCL-R and risk assessment: A reply to Gendreau, Goggin, and Smith. *Criminal Justice and Behavior, 31*, 203–243.

Hemphill, J. F., Hare, R. D., & Wong, S. C. P. (1998). Psychopathy and recidivism: A review. *Legal and Criminological Psychology, 3*, 139–170. doi:10.1111/j.2044-8333.1998.tb00355.x.

Hemphill, J. F., & Hart, S. D. (2003). Forensic and clinical issues in the assessment of psychopathy. In I. B. Weiner (Series Ed.) & A. M. Goldstein (Vol. Ed.), *Comprehensive handbook of psychology, Vol. 11: Forensic psychology*. New York: John Wiley & Sons.

Hicks, B. M., Markon, K. E., Patrick, C. J., Krueger, R. F., & Newman, J. P. (2004). Identifying psychopathy subtypes on the basis of personality structure. *Psychological Assessment, 16*, 276–288.

Hicks, B. M., & Patrick, C. J. (2006). Psychopathy and negative affectivity: Analyses of suppressor effects reveal distinct relations with trait anxiety, depression, fearfulness, and anger-hostility. *Journal of Abnormal Psychology, 115*, 276–287.

Hicks, B. M., Vaidyanathan, U., & Patrick, C. J. (2010). Validating female psychopathy subtypes: Differences in personality, antisocial and violent behavior, substance abuse, trauma, and mental health. *Personality Disorders: Theory, Research, and Treatment, 1*, 38–57.

Kennealy, P. J., Hicks, B. M., & Patrick, C. J. (2007). Validity of factors of the Psychopathy Checklist–Revised in female prisoners: Discriminant relations with antisocial behavior, substance abuse, and personality. *Assessment, 14*, 323–340.

Kennealy, P. K., Skeem, J. L., Walters, G. D., & Camp, J. (2010). Do core interpersonal and affective traits of PCL-R psychopathy interact with antisocial behavior and disinhibition to predict violence? *Psychological Assessment, 22*, 569–580.

Kotler, J. S., & McMahon, R. J. (2010). Assessment of child and adolescent psychopathy. In R. T. Salekin & D. R. Lynam (Eds.), *Handbook of child and adolescent psychopathy* (pp. 79–109). New York: Guilford Press.

Kraepelin, E. (1904, 1915). *Psychiatrie: Ein lehrbuch* (7th ed., 1904; 8th ed., 1915). Leipzig, Germany: Barth.

Krueger, R. F., Hicks, B., Patrick, C. J., Carlson, S., Iacono, W. G., & McGue, M. (2002). Etiologic connections among substance dependence, antisocial behavior, and personality: Modeling the externalizing spectrum. *Journal of Abnormal Psychology, 111*, 411–424.

Lally, S. J. (2003). What tests are acceptable for use in forensic evaluations? A survey of experts. *Professional Psychology: Research and Practice, 34*, 491–498.

Leistico, A. R., Salekin, R. T., DeCoster, J., & Rogers, R. (2008). A large-scale meta-analysis relating the Hare measures of psychopathy to antisocial conduct. *Law and Human Behavior, 32*, 28–45. doi:10.1007/s10979-007-9096-6.

Lilienfeld, S. O., & Andrews, B. P. (1996). Development and preliminary validation of a self report measure of psychopathic personality traits in noncriminal populations. *Journal of Personality Assessment, 66*, 488–524.

Lilienfeld, S. O., & Fowler, K. A. (2006). The self-report assessment of psychopathy: Problems, pitfalls, and promises. In C. J. Patrick (Ed.), *Handbook of psychopathy* (pp. 107–132). New York: Guilford Press.

Lilienfeld, S. O., & Widows, M. R. (2005). *Psychopathic Personality Inventory–Revised (PPI-R) professional manual.* Odessa, FL: Psychological Assessment Resources.

Lorenz, A. R., & Newman, J. P. (2002). Deficient response modulation and emotion processing in low-anxious Caucasian psychopathic offenders: Results from a lexical decision task. *Emotion, 2*, 91–104.

Lykken, D. T. (1995). *The antisocial personalities.* Hillsdale, NJ: Lawrence Erlbaum Associates.

Lynam, D. R., & Derefinko, K. J. (2006). Psychopathy and personality. In C. J. Patrick (Ed.), *Handbook of psychopathy* (pp. 133–155). New York: Guilford Press.

Marcus, D. K., Fulton, J. J., & Edens, J. F. (2012). The two-factor model of psychopathic personality: Evidence from the Psychopathic Personality Inventory. *Personality Disorders: Theory, Research, and Treatment.*

McCord, W., & McCord, J. (1964). *The psychopath: An essay on the criminal mind.* Princeton, NJ: Van Nostrand.

Neumann, C. S., & Hare, R. D. (2008). Psychopathic traits in a large community sample: Links to violence, alcohol use, and intelligence. *Journal of Consulting and Clinical Psychology, 76*, 893–899. doi:10.1037/0022-006X.76.5.893.

Partridge, G. E. (1928a). Psychopathic personalities among boys in a training school for delinquents. *American Journal of Psychiatry, 8*, 159–186.

Partridge, G. E. (1928b). A study of 50 cases of psychopathic personality. *American Journal of Psychiatry, 7*, 953–973.

Patrick, C. J. (2006). Back to the future: Cleckley as a guide to the next generation of psychopathy research. In C. J. Patrick (Ed.), *Handbook of psychopathy* (pp. 605–617). New York: Guilford Press.

Patrick, C. J., & Bernat, E. M. (2009). Neurobiology of psychopathy: A two-process theory. In G. G. Berntson & J. T. Cacioppo (Eds.), *Handbook of neuroscience for the behavioral sciences* (pp. 1110–1131). New York: John Wiley & Sons.

Patrick, C. J., Edens, J. F., Poythress, N., Lilienfeld, S. O., & Benning, S. D. (2006). Construct validity of the PPI two-factor model with offenders. *Psychological Assessment, 18*, 204–208.

Patrick, C. J., Fowles, D. C., & Krueger, R. F. (2009). Triarchic conceptualization of psychopathy: Developmental origins of disinhibition, boldness, and meanness. *Development and Psychopathology, 21*, 913–938.

Patrick, C. J., Hicks, B. M., Krueger, R. F., & Lang, A. R. (2005). Relations between psychopathy facets and externalizing in a criminal offender sample. *Journal of Personality Disorders, 19*, 339–356.

Pinel, P. (1962). *A treatise on insanity* (D. Davis, Trans.). New York: Hafner. (Original work published 1806)

Poythress, N. G., Lilienfeld, S. O., Skeem, J. L., Douglas, K. S., Edens, J. F., Epstein, M., & Patrick, C. J. (2010). Using the PCL-R to help estimate the validity of two self-report measures of psychopathy with offenders. *Assessment, 17*, 206–219.

Prichard, J. C. (1835). *A treatise on insanity and other disorders affecting the mind.* London: Sherwood, Gilbert & Piper.

Quinsey, V. L., Harris, G. T., Rice, M. E., & Cormier, C. (1998). *Violent offenders: Appraising and managing risk.* Washington, DC: American Psychological Association.

Reardon, M. L., Lang, A. R., & Patrick, C. J. (2002). An Evaluation of Relations Among Antisocial Behavior, Psychopathic Traits, and Alcohol Problems in Incarcerated Men. *Alcoholism: Clinical and Experimental Research, 26*, 1188–1197.

Rice, M. E., & Harris, G. T. (1997). Cross-validation and extension of the Violence Risk Appraisal Guide for child molesters and rapists. *Law and Human Behavior, 21*, 231–241.

Richards, H. J., Casey, J. O., & Lucente, S. W. (2003). Psychopathy and treatment response in incarcerated female substance abusers. *Criminal Justice & Behavior, 30*, 251–276.

Robins, L. N. (1966). *Deviant children grown up.* Baltimore, MD: Williams & Wilkins.

Robins, L. N. (1978). Sturdy predictors of adult antisocial behaviour: Replications from longitudinal studies. *Psychological Medicine, 8*, 611–622.

Ross, S. R., Benning, S. D., Patrick, C. J., Thompson, A., & Thurston, A. (2009). Factors of the Psychopathic Personality Inventory: Criterion-related validity and relationship to the BIS/BAS and Five-Factor models of personality. *Assessment, 16*, 71–87.

Salekin, R. T. (2006). Psychopathy in children and adults: Key issues in conceptualization and assessment. In C. J. Patrick (Ed.), *Handbook of psychopathy* (pp. 389–414). New York: Guilford Press.

Salekin, R. T., Brannen, D. N., Zalot, A. A., Leistico, A., & Neumann C. S. (2006). Factor structure of psychopathy in youth: Testing the applicability of the new four-factor model. *Criminal Justice and Behavior, 33*, 135–157.

Salekin, R., Rogers, R., & Sewell, K. (1996). A review and meta-analysis of the Psychopathy Checklist and Psychopathy Checklist–Revised: Predictive validity of dangerousness. *Clinical Psychology: Science and Practice, 3*, 203–215. doi:10.1111/j.1468-2850.1996.tb00071.x.

Salekin, R. T., Rogers, R., Ustad, K. L., & Sewell, K. W. (1998). Psychopathy and recidivism among female inmates. *Law and Human Behavior, 22*, 109–128. doi:10.1023/A:1025780806538.

Schneider, K. (1934). *Die psychopathischen personlichkeiten* (3rd ed.). Vienna: Deuticke.

Serin, R. C., Peters, R. D., & Barbaree, H. E. (1990). Predictors of psychopathy and release outcome in a criminal population. *Psychological Assessment: A Journal of Consulting and Clinical Psychology, 2*, 419–422.

Singh, J. P., Grann, M., & Fazel, S. (2011). A comparative study of violence risk assessment tools: A systematic review and metaregression analysis of 68 studies involving 25,980 participants. *Clinical Psychology Review, 31*, 499–513. doi:10.1016/j.cpr.2010.11.009.

Skeem, J. L., & Cooke, D. J. (2010). Is criminal behavior a central component of psychopathy? Conceptual directions for resolving the debate. *Psychological Assessment, 22*, 433–445. doi:10.1037/a0008512.

Skeem, J. L., Johansson, P., Andershed, H., Kerr, M., & Eno Louden, J. (2007). Two subtypes of psychopathic violent offenders that parallel primary and secondary variants. *Journal of Abnormal Psychology, 116*, 395–409.

Skeem, J. L., & Monahan, J. (2011). Current directions in violence risk assessment. *Current Directions in Psychological Science, 20*, 38–42. doi:10.1177/0963721410397271.

Skeem, J. L., & Mulvey, E. P. (2001). Psychopathy and community violence among civil psychiatric patients: Results from the MacArthur Violence Risk Assessment study. *Journal of Consulting and Clinical Psychology, 69*, 358–374. doi:10.1037/0022-006X.69.3.358.

Skeem, J. L., Polaschek, D. L. L., Patrick, C. J., & Lilienfeld, S. O. (2011). Psychopathic personality: Bridging the gap between scientific evidence and public policy. *Psychological Science in the Public Interest, 12*, 95–162. doi:10.1177/1529100611426706.

Tengstrom, A., Grann, M., Langstrom, N., & Kullgren, G. (2000). Psychopathy (PCL-R) as a predictor of violent recidivism among criminal offenders with schizophrenia. *Law and Human Behavior, 24*, 45–58.

Uzieblo, K., Verschuere, B., Van den Bussche, E., & Crombez, G. (2010). The validity of the Psychopathic Personality Inventory–Revised in a community sample. *Assessment, 17*, 334–346. doi:10.1177/1073191109356544.

Vaughn, M. G., Howard, M. O., & DeLisi, M. (2008). Psychopathic personality traits and delinquent careers: An empirical investigation. *International Journal of Law and Psychiatry, 31*, 407–416.

Venables, N. C., & Patrick, C. J. (2012). Validity of the Externalizing Spectrum Inventory in a criminal offender sample: Relations with disinhibitory psychopathology, personality, and psychopathic features. Psychological Assessment, 24, 88–100.

Verona, E., Hicks, B. M., & Patrick, C. J. (2005). Psychopathy and suicidal behavior in female offenders: Mediating influences of temperament and abuse history. *Journal of Consulting and Clinical Psychology, 73*, 1065–1073.

Verona, E., Patrick, C. J., & Joiner, T. E. (2001). Psychopathy, antisocial personality, and suicide risk. *Journal of Abnormal Psychology, 110*, 462–470.

Walsh, T., & Walsh, Z. (2006). The evidentiary introduction of Psychopathy Checklist–Revised assessed psychopathy in U.S. Courts: Extent and appropriateness. *Law and Human Behavior, 30*, 493–507. doi:10.1007/s10979-006-9042-z.

Walsh, Z., & Kosson, D. S. (2008). Psychopathy and violence: The importance of factor level interactions. *Psychological Assessment, 20*, 114–120.

Walters, G. D. (2003a). Predicting criminal justice outcomes with the Psychopathy Checklist and Lifestyle Criminality Screening Form: A meta-analytic comparison. *Behavioral Sciences and the Law, 21*, 89–102.

Walters, G. D. (2003b). Predicting institutional adjustment and recidivism with the Psychopathy Checklist factor scores: A meta-analysis. *Law and Human Behavior, 27*, 541–558. doi:10.1023/A:1025490207678.

Walters, G. D., Knight, R. A., Grann, M., & Dahle, K. P. (2008). Incremental validity of the Psychopathy Checklist facet scores: Predicting release outcome in six samples. *Journal of Abnormal Psychology, 117*, 396–405.

Webster, C. D., Douglas, K. S., Eaves, D., & Hart, S. D. (1997). *HCR-20: Assessing Risk for Violence (Version 2)*. Burnaby, British Columbia, Canada: Mental Health, Law, and Policy Institute, Simon Fraser University.

Yang, M., Wong, S. C. P., & Coid, J. W. (2010). The efficacy of violence prediction: A meta-analytic comparison of nine risk assessment tools. *Psychological Bulletin, 136*, 740–767. doi:10.1037/a0020473.

Zinger, I., & Forth, A. E. (1998). Psychopathy and Canadian criminal proceedings: The potential for human rights abuses. *Canadian Journal of Criminology, 40*, 237–276.

CHAPTER THIRTEEN

Guidelines for the Evaluation and Interpretation of Psychopathy Research Findings

Carl B. Gacono

Labels for personality and behavior patterns consistent with psychopathy exist in most cultures (Cooke, 1998; Murphy, 1976). For example, the word *Kunlangeta*, in the Inuit (Northwest Alaska) community, describes "a man who . . . repeatedly lies and cheats and steals things and does not go hunting and, when the other men are out of the village, takes sexual advantage of many women—someone who does not pay attention to reprimands and who is always being brought to the elders for punishment" (Murphy, 1976, p. 1026). In rural Nigeria, the term *Aranakan* describes an individual who "always goes his own way regardless of others, who is uncooperative, full of malice, and bullheaded" (Murphy, 1976, p. 1026).

To gain further insight into the culturally shared concept of psychopathy, a historic conference was held in Alvor, Portugal, from November 27 to December 7, 1995. Under the support of a North Atlantic Treaty Organization Advanced Study Institute (NATO ASI), 85 participants from 15 countries met to share research findings on the current state of psychopathy (Gacono, 2000a). Difficult concepts crystallized as authors articulated the process through which their research had unfolded. Participants were informed of "What we currently know" and challenged concerning "What we yet need to learn" (Gacono, 2000a). It was exciting to discover that the majority of the NATO countries shared a similar view of psychopathy (Cooke, Forth, & Hare, 1998; Cooke, Forth, Newman & Hare, 1996).

The Alvor research supported cultural observations, suggesting the existence of a unique phenotype of human personality as distinct and uniform as that of, say, a primary color. Whereas there are, for example, many shades of blue, no shade of blue is likely to mistaken for yellow. Likewise, one may observe many forms of antisocial personality traits and aberrant behavior, but none match the unique constellation of both traits and behaviors found in psychopathy. The consensus among the NATO countries could be directly attributed to the development of the Psychopathy Checklists (Hare, 1991, 2003) and their ability to measure psychopathy in a reliable and valid manner. The PCL-R provides a method for differentiating among individuals based on their psychopathy level. High PCL-R scores correlate with increases in quantity and variety of offenses committed, frequency of violent offenses, higher recidivism rates, poor treatment response (Ogloff, Wong, & Greenwood, 1990; Rice, Harris, & Cormier, 1992), and institutional misbehavior (Gacono, Meloy, Sheppard, Speth, & Roske, 1995; Gacono, Meloy, Speth, & Roske, 1997). These findings remain stable even when culture, gender, and the presence or absence of a major mental disorder is controlled (Cooke, Forth, & Hare, 1998).

While Hare (1996) described psychopathy as "a clinical construct whose time has come," the translation of theory and research into clinical/forensic practice was less evident at the time of the NATO conference in 1995. There were notable gaps between the "ivory tower" and the clinic. Clinically oriented participants were challenged to adopt the research for clinical/forensic practice. The publication of *The Clinical and Forensic Assessment of Psychopathy: A Practitioner's Guide* (Gacono, 2000a) was a direct result of that challenge. It was also clear that the Psychopathy Checklists had catalyzed, and would continue to catalyze, psychopathy research (Hare, 1966, 1996, 1998a, 1998b), as they have for the past 11 years.

Although the Alvor conference confirmed a significant cross-cultural consensus in the construct of psychopathy, not all subsequent studies have been well designed. In fact, a considerable number of studies contain similar conceptual and/or methodological errors. As these studies have found their way into the published literature, rather than increasing our understanding of psychopathy, they have only added confusion. This chapter discusses key issues in understanding psychopathy and provides criteria for evaluating psychopathy research.

Sociopathy, Antisocial Personality, and Psychopathy

How has our understanding of psychopathy developed? Evolving from Pinel's first clinical observations, through Cleckley's refined criteria and the empirical design of Hare, the object relations understanding of the psychopath's "inner life" (Meloy, 1988; Meloy & Gacono, 1998), and the use of empirical measurement to flesh out the inner dynamics of the psychopath (Gacono & Meloy, 1994, 2009), each step has refined, added to, and clarified our understanding. In fact, antisocial syndromes, and particularly psychopathy, have enjoyed more attention and research than any other character disorder.

Yet despite a wealth of published research (Hare, 1966, 1996, 1998a, 1998b), terms such as sociopathy, Antisocial Personality Disorder (ASPD), and psychopathy are often inappropriately viewed as synonymous (Losel, 1998; Millon, Simonsen, Birket-Smith, & Davis, 1998). Originating from separate theoretical lines, these constructs manifest empirically measurable and clinically relevant differences.

Sociopathy (American Psychiatric Association [APA], 1952) and Antisocial Personality Disorder (APA, 1994) are terms used in various editions of the American Psychiatric Association's *Diagnostic and Statistical Manual of Mental Disorders* (DSM). Lacking contemporary clinical meaning, sociopathy was used in the first DSM (APA, 1952) to describe a variety of conditions such as sexual deviation, alcoholism, and "dissocial" and "antisocial" reactions. Characteristics of the classic psychopath were most visible in the "antisocial reaction" criteria. In the DSM-II (APA, 1968), sociopathy was replaced by ASPD. Many of the traditional characteristics of psychopathy disappeared from ASPD in the DSM-III (APA, 1980). Subsequent versions of the DSM (APA, 1980, 1987, 1994) have reflected the influence of a social deviancy model (Robins, 1966) through the continued reliance on behavioral criteria.

Unlike ASPD, psychopathy (Cleckley, 1941/1976; Meloy, 1988; Hare, 1996; see Table 13.1) is comprised of both trait and behavioral criteria. As measured by the Psychopathy Checklists (Forth, Kosson, & Hare, 2003; Hare, 1991; Hart, Cox & Hare, 1995), psychopathy contains two stable, oblique factors. The first factor, "callous, remorseless use of others" (Factor 1), is characterized by egocentricity, callousness, and remorselessness, and correlates with Narcissistic and Histrionic Personality Disorders, low anxiety, low empathy, and self-report measures of Machiavellianism and narcissism (Hare, 2003). The second factor, "antisocial lifestyle" (Factor 2), represents an irresponsible, impulsive, thrill-seeking, unconventional, and antisocial lifestyle and correlates most strongly with

Table 13.1 Psychopathic Traits and Behaviors

*1. Glibness/superficial charm
*2. Grandiose sense of self-worth
+3. Need for stimulation/proneness to boredom
*4. Pathological lying
*5. Conning/manipulative
*6. Lack of remorse or guilt
*7. Shallow affect
*8. Callous/lack or empathy
+9. Parasitic lifestyle
+10. Poor behavioral controls
11. Promiscuous sexual behavior
+12. Early behavioral problems
+13. Lack of realistic long-term goals
+14. Impulsivity
+15. Irresponsibility
*16. Failure to accept responsibility for own actions
17. Many short-term marital relationships
+18. Juvenile delinquency
+19. Revocation of conditional release
20. Criminal versatility

Sources: Hare (1980); Hare, Harpur, Hakstian, Forth, Hart, & Newman (1990)
*PCL-R Factor 1
+PCL-R Factor 2

criminal behaviors, lower socioeconomic background, lower IQ, less education, self-report measures of antisocial behavior, and the diagnoses of Conduct Disorder and Antisocial Personality (Hare, 1991, 2003). In summary, while most criminal psychopaths meet criteria for ASPD, the majority of ASPD individuals are not psychopaths.

Caveats for Understanding and Evaluating the Psychopathy Research

Understanding that "psychopathy" can be conceptualized in both a dimensional and categorical (taxon; PCL-R $\geq$ 30) manner is essential to interpreting research findings (Gacono & Bodholdt, 2001; Gacono & Gacono, 2006). Research findings are frequently obscured when authors make categorical inferences (discuss psychopathy; PCL-R $\geq$ 30) from studies utilizing dimensional research designs (e.g., correlations of behavior with total PCL-R scores, and/or absence of a psychopathic group, > 29 scorers).

When used dimensionally, psychopathy is conceptualized as existing along a continuum of severity. Clinically, one is more interested in determining what ranges of PCL-R scores are best at predicting behavior, than in whether or not a given individual meets the threshold score for a designation of *psychopathy* (PCL-R $\geq$ 30; Gacono & Bodholdt, 2001). For example, the VRAG and SORAG (Quinsey, Harris, Rice, & Cormier, 1998) are forensic instruments that use differing PCL-R cutting scores as part of a "weighted" formula for predicting violence and sexual violence risk. PCL-R scores, rather than a diagnosis (category), become one of several factors in decision making.

For research purposes, our understanding of psychopathy (category) is enhanced when groups of psychopaths (PCL-R $\geq$ 30) are compared to groups of non-psychopaths (PCL-R < 30) or, at minimum, when there are sufficient numbers of PCL-R $\geq$ 30 scorers in a given study. What might seem obvious—for a study to make inferences about *psychopathy*, it must have *psychopaths* in it—is frequently overlooked. Two common research procedures that can create samples without psychopaths involve using the PCL:SV, or a self-report measure for creating a "psychopathic group"; and/or lowering PCL-R cutoff scores to form a "psychopathic" group (Gacono & Gacono, 2006).

The PCL:SV is for screening purposes only. It is not a substitute for the PCL-R. Unlike the PCL:SV, the PCL-R allows for a categorical designation of psychopathy (PCL-R $\geq$ 30). Although the PCL:SV is appropriate for examining relative differences within a given sample, it cannot be used to make inferences about psychopaths when used as the independent measure for forming "psychopathy groups."

A similar argument can be made for the use of self-report measures of psychopathy (Lilienfeld & Andrews, 1996). These instruments suggest that *individual traits* (dimensional—inherent in any one of a number of disorders and non-disorders) are individually *psychopathic* (category). In reality, a designation of *psychopath* is appropriate only when a sufficient number of individual traits are fully present. It is the aggregate of traits, rather than an individual trait, that determines the presence of a psychopath. With some exceptions, self-report measures assess "traits" or dimensions, as opposed to "categories" (presence of a psychopath). Mislabeling traits, such as self-centeredness, impulsivity, impaired empathy, and irresponsibility, as inherently "psychopathic" returns psychology to the pre-1900s trend of including all personality disorders under the rubric of psychopathy. Even established self-report measures, such as the MMPI-2, are not appropriate for establishing *psychopathic* groups (Hare, 1991, 2003).

A related concern involves lowering PCL-R cutoff scores to form a "psychopathic" group. Researchers do this for one reason—their samples do not contain sufficient numbers of actual psychopaths (PCL-R $\geq$ 30).

While this can be part of an acceptable research design, the author(s) must refrain from making inferences about psychopaths (category) when they have few, if any, psychopaths in their sample. When lowered PCL-R cutoff scores are used to establish groups, the best that can be inferred is relative differences among high versus low scorers only *within that sample*.

Clearly, the methods used for creating a psychopathy group have direct bearing on the types of inferences that can be made; moreover, these methods are critical to the evaluation of the studies' generalizability. Results across studies can only be compared appropriately when psychopathy has been defined by a PCL-R score ≥ 30 (measurement error notwithstanding), and other relevant confounds are controlled. Divergent study findings can frequently be explained not by true differences, but by the simple fact that the study has few or no *psychopaths* in it, and/or no differences would be expected due to uncontrolled confounds (factors such as gender, IQ, presence of a mental illness, which may affect data from the dependent measure). Additionally, statistical approaches that use simple correlational methods to compare dependent variables to individual PCL-R scores (dimensional application) fail to capture true between-group differences. When evaluating research findings that present conclusions about *psychopathy*, the reviewer must always examine the mean, standard deviation, frequencies, and ranges of PCL-R scores for the sample. These data should always be provided by the researcher. Given an acceptable methodology, this data will allow a determination of whether there were enough *psychopathic subjects* (PCL-R ≥ 30) to justify the studies' conclusions. For inferences to be made regarding *psychopathy* (category), the PCL-R or the PCL:YV must be used as the independent measure, and there must be sufficient numbers of ≥ 30 scorers in the samples analyzed.

Gacono, Loving, and Bodholdt (2001; see also Gacono, Evans, & Viglione, 2008; Gacono & Gacono, 2006) offered five conceptual and four methodological considerations for evaluating psychopathy research. The following conceptual issues are essential to consider when evaluating a study's findings:

1. Antisocial personality disorder (ASPD; APA, 1994) and psychopathy are related but distinct constructs, differing from each other along important historical, theoretical, and definitional lines.
2. Psychopathy may be conceptualized both in dimensional terms (i.e., along a continuum of severity) and in categorical terms (i.e., as a taxon or discrete syndrome), and applying one of these approaches versus the other to PCL-R scores affects research findings.

3. Psychopathy may manifest in varying forms across various populations (e.g., across gender or throughout development from youth into adulthood).
4. Personality testing is only one facet of both psychological assessment and diagnosis. It contributes to the assessment of the dimensional aspects of psychopathy.
5. The generalizability of a study's findings depends on consideration of the above four conceptual issues and should be of concern when designing studies, presenting findings, or offering discussion that includes comparison to other studies. Authors must account for confounds related to both their conceptual formulations and their measurement tools.

Treating ASPD and psychopathy as synonymous, failing to distinguish between dimensional and categorical understandings of psychopathy, failing to consider the influence of age and gender, equating diagnosis with assessment, and so on all contribute to a study's design and, ultimately, to both the validity of the conclusions and the generalizability of the findings (Gacono, Bodholdt, & Loving, 2001; Gacono & Evans, 2004; Gacono & Gacono, 2006; Gacono et al., 2008).

In addition to outlining five conceptual issues, Gacono et al. (2001) offered four methodological criteria for reviewing individual psychopathy studies. A reviewer might ask:

1. Did the authors treat psychopathy as a taxon and validate groups with an appropriate measure (e.g., the PCL-R with adults, the PCL:YV for adolescents [or a PCL:YV prepublication–modified version of the PCL-R])? Did they use the accepted cutoff scores (PCL-R ≥ 30)?
2. Did the authors account for (control or delineate) the limitations imposed by factors such as gender, sexual deviance, concurrent Axis I psychosis, age, IQ, testing setting, and legal status? The weight of these varies dependent on the instrument utilized.
3. If the dependent measure was the Rorschach, was R (number of responses) considered? Increased R is found in certain sex offender groups (Bridges, Wilson, & Gacono, 1998; Gacono et al., 2000), whereas low R is typical among many criminal groups. Thus, R can act as a moderator influencing the relationship between Rorschach variables and criterion variables.
4. Was response style considered (Bannatyne, Gacono, & Greene, 1999) when interpreting findings? With the Rorschach, for example, IQ and variables such as R, Lambda, Extratensiveness, and Introversiveness can impact the production of certain variables (Exner, 1995).

Understanding these five conceptual and four methodological issues will allow a reviewer to assess the validity of any given study.

Inconsistencies that result from the failure to account for these issues are easily impeached. Studies that result in no significant differences and/or unexpected findings, and/or those that are at odds with a body of well-controlled studies, can often be explained by errors that result from the presence of one or several of the above issues.

An article by Wood and colleagues (2010) provides an excellent example of these errors. Seventy percent of the studies used in their meta-analysis contained one or more of these errors (Cunliffe et al., 2011). This number does not account for studies that concurrently included inappropriate administrations (for a standardized interview format, see Gacono, 2005; Gacono & Hughes, 2006), inappropriate modifications of instruments, and failure to report significant information such as interrater reliabilities for one or more of the instruments utilized, mean IQ scores for the subjects studied, and so on. Poorly designed studies, such as the Wood et al. (2010) meta-analysis, tell us little about psychopathy or the Rorschach.

Conclusion

As a construct, psychopathy has journeyed beyond confusing origins and a mishmash of labels into an empirically measurable syndrome (Hare, 1991, 2003). Psychopathy is no longer understood as a disorder that is a step beyond our comprehension (Cleckley, 1941/1976). Empirically sound research adds to our understanding of the disorder. Since the 1995 NATO conference, a considerable amount of not-so-useful data has been disseminated. Misleading or not, this data finds its way into the court rooms, impacting forensic decisions and adding confusion to our clinical ones.

The strength of psychopathy assessment lies in the requirement for researchers and clinicians to work together. Nomothetic, empirically based research findings inform and guide individual clinical decisions, while clinical observations suggest the need for research related to individual differences. Nomothetic and idiographic data coalesce in clinical/forensic decisions. For example, an additional clinical tool, besides the PCL-R, may be needed for assessing psychopathy in community versus institutional settings. One need only look to Babiak's (2000) work to organize this discussion within an empirical context. In corporate settings, Babiak (2000) discovered that individuals whose disruptive behavior brought them to the attention of the organization were high PCL-R scorers. Five "noncriminal" male subjects received scores of 27.8, 29.4, 29.4, 30.6, and 31.3. Certainly, these findings are not conclusive. However,

Babiak's findings suggest that the PCL-R may be useful in identifying psychopathy outside of criminal settings and that, dependent on further study, an additional tool is not necessary. Perhaps it is only the paucity of collateral information, and not the specific setting, that limits the usefulness of the PCL-R.

One of many continuing challenges for clinicians is applying nomothetic findings to individual (idiographic) cases. Optimal PCL-R dimensional scores for various risk paradigms (i.e., treatability, violence, institutional management, recidivism) within specific settings must be determined (Bodholdt, Richards, & Gacono, 2000; Gacono, Nieberding, Owen, Rubel, & Bodholdt, 2001). In this regard, dimensional scores are preferable to taxonomic designations, multi-methods of assessment are recommended, and sensitivity to age, gender, and ethnicity are preferred (Gacono, 2000a, 2000b). While comparative data from like-settings and similar subject populations is essential to clinical work, the work of Quinsey et al. (1998; VRAG & SORAG), provides a useful conceptual model for integrating psychopathy data into clinical practice. This actuarial approach provides a template for further research and developing models to inform other clinical decisions (Gacono & Meloy, 2009).

Beyond serving as a guide to the presence or absence of psychopathy (taxon) or as one point in an actuarial risk assessment, PCL-R data provides a rich yield with valuable information concerning treatment planning and characterological diagnosis in "nonpsychopathic offenders" (Gacono, 1998; Gacono & Hughes, 2006; Gacono, Jumes, & Gray, 2008). Determining the relevance of individual PCL-R item scores to such clinical issues has only begun and begs further study (Gacono & Hutton, 1994; Gacono, 1998; Gacono et al., 2008). Despite its infancy, clinical item and cluster analysis provide a useful model for broadening the PCL-R's scope of application.

Since the NATO conference, research has supported the importance of the Psychopathy Checklists (PCL, PCL-R, PCL:SV, PCL:YV, PSD) to psychopathy assessment and to both research and clinical practice. These instruments not only inform and guide our thinking, but comprise a significant step toward aiding the clinical-forensic issues of prediction and risk, including violent recidivism, treatability, and management (Gacono, 2000a; Gacono & Bodholdt, 2001). While sophistication is required for separating the research wheat from the chaff within the psychopathy literature, we might echo Hare's (1996) "Psychopathy [was]: a clinical construct whose time has come," with Gacono's (2000), "Psychopathy is a construct that is likely here to stay" (p. 407).

References

American Psychiatric Association (1952). *Diagnostic and statistical manual of mental disorders*. Washington, DC: Author.

American Psychiatric Association. (1968). *Diagnostic and statistical manual of mental disorders* (2nd ed.). Washington, DC: Author.

American Psychiatric Association. (1980). *Diagnostic and statistical manual of mental disorders* (3rd ed.). Washington, DC: Author.

American Psychiatric Association. (1987). *Diagnostic and statistical manual of mental disorders* (3rd ed.,rev.). Washington, DC: Author.

American Psychiatric Association. (1994). *Diagnostic and statistical manual of mental disorders* (4th ed.). Washington, DC: Author.

Babiak, P. (2000). Psychopathic manipulation at work. In C. B. Gacono (Ed.), *The clinical and forensic assessment of psychopathy: A practitioner's guide* (pp. 287–312). Mahwah, NJ: Lawrence Erlbaum Associates.

Bannatyne, L. A., Gacono, C. B., & Greene, R. (1999). Differential patterns of responding among three groups of chronic psychotic forensic outpatients. *Journal of Clinical Psychology, 55*(12), 1553–1565.

Bodholdt, R. H., Richards, H. R., & Gacono, C. B. (2000). Assessing psychopathy in adults: The Psychopathy Checklists, Revised and Screening Version. In C. B. Gacono (Ed.), *The clinical and forensic assessment of psychopathy: A practitioner's guide* (pp. 55–86). Mahwah, NJ: Lawrence Erlbaum Associates.

Bridges, M., Wilson, J., & Gacono, C.B. (1998). A Rorschach investigation of defensiveness, self-perception, interpersonal relations, & affective states in incarcerated pedophiles. *Journal of Personality Assessment, 70*(2), 365–385.

Cleckley, H. (1976). *The mask of sanity* (5th ed.). St. Louis, MO: Mosby. (Original work published 1941)

Cooke, D.J. (1998). Cross-cultural aspects of psychopathy. In T. Millon, E. Simonsen, M. Birket-Smith, & R. Davis (Eds.), *Psychopathy: Antisocial, criminal, and violent behavior* (pp. 260–276). New York: Guilford Press.

Cooke, D. J., Forth, A. E., & Hare, R. D. (1998). *Psychopathy: Theory, research and implications for society*. London: Kluwer Academic Publishers.

Cooke, D. J., Forth, A. E., Newman, J., & Hare, R. D. (Eds.). (1996). International perspectives on psychopathy: Abstracts from the Alvor NATO ASI on psychopathy. In *Issues in criminology and legal psychology No. 24*. Leicester, England: British Psychological Society.

Cunliffe, T. B., Gacono, C. B., Meloy, J. R., Smith, J. M., Taylor, E. E., & Landry, D. (2011). Psychopathy and the Rorschach: A response to Wood et al. (unpublished).

Exner, J. E. (1995). *A Rorschach workbook for the Comprehensive System* (4th ed.). Asheville, NC: Rorschach Workshops.

Forth, A. E., Kosson, D. S., & Hare, R. D. (2003). *The Hare Psychopathy Checklist: Youth Version*. Toronto, Ontario, Canada: Multi-Health Systems.

Gacono, C. B. (1990). An empirical study of object relations and defensive operations in antisocial personality. *Journal of Personality Assessment, 54*, 589–600.
Gacono, C. B. (1998). The use of the Psychopathy Checklist–Revised (PCL-R) and Rorschach for treatment planning with antisocial personality disordered patients. *International Journal of Offender Therapy and Comparative Criminology, 42*(1), 49–64.
Gacono, C. B. (2000a). *The clinical and forensic assessment of psychopathy: A practitioner's guide*. Mahwah, NJ: Lawrence Erlbaum Associates.
Gacono, C. B. (2000b). Suggestions for the implementation and use of the Psychopathy Checklists in forensic and clinical Practice. In C. B. Gacono (Ed.), *The clinical and forensic assessment of psychopathy: A practitioner's guide* (pp. 175–202). Mahwah, NJ: Lawrence Erlbaum Associates.
Gacono, C. B. (2005). *The clinical and forensic interview schedule for the Hare Psychopathy Checklist: Revised and Screening Version*. Mahwah, NJ: Lawrence Erlbaum Associates.
Gacono, C. B., & Bodholdt, R. (2001). The role of the Psychopathy Checklist–Revised (PCL-R) in risk assessment. *Journal of Threat Assessment, 1*(4), 65–79.
Gacono, C. B., & Evans, F. B. (2004). Entertaining reading but not science: Book review of *What's Wrong with the Rorschach*. *International Journal of Offender Therapy and Comparative Criminology, 48*(2), 253–257.
Gacono, C. B., Evans, F. B., Kaser-Boyd, N., & Gacono, L. A. (2008). *The handbook of forensic Rorschach assessment*. Mahwah, NJ: Lawrence Erlbaum Associates.
Gacono, C. B., Evans, F. B., & Viglione, D. J. (2008). Essential issues in the forensic use of the Rorschach. In C. Gacono, B. Evans, N. Kaser-Boyd, & L. Gacono (Eds.), *The handbook of forensic Rorschach assessment* (pp. 3–20). Mahwah, NJ: Lawrence Erlbaum Associates.
Gacono, C. B., & Gacono, L. A. (2006). Some caveats for evaluating the research on psychopathy. *The Correctional Psychologist, 38*(2), 7–9.
Gacono, C. B., Gacono, L. A., & Evans, F. B. (2008). *The Rorschach and antisocial personality*. In C. Gacono, B. Evans, N. Kaser-Boyd, & L. Gacono (Eds.), *The handbook of forensic Rorschach assessment* (pp. 323–360). Mahwah, NJ: Lawrence Erlbaum Associates.
Gacono, C. B., & Hughes, T. L. (2006). The clinical and forensic interview schedule for the Hare Psychopathy Checklist Youth Version (with an optional section for the school psychologist). Unpublished manuscript.
Gacono, C. B., & Hutton, H. E. (1994). Suggestions for the clinical and forensic use of the Hare Psychopathy Checklist–Revised (PCL-R). *International Journal of Law and Psychiatry, 17*(3), 303–317.
Gacono, C. B., Jumes, M. T., & Gray, B. T. (2008). Use of the Rorschach in forensic treatment planning. In C. Gacono, B. Evans, N. Kaser-Boyd, & L. Gacono (Eds.), *The handbook of forensic Rorschach assessment* (pp. 211–232). Mahwah, NJ: Lawrence Erlbaum Associates.

Gacono, C. B., Loving, J., & Bodholdt, R. (2001). The Rorschach and psychopathy: Toward a more accurate assessment of the research findings. *Journal of Personality Assessment, 77*(1), 16–38.

Gacono, C. B., & Meloy, J. R. (1991). A Rorschach investigation of attachment and anxiety in antisocial personality. *Journal of Nervous and Mental Disease, 179*, 546–552.

Gacono, C. B., & Meloy, J. R. (1994). *The Rorschach assessment of aggressive and psychopathic personalities*. Hillsdale, NJ: Lawrence Erlbaum Associates, Publishers.

Gacono, C.B., Meloy, J.R., & Bridges, M.R. (2000). A Rorschach comparison of psychopaths, sexual homicide perpetrators, and nonviolent pedophiles: Where angels fear to tread. *Journal of Clinical Psychology*, *56*(6), 757–777.

Gacono, C. B., & Meloy, J. R. (2009). Assessing antisocial and psychopathic personalities. In J. Butcher (Ed.), *The Oxford handbook of personality assessment*. Oxford, UK: Oxford University Press.

Gacono, C. B., Meloy, J. R., & Heaven, T. (1990). A Rorschach investigation of narcissism and hysteria in antisocial personality disorder. *Journal of Personality Assessment, 55*, 270–279.

Gacono, C. B., Meloy, J. R., Sheppard, K., Speth, E., & Roske, A. (1995). A clinical investigation of malingering and psychopathy in hospitalized insanity acquittees. *Bulletin of the American Academy of Psychiatry and the Law, 23*(3), 387–397.

Gacono, C. B., Meloy, J. R., Speth, E., & Roske, A. (1997). Above the law: Escapes from a maximum security forensic hospital. *Bulletin of the American Academy of Psychiatry and the Law, 25*(4), 547–550.

Gacono, C. B., Nieberding, R., Owen, A., Rubel, J., & Bodholdt, R. (2001). Treating juvenile and adult offenders with conduct-disorder, antisocial, and psychopathic personalities. In J. Ashford, B. Sales, & W. Reid (Eds.), *Treating clients with special needs* (pp. 99–130). Washington DC: American Psychological Association.

Hare, R. D. (1966). Psychopathy and choices of immediate and delayed punishment. *Journal of Abnormal Psychology, 71*, 25–29.

Hare, R. D. (1991). *The Hare Psychopathy Checklist–Revised*. Toronto, Ontario, Canada: Multi-Health Systems.

Hare, R. D. (1996). Psychopathy: A clinical construct whose time has come. *Criminal Justice and Behavior, 23*(1), 25–54.

Hare, R. D. (1998a). Psychopaths and their nature: Implications for the mental health and criminal justice systems. In T. Millon, E. Simonsen, M. Birket-Smith, & R. Davis (Eds.), *Psychopathy: Antisocial, criminal, and violent behavior* (pp. 188–212). New York: Guilford Press.

Hare, R. D. (1998b). The Alvor Advance Study Institute. In D. J. Cooke, A. E. Forth, & R. D. Hare (Eds.), *Psychopathy: Theory, research and implications for society* (pp. 1–11). London: Kluwer Academic Publishers.

Hare, R. D. (2003). *The Hare Psychopathy Checklist–Revised.* Toronto, Ontario, Canada: Multi-Health Systems.

Hart, S. D., Cox, D. N., & Hare, R. D. (1995). *The Hare Psychopathy Checklist: Screening Version.* North Tonawanda, NY: Multi-Health Systems.

Lilienfeld, S., & Andrews, B. (1996). Development and preliminary validation of a self-report measure of psychopathic personality traits in noncriminal populations. *Journal of Personality Assessment, 66*, 488–534.

Losel, F. (1998). Treatment and management of psychopaths. In D. Cooke, A. Forth, & R. Hare (Eds.), *Psychopathy: Theory, research and implications for society* (pp. 303–354). NATO ASI Series. Netherlands: Kluwer Academic Publishers.

Meloy, J. R. (1988). *The psychopathic mind: Origins, dynamics, and treatment.* Northvale, NJ: Aronson.

Meloy, J. R., & Gacono, C. B. (1998). The internal world of the psychopath: A Rorschach investigation. In T. Millon, E. Simonsen, M. Birket-Smith, & R. Davis (Eds.), *Psychopathy: Antisocial, criminal, and violent behavior.* New York: Guilford Press.

Millon, T., Simonsen, E., Birket-Smith, M., & Davis, R. (1998). *Psychopathy: Antisocial, criminal, and violent behavior.* New York: Guilford Press.

Murphy, J. (1976). Psychiatric labeling in cross-cultural perspective. *Science, 191*, 1019–1028.

Ogloff, J. R., Wong, S., & Greenwood, A. (1990). Treating criminal psychopaths in a therapeutic community. *Behavioral Sciences and the Law, 8*, 181–190.

Quinsey, V., Harris, G., Rice, M., & Cormier, C. (1998). *Violent offenders: Appraising and managing risk.* Washington, DC: American Psychological Association.

Rice, M. E., Harris, G., & Cormier, C. (1992). An evaluation of a maximum security therapeutic community for psychopaths and other mentally disordered offenders. *Law and Human Behavior, 16*, 399–412.

Robins, L. (1966). *Deviant children grown up: A sociological and psychiatric study of sociopathic personality.* Baltimore, MD: Williams & Wilkins.

Smith, A. M., Gacono, C. B., & Kaufman, L. (1997). A Rorschach comparison of psychopathic and non-psychopathic conduct disordered adolescents. *Journal of Clinical Psychology, 53*, 289–300.

Wood, J. M., Lilienfeld, S. O., Nezworski, M. T., Garb, H. N., Holloway Allen, K., & Wildermuth, J. L. (2010). Validity of Rorschach inkblot scores for discriminating psychopaths from nonpsychopaths in forensic populations: A meta-analysis. *Psychological Assessment, 22*(2), 336–349.

CHAPTER FOURTEEN

Psychopathic Aggression: Will or Determinism?

George B. Palermo

Psychopathic aggressive behavior is extremely antisocial, and its destructiveness can be appalling. Throughout the past and still at present, psychopathy has been the topic of descriptive, psychodynamic, genetic and biological investigations. This chapter addresses the question of whether psychopaths are free in their decisional capacity or whether their criminal acts are subjected to determinism. A brief review of the history of psychopathy, psychopathic aggressivity, and pertinent psychoanalytic views are presented, along with philosophical theories of free will and determinism. Recent findings of brain neuroimaging of psychopaths are discussed. Special regard is given to Libet's theory of free will. The criminal responsibility of psychopaths is considered in view of free will and determinism.

History of Psychopathy

The *Diagnostic and Statistical Manual-IV-TR* (American Psychiatric Association, 2000) includes under the heading "Antisocial Personality Disorder" some of the basic characteristics of the psychopathic personality. However, the consensus among mental health professionals is that a distinction should be made between the two. The majority of persons with an antisocial personality disorder can be viewed as reactors to social stresses, while the psychopaths are "real" actors, planning and initiating an antisocial action. The characteristics of the latter, as reported by Hare

(1993), seem to retrace Cleckley's (1941/1955) description of psychopaths as self-centered, callous, and remorseless persons, profoundly lacking in empathy, and with an inability to form warm relationships with others, persons who function without the restraint of a conscience. The recidivism of criminal psychopaths is well known and their treatability is questionable.

Historically, the concept of psychopathy dates back to the time of Pinel (1801/1962) and Lombroso (1889)—to Pinel, with his emphasis on the lack of morals in the psychopath, and to Lombroso, with his characterization of the psychopath as a *born criminal*. Many scholars have stressed the etiology of psychopathy, presenting it variously as congenital, biological, personal, or environmental. Pinel considered psychopaths to be mentally ill, suffering from a *manie sans delire* and in need of moral treatment; Rush (1812) proposed organic causes for psychopathy, which he considered a disease; and Prichard (1835) described it as a disorder of a person's feelings and attitudes, without the involvement of higher mental functions, but with a predisposition to behave as a morally insane person without the human capacity for empathy. Koch (1891) coined the term "psychopathic inferior," and he considered psychopathy to be a hereditary disease, with emotional and moral aberrations and abnormal behaviors. Maudsley (1896) thought psychopaths to be suffering from moral imbecility due to a cerebral dysfunction; von Krafft-Ebing (1922) viewed them as "savages" and believed that they were in need of isolation and treatment for their own sake and that of society; and Kraepelin (1915) described them as manipulators and charming liars, impulsive and remorseless (Arrigo & Shipley, 2001).

Cleckley (1941/1955), in his seminal work *The Mask of Sanity*, described psychopaths as grandiose, arrogant, callous, superficial, and manipulative. He reported their conduct to vary in severity "from a mild or borderline degree up through a great degree of disability" (p. 279), and he believed the disability to be genuine. He also pointed out their recidivistic criminal tendencies and their frequent outward appearance of normality. In the psychopaths we are indeed confronted, as Cleckley wrote, with a *mask of sanity*, and "all the outward features of this mask are intact. . . . The thought processes retain their normal aspect under psychiatric investigation and in technical tests . . . [an example of] *la folie lucid*" (p. 423). Their expressions, tone of voice, and general demeanor seem normal, but they fail "altogether when [they are] put into the practice of actual living" (p. 424). The personal and social failures of psychopaths are so pervasive that they can only be explained, as Cleckley wrote, by their being *madmen*, or by their being incapable of grasping the meaning of their thoughts or feelings. The concept of their functioning, said Cleckley, "postulates a selective defect . . . which prevents important components of normal experience from being integrated into the whole human reaction, particularly an elimination or attenuation of those strong affective components that ordinarily arise in major personal and social issues" (p. 428). The distorted affectivity of psychopaths, their tragic persistence in antisocial behavior, and their inability to learn from mistakes is akin to a profound childish immaturity, which causes them to move, without reflection, from thought to action, without appraising and discerning what type of decision they should make and act upon.

The emotions of psychopaths can be described as pseudo-emotions. They use a pantomime of feelings. They are full of rationalizations, their judgment is poor, and their sense of value is almost inexistent. Their outward behavior seems to be the result of a deeply distorted inner personality, similar to that of the schizophrenic, at times largely concealed by apparently good reasoning and their ability to live their lives in a quasi-sane manner (Palermo, 2004).

Macdonald (1961) described psychopaths as lacking empathy, impulsive and intolerant of frustration. They are usually of average or above-average intelligence, have an apparent lack of guilt, and do not learn from experience. Alexander and Ross (1952) believed that at the basis of psychopaths' symptomatic self-destructive behavior is the presence of unconscious neurotic conflicts, even of an incestuous or patricidal nature. The psychopath may project his unacceptable aggressive feelings outwardly; and for him the world suddenly becomes a hostile place in which to live, and at times he acts out against it. Halleck (1967) posited that the psychopath violates the law "in his efforts to suit the world to his own needs" (p. 109). The crimes could be a way to control a fear of psychological disintegration.

Arieti (1967) attributed the impulsiveness of psychopaths and their desire for immediate gratification to an attempt to overcome unbearable inner tension due to short-circuited anxiety. They are "unable to change, repress, postpone or neutralize [their] need for hostility," he stated (p. 248), and their criminal acting out may be in the form of murder, rape, seduction in men, or promiscuity and prostitution in women. More important and relevant to this discussion, however, is Arieti's reflection on the paranoid psychopath. Psychopathic traits or behavior "generally preceded a definite paranoiac symptomatology, or, in some cases, periods of acting out with no freely expressed delusions alternating with obvious delusional periods" (p. 248).

Psychopaths have a reduced sensitivity or no response to displays of distress in others, are distractible, have a desire for immediate gratification without a balance between immediate and long-term gratification, and have linguistic deficits (Schneider & Nussbaum, 2007). Already in 1993, Robert Hare reported that linguistically, the psychopath's speech is syntactically and semantically disordered, with disconnected components that are, nevertheless, masked by a superficially grammatical orderly structure.

In summary, psychopaths are self-indulgent and interpersonally intrusive (Yochelson & Samenow, 1976). When acting out criminally, they are remorseless and callous. Their transgressions of societal rules bring harm to others and show their inability to process moral issues in a mature way. They are "oblivious and insensitive to affective moral valences and therefore the prospect of being governed by those aspects of life is not even a possibility" (Schneider & Nussbaum, 2007, p. 180). They seem to be fixed at a preconventional level of moral development (Kohlberg, 1984; Piaget, (1932/1965). Psychological and neurological studies support the clinical findings that psychopaths show diminished emotional responsiveness to the suffering of the people they victimize. They seem to be unable to understand their victim's fear as reflected in their facial expression (theory of mind), and that worsens their aggressive violence (Blair, 2001). They show a diminished appreciation of moral codes. They are extremely impulsive and act without reflecting on the consequences of their behavior. This raises the question of whether they are morally or legally responsible for their actions.

At times psychopaths show feature of a borderline personality disorder. In those cases their symptomatology is even more complex. They may go through sudden mood changes, such as anger, depression, anhedonia, sense of futility, loneliness, and isolation. They resort to primitive defense mechanisms, such as ambivalence, projective identification, and feelings of omnipotence, denial, idealization, and devaluation. Their behavior is more marginal, transient and ego-dystonic, and their interpersonal relationships appear to be good only on the surface. At times they may suffer from transitory and fleeting hallucinations or delusions. They even seem unable to control their impulses because of sudden psychotic thinking due to internal and external stress. In such cases they fall into Otto Kernberg's (1992) classification of psychotic personality organization.

Psychopathic Aggression

Research has found a strong relationship between psychopathy and aggressive behavior in offenders throughout their criminal careers. Hare and Jutai (1983) supported the propensity for violent aggression by psychopathic offenders who, they found, committed crimes twice as often as non-psychopaths. Similar percentages were found by Porter, Birt, and Boer in another later study (2001).

In general, aggression driven by anger and hostility can be viewed as a progressive manifestation of the displeasure felt in and about life and people by a person with a shaky emotional equilibrium. It can be distinguished as primary aggression and reactive aggression. Blackburn (1993) described aggressive psychopathic behavior as primary—that of the classical psychopath, hostile and destructive in character, with many constitutional deficits—or secondary—as reactive to psychosocial factors, generally frustrating life experiences. Aggression also can be subdivided into premeditated aggression, impulsive aggression, and aggression caused by medical illnesses (Glenn & Raine, 2009). The aggression of psychopaths has in itself a varied degree of impulsivity.

Impulsivity may be viewed as a complex act by a person "without the ability to consider the consequences to [himself] or others. . . . a failure of a normal process by which, over about one-third of a second, a potential behavior is screened before it enters conscious awareness" (Swann, 2003, p. 26). Even though psychopaths seem to function normally, their quick decision-making, lacking reflection before acting, makes their decisional capacity defective. To this effect, Wilson and Herrnstein (1985) stated: "Impulsiveness can be thought of as either the cause or the effect of the poor conditionability of the psychopath" (p. 204). They show a lack of self-criticism and "[w]ithout the internal monologue, time horizons shrink; behavior becomes more tied to its immediate consequences" (p. 205). Strong unsublimated impulses are disruptive, and self-control is essential for a person in order to avoid giving vent to unbridled impulsivity.

From a philosophical point of view, impulses were viewed by Friedrich Nietzsche (1998) as important in a person's behavior. He wrote that "a man without impulses could not do the good or create the beautiful any more than a castrated man could beget children" (in Kaufmann, 1974, p. 224). Nevertheless, impulses need control, and he viewed the man who is able to master his passions as powerful—a superman (*übermann*)—able to organize his self and, in so doing, give style to his character. As Kaufmann wrote (1974), Nietzsche believed that the man who imposes restraints on himself is not only "a 'rational' animal, but also a 'moral' animal" (p. 213). The two may coexist. On the other hand, he viewed the man who strives for power over others through bullying and criminal activity as a weak person, deeply frustrated. Nietzsche believed firmly that true existence is not a passive accident but is a personal, progressive achievement toward bettering oneself, attempting to achieve those higher models of behavior one should aim for in order to become one's true self: "You shall become who you are [*Du sollst der werden, der du bist*]" (Kauffman, 1974, p. 159). He well portrayed the criminal's restless, morally unhealthy personality when he wrote, "What is this man? He's a heap of diseases, which through his spirit, reach out into the world: there they want to catch their prey ... a ball of wild snakes, which rarely enjoy rest from each other: so they go forth singly and seek prey in the world" (Nietzsche, 1978, p. 39). His stark description is typical of the criminal psychopath.

Baruk, the French psychiatrist, viewed the total lack of moral values, present in the psychopathic offenders, as "one of the worst calamities that can affect a human being, because of its personal and social consequences" (cited in Di Tullio, 1971, p. 41), one of the most serious of which is their aggressive acting-out behavior. Aggressivity, in its destructive form, is frequently connected with explosive impulsivity. During such explosive reactions, some individuals, unable to contain their feelings, behave in a socially unacceptable way and, careless of the boundaries of good interpersonal civilized conduct, do not weigh their thoughts or their feelings before acting out. These antisocial behaviors are at times observed in persons suffering from antisocial personality, passive-aggressive, paranoid, or borderline personality disorders, but they are more frequently seen in psychopaths. Their behaviors are immature, remindful of children who are unable to exercise their reflective capacity and control over their impulses. As Daniel Goleman (1995) wrote, "There is perhaps no psychological skill more fundamental than resisting impulse. It is the root of all emotional self-control, since all emotions, by their very nature, lead to one or another impulse to act" (p. 81). Sudden acting out may signify a call for attention or acknowledgment, or may be simple surrender to evildoing.

The impulsive act of psychopathic aggression is frequently out of proportion to the contextual situation. It has been proposed that at the basis of impulsive hostility and aggressivity may be frustrated feelings of dependency, a craving for love, a way to recapture a primitive maternal relationship, a sense of helplessness, and a wish to control the other (Winnicott, 1953). The negative feelings of psychopaths are usually long-standing and deeply buried within the unconscious or the subconscious. Their hostile and aggressive feelings are ego-dystonic, and they try to control them in order to avoid real or fantasized narcissistic injuries. In trying to maintain their psychological homeostasis, they exercise repression but often are unable to do so. At times, confused irrational behavior or an upsurge of feelings of frustration precedes destructive acting-out.

Psychopaths are "less likely to be affected by punishment [which frequently produces moral socialization] and thus are more likely to continue to engage in the punished action in the future" (Daversa, 2010, p. 9).

Psychopathy itself predicts aggressive behavior. Lacking remorse and empathy, and because of a tendency to uninhibited behavior, they qualify as intraspecies predators, using aggressivity to obtain sexual pleasure and employing power and control in crimes that may include murder and sadistic behaviors. In their homicidal fury or sexual orgies, they are ruthless.

Although, psychopathic aggression may be reactive, it is more likely to be instrumental, premeditated, and well organized. The behavior is occasionally interspersed with lack of control. Cleckley (1941/1955) asserted that psychopathic violence is more instrumental and is motivated by material gain, unrestrained sexual drives, and destructive hostility, thrill-seeking motivation, and a lack of emotional arousal. Psychopaths are found in every social stratum, from the lowest to the highest, and include professionals, political leaders, and financiers. They often have a behavioral façade of normalcy, which deceives others. They tend to downplay their actions and exculpate themselves, minimizing their planned violence in favor of reactive behavior. Prostitution, drug addiction, and drug trafficking are frequently observed in these persons, who have a strong tendency to exploit others.

Psychoanalytic Theories of Aggression

Various scholars have contributed to the understanding of the development of human aggression. Freud, in *Civilization and Its Discontents* (1961), wrote, "Men are not gentle creatures who want to be loved, and who at the most can defend themselves if they are attacked; they are, on the contrary, creatures among whose instinctual endowment is to be reckoned a powerful share of aggressiveness" (p. 68). He hypothesized that at the basis of some criminal actions there may be a conflict at the level of the Oedipal relationship. The crime could be the means to call upon oneself punishment for the Oedipic guilt. Alexander (1948) described psychopaths as a group of offenders who, because of intense guilt feelings over removed early life experiences, engage in antisocial, aggressive behavior in order to be apprehended and punished.

Several theories on the psychological development of the infant shed light on the development and understanding of aggressive behavior. Schilder (1942) proposed that as the child grows in the definition of his body image, he becomes more active and tries to master the world around himself. That requires a certain amount of aggressivity, which at times is mixed with sexuality. Eventually, however, helped by the positive controlling influence of the family and social mores, the child masters this aggressivity. Kohut (1971) theorized that a child achieves individuation and self-esteem when he is able to tame the archaic, grandiose, and exhibitionistic self. Kohut believed that this is a necessary step in order to achieve an ego-syntonic, purposeful adult personality development. However, he also thought that at times, due to a narcissistic trauma suffered in early infancy, the child may not progress toward maturation and may still retain within himself the presence of a disappointing parental imago. At the core of his psychological self, even during his adult life, there would then be the presence of what Kohut refers to as an archaic transitional self-object, usually required for the maintenance of a narcissistic homeostasis. When venting his aggression against others, the psychopath attempts to keep under control the disappointing parental imago, which threatens his narcissistic homeostasis.

One of the most influential object relations theorists, Kernberg (1992) posited the idea that the infant is prewired to form destructive schemes of himself and others. Cognitive and affective potentials facilitate, he said, the relationship of the infant with his mother. Object relations are initiated by "a central biological function of inborn affective patterns with their behavioral, communicative, and psychophysiological manifestations" (p. 15). Kernberg postulated that the infant's affective memories of earlier experiences (good and bad mother perceptions) are stored in the limbic system and that they may be reactivated later in specific relationships.

It is assumed that the infant has many gratifying and concrete experiences with his mother, and the environment that will form a complex world of affective object relations, which are internalized as good-object relations. According to Kernberg (1992), "Love and hate thus become stable intrapsychic structures . . . for organizing psychic experience and behavioral control . . . through various developmental stages" (p. 20). That gives birth to libido and aggression, which will later become driving affects. In the normal formation of character, defenses "push the dynamic unconscious deeper and deeper into the psychic apparatus" (p. 19), contributing to the concomitant formation of ego and id. This dynamic unconscious and its pathological primitive complexes at times erupt into consciousness, especially in persons with severe personality disorders, such as psychopathic and borderline individuals, as well as in those with psychoses.

On the basis of object relations theories, it could be claimed that the violent psychopaths, especially those that kill, are unable to tame their archaic, grandiose, exhibitionistic self, as Kohut (1971) and Mahler (1972) asserted. Or, as Klein (1935) stated, their repressed bad imagoes are projected onto the outside world and their desire to destroy them ensues; or even that, as in a narcissistic crisis, the repressed pathological complexes come to the fore, and in aggressively acting out, they destroy the frustrating object. It could be postulated that in those moments, at the time of the killings, these killers are victims of their pathological, irrational unconscious.

Will or Determinism: A Metaphysical Debate

The metaphysical debate regarding will and determinism spans almost three millennia of the history of Western civilization. This debate is important in the discussion of psychopathic aggressivity. It follows the evolution of human thinking from a concrete understanding of the world and the self to the present-day, highly sophisticated scientific climate. It goes from a deterministic view of the physical world and a self under partial control by anthropomorphic gods to the self as a free individual, master of his own destiny.

In the beginning, humans had no concept of the self as an agent to will, and the gods were thought to frequently intrude into their lives, guiding their conduct. Bible narratives, estimated to have been written around 3,500 years ago, seem to testify to the Jewish belief that the god of the Jews, Yaweh, created humans with a free will when, in Genesis, it is recounted that if Adam and Eve disobeyed God's commands, they would be punished. It seems reasonable to interpret those words as meaning that they had a choice to exercise their own will. In Deuteronomy, the same recommendation is given to Cain and the people of Israel. This indicates that already at the time of the biblical recounting, people believed that they possessed freedom of action and accountability.

In Homer's *Iliad* (c. 800 BCE), the many heroes often justified their deeds, both good and bad, by claiming that the gods had intervened to influence their actions. Agamemnon, king of Mycenae, for example, justified his abduction of Briseis, Achilles's beloved, by attributing his lustful action to the gods who blinded his judgment. Both the *Iliad* and the *Odyssey* (c. 750 BCE) portray numerous episodes in which human behavior is portrayed as due to the interference of the gods. Thus, there was only an appearance of freedom, since the actions were quasi-predetermined.

As early Greek philosophers began to speculate about the origins and meanings of life, Protagoras (c. 481–420 BCE) came to believe that man is the measure of all things. During the same period, philosophers of the atomistic school (Leucippus [c. 480–420 BCE] and Democritus [c. 470–370 BCE]), theorized that humans, as well as the cosmos, are made of indivisible particles, which they called atoms. They believed that in humans, the atoms were in continuous movement, and when they collided with one another, they generated their free will. This theory, even though deterministic when concerning cosmic events (a concatenation of immutable repetitive events), was at the basis of the Epicurean theory of Lucretius (94–55 BCE), who believed that humans possess free will. Socrates, Plato, and Aristotle (fourth century BCE) all believed in free will, the first two also accepting moral determinism, since they thought that people did not act against what they believed to be good. In his *Nicomachean Ethics*, Aristotle wrote that "man is the origin of his actions" (III, iii, 15, p. 139), capable of a voluntary act following a deliberate choice. But he added that "acts done from passion seem very far from being done of deliberate choice" (III, ii, 6, p. 131). The Stoics (early third century BCE), on the other hand, including the later Roman orator Cicero (106 BCE–43 BCE) and the Roman emperor Marcus Aurelius (121 CE–180 CE), believed not in free will but in strict determinism, and they claimed that this belief was supported by logic.

Greek tragedians (e.g., Euripides, Aeschylus, and Sophocles) believed in free will and attempted to enlighten people through their works to a nondeterministic view of human behavior. They stressed human decisional capacity and personal responsibility for actions. Euripides's Medea admits that with her own hands, she killed her children in an act of revenge against her unfaithful husband, disclaiming any interference from the gods in her decision. Aeschylus, in his tragedy *Seven against Thebes*, strongly advised that people stop blaming the gods for their deeds and accept their responsibility, especially for their loss of moral control. The struggle between god-driven fate and personal decision making continued in the tragedies of Sophocles. In *Oedipus Rex*, Oedipus admits that his actions were his own decision and accepts the responsibility for them, stating that the hand that struck his victims was his own.

During early Christianity, two religious scholars were prominent in the debate on free will and determinism. Pelagius (fourth century CE) rejected the thesis of original sin and argued that humans had the power to choose and to decide, and their choices would determine whether they would go to Heaven or to Hell. During the same period, Augustine, Bishop of Hippo, argued that humans carry the original sin of Adam and Eve, the early transgressors of God's commands; but that through an act of grace, God grants freedom of choice to those people who are good Christians. He maintained that God in his omniscience, even though knowing what decisions would be made, does not interfere with them. Later, St. Thomas Aquinas (1225–1274) made a distinction between a natural *unfree* will (the acceptance of naturally and necessarily desirable truths such as justice and peace) and a deliberate or free will, which helps one to evaluate choices before deciding.

During the Renaissance and beyond, philosophers continued to question whether man's actions are free or determined. Descartes (1596–1650), for example, who is famous for his dictum *Cogito ergo sum*, firmly believed in human free will. He thought it essential for the making of moral choices and important in assessing responsibility for a person's actions. He thought of free will as the ability of humans to do or not to do something without constraint, after having had the opportunity and capacity to reflect on alternative choices and consequences. In *The Passions of the Soul*, he wrote, "But the will is by its nature so free that it can never be constrained" (Descartes, 1999, p. 343). More pertinent to the present discussion, he also wrote: "[By] understanding one is enabled to entertain certain propositions, but understanding by itself neither affirms, denies, neither chooses nor rejects. The role is reserved for the will" (Taylor, 1972, p. 365).

Among the humanistic scholars, Voltaire (1694–1778) and Rousseau (1712–1778) upheld free will and the idea that people make choices for which they assume responsibility. Free will was seen as the expression of human autonomy and dignity of the willer. Kant (1724–1804) also asserted in *The Critique of Practical Reason* (2008) that humans have free will, and he believed that their actions are intentional and self-determined. Schopenhauer (1788–1860) (2003) asserted that the will is the dominant force in a person's life. Later, James (1842–1910), arguing that humans exercise free will, rejected scientific determinism (Boas, 1972). And in the twentieth century, Sartre (1956), strongly supporting free will, contended that to deny one's own free will is to make excuses for one's behavior.

Contrary to free will, determinism is based on the belief that any decision or action is predetermined: it is viewed as the resultant of a concatenation of events, each caused by the preceding one and causing the subsequent one. Among the most famous determinists, one finds the formerly mentioned Stoics, who believed that every event has a cause and that the cause is rational. By the time of the late Renaissance, Luther (1483–1546) and Calvin (1509–1564) firmly believed that man's actions are predetermined. Spinoza (1632–1677) asserted his belief that feelings of free will are due to being conscious of one's actions, but he was basically unaware of the concatenation of causes that determine those actions. The French philosopher d'Holbac (1723–1789) stated that every thought or action is determined by prior ones and, more specifically, that man's desires are outwardly and inwardly motivated.

Scholars of the compatibilistic school of philosophy generally accepted natural causation of events but admitted the possibility of free choice.

Among the most important scholars of compatibilism are Hobbes (1588–1679) and Hume (1711–1776). Although upholding determinism, Hobbes did not reject free will, believing that a voluntary act is caused by an act of the will and is no less voluntary because the act of will is caused. Hume believed that people are free and responsible for exercising their free will. However, he also held a deterministic view of human actions, because the same motives produced the same actions. Others, such as Darwin (1809–1882), not believing in free will, asserted that no one deserves credit for anything.

The long debate on free will and determinism continued into the twentieth century, and even quantum theory has been used in support of free will. In that regard, Cashmore (2010) wrote that Eccles (1989) had suggested "in the interaction between mind and soul . . . [Man] achieves the capacity to 'swerve atoms'—a requirement for free will (as noted by Epicurus) by taking the 'magic of the soul' afforded by the dualism of Descartes and combining it with Heisenberg's uncertainty principle" (p. 2).[1] Frankfurt (1969, 1988) made a distinction between acting freely and having free will, believing that although people can and do act freely, they still do not have free will. Free will, he said, is present only when an individual who knows that what he wishes to do is wrong decides not to do it. It is then that free will is exercised. A man is only free when he is able to choose or to take the initiative to deliberate responsibly. Other twenty-first-century philosophers do not believe in free will. Pereboom (2001) believes that people should not be held responsible for their actions, Smilansky (2000), in a utilitarian fashion, stated that even though there is no free will, people should not stop believing in it, because it would destroy cardinal tenets of law, such as findings of guilt or innocence and therefore annul punishment for wrongdoing. And Wilson (1998), even though admitting that there is no certainty of its existence, wrote "[W]ithout it the mind, imprisoned by fatalism, would slow and deteriorate" (p. 120).

Biological and Neuroimaging Findings in Psychopathy

The prevalence rate of brain dysfunction in the general population is 3%, but "neuropsychological studies show that the prevalence rate of brain dysfunction among the criminal population is extremely high, with prevalence rates of ninety-four percent among homicide offenders, sixty-one percent among habitually aggressive adults, forty-nine to seventy-eight percent among sex offenders, and seventy-six percent among juvenile offenders" (Redding, 2006, p. 57), many of whom are psychopathic offenders. From a biological point of view, psychopathic aggressive behavior is influenced by the interplay of multiple genes. These genes, together with hormones and neurotransmitters, act upon various biochemical circuits. Genetics, biological, and environmental correlates of aggressive behavior have been pointed out by twin studies, adoption studies, electroencephalographic studies, low arousal theory, heart rate studies, skin conductivity tests, and gene mutations, such as MAOA activity, testosterone, and cortisol levels (Palermo, 2010). Antisocial psychopathic aggression should therefore be viewed as the resultant of a biological predisposition and environmental factors and their effect on the brain. At present, neural factors at the basis of abnormal behavior, from depression and schizophrenia to personality disorders and psychopathic criminal conduct, may be detected by recent neuroimaging techniques (various scans including CAT, MRI, fMRI, MRA, and PET).

The areas of the brain principally identified as dysfunctional in the psychopath include the prefrontal cortex, the temporal cortex, the amygdala, the hippocampus complex, the corpus callosum, and the angular gyrus. In addition, the neurotransmitters dopamine and serotonin are involved in the uninhibited (impulsive) behavior of the psychopath. The frontal inhibitory system is under the effect of serotonin. If serotonin is deficient, dopamine takes over and increases the tendency to immediate reward, with a lack of encoding or moral appreciation (Palermo, 2010).

Aggressive behavior is due in part to hypofunctionality of the frontal lobes and hyperfunction of the limbic system, especially the amygdala nuclei. The frontal lobes, with their discriminating, controlling, and executive capacities, keep the amygdala, primarily involved in emotional reactivity, in check. The neurotransmitter serotonin is also involved in this interplay. A lack of serotonin, indeed, increases the amygdala-neuronal reactivity as reported by Hariri et al. (2002, 2005) (as cited in Rutter, 2006).

The amygdala, an almond-shaped cerebral structure, is involved not only in aggression and emotional reactions, but also in emotional memory. Its activities are modulated by connections with various parts of the frontal cortex (medial, orbital, and dorso-lateral regions). In fear-inducing situations, the amygdala reacts and initiates a chain of neuronal events through the hypothalamic-pituitary axis, which leads to instrumental aggressivity. The Island of Reil, another brain structure, also contributes to emotional reactivity, with its involvement in the feelings of humiliation and lust that frequently are associated with aggressive behavior.

Frontal lobe lesions diminish an individual's capacity to discriminate, to execute complex tasks, and, most importantly, to differentiate right from wrong. Their detection plays a major role in forensic psychiatry in the determination of competency and legal responsibility. Criminal psychopaths at times show cognitive impairment due to old, traumatic frontal lobe lesion and emotional disinhibition with rage and violence, the consequence of limbic system pathology (Volavka, 1995). The above pathological behaviors, cognitive impairment and emotional disinhibition, are also observed in brainstem lesions (Goldberg, 2001). In addition, the cerebral gray matter has been found to be frequently reduced in criminal psychopaths (Raine et al., 1998), together with impulsivity, disinhibited rage and occasional post-crime depression. The behavior of psychopaths, particularly those with borderline features, also may be due to a possible disruption of four important brain-emotional circuits: ACC (the anterior cingulate cortex), OXC (the orbital frontal cortex), VMC (the ventromedial prefrontal cortex), and DLPFC (the dorsolateral prefrontal cortex) (Goodman, Triebwasser, Shah, & New, 2007). A study by Raine, Lencz, Bihrle, LaCasse, and Colletti (2007) noted in individuals with a high degree of psychopathy a diminution of the gray matter in the prefrontal lobes as well as a smaller amygdala. One study found that fMRI showed decreased activity in various parts of the brain in psychopaths, including "the amygdala, hippocampal formation, parahippocampal gyrus, ventral striatum and anterior and posterior cingulated gyrus" (Goodman et al., 2007, p. 103).

In addition to biological and genetic explanations for psychopathic behaviors, it has been theorized that environmental and psychosocial factors may also be at the basis of their development. Indeed, the continuous stress of maltreatment by caregivers, nonresponsive parental attitudes, rejection, and abuse (psychological, physical, or sexual) may cause an affective disregulation. This disregulation in mediated by a hormonal cascade, enhanced by monoamine oxidase A genotype involving the brain, especially the functions of the amygdala and hypothalamus (Caspi et al., 2002). The affective neural network disregulation in the growing child over time will produce typical psychopathic behaviors, such as a lack of affective responsivity or distant or arrogant and antisocial interpersonal relationships (Daversa, 2010).

The Libet Experiment

In 1965, researchers in Germany, using human EEG tracings, reported that just before (0.4–4.0 seconds) consciously initiating a voluntary movement of the hand or foot, the electrical pattern of brain activity of the participants in their study shifted (Kornhuber & Deecke, 1965). They termed the shift readiness potential (*Bereitschaftspotential*), believing that it was related to the process of preparing the body to make the movement. Libet, Gleason, Wright, and Pearl (1983) replicated the experiment, employing neuroimaging to pinpoint the exact moment when the subject became consciously aware of his intention to act. They were able to demonstrate that the *readiness potential* began 550 milliseconds before the muscles were activated to perform the act. However, the readiness potential was not always followed by movement. They noted that "[t]he brain was evidently beginning the volitional process of the act well before the activation of the muscle that produced movement" (p. 49). In addition, they wrote, the muscle activation took place after too long a time to assume that it was due to a motor command to the muscle. The study confirmed that individuals became aware of their desire to move the hand 350 milliseconds before the readiness potential unconsciously took place, but 200 milliseconds before the motor act itself.

The above experiments support the idea that the unconscious readiness potential takes place before individuals are aware of having the will to act. That would be contrary to the assumption that their free will initiated the action, because the action apparently started in the brain 350 milliseconds before the act, and 200 milliseconds before the subjects' awareness. Libet et al. (1983) theorized that although the will does not initiate the action, it may exercise a veto of the entire process if the subjects do not wish to continue a specific action. As Schwartz and Begley (2003) wrote, Libet had noted that the veto of an urge to act is a common experience. Therefore, even though the urge to move the hand is unconsciously initiated, the will is still in control and carries on the act in the way the individual decided. In other words, they note, refraining from acting is as much of an act as committing one, as Sherrington (1933) had written decades earlier.

Libet et al.'s (1983) findings support the idea that free will does not initiate a voluntary act but allows it or suppresses it because of the specific desire of the subject or because of its socially unacceptable consequences. He clearly stated that the volitional process is initiated unconsciously, but added that free will is not excluded because it can veto the act. That is, the final decision to carry out an act is consciously controlled, and the unconscious initiative for an action may either proceed or may be aborted by the veto of the free will, which, in that case, acts as a gatekeeper or censor; that is, the veto capacity is not the result of a preceding unconscious process. However, what is necessary for gatekeeping is attention (will)—a mental force that actively engages the wisdom of the executive discrimination of the prefrontal cortex. Schwartz and Begley (2003) commented that the will acting as a gatekeeper has long been present in religious and ethical dicta as *Do not do that*, or *Control thyself*.

Libet later wrote (1999), "Given the speculative nature of both determinism and non-determinist theories, why not adapt the view that we do have a free will (until some real contradictory evidence may appear, if it ever does). Such a view would at least allow us to proceed in a way that accepts and accommodates our own deep feelings that we do have free will" (p. 56). In this way, man would not view himself as an automaton.

It has been asserted that advances in neuroscience will not undermine our intuitive notions of free will and moral responsibility. Thus far, wrote Roskies (2006), they have not established whether we live in a determinate world but have brought into the debate random or probabilistic processes. Further, she wrote that "[d]eterminism is an assumption that many scientists adhere to, but it is likely always to remain an assumption" (p. 421). Assumptions are, obviously, not facts. The same cannot be said of biological mechanisms and their effects on humans as responsible agents. Studies have shown that volitional activity activates the prefrontal cortex, just as automatic clenching of the hands activates the motor cortex. It can be safely said that the dorsolateral prefrontal region has as a primary role in the free selection of behavior, "choosing from a number of possible actions by inhibiting all but one and focusing the attention on the chosen one" (Schwartz & Begley, 2003, p. 312). If lesions are present in those areas of the brain, they make the subject similar to an automaton, diminishing spontaneous activity and selective attention. It is to be hoped that more extensive knowledge of neuroscience will facilitate the shaping of views on responsibility, reconciling intuitive and legal notions within the framework of a compatibilistic view of brain and mind working together. As Kawohl and Habermeyer (2007), reacting to Libet's paper, suggested, in dealing with offenders, psychoforensic experts should use a psychopathological approach based on cognition, motivation, personality, and personality values rather than the data from Libet's experiments.

Free Will, Decisional Capacity, and Criminal Responsibility

The concept of free will in criminal responsibility and *mens rea*, introduced into the legal system in England around the eleventh century, was emphasized in the following centuries by various scholars, including de Bracton (thirteenth century), Hale (seventeenth century), and Blackstone (eighteenth century). For any decision to be free, an adult individual must be aware of his surroundings (the reality around him), of his own and other's behavior, and of the consequences of his actions or nonactions. Further, he must have the cognitive capacity to be able to make choices in conformity to the laws, ethics, and moral and social standards of the society in which he lives, and to recognize the social value of the acts he is performing.

Cognitive capacity is understood as the capacity to assess one's own actions. This capacity may be impaired because of damage to particular brain areas, usually involving the frontal and prefrontal regions of the brain, the seats of cognitive processing that can signal and trigger prepackaged emotional reactions. Cognition facilitates the presence of emotions by "giving us the ability to make decisions about what kind of action should occur next, given the situation in which we find ourselves now. ... [and] it allows this shift from reaction to action" (Le Doux, 1996, p. 175). Integrating cognitive capacity, decisional—or volitional—capacity, is the ability to reach a free and voluntary intent to act out what one chooses. It includes a deliberating process that requires prior reflection and the choice of a given course of action, which may or may not be executed. In forensics, free decisional capacity determines responsibility.

There are mental disorders in which the decisional capacity is clearly involved. These include the obsessive-compulsive neurosis, in which the compulsion to act does not allow reflection before acting or obsessive thinking does not allow deliberation; the disinhibited behaviors of the psychopath who acts out in an impulsive manner, without prior reflection; or the disinhibited, unreflective decision making of persons under the effects of alcohol or drugs. At times, inner suspiciousness in persons with severe personality disorders may cause a misinterpretation of facts that contributes to impairment in decision making. People with schizoid and schizotypal personalities who are severely withdrawn may also show decisional impairment, not being totally aware of the many facets of a social situation. This becomes more evident when they are under stress. Cognitive and decision-making capacities (understanding and will) normally integrate each other. However, they are frequently impaired in people who are psychotic, disrupting their capacity for clear reasoning and choice.

In one of the most well-known criminal cases of the twentieth century, the defense attorney pointed out the presence of many factors, known and unknown, that may undermine an individual's cognition and decisional capacities. His voice echoed in the courtroom as he asked why the defendants had attacked their victim. The answer, he said, "was self-explanatory, not for money, not out of spite, not for hate. They killed him as they might kill a spider, a fly, for the experience. They killed him because they were made that way. Because somewhere in the infinite processes that go to the making up of the boy or the man, something slipped" (Famous American Trials, 2010). Those were the words of Clarence Darrow and his main argument in his defense of Nathan Leopold and Richard Loeb, both teenagers, who killed 14-year-old Bobby Franks. In his final closing statement, Darrow claimed that the two defendants were not fully responsible for their act. Their behavior, he asserted, might have been the consequence of peculiar and immature thinking, possibly due to psychological, biological, or genetic factors. His defense was upholding determinism in a court of law, and it was his belief that the future would support his assertion. He shifted the debate of will and determinism from the metaphysical arena to the scientific/forensic one. Darrow was anticipating what 80 years later is taking place: the contributions of neuropsychological assessments and neuroimaging technology to forensics and to findings of legal accountability.

Legal accountability theory attempts to determine whether the individual/agent has *mens rea*—the capacity to form intent and the mental capability of controlling his own actions: the actor should have the capacity to act differently on the basis of a selection of choices. Accountability theory views the miscreant as responsible for his actions unless his mental state at the time of a crime made him unable to appreciate the wrongfulness, the quality, or the consequences of his actions, and to behave according to the dictates of the law (American Law Institute Model Penal Code)—in other words, he isin control of his volitional capacity. The presumption of free will underlies all tests for criminal responsibility: are criminal actions the result of the exercise of free will, or the consequence of deterministic factors? Wilson and Herrnstein (1985) wrote, "The recurrent theme for the concept of responsibility . . . is behavior freely and intentionally engaged in" (p. 504).

Determinism, as described previously, means that behavior is due to a concatenation of causes, and as Juth and Lorentzon (2010) wrote, "Everything that happens is taken to be sufficiently determined by prior states, hence there could never have been any real attenuations to what actually happened" (p. 2). On the basis of pure (hard) determinism, psychopaths would not be responsible for aggressive behavior because they did not exercise free will. However, present-day forensic legislation reflects the largely accepted assumption that "people have a relatively unhindered capacity to make choices and to decide what they will do" (Felthous, 2008, p. 1). Indeed, in addition to cognition, the 1962 American Law Institute Model Penal Code for the insanity defense stressed volitional capacity.

Juth and Lorentzon (2010), avoiding involvement in a metaphysical dispute on free will and determinism, suggest substituting free will with gradual autonomy, making accountability a matter of degree. They explain that the interplay of will, decision, and action, which are part of the autonomous self, would stress "responsibility and accountability in terms of control and control in terms of a conception of autonomy" (p. 5). Their concept of autonomy is remindful of Bandura's (2006) view of people as a human agency with the unique capacity to mold their life circumstances and the course that their life takes. This idea also is stressed by Felthous (2008), who stated that people are agents with a locus of control and that in spite of "the concatenation of natural causes for decision and action . . . [they] must be treated as individuals" (p. 9). People possess a will, he added, that allows them to exercise necessary control of decisions and actions in their social life, which enables society to function.

Legal scholar Morse (2007) argued that free will is not a necessary part of the assessment of criminal responsibility, because the test required by the courts is a rationality test. The rationality test is basic to the assessment of competency to stand trial, but a complete assessment of criminal responsibility includes the will (or decisional capacity), necessary in deliberating and acting upon a specific intent. An individual's will includes the following faculties: to control, to choose, to decide, to have knowledge of consequences, and to be accountable for actions. It is necessary for rational interaction with others and the environment. The thinking of psychopaths is frequently irrational at a deeper level, so much so that their cognitive capacity is often impaired. As Schneider and Nussbaum (2007) stated, they have difficulty in "processing and responding appropriately to the emotional and moral dimensions of a situation" (p. 167), and they show deficits in the cognitive and emotional spheres.

Some legal scholars question the rationality test that Morse stated is at the basis of the legal system approach to criminal responsibility. Felthous (2009) seems to disagree with a pure rationality principle, writing that "[t]he law's approach to mental criminal responsibility . . . can best be described as normative functionalism on the basis of presence or absence of certain capacities or functional abilities or by the specific actual, active functions such as specific intent and deliberation" (p. 8). Those normative functions important for a finding of criminal responsibility are functional parts of the will: consciousness, self-control, rationality, intentionality, choice, and deliberation.

Cognitive and volitional factors, essential in the determination of free will and necessary for normal human interactions, are basic in the assessment of psychopathic offenders' legal responsibility for criminal acts. When those assessments conclude that offenders are legally insane, the findings should be based on the fact that they have been found to be suffering from impairment of those factors. To this effect, Buchanan (2008) wrote, "Criminal responsibility requires, broadly speaking, the same kind of mental [cognitive] abilities that are required before someone can validly enter into a contract or make a will . . . [so] we want people to have been making a proper choice to act as they did before we hold them responsible, or, at least, fully responsible" (p. 26).

The aggressive behavior of psychopaths is central to a discussion of their criminal responsibility. As discussed throughout this chapter, they show poor control of their aggressive instincts. Their aggression is mostly instrumental and goal directed (Blair, 2001) and "[t]hey show severe difficulties in aversive conditioning and instrumental learning. . . . [and] in processing the fearfulness and sadness of others (Blair, 2003, p. 5). Their aggressivity and degree of psychopathy is supported by various studies showing changes in some brain structures and functions (e.g., Kiehl et al., 2001; Raine et al., 2000; Tiihonen et al., 2000). Consideration of biological correlates and neuroimaging findings are important in the assessment of criminal responsibility, and when used in the forensic assessment, they bring a paradigm shift from a neurophilosophical perspective to a brain-behavior one (Witzel, Walter, Bogerts, & Northoff, 2008). It is probable that in the future they will become ever more helpful, as, for example, DNA has been in determining criminal responsibility; and even at present, they should be an essential adjunct in the clinical decision making used to assess responsibility, responsibility that ultimately should be based on a free and voluntary act. But the workings of the human mind are more complex and complicated than is revealed by new technologies. In view of the gross impact that neuroscience seems to have on criminal law at present one should opt for prudence in its application. The self cannot be totally described on the basis of technology, and behavior is not limited to states of the brain, isolated from the world. Mental states are a dynamic process dealing with beliefs and desires. In the process of the volitional activity, the individual self is moved by intentions and emotions.

Conclusion

Although it is commonly accepted that the universe obeys natural laws, humans have intuitive feelings that they are endowed with the capacity to freely choose what they want to do and whether they want to control their actions. Compatibilistic theorists believe that human beings, even though partially subjected to determinism in their behaviors, are still able to make free and conscious decisions. According to the explanations of Libet (1983, 1999), they are able to make a conscious decision to veto (or not veto) whatever their unconscious had prepared them to decide or to will. "The role of conscious free will would be, then, not to initiate a voluntary act, but rather to control whether the act takes place" (Libet, 1999, p. 54). It is an act of selection by the conscious will and decision about which one of the unconscious initiatives should be vetoed or should go forward to action.

This is not unusual for the workings of the mind; the unconscious generally does the groundwork for the conscious. The conscious ego frequently only decides or wills behavior. Without the unconscious, the conscious mind would be a chaotic arena, inundated by numerous informative facts, requirements, or rearrangements, and the self could not function. That is why the unconscious is also important. It is where the brain stores and uses information and prepares solutions for the signature of the self and where much thinking is done.

Psychopaths, in their life course and specifically in their aggressive behavior, are certainly under the effect of genetic-biological factors and environmental stimuli, and they seemingly lack control and are prey to impulsivity, even though their aggression is generally considered instrumental. They place themselves above the laws of society, possibly due to inner feelings of inadequacy and previous rejection. They basically know, but obviously disregard, the entity, quality, and consequences of their actions. Even though he had deep psychiatric problems, Jeffrey Dahmer, the serial killer, was the epitome of the above (Palermo, 2004).

In summary, psychopathic criminal behavior is due not only to a personal decision to act (or a decision not to act), but also to predisposing factors—biological, genetic, and environmental. Therefore, their aggressive behavior should be viewed within a compatibilistic theoretical approach (the coexistence of free will and determinism) and, if found guilty, the question of diminished responsibility should be considered before deciding their punishment.

Punishment should be, ideally, proportionate to the crime committed. In the utilitarian theory, punishment is right if it produces a positive outcome (Bentham, 1830). Its purpose should be to make offenders reflect that what they did was wrong or is considered wrong, is not to be repeated, and obviously to be corrected in any future behavior. Kant ([1797] 1985), the most famous proponent of retributive punishment, believed that punishing offenders is a "must" and that not to punish them is morally wrong. Society, however, argues Grachek (2006), should not punish those who cannot profit from it, such as the mentally ill who, in spite of punishment, continue to be unable to conform their conduct to the law, in which case it would serve no purpose. Indeed, even though retribution has beneficial effects for some, psychopathic offenders, though deserving punishment for their criminal acts, need a different, perhaps more lenient, kind of punishment than criminals found to be legally sane, one that takes into consideration the unique factors that contributed to their criminal misconduct.

Note

1. Werner Heisenberg's principle states that it is impossible to determine simultaneously both the position and velocity of an electron or any other article with any great degree of accuracy or certainty.

References

Alexander, F. (1948). *Fundamentals of psychoanalysis*. New York: Norton.

Alexander, F., and Ross, H. (1952). *Dynamic psychiatry*, Chicago, IL: University of Chicago Press.

American Law Institute. (1962). American Law Institute Model Penal Code.

American Psychiatric Association. (APA). (2000). *Diagnostic and statistical manual of mental disorders* (4th ed., text rev.). Washington, DC: Author.

Arieti, S. (1967). *The intrapsychic self*. New York: Basic Books.

Aristotle. (1975). *The Nicomachean ethics* (The Loeb classical library; G. P. Goold, Ed.; H. Rackham, Trans.) London: William Heinemann.

Arrigo, B. A., & Shipley, S. (2001).The confusion over psychopathy (I): Historical considerations. *International Journal of Offender Therapy and Comparative Criminology, 45*, 325–344.

Bandura, A. (2006). Toward a psychology of human agency. *Perspectives on Psychological Sciences, 1*(2). 164–180. Retrieved from http://des.emory.edu/mfp/Bandura2006PPS.pdf.

Bentham, J. (1830). *The rationale of punishment*. London: R. Heward.

Blackburn, R. (1993). *The psychology of criminal conduct: Theory research and practice*. New York: John Wiley & Sons.

Blair, R. J. R. (2001). Advances in neuropsychiatry: Neurocognitive disorders, and psychopathy models of aggression, the antisocial personality disorders and psychopathy. *Journal of Neurology, Neurosurgery and Psychiatry, 71*, 727–731.

Blair, R. J. R. (2003) Editorial: Neurological basis of psychopathy. *The British Journal of Psychiatry, 182*, 5–7.

Boas, G. (1972). French philosophy. In P. Edwards (Ed.), *The encyclopedia of philosophy* (Vols. 1 & 2; pp. 238–249). New York: Macmillan & The Free Press.

Buchanan, A. (2008). Commentary: Freedom and function. *Journal of the American Academy of Psychiatry and Law, 36*(1), 25–26.

Cashmore, A. R. (2010). *The Lucretian swerve: The biological basis of human behavior and the criminal justice system*. Retrieved from http://www.pnas.org/content/early/2010/02/04/0915161107.

Caspi, A., McClay, J., Moffitt, T. E., Mill, J., Martin, J., Craig, I. W., . . . R. Poulton. (2002). Role of genotype in the cycle of violence in maltreated children. *Science, 297*, 851–854.

Cleckley, H. (1955). *The mask of sanity: An attempt to clarify some issues about the so-called psychopathic personality*. St. Louis, MO: Mosby. (Original work published 1941)

Daversa, M. T. (2010). Early environmental predictors of the affective and interpersonal constructs of psychopathy. *International Journal of Offender Therapy and Comparative Criminology, 54*, 6–21.

Descartes, R. (1999). *The philosophical writings of Descartes* (Vol. 1; J. Cottingham, R. Stoothoff, & D. Murdoch, Trans.). Cambridge, UK: Cambridge University Press.

Di Tullio, B. (1971). *Principii di criminologia generale e clinica e psicopatia sociale* [*Principles of general and clinical criminology and social psychopathy*]. Rome: Istituto di Medicina Sociale.

Eccles, J. C. (1989). *Evolution of the brain*. New York: Routledge.

Famous American Trials: *Illinois v. Nathan Leopold and Richard Loeb*. 1924. Retrieved from http://www.law.umkc.edu/faculty/projects/ftrials/leoploeb/leopold.htm.

Felthous, A. R. (2008). The will: From metaphysical freedom to normative functionalism. *Journal of the American Academy of Psychiatry and the Law, 35*, 16–24.

Frankfurt, H. (1969). Alternate possibilities and moral responsibility. *Journal of Philosophy, 66*, 829–839.

Frankfurt, H. (1988). *The importance of what we care about: Philosophical essays*. New York: Cambridge University Press.

Freud, S. (1961). *Civilization and its discontents* (J. Strachey, Trans). New York: Norton.

Glenn, A. L., & Raine, A. (2009). Psychopathy and instrumental aggression: Evolutionary, neurobiological, and legal perspectives. *International Journal of Law and Psychiatry, 32*, 253–258.

Goldberg, E. (2001). *The executive brain: Frontal lobes and the civilized mind*. New York: Oxford University Press.

Goleman, D. (1995). *Emotional Intelligence*. New York: Bantam Books.

Goodman, M., Triebwasser, J., Shah, S., & New, A. S. (2007). Neuroimaging in personality disorders: Current concepts, findings and implications. *Psychiatric Annals, 37*, 100–108.

Grachek, J. E. (2006). The insanity defense in the twenty-first century: How recent United States Supreme Court case law can improve the system. *Indiana Law Journal, 81*, 1479–1501.

Halleck, S. L. (1967). *Psychiatry and the dilemma of crime*. New York: Harper and Row/Hoeber Medical Books.

Hare, R. D. (1993). *Without conscience: The disturbing world of the psychopaths among us*. New York: Simon & Schuster.

Hare, R. D., & Jutai, J. W. (1983). Criminal history of the male psychopath: Some preliminary data. In K. T. Van Dusen & S. A. Mednick (Eds.), *Prospective studies of crime and delinquency: Longitudinal research in the behavioral, social and medical studies* (pp. 225–236). Boston, MA: Kluwer-Nijhoff.

Hariri, A. R., Drabant, E. M., Munoz, K. E., Kolachana, B. S., Mattay, V. S., Egan, M. F., & Weinberger, D. R. (2005). A susceptibility gene for affective disorders and the response of the human amygdala. *Archives of General Psychiatry, 62*, 146–152.

Hariri, A. R., Mattay, V. S., Tessitore, A., Kolachana, B., Fera, F., Goldman, D., . . . Weinberger, D. (2002). Serotonin transporter genetic variation and the response of the human amygdala. *Science, 297*, 400–403.

Juth, N., & Lorentzon, F. (2010). The concept of free will and forensic psychiatry. *International Journal of Law and Psychiatry, 33*, 1–6.

Kant, I. ([1797] 1985). The right to punish. In J. G. Murphy (Ed.), *Punishment and rehabilitation* (2nd ed., pp. 20–23). Belmont, CA: Wadsworth.

Kant, I. (2008). *Kant's critiques: The critique of pure reason the critique of practical reason, the critique of judgement*. Radford, VA: A & D Publishing.

Kaufmann, W. (1974). *Nietzsche: Philosopher, psychologist, antichrist* (4th ed.). Princeton, NJ: Princeton University Press.

Kawohl, W., & Habermeyer, E. (2007). Free will: Reconciling German civil law with Libet's neurophysiological studies on the readiness potential. *Behavioral Sciences and the Law, 25*, 309–320.

Kernberg, O. F. (1992). *Aggression in personality disorders and perversions*. New Haven, CT: Yale University Press.

Kiehl, K. A., Smith, A. M., Hare, R. D., Mendrek, A., Forster, B. B., Brink, J., & Liddle, P. F. (2001). Limbic abnormalities in affective processing by criminal psychopaths as revealed by functional magnetic resonance imaging. *Biological Psychiatry, 50*, 677–684.

Klein, M. (1935). A contribution to the psychogenesis of manic-depressive states. *International Journal of Psychoanalysis, 16*, 145–174.

Koch, J. L. (1891). *Die psychopathischen Mindwertigkeite [The psychopathic inferiorities]*. Ravensburg, Germany: Ravensburg.

Kohlberg, L. (1984). *The psychology of moral development: The nature and validity of moral stages*. San Francisco, CA: Harper & Row.

Kohut, H. (1971). The psychoanalytic study of the child. Monograph No. 4. In *The analysis of the self*. New York: International University Press.

Kornhuber, H., & Deecke, L. (1964). Hirnpotentialanderungen bei willkurbewegungen und passive bewegunmgen des menschen: Bereitschaftspotential un reafferente potentiale. *Pflügers Arch Gesamte Physiol Menschen Tiere [Pflüger Archv: European Physiology], 248*, 1–17.

Kraepelin, E. (1915). *Psychiatrie: Ein lehrbuch [Psychiatry: A textbook]* (8th ed., Vol. 4.) Leipzig, Germany: Barth.

Le Doux, J. (1996). *The emotional brain: The mysterious underpinning of emotional life*. New York: Simon & Schuster.

Libet, B. (1999). Do we have free will? *Journal of Consciousness Studies, 6*, 47–57.

Libet, B., Gleason, C. A., Wright, E. W., & Pearl, D. K. (1983). Time of conscious intention to act in relation to onset of cerebral activity (readiness potential: The unconscious initiation of a freely voluntary act. *Brain, 106*, 623–642.

Lombroso, C. (1889). *L'uomo delinquente* [*The criminal man*] (4th ed.). Turin, Italy: Bocca.

Macdonald, J. M. (1961). *The murderer and his victim*. Springfield, IL: Charles C. Thomas.

Mahler, M. (1972). A study of the separation-individuation process. *Psychoanalytic Study of the Child, 26*, 403–424.

Maudsley, H. (1896). *Responsibility in mental disease*. New York: D. Appleton & Co.

Morse, S. (2007). The non-problem of free will, in forensic psychiatry and psychology. *Behavioral Sciences and the Law, 25*, 203–220. Retrieved from http://lsr.nellco.org/cgi/viewcontent.cgi?article=1161&context=upenn_wps

Nietzsche, F. (1978). *Thus spoke Zarathustra: A book for none and all* (W. Kaufmann, Ed. & Trans.). New York: Penguin Books.

Nietzsche, F. (1998). *Beyond good and evil: Prelude to philosophy of the future* (M. Faber, Ed. & Trans.) New York: Oxford University Press.

Palermo, G. B. (2004). *The faces of violence* (2nd ed.). Springfield, IL: Charles C. Thomas.

Palermo, G. B. (2010). Environmental correlates of aggressive behavior. *Journal of Forensic Psychology Practice, 10*, 300–324.

Pereboom, D. (2001). *Living without free* will. Cambridge, UK: Cambridge University Press.

Piaget, J. (1932/1965). *The moral judgment of the child* (M. Gabain, Trans.). London: Routledge & Kegan Paul.

Pinel, P. (1801/1962). *A treatise on insanity* (D. Davis, Trans.). New York: Hafner.

Porter, S., Birt, A. R., & Boer, D. P. (2001). Investigation of the criminal and conditional release profiles of Canadian federal offenders as a function of psychopathy and age. *Law and Human Behavior, 25*, 647–661.

Prichard, J. C. (1835). *A treatise on insanity and other disorders affecting the mind*. London: Sherwood, Gilbert, & Piper.

Raine, A., Lencz,T., Bihrle, S., LaCasse, L., & Colletti, P. (2000). Reduced prefrontal grey matter volume and reduced autonomic activity in antisocial personality disorder. *Archives of General Psychiatry, 57*, 119–127.

Raine, A., Meloy, J. R., Bihrle, S., Stoddard, J., LaCasse, L., & Buchsbaum, M.S. (1998). Reduced prefrontal and increased subcortical brain functioning assessed using positron emission tomography in predatory and affective murderers. *Behavioral Sciences and the Law, 16*, 319–332.

Redding, R. E. (2006). The brain disordered defendant: Neuroscience and legal insanity in the twenty-first century. *Villanova Public Law and Legal Theory Working Paper Series, No. 2006-17* (pp. 1–78). Retrieved from http://papers.ssrn.com/sol3/papers.cfm?abstract_id=937349

Roskies, A. (2006). Neuroscientific challenges to free will and responsibility. *Trends in Cognitive Sciences, 10* (9), 419–423.

Rush, B. (1812). *Medical inquiries and observations upon the diseases of the mind.* Philadelphia, PA: Kimber & Richardson.

Rutter, M. (2006). *Genes and behavior: Nature-nurture interplay explained.* Oxford, UK: Blackwell.

Sartre, J. P. (1956). *Being and nothingness.* New York: Washington Square Press.

Schilder, P. (1942). *Goals and desires of man: A psychological survey of life.* New York: Columbia University Press.

Schneider, R., & Nussbaum, D. (2007). Can the mad be bad? *Criminal Law Quarterly, 53*, 162–182.

Schopenhauer, A. (2003). *Prize essay on the freedom of the will* (G. Zoller, Ed.; E. F. J. Payne, Trans.). Cambridge, UK: Cambridge University Press.

Schwartz, J. M., & Begley, S. (2003). *The mind and the brain: Neuroplasticity and the power of mental force.* New York: HarperCollins.

Sherrington, C. (1933). *The brain and its mechanism.* Cambridge, UK: Cambridge University Press,

Smilansky, S. (2000). *Free will and illusion.* New York: Oxford University Press.

Swann, A. C. (2003). Neuroreceptor mechanisms of aggression and its treatment. *Journal of Clinical Psychiatry, 64*, 26–35.

Taylor, R. (1972). Determinism. In P. Edwards (Ed.), *The encyclopedia of philosophy* (Vols. 1 & 2, pp. 359–373). New York: Macmillan & The Free Press.

Tiihonen, J., Hodgins, S., Vaurio, O., Laakso, M., Repo, E., Soininen, H., ... Savolainen, L. (2000). Amygdaloid volume loss in psychopathy [Abstract]. *Society for Neuroscience Abstracts*, 2017.

Volavka, J. V. (1995). *Neurobiology of violence.* Washington, DC: American Psychiatric Press.

von Krafft-Ebing, R. (1922). *Psychopathia Sexualis with a special reference to the antipathic sexual instinct: A medico-forensic study* (Rev. ed.; F. J. Rebman, Trans.) New York: Medical Art Agency.

Wilson, E. O. (1998). *Consilience. The unity of knowledge.* New York: Alfred A. Knopf.

Wilson, J. Q., & Herrnstein, R. J. (1985). *Crime and human nature: The definitive study of the causes of crime.* New York: Basic Books.

Winnicott, D. (1953). Transitional objects and transitional phenomena. *International Journal of Psychoanalysis, 34*, 89–97.

Witzel, J., Walter, M., Bogerts, B., & Northoff, G. (2008). Neurophilosophical perspectives of neuroimaging in forensic psychiatry—giving way to a paradigm shift? *Behavioral Sciences and the Law, 26*, 113–130.

Yochelson, S., & Samenow, S. E., (1976). *The criminal personality, Vol. 1: A profile for change.* New York: Jason Aronson.

CHAPTER FIFTEEN

Career Criminality, Childhood Experiences, and Adult Personality among Forensic Patients in the Netherlands

Stefan Bogaerts, Marinus Spreen, Zsuzsanna Horváth, Machiel S. Polak, and Maaike Cima

Introduction

Research into personality disorders in relationship to clinical factors such as insight into problem behavior, (lack of) empathy, and the quality of coping skills is often done in the past. However, these studies are primarily focused on the question of whether individuals with a specific personality disorder differ on these clinical factors compared to individuals without personality disorders. Unfortunately, within forensic psychology and psychiatry, the severity of the personality disorder, more particularly the presence of multiple personality disorders in individuals in relationship to clinical factors, is very rarely examined. In addition, from developing psychological research, it is known that relevant factors in the past, such as conduct disorders and experiences of neglect and abuse in youth, are strong predictors for the development of a problematic personality structure. This gap in forensic scientific research has obvious implications for the treatment, the social reintegration of forensic psychiatric patients, and the likelihood of recidivism. In this chapter, the relationship is examined between the severity of personality disorders (past and present) in relationship to empathy and coping skills in adulthood and negative childhood experiences and conduct disorder.

Personality disorders are linked to impaired functioning in many areas of daily life, such as poor job performance, problematic romantic relationships, usage of maladaptive coping strategies, social isolation, and violence (e.g., Haw & Hawton, 2008; Skodol et al., 2002). The DSM-IV (APA, 1994, p. 629) describes personality disorders as characterized by "An enduring pattern of inner experience and behaviour that deviates markedly from the expectations of the individual's culture, is pervasive and inflexible, has an onset in adolescence or early adulthood, is stable over time, and leads to distress and impairment." The current version of the DSM-IV-TR (APA, 2000) differentiates between 10 types of personality disorders that are categorized in three clusters based on the common characteristics of the disorders: cluster A (paranoid, schizoid, and schizotypal personality disorder), characterized by odd and eccentric behaviors; cluster B (antisocial, borderline, histrionic, and narcissistic personality disorder), described by flamboyant, dramatic, or emotional behavior; and cluster C (avoidant, dependent, and obsessive-compulsive personality disorder), represented by anxious or fearful behavior. To be diagnosed with a certain disorder, the patients must meet usually four or five out of the seven, eight, or nine criteria by which the disorder is described (see DSM-IV-TR, APA, 2000).

The Absence of Severity Measures of Personality Disorders

Current DSM-IV classifications of personality disorders do not involve severity-based distinction (Yang, Cold, & Tyrer, 2010). There is a major lack of studies that have investigated the severity of personality disorders among forensic psychiatric patients. However, the severity of personality disorders influences other domains of daily functioning such as cognitive executive functioning (Bergvall, Nilsson, & Hansen, 2003) and causes deficits of working memory, planning, attention, inhibition, and set-shifting (Roberts, Robbins & Weiskrantz, 1996; Smith & Jonides, 1999). Bergvall, Nilsson, and Hansen (2003) studied the relationship between personality deviations and deficits in cognitive executive function among a group of forensic patients. They concluded that personality-disordered individuals performed worse on the attentional shift task than healthy counterparts. Moreover, significant differences were found between violent offenders with personality disorder and those without personality

Table 15.1 Classifying the Severity of Personality Disorder

Level	Classification	Description
0	No personality disorder	Good capacity to form relationship and to withstand stress
1	Personality difficulty	Social functioning impaired in times of stress but not otherwise
2	Simple personality disorder	Meeting criteria for one or more personality disorders according to ICD-10 or DSM-IV within a single cluster
3	Complex personality disorder	Meeting criteria for personality disorders occurring in more than one cluster
4	Severe personality disorder	Meeting criteria for two or more personality disorders from different clusters (including B) plus gross social disturbance

Source: Tyrer & Johnson (1996)

disorder regarding self-directedness and cooperativeness. Besides the behavioral manifestations, abnormalities in the brain structure, namely a decrease in gray matter in both frontal and temporal brain regions, were also found (Müller et al., 2008). Based on the study of Yang, Cold, and Tyrer (2010), further influential factors that can contribute to the development of a more severe personality disorder are: younger age, childhood institutional care, negative childhood experiences, expulsion from school, contacts with the criminal justice system, economic inactivity, and more DSM-IV axis I comorbidity (all $p < 0.001$). However, because of the small sample size, this study may lack external validity.

The following question has arisen in literature: What is considered to be severe? Tyrer and Johnson (1996) argue that individuals with severe personality disorders meet the criteria of almost all clusters of the DSM-IV classification system. Since there is an overlap between the different personality disorder categories, it is very difficult to find a proper classification. Therefore in an earlier stage, Tyrer and Johnson (1996) have suggested this complexity to be an indicator of severity. Disorders that have common characteristics have been classified into common personality disorder clusters, and as the overlap between clusters increases, so does the disturbance (Duggan, 2005) (see Table 15.1).

During forensic assessments it is crucial to be aware of the clinical factors, since they are the closest to the offense in time, they describe the current state of the offender the most accurately, and hence they are closely related the circumstances and causes of the offense. The clinical factors of the HKT-30 (see "Instrument" later in this chapter) are related to the probability of committing a crime and to the likelihood of recidivism (Bogaerts, 2010). The HKT-30 places emphasis on the clinical variables; thus the instrument is also used recently as a treatment evaluation instrument (Routine Outcome Monitoring). The current study examines the contribution of four HKT-30 factors—namely two clinical factors, coping skills and lack of empathy; and two historical factors, namely conduct disorder before age 12 and abuse and neglect before age 18—to the occurrence of the severity of personality disorders. The historical factors, due to their association with crime and their relationship to the two clinical factors, are also studied.

Coping Skills and Lack of Empathy

Coping refers to the individual differences in reactions to stressful situations. In response to stress, some individuals become distressed and perform poorly, whereas others remain calm and perform well. Taking into account the individual differences, there is a substantial literature on the relationship between coping and personality (Beauchamp, Lecomte, Lecomte, Leclerc, & Corbiere, 2011; Beutler, Harwood, Kimpara, Verdirame, & Blau, 2011; Suls, David, & Harvey, 1996). However, there is only a limited amount of empirical research on the relation between coping and DSM Axis II personality disorders (Bijttebier & Vertommen, 1999; Coolidge, Segal, Hook, & Stewart, 2000). The findings of the existing studies imply that there is a deficit in coping style among personally disordered patients, such as active, problem-focused coping and social support seeking, together with an excess of behavioral passivity, mental disengagement, and uncontrolled discharge of emotions (Bijttebier & Vertommen, 1999; Vitaliano et al., 1990; Vollrath, Alnaes, & Torgersen, 1994). Bijttebier and Vertommen (1999) have compared the coping strategies of psychiatric inpatients who meet the criteria for a specific personality disorder with those without personality disorder, and found a smaller amount of social support seeking and a greater amount of avoidance in patients diagnosed with paranoid personality disorder, schizoid personality disorder, schizotypal personality disorder, borderline personality disorder, or avoidant personality disorder. They also found that there is a smaller amount of social support seeking in patients diagnosed with antisocial personality disorder. Similar pattern of coping styles is found within forensic patients. The relevant literature on the relationship between coping skills and offense shows that the coping strategies used by forensic patients are linked to psychological distress or denial (e.g., Negy, Woods, & Carlson, 1997; Van Harreveld, Van Der Pligt, Claassen, & Van Dijk, 2007). Van Harreveld et al. (2007) found that male prisoners with passive coping style, such as avoidance, reported greater experience of guilt, fear, and regret. Negy et al. (1997) reported that female prisoners using denial and behavioral disengagement to adapt to the prison environment were less able to adjustment to prison environment. Ireland, Brown and Ballarini (2006) developed a model to explain the association among maladaptive personality traits, maladaptive coping (emotional and avoidant coping), and psychological distress. They found maladaptive personality traits to be associated with maladaptive coping and greater psychological distress. Furthermore, their model implies a three-factor structure among maladaptive personality traits, with correlated factors giving emphasis to antisocial and asocial personality and a third indicating anxious/dramatic personality. These studies provide a basis for further exploration into the link between personality disorders and coping (Xuereb, Ireland, & Davies, 2009).

Empathy has been defined as the "[c]apacity to understand others and experience their feelings in relation to oneself" (Decety & Jackson, 2004, p. 71). The affective component of empathy is considered to be responsible for one's emotional response to others' mental states; whereas the cognitive component refers to one's ability to understand the others' mental states (Henry, Bailey, & Rendell, 2008). This ability plays a crucial role in human social interaction, and it supports long-term social commitment (Baron-Cohen & Wheelwright, 2004). Social and behavioral abnormalities are among the most common features of personality disorders such as borderline personality disorder, narcissistic personality disorder, and schizotypal personality disorder. Harari, Shamay-Tsoory, Ravid, and Levkovitz (2010) studied the differences between cognitive and affective empathic abilities of patients with borderline personality disorder compared to healthy controls, and they found that controls had higher scores on cognitive empathy compared with affective empathy scores, while the borderline personality disorder group showed the opposite pattern. Similar conclusions can be drawn based on the study of Ritter et al. (2011), who found that narcissistic personality disorder only involves emotional empathy impairments, but cognitive empathy seems to be intact. However, Asai, Mao, Sugimori, and Tanno (2011) found evidence that people who experience a stronger rubber hand illusion (participants observe a rubber hand being touched, their sense of touch was activated) might have stronger empathic and schizotypal personalities at the same time.

Empathy and aggression appear to be inversely related (Miller & Eisenberg, 1988). Empathy studies arrived to the conclusion that empathy is a motivator in eliciting altruism and inhibiting aggression (Hastings, Zahn-Waxler, Robinson, Usher, & Bridges, 2000; Zahn-Waxler & Radke-Yarrow, 1990). These studies are based on the theory that if a person is able to feel empathy, he or she will take the responsibility for his or her actions and therefore will be less likely to harm others. Consequently, empathy can be described as a "protective factor" against aggression. According to Hastings, Zahn-Waxler, Robinson, Usher, and Bridges (2000), in case of an aggressive act, empathy makes the perpetrator aware of the negative consequences of his or her violence (the suffering of the other), and so immediately discourages this harmful behavior. Hinchey and Gavelek (1982) link violent behavior to family history by suggesting that children from violent homes have lower levels of empathy than control samples. Violence and lack of empathy are typical characteristics of clinical psychopathy, which occurs very frequently among forensic patients. Clinical psychopathic individuals show a selective empathic deficit in recognizing sad and fearful facial expressions (e.g., Alia, Amorima, & Chamorro-Premuzic, 2009). Boulanger, Habib and Lançon (2008) found a selective impairment for cognitive flexibility, cognitive empathy, and decision making in the psychopathic, but not in the control group. According to Blair (1995, 1999), there is a difference between primary and secondary psychopathy; individuals with high primary psychopathic traits experience more pleasure and less empathy, when seeing someone suffer, than secondary psychopaths, as they show a selective emotional empathy dysfunction by not processing sad and fearful expressions appropriately. Lack of empathy seems to be a common characteristic of both individuals with personality disorder and aggressive tendencies.

Conduct Disorder and Abuse and Neglect in Youth

The DSM-IV describes conduct disorder as a repetitive and persistent pattern of antisocial behaviors, characterized by aggression, deceitfulness, and violation of the rules (DSM-IV, APA, 1994). A diagnosis of conduct disorder before the age of 15 is based on the C criterion for antisocial personality disorder as stated in the Structured Clinical Interview for DSM-IV Axis II Personality Disorders (SCID-II) (First, Gibbon, Spitzer, Williams, & Smith, 1997). Furthermore, conduct problems with childhood-onset disruptive behavior have been most frequently associated with antisocial behaviors in adulthood (Lahey & Loeber, 1997; Gelhorn, Sakai, Price, & Crowley, 2007). Therefore, high occurrence of conduct disorder is expected in forensic samples. However, antisocial behavior in childhood does not necessarily lead to antisocial behavior in adulthood (Gelhorn et al., 2007; Robins, 1978). There is an uncertainty in literature about discriminating adolescents with a transient versus a persistent pattern of antisocial behavior, which is partly due to the heterogeneous etiology of antisocial behavior (Eaves et al., 1993). Research on persistent antisocial behavior argues that an early childhood onset may predict persistence (Farrington et al., 1990), as well as pervasiveness (Brooner, Schmidt, Felch, & Bigelow, 1992) of adult antisocial behavior. Other studies disagree, stating that earlier age of onset cannot be considered as a predictor of adult antisocial behavior (Sanford, Boyle, Szatmári, Offord, Jamieson, & Spinner, 1999), and that antisocial adults both with and without prior conduct disorder diagnoses have similar levels of psychopathological risk factors (Bogaerts, Vervaeke, & Goethals, 2004; Marmorstein, 2006).

Infants and young children are weak and vulnerable emotionally; therefore the exposure to violence or abuse can diminish personality qualities such as self-worth and confidence and lead to suspiciousness, to intimidation in the short run, and to violent behavior or severe personality pathology in adult life (Becker & Kaplan, 1991; Roza, Hofstra, Van der Ende, & Verhulst, 2003, in De Clercq, Fruyt, & Widiger, 2009). Despite the importance of this issue, the role of childhood antecedents for personality disorders is only slightly mentioned in the DSM-IV-TR (APA, 2000). However, there are a few published studies that show evidence for the developmental etiology of personality disorders, including the schizoid (e.g., Wolf, 1966), schizotypal (Caplan & Guthrie, 1992), avoidant (Francis, Last, & Straus, 1992), narcissistic (Hilsenroth, 1996), antisocial personality disorder (Burgess, Hartman, & McCormack, 1987; Pollock et al., 1990) and borderline personality disorders (Zanarini, Gunderson, Marino, Schwartz, & Frankenburg, 1989). The incomplete literature about the childhood antecedents of most personality disorders is due to the lack of empirical documentation (De Clercq et al., 2009). Consequently, it is difficult to find systematic research on the childhood history of the DSM-IV-TR personality disorders. Interestingly, evidence suggests that individuals with borderline personality disorder have an extremely high incidence of childhood sexual abuse (Paris, 1994), whereas persons with antisocial traits have high prevalence of physical abuse (Johnson, Cohen, & Brown, 1999; Luntz & Widom, 1994).

A child who has faced aggression, abuse, or other trauma from their parents in early childhood is likely to encounter with similar difficulties in adolescence, such as hostility and anger (Sappington, Pharr, Tunstall, & Rickert, 1997). Studies found that physical abuse in childhood can lead to violent behavior in adulthood. Becker et al. (1995) suggested that there is a relationship between childhood abuse, adult criminality, and recidivism. The violent and homicidal patients of psychiatric and drug/alcohol clinics are more likely to have been physically abused in their past (Malinosky-Rummell & Hansen, 1993). Furthermore, about one-third of individuals who were abused as children later abuse their own children (Widom, 1989). According to Doumas, Margolin, and John (1994) physical abuse in one generation predicts physical abuse in the family two generations later. Consequently, a self-perpetuating sequence of violence is very likely to occur. However, despite the decades of studying child abuse, research on this field has to face with considerable drawbacks that stem from methodological problems (Widom, 1989). Most of the studies that aim to understand the relationship between child abuse and physical or mental health problems are limited to self-report measures, rather than longitudinal designs (Widom, 1995). Nevertheless, it is essential to measure the onset and course of personality disorders with repeated examinations from youth and adulthood.

The empirical literature points toward the past events as important influential factors in one's life, suggesting that besides the current clinical factors such as coping skills or empathic abilities, life history including childhood traumas and conduct problems also must be taken into account during a forensic evaluation. Based on this assumption, interrelationships among these concepts are expected when predicting the occurrence and severity of personality disorders in forensic patients. Various studies support this theory. Kunitz, Levy, McCloskey, and Gabriel (1998) found abuse to be a risk factor for conduct disorder and for being involved in domestic violence either as perpetrator or as victim. Leitenberg, Gibson, and Novy (2004) demonstrated that undergraduate women with abusive histories are at risk of using maladaptive coping strategies to deal with stress later in their life. Runtz and Schallow (1997) suggest that there is a relationship between past childhood sexual and physical maltreatment and current psychological adjustment strongly mediated by coping strategies. Sterzer, Stadler, Poustka, and Kleinschmidt (2007) examined the neural correlates of empathy and conduct disorder and found reduced gray-matter volume in bilateral anterior insular cortex and the left amygdala in conduct disorder patients compared to the healthy control group. Moreover, a significant correlation was found between the bilateral anterior insular gray-matter volume in conduct disorder patients and empathy scores in conduct disorder patients. The association between empathy and Plutchik's coping style was also studied. Rim (1995) suggested empathy to be correlated positively with minimization, seeking succorance and replacement for men, and negatively with minimization, replacement, mapping, and reversal for women. However, the literature lacks studies examining the effect of being abused as a child on the individual's empathic skills in adulthood, the main focus of the existing studies is on the empathic skills of abusive parents. Furthermore, there is a lack in the literature about the effect of having conduct disorder as a child on the usage of certain coping strategies.

In summary, the empirical literature suggests that the above-mentioned concepts are intercorrelated, and their joint contribution might contribute to a better understanding of personality disorders in forensic patients. Based on the relevant literature, the current research attempts to shed some light on historical factors measured by abuse and neglect before age 18 and conduct disorder before age 12 in connection with the severity of personality disorders (measured in the past), and on clinical factors measured by empathy and coping skills in relation to the occurrence of personality disorders (measured in the present).

The following hypotheses were addressed: (1) the two historical factors of the HKT-30—abuse and neglect before age 18, and conduct disorder before age 12—and the two clinical factors of the HKT-30—lack of empathy and coping skills—are expected to be correlated with each other; (2) the existence of the clinical and historical factors of the HKT-30 is expected to be confirmed; (3) the two clinical factors and the two historical factors of the HKT-30 are expected to significantly contribute to the estimation of the occurrence of personality disorders in adulthood; (4) the two historical factors of the HKT-30 are expected to significantly contribute to the estimation of the severity of personality disorders; and (5) the severity of personality disorder (measured in the past) and the occurrence of personality disorder (measured in the present) are expected to be highly correlated (since personality disorders are considered to be stable over time).

Method

Participants and Procedure

The sample consisted of 378 male violent offenders who were hospitalized in two Dutch forensic psychiatric hospitals in the Netherlands (Kijvelanden at Poortugaal, and Dr. S. van Mesdag at Groningen). Seventy-two percent of the offenders were born in the Netherlands, 15% in Suriname, 2% in Morocco, and 11% in the Netherlands Antilles. The mean age of the patients was 39.1 years old (SD = 7.9; range 20–69 years). The index offenses: 55% (attempted) homicide, 10% assault, 20% extortion, robbery with violence, and 15% for arson. The average age at first conviction was 22 years and 8 months (SD = 8.2), the average number of previous convictions was 5.1 (SD = 4.5). Data were retrieved from scores of the patient on the HKT-30, which is part of the electronic patient records. Patients were also examined by a psychiatrist and a (clinical) psychotherapist and were diagnosed with personality disorders based on the DSM-IV-TR.

The Severity Measures of the Historical and Clinical Factors

The severity of conduct disorder before age 12 is defined as: 0 = no conduct disorder; 1 = behavior problems mentioned but not concrete; 2 = conduct disorder but no violent behavior; 3 = conduct disorder (with or without violent behavior) caused serious problems in school and/or family; 4 = severe conduct disorder (with or without violent behavior), response to placement in an institution. The history of childhood abuse and neglect before age 18 is defined as: 0 = never victim/witness of family violence; 1 = witnessed family violence; 2 = victim of neglect (emotional/physical); 3 = victim of chronic neglect and incidental abuse; 4 = victim of systematic abuse and chronic neglect. Empathic abilities are defined as: 0=capable to be empathic and emotional connected with others; 1 = severity between 0 and 2; 2 = difficult to empathize with others, is capable to think about it or can follow instructions and acts to be more empathetic; 3 = severity between 2 and 4; and 4 = shows no empathy and compassion, is unable to empathize with others, is only interested in own benefits. Coping is defined as 0 = adequate coping; 1 = enough adequate coping but low stability; 2 = low coping skills, adequate in dealing with current conditions; 3 = Insufficient or inadequate coping skills; and 4 = Insufficient/inadequate coping skills, risk of destabilization and chronic feelings of anger were obtained from (hetero-)anamnesis.

Severity of personality disorder in the past was defined by the classification system of Tyrer and Johnson (1996): 0 = No PD; 1 = pathological trait but no PD concerning DSM-IV; 2 = 1 PD, but no cluster B; 3 = 1 (or more) PD with 1 cluster B; 4 = 2 (or more) PD cluster BB or cluster BA). The occurrence of personality disorders in the present was used as a binary variable: 0 = No PD; 1 = PD (cluster B: 1 or more). Furthermore, it was confirmed whether there had been a history of crime in the past. If so, the kind of committed crime was obtained by probation (an organization that holds the jurisdiction for resocialization in the Netherlands). Severity of crime was classified according to the degree of penalty constituted by the Dutch department of security and justice in 2011.

Instrument

The HKT-30 is a risk assessment instrument developed for the 13 Dutch forensic psychiatric centers and used for the prediction of future recidivism and recently for treatment evaluation. The HKT-30 is based on structured clinical assessment of psychologists and psychiatrists, rather than on self-report; therefore it provides a more objective framework of the forensic patients' current psychological and mental state, and of effectiveness of the treatment they have received. The HKT-30 consists of 11 historical and static factors, and 13 clinical and 6 dynamic future management items. The 19 dynamic items are potentially convertible by treatment and counseling. The three scales have a reasonable predictive validity in violent recidivism (Hildebrand, Hester, Spreen, & Nijman, 2005). The HKT-30 is based on a five-point scale, ranging from "0" to "4" (0 = not present, 1 = unclearly present, 2 = partially present, 3 = almost present, and 4 = clearly present) and is sensitive for small differences among patients; hence, it appears to be a useful tool in making clinical decisions concerning termination or prolongation of a particular treatment. The three scales have a reasonable predictive validity in violent recidivism (Hildebrand et al., 2005). The interrater reliability of the H-, K-, and T-scale scores was calculated using correlations and is 0.76, 0.71, and 0.64, respectively. Correlations between 0.60 and 0.80 are encouraging. The internal consistency of the H-, K-, and T-scale is 0.62, 0.87, and 0.88, respectively. The HKT-30 has agreements with the HCR-20 (Webster, Douglas, Eaves & Hart, 1997) but there are differences (Spreen et al., 2009). The HCR-20 consists of 5 clinical items, while the HKT-30 has 13 clinical items. Eight extra-clinical items—empathy, hostility, social relational skills, self-reliance, acculturation problems, responsibility for the offense, sexual preoccupation, and coping skills—are included in the HKT-30 and not in the HCR-20. The HCR-20 is based on a three-point scale for each item, while the HKT-30 is based on a five-point scale. We assume a five-point scale is more sensitive for small differences that are important in the character of formalizing clinical decisions concerning prolongation for further rehabilitation.

Statistical Analyses

Descriptive statistics were computed for each of the analyzed variables. Bivariate Pearson correlation was performed to determine the interrelationships among the variables. Factor analysis was performed to determine the factors. Binary logistic regression was used to determine the contribution of coping skills, lack of empathy, abuse and neglect before age 18, and conduct disorder before age 12 in predicting the severity of personality disorders. Since the interest of the study lies in examining how much each independent variable contributes to the dependent variable, instead of using the factor scores, the individual variables were used in the analysis—especially because saving the factor scores, and using the saved scores in secondary analysis, leads to an attenuation effect (Croon, 2002).

Results

Pearson correlation indicated a significant relationship between conduct disorder before age 12 and abuse and neglect before age 18, r = .25, p (one-tailed) < .01. Conduct disorder before age 12 was also significantly related to coping skills, r = .19, p (one-tailed) < .01; and to lack of empathy, r = .11, p (one-tailed) < .05. There was a significant association between abuse and neglect before age 18 and coping skills, r = .12, p (one-tailed) < .05, and coping was significantly related to lack of empathy, r = .35, p (one-tailed) < .001. (There was no significant relationship between abuse and neglect before age of 18 and lack of empathy).

Principal component analysis (PCA) (N = 363) was conducted on the four independent variables with orthogonal rotation (Varimax). The Kaiser-Meyer-Olkin (KMO) measure confirmed the sampling adequacy for the analysis as .57, which is considered to be mediocre (Field, 2009), and all KMO values for individual variables were > .64, which is above the satisfactory limit of .50 (Field, 2009). Bartlett's test of sphericity χ^2; (6) = 218,32, p < .001, indicated that correlations between the variables were sufficiently large for PCA. An initial analysis was run to obtain eigenvalues for each component in the data. Four components had eigenvalues over Kaiser's criterion of 1 and in combination explained 65% of the variance. The scree plot was obvious, indicating to retain both components 1 and 2 in the final analysis. Table 15.2 shows the factor loadings after rotation. The variables clustered on the same components suggest that component 1 represents the clinical factors, component 2 the historical factors.

Binary logistic regression analysis (N = 327) was carried out on the data for the entire sample with the severity of personality disorder (measured in the present) as dependent variable and coping, lack of empathy, abuse and neglect before age 18, and conduct disorder before age 12 as predictor variables. The binary logistic regression analysis examined whether the four predictors have an effect on the odds of the occurrence of personality disorders. The model fit indices (−2 LL = 518,11; χ^2 (4) = 71.53,

Table 15.2 Rotated Component Matrix Using Principal Component Analysis as Extraction Method and Varimax with Kaiser Normalization as Rotation Method

	Component	
Historical and clinical factors	1	2
CD before age 12	.11	.74
abuse and neglect before age 18	−.02	.79
lack of empathy	.81	−.03
coping skills	.78	.14

$p < 0.001$) show that the model fits the data well, the explained variance by the model is 15% (Cox & Snell R2 = .15, Nagelkerke R2 = .21). Lack of empathy, conduct disorder before age 12 and abuse and neglect before age 18 proved to be significant predictors of the occurrence of personality disorders ($p < .001$) as shown in Table 15.3. It can be concluded that the odds of the occurrence of personality disorders is 43% higher than not having a personality disorder with an increase of one step on the abuse and neglect before age 18 scale, 40% higher than not having a personality disorder with an increase of one step on the conduct disorder before age 12 scale, 45% higher than not having a personality disorder with an increase of one step on the on the lack of empathy scale. With 95% certainty, we can say that the odds of having a personality disorder is 23%–65% higher than the odds of not having a personality disorder with an increase of one step on the abuse and neglect before age 18 scale, 20%–62% higher than the odds of not having a personality disorder with an increase of one step on the conduct disorder before age 12 scale, and 14%–84% higher than the odds of not having a personality disorder with an increase of one step on the lack of empathy scale (Table 15.3).

Ordinal logistic regression (N = 368) analysis was carried with the severity of personality disorder (measured in the past) as dependent variable and abuse and neglect before age 18, and conduct disorder before age 12 as predictor variables. The ordinal logistic regression analysis tested whether the two variables (conduct disorder before age 12 and abuse and neglect before age 18) have an effect on the odds of one step increase on the severity of personality disorder scale. The model fit indices ($-2\ LL = 359.375$; $\chi^2 (4) = 77.484$, $p < 0.001$) demonstrate that the model fits the data well; the explained variance by the model is 11% (Cox & Snell R2 = .11, Nagelkerke R2 = .13). Conduct disorder before age 12 and abuse and neglect before age 18 proved to be significant predictors of severity of personality disorder ($p < .001$), as shown in Table 15.4. It can be

Table 15.3 Parameter Estimates of the Effect of Abuse and Neglect before Age 18, Conduct Disorder before Age 12, Lack of Empathy, and Coping Skills on the Occurrence of Personality Disorder

			95% Confidence Interval				95% Confidence Interval for Exp(B)	
Parameter	B	Std. Error	Lower	Upper	Sig.	Exp(B)	Lower	Upper
(intercept)	−815	.3782	−1.555	−.072	.032	.439	.211	.931
Abuse and neglect	.352	.0739	.212	.501	.000	1.418	1.236	1.651
conduct disorder	.325	.0775	.178	.482	.000	1.387	1.195	1.619
lack of empathy	.372	.1212	.132	.607	.002	1.451	1.141	1.835
coping skills	−.154	.1152	−.378	.074	.187	.862	.685	1.077

Table 15.4 Parameter Estimates of the Effect of Abuse and Neglect before Age 18 and Conduct Disorder before Age 12 on the Severity of Personality Disorder

			95% Confidence Interval				95% Confidence Interval for Exp(B)	
Parameter	B	Std. Error	Lower	Upper	Sig.	Exp(B)	Lower	Upper
threshold 0	−1.690	.1657	−2.015	−1.366	.000	.191	.133	.255
threshold 1	−.582	.1358	−.848	−.315	.000	.572	.428	.730
threshold 2	.925	.1364	.658	1.192	.000	2.544	2.002	3.295
threshold 3	3.336	.1863	2.971	3.702	.000	28.121	19.662	40.509
H03gedragsproblvr12	.285	.0491	.189	.381	.000	1.326	1.212	1.464
H04violate18	.222	.0473	.129	.315	.000	1.245	1.142	1.370

concluded that with an increase of one step on the abuse and neglect before age 18 scale, the odds of one step increase on the severity of personality disorder scale is 33% higher than in one category below; with an increase of one step on the conduct disorder scale before age 12, the odds of one step increase on the severity of personality disorder scale is 25% higher than in one category below. With 95% certainty, we can say that with an increase of one step on the abuse and neglect before age 18 scale, the odds of one step increase on the severity of personality disorder scale is 21%–46% higher than in one category below; and with an increase of one step on the conduct disorder before age 12 scale, the odds of one step increase on the severity of personality disorder scale is 14%–37% higher than in one category below (see also Table 15.4).

Pearson correlation (N = 301) indicated a significant relationship between the severity of personality disorder (measured in the past) and the occurrence of personality disorder (measured in the present), $r = .940$, p (one-tailed) $< .01$.

Discussion and Conclusion

The aim of the study was to examine the role of abuse and neglect before age 18 and conduct disorder before age 12 besides lack of empathy and coping skills in the occurrence and severity of personality disorders in a sample of hospitalized forensic patients. The findings suggest significant association between abuse and neglect before age 18; conduct disorder before age 12; lack of empathy, coping skills, but not between abuse and neglect before age 18; and lack of empathy. However, the literature also lacks information about the relationship between these two concepts. The results confirm the existence of the clinical and historical factors of the HKT-30.

The results indicate that all the variables except coping skills (what is an executive function), significantly contributed to the occurrence of personality disorders. The history of childhood abuse, conduct disorder, and empathy problems increase the probability of the occurrence of personality disorders. Lack of empathy appears to have the greatest contribution to the prediction of the occurrence of personality disorders, which is in line with the expectations of the current study and is closely related to the forensic characteristics of the sample, given that there is an inverse relationship between aggression and empathy (Miller & Eisenberg, 1988). Lack of empathy is typically associated with antisocial personality disorder, which is characterized by manipulative behavior and the absence of feelings such as guilt or remorse. Previous studies also found that criminal offenders displayed low levels of empathy (Heilbrun, 1982). The lack of empathy variable of the HKT-30 mainly refers to emotional empathy; thus the results are also consistent with the findings of Ritter et al. (2011), who found emotional empathy impairment in individuals with narcissistic personality disorder. Our data suggest both abuse and neglect before age 18 and conduct disorder before age 12 to be significant predictors of the severity of personality disorders, with other words: individuals who were abused or had conduct disorder in their childhood are more likely to develop more severe personality disorders than those without the history of abuse and/or conduct disorder. Moreover, conduct disorder seems to be the strongest predictor of the development of more severe personality disorders, which is in line with the expectations of the present study, and with the findings of previous studies. Gelhorn et al. (2007) found conduct disorder to be a useful indicator of the severity and persistence of antisocial personality disorder with victim-oriented, aggressive behavior. Conduct problems have also been linked to adult crime and psychopathy (Vitelli, 1996); thus the forensic nature of the sample was dominant in this analysis as well. Finally, personality disorders, in general, are considered to be stable over time. In line with this assumption, the present study shows that the severity of personality disorders (measured in the past) and the occurrence of personality disorders (measured in the present) are highly correlated, but not identical. The slight difference could be because the DSM-IV criteria for Axis II personality disorders vary in their longitudinal prevalence and stability within disorder.

The present study has some limitations. First, the most important limitation of this study is that the severity of personality disorders is not measured in the present, but only in the past. Therefore, it was not possible to look at the association between the clinical factors happening in the present and the severity of personality disorders because it was only measured in the past. Second, the different levels of the HKT-30 items do not indicate the different subtypes of a certain variable such as differences in coping skills or distinction between emotional and cognitive empathy. Finally, the types of personality disorders are not specified in the HKT-30. Although, the severity (measured in the past) shows us to which clusters the participant belongs, the presence of personality disorders (measured in the present) only indicates whether a participant has the disorder or not. Despite the limitations, the HKT-30 seems to be a very useful tool during forensic evaluations as it is not based on self-report, but on objective assessment of forensic psychologists and psychiatrists.

References

Alia, F., Amorima, I. S., & Chamorro-Premuzic, T. (2009). Empathy deficits and trait emotional intelligence in psychopathy and Machiavellianism. *Personality and Individual Differences, 47*(7), 758–762.

Asai, T., Mao, Z., Sugimori, E., & Tanno, Y. (2011). Rubber hand illusion, empathy, and schizotypal experiences in terms of self-other representations. *Consciousness and Cognition, 20*, 1744–1750.

American Psychiatric Association. (APA). (1994). *Diagnostic and statistical manual of mental disorders* (4th ed.). Washington, DC: Author.

American Psychiatric Association. (APA). (2000). *Diagnostic and statistical manual of mental disorders* (4th ed., text rev. [DSM-IV-TR]). Washington, DC: Author.

Baron-Cohen, S., & Wheelwright, S., 2004. The Empathy Quotient: An investigation of adults with Asperger syndrome or high functioning autism and normal sex differences. *Journal of Autism and Developmental Disorders, 34*, 163–175.

Beauchamp, M. C., Lecomte, T., Lecomte, C., Leclerc, C., & Corbiere, M. (2011). Personality traits in early psychosis: Relationship with symptom and coping treatment outcomes. *Early Intervention in Psychiatry, 5*(1), 33–40.

Becker, V. J., Alpert, J. L., Bigfoot, D. S., Bonner, B. L., Geddie, L. F., Henggeler, S. W., . . . Walker, C. E. (1995). Empirical research on child abuse treatment: Report by the child abuse and neglect treatment working group. American Psychological Association. *Journal of Clinical Child Psychology, 24*, 23–46.

Becker, V. J., & Kaplan, S. M. (1991). The incidence of depressive symptomatology in juvenile sex offenders with a history of abuse. *Sexual Child Abuse and Neglect, 15*, 531–536.

Bergvall, A. H., Nilsson, T., & Hansen, S. (2003). Exploring the link between character personality disorder, and neuropsychological function. *European Psychiatry, 18*(7), 334–344.

Beutler, L. E., Harwood, M. T., Kimpara, S., Verdirame, D., & Blau, K. (2011). Adapting psychotherapy to the individual patient: Coping style. *Journal of Clinical Psychology, 67*(2), 176–183.

Bijttebier, P., & Vertommen, H. (1999). Coping strategies in relation to personality disorders. *Personality and Individual Differences, 26*, 847–856.

Blair, R. J. R. (1995). A cognitive developmental approach to morality: investigating the psychopath, *Cognition, 57*, 1–29.

Blair, R. J. R. (1999). Responsiveness to distress cues in the child with psychopathic tendencies. *Personality and Individual Differences, 27*, 135–145.

Bogaerts, S. (2010). Emerging international perspectives in forensic psychology: Individual level analyses. *Journal of Forensic Psychology Practice, 10*, 1–4.

Bogaerts, S., Vervaeke, G., & Goethals, J. (2004). A comparison of relational attitude and personality disorders in the explanation of child molestation. *Sexual Abuse: A Journal of Research and Treatment, 16*, 1.

Boulanger, C., Habib, M., & Lançon, C. (2008). Impaired making-decision and empathy disorder in psychopathy. *European Psychiatry, 23*(2), S92.

Brooner, R. K., Schmidt, C. W., Felch, L. J., & Bigelow, G. E. (1992). Antisocial behavior of intravenous drug abusers: Implications for diagnosis of antisocial personality disorder. *American Journal of Psychiatry, 149*(4), 482–487.

Burgess, A. W., Hartman, C. R., & McCormack, A. (1987). Abused to abuser: Antecedents of socially deviant behavior. *American Journal of Psychiatry, 144*, 1431–1436.

Caplan, D. M. R., & Guthrie, D. (1992). Communication deficits in childhood schizotypal personality disorder. *Journal of the American Academy of Child and Adolescent Psychiatry, 31*(5), 961–967.

Coolidge, F. L., Segal, D. L., Hook, J. N., & Stewart, S. (2000). Personality disorders and coping among anxious older adults. *Journal of Anxiety Disorders, 14* (2), 157–172.

Croon, M. A. (2002). Using predicted latent scores in general latent structure models. In G. A. Marcoulides & I. Moustaki (Eds.), *Latent variable and latent structure models* (pp. 195–224). Mahwah, NJ: Lawrence Erlbaum Associates.

Decety, J., & Jackson, P. L. (2004). The functional architecture of human empathy. *Behavioral and Cognitive Neuroscience Reviews, 3*, 71–100.

De Clercq, B., Fruyt, D. F., & Widiger, T. A. (2009). Integrating a developmental perspective in dimensional models of personality disorders. *Clinical Psychology Review, 29*, 154–162.

Doumas, D., Margolin, G., & John, R. (1994). The intergenerational transmission of aggression across three generations. *Journal of Family Violence, 9*, 157–175.

Duggan, C. (2005). *The treatment of severe personality disorder*. Kidlington, Oxford: The Medicine Publishing Company.

Eaves L. J., Silberg, J. L., Hewitt, J. K., Rutter, M., Meyer, J. M., Neale, M. C., & Pickles, A. (1993). Analyzing twin resemblance in multisymptom data: Genetic applications of a latent class model for symptoms of conduct disorder in juvenile boys. *Behavior Genetics*, 23(4), 5–19.

Farrington, D. P., Loeber, R., Elliot, D. S., Hawkins, D. J., Kandel, D. B., Klein, M. W., ... Tremblay, R. E. (1990). Advancing knowledge about the onset of delinquency and crime. In: B. Lahey & A. Kazdin (Eds.), *Advances in clinical child psychology* (pp. 231–342). New York: Plenum Press.

Field, A. (2009). *Discovering statistics using SPSS* (3rd ed.). London: Sage Publications.

First, M. B., Gibbon, M., Spitzer, R. L., Williams, J. B., & Smith, B. L. (1997). Structured clinical interview for DSM-IV Axis II personality disorders (SCID-II). Washington, DC: American Psychiatric Press.

Francis, G., Last, G. C., & Strauss, C. C. (1992). Avoidant disorder and social phobia in children and adolescents. *Journal of the American Academy of Child & Adolescent Psychiatry, 31*(6), 1086–1089.

Gelhorn, L. H., Sakai, T. J., Price, K. R., & Crowley, J. T. (2007). DSM-IV conduct disorder criteria as predictors of antisocial personality disorder. *Comprehensive Psychiatry, 48*, 529–538.

Harari, H., Shamay-Tsoory, S. G., Ravid, M., & Levkovitz, Y. (2010). Double dissociation between cognitive and affective empathy in borderline personality disorder. *Psychiatric Research, 175*, 277–279.

Hastings, P. D., Zahn-Waxler, C., Robinson, J., Usher, B., & Bridges, D. (2000). The development of concern for others in children with behavior problems. *Developmental Psychology, 36*(5), 531–546.

Haw, C., & Hawton, K. (2008). Life problems and deliberate self-harm: Associations with gender, age, suicidal intent and psychiatric and personality disorder. *Journal of Affective Disorders 109*(1–2), 139–148.

Heilbrun, A. B. (1982). Cognitive models of criminal violence based upon intelligence and psychopathy levels. *Journal of Consulting and Clinical Psychology*, 50, 546–557.

Henry, D. L., Bailey, E. P., & Rendell, G. P. (2008). Empathy, social functioning and schizotypy. *Psychiatry Research, 160*, 15–22.

Hildebrand, M., Hesper, B. L., Spreen, M., & Nijman, H. L. I. (2005). *De waarde van gestructureerde risicotaxatie en van de diagnose psychopathie: een onderzoek naar de betrouwbaarheid van de HCR-20, HKT-30 en PCL-R* 2005. Utrecht: Expertisecentrum Forensische Psychiatrie (EFP).

Hilsenroth, J. M. (1996). Assessment of narcissistic personality disorder: A multimethod review. *Clinical Psychology Review, 16*(7), 655–683.

Hinchey, F. S., & Gavelek, J. R. (1982). Empathic responding in children of battered mothers. *Child Abuse and Neglect, 6*(4), 395–401.

Ireland, J. L., Brown, S. L., & Ballarini, S. (2006). Maladaptive personality traits, coping styles and psychological distress: A study of adult male prisoners. *Personality and Individual Differences, 41*, 561–573.

Johnson, J. G., Cohen, P. A., & Brown, J., (1999). Childhood maltreatment increases risk for personality disorders during early childhood. *Archives of General Psychiatry, 56*, 600–606.

Kunitz, J. S., Levy, E. J., McCloskey, J., & Gabriel, R. K. (1998). Alcohol dependence and domestic violence as sequelae of abuse and conduct disorder in childhood. *Child Abuse and Neglect, 22*(11), 1079–1091.

Lahey, B. B., & Loeber, R. (1997). ADHD and antisocial behavior. In D. M. Stoff (Ed.), *Handbook of antisocial behavior* (pp. 243–254). New York: John Wiley and Sons.

Leitenberg, H., Gibson, L. E., & Novy, P. L. (2004). Individual differences among undergraduate women in methods of coping with stressful events: the impact of cumulative childhood stressors and abuse. *Child Abuse and Neglect*, 28, 181–192.

Luntz, B. K., & Widom, C. S. (1994). Antisocial personality disorder in abused and neglected children grown up. *American Journal of Psychiatry, 151*, 670–674.

Malinosky-Rummell, R., & Hansen, D. J. (1993). Long term consequences of childhood physical abuse. *Psychological Bulletin, 114*, 68–79.

Marmorstein, N. R. (2006). Adult antisocial behavior without conduct disorder: Demographic characteristics and risk for co-occurring psychopathology. *Canadian Journal of Psychiatry, 51*, 226–233.

Miller, P. A., & Eisenberg, N. (1988). The relation of empathy to aggressive and externalizing/antisocial behavior. *Psychological Bulletin, 103*(3), 324–344.

Monahan, J. (1992). Mental disorder and violent behavior: Perceptions and evidence. *American Psychologist, 47*(4), 511–521.

Müller, J. L., Gänssbauer, S., Sommer, M., Döhnel, K., Weber, T., Schmidt-Wilcke, T., & Hajak, G. (2008). Gray matter changes in right superior temporal gyrus in criminal psychopaths. Evidence from voxel-based morphometry. *Psychiatry Research: Neuroimaging, 163*(3), 213–222.

Negy, C., Woods, D. J., & Carlson, R. (1997). The relationship between female inmates' coping and adjustment in a minimum-security prison. *Criminal Justice and Behavior, 24*(2), 224–233.

Paris, J. (1994). *Borderline personality disorders: A multidimensional approach.* Washington, DC: American Psychiatric Press.

Pollock, V. E., Briere, J., Schneider, L., Knop, J., Mednick, S. A., & Goodwin, D. W. (1990). Childhood antecedents of antisocial behavior: Parental alcoholism and physical abusiveness. *American Journal of Psychiatry, 147*, 1290–1293.

Rim, Y. (1995). Notes and shorter communications—coping styles, impulsiveness, venturesomeness and empathy. *Personality and Individual Differences, 18* (1), 159–160.

Ritter, K., Dziobek, I., Preißler, S., Rüter, A., Vater, A., Fydrich, T., . . . Roepke, S. (2011). Lack of empathy in patients with narcissistic personality disorder. *Psychiatry Research, 187*, 241–247.

Roberts, A. C., Robbins, T. W., & Weiskrantz, L. (1996). Executive and cognitive functions of the prefrontal cortex. *Philosophical Transactions of the Royal Society B, 351*, 1387–1527.

Robins, L. N. (1978). Sturdy childhood predictors of adult antisocial behaviour: replications from longitudinal studies. *Psychological Medicine, 8*, 611–622.

Runtz, M. G., & Schallow, J. R. (1997). Social support and coping strategies as mediators of adult adjustment following child maltreatment. *Child Abuse and Neglect, 21*, 211–226.

Sanford, M., Boyle, M. H., Szatmári, P., Offord, D. R., Jamieson, E., & Spinner, M. (1999). Age-of-onset classification of conduct disorder: reliability and validity in a prospective cohort study. *Journal of American Academy of Child Adolescent Psychiatry, 38*(8), 992–999.

Sappington, A. A., Pharr, R., Tunstall, A., & Rickert, E. (1997). Relationships among child abuse, date abuse, and psychological problems. *Journal of Clinical Psychology, 53*, 1–11.

Skodol, A. E., Gunderson, J. G., McGlashan, T. H., Dyck, I. R., Stout, R. L., Bender, D. S., . . . Oldham, J. M. (2002). Functional impairment in patients with schizotypal, borderline, avoidant, or obsessive-compulsive personality disorder. *American Journal of Psychiatry, 159*, 276–283.

Smith, E. E., & Jonides, J. (1999). Storage and executive processes in the frontal lobes. *Science, 283*, 1657–1661.

Spreen, M., Ter Horst, P. R. M., Bogaerts, S., Lammers, S. M. M., Hochstenbach, J., Soe-Agnie, S. E., & Reubsaet, R. J. (2009). Risicotaxatie aan de hand van de HCR-20 en de HKT-30: Een vergelijking tussen beide instrumenten. In T. I. Oei & M. S. Groenhuijsen (Eds.), *Forensische psychiatrie en haar grensgebieden: Actualiteit, geschiedenis en toekomst* (pp. 459–476). Alphen aan den Rijn: Kluwer.

Sterzer, P., Stadler, C., Poustka, F., & Kleinschmidt, A. (2007). A structural neural deficit in adolescents with conduct disorder and its association with lack of empathy. *NeuroImage, 37*, 335–342.

Suls, J., David, J. P., & Harvey, J. H. (1996). Personality and coping: Three generations of research. *Journal of Personality, 64*(4), 711–735.

Tyrer, P., & Johnson, T. (1996). Establishing the severity of personality disorder. *American Journal of Psychiatry, 153*, 1593–1597.

Van Harreveld, F., Van Der Pligt, J., Claassen, L., & Van Dijk, W. W. (2007). Inmate emotion doping and psychological and physical well-being: The use of crying over spilled milk. *Criminal Justice and Behavior, 34*, 697–708.

Vitaliano, P. P., Maiuro, R. D., Russo, J., Katon, W., De Wolfe, D., & Hall, G. (1990). Coping profiles associated with psychiatric, physical health, work and family problems. *Health Psychology, 9*(3), 348–376.

Vitelli, R. (1996). Prevalence of childhood conduct and attention-deficit hyperactivity disorder in adult maximum-security inmates. *International Journal of Offender Therapy and Comparative Criminology, 40*(4), 263–271.

Vollrath, M., Alnaes, R., & Torgersen, S. (1994). Coping and MCMI-II personality disorders. *Journal of Personality Disorders, 8*(1), 53–63.

Webster, C. D., Douglas, K. S., Eaves, D., & Hart, S. D. (1997). *HCR-20: Assessing the Risk for Violence (Version 2)*. Vancouver, British Columbia, Canada: Mental Health, Law, and Policy Institute, Simon Fraser University.

Widom, C. S. (1989). Does violence beget violence?: A critical examination of the literature. *Psychological Bulletin, 106*, 3–28.

Widom C. S. (1995). Alcohol abuse in abused and neglected children followed-up: Are they at increased risk? *J Studies Alc, 56*, 207–217.

Wolf, E. (1966). Psychogenic disorders and interpersonal behaviour. *Psychosomatic Research, 10*, 119–126.

Xuereb, S., Ireland, J. L., & Davies, M. (2009). Chronic and offence-related factors and coping styles in offenders. *Personality and Individual Differences, 46*, 465–471.

Yang, M., Cold, J., & Tyrer, P. (2010). Personality pathology recorded by severity: national survey. *British Journal of Psychiatry, 197*(3), 193–199.

Zahn-Waxler, C., & Radke-Yarrow, M. (1990). The origins of empathic concern. *Motivation and Emotion, 14*(2), 107–130.

Zanarini, C. M., Gunderson, G. J., Marino, F. M., Schwartz, O. E., & Frankenburg, R. F. (1989). *Comprehensive Psychiatry, 30*(1), 18–25.

CHAPTER SIXTEEN

A Proposed Sexual Homicide Category: The Psychopathic–Sexually Sadistic Offender

Shayne Jones, Heng Choon (Oliver) Chan, Wade C. Myers, and Kathleen M. Heide

Documented cases of sexual homicide in the United States and in other countries where data exist are rare. Sexual homicide constituted less than 1% of all homicides in the United States during the 30-year period from 1976 to 2005 (Chan, Myers, & Heide, 2010). Despite public concern and legislative action in this area, research on sexual homicide has been limited. In a comprehensive review of the literature, Chan and Heide (2009) found that fewer than 40 empirical studies had been published on sexual homicide prior to 2009. Research efforts have been limited by the lack of reliable national crime statistics and a standardized definition of sexual homicide (Chan & Heide, 2009; Myers, 2004). In recent years, efforts have intensified to study this phenomenon (Chan & Heide, 2009). As a result, the field has developed a better understanding of several of the important issues surrounding sexual homicide.

Sexual homicide is a distinct type of murder. According to Meloy (2000), most sexual murders involve male offenders who commit their first sexual homicide prior to the age of 30 years. Females (Van Patten & Delhauer, 2007) and adults (Chan & Heide, 2008) comprise the overwhelming majority of the victims. Sexual homicide is primarily an intra-racial offense, particularly among white offenders. During the period 1976–2005, almost all sexual homicides committed by white offenders in the United States involved white victims. Black offenders were significantly more likely than white offenders to murder inter-racially as the age of the victim increased. Still, more than half of the child, adolescent, and adult victims killed by both juvenile and adult black offenders were of the same race. However, one exception to this intra-racial "rule"—that sexual homicide offenders (SHOs) usually kill intra-racially—was observed in the case of juvenile or adult black offenders who killed elderly victims—their victims were white in more than half of the cases (Chan, Myers, & Heide, 2010).

Regarding their methods of killing, analysis of 29 years of U.S. Supplementary Homicide Report (SHR) data revealed that both juvenile and adult SHOs were far more likely to use close-contact weapons, such as personal weapons and contact and edged weapons (Chan & Heide, 2008), than nonsexual murderers, who were likely to employ firearms to kill their victims (Fox & Levin, 1991). One theory posits that the use of personal weapons allows for a more "intimate," and thus more gratifying, experience for some of these killers (Krafft-Ebing, 1898/1965; Van Patten & Delhauer, 2007).

The recidivism rate in SHOs has not been widely researched, although some recent studies do provide estimates. Hill, Habermann, Klussman, Berner, and Briken (2008) conducted one of the first comprehensive recidivism studies of SHOs. They noted that the combined rate of violent recidivism, sexual or nonsexual, in a 10-year follow-up period of 90 SHOs was higher in offenders who committed their first sexual homicide under the age of 21 years and who were released back to the community after short periods of incarceration. Three men (3%) out of the 90 subjects were reconvicted for either attempted (two subjects) or completed (one subject) homicides; two of these offenses were sexual in nature. Myers, Chan, Vo, and Lazarou (2010) recently found that 55% of their sample of 11 juvenile SHOs recidivated in either sexual, nonsexual, or violent offenses within five years after release, and 27% of these 11 became sexual murderers. Clearly more work needs to be conducted regarding recidivism before reliable estimates can be ascertained.

Although much has been learned about SHOs generally, obstacles remain that impede a more refined understanding of this dangerous group of offenders. One means of achieving greater clarity is to explore whether there are differences among SHOs. Ressler, Burgess, and Douglas (1988) were among the first to classify SHOs largely based on the offenders' motivation to sexually perpetrate their victims. Although there are references in the literature to serial murderers as psychopathic sexual sadists, little attention has focused on systematically exploring the combined roles of sadism and psychopathy in sexual homicide offenders (Geberth, 1995). Rather, most of the efforts have largely relied on an analysis of crime scene characteristics to classify offenders. In the current chapter, a different approach is taken whereby the focus is on specific psychological factors.

Several studies have examined whether SHOs demonstrate distinct forms of psychopathology. Despite the disturbing nature of sexual homicide, these offenders are in the great majority of cases rational beings who understand the nature of their actions. Scholars and clinicians agree that SHOs are rarely psychotic. Schizophrenia and other psychoses have been infrequently diagnosed in SHOs (Hill, Habermann, Berner, & Briken, 2007; Meloy, Gacono, & Kenney, 1994). In contrast, personality disorders are quite common among SHOs (Langevin, Ben-Aron, Wright, Marchese, & Handy, 1988). Psychopathy, in particular, is a common personality disturbance in this population. Previous research suggests a strong link between sexual homicide and psychopathy (Beauregard, Proulx, & St-Yves, 2007; Chan & Heide, 2009; Firestone, Bradford, Greenberg, & Larose, 1998a; Firestone, Bradford, Greenberg, Larose, & Curry, 1998b; Hakkanen-Nyholm, Repo-Tiihonen, Lindberg, Salenius, & Weizmann-Henelius, 2009; Heide, Beauregard, & Myers, 2009; Juodis, Woodworth, Porter, & ten Brinke, 2009; Meloy, 2000; Myers & Blashfield, 1997; Myers, Chan, Vo, & Lazarou, 2010; Myers, Eggleston, & Smoak, 2003; Porter, Demetrioff, & ten Brinke, 2010; Porter, Woodworth, Earle, Drugge, & Boer, 2003, Stone, 2001). Importantly, and more pertinent to this chapter, the role of psychopathy appears to be an important component that can help distinguish among different types of SHOs, particularly when coupled with sexual sadism.

To date, few studies have examined in detail the interconnections between psychopathic traits, sadism, and sexual homicide. The purpose of this chapter is to make more explicit these linkages by synthesizing key aspects from these literatures, with the aim of describing the distinctive psychological profile of the sexually sadistic and psychopathic SHO. Toward this end, this chapter includes the pertinent literature on psychopathy and how this disorder has been linked to sexual offending, sadism, and SHO. Thereafter, the characteristics of a proposed type of psychopathic–sexually sadistic SHO are illustrated in a case study of this distinctive type of SHO.

Psychopathy

Psychopathy is a personality disorder characterized by interpersonal and affective deficits as well as by specific lifestyle and antisocial tendencies. Interpersonally, psychopathic individuals are grandiose, manipulative, and superficial. Affectively, they lack remorse and are callous. Their lifestyle often lacks direction, and they tend to be parasitic, impulsive, and irresponsible. Moreover, many psychopathic individuals have a marked history of antisocial and aggressive behaviors. These features are routinely assessed with the Psychopathy Checklist–Revised (PCL-R; Hare, 2003).

Psychopathy is rare among nonoffenders; only approximately 1% of the general population would meet the diagnostic criteria for this disorder (Blair, Mitchell, & Blair, 2005; Hare, 1999, Hare & Neumann, 2006). The prevalence in offender populations is much higher. For example, between 15% and 25% of male offenders in the Canadian federal correctional system meet current diagnostic criteria for psychopathy (Hare, 1996; see also Porter et al., 2000). Importantly, psychopathy has proven to be a robust correlate of antisocial, aggressive, and offending behavior, and appears to be particularly related to violence (for recent studies, e.g., Murrie et al., 2007; Reidy, Zeichner, & Martinez, 2008; Reidy, Zeichner, & Seibert, 2011). As will be elaborated below, psychopathic individuals are more likely to engage in sexual violence (Knight & Guay, 2006) as well as sexual homicides (Porter & Woodworth, 2006).

Before proceeding, it is important to make clear how we will be discussing psychopathy and why. Although there is debate surrounding the precise factor structure of psychopathy, especially when defined by the PCL-R, the more traditional factor structure is defined by the interpersonal and affective features as comprising Factor 1, and the lifestyle and antisocial features comprising Factor 2. We recognize that some have argued for a three-factor model (Cooke & Michie, 2001) and a four-factor model (Hare & Neumann, 2006). This issue is an important one that deserves continued attention, but this debate lies well beyond the scope of this chapter. Because much of the literature we review is based on the two-factor model, we will refer to psychopathy in this manner in those instances where the factor structure is explicitly referenced.

Psychopathy and Sexual Homicide

Although most sexual offenders are not psychopathic individuals (Porter et al., 2000), some degree of psychopathic traits is common in this population. Likewise, psychopaths commit sexual crimes at a markedly higher rate than those without psychopathy (Harris, Rice, Hilton, Lalumiere, & Quinsey, 2007). It is the intersection of these two concepts—sexual offending and psychopathy—that brings about even greater concern, with sexual violence a not-uncommon result. In its more extreme form, sexual violence can lead to the death of the victim. When the victim dies, the offense can be classified as sexual homicide. In discussing SHOs with psychopathic traits, Porter, Campbell, Woodworth, and Birt (2002) coined the term "sexual psychopaths" to describe this unique class of violent offenders.

Many scholars have found that their samples of SHOs scored significantly higher than non-SHOs on the PCL-R, with mean scores commonly in the mid-20s or higher (PCL-R score range 0–40) (Beauregard et al., 2007; Firestone et al., 1998a; Firestone, et al., 1998b; Hakkanen-Nyholm et al., 2009; Meloy, 2000; Meloy et al., 1994; Myers & Blashfield, 1997; Myers & Monaco, 2000; Myers et al., 2003; Myers et al., 2010; Porter et al., 2003; Stone, 2001; Woodworth & Porter, 2002). SHOs also scored higher than non-SHOs on both Factors 1 and 2 of the PCL-R. According to Hakkanen-Nyholm and colleagues (2009), psychopaths who committed sexual homicides tended to lack empathy, lie pathologically, and be manipulative and remorseless. In addition, they were likely to have a higher prevalence of previous sexual crimes than non-SHOs (Hakkanen-Nyholm et al., 2009).

The offending methods of psychopathic SHOs generally suggest more planning than that observed in non-psychopathic SHOs (Hakkanen-Nyholm et al., 2009; Juodis et al., 2009; Porter et al., 2003; Warren, Hazelwood, & Dietz, 1996; Woodworth & Porter, 2002). The nature of this planning may reflect the presence of deviant sexual fantasies (Chan & Heide, 2009; Chan, Heide, & Beauregard, 2010). The evidence suggests that these offenders were primarily motivated by the need to express power and anger through humiliation and degradation of the victims. Psychopathic SHOs typically derive sexual gratification from the victim's suffering; the victim's suffering is sexually arousing in addition to the satisfaction that is experienced from the sexual act itself (Hazelwood & Warren, 2000). Sexual sadism, a type of paraphilia, has been linked to psychopathic personality, particularly in the SHO population.

The literature indicates that most SHOs who recidivated were diagnosed with psychopathy, or at least possessed several psychopathic traits. The risk of reoffending, particularly sexual recidivism, is closely associated with the presence of psychopathic personality (Hanson & Bussiere, 1998; Hill et al., 2008; Kosson, Kelly, & White, 1997; Myers et al., 2010; Rice & Harris, 1997) and sexual sadism (Berner, Berger, & Hill, 2003; Myers et al., 2010) in the individual. Sexual recidivism is strongly predicted by a combination of a high PCL-R score and deviant sexual arousal (Hanson & Bussiere, 1998). As this discussion suggests, the role of sexual sadism, like psychopathy, appears to be an important factor in differentiating specific types of SHOs.

Sexual Sadism

Krafft-Ebing (1898/1965) introduced the term "sadism" and classified sexually sadistic homicide as "lust murder." MacCulloch, Snowden, Wood, and Mills (1983) further expanded the work of Krafft-Ebing and defined sadism as "the repeated practice of behavior and fantasy which is characterized by a wish to control another person by domination, denigration, or inflicting pain, for the purpose of producing mental pleasure, and sexual arousal (whether or not accompanied by orgasm) in the sadist" (p. 20). DSM-IV-TR (American Psychiatric Association, 2000) diagnostically defined sexual sadism as involving "recurrent, intense sexually arousing fantasies, sexual urges, or behaviors involving acts (real, or simulated) in which the psychological or physical suffering (including humiliation) of the victim is sexually exciting to the person" for at least six recurrent months (p. 530). Sexual sadism is one of several types of paraphilias (American Psychiatric Association, 2000), which are frequently identified in lust murderers (see Purcell & Arrigo, 2006).

Despite the many different definitions stated by various parties aside from the three aforementioned widely used definitions, disagreement continues to exist regarding the subjective defining and diagnostic criteria of sexual sadism, particularly on the motives that drive sexual sadists (for review, see Marshall & Kennedy, 2003). Hence, reliability of sexual sadism diagnosis across diagnosticians is difficult to achieve even after years of empirical efforts (e.g., Berner et al., 2003; Gratzer & Bradford, 1995; Knight, 1989; Knight & Prentky, 1990; Marshall & Hucker, 2006a, 2006b; Marshall, Kennedy, & Yates, 2002). Nevertheless, researchers in recent years have attempted to develop a more objective dimensional approach in identifying the important behavioral features of sexual sadists (see Marshall & Hucker, 2006a, 2006b; Nitschke, Osterheider, & Mokros, 2009).

Nitschke and colleagues (2009) put forth an 11-item set of the Severe Sexual Sadism scale reprinted below. At least 4 of the 11 criteria have to be met to be classified as a sexual sadist. In addition, at least three of these criteria have to belong to the core criteria proposed by Marshall, Kennedy, and Yates (2002): "(a) offender is sexually aroused by the act, (b) offender exercises power/control/domination over the victim, (c) offender humiliates or degrades the victim, (d) offender tortures the victim or engages in acts of cruelty to the victim, and (e) offender mutilates sexual parts of the victim's body" (Nitschke et al., 2009, p. 273).

1. Offender engages in gratuitous violence toward or wounding of the victim.
2. Offender exercises power/control/domination over the victim.

3. Offender humiliates or degrades the victim.
4. Offender is sexually aroused by the act.
5. Offender tortures the victim or engages in acts of cruelty to the victim.
6. Evidence of ritualism in offense.
7. Victim is abducted or confined.
8. Insertion of object(s) into victim's bodily orifice(s).
9. Offender mutilates sexual parts of the victim's body.
10. Offender mutilates nonsexual parts of the victim's body.
11. Offender keeps trophies (e.g., hair, underwear, ID) of the victim or keeps records of the offense.

Sadism and Sexual Homicide

The expression of sexually sadistic interests ranges from mild in nature, such as harmless sadomasochistic sexual activity between consenting partners, to "bizarre and grotesque" serial killings (Drukteinis, 1992). Population surveys (e.g., see Kinsey, Pomeroy, Martin, & Gebhard, 1953) indicate that sadomasochistic interests are not uncommon in the general population. However, it is also important to note that sexual sadists are relatively rare among sex offenders, accounting for just 2% to 5% of the sex offender population (Langevin, 2003). Nonetheless, they do represent a meaningful group worthy of scholarly and clinical attention. For instance, Myers, Husted, Safarik, and O'Toole (2006) proposed a new DSM diagnosis of "Sexual Sadism, Homicidal Type" to address those sexually sadistic serial murderers.

Engaging in sexual sadistic behavior may increase the motivation of the offender to commit sexual homicide. SHOs who perform sadistic acts usually fantasize about them before and after acting upon them. Collecting sadistic pornographic material is fairly frequent among sexual sadists generally, and is even more prevalent among sadistic SHOs (Brittain, 1970; Chan & Heide, 2009; Dietz, Harry, & Hazelwood, 1986; Langevin, 2003). With time, the SHO may become habituated to pornographic material, and thus will seek alternative and more fulfilling sources of stimulation to achieve fulfillment.

When engaging in sadistic fantasies about human victimization becomes less sexually gratifying, sadistic sex offenders may progress to the actual execution of sadistic acts on humans, resulting in murder (Palermo, 1994; Purcell & Arrigo, 2006). This assertion is in line with MacCulloch, Gray, and Watt's (2000) two important cognitive-behavioral features of the "Sadistic Murderer Syndrome." That is, these murderers (or those who will murder) engage in extreme sadistic fantasies, often act out their sadistic attacks in incremental fashion, and, over time, their expression of violence escalates as the act of fantasizing becomes less satisfying. On occasion, sadistic SHOs may practice their sadistic acts on consenting partners (Hazelwood, Warren, & Dietz, 1993) as a way to try out their sadistic fantasies for the first time or to improve their modus operandi. As this discussion suggests, there appears to be a progression among some sadistic sex offenders in terms of escalating violence. As detailed in subsequent sections of this chapter, it may also be true that specific types of sexual sadists—those with psychopathic traits—may engage in more violence over time to increase their psychological and sexual arousal.

Prevalence of Sexual Sadism in Psychopathic Sexual Homicide Offenders

There is burgeoning speculation that the elements of psychopathy, sadism, and sexual violence may combine to produce sexual homicides. The comorbidity of psychopathy and sexual sadism was found to be high among SHOs as noted earlier. This suggests that both elements—psychopathy and sadism—are important in understanding SHOs.

The most common underlying motivation of sadistic SHOs is to exert control, domination, and power upon the victim for sexual pleasure (Chan & Heide, 2009). In addition, sadistic sexual offenders are likely to use the execution of sadistic acts as an outlet for their unexpressed internal distress (Heide et al., 2009; Proulx, McKibben, & Lusignan, 1996). Kirsch and Becker (2007) posited that psychopaths with sexual sadism may experience victim distress as sexually arousing. One major distinction addressed by Kirsch and Becker between psychopaths and psychopathic-sadists was that psychopaths likely disregard their victim's suffering, whereas sadists with psychopathy are likely sexually excited and aroused in response to their victim's suffering. Sadists with psychopathy are likely to be more violent and lethal than psychopaths without sadistic traits and sadists without psychopathic personalities.

Although limited, available findings suggest that sadistic SHOs with psychopathic personality are likely to be at higher risk of reoffending, compared to nonsadistic SHOs and other nonsexual violent offenders (Beauregard & Proulx, 2002; Chan & Heide, 2009; Firestone et al., 1998a; Hill et al., 2007; Hill et al., 2008; Myers, 2004; Myers et al., 2010). This type of SHO, although small in number, is extremely dangerous and the one most feared by the public, particularly by those who are parents with small children (Heide et al., 2009).

As the discussion illustrates, there are some aspects of the sadistic psychopathic SHO that are known. What is less clear is a how best to conceptualize this specific type of offender. In the following section, different conceptualizations of the sadist, psychopath, and violent sexual offender are discussed, and a proposal is set forth that ties them together.

Conceptual Basis for Psychopathic–Sexually Sadistic SHO

For several years, Knight and Prentky (1990) have worked to develop an offender classification system for sexual offenders. This classification has been revised several times, based on continued evaluation of empirical evidence, in an effort to better differentiate types of sexual offenders. Although nine different types have emerged, of particular interest in the current chapter is the sadistic type. Knight and Guay (2006) noted that the sadistic sexual offender possesses three core attributes. The first two are psychopathic traits; namely the affective-interpersonal deficits (Factor 1) and impulsivity-antisociality (Factor 2). The third feature is sexualization, which refers to the "combination of sexual preoccupation, a frequent need for sexual activity (i.e., a high total sexual outlet), extensive use of pornography, and the presence of paraphilic fantasies and behavior" (p. 523). Thus, it is the combination of all three elements that produces the sadistic sexual offender. This offender fuses sexual and aggressive drives and is described as angry. He receives sexual satisfaction through the use of extreme physical force and the consequent physical damage inflicted upon the victim. To be clear, Knight and Guay are referring to a violent sexual offender, and not a homicide offender. However, as articulated below, there are reasons to suspect that this type of offender's behavior can relatively easily lead to the death of the victim.

Beyond sexual aggression specifically, the link between psychopathy and sadism has been extensively noted in the literature as well (as discussed above). In a review of this literature, Porter and Woodworth (2006) arrived at the conclusion that psychopathic offenders may derive pleasure from inflicting physical and emotional harm on others. That is, those with elevated psychopathic traits are sadists. Further, they indicated that SHOs may typify the link between psychopathy and sadism. They suggested that a key element to understanding why psychopathic offenders are more likely to be sadistic is their need for intense stimulation, or thrill seeking, along with their affective deficits. In the PCL-R (Hare, 2003), the item "need for stimulation/proneness to boredom" loads on Factor 2 (of the two-factor model). It is somewhat unclear whether this PCL-R item is synonymous with the type of thrill seeking discussed by Porter and Woodworth. However, and similar to Knight and Guay, there appear to be items stemming from both psychopathy factors that, when combined with the element of sadism, describe a particularly dangerous type of offender.

Each of these notions—psychopathy, sadism, sexualization, thrill seeking—provides some potential insights into the traits and characteristics of the psychopathic–sexually sadistic SHO. What remains elusive is why this type of offender engages in his crime. Recent work by Blair provides a possible explanation. Blair, Mitchell, and Blair (2005) suggested that the core dysfunction of psychopathic individuals is an affective deficit—they have difficulty in processing and learning emotional stimuli. Several studies suggest that the reason for this difficulty is amygdala impairment/abnormality. The amygdala is crucial for learning, especially emotional learning. Blair and colleagues suggested that the amygdala impairment characteristic of psychopathic individuals compromises their ability to recognize sadness and fearfulness in the expression of others. According to these researchers, this recognition is critical to inhibiting violence. Stated differently, for individuals with a properly functioning amygdala, the sadness and fearfulness of a victim is recognized and is perceived as an aversive stimulus. This negative affective reaction, in turn, will lead to an interruption of the violent behavior, or prevent it from occurring in the first place. Among psychopathic individuals, however, the distress evinced by a victim's sad or fearful expressions is not perceived as readily, leading to a greater likelihood that the violence will continue unabated.

This theoretical perspective appears to shed some light on the development of psychopathy. Specifically, psychopathic individuals will not perceive sadness and fearfulness as easily as non-psychopathic individuals. Psychopathic individuals who are also sadists have a desire to perceive these reactions in others. Accordingly, they inflict considerably greater harm on a victim, which will lead to greater expressions of sadness and fearfulness. Thus, the necessary violence that must be enacted by the sadistic psychopath to satisfy his sadistic desires might lead to the death of the victim. Although not yet empirically validated for psychopathic–sexually sadistic SHOs, this perspective holds promise in better understanding the neurocognitive mechanisms that might explain why this type of offender engages in sexual homicides. (Note that several other regions of the brain, including the orbital frontal cortex and areas of the temporal cortex, have also been implicated in psychopathy.)

Case Study of a Psychopathic–Sexually Sadistic Sexual Homicide Offender

Mr. Krewel's childhood was notable for his father being an alcoholic and verbally abusive toward his wife when he was drunk. His parents divorced when Mr. Krewel was an early teenager. His school grades were unremarkable and his IQ fell within the average range. As a teenager, he engaged in stealing and fighting, and he had an arrest for underage drinking. He denied aberrant sexual practices while a juvenile, and there was no history of sexual or physical abuse.

After high school, Mr. Krewel did some limited college coursework and then enlisted in the armed forces for several years. He alluded to knowing about some perverse, fatal sexual activities involving captive women that occurred while he was stationed overseas, but he declined to elaborate. He paradoxically smiled as he reminisced about their fate. Around this time in his early adulthood, he exhibited other sexually sadistic tendencies. For instance, a woman with whom he was on a date passed out from drinking too much. He cut her clothes off with a knife and raped her while she was unconscious.

Mr. Krewel was married for a brief time, but his wife left him as she was frightened by his volatile temper and abusive episodes. On several occasions, she thought he had tried to kill her. Adding to her concerns were his heavy drinking, constant demands for sex, and extramarital affairs.

Mr. Krewel had multiple arrests as an adult. His criminal activity included trespassing, vandalism, theft, burglary, drug offenses, child molestation, sexual assault, and battery. Law enforcement also suspected him in a handful of sexual homicides, but he denied involvement, and there was no physical evidence and no witnesses to connect him to these unsolved crimes. Additionally, a woman with whom Mr. Krewel was temporarily staying died in her home from head trauma. Despite these mysterious circumstances, the possibility of her death being accidental could not be sufficiently excluded by the authorities to proceed ahead with prosecution.

When a middle-aged man, Mr. Krewel was finally arrested and successfully prosecuted for the sexual murder of a woman. In addition to sexually assaulting the victim, he also stabbed her repeatedly, beheaded her, posed her corpse, and dissected out her genital region and took it home to eat at a later time. Her clothes had been cut off her body with a knife.

Diagnostically, Mr. Krewel had a psychopathic personality and met DSM-IV-TR criteria for sexual sadism (American Psychiatric Association, 2000). On the Psychopathy Checklist–Revised (PCL-R), he had a score of 29 (scores of 25 or 30 are generally identified as the cutoff for the presence of a psychopathic personality; Hare, 2003).

The *SADSEX-SH*, a recently developed 10-item rating scale designed to dimensionally estimate the degree of offender sexual sadism in cases of sexual homicide, was applied to Mr. Krewel's case. Each item is scored

Table 16.1 Mr. Krewel's SADSEX-SH Rating Scale

SADSEX-SH RATING SCALE*

Item	Not Present/ Unknown	Possibly Present/ Some Evidence	Present
1. Sexual excitement from the victim's pain or suffering			X
2. Recurrent sexually sadistic fantasies	X		
3. Sexual domination of the victim through the use of bondage, asphyxia, blindfolding, a knife, etc.		X	
4. Physical or psychological torture of victim		X	
5. Victim forced to verbally or physically engage in sexually degrading, humiliating behavior			X
6. Gratuitous violence, excessive injury, biting, cutting, or other acts of physical cruelty inflicted on the victim			X
7. Anal or oral sex forced upon victim			X
8. Use of an inanimate object(s) to sexually penetrate victim	X		
9. Sexual mutilation of the victim			X
10. Souvenirs or trophies taken from the victim			X

*Dimensionally measures probable degree of sexual sadism in cases of sexual homicide.
Scoring: Not Present or Unknown = 0 points
Possibly Present/Some Evidence = 1 point
Present = 2 points
Sexual Sadism Score (Items 1–10) = *14* (range 0–20)

in terms of no evidence present (0), some evidence present (1), and evidence present (2). It is scored using crime scene and other all available investigative information. Mr. Krewel's case scored a 14 out of 20 (see Table 16.1), supportive of a robust degree of sexual sadism according to preliminary norms described below.

The *SADSEX-SH* was constructed by author Wade Myers based on the violent sexual sadism literature and clinical experience (e.g., Dietz, Hazelwood, & Warren, 1990; Federoff, 2008; Gratzer & Bradford, 1995; Marshall, Kennedy, & Yates, 2002; Nitschke et al., 2009). Preliminary norms for the *SADSEX-SH* indicate that it may have some usefulness in predicting offender sexual sadism in sexual homicides. Five adult male sexual murderers with the diagnosis of sexual sadism who had killed adult females were randomly selected from the author's case files. These five men all had moderate to high levels of psychopathy, with a mean PCL-R score of 26.8 ± 6.5 (range 20–36), and thus were considered "psychopathic–sexually sadistic SHOs." They were then matched with five male adult sexual murderers without sexual sadism who also had killed adult females. Both groups were then rated using the *SADSEX-SH*. Comparisons made on basic demographic variables found no significant differences based on age at the time of the murder (31.6 years ± 14.9 versus 34.2 years ± 9.6, $t = 0.33$, $p = .751$), race (60% vs. 40% white, Fisher's Exact, $p = 1.000$) or IQ (98.8 ± 15.8 versus 92.2 ± 9.9, $t = -0.79$, $p = .453$). There was a significant difference between the two groups on their *SADSEX-SH* scores (13.8 ± 3.6, range = 10–18, versus 3.2 ± 1.6, range = 1–5, $t = -5.94$, $p < .001$). Using a preliminary cutoff score of 8, all 10 individuals were correctly identified as having sexual sadism or not.

Discussion

This proposed category of SHO—the Psychopathic–Sexually Sadistic Offender—brings together the distinctive characteristics of psychopathic personality and sexual sadism. Some available typologies in the literature subsume, without differentiating, the psychopathic personality type and sexual sadism under the same category. For instance, the organized/disorganized sexual murderer taxonomy as proposed by Ressler and colleagues (1986) fails to explicate the presence or lack of psychopathic traits or sexual sadism for either of these categories.

The anger-excitation rape-murderer profile suggested by Keppel and Walter (1999) resembles in some respects of our proposed Psychopathic–Sexually Sadistic Offender category. The anger-excitation rape-murderer is typically motivated by intense hatred, and likewise the sadistic sexual homicide offender may seek to gratify his lust for domination and control through anger expression. Besides the expression of rage and anger, the victim's suffering as a result of sadistic acts can be sexually exciting and arousing (Kirsch & Becker, 2007; Myers et al., 2006). The suffering may be not only a matter of power and control.

The current proposed Psychopathic–Sexually Sadistic SHO profile also bears a resemblance to several other scholars' SHO profiles. The current psychological profile is comparable with Schlesinger's (2007) planned compulsive sexual murderer and Geberth's (1996) homosexual lust murderer. What we have attempted to do in this chapter is provide a conceptual framework by which to understand the behavior of the Psychopathic–Sexually Sadistic SHO. We have included a focus on neurocognitive mechanisms.

Beauregard and Proulx's (2002) typology of sexual murderers, developed to address non-serial sexual homicide, includes a sadistic sexual murderer profile, which shares some similarities with the proposed type of SHO. The SHO with psychopathic traits is more likely to plan and carry out his attack in an organized method to elude apprehension. His careful attention to avoiding arrest can make apprehension difficult. The Psychopathic–Sexually Sadistic Offender is prone to operate in a serial fashion. One clear distinction between Beauregard and Proulx's (2007) sexual predator profile and the proposed Psychopathic–Sexually Sadistic SHO profile is that the former offender profile is homosexual in sexual orientation. The current offender profile includes both heterosexual and homosexual SHOs.

Implications for Research, Practice, and Policy

The new category proposed in this chapter, the Psychopathic–Sexually Sadistic Offender, is based on research that has shown that psychopathy and sadism are frequently found among SHOs. It is unknown, however, what percentage of SHOs would fit into this category. Future research efforts should be undertaken to extend the field's efforts to measure psychopathy and sexual sadism in sex offenders and SHOs. With further development, a more comprehensive offender typology could be yielded and different subtypes may emerge. This, in turn, might also assist law enforcement in the profiling and apprehension of these dangerous offenders.

Research assessing differences in psychopathic and sadistic traits among offenders, particularly if shown to be significantly correlated with lethal violence, has direct practical implications. Mental health professionals, in their assessments of sex offenders, could consider whether the individual being evaluated meets the diagnostic profile of the Psychopathic–Sexually Sadistic SHO. If so, the clinician could advise the appropriate agency or body (e.g., court, correctional authority, parole board, clemency board) that the offender is dangerous and that the prognosis for successful reintegration into the community is poor.

Additionally, this research has direct relevance to policy. The public is concerned about sex offenders reoffending and their crimes escalating into more violent assaults. Sadly, there are cases in which convicted sex offenders with psychopathic and sadistic traits have been released back into the community and have subsequently sexually assaulted and killed victims (see, e.g., Heide, Beauregard, & Myers, 2009). Sentences need to be based on accurate risk assessments of sex offenders in addition to crime severity. Legislation in many states allows for civil commitment of sex offenders. In an era in which civil liberties, public safety, and fiscal realities compete, decisions as to which offenders need to be confined indefinitely should be based on science. In some cases, sex offenders can be treated and successfully reintegrated into society. At the same time, the public needs to be protected from sex offenders for whom the likelihood of sexually reoffending and of increased violence are high. At a time when the economies of the United States and in many nations around the globe are in an economic downturn, it is impractical to lock up those sex offenders who, with effective treatment and monitoring, could be safely released back into the community. Future studies should focus on building a complete sex offender typology that takes into account other, less extreme types of SHOs, while refining our ability to identify risk factors and more accurately predict which offenders will progress to the most extreme forms of sexual violence.

References

American Psychiatric Association. (2000). *Diagnostic and statistical manual of mental disorders* (4th ed. text rev.). Washington, DC: Author.

Beauregard, E., & Proulx, J. (2002). Profiles in the offending process of nonserial sexual murderers. *International Journal of Offender Therapy and Comparative Criminology, 46*(4), 386–399.

Beauregard, E., & Proulx, J. (2007). A classification of sexual homicide against men. *International Journal of Offender Therapy and Comparative Criminology, 51*(4), 420–432.

Beauregard, E., Proulx, J., & St-Yves, M. (2007). Angry or sadistic: Two types of sexual murderers. In J. Proulx, E. Beauregard, M. Cusson, & A. Nicole (Eds.), *Sexual murderers: A comparative analysis and new perspectives* (pp. 123–141). Hoboken, NJ: Wiley.

Berner, W., Berger, P., & Hill, A. (2003). Sexual sadism. *International Journal of Offender Therapy and Comparative Criminology, 47*, 383–395.

Blair, J., Mitchell, D., & Blair, K. (2005). *The psychopath: Emotion and the brain*. Malden, MA: Blackwell.

Brittain, R. P. (1970). The sadistic sexual murderers. *Medicine, Science, and the Law, 10*, 198–207.

Chan, H. C., & Heide, K. M. (2008). Weapons used by juveniles and adult offenders in sexual homicides: An empirical analysis of 29 years of US data. *Journal of Investigative Psychology and Offender Profiling, 5*(3), 189–208.

Chan, H. C., & Heide, K. M. (2009). Sexual homicide: A synthesis of the literature. *Trauma, Violence, and Abuse, 10*(1), 31–54.

Chan, H. C., Heide, K. M., & Beauregard, E. (2010). What propels sexual murderers: A proposed integrated theory of social learning and routine activities theories. *International Journal of Offender Therapy and Comparative Criminology, 55* (2), 228–250.

Chan, H. C., Myers, W. C., & Heide, K. M. (2010). An empirical analysis of 30 years of U.S. juvenile and adult sexual homicide offender data: Race and age differences in the victim-offender relationship. *Journal of Forensic Sciences, 55*(5), 1282–1290.

Cooke, D. J., & Michie, C. (2001). Refining the construct of psychopathy: Towards a hierarchical model. *Psychological Assessment, 13*, 171–188.

Dietz, P., Harry, B., & Hazelwood, R. (1986). Detective magazines: Pornography for the sexual sadist? *Journal of Forensic Sciences, 31*, 197–211.

Dietz, P. E., Hazelwood, R., & Warren, J. (1990). The sexually sadistic criminal and his offenses. *Bulletin of the American Academy of Psychiatry and the Law, 18*, 163–178.

Drukteinis, A. (1992). Serial murder: The heart of darkness. *Psychiatry Annals, 22*, 532–538.

Federoff, J. P. (2008). Sadism, sadomasochism, sex, and violence. *The Canadian Journal of Psychiatry*, 53, 637–646.

Firestone, P., Bradford, J. M., Greenberg, D. M., & Larose, M. R. (1998a). Homicidal sex offenders: Psychological, phallometric, and diagnostic features. *Journal of American Academy Psychiatry and Law, 26*(4), 537–552.

Firestone, P., Bradford, J. M., Greenberg, D. M., Larose, M. R., & Curry, S. (1998b). Homicidal and nonhomicidal child molesters: Psychological, phallometric, and criminal features. *Sexual Abuse: A Journal of Research and Treatment, 10*, 305–323.

Forth, A. E., & Hare, R. D. (1989). The contingent negative variation in psychopaths. *Psychophysiology, 26*, 676–682.

Fox, J., & Levin, J. (1991). Homicide against the elderly: A research note. *The Criminologist, 29*, 317–327.

Geberth, V. J. (1995, April). Psychopathic sexual sadists. *Law and Order, 43*(4). Retrieved from http://www.practicalhomicide.com/articles/psexsad.htm.

Geberth, V. J. (1996). *Practical homicide investigation: Tactics, procedures, and forensic techniques* (3rd ed.). Boca Raton, FL: CRC Press.

Gratzer, T., & Bradford, J. M. W. (1995). Offender and offense characteristics of sexual sadists: A comparative study. *Journal of Forensic Sciences, 40*, 450–455.

Hakkanen-Nyholm, H., Repo-Tiihonen, E., Lindberg, N., Salenius, S., & Weizmann-Henelius, G. (2009). Finnish sexual homicides: Offense and offender characteristics. *Forensic Science International, 188*, 125–130.

Hanson, R. K., & Bussiere, M. T. (1998). Predicting relapse: A meta-analysis of sexual offender recidivism studies. *Journal of Consulting and Clinical Psychology, 66*(2), 348–362.

Hare, R. D. (1970). *Psychopathy: Theory and research*. New York: John Wiley and Sons.

Hare, R. D. (1986). Twenty years of experience with the Cleckley psychopath. In W. H. Reid, D., Dorr, J. I. Walker, & J. W. Bonner, III (Eds.), *Unmasking the psychopath: Antisocial personality and related syndromes* (pp. 3–27). New York: Norton.

Hare, R. D. (1991). *The Hare Psychopathy Checklist–Revised*. Toronto, Ontario, Canada: Multi-Health Systems.

Hare, R. D. (1996). Psychopathy: A clinical construct whose time has come. *Criminal Justice and Behavior, 23*, 25–54.

Hare, R. D. (1999). Psychopathy as a risk factor for violence. *Psychiatric Quarterly, 70*, 181–197.

Hare, R. D. (2003). *The Hare Psychopathy Checklist–Revised* (2nd ed.). Toronto, Ontario, Canada: Multi-Health Systems.

Hare, R. D., & Neumann, C. S. (2006). The PCL-R assessment of psychopathy: Development, structural properties, and new directions. In C. J. Patrick (Ed.), *Handbook of psychopathy* (pp. 58–88). New York: Guilford.

Harris, G. T., Rice, M. E., Hilton, N. Z., Lalumiere, M. L., & Quinsey, V. L. (2007). Coercive and precocious sexuality as a fundamental aspect of psychopathy. *Journal of Personality Disorders, 21*, 1–27.

Hazelwood, R. R., & Warren, J. (2000). The sexually violent offender: Impulsive or ritualistic? *Aggression and Violent Behavior, 5*(3), 267–279.

Hazelwood, R., Warren, J., & Dietz, P. (1993). Compliant victims of the sexual sadist. *Australian Family Physician, 22*, 474–479.

Heide, K. M., Beauregard, E., & Myers, W. C. (2009). Sexually motivated child abduction murders: Synthesis of the literature and case illustration. *Victims and Offenders, 4*, 58–75.

Hill, A., Habermann, N., Berner, W., & Briken, P. (2007). Psychiatric disorders in single and multiple sexual murderers. *Psychopathology, 40*, 22–28.

Hill, A., Habermann, N., Klussman, D., Berner, W., & Briken, P. (2008). Criminal recidivism in sexual homicide perpetrators. *International Journal of Offender Therapy and Comparative Criminology, 52*(1), 5–20.

Juodis, M., Woodworth, M., Porter, S., & ten Brinke, L. (2009). Partners in crime: A comparison of individual and multi-perpetrator homicides. *Criminal Justice and Behavior, 36*(8), 824–839.

Keppel, R. D., & Walter, R. (1999). Profiling killers: A revised classification model for understanding sexual murder. *International Journal of Offender Therapy and Comparative Criminology, 43*(4), 417–437.

Kinsey, A. C., Pomeroy, W. B., Martin, C. E., & Gebhard, P. H. (1953). *Sexual behavior in the human female*. Philadelphia, PA: Saunders.

Kirsch, L. G., & Becker, J. V. (2007). Emotional deficits in psychopathy and sexual sadism: Implications for violent and sadistic behavior. *Clinical Psychology Review, 27*(8), 904–922.

Knight, R. A. (1989). An assessment of the concurrent validity of a child molester typology. *Journal of Interpersonal Violence, 4*(2), 131–150.

Knight, R. A., & Guay, J. P. (2006). The role of psychopathy in sexual offenders against women. In C. J. Patrick (Ed.), *Handbook of psychopathy* (pp. 512–532). New York: John Wiley.

Knight, R. A., & Prentky, R. A. (1990). Classifying sexual offenders: The development and corroboration of taxonomic models. In W. L. Marshall, D. R. Laws, & H. E. Barbaree (Eds.), *Handbook of sexual assault: Issues, theories, and treatment of the offender* (pp. 27–52). New York: Plenum.

Kosson, D. S., Kelley, J. C., & White, J. W. (1997). Psychopathy-related traits predict self-reported sexual aggression among college men. *Journal of Interpersonal Violence, 12*, 241–254.

Krafft-Ebing, R. V. (1965). *Psychopathia sexualis* (H. Wedeck, Trans.). New York: Putnam. (Original work published 1898)

Langevin, R. (2003). A study of the psychosexual characteristics of sex killers: Can we identify them before it is too late? *International Journal of Offender Therapy and Comparative Criminology, 47*, 366–382.

Langevin, R., Ben-Aron, M. H., Wright, P., Marchese, V., & Handy, L. (1988). The sex killer. *Annals of Sex Research, 1*(2), 263–302.

Laws of Florida, 2005-28. (2005). *House Bill 1877*. Retrieved July 14, 2008, from http://laws.flrules.org/files/Ch_2005-028.pdf.

MacCulloch, M., Gray, N., & Watt, A. (2000). Brittain's sadistic murderer syndrome reconsidered: An associative account of the etiology of sadistic sexual fantasy. *The Journal of Forensic Psychiatry, 11*(2), 401–418.

MacCulloch, M. J., Snowden, P. R., Wood, P. J. W., & Mills, H. E. (1983). Sadistic fantasy, sadistic behavior, and offending. *British Journal of Psychiatry, 143*, 20–29.

Marshall, W. L., & Hucker, S. J. (2006a). Issues in the diagnosis of sexual sadism. *Sexual Offender Treatment, 1*(2), 1–5.

Marshall, W. L., & Hucker, S. J. (2006b). Severe sexual sadism: Its features and treatment. In R. D. McAnulty & M. M. Burnette (Eds.), *Sex and sexuality: Vol. 3. Sexual deviation and sexual offenses* (pp. 227–250). Westport, CT: Praeger.

Marshall, W. L., & Kennedy, P. (2003). Sexual sadism in sexual offenders: An elusive diagnosis. *Aggression and Violent Behavior, 8*, 1–22.

Marshall, W. L., Kennedy, P., & Yates, P. (2002). Issues concerning the reliability and validity of the diagnosis of sexual sadism applied in prison settings. *Sexual Abuse: A Journal of Research and Treatment, 14*, 301–311.

Meloy, J. R. (2000). The nature and dynamics of sexual homicide: An integrative review. *Aggression and Violent Behavior, 5*(1), 1–22.

Meloy, J. R., Gacono, C. B., & Kenney, L. (1994). A Rorschach investigation of sexual homicide. *Journal of Personality Assessment, 62*(1), 58–67.

Murrie, D. C., Marcus, D. K., Douglas, K. S., Lee, Z., Salekin, R. T., & Vincent, G. (2007). Youth with psychopathic features are not a discrete class: A taxometric analysis. *Journal of Child Psychology and Psychiatry, 48*, 714–723.

Myers, W. C. (2004). Serial murder by children and adolescents. *Behavioral Sciences and the Law, 22*, 357–374.

Myers, W. (1994). Sexual homicide by adolescents. *Journal of the American Academy of Child and Adolescent Psychiatry, 33*, 962–969.

Myers, W. C., & Blashfield, R. (1997). Psychopathology and personality in juvenile sexual homicide offenders. *Bulletin of the American Academy of Psychiatry and Law, 25*, 497–508.

Myers, W. C., Chan, H. C., Vo, E. J., & Lazarou, E. (2010). Sexual sadism, psychopathy, and recidivism in juvenile sexual murderers. *Journal of Investigative Psychology and Offender Profiling, 7*(1), 49–58.

Myers, W. C., Eggleston, C. F., & Smoak, P. (2003). A media violence-inspired juvenile sexual homicide offender 13 years later. *Journal of Forensic Sciences, 48*, 1–5.

Myers, W. C., Husted, D. S., Safarik, M. E., & O'Toole, M. E. (2006). The motivation behind serial sexual homicide: Is it sex, power, and control, or anger? *Journal of Forensic Sciences, 51*, 900–907.

Myers, W. C., & Monaco, L. (2000). Anger experience, styles of anger expression, sadistic personality disorder, and psychopathy in juvenile sexual homicide offenders. *Journal of Forensic Sciences, 45*(3), 698–701.

Nitschke, J., Osterheider, M., & Mokros, A. (2009). A cumulative scale of severe sexual sadism. *Sexual Abuse: A Journal of Research and Treatment, 21*(3), 262–278.

Palermo, G. B. (1994). *The faces of violence*. Springfield, IL: Charles C. Thomas.

Porter, S., Campbell, M. A., Woodworth, M., & Birt, A. R. (2002). *A new psychological conceptualization of the sexual psychopath. Advances in psychology research* (Vol. 7). New York: Nova Science.

Porter, S., Demetrioff, S., & ten Brinke, L. (2010). Sexual psychopath: Current understanding and future challenges. In A. Schlank (Ed.), *The sexual predator* (Vol. 4, pp. 13.1–13.12). Kingston, NJ: Civic Research Institute.

Porter, S., Fairweather, D., Drugge, J., Herve, H., Birt, A., & Boer, D. P. (2000). Profiles of psychopathy in incarcerated sexual offenders. *Criminal Justice and Behavior, 27*, 216–233.

Porter, S., & Woodworth, M. (2006). Psychopathy and aggression. In C. J. Patrick (Ed.), *Handbook of Psychopathy* (pp. 481–494). New York: Guilford

Porter, S., Woodworth, M., Earle, J., Drugge, J., & Boer, D. (2003). Characteristics of sexual homicides committed by psychopathic and nonpsychopathic offenders. *Law and Human Behavior, 27*, 459–470.

Proulx, J., McKibben, A., & Lusignan, R. (1996). Relationship between affective components and sexual behaviors in sexual aggressors. *Sexual Abuse: A Journal of Research and Treatment, 8*, 279–289.

Purcell, C. E., & Arrigo, B. A. (2006). *The psychology of lust murder*. Burlington, MA: Academic Press.

Reidy, D. E., Zeichner, A., & Martinez, M. A. (2008). Effects of psychopathy traits on unprovoked aggression. *Aggressive Behavior, 34*, 319–328.

Reidy, D. E., Zeichner, A., & Seibert, L. A. (2011). Unprovoked aggression: Effects of psychopathic traits and sadism. *Journal of Personality, 79*(1), 75–100.

Ressler, R. K., Burgess, A. W., & Douglas, J. E. (1988). *Sexual homicide: Patterns and motive*. New York: Free Press.

Ressler, R. K., Burgess, A. W., Douglas, J. E., Hartman, C. R., & D'Agostino, R. B. (1986). Sexual killers and their victims: Identifying patterns through crime scene. *Journal of Interpersonal Violence, 1*, 288–308.

Rice, M. E., & Harris, G. T. (1997). Cross-validation and extension of the Violence Risk Appraisal Guide for child molesters and rapists. *Law and Human Behavior, 21*, 231–241.

Schlesinger, L. B. (2007). Sexual homicide: Differentiating catathymic and compulsive murders. *Aggression and Violent Behavior, 12*, 242–256.

Stone, M. H. (2001). Serial sexual homicide: Biological, psychological, and sociological aspects. *Journal of Personality Disorders, 15*(1), 1–18.

Swigert, V. L., Farrell, R. A., & Yoels, W. C. (1976). Sexual homicide: Social, psychological, and legal aspects. *Archives of Sexual Behavior, 5*(5), 391–401.

Van Patten, I. T., & Delhauer, P. Q. (2007). Sexual homicide: A spatial analysis of 25 years of deaths in Los Angeles. *Journal of Forensic Sciences, 52*, 1129–1141.

Warren, J. I., Hazelwood, R. R., & Dietz, P. E. (1996). The sexually sadistic serial killer. *Journal of Forensic Sciences, 41*, 970–974.

Woodworth, M., & Porter, S. (2002). In cold blood: Characteristics of criminal homicides as a function of psychopathy. *Journal of Abnormal Psychology, 111*, 436–445.

CHAPTER SEVENTEEN

Are Male and Female Psychopaths Equivalent? A Rorschach Study*

Ted Cunliffe, Carl B. Gacono, J. Reid Meloy, and Enna Taylor

Female offenders comprise a growing, yet misunderstood offender population. Currently there are an estimated 114,852 women housed in state and federal facilities in the United States, up from 13,420 in 1980 (U.S. Department of Justice, Bureau of Justice Statistics, 1999, 2008). Thus, between 1980 and 2008, the female state and federal prison populations increased 756%, compared to a 373% increase for men during the same period. Despite this increase, incarcerated populations continue to be predominantly male. Therefore, the focus of state and federal correctional authorities from a management and policy perspective has centered upon the male population given the significantly greater numbers. However, female offenders present singular management, control, and treatment challenges to the legal and correctional systems. Given identified gender differences in cognition, self-concept, and interpersonal behavior between all individuals and, more specifically, male and female offenders, increased study is needed to enhance the current understanding of female criminals to address these management, adjudicative, and policy concerns.

*Portions of this chapter are reprinted and adapted from "A Rorschach Understanding of Antisocial and Psychopathic Women," *The Handbook of Forensic Rorschach Assessment* by Gacono et al. Copyright © 2008. Reproduced by permission of Taylor and Francis Group, LLC, a division of Informa plc.

The interaction between biological and social variables in the development of gender-related self-concept and sex-role orientations (Krampen, Effertz, Jostock, & Muller, 1990) is an important consideration in female offenders. Current research findings suggest a link between biological variables, personality traits, and gender differences. For example, studies examining the relation between the heredity of personality traits (i.e., dominance and aggression) and physiological variables may be due to biological sex differences in gonadal hormones (Eysenck, 1992; Zuckerman, 1991). These differences contribute to an increased vulnerability to depression in women (Nolen-Hoeksema, 1987; Perris, 1966; Winokur & Tanna, 1969) and gender differences in socialization (Block, 1983), physical attractiveness (Feingold, 1994), neuroticism/extroversion /psychoticism (Lynn & Martin, 1997), and other personality variables (Krampen et al., 1990). However, cognitive dysfunction, compulsive behavior, conduct problems, suspiciousness, callousness, and self-harm have been reported less frequently in women than men (Jang, Livesley, & Vernon, 1997).

Differences in traditional female and masculine roles may be attributed, in part, to the woman's greater responsibility for childcare (Chodorow, 1975). Compared to males, the development of the female personality comes to be defined by the increased levels of contact and connection to other people, like mother. On the other hand, boys tend to define themselves as masculine and separate from their mothers: what is not mother/feminine. Therefore, when a young girl is placed in a moral dilemma, she will situate herself in relation to the world and will choose to help others (group orientation), while a boy faced with a similar circumstance will place the world in relation to himself ("self orientation"; Gilligan, 1982). Perhaps too simply, male development is linked to empathic individuation and a defensive firming of ego boundaries, while female development depends upon communion with others and enhanced interpersonal contact and communication. Males exhibit a higher degree of self-orientation (narcissism), while a women's orientation consists of an interpersonal web characterized by a succession of relationships and connections with others. From this perspective, in women, autonomy as a replacement for attachment is viewed as dangerous and incongruent with a group orientation (Gilligan, 1982).

Millon's (Millon & Davis; 1996) conceptualization of histrionic personality disorder (HPD) adds to our understanding of the hypothesized gender differences when viewed as psychopathology (i.e., extreme end of the personality trait continuum). The HPD person's reliance on others involves an active solicitation in order to satisfy her pronounced needs for affiliation and attention (active/dependent style; Millon & Davis,

1996). Additionally, hysterical character has been hypothesized to defend against a consciously experienced depression and a negative self-concept (Lazare & Klerman, 1968; Pfohl, 1991; Shapiro, 1965). Consistent with Gacono & Meloy's (1994) conceptualization of the female psychopath, women have been found to score higher on measures of histrionic, dependent, and avoidant dimensional personality disorder scales, while men tend to score higher on paranoid, compulsive, schizoid, and narcissistic scales (Jang et al., 1997).[1] Research indicates higher prevalence rates of these particular personality disorders within male and female populations (Alnaes & Torgersen, 1988; Golomb, Fava, Abraham, & Rosenbaum, 1995; Grilo, Becker, Fehon, & Walker, 1996; Jackson, Whiteside, Bates, & Bell, 1991; Jang et al, 1997; Kass, Spitzer, & Williams, 1983; Robins, 1984).

Gendered information (Bem, 1981) also affects the self-concept, personality, and social behavior of all individuals (Block, 1983; Feingold, 1990, 1991, 1992, 1994) as a function of the distinct psychological and behavioral early childhood experiences of men and women. Although the male role has been putatively characterized as self-focused, the female role involves an increased sensitivity to the concerns of both self and others. Further, sex-differentiated socialization is hypothesized to impact the cognitive development of males and females as evidenced by differences in interpersonal interaction (Bem, 1981). In males, high levels of self-assertion, dominance, and agency result in an inclination toward forceful, aggressive, or violent compensatory strategies; while in women, low levels give rise to increased cooperation and group membership (Eagly & Steffen, 1986; Shapiro & Mahajan, 1986).

Pollak and Gilligan (1982) examined gender-based differences in violence and aggression and concluded: (1) women view the world in terms of maintaining relationships, and are usually prone to less violence; and (2) aggression is frequently seen as a failed connection by females. Thus, when women do express aggression, it is less commonly manifested through overt or violent behaviors; but rather, it is more likely to be conveyed via manipulative strategies characterized by social ostracism (Werner & Crick, 1999). These effects play a significant role in the gender-linked expression of violence and criminal behavior when extended to antisocial patterns. Female offenders would be less likely to exhibit a dominant, physically aggressive interpersonal style or engage in violent criminal behavior (U.S. Department of Justice, Bureau of Justice Statistics, 2008).

Male psychopaths are responsible for a disproportionate number of serious behavioral problems (Hare & McPherson, 1984), are difficult to manage within correctional and forensic hospital settings (Gacono, Meloy, Sheppard, Speth & Roske, 1995; Gacono, Meloy, Speth, &

Roske, 1997; Ogloff, Wong, & Greenwood, 1990; Rice, 1997; Rice, Harris, & Cormier, 1992) and commit a greater number of offenses compared to non-psychopathic offenders (Hare, 2003). While male psychopathy has been studied extensively over the past 50 years, comparatively little is known about female psychopathy (Cunliffe & Gacono, 2008; Gacono, 2000a; Verona & Vitale, 2006).

Although the number of incarcerated women has increased in recent years, state and federal inmates are predominately male (93%; Bureau of Justice Statistics, 2008). Female psychopaths have been found to be more prone to affective rather than predatory violence (Cunliffe & Gacono, 2005; Meloy, 2006), offend against intimates and associates (relational violence; U.S. Department of Justice, Bureau of Justice Statistics, 1999), and experience increased rates of psychopathology and maladjustment to correctional and forensic psychiatric facilities (Hicks, Vaidyanathan, & Patrick, 2010) compared to non-psychopathic females. While the knowledge base for female offenders is growing, the appropriate management, assessment, and treatment of this population necessitates a comprehensive understanding of the personality functioning and interpersonal behavior of female offenders, in general, and female psychopaths, in particular.

Psychopathology is also likely to accentuate normal gender differences. It follows that psychopathy would present differently as a function of gender and identification with traditional gender roles. Rather than the cold, remorseless, and callous outward presentation seen in males, the female psychopath would be expected to present an outward appearance of increased interpersonal interest, connection, and group affiliation. Further, her behavior would be expected to be characterized by increased contact with others rather than the solitary detachment (Rorschach elevated T) and isolation described for male psychopathy (Hare, 2003; Gacono & Meloy, 1994).

While male and female psychopaths display similar behaviors and share a comparable personality organization (borderline or psychotic), both Rorschach research and other findings suggest that the syndrome is not equivalent across gender (Gacono & Meloy, 1994; Cunliffe, 2002; Cunliffe & Gacono, 2005; Verona & Vitale, 2006). Rorschach findings with male psychopaths suggest a grandiose (Gacono & Meloy, 1994; Gacono, Meloy, & Heaven, 1990; Meloy, 1988), detached, narcissistic, interpersonal style (Kernberg, 1975; Millon & Davis, 1996), and correlations with several of the DSM-IV (APA, 1994) Cluster B Personality Disorders, specifically narcissistic (NPD), histrionic (HPD), and antisocial personality disorders (ASPD) have been found (Hare, 2003; Gacono & Meloy, 1994). Rorschach studies with female psychopaths have suggested that hysteria, rather than narcissism, is the comorbid character style (Cunliffe, 2002; Cunliffe & Gacono, 2005; Gacono & Meloy, 1994). These findings are consistent with expected gender differences.

Female Psychopathy and the PCL-R

Although there has been much research using the Psychopathy Checklists with male offenders, there has been less with females (Nicholls, Odgers, & Cooke, 2007; Verona & Vitale, 2006). This discrepancy is likely an artifact of the relatively low numbers of incarcerated women, which limits the opportunity for study with female offenders (e.g., 93% of state and federal inmates are male; U.S. Department of Justice, Bureau of Justice Statistics, 2008) and a relative disinterest among researchers to study female offenders over the years.

Many of the existing female psychopathy studies include methodological problems that limit their usefulness (Cunliffe, Gacono, Meloy, Smith, Taylor, & Landry, submitted; Gacono & Gacono, 2006; Gacono, Loving, & Bodholdt, 2001; Gacono, Loving, Evans, & Jumes, 2002; Gacono, in press). Some researchers have utilized the PCL:SV (Hart, Cox, & Hare, 1995) to designate "psychopathy" (Rogers, Johansen, Chang, & Salekin, 1997; Salekin, Rogers, & Sewell, 1998), despite the fact that the PCL:SV (Screening Version) is not designed to make a categorical designation (Bodholdt, Richards, & Gacono, 2000; Gacono et al., 2001). Other studies have lowered PCL-R cutoff scores (Peaslee, Fleming, Baumgardner, Silbaugh, & Thackrey, 1992) and/or had few psychopaths (PCL-R $\geq$ 30) in their samples (Vitale & Newman, 2001; Vitale, Smith, Brinkley, & Newman, 2002). Investigators have discussed ASPD and psychopathy as synonymous constructs or attempted to discuss specific items on the PCL-R as indicative of psychopathy (Shipley & Arrigo, 2004). This "psychopathic traits" approach marks a return to research practices prior to the PCL-R and has been sharply criticized (Gacono, 2000a; Gacono & Gacono, 2006; Gacono, Chapter 13 of this volume; Hare, 2003).

Findings with male psychopaths or female ASPDs may also not be generalizable to female psychopaths (Gacono et al., 2001). Forouzan and Cooke (2005) highlighted a number of concerns related to the assessment of psychopathy with female populations: (1) whether the same criteria developed with male samples were being used to diagnose the syndrome in females, (2) the equivalence of the construct across gender, (3) the behavioral expression of psychopathy as a function of gender, and (4) the diagnostic forensic utility of psychopathy with female offenders. Additionally, Bolt, Hare, Vitale, and Newman (2004) found differential item functioning for a number of PCL-R items: 5 (Conning/Manipulative), 12 (Early Behavioral Problems), 18 (Juvenile Delinquency), and 20 (Criminal Versatility). Further, Hicks et al. (2010) found that incarcerated female psychopaths (PCL-R $\geq$ 30) scored higher on measures of stress reaction and poor behavioral control compared to male psychopathic offenders, and lower scores on measures of agency and aggression. Specifically, the authors found that female secondary psychopaths (PLC-R $\geq$ 30 with high levels of negative emotions, impulsivity, and aggression combined with lower levels of callousness and lack of empathy scores) exhibited higher scores on measures of absorption (risk factor for dissociative symptoms) and suggested a relationship between female psychopathy, borderline personality disorder (APA, 2000), and post-traumatic stress disorder (APA, 2000).

Most importantly, the study of female psychopathy requires a careful consideration of how the PCL-R items are best assessed in female offenders. In our empirical and clinical work with female offenders (Cunliffe & Gacono, 1995, 2008; Gacono & Meloy, 1994), the presentation of female psychopathic and non-psychopathic offenders were significantly different than that described by Hare (1991, 2003) for males. PCL-R use with women may require a different scoring and interpretation of specific PCL-R items and factors. Just as a well-informed knowledge of base rates for behavior is necessary to assess symptoms present in any clinical population, the differential PCL-R scores may also be a reflection of the lack of knowledge of the female offender population as a whole by those scoring the measure. However, the issue of a possible gender difference in psychopathy and PCL-R scores remains unresolved.

The Rorschach Study

The Rorschach was used as a dependent measure for understanding female antisocial personality disorder (ASPD) and psychopathy (see Gacono & Meloy, 1994). Compared to non-psychopathic ASPD women, the ASPD female psychopaths would be expected to produce significant differences on Rorschach variables related to self-perception (3r + (2)/R; MOR), affect modulation (FC: CF + C; DEPI; Afr), mediation (P; X – %; X + %; Level 2 Special Scores) and interpersonal behavior (COP; T; H). Comprehensive System (Exner, 1993) data for female psychopaths are provided herein to aid examiners evaluating similar patients. The Rorschach differences between psychopathic and non-psychopathic ASPD women are also presented and discussed. Finally, conceptual and practical issues related to the assessment of the female antisocial and psychopathic individual are explored.

Comprehensive System Rorschach Data for Female Psychopaths (n = 27)

The sample of psychopathic women presented here are part of a small database of ASPD females (N = 69; see Gacono & Meloy, 1994). While our sample size is small and caution dictates careful interpretation, the data suggest interesting trends. Our sample was analyzed by Rorschach Workshops using RIAP4 Plus (Exner, Weiner, & Par Staff, 2002). Understanding the Rorschach core characteristics, controls, stress tolerance, affect, self-perception, thinking and processing, and interpersonal data from these psychopathic women adds to our understanding of their personality functioning. When appropriate our group data is compared to Exner (2001) nonpatient group data (NP, N = 600). Significant differences between the groups were assessed with Wilcoxon U, and Chi Squares were utilized for non-parametric data (Rorschach) and Spearman Rank Correlations (rho) and descriptive analyses (means, S_d) were used for parametric data (PCL-R data). Additionally, Pearson Product Moment Correlations were used to assess effect size for significant comparisons. Effect size was interpreted in accordance with Cohen's (1988) recommendations for the evaluation of effect size (small, $r = 0.1–0.23$; medium, $r = 0.24–0.36$; large, $r = 0.37$ or larger). Consequently, an effect size below a value of $r = 0.1$ was interpreted as not significant (ns).

Core Characteristics, Controls, and Stress Tolerance

Female psychopaths produce less than a normative number of responses (M = 19.86; NP, M = 22.32). They are more likely to be ambitent (39%) or extratensive (21%) rather than introversive (4%). Their diminished psychological resources (EA, M = 7.30) and reduced stress tolerance (CDI ≥ 4 = 36%, D score = 0, 54%, Adj D = 0, 43%) underscore an alloplastic adaptation to the environment. These personality characteristics are conducive to acting out which reduces the female psychopath's levels of experienced stress related distress (FM + m = M = 3.96, es = M = 9.96). Both the psychopathic and non-psychopathic females do not differ significantly on measures of control apart from the greater proportion of *non-psychopathic* women producing CDI ≥ 4 (See Table 17.1).

Affect

Difficulty modulating affect is a hallmark of histrionic and borderline personality disorders and a predominate trait for female psychopaths (FC: CF + C = .93:2.96). The internal world of the psychopathic female is characterized by dysphoria (DEPI ≥ 5=41%; C', M = 1.89, V, M = 2.04), and anger (S > 2 = 43%). Affective avoidance (Afr < .40 & .50 = 29% & 61%) and

Table 17.1 Female Psychopaths (*N.* = 27) Group Mean and Frequencies for select Ratios, Percentages, and Derivations

R = 19.86 (SD = 6.66)	L = .71 (SD = .48)
EA = 7.30 (SD = 4.16)	
es = 10.00 (SD = 6.60)	
FM + m < SUMShading 14	(50%)
D Score = −1.04 (SD = 2.05)	AdjD = −0.54 (SD = 1.69)
EB STYLE	
Introversive......................1	4%
Ambitent..................11	39%
Extratensive..................6	21%
EA - es DIFFERENCES:D-SCORES	
D Score > 0..............3	11%
D Score = 0.............15	54%
D Score < 0.............10	36%
D Score < −1............ 9	32%
AdjD Score > 0..........6	21%
AdjD Score = 0.........12	43%
AdjD Score < 0.........10	36%
AdjD Score < −1.........4	14%
AFFECT	
FC: CF + C = .93 : 2.96	
Pure C = .46 (SD = .58)	(Pure C > 0 = 43%; Pure C > 1 = 4%)
FC > (CF + C) + 2..........1	4%
FC > (CF + C) + 1..........2	7%
(CF + C) > FC + 1.........16	57%
(CF + C) > FC + 2.........11	39%
SumC′ = 1.89	(SD = 1.95)
SumV = 2.04 (SD =2.56)	
SumY = 1.36 (SD =1.42)	
Afr = .54 (SD = .23)	(Afr < .40 = 8, 29%; Afr < .50 = 17, 61%)
S = 2.64 (SD = 1.97)	(S > 2 = 12, 43%)
Blends: R = 4.64 : 19.86	
CP = .04 (SD = .19)	
INTERPERSONAL	
COP = 1.39 (SD = 1.37)	(COP = 0 = 11, 39%; COP > 2 = 5, 18%)
AG = . 57 (SD = .92)	(AG = 0 = 17, 61%; AG > 2 = 1, 4%)
Food = .43 (SD = .79)	
Isolate/R = .17 (SD = .13)	
H:(H)+Hd+(Hd) = 2.36 : 3.82	(H = 0=4, 14%; H < 2 =9, 32%)

Table 17.1 (Continued)

R = 19.86 (SD = 6.66)	L = .71 (SD = .48)
(H)+(Hd):(A)+(Ad) =2.07 :.72	
H+A:Hd+Ad = 9.90 : 2.79	
Sum T = .75 (SD = 1.21)	(T = 0 = 16, 57%; T > 1 = 4, 14%)
SELF-PERCEPTION	
3r+(2)/R = .40 (SD = .16)	(3r+(2)/R < .33 = 12, 43%; 3r + (2)/ R > .44 = 9, 32%)
Fr+rF = .54 (SD = 1 .04)	(Fr + rF > 0 = 8, 29%) (FrrF = 0 and 3r + (2) ≥ .44 = 5, 18.5%)
FD = .18 (SD = .39)	
An+Xy = 2.04 (SD = 2.14)	
MOR = 2.39 (SD = 2.46)	(MOR > 2 = 11, 39%)
IDEATION	
a:p = 4.50 : 3.25	(p > a+1 = 5, 18%)
Ma:Mp = 1.93 : 1.82	(Mp > Ma = 9, 32%)
M = 3.64 (SD = 2.44)	(M– = .71, SD = 1.27; M none = 25%)
FM = 2.50 (SD = 1.64)	m = 1.46 (SD = 1.57)
2AB + Art + Ay = 2.57 (S.D. = 2.60)	2AB + Art + Ay > 5 = 3, 11%
Sum6 = 7.68 (S.D. = 6.04)	WSum6 = 24.0 (SD = 20.69)
(Level 2 Special Scores > 0 = 12, 43%)	
MEDIATION	
Populars = 4.61 (SD = 2.20)	(P < 4 = 9, 32%; P > 7 = 2, 7%)
XA% = .73 (SD = .15)	
WDA% = .76 (SD = .16)	
X+% = .51 (SD = .14)	
X–% = .25 (SD = .15)	
Xu% = .22 (SD = .11)	
S– = 1.25 (SD = 1.17)	
XA% > .89. 1	4%
XA% < .70. 9	32%
WDA% < .85. 17	61%
WDA% < .75. 11	39%
X+% < .55. 15	54%
Xu% > .20. 15	54%
X–% > .20. 14	50%
X – % > .30. 7	25%
PROCESSING	
Zf = 10.82 (SD = 3.70)	
Zd = .61 (SD = 3.52)	(Zd > +3.0 = 6, 21%; Zd < –3.0 = 4, 14%)
W:D:Dd = 8.92:8.52:2.19	
W:M = 8.86 : 3.64	

(continued)

Table 17.1 (Continued)

R = 19.86 (SD = 6.66)	L = .71 (SD = .48)
DQ+ = 5.29 (SD = 3.02)	
DQv = 2.64 (SD = 2.16)	(DQv > 2 = 13, 46%)
CONSTELLATIONS	
PTI = 5.....0 0% DEPI = 7...2 7%	CDI = 5...1 4%
PTI = 4.....4 14% DEPI = 6...5 18%	CDI = 4...9 32%
PTI = 3.....0	0% DEPI = 5...4 14%
S-Constellation Positive.......1	4%
HVI Positive........................0	0%
OBS Positive.................. 0	0%

emotional constriction (Blends = 4.64) are natural developmental reactions to an inability to deal with strong affect. Emotional constriction, avoidance, and acting out are similar to what is found in male psychopaths.

Thinking and Processing

Psychopathic women do not see the world as others do. They tend to miss important details essential to effective information processing. Their thinking contains fluidity, lacking structure and boundaries (DQv = 2.64; DQv > 2 = 46%). They are prone to misperceptions and unconventionality (P < 4 = 32%). Cognitive slippage abounds in psychopathic women (Level 2 Special Scores > 0 = 43%), as do other indicators of mild to moderate formal thought disorder.

Self-Perception

Poor controls, problems managing affect, and unconventional and distorted thinking all contribute to almost half of the sample's negative evaluation of self (3r + (2)/R < .33 = 43%). Healthy self-esteem is not expected without emotional mastery. The grandiose self-structure found in the adult male psychopath (Kernberg, 1975; Meloy, 1988) is not manifested in the same way in female psychopaths. These women perceive themselves as "damaged" (MOR, M = 2.39, MOR > 2 = 39%); and although they possess a corresponding self focus to males, the female psychopath's self-perception is characterized by poor self-regard and chronic self-criticism (3r + (2)/R < .33 = 43%; SumV, M = 2.04).

Interpersonal

As expected, psychopathic women do not experience cooperation as a natural result of interpersonal interactions (COP = 0 = 39% &

COP > 2 = 18%). Perhaps a combination of biological predisposition and severe disappointments (narcissistic wounding) contribute to reduced affectional relatedness ($T = 0 = 57\%$) and a diminished interest in others (H = 0 = 14% & H < 2 = 32%). Certainly, low or inflated self-worth and misinterpretations of interpersonal cues further weaken the opportunity for positive interpersonal experience (Gacono & Meloy, 1994). As a result, psychopathic women have poor interpersonal experiences (CDI ≥ 4=37%; GHR = 3.18; PHR = 3.36; GHR > PHR = 32%). All of these factors ultimately coalesce into an increasingly detached and exploitative view of interpersonal relations in a manner quite similar to Sullivan's (1953) concept of malevolent transformation.

A Comparison of Psychopathic and Non-Psychopathic ASPD Women

Procedure

All participants were unpaid volunteers. Half of the incarcerated population at the facilities (665 female inmates) randomly selected to receive a flyer requesting their participation in the study. Exclusion criteria for selection were IQ < 80, previous diagnosis of a major mental illness, pending release from the institution (< 2 months), and/or a lack of fluency in the English language.

Potential participants were informed of the purpose, procedures, risks and benefits, and limits to confidentiality were reviewed. Of the 103 women who volunteered for the study, 20 (19.6%) were eliminated due to language problems, 2 (2%) had a history of schizophrenia, 3 (3%) had a history of bipolar disorder, 1 (1%) expressed suicidal ideation and intent, 1 (1%) woman was transferred from the institution before testing could be completed, and 1 (1%) individual withdrew. Seventy-five participants completed the study procedures. Unfortunately, 48 (64%) of the original 75 subjects were excluded from the study due to inadequate Rorschach administration (Gacono, Evans, & Viglione, 2002).[2] Of the remaining 27 women, 22 were medium- to maximum-security inmates and 5 were low-security work camp inmates. Four women were not included in our analyses because their PCL-R scores fell between 25 and 29.

Prior to being interviewed, the institutional, psychological, legal, and medical files of each inmate were reviewed. PCL-R interviews and ratings were conducted by 2 PhD-level graduate students trained in the administration, scoring, and interpretation of the measure. Next, Rorschach protocols were administered following Comprehensive System Guidelines (Exner, 1993) and scored by a PhD-level graduate student. The sample was supplemented with 17 records selected from a database of incarcerated females collected in Wyoming (Gacono & Meloy, 1994; Peaslee et al, 1992) and another 5 protocols from the Gacono and Meloy database.

Participants scoring ≥ 30 on the PCL-R (N = 27) were assigned to the psychopathic ASPD group (P-ASPD), and those scoring < 25 comprised the non-psychopathic ASPD group (NP-ASPD; N = 18). Upon completion of the data collection phase of the study, all Rorschach protocols were sent to an independent rater for re-scoring (blind to PCL-R score) to be used in the calculation of interrater reliability. Twenty Rorschachs and PCL-Rs were chosen at random for the calculation of the interrater reliability.

Although the required discarding of the Rorschach protocols and PCL-R data for the above 48 participants is a limitation of the study in terms of the representativeness of the sample, given the comparison of psychopaths versus non-psychopaths conducted, the deletion of this data from the sample is unlikely to have a significant impact. For instance, the data presented here is descriptive in nature used to understand the personality dynamics present in female psychopathic and non-psychopathic offenders rather than an examination of variables predictive of the female offender population as a whole or future behaviors (recidivism, treatment amenability).

Our comparison samples were comprised of 40 participants from 3 women's correctional facilities and 5 subjects from Gacono and Meloy's (1994) ASPD female offender files. Twenty-three were collected from 2 low-medium security women's federal prisons in northern California (Federal Correctional Institution–Dublin [FCI-Dublin], Federal Prison Camp–Dublin [FPC-Dublin]) and 17 were collected from a larger sample of women incarcerated in a female prison in Wyoming (see Gacono & Meloy, 1994; Peaslee, 1993). While the 17 subjects from the Peaslee (1993) sample and the 5 subjects from the Gacono and Meloy (1994) ASPD sample were previously presented as part of ASPD group data (N = 38; Gacono & Meloy, 1994), none of these 22 subjects have been previously used in comparisons of PCL-R identified psychopathic (PCL-R ≥ 30) and low scoring female ASPD offenders (PCL-R < 25). The combined sample consisted of two distinct groups: psychopathic (PCL-R ≥ 30; n = 27) and non-psychopathic (PCL-R < 25; n = 18) offenders.

The ethnicity of the combined female sample was 65% Caucasian, 15% African American, 15% Hispanic, and 2% Asian. Ages ranged from 21 to 70 years (M = 32.40, SD = 10.70), IQ estimates fell between 80 and 155 (M = 106.12, SD = 14.37), and over 50% of the women possessed a high school diploma or GED. The psychopathy group (PCL-R ≥ 30) contained 14 Caucasians (52%), 7 African Americans (26%), 5 Hispanics (18%), and 1 participant of unidentified racial origin (4%); while the non-psychopathy group was comprised of 14 Caucasians (78%), 2 Asians (11%) and 2 Hispanics (11%). The study participants were incarcerated for violence (35%), drugs (37%), fraud (26%), theft (15%), sex offenses (11%), and unknown (13%). All participants met the DSM-IV (APA, 1994) criteria for ASPD. Although an actuarial assessment of other DSM-IV personality disorders was not conducted, based upon clinical interviews conducted for the purpose of the PCL-R, a high percentage of subjects also met the criteria for HPD and borderline personality disorder (BPD). Participants who produced PCL-R scores $\geq$ 30 were included in the psychopathic group (P-APSD) while individuals scoring $\leq$ 24 were included in a non-psychopathic group (NP-ASPD).

The Shipley Institute of Living Scale (SILS), PCL-R, and Rorschach Inkblot Method (RIM; Rorschach, 1921) were administered to 75 incarcerated women. The measures were administered in accordance with procedures outlined for the SILS (Zachary, 1986), PCL-R (Gacono, 2000b; Hare, 2003), and Rorschach (Exner, 1993). The SILS was used to screen out participants with an estimated IQ score of < 80.

The PCL-R was used to assess each participant's level of psychopathy. Participants with PCL-R scores $\geq$ 30 were included in the psychopathy group. PCL-R administration and scoring entails an intensive review of the participant's medical, legal, and institution files succeeded by a detailed semi-structured interview and rating of the individual's personality and antisocial behaviors. Gacono's (2000b, 2005) Clinical and Forensic Interview Schedule was used to organize record and interview information. Record review produced a 100% agreement between the authors for the ASPD diagnosis.

The Rorschach protocols were scored for Fr/rF (self-focus), PER (defensiveness, aggrandizement), (2), MOR (sense of self-damage), V (painful rumination), FD $\geq$ 1 (psychological mindedness), T (affectional relatedness), COP (expectations of cooperative human interactions), Fd (neediness), X − % (reality testing), X + % (perceptual accuracy) and the Human Experience Variable (HEV; Perry & Viglione, 1991). The HEV relates to the quality of interpersonal relatedness (Burns & Viglione, 1996)

Results

Of the original 75 participants, PCL-R mean scores for the FCI-Dublin Sample were 25.46 (SD = 6.38), while the scores for the sample of 45 participants used in this study ranged from 11.60 to 39 (M = 27.80, SD = 6.37). The P-ASPD group (N = 27) had a mean PCL-R score of 32.69 (SD = 2.81), while the NP-ASPD group (N = 18) had a mean PCL-R score of 20.73 (SD = 3.38). PCL-R interrater reliability analyses yielded Spearman Rhos of .98 (Total scores), .93 (Factor 1), and .92 (Factor 2).

No significant differences in age or IQ were noted. The P-ASPD group contained 14 Caucasians (50%), 7 African Americans (25%), 5 Hispanics (18%), and 1 Asian (3.5%) while the NP-ASPD group contained 16 Caucasians (89%) and 2 African Americans (11%) with no Asian or Hispanic participants. Both groups contained significantly more Caucasians than other ethnicities ($X^2 = 22.26$, $p < .001$).

P-ASPDs were incarcerated for violence (54%), drugs (50%), sex (25%), fraud (21%), and theft (21%) convictions; NP-ASPDs were incarcerated for violence (6%), drugs (25%), sex (6%), fraud (39%), and theft (17%) convictions. The P-ASPD group contained significantly more violent offenders ($X^2 = 4.79$, $p = .029$) while the NP-ASPD group contained significantly more women incarcerated for fraud ($X^2 = 7.68$, $p = .006$). This is consistent with the positive correlations between psychopathy level and violence in male offender samples. Studies, however, have found women to be less likely to engage in predatory violence (typically found in male psychopaths; Hare and McPherson, 1984; Meloy, 2001, 2006, in press) and more liable to exhibit affectively based or reactive aggression (i.e., reacting to emotion evoked by a lesbian love triangle).

Rorschach Results

There were no significant differences in the number of Rorschach responses between the groups (P-ASPD: M = 19.86; NP-ASPD: M = 17.66). An overall 88% agreement was obtained for coding. For individual Rorschach variables, percentage agreement was as follows: Reflections (100%), Personals (84%), Morbid (88%), Pairs (89%), Vista (85%), Form Dimension (96%), Texture (84%), Cooperative Human Movement (89%), Food Content (84%), and Cognitive Special Scores (79%) (See Table 17.2).

Self-Perception

There were no significant differences in the proportions or frequencies of Reflection responses or PER responses. While there were no differences in the total number of Pair responses (2), significantly more psychopaths produced 11 or more Pairs (P = 22%; NP = 5%; $p = .001$; $r = .32$) and elevated Egocentricity Ratios ($\geq$ .44) without a Reflection response (P-ASPD = 18.5%; NP-ASPD = 11%; p = < .001; $r = .10$).

Table 17.2 Select Structural Variables for Psychopathic and Non-Psychopathic Incarcerated Females

Psychopaths (n = 27)				Non-Psychopaths (n = 18)				
Self-Perception								
	M	S_d	Freq	M	S_d	Freq	Effect Size (r)	P Value
Fr/rF	.44	.79	8	.72	1.03	7	ns	< .001
PER			18			14	ns	ns
(2) > 10			5			1	.32	< .001
Ego > .44			5			2	.10	< .001
Fr/rF = 0								
MOR > 2			10			4	.11	.006
V > 0			11			3	.11	< .001
FD > 1			4			5	.19	< .001
Interpersonal Relationships								
	M	S_d	Freq	M	S_d	Freq	Effect Size (r)	P Value
T = 0			15			14	.26	< .001
T = 1			8			3	.26	< .001
T > 2			4			1	.27	< .001
Prt Obj T			5			0	.28	< .001
COP			27			18	.18	.003
COP ≥ 2			13			4	ns	ns
COP (spoil)			27			11	.20	< .001
COP (good)			9			8	.10	< .001
Fd			6			1	.33	.20
HEV	−.20	1.41	7	−.24	2.09	8	.24	ns
Reality Testing								
	M	S_d	Freq	M	S_d	Freq	Effect Size (r)	P Value
X + % < .61	.51	.14	21	.57	.14	10	.23	.029
X − % > .15	.24	.15	6	.16	.89	2	.29	.057
X + % < .61 + X − % > .15			18			4	.27	<.001

P-ASPDs also produced more protocols with ≥ 2 MORs (P-ASPD = 37%, NP-ASPD = 22%; p = .006; r = .11). The difference between mean Vs (P-ASPD, M = 1.66; NP-ASPD, M = 2.23) was not significant; however, a significantly greater number of psychopaths produced > 1 Vista response (P-ASPD = 41%; NP-ASPD = 17%; X^2 = 68.08, p = < .001; r = .11). Fewer psychopaths [4, (15%)] produced at least 1 FD compared to 5 (28%) of NP-ASPDs (X^2 = 49.32, p < .001; r = .19).

Interpersonal Relationships

P-ASPDs produced the following distribution of Texture (T) responses: T = 0 (56%), T = 1 (30%), and T ≥ 2 (15%), and NP-ASPD T=0 (78%), T=1 (17%) and T≥2 (6%). (P-ASPD, M = .75; NP-ASPD, M = .28; X^2 = 23.66, < .001; r = .26). P-ASPDs also produced significantly more part object T responses (T with Ad or Hd content) compared to the NP-ASPDs (X^2 = 28.17, p < .001; r = .28). Additionally, P-ASPDs produced a significantly higher mean number of Fd responses (Wilcoxon U = 199.5; p = .020) and a larger proportion of Fd (X^2 = 23.17; p < .001; r = .33). Of note, 83% of the 6 Fd responses produced by P-ASPDs were spoiled (poor form quality; Gacono & Meloy, 1991).

The P-ASPD group produced 36 COP responses while NP-ASPDs produced 19 (X^2 = 16.30, p = .003; r = .18). Thirteen (48%) P-ASPDs produced ≥ 2 COP compared to 4 (22%) (X^2 = 3.13, p = .08; ns). Although not significant, a trend between psychopathy and increased COP production was observed. Significantly more P-ASPDs produced spoiled (poor form quality; P, 27 [75%]; NP, 11 [58%]; X^2 = 19.56; p < .001; r = .20) and fewer good quality COP (P, 9 [25%]; NP, 8 [42%]; X^2 = 27.96, p = < .001; r = .10) responses. The P-ASPD group had a mean Human Experience Variable (HEV; Perry & Viglione, 1991) of −.20 (SD = 1.41) compared to a mean of −.24 (SD = 2.09) for the NP-ASPD group (Mann-Whitney U = 222.00; ns). Significantly fewer psychopaths scored in the high range of interpersonal relatedness (P-ASPD = 22%, NP-ASPD = 44%, X^2 = 7.04, p = .008; r = .24).

Reality Testing

There were no significant differences found between the mean X + % values. However, significantly more of the P-ASPDs (78%) had X + % values below .61 (NP-ASPDs, N = 11; 61%; X^2 = 4.79, p = .029; r = .23). While both groups evidenced problems with reality testing (X − % > .15), P-ASPDs exhibited greater impairment [Mann-Whitney U = 167.5, p = .057; r= .29). Significantly more psychopaths produced an X − % value greater than .29 (X^2 = .45, p < .001; r = .29). Eighteen (67%) psychopaths had an X + % < .61 and X − % > .15 compared to 8 (44%) of the low psychopathy group (p < .001; r = . 27).

Discussion

The mean PCL-R score (M = 27.80) of our sample was greater than previously reported for females (M = 23.37, Hare, 2003; M = 21.1, Neary, 1990; M = 24.49, Strachan, 1993). Specifically, there were proportionately more psychopaths (PCL-R $\geq$ 30) in our sample. This may be due to two factors. First, other researchers have included fewer female psychopaths (PCL-R $\geq$ 30) in their samples. Secondly, previous studies have included subjects from the entire inmate population. In this study, we included only those female offenders with a concurrent ASPD diagnosis; thereby, elevating the mean PCL-R scores for the sample.

Our findings suggest that female psychopaths differ from their non-psychopathic ASPD counterparts in a number of areas: self-perception, interpersonal relatedness, and reality testing. Additionally, moderate- to large-effect sizes were found for a number of specific Rorschach variables [(2) > 10; T; Fd; HEV; X – % > .15; X + % < .61 + X – % > .15], which indicates the importance of these particular variables in female offenders. Compared to NP-ASPDs, the psychopaths experienced marked disturbances in self-perception (negative self-image), dysphoric affect, poor self-regard, limited capacity for introspection, poor interpersonal relatedness (superficial interpersonal relations), limited understanding of the motivations of others, lack of empathy, and poor reality testing (cognitive distortion and unconventionality).

The greater number of female P-ASPDs who produced elevated Egocentricity Ratios without a Reflection is noteworthy. While high Egocentricity Ratios suggest an inordinate self-focus, high ratios without Reflection indicate a sense of displeasure in doing so (Weiner, 1998). Male psychopaths look at themselves exalting in self-admiration and grandiosity (high Reflections, high Egocentricity Ratio). In contrast, our female psychopaths appear to experience distress while engaging in the same process (high Egocentricity Ratio without Reflections). Individuals with a pattern of no Reflections, high Egocentricity Ratios, and Vistas possess a situation-specific type of self-criticism not related to a true sense of remorse or guilt (Weiner, 1998). This pattern suggests chronic self-criticism and shame. Rather than remorse or guilt, the self-critical, unhappy, and dissatisfied presentation of the female psychopath may be viewed as an insidious negative self-image arising from long-standing frustration over unmet needs for attention and contact with others.

The similar frequencies for Reflection responses in our groups argue against the presence of the grandiose self-structure operating in male psychopaths (Gacono et al., 1990; Loving & Russell, 2000; Smith, Gacono, &

Kaufman, 1995; Young, Justice, Erdberg, & Gacono, 2000).[3] Rather, the female psychopath appears to need attention and acceptance (Millon & Davis, 1996) in order to mediate the effects of chronic dissatisfaction and self-criticism. Their increased COP, V, Fd, and T combined with larger proportions of spoiled COP and part T responses highlight the tenuousness of a pattern reliant on others to regulate self-esteem and mood. Compared to the independent detached interpersonal style noted in male psychopaths, the female's increased superficial need for attention and interpersonal contact renders her more dependent on the views and approval of others, resulting in a chronic, negative sense of self.

The larger numbers of female psychopaths who produced white Space ($S > 0$; P-ASPD = 44%; NP-ASPD = 22%; $X^2 = 23.17$, $p < .001$) and Sum shading > FM + m (dysphoric affect; P-ASPD = 48%; NP-ASPD = 7%; $X^2 = 4.79$, $p = .029$) contrasted with the NP-ASPDs production of increased C' (P-ASPD = 18%; NP-ASPD = 33%; $X^2 = 13.30$, $p < .001$) suggest that, in addition to the negative self-image and limited capacity for introspection ($FD \geq 1$; P-ASPD = 15%, NP-ASPD = 28%, $X^2 = 7.89$, $p < .001$), female psychopaths appear to experience increased dysphoric affect and negative, oppositional feelings. Since other signs of a deeper, more consciously experienced depression are absent—social isolation (COP < 2), low energy (suggested by Blends < 4), anhedonia, and difficulties sorting out their feelings (Color-Shading Blends > 0) while experiencing more painful internalized affect (Sum C' > 2)—it is likely that their sadness and "depression" arise from character pathology rather than true depression. Consistent with theory (Gacono & Meloy, 1994; Lazare & Klerman, 1968), the chronic self-preoccupied, critical, and negative self-image exhibited by the female psychopaths in our study supports the assertion that their regulatory mechanisms fail to bolster self-esteem. This may represent an important gender difference between male and female psychopaths.

Although the female psychopaths displayed greater needs for "affectional relatedness" than the non-psychopaths, further analyses of the psychopaths' COP, Food content, and T responses suggest that their poor understanding of the motivations and desires of those around them severely compromise their ability to engage in genuine and reciprocal relations with others. Despite her heightened interest in others, the female psychopath exhibits a reduced capacity for interpersonal relatedness. Our findings support the superficial, shallow, and insincere character of these women, while predicting the female psychopath's preference for more frequent, superficial interpersonal contacts.

The female psychopath's interest in others is not based on a desire for greater intimacy, but rather is motivated by a need to be the center of attention. Self-focus is sought in the interests of providing a distraction from ruminative self-criticism, a sense of insecurity, a negative sense of self, and the experience of dysphoric affect. Thus, an examiner should not confuse this increased need for "connection" with empathy or caring, but instead should interpret it as an attempt to satisfy her needs for attention. Additionally, the female psychopath's diminished capacity for introspection (FD = 15%) further reduces her ability to establish and maintain healthy relations with others.

Millon and Davis (1996) characterized HPD as an amalgam of active-dependent characteristics and sensation-seeking behavior. The histrionic personality was distinguished from the dependent personality disorder (DPD) by the manner in which the histrionic person *actively* solicits attention and admiration through sexually seductive, entertaining, and manipulative behaviors. Although both styles exhibit dependency, the histrionic presentation is characterized by a gregarious, extroverted attempt to garner the attention and support of the intended person or group rather than by more indirect means typically employed by DPD individuals. That is, DPD individuals will employ a more passive and helpless presentation to elicit caring and attending behavior from the other person; while the HPD person, on the other hand, will gain the desired contact and attention via entertaining, dramatic, sexual, and emotionally expressive displays. The pseudo-dependency of the female psychopath is reflected in her increased production of texture, food content, and COP responses. Her decreased interpersonal relatedness and limited capacity for genuine intimacy is consistent with HPD theory (Chodoff & Lyons, 1958; Millon & Davis, 1996; Phohl, 1991).

Poor interpersonal judgment and the misperception of interpersonal cues are highlighted by the Rorschach findings. Investigators have previously emphasized the problems hysterical or histrionic individuals display with reality testing (Chodoff & Lyons, 1958; Pfohl, 1991). The female psychopaths produced elevated scores on Rorschach indices indicating impaired reality testing. Two of the DSM-IV HPD criteria are relevant here: "7) is suggestible, i.e., easily influenced by others and circumstances; and 8) considers relationships to be more intimate than they actually are" (APA, 1994, p.658). The histrionic person's misinterpretation of intimacy and increased suggestibility reflect the interaction of poor reality testing (distorted thinking) and interpersonal dependency.

The current conceptualization of male psychopathy is an amalgam of a self-centered, grandiose, and narcissistic personality style and a criminal, antisocial lifestyle. The female psychopath's PCL-R profile suggests a person who is less grandiose, more interested in others, and behaviorally less violent. Both genders do, however, exhibit similar degrees of conning and manipulative behavior (PCL-R Item 5), pathological lying (Item 4), and antisocial (Items 3, 9, 10, 14, and 15) and criminal activity (Items 18–20). This female PCL-R profile suggests that although it might first appear that she is more interested in relations with others, this interest is likely to be superficial and immature.

Gender differences are also reflected in the differing patterns of aggression and violence displayed by men and women. Women serving a sentence for a violent offense have been found to be two times more likely to have committed their offense against an acquaintance (U.S. Department of Justice, Bureau of Justice Statistics, 1999). Again, this indicates the importance of others in the lives of female criminals. Heightened interpersonal dependency, poor understanding of others, and limited capacity for introspection increase the risk of the female psychopath offending against her family, friends, and acquaintances. Male psychopaths, on the other hand, exhibit a detachment from others reflected in their acts of violence against strangers (Hare & McPherson, 1984). Integration of cross-sectional findings with studies of aggression, suggest that male violence is driven by narcissism (Gacono & Meloy, 1994). That is, while Factor 2 (antisocial lifestyle) PCL-R scores may decline slightly over the life span, Factor 1 scores (narcissism or affective deficiency) do not.

A number of pertinent issues and constructs have been identified in the female developmental literature that relate directly to female psychopathy. Meloy (1988) posited that the symptoms subsumed within psychopathy may be seen as extreme variants of personality traits and socially deviant behaviors present in all individuals. A number of investigators (Gilligan, 1982; Krampen et al., 1990; Zuckerman, 1991) have highlighted the interactive relation between biological and socialization variables that can be understood to have important implications for the assessment of psychopathy and the scoring of the PCL-R. Specifically, biologically linked variables such as the expression of aggression, agency, and detachment and socialization variables such as intimate and familial relationships, parenting, problem-solving styles, and individual-group orientation would be expected to affect how data for certain PCL-R items would be assessed, scored, and interpreted.

Implications for the PCL-R with Female Offenders

Our findings have implications for the administration, scoring, and interpretation of the PCL-R with women. As with all PCL-R administrations, it is important to gain as much record information as possible before the structured interview portion of the measure is conducted (Gacono & Hutton, 1994; Gacono, 2000, 2005). This is a particularly pertinent factor in the PCL-R administration of female offenders given their high needs for impression management and praise from others, something not seen as frequently in male offenders, whereby their interest in being seen in a positive light is in the interests of manipulating others rather than attention (females).

The naïve or inexperienced rater should not interpret dysphoric affect (as reflected in Rorschach data presented in Tables 17.1 and 17.2) and "depression" as guilt (PCL-R Item 6) or evidence against the presence of shallow affect (PCL-R Item 7). As always, accurate scoring requires a full exploration of the nature of the reported symptoms (Gacono, 2000b). A chronic negative sense of self, shame, and dissatisfaction are distinct from the experience of a true depression or remorse. These latter affective states involve a sense of guilt for past behavior and a depressive presentation characterized by low energy, problems sleeping/eating, and/or anhedonia. It is suggested that the female psychopath's affective displays are more akin to trait-based rumination and self-pity than true remorse.

Incorrect PCL-R scoring may also be compounded when the examiner discovers a history of treatment for depression or "suicide attempts" noted in medical or mental health records and mistakes these behavioral markers as indicators of actual depression or a full range of affect. A careful exploration of the history is essential to distinguish between possible cutting behavior for the purposes of escaping dysphoric affect and rumination (an aspect of hysteria and, perhaps, borderline personality disorder), feigned suicidal behavior for the purposes of secondary gain, and bona fide suicide attempts, whereby the individual suffers severe depression, guilt, or remorse for her past actions. That is, the examiner must take care to discriminate true depressive symptoms from the experience of inner emptiness (a chronically unhappy, dissatisfied person frustrated by failed attempts to elicit attention from others). Specifically, length of stay within a mental health treatment setting is suggested as a significant marker of an attempt at manipulation or a more chronic, inflexible, and maladaptive personality functioning rather than actual depression. Thus, characterological presentations would not be viewed by clinical staff as in need of intensive treatment or intervention, while true depressive symptoms would require more extensive clinical attention. This determination may be made on the basis of an intensive examination of inpatient or outpatient treatment reviews, treatment contacts, and disciplinary actions taken by security staff against the inmate relating to their solicitation of medical or mental health staff (i.e., lying to staff or feigning illness) or inappropriate behavior within the institution.

The female psychopath's increased desire for contact with others may also complicate PCL-R scoring on a number of items. At first glance, it may appear that her increased interest in others or stated love for her children is evidence of a capacity for attachment or empathy for others (PCL-R Item 8). Further, the greater interest in others may also be misconstrued as a data point against a high score on grandiose sense of self-worth (PCL-R Item 2). Similarly, it is suggested that an inexperienced rater or person less familiar with female offenders might make incorrect attributions related to parasitic lifestyle (PCL-R Item 9) as well. Since the female psychopath would be expected to be more likely to "play the sympathy card" as a function of their increased need for contact and positive evaluation by others, the clinician or rater must be particularly on guard against a number of sources of clinical bias: (1) affective, availability, and representativeness heuristics (Gilovich, Griffin, & Kahneman, 2002), (2) illusory correlation (Chapman & Chapman, 1967), and (3) confirmatory bias (Garb, 1998).

The female developmental literature may assist in improving the understanding of female psychopathy as a whole and more specifically, how female offenders may present on the PCL-R. Based upon an understanding of the female psychopathy literature, our extensive clinical/forensic experience with female psychopaths, and our research findings, we identified nine PCL-R items that may require special consideration when scoring the measure with females: (1) Glibness-Superficial Charm, (2) Grandiose Sense of Self-Worth, (3) Conning/Manipulative, (4) Callous–Lack of Empathy, (5) Parasitic Lifestyle, (6) Early Behavioral Problems, (7) Juvenile Delinquency, (8) Revocation of Conditional Release, and (9) Criminal Versatility.

Glibness/Superficial Charm

As defined by Hare (2003), this item involves a "verbally facile individual who exudes an insincere and superficial sort of charm . . . always ready with a clever and quick comeback . . . seems too slick and smooth to be entirely believable" (p. 35). Male glibness presents in a boastful and swaggering fashion. The corresponding female manifestation is likely to be characterized by a coy, coquettish, and seductive interpersonal style. Rather than the more physically and interpersonally dominant behavior of the male psychopath, the female would be more likely to present as a "damsel in distress" to charm the interviewer. On the Rorschach, this style was highlighted in our female psychopathic sample by the elevated FC: CF + C, the female's increased need for contact with others (COP, Fd, and T responses) and diminished capacity of introspection (FD). Combined with fewer indicators of dominance (i.e., lack of narcissism, lower Fr), the female psychopath is less prone to physical control and intimidation and more likely to manipulate others through dramatic, demure, and seductive displays.

Additionally, this greater need for contact is also reflected in the higher incidence of relational and affective violence found in our study. From a developmental perspective, this need to be seen in a positive light may be understood as a reflection of the female psychopath's identification with female gender roles and her desire to garner the approval of others (i.e., group orientation). Therefore, the seduction on her part would be more likely to manifest in an attempt to elicit sympathy rather than the charming, slick, and smooth attempts by the male psychopath to impress and cajole the evaluator.

Grandiose Sense of Self-Worth

Item 2 is characterized as "a grossly inflated view of his abilities and self-worth . . . may impress as a braggart . . . appears self-assured, opinionated, and cocky during the interview . . . perhaps giving the impression he is performing or giving a press conference" (Hare, 2003, p. 36). In males, this item on Factor 1 has a strong relationship to the diagnosis of narcissistic personality disorder (NPD; APA, 2000) and describes an individual who is arrogant, self-centered, and overvalues his self-worth. However, base rates for NPD in women have been found to be significantly lower than in male samples (Stinson et al., 2008) while the prevalence for borderline and histrionic personality disorders (BPD; HPD; APA, 2000) have been found to be significantly higher in women than in men. This lack of an individualistic orientation may also be understood as a reflection of Gilligan's (1982) suggestion that autonomy (separation from the group) would be more likely to be viewed by women as dangerous and contrary to a desire to maximize group affiliation. Thus, NPD is the more likely diagnosis with male samples while BPD and HPD are more likely to be found in females.

On the Rorschach, the Reflection Response has been found to be indicative of self-focus, grandiosity, and narcissism (Exner, 1986; Gacono & Meloy, 1994) and is one component of the Egocentricity Index along with the Pair Response. Gacono and Meloy (1994) found that psychopathic ASPD samples produced up to 50% frequencies of individuals with at least one reflection response (see Gacono, Meloy, & Bridges, 2008). Our findings revealed that a significant number of the female psychopathic sample (P-ASPD = 43%; NP-ASPD = 13%) exhibited elevated Egocentricity Index scores in the absence of a Reflection Response; and in addition, tended to perceive themselves as damaged (P MOR, M = 2.39; NP MOR, M = .79).

As discussed earlier, Weiner (1998) characterized the individual who presents this pattern, an elevated Egocentricity Index in the absence of a reflection, as a self-focused individual who does not experience the corresponding self-adulation seen in a narcissistic process and tends to not be "taking any special pleasure in their self-focusing" (p. 155). Thus, our psychopathic women possessed a pathological self-focus; but rather than self-adulation, they exhibited signs suggestive of a sense of self as "damaged" (MOR), and consequently, the focus upon themselves was not the type of self-aggrandizement found in male psychopaths, but rather, a preoccupation with themselves driven by a desire to understand and possibly overcome their perceived shortcomings. The lack of pleasure associated with self-evaluation is also evidenced in the female psychopath's problems with negative self-image, dysphoric affect, and poor self-regard.

These findings have significant implications for the collection of data needed to score and interpret this item. PCL-R interview data collection and interpretation should be less focused on the arrogant, grandiose, and haughty behavior described by Hare (1991, 2003) in the PCL-R manual for males, but rather, clinicians should assess behavioral and interpersonal indicators of a preoccupation with how she is perceived by others, a tendency toward self-dramatization, and impressionistic (lacking in detail) speech. Additionally, as reflected in the lower observed levels of agency found in female offender samples (Hicks et al., 2010), a female offender would not be expected to present as "self-assured, opinionated, and cocky" (Hare, 2003, p. 36) but instead would be more likely to engage the examiner in a more passive, subdued way. For example, contrary to bragging or engaging, active displays designed to impress the examiner or take control of the interview (males), a subtle glance or seductive body posture might be employed to lure the object of their attention. However, the examiner should not be surprised by a defensive, hostile reaction displayed by the female psychopath when their "grandiosity" (manifest in fabricated stories and direct lying) is confronted. A failure to consider how the construct captured by Item 2 might manifest differently in a female would likely result in a lower score on the item.

Conning/Manipulative

Item 5 is described as "the use of deceit and deception to cheat, bilk, defraud, or manipulate others ... use of schemes and scams motivated by a desire for personal gain ... carried off in a cool, self-assured, and brazen manner" (Hare, 2003, p. 37). Item 5 has been identified by a number of investigators (Bolt et al., 2004; Hicks et al., 2010) as a poor descriptor of psychopathy in females. Lower levels of agency and a greater likelihood of an active-dependent orientation (Millon & Davis, 1996) would contribute to a more accurate appreciation of how this particular item might manifest in women. Hare's (1991, 2003) depiction of the prototypic presentation on the item connotes an individual who is actively attempting to dominate another person by manipulative means as evidenced by their "brazen manner" and the use of "schemes and scams." The female presentation is likely to occur in a much more subtle form. Raters should pay special attention to record review information found in disciplinary reports involving staff and other inmates rather than the elaborate schemes to defraud others. Third-party interviews (i.e., housing and program staff) may also be helpful. Specifically, clinicians should be on the lookout for staff misconduct involving an inmate, which may reveal evidence of manipulation or conning behavior present in less severe infractions (i.e., inappropriate seductive behavior toward staff). Given the psychopath's needs for attention and desired positive evaluation, a greater emphasis should be placed on the record review rather than her statements during the interview.

Callous/Lack of Empathy

Hare (2003) described Item 8 as "attitudes and behavior indicate a profound lack of empathy and callous disregard for the feelings, rights, and welfare of others ... he is cynical and selfish" (p. 39). The female psychopath's increased needs for affiliation and contact (albeit superficial due to increased dependency as evidenced in T > 2 responses) may be easily misconstrued as evidence of a genuine connection to other people. Secondly, driven by her desire for acceptance, she will frequently characterize herself as a "good mother" or a "good person" in the interests of maintaining her status within the larger group of women (group orientation). However, consider if the children have been placed on the individual's visiting list, the frequency of the visits, letters received, and their behavior toward others in their social milieu (behavior in court, statements about their crime/victims, conduct in the institution, and past relationships) when making this determination. In some cases, the female psychopath may use the separation from her children as a means to garner sympathy from others and draw attention to herself. Upon more careful investigation, it may be revealed that she has little interest in her children or their activities, and that she has not made any significant attempts to maintain contact with them. Third, her expected increased impression management is also likely to affect the scoring of this item, since she would be unlikely to present in a cynical fashion or exhibit signs of contempt as frequently seen in male psychopaths. Rather, she would be likely to present in a "gentle and friendly" fashion as a function of her less overt or dominant attempts to manipulate the examiner. The female psychopath's increased, yet superficial and self-serving, interest in others may cause less experienced or naïve clinicians to misinterpret or project their own feelings brought about by empathizing with the situation presented by the psychopath onto their assessment, and thereby overvalue the quality or depth of her affective life and interpersonal relationships, resulting in an overestimation of the inmate's capacity for empathy.

Parasitic Lifestyle

Item 9 captures an interpersonal style characterized by "financial dependence on others is an intentional part of his lifestyle . . . although able-bodied, he avoids steady, gainful employment; instead he continually relies on family, relatives, friends, or social assistance" (Hare, 2003, p. 40). The parasitic lifestyle item has also been identified by some investigators (Bolt et al., 2004; Hicks et al., 2010) as poorly discriminating or not well suited to female offender samples. The scoring of the item is complicated by a number of factors: (1) financial dependence may prove to be difficult to accurately assess in women, (2) traditional female gender roles may influence interpretation, and (3) the nature of the offenses they commit. However, depending upon the quality and level of detail present in the record review material, these issues may be overcome. For these reasons, particular attention to detail and careful discernment of the data present in available records and third-party information is necessary.

Given the female psychopath's increased levels of pseudo-dependency, concern about presenting herself in a positive light, and desire to be accepted or approved by others, the examiner must carefully assess the quality of the record review information. For example, an individual who receives money from family or social assistance for childcare should be assessed as to whether the funds were spent for the purpose intended rather than on their own, often selfish, needs. A revocation of benefits due to inappropriate spending practices could be seen as a data point for this item. Secondly, traditional female gender roles are related to the adoption of a primary caregiver or homemaker function within a traditional home (Gilligan, 1982). However, as with Item 8, a careful examination of the quality of the relationship with her children could be instructive and give clues to the extent to which she may have been using her children as a means of garnering financial support. Finally, a careful review of the female psychopath's criminal record and court documents is a necessary element of a correct scoring of the item. For example, due to the female's lack of physical strength and prowess compared to males, in order to achieve her interpersonal and criminal goals, she would be more likely to enlist the assistance of a more dominant male codefendant. Therefore, a careful review of these records could reveal the extent to which she has been engaging in parasitic behavior and rejecting financial responsibilities via her association with a male codefendant. However, it is clear that complete and comprehensive legal, institutional, and medical records are essential to scoring this item combined with any applicable third-party information (i.e., interviews with family, institutional staff). In situations in which this detailed information is not available, the item should be omitted since interview data is likely to be less important or helpful when scoring the item.

Sexual Promiscuity and Early Behavioral Problems

Sexual Promiscuity (Item 11) is described as "sexual relations with others are impersonal, casual, or trivial ... indiscriminate sex partners" (Hare, 2003, p. 41) and Early Behavioral Problems (Item 12) as "serious behavioral problems as a child ... persistent lying, cheating, theft, robbery, fire-setting, disruption of classroom activities ... violence, bullying, running away from home" (Hare, 2003, p. 41). Higher base rates for sexual promiscuity and antisocial behavior in childhood for men and boys have been observed within both offender and non-offender male samples (APA, 2000; Grant et al., 2004). Although male and female psychopaths possess corresponding levels of detachment as evidenced by a lack of relationship in males (T = 0) and a superficial (albeit frequent) attachment in females (T > 2, COP, low interpersonal relatedness), the males tend toward pathological independence while females tend toward enmeshment.

Although the male psychopath would be likely to present the type of behaviors described in these items with a sense of pride (due to heightened narcissism), the female psychopath would be less likely to endorse them due to their pseudo-dependent character style, need to be seen in a positive light, and gender role endorsement. Anecdotally, interview data from our sample revealed that both the psychopathic and non-psychopathic females tended to view discussions around sexual activity and deviant behavior with a sense of embarrassment or reticence. This is reflected in the high numbers of female psychopaths with elevated egocentricity indexes in the absence of reflection responses and elevated MOR scores (sense of self as damaged and preoccupied with shortcomings). This may also be affected or exacerbated by a self-appraisal or characterization of themselves as deviant or disordered compared to other women. The influence of societal norms and gender and sex roles upon the clinical and legal interpretation of female antisocial behavior is evidenced in the general perception that aggressive and criminal acts leading toward incarceration are viewed as more deviant in women than in men. This is reflected by the low base rates of incarceration for women and the greater number of female offenders with mental health needs and institutional maladjustment (Hicks et al., 2010).

Therefore, a "data driven" approach is an important consideration when administering the PCL-R with women. A focus upon intensive record review or third-party interviews is likely to be a more reliable and valid means of scoring/interpreting the measure and serves to limit potential sources of bias inherent in the evaluation of psychopathic women. Secondly, a more engaging, supportive, and empathic interview style may be more successful in eliciting the information given the female's greater needs for affiliation and concerns for how she is being perceived. Given her heightened interpersonal sensitivity and levels of impression management, the female psychopath may be more likely to withdraw from or avoid a discussion of this item not out of shame or guilt, but rather out of a fear that she is likely to be viewed as deviant or disordered. Thus, she may disengage due to a perceived loss of status and approval.

Juvenile Delinquency, Revocation of Conditional Release, and Criminal Versatility

The PCL-R (Hare, 1991, 2003) considers a number of criminal history variables: juvenile delinquency (serious antisocial behavior or arrests as an adolescent), revocation of conditional Release (violation of conditional release or escape), and criminal versatility (charges and convictions for a variety of offenses). Female offenders have been found to have lower rates of incarceration and arrest than male samples (U.S. Department of Justice, Bureau of Justice Statistics, 1999, 2008). However, it is unclear if these findings are due entirely to lower base rates of criminal activity, or to lower rates of arrest and adjudication for antisocial and illegal behaviors. Secondly, gender and sex role concerns also limit the degree to which females engage in a variety of criminal activity. Once again, careful record review is necessary to determine the exact circumstances of arrest, presence of codefendants, and courtroom behavior. It is clear that criminal activity in women occurs at a much lower rate than that for men (APA, 2000; Grant et al., 2004; U.S. Department of Justice, Bureau of Justice Statistics, 2008); and given the current evidence, it is likely that criminal female psychopaths comprise a more deviant, impaired population (as evidenced by increased utilization of mental health services and psychiatric treatment; Hicks et al., 2010) than their male counterparts.

Despite these concerns, special care must be taken when evaluating antisocial behavior in women to guard against errors in clinical judgment.

A number of investigators have identified the evidence of gender bias in relation to ASPD, and Borderline and Histrionic Personality Disorders (APA, 2000; Jane, Oltmanns, South, & Turkheimer, 2007; Skodol & Bender, 2003; Samuel & Widiger, 2009). Further, Flanagan and Blashfield (2003) studied the influence of gender-based social stereotypes on the diagnosis of personality disorders and found that when no gender associations were taught to novice clinicians, gender did not affect the diagnosis. However, when gender-based stereotyped information was highlighted, evidence of gender bias was found for DSM-IV Cluster B personality disorders. The same type of bias has been found to occur when evaluating violence and criminal behavior in female samples. For example, evidence of gender bias has been suggested by a lower likelihood of females being removed from the home in post-adjudicative dispositions (Espinosa, Belshaw, & Osho, 2008) and a tendency for female offenders to be handled more informally at the entry level of the justice system (McDonald & Chesney-Lind, 2001) compared to males.

Although the female offender may be less likely to be the direct perpetrator of violent acts (due to less physical strength), they are more likely to enlist the assistance or accompany a violent, dominant male codefendant (by stander crime). Therefore, the criminal offense data used for the PCL-R record review must be carefully evaluated when administering the measure to female offenders in order to correctly assess their history of convictions. It is suggested that the rater carefully examine the circumstances of the offenses, the female offender's involvement in all aspects of the crime (i.e., planning, commission, and evasion of prosecution), presence of a codefendant, and court decisions since some offenses may have been dismissed or lessened due to a court's leniency related to the sources of bias discussed above.

Conclusion

While the prototypical presentation of psychopathy results from the study of the male psychopath, research with female psychopaths is, comparatively speaking, in its infancy. The psychopathic interpersonal style of a narcissistic, detached, cold, calculating, hostile, and remorseless individual has evolved from studying male psychopathy (Gacono, 2000; Hare, 2003). In many respects, the female psychopath's presentation of an interpersonally needy, gregarious, superficially friendly, and self-critical individual is, at first blush, at odds with this prototypic image. The engaging style of the female psychopath may catch the inexperienced or naïve rater off guard. It is essential for the examiner to carefully consider the inmate's relations with others as evidenced by her actions, behaviors, and interpersonal reactions rather than her verbal reports.

The male and female expressions of psychopathy differ from one another in two separate but related dimensions: interpersonal relatedness and self-perception. The female psychopath's pronounced needs for "relatedness" and attention from others form the cornerstone of her histrionic character. Her interpersonal connections are focused on attempts to overcome her negative self-concept and dysphoric feelings that have arisen from her perceived alienation from those around her. The very dysphoria, and feelings of anger and irritation she seeks to escape have their roots in unmet needs for affiliation, approval, and desire to be "entertained." The female psychopath lacks the grandiose self-structure and detachment noted in males, and although she may lack the male psychopaths' desire for domination and humiliation of others, she displays a corresponding incapacity for empathy and perspective taking. The females also exhibit similar problems empathizing with others when compared to males; but rather than a detached, contemptuous devaluation of their victims, they display a clear disregard for the welfare of others despite an outward appearance of interrelatedness.

Our findings offer preliminary support for the hypothesized histrionic character of the female psychopath (Gacono & Meloy, 1994). Additionally, they provide important clues into her interpersonal and personality functioning and highlight the need for continued study of female offenders in general, and female psychopaths in particular. Further, they highlight the importance of considering a number of key issues in the correct administration, scoring, and interpretation of the PCL-R with female offenders.

Notes

1. There is also a long line of research throughout history linking hysteria and psychopathy in general (Meloy, 1988).

2. All of the discarded Rorschach protocols had been administered by a single examiner. It was also discovered that several had been administered per day. A review of the verbatim protocols indicated inadequate inquiry, perhaps due, in part, to the rapid administration. Although a tempting method for increasing our N, rather than picking out potentially "valid" protocols, and thereby biasing the subject selection process, we eliminated all protocols administered by the single examiner.

3. While female offenders have been found to be four times as likely to produce a Reflection response (related to self-focus) when compared to nonpatient females (Gacono & Meloy, 1994; Peaslee, 1993), they produce fewer

Reflections than male psychopaths. Gender differences have also been observed with adolescents; whereby, males were found to produce more animal than human Reflection responses and females produced Reflections involving more scenes, mirrors, and trees (Ames, Metraux, & Walker, 1959).

References

Alnaes, R., & Torgersen, S. S. (1988). DSM-III symptom disorders (Axis I) and personality disorders (Axis II) in an outpatient population. *Acta Psychiatrica Scandinavica, 78*(3), 348–355. doi:10.1111/j.1600-0447.1988.tb06346.x

American Psychiatric Association. (1994). *Diagnostic and statistical manual of mental disorders* (4th ed.). Washington, DC: Author.

American Psychiatric Association. (2000). *Diagnostic and statistical manual of mental disorders* (4th ed., text rev.). Washington, DC: Author.

Ames, L., Metraux, R., & Walker, R. (1959). *Adolescent Rorschach responses.* New York: Hoeber.

Bem, S. L. (1981). Gender schema theory: A cognitive account of sex typing. *Psychological Review, 88*(4), 354–364.

Block, J. H. (1983). Differential premises arising from differential socialization of the sexes: Some conjectures. *Child Development, 54*(6), 1335–1354. doi:10.1111/1467-8624.ep12418464

Bodholdt, R. H., Richards, H. R., & Gacono, C. B. (2000). Assessing psychopathy in adults: The Psychopathy Checklist–Revised and screening version. In C. B. Gacono (Ed.), *The clinical and forensic assessment of psychopathy: A practitioner's guide* (pp. 55–86). Mahwah, NJ: Lawrence Erlbaum Associates.

Bolt, D. M., Hare, R. D., Vitale, J. E., & Newman, J. P. (2004). A multigroup item response theory analysis of the Psychopathy Checklist–Revised. *Psychological Assessment, 16*(2), 155–168.

Burns, B., & Viglione, D. J. (1996). The Rorschach human experience variable, interpersonal relatedness, and object representation in nonpatients. *Psychological Assessment, 8*(1), 92–99.

Chapman, L. J. Illusory correlation in observational report. *Journal of Verbal Learning and Verbal Behavior*, 1967, 6, 151–155.

Chodoff, P., & Lyons, H. (1958). Hysteria, the hysterical personality, and "hysterical" conversion. *American Journal of Psychiatry, 114*, 734–740.

Chodorow, N. J. (1975, July). Family structure and feminine personality: The reproduction of mothering. *Dissertation Abstracts International*, 36. Retrieved from EBSCO*host*.

Cohen, J. (1988). *Statistical power analysis for the behavioral sciences* (2nd ed.). Hillsdale, NJ: Lawrence Erlbaum Associates.

Cunliffe, T. (2002). *A Rorschach investigation of incarcerated female psychopaths* (Unpublished doctoral dissertation). Pacific Graduate School of Psychology, Palo Alto, CA.

Cunliffe, T., & Gacono, C. (2005). A Rorschach investigation of incarcerated antisocial personality disordered female offenders. *International Journal of Offender Therapy and Comparative Criminology, 49*, 530–547.

Cunliffe, T., & Gacono, C. B. (2008). A Rorschach understanding of antisocial and psychopathic women. In C. B. Gacono & F. B. Evans (Eds.), *The handbook of forensic Rorschach assessment* (pp. 361–378). New York: Routledge/Taylor & Francis Group.

Cunliffe, T. B., Gacono, C. B., Meloy, J. R., Smith, J. M., Taylor, E. E., and Landry, D. (Manuscript submitted). Psychopathy and the Rorschach: A response to Wood et al. (2010). *Archives of Assessment Psychology*.

Eagly, A. H., & Steffen, V. J. (1986). Gender and aggressive behavior: A meta-analytic review of the social psychological literature. *Psychological Bulletin, 100*(3), 309–330. doi:10.1037/0033-2909.100.3.309

Espinosa, E. M., Belshaw, S. H., & Osho, G. S. (2008). Justice by gender: Understanding the role of gender in disposition decisions involving out of home placement for juvenile offenders. *American Journal of Criminal Justice, 33*(2), 267–281.

Exner, J. E. (1986). Some Rorschach data comparing schizophrenics with borderline and schizotypal personality disorders. *Journal of Personality Assessment, 50*(3), 455–471.

Exner, J. E. (1993). *The Rorschach: A comprehensive system: Vol. 2 Basic foundations* (3rd ed.). New York: Wiley.

Exner, J. E. (2001) *A Rorschach workbook for the comprehensive system* (5th ed.). Asheville, NC: Rorschach Workshops.

Exner, J. E., Weiner, I. B., & Par Staff (2002). *Rorschach interpretation assistance program: Version 4 plus for Windows*. Lutz, FL: Psychological Assessment Resources.

Eysenck, M. W. (1992). The nature of anxiety. In A. Gale & M. W. Eysenck (Eds.), *Handbook of individual differences: Biological perspectives* (pp. 157–178). Oxford, UK: John Wiley & Sons. Retrieved from EBSCO*host*.

Feingold, A. (1990). Gender differences in effects of physical attractiveness on romantic attraction: A comparison across five research paradigms. *Journal of Personality and Social Psychology, 59*(5), 981–993. doi:10.1037/0022-3514.59.5.981.

Feingold, A. (1991). Sex differences in the effects of similarity and physical attractiveness on opposite-sex attraction. *Basic and Applied Social Psychology, 12*(3), 357–367. doi:10.1207/s15324834basp1203_8.

Feingold, A. (1992). Gender differences in mate selection preferences: A test of the parental investment model. *Psychological Bulletin, 112*(1), 125–139. doi:10.1037/0033-2909.112.1.125.

Feingold, A. (1994). Gender differences in personality: A meta-analysis. *Psychological Bulletin, 116*(3), 429–456. doi:10.1037/0033-2909.116.3.429.

Flanagan, E. H., & Blashfield, R. K. (2003). Gender bias in the diagnosis of personality disorders: The roles of base rates and social stereotypes. *Journal of Personality Disorders, 17*(5), 431–446.

Forouzan, E., & Cooke, D. J. (2005). Figuring out la femme fatale: Conceptual and assessment issues concerning psychopathy in females. *Behavioral Sciences and the Law, 23*, 765–778.

Gacono, C. B. (Ed.). (2000a). *The clinical and forensic assessment of psychopathy: A practitioner's guide*. Mahwah, NJ: Lawrence Erlbaum Associates.

Gacono, C. B. (2000b). Suggestions for implementation and use of the psychopathy checklists in forensic and clinical practice. In C. B. Gacono (Ed.), *The clinical and forensic assessment of psychopathy: A practitioner's guide*. Mahwah, NJ: Lawrence Erlbaum Associates.

Gacono, C. B. (2005). *A clinical and forensic interview schedule for the Hare Psychopathy Checklist–Revised and Screening Version*. Mahwah, NJ: Lawrence Erlbaum Associates.

Gacono, C. B., Evans, B., & Viglione, D. (2002). The Rorschach in forensic practice. *Journal of Forensic Psychology Practice, 2*(3), 33–53.

Gacono, C. B., & Gacono, L. A. (2006). Some caveats for evaluating the research of psychopathy. *The Correctional Psychologist, 38*(2), 7–9.

Gacono, C. B., Loving, J., & Bodholdt, R. (2001). The Rorschach and psychopathy: Toward a more accurate understanding of the research findings. *Journal of Personality Assessment, 77*(1), 16–38.

Gacono, C. B., Loving, J., Evans, B., & Jumes, M. (2002). The Psychopathy Checklist–Revised: PCL-R testimony and forensic practice. *Journal of Forensic Psychology Practice, 2*(3), 33–53.

Gacono, C. B., & Meloy, J. R. (1991). A Rorschach investigation of attachment and anxiety in antisocial personality. *Journal of Nervous and Mental Disease, 179*, 546–552.

Gacono, C. B., & Meloy, J. R. (1994). *The Rorschach assessment of aggressive and psychopathic personalities*. Hillsdale, NJ: Lawrence Erlbaum Associates.

Gacono, C. B., & Meloy, J. R. (1997). Rorschach research and the psychodiagnosis of antisocial and psychopathic personalities. *Rorschachiana, 22*, 130–145.

Gacono, C. B., Meloy, J. R., & Berg, J. (1992). Object relations, defensive operations, and affective states in narcissistic, borderline, and antisocial personality disorder. *Journal of Personality Assessment, 59*, 32–59.

Gacono, C. B., Meloy, J. R., & Bridges, M. R. (2008). A Rorschach understanding of psychopaths, sexual homicide perpetrators, and nonviolent pedophiles. In C. B. Gacono, F. Evans, N. Kaser-Boyd, & L. Gacono (Eds.), *The handbook of forensic Rorschach assessment* (pp. 379–393). New York: Routledge/Taylor & Francis Group.

Gacono, C. B., Meloy, J. R., & Heaven, T. R. (1990). A Rorschach investigation of narcissism and hysteria in antisocial personality disorder. *Journal of Personality Assessment, 55*, 270–279.

Gacono, C. B., Meloy, J. R., Sheppard, K., Speth, E., & Roske, A. (1995). A clinical investigation of malingering and psychopathy in hospitalized insanity acquittees. *Bulletin of the American Academy of Psychiatry and the Law, 23*(3), 387–397.

Gacono, C. B., Meloy, J. R., Speth, E., & Roske, A. (1997). Above the law: Escapes from a maximum security forensic hospital and psychopathy. *Journal of the American Academy of Psychiatry and the Law, 25*, 547–550.

Garb, H. N. (1998). *Studying the clinician: Judgment research and psychological assessment*. Washington, DC: American Psychological Association.

Gilligan, C. (1982). *In a different voice: Psychological theory and women's development*. Cambridge, MA: Harvard University Press.

Gilovich, T., Griffin, D., & Kahneman, D. (2002). Hueristics and biases: The psychology og intuitive judgment. Cambridge: Cambridge University Press.

Golomb, M., Fava, M., Abraham, M., & Rosenbaum, J. F. (1995). Gender differences in personality disorders. *American Journal of Psychiatry, 152*(4), 579–582. Retrieved from EBSCO*host*.

Grant, B. F., Hasin, D. S., Stinson, F. S., Dawson, D. A., Chou, S., Ruan, W., & Pickering, R. P. (2004). Prevalence, correlates, and disability of personality disorders in the United States: Results from the National Epidemiologic Survey on Alcohol and Related Conditions. *Journal of Clinical Psychiatry, 65*(7), 948–958.

Grilo, C. M., Becker, D. F., Fehon, D. C., & Walker, M. L. (1996). Gender differences in personality disorders in psychiatrically hospitalized adolescents. *American Journal of Psychiatry, 153*(8), 1089–1091. Retrieved from EBSCO*host*.

Hare, R. D. (1991). *The Hare Psychopathy Checklist–Revised*. Toronto, Ontario, Canada: Multi-Health Systems.

Hare, R. D. (2003). *The Hare Psychopathy Checklist–Revised* (2nd ed.). Toronto, Ontario, Canada: Multi-Health Systems.

Hare, R. D., & McPherson, L. M. (1984). Violent and aggressive behavior by criminal psychopaths. *International Journal of Law and Psychiatry, 7*, 35–50.

Hart, S. D., Cox, D. N., & Hare, R. D. (1995). *Manual for the Psychopathy Checklist: Screening Version (PCL:SV)*. Toronto, Ontario, Canada: Multi-Health Systems.

Hicks, B. M., Vaidyanathan, U., & Patrick, C. J. (2010). Validating female psychopathy subtypes: Differences in personality, antisocial, and violent behavior, substance abuse, trauma, and mental health. *Personality Disorders, Theory, Research, and Treatment, 1*(1), 38–57.

Jackson, H. J., Whiteside, H. L., Bates, G. W., & Bell, R. R. (1991). Diagnosing personality disorders in psychiatric patients. *Acta Psychiatrica Scandinavica, 83*(3), 206–213. doi:10.1111/j.1600-0447.1991.tb05526.x.

Jane, J., Oltmanns, T. F., South, S. C., & Turkheimer, E. (2007). Gender bias in diagnostic criteria for personality disorders: An item response theory analysis. *Journal of Abnormal Psychology, 116*(1), 166–175. doi:10.1037/0021-843X.116.1.166.

Jang, K. L., Livesley, W., & Vernon, P. A. (1997). Gender-specific etiological differences in alcohol and drug problems: A behavioural genetic analysis. *Addiction, 92*(10), 1265–1276. doi:10.1111/j.1360-0443.1997.tb02846.x.

Kass, F., Spitzer, R. L., & Williams, J. B. (1983). An empirical study of the issue of sex bias in the diagnostic criteria of DSM-III Axis II Personality Disorders. *American Psychologist, 38*(7), 799–801. doi:10.1037/0003-066X.38.7.799.

Kernberg, O. (1975). *Borderline conditions and pathological narcissism.* New York: Jason Aronson.

Krampen, G., Effertz, B., Jostock, U., & Müller, B. (1990). Gender differences in personality: Biological and/or psychological? *European Journal of Personality, 4*(4), 303–317. Retrieved from EBSCO*host*.

Lazare, A., & Klerman, G. L. (1968). Hysteria and depression: The frequency and significance of hysterical personality features in hospitalized depressed women. *American Journal of Psychiatry, 124*(11), 48–56.

Loving, J., & Russell, W. (2000). Selected Rorschach variables of psychopathic juvenile offenders. *Journal of Personality Assessment, 75*, 126–142.

Lynn, R., & Martin, T. (1997). Gender differences in extraversion, neuroticism, and psychoticism in 37 nations. *Journal of Social Psychology, 137*(3), 369–373. Retrieved from EBSCO*host*.

McDonald, J. M., & Chesney-Lind, M. (2001). Gender bias and juvenile justice revisited: A multiyear analysis. *Crime and Delinquency, 47*(2), 173–195.

Meloy, J. R. (1988). *The psychopathic mind.* Northvale, NJ: Jason Aronson.

Meloy, J. R. (2001). *The mark of Cain: Psychoanalytic insight and the psychopath.* Hillsdale, NJ: Analytic Press.

Meloy, J. R. (2006). The empirical basis and forensic application of affective and predatory violence. *Australian and New Zealand Journal of Psychiatry, 40*, 539–547.

Meloy, J. R. (2012). Predatory violence and psychopathy. In H. Hakkanen-Nyholm & J. Nyholm (Eds.), *Psychopathy and law.* London: Wiley.

Millon, T., & Davis, R. (1996). *Disorders of personality: DSM-IV and beyond.* New York: Wiley.

Neary, A. (1990). *DSM-III and psychopathy checklist assessment of antisocial personality disorder in black and white female felons* (Unpublished doctoral dissertation). University of Missouri, St. Louis, MO.

Nicholls, T., Odgers, C., & Cooke, D. (2007). Women and girls with psychopathic characteristics. In A. Felthous & H. Sass (Eds.), *International handbook on psychopathic disorders and the law* (Vol. 1, pp. 347–366). New York: Wiley.

Nolen-Hoeksema, S. (1987). Sex differences in unipolar depression: Evidence and theory. *Psychological Bulletin, 101*(2), 259–282. doi:10.1037/0033-2909.101.2.259.

Ogloff, J., Wong, S., & Greenwood, A. (1990). Treating criminal psychopaths in a therapeutic community program. *Behavioral Sciences and the Law, 8*, 81–90.

Peaslee, D. (1993). *An investigation of incarcerated females: Rorschach indices and Psychopathy Checklist scores* (Unpublished doctoral dissertation). California School of Professional Psychology, Fresno, CA.

Peaslee, D., Fleming, G., Baumgardner, T., Silbaugh, D., & Thackrey, M. (1992). *An explication of female psychopathy: Psychopathy Checklist scores, Rorschach manifestations, and a comparison of male and female offenders with moderate and severe psychopathy*. Unpublished manuscript.

Perris, C. (1966). Community psychiatric service and after-care of the patients returned to the community in the organization of a Swedish mental hospital. *International Journal of Social Psychiatry, 12*(4), 293–298. doi:10.1177/002076406601200408.

Perry, W., & Viglione, D. J. (1991). The ego impairment index as a predictor of outcome in melancholic depressed patients treated with tricyclic antidepressants. *Journal of Personality Assessment, 56*(3), 487–501.

Pfohl, B. (1991). Histrionic personality disorder: A review of available data and recommendations for DSM-IV. *Journal of Personality Disorders, 5*(2), 150–166.

Pollak, S., & Gilligan, C. (1982). Images of violence in Thematic Apperception Test stories. *Journal of Personality and Social Psychology, 42*(1), 159–167. doi:10.1037/0022-3514.42.1.159

Rice, M. E. (1997). Violent offender research and implications for the criminal justice system. *American Psychologist, 52*, 414–423.

Rice, M. E., Harris, G., & Cormier, C. (1992). An evaluation of a maximum security therapeutic community for psychopaths and other mentally disordered offenders. *Law and Human Behavior, 16*, 399–412.

Robins, L. (1984). Lifetime prevalence of specific psychiatric disorders in three sites. *Archives of General Psychiatry, 41*(10), 949–958. Retrieved from EBSCO*host*.

Rogers, R., Johansen, J., Chang, J. J., & Salekin, R. T. (1997). Predictors of adolescent psychopathy: Oppositional and conduct-disordered symptoms. *Journal of the American Academy of Psychiatry and the Law, 25*, 261–271.

Rorschach, H. (1921). *Psychodiagnostik*. Bern, Switzerland: Bircher (translation Hans Huber Verlag, 1942).

Salekin, R., Rogers, R., & Sewell, K. (1998). Construct validity of psychopathy in a female offender sample: A multitrait-multimethod evaluation. *Journal of Abnormal Psychology, 106*, 576–585.

Samuel, D. B., & Widiger, T. A. (2009). Comparative gender biases in models of personality disorder. *Personality and Mental Health, 3*(1), 12–25. doi:10.1002/pmh.61

Shapiro, D. (1965). *Neurotic styles*. New York: Basic Books.

Shapiro, R. Y., & Mahajan, H. (1986). Gender differences in policy preferences: A summary of trends from the 1960s to the 1980s. *Public Opinion Quarterly, 50*(1), 42–61. Retrieved from EBSCO*host*.

Shipley, S. L., & Arrigo, B. A. (2004). *The female homicide offender: Serial murder and the case of Aileen Wuornos*. Upper Saddle River, NJ: Prentice Hall.

Skodol, A. E., & Bender, D. S. (2003). Why are women diagnosed borderline more than men? *Psychiatric Quarterly, 74*(4), 349–360. doi:10.1023/A:1026087410516

Smith, A., Gacono, C. B., & Kaufman, L. (1995). A Rorschach comparison of psychopathic and nonpsychopathic conduct disordered adolescents. *Journal of Clinical Psychology, 53*, 289–300.

Stinson, F. S., Dawson, D. A., Goldstein, R. B., Chou, S. P., Huang, B. Smith, S. M., . . . Grant, B. F. (2008). Prevalence, correlates, disability, and comorbidity of DSM-IV narcissistic personality disorder: Results from the wave 2 national epidemiologic survey on alcohol and related conditions. *Journal of Clinical Psychiatry*, *69*(7), 1033–1045.

Strachan, C. (1993). *The assessment of psychopathy in female offenders* (Unpublished doctoral dissertation). Department of Psychology, University of British Columbia, Vancouver, British Columbia, Canada.

Sullivan, H. S. (1953). *The interpersonal theory of psychiatry*. New York: Norton.

U.S. Department of Justice, Bureau of Justice Statistics (1999). *Women Offenders (Bureau of Justice Statistics Bulletin)*. Rockville, MD: U.S. Department of Justice.

U.S. Department of Justice, Bureau of Justice Statistics (2008). *Prisoners in 2008 (Bureau of Justice Statistics Bulletin)*. Rockville, MD: U.S. Department of Justice.

Verona, E., & Vitale, J. (2006). Psychopathy in women. In C. J. Patrick (Ed.), *Handbook of psychopathy* (pp. 415–436). New York: Guilford Press.

Vitale, J. E., & Newman, J. P. (2001). Response perseveration in psychopathic women. *Journal of Abnormal Psychology, 110*(4), 644–647.

Vitale, J. E., Smith, S. S., Brinkley, C. A., & Newman, J. P. (2002). The reliability and validity of the Psychopathy Checklist–Revised in a sample of female offenders. *Criminal Justice and Behavior, 29*(2), 202–231.

Weiner, I. B. (1998). *Principles of Rorschach interpretation*. Mahwah, NJ: Lawrence Erlbaum Associates.

Young, M. H., Justice, J. V., Erdberg, P. S., & Gacono, C. B. (2000). The incarcerated psychopath in psychiatric treatment: Management of treatment? In C. B. Gacono (Ed.), *The clinical and forensic assessment of psychopathy: A practitioner's guide* (pp. 313–332). Mahwah, NJ: Lawrence Erlbaum Associates.

Werner, N. E., & Crick, N. R. (1999). Relational aggression and social-psychological adjustment in a college sample. *Journal of Abnormal Psychology, 108*(4), 615–623. doi:10.1037/0021-843X.108.4.615

Winokur, G., & Tanna, V. L. 1969. Possible role of X-linked dominant factor in manic depressive disease. *Diseases of the Nervous System, 30*(2), 89–94. Retrieved March 8, 2011, from *PsycINFO*, EBSCO*host*.

Zachary, R. (1986). *Shipley Institute of Living Scale: Revised manual*. Los Angeles, CA: Western Psychological Services.

Zuckerman, M. (1991). Biotypes for basic personality dimensions? "The Twilight Zone" between genotype and social phenotype. In J. Strelau, A. Angleitner, J. Strelau, & A. Angleitner (Eds.), *Explorations in temperament: International perspectives on theory and measurement* (pp. 129–146). New York: Plenum Press.

CHAPTER EIGHTEEN

Psychopathy, Borderline Personality Disorder, and Domestic Violence: An Empirical Review

Ted Cunliffe, Elizabeth A. Johnson, and Donna E. Weiss

Intimate partner violence (IPV) accounts for more than 18.5 million mental health care visits annually and almost one-third of female homicide victims in the United States (National Center for Injury Prevention and Control, 2003). Additionally, worldwide estimates of IPV reveal that in the majority of countries around the globe, between 30% and 60% of women who have ever been in an intimate relationship report histories of physical or sexual violence or both at some point in their lives (Garcia-Moreno, Jansen, Ellsberg, Heise, & Watts, 2006). In a large urban county in the northeastern United States, Fantuzzo, Fusco, Mohr, and Perry (2007) found that 48% of all assaults were domestic violence events, children were present in 50% of the cases studied, and 23% of responses by police resulted in an arrest. In the United States, current estimates are that in approximately 70% to 80% of intimate partner homicides, irrespective of the partner murdered, the woman was being physically abused prior to the murder (Campbell et al., 2003). Further, domestic violence has been found to be responsible for approximately 43% of children's injuries treated by pediatricians (American Academy of Pediatrics, Committee on Child Abuse and Neglect, 1998) and related to increased rates of low birth weight and preterm births (Shah & Shah, 2010). In 1995 (U.S. Department of Justice, Bureau of Justice Statistics, 1995), the annual cost of IPV was estimated to be in excess of $5.8 billion, with approximately $4.1 billion due to medical and mental health services. If this figure is adjusted to 2011 dollars, the value is in excess of $8.4 billion.

Thus, IPV is emerging as an area of clinical, legal, and public health importance. IPV gained federal support with the signing of the Violence Against Women Act of 1994, whereby funding was provided to enhance the investigation and prosecution of those perpetrating violent crimes against women, increased pretrial detention of the accused, imposed automatic and mandatory restitution upon those convicted, and allowed civil redress in those cases in which prosecutors elected not to pursue adjudication. The National Institute of Justice (2007) defines IPV as physical, sexual, or psychological harm by a current or former intimate partner or spouse, occurring between heterosexual and homosexual couples. The increasing awareness of the issue is evidenced in the greater number of community-based and court-ordered treatment programs and services (Walker, 1999). It is suggested that in order to impact the incidence, severity, and perception of IPV, a clear understanding of the motivations, psychological functioning, and associated risk for future violence of domestically violent offenders is needed. Therefore, in the interests of efficacious, realistic, and cost-effective treatment planning, a determination of the treatment needs of the battering population has become increasingly important and is predicated on an empirically based and comprehensive understanding of the self-concept, interpersonal, and mediation capacities of the male batterer.

Epidemiological data from 2002 revealed that the majority of IPV cases involved a male defendant and a female victim (84%), 12% were concerned with a female defendant and a male victim, and 4% occurred in same-sex relationships (U.S. Department of Justice, Bureau of Justice Statistics, 2009). Although a comprehensive understanding of the physical and psychological effects of IPV on the victim has been amassed and continues to grow, a clear conceptualization and delineation of the male batterer has remained elusive. Although sources of bias (i.e., gender, clinical judgment, and cognitive heuristics biases) continue to hamper the study, conceptualization, and measurement of the phenomenon, explanations of intimate partner abuse have centered upon the neurological, biological, and psychological causes (Dutton, 2007). Within the past 25 years of research, a litany of batterer subtypes has been suggested, and comprise various DSM (APA, 1968, 1980, 1987, 1994, 2000) personality disorders including antisocial, narcissistic, schizoid, borderline, dependent, and obsessive-compulsive in addition to DSM Axis I diagnoses (i.e., mood, psychotic, and substance-related disorders; Dutton, 2007). The heterogeneous qualities of borderline personality disorder (BPD), antisocial personality disorder (ASPD), and psychopathy have been highlighted. Further, the constructs of BPD and psychopathy have been determined to have overlapping dimensions related to IPV captured by battering subtypes, attachment styles, and deficits in affective processing and interpretation. This overlay presents an opportunity to explore the possibility of the borderline psychopath in IPV. Given the much greater numbers of male perpetrators and data available, the focus of this chapter will be upon male batterers.

Domestic Violence

Although various definitions of domestic violence have been proposed, investigators studying IPV have often used the terms "violence" and "abuse" interchangeably (Walker, 1999). Additionally, when clarification of the concept of domestic violence was provided, authors frequently focused upon the physical, sexual, and/or psychological abuse suffered by the victim rather than the characteristics of the perpetrator or offender. Although Walker (2000, 2009) conceptualized domestic violence as a learned behavior that was directed toward the maintenance of power and control over the victim, the emphasis upon the word "violence" in the popular press and scientific literature has led to misleading characterizations of the dynamics of the construct. That is, the true impact on victims was determined to be the psychological effects of repeated humiliation and physical/emotional dominance of the victims evidenced in their surrender of control, power, and autonomy rather than the physical violence alone (Walker 2000, 2009). Consistent with this conceptualization, the American Psychological Association's Task Force on Violence and the Family (American Psychological Association, 1996) defined domestic violence as a pattern of abusive behavior characterized by physical, sexual, and psychological maltreatment by an individual in an intimate relationship against another to gain or maintain power, control, and authority. The American Psychological Association's definition of domestic violence reflects an abusive intimate relationship between two individuals and thereby closely resembles that of IPV. Moreover, the focus on "abuse" rather than on "violence" more accurately captures the nature, severity, and dynamics of the relationship, placing an emphasis on the abusive quality rather than solely on the presence of physical violence.

At the forefront of the modern conceptualization of domestic violence, Lenore Walker (1979, 1994, 2000, 2009) initiated the exploration of the relationship dynamics between the batterer and the victim(s) and postulated that violence and manipulation generally grow in intensity and frequency over time. Walker (cycle of violence; 1979) hypothesized that although IPV initially appeared random, the violence may be conceptualized as occurring in a multistage cycle whereby a process of tension reduction gives rise to three recurring stages of battering: (1) tension-building, (2) the acute battering incident, and (3) loving-contrition. According to Walker, following the courtship, the abuser is unusually loving and attentive (beginning of the tension-building phase) leading to a gradual buildup of tension in which the batterer engages in acts that cause increased friction in the relationship (i.e., name-calling or physical violence). The victim is usually aware of a change in their partner's behavior and attempts to quell the strain on the relationship through a variety of appeasement or distraction strategies. These initially successful attempts to "keep the peace" may be temporarily effective in reducing the violence and thereby reinforce the victim's unrealistic or inaccurate belief that she is capable of controlling the violence or abusive behavior (Walker, 2000). Walker (1979, 2000) suggested that unless some form of intervention occurs within this phase, the acute battering incident (second phase) will arise whereby the tension is discharged through a violent attack upon the intimate partner, resulting in injury and police involvement. The second part of the cycle typically concludes with a sharp physiological reduction in tension giving rise to contrite, caring behavior (loving-contrition stage; Walker, 2009). This phase of the cycle is characterized by profuse apologies, gift-giving, declarations of love, solemn assurances that the attack will never again transpire, and seemingly apparent concerns for the victim's well-being. Therefore, this "honeymoon" period is most often exemplified by an absence of tension and provides the reinforcement for the victim to remain in the relationship.

Walker (2009) found empirical support for the cycle of violence in her sample of battered women, where she observed the presence of the tension-building phase in 65% of all cases and the loving-contrition phase in 58%. However, Follingstad (2003) noted that the data suggests that a minority of battered women endorse experiencing all three phases. Dutton (1992) indicated that other unique patterns of abuse may occur that represent variations from the cycle of violence and suggested that abuse cannot be precisely predicted. Further, the psychological constructs underlying the cycle, such as learned helplessness, low self-esteem, interpersonal disturbance, and self-blame, have received inconsistent empirical support (Follingstad, 2003). Additionally, Dutton and Painter (1993) posited that it may not be the cyclical nature of the abusive incidents, but rather, the intermittent frequency of the abuse that predicts distress and psychological symptoms leading to a sense of hopelessness or lack of control. While the clinical utility of the cycle of violence is established, the differential expression of IPV may reflect a number of subtypes of batters (dimensional versus categorical conceptualization) rather than a representation of a universal relationship dynamic common to all batterers (Dutton, 2007). Specifically, the dynamics of a borderline batterer subtype is evidenced in some descriptions of battering behavior (Dutton, 2007).

Modern conceptualizations of intimate partner abuse have begun to explore and delineate the personality characteristics of male batterers. A consideration of the complex dynamics that underlie the batterer's behavior, stemming from significant developmental attachment problems, poor socialization, and biological or genetic variables, contributes to the identification of specific personality configurations. A number of investigators (Boyle, O'Leary, Rosenbaum, & Hassett-Walker, 2008; Holtzworth-Munroe, Meehan, Herron, Rehman, & Stuart, 2000; Holtzworth-Munroe & Stuart, 1994; Huss & Langhinrichsen-Rohling, 2006; Jacobson & Gottman, 1998; Mauricio & Lopez, 2009; Tweed & Dutton, 1998; Waltz, Babcock, Jacobson, & Gottman, 2000) have identified different subgroups of batterers, each exhibiting distinct patterns of interpersonal violence differing along personality dimensions. Further, BPD, ASPD, and anxious and avoidant attachment styles have been found to be prominent among empirically differentiated batterer subgroups (Mauricio & Lopez, 2009).

Dutton (2007) characterized battering men along four dimensions of violence: (1) overcontrolled, (2) undercontrolled, (3) impulsive, and (4) instrumental. The overcontrolled individual denies their anger, resulting in chronic frustration and resentment, while the undercontrolled is characterized by frequent violent outbursts. The instrumental batterer utilizes violence to achieve specific objectives, whereas the impulsive perpetrator responds violently in order to extinguish inner tension. Gottman et al. (1995) proposed two types (I & II) of batterers, which closely resemble antisocial and borderline personality disorders (APA, 2000), respectively. In addition, they noted a physiological difference wherein the type II group experienced elevated heart rate in response to marital violence, while type I displayed decreased heart rate reactivity, echoing findings with male psychopaths (Hare & McPherson, 1984). This spawned the "cobra" and "pit bull" typologies discussed by Jacobson and Gottman (1998). Cobras, those whose heart rates decreased, were more likely to engage in instrumental violence and displayed evidence of severe antisocial traits suggestive of

ASPD or psychopathy. Pit bulls, on the other hand, presented as insecure and emotionally labile, and had unstable relationships reflective of BPD. Similarly, Tweed and Dutton (1998) categorized those with more severe IPV and antisocial traits/behavior as the instrumental subtype, while individuals presenting with less severe and more remorseful behavior (BPD features) were classified as impulsive. Notably, while both types reported preoccupied attachment styles, the impulsive subgroup also exhibited a fearful attachment.

Holtzworth-Munroe and Stuart (1994) identified three batterer subtypes (family only, borderline-dysphoric, and generally violent-antisocial) conceptualized across three interrelated descriptive dimensions: severity of marital physical violence, generality of violence, and psychopathology. Family-only (FO) batterers engage in the least severe violence, are limited to the household, and exhibit low levels of psychopathology. Borderline-dysphoric (BD) batterers engage in moderate to severe spousal abuse, evidence some degree of extrafamilial violence, and are hypothesized to be prone to exhibiting psychological distress and increased rates of substance abuse and dependence. Those in the generally violent-antisocial (GVA) category are more likely to commit moderate to severe IPV and have the highest levels of extrafamilial aggression, criminal behavior, and substance abuse. The model differentiated the subgroups via an integration of existing interpersonal models of aggression and IPV and highlighted distal (early childhood and deviant peer and family experiences in childhood and adolescence) and proximal (attachment in adulthood leading to problems in impulsivity, social skills, antisocial attitudes, and beliefs related to violence in adult partner relationships) factors hypothesized to influence the development of violent behaviors in intimate relationships (Waltz et al., 2000). Further, when empirical tests of the theoretical model were conducted with a community sample, Holtzworth-Munroe, Meehan, Herron, Rehman, and Stuart (2000) identified a fourth, low-level antisocial (LLA) group, similar to the FO. Across the different descriptive dimensions, the LLA batterers fell between the family only and generally violent/antisocial groups. The presence of four, rather than three, distinct subgroups was replicated by Huss and Langhinrichsen-Rohling (2006) and demonstrated reasonable long-term consistency in a follow-up study by Holtzworth-Munroe, Meehan, Herron, Rehman, and Stuart (2003).

According to Holtzworth-Munroe et al. (2003), FO batterers are characterized as having the fewest risk factors for violent behavior resulting from poor coping skills and the influence of low-level risk factors such as childhood exposure to marital violence and limited relationship skills.

Following incidences of IPV, their low level of psychopathology, positive attitudes toward women, and negative attitudes toward violence tend to inhibit the escalation and frequency of abuse. Consistent with a borderline personality organization (Kernberg, 1984), the BD subtype is hypothesized to be related to histories of parental abuse and rejection. Therefore, they have difficulty forming secure attachments in intimate relationships and are characterized as highly dependent, preoccupied with abandonment, jealous, and lacking in marital relationship skills. These individuals also tend to harbor hostile attitudes toward women and subscribe to attitudes moderately supportive of violence. The GVA subgroup individuals were found to have a greater frequency of violence in their family of origin and more association with deviant peers compared to the other subtypes. They were described as impulsive, lacking in interpersonal skills, more likely to subscribe to hostile attitudes toward women, and tended to view violence as an acceptable solution to overcoming challenges to self-esteem and interpersonal problems. Further, they exhibited an insecure and dismissive attachment style leading to increased aggression and antisocial behavior.

Borderline Personality Disorder

According to the *Diagnostic and Statistical Manual*, Fourth Edition, Text Revision (DSM-IV-TR; APA, 2000), a personality disorder is a pervasive, inflexible, maladaptive, and stable pattern of inner experience and interpersonal behavior. BPD is characterized by a pattern of instability in interpersonal relationships, affect, identity disturbance, and marked impulsivity across a number of potentially self-damaging areas. Additionally, episodic dysphoric affect, anxiety, irritability, anger, and chaotic and intense relationships as well as pronounced fears of abandonment have been identified as essential elements. Further, Linehan (1993) characterized emotional reactivity, emotional dysregulation, and poor distress tolerance as primary characteristics. Given the salience of intrapersonal and interpersonal disturbances in BPD, some developmental psychologists have postulated that many aspects of the disorder result from disruptions in early attachment (Levy, 2005). Additionally, a significant negative relationship exists between the level of aggressiveness and the degree of attachment security in BPD individuals (Fossati et al., 2005). Therefore, prominent contemporary approaches to BPD treatment emphasize the importance of skill development in these domains (Linehan, 1993).

Trauma experts have established that a majority of traumatized individuals also carry a diagnosis of BPD and have suggested that a significant number of BPD-diagnosed individuals have histories of childhood trauma such as physical abuse, sexual abuse, and witnessing domestic violence (Gold, 2000; Herman, Perry, & van der Kolk, 1989; Lewis & Grenyer, 2009). This has led some to conclude that trauma is a causative factor in the development of BPD (Herman et al., 1989). Although there is a high comorbidity between BPD and post-traumatic stress disorder (PTSD) in traumatized individuals (Gold, 2000; Herman et al., 1989), other investigators have also highlighted the presence of the disorder in the non-traumatized population (Golier et al., 2003). Since survivors of chronic childhood trauma often develop complex symptoms that are not fully represented by a PTSD diagnosis alone, diagnostic criteria for complex PTSD (CP), also referred to as complicated PTSD, disorders of extreme stress (DES), and disorders of extreme stress not otherwise specified (DESNOS) have also been proposed (Roth, Newman, Pelcovitz, van der Kolk, & Mandel, 1997).

CP is comprised of seven symptom clusters: (1) difficulty with affect regulation and impulse control, (2) alterations in consciousness including dissociative experiences, (3) poor self-perception, (4) distorted perception of the perpetrator, (5) disturbed interpersonal relationships, (6) somatic symptoms, and (7) alterations in systems of meaning (Roth et al., 1997). Battered woman syndrome (BWS; Walker, 1979, 2000, 2009) includes the three major symptom clusters that form a PTSD diagnosis in addition to disturbed interpersonal relationships, body image distortion and/or somatic complaints, and sexual intimacy issues. However, symptom overlap exists between BPD, BWS, and CP, all of which are etiologically related to trauma. Therefore, it has been suggested that BWS is not a distinct syndrome and should be subsumed under a PTSD or complex PTSD diagnosis, since symptoms exhibited by battered women are similar to those that other trauma survivors experience (Follingstad, 2003). Debate has arisen concerning BWS since it has not been designated as a distinct diagnostic category in the DSM-IV-TR (APA, 2000), not all battered women experience the syndrome, and some critics of the construct have suggested that expert testimony on BWS has promoted the stereotype that battered women are pathological (Russell, 2010).

The variability within the population of individuals diagnosed with BPD has led investigators to examine possible sub-patterns of BPD that can be reliably distinguished. Attempts to differentiate between levels of functioning in BPD patients were based on the awareness that the impulsivity, affective lability, and self-defeating actions occur in an interpersonal context, following triggers from real or imagined events in relationships (Levy, 2005). Further, it has been suggested that BPD-diagnosed individuals exhibit an elevated sensitivity to environmental cues (Sieswerda, Arntz, Mertens, & Vertommen, 2007). Thus, dimensional conceptualizations of the disorder have been proposed to account for a large proportion of the variance within BPD-diagnosed individuals (Hopwood et al., 2009).

Trull (1995) developed an identification strategy for sub-syndromal and syndromal levels of BPD utilizing the Personality Assessment Inventory Borderline Features Subscale (PAI-BOR; Morey, 1991). The sub-syndromal type was described as those who scored above a threshold that indicates the presence of significant BPD features while failing to meet full DSM-IV (APA, 1994) diagnostic criteria. Linehan (1993) described two interpersonal patterns in BPD: (1) "butterfly-like" and (2) "attached." The former has difficulty developing attachments, tending to "flutter" in and out of relationships, while the "attached" type quickly develops stormy and intense relationships. Leihener and colleagues (2003) provided data supporting an empirical model for grouping BPD patients according to their interpersonal characteristics whereby they identified two subgroups, termed "autonomous" and "dependent." Interestingly, the patterns that emerged were similar to the clinical groups identified by Linehan (1993). Ryan and Shean (2007) attempted to determine if college students who met Trull's (1995) criteria for sub-syndromal levels of BPD symptoms would also be divided into the "autonomous" and "dependent" subtypes identified by Leihener et al. (2003). Within the high-BPD trait group, two distinct subgroups that resembled those identified by Leihener et al. (2003) emerged from the cluster analysis. The "autonomous" subtype evidenced interpersonal problems associated with being domineering, controlling, overly assertive, self-centered, vindictive, and emotionally distant. On the other hand, the "dependent" subtype presented as being overly accommodating and submissive, having little influence over others, difficulty conveying needs to others, and low self-confidence.

Affective recognition has received little empirical attention in the literature on BPD despite findings suggestive of a heightened sensitivity to facial expressions in individuals with the disorder (Lynch et al., 2006; Wagner & Linehan, 1999), deficits in recognizing negative expressions (Levine, Marziali, & Hood, 1997), misattribution of negative emotionality (Wagner & Linehan, 1999), bias toward perception of anger (Domes et al., 2008), or no difficulty with affective recognition (Domes et al., 2008). Domes, Schultz, and Herpertz (2009) hypothesized that the inconsistency across studies relates to the interference of enhanced emotional arousal during the cognitive evaluation of the emotional facial expressions. In addition, methodological differences may have prevented evaluation of subtle discrepancies in recognition of emotional expression (Domes, Schultz, & Herpertz, 2009). For example, in one study (Lynch et al., 2006), subjects were permitted to change their responses, while in another, each trial was discontinued immediately following a single response (Domes et al., 2008). Response options differed as well, with some studies utilizing a forced-choice format (Levine et al., 1997) as opposed to allowing participants to spontaneously respond verbally (Wagner & Linehan, 1999). In either case, discrepancies across multiple studies in emotional recognition occur frequently in the BPD population, although the exact nature and quality of this disparity remains poorly defined.

Since the capacity to accurately identify the mental state of others through external cues is essential to governing one's behavior and regulating emotional states, facial recognition could be considered the cornerstone for intact social functioning since misinterpretation may lead to impaired functioning in both the social and emotional domains (Domes et al., 2009). Intimate partner abusers have been found to consistently misperceive emotional displays (Holtzworth-Munroe & Hutchinson, 1993) whereby violent men were found to be more likely to attribute negative intent to their spouses compared to controls. Thus, situations involving jealousy, potential abandonment, and public humiliation were more likely to elicit greater negative attribution of intent (Holtzworth-Munroe & Hutchinson, 1993). Similarly, provocative dating situations elicited greater negative intent attributions (Moore, Eisler, & Franchina, 2000). Further, intimate partner abusers were less likely to offer comfort and support and more likely to report irritation when presented with stimuli depicting sad or anxious wives compared to non-distressed and distressed non-IPV men (Holtzworth-Munroe & Smutzler, 1996).

Babcock, Green, and Web (2008) evaluated facial affect recognition among IPV couples classified according to the Holtzworth-Munroe and Stuart (1994) typology of batterers in a community sample. Deficits in labeling facial affect displays differed by abuser subgroup. Men who were generally violent with traits suggestive of psychopathy (GVP batterers) displayed deficits in recognition of angry, happy, surprised, and neutral expressions. Interestingly, the pattern of errors suggested a tendency to label neutral and positive emotional cues negatively, while those with borderline personality characteristics evidenced little difficulty identifying facial expressions. The authors noted that although this accurate interpretation may appear positive, it could also serve as a risk factor for interpersonal violence, especially among those prone to aggressive behavior and impulsivity. Schweinle and Ickes (2007) suggested that contemptuous emotions, pronounced criticism/rejection bias, and deficits in empathy may characterize both antisocial and borderline batterers, but to differing degrees.

Psychopathy

Psychopathy is one of the oldest psychological constructs in the literature, with roots dating back to the ancient Greeks (Millon, Simonsen, & Birket-Smith, 1998). Current conceptualizations of psychopathy have identified three distinct but related dimensions: (1) affective (shallow emotions, lack of empathy, guilt, remorse, and a failure to accept responsibility), (2) interpersonal (glib/superficial charm, conning and manipulative behavior, deceitfulness, and a grandiose sense of self-worth), and (3) behavioral (impulsivity, irresponsibility, parasitic lifestyle, poor behavioral controls, and antisocial/criminal behavior). Although diagnostic confusion has existed over the years between the related but distinct constructs of ASPD, sociopathy, and psychopathy, extensive empirical findings have revealed that although the disorders share some characteristics in common, they diverge along historical, developmental, and diagnostic lines (Gacono, Chapter 13 this volume). With the advent of the Psychopathy Checklists (Hare, 1980, 1991, 2003), the reliability and validity of the construct has been demonstrated.

Karpman (1941) proposed a distinction between primary and secondary psychopathy and suggested that although the two subtypes within the construct are interrelated, they may be distinguished from one another. He hypothesized that although both subtypes present with elevations across all the dimensions, the primary psychopath is concentrated around symptoms related to a severe affective deficit, while the secondary psychopath is based on a highly impulsive interpersonal style. Blackburn, Logan, Donnelly, and Renwick (2008) suggested that the degree of withdrawal or detachment may be viewed as the chief distinction between primary and secondary psychopathy. Notably, Blackburn et al. (2008) identified four profile classes of psychopathy among forensic psychiatric patients: the primary (extraverted, self-confident, impulsive, hostile), secondary (impulsive, hostile, socially anxious, withdrawn, moody), inhibited (introverted, withdrawn, controlled, depressed) and controlled (defensive, conforming sociable, unemotional). While both the primary and secondary psychopathic groups were similarly impulsive, aggressive, and undersocialized, the secondary psychopath group was more introverted and evidenced higher levels of PTSD and increased incidence of abuse. Thus, it was suggested that the controlled psychopath group was a variation of the primary psychopath. Similar to the successful psychopath described by Hare (1998), they displayed low anxiety, high self-esteem, and agreeableness as well as marked histrionic and narcissistic traits. This group also demonstrated the lowest degree of Axis I anxiety disorders and traits of Cluster B personality disorders, specifically, indicators of BPD. Similarly, Poythress and colleagues (2010) conducted a cluster analysis involving 1,413 male offenders with moderate (ASPD) and high levels of psychopathy and delineated four subgroups (including primary and secondary psychopathy subsets) that differed significantly in their patterns of antisocial behavior.

Psychopathy, as measured by the Psychopathy Checklist–Revised (Hare, 1991, 2003), is composed of two broad, correlated factors: (1) Interpersonal/Affective and (2) Socially Deviant Lifestyle. Although Factor 2 may be viewed as an operationalization of ASPD, Factor 1 encompasses a number of DSM-IV-TR (APA, 2000) Axis II personality disorders, including BPD. Robust empirical findings related to the brain function of psychopathic individuals (Blair, Mitchell, & Blair, 2005; Harenski, Harenski, Shane, & Kiehl, 2010; Rogers, 2006) have found evidence for deficits in processing of affect (Ali, Amorim, & Chamorro-Premuzic, 2009; Del Gaizo & Falkenbach, 2008) and decision making (Koenigs, Kruepke, & Newman, 2010). Skeem, Poythress, Edens, Lilienfeld, and Cale (2003) suggested that the secondary psychopath includes borderline personality traits that may be useful in distinguishing the subtypes of psychopathy. Thus, when the constellation of psychopathic characteristics is considered, it is clear that some individuals high in psychopathy would be expected to carry a comorbid BPD diagnosis. Further, when men who batter are viewed from a personality perspective, psychopathy and borderline characteristics would be expected to exist within some members of this population (Dutton & Golant, 1995). This is also reflected in the considerable comorbidity between ASPD, psychopathy, and BPD within some populations (Andrulonis, 1991; Charbrol & Leichsenring, 2006; Herpertz et al., 2001). Despite this overlap of symptoms, little research has been conducted evaluating the possible relationship between these constructs and IPV.

Among violent offenders, secondary psychopaths display more deficient interpersonal (irritability, social withdrawal, lack of assertiveness), and psychological (major mental disorder) functioning than primary psychopaths (Skeem, Johansson, Andershed, Kerr, & Louden, 2007). In comparison to a violent but non-psychopathic group, the secondary psychopathic group presented as emotionally unstable and withdrawn (Skeem et al., 2007). Additionally, Langhinrichsen-Rohling, Huss, and Ramsey (2000) found that the GVA battering subgroup, relative to other batterer subgroups, were least likely to successfully terminate from group treatment and were rated as more likely to engage in violence six months post treatment (poor treatment amenability in psychopathic populations), mirroring findings with male psychopaths measured with the PCL-R (Hare, 1991, 2003). Given the overlap between the two batterer typologies (instrumentally violent versus impulsively violent) and connections to the psychopathy literature, a conceptualization of a borderline psychopathic batterer is appropriate.

Impulsivity (a hallmark of the BPD diagnosis) has become a focal point for the study of BPD, and recent laboratory studies have begun to clarify the nature of impulsivity within this population. Stevenson, Meares, and Comerford (2003) found impulsivity to be the only facet of BPD, which is negatively correlated with age (in accordance with findings with male psychopaths; Harpur & Hare, 1994). Chapman, Leung, and Lynch (2008) examined the effect of emotional states on impulsivity on a passive avoidance learning (PAL) task among individuals with BPD. Similar to previous work with male primary psychopaths (Newman, 1987), high-BPD individuals committed a larger number of impulsive responses than low-BPD individuals. Although high-BPD participants reported difficulty in several domains of emotional regulation, laboratory findings suggested that negative emotional states did not potentiate impulsivity. Instead, among persons with BPD features, negative emotional states were found to facilitate performance on tasks that involve learning to avoid negative consequences.

Although BPD and psychopathy share a constellation of features including intense interpersonal relationships, impulsivity, anger, violence, and affective explosiveness, limited study of the co-occurrence of the two disorders has been conducted. However, some investigators have demonstrated that BPD may be associated with level of psychopathy (Cunliffe & Gacono, 2005; Newhill, Vaughn, & DeLisi, 2010). Consistent with past studies and theoretical constructs, Fossati et al. (2004) found that BPD and ASPD are linked to impulsivity and aggressiveness. Motoric impulsivity presented as the impulsivity component predictive of both ASPD and BPD symptoms; while emotional aggressiveness, on the other hand, was only predictive of BPD (relational or affective violence). Further, both physical and indirect aggression and oppositional behavior were predictive of ASPD symptoms. Fossati et al. (2005) assessed adult attachment, BPD, impulsivity, and aggressiveness from a dimensional perspective in a clinical population, and results suggested that adult attachment is involved in the regulation of the interaction between BPD, impulsivity, and aggressiveness. Insecure attachment emerged as the prominent risk factor for BPD symptomatology, since it is a significant predictor of aggressiveness and, to a lesser degree, impulsivity. Thus, although, psychopathy and ASPD are not synonymous terms, the findings are suggestive of a link between psychopathy and BPD, since BPD and ASPD appear to share genetic and environmental risk factors beyond those common to all four Cluster B personality disorders (Torgersen et al., 2008).

Similarities exist between the characteristics of the secondary psychopath and the BD subgroup described by Holtzworth-Munroe and Stuart (1994). This is also evidenced by similar histories of trauma and insecure attachment observed in literature with BD batterers, BPD, and secondary psychopathy (Blackburn et al., 2008; Holtzworth-Munroe & Stuart, 1994; Holtzworth-Munroe et al., 2000; Murphy & Vess, 2003; Poythress et al., 2010; Waltz et al., 2000). Similar findings have been reported in relation to affective processing in BD batters and secondary psychopathy (Babcock et al., 2008; Del Gaizo & Falkenbach, 2008). Further, GVA batterers have been found to evidence difficulty accurately recognizing angry, happy, surprised, and neutral expressions, similar to the deficits seen in primary psychopaths (Babcock et al., 2008; Del Gaizo & Falkenbach, 2008; Schweinle & Ickes, 2007). These findings provide preliminary evidence that GVA batterers and primary psychopaths may be highly similar, while a corresponding resemblance may exist between BD batters and secondary psychopaths.

Conclusions and Implications for Forensic Practice

In this chapter, we have explored the connections between three separate related dimensions: psychopathy, BPD, and IPV. Although rarely considered as comorbid constructs, all three have been studied within different contexts, etiologies, and conceptual frameworks by researchers and clinicians within their respective areas of psychology. However, an integration of the constructs has yet to be considered. Although significant links between subtypes of batterers and psychopathy have been identified, significant challenges remain to gain a full, comprehensive understanding of the construct of male-female violence within intimate relationships. During this review, we have identified significant overlap between psychopathy, IPV, and BPD, determined areas in need of further research, and developed a conceptualization of battering behavior that integrates the three different literatures in the hopes of a more comprehensive exploration of the nature of male-female violence, in general, and the conceptualization of the male batterer, in particular.

Many previous empirical studies have examined the relationship of BPD, ASPD, and psychopathy to aggression, impulsivity, etc., with nonclinical samples, college students, and minute sample sizes. While these samples are convenient and more readily available, the inferences drawn are inherently flawed, and generalization to other well-designed studies is not warranted. In addition, attempts to investigate psychopathy among domestic violence perpetrators has been done with significant limitations; most notably, the application of self-report measures of psychopathy (Holtzworth-Munroe et al., 2000). Given the elevated base rates of manipulative behavior, deceitfulness, and lying common in antisocial populations (particularly primary and secondary psychopathy), the use of self-report measures is highly questionable and ill advised. Thirdly, very few studies have integrated psychopathy (as measured by the PCL-R), BPD, and IPV, which has led to misleading conclusions since the constructs are likely to be mutually confounding variables. That is, in studies of incarcerated male offenders, a failure to consider their offense for domestic violence may lead to incorrect or misinformed conclusions concerning their presentation, since batterers are widely known to comprise a distinct subset within offender populations. Similar problems also exist within the IPV and personality disorder research literatures. Further, it is acknowledged that our review did not explore the related but less frequently occurring female-male, male-male, or female-female domestic violence perpetrators. Although these populations are worthy of study, as yet, they remain comparatively unstudied in an organized, empirical, and quantitative manner.

Courts are increasingly being called upon to provide rulings in cases related to domestic violence in general, and IPV in particular. Therefore, requests for the expertise of psychologists with specialized knowledge of domestic violence, IPV, violence risk, and forensic mental health (treatment amenability, assessment of juvenile offenders transferred to adult court, and death penalty mitigation) to inform legal decisions are more frequent. The construct of psychopathy is one of the most powerful predictors of continued criminal behavior and violence across a variety of samples and cultures (Hare, 1991, 2003) and, as a result, should play a prominent role in the assessment of all offenders, particularly batterers. Therefore, an actuarial assessment of BPD and psychopathy combined with collateral reports from the batterer's partner should be routinely obtained (Holtzworth-Munroe et al., 2000).

In their work with batterers and their spouses, Holtzworth-Munroe et al. (2003) found that when assessing attachment, perpetrators' reports of attachment were more useful than those of their spouses in distinguishing subtypes, while the partner's reports of attitudes toward violence were more accurate than that acknowledged by the batterer. This highlights problems with relying solely upon the often inaccurate report of only one partner and points to the importance of third-party record review (police reports, prior arrest history, victim statements, and mental health treatment records) in the assessment of this population. Secondly, it indicates the need for an assessment of deception in domestic violence evaluations. It behooves the clinician to assume that the batterer will minimize his violence as a function of the above personality dimensions in addition to being influenced by contextual variables inherent in the adjudication or incarceration process (secondary gain). Further, obtaining valid psychological test results is dependent upon the test-taker presenting an accurate symptom picture and putting forth adequate effort. Although estimates of base rates of malingering of psychiatric symptoms vary widely, one study found that 54.3% of criminal defendants referred for neuropsychological evaluation met criteria for probable or definite malingering of neurocognitive dysfunction (Ardolf, Denney, & Houston, 2006). The increasing involvement of mental health professionals in forensic settings has led to an explosion of malingering research and the development of numerous screening instruments and psychological tests to assess malingering of cognitive and psychiatric symptoms. Given the high base rates of malingering in forensic and correctional settings, an ethical evaluation of the batterer should incorporate specific measures of deception and/or malingering. Due to the negative connotations and far-reaching consequences associated with a diagnosis of malingering, malingering assessment must be thorough and accurate.

Responsible evaluation of psychopathy requires the use of the PCL-R (Hare, 2003), the gold standard for the assessment of psychopathy in adult populations. PCL-R administration and scoring entails an intensive review of the participant's medical, legal, and institutional files succeeded by a detailed semi-structured interview and rating of the individual's personality and antisocial behaviors on a three-point ordinal scale. Gacono (Chapter 13 this volume) commented that although categorical understandings of psychopathy are useful for research purposes, a dimensional perspective is more appropriate for clinical applications. Therefore, the important question in psychopathy assessment is not whether the individual is psychopathic or not, but rather, how closely he or she approximates the psychopathic prototype (PCL-R $\geq$ 30). That is, the level of psychopathy or PCL-R score is related to behavioral correlates at differing degrees of the syndrome identified in the literature. Secondly, given the high negative connotative association to the term "psychopath" and the fact that psychopathy is not a formally recognized diagnosis, it is suggested that the phrase "ASPD in the severe range" be used to reduce the possibility of bias.

Given the correlation between Cluster B diagnoses and psychopathy, Huchzermeier et al. (2007) recommend administering a PCL-R, specifically in forensic populations, when a Cluster B diagnosis has been given. For the evaluation of clients not otherwise involved in the criminal justice system, the use of non-forensic specific psychological testing (Minnesota Multiphasic Personality Inventory–2 [Butcher et al., 1992]; Personality Assessment Inventory–2 [Morey, 2007]; Wechsler Adult Intelligence Scales–Fourth Edition [Wechsler, 2009]) will aid in the determination of psychological functioning and dynamics while forensic assessment instruments and forensically relevant instruments will assist in specific questions to be addressed per the court (domestic violence measures, violence risk measures, etc.). Given the significant trauma histories observed in BPD, BD batterers, and secondary psychopathy, a formal assessment of the DSM-IV-TR criteria for PTSD is warranted via structured interview (i.e., Clinician-Administered PTSD Scale [Weathers, Blake, Schnurr, & Charney, 2004]) in addition to the assessment of trauma symptomatology with trauma-specific psychological testing (Detailed Assessment of Posttraumatic Stress [Briere, 2001] and Trauma Symptom Inventory–2 [Briere, 2011]). Accurate assessment is needed in order to address treatment and placement concerns.

Treatment programs currently make no attempt to match the offender to a specific treatment modality or approach (Cavanaugh & Gelles, 2005). However, the treatment of personality disordered offenders, separate from those low in psychopathology, may result in improved outcomes for the less pathological batterers (Mauricio & Lopez, 2009). Cognitive-behavioral and behavioral interventions have been suggested as the most successful treatment modality for those classified as GVA (Holtzworth-Munroe et al., 2000). Evaluation of therapeutic community programs and maximum-security therapeutic community samples reveal that recidivism for non-psychopaths decreased while the symptoms reflective of psychopathy and recidivism rates increased for those scoring greater than 30 on the PCL-R (psychopaths; Rice & Cormier, 1994; Rice, Harris & Cormier, 1992). Therefore, since it has been suggested that a subset of GVA batterers would meet the criteria for psychopathy (Holtzworth-Munroe et al., 2000; Huss & Langhinrichsen-Rohling, 2000), a comprehensive screening should be implemented to guard against problems inherent in attempting to treat psychopaths in a group format (very poor treatment amenability in group insight-oriented therapy). Murphy and Vess (2003) suggest this group could best be treated from a behavioral management standpoint, suggesting that some psychopaths learned to recognize that while their behavior may be egosyntonic, it does not serve their best interests in the long run. However, although secondary psychopaths have been found to display less clinician-rated disruptive behaviors and higher treatment motivation in a drug treatment program (Poythress et al., 2010), treating primary psychopaths, particularly in a group, insight-oriented format is not recommended. Further, the BPD symptoms would be best treated with Linehan's (1993) Dialectical Behavior Therapy (DBT) cognitive-behavioral approach to treatment of BPD. DBT has also been utilized to treat complex PTSD and should be incorporated into the treatment protocols of batterers with significant trauma histories. Finally, a substance abuse treatment component is also suggested due to the high base rates for substance dependence and abuse among IPV populations (Holtzworth-Munroe et al., 2000).

From a preventative perspective, programs for at-risk populations may be warranted in the juvenile population. Based on the positive correlation between violence in the family of origin and borderline and antisocial personality organization in batterers combined with the high base rates for the presence of children in the home during domestic violence events, secondary prevention and early intervention programs for at-risk children (child protective services, families receiving assistance at domestic violence shelters, and police response to domestic violence complaints) is warranted (Boyle et al., 2008). Research also supports the importance of interventions aimed toward juveniles identified as delinquent or diagnosed with conduct disorders to prevent future violence against intimate partners (Boyle et al., 2008). A thorough assessment of trauma exposure and symptomatology is of critical importance with this population since delinquent juveniles have been found to be at increased risk of experiencing high rates of abandonment, neglect, and physical and sexual abuse (Beyer, 2006; Garbarino, 1999; Widom, 1989). Further, trauma-exposed juveniles who are arrested at an early age are more likely to become chronic, repeat violent offenders (Woolard, 2009). Early intervention with traumatized conduct-disordered youth could be an important component for reducing recidivism in court-involved adolescents. Further, the juvenile justice system is often not equipped to adequately address the treatment needs and complex psychological symptoms that accompany early victimization.

Research supports the consideration of a relation between BPD and psychopathy as evidenced by concordance and overlap with the Holtzworth-Munroe and Stuart (1994) borderline batterer typology. While the suggested connection between these constructs remains preliminary, it is a promising area of future research with significant implications for the assessment, placement, and treatment of perpetrators of intimate violence within the community, legal, and correctional systems.

References

Ali, F., Amorim, I. S., & Chamorro-Premuzic, T. (2009). Empathy deficits and trait emotional intelligence in psychopathy and Machiavellianism. *Personality and Individual Differences, 47*, 758–762.

American Academy of Pediatrics, Committee on Child Abuse and Neglect. (1998). The role of the pediatrician in recognizing and intervening on behalf of abused women. *Pediatrics, 101*, 1091–1092.

American Psychiatric Association. (APA). (1968). *Diagnostic and statistical manual of mental disorders* (2nd ed.). Washington, DC: Author.

American Psychiatric Association. (APA). (1980). *Diagnostic and statistical manual of mental disorders* (3rd ed.). Washington, DC: Author.

American Psychiatric Association. (APA). (1987). *Diagnostic and statistical manual of mental disorders* (3rd ed., rev.). Washington, DC: Author.

American Psychiatric Association. (APA). (1994). *Diagnostic and statistical manual of mental disorders* (4th ed.). Washington, D.C.: Author.

American Psychiatric Association. (APA). (2000). *Diagnostic and statistical manual of mental disorders* (4th ed., text rev.). Washington, DC: Author.

American Psychological Association. (1996). *Violence and the family: Report of the American Psychological Association Presidential Task Force on violence and the family*. Washington, DC: Author.

Andrulonis, P. A. (1991). Disruptive behavior disorders in boys and the borderline personality disorder in men. *Annals of Clinical Psychiatry*, 3(1), 23–26 [Abstract].

Ardolf, B. R., Denney, R. L., & Houston, C. M. (2007). Base rates of negative response bias and malingered neurocognitive dysfunction among criminal defendants referred for neuropsychological evaluation. *The Clinical Neuropsychologist, 21*, 899–916.

Babcock, J. C., Green, C. E., & Webb, S. A. (2008). Decoding deficits of different types of batterers during presentation of facial affect slides. *Journal of Family Violence, 23*, 295–302. doi:10.1007/s10896-008-9151-1.

Beyer, M. (2006). Fifty delinquents in juvenile and adult court. *American Journal of Orthopsychiatry, 76*, 206–214.

Blackburn, R., Logan, C., Donnelly, J. P., & Renwick, S. J. D. (2008). Identifying psychopathic subtypes: Combining an empirical personality classification of offenders with the Psychopathy Checklist–Revised. *Journal of Personality Disorders, 22*(6), 604–622.

Blair, R. J. R., Mitchell, D. G. V., & Blair, K. S. (2005). *The psychopath: Emotion and the brain*. Malden, MA: Blackwell Publishing.

Boyle, D. J., O'Leary, K. D., Rosenbaum, A., & Hassett-Walker, C. (2008). Differentiating between generally and partner-only violent subgroups: Lifetime antisocial behavior, family of origin violence and impulsivity. *Journal of Family Violence, 23*, 47–55. doi:10.1007/s10896-007-9133-8.

Briere, J. (2001). *Detailed assessment of posttraumatic stress: Professional manual.* Odessa, FL: Psychological Assessment Resources.

Briere, J. (2011). *Trauma symptom inventory-2: Professional manual.* Lutz, FL: Psychological Assessment Resources.

Butcher, J. N., Williams, C. L., Graham, J. R., Archer, R. P., Tellegen, A., Ben-Porath, Y. S., & Kaemmer, B. (1992). *Minnesota Multiphasic Personality Inventory-Adolescent Version (MMPI-A): Manual for administration, scoring and interpretation.* Minneapolis, MN: University of Minnesota Press.

Campbell, J. C., Webster, D., Koziol-McLain, J., Block, C. B., Campbell, D., Curry, M. A., . . . Wilt, S. A. (2003). Assessing risk factors for intimate partner homicide. *NIJ Journal*, 250, 14–19.

Cavanaugh, M. M., & Gelles, R. J. (2005). The utility of male domestic violence offender typologies: New directs for research, policy and practice. *Journal of Interpersonal Violence, 20*(2), 155–166. doi:10.1177/0886260504268763.

Chapman, A. L., Leung, D. W., & Lynch, T. R. (2008). Impulsivity and emotion dysregulation in borderline personality disorder. *Journal of Personality Disorders, 22*(2), 148–164.

Charbrol, H., & Leichsenring, F. (2006). Borderline personality organization and psychopathic traits in nonclinical adolescents: Relationships of identity diffusion, primitive defense mechanisms and reality testing with callousness and impulsivity traits. *Bulletin of the Menninger Clinic, 70*, 160–170.

Cunliffe, T., & Gacono, C. (2005). A Rorschach investigation of incarcerated antisocial personality disordered female offenders. *International Journal of Offender Therapy and Comparative Criminology, 49*, 530–547.

Del Gaizo, A. L., & Falkenbach, D. M. (2008). Primary and secondary psychopathic-traits and their relationship to perception and experience of emotion. *Personality and Individual Differences, 45*, 206–212.

Domes, G., Czieschneck, D., Weidler, F., Berger, C., Fast, K., & Herpertz, S. C. (2008). Recognition of facial affect in borderline personality disorder. *Journal of Personality Disorders, 22*(2), 135–147. doi:10.1521/pedi.2008.22.2.135.

Domes, G., Schultz, L., & Herpertz, S. C. (2009). Emotional recognition in borderline personality disorder—a review of the literature. *Journal of Personality Disorders, 23*(1), 6–19.

Dutton, D. G. (2007). *The abusive personality: Violence and control in intimate relationships* (2nd ed.). New York: Guilford Press.

Dutton, D. G., & Golant, S. K. (1995). *The batterer: A psychological profile.* New York: Basic Books.

Dutton, D. G., & Painter, S. (1993). The battered women syndrome: Effects of severity and intermittence of abuse. *American Journal of Orthopsychiatry, 63* (4), 614–622.

Dutton, M. A. (1992). *Empowering and healing the battered woman.* New York: Springer.

Fantuzzo, J. W., Fusco, R. A., Mohr, W. K., & Perry, M. A. (2007). Domestic violence and children's presence: A population-based study of law enforcement surveillance of domestic violence. *Journal of Family Violence, 22*, 331–340.

Follingstad, D. R. (2003). Battered women syndrome in the courts. In A. M. Goldstein & I. B. Weiner (Eds.), *Handbook of psychology: Volume 11, forensic psychology* (pp. 485–507). Hoboken, NJ: John Wiley & Sons.

Fossati, A., Barratt, E. S., Carretta, E., Leonardi, B., Grazioli, F., & Maffei, C. (2004). Predicting borderline and antisocial personality disorder features in nonclinical subjects using measures of impulsivity and aggressiveness. *Psychiatry Research, 125*, 161–170. doi:10.1016/j.psychres.2003.12.001.

Fossati, A., Feeney, J. A., Carretta, I., Grazioli, F., Milesi, R., Leonardi, B., & Maffei, C. (2005). Modeling the relationships between adult attachment patterns and borderline personality disorder: The role of impulsivity and aggressiveness. *Journal of Social and Clinical Psychology, 24*(4), 520–537.

Garbarino, J. (1999). The effects of community violence on children. In L. Balter & C. S. Tamis- LaMonda (Eds.), *Child psychology: A handbook of contemporary issues* (pp. 412–428). Philadelphia, PA: Psychology Press.

Garcia-Moreno, C., Jansen, H. A., Ellsberg, M., Heise, L., & Watts, C. H. (2006). Prevalence of intimate partner violence: Findings from the WHO multi-country study on women's health and domestic violence. *Lancet, 368*, 1260–1269.

Gold, S. N. (2000). *Not trauma alone: Therapy for child abuse survivors in family and social context*. Philadelphia, PA: Taylor & Francis.

Golier, J., Yehuda, R., Brierer, L. M., Mitropoulou, V., New, A. S., Schmeidler, J., . . . Siever, L. J. (2003). The relationship of borderline personality disorder to posttraumatic stress disorder and traumatic events. *American Journal of Psychiatry, 160*(11), 2018–2024.

Gottman, J. M., Jacobson, N. S., Rushe, R., Shortt, J. W., Babcock, J., La Taillade, J. J., & Waltz, J. (1995). The relationship between heart rate reactivity, emotionally aggressive behavior, and general violence in batterers. *Journal of Family Psychology, 9*(3), 227–248.

Hare, R. D. (1980). A research scale for the assessment of psychopathy in criminal populations. *Personality and Individual Differences, 1*, 111–120.

Hare, R. D. (1991). *The Hare Psychopathy Checklist–Revised*. Toronto, Ontario, Canada: Multi-Health Systems.

Hare, R. D. (1998). *Without conscience: The disturbing world of psychopaths among us*. New York: Guilford Press.

Hare, R. D. (2003). *Manual for the revised psychopathy checklist* (2nd ed.). Toronto, Ontario, Canada: Multi-Health Systems.

Hare, R. D., & McPherson, L. M. (1984). Psychopathy and perceptual asymmetry during verbal dichotic listening. *Journal of Abnormal Psychology, 93*(2), 141–149.

Harenski, C. L, Harenski, K. A., Shane, M. S., & Kiehl, K. A. (2010) Aberrant neural processing of moral violations in criminal psychopaths. *Journal of Abnormal Psychology, 119*(4), 863–874.

Harpur, T. J., & Hare, R. D. (1994). The assessment of psychopathy as a function of age. *Journal of Abnormal Psychology, 103*, 604–609.

Herman, J. L., Perry, J. C., & van der Kolk, B. A. (1989). Childhood trauma in borderline personality disorder. *American Journal of Psychiatry, 146*, 490–495.

Herpertz, S. C., Werth, U., Lukas, G., Qunaibi, M., Schuerkens, A., Kunert, H. J., . . . Sass, H. (2001). Emotions in criminal offenders with psychopathy and borderline personality disorder. *Archives of General Psychiatry, 58*, 737–745.

Holtzworth-Munroe, A., & Hutchinson, G. (1993). Attributing negative intent to wife behavior: The attributions of maritally violent versus nonviolent men. *Journal of Abnormal Psychology, 102*(2), 206–211.

Holtzworth-Munroe, A., Meehan, J. C., Herron, K., Rehman, U., & Stuart, G. L. (2000). Testing the Holtzworth-Munroe and Stuart (1994) batterer typology. *Journal of Consulting and Clinical Psychology, 68*(6), 1000–1019. doi:10.1037// 0022-006X.68.6.1000.

Holtzworth-Munroe, A., Meehan, J. C., Herron, K., Rehman, U., & Stuart, G. L. (2003). Do subtypes of martially violent men continue to differ over time? *Journal of Consulting and Clinical Psychology, 71*, 728–740.

Holtzworth-Munroe, A., & Smutzler, N. (1996). Comparing the emotional reactions and behavioral intentions of violent and nonviolent husbands to aggressive, distressed, and other wife behaviors. *Violence and Victims, 1*, 319–339.

Holtzworth-Munroe, A., & Stuart, G. L. (1994). Typologies of male batterers: Three subtypes and the differences among them. *Psychological Bulletin, 116* (3), 476–497.

Hopwood, C. J., Newman, D. A., Donnellan, M. B., Markowitz, J. C., Grilo, C. M., Sanislow, C. A., . . . Morey, L. C. (2009). The stability of personality traits in individuals with borderline personality disorder. *Journal of Abnormal Psychology, 11*(4), 806–815.

Huchzermeier, C., Friedemann, G., Bruß, E., Godt, N., Kohler D., Hinrichs, G., & Aldenhoff, J. B. (2007). The relationship between DSM-IV Cluster B personality disorders and psychopathy according to Hare's criteria: Clarification and resolution of previous contradictions. *Behavioral Sciences and the Law, 25*, 901–911. doi:10.1002/bsl.722.

Huss, M. T., & Langhinrichsen-Rohling, J. (2000). The identification of the psychopathic batterer: Clinical, legal, and policy implications. *Aggression and Violent Behavior, 5*, 403–422.

Huss, M. T., & Langhinrichsen-Rohling, J. (2006). Assessing the generalization of psychopathy in a clinical sample of domestic violence perpetrators. *Law and Human Behavior, 30*, 571–586. doi:10/1007/s10979-006-9052-x.

Jacobson, N. S., & Gottman, J. M. (1998). *When men batter women: New insights into ending abusive relationships*. New York: Simon & Schuster.

Karpman, B. (1941). On the need for separating psychopathy into two distinct clinical types. *Journal of Criminology and Psychopathology, 3*, 112–137.

Kernberg, O. (1984). *Severe personality disorders: Psychotherapeutic strategies*. New Haven, CT: Yale University Press.

Koenigs, M., Kruepke, M., & Newman, J. P. (2010). Economic decision-making in psychopathy: A comparison with ventromedial prefrontal lesion patients. *Neuropsychologia, 48*(7), 2198–2204.

Langhinrichsen-Rohling, J., Huss, M. T., & Ramsey, S. (2000). The clinical utility of batterer typologies. *Journal of Family Violence, 15*(1), 37–53. doi:10.1023/A:1007597319826.

Leihener, F., Wagner, A., Haaf, B., Schmidt, C., Lieb, K., Stieglizt, R., & Bohus, M. (2003). Subtype differentiation of patients with borderline personality disorder using a circumplex mode of interpersonal behavior. *Journal of Nervous and Mental Disease, 191*(4), 284–254. doi:10.1097/00005053-200304000-00006.

Levine, D., Marziali, E., & Hood, J. (1997). Emotional processing in borderline personality disorder. *Journal of Nervous and Mental Disease, 185*(4), 240–264.

Levy, K. N. (2005). The implications of attachment theory and research for understanding borderline personality disorder. *Development and Psychopathology, 17*, 959–986.

Lewis, K. L., & Grenyer, B. F. (2009). Borderline personality disorder or complex posttraumatic stress disorder? An update on the controversy. *Harvard Review of Psychiatry, 17*(5), 322–328.

Linehan, M. M. (1993). *Cognitive-behavioral treatment of borderline personality disorder*. New York: Guilford Press.

Lynch, T. R., Rosenthal, M. Z., Kosson, D. S., Cheavens, J. S., Lejuez, C. W., & Blair, R. J. R. (2006). Heightened sensitivity to facial expressions of emotion in borderline personality disorder. *Emotion, 6*, 647–655. doi:10.1037/1528-3542.6.4.647.

Mauricio, A. M., & Lopez, F. G. (2009). A latent classification of batterers. *Violence and Victims, 24*(4), 419–438. doi:10.1891/0886-6708.4.4.419.

Millon, T., Simonsen, E., & Birket-Smith, M. (1998). Historical conceptions of psychopathy in the United States and Europe. In T. Millon, E. Simonsen, M. Birket-Smith, & R. D. Davis (Eds.), *Psychopathy: Antisocial, criminal, and violent behavior* (pp. 3–31). New York: Guilford Press.

Moore, T., Eisler, T., & Franchina, J. (2000). Causal attributions and affective responses to provocative female partner behavior by abusive and nonabusive males. *Journal of Family Violence, 15*(1), 69–80.

Morey, L. (1991). *Personality Assessment Inventory*. Lutz, FL: Psychological Assessment Resources.

Morey, L. (2007). *Personality Assessment Inventory* (2nd ed.). Lutz, FL: Psychological Assessment Resources.

Murphy, M., & Vess, J. (2003). Subtypes of psychopathy: Proposed differences between the narcissistic, borderline, sadistic and antisocial psychopaths. *Psychiatric Quarterly, 74*(1), 11–29.

National Center for Injury Prevention and Control. (2003). *Costs of Intimate Partner Violence Against Women in the United States*. Atlanta, GA: Centers for Disease Control and Prevention.

National Institute of Justice. (2007). *Intimate partner violence*. Retrieved from http://www.ojp.usdoj.gov/nij/topics/crime/intimate-partner-violence/welcome .htm .

Newhill, C. E., Vaughn, M. G., & DeLisi, M. (2010). Psychopathy scores reveal heterogeneity among patients with borderline personality disorder. *Journal of Forensic Psychiatry and Psychology, 21*, 202–220. doi:10.1080/147899409 03281157.

Newman, J. P. (1987). Reaction to punishment in extraverts and psychopaths: Implications for the impulsive behavior of disinhibited individuals. *Journal of Research in Personality, 21*, 464–480.

Poythress, N. G., Edans, J. F., Skeem, J. L., Lilienfeld, S. O., Douglas, K. S., Frick, P. J., . . . Wang, T. (2010). Identifying subtypes among offenders with antisocial personality disorder: A cluster-analytic study. *Journal of Abnormal Psychology, 119*(2), 389–400. doi:10.1037/a0018611.

Rice, M. E., & Cormier, C. A. (1994). Psychopaths: Is a therapeutic community therapeutic? *Therapeutic Communities, 15*(4), 283–299.

Rice M. E., Harris, G. T., & Cormier, C. A. (1992). An evaluation of a maximum security therapeutic community of psychopaths and other mentally disordered offenders. *Law and Human Behavior*, *16*(4), 399–412.

Rogers, R. (2006). The functional architecture of the frontal lobes: Implications for research and psychopathic offenders. In C. J. Patrick (Ed.), *Handbook of psychopathy*. New York: Guilford Press.

Roth, S., Newman, E., Pelcovitz, D., van der Kolk, B., & Mandel, F. S. (1997). Complex PTSD in victims exposed to sexual and physical abuse: Results from the DSM-IV field trial for posttraumatic stress disorder. *Journal of Traumatic Stress, 10*(4), 539–555.

Russell, B. L. (2010). *Battered woman syndrome as a legal defense: History, effectiveness and implications*. Jefferson, NC: McFarland & Company.

Ryan, K., & Shean, G. (2007). Patterns of interpersonal behaviors and borderline personality characteristics. *Personality and Individual Differences, 42*, 193–200. doi:10:1016/j.paid.2006.06.010.

Schweinle, W. E., & Ickes, W. (2007). Role of men's critical/rejecting overattribution bias, affect, and attentional disengagement in marital aggression. *Journal of Social and Clinical Psychology, 26*(2), 173–198.

Shah, P. S., & Shah, J. (2010). Maternal exposure to domestic violence and pregnancy and birth outcomes: A systematic review and meta-analyses. *Journal of Women's Health, 19*, 2017–2031.

Sieswerda, S., Arntz, A., Mertens, I., & Vertommen, S. (2007). Hypervigilance in patients with borderline personality disorder: Specificity, automaticity, and predictors. *Behavior Research and Therapy*, *45*(5), 1011–1024.

Skeem, J., Johansson, P., Andershed, H., Kerr, M., & Louden, J. E. (2007). Two subtypes of psychopathic violent offenders that parallel primary and secondary variants. *Journal of Abnormal Psychology, 16*(2), 395–409. doi:10.1037/ 0021-843X.116.2.395.

Skeem, J. L., Poythress, N. G., Edens, J. F., Lilienfeld, S. O., & Cale, E. M. (2003). Psychopathic personality or personalities? Exploring potential variants of psychopathy and their implications for risk assessment. *Aggression and Violent Behavior, 8*(5), 513–546.

Stevenson, J., Meares, R., & Comerford, A. (2003). Diminished impulsivity in older patients with borderline personality disorder. *American Journal of Psychiatry, 160*(1), 165–166.

Torgersen, S., Czajkowski, N., Jacobson K., Reichborn-Kjennerud, T., Roysamb, E., Neale, M. C., & Kendler, K. S. (2008). Dimensional representations of DSM-IV Cluster B personality disorders in a population-based sample of Norwegian twins: A multivariate study. *Psychological Medicine, 38*, 1617–1625.

Trull, T. J. (1995). Borderline personality disorder features in non-clinical young adults: 1. Identification and validation. *Psychological Assessment, 7*, 33–41.

Tweed R., & Dutton, D. G. (1998). A comparison of impulsive and instrumental subgroups of batterers. *Violence and Victims, 13*(3), 217–230.

U.S. Department of Justice, Bureau of Justice Statistics. (1995). *Intimate partner violence*. Washington, DC: Author.

U.S. Department of Justice, Bureau of Justice Statistics. (2009). *Profile of intimate partner violence cases in large urban counties*. Washington, DC: Author.

Violence Against Women Act, 18 U.S.C. § 2261 *et seq*. (1994).

Wagner, A. W., & Linehan, M. M. (1999). Facial expression recognition ability among women with borderline personality disorder: Implications for emotional regulation?*Journal of Personality Disorders, 13*(4), 329–344.

Walker, L. E. A. (1979). *The battered woman*. New York: Harper & Row.

Walker, L. E. A. (1994). Battering. In *Abused women and survivor therapy: A practical guide for the psychotherapist* (pp. 55–79). Washington, DC: American Psychological Association. doi:10.1037/10153-003.

Walker, L. E. A. (1999). Psychology and domestic violence around the world. *American Psychologist, 54*(1), 21–29.

Walker, L. E. A. (2000). *The battered woman syndrome* (2nd ed.). New York: Springer.

Walker, L. E. A. (2009). *The battered woman syndrome* (3rd ed.). New York: Springer.

Waltz, J., Babcock, J. C., Jacobson, N. S., & Gottman, J. M. (2000). Testing a typology of batterers. *Journal of Consulting and Clinical Psychology, 68*, 658–669.

Wechsler, D. (2009). *Wechsler Adult Intelligence Scales* (4th ed.). Minneapolis, MN: Pearson Assessments.

Weathers, F. W., Blake, D. D., Schnurr, P. P., & Charney, D. S. (2004). *Clinician-administered PTSD scale*. Los Angeles, CA: Western Psychological Services.

Widom, C. S. (1989). Does violence beget violence? A critical examination of the literature. *Psychological Bulletin, 106*, 3–28.

Woolard, J. (2009). *Adolescent development module 1: Toward developmentally appropriate practice: A juvenile court training curriculum*. Washington, DC: National Juvenile Defender Center.

CHAPTER NINETEEN

A Rorschach Understanding of Antisocial and Psychopathic Personalities*

Carl B. Gacono and J. Reid Meloy

Search for clinical knowledge of psychopathy and aggression generates questions of motivation and meaning that call for inquiry into the thought, organization, affective life, impulses, defensive operations, and object relations of psychopaths and other aggressive individuals (Gacono & Meloy, 1994). The PCL-R (1991, 2003) has catalyzed research over the past 20 years and has provided a reliable and valid method for classifying psychopathy. Our work examining the Rorschach as a dependent measure using the PCL-R (1991, 2003) as an independent classification offers a contribution to understanding psychopathy and aggression as a way to psychometrically "map" the intrapsychic life of these individuals.

Two points are essential for understanding the Rorschach's use in studying personality disorders. First, although personality disorders are currently coded as discrete categories (DSM-IV; APA, 1994), there is considerable overlap among them (e.g., Gunderson & Ronningstam, 2001;

---

*Portions of this chapter are reprinted and adapted from Gacono, Carl B., J. Reid Meloy, and Michael R. Bridges, "A Rorschach comparison of psychopaths, sexual homicide perpetrators, and nonviolent pedophiles: Where angels fear to tread," *Journal of Clinical Psychology* Volume 56, Issue 6, pages 757–777, June 2000.

Morey, 1988; Plakun, Muller, & Burkhardt, 1987). Paranoid and compulsive persons share similarities in cognitive style; narcissistic and paranoid individuals evidence grandiosity; and hysteric and narcissistic people share a need for attention. This overlap must be considered when predicting Rorschach differences between groups. For example, Gacono, Meloy, and Bridges (2000, 2008) predicted and found similar frequencies of Rorschach reflection responses among sexual homicide perpetrators, psychopaths, and pedophiles. Rather than viewing reflections responses as a diagnosis (category, psychopathy), the authors conceptualized them as measuring a personality trait (dimensional, self-focus, or narcissism). This finding was consistent with theory, as each of these groups is thought to be narcissistic and/or self-absorbed.

Secondly, each personality disorder contains some amount of heterogeneity; that is, each contains potentially identifiable subgroups. This heterogeneity is most evident when examining extremes within a given category, such as an ASPD patient with a concurrent avoidant personality disorder, contrasted with an ASPD patient with a narcissistic personality disorder. Consequently, additional *independent* measures are necessary when studying personality disorders. Without a doubt, psychopathy is the ancillary construct most relevant to studying antisocial personality disorder.

Psychopathy is not synonymous with antisocial personality disorder. Antisocial personality disorder (ASPD; DSM-IV; APA, 1994) evolved from a social deviancy model (Robins, 1966) and the term sociopathy (DSM; APA, 1952). Appearing in the first DSM (APA, 1952), sociopathy included a variety of conditions such as sexual deviation, alcoholism, and "dyssocial" and "antisocial" reactions. While only the antisocial reaction was similar to psychopathy, the replacement of "Sociopathy" with ASPD in DSM-II (APA, 1968) and the increased focus on behavioral criteria would widen the gap between ASPD and psychopathy.

Psychopathy, although its generic roots extend back several centuries (Meloy, 1988), emerged as a discrete character type from Cleckley's (1976) traditional psychiatric conceptualization that included a combination of personality traits and behaviors (two-factor model; see Table 19.1). From a DSM-IV perspective, psychopathy can be understood as a disorder comprised of selected behavioral and affective features of several Cluster B syndromes, including narcissistic, histrionic, and borderline personality disorders (Gacono, Nieberding, Owen, Rubel, & Bodholdt, 2001). In DSM-V, it will likely stand as one of five personality *dimensions*.

Several caveats spring from psychopathy's two-factor structure versus the single factor associated with ASPD (Gacono, Loving, & Bodholdt,

Table 19.1 Diagnostic Criteria for Antisocial Personality Disorder and Psychopathy

DSM-IV Antisocial Personality Disorder

A. At least 3 of the following since age 15:
   1. Arrestable Acts
   2. Lies
   3. Impulsive
   4. Fights & Assaults
   5. Reckless
   6. Irresponsible
   7. Lacks remorse
B. Current age at least 18
C. Conduct Disorder, onset before 15
D. Antisocial behavior not exclusively during Schizophrenia or Manic Episode.

Psychopathic Traits and Behaviors (Hare, 1980; Hare et al., 1990)

1) *Glibness/Superficial Charm
2) *Grandiose Sense of Self Worth
3) Need for Stimulation/Proneness to Boredom
4) *Pathological Lying
5) *Conning/Manipulative
6) *Lack of Remorse or Guilt
7) *Shallow Affect
8) *Callous/Lack of Empathy
9) Parasitic Lifestyle
10) Poor Behavioral Controls
11) Promiscuous Sexual Behavior
12) Early Behavioral Problems
13) Lack of Realistic, Long-term Goals
14) Impulsivity
15) Irresponsibility
16) *Failure to Accept Responsibility for Own Actions
17) Many Short-term Marital Relationships
18) Juvenile Delinquency
19) Revocation of Conditional Release
20) Criminal Versatility

*PCL-R Factor.

2001). First, whereas one can arrive at the ASPD diagnosis by a virtually unlimited number of criteria combinations, so that vastly different individuals are included in this single diagnosis, psychopathy constitutes a more homogeneous syndrome. As a result, base rates for ASPD and psychopathy are significantly different. While ASPD community rates are estimated at 5.8% of males and 1.2% of females, forensic populations in maximum-security settings will typically have rates of 50% to 80%. Psychopaths will comprise only 15% to 25% of the same forensic population. Finally, in terms of predictive validity, psychopathy assessment has important clinical and forensic implications (Gacono & Bodholdt, 2001; Gacono, Loving, Evans, & Jumes, 2002). High PCL or PCL-R scores have been associated with a higher frequency and wider variety of offenses committed (Hare, 2003); higher frequency of violent offenses (Hare, 2003); higher reoffense rates (Hare, 2003); poor treatment response (Ogloff, Wong, & Greenwood, 1990; Rice, Harris, & Cormier, 1992); and more serious and persistent institutional misbehavior (Gacono, Meloy, Sheppard, Speth, & Roske, 1995; Gacono, Meloy, Speth, & Roske, 1997; Heilbrun et al., 1998). The ASPD diagnosis is not associated with these same outcomes (Lyon & Ogloff, 2000).

Equally important for understanding the role of psychopathy in studying ASPD is the fact that it can be conceptualized both in dimensional terms (i.e., along a continuum of severity) and categorical terms (i.e., as a taxon or discrete syndrome). When concerned with how psychopaths nomothetically differ from non-psychopaths, the researcher is using psychopathy as a category or taxon and should use the appropriate PCL-R cutoff (as a group, PCL-R $\geq$ 30 for psychopathy; see Gacono, Loving & Bodholdt, 2001; Gacono & Gacono, 2006; and/or Gacono, Chapter 13 of this volume for caveats for understanding the psychopathy/Rorschach literature). Our independent research measures have mostly included both a DSM diagnosis (character disorder or ASPD) and a determination of psychopathy (PCL-R $\geq$ 30).

The Rorschach and Psychopathy

Robert Lindner (1943) pioneered the use of the Rorschach with antisocial and psychopathic personalities. Along with others, such as Samuel Beck, he believed that the Rorschach would aid in understanding these disorders. Lindner did not espouse a "sign" approach for interpreting psychopathic Rorschachs. Rather, he hypothesized that at least one psychopathic group produced Rorschach protocols, characterized by superficiality, avoidance, explosiveness, incompleteness, and egocentricity (Lindner, 1943). The state of psychology in the 1940s and 1950s did not allow Lindner to fully test his beliefs. His untimely death in 1956 prevented him from seeing the measurement of his clinical observations (Gacono & Meloy, 1992).

Since the 1950s, advances in psychological assessment, technology, and theory have made a more sound approach to the Rorschach study of antisocial and psychopathic personalities possible. First, the development of the Psychopathy Checklists has provided a reliable and valid method for distinguishing psychopaths from non-psychopaths—creating clearly delineated psychopathic groups (PCL-R & PCL:YV scores of $\geq$ 30; Forth, Kosson, & Hare, 2003; Hare, 2003). Secondly, Rorschach advances, such as the development of the Comprehensive System (Exner, 1986, 2003) and systems for scoring defenses (Cooper & Arnow, 1986; Lerner & Lerner, 1980), object relations (Kwawer, 1980), and aggression (Gacono & Meloy, 1994; Gacono, Gacono, Meloy, & Baity, 2005, 2008), have allowed researchers to study dimensional aspects of psychopathy. Thirdly, advances in computer technology have provided the means for analyzing these data. Finally, developments in ego psychology and object relations theory have provided a map for the disorder's underlying intrapsychic and interpersonal personality organization (Meloy, 1988, 2001; Gacono & Meloy, 1994). In particular, Kernberg's (1975) conceptualization of antisocial personality disorder proper as a detached, pathological, and aggressive variant of narcissistic personality disorder organized at a borderline level of personality has formed the theoretical basis of our empirical work (Gacono, 1988, 1990; Gacono & Meloy, 1994; Gacono, Gacono, & Evans, 2008; Meloy, 1988).

Utilizing these advances, along with several colleagues, we conducted a series of studies exploring the antisocial, aggressive, and psychopathic personalities (Bannatyne, Gacono, & Greene, 1999; Bridges, Wilson, & Gacono, 1998; Cunliffe & Gacono, 2005, 2008; Gacono, 1988, 1990; Gacono, Meloy, & Heaven, 1990; Gacono & Meloy, 1991, 1992; Meloy & Gacono, 1992; Meloy, Kenney, Gacono, 1994; Smith, Gacono, & Kaufman, 1997; Weber, Meloy, & Gacono, 1992). Summarized in *The Rorschach Assessment of Aggressive and Psychopathic Personalities* (Gacono & Meloy, 1994), this body of work considered developmental issues, gender, sexual deviation, and concurrent Axis I psychopathology in studying the antisocial spectrum. We turn to a summary of that work now.

Comparative Rorschach Findings

In our Rorschach studies, we sought to answer several questions (Gacono & Meloy, 1994, 1997a; Meloy & Gacono, 1998):

1) Would the Rorschach empirically validate Kernberg's (1975) psychoanalytic constructs associated with psychopathy? Kernberg hypothesized that the

psychopath was a detached, aggressive variant of narcissistic personality disorder organized at a borderline level of personality functioning.

2) Given the behavioral differences among offenders, as noted by Lindner (1943), could the Rorschach discriminate among ASPD groups by psychopathy level?
3) Could the Rorschach also discriminate between ASPD and other Cluster B personality disorders?
4) Regarding the first three questions, would there be gender differences for ASPD and psychopathy and could the Rorschach measure them? Would these differences be consistent with our observations that while the male psychopath fit the Kernberg description of malignant narcissism, the female psychopath would more follow a pattern of malignant hysteria (Gacono & Meloy, 1994)?
5) Would the Rorschach be sensitive in measuring the theoretical differences between offenders with histories of sexual deviance (nonviolent pedophiles), those with violence histories and absent sexual deviance (psychopaths), and those with both a sexual deviant and violent history (sexual homicide perpetrators)?

What follows is a summary of our Rorschach findings related to borderline personality organization, pathological narcissism, attachment deficits and aggression. Additionally, our studies comparing male and female ASPD and psychopathic subjects to other personality disorders and those comparing various sexually deviant subjects are summarized.

Borderline Personality Organization

Gacono (1988, 1990) compared the object relations and defensive operations of 14 psychopathic male antisocial personality disordered subjects (P-ASPD; PCL-R $\geq$ 30) and 19 non-psychopathic male antisocial personality disordered subjects (NP-ASPD; PCL-R $<$ 30). While specific defenses failed to differentiate between the groups, this study did find that ASPDs relied on devaluation, primitive denial (Lerner & Lerner, 1980), splitting, projective identification, and devaluation (Cooper & Arnow, 1986). The presence of these primitive defenses, along with the notable absence of neurotic-level defenses and idealization (Lerner & Lerner, 1980), combined with a plethora of borderline object relations (Kwawer, 1980), supported the hypothesis of a common borderline level of functioning for male ASPD subjects (see also Gacono & Meloy, 1992, 1997a).

Surprisingly, Kwawer's (1980) primitive (borderline) modes of interpersonal relating were produced in a proportionally greater amount by the P-ASPD group. Finding significant between-group differences was surprising, since the majority of these ASPD subjects produced PCL-R scores of less than 20. A randomly obtained prison population would be more diverse (psychopathy level), including non-ASPD subjects and low scoring PCL-R subjects. When studying offenders, expanding the range of psychopathy scores (including non-ASPD subjects) allows for the creation of more dissimilar groups (psychopaths, PCL-R > 30, and low scorers, PCL-R < 20) thereby increasing the probability of obtaining significant between group differences.

We also found similar patterns in female ASPD subjects (N = 38; Gacono & Meloy, 1994). They produced Kwawer's (1980) primitive modes of relating with the following frequencies: Malignant Internal Processes (40%), Violent Symbiosis (37%), Narcissistic Mirroring (26%), Boundary Disturbance (26%), Symbiotic Merging (24%), and Separation-Division (16%). Comparatively, male ASPD psychopaths (N = 33) tended to produce greater frequencies of Narcissistic Mirroring (45%), Boundary Disturbance (39%), and less Malignant Internal Processes (15%). Despite these differences, 79% of the female subjects produced at least one of the Kwawer indices, supporting the notion that ASPD females and ASPD and psychopathic males share a borderline level of personality.

Pathological Narcissism

Gacono, Meloy, and Heaven (1990) examined the relationship between psychopathy, pathological narcissism (Harpur, Hare, & Hakstian, 1989; Kernberg, 1975), and hysteria (Guze, 1976; Guze, Woodruff, & Clayton, 1971). Twenty-one male P-ASPD subjects were compared to 21 male NP-ASPD subjects on the relevant Comprehensive System (1986) measures of Pair (2), Reflection (rF, Fr), Personal Responses (PER), and Egocentricity Index (3r+(2)/R). The Impressionistic Response[1] (IMP; Gacono, 1988, 1990) was used as a measure of hysterical mechanisms (Shapiro, 1965). The mean number of Pair and Impressionistic Responses did not significantly differ between the two Antisocial groups. P-ASPD males did exhibit a significantly greater mean number of Reflections ($p < .05$) and Personal Responses ($p < .05$). The Egocentricity Index scores were also significantly different ($p < .01$) with P-ASPDs producing much larger ratios (M = .46, SD = .18), along with increased Reflections and Personal Responses, than the NP-ASPD males (M = .30, SD = .14). These differences supported the hypothesis of greater pathological narcissism among the P-ASPDs. The low Egocentricity Ratios produced by the NP-ASPDs suggested "a reduced effectiveness for bolstering grandiosity and warding off the disruptive effects of internal (anxiety) and external (incarceration) threat. The internal regulating mechanisms of the severe psychopath are less tenuous" (Gacono et al., 1990, pp. 275–276).

In two related adolescent studies, Loving and Russell (2000) found that psychopaths were more likely to have produced a Reflection Response than non-psychopaths; and, while Smith, Gacono, and Kaufman (1997) failed to replicate a significant difference for *PERs* and *Reflections*, they did discover that a significantly greater number of psychopathic conduct disordered youths (P-CDs) produced Egocentricity Ratios greater than .54 (P-CDs = 42%; NP-CDs = 9%). It should be noted that the Smith et al. (1997) sample contained predominately high Lambda subjects, which can impact the production of certain Rorschach variables such as Reflections (Bannatyne et al., 1999).

Cunliffe and Gacono (2005) compared female P-ASPDs (N = 27; PCL-R Mean = 32.69 [SD = 2.81]) with female NP-ASPDs (N = 18; mean PCL-R = 20.73 [SD = 3.38]). Proportions or frequencies of Reflection responses or PER responses did not differentiate between the groups. Significantly more female psychopaths produced 11 or more Pairs (P = 22%; NP = 5%) and elevated Egocentricity Ratios ($\geq$ .44) without a Reflection response (P-ASPD = 18.5%; NP-ASPD = 11%). P-ASPD females also produced a greater number of $\geq$ 2 MORs (P-ASPD = 37%, NP-ASPD = 22%), more protocols with > 1 Vista response (P-ASPD = 41%; NP-ASPD = 17%) and fewer FD responses [P-ASPD = 4, (15%); NP-ASPD = 5, 28%).

Concerning the ASPD females' production of elevated Egocentricity Ratios without a Reflection response Cunliffe and Gacono (2005) wrote:

> While high Egocentricity Ratios suggest an inordinate self-focus, high ratios without Reflection indicate a sense of displeasure in doing so (Weiner, 1998). Male psychopaths look at themselves exalting in self-admiration and grandiosity (high Reflections, high Egocentricity Ratio). In contrast, our female psychopaths appear to experience distress while engaging in the same process. Individuals with a pattern of no Reflections, high Egocentricity Ratios, and Vistas possess a situation-specific type of self-criticism not related to a true sense of remorse or guilt (Weiner, 1998). This pattern suggests chronic self-criticism and shame. Rather than remorse or guilt, the self-critical, unhappy, and dissatisfied presentation of the female psychopath may be viewed as an insidious negative self-image arising from longstanding frustration over unmet needs for attention and admiration. (539–540)

The frequency of and lack of difference for Reflection responses between the two female groups, coupled with a reduced frequency or reflections compared to male psychopaths, argues against the presence of the grandiose self-structure found in male psychopaths operating in the female psychopath (Gacono et al., 1990; Loving & Russell, 2000; Smith et al., 1997; Young, Justice, Erdberg, & Gacono, 2000).[2] Unlike the male psychopath, the female struggles with a hysterical need for attention and admiration in order to mediate the effects of chronic dissatisfaction and self-criticism. Compared to the independent, detached interpersonal style noted in male psychopaths, the female's increased need for attention and interpersonal contact renders her more dependent on the views and approval of others, resulting in a chronic, negative sense of self (Cunliffe & Gacono, 2005).

Attachment Deficits

Emotional detachment is another characteristic of psychopathy (Cleckley, 1976; Meloy, 1988). Through a comparison of Rorschach Comprehensive System variables of Texture (T, TF, FT), Diffuse Shading (Y, YF, FY), Vista (V, VF, FV), D scores (D) and Adjusted D scores (Adj-D) between male P-ASPDs (N = 21) and male NP-ASPDs (N = 21), Gacono and Meloy (1991) investigated Rorschach manifestations of attachment and anxiety. Vista frequencies did not differ significantly between the groups. As expected, Texture ($p < .01$) and Shading ($p < .001$) frequencies were significantly less in the P-ASPDs than the NP-ASPDs. Additionally, though not reaching significance, important trends were noted with D and AdjD, with NP-ASPDs results suggesting more situational and chronic levels of stress, and P-ASPDs indicating that their chaotic lifestyles were more ego-syntonic.

The somewhat surprising presence of Vista in male psychopaths was interpreted as representing failed grandiosity (Fr, rF, r) and perhaps self-pity (Gacono & Meloy, 1991), rather than representing guilt and remorse. Lower amounts of Diffuse Shading in the P-ASPDs, coupled with the normal D and AdjD score patterns suggested an absence of anxiety and helplessness, while the lower Egocentricity Ratios for NP-ASPDs pointed to the tenuous nature or vulnerability of the grandiose self structure in non-psychopaths. A troubling implication of these findings was that the psychopaths' particular form of character pathology seemed to be effective in regulating their self-structure and narcissism, thus reducing anxiety and conflict about their antisocial behavior.

The virtual absence of T in male psychopaths (5% versus 60%–82% nonpatient adults) empirically supported the hypothesis of profound emotional detachment (Gacono & Meloy, 1997b), consistent with a growing body of research on the dismissive attachment style of the antisocial personality (Meloy, 2002; Meloy & Shiva, 2007). Three related studies with adolescents added to these findings. Weber, Meloy, and Gacono (1992) found that CD inpatient subjects evidenced less attachment capacity (71%, T = 0), were less anxious (48%, Y = 0), and showed less interest in others (33%, Pure H = 0) than dysthymic and nonpatient adolescents. Smith et al. (1997) found similar results with P-CD adolescents (P-CD; 79%, T = 0; 75%, Y = 0). Further, Loving and Russell (2000) found that T differentiated among CD groups with psychopaths producing the lowest frequency.

Related studies found that ASPD females were less likely to produce *T* (T ≥ 1 = 29%) than Borderline females (T ≥ 1 = 100%; Berg, Gacono, Meloy, & Peaslee, 1994) and P-ASPD males evidenced less attachment capacity (*T*) and experienced less anxiety (*Y*) than NP-ASPD males, Narcissistic (NPD) or Borderline Personality Disordered males (BPD) (Gacono, Meloy, & Berg, 1992). When differentiated based on their level of psychopathy, ASPD women produced the following distribution of T: P-ASPD, T = 0 (56%), T = 1 (30%), T ≥ 2 (5%); and NP-ASPDs, 78% T = 0, 17% T = 1, and 6% ≥ 2 (P-ASPD, M = .75; NP-ASPD, M = .28). P-ASPD females also produced significantly more part object T responses (T with Ad or Hd content) and a significantly higher number of Fd responses (83% of 6 Fd responses were spoiled; Gacono & Meloy, 1991).

The female psychopaths also produced 36 COP responses compared to 19 responses for the non-psychopaths. Forty-eight percent of the psychopaths produced ≥ 2 COP compared to 22% of the non-psychopaths. COPs for the psychopaths tended to be spoiled (poor form quality; P; 27 [75%]; NP; 11 [58%]). Significantly fewer psychopaths (22%) scored in the high range of interpersonal relatedness (NP-ASPD = 44%; Perry & Viglione, 1991).

In summary, regardless of gender or concurrent Axis I pathology, there was significant evidence of attachment deficits in CD and ASPD subjects, as they rarely produce Texture responses (*T* = 0 found in 88% of CD children, 86% of CD adolescents, 71% of ASPD females, and 91% of psychopathic males; Gacono & Meloy, 1994). The pattern of Texture responses in the ASPD psychopathic women were of note since they were bimodally distributed (T = 0 and T > 1). Findings with Y, the CS variable associated with helplessness, were equivocal, but consistent with acting out as a defense against anxiety.

Aggression

Aggression plays a crucial role in the development and functioning of conduct and antisocial personality disorder and has been identified as a discriminating variable between the psychopathic and narcissistic disorders (Kernberg, 1975; Meloy, 1988). Based on their observations, Gacono (1988) and Heaven (1988) realized the limitations of the Exner (1986) Aggressive Movement response (AG) for capturing the range and intensity of aggressive drive derivatives produced by ASPD subjects on the Rorschach. Interestingly, and counter to expectations, CD and ASPD samples uniformly produce less AG than nonpatients (Gacono, 1997; Gacono et al., 2005; Smith et al., 1997), strongly suggesting the Aggressive Movement variable is not a reliable measure of aggressive behavior in these populations. Although initially speculated about the presence of active censoring of AG in ASPD subjects, we have come to believe that the ego-syntonic nature of the aggressive impulse and a pattern of acting out aggression for ASPDs contribute to its absence on the Rorschach (Gacono et al., 2005, 2008), since it does not need to be symbolized as a contained tension state.

Despite the paucity of AG responses in ASPD records, other types of aggressive imagery were present. This additional imagery led to the development (Gacono, 1988, 1990, 1997) and refinement (Gacono & Meloy, 1994; Meloy & Gacono, 1992) of five additional scoring categories: Aggressive Content (AgC), Aggressive Past (AgPast), Aggressive Potential (AgPot), Aggressive Vulnerability (AgV), and Sado-Masochism (SM) (Gacono, Bannatyne-Gacono, Meloy, & Baity, 2005; Gacono, Gacono, Meloy, & Baity, 2008). In Meloy and Gacono (1992), these experimental aggression scores, were compared between P-APSDs (N = 22) and NP-ASPDs (N = 21), with psychopaths producing greater frequencies of SM. Huprich, Gacono, Schnieder, and Bridges (2004) found that sexual homicide perpetrators produced higher frequencies of AgPot and SM and less AgPast than nonviolent pedophiles (SM = 24%, 3% respectively). Female ASPD subjects (N = 38) tend to produce similar mean and frequencies for AG, AgC, AgPast, and AgPot as male subjects (Gacono & Meloy, 1994). While essential for understanding the psychology of aggressive patients, these scores warranted and received further study (Gacono et al., 2005, 2008). AgC, AgPast, AgPot, and SM have been incorporated into the ROR-SCAN Version 6 Rorschach Interpretive Scoring System (Caracena, 2002) and, due to its robustness in subsequent reliability and incremental validity studies, AgC has been adopted into the R-PAS system (Katko, Meyer, Mihura, & Bombel, 2010).

Comparison to Cluster B Personality Disorders

Could the Rorschach elucidate the nuances that differentiate similar personality disordered groups? In order to test this hypothesis, Gacono,

Meloy, and Berg (1992) compared male psychopathic (P-ASPD) and nonpsychopathic ASPD subjects with male Narcissistic (N = 18) and Borderline (N = 18) outpatient personality disordered subjects.

Important differences and similarities emerged among these Cluster B groups. While both P-ASPDs (N = 22) and NPDs were highly narcissistic (elevated Fr + rF responses & EgoC), NPDs were more anxious (Y, YF, FY), evidenced greater attachment capacity (Sum T), and produced fewer borderline object relations (Kwawer, 1980) and damaged content scores (MOR, AgPast). BPDs were less narcissistic than P-ASPDs and NPDs, and showed equal numbers of borderline object relations scores with P-ASPD subjects. BPD individuals were more anxious, produced more unsublimated aggressive (AG) and libidinal (Sx) material, and evidenced greater potential for attachment (T) than P-ASPDs. NP-ASPDs showed less borderline functioning than P-ASPDs or BPDs, were less narcissistic than NPD and P-ASPDs, produced less evidence of attachment capacity than the outpatient groups (though more than P-ASPDs), and were similar to BPDs in their proneness to anxiety. Consistent with Lerner's (1991) schema, the NPDs and BPDs also produced more idealization responses than the ASPDs. This difference was consistent with the outpatient subjects' capacity for forming pseudo-sublimatory channels (evident in their interpersonal attachments and consistent work career).

In comparing ASPD females (N = 38) with BPD females (N = 32), Berg, Gacono, Meloy, and Peaslee (1994) found, "both groups [to be] significantly psychopathologic when affect states, object relations, and perceptual accuracy are measured. The damage, dysphoria, and anxiety of both groups is only distinguished by the borderline females' capacity to bond (T) and a greater amount of affect (CF > BPD), positive treatment indicators that also portend a tumultuous tie to the psychotherapist. Object relations will be pre-oedipal in both groups, but much more apparent in the Borderline female. Symbiotic rather than autistic developmental themes are likely (Mahler, Pine & Bergman, 1975). Both groups will be characterologically rigid, self-absorbed, and likely to express a narcissistic sense of entitlement: the Borderline females' wish to be taken care of, the Antisocial female's wish to take" (Berg et al., 1994, pp. 18–19). While differences emerged in the females, none were as striking as those when comparing any of the groups to psychopathic antisocial personality disordered males.

Sexual Deviance

Studies of sexual offenders have found that psychopathy and sexual deviance contribute to most of the variance in reoffense rates (Quinsey,

Harris, Rice, & Cormier, 1998; Rice, Harris, & Quinsey, 1990; Rice, Quinsey, & Harris, 1991; Rice & Harris, 1997). Through several studies we sought to determine the extent to which the Rorschach would aid in understanding the psychodynamics of these individuals.

In a preliminary study, we compared a small samples of *nonsexually* offending, violent psychopaths (N = 23) and sexual homicide perpetrators (SHP, N = 18) to determine if the Rorschach would discriminate based on the presence or absence of a sexual deviation (Meloy, Gacono, & Kenney, 1994). While both groups shared similar levels of narcissism (Fr + rF) and anger (S, extended Ag scores), the SHP were found to evidence a bimodal distribution of Texture, more severe cognitive slippage, greater levels of obsessional thought (FM), and a greater interest in others (H & COP). These Rorschach differences suggested five core psychodynamic characteristics for sexual homicide perpetrator (Gacono & Meloy, 1994): chronic anger, entitlement and grandiosity, abnormal bonding, borderline or psychotic reality testing, and formal thought disorder. We later added a sixth, obsessional thought.

In a subsequent study, we found similar degrees of pathological self-focus (Fr + rF $\geq$ 1) and abnormal bonding (T = 0 or T > 1) between mixed pedophiles and other offenders. Consistent with sexual offending theories, Rorschach variables related to anxiety, painful introspection, distorted view of others, characterological anger, and primitive dependency were produced significantly more often by the pedophile (Bridges, Wilson, & Gacono, 1998).

Next, we compared violent psychopaths (N = 32), sexual homicide perpetrators (N = 38), and nonviolent pedophiles (N = 39; Gacono, Meloy, & Bridges, 2000, 2008) in order to ascertain whether the Rorschach would discriminate among them and aid in understanding their internal worlds. The rigidity and simplicity of the pedophiles' cognitive style (high Lambda) facilitates repetition of their deviant sexual behavior. Their high Lambdas support their belief that others or situational factors are to be blamed for their behaviors (Marshall, 1997). High levels of dysphonic affect (V, DEPI) and primitive need states (FM, Fd, T) drive their sexual acting out (Pithers, 1999). While interest in others (H) is suggested, their perceptions are based more on imagination than reality (H < [Hd] + Hd + [Hd]) and are contaminated by formal thought disorder (WSum6), borderline reality testing (X – %), and pathological narcissism (Rf, PER, EgoC). The pedophile feels entitled to gratify his sexualized desires for human connection through the part-object (Hd) of a child. A preponderance of cartoon, science-fiction, and fairy-tale figures produced by pedophiles may reflect a narcissistic identification with children and characters associated with childhood (Bridges et al., 1998).

Pedophiles are distinguished from the nonsexually offending psychopaths by introversiveness and a tendency toward dysphoric rumination. The latter group is characterized by a conflict-free, remorseless dynamic state—which contributes to the absence of violence in pedophiles and its presence in psychopaths. Pedophiles are, however, significantly more characterologically angry (S) than the other two groups. Their anger may be caused by inadequacy, less antisocial avenues for acting out, and the pedophiles' introversive inability to gratify their needs.

Around 50% of each group produced reflection responses. Additionally, pedophiles were found to be susceptible to negative affect or a damaged sense of self (V > 0, Y > 1, m > 1, or MOR > 1) in the context of their failed narcissistic defenses (Bridges et al., 1998). At a preconscious level, nonpsychopathic pedophiles are aware that their grandiosity is a sham. Feelings of damage and ineptness contribute to their difficulties developing and maintaining intimate adult relationships.

Psychopaths are the least internally troubled of the three groups (less FM, T, Fd, V, S). They are less interested in others (T = 0, H), have little expectation of interpersonal cooperation (COP), and evidence less oral dependency (Huprich, Gacono, Schneider, & Bridges, 2004). They use people in a self-serving manner (Fr + rF) and are unfettered by remorse, guilt (V), or sustained reflection (FD; introversion). Like the pedophiles, psychopaths' perceptual and cognitive distortions (WSum6, X – %) add to their poor interpersonal judgment, and when combined with self-centeredness (Fr + rF), may contribute to a sense of entitlement. Psychopaths avoid genuine affective involvement, and although many might be characterized as moving toward gregariousness and sensation-seeking (one-third are extratensive), pleasure in others versus pleasure in self is experienced when others serve as an adequate mirror.

For our sexual homicide perpetrators, of whom two-thirds are likely psychopaths (PCL-R scores are available for only a portion of these subjects), their sexual deviance appears to emotionally disrupt their narcissistic equilibrium. Unlike nonsexually offending psychopaths, sexual homicide perpetrators are internally troubled. Their high levels of internal dysphoria, yearning, obsession, and dependency needs (V, T, FM, Fd) push behaviors, while other defenses operate to distance or disengage from the environment (Lambda, R). External stimuli that resonate with their sexual deviance are appealing and literally irresistible. The intensity of this push-pull effect is exacerbated by less than optimal controls (D = −1.45, AdjD = −.58; R). High levels of ideational noise, or obsessional thought (FM), absent in the simple psychopathy, are ubiquitous for the sexual homicide perpetrator. Like pedophiles, they are interested and perhaps drawn to others; however, their attraction is colored by the self-centeredness (Fr + rF) and severe perceptual (X − %) and cognitive distortions (WSum6) which characterize all three groups. Isolation is also a common defense utilized by these groups (SHP = 31.6% > .33; PED = 28.2% > .33; P = 25% > .33).

Nonsexually offending psychopaths tend to produce T-less protocols. In contrast, within the sexual homicide group, there was little relationship between psychopathy level and T. Psychopathic sexual homicide perpetrators were just as likely to produce one or more Ts as their non-psychopathic counterparts. The texture response has been interpreted as a measure of interpersonal closeness or affectional relatedness (Exner, 1986; Klopfer, 1938; Schachtel, 1966). Meloy (1988) also theorized that T was a somatosensory analog for early skin contact with the mother. Schachtel (1966) believed that in some cases texture responses indicated ambivalence surrounding attachment and perhaps a fear of unpleasant skin contact ("negated T" response; Gacono & Meloy, 1991, 1994). Texture may actually constitute an intrapsychic irritant that, when coupled with sexual deviance and a propensity for violence, "energizes" the interpersonal behavior of these sexual murderers. Their affectional hunger surfaces in the need for direct skin contact with the victim; subsequently, ritualistic elements in the crime scene provide a canvass for the expression of their internal and stable psychosexual fantasies (the crime "signature," which may link one victim with another in a case of serial sexual murder; Meloy, 2000).

The Forensic Rorschach Database

In the process of conducting research, we began to accumulate a forensic Rorschach database that was first summarized in *The Rorschach Assessment of Aggressive and Psychopathic Personalities* (Gacono & Meloy, 1994). Since publication of our 1994 text, the forensic Rorschach database has grown. As presented in the *Handbook of Forensic Rorschach Assessment* (Gacono, Evans, Kaser-Boyd, & Gacono, 2008) it is now comprised of 2,059 criminal and civil Rorschach protocols. The database is made up of three primary groups: Group 1 includes 528 subjects, mostly nonrandomly, selected from various outpatient, jail, prison, hospital, and forensic hospital populations throughout the United States who met criteria for conduct disorder (CD) in children and adolescents or ASPD in adults. Seventy-two CD children (mostly solitary aggressive type); 179 CD adolescents; 69 ASPD females; 108 ASPD males; and 100 ASPD male schizophrenics (mostly paranoid schizophrenics; see Gacono, Gacono, & Evans, 2008) are included in this data set. Approximately 80 of the adult ASPD subjects obtained PCL-R scores ≥ 30.

Group 2 (N = 304) includes 38 sexual homicide perpetrators (SHP), 39 nonviolent pedophiles (PED; see Gacono, Meloy, & Bridges, 2008), and 90 paranoid schizophrenic, 59 schizoaffective, 40 bipolar, and 38 undifferentiated schizophrenic CONREP (conditional release) patients (see Bannatyne et al., 1999; L. Gacono & C. Gacono, 2008; Nieberding et al., 2003). The nonviolent PEDs were selected from a larger sample (N = 60; Bridges et al., 1998) of subjects whose IQs were ≥ 80, and absent psychosis, organicity, diagnosed depression, or ASPD or psychopathy (Gacono, Meloy, & Bridges, 2000; Huprich et al., 2004). All SHP subjects had to commit at least one sexual homicide and none were psychotic at the time of testing (Gacono et al., 2000). The majority met the criteria for ASPD, and approximately two-thirds scored ≥ 30 on the PCL-R (see Gacono et al., 2000; Huprich et al., 2004).

Group 3 subjects (N = 1,227) includes three samples: forensic psychiatric inpatients (N = 259; Young, Erdberg, & Justice, 2008), child custody litigants (N = 728; Singer, Hoppe, Lee, Olesen, & Walters, 2008), and, disruptive professionals (N = 240; Stacey, Graham, & Athey, 2008).

All 2,059 of these forensic Rorschach protocols were administered using the Exner Comprehensive System guidelines (Exner 1991, 1993), with each protocol being scored for Comprehensive System variables multiple times by one of several researchers. In all cases, the interjudge reliability (% agreement and kappa coefficients) of Rorschach scoring was satisfactory (see Gacono et al., 2000; Gacono et al., 2008). Consistent with Exner's (1990) new Comprehensive System data sets, protocols with fewer than 14 responses (Exner, 1988) were excluded from all the samples (except the SHP sample).[3]

This group data (N = 2,059 subjects; see Gacono et al., 2008) has influenced, at times surprised, at other times confirmed our thinking regarding the antisocial personality spectrum. It forms the backbone of the applied, empirical, and theoretical use of the Rorschach. We concur with Martin Orne, MD, PhD, who stated, "In God we trust: all others must have data." It should be noted that many of the CD and ASPD subjects were nonrandomly selected. Consequently, while their Rorschach patterns are consistent with theory, they may not represent all antisocial or psychopathic individuals. Some of our comparison studies utilized the same or expanded subject groups, increasing the possibility of type 1 errors. Some subjects were gathered by different researchers in different locations at different times, raising the probability of confounding variables. Some differences in scoring decisions did exist despite the good to excellent interrater reliability statistics for all samples. Also, when utilized, the statistical analyses were simple and straightforward, but did not utilize effect sizes, odds ratios, and confidence intervals. Despite these potential limitations, this forensic Rorschach database is the largest of its kind, and provides a wealth of data (most published in peer-reviewed scientific journals and professional books) for psychologists who utilize the Rorschach in forensic settings. Most importantly, all the variables within this database (included in the R-PAS) will still provide accurate interpretive data since the mean R across virtually all the samples is within the optimal range.

Conclusions

Our findings have supported Lindner's (1943) hypotheses concerning the usefulness of the Rorschach for understanding the antisocial and psychopathic syndromes and provided modest empirical support for Kernberg's formulations of antisocial personality disorder proper (Kernberg, 1984). Patterns emerged from the group data that were able to differentiate between male P-ASPDs from NP-ASPDs. The group Rorschach data suggested that central to the disorders studied—CD, ASPD, sexually deviant and psychopathic—are difficulties dealing with complexity, a propensity to being easily overwhelmed, defensive grandiosity, affect avoidance, severe interpersonal difficulties, and highly idiosyncratic and disturbed cognitive function.

An important discovery is that male and female psychopathy differs in two separate but related dimensions: interpersonal relatedness and self-perception (Cunliffe & Gacono, 2005). Consistent with Gacono and Meloy's (1994) conceptualization of malignant hysteria, the female psychopath's pronounced needs for "relatedness" and adulation from others form the cornerstone of her character. Her interpersonal connections are focused on attempts to overcome her negative self-concept and dysphoric feelings that have arisen from her perceived alienation from those around her. The very dysphoria and feelings of anger and irritation she seeks to escape have their roots in unmet needs for affiliation and desire to be "entertained" by others. The female psychopath lacks the grandiose self-structure and detachment noted in males, and although she may lack the male psychopaths' desire for domination and humiliation of others, she displays a corresponding incapacity for empathy and perspective taking. The females also exhibit similar problems empathizing with others when compared to males, but rather than a detached, devaluation of their victims, they display a clear disregard for the welfare of others despite an outward appearance of interrelatedness (Cunliffe & Gacono, 2005).

The frequency of and lack of difference for Reflection responses between the female psychopathic and non-psychopaths argues against the presence of the grandiose self-structure operating in male psychopaths (Gacono et al., 1990; Loving & Russell, 2000; Smith et al., 1997; Young et al., 2000). Their increased COP, V, Fd, and T combined with larger proportions of spoiled COP and part T responses highlight the tenuousness of a pattern reliant on others to regulate self-esteem and mood. Compared to the independent, detached interpersonal style noted in male psychopaths, the female's increased superficial need for attention and interpersonal contact renders her more dependent on the views and approval of others, resulting in a chronic, negative sense of self (Cunliffe & Gacono, 2005).

The psychological operations of sexual homicide perpetrators, psychopaths, and nonviolent pedophiles show similarities and differences.[4] Two of the groups are sexually deviant (PED, SHP), and two are criminally inclined (SHP, P). The construct of pathological narcissism helps to understand the antisocial behavior, abnormal bonding, and cognitive problems of all the subjects, but between each group there are notable differences. Sexual deviance adds to the mix, and although we did not measure sexual arousal directly, it appears to further disorganize all psychopathologies, with the most sexually aggressive and dangerous group being the sexual homicide perpetrators (Aggrawal, 2009, 2011; Schlesinger, 2004).

Our findings are also consistent with recent theories relating disturbed attachment styles to sexual offending and psychopathy (Fonagy et al., 1997; Marshall, 1997). The psychopath corresponds to Bowlby's "affectionless" style in that the individuals capacity for attachment has been so disrupted that any basic capacity for bonding and empathy have been obliterated ($T = 0$, $H < 2$), while the pedophiles appear more "anxious/ambivalent" or "preoccupied" ($T > 1$, Fd, Y, V, m). Some, but not all, of the sexual homicide perpetrators seem to experience high levels of cognitive slippage, poor reality testing, and dyscontrol in the context of interpersonal relationships (WSum6, X – %, M–). This pattern corresponds to the "disorganize/disoriented" attachment style (which is etiologically based in trauma).

Our findings expand and clarify the differences between the nonsexually offending psychopaths and sexual homicide perpetrators. Nonsexually offending psychopaths are not interested in others, lack attachment capacity, lack the channeled sexual arousal to extreme violence, and are not aggressively motivated by dysphoria, obsession, or affectional hunger. Pedophiles display the sexual deviance integral to their offenses, but lack the emotional detachment noted in the psychopaths and evidence better controls than the sexual homicide perpetrators.

A careful evaluation of the Rorschach and psychopathy literature also provides caveats for interpreting divergent findings as well as conducting future CD and ASPD research (Gacono, Loving, & Bodholdt, 2001; Gacono, Chapter 13 of this volume). Several of these are:

1) CD and ASPD are comprised of heterogeneous groups of individuals. Whenever possible, comparative studies that treat psychopathy as a taxon must include psychopathy as an independent measure (evaluated with either the PCL-R, a "recommended" modified version of the PCL-R for adolescents, or the PCL:YV) and use the accepted cutoff scores (Gacono & Gacono, 2006).
2) Studies need to control or discuss the limitations imposed by such variables as gender, sexual deviance, concurrent Axis I functional psychosis, age, IQ, testing setting, and legal status. These factors can also influence the production of certain Rorschach variables.
3) The influence of R (number of responses) must always be considered in Rorschach research (Meyer, 1992). With particular reference to psychopathic and antisocial personalities, with certain sex offender groups, increased *R* is predicted (Bridges et al., 1998; Gacono et al., 2000). While *R* is always important related to constellations and certain variables, its interpretation is relative for others. As we expect a greater likelihood of a variable occurring when *R* is elevated, in studies where *R* is low and a low base rate variable is high (*Fr* or *T*) the interpretation that the presence of the variable represents a characterological marker of the disorder is strengthened. For example, in a group with a mean *R* of 14, the mean *Fr* of .50 (frequency of 50% producing at least one) provides striking evidence of self focus as a predominant trait of this group. Likewise, the absence of a variable in a high *R* sample similarly adds weight to its interpretation. The new R-PAS system optimizes R through more controlled administration of the test to address this problem.
4) Response style must be considered when discussing the generalizability of findings across studies (Bannatyne et al., 1999).

Exner (1995) has clearly demonstrated that response style—i.e., Extratensive, Ambitent, and Introversive styles—as well as R and high Lambda can significantly impact the production of certain Rorschach variables. For example, in a high Lambda psychopathic ASPD group (PCL-R $\geq$ 30) with low mean IQs, a paucity of reflection responses should never be attributed with certainty to "failed replication" of previous findings with other ASPD groups. High Lambda and low IQ can both constrict the production of certain Rorschach variables. On the other hand, an elevation of Reflection responses in this same "constricted" group would impressively strengthen the weight of these findings. Other factors such as the presence of Schizophrenia can impact the manifestation of traits; Schizophrenic psychopathic ASPDs are not expected to produce as many Reflection responses as psychopathic ASPDs without psychosis (Gacono & Meloy, 1994).

The Rorschach demonstrates a capacity for assessing subtle, highly nuanced differences in self-functions, object relations, and capacity for attachment between seemingly similar, but distinct, personality disorder manifestations. While sign approaches and making "a diagnosis" based solely on the Rorschach are likely never to be fruitful endeavors, the Rorschach data allow us to assess crucial dimensional aspects of the antisocial and psychopathic spectrums (Gacono, Loving, & Bodholdt, 2001; Gacono et al., 2002; Gacono & Meloy, 2009). As such, the Rorschach's capacity to do so can significantly add to dimensionally based psychological assessment in both clinical and forensic settings.

Notes

1. The *Impressionistic Response* (IMP; Gacono 1988, 1990; Gacono, Meloy, & Heaven, 1990), identifies responses stimulated by color that contain abstract concepts or events (Gacono et al., 1990). It is coded by scoring achromatic (including shading) or chromatic color and an *Abstraction* (AB). *IMP* responses may be "sensitive indicator[s] of the degree to which certain patients organized at a borderline level split off affect into rapid and diffuse symbolization" (Gacono et al., 1992, p. 45).

2. Female offenders have been found to be four times as likely to produce a Reflection response (related to self-focus) when compared to nonpatient females (Gacono & Meloy, 1994). They produce fewer Reflections than male psychopaths. Interestingly, adolescent males were found to produce more animal than human Reflection responses and females produced Reflections involving more scenes, mirrors, and trees (Ames, Metraux, & Walker, 1959).

3. In the SHP sample, two low-response protocols were deemed valid (low Lambda, elevated Blends with ≤ 12 responses) and kept in the sample (both psychopaths). One psychopathic response style involves a reduction in *R* without other constriction. The psychopaths grandiosity is reflected in an attempt to produce "perfect" *W* responses for all 10 cards (Gacono, 1997); or, in a paranoid fashion, increased *W*s results from the need to maintain imaginary control over all perceptual aspects of the blot. This characterological constriction can result in a valid < 14 response protocol (caution in interpreting the constellations; Gacono, 1997; Gacono et al., 1990).

4. While these *group* differences are clinically useful and consistent with the literature on sexual deviance and psychopathy in accurately portraying the major personality constructs and traits associated which each of the groups (Marshall,

1997; Gacono & Meloy, 1994) and therefore describe the *typical* group member, we are not suggesting that the emergent Rorschach profiles distinguish *all* psychopaths, pedophiles or sexual homicide perpetrators. Each individual case will be different.

References

Aggrawal, A. (2009). *Forensic and medico-legal aspects of sexual crimes and unusual sexual practices*. New York: CRC Press.

Aggrawal, A. (2011). *Necrophilia: Forensic and medico-legal aspects*. New York: CRC Press.

American Psychiatric Association. (APA). (1952). *Diagnostic and statistical manual of mental disorders*. Washington, DC: Author.

American Psychiatric Association. (APA). (1968). *Diagnostic and statistical manual of mental disorders* (2nd ed.). Washington, DC: Author.

American Psychiatric Association. (APA). (1994). *Diagnostic and statistical manual of mental disorders* (4th ed.). Washington, DC: Author.

Ames, L., Metraux, R., & Walker, R. (1959). *Adolescent Rorschach Responses*. New York: Hoeber.

Bannatyne, L. A., Gacono, C. B., & Greene, R. (1999). Differential patterns of responding among three groups of chronic psychotic forensic outpatients. *Journal of Clinical Psychology, 55*(12), 1553–1565.

Berg, J., Gacono, C., Meloy, J., & Peaslee, D. (1994). A Rorschach comparison of borderline and antisocial females. Unpublished manuscript.

Bodholdt, R., Richards, H., & Gacono, C. B. (2000). Assessing psychopathy in adults: The Psychopathy Checklists, Revised and Screening Version. In C. B. Gacono (Ed.), *The clinical and forensic assessment of psychopathy: A practitioner's guide* (pp. 55–86). Mahwah, NJ: Lawrence Erlbaum Associates.

Bridges, M., Wilson, J., & Gacono, C. B. (1998). A Rorschach investigation of defensiveness, self-perception, interpersonal relations, and affective states in incarcerated pedophiles. *Journal of Personality Assessment, 70*(2), 365–385.

Caracena, P. F. (2002). *ROR-SCAN Version 6 Rorschach Interpretive System*. Laredo, TX: ROR-SCAN.

Cleckley, H. (1976). *The mask of sanity* (5th ed.). St. Louis, MO: Mosby. (Original work published 1941).

Cooper, S., & Arnow, D. (1986). An object relations view of the borderline defenses: A Rorschach analysis. In M. Kissen (Ed.), *Assessing object relations phenomena* (pp. 143–171). Madison, CT: International Universities Press.

Cunliffe, T., & Gacono, C. B. (2005). A Rorschach investigation of psychopathy and hysteria in incarcerated antisocial personality disordered female offenders. *International Journal of Offender Therapy and Comparative Criminology, 49*(5), 530–546.

Cunliffe, T., & Gacono, C. B. (2008). A Rorschach understanding of antisocial and psychopathic women. In C. B. Gacono, F. B. Evans, L. A. Gacono, &

N. Kaser-Boyd (Eds.), *The handbook of forensic Rorschach psychology* (pp. 361–378). Mahwah, NJ: Lawrence Erlbaum Associates.

Ephraim, D., Occupati, R., Riquelme, J., & Gonzales, E. (1993). Gender, age and socioeconomic differences in Rorschach thematic content scales. *Rorschachiana, 18*, 68–81.

Exner, J. E. (1986). *The Rorschach: A Comprehensive System, Vol. I: Basic foundations* (2nd ed.). New York: John Wiley & Sons.

Exner, J. E. (1988). *COP* [Alumni newsletter]. Asheville, NC: Rorschach Workshops.

Exner, J. (1991). *A Rorschach workbook for the Comprehensive System* (3rd ed.). Asheville, NC: Rorschach Workshops.

Exner, J. (1993). *The Rorschach: A Comprehensive System, Vol. I: Basic Foundations* (3rd ed.). New York: John Wiley & Sons.

Exner, J. (1995). *A Rorschach workbook for the Comprehensive System* (4th ed.). Asheville, NC: Rorschach Workshops.

Exner, J. E. (2000). *A primer for Rorschach interpretation*. Asheville, NC: Rorschach Workshops.

Exner, J. E. (2003). *The Rorschach: A Comprehensive System* (4th ed.). Hoboken, NJ: John Wiley & Sons.

Fonagy, P., Target, M., Steele, M., et al (1997) Morality, disruptive behavior, borderline personality disorder, crime, and their relationship to security of attachment. In L. Atkinson & K. J. Zucker (Eds.), *Attachment and psychopathology* (pp. 233– 274). New York: Guilford Press.

Forth, A. E., Kosson, D. S., & Hare, R. D. (2003). *The Hare Psychopathy Checklist: Youth Version*. Toronto, Ontario, Canada: Multi-Health Systems.

Gacono, C. (1988). *A Rorschach analysis of object relations and defensive structure and their relationship to narcissism and psychopathy in a group of antisocial offenders* (Unpublished doctoral dissertation). United States International University, San Diego, CA.

Gacono, C. (1990). An empirical study of object relations and defensive operations in antisocial personality. *Journal of Personality Assessment, 54*, 589–600.

Gacono, C. B. (1997). Is the Rorschach Aggressive Movement Response enough? *British Journal of Projective Psychology, 42*(2), 5–11.

Gacono, C. B., & Bodholt, R. (2001). The role of the Psychopathy Checklist–Revised (PCL-R) in risk assessment. *Journal of Threat Assessment, 1*(4), 65–79.

Gacono, C. B., Evans, B., Kaser-Boyd, N., & Gacono, L. A. (2008). *The handbook of forensic Rorschach assessment*. Mahwah, NJ: Lawrence Erlbaum Associates.

Gacono, C. B., & Gacono, L. A. (2006). Some caveats for evaluating the research on psychopathy. *The Correctional Psychologist, 38*(2), 7–9.

Gacono, C. B., Gacono, L. A., & Evans, B. F. (2008). The Rorschach and antisocial personality. In C. B. Gacono, F. B. Evans, L. A. Gacono, & N. Kaser-Boyd (Eds.), *The handbook of forensic Rorschach assessment* (pp. 323–360). Mahwah, NJ: Lawrence Erlbaum Associates.

Gacono, C. B., Bannatyne-Gacono, L. A., Meloy, J. R., & Baity, M. R. (2005). The Rorschach extended Aggression Scores. *Rorschachiana, 27*, 164–190.

Gacono, C. B., Gacono, L. A., Meloy, J. R., & Baity, M. R. (2008). The Rorschach assessment of aggression: The Rorschach Extended Aggression Scores. In C. B. Gacono, F. B. Evans, L. A. Gacono, & N. Kaser-Boyd (Eds.), *The handbook of forensic Rorschach assessment* (pp. 543–560). Mahwah, NJ: Lawrence Erlbaum Associates.

Gacono, C. B., Loving, J. L., & Bodholdt, R. (2001). The Rorschach and psychopathy: Toward a more accurate understanding of the research findings. *Journal of Personality Assessment, 77*(1), 16–38.

Gacono, C. B., Loving, J. L., Evans, F. B., & Jumes, M. (2002). The Rorschach in forensic practice. *Journal of Forensic Psychology Practice, 2*(3), 33–53.

Gacono, C. B., & Meloy, J. R. (1991). A Rorschach investigation of attachment and anxiety in antisocial personality. *Journal of Nervous and Mental Disease, 179*, 546–552.

Gacono, C. B., & Meloy, J. R. (1992). The Rorschach and the DSM-III-R antisocial personality: A tribute to Robert Lindner. *Journal of Clinical Psychology, 48*(3), 393–405.

Gacono, C. B., & Meloy, J. R. (1994). *The Rorschach assessment of aggressive and psychopathic Personalities*. Hillsdale, NJ: Lawrence Erlbaum Associates.

Gacono, C. B., & Meloy, J. R. (1997a). Rorschach research and the psychodiagnosis of antisocial and psychopathic personalities. *Rorschachiana*, 22, 130–145.

Gacono, C. B., & Meloy, J. R. (1997b). Attachment deficits in antisocial and psychopathic personalities. *British Journal of Projective Psychology, 42*(2), 47–55.

Gacono, C. B., & Meloy, J. R. (2002). Assessing the psychopathic personality (2nd edition). In J. Butcher (Ed.), *Clinical personality assessment* (pp. 361–375). New York: Oxford University Press.

Gacono, C. B., & Meloy, J. R. (2009). Assessing antisocial and psychopathic personalities. In J. Butcher (Ed.), *The Oxford handbook of personality assessment*. Oxford, UK: Oxford University Press.

Gacono, C. B., Meloy, J. R., & Berg, J. (1992). Object relations, defensive operations, and affective states in narcissistic, borderline, and antisocial personality. *Journal of Personality Assessment, 59*, 32–49.

Gacono, C. B., Meloy, J. R., & Bridges, M. (2000). A Rorschach comparison of psychopaths, sexual homicide perpetrators, and nonviolent pedophiles: Where angels fear to tread. *Journal of Clinical Psychology, 56*(6), 757–777.

Gacono, C. B., Meloy, J. R., & Bridges, M. (2008). A Rorschach understanding of psychopaths, sexual homicide perpetrators, and nonviolent pedophiles. In C. B. Gacono, F. B. Evans, L. A. Gacono, & N. Kaser-Boyd (Eds.), *The handbook of forensic Rorschach assessment* (pp. 379–402). Mahwah, NJ: Lawrence Erlbaum Associates.

Gacono, C. B., Meloy, J. R., & Heaven, T. (1990). A Rorschach investigation of narcissism and hysteria in antisocial personality disorder. *Journal of Personality Assessment, 55*, 270–279.

Gacono, C. B., Meloy, J. R., Sheppard, K., Speth, E., & Roske, A. (1995). A clinical investigation of malingering and psychopathy in hospitalized insanity acquittees. *Bulletin of American Academy of Psychiatry and the Law*, 23(3), 387–397.

Gacono, C. B., Meloy, J. R., Speth, E., & Roske, A. (1997). Above the law: Escapes from a maximum security forensic hospital and psychopathy. *American Academy of Psychiatry and the Law, 25*(4), 1–4.

Gacono, C. B., Nieberding, R., Owen, A., Rubel, J., & Bodholdt, R. (2001). Treating juvenile and adult offenders with conduct-disorder, antisocial, and psychopathic personalities. In J. Ashford, B. Sales, & W. Reid (Eds.), *Treating adult and juvenile offenders with special needs* (pp. 99–130). Washington, DC: American Psychological Association.

Gacono, L. A., & Gacono, C. B. (2008). Some considerations in assessing outpatient forensic psychiatric patients. In C. B. Gacono, F. B. Evans, L. A. Gacono, & N. Kaser-Boyd (Eds.), *The handbook of forensic Rorschach assessment* (pp. 421–444). Mahwah, NJ: Lawrence Erlbaum Associates.

Gunderson, J. G., & Ronningstam, E. (2001) Differentiating narcissistic and antisocial personality disorders. *Journal of Personality Disorders, 15*, 103–109.

Guze, S. (1976). *Criminality and psychiatric disorders*. New York: Oxford University Press.

Guze, S., Woodruff, R., & Clayton, P. (1971). Hysteria and antisocial behavior: Further evidence of an association. *American Journal of Psychiatry, 127*, 957–960.

Hare, R. (2003). *Manual for the revised Psychopathy Checklist* (2nd ed.). Toronto, Ontario, Canada: Multi Health Systems.

Harpur, T., Hare, R., & Hakstian, R. (1989). Two-factor conceptualization of psychopathy: Construct validity and assessment implications. *Psychological Assessment: A Journal of Consulting and Clinical Psychology, 1*, 6–17.

Heaven, T. (1988). Relationship between Hare's Psychopathy Checklist and selected Exner Rorschach variables in an inmate population (Unpublished doctoral dissertation). United States International University, San Diego, CA.

Heilbrun, K., Hart, S. D., Hare, R. D., Gustafson, D., Nunez, C., & White, A. J. (1998). Inpatient and post-discharge aggression in mentally disordered offenders: The role of psychopathy. *Journal of Interpersonal Violence, 13*, 514–527.

Huprich, S. K., Gacono, C. B., Schnieder, R. B., & Bridges, M. R. (2004). Rorschach oral dependency in psychopaths, sexual homicide perpetrators, and nonviolent pedophiles. *Behavioral Sciences and the Law, 22*, 345–356.

Katko, N., Meyer, G., Mihura, J., & Bombel, G. (2010). A principal components analysis of Rorschach aggression and hostility variables. *Journal of Personality Assessment, 92*, 594–598.

Kernberg, O. (1975). *Borderline conditions and pathological narcissism*. New York: Jason Aronson.

Kernberg, O. (1984). *Severe personality disorders*. New Haven, CT: Yale University Press.

Klopfer, B. (1938). The shading responses. *Rorschach Research Exchange, 2*, 76–79.

Kwawer, J. (1980). Primitive interpersonal modes, borderline phenomena and Rorschach content. In J. Kwawer, A. Sugarman, P. Lerner, & H. Lerner (Eds.), *Borderline phenomena and the Rorschach test* (pp. 89–109). New York: International Universities Press.

Lerner, P. (1991). *Psychoanalytic theory and the Rorschach*. Hillsdale, NJ: Analytic Press.

Lerner, P., & Lerner, H. (1980). Rorschach assessment of primitive defenses in borderline personality structure. In J. Kwawer, A. Sugarman, P. Lerner, & H. Lerner (Eds.), *Borderline phenomena and the Rorschach test* (pp. 257–274). New York: International Universities Press.

Lindner, R. (1943, July). The Rorschach test and the diagnosis of psychopathic personality. *Journal of Criminal Psychopathology*, 69–93.

Loving, J. L., & Russell, W. (2000). Selected Rorschach variables of psychopathic juvenile offenders. *Journal of Personality Assessment, 75*(1), 126–142.

Lyon, D. R., & Ogloff, J. R. (2000). Legal and ethical issues in psychopathy assessment. In C. B. Gacono (Ed.), *The clinical and forensic assessment of psychopathy: A practitioner's guide* (pp. 139–174). Mahwah, NJ: Lawrence Erlbaum Associates.

Mahler, M., Pine, F., & Bergman, A. (1975). *The psychoanalytic birth of the human infant*. New York: Basic Books; Mahwah, NJ: Lawrence Erlbaum Associates.

Marshall, W. L. (1997). Pedophilia: Psychopathology and theory. In D. R. Laws & W. O'Donohue (Eds.), *Sexual deviance: Theory, assessment, and, treatment* (pp. 152–174). New York: Guilford Press.

Meloy, J. R. (1988). *The psychopathic mind: Origins, dynamics, and treatment*. Northvale, NJ: Jason Aronson.

Meloy, J. R. (2000). The nature and dynamics of sexual homicide: An integrative review. *Aggression and Violent Behavior, 5*, 1–22.

Meloy, J. R. (2001). *The mark of Cain: Psychoanalytic insight and the psychopath*. Mahwah, NJ: Analytic Press.

Meloy, J. R. (2002). Pathologies of attachment, violence, and criminality. In A. Goldstein (Ed.), *Comprehensive handbook of psychology, Volume 11: Forensic psychology*. New York: Wiley.

Meloy, J. R., & Gacono, C. B. (1992). The aggressive response and the Rorschach. *Journal of Clinical Psychology 48*(1), 104–114.

Meloy, J. R., & Gacono, C. B. (1998). The internal world of the psychopath: A Rorschach investigation. In T. Millon, E. Simonsen, M. Birket-Smith, & R. D. Davis (Eds.), *Psychopathy: Antisocial, criminal, and violent behaviors* (pp. 95–109). New York: Guilford Press.

Meloy, J. R., Gacono, C. B., & Kenney, L. (1994). A Rorschach investigation of sexual homicide. *Journal of Personality Assessment, 62*, 58–67.

Meloy, J. R. & Shiva, A. (2007). A psychoanalytic view of the psychopath. In A. Felthous & H. Sass (Eds.), *International handbook on psychopathic disorders and the law* (pp. 335–346). New York: Wiley.

Meyer, G. J. (1992). Response frequency problems in the Rorschach: Clinical and research implications with suggestions for the future. *Journal of Personality Assessment, 58*, 231–244.

Morey, L. C. (1988). Personality disorders in DSM-III and DSM-III-R: Convergence, coverage, and internal consistency. *American Journal of Psychiatry, 145*, 573–577.

Nieberding, R., Gacono, C., Pirie, M., Bannatyne, L., Viglione, D., Cooper, B., . . . Frackowiak, M. (2003). MMPI-2 based classification of forensic psychiatric outpatients: An exploratory cluster analytic study. *Journal of Clinical Psychology, 59*(9), 907–920.

Ogloff, J., Wong, S., & Greenwood, A. (1990). Treating criminal psychopaths in a therapeutic community program. *Behavioral Sciences and the Law, 8*, 181–190.

Perry, W., & Viglione, D. J. (1991). The ego impairment index as a predictor of outcome in melancholic depressed patients treated with tricyclic antidepressants. *Journal of Personality Assessment, 56*(3), 487–501.

Pithers, W.D. (1999). Empathy: Definition, enhancement, and relevance to the treatment of sex abusers. *Journal of Interpersonal Violence, 14*(3), 257–284.

Plakun, E. M., Muller, J. P. & Burkhardt, P. E. (1987). The significance of borderline and schizotypal overlap. *Hillside Journal of Clinical Psychiatry, 9*, 47–54

Porter, S., Woodworth, M., Earle, J., Drugge, J., & Boer, D. (2003). Characteristics of violent behavior exhibited during sexual homicides by psychopaths and non-psychopaths. *Law and Human Behavior, 31*, 91–107.

Quinsey, V. L., Harris, G. T., Rice, M. E., & Cormier, C. A. (1998). *Violent offenders: Appraising and managing risk*. Washington, DC: American Psychological Association.

Rice, M. E., & Harris, G. T. (1997). Cross-validation and extension of the Violence Risk Appraisal guide for child molesters and rapists. *Law and Human Behavior, 21*, 231–241.

Rice, M. E., Harris, G. T., & Cormier, C. A. (1992). An evaluation of a maximum security therapeutic community for psychopaths and other mentally disordered offenders. *Law and Human Behavior, 16*, 399–412.

Rice, M. E., Harris, G. T., & Quinsey, V. L. (1990). A follow-up of rapists assessed in a maximum security psychiatric facility. *Journal of Interpersonal Violence, 5*, 435–448.

Rice, M. E., Quinsey, V. L., & Harris, G. T. (1991). Sexual recidivism among child molesters released from a maximum security psychiatric facility. *Journal of Consulting and Clinical Psychology, 59*, 381–386.

Riquelme, J., Occupati, R., & Gonzales, E. (1991). Rorschach: Study of the content: Normative data for nonpatient subjects from the greater Caracas area: According to Exner's Comprehensive System. Unpublished data.

Robins, L. N. (1966). *Deviant children grown up*. Baltimore, MD: Williams & Wilkins.

Rogers, R., Salekin, R. T., Sewell, K. W., & Cruise, K. R. (2000). Prototypical analysis of antisocial personality disorder: A study of inmate samples. *Criminal Justice and Behavior, 27*, 234–255.

Rorschach, H. (1942). *Psychodiagnostics*. New York: Grune & Stratton. (Original work published 1921).

Schachtel, E. (1966). *Experiential foundations of Rorschach's test*. New York: Basic Books.

Schlesinger, L. (2004). *Sexual murder: Catathymic and compulsive homicides*. New York: CRC Press.

Shapiro, D. (1965). *Neurotic styles*. New York: Basic Books.

Singer, J., Hoppe, C., Lee, M., Olesen, N., & Walters, M. (2008). Child custody litigants: Rorschach data from a large sample. In C. B. Gacono, F. B. Evans, L. A. Gacono, & N. Kaser-Boyd (Eds.), *The handbook of forensic Rorschach assessment* (pp. 445–466). Mahwah, NJ: Lawrence Erlbaum Associates.

Smith, A. M., Gacono, C. B., & Kaufman, L. (1997). A Rorschach comparison of psychopathic and nonpsychopathic conduct disordered adolescents. *Journal of Clinical Psychology, 53*, 289–300.

Stacey, S., Graham, P., & Athey, G. (2008). The use of the Rorschach in professional fitness to practice evaluations. In C. B. Gacono, F. B. Evans, L. A. Gacono, & N. Kaser-Boyd (Eds.), *The handbook of forensic Rorschach assessment* (pp. 505–526). Mahwah, NJ: Lawrence Erlbaum Associates.

Sullivan, H.S. (1953). *Interpersonal theory of psychiatry*. New York: Norton.

Weber, C., Meloy, J. R., & Gacono. C. B. (1992). A Rorschach study of attachment and anxiety in inpatient conduct disordered and dysthymic adolescents. *Journal of Personality Assessment, 58*(1), 16–26.

Weiner, I. (1998). *Principles of Rorschach interpretation*. Mahwah, NJ: Lawrence Erlbaum Associates.

Winnicott, D. (1958). *The antisocial tendency*. Collected Papers. London: Tavistock Publishers.

Young, M., Erdberg, P., & Justice, J. (2008). Inmates in prison psychiatric treatment: A multimethod description. In C. B. Gacono, F. B. Evans, L. A. Gacono, & N. Kaser-Boyd (Eds.), *The handbook of forensic Rorschach assessment* (pp. 403–420). Mahwah, NJ: Lawrence Erlbaum Associates.

Young, M., Justice, J., Erdberg, P., & Gacono, C. B. (2000). The incarcerated psychopath in psychiatric treatment: Management or treatment? In C. B. Gacono (Ed.), *The clinical and forensic assessment of psychopathy: A practitioner's guide* (pp. 313–332). Mahwah, NJ: Lawrence Erlbaum Associates.

CHAPTER TWENTY

The Popular Conception of the Psychopath: Implications for Criminal Justice Practice

Jacqueline B. Helfgott

Introduction

Psychopathy is a scientific construct that refers to a human condition characterized by the inability to attach to others, predatory aggression, and antisocial behavior (Hare, 1993; Meloy, 1988). Research conducted over the past several decades suggests that psychopathy is a unique clinical condition characterized by the "juxtaposition of affective interpersonal traits with antisocial behavior" (Hare & Neumann, 2006, p. 84) that is empirically associated with criminal behavior and violent recidivism. The phenomenon has been explored for well over two centuries, predominantly by psychiatrists and psychologists, who recognize the condition as a disorder of personality associated with criminal and immoral behavior.

The scientific conception of psychopathy has become crystal clear in recent years as researchers have reached consensus regarding the understanding and assessment of the condition. Psychometric tests to measure the condition have been developed, standardized, and validated (Hare, 1996, 2003, 2007); and there has been what amounts to a research explosion on a range of aspects of psychopathy, from psychometric properties of the PCL-R, to brain structure and function and manifestation of the condition across culture (Patrick, 2006), to philosophical perspectives and the moral responsibility of the psychopath (Malatesti & McMillan, 2010). In fact, in the last 15 years, there have been over 500 scientific publications and many books and edited volumes on the subject, and the condition is now considered by many to be the most useful psychological constructs applied in the criminal justice system and the most important forensic concepts in the twenty-first century (Hare & Neumann, 2010). There has been so much attention to psychopathy and the PCL-R in recent years that books have now been published on how to "pass" the PCL-R (Gentry, 2011).

On the other hand, the popular conception of the psychopath is not so clear. Psychopaths depicted in media and popular culture are an interesting mix of coldblooded, evil, likable, genius, and bizarre. Popular TV shows like *Dexter* show a likable character who carries a baby around to crime scenes who, after putting the little one to bed, sneaks off to bind, torture, and eviscerate deserving victims. Or Linda Fiorentino's neonoir femme fatale character in the *The Last Seduction* (Gorog et al. & Dahl, 1994), a glamorous and beautiful woman who outsmarts and outseduces every man in her path. A far-cry psychopathic icon, *Silence of the Lambs*' (Bozman et al. & Demme, 1991) Hannibal Lecter, became the cinematic poster boy for psychopathy in the 1990s.

Beyond scientific discourse, the term psychopath is used by criminal justice professionals, the media, and the general public. In the past decade, there has been widespread application of the construct of psychopathy in the criminal justice system with increased attention to issues associated with expert testimony on the relationship between psychopathy and general and violent recidivism in criminal and civil courts (Lyon & Ogloff, 2000), misuses of the PCL-R in court (Edens, 2001), the use of the label "psychopath" as a legal synonym of evil (Ruffles, 2004), and the impact of the negative connotation of the term psychopath in correctional contexts (Rhodes, 2002, 2004), the juvenile justice system (Murrie, Cornell, & McCoy, 2005) and on juries and in death penalty decisions (Edens, Desforges, Fernandez, & Palac, 2004).

The cultural meaning of the term has received minimal attention in the literature. The purpose of the present study is to determine what the popular conception of the psychopath is, and to discuss how this conception may shape criminal justice policy and practice.

The Scientific Conception of the Psychopath

The American Psychiatric Association (APA) abandoned the term "psychopath" 50 years ago, replacing it in successive editions of the

Diagnostic and Statistical Manual of Mental Disorders (DSM; APA, 1952, 1968, 1980, 1987, 1994, 2000) with the terms "sociopathic personality," "dyssocial personality," "antisocial personality," and presently, "antisocial personality disorder." Despite the APA's abandonment of the term, researchers agree that the concept of psychopathy has not been adequately conveyed through the diagnostic categories in the DSM and continue to use the term "psychopath" in discussion and empirical study in reference to a distinct phenomenon that is not synonymous with associated terms used over time in the DSM, DSM-II, DSM-III, DSM-III-R, or, at present, in the DSM-IV.

The concept of psychopathy became operational for use in empirical research with the advent and standardization of the Psychopathy Checklist (PCL; Hare, 1980) and subsequent Psychopathy Checklist Revised (PCL-R; Hare, 1991, 2003). The development and widespread use of the PCL-R has radically transformed the state of the research on psychopathy and its relevance to criminal behavior and criminal justice. The PCL-R differs from the DSM-IV-TR Antisocial Personality Disorder (ASPD) in that its criteria capture both the behavioral and personality features of traditional concept of psychopathy based on the work of Cleckley (1941, 1988) (Hare, Hart, & Harpur, 1991; Hare, 1996; Hare & Neumann, 2006).[1] The PCL-R is regarded as the first reliable and valid measure of psychopathy, offering researchers a long-awaited and robust tool with which to empirically study and clinically assess the condition (Hare, 1993; Hare & Neumann, 2010), and it can be safely said that the clinical conception of the construct of psychopathy has come (Hare, 1996) and is here to stay (Hare, 2007).

There is a single thread joining the differing explanations of the disorder throughout the history of the evolution of the scientific concept of psychopathy. Every theory, researcher, and clinician has addressed the psychopath's inability to connect emotionally with others. This feature has been referred to as "lack of empathy," "lack of remorse," and "absence of conscience" (Hare, 2003), "defect in affect" (Cleckley, 1941/1988), "failure to put oneself in another's position" (Yochelson & Samenow, 1977), lack of attachment, affect hunger, and unconscious identification with the "predator part-object" (Meloy, 2001), "human disidentification," and a "reptilian nature that is void of human affect" (Meloy, 1988). Debate regarding the centrality of personality versus antisocial and criminal behavior features of the disorder has persisted for decades. Researchers continue to suggest that the criminal behavior component of psychopathy is a correlate rather than a fundamental component of the disorder (Skeem & Cooke, 2010) however the emotional deficit (Blair,

2005), qualitative difference in the emotional experience of the psychopath (Steuerwald & Kosson, 2000; Patrick, 2007), and inability to experience human emotion and empathy (Baron-Cohen, 2011).

The Popular Conception of the Psychopath

The popular conception of the psychopath has not been empirically studied.[2] The term floats about in culture, in films, true crime novels, the news media, and everyday conversation. It is unclear how popular images of, and references to, the psychopath shape people's general understanding of psychopathology and crime and how this understanding shapes legislative decisions and criminal justice policy. Much of the scientific literature on psychopathy is clinical and technical, and not likely to be read by the ordinary person. Media representations of psychopathologies in general are often inaccurate because the media must conform to the constraints of art, not science (Miller, 1987). The general public is bombarded with true crime novels, television cop shows, infomercials, and news programs that use the term "psychopath" interchangeably with "sociopath," "psychotic," "lunatic," "deranged," "insane," "narcissist," and "criminal."[3]

A number of authors have offered analyses of psychopaths in film, literature, art, and popular culture (Black, 1991; Neroni, 2005; Sargeant, 1996, Simpson, 2000; Wilson, 1999). However, depictions of, and what has been written about, psychopaths in film includes a confusing hodgepodge of "serial killer," "psycho," or "psychopath." Rafter (2006) suggests that these "sensationalistic, overlapping categories tell us little about either psychopaths or movies and that "the clinical literature on the condition of psychopathy offers us a way out of this definitional morass," and the PCL-R and scientific conception of the psychopath offers a means to more precisely define what is meant by a psychopathic movie as "films in which the main character lacks a conscience and exhibits other symptoms of psychopathy" (p. 94). Given this definitional confusion in the film studies literature, it is unlikely that the general public has the same understanding of who a psychopath is as do social scientists.

In addition to media influences, popular conceptions are influenced by scientific theories, professional terminology, and everyday practices used within the criminal justice system. In turn, views held by the general public enter the justice system through political rhetoric, legislation, jury decisions, and victim impact statements (in sentencing, parole, and community supervision). At every stage of the criminal justice process, from arrest through release, popular conceptions play a vital role. Along these lines, Garland (1990) states:

> When the penal system adopts a particular conception of criminals and criminality, or a specific way of classifying criminals, or a particular psychology of motivation and reform; or when it begins to use a particular vocabulary to describe offenders and to characterized their conduct, such conceptions and vocabularies are never confined to the in-house activities of expert practitioners. Instead they feed back into the wider society, and frequently enter into conventional wisdom and general circulation. Terms such as "degenerate," "feeble-minded," "imbecile," "delinquent," "kleptomaniac," "psychopath," and "career criminal" quickly become common currency after only a few years of official use. (p. 257)

Of the terms Garland refers to, "psychopath" is perhaps the most derogatory and the most threatening to individual liberty because it connotes (through its literal meaning) an inherently "sick (twisted, dangerous) mind" that is unchangeable. Used incorrectly (some may argue if used at all), in reference to criminality, the label carries serious ramifications. The term psychopath, originally used in medical, mental health, and criminal justice circles to refer to a condition characterized by moral depravity without cognitive defect, has become common currency. Yet, it is unclear how this popular conception of the psychopath "feeds back" into criminal justice policy and practice. Punishment (and all of the criminal justice practices of which it is comprised) can be viewed as "a complex cultural artifact, encoding the signs and symbols of the wider culture in its own practices" (Garland, 1990, p. 198). In an age of "actuarial justice" (Garland, 2002) when all stages of the criminal justice decision points rely on forensic assessment and actuarial tools (Harcourt, 2007), it seems of timely and critical importance to identify what the popular conception of psychopathy is and how it is used in everyday life, society, and culture, and in criminal justice policy and practice where an individual's liberty can be taken away with varying degrees of evidence to suggest he or she is a threat to public safety.

In 1993, Richard Allen Davis kidnapped 12-year-old Polly Klaas from a slumber party at her home in California. Her body was found two months later after Davis confessed to her murder when his fingerprints were identified as those of the kidnapper after being arrested for drunk driving. At the time of Polly Klaas's murder, Davis was on parole after serving 8 years of a 16-year sentence for a prior kidnapping. On August 5, 1996, the jury verdict was delivered, and on September 26, 1996, Davis was sentenced to death by a California judge. Following the verdict, Davis turned to the TV cameras and courtroom audience and, with a glaring smirk and without a flicker of remorse, raised his middle finger, assuring the world that the jury had made the right decision. Later, Polly's father, Marc Klaas, told reporters, "It will be nice to see him go down. . . . nobody likes to see death, except people like Davis" (Golden, 1996). In a later television interview, Marc Klaas said that he hoped the verdict would send a message to "all of the other psychopaths out there" (King 5 News, August 5, 1996). The news broadcasting of the judge's decision to sentence Davis to death strongly reinforced the idea in most people's minds that psychopaths are, in fact, monsters. Upon hearing the verdict on Davis's capital sentence, Marc Klaas said to Davis, "When you get where you're going, say hello to Dahmer, say hello to Bundy, say hello to Hitler." When the judge asked Davis if he had anything to say, he said, "The main reason I believe I did not commit a lewd act is because of what Polly Klaas told me while we were going up the embankment. . . . She said 'just don't do me like my dad' " (Kennedy, September 27, 1996). Following this statement, screams could be heard in the courtroom, Marc Klaas had to be restrained and escorted out, and the judge told Davis that his actions made the decision to impose the death sentence a very easy decision to make. As of 2012, Richard Allen Davis still sits on San Quentin death row, he has a website,[4] and his death sentence was recently unanimously upheld by the California Supreme Court (Egelko, 2009).

Marc Klaas appeared to have no trouble identifying his daughter's murderer as a psychopath. Perhaps more interesting is his implication that the psychopaths "out there" would be deterred by the verdict, and if not, that the justice system would be able to identify and to subsequently execute them. This view that psychopaths are easy to identify and that their behavior can be deterred by the fear of a death sentence flies in the face of findings in the scientific literature. Since the inception of the term in the 1800s, forensic psychologists, psychiatrists, and criminologists have had a difficult time reaching consensus on the definition of psychopathy. To date the PCL-R is the only standardized assessment tool available to diagnose the condition (and can be administered for clinical purposes only by clinical psychologists), and studies have consistently shown that punishment or the threat of it has no impact on the behavior of psychopaths (Cleckley, 1941/1988; Fowles & Dindo, 2006; Hare, 1991, 1993, 2003; Meloy, 1988; Wallace et al., 2000; Yochelson & Samenow, 1977). Furthermore, Klaas's implication that psychopaths "like Davis" are the offenders who most would like to see executed, sends a powerful message—that there are certain individuals we can all feel comfortable executing.

The ways in which psychopathy is understood, imagined, and communicated in culture in films, TV programs, the news media, and everyday conversation suggests may contribute a great deal to the scientific knowledge of the phenomenon and its relevance to the study of crime and the development of criminal justice policy. What comes to people's minds when they hear the word "psychopath?" As Marc Klaas's statement suggests, use of the term psychopath is common in everyday language. We think we know who Klaas was talking about. Some may not know the psychological terms or how to objectively diagnose personality disorders, but we know what it feels like when the hair raises on the backs of our necks. And when it comes to making decisions about crime, it is this feeling that drives us.

Psychopathy and Criminal Justice Policy

There are two ways of looking at the role psychopathy plays in the criminal justice system. First, the condition itself presents special challenges for criminal justice decision makers. Individuals such as Ted Bundy, Gary Ridgway, Dennis Rader, Jeffrey Dahmer, Kevin Coe, Susan Smith, and Aileen Wuornos appear to be extremely disordered, yet because they "know" right from wrong and have been convicted of their crimes and have not been determined not guilty by reason of insanity. In the correctional system, such individuals can be difficult to manage and present as much of a threat to other prisoners and correctional staff as they did to society at large prior to incarceration. Understanding and treating the psychopath is not the primary function of the correctional system, but corrective (punitive) sanctions do not deter the psychopath. The complex nature of the condition commands sophisticated decisions about how these individuals should be interrogated by the police, understood by the courts, and managed in correctional settings. Second, scientific and popular conceptions of the psychopath influence decisions at every stage of the criminal justice process. Scientific conceptions of the psychopath are at the root of laws of insanity (Goldstein, 1967; Low, Jeffries, & Bonnie, 1986) and sexual predator/psychopath statutes (Minnesota Office of the Legislative Auditor, 1994)[5] and are used in police profiling (Harcourt, 2007; Holmes & Holmes, 2002; O'Toole, 2007; Turvey, 2011), predictions of dangerousness in release decisions (Harris, Rice, & Cormier, 1991; Quinsey, 1995; Serin & Amos, 1995; Serin, Peters, & Barbaree, 1990) and capital sentencing decisions (Edens et al., 2004, Ewing, 1983), and in correctional classification (Van Voorhis, 1994) and treatment (Stevens, 1994) and other legal and forensic contexts (Edens & Petrila, 2006; Lyon & Ogloff, 2000; Malatesti & McMillan, 2010).

The 1990s was a decade of unprecedented "get tough" on crime campaigns. Washington State, California, and states around the country enacted "Three Strikes" legislation (California's spurred in part by the murder of Polly Klaas). Some states enacted "Two Strikes" sentencing provisions and, in addition to Three Strikes legislation, Washington (and other states) enacted sex offender registration, civil commitment of sexually violent predators, and a "Two Strikes" provision for sex offenders. This punitive approach toward crime has gained support largely through the ways in which the problem of crime is presented to and understood by the general public and the notion that a small, identifiable subpopulation of offenders is responsible for the majority of crime, especially violent predatory crime.

According to Best (1994), the rhetoric with which a social problem is constructed plays an important role in the acknowledgment of, and decisions about, the problem in the larger social context. Decisions about social problems are founded on particular definitions, on the ways in which symbols influence people, and on the mood of the times, rather than on the nature of the problem itself. For example, Jenkins (1994) suggests that growing public interest in serial murder did not correspond to a rise in this type of crime, but rather "coincided exactly with a strong political trend toward the reevaluation of the etiology of social problems, a general tendency toward viewing wrongdoing and deviancy as issues of personal sin and evil rather than social or economic dysfunction" (p. 9). This changing view of crime and deviance has shaped criminal justice policy through renewed interest in psychological and metaphysical perspectives that locate the source of extreme criminality within individual personality and outside of human nature.

Psychopathy, like serial murder, is equated with evil in the public mind and conveyed through well-designed atrocity tales. In the case of the serial murder, an enormous gap exists between the objective reality and the subjective definition of the problem, and public fear of serial murder is disproportional to the statistical likelihood of falling victim to such a crime (Jenkins, 1994). Unlike serial murder (a behavior), psychopathy (a personality disorder) is not as overtly observable and may be more prevalent than most people believe. At least two million psychopaths live in North America alone (Hare, 1993), and though information about psychopaths is generally obtained through notorious media cases, true crime novels, and films, psychopaths are said to exist in all segments of society (Cleckley, 1941/1988; Hare, 1993). Media portrayals of extreme criminal psychopaths may have generated confused public ideas among the about relationship between psychopathy, psychosis and other forms of psychopathology, and criminal behavior. Cultural (subjective) and scientific (objective) definitions of psychopathy are likely to influence the social context within which crime and deviance are understood and the policies through which such behavior is controlled. In the understanding of psychopathy, subjective definition may be just as important objective reality.

A Survey on the Public View of Psychopathy

This chapter reports previously unpublished results from a general public survey conducted in 1997 (Helfgott, 1997). The study attempted to answer the question, "What is the popular conception of the psychopath?" The following sub-questions are specifically addressed: (1) *Is there consensus among the general public regarding what psychopathy means?* (2) *Does the popular conception of the psychopath differ from the scientific conception?* (3) *How might attitudes and beliefs about psychopaths influence decision points in the criminal justice process?*

Method

Respondents

Data were collected through a telephone survey of the general public in the Seattle metropolitan area. Respondents' phone numbers were chosen randomly from a sample of 5,430 numbers drawn from local prefixes listed in the 1997 *US West Seattle Telephone Directory*. The numbers were generated through random digit dialing to insure anonymity and inclusion of unlisted numbers. From the larger sample, 2,670 numbers were selected. Of the 2,670 numbers called, 353 (13.2%) respondents agreed to complete the survey. Of the 353 respondents who participated, 188 (55%) were female and 155 (45%) were male (10 respondents declined to offer all or part of the background information, and gender was not recorded). Respondents ranged in age from 16 to 75 ($n = 339$, $M = 39.4$, $SD = 17.6$), and in education from below high school to professional/graduate degree ($n = 336$, $M = 13.7$ years education, $SD = 2.2$). Incomes of the respondents ranged from \$12,000 to \$100,000 ($n = 290$, $M = 34{,}640$, $SD = 20{,}450$).[6] Of the respondents who reported their political affiliation ($n = 311$), 135 (43.4%) reported that they were Democrats, 68 (21.9%) Republicans, 82 (26.4%) independent, and 26 (8%) reported "other." Of the respondents who reported their political perspective ($n = 313$), 103 (32.9%) said they were liberal, 129 (41.2%) said they were moderate, 60 (19.2%) said they were conservative, and 20 (6.4%) reported "other." Of the respondents who reported their marital status ($n = 342$), 127 (37.1%) were single, 148 (43.3%) were married, 28 (8.2%) were divorced, 18 (5.3%) were living with someone (common law), and 21 (6.1%) were widowed. Of the respondents who reported whether or not they had children (n = 307), 170 (54.3%) said yes, and 137 (43.8%) said no. Of the respondents who reported their ethnicity (n = 311), 251 (80.7%) were white, 26 (8.4%) were African American, 14 (4.5%) were Asian/Pacific Islander, 9 (2.9%) were Latino/Hispanic, 3 (1%) were Native American, 2 (.6%) were East Indian, and 6 (1.9%) reported "other."

Materials

A survey was developed to determine what the term "psychopath" means to people and how understanding of the term shapes views about the use of the concept of psychopathy in criminal justice policy, consisting of nine questions (including sub-questions). Questions were developed and included based on issues historically reflected in the scientific literature on psychopathy, such as lack of consensus on the definition and terminology, terminology, sex-based classification in DSM diagnoses, treatment, psychopathy in children and adolescents, and the use of the PCL-R in the criminal justice system. Of the nine questions, four were open-ended, designed to obtain general information about what the term means to people. These four questions were organized such that the first was broad (i.e., "When you hear the word 'psychopath,' what is the first thing that comes to mind?") and the three following became successively more specific (i.e., "What does 'psychopath' mean to you?" "If I asked you to think of a typical psychopath who would come to mind?" "Are there other terms you would use to refer to someone who you believe is a psychopath?"). The fifth question solicited information regarding what terms respondents would generally use as synonyms for psychopath. Respondents were read a list of 23 terms and asked to say "yes," "no," or "pass" to each. Terms included in this list were drawn from terms used in reference to the psychopath in the scientific literature (e.g., antisocial personality, histrionic personality, sociopath) and pop culture (e.g., psycho, evil, lunatic). Question six solicited Likert-scale responses. Respondents were asked whether they strongly agree, somewhat agree, somewhat disagree, or strongly disagree with 20 statements about psychopaths. Statements included in this section were design to solicit information about attitudes and beliefs regarding the etiology, nature, and prevalence of psychopathy (e.g., "Some children are psychopaths," "Psychopaths can't tell the difference between right and wrong," "Psychopaths feel remorse and guilt, they just don't show it," "Female psychopaths are rare," "It's hard to tell who is and who is not a psychopath,"

"Some non-psychopaths engage in psychopathic acts"). Question seven solicited Likert-scale responses to the following question:

> There is a test called the Psychopathy Checklist that social scientists agree can confidently determine whether or not a person is a psychopath. This test is beginning to be used to make various criminal justice decisions. I am going to read you a list of examples of the ways in which this test might be used and I would like you to tell me if you strongly agree, somewhat agree, somewhat disagree, or strongly disagree.

Seventeen examples were included in this section, ranging from use of the test in police interrogations to sentencing decisions to correctional classification, to child custody decisions. Question eight solicited information about whether or not the respondent had ever been personally affected by a psychopath, and question nine solicited information about sources influencing respondents' understanding of psychopathy (see the Appendix at the end of this chapter).

Procedure

The survey was administered by eight undergraduate research assistants. Institutional Review Board approval was obtained. Seventy-five surveys (both telephone and in person) were conducted as a pretest, and the survey was modified accordingly. Research assistants were trained through multiple practice administrations. The survey was conducted from October 1996 through January 1997, Monday through Saturday during both daytime (11 a.m.–3 p.m.) and evening hours (4 p.m.–8 p.m.). The interviewers introduced themselves as Seattle University student research assistants. Respondents were told that the survey was about public conceptions of the psychopath and that it would take 10–15 minutes to complete. Upon agreeing to participate, respondents were informed that there were no right or wrong answers and that if they had any questions during the course of the survey, the research assistant would be happy to answer them at the end of the survey. Qualitative data from open-ended questions were numerically coded. Frequencies were conducted to identify the most popular responses on the questions. Chi square tests were conducted to determine differences in responses with respect to gender, political affiliation, and political perspective, and t-tests to determine differences in responses with respect to age, education, and income. Chi square tests were also conducted to identify if there

Table 20.1 Frequency and Percent of Responses to the Question, "When you hear the word 'psychopath,' what is the first thing that comes to mind?"

Value Label ($N = 348$)	Frequency	Percent
Real Serial Killer	38	10.9
Murderer (General)	28	8.0
Criminal	17	4.9
Violent/Dangerous	16	4.6
Antisocial	10	2.9
Fictional Serial Killer	9	2.6
Sexual Predator	2	.6
Stalker	1	.3
Total for "Criminal Behavior"	**121**	**34.8**
Slang for Crazy	111	31.9
Mentally Ill	67	19.3
Insane	14	4.0
Psychotic	7	2.0
Appears Sane but Isn't	5	1.4
Total for "Mental Disorder"	**204**	**58.6**
Other	23	6.6
Missing	7	–
Total Number of Respondents	353	100

was any relationship between answers given to questions one through six and those given to question seven.

Results

Results show that the majority of respondents associate the term psychopath with mental disorder. Responses to questions "*When you hear the term psychopath, what comes to mind?*" "*What does the word psychopath mean to you?*" and "*Are there any other terms you would use to refer to someone who you believe is a psychopath?*" indicate that over 50% of the respondents said that the first thing that comes to mind, the meaning of the term, and other terms they would use are "mental illness," or "crazy."[7] Table 20.1 shows responses to the question, "When you here the term 'psychopath,' what is the first thing that comes to mind?"

When collapsing the categories associated with criminality into one category called "criminal behavior," and those associated with mental illness into "mental disorder," 34.8% ($n = 121$) of the respondents indicated that the first thing that came to mind when they hear the word psychopath is criminal behavior and 58.6% ($n = 204$) indicated mental disorder.

Table 20.2 Frequency and Percent of Responses to the Question, "What does 'psychopath' mean to you?"

Value Label (*N* = 348)	Frequency	Percent
Serial Murderer	26	7.6
Antisocial	19	5.5
Violent/Dangerous	14	4.0
Criminal	10	2.9
Sociopath	5	1.5
Sexual Predator	2	.6
Total for "Criminal Behavior"	**76**	**22.1**
Mentally Ill	159	46.4
Slang for Crazy	45	13.1
Insane	17	5.0
Appears Sane but Isn't	15	4.4
Psychotic	9	2.5
Total for "Mental Disorder"	**253**	**71.5**
Total for "Evil"	**8**	**2.4**
Other	14	4.0
Missing	10	–
Total Number of Respondents	353	100

Responses to the question, "*What does the word 'psychopath' mean to you?*" are shown in Table 20.2. Responses were collapsed into three categories—"criminal behavior," "mental disorder," and "evil." Results show that 23.1% ($n = 76$) associate psychopathy with criminal behavior, 71.6% ($n = 235$) with mental disorder, and 5.2% ($n = 17$) with evil.

Respondents who associated psychopathy with criminality (on the question, "*What does the word psychopath mean to you?*") and those who associated psychopathy with mental disorder on questions one and two differed significantly with respect to the use of the PCL-R at several stages of the criminal justice process. When comparing the two groups (respondents who said psychopathy means criminality, and those who said psychopathy means mental disorder), those who indicated that psychopathy means criminality were more likely to agree that psychopaths cannot change ($t = -2.59$, $df = 301$, $p \leq .01$), that psychopaths should not be allowed to use the insanity defense ($t = 1.93$, $df = 309$, $p < .05$), and to disagree that psychopaths should be confined in a special prison ($t = 2.85$, $df = 320$, $p < .01$).

Responses to the question, "If I asked you to think of an example of the typical psychopath, who comes to mind?" show that most of the respondents associate psychopathy with serial murder, offering Ted Bundy (27.9%, $n = 95$), Jeffrey Dahmer (21.2%, $n = 72$), Charles Manson

Table 20.3 Frequency and Percent of Responses to the Question, "If I asked you to think of an example of the typical psychopath, who comes to mind?"

Value Label ($N = 340$)	Frequency	Percent
Ted Bundy	95	27.9
Jeffrey Dahmer	72	21.2
Charles Manson	40	11.8
Real Serial Killer	31	9.1
O. J. Simpson	8	2.4
Unabomber	9	2.6
Real Mass Murderer	9	2.6
Total for "Real Killers"	**264**	**77.6**
Fictional Serial Killer/Other	16	4.7
Hannibal Lecter	8	2.4
Norman Bates	5	1.5
Total for "Fictional Killers"	**29**	**8.6**
Other	18	5.3
Friend/Relative/Self	12	3.5
Celebrities/Other	9	2.6
Real Sexual Predator/Other	5	1.5
Politicians	3	.9
Missing	13	–
Total Number of Respondents	353	100

(11.8%, $n = 40$), or the name of another violent criminal or murderer who has been in the news over the past several years[8] (9.1%, $n = 31$) as examples of the typical psychopath. Of those who reported the name of a serial (or other) murderer as the typical psychopath ($n = 264$), 77.6% reported a real killer, and 8.6% ($n = 29$) reported a fictional killer. Hannibal Lecter from the film *Silence of the Lambs* and Norman Bates from the film *Psycho* were reported by more respondents than were other fictional killers (see Table 20.3).

When asked what other terms they would use to refer to someone who they believe to be a psychopath, respondents indicated that they would use the terms "serial murderer" (90.6%, $n = 319$), "psycho" (81.5%, $n = 287$), "mass murderer" (78.7%, $n = 277$) "psychotic" (75.6%, $n = 266$), "mentally ill" (69.3%, $n = 244$), "sexual predator" (67.4%, $n = 238$), "evil" (65.6%, $n = 231$), "monster" (64.2%, $n = 226$), "insane" (65.3%, $n = 230$), "criminal" (63.4%, $n = 223$), "lunatic" (59.9%, $n = 211$), "sociopath" (57.1%, $n = 201$), and "antisocial personality" (55.7%, $n = 196$). Table 20.4 shows yes/no responses for the terms used to refer to a psychopath listed from the most to the least popular.

Table 20.4 Terms Respondents Said They Would Use to Refer to a Psychopath Ranked from Most to Least Popular

Terms Read to Respondents	Frequency	Percent
Serial Murderer	319	90.6
Psycho	287	81.5
Mass Murderer	277	78.7
Psychotic	266	75.6
Mentally Ill	244	69.3
Sexual Predator	238	67.4
Evil	231	65.6
Insane	230	65.3
Monster	226	64.2
Criminal	223	63.4
Lunatic	211	59.9
Sociopath	201	57.1
Antisocial Personality	196	55.7
Morally Bankrupt	173	49.1
Multiple Personality	158	44.9
Schizophrenic	134	38.2
Obsessive-Compulsive	133	37.8
Genius	121	34.4
Chameleon	95	27.0
Narcissist	92	26.1
Reptile	64	18.2
Femme Fatale	58	16.5
Histrionic Personality	43	12.2

Means were analyzed for Likert-scale questions regarding attitudes and beliefs about psychopaths and the use of the PCL-R in the criminal justice system. Tables 20.5 and 20.6 show means for the Likert-scale questions and the percentage of respondents who agreed and disagreed with each (collapsing "strongly" and "somewhat agree" into "agree" and "strongly" and "somewhat disagree" into "disagree").

The information sources cited most frequently by respondents were news (78%), conversations with others (73%), films (69%), television programs (67%), and academic education (61%).

Discussion

The results from the present study suggest that the popular conception of the psychopath is someone who is mentally ill, out of control, out of

Table 20.5 Percentage of Respondents Who Agreed with Statements about Psychopaths with Mean Responses to Likert-Scale Questions Regarding Statements about Psychopaths (1 = Strongly Agree, 2 = Somewhat Agree, 3 = Somewhat Disagree, 4 = Strongly Disagree)

Statement	*M*	*SD*	*n*
Psychopaths come from all racial, gender, and/or cultural backgrounds (81.6)	1.71	.98	347
It's hard to tell who is and who is not a psychopath (77.2)	1.85	.91	351
Some non-psychopaths engage in psychopathic acts (70.9)	2.06	.97	347
There are more psychopaths in America today than in past (61.0)	2.23	1.07	344
Psychopaths can't tell the difference between right/wrong (58.7)	2.27	1.09	351
The only way to protect society from psychopaths is to provide them with mental health treatment (58.7)	2.30	1.10	349
Most psychopaths are victims of childhood abuse (60.9)	2.35	1.02	340
Some children are psychopaths (58.9)	2.41	1.06	350
Female psychopaths are rare (50.4)	2.54	1.10	339
There are more psychopaths in America than in other cultures (51.2)	2.54	1.00	334
Psychopaths can't change their personality or behaviors (50.0)	2.57	1.05	340
Most psychopaths are white (46.6)	2.65	1.09	339
Most psychopaths are in prison, or will end up there (37.9)	2.78	1.09	343
As women gain equal rights with men, we will see more female psychopaths (39.1)	2.80	1.06	345
Psychopaths are in touch with reality (36.1)	2.93	1.04	346
Psychopaths feel remorse, they just don't show it (31.5)	2.94	1.03	340
Female psychopaths are more violent than male psychopaths (26.3)	3.04	.93	339
A person has to have some psychopathic characteristics to be successful in America (32.1)	3.04	1.02	349
The only way to protect society from psychopaths is to execute them (29.3)	3.05	1.04	348
Most people in prison are psychopaths (27.7)	3.08	.96	350

Note: Percentages are based on the number of respondents who indicated "Somewhat Agree" or "Strongly Agree."

Table 20.6 Percentage of Respondents Who Agreed with Statements about the Use of the Psychopathy Checklist–Revised (PCL-R) at Various Criminal Justice Decision Points with Mean Responses to Likert-Scale Questions Regarding the Use of the PCL-R (1 = Strongly Agree, 2 = Somewhat Agree, 3 = Somewhat Disagree, 4 = Strongly Disagree)

Statement	*M*	*SD*	*n*
To sentence to a special prison for psychopaths that provides psychiatric/psychological treatment (78.7)	1.85	.96	348
As criteria for civil commitment to a mentalinstitution (70.4)	1.87	.96	346
To impose strict restrictions/conditions in community supervision (78.8)	1.91	.99	349
To impose community notification/offender registration (74.0)	1.98	1.02	346
To aid police in investigations (73.1)	2.00	.94	349
To imprison in a high security prison (70.1)	2.08	1.03	348
As an indication that the individual should receive mental health treatment rather than a prison sentence (68.4)	2.14	1.06	342
To allow the state to take away custody of a child (64.7)	2.19	1.06	346
To help police interrogate suspects (64.4)	2.21	1.05	348
To justify denying bail (63.2)	2.22	1.04	348
To deny plea bargaining (58.6)	2.35	1.08	345
To impose a Three Strikes sentence (55.7)	2.42	1.11	345
As evidence in court to help jury members make decisions about a defendant's guilt/innocence (55.5)	2.43	1.13	346
As an indication that the person should be permitted to use the insanity defense (44.3)	2.71	1.08	348
To impose the death penalty (42.7)	2.80	1.12	347
To impose a 2 Strikes sentence (37.6)	2.91	1.09	348
To impose a 1 Strike sentence (28.9)	3.09	1.09	348

Note: Percentages are based on the number of respondents who indicated "Somewhat Agree" or "Strongly Agree."

touch with reality, violent, and dangerous. The majority of the respondents associate psychopathy with mental disorder and serial murder. The first thing that came to mind for most when they heard the word "psychopath" was a real-life serial killer. The most popular real-life psychopath was Ted Bundy and the most popular fictional psychopath was Hannibal Lecter. There was a significant difference in beliefs about how the PCL-R and the construct of psychopathy should be used in the criminal justice system between respondents who viewed psychopaths as mentally ill versus those who viewed psychopaths as criminal, with the latter more likely to agree with statements regarding punitive sanctions.

The popular conception of the psychopath as mentally ill and out of touch with reality markedly differs from the scientific conception of the psychopath in that the personality organization of the clinical psychopath is characterized by adequate reality testing (Kernberg, 1967; Meloy, 1988) and psychopaths who meet the criteria for antisocial personality disorder are specifically exempt from the insanity defense in most states (Smith & Meyer, 1987). However, the popular conception is consistent with research findings (e.g., Cleckley, 1941/1988; Gacono & Meloy, 1994; Gorenstein, 1991; Meloy, 1988; Reiber & Green, 1989; Reiber & Vetter, 1995) that suggest that the classification of psychopaths as "sane" is an oversimplification of the dynamics of the condition.

The finding that there is a significant difference between respondents who viewed psychopaths as mentally ill versus those who viewed psychopaths as criminal with the latter more likely to agree with statements regarding punitive sanctions suggests that when people view psychopaths as mentally ill, they are more inclined to favor more lenient treatment in the criminal justice system. Thus, the more people believe that psychopaths are cognitively intact, the more likely they are to agree with statements regarding punitive sanctions such as capital punishment and habitual offender laws. This finding has direct implications for forensic practice given the studies that have found juror inclinations to enter guilty verdicts when psychologist and psychiatrist testimony on psychopathy is presented in court (Edens et al., 2004) and the tendency of courts to use psychopathy as an aggravating rather than mitigating factor (Lyons & Ogloff, 2000).

It is not clear from the results whether or not a consensus exists regarding the conception of the psychopath among the general public. Although the majority of respondents in the present study associated psychopathy with mental disorder, the spectrum of terms people used to refer to a psychopath was so wide (over 200 different terms were mentioned) that is difficult to identify any sort of consensus beyond the common thread of "crazy" that seemed to link many of the terms used. This parallels Stevens's (1994) findings on correctional and forensic practitioners' understanding of psychopathy and antisocial personality disorder. According to Stevens, one psychiatrist said, "If you asked 15,000 psychiatrists for their definitions (of antisocial personality disorder), you would probably get 15,000 definitions" (p. 169).[9]

The respondents' association of the term serial murderer with psychopathy suggests, as Cleckley (1941/1988) and Hare (1993) point out, that though psychopaths are far from rare in the noncriminal population, most people continue to think of psychopaths as the most extreme type of criminal. One explanation for the association between serial murder and psychopathy is the media focus that has magnified the serial murder problem in the minds of many citizens (Jenkins, 1994). Furthermore, the relationship between serial murder and psychopathy is far from clear in the scientific literature. Many researchers indicate that most psychopaths are not serial killers (Hare, 1993, Hickey, 2009; Meloy, 1988, Yochelson & Samenow, 1977) but some also suggest that most (if not all) serial murderers are psychopaths (Egger, 1990; Holmes & Holmes, 2002).

The finding that Ted Bundy, Jeffrey Dahmer, and Charles Manson head the pack as examples of the "typical" psychopath in the public mind is not surprising (and echoes Marc Klaas's statement to Richard Allen Davis when he said to Davis, "Say Hello to Bundy, say hello to Dahmer, say hello to Hitler"—though surprisingly, Hitler was mentioned as the typical psychopath by only one respondent). The frequency with which Bundy's and Dahmer's names were mentioned in the study suggest that the popular news media is a primary influence of the popular conception of the psychopath, and that real-life images of psychopathy and serial murder may have a more powerful impact on people than do their fictional counterparts (i.e., Hannibal Lecter and Norman Bates) which offers some empirical data to the literature media effects and copycat crime (Coleman, 2004; Surette, 1990, 1992, 2004) where some have suggested that perhaps fictional representations may be more powerful than real life (Black, 1991; Fister, 2005). Perhaps, fictional representations of serial killers, psychopathic criminals, and other offenders are more influential to a small percentage of individuals who, as some have suggested in the literature, have lack of identity integration and blurred boundaries between reality and fantasy (Black, 1991; Helfgott, 2008).[10]

One of the more interesting findings in the present study is the gender differences in attitudes and beliefs about psychopaths. Why men are more likely than women to agree that female psychopaths are more violent than male psychopaths, and to disagree that female psychopaths are rare, suggests that women, more so than men, resist the labeling of females as psychopaths. Given the discourse in the 1990s that has continued through today on the rise of the violent and "deadlier than the male" female (Krista, 1994; Valentis & Devane, 1994) and issues raised in the literature regarding media distortion of motive in male/female copycat offenders with attribution of blame and agency placed on male perpetrators, even when factual evidence exists to the contrary (Boyle, 2001), further examination of the ways in which female psychopaths are portrayed and perceived by the public would offer valuable information that would have particular relevance in real-life cases involving jury trials, parole board decisions, or death penalty cases involving female offenders who are referred to by expert witnesses or others as psychopaths (e.g., Diane Downs, Susan Smith, Amanda Knox, Casey Anthony, and Aileen Wuornos). Gender aside, though 81% of the respondents said that psychopaths come from all different race, ethnic, gender, and cultural backgrounds, most did not associate psychopathy with the female gender. This is evident by the finding that the terms "femme fatale" and "Histrionic Personality" (a personality disorder that many researchers have long considered to be a sex-typed manifestation of psychopathy—e.g., Ford & Widiger, 1989; Horowitz, 1977/1991; Kass, Spitzer, & Williams, 1983; Spalt, 1980; Warner, 1978) are the least popular terms used to refer to a psychopath.

There are a number of limitations with this study. First, the sample was small, regional (Seattle), and with a low response rate (13.2%), and may not be generalizable to the general public at large. Second, the study was collected in 1996–1997, and the findings may be considerably different today, especially with the rapid increase in research on psychopathy, its dissemination, and technological advances (e.g., the Internet) that have made this information much more accessible to the average person. It could be the case that, given the enormous amount of information now available on the scientific conception of psychopathy, if the study were to be conducted today, the gap between the scientific and popular conceptions could be much smaller. In addition, given that the study was conducted several years after enactment of high-profile legislation in Washington State (Three Strikes, sex offender registration, and civil commitment) and in the same year Two Strikes for sex offenders was enacted, this was a time period in which a great deal of media attention had been directed toward individuals who were presented in the media as psychopathic superpredators. Replication of the study in a different region, during a different time period, may yield different results.

However, the results from the present study offer a glimpse of how the public viewed psychopaths during a particular time period and in a location of legislative change involving high-risk offenders presented by the media (and, in some cases, also by forensic psychologists and criminal justice practitioners) as psychopathic criminals, and a time in which there was a rapid rise in research attention to the construct of psychopathy, publication, and widespread use of forensic assessment tools in the criminal justice system (designed to measure psychopathy—e.g., the PCL-R—to predict dangerousness—e.g., the VRAG, SORAG, RRASOR, LSI-R, Static-99—and others).[11] The findings suggest that the popular media shapes the public's conception of the psychopath, and that attitudes and beliefs about psychopaths may influence criminal justice policy and practice.

Results regarding respondents' beliefs about the use of the PCL-R at different stages of the criminal justice process suggest that the popular conception of the psychopath may influence public support for the use of the concept of psychopathy (through the PCL-R) at virtually every discretion point in the criminal justice system. Respondents' agreement with the use of the PCL-R in police investigations, prosecutorial decisions, sentencing, community supervision, and child custody and civil commitment decisions suggests that the general public may be willing to support infringement of due process rights, harsher crime control initiatives, and more punitive sanctions for individuals who score high on psychometric assessments of psychopathy.

We are in an era that relies so heavily on forensic assessment and actuarial tools in criminal justice decision-making and "the term 'psychopath' is a powerful label that can have a profound impact on how individuals are perceived and treated in the legal system" (Edens & Petrila, 2006, p. 585). Further exploration is needed on the popular conception of the psychopath and the ways in which ideas and beliefs people hold about psychopathy influence their decisions in the voting booth, on juries, in everyday life, and (for those who work in the criminal justice, social service, mental health, or forensic settings) in the workplace. There is a reflexive relationship between criminal justice legislation, sanctions, and punishment practices and culture (Garland, 1990, 2002; Ferrell, 1995; Ferrell, Hayward, & Young, 2008; Ferrell & Sanders, 1995). Future research is needed on the nature and dynamics of the reciprocity between the concordance of scientific and popular conceptions of psychopathy and the impact of both in criminal justice legislation, policy, and practice.

Acknowledgments

The author would like to thank Edwin Aleman, Mary Jackson, Doug Johnson, Christina Kirkpatrick, Kelvin Kirkpatrick, John Parry, Jean Woods, and Karla V. Zamora, who conducted the data collection and assisted with other phases of this project. The study could not have been completed without them.

Notes

1. Hare, Hart, and Harpur (1991) proposed the use of the PCL-R criteria years ago, but after 15 years of theory, research, and discussion, the construct of psychopathy is still not reflected in the current version of the DSM—DSM-IV-TR—and it is unclear how or if the psychopathy construct will make its way into the DSM-IV (Hare & Neumann, 2010).

2. A number of studies explore popular conceptions of criminals (see Gabor, 1994), but few (if any) specifically address the popular conception of the psychopath.

3. See the film *Natural Born Killers* for an excellent illustration of the hodgepodge of terms used in popular culture as synonyms for psychopath (Hamsher, Murphey, Townsend, & Stone, 1995; Kiselyak, 1996).

4. See Helfgott (2008, pp. 407–408) for a discussion of Davis's website (http://www.ccadp.org/richarddavis.htm), hosted by the Canadian Coalition against the Death Penalty (CCADP), and other prisoner websites.

5. Many states have sexual psychopath statutes whereby sex offenders deemed to be psychopathic or predatory can be sentenced indeterminately. For example, Washington State's Community Protection Act of 1990 states that "sexual predators" can be civilly committed for an indeterminate period of time. Minnesota has a similar law called the "Psychopathic Personality Commitment Law." Both laws have been (and continue to be) challenged in court, and to date, have been upheld.

6. Means and standard deviations for age, education, and income are approximated from data obtained from ranges.

7. There were so many different, though similar, answers to these questions (e.g., deranged, lunatic, disordered, disturbed, looney, emotionally unbalanced, mentally sick, nut, irrational, maniac, crazy white person, crazy male, someone in a padded room and a straitjacket, somebody who is a few fries short of a happy meal, people who talk to themselves) that many that could be considered synonymous for crazy were collapsed into one category labeled "slang for crazy."

8. Some of the names mentioned were John Hinckley, George Russell, John Wayne Gacy, Adolf Hitler, the Green River Killer, and several local teenagers charged with multiple homicides who have recently been in the news—namely Alex Baranyi, who is one of two teenagers accused of killing a family of four in Bellevue, Washington, in early 1997; and Barry Loukaitis, a teenager who went on a shooting spree, killing several students and teachers, in his Moses Lake, Washington, middle school in 1996.

9. This study surveyed correctional psychologists working in the prison setting before the PCL-R had been published and made available for widespread use. It is unlikely that the same lack of consensus would be found among forensic psychologists working in prison today.

10. John Hinckley, who attempted to assassinate Ronald Reagan; Mark David Chapman, who murdered John Lennon; and Robert Bardo, who stalked and

murdered actress Rebecca Schaeffer and other celebrity stalkers, are examples. See Black (1991) and Harvey (2002).

11. See Helfgott (2008) and Bernat, Helfgott, and Godlove (Volume 3, Chapter 4 of this reference set) for overview and discussion of these instruments.

References

Adler, F., Mueller, G. O. W., & Laufers, W. S. (1994). *Criminal justice*. New York: McGraw-Hill.

Ainsworth, M. D. S. (1989). Attachments beyond infancy. *American Psychologist, 44*, 709–716.

American Psychiatric Association. (APA). (1952). *Diagnostic and statistical manual of mental disorders* (DSMI). Washington, DC: Author.

American Psychiatric Association. (APA). (1968). *Diagnostic and statistical manual of mental disorders* (2nd ed.; DSM-II). Washington, DC: Author.

American Psychiatric Association. (APA). (1980). *Diagnostic and statistical manual of mental disorders* (3rd ed.; DSM-III). Washington, DC: Author.

American Psychiatric Association. (APA). (1987). *Diagnostic and statistical manual of mental disorders* (3rd ed., rev.; DSM-III-R). Washington, DC: Author.

American Psychiatric Association. (APA). (1994). *Diagnostic and statistical manual of mental disorders* (4th ed.; DSM-IV). Washington, DC: Author.

American Psychiatric Association. (APA). (2000). *Diagnostic and statistical manual of mental disorders* (4th ed., text rev.; DSM-IV-TR). Washington, DC: Author.

Baron-Cohen, S. (2011). *The science of evil: On empathy and the origins of cruelty*. New York: Basic Books.

Best, J. (1994). Rhetoric in claims-making: Constructing the missing children problem. In P. A. Adler & P. Adler (Eds.), *Constructions of deviance: Social power, context, and interaction* (pp. 105–121). Belmont, CA: Wadsworth.

Black, J. (1991). *The aesthetics of murder: A study in romantic literature and contemporary culture*. Baltimore, MD: Johns Hopkins University Press.

Boyle, K. (2001). What's natural about killing: Gender, copycat violence, and natural born killers. *Journal of Gender Studies, 10* (3), 311–321.

Bozman, R. M., Saxon, E., & Utt, K. (Producers); Blake, G., & Goetzman, G. (Associate Producers); & Demme, J. (Director). (1991). *Silence of the lambs* [Motion picture]. USA: Orion Pictures.

Cleckley, H. (1941/1988). *The mask of sanity*. Augusta, GA: Emily S. Cleckley.

Coleman, L. (2004). *The copycat effect: How the media and popular culture trigger mayhem in tomorrow's headlines*. New York: Paraview Pocket Books.

Edens, J. F. (2001). Misuses of the Hare Psychopathy Checklist–Revised in court. *Journal of Interpersonal Violence, 16*(10), 1082–1093.

Edens, J. F., Desforges, D. M., Fernandez, K., & Palac, C. A. (2004). Effects of psychopathy and violence risk testimony on mock juror perceptions of dangerousness in a capital murder trial. *Psychology, Crime, and Law, 10*(4), 393–412.

Edens, J. F., & Petrila, J. (2006). Legal and ethical issues in the assessment and treatment of psychopathy. In C. J. Patrick (Ed.), *Handbook of psychopathy* (pp. 573–588). New York: Guilford Press

Egger, S. A. (1990). *Serial murder: An elusive phenomenon*. New York: Praeger.

Egelko, B. (2009, June 2). "Death sentence upheld for Polly Klaas's killer." *San Francisco Chronicle*. Retrieved from http://www.sfgate.com/cgi-bin/article.cgi?f=/c/a/2009/06/01/BAFM17UPVC.DTL.

Ewing, C. P. (1983). "Dr. Death" and the case for an ethical ban on psychiatric and psychological predictions of dangerousness in capital sentencing proceedings. *American Journal of Law and Medicine, 8*, 407–428.

Ferrell, J. (1995). Culture, crime, and cultural criminology. *Journal of Criminal Justice and Popular Culture, 3*(2), 25–42.

Ferrell, J., Hayward, K., & Young, J. (2008). *Cultural criminology*. Thousand Oaks, CA: Sage.

Ferrell, J., & Sanders, C. R. (1995). *Cultural criminology*. Boston, MA: Northeastern University Press.

Fister, B. (2005). Copycat crimes: Crime fiction and the marketplace of anxieties. *Clues, 23*(3), 43–56.

Ford, M., & Widiger, T. (1989). Sex bias in the diagnosis of histrionic and antisocial personality disorders. *Journal of Consulting and Clinical Psychology, 57*, 301–305.

Fowles, D. C., & Dindo, L. (2006). A dual deficit model of psychopathy. In C. J. Patrick (Ed.), *Handbook of psychopathy* (pp. 14–34). New York: Guilford.

Gabor, T. (1994). *Everybody does it! Crime by the public*. Toronto, Ontario, Canada: University of Toronto Press.

Gacono, C. B., & Meloy, J. R. (1994). *The Rorschach assessment of aggressive and psychopathic personalities*. Hillsdale, NJ: Lawrence Erlbaum Associates.

Garland, D. (1990). *Punishment and modern society: A study in social theory*. Chicago: University of Chicago Press.

Garland, D. (2002). *The culture of control: Crime and social order in contemporary society*. Chicago: University of Chicago Press.

Gentry, A. (2011). *Pass the PCL-R: Your guide to passing the Hare Psychopathy Checklist–Revised aka the psychopath test*. Charleston, SC: Create Space (DBA of On-Demand Publishing LLC, part of the Amazon group of companies).

Golden, T. (1996, August 6). Jury recommends death for killer of Polly Klaas. *New York Times*.

Goldstein, A. S. (1967). *The insanity defense*. New Haven, CT: Yale University Press.

Gorenstein, E. E. (1991). A cognitive perspective on antisocial personality. In P. A. Magaro (Ed.), *Cognitive bases of mental disorders. Annual review of psychopathology*, Vol. 1. Newbury Park, CA: Sage.

Gorog, M. C., Shestack, J., & Stone, N. R. (Producers), & Dahl, J. (Director) (1994). *The last seduction* [Motion picture]. USA: Incorporated Television Company.

Hamsher, J., Murphey, D., Townsend, C. (Producers), & Stone, O. (Director) (1995). *Natural born killers* [Motion picture]. USA: Warner Brothers.

Harcourt, B. E. (2007). *Against prediction: Profiling, policing, and punishing in an actuarial age.* Chicago: University of Chicago Press.

Hare, R. D. (1980). A research scale for the assessment of psychopathy in criminal populations. *Personality and Individual Differences, 1*, 111–119.

Hare, R. D. (1985a). Comparison of procedures for the assessment of psychopathy. *Journal of Consulting and Clinical Psychology, 53*, 7–16.

Hare, R.D. (1985b). *The psychopathy checklist.* Unpublished manuscript. Vancouver, British Columbia, Canada: University of British Columbia.

Hare, R. D. (1991). *Manual for the Revised Psychopathy Checklist.* Toronto, Ontario, Canada: Multi-Health Systems.

Hare, R. D. (1993). *Without conscience.* New York: Simon & Schuster.

Hare, R. D. (1996). Psychopathy: A clinical construct whose time has come. *Criminal Justice and Behavior, 23*(1), 25–54.

Hare, R. D. (2007). Forty years aren't enough: Recollections, prognostications, and random musings. In H. Herve & J. C. Yuille (Eds.), *The psychopath: Theory, research, and practice* (pp. 3–28). Mahwah, NJ: Lawrence Erlbaum Associates.

Hare, R. D., & Neumann, C. S. (2006). The PCL-R assessment of psychopathy: Development, structural properties, and new directions. In C. J. Patrick (Ed.), *Handbook of psychopathy* (pp. 58–88). New York: Guilford Press.

Hare, R. D., & Neumann, C. S. (2010). Psychopathy: Assessment and forensic implications. In L. Malatesti & J. McMillan (Eds.), *Responsibility and psychopathy: Interfacing law, psychiatry, and philosophy* (pp. 93–123). Oxford, UK: Oxford University Press.

Hare, R. D., Hart, S. D., & Harpur, T. (1991). Psychopathy and the DSM-IV criteria for antisocial personality disorder. *Journal of Abnormal Psychology, 100*(3), 391–398.

Harpur, T. J., Hakstian, R. A., & Hare, R. D. (1988). Factor structure of the psychopathy checklist. *Journal of Counseling and Clinical Psychology, 56*(5), 741–747.

Harris, G. T., Rice, M. E., & Cormier, C. A. (1991). Psychopathy and violent recidivism. *Law and Human Behavior, 15*(6), 625–637.

Harvey, D. (2002). *Obsession: Celebrities and their stalkers.* Dublin, Ireland: Merlin Publishing.

Helfgott, J. B. (1997, March). The popular conception of the psychopath: Implications for criminal justice policy and practice. Paper presented at the annual convention of the Academy of Criminal Justice Sciences, Louisville, KY.

Helfgott, J. B. (2008). *Criminal behavior: Theories, typologies, and criminal justice.* Thousand Oaks, CA: Sage Publications.

Hickey, E. W. (1997, 2009). *Serial murderers and their victims.* Belmont, CA: Wadsworth.

Holmes, R. M., & Holmes, S. T. (2002). *Profiling violent crimes: An investigative tool*. Newbury Park, CA: Sage.

Horowitz, M. J. (1977/1991). *Hysterical personality style and the histrionic personality disorder*. Northvale, NJ: Jason Aronson.

Jenkins, P. (1994). *Using murder: The social construction of serial homicide*. New York: Aldine de Gruyter.

Johannessen, C. (Producer). (2006–). *Dexter* [Television series]. New York:

Kass, F., Spitzer, R., & Williams, J. (1983). An empirical study of the issue of sex bias in the diagnostic criteria of DSMIII Axis II personality disorders. *American Psychologist, 38*, 799–801.

Kennedy, H. (September 27, 1996). "A murderer's final blow." *New York Daily News*. Retrieved from: http://articles.nydailynews.com/1996-09-27/news/18011997_1_richard-allen-davis-polly-klaas-lorena-chandler.

Kernberg, O. F. (1967). Borderline personality organization. *Journal of the American Psychoanalytic Association, 15*, 641–685.

King 5 News (August 5, 1996). Interview with Mark Klaas re Richard Allen Davis sentencing.

Kirsta, A. (1994). Deadlier than the male: Violence and aggression in women. Hammersmith, London: HarperCollins.

Kiselyak, C. (Producer, Director) (1996). *Natural Born Killers–Director's cut* [Film]. Pioneer Entertainment.

Lyon, D. R., & Ogloff, J. R. P. (2000). Legal and ethical issues in psychopathy assessment. In C. B. Gacono (Ed.), *The clinical and forensic assessment of psychopathy* (pp. 139–173). Mahwah, NJ: Lawrence Erlbaum Associates.

Low, P. W., Jeffries, J. C., & Bonnie, R. J. (1986). *The trial of John W. Hinckley, Jr. A case study in the insanity defense*. New York: Foundation Press.

Malatesti, L., & McMillan, J. (Eds.). (2010). *Responsibility and psychopathy: Interfacing law, psychiatry, and philosophy*. Oxford, UK: Oxford University Press.

Meloy, J. R. (1988). *The psychopathic mind: Origins, dynamics, and treatment*. Northvale, NJ: Jason Aronson.

Meloy, J. R. (1992). *Violent attachments*. Northvale, NJ: Jason Aronson.

Meloy, J. R. (2001). *The mark of Cain: Psychoanalytic insight and the psychopath*. Hillsdale, NJ: Analytic Press.

Miller, L. (1987). Classification of psychopathology according to a scientific (psychology and psychiatry) and an artistic (film noir) perspective. *Psychological Reports, 61*, 287–299.

Minnesota Office of the Legislative Auditor (1994, February 25). *Psychopathic Personality Commitment Law: Executive summary* [Online]. Retrieved from http://www.auditor.leg.state.mn.us/PSYCHO.htm

Murrie, D. C., Cornell, D. G., & McCoy, W. K. (2005). Psychopathy, conduct disorder, and stigma: Does diagnostic labeling influence juvenile probation officer recommendations? *Law and Human Behavior, 29*(3), 323–341.

Neroni, H. (2005). *The violent woman: Femininity, narrative, and violence in contemporary American cinema*. Albany, NY: State University of New York Press.

O'Toole, M. E. (2007). Psychopathy as a behavioral classification for violent and serial crime scenes. In H. Herve & J. C. Yuille (Eds.), *The psychopath: Theory, research, and practice* (pp. 301–325). Mahwah, NJ: Lawrence Erlbaum Associates.
Patrick, C. J. (Ed.). (2007). *Handbook of psychopathy*. New York: Guilford Press.
Patrick, C. J. (2007). Getting to the heart of psychopathy. In H. Herve & J. C. Yuille (Eds.), *The psychopath: Theory, research, and practice* (pp. 207–252). Mahwah, NJ: Lawrence Erlbaum Associates.
Quinsey, V. L. (1995). The prediction and explanation of criminal violence. *International Journal of Law and Psychiatry, 18*, 117–127.
Rafter, N. (2006). *Shots in the mirror: Crime films and society*. Oxford, UK: Oxford University Press.
Reid, W. (1985). The antisocial personality: A review. *Hospital and Community Psychiatry, 36*(8), 831–837.
Rhodes, L. A. (2002). Psychopathy and the face of control in supermax. *Ethnography, 3*(4), 442–466.
Rhodes, L. A. (2004). *Total confinement: Madness and reason in the maximum security prison*. Berkeley, CA: University of California Press.
Rieber, R. W., & Green, M. (1989). The psychopathy of everyday life: Antisocial behavior and social distress. In R. W. Rieber (Ed.), *The individual, communication, and society* (pp. 48–89). Cambridge, UK: Cambridge University Press.
Rieber, R. W., & Vetter, H. J. (1995). The language of the psychopath. In R. W. Rieber (Ed.), *The psychopathology of language and cognition*. New York: Plenum Press.
Ruffles, J. (2004). Diagnosing evil in Australian courts: Psychopathy and antisocial personality disorder as legal synonyms of evil. *Psychiatry, Psychology, and the Law, 11*(1), 113–121.
Sargeant, J. (1996). *Born bad: The story of Charles Starkweather and Caril Ann Fugate*. London: Creation Books.
Serin, R. C., & Amos, N. L. (1995). The role of psychopathy in the assessment of dangerousness. *International Journal of Law and Psychiatry, 18*, 231–238.
Serin, R. C., Peters, R. D., & Barbaree, H. E. (1990). Predictors of psychopathy and release outcome in a criminal population. *Psychological Assessment: A Journal of Consulting and Clinical Psychology, 2*, 419–422.
Simpson, P. L. (2000). *Psychopaths: Tracking the serial killer through contemporary American film and fiction*. Carbondale, IL: Southern Illinois University Press.
Skeem, J. L. & Cooke, D.J. (2010). Is criminal behavior a central component of psychopathy? Conceptual directions for resolving the debate. *Psychological Assessment, 22*(2), 433-445.
Smith, S. R., & Meyer, R. G. (1987). *Law, behavior, and mental health: Policy and practice*. New York: New York University Press.
Spalt, L. (1980). Hysteria and antisocial personality: A single disorder? *Journal of Nervous and Mental Disease, 168*(8), 456–464.
Stevens, G. F. (1994). Prison clinicians' perceptions of antisocial personality disorder as a formal diagnosis. *Journal of Offender Rehabilitation, 20*, 159–185.

Steuerwald, B. L. & Kosson, D. S. (2000). Emotional experiences of the psychopath. In C. B. Gacono (Ed.), *The clinical and forensic assessment of psychopathy* (pp. 111–135). Mahwah, NJ: Erlbaum.

Surette, R. (1990). Estimating the magnitude and mechanisms of copycat crime. In R. Surette (Ed.), *The media and criminal justice policy: Recent research and social effects*. Springfield, IL: Charles C. Thomas.

Surette, R. (1998). *Media, crime, and criminal justice: Images and realities*. Belmont, CA: Wadsworth.

Surette, R. (2002). Self-reported copycat crime among a population of serious and violent adult offenders. *Crime and Delinquency, 48*(1), 46–69.

Turvey, B. E. (2011). *Criminal profiling: An introduction to behavioral evidence analysis*. San Diego, CA: Academic Press.

Valentis, M., & Devane, A. (1994). *Female rage: Unlocking its secrets and claiming its power*. New York: Carol Southern Books.

Van Voorhis, P. (1994). *Psychological classification of the adult male prison inmate*. New York: State University of New York Press.

Wallace, J. F., Schmitt, W. A., Vitale, J. E., & Neman, J. P. (2000). Experimental investigations of information-processing deficiencies in psychopaths: Implications for diagnosis and treatment. In C. B. Gacono (Ed.), *The clinical and forensic assessment of psychopathy* (pp. 87–109). Mahwah, NJ: Lawrence Erlbaum Associates.

Warner, R. (1978). The diagnosis of antisocial and hysterical personality disorders. *Journal of Nervous and Mental Disease, 166*, 839–845.

Wilson, W. (1999). *The psychopath in film*. Lanham, MD: University Press of America.

Yochelson, S., & Samenow, S. E. (1977). *The criminal personality. Volumes 1-3*. New York: Jason Aronson.

Appendix

Subject #____

____

Phone#/Location____________________**Date/Day:**__________/__________

Start time:__________________**Interviewer:**__________________________

Introduction: *Hi, my name is ___. I'm a student research assistant at Seattle University and I'm conducting a survey on public conceptions of the psychopath. Would you be willing to take 15 minutes to answer some questions?* ***Instructions:*** *There are no right or wrong responses to the questions I am going* *to ask. If you have questions about the study, I will be happy to answer them at the end of the survey.*

Survey Questions

1) When you hear the word "psychopath," what is the first thing that comes to mind?

2) What does "psychopath" mean to you? (*If answer is vague, probe for more info — Could you elaborate on that?*)

3) If I asked you to think of an example of the typical psychopath, who comes to mind?

4) Are there other terms you would use to refer to someone who you believe is a psychopath? (*Get S to offer at least three examples*)

5) I am going to read a list of terms. As I read each one, please indicate by saying yes or no, which, in addition to the term(s) you just mentioned, you might use to refer to someone who you think is a psychopath? If you would never think of using the term because you don't know what it means, just say "pass" (*Check for each yes response. If "Pass" write "P," DO NOT EXPLAIN TERMS*)

   Reptile/Snake_____ Serial murderer_____ Sociopath_____ Narcissist_____ Multiple personality_____ Monster_____ Psychotic_____ Antisocial personality_____ Sexual

predator_____Lunatic_____ Histrionic_____Evil_____ Psycho_____ Chameleon_____Mass Murderer_____ Criminal_____Femme Fatale_____ Schizophrenic_____Obsessive compulsive_____Insane_____Genius_____ Morally bankrupt_____ Mentally ill_____Others????
____

6) I am going to read several statements. As I read each, I would like you to tell me if you strongly agree (=*1*), somewhat agree (=2), somewhat disagree (=3), strongly disagree (=4) with each (*Mark each with appropriate #*).
Some children are psychopaths_____Psychopaths can't tell the difference between right and wrong_____Female psychopaths are rare____ There are more psychopaths in America today than there have been in the past_____Most psychopaths are White_____It's hard to tell who is and who is not a psychopath_____Some nonpsychopathic people engage in psychopathic acts____Most people in prison are psychopaths____Psychopaths can't change their personality or their behaviors_____Most psychopaths are victims of childhood abuse_____There are more psychopaths in America than there are in other cultures_____The only way to protect society from psychopaths is to provide them with mental health treatment_____As women gain equal rights with men, we will see more female psychopaths_____Psychopaths feel remorse and guilt, they just don't show it_____The only way to protect society from psychopaths is to execute them_____Female psychopaths are more violent than male psychopaths_____A person has to have some psychopathic characteristics to be successful in America_____Psychopaths are in touch with reality_____Most psychopaths are in prison, or will end up there____Psychopaths come from all racial, ethnic, gender, and/or cultural backgrounds.

7) There is a test called the Psychopathy Checklist that social scientists agree can confidently determine whether or not a person is a psychopath. This test is beginning to be used to help make various decisions in the criminal justice system. I'm going to read a list of examples of the ways in which information from this test might be used and I would like you to tell me if you strongly agree (=*1*), somewhat agree (=2), somewhat disagree (=3), strongly disagree (=4) with each (*Mark each with appropriate #*).

If a person scores high on the test, this information should be used:
to aid police in investigations_____to help police interrogate suspects_____to justify denying bail_____to deny plea bargaining_____as evidence in court to help jury members make decisions about a defendant's guilt or innocence_____to impose a "3 strikes" sentence_____ "2 strikes"_____ "1 strike"_____to imprison in a high security prison_____to impose the death penalty_____as indication that an individual should receive mental health

treatment rather than a prison sentence_____to sentence to special prison for psychopaths that provides psychiatric/psychological treatment_____as an indication that the person should be permitted to use the insanity defense_____ to impose strict restrictions/conditions in community supervision_____to impose community notification/offender registration_____to allow the state to take away custody of person's child_____as criteria for civil commitment to a mental institution_____.

8) Have you ever been personally affected by someone you would consider to be a psychopath? (*Check one*) Yes_____No_____Don't know_____
If "Yes," Can you describe your experience with this person(s)?

9) Which of the following sources of information have influenced your understanding of the psychopath? (*Check each one that applies*)

News media_____TV Programs_____Personal experiences_____Academic education_____Fictional novels_____ Mythology_____ Bible_____True-crime novels_____Conversations with others_____Films_____Scholarly journals_____ Magazines_____ Radio____Comic books_____ Cartoons_____
*Others?*_______________________________________

____

Background Information: This information is needed for statistical purposes. If you do not feel comfortable providing any of the information, feel free to say "Pass."
Gender: M_____ F_____

Age: 18–24_____ 25–34_____ 35–49_____ 50–64_____ 65+_____

Education: <HS_____ HS/GED_____Some College_____ AA_____ BA/BS_____ MA/MS_____ Ph.D./Professional Degree____

Income: <20,000_____ 20–30,000_____ 31–50,000_____ 51–80,000_____ 80,000+_____

Political Affiliation: Democrat_____Republican_____Independent_____
Other_______________________________________

Political Perspective: Liberal________Moderate________Conservative______
Other__________________

Marital Status: Single______Married______Divorced______Living w/someone (Common law)______Widow(er)______

Children? (*Mark # of children in each age group*): <18______ >18______
No children______________

Occupation: ____

Cultural/Ethnic
Background: ____

**Would you be willing to be contacted for a telephone interview at a later date?

Name:____

Phone:__________________________/ Good time to call?________________

____

NOTES:

____

Time interview completed:__________Minutes to complete:__________

About the Editor and Contributors

The Editor

Jacqueline B. Helfgott is Professor and Chair of the Criminal Justice Department at Seattle University. She has a PhD and MA in Administration of Justice with a graduate minor in psychology from Pennsylvania State University and a BA from the University of Washington in Psychology and Society & Justice. Her research interests include criminal behavior, psychopathy, correctionsand offender reentry, and victim impact in criminal justice decision-making. She is author of *Criminal Behavior: Theories, Typologies, and Criminal Justice* (Sage Publications, 2008). Her work has been published in journals including *Journal of Police and Criminal Psychology*, *Journal of Forensic Psychology Practice, International Journal of Offender Therapy and Comparative Criminology, Criminal Justice and Behavior, International Review of Victimology*, and the *Encyclopedia of Prisons and Correctional Facilities* and the *Encyclopedia of Street Crime in America*. She has been involved in research and service in correctional settings since 1987. From 1997 to 2000, she was principal investigator on a project funded by the Soros Open Society Institute's Center on Crime, Communities and Culture that involved development, implementation, and evaluation of *Citizens, Victims, and Offenders Restoring Justice* (CVORJ), a prison-based encounter program at the Washington State Reformatory. Her current/forthcoming work includes *No Remorse: Psychopathy and Criminal Justice* (Sage Publications) and coauthor of *Success on the Streets: Creating Opportunities for Offender Reentry* (Lynne Rienner Publishers) and applied research evaluating the Seattle Police Crisis Intervention Team/Mental Health Practitioner Pilot Project. She has served on the Advisory Board for the Washington State Department of Social and Health

Services Special Commitment Center at McNeil Island that houses civilly committed sexually violent predators and currently serves on the Board of Directors for Interaction Transition (a nonprofit, ex-offender transition agency) and the Virginia Mason Separation and Loss (support services for family members following violent death).

The Contributors

Robert Agnew is Samuel Candler Dobbs Professor of Sociology at Emory University. His research focuses on the causes of crime and delinquency, particularly his general strain theory of delinquency. Recent works include *Pressured into Crime: An Overview of General Strain Theory* (Oxford, 2006); *Why Do Criminals Offend: A General Theory of Crime and Delinquency* (Oxford, 2005); and *Toward a Unified Criminology: Integrating Assumption about Crime, People and Society* (NYU Press, 2011).

Stefan Bogaerts is a full Professor of forensic psychology and victimology at Tilburg University (The Netherlands) and the University of Leuven (Belgium). At Tilburg University, he is responsible for the master training in forensic psychology and the forensic psychological research program. He is also the head of Kijvelanden Academy for Research, Innovation and Development, Forensic and Poli-clinic Psychiatric Centre in the Netherlands. He specializes in forensic diagnostics, offender and victim risk assessment and management and treatment. In his research, he combines offender and victim related characteristics and more specific, psychological traumatology. Together with Dr. Marinus Spreen, the head of the forensic psychiatric Centrum Dr. S. van Mesdag in Groningen, the Netherlands, and in cooperation with Tilburg University and the Kijvelanden, Professor Bogaerts is currently doing neuropsychological research in the context of sexual and aggressive delinquent behavior. Bogaerts is the (co)author of numerous international peer-reviewed articles and book chapters.

Michele L. Borynski is a Chief Psychologist at North Texas State Hospital–Vernon Campus, Maximum Security Unit, on a unit for individuals found not guilty by reason of insanity or incompetent to stand trial for violent felonies. She earned her bachelor's degree in psychology at Winthrop University in Rock Hill, South Carolina, and her master's degree at Illinois State University. She earned her doctorate in clinical psychology at Central Michigan University in 2006. Her clinical practice interests are in working with individuals with serious mental illness, particularly those with histories of high-lethality/low-frequency violence.

Heng Choon (Oliver) Chan is a doctoral candidate in the Criminology program at the University of South Florida, Tampa, Florida, where he was awarded the Criminology Asian Scholarship to fund his studies. Currently, he is a full-time criminology researcher at the University of Hong Kong, Hong Kong, SAR, an adjunct criminology lecturer at the City University of Hong Kong, Hong, Kong, SAR, and an adjunct criminology instructor at the University of South Florida. Mr. Chan received his master of arts degree in forensic psychology from Marymount University, Virginia, and his bachelor of arts degree in psychology from Bemidji State University, Minnesota. Mr. Chan's research is focused primarily in the areas of sexual homicide, offender profiling, and criminological issues concerning the Asian population. He has published in a number of top-tier and SSCI-/SCI-indexed scholarly journals, and presented his research in international and regional academic conferences.

Maaike Cima started her study in biological psychology at Maastricht University in 1996, with two specializations—neuropsychology and clinical psychology. In 2000 she was a scientific researcher at Rhinic Clinics Düren, Germany, where she also performed her PhD research. In 2002, she was appointed as assistant professor at the Open University Heerlen, the Netherlands. In 2003 she defended her PhD thesis, "Faking Good, Bad, and Ugly; Malingering in Forensic Psychiatric Inpatients," and she was appointed as Assistant Professor at Maastricht University, the Netherlands. Her research focused more into the development of antisocial behavior. In 2009, she was appointed as associate professor at Tilburg University. In addition, she has an honorary appointment at the Juridical Youth Institution, het Keerpunt, the Netherlands. Furthermore, she also works at the Forensic Psychiatry Centre, The Rooyse Wissel, the Netherlands were she is head of the research department and is also involved with the treatment of several patients with antisocial personality disorder.

Ted Cunliffe, PhD, is a psychologist licensed to practice in the state of Florida. Currently, he is a core faculty member and Assistant Professor and the director of the Forensic Psychology Training Program and at Carlos Abizu University in Doral, Florida. His research interests include the forensic use of the Psychopathy Checklist–Revised, the Rorschach

Inkblot Test, criminal thinking and decision-making, violence risk assessment, and criminal recidivism. He has published articles and book chapters in the areas of social skills training with juvenile offenders, jail suicide, and incarcerated adult female psychopaths. Clinically, Dr. Cunliffe has worked with forensic populations in a variety of settings including juvenile detention centers, adult prisons, juvenile probation, and outreach programs in the community for over 30 years, in addition to expert witness services in the areas of psychopathy assessment, violence risk, and suicide/wrongful death litigation in Florida and California.

Jérôme Endrass is Professor of forensic psychology at the University of Konstanz (Germany) and head of the research department at the Zurich Office of Corrections (Switzerland). This division conducts research relevant to forensic practice. Its main foci lie in the evaluation and development of risk assessment instruments for violent and sex offenders and in the evaluation of the effectiveness of threat management and offense-oriented therapeutic interventions. Professor Endrass has taught at the University of Zurich since 2001 and at the University of Constance, Germany, since 2007.

Carl B. Gacono is a diplomate in assessment psychology, ABAP, and fellow of the Society for Personality Assessment. Formerly the assessment center director at Atascadero State Hospital and later, the chief psychologist at the Federal Correctional Institution, Bastrop, Texas, he is now involved in the full-time independent practice of clinical and forensic psychology in Austin, Texas. He is author of *The Clinical and Forensic Interview Schedule for the Hare Psychopathy Checklist–Revised and Screening Version* (LEA, 2005), coauthor of *The Rorschach Assessment of Aggressive and Psychopathic Personalities* (LEA, 1994), coeditor of *Contemporary Rorschach Interpretation* (LEA, 1997), editor of *The Clinical and Forensic Assessment of Psychopathy: A Practitioner's Guide* (LEA, 2000), senior coeditor of *The Handbook of Forensic Rorschach Assessment* (LEA, 2007), and has authored or coauthored over 80 scientific articles and book chapters. He is the 1994 recipient of the Samuel J. and Anne G. Beck Award for excellence in early career research and the 2000 recipient of the Walter G. Klopfer Award. Dr. Gacono is sought as an expert in the area of personality disorders, criminal behavior, psychopathy, and clinical, forensic, and research applications of the Rorschach and Psychopathy Checklists.

Juliane Gerth studied psychology and criminology at Martin-Luther-University Halle-Wittenberg (Germany). Since 2008, she works as a research assistant and, since 2010, as research associate in a crime prevention research unit of the Psychiatric/Psychological Service (PPS) of the Zurich Office of Corrections. She teaches at the University of Constance and is intending to earn her doctoral degree on the evaluation of forensic-psychological risk-assessment tools for violent and sexual offenders.

Jason R. Hall is a visiting research Assistant Professor in the Department of Mental Health Law and Policy at the University of South Florida. He received his BA in psychology at Emory University, and later completed his graduate studies in clinical psychology at the University of Minnesota, under the supervision of Dr. Christopher Patrick. Dr. Hall's program of research is focused on elucidating the neurobehavioral systems that give rise to varying forms of psychopathology, with a particular emphasis on psychopathy, antisocial behavior, and substance use disorders.

Kathleen M. Heide is a Professor in the Department of Criminology at the University of South Florida. Dr. Heide has authored or coauthored more than 100 publications. She is the author of two widely acclaimed books on juvenile homicide, *Why Kids Kill Parents: Child Abuse and Adolescent Homicide* and *Young Killers: The Challenge of Juvenile Homicide*, and (coauthored with Linda Merz-Perez) *Animal Cruelty: Pathway to Violence against People*. She is a licensed mental health counselor and a court-appointed expert in matters relating to homicide, sexual battery, and children and families. Dr. Heide is a frequent consultant to the national print and electronic media and numerous international newspapers and magazines on matters relating to juvenile crime and youth violence. She is a member or former member of more than 10 community and state boards of directors, councils, or task forces.

Zsuzsanna Horváth was born in Hungary and is currently studying at Tilburg University, pursuing a master's in research psychology. She researches the severity of personality disorders among criminals. She is also involved in a nationwide study on victimization and perpetration among psychiatric patients with a severe mental illness in the Netherlands.

Elizabeth A. Johnson is a doctoral candidate at Carlos Albizu University. She is pursuing her PsyD in clinical psychology, specializing in the evaluation and treatment of forensic populations. She received her master's in forensic psychology from the Chicago School of Professional Psychology. Ms. Johnson is primarily interested in the areas of intimate partner violence, psychopathy, and sex offenders.

Shayne Jones is an Associate Professor of criminology at the University of South Florida. He received his PhD at the University of Kentucky, and completed postdoctoral training at the University of Pittsburgh. His research focuses on the relationship between personality and antisocial behavior, as well as the factors that mediate and moderate this relationship. He also researches factors that influence legal judgments and evaluations, including jury and judicial decision-making.

Alex Kigerl is a PhD student in criminal justice and criminology at Washington State University. His research interests are in cybercrime and personality, and he has authored studies on e-mail spam and phishing, which appear in *Social Science Computer Review* and the *International Journal of Cyber Criminology*. He plans to continue his research on e-mail spam and deterrence as part of his doctoral dissertation.

Richard N. Kocsis is a consultant medicolegal psychologist in private practice. Over his career, Dr. Kocsis has produced five books (his latest text is entitled *Applied Criminal Psychology*) and is the author/coauthor of approximately 100 scholarly publications (articles, book chapters, etc.) on topics such as criminal profiling, serial violent offenders, and forensic psychological practice. He has served as an expert consultant to law enforcement, emergency, and prosecution agencies as well as various law firms. In addition to his clinical and forensic work, he has held various academic positions in the areas of forensic psychology and criminology. In 2000, he was awarded the Australian Museum's prestigious Eureka Prize for critical thinking in recognition of his scientific research in the area of criminal profiling.

J. Reid Meloy is a diplomate in forensic psychology of the American Board of Professional Psychology, and consults on criminal and civil cases throughout the United States and Europe. He is a Clinical Professor of psychiatry at University of California, San Diego, School of Medicine, and a faculty member of the San Diego Psychoanalytic Institute. He is a fellow of the American Academy of Forensic Sciences and is past president of the American Academy of Forensic Psychology. He has received a number of awards from various professional organizations and is chairman of

Forensis, Inc., and Forensis Europa, Inc., two nonprofit, public benefit corporations devoted to forensic psychiatric and psychological research (http://www.forensis.org). Dr. Meloy has authored or coauthored over 200 papers published in peer-reviewed psychiatric and psychological journals, and has authored, coauthored or edited 10 books. His first book, *The Psychopathic Mind* (Aronson, 1988), was an integration of the biological and psychodynamic understanding of psychopathy, His most recent edited book, *Stalking, Threatening and Attacking Public Figures* (Oxford University Press, 2008), led to a commissioned study for the National Academy of Sciences on threats toward public figures published in March, 2011 (http://www.nap.edu). Dr. Stephen White and he created the WAVR-21 (Specialized Training Services, 2007), the first scientifically based structured professional judgment instrument for workplace targeted violence assessment. His forthcoming edited book with Dr. Jens Hoffman, *The International Handbook of Threat Assessment*, will be published by Oxford University Press in 2013. Dr. Meloy is also a consultant to the counterintelligence division of the FBI and intermittently teaches at the Behavioral Analysis Units in Quantico. He is a member of the Fixated Research Group for the United Kingdom's Home Office concerning threats to the Royal Family and British political figures, and also teaches for the Netherlands National Police. He has been a technical consultant to the television program *CSI* since its inception in 2001.

Andreas Mokros studied psychology at the universities of Bochum, Liverpool, and Wuppertal and holds degrees of Dipl.-Psych. (German master's equivalent in psychology), MSc in investigative psychology, and PhD. Dr. Mokros has worked in forensic mental health for eight years, currently as a quality assurance and research representative, Center for Forensic Psychiatry, at the Psychiatric University Hospital, Zurich, Switzerland. Dr. Mokros's primary research interests include experimental diagnostics of sexual preference disorders through attentional tests, forensic case analysis and offender profiling, measurement models of psychopathy, prediction of violence, item response theory. Dr. Mokros has been a consultant to police forces and an expert witness for psychological assessment in court.

Wade C. Myers is a Professor in the Department of Psychiatry and Human Behavior at the Alpert Medical School of Brown University and Director of Forensic Psychiatry for Rhode Island Hospital. His primary research interests are in juvenile and adult homicide, sexual homicide, and detection of malingering in murderers. He is the author of 95 publications and the book *Juvenile Sexual Homicide*. Dr. Myers regularly serves as a forensic psychiatry consultant to attorneys and courts in homicide cases. Additionally, he is a member of a Sheriff's Office Homicide Cold Case Team.

R. Thomas Naylor is Professor of economics at McGill University, and an associate faculty member at the McGill School of Environment in Montreal, Quebec. His main research concerns are international black markets, smuggling (particularly of arms, drugs, wildlife and artworks), money laundering, "terrorist financing," and environmental crime with particular reference to toxic waste dumping and wildlife poaching. He has consulted for and lectured to government agencies involved in tax and criminal justice enforcement issues, and to forensic accounting firms involved in investigating financial fraud. His published work appears regularly in, among other journals, *Crime, Law and Social Change*, of which he was until recently a senior editor. He is the author of 10 books, of which the best known are: *Hot Money and the Politics of Debt*; *Economic Warfare: Sanctions, Embargo Busting and State-Sponsored Crime*; *Wages of Crime: Black Markets, Illegal Finance and the Underworld Economy*; *Satanic Purses: Money, Myth and Misinformation in the War on Terror*; and, most recently, *Crass Struggle: Greed, Glitz and Gluttony in a Wanna-Have World*. He is currently at work on a book entitled *The Rise and Fall of the Carbon Economy*.

George B. Palermo graduated from the University of Bologna Medical School, Bologna, Italy, and was trained in general medicine and psychiatry in the United States. He received a master of science degree in criminology from the University of Rome, La Sapienza, and a PhD in forensic psychiatry from Erasmus University, Rotterdam, the Netherlands. He is a diplomate of the American Board of Psychiatry and Neurology in Psychiatry, a fellow of the American College of Forensic Examiners, and a diplomate of the American Board Forensic Medicine. He is Clinical Professor of Psychiatry at the University of Nevada School of Medicine and the Medical College of Wisconsin, and Professor Adjunct of Criminology and Law Studies at Marquette University. He is also on the faculty of La Sapienza University of Rome, Italy. He is editor-in-chief of *International Journal of Offender Therapy and Comparative Criminology*. In addition, he is on the editorial and review boards of various national and international psychiatric and criminological journals. He has published numerous articles, books and book chapters on forensic psychiatry and criminology.

Christopher J. Patrick is a Professor of clinical psychology at Florida State University. His scholarly interests include psychopathy, antisocial behavior, substance abuse, personality, fear and fearlessness, psychophysiology, and affective and cognitive neuroscience. He is author of more than 160 articles and book chapters, and editor of the *Handbook of Psychopathy* (Guilford Press, 2006). Since 2008, he has served as a scientific advisor to the DSM-V Personality and Personality Disorders (PPD) Work Group, and in 2010, he served as a workgroup member for the National Institute of Mental Health's Research Diagnostic Criteria (RDoC) initiative. A recipient of Early Career awards from the American Psychological Association and the Society for Psychophysiological Research (SPR), Dr. Patrick is currently President of SPR, and is a Past President of the Society for Scientific Study of Psychopathy.

Machiel S. Polak is the supervisory board chairman at the Sinai Centre in Rotterdam Area, the Netherlands and is a psychiatrist and chairman of the board at the FPC Kijvelanden.

Stephen K. Rice is an Assistant Professor in the Department of Criminal Justice at Seattle University. His research focuses on deference and defiance in individuals' interactions with the justice system. For example, his recent work has focused on areas to include procedural and restorative justice, racial profiling, radicalization, final statements of the condemned, and criminological theories which inform these processes. His publications have appeared in outlets including *Criminology*, *Justice Quarterly*, *Deviant Behavior*, and the *Journal of Quantitative Criminology*. He is also lead editor of *Race, Ethnicity, and Policing: New and Essential Readings* (NYU Press, 2010). At Seattle University he teaches undergraduate and graduate courses in punishment and social theory, senior synthesis, organizational theory in criminal justice, and qualitative research methods.

Henry Richards received his doctorate from Loyola University of Chicago. His doctoral internship was conducted under the auspices of NIMH at St. Elizabeths Hospital in Washington, D.C., where his internship and post-doctoral studies focused the assessment and treatment of NGRI patients. He was later contracted by the Department of Justice to review the status of care of all White House cases at St. Elizabeths Hospital. He directed clinical services at Patuxent Institution, Maryland and was executive director of the Special Commitment Center, McNeil Island, Washington. His publications are in the areas of addiction, psychopathy and other personality disorders, and sexual offending. He currently cochairs the Washington State Public Safety Review Panel, which advises the state hospitals and courts regarding the risk posed by potential releases of patients found NGRI for felonies. His forensic practice is in Seattle Washington, where he is on the adjunct faculty of the University of Washington, and Seattle University.

Jeffrey Ian Ross is an Associate Professor in the School of Criminal Justice, College of Public Affairs, and a research fellow of the Center for International and Comparative Law at the University of Baltimore. He has researched, written, and lectured on corrections, policing, political crime (esp., terrorism and state crime), violence (esp., criminal, political, and religious), cybercrime, extreme/ abnormal criminal behavior, and crime and justice in Indian Country for over two decades. Ross's work has appeared in many academic journals and books, as well as popular media. He is the author, coauthor, editor, or coeditor of 16 books, most recently *Policing Issues: Challenges and Controversies* (Jones & Bartlett Learning, 2011). Ross is a frequent and respected subject matter expert for local, regional, national and international news media. He has made live appearances on CNN, CNBC, and Fox News Network. Additionally Ross has written op-eds for *The (Baltimore) Sun, The (Maryland) Daily Record, The Gazette* (weekly community newspapers serving Maryland's Montgomery, Frederick, Prince Georges and Carroll counties), the *Baltimore Examiner*, and the *Tampa Tribune*. From 1995 to 1998, Ross was a social science analyst with the National Institute of Justice, a Division of the U.S. Department of Justice. In 2003, he was awarded the University of Baltimore's Distinguished Chair in Research Award. During the early 1980s, Ross worked for almost four years in a correctional institution. His website is http://www.jeffreyianross.com.

Astrid Rossegger studied psychology and criminology at the University of Constance (Germany). Since 2000 she has worked as a research associate in the crime prevention research unit of the Psychiatric/Psychological Service (PPS) of the Zurich Office of Corrections, becoming deputy head of the unit in 2005. Since 2007, Rossegger has taught at the Universities of Zurich and Constance. Her research foci lie within the development and validation of risk-assessment tools as well as the evaluation of therapeutic interventions for the prevention of repeat offending.

Stacey L. Shipley obtained her doctorate in clinical/forensic psychology from California School of Professional Psychology in Fresno,

California. She is the Director of psychology at North Texas State Hospital, the only maximum-security forensic hospital in Texas. She specializes in the areas of forensic and clinical assessment, violence risk assessment, and evaluating and treating maternal filicide offenders and offenders with severe mental illness. She serves as a consulting expert witness and conducts assessments of competency to stand trial and sanity. She is trained in the investigation and evaluation of violent crimes and offenders, serial crimes, linkage analysis, and threat communications. She has published in the areas of psychopathy, homicide, women and crime, maternal filicide, forensic case formulation for sexual offenders, and serial murder and serial rape typologies. Dr. Shipley is the first author of *Introduction to Forensic Psychology: Court, Law Enforcement, and Correctional Practices* (3rd ed., in press) with Elsevier/Academic Press.

Marinus Spreen was born in Groningen and is the head of the Research Department of the Forensic Psychiatric Centre in the Netherlands. He is also appointed as Lector Social Work & Arts Therapies, Stenden University, Leeuwarden, the Netherlands. Dr. Spreen completed his PhD at Maastricht University and is an expert in the field of forensic social network analysis. Currently, he is working on the revision of the risk assessment instrument, HKT-30.

Ray Surette has a doctorate in criminology from Florida State University and is a Professor of criminal justice at the University of Central Florida. His crime and media research interests revolve around the media's effect on perceptions of crime and justice and media-generated crime and criminal justice policies. He has published numerous articles and books on media, crime, and criminal justice topics and is an internationally recognized scholar in the area. In addition to interest in copycat crime, he has published research on the use of public information officers in criminal justice agencies, crime and justice infotainment programming, media-oriented terrorism, the effect of crime news coverage on similarly charged non-covered trials and the effect of coverage of corrections on municipal jail population trends, and media use, fear of crime, and criminal justice policy support within the general public. He is currently involved in studying the use of police surveillance camera systems in public spaces and associated media portraits and public acceptance of these systems. He is also currently working on a book on copycat crime.

Enna Taylor is a researcher at Carlos Albizu University, Miami campus.

Noah C. Venables is a graduate student in the clinical psychology doctoral program at Florida State University. He received his BA in psychology and sociology of law, criminology, and deviance from the University of Minnesota. His research interests include issues related to the conceptualization, assessment, and neurobiology of psychopathy and externalizing traits and behaviors such as impulsivity, aggression, and criminality.

Donna E. Weiss is a Florida-licensed psychologist who specializes in forensic psychology. She is the founder of Forensic Psychology & Trauma, LLC, a private practice located in Fort Lauderdale, Florida, specializing in the assessment of trauma in forensic contexts. She has performed hundreds of forensic evaluations with adults and juveniles in criminal, civil, and family law cases. She is regularly qualified as an expert witness in state and federal courts. Her areas of expertise include post-traumatic stress disorder, dissociative disorders, battered woman's syndrome, domestic violence, childhood sexual and physical abuse, juveniles transferred to adult court, juvenile and adult homicide, death penalty mitigation, competency to proceed to trial, competency to waive Miranda rights, sanity, violence risk assessment, and malingering. She has published articles and book chapters in the areas of childhood sexual abuse, dissociative identity disorder, psychopathy, and chronic fatigue syndrome.

Index

Note: Page numbers followed by f or t refer to Figures or Tables

Absolute contraband, 169
Action plans, 150–51
Action tendencies, 149
Active imagination, 154
Adolescents: conduct disorder and, 386–89; crime and, 116; sexual fantasies and, 130–31, 145–46
Advance fee fraud, 231, 242
Aeschylus, 364
Age factors: in cybercrime, 237; life-course criminology and, 115–16; prison violence and, 115
Aggression: antisocial personality disorder and, 496–97; criminal responsibility and, 374; empathy and, 385–86; by females, 425–26; meanness and, 295; psychoanalytic theories of, 361–63; psychopathy and, 287–88, 299, 358–61, 366–68; Rorschach and, 496–97. *See also* Violence/violent crimes
Alcohol, tobacco, fuel illegal markets, 186t
Alcohol use and abuse. *See* Substance use disorders
al-Qaeda, 217–19, 221
al-Zawahiri, Ayman, 221
American Psychiatric Association, 12
Amydala, 412
Anger excitation typology, 23
Anger retaliatory typology, 23
Anomic theory of deviance, 202
Antisocial personalities, 22–23
Antisocial personality disorder (ASPD): aggression and, 496–97; attachment deficits and, 495–96; borderline personality disorder and, 473–74, 492–93, 497–98; conduct disorder and, 386–89; DSM and, 280, 281, 315, 355–56; gender differences, 427–28; intimate partner violence and, 465; pathological narcissism and, 493–95; psychopathic versus non-psychopathic women, 433–36, 437t, 439–42; psychopathy and, 82–85, 343–44, 346–47, 487–90, 488–90; Rorschach and, 505–6
Antisocial Process Screening Device (APSD), 282–83, 292, 295–96, 318–19
Antisocial/Vindictive pathway, 142
Anxiety, 288, 300, 320–21
Anxiety disorders, 71–72
APSD. *See* Antisocial Process Screening Device (APSD)
Arab Spring, 215
Aranakan, 341
Aristotle, 364
Art and antiquities illegal markets, 186t
ASPD. *See* Antisocial personality disorder (ASPD)
Associational drives, 208
Attachment deficits, 495–96, 504

Autonomy, 372–73
Auto theft, 195
Azzam, Abdullah, 221

Basque Homeland and Liberty, 219
Battered woman syndrome (BWS), 468
Beck, Samuel, 490
Behavioral Sciences Unit (BSU), 47–48
Berlin Crime study, 116
Bible narratives, 363
bin Laden, Osama, 217–18, 220, 221
Biological typologies, 17–19
Boldness, 293–94, 298, 299, 300, 301
Bootlegging, 189–91
Borderline personality disorder (BPD): antisocial personality disorder and, 473–74, 492–93, 497–98; child abuse and, 387; empathy and, 385; intimate partner violence and, 463, 465, 467–71, 474–78; psychopathy and, 473–74; Rorschach and, 492–93
Boston Strangler, 45
Botnets, 230–32
Bouazizi, Mohamed, 215
BPD. *See* Borderline personality disorder (BPD)
Brain dysfunction, 366–68, 388
BSU. *See* Behavioral Sciences Unit (BSU)
Bundy, Ted, 21, 521, 533
Busic, Zvaonko, 220
BWS. *See* Battered woman syndrome (BWS)

Callousness: antisocial personality disorder and, 283; life-course violence and, 116; meanness and, 294–95, 297–98; psychopathy and, 84, 280–81, 285, 287, 358
Calvin, 365
Career criminals, 115–16, 288–89, 300
Central systematic processing, 252–54, 257–58
Cerebrotonic temperament, 18
Child abuse/neglect: borderline personality disorder and, 467–68; conduct disorder and, 387–89, 393–97; intimate partner violence and, 478; violent offending and, 112
Child Psychopathy Scale (CPS), 282, 295
Cho, Seung-Hui, 10
CIA. *See* Criminal Investigative Analysis (CIA)
Civilization and Its Discontents (Freud), 361
Cleckley, Hervey, 22, 279–80, 285, 286–90, 293, 313–16, 356–57
The Clinical and Forensic Assessment of Psychopathy: A Practitioner's Guide (Gacono), 342
Coe, Kevin, 521
Cognitive violence, 217
Coldheartedness, 284–85, 294
Commercial economic crimes: criminal association and, 180–81; definition and overview, 171–72; effect on GDP, 174; fiscal implications, 176–77; proceeds of, 175; summary, 173t; violence and, 183
Commonwealth v. DeStafano, 56
Compatibilistic theorists, 374–75
Complex posttraumatic stress disorder (CP), 468
Computer-assisted/computer-focused crimes, 229–30. *See also* Cybercrimes
Conduct disorder: child abuse/neglect and, 386–89; Netherlands forensic patients study, 389–97; Rorschach and, 494, 496–97, 501–3, 505
Coping, 221–22, 384–85, 388–89, 396
Copycat crimes: acquisition of crime knowledge, 256–57; appraisal and adoption decision, 262–63; at-risk individuals, 267–68; attempting, 263–64; central systematic processing path, 252–54, 257–58; composite behavior model and, 255; consequences, 264–66; definition and overview, 251–52; exposure to a media generator and, 255; features of, 8t; heuristic peripheral processing path, 253–54, 258–59; narrative persuasion path, 253–54, 259–60; paths to, 252–54; personality, situation and internal state, 255–56; priming and script activation, 261–62; social effects and feedback, 266–67
Core fantasies, 147–49
Corporate crime, 180–81, 196, 233
Corruption, 178–79
Cost-benefit calculations, 209, 222

CP. *See* Complex posttraumatic stress disorder (CP)
CPI Socialization Scale, 283
CPS. *See* Child Psychopathy Scale (CPS)
Credential goods, 232
Credit card theft, 192–93
Crime Action Profiling (CAP), 50
Crime Classification Manual (FBI), 21, 23
Crime prevention, 7
Crime Profiles (Miethe, McCorkle, & Listwan), 24
Crime types, 6–9
Crimeware and services, 232
Criminal association, 179–81
Criminal behavior, 5–6, 10–16
Criminal Behavior Systems (Clinard, Quinney, & Wildeman), 24
Criminal Investigative Analysis (CIA), 47–49
Criminal justice, 55–57, 521–23
Criminal personality profiling, 44
Criminal profiling: Crime Action Profiling, 50; Criminal Investigative Analysis, 47–49; definition and overview, 43–45; Diagnostic Evaluations, 46–47; geographic profiling, 51–52; Investigative Psychology, 49–50; use in courtrooms, 55–57; validity and utility of, 52–55
Criminal responsibility, 370–74
The Critique of Practical Reason (Kant), 365
Crowley, Aleister, 155–56
Culture, 341–42
Cyberbullying, 242
Cybercrimes: features of, 8t; overview, 227–33; profile of a cybercriminal, 233–39; routine activity theory and, 240–44

Dahmer, Jeffrey, 21, 375, 521, 533
Dark Triad traits, 143–44
Darrow, Clarence, 371–72
Davis, Richard Allen, 519–20, 533
DE. *See* Diagnostic Evaluations (DE)
Decisional capacity, 370–74, 374–75
Deinstitutionalization, 87–88
Deprivation, 217
DES. *See* Disorders of extreme stress (DES)
Descartes, 365
DESNOS. *See* Disorders of extreme stress not otherwise specified
Determinism and will, 363–66, 370, 372–73
Dexter, 516
Diagnostic and Statistical Manual of Mental Disorders (DSM): antisocial personality disorder, 280, 281, 315, 343–44, 355–56; childhood antecedents, 387; conduct disorder, 386; coping skills and, 384–85; intimate partner violence and, 462–63; paraphilias defined, 132, 134, 135–37; personality disorders, 382; psychopathy and, 488–90, 516–17; sexual sadism, 408; sociopathic personality disorder, 279, 488; as a typology, 12–14, 21
Diagnostic Evaluations (DE), 46–47
Differential association theory, 204–5, 210, 261
Disaffiliated agency, 294
Disinhibition, 291–93, 297, 299, 300, 301, 371
Disorders of extreme stress (DES), 468
Disorders of extreme stress not otherwise specified (DESNOS), 468
Distributed denial of service (DDoS) attacks, 230
Divine Comedy, 154
DNA profiling, 43–44
Domestic violence, 106–8. *See also* Intimate partner violence
Dominance fantasies, 139, 143, 410
Drug use/abuse. *See* Substance use disorders
DSM. *See Diagnostic and Statistical Manual of Mental Disorders* (DSM)

Economic crimes: ambiguity in, 191–95; corruption, 178–79; criminal association, 179–81; features of, 8t; money laundering, 175; tax evasion, 175–77; terminology, 164–66; violence and, 181–83; wealth distribution and, 172–74. *See also* Commercial economic crimes; Market-based economic crimes; Predatory economic crimes

Ectomorphs, 18
Elemental Psychopathy Assessment (EPA), 283, 284
Emotions: attachment deficits, 495–96; terrorism and, 216–19
Empathy, 385–86, 388–89, 396–97
Endomorphs, 18
England/Wales violent crime rates, 102–5
Entertainment education theory, 252, 260–61, 270
Environmental psychology, 52
EPA. *See* Elemental Psychopathy Assessment (EPA)
Erotomania, 156–57
ESI. *See* Externalizing Spectrum Inventory (ESI)
Executive function, 382–83
Exhaustive/exclusive typologies, 34–35
Expressive violence, 105
Externalizing, 292–93, 295–96, 312
Externalizing Spectrum Inventory (ESI), 297

Facial affect recognition, 469–71
Facilitating traits, 207
Falling, Christine, 21
Fantasy scripts, 150
FBI, 23–24, 47–48
Fearlessness, 293–94, 301–2
Felonies, 19, 34
Female criminal behavior: antisocial personality disorder/psychopathy and, 428–29; maternal filicide and, 78–82; psychopathy and violence and, 85, 425–27, 427–28; violent crimes, 108–9. *See also* Gender differences; Rorschach
Filicide, 78–82
Fiorentino, Linda, 516
Fiscal contraband, 168
Five-Factor Model of personality, 145, 284
Forensic Rorschach database, 501–3
Franks, Bobby, 372
Free will, 363–66, 369–70, 370–74, 372–73, 374–75
Frustration-aggression, 207
Frye v. United States, 56

Gambling, 186t
Gender differences: in attitudes and beliefs about psychopaths, 533–34; in biological and social variables, 424–25; in cybercrime, 236–37; pathological narcissism and, 494–95; psychopathy and, 503–4; in psychopathy and violence, 85; sexual fantasies and, 137–41; in violent crimes, 109, 425–27. *See also* Female criminal behavior
General Aggression Model, 252, 270
General learning model (GLM), 255, 262
General strain theory, 219–22
Genetics, 367
Geographic Information Systems (GIS), 51
Geographic profiling, 51–52
German violent crime rates, 102–5
Giffords, Gabrielle, 10
GIS. *See* Geographic Information Systems (GIS)
GLM. *See* General learning model (GLM)
Guiding fantasies, 148–50
Guns. *See* Weapons use

Hackers, 237–38, 243
Hallucinations, 75, 81
Hamas, 219
Handbook of Forensic Rorschach Assessment (Gacono et al.), 501
Hare Psychopathy Checklist–Revised. *See* Psychopathy Checklist–Revised (PCL-R)
Hare, Robert, 280, 294
Hare Self-Report Psychopathy Scale (HSRP), 283
HCR-20. *See* Historical, Clinical, and Risk Management Violence Risk Assessment Scheme (HCR-20)
Heuristic peripheral processing, 253–54, 258–59
Hezbollah, 219
Hinckley, John, 10
Hirstein, William, 152–53
Historical, Clinical, and Risk Management Violence Risk Assessment Scheme (HCR-20), 113, 328–29, 391
Histrionic personality disorder (HPD), 424–25, 441
Hitler, Adolf, 45
HKT-30, 384, 389, 391
Hobbes, 366

Homer, 363
Homicides, 65–66, 73, 111, 461. *See also* Violence/violent crimes
Homogenous/heterogeneous typologies, 32, 34
Horney, Julie, 5
Hostile aggression, 105
HPD. *See* Histrionic personality disorder (HPD)
HSRP. *See* Hare Self-Report Psychopathy Scale (HSRP)
Human rights violations, 210
Hume, 366
Humiliated fury, 216–19

Iliad (Homer), 363
Implicit planning, 149–50
Impulsivity/impulse control, 291–93, 302, 359–60, 473
Individual-situation interaction, 6
In-group love, 221
Inpatient settings, 77–78, 87
Instrumental aggression, 105, 115
Integrated view of oppositional political terrorism, 206–9
Intellectual property crime, 186t, 193
Intimate partner violence (IPV): borderline personality disorder and, 463, 465, 467–71; characteristics of batterers, 465–67; cycles of, 464–65; domestic violence versus, 463; forensic practice and, 474–78; prevalence and overview, 461–63; psychopathy and, 463, 471–74
Investigative Psychology (IP), 49–50
IPV. *See* Intimate partner violence (IPV)
Irish Republican Army, 219, 221

Jack the Ripper, 45
Japanese violent crime rates, 102–5
Jung, Carl, 154

Kant, 365
Kernberg, Otto, 155
Klaas, Marc, 520–21, 533
Klaas, Polly, 519–20
Knight and Prentky typology of sex offenders, 29–32, 33f
Koch, J. L., 278
Kunlangeta, 341

The Last Seduction, 516
Learning opportunities, 208–9
Legal accountability theory, 372
Legalistic typologies, 19–20
Leopold, Nathan, 372
Level of Service Inventory–Revised (LSI-R), 328–29
Levenson Self-Report Psychopathy Scale (LSRP), 283
Libet experiment, 368–70
Life-course criminology, 115–16
Lindbergh kidnapping, 45
Lindner, Robert, 490
Loan sharking, 192
Loeb, Richard, 372
Lombroso, Cesare, 17–18
The Looming Tower: Al-Qaeda and the Road to 9/11 (Wright), 217–18
Loughner, Jared, 10
LSI-R. *See* Level of Service Inventory–Revised (LSI-R)
LSRP. *See* Levenson Self-Report Psychopathy Scale (LSRP)
Lucas, Henry Lee, 21
Luther, 365
Luxury products smuggling, 186t
Lykken, David, 279–80, 290

MacArthur Study of Mental Disorder and Violence, 15–16
Mad Bomber of New York, 45
Maladaptive personality traits, 385
Malware, 232, 235, 241–43
Manson, Charles, 533
Market-based economic crimes: definition and overview, 167–70; effect on GDP, 173–74; fiscal implications, 176; organized crime and, 179–80; proceeds of, 175; summary, 173t; violence in, 184–91
MASA. *See* Multidimensional Assessment of Sex and Aggression (MASA)
The Mask of Sanity (Cleckley), 22, 279, 289, 313, 356
Massachusetts Treatment Center Rapist Typology Version 3 (MTC:R3), 141–42
Mass communication theory, 257
Masturbation, 132

Maternal filicide, 78–82
MCMI Antisocial Scale, 283
MDS. *See* Multidimensional scaling (MDS)
Meanness, 294–96, 297, 299, 300, 301
Media generator crimes, 255, 262
Media immersion, 267–69
Media violence. *See* Copycat crimes
Mens rea, 370
Mental disorders: criminal behavior and, 10–16; Michael case study, 64–65; prevalence of, 67–69; victims known to offenders and, 106; violent crime and, 69–71, 86–88, 110–11. *See also specific disorders, such as* Personality disorders
Mesomorphs, 18
Migrants illegal markets, 186t
Misdemeanors, 19, 34
MMPI Psychopathic Deviate scale, 283
Mobility typology, 20–21
Money laundering, 175
Mood disorders, 71–72
Moral outrage, 216–17
Moral values, 194, 315, 356, 358, 360, 370
Motivational approach, 105
MTC:R3. *See* Massachusetts Treatment Center Rapist Typology Version 3 (MTC:R3)
Multidimensional Assessment of Sex and Aggression (MASA), 144
Multidimensional scaling (MDS), 49
Multi-trait typologies, 24–26
Musharraf, Pervez, 221

Narcissism-aggression, 207–8
Narcissistic personality disorder, 385. *See also* Pathological narcissism
Narcotics market, 186t, 188
Narrative persuasion, 253–54, 259–60
Negative affect, 216, 220, 222–23
Netherlands forensic patients study, 389–97
Neuroimaging, 366–68
Neuroticism, 144, 287
Neutralization techniques, 11, 235–36
Nicomachean Ethics (Aristotle), 364
Nietzsche, Friedrich, 359–60
Normal offenders, 22–23

Object relations theories, 362–63
Observational learning, 256–57
Obsessive compulsive disorder (OCD), 134, 371
Oedipus Rex, 364
Offender profiling, 44
Operational utilitarian argument, 52–53
Oppositional political terrorism, 206–9
Organized crime, 179–81
Organized/disorganized typology, 23–24, 35–37, 48–49
Organ trafficking, 186t
Orne, Martin, 502

PAI-BOR. *See* Personality Assessment Inventory Borderline Features Subscale (PAI-BOR)
Pakistan, 102
Paranoia, 76–77
Paraphilia, 132–35, 135–37
The Passions of the Soul (Descartes), 365
Pathological narcissism, 493–95. *See also* Narcissistic personality disorder
PCL-R. *See* Psychopathy Checklist–Revised (PCL-R)
PCL:SV. *See* Psychopathy Checklist: Screening Version (PCL:SV)
PCL:YV. *See* Psychopathy Checklist: Youth Version (PCL:YV)
Peak shift effect, 153
Pedophilia, 156–57, 499–500
Peer influences, 236
Perceived injustice, 221
Personality Assessment Inventory Borderline Features Subscale (PAI-BOR), 469
Personality disorders: conduct disorder, 386–89; coping skills and, 384–85; Dark Triad traits, 143–44; DSM and, 382; empathy and, 385–86, 388–89, 396–97; histrionic personality disorder, 424–25, 441; mental disorders and, 13–14; narcissistic personality disorder, 385; Rorschach use in, 487–88, 497–98; severity measures and, 382–84; sociopathic personality disorder, 279, 312, 343–44, 488; violence and, 82–83. *See also* Antisocial personality disorder; Borderline personality disorder

Personality traits: copycat crimes and, 255–56; of cybercriminals, 228, 233–38, 243–45; gender differences, 424–25; of terrorists, 207
Phishing, 231, 242
Pinel, Philippe, 278, 356
Piracy (of software), 235–36, 241
Political crimes: definition and overview, 199–200, 201–2; features of, 8t; obstacles to understanding and interpreting, 200–201; oppositional political terrorism, 206–9; psychological interpretation, 203–5; theories of, 202–3
Pornography, 131
Portugal, 101
Postpartum psychosis, 78–82
Posttraumatic stress disorder (PTSD), 468
Power assertive typology, 23
Power reassurance typology, 23
PPI. *See* Psychopathic Personality Inventory (PPI)
Predatory economic crimes: criminal association and, 179; definition and overview, 166–67; effect on GDP, 173; fiscal implications, 175–76; proceeds of, 175; summary, 173t; violence and, 183
Present internal state, 256
Priming, 261
Primitive borderline defenses, 11
Prisoner adaptation, 20
Prison hierarchies, 20
Prison violence, 114–15
Profilers, 43
Profiling. *See* Criminal profiling
Prohibition, 189–91
Psychoanalysis, 128, 361–63
Psychological profiling, 44
Psychological typologies, 21–24
The Psychopath: An Essay on the Criminal Mind (McCord & McCord), 315
Psychopathic Personality Inventory (PPI), 283, 284–85, 292, 294, 301, 302, 321–22, 326
Psychopathic-Sexually Sadistic Offenders, 415–17
Psychopathy: aggression and, 287–88, 299, 358–61, 366–68; antisocial personality disorder and, 82–85, 343–44, 346–47, 355–56, 487–90, 488–90; anxiety and, 288, 300, 320–21; behaviors of, 358; biological and neuroimaging findings, 366–68; borderline personality disorder and, 473–74; career criminals and, 116, 288–89, 300; controversy about, 286–90; criminal justice policy and, 521–23; criminal responsibility and, 374; culture and, 341–42; DSM and, 488–90, 516–17; free will, decisional capacity, responsibility, 370–74; gender differences, 85, 425–27 (*see also* Female criminal behavior); historical conceptions of, 278–79, 312–16, 355–58; intimate partner violence and, 463, 471–74, 474–78; language and, 11; Libet experiment, 368–70; as masked psychological disturbance, 279–80; noncriminal, 283–86; popular conception of, 518–21; Psychopathic-Sexually Sadistic Offenders category, 415–17; public view of (survey), 523–35; recidivism and, 85, 323–28; research, 344–48; risk assessment and, 328–30; Rorschach and, 490–92, 500; scientific conception of, 515–18; as severe, persistent criminal deviance, 280–81; sexual fantasies and, 143–44; sexual homicide offenders and, 405–7; sexual sadism and, 410–17; sociopathy and, 343–44, 488; successful, 289–90, 301–2; triarchic model of, 290–91, 299–302; boldness, 293–94; disinhibition, 291–93; meanness, 294–96; violence and, 82–85, 287–88, 299, 323–28. *See also* Child Psychopathy Scale; Elemental Psychopathy Assessment; Levenson Self-Report Psychopathy Scale; MMPI Psychopathic Deviate scale; Psychopathic Personality Inventory; Psychopathy Checklist–Revised (PCL-R); Psychopathy Checklist: Youth Version (PCL:YV);Triarchic Psychopathy Measure
Psychopathy Checklist–Revised (PCL-R): anxiety and, 300, 320–21; boldness and, 294, 298; clinical assessment and, 316–19; criminality and, 287–88;

culture and, 341–42; development of, 84, 281–83, 517; disinhibition and, 297; externalizing and, 292; fearlessness and, 301; female offenders and, 442–51; forensic practice and, 476–77; gender differences, 427–28, 441–42; meanness and, 295; measures of, 472; multidimensionality and, 285–86; in noncriminal settings, 348–49; predictive validity of, 328–32; recidivism and, 114, 323–28; research studies and, 344–48; sexual entitlement pathway and, 142; sexual homicide offenders and, 407; structure and external correlates, 319–21; utility of, 311–12; violent inmates and, 115
Psychopathy Checklist: Screening Version (PCL:SV), 317–18, 345, 349
Psychopathy Checklist: Youth Version (PCL:YV), 282, 288, 295, 318–19, 349
Psychosis: maternal filicide and, 78–82; recidivism and, 113; violence and, 73–78, 110–11
Psychotic offenders, 22–23
PTSD. *See* Posttraumatic stress disorder (PTSD)
Public order crimes, 8t
Punishment: copycat crimes and, 264–66; psychopathy and, 360–61, 375–76

Race, 68
Racial profiling, 44
Rader, Dennis, 521
Radicalization, 215–22
Ramachandran, V. S., 152–53
Rape and rapists, 21, 141. *See also* Sex crimes/offenders; Sexual homicide offenders
RAT. *See* Routine activity theory (RAT)
Rationality test, 373
Readiness potential, 369
Reagan, Ronald, 10
Reasoned actions, 257
Recidivism: child abuse and, 387–88; psychopathy and, 85, 323–28; rates of, 70, 112; risk factors, 112–14; sexual homicide offenders and, 404, 407
Regulatory environment, 182–83
Relative contraband, 168
Ridgway, Gary, 21, 521
Risk assessment, 328–30
Risk-taking, 234–35, 236, 238, 242
r/K selection theory, 19
Role-career model, 20
Roll, John, 10
Rorschach: aggression and, 496–97; attachment deficits and, 495–96; borderline personality disorder and, 492–93; Cluster B personality disorders and, 497–98; forensic Rorschach database, 501–3; pathological narcissism and, 493–95; psychopathic women and (*see* Rorschach, psychopathic women and); psychopathy and, 490–92; sexual offenders and, 498–501
Rorschach, psychopathic women and: affect, 429, 432; comparison of psychopathic and non-psychopathic ASPD, 433–36, 437t, 439–42; core characteristics, controls, stress tolerance, 429; female antisocial personality disorder and psychopathy, 428–29; gender differences, 426–27; group mean and frequencies, 430t–432t; implications for the PCL-R, 442–51; interpersonal, 432–33, 438; reality testing, 439; self-perception, 432, 436, 438; thinking and processing, 432
The Rorschach Assessment of Aggressive and Psychopathic Personalities (Gacono & Meloy), 501
Rousseau, 365
Routine activity theory (RAT), 240–44

Sadism. *See* Sexual sadism
SADSEX-SH rating scale, 413–15
SARA. *See* Spousal Assault Risk Assessment Guide (SARA)
Schizophrenia, 75–76, 106, 110–11, 146–47
Script activation, 262
Self-control theory, 234
Self-efficacy, 262
Sensation seeking, 145
Seven against Thebes (Aeschylus), 364
Severe Sexual Sadism scale, 408–9

Sex crimes/offenders: compulsive offenders and, 151–53; features of, 8t; Knight and Prentky typology of, 29–32, 33f; Rorschach and, 498–501; sexual fantasies and, 141–43; transcendence and, 154–57; violence and, 186t, 188. *See also* Sexual homicide offenders
Sexual Entitlement pathway, 142
Sexual fantasies: adolescents and, 130–31, 145–46; behaviorism and, 128; cognitive-behavioral theory and, 128–29; compulsive offenders and, 151–53; core fantasies, 147–49; definitions, 132–35; effects on behavior, 143–45; empirical research and, 127–28; in everyday life, 137–41; guiding fantasies, 148–50; overview, 130–32; psychiatric diagnoses and, 135–37; psychoanalysis and, 128; sadistic, 409–10; schizophrenia and, 146–47; sex crimes and, 141–43; Sexual Fantasy Structural Properties Model and, 129; transcendental function of, 153–57
Sexual Fantasy Structural Properties Model (SFSPM), 129
Sexual homicide offenders (SHOs): case study, 412–15; overview, 403–5; Psychopathic-Sexually Sadistic Offenders category, 415–17; psychopathy and, 405–7; recidivism and, 404, 407; Rorschach and, 498–500, 504–5; sexual sadism and, 408–12; typology, 26
Sexualization pathway, 141–42
Sexual sadism, 155, 408–12, 410–17, 413–15, 415–17
Sexual scripts, 150
Sheldon, William, 18
Sherman, Lawrence, 215
Shining Path, 219
Silence of the Lambs, 516
Simple/complex typologies, 35–37
Smith, Susan, 521
Social bond theory, 11
Social control, 222
Social engineering, 231
Social justice perspective, 200
Social learning model, 252, 266–67
Social mobilization, 216
Socioeconomic levels, 68–69, 113
Sociological typologies, 20–21
Sociopathic personality disorder/sociopathy, 279, 312, 343–44, 488
Software cracking, 236–37
Somotonic temperament, 18
Spam, 230–32
Spamvertising, 231
Spinoza, 365
Spousal Assault Risk Assessment Guide (SARA), 113
State v. Fortin, 56
Stereotypes, 27
Stolen goods, 195–96
Stress, 384–85
Structural conflict theory, 203
Submission fantasies, 140–41, 143
Substance use disorders, 72–73, 107, 111
Swiss violent crime rates, 102–5

Tamil Tigers, 220
Tax evasion, 175–77
Technical cybercrimes, 230–31
Terrorism: definition and overview, 215–16; emotions and radicalization and, 216–19; general strain theory and, 219–22; psychological explanations of, 206–9
Theory of violent attachments, 11
Threat/control-override symptoms, 75
Three Strikes legislation, 521–22
Toole, Otis, 21
Toxic waste illegal markets, 186t
Treatment programs, 477–78
Triarchic Psychopathy Measure (TriPM), 296–99
Tübinger Young Offenders Study, 116
Typologies: biological, 17–19; construction of, 27–29; crime types, 6–9; definition and overview, 4–5; evaluation of, 32, 34–37; Knight and Prentky example, 29–32; legalistic, 19–20; mental disorders and criminal behavior, 10–16; multi-trait, 24–26; psychological, 21–24; situational specificity of criminal behavior and, 5–6; sociological, 20–21; theory and purpose, 16–17, 18f

UCR. *See Uniform Crime Reports* (UCR)
Unemployment, 238–39
Uniform Crime Reports (UCR), 19–20, 35
U.S. violent crime rates, 102–5

Victim services, 7
Victims known to offenders, 105–6
Violence Against Women Act of 1994, 462
Violence Risk Appraisal Guide (VRAG), 113–14, 115, 328–29
Violence/violent crimes: adverse childhood experiences and, 112; antisocial personality disorder and, 82–85; anxiety disorders and, 71–72; child abuse and, 387–88; cognitive violence, 217; defined, 99; domestic violence, 106–8; in economic crimes, 181–83; empathy and, 385–86; features of, 8t; of females, 108–9; gender differences, 425–26; life-course persistence and, 115–16; in market-based economic crimes, 184–91; mental disorders and, 69–71, 86–88, 110–11; motivational background of, 105; offense characteristics, 105–6; prevalence of, 65–66, 100–102; in prisons, 114–15; psychopathy and, 287–88, 299, 323–28; psychosis and, 73–78; recidivism and, 112–14; regulatory environment and, 182–83; risk factors, 109–10; substance use disorders and, 72–73, 111; U.S., Japan, England/Wales, Germany, Switzerland, 102–5. *See also* Aggression
Virginia Tech school shooting, 10
Viscerotonic temperament, 18
Vocabulary of rapists, 11
Voltaire, 365
VRAG. *See* Violence Risk Appraisal Guide (VRAG)

Walker, Lenore, 464
Weapons illegal markets, 186t, 196
Weapons use, 106
White-collar crimes, 233–35, 239. *See also* Cybercrimes
Wildlife illegal markets, 186t
Will and determinism, 363–66
Wright, Lawrence, 217–18
Wuornos, Aileen, 521

Yates, Andrea, 10, 78–79
Youth Psychopathic Traits Inventory (YPI), 283–84
YPI. *See* Youth Psychopathic Traits Inventory (YPI)

Criminal Psychology

Criminal Psychology

Volume 3: Implications for Forensic Assessment, Policing, and the Courts

Jacqueline B. Helfgott, PhD, Editor

Foreword by J. Reid Meloy

PRAEGER

AN IMPRINT OF ABC-CLIO, LLC
Santa Barbara, California • Denver, Colorado • Oxford, England

Library of Congress Cataloging-in-Publication Data

Criminal psychology / Jacqueline B. Helfgott, PhD, editor ; foreword by J. Reid Meloy.
volumes ; cm
Includes bibliographical references and index.
ISBN 978–0–313–39607–6 (hbk. : alk. paper) — ISBN 978–0–313–39608–3 (ebk.)
1. Criminal psychology. I. Helfgott, Jacqueline B.
HV6080.C7335 2013
364.3—dc23 2012051076

ISBN: 978–0–313–39607–6
EISBN: 978–0–313–39608–3

17 16 15 14 3 4 5

This book is also available on the World Wide Web as an eBook.
Visit www.abc-clio.com for details.

Praeger
An Imprint of ABC-CLIO, LLC

ABC-CLIO, LLC
130 Cremona Drive, P.O. Box 1911
Santa Barbara, California 93116-1911

This book is printed on acid-free paper ∞

Manufactured in the United States of America

For my parents, Esther & Oscar

Contents

Foreword by J. Reid Meloy *xi*

Preface by Jacqueline B. Helfgott *xv*

Section I: Forensic Assessment and Risk Prediction

Chapter One: Forensic Assessment of Risk in Criminal Justice 3
Arthur J. Lurigio and Faye S. Taxman

Chapter Two: A Classification of Violent and Other Serious Juvenile Offenders into Subgroups: From Statistical Analyses to Clinical Practice 21
Eva Mulder, Eddy Brand, Ruud Bullens, and Hjalmar J. C. van Marle

Chapter Three: Statistical Controversies in the Sexually Violent Predator Evaluation (SVPE) Practice Community: Bayesian Departure and Polarization 41
Henry Richards

Chapter Four: Sexually Violent Predators and State Appellate Courts' Use of Actuarial Tests in Civil Commitments 87
Frances P. Bernat, Jacqueline B. Helfgott, and Nicholas Godlove

Chapter Five: Actuarial Prediction in Determinate-Plus Sex Offender Release Decisions 113
Jacqueline B. Helfgott and Beck M. Strah

SECTION II: LAW ENFORCEMENT AND PUBLIC SAFETY

Chapter Six: Crisis Intervention and Police Interactions with Individuals with Mental Illness 139
Elizabeth Neidhart

Chapter Seven: The Elements of Hostage (Crisis) Negotiation 169
Lisbeth Eddy and Stanley W. Patrzalek

Chapter Eight: Criminal Profiling: Empirical Evidence on Skills and Accuracy 195
Richard N. Kocsis

Chapter Nine: Linkage Analysis of Serial Murder Cases Involving Prostitute Victims 211
C. Gabrielle Salfati

Chapter Ten: Profiling Psychopathic Traits in Serial Sexual Homicide: A Case Study of the Personality and Personal History of the Green River Killer, Gary Leon Ridgway 229
Loren T. Atherley

Chapter Eleven: Forensic Psychological Evaluations for Behavioral Disorders in Police Officers: Reducing Negligent Hire and Retention Risks 253
Ronn Johnson

SECTION III: CRIMINAL LAW AND THE COURTS

Chapter Twelve: Competency to Stand Trial: Legal Foundations and Practical Applications 281
Stacey L. Shipley

Chapter Thirteen: Insanity Defense 307
Arthur J. Lurigio and Lauran Babchuk

Chapter Fourteen: The Psychology of Criminal Behavior and Sentencing 333
Olaoluwa Olusanya

Chapter Fifteen: Mental Health Court: One Approach for Addressing the Problems of Persons with Serious Mental Illnesses in the Criminal Justice System 367
Matthew W. Epperson, Kelli E. Canada, and Arthur J. Lurigio

Chapter Sixteen: Mental State at the Time of the Offense Forensic Psychological Evaluation: Teresa Lewis Death Penalty Case 393
Ronn Johnson

About the Editor and Contributors 423

Index 433

Foreword

J. Reid Meloy

Ever since the eighteenth and nineteenth centuries—when Franz Gall and Cesare Lombroso, in phrenological leaps of faith, studied the shape of criminal skulls, and Ernst Kretschmer and William Sheldon, in morphological moments of insight, kindled an interest in the physical habitus of the criminal's body—philosophers, biologists, theologians, and psychologists have attempted to discern the criminal's mind. Introducing the unconscious world of psychodynamics shortly thereafter—and challenging a pure biological determinism—Sigmund Freud wrote at the beginning of the twentieth century:

> Two traits are essential in a criminal: a boundless egoism and a strong destructive urge. Common to both of these, and a necessary condition for their expression, is the absence of love, the lack of an emotional appreciation of (human) objects. (Standard Edition, Vol. XXI, p. 178)

None of these pioneers would have imagined the enormity and complexity of criminal psychology at the dawn of the twenty-first century. Jacqueline Helfgott did, and undertook what others might perceive as a Sisyphean task for which she was clearly capable: assemble a multivolume understanding of criminal psychology based upon contemporary theory and empirical research, with the breadth and depth it both required and deserved. She has achieved this remarkable goal with the help of over 100 very accomplished, and in some cases internationally known, contributors.

Dr. Helfgott is a professor and chair of the Criminal Justice Department at Seattle University. We first met in 1989 when she was a young doctoral student at Pennsylvania State University, and had taken an interest in some of our early writing on conscious cognitive processes and psychopathy. She readily understood that there are both unconscious psychodynamics and neurobiological processes that may shape the criminal's conscious thinking—a perspective often lost in some psychology professionals' treatment of choice for criminals, such as a heavy reliance on just cognitive behavioral therapy. To avoid the fundamental attribution error, our tendency to overweight the contribution of personality to motivation and underweight the contribution of the environment, she also paid close attention to both criminology and social psychology. But to really leave a footprint in her profession, she embraced the dynamic interplay between theory and research. Without theory, empirical research is just counting; and without empirical research, theory is just speculation. Or as the British astrophysicist Arthur Eddington once wrote, "No experiment should be believed until it has been confirmed by theory." Dr. Helfgott's early work resulted in two important papers (Helfgott, 1997, 2004) which empirically tested the theory of the relationship between conscious cognitive processes and unconscious psychodynamics in psychopaths, and also applied such findings to the field of forensic psychology practice.

She continues to recognize the importance of engaging both the ivory tower and the street. She has managed the authors and guided in the production of these scholarly volumes; and at the same time, she continues her work on other applied research projects, advisory boards, and various boards of directors concerning treatment of both perpetrators and victims of crime in the Seattle and surrounding Washington State.

When I open a professional or technical book for the first time, I conduct a test that consists of three parts. First, I read something from the book I know a lot about to see how accurate and well referenced it is. Second, I then read something I know nothing about to see if I will learn something new. Finally, I check to see if the writing style delivers the content in a pleasurable manner, or if it is an impediment to learning. In other words, do I have to struggle with poor grammatical choices, moments of illogic, occasional meandering thinking, and awkward syntax to glean something useful from the text? Are there any sentences that approach, for instance, the most elegant and poetic understanding of transference ever written: "So we beat on, boats against the current, borne back ceaselessly into the past"? Probably not, but textbooks should not drive us away, longing for the novels of F. Scott Fitzgerald.

I remember once hearing a well-known forensic psychiatrist testify in a criminal case. His testimony followed a psychiatrist for the defense who had talked in detail about the defendant's propensity to sexually assault his victims only late at night, and his habit of sleeping, instead, throughout the day. He went on with great erudition, his technical use of terms, such as the circadian rhythm sleep disorder of this defendant, superseded only by his boring delivery. When the opposing psychiatrist took the stand and was asked the same question, he responded, "the defendant is a nocturnal predator." Clarity of thought; luminescence in the mind of the listener.

Criminal Psychology, if measured by my admittedly simple yardstick, is a resounding success. The readers of this four-volume set, whether graduate student or seasoned professional, practitioner or academic, will be assured of their existing knowledge, learn much that is new, creative, and scientifically sound, and find it a pleasure to deepen their own thinking.

References

Helfgott, J. (1997). The unconscious defensive process/conscious cognitive style relationship in psychopaths. *Criminal Justice and Behavior, 24*, 278–293.

Helfgott, J. (2004). Primitive defenses in the language of the psychopath: Considerations for forensic practice. *Journal of Forensic Psychology Practice, 4*, 1–29.

J. Reid Meloy is a clinical professor of psychiatry at UC San Diego School of Medicine, and a faculty member of the San Diego Psychoanalytic Institute.

Preface

Jacqueline B. Helfgott

My interest in criminal psychology began sometime around the late 1970s/early 1980s. I'm not sure if I can identify exactly what led me to willingly want to spend the majority of my adult life and most of my waking hours reading, writing, thinking about crime, violence, and psychopathy, and conducting research and programs inside prisons and other criminal justice contexts. When I think back, I guess it was probably a mix of popular culture and personal experiences that made me so interested in the intersection of psychology and criminology/criminal justice. I grew up in the Northwest with a single mother in graduate school, a social activist grandmother, and two younger brothers. I watched a good amount of TV (mostly *I Dream of Jeannie* and *The Brady Bunch*, and shows my brothers wanted to watch such as *Speed Racer*), but not a lot of crime shows. The crime shows on TV at the time were nothing like they are today. Most of the pop cultural crime and violence I was exposed to growing up was on Saturday morning superhero cartoons such as *Wonder Woman* and *Batman*, *ABC After-School Specials*, or shows such as *Charlie's Angels*, *The Six Million Dollar Man*, and *The Bionic Woman* and in the *Hardy Boys* and *Nancy Drew* books. It was well before the era of the serial murder film, and the most memorable depiction of film violence I was allowed to see as a kid was Sissy Spacek's character in *Carrie* when she unleashed her torment on her classmates at the prom after being publicly doused with pig's blood.

One of my earliest memories of being aware of real-life crime was at the breakfast table sometime in the 1970s while eating cereal with my brothers. The little kid on the back of the milk carton was missing, and there had been a lot of stuff in the news around that time about missing children. A couple of years later, my youngest brother's five-year-old friend was found dead, hung in his mother's closet, murdered by a man who was renting a room from his mom. I knew people growing up who shoplifted, used drugs, did time in juvenile detention, and dropped out of school. At my high school graduation, when everyone threw up their hats to hug their friends, I looked around and realized that everyone I knew had dropped out. I wondered why I continued on to college while all of my close friends from that time did not, and a few of them even ended up spending time in jail or prison. I attributed my own trajectory of academic success and crime desistance to the fact that I grew up seeing my mom studying and reading all the time and my grandma fighting for this or that social cause. But I wondered if it could be that simple.

At the time I graduated from high school, my old high school boyfriend came home to find his mother stabbed to death multiple times—the guy who did it was a drug dealer she knew who was caught shortly after. A couple of years later, I bumped into a neighbor friend who lived across the street, who told me that his younger sister was missing and was determined by police to be a victim of the Green River killer. Some years after that, an 83-year-old woman I knew was attacked with lawn sheers and butcher knives by her schizophrenic son who had gone off his meds. He attacked her for hours, stabbed her in the head, and cut her throat from ear to ear. I helped clean the mess that remained after the police and medics left. She survived the attack, and her son was sent to Western State Hospital upon a "Not Guilty by Reason of Insanity" verdict. He was released to his mother's—his victim's—care five years later. These and other incidents and experiences have made criminal behavior and its response in both the mental health and criminal justice systems very real for me.

I decided to study criminal justice and psychology in college after starting out as an art major and deciding that I would not be able to draw under pressure and that it would probably be more realistic to do something else for a living. I waited tables through college and got to know police officers who came into the restaurants where I worked and who took me on ride-alongs. I completed an internship in community corrections working with an officer in charge of a sex-offender caseload and read case files filled with accounts of bizarre acts of sexual deviancy. I went on tours of prisons and halfway houses and on work releases. I took courses from inspirational faculty, many of whom were leading-edge scholars at the forefront of forensic psychology and criminology, some of the most prominent scholars in the field—cognitive psychologist Elizabeth Loftus, now one of the most cited psychologists in history; Dale Smith, a psychologist who had published work with Hans Toch on inmate adjustment; and criminology and criminal justice with George Bridges, whose lecture style of story after story made academic criminology seem like one of the most important callings. I took a tour of the Washington State Penitentiary in Walla Walla, where I saw Kevin Coe, the subject of Jack Olsen's book *Son: A Psychopath and His Victims*, soon after he was convicted, standing only feet away from me. I conducted a study on psychologists' views on psychopathy and had the opportunity to interview Seattle-area psychologists who worked in the intersection of criminal justice and mental health, including psychologists who later would go on to evaluate infamous serial killers such as Wesley Dodd. My personal experiences learning about crime from people I knew who were victims or offenders were shaped and explained in a new way through learning from practitioners in the field and academic research.

In my senior year of college in the late 1980s, while finishing up my undergraduate degrees in psychology and society and justice, I read books that to this day I have not been able to get out of my head—Wambaugh's (1987) *The Onion Field*; Olsen's (1983) *Son: A Psychopath and His Victims*; Rule's (1987) *Small Sacrifices*; Cleckley's (1941) *The Mask of Sanity*; Lindner's (1945) *Rebel without a Cause*; McCoy's (1981) *Concrete Mama: Prison Profiles from Walla Walla*; Hare's (1970) *Psychopathy: Theory and Research*; Yochelson and Samenow's (1977) *The Criminal Personality, Volumes 1–3*; Goffman's (1963) *Stigma*; Meloy's (1988) *The Psychopathic Mind*; and Johnson's (1987) *Hard Time: Understanding and Reforming the Prison*. These and other works I read at the time created great intrigue for me, raising question after question at the nexus of psychology and criminology/criminal justice—*What makes a person a law-abiding citizen versus a home invasion robber or a rapist or a murderer? How do police and corrections officers mentally process their jobs and their interactions with offenders? How do the mental health and criminal justice systems work together to respond to criminal behavior? How do victims of crime move on in the aftermath of criminal behavior? What makes a person incapable of feeling and able to hurt other people without feeling any guilt or concern for their welfare? What kinds of things go on in people's minds when they steal, vandalize, kidnap, rape, and murder? How do prison inmates adjust to long-term confinement? Where do fantasies about hurting other people come from in the first place? What is a psychopath, and how do you tell who is and who is not one? If psychopaths and other persistent offenders are so impervious to treatment, what should be done with them? How were psychologists so certain they could tell the difference between a criminal psychopath and a criminal who was just down on his luck? What mental mechanisms are at work when people commit minor crimes like shoplifting and major crimes like child abduction and serial murder? Once a person develops a deviant or criminal identity, what hope is there that the person can change to be a law-abiding citizen?*

In the late 1980s, there were few quick or definitive answers to most of these questions. Forensic psychology did not yet exist in the form of formal academic programs (beyond a few joint psychology and law programs). Computers were just becoming accessible on college campuses, and there was no Internet or Google. I typed my graduate school applications on a typewriter and picked schools I thought sounded good in places I thought I might like to go. I had read Bob Hare's book *Psychopathy*, but as a naïve undergraduate who was working three waitress jobs while going to school full time, it somehow eluded me (until a couple of years later when across the country in graduate school) that he was only 150 miles away at the University of British Columbia. I recall calling and speaking with Stanton Samenow on the phone as I prepared my graduate applications. I don't remember what I asked him or what we discussed, but he was nice enough to speak to a know-nothing college student just starting out. I had no idea where to apply to graduate school. All I knew was that I wanted to study psychopaths and the intersection of criminal justice and psychology. I applied to programs in psychology and criminal justice and landed at Penn State. I had applied to the Psychology Department there but had written a cover letter about wanting to study psychopathy and the intersection of mental health and criminal justice. The Psychology Department called and asked if I minded if they sent my file to the Administration of Justice Department. I got a call the next day with an enthusiastic offer of a research and teaching assistantship in administration of justice with a graduate minor in psychology that would allow me to pursue my research interests, which I gladly accepted.

I did my master's thesis and dissertation in the early 1990s on the unconscious defensive process/conscious cognitive style relationship in psychopaths. When I got to graduate school and started doing research for my master's thesis, I came across Gacono and Meloy's (1988) article, "The Relationship between Conscious Cognitive Style and Unconscious Defensive Process in the Psychopath," published in *Criminal Justice and Behavior*. I still remember the day I got my hands on the article and sat in the library reading it. I was so enthralled that soon after, I began the process of pulling together my thesis and dissertation committee and developing a study to empirically test the hypothetical rape scenario and levels hypothesis on the UDP/CCS relationship in psychopaths proposed in the article. My dissertation committee consisted of two psychologists (Lynne Goodstein, who had done work on inmate adjustment and long-term imprisonment, and Juris Draguns, whose research focused on cross-cultural psychology and personality), a lawyer (Daniel Katkin), and a former probation officer turned professor (William Parsonage). I took courses with Philip Jenkins (who some years later went on to write highly influential work on moral panic theory), Fran Bernat (now the editor of *Women and Criminal Justice*), and was fortunate to have assistance from Bob Hare, Carl Gacono, and Reid Meloy during the process of completing my dissertation. I received training in administering the PCL-R through the old-school method, which involved receiving large cardboard boxes in the mail from Bob Hare and colleagues containing videotapes and files that I was to review, score, and mail back for interrater reliability scores. Juris Draguns taught me how to administer the Rorschach. In my graduate school years, Faith Lutze, who went on to do important work in corrections and offender reentry, and Bruce Arrigo (now editor of the *Journal of Forensic Psychology Practice*), who has made prolific and key contributions in forensic psychology, were classmates; and I had the opportunity to meet other scholars whose work I admired at conferences, such as Adrian Raine, Robert Johnson, Kathleen Heide, and many others. Later, as a newly minted assistant professor, I invited my favorite true crime authors Jack Olsen and Ann Rule to campus to speak and had the opportunity to get to know them as well, especially Jack Olsen, who I consider the greatest true crime writer of all time.

Since those early years that shaped my academic career, I have had the opportunity to engage in research in law enforcement and corrections that has further shaped my perspective and academic pursuits. I have spent a good part of my career teaching courses and conducting research at the intersection of psychology and criminal justice. I have also been fortunate to be able to combine some of my other interests into my work. I have coordinated art and other programs in prisons for most of my career, which has allowed me to spend great amounts of time working directly with people who have committed crimes and who have served long sentences, both in and out of confinement. I have been involved in applied research that has kept me constantly aware of the real issues confronting practitioners and the responsibility academics have to make theory and research accessible to practice. I have worked with truly amazing students, from whom I have learned and who have helped me to expand my views and the questions I ask. Through some of these experiences, I have had been able to learn about the psychology of crime and criminal justice in ways that more formal research endeavors have not allowed. It has always been a bit surprising to me how much more I have learned about crime while painting a mural with a group of Lifers or riding around town with police officers than by analyzing data from psychometric tests and self-reports.

I sometimes find myself envious of the opportunities my students have today for the great many academic programs in forensic psychology. In the 1980s, the field of forensic psychology did not yet exist in the form of established academic programs, scholarly journals, or professional organizations. The academic discipline of criminal justice/criminology was only a generation old, if that. Library research on topics such as "psychopaths," "criminal psychology," or "criminal profiling" at that time resulted in a confusing absence of consensus and muddled terminology that had the potential to generate more frustration than new ideas or frameworks for empirical research. Today, there are a range of opportunities to study the intersection of psychology and crime, with many academic programs in forensic psychology and criminology/criminal justice, and there is disciplinary integration that did not exist 20 years ago.

However, I feel fortunate to have learned from, worked with, and/or gone to school with some of the brightest minds in the field responsible for shaping the study of criminal and forensic psychology today. Many of these scholars have contributed their work to this reference set. The study of criminal psychology and criminal behavior has come incredibly far in a very short time. Theory and anecdote have been tested by empirical research; forensic assessment tools have been developed, standardized, and validated; and much of the important theoretical and empirical work that has been done in the intersection of psychology and criminology/criminal justice is now making its way into practice in law enforcement agencies, courts, prisons and halfway houses, juvenile detention facilities, schools, victim services, and communities.

The volumes and chapters included in *Criminal Psychology, Volumes 1–4* reflect the state of the science of criminal psychology and criminal behavior written by the best and brightest minds in the academic criminology and forensic psychology, practitioners at the front end of the criminal justice and forensic settings, and scholars engaged in creative cutting-edge work. The work is organized into four volumes: Volume 1: Theory and Research; Volume 2: Typologies, Mental Disorders, and Profiles; Volume 3: Implications for Forensic Assessment, Policing, and the Courts; and Volume 4: Implications for Juvenile Justice, Corrections, and Reentry. Volume 1 offers an overview of theory, research, and key findings on criminal psychology and criminal behavior. Volume 2 addresses the utility of criminal typologies and profiles, presents research on specific crime types and psychopathy. The chapters included in Volumes 3 and 4 illustrate how theory and research on criminal psychology enter the criminal justice system in forensic assessment and prediction of dangerousness, law enforcement, criminal law, the courts, and sentencing, juvenile justice, institutional and community corrections, and offender reentry. I am proud of this mix of key and prominent researchers and theorists, whose work is the brick and mortar of today's criminal psychology joined by scholars just starting out in the field and practitioners who have a front-line vantage point. I am grateful to their willingness to contribute their work in this comprehensive, timely, and important collection on criminal psychology and criminal behavior. We have seen an unprecedented amount of attention to criminal psychology in the last 20 years, in all realms—academic, popular culture, and real-world practice. I hope the work contained in this set raises new questions and helps set the stage for what promises to be an era of greater refinement of theory, research, and practice that will provide answers that will help whittle away at the complex underpinnings and sometime tragic effects of criminal behavior.

A project like this is an enormous undertaking that requires the collaboration of many people. I am grateful to the many authors who have contributed their work and would like to thank each one of them individually. There are a number of people who deserve special acknowledgment. First and foremost, my research assistant Teneshia Thurman, who corresponded with over 100 authors, edited 61 chapters, and assisted with all aspects of the project. Teneshia's contributions to this project were enormous and invaluable and required extraordinary patience and attention. I could not have completed the project without her. I would also like to thank Praeger/ABC-CLIO senior editor Debbie Carvalko for her assistance with the project and her advice, contributions, and good humor at key points in the process, and Praeger/ABC-CLIO acquisitions editor Alicia Merritt for inviting me to serve as editor for this set. Special thanks to the energetic and supportive faculty and students I work with in the Criminal Justice Department at Seattle University; to George Palermo (editor of the *International Journal of Offender Therapy and Comparative Criminology*), Carl Gacono and Kathleen Heide, who, in addition to contributing their own work, were instrumental in linking me to other authors; and to Reid Meloy for both contributing work and for writing the foreword. I don't think a single student has completed one of my courses during the course of my career who hasn't heard me say that I think Reid Meloy is the most brilliant theorist that has ever written in the field of criminal psychology. To have him write the foreword for this set is an incredible honor, and I can't think of a more perfect way to introduce to the subject of criminal psychology and the work and authors contained in this collection.

Finally, I would like to thank my family and friends who provided a huge amount of support in the three years it took to complete this project, especially: my daughter Zalia, who saves me from embarrassing myself on a daily basis and has spent many more hours than I would have liked talking to me behind a computer screen; my brothers Ian and Scott; and my parents Esther Helfgott and Oscar Feit, to whom this work is dedicated. My mom is a never-ending source of inspiration. She is my flagger at the fork at the end of the road and the reason I took the right turn instead of the wrong one. My dad died during the course of this project. Even after he had a heart attack and was struggling to recuperate, he was always trying to send me on my way, saying, "Go write your books . . ." He died sitting in his living room chair. When we cleaned out his apartment, there were three books in the little cabinet right next to his chair—a Bible, my dissertation, and the *Criminal Behavior* textbook I wrote a few years ago (Helfgott, 2008). I think he would have enjoyed reading this.

References

Cleckley, H. (1941, 1976, 1988). *The mask of sanity*. St. Louis, MO: Mosby.

Goffman, E. (1963). *Stigma: Notes on the management of spoiled identity*. Englewood Cliffs, NJ: Prentice-Hall.

Hare, R. D. (1970). *Psychopathy: Theory and research*. New York/London: John Wiley & Sons.

Helfgott, J. B. (2008). *Criminal behavior: Theories, typologies, and criminal justice*. Thousand Oaks, CA: Sage.

Johnson, R. (1987). *Hard time: Understanding and reforming the prison*. Belmont, CA: Brooks/Cole.

Lindner, R. M. (1945). *Rebel without a cause*. London: Research Books.

McCoy, J. (1981). *Concrete mama: Prison profiles from Walla Walla*. Columbia, MO: University of Missouri Press.

Meloy, J. R. (1988). *The psychopathic mind: Origins, dynamics, and treatment*. New Jersey/London: Jason Aronson.

Olsen, J. (1983). *Son: A psychopath and his victims*. New York: Macmillan Press.

Rule, A. (1987). *Small sacrifices: A true story of passion and murder*. New York: New American Library.

Wambaugh, J. (1987). *The onion field*. New York: Dell.

Yochelson, S., & Samenow, S. E. (1977). *The criminal personality: Volumes 1–3*. New York: Jason Aronson.

SECTION I

Forensic Assessment and Risk Prediction

CHAPTER ONE

Forensic Assessment of Risk in Criminal Justice

Arthur J. Lurigio and Faye S. Taxman

This chapter discusses forensic risk assessment in criminal justice and is divided into five sections. The first section introduces the concept of risk assessment and its general application in various decision-making domains, such as medicine. Forensic risk assessments are conducted in court and correctional settings for the purpose of predicting human behavior, most commonly, criminal recidivism. The next section explores four generations of forensic risk assessment, which employ different mechanisms for predicting outcomes. The oldest method, clinical decision-making, consists of subjective judgments and impressions that are formulated through record analyses and unstructured clinical interviews.

In the area of forensic risk assessment, clinicians have been asked to predict "dangerousness." Research has showed that clinicians perform poorly at this task, yet the Supreme Court has ruled that predictions of violence are admissible as evidence in criminal and civil proceedings. Clinical models have been largely supplanted by statistically derived instruments, which are more structured and accurate. However, statistical tools often fail to consider criminogenic needs as well as offenders' amenability to change during the supervisory process. Therefore, forensic risk assessment now includes evaluations of dynamic factors and criminogenic needs. The most recent generation of forensic risk assessment, known as structured professional judgment, melds statistical and clinical techniques.

The third section briefly describes several forensic risk assessment tools, including examples of instruments that combine approaches to risk evaluation (statistical and clinical). The fourth section discusses the obstacles to adopting risk assessment tools (e.g., individual, organizational, perceptual, and practical) and suggests ways to improve the implementation of risk/need evaluation in the criminal justice system. The final section explores directions for future research and practices in forensic risk assessment. Predictions that are rendered about specific, rather than general, outcomes are usually more useful to decision makers and their clients. Forensic risk assessment can be an opportunity for prevention and behavioral change, altering offenders' criminality and penetration into the criminal justice system.

Risk Assessment: An Overview

Risk assessment is broadly defined as a process in which information is collected and synthesized for the purpose of predicting adverse events. These predictions are often used in attempts to prevent such events or to minimize their consequences (McNiel et al., 2002). The risk assessment process involves an estimation of the likelihood of an event and its potential ramifications (Janus & Meehl, 1997). Risk assessments are conducted in numerous decision-making domains, such as meteorology, actuarial science, and medicine (Fischoff, 1994; Hayakawa, Fischbeck, & Fischoff, 2000).

In medicine, for example, cardiologists assess patient risk for a heart attack (the adverse event) by examining the patient and studying the results of diagnostic tests to determine the severity of heart disease (the evaluation). If a heart attack appears imminent, and thus the risk is high (i.e., the risk assessment shows severe blockages in the coronary arteries), the physician orders emergency surgery or other interventions designed to avert a myocardial infarction (preventive measures). If a heart attack has already occurred, the physician conducts a risk assessment to create a treatment plan for minimizing the damage caused by the heart attack (harm reduction) as well as halting or reversing the progression of cardiovascular disease. Interventions to reduce the odds of a subsequent heart attack are an example of the linkage between risk assessment and prevention.

Forensic risk assessments are performed in a variety of legal and correctional settings and concentrate on predictions of the likelihood of reoffending (Fulero & Wrightsman, 2009). People's future actions are typically more difficult to forecast and forestall than diseases or natural disasters; hence, the prediction and prevention of adverse events in forensic risk assessment are much less certain than they are in medicine or the basic sciences. For example, a psychiatrist evaluates a patient who has been confined to a maximum-security facility after being found not guilty by reason of insanity for stabbing a victim in a psychotic rage. The forensic examiner assesses the patient's risk for violence in the community (the adverse event) by interviewing the patient and reviewing his records, including the patient's behavior on the locked unit (the evaluation). If the subject is judged a risk for future violence, the psychiatrist can recommend continued confinement (the preventive measure). However, unlike the field of cardiology, the forensic examiner operates in a complex, multifactorial decision-making environment with no definitive tests for predicting criminal activity.

The preceding example illustrates the primary purpose of forensic risk assessment, which is to evaluate people for the purpose of predicting their future behavior, particularly any of their activities that are harmful to others. Forensic risk assessments consist of several basic components. These include a decision maker (e.g., psychologist, psychiatrist, probation officer, social worker, or parole administrator); a subject (e.g., inmate, pretrial detainee, probationer, or patient); a predicted behavior (e.g., criminal activity, recidivism, sex offense, or parole violation); a decision (e.g., preventive detention, sentencing, case management, or treatment); information for arriving at the decision (e.g., criminal and psychiatric records, interview responses, or histories of substance use or violence); a process for weighing and combining information (e.g., risk scales); and a setting in which a decision is rendered (e.g., courtroom, jail, prison, or parole office).

As discussed in this chapter, decision makers can adopt different methodologies for collecting and integrating information used to predict an outcome. These strategies have varying degrees of predictive validity or accuracy; some focus on highly specific behaviors (e.g., sex offending), others on more general behaviors (e.g., recidivism). After a prediction is generated, decision makers can recommend interventions that affect the future status, freedom, or behavior of a subject. The predictive criterion or outcome most common in forensic risk assessment is the commission of violent or sex offenses (Lurigio & Harris, 2009).

Generations of Forensic Risk Assessment

First Generation: Clinical Models

Psychodynamics

Forensic risk assessment has evolved through four generations of decision making, which are characterized by different philosophies and processes. The first generation, clinical risk assessment, is usually performed by psychologists and psychiatrists trained in psychodynamic or medical models of psychopathology (e.g., violence, addiction, or criminal behavior). Based primarily on interviews and historical analyses of subjects' early experiences and records of treatment and confinement, clinical evaluations are also performed by non-clinicians, such as probation and correctional officers (Meehl, 1954).

Clinical assessments are often grounded in theoretical frameworks or paradigms (psychoanalytic, humanistic, and behavioral). Within these comprehensive frameworks, clinicians draw on their instincts and impressions when judging subjects' predilections and motivations; these insights provide the foundation for prediction. Although clinical decision-makers might share the same orientations, clinical decision-making is highly idiosyncratic and therefore highly unreliable. Decisions are unstructured and made on a case-by-case, intuitive basis with little or no statistical information, such as base rates, which can greatly improve the accuracy of prediction (Andrews, Bonta, & Wormith, 2006; Lurigio & Harris, 2009; Taxman, Cropsey, Young, & Wexler, 2007). Furthermore, clinical decision-making can consider variables that are unrelated statistically to the outcome and therefore add no predictive value, frequently leading to systematic errors and introducing biases (e.g., gender, race, and age) into the assessment process (Taxman, Cropsey, et al., 2007). In addition, clinical decision-making employs no standard protocols that allow the judgment process to be replicated or tested for immediate or long-term validity (Bonta, 2002).

Dangerousness

The earliest forensic risk assessments were of "dangerousness" (Fulero & Wrightsman, 2009). Many of these evaluations were performed to determine whether to release prison inmates or people with mental illness who were institutionalized for violent acts. The assumption was that such "dangerous" individuals pose a risk to public safety when released into the community. In *Baxstrom v. Herold* (1966), the U.S. Supreme Court questioned the validity and constitutionality of assessments of dangerousness conducted for the purpose of involuntary psychiatric commitment. At the time the case was heard, Baxstrom was civilly committed to the Dannemora State Hospital, a maximum-security correctional hospital in upstate New York, after he had served his criminal sentence. The court ruled that indefinite confinement was a violation of the equal protection safeguards that extend to involuntarily committed psychiatric patients.

As a result of the *Baxstrom* decision, 967 civilly committed offenders in New York State were released following the completion of their prison sentences. Research showed that the rate of reoffending among these releasees was very low (Steadman & Cocozza, 1974)—a finding that was replicated within the forensic populations of other states, such as Pennsylvania (Thornberry & Jacoby, 1979). The *Baxstrom* case and its aftermath fostered lingering doubts about clinicians' ability to accurately predict violence and uncovered their tendency to overpredict recidivism (i.e., to commit false-positive errors) (Steadman & Cocozza, 1974).

A comprehensive review of research on the predictive validity of dangerousness assessments concluded that "psychiatrists and psychologists are accurate in no more than one out of three predictions of violent behavior over a several-year period among institutionalized populations that had both committed violence in the past (and thus had a high base rate for it) and who were diagnosed as mentally ill" (Monahan, 1982, p. 77). Following the Baxstrom study and other widely cited investigations, researchers and legal scholars began expressing serious concerns about the constitutionality and accuracy of clinical predictions of violent behavior (Ennis & Litwack, 1974). Thus, "as the concept of dangerousness began to fall into disfavor in the scientific community, a new risk assessment model began to emerge" (Fulero & Wrightsman, 2009, p. 135). Nonetheless, in *Barefoot v. Estelle* (1983), the court ruled that experts may proffer opinions about a defendant's tendency to commit future violent or criminal acts, asserting that triers-of-fact can properly weigh the probative value of such evidence.

Second Generation: Statistical Models

Background

Statistical or actuarial techniques—the second generation of forensic risk assessment—rely on data from large samples of cases in order to develop objective instruments that produce more precise predictions and fewer systematic biases than clinical risk assessments (Otto, 1992). Prediction can be stated as a probability (e.g., this parolee has a 20% likelihood of violating the conditions of release) or a frequency (e.g., of 100 such parolees, 20 will violate the conditions of release) (Heilbrun, Douglas, & Yasuhara, 2009). Actuarial prediction is a formal, mechanistic method that "uses an equation, a formula, a graph, or an actuarial table to arrive at a probability or expected value of some outcome" (Grove & Meehl, 1996, p. 294).

The construction of statistical prediction tools involves a threefold process (Gottfredson, 1987; Holsinger, Lurigio, & Latessa, 2001). In the first phase, researchers select variables (e.g., number of previous arrests, employment, educational background, marital status, and drug use history) that are deemed to be related to the predicted outcome (e.g., rearrest, technical violation, on parole). These variables are coded from closed cases in which the outcome is known (e.g., arrest/no arrest while on parole). Multivariate analyses are performed to identify variables that differentiate between those rearrested and those not (or any outcome of interest). Variables that bear a statistical relationship to the outcome are weighted according to their power to accurately retrodict membership in the groups. In the second phase, the variables are built into an assessment tool with specific directions for scoring subjects on each factor. These scores are summed to arrive at a prediction of rearrest or other criteria. On the basis of the assessed risk of rearrest, subjects are placed into categories for supervision. In the third phase, the variables in the constructed assessment tool are then tested on a new sample of closed cases (or sometimes a bootstrap sample of randomly selected subgroups of closed cases) to validate the outcomes. The validation process demonstrates whether a risk instrument has sufficient predictive validity.

The development of one of the second-generation risk tools to predict violence involved the coding of several variables from the files of more than 600 men once confined to a maximum-security hospital in Canada (Harris, Rice, & Quinsey, 1993). These variables included marital status, intelligence, early separation from parents, elementary school maladjustment, and history of alcohol abuse. Patients were scored on each of the variables. The scores were summed and the total score was used to predict whether releasees were subsequently rearrested for a violent crime following discharge. The variables that distinguished between violent arrestees and nonarrestees were built into a structured assessment tool for predicting violence among future patients evaluated for release.

Statistical decision-making is superior to clinical decision-making for several reasons. Specifically, the former uses information from a large number of cases to create assessment protocols that take advantage of the robust statistical relationships between predictors and outcomes. The latter uses information from clinical experiences that are tinged with biases, heuristics, and shortcomings intrinsic to human judgment and decision making. The vast superiority of actuarial over clinical models of prediction has been demonstrated consistently since the 1950s (Grove & Meehl, 1996), and actuarial models have dominated the field of forensic risk assessment since the 1970s (Holsinger et al., 2001).

Third Generation: Criminogenic Needs/Dynamic Models

Overview

Second-generation forensic risk assessment tools were developed primarily for predicting recidivism, not for informing treatment or intervention plans. Such tools consisted mostly of static (unchangeable) predictors, such as criminal history and early behavioral problems (Wong, Gordon, & Gu, 2007; Taxman, Cropsey, et al., 2007). The tools were more effective than clinical evaluations at predicting risk, but many failed to adequately address offenders' service needs or their readiness or capability to change. Second-generation instruments also performed poorly at measuring changes in risk levels over time (Douglas & Skeem, 2005).

Third-generation tools recognize that offenders can modify their behaviors during the course of supervision, and therefore, such instruments also consist of dynamic (mutable) factors, such as employment, drug use, and educational attainment. In addition, third-generation models incorporate the principles of risk, need, and responsivity, which provide the groundwork for developing case management plans for reducing the risk of recidivism. Correctional treatments that build explicitly on addressing criminogenic needs are generally more effective in changing offenders than those that ignore such principles (Andrews et al., 1990; Andrews & Bonta, 2003).

Risk and Need

The risk principle indicates that levels of supervision (or correctional control) should match clients' predicted level of risk. Specifically, offenders judged as exhibiting "high," "medium," or "low" risk should participate in case management programming that is commensurate with those risk levels. The need principle indicates that an offender's criminogenic needs—which are associated with violence or criminality, such as criminal attitudes, associates, and thinking as well as drug use, impulsivity, and family dysfunction—must be evaluated and targeted for services. Other factors such as mental health status, employment, and education, which are not determinants of criminal behavior, should be considered in order to stabilize the offender in the treatment and control process. Effective correctional treatments ameliorate criminogenic needs, thereby reducing risk and further criminal involvement. Interventions that fail to address criminogenic needs have little or no effect on risk or propensity for rearrest (Andrews & Bonta, 2003; Andrews & Dowden, 2005; Wong et al., 2007). Moreover, correctional interventions that respond to the noncriminogenic needs of low-risk offenders can increase recidivism (Andrews & Bonta, 2006; Lowenkamp, Latessa, & Holsinger, 2006).

Responsivity

The responsivity principle indicates that treatment effectiveness is maximized when interventions are tailored to offenders' intellectual abilities, learning style, motivation to change, readiness for treatment, and cultural backgrounds. Responsivity refers to individual characteristics that must be considered in case management planning to ensure that treatment and monitoring schemes are precisely matched to offenders' strengths and preparedness to benefit from services (Wong & Hare, 2005). Another issue related to responsivity is the degree to which criminogenic needs are being addressed by treatment programs. Programs that attend to three or more criminogenic needs are more likely to improve outcomes by dealing with an offender's criminal lifestyle (Andrews et al., 2006).

Fourth Generation: Structured Clinical Judgment Models

The advantages of second- and third-generation risk assessment models lie in their structured and statistical nature. The former enhances the reliability of the tools—the latter, their validity. As noted earlier, in the long term and with a large number of clients, these instruments lead to greater success in prediction than clinical evaluations. Statistical tools were improved with the inclusion of dynamic factors, which examine changes in risk levels and underscore the importance of servicing criminogenic needs in highly individualized case management plans that account for treatment readiness as well as gender, cultural, and other types of sensitivities. Despite these obvious strengths, recent generations of risk assessment have neglected the obvious contribution of clinical judgments. In contrast, fourth-generation (anamnestic) tools encompass clinical judgments within a risk management framework that seeks to prevent crime and violence through the identification and mitigation of immediate risk factors (Andrews et al., 2006; Heilbrun, 1997).

As suggested above, fourth-generation risk assessment strategies are designed to bridge the actuarial-clinical divide; such strategies meld actuarial methods, which are heavily reliant on static variables and focus on long-term risk, with clinical methods, which are heavily reliant on individualized factors and focus on short-term risk (Dvoskin & Heilbrun, 2001). Traditional actuarial models limit the flexibility needed to make impromptu adjustments in risk appraisals based on immediate circumstances, which are typically beyond the scope of standard risk-assessment metrics. "A major goal of the fourth-generation instruments is to strengthen adherence with the principles of effective treatment and to facilitate clinical supervision devoted to enhance public protection from recidivistic crime" (Andrews et al., 2006, p. 8). As such, fourth-generation risk assessment views actuarial and clinical decision-making techniques as comparable strategies.

Once criticized as arbitrary and unstructured, the role of professional judgment has shifted dramatically with the development of empirically guided instruments that infuse clinical expertise into the risk assessment process. Structured clinical or professional assessment tools prompt the evaluator to consider a range of statistically valid risk factors, which are then viewed as more or less applicable in estimating risk in particular cases (Webster, Douglas, Eaves, & Hart, 1997). In contrast to the prescriptive nature of pure actuarial instruments, structured professional judgments are more elastic and therefore provide examiners with more discretion in the inclusion, weighting, and combination of specific risk factors.

The clinical-actuarial debate made a clear distinction between unstructured, impressionistic evaluations, which predict risk on the basis of subjective judgments, and objective, standardized measures, which predict risk on the basis of statistical formulations (Dawes, Faust, & Meehl, 1989). However, a more balanced, hybrid approach to risk assessment has recently appeared: clinical methods have become increasingly evidenced-based (Webster et al., 1997), and actuarial methods that more closely mirror clinical decision-making (Monahan et al., 2005). Hybrid risk assessment tools are referred to as structured clinical or professional judgments.

Risk Assessment Tools

Violence Risk Appraisal Guide

Featured in the above example of the construction of a risk assessment tool, the Violence Risk Appraisal Guide (VRAG) is a prominent actuarial instrument. It was validated in a longitudinal study of 800 offenders released from a maximum-security Canadian psychiatric facility (Quinsey, Harris, Rice, & Cormier, 1998). The VRAG consists of 12 items that are scored and summed in order to predict the likelihood that an individual will commit a violent act in the community. One of the VRAG's core predictive factors is psychopathy, which is measured by the Hare Psychopathy Checklist–Revised (PCL-R; Hare, 1991). This measure is embedded in several other actuarial risk scales and has been shown to be a valid predictor of violence.

Historical/Clinical/Risk Management-20

The blending of clinical and statistical approaches is embodied in a guided clinical evaluation tool known as the Historical/Clinical/Risk Management-20 (HCR-20). Originally developed in 1995 and revised in 1997, the instrument became a prototype for structured clinical decision-making, providing an alternative to more rigid actuarial models such as the VRAG. The HCR-20 contains many of the factors measured in the PCL-R and is balanced in terms of static, stable, and dynamic variables. Its 20 items (rated on a 0–2 scale like the PCL-R) are divided into three sections that integrate information that pertains to the past (historical), present (clinical), and future (risk management) (Webster et al., 1997).

Iterative Classification Tree

Perhaps the most ambitious attempt to bridge the clinical-actuarial divide is the Iterative Classification Tree (ICT) and its companion tool known as the Classification of Violence Risk (COVR). Stemming from the MacArthur Violence Risk Assessment Study, the ICT and COVR introduced a new paradigm for evaluating the risk of violence, addressing many of the methodological shortcomings that have affected previous studies of risk assessment (Banks et al., 2004; Monahan et al., 2000; Monahan et al., 2005).

The ICT is consistent with a new vision for violence risk assessment; predicated on a more nuanced and interactive view of violence and its causes; and attentive to that fact that actuarial tools, in general, have been embraced by researchers but resisted by clinicians. This resistance can be explained, in part, by the reliance of actuarial tools on linear regression-based models that place people in categories of risk and ignore critical differences among the people within those categories. The ICT parallels the clinical decision-making process by using decision trees and setting thresholds for high- and low-risk cases (Steadman et al., 2000).

Based on the ICT process, MacArthur researchers developed and validated the COVR, which is a computer-based application (Monahan et al., 2005). Research has demonstrated that the COVR differentiates successfully between low- and high-risk populations but is less accurate in identifying moderate-risk cases. To date, the COVR has been validated with only psychiatric populations. However, the tool's conceptual, methodological, and operational advantages are promising. Through its multidimensional evaluation of risk and its technology-supported administration, the COVR can also be implemented in the fields of community corrections and law enforcement.

Level of Service Inventory–Revised

The Level of Service Inventory–Revised (LSI-R) assesses risk by combining dynamic and static factors (Andrews & Bonta, 1995). The LSI-R covers 10 domains, including criminal history, education, employment, and financial resources. This tool provides useful information on clients' risk and criminogenic needs, but it does not assess the key responsivity issue of treatment readiness. It is also unclear about how to relate treatment changes with changes in needs (i.e., the specific behaviors that signify changes in these domains). For example, in the LSI-R, finances and employment can be measured if the offender was recently working in the community. However, changes in the domain are difficult to assess if the individual has been incarcerated and out of the workforce (Wong et al., 2007).

Violence Risk Scale

The Violence Risk Scale (VRS) incorporates the principles of risk, need, and responsivity (Andrews & Bonta, 2003; Wong & Gordon, 2006). The VRS also tracks reductions in risk as a function of progress in treatment. The VRS consists of 6 static and 20 dynamic variables, which are each rated on a four-point scale (0, 1, 2 or 3) based on data collected from offender files and a semi-structured interview. The VRS's static variables predict general and violent recidivism. Higher ratings on the static variables reflect histories of dysfunctional and antisocial behavior. The dynamic variables include interpersonal aggression and criminal attitudes; they can be used as targets of treatment and measures of changes in risk levels. Higher ratings (2 or 3) on dynamic variables predict a greater likelihood of violence and are focal points for treatment (need principle). The sum of the ratings of the static and dynamic variables indicate a subject's overall level of violence risk; the higher the score, the higher the risk. Those with higher VRS scores are candidates for higher intensity interventions (risk principle). The VRS can also be used to assess a client's current risk of violence (risk management).

Improving the Adoption of Risk Assessment Tools in the Criminal Justice System

Although actuarial risk assessment tools have been used to make criminal justice decisions since the 1920s, they are still evolving slowly. In a national survey, fewer than 30 percent of correctional administrators reported that their agencies have adopted a risk assessment tool as part of routine practices (Taxman, Perdoni, & Harrison, 2007). The obstacles that interfere with the implementation of risk assessment tools include clinical overrides, the interplay between risk and needs, and agency costs. Organizational culture, staff attitudes, alignment with current practices, and the perceived value of new technology also affect the implementation of risk assessment practices.

Overriding Clinical Judgment

The tension between clinically based and actuarially based judgments still looms large in the field of corrections. Third- and fourth-generation models of risk assessment have eased the conflict between clinical and purely actuarial judgments. Nevertheless, correctional staffs believe in the power of subjective decision-making. Agencies have used the number of overrides (e.g., the percentage of cases in which staff members reject a tool-recommended risk level) to ascertain the degree to which staff members devalue the risk tool employed in their agency. The rule of thumb is that when staff members override a tool in 10% of decisions, they are probably distrustful of the tool's recommended levels of supervision (Taxman, Perdoni, et al., 2007).

Frequent overrides indicate that agency staff members are using a tool inappropriately. In such instances, administrators should examine the legitimacy of staff members' concerns regarding cutoff or placement levels and the need for further training in order to enhance their understanding of the instrument or a particular set of questions (or domain area) in the instrument. Agencies often ignore the degree to which overrides occur; still, such information can be valuable in helping organizations use risk assessment strategies to their full extent and potential.

Combining Risk and Needs: A Problem of Interpretation

The combining of risk and needs into one instrument encourages the incorporation of the results of risk assessment into classification and treatment decisions. However, the scoring of such instruments can be problematic. For example, a major problem with a combined risk and need instrument (third- and fourth-generation) is that the resultant score can be misleading (Baird, 2009). Specifically, static factors (second-generation) predict recidivism or other negative outcomes; whereas criminogenic need factors are useful for making treatment decisions, although they are less useful in predicting negative outcomes. In fact, the combined score can actually overemphasize static risk factors over need factors.

For needs assessment to be useful in treatment, placement, or case management decisions, the instrument must identify areas in which individuals experience varying degrees of difficulties or problems (Taxman, 2006). For example, a substance-abusing offender is different from a substance-dependent offender. A stalker is different from an individual who is verbally aggressive toward a target. Total scores on an instrument can obscure these differences, which ultimately undermines the usefulness of a risk and need assessment tool. Total scores also can deemphasize risk factors. Hence, a growing trend in the field is the production of at least two scores: one for risk, the other for needs (or criminogenic needs). The separation of these scores helps users identify risk and various need levels in different problem domains.

Perceived Costs and Benefits

The utility and value of risk assessment protocols are determined, in part, by the degree to which the instruments are actually used by the organization. Innovation diffusion can be explained by an economic framework (Coiera, 2003). New assessment tools will have a low rate of adoption unless the staff perceives such strategies as beneficial. Only when the benefit-cost ratio shifts to perceived benefit will a practice be accepted and used. To encourage implementation, administrators and staff must consider strategies to increase the value of using risk assessment tools, which are a prime example of a technology that has been readily available for nearly six decades but not yet fully adopted by criminal justice agencies.

The clinical-versus-actuarial debate has affected the perceived value of risk assessment tools. These tools are most useful for allocating resources for treatment and supervision but are typically underused for this purpose. As more agencies begin to focus on responsivity and treatment-matching practices, the costs of using instruments will be perceived to be lower than the benefits. The benefits of responsivity are unlikely to be appreciated, given the paucity of programming in the criminal justice system, with fewer than 10% of offenders involved in services on a daily basis. Hence, programming resources must be expanded in order to further promote the use of risk assessment tools.

Future Considerations

Forensic risk assessment is a critical component of many aspects of criminal justice decision-making practices. Evaluations are conducted in numerous settings and adopt techniques from each of the generations of assessments presented in this chapter. As the field has progressed, increasingly sophisticated techniques have been created to improve the accuracy, efficiency, and usefulness of the prediction process, which still remains limited in its power to forecast or change offender behavior. Indeed, the use of forensic risk assessment for prediction only reduces the value of such evaluations. Therefore, most risk assessments also provide the basis for case management planning, which includes blueprints for supervision and service brokerage. Nonetheless, the prediction of offender behaviors will always be a challenge; evaluations can afford only a snapshot of clients and yield a best guess about their predilections. Although past behavior can inform judgments about future behavior, such inferences can be misleading and inaccurate—people and their life circumstances can change, sometimes dramatically. In addition, the particular factors that trigger criminal or violent behavior in a subject's life might not be included in an evaluation tool or in a clinician's standard evaluation protocol.

Forensic risk assessment in criminal justice serves as an opportunity to develop interventions for remediating the factors that elevate the risk of crime and violence, which is akin to the use of such evaluations in medicine. The LSI-R, for example, is used by correctional professionals to develop comprehensive case management plans aimed at changing probationers' behaviors and lowering their risk for future crime. If an offender is unlikely or unwilling to benefit from services, the instrument can be used to establish a schedule of supervision that protects public safety by preventing future offenses or minimizing the consequences of illegal behaviors. In addition, evaluations should be regularly updated to take into account offenders' progress in services and their changing environments. As suggested throughout this chapter, "risk and dangerousness are not fixed parameters but will change with contact and the passage of time and they should be regarded as such in any assessment" (Howitt, 2009, p. 481). Research has shown that changes in risk scores during supervision are associated with changes in recidivism rates (Andrews & Bonta, 1995). Therefore, reassessments of risk should be performed periodically to chart offender progress and to retool supervision plans to enhance their effectiveness.

References

Andrews, D. A., & Bonta, J. (1995). *The Level of Service Inventory–Revised.* Toronto, Ontario, Canada: Multi-Health Systems.

Andrews, D. A., & Bonta, J. (2003). *The psychology of criminal conduct* (3rd ed.). Cincinnati, OH: Anderson.

Andrews, D. A., Bonta, J., & Wormith, J. S. (2006). The recent past and near future of risk and/or needs assessment. *Crime and Delinquency, 52*, 7–27.

Andrews, D. A., & Dowden, C. (2005). Managing correctional treatment for reduced recidivism: A meta-analytic review of program integrity. *Legal and Criminological Psychology, 10*, 173–187.

Andrews, D. A., Zinger, I., Hoge, R. D., Bonta, J., Gendreau, P., & Cullen, F. T. (1990). Does correctional treatment work? A psychologically informed meta-analysis. *Criminology, 28*, 369–404.

Baird, C. (2009). *A question of evidence: A critique of risk assessment models used in the justice system*. Oakland, CA: National Council on Crime and Delinquency.

Banks, S., Robbins, P. C., Silver, E., Vesselinov, R., Steadman, H. J., Monahan, J., . . . Roth, L. H. (2004). A multiple-models approach to violence risk assessment among people with mental disorder. *Criminal Justice and Behavior, 31*, 324–340.

Barefoot v. Estelle, 463 U.S., at 921 (1983).

Baxstrom v. Herold, 383 U.S., at 107 (1966).

Bonta, J. (2002). Offender risk assessment: Guidelines for selection and use. *Criminal Justice and Behavior, 29*, 355–379.

Coiera, E. (2003). Disseminating and applying protocols. In E. Coiera (Ed.), *Guide to health informatics* (2nd ed., pp. 171–179). London: Arnold.

Dawes, R. M., Faust, D., & Meehl, P. E. (1989). Clinical versus actuarial judgment. *Science, 243*, 1668–1674.

Douglas, K., & Skeem, J. (2005). Violence risk assessment: getting specific about being dynamic. *Psychology, Public Policy, and Law, 11*, 347–383.

Dvoskin, J., & Heilbrun, K. (2001). Risk assessment and release decision-making: Toward resolving the great debate. *Journal of the American Academy of Psychiatry and Law, 29*, 6–10.

Ennis, B. J., & Litwack, T. R. (1974). Psychiatry and the presumption of expertise: Flipping coins in the courtroom. *California Law Review, 62*, 693–752.

Fischoff, B. (1994). What forecasts (seem to) mean. *International Journal of Forecasting, 10*, 387–403.

Fulero, S. M., & Wrightsman, L. S. (2009). *Forensic psychology*. Belmont, CA: Wadsworth.

Gottfredson, D. M. (1987). Prediction and classification in criminal justice decision making. In D. Gottfredson & M. Tonry (Eds.), *Crime and justice: A review of research* (pp. 1–20). Chicago: University of Chicago Press.

Grove, W. M., & Meehl, P. E. (1996). Comparative efficiency of informal (subjective, impressionistic) and formal (mechanical, algorithmic) prediction procedures: The clinical-statistical controversy. *Psychology, Public Policy, and Law, 2*, 293–323.

Hare, R. (1991). *The Hare Psychopathy Checklist–Revised: Manual*. North Tonawanda, NY: Multi-Health Systems.

Harris, G. T., Rice, M. E., & Quinsey, V. L. (1993). Violent recidivism of mentally disordered offenders: The development of a statistical prediction instrument. *Criminal Justice and Behavior, 20*, 315–335.

Hayakawa, H., Fischbeck, P., & Fischoff, B. (2000). Mental models of auto risks and insurance: Japanese and American motorists. *Journal of Risk Research, 3*, 51–67.

Heilbrun, K. (1997). Prediction vs management models relevant to risk assessment: The importance of legal decision-making context. *Law and Human Behavior, 21*, 347–359.

Heilbrun, K., Douglas, K. S, & Yasuhara, K. (2009). Controversies in violence risk assessment. In J. L. Skeem, K. S. Douglas, & S. O. Lilienfeld (Eds.), *Psychological science in the courtroom: Controversies and consensus* (pp. 333–356). New York: Guilford.

Holsinger, A. M., Lurigio, A. J., & Latessa, E. J. (2001). Practitioner's guide to understanding the basis of assessing offender risk. *Federal Probation, 65*, 46–50.

Howitt, D. (2009). *Introduction of forensic and criminal psychology*. New York: Pearson.

Janus, E. S., & Meehl, P. (1997). Assessing the legal standard for predictions of dangerousness in sex offender commitment proceedings. *Psychology, Public Policy, and Law, 3*, 33–64.

Lowenkamp, C. T., & Latessa, E. J. (2005). Increasing the effectiveness of correctional programming through the risk principle: Identifying offenders for residential placement. *Criminology & Public Policy, 4*, 263–289.

Lowenkamp, C. T., Latessa, E. J., & Holsinger, A. M. (2006). The risk principle in action: What have we learned from 13,676 offenders and 97 correctional programs? *Crime and Delinquency*, *52*, 77–93.

Lurigio, A. J., & Harris, A. J. (2009). Mental illness, violence, and risk assessment. *Victims and Offenders, 4*, 341–347.

McNiel, D., Borum, R. Douglas, K. Hart, S., Lyon, D., Sullivan, L., & Hemphill, J. (2002). Risk assessment. In J. R. P. Ogloff (Ed.), *Taking psychology and law into the 21st century: Perspectives in law and psychology* (pp. 182–202). New York: Plenum Publishing.

Meehl, P. (1954). *Clinical versus statistical prediction: A theoretical analysis and a review of the evidence*. Minneapolis: University of Minnesota Press.

Monahan, J. (1982). Clinical prediction of violent behavior. *Psychiatric Annals, 12*, 509.

Monahan, J., Steadman, H. J., Robbins, P. C., Silver, E., Appelbaum, P., Grisso, T., . . . Roth, L. H. (2000). Developing a clinically useful actuarial tool for assessing violence risk. *British Journal of Psychiatry, 176*, 312–319.

Monahan, J., Steadman, H., Silver, E., Appelbaum, A., Robbins, P., Mulvey, E., . . . Banks, S. (2001). *Rethinking risk assessment: The MacArthur study of mental disorder and violence*. New York: Oxford University Press.

Monahan, J., Steadman, H. J., Robbins, P. C., Appelbaum, P., Banks, S., Grisso, T., . . . Silver, E. (2005). An actuarial model of violence risk assessment for persons with mental disorders. *Psychiatric Services, 56*, 810–815.

Otto, R. (1992). Prediction of dangerous behavior: A review and analysis of "second generation" research. *Forensic Reports, 5*, 103–133.

Quinsey, V. L., Harris, G. T., Rice, M. E., & Cormier, C. (1998). *Violent offenders: Appraising and managing risk*. Washington, DC: American Psychological Association.

Steadman, H. J., & Cocozza, J. J. (1974). *Careers of the criminally insane: Excessive social control of deviance*. Lexington, MA: Lexington Books.

Steadman, H. J., Silver, E., Monahan, J., Appelbaum, P., Robbins, P. C., Mulvey, E. P., . . . Banks, S. (2000). A classification tree approach to the development of actuarial violence risk assessment tools. *Law and Human Behavior, 24*, 83–100.

Taxman, F. S. (2006). Assessment with a flair. *Federal Probation, 70*, 3–15.

Taxman, F. S., Cropsey, K. L., Young, D. W., & Wexler, H. (2007). Screening, assessment, and referral practices in adult correctional settings: A national perspective. *Criminal Justice and Behavior, 34*(9), 1216–1234. PMID: 18458758.

Taxman, F. S., Perdoni, M., & Harrison, L. (2007). Drug treatment services for adult offenders: The state of the state. *Journal of Substance Abuse Treatment, 32*(3), 239–254. PMID: 17383549.

Thornberry, T. P., & Jacoby, J. E. (1979). *The criminally insane: A community follow-up of mentally ill offenders*. Chicago: University of Chicago Press.

Webster, C., Douglas, K., Eaves, D., & Hart, S. (1997). *Manual for the HCR-20: Assessing risk for violence*. Burnaby, British Columbia, Canada: Mental Health Law and Policy Institute, Simon Fraser University.

Wong, S. C. P., & Gordon, A. (2006). The validity and reliability of the Violence Risk Scale: A treatment friendly violence risk assessment tool. *Psychology, Public Policy, and Law, 12*, 279–309.

Wong, S. C. P., Gordon, A., & Gu, D. (2007). Assessment and treatment of violence-prone forensic clients: An integrated approach. *The British Journal of Psychiatry, 190*, 66–74.

Wong, S. C. P., & Hare, R. D. (2005). *Guidelines for a psychopathy treatment program*. Toronto, Ontario, Canada: Multi-Health Systems.

CHAPTER TWO

A Classification of Violent and Other Serious Juvenile Offenders into Subgroups: From Statistical Analyses to Clinical Practice

Eva Mulder, Eddy Brand, Ruud Bullens, and Hjalmar J. C. van Marle

Serious juvenile offenders are responsible for a large part of crime committed by juveniles (Loeber, Slot, & Sergeant, 2001) and they are at risk of becoming chronic offenders (Moffitt, 1993; Moffitt, Caspi, Harrington & Milne, 2002). Over the years there has been a substantial amount of research on risk factors for persistence of offending behavior in juvenile offenders. In research on effectiveness of interventions, the What Works principles are the leading principles when it comes to maximizing treatment effect (Andrews & Bonta, 1995). The What Works *risk principle* implies that intensity of treatment should depend on the risk for recidivism: the higher the risk, the higher treatment intensity is needed. The risk factors that predict recidivism are the first ones that should be targeted during intervention to maximize treatment effect according to the What Works *needs principle*. However, previous research showed that serious juvenile offenders are a heterogeneous group that can be subdivided in subgroups, each with its specific needs. To maximize the effectiveness of interventions, it is important to adjust the interventions to the needs of distinct subgroups of juvenile delinquents.

In previous research on the heterogeneity of serious juvenile offenders, subgroups of juvenile offenders were distinguished. One way of classifying serious juvenile offenders is on the basis of *past offending behavior*. For instance, some studies found distinct subtypes of sex offenders on the basis of offense characteristics (Långström, Grann & Lindblad, 2000; Parks & Bard, 2006). In other studies, subgroups with distinct criminal careers were also defined by the age at onset, the level of problem behavior, and whether or not the problem behavior continued into adulthood. Differences between subgroups were found on personality and background characteristics (Chung, Hill, Hawkins, Gilchrist & Nagin, 2002; Nagin & Tremblay, 1999; Van der Geest & Bijleveld, 2008).

Another way of classifying juvenile offenders into subgroups is primarily on the basis of background characteristics (instead of offense data). Several studies found subgroups on the basis of characteristics they have in common, such as the amount of risk factors, personality characteristics, or psychopathic features (Juon, Doherty, & Ensminger, 2006; Wareham, Dembo, Poythress, Childs, & Schmeider, 2009).

Although there has been some research aimed at identifying subgroups of offenders, either on the basis of offense data or on background characteristics, differences in recidivism as well as differences in risk factors for recidivism between subgroups are still to be researched. Most studies on risk factors for recidivism focus on one subgroup, such as sex offenders or violent offenders (Kjelsberg, 2002; Loeber & Farrington, 2001; Nisbet, Wilson, & Smallbone, 2004; Resnick, Ireland & Borowski, 2004; Vandiver, 2006; Waite et al., 2005). However, by focusing on one specific subgroup, there is no possibility of comparing subgroups of offenders, with the consequence that specificity has been lost with regard to special profiles of risk factors. A classification in subgroups on the basis of both their criminal careers and their risk profiles would provide extra information that is useful for both risk assessment and treatment (Mulder, Brand, Bullens, & van Marle, 2011).

In previous research we found that serious juvenile offenders can be divided in several homogeneous subgroups. Both a classification on the basis of offending behavior and a classification on the basis of the risk factors that subgroups have in common were found and combined with a joint classification in 18 subgroups as a result (Mulder, Brand, Bullens & van Marle, 2010; Mulder, Brand, et al., 2011; Mulder, Vermunt, Brand, Bullens & van Marle, 2011). Classifying serious juvenile offenders in subgroups, not only on the basis of clinical interpretability but with latent class analysis and cluster analysis to ensure statistical significance, enabled us to examine which risk factors predict recidivism in each subgroup. In this way we can fine-tune interventions, with the goal being to improve risk assessment and to maximize treatment effect.

The aim of this study was to build a bridge from a statistically significant classification of serious juvenile offenders to clinical practice. The risk factors that predict severity of recidivism in each subgroup are the ones that should be targeted in the first place during intervention. The highest-risk subgroups need the highest treatment intensity. The results are used to formulate what is needed in terms of interventions. Recommendations are given for the improvement of existing interventions and the development of new interventions.

Methods

Participants

Participants in this study were male adolescents aged 12–22 years, sentenced to placement in a Dutch juvenile institution for mandatory treatment between 1995 and 2004 (n = 1,179). A mandatory treatment order can last from two to six years and is the most severe measure in the Dutch juvenile justice system, which is applied to juveniles between 12 and 18 years old (Lodewijks, Doreleijers, & de Ruiter, 2008).

Measuring Severity of Crime and Recidivism

To measure recidivism, all convictions starting at release from the institution were registered, together with the date and type of the offense committed. The choice for official reconviction data is straightforward, but it does have some limitations. The most important limitation is that an unknown number of offenses will get lost, as only those that have led to a conviction are counted. Using self-report would probably lead to higher recidivism rates than official records. Another limitation is the possible influence of changes in policy on reconviction (Friendship, Beech, & Browne, 2002). Despite these limitations, official reconviction data were used because they provide an objective and clear measure for recidivism (Heilbrun et al., 2000). We classified recidivism in two ways: overall recidivism (recidivism versus no recidivism) and serious recidivism (violent recidivism versus no violent recidivism).

The criminal records of the subjects were collected in June 2008. Previous research shows that within one year after release, a high percentage of reconviction is found (most recidivists have already reoffended), but the recidivism rate continues to rise in the first five to eight years after release (Wartna, Harbachi, & Van der Laan, 2005). We included only those juveniles with a time at risk of more than two years (n = 695) to make sure that juvenile offenders that were included in the sample had enough time to reoffend. The mean age at release from the treatment facility was 20 years (*SD* = 1.63). Time until first reoffense ranged from 0 to 8.08 years (*M* = 1.2; *SD* = 1.5). The minimum time at risk (time after date of liberation) was two years, and the mean time at risk in our study was 5.83 years (*SD* = 2.39, range 2 years–11.17 years).

Instruments

Juvenile Forensic Profile (FPJ)

A list of 70 risk factors was assessed with the FPJ (Juvenile Forensic Profile; Brand & Van Heerde, 2004), an instrument that was especially developed for forensic research based on file data. This instrument was derived from existing internationally and nationally validated instruments for risk assessment and for measuring problem behavior (e.g., Child Behaviour Check List, Structured Assessment of Violence Risk in Youth, Psychopathy Checklist: Youth Version, Juvenile-Sex Offender Assessment Protocol, HCR-20 Violence Risk Assessment Scheme). The list contains risk factors concerning seven domains: "history of criminal behavior," "family and environment," "offense-related risk factors and substance use," "psychological factors," "psychopathology," "social behavior/interpersonal relationships," and "behavior during stay in the institution." Each risk factor is measured on a three-point scale, with 0 = no problems, 1 = some problems, and 2 = severe problems. Previous research on the FPJ list showed that the available file information was thorough and complete enough to be able to score the instrument (Van 't Hoff, Brand, Van Parijs, & Van Heerde, 2002). The interrater-reliability was tested (double scoring of 80 files, r = 0.73; K = 0.61) and a high convergent validity of the FPJ list with the SAVRY was found (Van Heerde, Brand, Van 't Hoff, & Mulder, 2004). The predictive validity of the instrument was tested in the first sample of 102 boys (AUC of .803 with a sum-score of nine risk factors). In sum, the psychometric qualities of the instrument were found to be satisfactory (Brand, 2005a, 2005b; Van Heerde & Mulder, 2005).

Procedure

The study was approved by the Medical Ethical Commission of Erasmus University Medical Centre in Rotterdam, the Netherlands. After one year of treatment in the juvenile institution, the files were scored with the FPJ list. We measured after this period to be able to include risk factors *during* treatment. All files (n = 695) were read and scored with the FPJ list by master-students (in psychology or criminology). Before scoring the files, the students received three weeks of training.

Statistics

All statistics were calculated with SPSS 15.0 for Windows. In previous research we found subgroups of offenders in two ways: with latent class analysis (Francis, Soothill, & Fligelstone, 2004; Magidson & Vermunt, 2004) and cluster analysis (Milligan & Cooper, 1985). With latent class analysis we identified four subgroups on the basis of the types of offenses committed in the past and the frequency of offending (Mulder, Vermunt, et al., 2011). Six subgroups, based on combinations of risk factors they have in common, have been identified with cluster analysis (Mulder, Brand, et al., 2011). Next, the overlap of both classifications was studied with a cross tabulation. A classification in 18 subgroups was suggested that makes use of the strengths of both classifications. Descriptive statistics were used for analyses of the recidivism rates in each subgroup. The results of multiple linear regression analysis for all subgroups show which risk factors predict severity of recidivism. The risk factors that predict severity of recidivism in each subgroup are in this study listed and combined into clinically relevant risk domains that can be targeted during intervention. In Figure 2.1, the different steps preceding this study are shown. On the basis of the risk factors for severity of recidivism in each subgroup, recommendations for treatment are given.

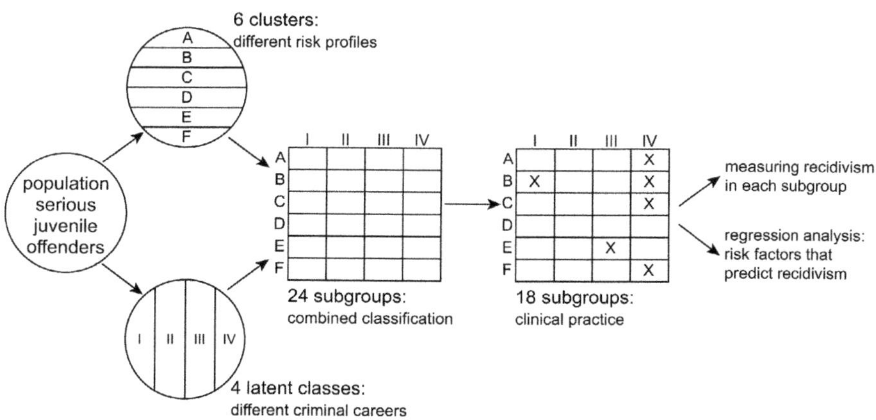

Figure 2.1 From a classification in subgroups, with risk factors for recidivism, towards clinical practice. X = subgroup does not exist in clinical practice.

Results

Results of Previous Research

A Combination of Two Classifications of Serious Juvenile Offenders

In previous research, two classifications of serious juvenile offenders were found: one on the basis of criminal behavior in the past, and one on the basis of risk profile. In Figure 2.2, the combined classification is shown: a classification in six risk profiles, each with one out of four patterns of offending behavior. Six of the 24 theoretical subgroups were too small to take into consideration and were therefore left out of the model. As a result, 18 subgroups do actually occur in clinical practice (Figure 2.2).

Recidivism and Serious Recidivism in 18 Subgroups of Offenders

Recidivism in the total sample of 695 serious juvenile offenders is 79.9% and serious recidivism is 62.9% in the total sample. For all 18 subgroups, the rates of recidivism and serious recidivism have been analyzed. In Figure 2.3, the differences in risk for recidivism are shown for all 18 subgroups. Some subgroups score considerably higher on recidivism and severity of recidivism than the total population:

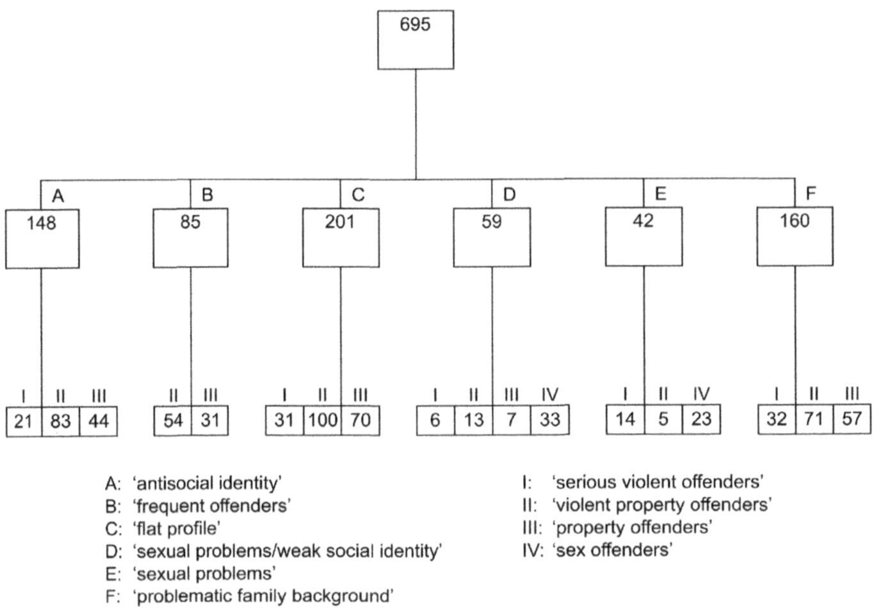

Figure 2.2 Combined classification of serious juvenile offenders in subgroups.

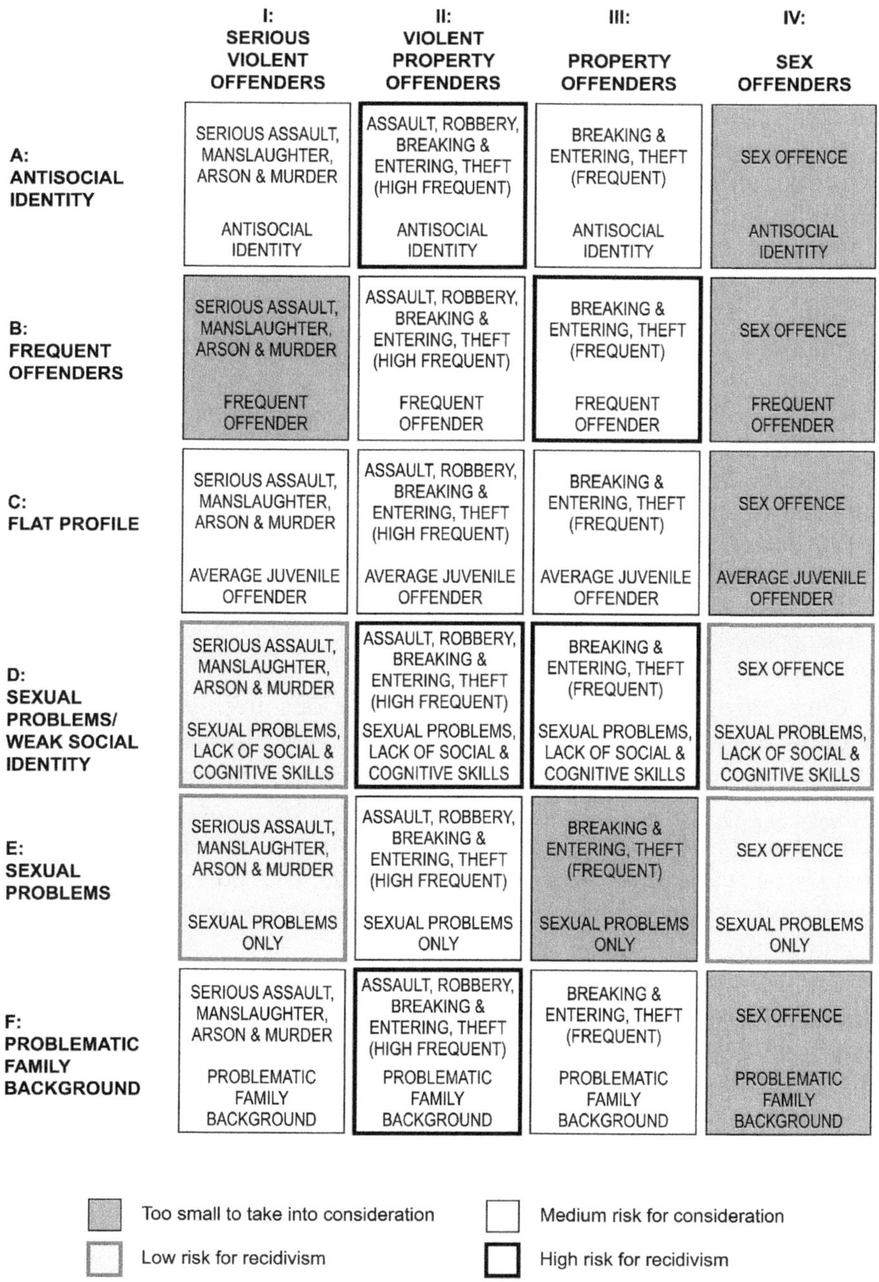

Figure 2.3 Risk for Recidivism in Eighteen Subgroups.

- IIA: Violent property offenders with an antisocial identity (90% recidivism, 82% serious recidivism)
- IID: Violent property offenders with sexual problems and a weak social identity (92% recidivism, 82% serious recidivism)
- IIF: Violent property offenders with a problematic family background (93% recidivism, 76% serious recidivism)
- IIID: Property offenders with sexual problems and a weak social identity (86% recidivism, 69% serious recidivism)

Some subgroups score considerably lower on recidivism than the total population:

- ID: Serious violent offenders with sexual problems and a weak social identity (50% recidivism, 33% serious recidivism)
- IE: Serious violent offenders with sexual problems (36% recidivism, 14% serious recidivism)
- IVE: Sex offenders with sexual problems only (52% recidivism, 30% serious recidivism)
- IVD: Sex offenders with sexual problems and a weak social identity (39% recidivism, 18% serious recidivism).

Considering the criminal careers of very serious juvenile offenders, the findings show that juveniles who combine violent offenses and property offenses are the highest-risk offenders in the sample, no matter what their risk profile is. We are dealing with generalizing behavior, which is apparently hard to influence. Another issue that should be noticed is the fact that serious violent offenders and sex offenders, who committed the most serious offenses *before* treatment have significantly lower rates of recidivism that the other subgroups *after* release.

Considering the risk profiles of very serious juvenile offenders, the findings show that the two clusters of juveniles with sexual problems contain both subgroups with significantly *higher* rates of recidivism (IID and IIID) than average, as well as subgroups with significantly *lower* rates of recidivism (ID, IE, IVD, and IVE). This result asks for careful assessment of serious juvenile offenders with sexual problems.

Risk Factors for Severity of Recidivism in 18 Subgroups

Risk factors for severity of recidivism were analyzed with multiple (stepwise) linear regression analysis for each of the four latent classes (for an extensive description, see Mulder, Vermunt, et al., 2011) and for each of the six clusters (for an extensive description, see Mulder, Brand, et al., 2011). Each latent class turned out to have a *specific* combination

Table 2.1 Risk Factors That Predict Severity of Recidivism in Total Population of 24 Subgroups. Time at risk $\geq$ 2 years, n = 695.

Dynamic Risk Factors	
1. Individual characteristics	**4. Peers/ the social network**
Conduct disorder	Defective social network
Lack of empathy	Involvement with antisocial peers
Authority problems	**5. Psychopathology**
Lack of positive coping skills	Absence of psychotic disorder
2. Treatment adherence	Absence of anxiety disorder
Incidents in the institution	Absence of autism spectrum disorder
Treatment compliance (medication faith)	**6. Substance abuse**
Lack of treatment motivation	Gambling
3. Family/ the parents	Drug abuse
Low accessibility of the parents	Alcohol abuse
Problems with parents parenting skills	**7. Offense-related risk factors**

of risk factors that predicts severity of recidivism, as did each cluster. The next step is to combine the risk profiles of all subgroups to decide which risk factors predict recidivism in 18 subgroups of offenders. The dynamic risk factors can be influenced during intervention. Therefore, the dynamic risk factors have been grouped in seven categories on the basis of clinical interpretability in Table 2.1. These categories can be aimed at during intervention: (1) individual characteristics, (2) treatment adherence, (3) family/ the parents, (4) peers/the social network, (5) psychopathology, (6) substance abuse, and (7) offense-related risk factors.

From Statistical Analyses to Clinical Practice

In Figure 2.4, all the results are combined with the aim to draw conclusions about the specific needs of serious juvenile offenders. The 18 different subgroup combinations are shown, together with the rates of serious recidivism per subgroup. In the last columns, the clinical risk categories that predict recidivism in each subgroup are shown. For 18 subgroups, 12 different combinations of risk categories occur.

Two Basic Risk Domains

Taking a closer look at the subgroups with their matching risk categories and recidivism rates, the first thing that should be noticed is that risk factors in the categories "individual" and "treatment adherence" predict recidivism in all eighteen subgroups. This implies that basic treatment should at least aim at these two risk categories: the individual (conduct

Sample	Tar >=2	RISK FACTOR-BASED SUBGROUPS		BEHAVIOR-BASED SUBGROUPS		18 subgroups	Overall recidivism	Severe recidivism	Individual	Treatment adherence	Parents	Network/Peers	Addiction	Psychopathology		MODULAR TREATMENT
1.024	709	Flat profile	203	Serious violent offenders	31	31	24 (77%)	14 (45%)	■				■		a	
				Violent property offenders	100	100	89 (89%)	70 (70%)	■	■		■	■		c	
				Property offenders	70	70	57 (81%)	45 (64%)	■	■			■	■	b	a Basic Addiction
				Sex offenders	2	x	—	—								b Basic Addiction Psychopath.
		Frequent offenders	91	Serious violent offenders	6	x	—	—								c Basic Addiction Network
				Violent property offenders	54	54	44 (81%)	37 (69%)	■	■		■	■		c	d Basic Addiction Network Psychopath.
				Property offenders	31	31	27 (87%)	22 (71%)	■	■		■	■	■	d	
				Sex offenders	0	x	—	—								
		Antisocial identity	150	Serious violent offenders	21	21	17 (81%)	13 (62%)	■		■			■	f	
				Violent property offenders	83	83	75 (90%)	68 (82%)	■	■	■	■		■	h	
				Property offenders	44	44	36 (82%)	30 (68%)	■	■	■			■	f	e Basic Parents
				Sex offenders	2	x	—	—								f Basic Parents Psychopath.
		Problematic family background	160	Serious violent offenders	32	32	23 (72%)	20 (63%)	■	■	■				e	g Basic Parents Network
				Violent property offenders	71	71	66 (93%)	54 (76%)	■	■	■	■			g	h Basic Parents Network Psychopath.
				Property offenders	57	57	47 (82%)	32 (56%)	■	■	■			■	f	
				Sex offenders	0	x	—	—								
		Sex. problems/weak social identity	59	Serious violent offenders	6	6	3 (50%)	2 (33%)	■	■		■			k	
				Violent property offenders	13	13	12 (92%)	9 (69%)	■	■		■			k	
				Property offenders	7	7	6 (86%)	6 (86%)	■	■		■		■	l	i Basic
				Sex offenders	33	33	13 (39%)	6 (18%)	■	■		■		■	l	j Basic Psychopath.
		Sexual problems	46	Serious violent offenders	14	14	5 (36%)	2 (14%)	■						i	k Basic Network
				Violent property offenders	5	5	4 (80%)	3 (60%)	■	■		■			k	l Basic Network Psychopath.
				Property offenders	4	x	—	—								
				Sex offenders	23	23	12 (52%)	7 (30%)	■	■				■	j	
	Total:		709		709	695	560 (81%)	440 (63%)	(100%)	(91%)	(44%)	(58%)	(41%)	(53%)		

Figure 2.4 Subgroups, Risks, and Needs.

disorder, lack of empathy, feelings of hostility before treatment, authority problems, lack of positive coping skills and academic achievement) and treatment adherence (incidents in the institution, treatment compliance/ medication faith, and lack of treatment motivation).

Psychopathology, Network, Parents, and Addiction

Next, we find four other risk categories than can be aimed at by treatment modules. First, problems with psychopathology occur in 6 of the 18 subgroups. This means that problems in this area are predictive for severity of recidivism in a large part of serious juvenile offenders. The same goes for the network, which also predicts severity of recidivism in six subgroups. The risk categories "parents" and "addiction" each predict severity of recidivism in 4 of the 18 subgroups. The subgroups with the highest risk for recidivism need attention in the highest number of risk categories. For each of these risk categories, an extra treatment module can be added on top of basic treatment described in the previous paragraph. In this way, modular treatment can be given that fits the specific needs of the subgroup to which a juvenile offender belongs.

Existing Interventions

In both the United States and the Netherlands, research has demonstrated the effectiveness of several interventions (Boonstra, Jonkman, Soeteman, & Van Busschbach, 2009; Breuk 2009; Curtis, Ronan, & Borduin, 2004). In Figure 2.5 an overview of existing interventions suitable for serious juvenile offenders is shown, which were judged to be effective or possibly effective by the Dutch Accreditation Panel of the Ministry of Justice. Each intervention is shown in Figure 2.5 with the risk factors that it aims to show in the upper part of the table. We have made an attempt to subdivide the symptoms these interventions aim at in the same risk categories that were described above on the basis of clinical interpretability. Not all dynamic risk factors that we found in our previous research are covered by existing accredited interventions. For instance, psychopathology, such as autism spectrum disorder, psychosis, or an anxiety disorder, is not included explicitly in any of the existing interventions, because—up until now—no intervention of these kinds has been acknowledged so far.

Discussion

The aim of this study was to build a bridge from empirically based statistical results to clinical practice. In previous research we built a combined classification of serious juvenile offenders in subgroups on the basis of

Emphasis	Intervention	Individual	Individual	Individual	Individual	Individual	Individual	Individual	Individual	Individual	Individual	Treatment adherence	Parents	Network / Peers	Network / Peers	Network / Peers	Addiction	Addiction	Addiction	Psychopathology
		Conduct disorder	Agression	Impulsivity	Empathy	Moral development	Making the right choices	Social skills	Coping	Negative thinking	Suicidal behavior	Motivation	Family	Social Network	School	Work	Alcohol abuse	Drug abuse	Gambling	
Individual	Learning from the offence	■	■		■			■												
	In Control!		■	■		■		■												
	Aggression training		■	■											■	■				
Individual + Treatment adherence	Dialectical behavioral therapy	■		■					■		■	■								
	Social skills training	■						■				■								
Parents	Functional Family Therapy (FFT)	■							■				■							
	Multisystemic Therapy (MST)	■							■				■	■	■					
	Multidimensional Family Therapy (MDFT)		■										■				■	■	■	
Network	New perspectives, resocialisation	■							■	■		■				■				
	Work-Wise														■	■				
	Working on your future			■			■		■						■	■				
Addiction	Brains 4 Use																■	■		

Summary

Intervention	Individual	Treatment adherence	Parents	Network / Peers	Addiction	Psychopathology
Learning from the offence	■					
In Control!	■					
Aggression training	■		■	■		
Dialectical behavioral therapy	■	■				
Social skills training	■	■				
Functional Family Therapy (FFT)	■		■			
Multisystemic Therapy (MST)	■		■	■		
Multidimensional Family Therapy (MDFT)	■		■		■	
New perspectives, resocialisation	■	■		■		
Work-Wise				■		
Working on your future	■			■		
Brains 4 Use	■				■	

Figure 2.5 Existing Interventions That Were Judged to Be Effective or Possibly Effective by the Accreditation Panel.

their criminal careers (types and frequency of offending behavior, latent class I–IV) and on the basis of their risk profile (combination of risk factors, cluster A–F). For each subgroup we found risk factors that predict severity of recidivism. The results in this study are useful for the application of the What Works risk and needs principles.

With respect to the risk principle, the results show that differences exist in risk for recidivism between subgroups. Several high-risk subgroups were identified, as well as several groups with a considerably lower risk. According to the risk principle, lower risk subgroups of sex offenders need a different kind of less intensive treatment than, for instance, violent property offenders, which is quite unexpected and remarkable considering the severity of sex offending. However, this conclusion is in line with the notion that sex offenses—though extreme in nature—may be during adolescence (at least for a large group of juveniles) a display of experimenting behavior that is limited to adolescence. We may have found a strong example of sex offenders with *adolescence-limited* offending behavior (Moffitt, 1993). At the same time, within juvenile offenders with sexual problems, next to subgroups with a considerably lower risk (specialists), several high-risk subgroups were also found (generalists). Juveniles in the high-risk subgroups combine sex offenses with violent and/or property offenses, thereby generalizing their criminal behavior, which is a strong predictor for new offenses. This finding asks for careful assessment of juvenile sex offenders to decide what the intensity and length of treatment should be.

Next to the generalist subgroups within sex offenders, the results show high-risk groups consisting of violent property offenders. These subgroups are in line with existing theoretical models, such as Loeber and Hay's developmental pathway model (Loeber, Farrington, Stouthamer Loeber, & Raskin White, 2008), which states that the more pathways of criminal behavior are followed, the higher the risk. Although serious violent offenders commit the most serious crimes before treatment, recidivism in these offenders is low. This may be explained by the fact that these subgroups had not developed an offending career yet before intervention, which is confirmed by the low frequency of offending before treatment. As a consequence, their offending behavior may have been easier to influence.

According to the needs principle, the risk factors that predict recidivism and severity of recidivism are the first ones that should be targeted during treatment. In Table 2.1 we listed the risk factors that predict severity of recidivism in the 18 subgroup combinations. The results showed that in all 18 subgroups, risk factors in the categories "individual" and "treatment adherence" predict severity of recidivism. These risk categories can be seen as the *basic needs* of serious juvenile offenders, which should be addressed in each intervention. In spite of the obvious importance of treatment adherence, this subject is not explicitly included in many of the existing interventions. The other categories of risk factors that predict severity of recidivism in subgroups of serious juvenile offenders are risk factors that have to do with family/parents, peers/social network, psychopathology, and substance abuse. For each of these categories, an extra treatment module should be added on top of basic treatment. In this way modular treatment can be applied that fits the needs of the specific subgroup to which a juvenile offender belongs.

If we aggregate sets of subgroups on the basis of their risk profile (clusters), several consistencies can be seen in the categories of risk factors that predict severity of recidivism. In each set of subgroups, we found that the higher the rate of recidivism, the more differently risk categories predict severity of recidivism and therefore should be aimed at during treatment. This is in line with both the risk principle and the needs principle. According to the risk principle, higher-risk subgroups should receive treatment with higher intensity, which means that extra treatment modules should be added on top of the basic module aiming at the individual and at treatment adherence. According to the needs principle, the choice of the modules that are added should be based on the specific categories of risk factors that predict severity of recidivism.

Another consistency is that within each set of subgroups, we found a specific category of risk factors that appears to be characteristic for this set of subgroups (Figure 2.4). In each set, psychopathology is a problem in the higher-risk subgroups. Psychopathology is apparently an important criminogenic factor if no treatment is applied.

In high-risk sex offenders (subgroups within clusters D and E), a problematic social network predicts severity of recidivism. This implies that in the subgroups of generalists that commit violent and property offences next to sex offenses, it is important to aim at the social network (peers), which apparently plays a role in their generalizing criminal behavior.

In all subgroups with antisocial identity offenders (A) and juvenile offenders with a problematic family background (F), severity of recidivism is predicted by risk factors in the category "family/parents" (Figure 2.4). This seems a logical aim for intervention in the subgroups with a problematic family background, which are of course characterized by problems in the family. Juvenile offenders with antisocial behavior might benefit from extra monitoring and adequate supervision by their parents; a so-called multisystemic approach is needed, aiming at both the juveniles and their parents.

In all subgroups with a flat profile or frequent offending (that is, subgroups BI, BII, BIII, CI, CII and CIII; see Figure 2.4) risk factors in the category addiction predict severity of recidivism. In these juvenile offenders, who are mainly characterized by their offending behavior or who can be characterized as average serious juvenile offenders, substance abuse plays an important role in their offending behavior and should therefore be a part of intervention.

After deciding what the needs of different subgroups of serious juvenile offenders are, *existing effective interventions* were listed. Several differences should be noticed between the demand and supply of interventions. First, not all the risk factors that were found to predict severity of recidivism in serious juvenile offenders are specifically included in existing interventions. Treatment adherence should be explicitly addressed during intervention, which is not the case in many of the existing interventions (see Figure 2.5).

Another example is psychopathology, which is not always integrated in existing interventions (see Figure 2.5). This implies that this module should be added to the existing range of interventions, or that new interventions that include psychopathology should be developed. In the Netherlands there is a chronic shortage of specialized psychiatrists for offender therapy (Council for the Administration of Criminal Justice and Protection of Juveniles, 2007). This asks for investments in training and recruiting psychiatrists and psychologists for treatment in juvenile justice institutions.

Another finding in this study that has implications for clinical practice is the importance of family factors. In juvenile justice institutions, treatment is applied to serious juvenile offenders, but their parents are often not or hardly in the picture. One cause is that parents are often not available or are living too far away from the institution, which is part of the problem. However, another cause is that intervention in juvenile justice institutions focuses mainly on the individual. Programs for aftercare and interventions in the family are being developed. However, the results of this study suggest that parents and aftercare should be an integrated part of treatment. After all, they are often the ones a juvenile offender returns to after release for living space or support.

One example of a treatment program that has been studied extensively, has been proven effective, and addresses family problems and parenting skills is Multisystemic Treatment (MST; Curtis, Ronan, & Borduin, 2004). The results of this study suggest that for serious juvenile offenders, MST might be quite appropriate. However, it may be even more appropriate as a module, when applied in combination with the basic modules that target other risk factors, such as the individual or treatment adherence. In this way all the needs of very serious juvenile offenders can be addressed.

This study has also several limitations. For one, the findings have been based on file information, attained with one measurement before treatment. However, the measurement that formed the basis for the data in this study was taken after one year of treatment. In this way we had a good clinical picture of the characteristics, abilities, and inabilities of the research population. For future research we plan to perform repeated measures with the FPJ list to include the development of dynamic risk factors during and after treatment as well.

Further, we formed hypothetical categories consisting of the risk factors that we found to predict severity of recidivism. Further research is needed to validate the risk categories that were found in this study. In addition to the risk categories, in future research the subgroups we found should be validated, and treatment effectiveness should be studied.

Conclusion

In conclusion, the results in this study are in line with the What Works principles, which set the terms for developing effective interventions. With respect to the risk principle, the results show differences in the level of risk between subgroups of serious juvenile offenders. The highest-risk subgroups need treatment with the highest intensity, consisting of several different treatment modules. With respect to the needs principle, the results show that the basic needs of serious juvenile offenders can be determined by deciding to which subgroup they belong. A classification of serious juvenile offenders in subgroups based on both their offending behavior and their risk profile can be used as a basis for decision making on which treatment modules should be applied to maximize treatment effect. The specific needs of individual juvenile offenders can be determined next, by combining the subgroup classification found in this study with clinical judgment. In future research this classification in subgroups should be validated.

References

Andrews, D. A., & Bonta, J. (1995). *The psychology of criminal conduct* (2nd ed.). Cincinnati, OH: Anderson.

Boonstra, C., Jonkman, C., Soeteman, D., & Van Busschbach, J. (2009). Multisystemic therapy for serious antisocial and delinquent juveniles: Two-year follow-up study. *Systeemtherapie*, *21*(2), 94–105.

Brand, E. F. J. M. (2005a). A measure for the quality of instruments for risk assessment. In M. F. Sjerps & J. A. Coster van Voorhout (Eds.), *The uncertain evidence. The use of statistics and probability in criminal law* (pp. 429–456). Deventer, the Netherlands: Kluwer.

Brand, E. F. J. M. (2005b). *Research study PIJ-files 2003C: Predictive validity of the FPJ-list*. The Hague: Department of Justice, National Agency of Correctional Institutions.

Brand, E. F. J. M., & Van Heerde, W. K. (2004). *Manual FPJ-lijst: Forensic profile-youth version*. The Hague: Department of Justice, National Agency of Correctional Institutions.

Breuk, R. (2009). *Breaking the cycle, day treatment for juvenile delinquents* (Unpublished doctoral dissertation). Vrije Universiteit, Amsterdam.

Chung, I. J., Hill, K. G., Hawkins, J. D., Gilchrist, L. D., & Nagin, D. S. (2002). Childhood predictors of offence trajectories. *Journal of Research in Crime and Delinquency, 39*(1), 60–90.

Council for the Administration of Criminal Justice and Protection of Juveniles (2007).

Juvenile Justice Institutions after 2010. Advice with respect to the report "A vision on juvenile justice institutions in juvenile criminal law." Retrieved November 28, 2009, from http://www.rsj.nl/Images/Visie op de JJI's na 2010 30-3-2007_tcm60-76859.pdf.

Curtis, N. M., Ronan, K. R. & Borduin, C. M. (2004). Multisystemic Treatment: A meta-analysis of outcome studies. *Journal of Family Psychology, 18*(3), 411–419.

Francis, B., Soothill, K., & Fligelstone, R. (2004). Identifying patterns and pathways of offending behaviour: A new approach to typologies of crime. *European Journal of Criminology, 1*(1), 48–87.

Friendship, C., Beech, A. R., & Browne, K. D. (2002). Reconviction as an outcome measure in research: A methodological note. *British Journal of Criminology, 42*, 442–444.

Heilbrun, K., Witte, G., Keeney, M., Brock, W., Westendorf, M., Waite, D., . . . Shumate, M. (2000). Risk factors for juvenile criminal recidivism: The postrelease community adjustment of juvenile offenders. *Criminal Justice and Behaviour, 27*(3), 275–291.

Juon, H. S., Doherty, E. E., & Ensminger, M. E. (2006). Childhood behaviour and adult criminality: Cluster analysis in a prospective study of African Americans. *Journal of Quantitative Criminology, 22*(3), 193–214.

Kjelsberg, E. (2002). Pathways to violent and non-violent criminality in an adolescent psychiatric population. *Child Psychiatry and Human Development, 33* (1), 29–42.

Långström, N., Grann, M., & Lindblad, F. (2000). A preliminary typology of young sex offenders. *Journal of Adolescence, 23*, 319–329.

Lodewijks, H. P. B., Doreleijers, T. A. H., & de Ruiter, C. (2008). Savry risk assessment in violent Dutch adolescents: relation to sentencing and recidivism. *Criminal Justice and Behaviour, 35*(6), 696–709.

Loeber, R., & Farrington, D. P. (2001). The significance of child delinquency. In *Child delinquents: Development, intervention and service needs* (pp. 1–21). Thousand Oaks, CA: Sage.

Loeber, R., Farrington, D. P., Stouthamer Loeber, M., & Raskin White, H. (2008). *Violence and serious theft: Development and prediction from childhood to adulthood.* Taylor & Francis Group.

Loeber, R., Slot, N. W., & Sergeant, J. A. (2001). *Serious and violent juvenile delinquency: Prevalence, causes and interventions.* Houten/Diegem: Bohn Stafleu Van Loghum.

Magidson, J., & Vermunt, J. K. (2004). Latent class models. In D. Kaplan (Ed.), *The Sage handbook of quantitative methodology for the social sciences* (pp. 175–198). Thousand Oaks, CA: Sage.

Milligan, G. W., & Cooper, M. C. (1985). An examination of procedures for determining the number of clusters in a data set. *Psychometrika, 50*(2), 159–179.

Moffitt T. E. (1993). Adolescence limited and life-course-persistent antisocial behaviour: A developmental taxonomy. *Psychological Review, 100*(4), 674–701.

Moffitt, T. E., Caspi, A., Harrington, H., & Milne, B. J. (2002). Males on the life-course-persistent and adolescence-limited antisocial pathways: Follow-up at age 26 years. *Development and Psychopathology, 14*(1), 179–207.

Mulder, E. A., Brand, E. F. J. M., Bullens, R. A. R., & van Marle, H. J. C. (2010). A classification of risk factors in serious juvenile offenders and the relation between patterns of risk factors and recidivism. *Criminal Behaviour and Mental Health, 20*(1), 23–38.

Mulder, E. A., Brand, E. F. J. M., Bullens, R. A. R., & van Marle, H. J. C. (2011). Towards an optimal classification of juvenile offenders: subgroups of serious juvenile offenders and severity of recidivism. *International Journal of Offender Therapy and Comparative Criminology*, advance online publication.

Mulder, E. A., Brand, E. F. J. M., Bullens, R. A. R., & van Marle, H. J. C. (submitted). A two-step classification of serious juvenile offenders into subgroups.

Mulder, E. A., Vermunt, J. K., Brand, E. F. J. M., Bullens, R. A. R., & van Marle, H. J. C. (2011). Subgroups of serious juvenile offenders: Different profiles, different risks? *Criminal Behaviour and Mental Health*, advance online publication.

Nagin, D., & Tremblay, R. E. (1999). Trajectories of boys' physical aggression, opposition, and hyperactivity on the path to physically and nonviolent juvenile delinquency. *Child Development, 70*(5), 1181–1196.

Nisbet, I. A., Wilson, P. H., & Smallbone, S. W. (2004). A prospective longitudinal study of sexual recidivism among adolescent sex offenders. *Sexual Abuse: A Journal of Research and Treatment, 16*(3), 223–234.

Parks, G. A., & Bard, D. E. (2006). Risk factors for adolescent sex offender recidivism: Evaluation of predictive factors and comparison of three groups based upon victim type. *Sexual Abuse: A Journal of Research and Treatment, 18*(4), 319–342.

Resnick, M. D., Ireland, M., & Borowski, I. (2004). Youth violence perpetration: What protects? What predicts? Findings from the national longitudinal study of adolescent health. *Journal of Adolescent Health, 35*(5), 424.e1–424.e10.

Van der Geest, V., & Bijleveld, C. (2008). Personal, background and treatment characteristics associated with offending after residential treatment: A 13-year follow up in adolescent males. *Psychology, Crime and Law, 14*(2), 159–176

Vandiver, D. M. (2006). A prospective analysis of juvenile male sex offenders: characteristics and recidivism rates as adults, *Journal of Interpersonal Violence, 21*, 673–688.

Van Heerde, W. K., Brand, E. F. J. M., Van 't Hoff, G. I. C. M., & Mulder, E. A. (2004). *Inter-rater reliability and convergent validity of the Juvenile Forensic Profile*. The Hague: Department of Justice, National Agency of Correctional Institutions.

Van Heerde, W. K., & Mulder, E. A. (2005). *Research study PIJ-files 2003-B. Clinical evaluation FPJ-list & SAVRY in Eikenstein and FORA*. The Hague: Department of Justice, National Agency of Correctional Institutions.

Van 't Hoff, G. I. C. M., Brand, E. F. J. M., Van Parijs, A. J., & Van Heerde, W. K. (2002). *Pilot study PIJ-files. From word to number*. The Hague: Department of Justice, National Agency of Correctional Institutions.

Waite, D., Keller, A., McGarvey, E. L., Wieckowski, E., Pinkerton, R., & Brown, G. L. (2005). Juvenile sex offender re-arrest rates for sexual, violent nonsexual and property crimes: A 10-year follow-up. *Sexual Abuse: A Journal of Research and Treatment, 17*(3), 313–331.

Wareham, J., Dembo, R., Poythress, N. G., Childs, K., & Schmeider, J. (2009). A latent class factor approach to identifying subtypes of juvenile diversion youths based on psychopathic features. *Behavioural Sciences and the Law, 27* (1), 71–95.

Wartna, B. S. J., Harbachi, S., & Van der Laan, A. M. (2005). *Youth in detention: Prevalence of recidivism in youth in juvenile justice institutions*. The Hague: WODC.

CHAPTER THREE

Statistical Controversies in the Sexually Violent Predator Evaluation (SVPE) Practice Community: Bayesian Departure and Polarization

Henry Richards

What Is Controversial about a Conditional Probability Theorem Dating from 1763?

This chapter on some controversial statistical issues in sexually violent predator evaluations (SVPEs) opens, perhaps unexpectedly, with a stop at the bookshelf near the author's back door, where *The Paul Meehl Reader* (Waller, Yonce, Grove, Faust, & Lenzenweger, 2006) is stationed perpetually awaiting its turn to be chosen for the author's next exit to a favored coffee shop, a routine retreat to break up the mental fog from processing thousands of pages of discovery (not atypical of SVPEs) by reading something intelligible, affirming, and written from the perspective of long experience and removed from the press of the currents of contemporary professional squabbling. The fact that four of the five coeditors/authors of the *Meehl Reader* knew Meehl personally increases the value of owning this solid tome by evoking a sense of pride in participation in an unbroken tradition of scientific psychology that now spans several generations. Meehl would have nodded knowingly at the emotional transferences that support such notions of apostolic succession. What Meehl called his little book (*Clinical and Actuarial Prediction*; Meehl, 1954) is the progenitor of the long lineage of literature assessing the relative accuracy of specialized expertise gained from training and experience versus the accuracy of mechanical mathematical models of decision making. Meehl himself held what seems an enlightened view: that together clinical and actuarial methods represent a seamless polarity in ways of knowing, and that each should have its due, where appropriate. This view was reflected in Meehl's work, which united his being an unwavering critic of many forms of clinical decision making that ignored or discounted statistical computation; while at the same time, he forcefully advocated for incorporating clinical judgments within actuarial models. Meehl also liked to point to his reputation among clinicians as a dust-bowl empiricist, and follow this by his reminding his audience that he was also a practicing psychoanalyst and a contributor to the psychodynamic theoretical framework, and was unapologetic about his conviction that ultimately the psychodynamic framework would not be conclusively falsified (given a future of continued theory-building and greatly improved measurement in models and technology).

Donald Kahneman's *Thinking, Fast and Slow* (Kahneman, 2011) recently joined *The Meehl Reader* on the same bookcase. In this book, Kahneman sums up his 30-year career (most of them spent arm in arm with colleague Amos Tversky) researching the psychology of judgment and decision making under conditions of uncertainty, the more general domain, which in this chapter will be narrowed, as far as possible, to the mere sliver of statistical and theoretical issues relevant to SVP assessment practice. To gauge Kahneman's accomplishment in making big-picture, complex, and counterintuitive ideas accessible, try to remember the last time a book featuring statistics in psychology was a best seller. (Perhaps, Nassim Taleb's *The Black Swan* qualifies, which has more to say about economics and investing than clinical decision-making.)

Kahneman acknowledges that Paul Meehl has been a hero to him starting from his early training as a psychologist. For my part (and perhaps somewhat oddly for someone with psychodynamic leanings similar to Meehl's), Tversky and Kahneman's cognitive heuristics and biases formed the inspirational core of my master's thesis and doctoral dissertation research projects. Seeing their work have its day in the sun of the general culture, through Kahneman's bestselling book, sparks the sense of being grounded in the praiseworthy tradition of intrepid thinking about thinking advanced by Meehl. To say that an enterprise is scientific is to praise it, to find it laudatory in some manner, if not superlative. Meehl withheld this laudatory designation from much of psychology, which he considered as having more in common with fashion and art than science. He viewed many of the fields of psychology as not progressing cumulatively, but changing sequentially, with the most basic assumptions of some fields being reinvented in less than a span of a decade, and the book remainders articulating the previous model are soon afterward sold at a steep discount, complete with dust covers announcing the model as a cutting-edge scientific breakthrough. Part Popperian sympathizer, Meehl was not afraid of bold hypotheses, and saw them as essential to science. One such hypothesis was his claim that, in contrast to what could be called the Psych-Lite disciplines of psychology, five truly "great, noble, and enduring" traditions in psychology would be building cumulative knowledge and theory a hundred years after this hypothesis was advanced (Meehl, 1978). Meehl's noble traditions are (a) descriptive clinical psychiatry, (b) psychometric assessment, (c) behavioral genetics, (d) behavior modification, and (e) psychodynamics. Although I would be loath to hand this canon to a social psychologist, forensic psychologists conducting SVPEs are unlikely to wince at reading it, and might be hard-pressed to add or eliminate traditions at a similar level that are routinely relied on in their work.

However, Meehl's bold prediction of lasting merit for psychological assessment did not anticipate the recent developments in forensic psychology that are the subject of this chapter. Although Meehl did not limit scientific statements to those that are falsifiable, his hypothesis of five enduring traditions of scientific psychology is and may be on the verge of being falsified, at least in the domain of SVPEs. This is not to predict that associations, journals, and careers dedicated to the subject matter of these traditions will soon cease to expand and begin to wither away, but to suggest that something integral to these traditions' resistance to the faddishness of the soft sciences is off kilter. Wenger (1998, 2004) coined the term community of practice to refer anthropologically to the interactions and institutions that support competent practice of a circumscribed art or skill, among practitioners that share ideas, methods, rules of conduct, and a subculture that allows for indoctrination, skill acquisition, status ranking, and professional satisfaction for its members. The community of practice formed by psychologists conducting SVPEs and related activities has suffered a loss of coherence in ideas, cohesiveness in affirmation of values, and consensus regarding methods and continuity with Meehl's five noble traditions. These changes are due not to paradigm drift, but to concerted efforts of a group of psychologists whose agenda is to undermine established thought and practice in assessment in order to advance a political agenda and a statistical philosophy that is strongly associated with a specific theory of science. Their political goal is to prevent the continued use of viable assessment methods to the extent that they can be no longer be used to support civil commitment determinations pursuant to sexually violent predator (SVP) laws.

The core ideology of this school, Bayesianism, is a philosophical extension of one of the two major approaches to probability theory, namely, Bayesian probability and statistical theory. Bayesianism is usually considered a form of philosophical subjectivism and fits nicely with views of philosophy of science that rely on historical perspectives, most famously developed in Thomas Kuhn's (1962) work on science that contributes to paradigm shifts versus normal science within an established paradigm. Kuhn's approach was later taken by others in the direction of both subjectivism and relativism, also consistent with some major variants of Bayesianism. Although most of the proponents of using these methods and tenets in conducting SVPEs frequently work as expert witnesses for the defense, many defense experts eschew the methods and obfuscations that typify some Bayesian practice, and it is clearly the case that nothing prevents experts working on either side of SVP cases from endorsing and using Bayesian principles within, and in support of, the noble traditions framework, which will be described at greater length later in this chapter.

At the onset, it is important to emphasize that the intent of this chapter is not to challenge the validity of Bayes's Theorem, or its appropriate application to issues related to SVP science and practice, or to denigrate Bayesian statistics or Bayesianism, per se. However, as is now obvious to the reader, the chapter is not neutral toward the views that are referred to here as Bayesianism to distinguish it from less extreme and at times necessary Bayesian methods, and it presents Bayesianism as a serious challenge to the integrity of forensic assessment practice and contends that SVPE practice is already straining the practice paradigm of scientific forensic assessment. Nevertheless, my goal is to provide, as accurately and fairly as possible, an informative overview of the methodological issues involved. Most of the issues concern statistics and their use and interpretation. Therefore, this overview will share all of the limitations of its author, who is neither a statistician nor a psychologist specializing in statistical methodology, and who has definite views of the issues that are addressed here. The goals of this chapter will be met if reading it serves to help readers to observe the aspects of assessment practice addressed here with greater curiosity and rigor, (and if the spirit so moves them) to attempt to disconfirm the patterns offered here as explanatory hypotheses for the schism that has developed in this practice area. The chapter's goals will be exceeded if it serves as an impetus for readers to go to the literature and investigate the issues for themselves, perhaps with the idea of setting the author straight on one issue or another.

Knowledge Destruction in SVPE Practice and Related Knowledge Domains

Since the controversy dealt with in this chapter is less related to statistical issues per se than to how those issues have come to polarize a community of practice and to undermine its coherence, cohesiveness, consensus, and continuity with its past, the concept of knowledge destruction techniques (KDTs) will be useful for understanding the current state of affairs in SVPEs, in which the foundations for much of the essential technology relied on has been under attack, not always from a frontal position, but as sabotage from within. Andrews and Bonta (2007) describe (KDTs) in criminal justice as attempts to undermine knowledge as it has developed over the decades in favor of some predetermined, biased point of view, often based on commitment to a specific theory or sociopolitical agenda. Andrews and Bonta (2007) trace, for the field of criminal justice policy and programs, the pendulum's swing from on one end of a polarity to another. The movement was away from an earlier era in which academics and bureaucrats touted a model in which social factors primarily were accountable for all crime, and idealized treatments or sociopolitical interventions were viewed as the necessary and sufficient solution. Proponents of a different view (in the minority for decades, but in the ascendance since the 1980s), which can be called the Nothing Works paradigm, were cynical regarding treatment, accepted permanent classification of some offenders as hardcore and essentially lost, and advocated that public support should go for incarceration expenses rather than toward the comparatively meager investment in correctional interventions, which were viewed as essentially a form of pandering to wrongdoers. Proponents of the second view, according to Andrews and Bonta (2007), resorted to a set of rhetorical techniques they described as knowledge destruction techniques, while Andrews and Bonta themselves argued for a move away from criminal justice framing within a Nothing Works paradigm (Martinson, 1974) toward a less extreme framing in which the paradigm is "What Works," their slogan for criminal justice paradigm in which pragmatic, evidence-based assessment and intervention are central. They developed lists of KDTs used by opponents to the What Works paradigm, and illustrated them in the course of presenting the literature and their own views regarding major criminal justice issues. For example, they demonstrated in detail how KDTs have been used in an attempt to undermine the reputation of the effectiveness of correctional interventions and acceptance of the predictive value of the concepts of antisocial personality disorder (ASPD) and psychopathy.

KDTs reflect an attitude toward knowledge and public discourse, but this attitude does not preclude inventiveness, making a definitive list of KDTs illusive. However, this author's list, generalized from Andrews and Bonta's (2007) book, include the following KDTs, framed here in regard to What Works, in lieu of established assessment practice:

- Asserting that human behavior is unpredictable, uncontrollable, and any attempt to predict or control it is an oppressive restriction on humanity.
- Enthusiastic endorsement and promotion of any finding or opinion consistent with skepticism regarding What Works.
- Asserting the inevitability of offending.
- Discounting evidence of intervention or prediction effects because they are judged as too small when judged from the bigger picture of society.
- Making *ad hominine* attacks on researchers or others based on their class status, financial interest, or general political orientation (often wrongly guessed at) and lack of objectivity.
- Attacking any research supporting What Works on the grounds that it was, of necessity, conducted by the biased individuals who deserved the treatment of the previous KDT in this catalog.
- Reviewing a literature that contains a substantial majority of findings supportive of elements of the What Works paradigm, and judging the whole body of literature as indicating the abysmal failure of the paradigm.
- When acknowledging that an intervention program or predictive scheme appears effective, pointing out that such interventions are too expensive, and are essentially frills that obscure the hopelessness of the system as a whole.

By addressing Bayesianism's threat to traditional practice, this chapter sharpens the opposite blade of the argument made by Prentky, Janus, Barbaree, Schwartz, and Kafka (2006) against what they saw as the intrusion of political bias into the scientific-legal arena of SVP commitment and the equivalent of KDTs. Their concern was primarily with experts working for the prosecution. Several quotes from Prentky et al. (2006), abridged through close ellipsis, are useful to exemplify their view of the effects of what they call "bad science" on "good science":

> Good science, in this context, refers to the faithful and rigorous adherence to the findings, the limitations, and the conclusions of published, peer-reviewed articles in scientific journals. Bad science refers to the intentional

> or uniformed distortion, misinterpretation, or selective reporting of findings from scientific articles. (p. 358) . . . the intrusion of bad science occurs with disturbing frequency in SVP cases. (p. 361) We are witnessing, in dramatic relief, the unfolding of two outcomes in SVP hearings: (a) the loss of integrity of the adjudicative process with testimony that is, at best, opaque, and, at worst dissimulative; and (b) the loss of the integrity of science itself. (p. 385). . . . the fact finder is frequently confronted by expert testimony that is energetic in spirit but naked in substance. (p. 386)

Prentky et al.'s (2006) conclusion was that in SVP forensic practice, bad science and irresponsible clinical practice had been disruptive to the judicial process, with this bad science entering through expert testimony aimed at perpetuating commitment, and in a misguided and destructive attempt to protect potential victims at the expense of scientific credibility and integrity, and resulting in clinically unsupportable commitments. This paper traces a similar disruption from the opposite direction—that is, from some experts who work unflinchingly to "defend" respondents in commitment proceedings, but produce the same effect on the community of SVPE practice and related knowledge domains.

It is my view that at the current time the balance of the evidence is that controversial and idiosyncratic science incorporated in the testimony and publications by a small group of psychologists are acting out Prentky et al.'s (2006) descriptions as though they were a script or prescription rather than what those authors intended them to be: a call to alarm and counteraction, a plea for returning to normal practice and to end further warping of the existing paradigm. What this small group of practitioners has in common is a subjectivist philosophy (Bayesianism) based on an isolated statistical concept (Bayes's Theorem), hence the term used here to describe them is SVP Bayesians. KDTs are frequent enough in the work of the SVP Bayesians that a separate chapter section could be written compiling their occurrence in testimony, presentations, and publications. However, instances of KDTs are presented fairly seamlessly with controversial Bayes's Theorem–related assertions in the work of SVP Bayesians who commit them (not all do) that they can be addressed in the course of treating their Bayesian-related ideas, methods, and assertions. For the purposes of this chapter, the main point to be conveyed here that there is significant damage being done to the entire endeavor of psychological assessment, and related domains.

One of the taboos of advertising is to attack one's competitor in ways that undermine the desirability everyone's goods. For Wendy's to confront their competition with "Where's the Beef?" was clever, humorous, and effective, but to have attempted to associate the competition's burgers with mad cow disease would have been fratricide as a prelude to suicide. The equivalent of this kind of mutual destruction has been taking place in the field of SVP assessment. One aspect of this destructive process is the turning of the KDT of complaining about the costliness of programs, assessment, and interventions into a self-fulfilling prophecy by the fostering of a cold war of escalating costs, a substantial proportion of which goes to hiring experts. Some opponents of SVP laws have stated that it is their strategy to make the law too expensive to survive, or to paraphrase, to force the law and its programs to strangle in their own excesses.

The Current Predicament in the SVPE Community of Practice

In a nutshell, the predicament for psychology stemming from SVP cases is not that psychologists retained for different sides of a commitment case may differ in their conclusions regarding the respondent, but that an increasingly widening gap has formed between methods and philosophical assumptions across the two sides. Thus the controversy regarding statistical methods and their interpretation is part of a broader development. Aiming at clarity, even a good description of a polarization that involves both ideas and practice tends to point to extremes and to leave out exceptions. One does not have to look very far to recover exceptions and middle cases in the form of individual practitioners who span the gap, and methods or assumptions shared on both sides of the divide. In this regard, the author will empathize with the reader's protests regarding either exaggeration or minimization of the degree of polarization in the SVP field.

Just as everything that exists does so to some degree, every development has a developmental history. Retrospective views over only two decades of SVP history prevent sweeping, all-inclusive generalizations, but the historical perspective of thinkers like Thomas Kuhn makes it possible to achieve a kind of metacognition regarding where the practice domain stands in the flow of history. Not surprisingly, I chose as a useful historical departure point, Paul Meehl's (1977) description of a tradition consisting of domains of knowledge and practice of lasting value in scientific psychology, and will use it as a touchstone to test how much the adversarial process has adulterated (or improved by alloying, depending on one's point of view) the methods and ideas in use by SVP practitioners relative to the thick vein of gold that, in his day, Meehl found running through the five noble domains.

First, consider how these five broad domains or knowledge and practice relate to the narrow domain of SVP practice. In addition to a history of qualifying sexual conduct, SVP laws have three prongs for proving an offender is committable: (1) presence of a current mental disorder or abnormality, (2) a finding that the offender's level of risk for future offending exceeds the statutory threshold, and (3) a causal/contributory nexus between the psychopathology and risk in the individual (Jackson & Richards, 2008). In terms of what the expert must engage in while performing a forensic psychological evaluation, these prongs equate to clinical determinations, each of which relies predominately one of Meehl's noble practice domains. Assessing the presence of a mental abnormality or personality disorder is applied descriptive psychiatry. The validity of diagnoses and their relevance to risk for future sex offending and the notion of volitional control versus psychiatrically compromised control are often issues in dispute in SVP determinations. Psychometric assessment is the practice domain related to the construction, improvement, and application of empirical predictive methods of risk estimation. Actuarial risk assessment instruments (ARAIs) have been developed for screening and assessment purposes. ARAIs render a mechanical estimation of an individual offender's risk by applying a mathematical algorithm to a table of observed recidivism.

Psychodynamic analyses trace the causal/contributing connection between mentation, affect, and habitual/automatic behavior (including self-selection of environments) with a specific class of problem behaviors. This is done by identifying a set of if-then behavioral patterns that explain past and present behavior. SVP experts engage in psychodynamics (although perhaps using a theoretical framework that eschews this term) when they describe the nexus between present mental abnormality and future risk.[1] Psychodynamics also entails assessing the significance of dynamic risk factors, and in determining whether there is psychiatric compromise to volitional controls.

Behavioral modification is the knowledge domain engaged when an evaluator incorporates treatment effects (including how enduring the changes are likely to be) into estimates of risk considerations, and this domain sometimes comes into play in regard to in diagnosis, when treatment may have contributed to reducing some behaviors below a diagnostic threshold.

Of Meehl's noble domains, behavioral genetics has the least relevance to SVP evaluations. However, behavioral genetics usually comes in through the back doors of the other domains. When there is strong evidence of a high proportion of genetic or neurobiological contribution to a syndrome (such as psychopathy and perhaps pedophilia), there may be an expectation on the part of the evaluator (with or without strong empirical support) of a higher base rate of that syndrome being manifested by more extreme and tightly clustered symptoms that are highly resistant to change. The combination of these expectations may raise the bar significantly in regard to what is taken as convincing evidence of change due to treatment or maturation, in behaviors that are used to assess psychodynamics and diagnosis.

Table 3.1 is intended as a heuristic for considering the validity of the proposition advanced here that polarization, almost to the point of creating a schism of competing factions, has occurred in SVP forensic psychology in these important practice domains. The table attempts to lay out how both sides have left behind the common ground of the previously shared methods and basic assumptions of Meehl's five noble domains of psychology, a shared ground that has washed away in the relentless beating waves of the adversarial process over the last two decades. This table contains depictions of positions taken by state's experts versus those taken by defense experts on issues that would have been much less polarized in the past. The first column depicts a traditional perspective from each of Meehl's noble domains. I have added the domain of philosophy of science, which does not include only moot issues when the discussion is limited, as it is here, to scientific psychology. Meehl was engaging this domain, somewhat informally, in posing the five-domain breakout from the rest of psychology, which he saw as developing more like fashion or art than like science. There, however, no row for a domain of inductive statistics and methods is included in the table, because this domain of knowledge was traditionally seen as part of the *hard core* (Lakatos, 1978) of each of the paradigmatic views. The various positions depicted for each of the noble domains serve to a certain extent as premises that predicate the selection of statistics and methods, and how these are to be weighed in decision making. Descriptions of the Prior Consensus column attempt to capture an aspect of the broad traditional perspective in a practice domain (hopefully one that Dr. Meehl would recognize) followed by the departures by the state's experts and defense experts in the next two columns. Depictions of the views of state experts immediately follow the depiction of the broader view of the traditional perspective. If the tradition of empirical psychology comprised of Meehl's noble domains is a compass needle denoting true magnetic north, departures by the experts identified with the two adversarial sides are not symmetrical, either in the angle of declination from true north or in the distance traveled away from it. This is reflected in the table by the depictions of the defense expert views residing in the column farthest away from the traditional perspective. This reflects the author's view that the assumptions and beliefs of the defense experts

Table 3.1 SVPE Community of Practice: Polarization and Departure from Hard Core of Key Paradigms

Domain	Prior Consensus	State Expert	Defense Experts
Descriptive Psychiatry	Although imperfect, shared diagnostic categories are useful for assisting in description of individuals conducting research and evaluating interventions.	DSM-IV-TR diagnoses can be reliably and meaningfully applied to cases in ways relevant to the legal criteria defining mental abnormalities.	DSM-IV-TR diagnoses are insufficiently reliable, and do not correlate statistically or have adequate conceptual overlap with legal criteria.
Psychometric Assessment	Enduring, and stable psychological and behavioral traits can be formulated as constructs for which reliable and valid measures can be designed, improved, and evaluated within limits of acceptable reliability and validity.	Findings from reliable and valid actuarial and psychological assessment instruments should serve as decision anchors for risk predictions.	ARAIs and psychological assessment instruments do not predict individual behavior or correctly characterized cases. The base rate (which is typically under the legal threshold) is the most defensible anchor.
Behavioral Genetics	Genetic inheritance plays a critical role in the formation of capacities for adaptive functioning in the development of vulnerabilities and resistances to psychopathology.	APD, and psychopathy, aggression, and dominance are life-persistent traits with significant genetic influences.	Aggression, dominance, and violence are life decisions pertaining mainly to the past and not generalizable to future behavior, particularly after intervening learning experiences such as punishment and treatment.
Behavior Modification	Behaviors involving homeostatic mechanisms are resistant to extinction and prone to spontaneous	In the absence of specifically targeted and effective counter-conditioning, deviant arousal	Deviant arousal and related cognitions often remit spontaneously or due to the

(continued)

Table 3.1 (Continued)

Domain	Prior Consensus	State Expert	Defense Experts
(Contingency Management)	recurrence. Nonetheless, they are modifiable by bottom-up contingencies and can be directed bytop-down executive controls (cognitive frameworks).	and related cognitions will persist or accelerate. Their spontaneous remission is rare and the passage of time is not predictive of their current intensity or influence over behavior.	passage of time, maturation, or due to cumulative learning from repeated negative consequences.
Psychodynamics	Human behavior is to a significant degree highly individualized, nuanced, and contextual. The interaction of mental states, behaviors, and manifesting situations form highly specific behavioral signatures of if-then patterns.	Psychologically meaningful explanations of past behavior will result in better prediction and intervention regarding future behavior. Clinical assessment can effectively identify and prioritize if-then patterns that are significantly related to offending.	There are so many ways to choose relevant clinical data and formulate cases that psychodynamic process is meaningless for prediction and weak for targeting interventions. The appeal to if-then patterns is an appeal to the authority of the clinician as soothsayer.
Philosophy of Science	[The received view from analytic philosophy of science.] The theory and methods of scientific psychology are quantitative, probabilistic, and bounded by formal logic. Qualitative information is progressively incorporated and subsumed within	The received view of scientific psychology holds for the long-range. In the midterm, where current practice is conducted, quantitative findings typically consist of a mixture of corroborating, disparate, and	The received view strongly limits legitimate scientific pronouncements about SVP cases. Clinical hypotheses without substantial empirical research support are simply unsupported assertions. The deductive logic of

this bounded structure, but usually at a slow pace, and supported by empirical studies that serve like "anchors" used to span distances in rock-climbing.	contradictory single-measure indicators with limited coverage of relevant domains. Qualitative data is useful for constructing evidence-based inductive linkages that support reasonable extrapolation from noisy quantitative sources.	falsification of theories applies to such claims, and raises the threshold for affirming them (as required by commitment statutes) beyond that attainable by current science. [Other views about the enterprise of psychology (humanistic/existential, constructivist, etc.) also preclude assertions supporting commitment, because they are predicated on the absence of volitional impairment in the absence of psychosis.]

in these cases depart more from the traditional perspective and may be, to some extent, a reaction to the assumptions and beliefs held by state experts. A disclaimer is offered here: traditional does not equate to good, superior, or right; each of these qualifiers requires the selection and judgment of evidence from a philosophical or practice-based stance. From the perspective of psychologists on the "right" side of the table, their positions are a legitimate critique of both the traditional perspective and the opposing experts' use of it, providing a Bayesian update to traditions to which they may view themselves as the legitimate heirs.

After ample description of one view of what is wrong with a campaign of single-minded Bayesianism, the chapter has not yet provided a requisite knowledge base, or refreshment of knowledge, regarding the appropriate, noncontroversial, and scientifically unavoidable uses of Bayes's Theorem. Before turning to the tenets and assertions the SVP Bayesians, and to the critique as applied to SVPEs, background information and substantive content regarding Bayes's Theorem (hopefully useful in many other contexts) is reviewed in the next section.

The Boy Who Cried Predator: A Pastoral Drama Featuring Bayes's Theorem

The foot in the door for Bayesian statistics is the extensive literature on heuristics and biases which demonstrates that persons naïve to probabilistic thinking tend to ignore base rate information in making estimates, perhaps due to a universal bias toward recognizing and processing unusual events. Weighing causal base rates over frequency base rates is another naturally naïve bias, which can be easily detected by comparing the divergent narratives and probability hunches most people construct upon reading "75% of the injuries at the archery range involved seniors" versus "the injuries occurred at an archery range where 75% of the members are seniors." Even psychologists adept at using statistical methods, such as significance testing, are not immune to such errors.

Kahneman and Tversky developed a hit-and-run accident scenario, which they named the cab problem, to use in research exposing common biases in probability estimation and to educate the probability naïve. The problem is presented here with the hit-and-run scenario changed in content to one often seen as typifying a scenario analogous to the situation of SVP evaluation process; that of crying wolf and credibility. We will see that scenarios like the cab problem (and this modified version of it) demonstrate Bayes's Theorem as a necessary corrective to intuitive probability estimates and the heuristic biases problem, and at the same time also foreshadow the hazards of making decisions that are overly reliant on an unquestioned probability rule, however indisputable that rule may be. The example will show how even the scenarios used to teach the importance of base rates in decision making have to be framed carefully to deliver the "right" lesson.

The modified version of the Kahneman and Tversky problem concerns Peter Jones (for some reason, the authors in the field of philosophy of science tend to pick on imaginary people named Jones) a skittish, almost timorous youth who lives with his father, a retired accountant who had worked for a commodities trader. In verdant Jones Valley, Jones family produces sheep to be sold for organic, free-range lamb. They also raise sheepdogs in large numbers to be sold for purposes other than those for which the sheep are sold. Mr. Jones, a retired accountant from a commodities firm, enjoys sheepherding and dog breeding, but he is a bit compulsive about all of his agricultural practices, going strictly by the book, and keeping meticulous records. It is Peter's job to watch over the sheep when they are allowed to stay overnight in a pasture with a rare nutrition-rich grass that will greatly increase their meat's market value as a gourmet item. Peter is to be particularly vigilant for signs of a wolf; since, historically, once a wolf enters the pasture, the flock is thinned out considerably before anything can be done about it, and there is an unknown risk of losing a skittish boy as well. Also, if a wolf is detected, either before or after a poaching incident, the flock must be moved to an enclosed pen and fed on hay, rather than eating the live green grass. Each day the flock spends in the pen erodes the Jones Valley Farm's reputation for a gourmet meat product and threatens its organic, free-range certification. Also, once a wolf in the pasture is confirmed, due to Jones's liberal views, a hunting party must be rounded up to capture it and eventually release it outside the sheepherding zone—another expensive sequence of endeavors. The stakes are exceedingly high for Mr. Jones, the sheep, the wolves, and Peter—who aspires to be an expert witness someday—hates to have his credibility and courage maligned by his father's reprimand for crying wolf when there is no wolf.

One dark and foggy night, Peter sprints home, breathlessly screaming "Wolf!" His father must make a decision, and fast. Was there "really" a wolf in the pasture, or was it one of the many wandering sheepdogs, which are never predatory of his sheep, that his skittish son has misidentified? Mr. Jones has previously decided that the probability of his son being right about any canid being a wolf must be greater than 50% for him to act on the boy's warning. In Jones Valley, there are 85% sheepdogs on the loose and 15% wolves. (We can trust Jones's counts; he is the stereotype of a compulsive accountant, after all, and he is sure there here are no foxes, coyote, jackals, or other canids in Jones Valley.) Jones knows from tabulating his journal notes that when his son sees a canid on these dark and foggy nights, the boy correctly identifies the animal as either a either *Canis lupus occidentalis* (Wolf) or a *Canis lupus familiaris* (Dog) 80% of the time. His son has just provided evidence in support of the hypothesis that the canid seen in the pasture was a wolf. Mr. Jones has decided that the probability of his son being right must be greater than 50% for him to act on the boy's warning. What probability estimate should Mr. Jones assign to the hypothesis: "Good God! A wolf has entered the pasture?"

For Kahneman's cab problem, which has the same numerical values as this modified version, the most common answer given by experimental subjects for the probability of a true positive was 81%. That would translate to Mr. Jones's situation as urgent advice that he better start herding the sheep toward the pen and rounding up the hunting party. However, Mr. Jones wants to avoid the kind of intuitive errors that are revealed in scenarios such as the one he exists in, so he studies up on Bayes's Theorem and then correctly applies the theorem to his dilemma. His research notes, reasoning and calculations are as follows:

Bayes's Theorem, or Bayes's Rule, is a law of conditional probability. The classic statement of Bayes's Theorem is:

$$P(H/E) = [P(E/H) \times P(H)] \div P(E)$$

Following from left to right in this equation are four different probability estimates.

1) P(H/E), the value we want to determine, is the posterior probability of the hypothesis (that what Peter saw was a Wolf). It is called the posterior probability because it is the probability of the hypothesis after taking into account the evidence of Peter claiming he saw a wolf. P(H/E) is also called an updated prior, because the right side of the equation shows us how to update our prior estimate, given the probability of the Evidence (that the Peter says it was a wolf). Our prior probability, that is our guess if we did not have the right side of the equation which will show us how to add new information, or update our belief, would be—thinking statistically—the base rate of Wolf, or 15% of the canid animals in the valley.
2) P(E/H) = .12. The Probability of the Evidence given the Hypothesis. This is how likely it is that the Peter will say an animal is a Wolf when the hypothesis that there is a Wolf in the pasture is true. It is a function of the Peter's reliability (.80) and the base rate of the hypothesis event, Wolf (.15), and in psychometric terminology, it is the rate of true positives.

3) P(H) = .15 The probability of the Hypothesis, or the base rate of Wolf, as already stated.
4) P(E) = .29. The probability of the Evidence. This can be thought of in several ways. It is the probability that the Peter will identify an animal as a Wolf irrespective of its true species. It is also a function of Peter's reliability because it is the combined probability of Peter saying a Dog is a Wolf (false positives) plus the probability of the Peter correctly identifying a Wolf (true positives). With reliability of .80 for detecting either species, Peter is likely to identify Dogs as Wolves with the probability of (1 – .80) × .85 = .17, the rate of false positives. At the same time, Peter will correctly identify Wolves with a probability of .80 × .15 = .12, the rate of true positives. Therefore, the probability of Peter crying Wolf (irrespective of the species that enters the pasture) is 17 + .12 = .29.
5) Plugging in Jones's values for each of the probabilities in on the right side of Bayes formula, we have:

   P (Wolf!) = (.80 * .15)/.29

   P(Wolf!) = .41379, or .41

With a Bayes's Theorem corrected estimate of a 41% likelihood that the canid was a wolf, Mr. Jones does not have to move his flock from open grazing, based on his decision criteria.

Mr. Jones has *updated* his prior belief in expectation of Peter being right about the seeing a wolf last night (which was the base rate of Wolf, .15) increasing it by .26 for a posterior probability estimate of .41. Mystery solved. Mr. Jones should believe that Peter's cry of wolf is testimony that is .41 percent likely to be true *if no other evidence comes in*. Since Mr. Jones will not let anxiety cause him to stray from his decision criterion, no search party will be launched, and the flock will continue to range free and graze on the good green stuff. However, if the wolves were to become 20% of the canid population, the probability Jones should assign to Peter's warning would be 50%, [(.80 × .20)/.32 = .50]. This would leave him with no statistically logical reason to choose between his two alternative courses of action. If he made a decision on anything other than a nonarbitrary basis (such as flipping a coin, or consulting his horoscope), he would be resetting his threshold criterion for a permissible risk. Jones should also realize that the base rate must exceed 1 minus the reliability quotient of any wolf crier (in the case of his son, 1 – .80, or .20) to exceed his 50% decision threshold. In the case of a wolf crier with 95% reliability of selection, the base rate must only exceed .05 to cross the 50% threshold of risk, but a crier with this level of accuracy has never been seen in Jones Valley.

Unpacking the allegory, an expert relying solely on ARAIs that are 80% reliable cannot rationally affirm that any offender tested is more likely than not to reoffend unless the reference group to which the offender has been matched for risk-relevant similarities has a base rate exceeding 20%. However, ARAIs work if, and only if, their scores validly segment the population into subgroups that have higher and lower base rates of offending than the larger general sex offender population. If the ARAI has been normed on multiple reference groups, matching the offender to the group he shares the most with, in terms of risk significant characteristics, will further improve the accuracy of the risk estimate.

All is well and good, in Jones Valley. But here is where is the uneasiness suggested in the introductory comments about this type of problem is realized. If you are like the author, you have some discomfort about the neat framing of the problem in the first place. It is too unrealistic, too much like a math problem; but the most common answer to this question is 81%, since most people ignore the base rates and rely on the eyewitness's testimony.

However, if we modify some starting assumptions of the problem frame, a different answer is needed. For example, if the frequency base rate of different canid species in the valley is unchanged, but we start off knowing that wolves are responsible for 85% of all canid intrusion into the fancy-grass pasture, because stray dogs hate the smell of the stuff, we must drastically update our P(H/E). Or, if we learn that when even one wolf moves into an area sheep are pasturing in, but not into the pasture itself, all the stray dogs are scared away for several days (update needed) and sometimes one or more dogs are eaten by the wolves (more updating). We have to calculate all the probabilities in the previous sentence, which requires lots of counts and estimates, some of which require knowledge beyond Jones's limited knowledge of dogs, sheep, and wolves from any study he has conducted; and the knowledge he does have comes with its own, often unknown, limits of reliability. Statistics is often complicated, but orderly; life is often complicated and messy. One of the major problems with founding all belief on Bayes's Theorem is the fact that information just keeps coming in, and much of it is quantitatively fuzzy (low reliability, low validity, or low on both) or qualitative in nature. Also, there is the problem of what counts as relevant, or even indispensable, information. When do we have to take a new fact or statistic seriously enough to do a new update?

Two Parallel Worlds of Statistics

Underlying the ballistics in journals and the courtroom is a cold war between two competing (and complementary) statistical worldviews: Bayesian statistics and frequentist statistics.[2] These two intellectual traditions in probability are something like the parallel worlds of physics theory—what is true in one world is similar, but oddly different in the other—but what is different from this analogy is that these two worlds are excruciatingly aware of each other, like mutually discontent Siamese twins. Frequentism is the simpler of the two approaches and has fewer philosophical assertions. Frequentism bases claims about probabilities on historically experienced frequencies. Frequentism is philosophically realistic, and there is strong current of Machian objectivism in frequentist statistics and philosophy, meaning that if something cannot be observed (hence measured) it has no meaningful existence; and until a measurement has been taken, there is little to discuss (Williams, 2001). Once the measurements or counts of meaningful events have been performed, the population base rate can be estimated from these observed base rates. Applying this process to sex offender recidivism, if similar methods of measurement are used, observed recidivism base rates across representative samples (i.e., whose members are believed to be similar in regard to important system variables, ecological variables, and individual characteristics) can be combined in a weighted average. For example, Harris and Hanson (2004) combined data on 4,724 offenders from 10 samples and obtained a pooled estimated recidivism rate over five years at risk of 14.0%, with the 95% CI being plus or minus 1.12% from this estimate. With no other data in hand, the best prediction of the recidivism risk for an offender considered to be adequately represented by the samples studied is the base rate, or 14% plus or minus 1.12%. With large samples, good variability in ARAI scores, and a short interval of observation/prediction, the confidence intervals of estimates can be quite narrow, as in the above example. However when these conditions are reversed (low sample size, constricted range of ARAI scores in the sample, and observation/prediction a short interval) the CIs become increasingly wide and relying on the estimate becomes increasingly less defensible.

Actuarial risk assessment instruments (ARAIs), when valid, can be used to predict an individual's risk more accurately than relying on the base rate alone. ARAIs are developed empirically by identifying offender characteristics associated with (but not necessarily causing) recidivism rates higher or lower than the base rate. These characteristics are represented by ARAI items, which are combined to form a total score. This may involve a weighting scheme based on the demonstrated strength of association of each variable to recidivism and the overlap in this association shared by the variables. The first stage of validating an ARAI is to demonstrate that higher scores on the ARAI are associated with recidivism higher than the base rate and that lower scores are associated with recidivism rates below the base rate. Analyses are performed to estimate the expected recidivism rate for each score or level of the ARAI from observed recidivism data. Because the criterion (predicted) variable, recidivism, is binary (yes or no for each individual in the sample—second bites at the apple are not usually allowed) and because any relationship between recidivism and a predictor variable can be framed in a linear model by employing coding schemes, log-linear regression is often used to estimate the risk associated with each score or level of the ARAI, usually expressed in percentages.

Frequentism is slower than Bayesian statistics, because new data has to be collected almost every time a new question is addressed. Frequentism has the strength of standing up to adversarial challenges when adversaries do not share assumptions. Frequentism does not claim to assert a philosophy, but some of its proponents have held that probability, in the form of propensity for future occurrence, is a property or quality of things, i.e., something in the world and not something we use to impose our need for order (Popper, 1959).[3]

Rather than ground probability in frequency counts, Bayesian probabilities are based on expectations, i.e., the degree to which one is confident of a statement about outcomes. Although this approach may be viewed as a form of subjectivism, clearly frequentist accounts also include considerations of whether a measurement is credible, given background information, understanding of the system producing outcomes, etc. Bayesian analysis can begin at the same place as frequentist analysis—that is, by simply determining probabilities from observed base rates. However, in situations that have not been sufficiently observed, Bayesian analysis can work from degrees of confidence in hypotheses about the base rate. Background experience may be used to set credible base rates. For example, rates may be generalized from one area of study to another, such as the rate of decrement in general criminality may be generalized to a credible estimate of an expected decrement in sexual offending. In the absence of sufficient background information to determine what is credible, the principle of indifference may be used—that is, equal probabilities can be assigned to all possible outcomes. In the middle case (when there is no preexisting model, yet it appears unlikely that all alternatives are equal), any anchoring estimate can be used as a starting point, as long as it is seen "reasonable." These anchors, or starting points, need only meet the most basic characteristics of quantitative analysis, and consist of simple relative frequency statements such as A is as probable as B, or A is more probable than B. From these priors (previous estimates of probability), we may tack our way through trial and error toward accuracy, the way a sailboat tacks against the main force of the wind, by overshooting and undershooting from what were only loosely informed, or even seriously mistaken, starting assumptions. Bayes's Theorem is used iteratively to calculate the probability of the starting assumption given the new outcome. This new information is used to "update" the original estimate, and probability of the updated estimate will be reevaluated from the next round of observations.

Such "probability calibration" (Griffin & Brenner, 2004) has proved very useful in exploratory studies in which there are strong practical incentives to move forward, and there is no need for proof. But the downside is that in Bayesian statistics, any premised prior (a belief based on prior knowledge or experience) is acceptable as long as the future promises opportunity for sufficient iterations of corrective trials to tack our way to accuracy. In other words, this faith in convergence-to-truth or merger-of-opinion outcomes (Howson & Urbach, 1993) anticipated by Bayesianism solves the problem of starting out in subjectivism in the long run. Critics of this approach may cite Keynes's famous rejoinder, "in the long run, we shall all be dead" (Keynes, 1923). Although faith in convergence to truth across studies may appear reasonable in fields that progress cumulatively, Bayesianism allows for the selection of priors that may be counterintuitive, or that may result in logically confounding inferences.

In summing up their review of Bayesianism principles and recent attempts to correct the problem noted above (and others) Hájek and Hall (2002) remarked that Bayesianism, even with various of these bells and whistles added, is still too permissive: "What is wanted is a justification of the "good" inductive inferences, *and no parallel justification of the "bad" ones*. These principles [of Bayesianism] do not seem to distinguish the good from the bad. Some of them, on the contrary, only seem to nurture the bad inferences" (p. 165, emphasis in the original).

Bayesianism, a merger of philosophical probabilism[4] and subjectivism,[5] also assigns prior probabilities to theories and other propositions. Here is one scholar's statement regarding strong Bayesianism:

> The claim that all propositions have probabilities is a philosophical doctrine, not a theorem of mathematics. This is where Bayesianism begins and Bayes's Theorem leaves off. But there is more to Bayesianism than this. Bayesianism in its strongest formulation, maintains not just that propositions have probabilities, but that all epistemological concepts that bear on empirical inquiry can be understood in terms of the probabilistic relationships described in Bayes's Theorem. (Sober, 2002, p. 21)

To be clear, even Bayesian statistics (less philosophical than Bayesianism) is not a simple matter of a different interpretation from frequentism. There are important circumstances where the Bayesian statistics and frequentist statistics result in both different interpretations and different numbers. This is markedly demonstrated in their divergent answers to the Behrens-Fisher problem of setting confidence intervals for the difference between the means of two or more independent variables calculated from different samples. In commenting on the divergent outcomes to this problem for Bayesian and frequentist statistics, David Williams (2001) explained how he as a textbook author had dealt with the dilemma of two versions of statistics throughout the textbook:

> To be sure there was a long period when furious arguments between Bayesians and Frequentists did Statistics no favors. These days, the politically correct thing is to ignore the controversy. But there have inevitably been some situations in this book (of which this is the most serious) when the philosophies disagree and even the numbers disagree. The Behrens-Fisher example will suggest to you many other important analogous situations . . . where there is a conflict my sympathies have tended to lie with the Frequentist school. A "schizophrenic" attitude is quite common. (Williams, 2001, p. 311)

The point here is that far from being a definitive solution to the problems of probability and statistics, Bayesian statistics (and even more so philosophical Bayesianism) is part of ongoing controversy in the fields of probability and statistics.

In Bayesianism, expectations are paramount over mere experience, resulting in an approach that is ultimately subjectivist. Even strong proponents of Bayesian statistics admit that there is strong subjectivist current in Bayesian statistics and philosophy (Dawid, 2002). Critics of Bayesianism give great weight to the problem of its subjectivism, which allows for different agents with the same evidence to rationally give different probabilities to the same hypotheses (Hájek & Hall, 2002). In establishing Bayesian priors, we may make what Reichenbach (1938) called volitional departures, decisions that are not compelled by logic or strong evidence. Bayesianism goes another step further and parallels a kind of idealism, where expectations and beliefs take on probabilities, theories have probabilities, and probabilities are based on our expectations (beliefs) and the restraints of mathematics and logical consistency.

The English Appeal Court on Bayesianism and Practical Reasoning

The potential of Bayesianism for cavalier indifference to what has actually been demonstrated through experience (established data) is the essential breakpoint between Bayesianism and individual assessment in forensic cases. For the individual respondent, the triers of law and fact usually have only one shot at it, not infinite iterations. The unfixed aspect of methods informed by Bayesianism—as well as level of complexity in concept and the slipperiness of application that can result in devastatingly wrong conclusions—led to what amounts to a judicial ban in the United Kingdom on jury instructions requiring that the jury use Bayesian methods. Two cases stand out as having led to the circumspection with which the British court regards Bayesian statistics, and they are worthy of consideration for their implications for SVP trials.

The first case is *Regina v. Sally Clark* (Dawid, 2002). Ms. Clark's three-month-old child died in her care, followed in the subsequent year by the death of her next-born child at the age of two months. Both children had signs of bruising and suffocation. It was the prosecution's contention that the children had been smothered by Ms. Clark and the defense's contention that the deaths were the result of Sudden Infant Death Syndrome (SIDS), with bruising explained as having resulted from the noble, if frantic and inept, attempts by the mother to resuscitate her failing children. The Crown's expert testified that those odds of two SIDS deaths occurring to one mother were 1 in 73 million. Ms. Clark was convicted of murder. The expert was later censured by the Royal Academy for unprofessional conduct. He had overlooked the counterbalancing probability of the two infanticides in one family, which Dawid (2002) calculated to be 100 times less likely than the two deaths due to SIDS. This is a dramatic example of the outcome (and credibility) of a Bayesian analysis hinging entirely on the assumptions and logical rigor of those applying it. As Phillip Dawid, a noted Bayesian statistician, put it: "The logic that identifies the correct statistical approach can be surprisingly subtle, and those who are not well versed in it frequently make errors" (Dawid, 2005, p. 8). Overlooking something could be simply catastrophic to the analysis, and to someone's life.

The second seminal case was *Regina v. Denis John Adams* (Dawid, 2002). Adams was charged with a rape in his neighborhood and the only evidence linking him to the crime was a DNA match to the crime scene evidence; all other evidence was in favor of acquittal. Expert opinion varied in regard to the rarity of the match, with estimates from 1 in 200 million (the Crown) to 1 in 2 million (the defense). The jury was extensively educated in Bayesian methods of evidence evaluation and were led to calculate that the risk (based on the number of suspicious males in the vicinity of the crime) was between .98 (based on the Crown experts estimate) and .36 (defense experts). Adams was convicted by the jury. The case was appealed, and the Appeal Court ordered a second trial, in which Adams was again found guilty. In its order, the Appeal Court chided the trial judge for having allowed the indoctrination of the jury with Bayesian methods. The Appeal Court typified the introduction of Bayes's Theorem *as a method of evidence evaluation* (that is, a philosophical overlay to the deliberation process, not the theorem itself) as tending toward preempting the traditional role of the jury in trying facts. In its order for a retrial, the Appeal Court addressed the nature of this role: "to evaluate evidence and reach a conclusion not by means of a formula, mathematical or otherwise, but by the joint application of their individual common sense and knowledge of the world to the evidence before them" (Dawid, 2002). Major among the concerns of the court was that the Bayesian methods used in the original trial would require that each piece of evidence be weighed separately in regard to its probability, whereas the Court's formulation of common sense involved weighing the totality of evidence and constructing and testing the strength of a chain of evidence.

Ultimately, the basic conflict between statistics and law is a conflict between rationalist and procedural approaches to evidence (Dawid, 2005). While law requires the exclusion of some kinds of evidence, rationalist statistics does not; for instance, while law may presume innocence, rationalist statistics can, and logically must, take into account the likelihood of guilt of the accused based in part on the fact that they have been accused, since a significant percentage of those charged with an offense are later found to be guilty.

Several philosophers of science have pointed out that the court's decision placed a strong and unjustifiable demarcation between science and common-sense, and that the court correctly identified that the Bayesian approach that was applied in the Adams trial reflected an individualistic epistemology in contrast to the jury's informal deliberative method, which is as an expression of communal knowledge (Kusch, 2001; Lynch & McNally, 2003). It is reasonable to view the Appeal Court order as reaffirming the common law view of evaluating evidence in the trying of facts—that is, the jury acts as a group of independent agents capable of reliable practical reasoning though a collaborative, communal process. Common sense is vulnerable to faulty assumptions and perceptions regarding probability and representativeness of samples (Kahneman, 2011; Tversky & Kahneman, 1974). However, it is reasonable to believe that cognitive biases affecting practical reasoning can be assuaged by providing appropriately formatted frequency information (Gigerenzer, 1991), providing information regarding corrective heuristics (Gigerenzer & Selten, 2001) and through instruction and education (Cox & Mouw, 1992). Clinical inference and reasoning as exercised by forensic psychologists is another form of practical reasoning that also has communal input and counterbalance through the psychologist's consideration of the state of established practice and science relevant to the evaluation task. The premise of this chapter is that by its tactics, the SVP Bayesian school undermines this communal counterbalance.

Categorizing Assertions and Methods Related to Bayes's Theorem

The development of Bayes's Theorem applications in SVP literature is traced and critiqued in the next section. A simplified typology of Bayesian concepts and practices found in this literature is provided here to assist the reader in categorizing methods and applications from this literature. Positions and assertions that utilized Bayes's Theorem or related concepts (related at times by being utilized to create an unorthodox statistical argument relative to SVP proceedings) can be characterized as direct applications of Bayes's Theorem, Bayesian statistics, philosophical Bayesianism, and other types of probabilistic inference. Nonproblematic Applications (NAs) are not contested by frequentists. Bayesian statistical analyses (BAs) based on high-quality frequency data using Bayesian methods can be referred to as soft Bayesianism, and often approximates frequentist solutions. Strong Bayesianism assertions (SBs) are based on constructing priors much more aggressively, and relies on a subjectivist epistemology. The works of the SVP Bayesians also assert some positions that undermine current practice in SVP evaluations and that are not grounded in Bayes's Theorem or Bayesianism as a philosophy. These constitute idiosyncratic methods (IMs) not typically found in psychology, and extra- statistical positions (XSs) that cluster with Bayesian concepts in SVP testimony and writing. Table 3.2 lists examples of positions, assertions, and methods from SVP literature and practice by these categories with source citations. This table's categories will be used to typify various methods and positions taking in regard to SVPEs.

From Nonproblematic Applications to a Revolutionary Subjectivist Agenda

The explicit introduction of Bayes's Theorem in SVP considerations began with simple, but illuminating analyses and conjectures from some of our most respected scientists and scholars. It has now devolved to constitute the efforts of those with a revolutionary agenda to overthrow established science and practice and to ensconce a subjectivist view of prediction for consumption by the courts. A purely cynical view would be that this is done only for the strategic purposes of constructing defenses for respondents, with the knowledge that in the long run, these ideas and methods cannot stand.

Table 3.2 Categorizing Positions Regarding Inferential Statistics, Bayes's Theorem and Philosophical Bayesianism

Nonproblematic Applications (NAs): General statistical principles & applications of Bayes's Theorem with minimum noncontroversial assumptions.
NA1: Actuarial scales developed for adult male offenders are not appropriate for juvenile offenders (Prentky, Janus, Barbaree, Schwartz, & Kafka, 2006). NA2: Each respondent should be compared to the base rate for the representative class for which stable relative frequencies are available, such as rapists specifically to rapists (Pretky et al., 2006). NA3: The effectiveness of an actuarial instrument is related to the base rate of recidivism in the population to which it is applied (Wollert, 2006). NA4: Actuarial tables can be used to calculate sample statistics and test operating characteristics (Donaldson & Wollert, 2008). NA5: Statistical prediction rules (algorithms) already incorporate prior probabilities and caution should be taken in ad hoc adjustments related to base rate considerations (Swetz et al., 2000).
Bayesian Analysis (BA): Bayesian statistical analysis based on premises that are not consensually held in the field of sex offender treatment and assessment
BA1: Actuarial instruments are "useless" in SVP evaluations because the relevant recidivism base rates are under 25% (Donaldson & Wollert, 2008). BA2: Actuarial instruments are "useless" because they do not fully take into account aging (Donaldson & Wollert, 2008). BA3: The effect of aging on sex offender recidivism risk is known and the effect size can be used to readjust actuarial tables without additional data collection and these new estimates can be applied to individuals to reduce their assessed risk (Wollert, 2007c). BA4: The reliability of paraphilia and personality disorder diagnoses is too low to support SVP determinations (Wollert, 2006). BA5: Relevant base rates of paraphilias rates are drastically in contradiction to the frequency they are diagnosed in SVP evaluations, and the evaluators are typically ignorant of the relevant base rate information (Wollert, 2007b).
Strong Bayesianism (SB): Subjectivist in approach, more aggressive in constructing priors, tendency to probabilistic reduction of phenomena or processes.

(*continued*)

SB1: Probabilistic logic based on Bayes's Theorem should displace current practices of clinical reasoning (Donaldson & Wollert, 2008; Wollert, 2007a).

SB2: Opinions regarding commitment status (and each element leading to or supporting such opinions) should be constrained to within a logic model based on Bayes's Theorem and null hypothesis testing: the Null Bates Logic Model (NBLM) (Wollert, 2007).

SB3: Case formulations that support dynamic risk considerations are to be impeached as speculation of the type "that "any verbally fluent and somewhat intelligent person can come up with" because they are not probabilistic algorithms (Wollert 2007a).

SB4: Base rates for disorders and recidivism can be estimated by experts who are informed in Bayesian methods and these estimates should displace "outdated" actuarial data, and the assumptions of clinicians and researchers who are not Bayesians (Donaldson & Wollert, 2008; Hart, Michie, & Cooke, 2008).

SB5: Subjectivist approaches should replace frequentist approaches in SVP applications because subjectivists notions are "more intuitively understandable" (Hart, Michie, & Cooke, 2007).

SB6: Psychologists should keep the number of diagnoses they assign in SVP cases to a minimum because of the product law of probability indicates lower confidence in a cluster of disorders than in a single disorder (Wollert, 2007b).

Idiosyncratic Method (IM): Not supported by Bayes's Theorem or Bayesianism and generally not found in psychological practice.

IM1: The legal "SVP construct" should be treated as a clinical construct, analogously to DSM disorders (Wollert, 2007a).

IM2: Each numerical total score for an ARAI should be treated as a separate group for which confidence intervals are calculated, with the result being some small N groups with very wide confidence intervals (Testimony and slides presented by R. Wollert, August 22, 2008, Snohomish County Court).

IM3: Formulas for calculating Confidence Intervals for group statistics should be calculated using n=1 for application to individual cases, with the result being unacceptably wide CIs (Hart, Michie, & Cooke, 2007).

IM4: Null hypothesis testing should be applied to individual diagnostic decisions and psycho-legal determinations, such as SVP status.

It appears that purely cynical strategy does not explain the fervor that is often shown in advancing Bayes's Theorem and Bayesian statistics as an all-inclusive breakthrough in the assessment of SVPs.

Although considerations of the relationship between base rates and selection accuracy for predictions have been long standing in sex offender assessment, Janus and Meehl (1997) may have been the first to advance systematic consideration of these issues in regard to civil commitment. They argued that the commitment standard applied by the courts can be quantitatively evaluated by estimating what the recidivism rate would be of those committed, the commitment class, if they were released. This estimation can be accomplished by applying "a small number of assumptions and non-problematic applications of Bayes's theorem" (p. 47) to models of the commitment selection process. Based on their review of the literature, they adopted the assumptions that the best selection process would have an upper limit of 75% accuracy and that the base rate of recidivism in the prison release population was somewhere between 20% and 45%. They concluded from their Bayesian analysis that a commitment standard of 50% was attainable under favorable assumptions but that a standard of 75% or higher "lies entirely outside the area of possible proof" (p. 55). Although their working assumptions and, therefore, conclusions have been challenged (Doren & Epperson, 2001), the decision models and Bayes's Theorem applications presented in Janus & Meehl (1997) are straightforward and noncontroversial. The implications of base rates for accurate predictions are illustrated in the body of the article, and notes and an appendix provide sufficient background and clarifying information regarding probability and statistics as well as a few relevant issues regarding philosophical aspects of probability theory. The spirit of the paper is that of empowering the courts through accessible statistical knowledge, "to hold sex offender commitment schemes to closer account" (p. 60).

In replying to Janus and Meehl (1997), with an analysis supporting the opposite conclusion, that the courts do employ their stated commitment standard, Doren and Epperson (2001) adopted different assumptions based on a different understanding of the state of research on sex offender recidivism and selection methods, but they felt comfortable using "the same mathematical analysis employed" (p. 51) by Janus and Meehl (1997). Thus, when Bayesian analysis was first systematically introduced in SVP discourse, it was done so authoritatively (Paul Meehl, after all) and non-controversially, with "a small number of assumptions and non-problematic applications of Bayes's theorem" (Janus & Meehl, 1997, p. 47). This conservative approach to using statistical concepts in general and Bayes's Theorem in particular is often found in articles responding to the SVP Bayesians, and it remains an ongoing theme in the SVP literature (additional examples include Harris & Rice, 2007; Mossman, 2006, 2008). In these contributions, Bayes's Theorem is used with little fanfare, and without encompassing claims.

In contrast, another stream of papers applying Bayes's Theorem in the SVP context, those reflecting SVP Bayesianism, has been less austere in assumptions and methods. Some of the SVP Bayesians are explicitly subjectivist in approach, and are unequivocally committed to promoting Strong Bayesianism.

Hart, Michie, and Cooke (2007), sounded the clarion cry of the SVP Bayesians as loudly and clearly as possible. In commenting on their findings of an admittedly "ad hoc" application of a group statistics to an individual estimate (Table 3.2, IM3) and acknowledging that "some readers may object" (p. 63) to the novelty of this approach,[6] these authors decried the meaningfulness of propensity for future violence (propensity being a frequentist term), as "a metaphysical abstraction" (p. 63) unrelated to the individual's behavior because that *future* behavior has not yet occurred. Having discarded one of the major modern attempts to form an inductive bridge from the past to the future, the concept of objective probability, these authors go on to proclaim:

> Our findings also suggest that people who develop and evaluate ARAIs should consider the potential benefits of conceptualizing violence risk from a subjectivist perspective, focusing on how evaluators do or should form beliefs about an individual's risk for future violence, especially in the light of uncertain information and decision errors with varying costs (e.g., Hájek, 2003). Although changing the discourse from frequentist to subjectivist will not make predictions any more accurate, it may provide ways of researching and communicating about the problem that are more intuitively understandable to mental health professionals and legal decision-makers alike (for an example, see Mossman, 2006). (p. 64)

This quote is solidly in the subjectivist vein of Bayesianism (Table 3.2, SB5). It is important to note that there is nothing on a close reading of Mossman (2006) that supports subjectivism. To the contrary, Mossman presented solid illustrations of the application of Bayes's Theorem to the issues of test efficiency under varying sample base rates (Table 3.2, NA3), applications to which the most purist frequentist would have difficulty objecting in principle.[7] Mossman and Sellke (2007), in responding to Hart, Michie, and Cooke (2007), stated:

> Using ARAIs raises serious moral problems as well as the valid scientific questions that Hart and colleagues mention. But in faulting ARAI's capacity to address an unspecified quantity called "individual risk," and in dressing up this notion with misapplied formulae or CIs, Hart and colleagues ultimately, create a muddle. (Electronic letter)

It is important to note that while Mossman is a psychometrically oriented psychiatrist, Sellke is one of the few academic statisticians weighing in on these issues.

Extreme Bayesianism in Practice

Richard Wollert, PhD, has been an active expert witness in SVP cases and a strong proponent of Bayesianism. Wollert (2006) argued that due to base rate considerations, the accuracy of actuarial prediction of sexual recidivism was only efficient for the youngest of offenders, and was otherwise "useless" for predicting likely recidivists (Table 3.2, BA1), and asserted that the base rate of qualifying diagnoses were too low to permit reliable positive determinations of commitment (Table 3.2, BA4). Starting from an age invariance principle (inverse correlation of age with recidivism) and an assumption of base rates of less than 25% among sex offenders released from prison, Wollert (2007a) later used Bayes's theorem to "respecify" Hanson's (2002) experience tables for the Static 99 (Table 3.2, BA3). Wollert justified his analyses on the clarifying power of Bayes's theorem, and bemoaned the neglect of the theorem by other trial experts:

> In spite of the clarifying power and very important implications of Bayes's Theorem, evaluators often do not discuss their Bayesian level of certainty when they are examined in court. They are also not often asked about this topic when they are cross-examined. Perhaps this avoidance stems from the fact that many expressions of the theorem include probability terms that are either discouragingly complex (Dawid, 2002; Fergusson et al., 1977; Swets et al., 2000) or difficult to remember because of the weak mnemonic connections with some of the variables of concern (Meehl & Rosen, 1955). It may also be due to a lack of knowledge about Bayes's Theorem or the steps involved in its calculation. Finally, it may be tedious and time consuming to estimate P, T, or F from available information. (Wollert, 2006, p. 64)

The publication of another paper by Wollert (2007b) marked a turning point for Bayesianism in the SVP literature. In this article, Wollert introduced his Null-Bayes Logic Model of forensic decision-making that had theretofore been disseminated through lengthy courtroom testimony supported by extensive PowerPoint presentations of logic models and statistical analyses. A major implication of the Nulls-Bayes Logic Model for SVP assessment, if accepted, is that the reliability for all components for the SVP decision model would have to be high for the enterprise of commitment to be empirically justified. Analyses reported by Packard and Levenson (2006) supported good to acceptable reliability for SVP diagnoses and commitment opinions. The rest of Wollert's article (beyond presentation of his model) undermines the accuracy and generalizability of these findings. Wollert asserted that the likelihood ratio (LR) was the correct measure of reliability for the analysis of these data and calculated the LR from the tables from Packard and Levenson. Using an application of Bayes's Theorem, Wollert then estimated the prior base rate expectations for each diagnosis. He concluded from this analysis that the mostly good to acceptable reliability measures previously reported in Packard and Levenson were evidence of "illusory certainty"—that is, the appearance of high reliability stemmed from the evaluators having shared an unrealistically high expectation of finding certain disorders (and committable evaluees) in the population evaluated for commitment proceedings. In the same article, Wollert reports a second study (to be addressed later in this article) intended to set more realistic, empirically grounded estimates of relevant diagnoses.

In contrast to Janus and Meehl (1997), Wollert's (2006) paper is based on theory-driven assumptions (i.e., age invariance principle), confuses empirically derived data with extrapolations, and makes far-reaching claims for Bayes's Theorem as a revelatory panacea. Wollert's (2007b) paper is replete with assumptions, often embedded in analyses or tables and otherwise imprecisely stated, and framed in a model (the Null-Bayes Logic Model of diagnosis and clinical reasoning) that is novel, idiosyncratic, and loosely specified. For example, the introduction of null hypothesis testing in the context of assessment of an individual is confounding (Table 3.2, IM4). Null hypothesis testing has been critical to psychological research since Fischer, Neymen, and Pearson developed the methods in the 1920s, but what does it have to do with assessing individuals? The null hypothesis is usually relied on in situations in which the notion of long-term relative frequency and the Strong Law of Large Numbers apply (Williams, 2001). In other words, aggregates of lots of data, usually on cases, but sometimes in many observations on the single case.

If framed as a null hypothesis, the question regarding ARAI is, does the risk category obtained for this individual represent a chance finding—i.e., is the statistically significant relationship between the ARAI and reoffending invalid in this case? This is a question of generalizability of the ARAI validation sample to this individual—or, conversely, the fit of the individual—as a member of the population represented by the validation sample. The answer to this question is the behavioral analysis and psychodynamic analysis of the individual. Efficiency measures such as AUC, on the other hand, are clear and unequivocal means to assess the likelihood of error in categorization based on the measure, since it includes the effects of reliability and generalizability for any new sample for which it is calculated.

The introduction of the null hypothesis in this context has a rhetorical and pretextual motivation; that is, the goal is to give the appearance of legitimacy to introducing the courtroom and judicial context at the earliest possible point of the clinical decision-making process, prior to the point that psycho-legal issues should be of any major consideration. Wollert (2006) does this by drawing an analogy between null hypothesis testing and the judicial determination of guilt or innocence, which in our system incorporates the principle of presumption of innocence.[8] As it should be, our legal system presupposes that an individual is innocent until proven guilty, and this principle has some parallel in the rule of placing the burden on the state to prove the necessity of civil commitments. The presumption of innocence appears to be similar in form to the null hypothesis in hypothesis testing because it precludes our increasing our belief in an assertion in the absence of strong evidence to the contrary, but the similarity is only superficial, and potentially misleading.

A second rhetorical or tactical motivation that appears to be at work is to confine the evaluator's task within a framework that can be defined in terms of simple decision rules to which probabilities appear directly relevant at the case level (Table 3.2, SB1, SB2). This limiting of the sample space is the first step in proselytizing for Bayesianism.

The Null Bayes Logic Model is not described with anything approaching an adequate level of detail in Wollert (2006) or elsewhere for assessing its usefulness in SVPE's. In fact, Wollert (2006) and Donaldson and Wollert (2008) dodge the precedent task of describing how practice is usually conceptualized before they attempt to radically modify and replace these conceptions. This can be easily accomplished, and any honest review of typical assessment process reveals something very different from what is proposed by Donaldson and Wollert (2008). Jackson and Hess (2007) surveyed 41 experts who conduct SVP evaluations to identify usual practice and found that "a great deal of agreement exists" (p. 441). Neither Bayes's Theorem nor the Null-Bayes Logic Model surfaced in the survey results. Jackson and Richards (2007) sought to explain the logic and methods of SVP evaluations as generally conducted. No reference was made to Bayes's Theorem or the Null-Bayes Logic Model as considerations for typical practice. Jackson, Rogers, and Shuman (2004) studied how professional psychologists use available data in case materials for making SVP determinations. Again, neither Bayes's Theorem nor the Null-Bayes Logic Model was viewed relevant to modeling typical practice. Beech, Fisher, and Thornton (2003) developed a model for thorough evaluation of sex offenders by identifying the domains of risk and surveying viable instruments and methods of assessment. Again, no Bayes's Theorem, no null hypothesis testing, and no Null-Bayes Logic Model. These descriptions of the evaluator's work serve to demonstrate how far away the complexity of the task is from framing it within a half-dozen boxes to cover the sample space for Bayesian analysis (Wollert, 2007a), yet at the same time, how transparent the process is to good old common sense and practical reasoning.

Donaldson and Wollert's article (2008) is one of the more recent publications that fit the SVP Bayesian prototype, and can be treated as an exemplary of this school's positions, methods, and tactics. It is ostensibly intended to demonstrate that when applied to fully specified recidivism tables, Bayes's Theorem can be used to deduce sample statistics (such as conditional probabilities for test score ranges and odd ratios) and test efficiency indices (such as sensitivity, specificity, and receiver operating characteristics) (Table 3.2, NA4). The central truth of the whole paper is summed up in one sentence "Bayes's Theorem is simply a probabilistic restatement of the way that frequency data are combined to arrive at whatever recidivism rates are paired with each test score in an actuarial table" (Donaldson & Wollert, 2008, p. 7).[9]

Although most readers will deal with the formulas in the article the way children deal with the broccoli on a plate that also contains macaroni and cheese, there will be readers, no doubt, who will check the math and formulae in hope that the authors (and editors) have nodded somewhere along the long line in delineating the proof. Looking for flaws in this paper is tempting in the same way that we postmodern thinkers are tempted to look for flaws when we encounter a medieval scholastic proof for the existence of God. We postmoderns (whether believers or nonbelievers) are somewhat entertained, but just are not convinced by the Gordian knot of logic and mathematics that is intended to hold us to a single conclusion. The authors rely on logic and syllogisms to force a point, but in the process, we sense (correctly) that the entire argument is vulnerable to both errors in logic and existential errors—situations when "it ain't necessarily so," even when apparently prescribed by an authoritative principle such as Bayes's Theorem.

Donaldson and Wollert (2008) could have ended with the quoted sentence supported by a long string of citations from the well-developed and uncontested literature applying Bayes's Theorem across many domains of practice in which a conclusion must be reached based on limited or partial evidence, or fallible methods of detection. For example, Dawid (1987) and Swets (1988) provided a general overview of the issues for screening and detection across several practice domains. In fact, all of these issues in regard to clinical prediction (including calculating probabilities from a frequency table and other probability concepts fundamental to diagnostic decisions and application of Bayes's Theorem) are covered adequately in two pages of text containing one table in Swets, Dawes, and Monahan (2000). Donaldson and Wollert could have referred us to Paul Meehl's (1955) classic paper "Antecedent Probability and the Efficiency of Psychometric Signs, Patterns, or Cutting Scores" as a starting point. This paper was recently reprinted posthumously in an edited book, with a chapter showing the specification of positive predictive value (PPV), negative predictive value (NPV), and the hit rate (HT) as illustrations of Bayes's Theorem. The chapter provides example sets with solutions, one of which uses Bayes's Theorem, to set the cut score for the Minnesota Sex Offender Screening Tool–Revised (MnSOST-R) at different "Bayesian coordinates" (Waller et al., 2006). They could have referred us to almost any graduate-level textbook in statistics and probability for the mathematical proof itself.

With this abundance of riches that are directly on point for the practice issues in civil commitment evaluations, why then are we treated to this mathematical proof, in this journal, at this time, and if not as a scholastic exercise, for what purpose? It appears that the tactical goal of what is ostensibly a redundant mathematical proof by Donaldson and Wollert (2008) is to insinuate (but not deliver), through yet another fragment, the promise of a forthcoming coherent integration of null hypothesis testing and Bayes's Theorem that will overthrow previously existing notions of assessment and diagnostic practice. If this coherent integration is ever successfully articulated—and it was not in this article, nor in Wollert's previous article (2007a), the primary published reference for the Null Bayes Logic Model—what could such a creature be called but a "novel and idiosyncratic method" of SVP assessment?

Novel and idiosyncratic methods may be exactly what are called for in some contexts. Viewed from Hans Reichenbach's (1938) distinction between a context of Discovery and a context of Justification, novel and idiosyncratic methods are critical to the context of discovery in science, and are particularly valuable when paradigms are stultifying, or prior to the point at which a field of study or practice has developed sufficiently encompassing and widely endorsed models. One can imagine experts in the SVPE domain asserting that the state of affairs in the field matches one of these extremes, while disagreeing about which positions bring us to which extreme. So, rather than criticizing Donaldson and Wollert's (2008) methods as novel and idiosyncratic (which they are in the extreme), it is more appropriate to complain that they have a more serious flaw: they are not coherently articulated, particularly in regard to how they relate to established thought and professional practice in the assessment field.

Donaldson and Wollert (2008) appeared to have been hanging a straw man in effigy. Put simply, no one holds the positions they launch proofs and diatribes against. There has been no serious challenge put forth against the proposition that probabilities can be derived from a recidivism table, nor has it been asserted that the inverse probabilities defined by Bayes's Theorem are irrelevant to diagnostic and prediction decisions made in sex offender evaluations. Because there are no contradicting claims to Bayes's Theorem per se or its relevance to actuarial tests and diagnostic decisions, the publication of this demonstration is redundant and unnecessary. Perhaps a redundant proof might have been necessary if the "anti-statistical" attitudes attributed by the authors to some expert evaluators in SVP cases in fact extended to the challenging the last few centuries of development in probability and statistics. But no one claims that a Gausian, Bayesian, papal, or other authoritative indulgence has been granted to SVP evaluators. It is difficult to take the statistical Luddites the authors referenced as the provocation for their mathematical demonstration as anything other than rhetorical straw men. In rushing to correct non-Bayesians, they miss something really essential. Statistics do not drive knowledge creation, especially an applied level like individual assessment decisions. In the context of empirical research, statistics and probability theory help us to assess our findings from the perspective of what is probable or rare given our model and our working assumptions. Our models and working assumptions should conform to certain constraints imposed by probability theory, but beyond this delimiting process, probability does not determine the model or working assumptions, let alone clinical and experimental methods (other than statistical methods), and certainly not the findings (Williams, 2001).

Bayesian reasoning is strongest in the context of a mutual admiration society, where assumptions are cozily shared. We find an invitation to this kind of cozy relationship in Donaldson and Wollert (2008), where in an extensive note (Note 3), the authors propose to limit the legitimacy of challenging Bayesian analyses to the range within foundational probabilities (priors), based on background understandings. Of course, these understandings are those of the authors. They are certainly not universally shared by the experts in the field of SVP evaluation, and even if they were, without the corrective of experience, they could simply be wrong.

With regard to examples of other forms of obfuscation, Wollert has persisted in misrepresenting the data and views of Karl Hanson in regard to the Static 99 and the relationship of this actuarial measure to age (Hanson, 2008). Wollert (2007c) distorted Hanson's attempt to shed light on whether the Static 99 accurately predicts recidivism among older offenders by declaring that the paper presents a new standardization table for age groups. Hanson pointedly warned against considering the values presented in that article as stable. He stressed (in good empirical frequentist fashion) the importance of awaiting the data of cross validation of differences; and, due to the cross-sectional nature of the samples studied, warned that older offenders in these samples are not merely the younger offenders grown up. Wollert consistently ignored these concerns. Wollert (2006) cited five sources supporting the idea that falling societal crime rates equates to falling sexual recidivism rates. Harris and Rice (2007) reported that, in fact, none of the cited sources supported this idea and one of them disconfirmed it.

For the art of data "correction," several examples can be provided. Wollert (2007c) adjusts the table's values by Bayesian arts such that the distribution of offenders in the youngest age category mirrors that of the group nearest to them in age. True, this might prevent some evaluators from testifying that 25- to 40-year-old high-risk group had higher recidivism than the youngest group, a violation of the "age invariance principle" criminology, which is not allowed in our Bayesians' theoreticism; but here the principle of age invariance is saved at the cost of fabricating data. Even if one accepted the approach, without the full data set (which Hanson was rightfully loath to relinquish to researchers who are eager to condition it with their personal priors) the calculations are not credible. For example, some of the subjects were lost to follow up, and are cannot be categorized as recidivists or non-recidivists. The Hanson data was generated by Cox survival analysis. The table produced by Wollert does not indicate what the "recid" column consists of, but the recidivism rates and confidence intervals could not possibly be generated from a Cox survival analysis because Wollert did not have sufficient case-level data to perform such analyses after their "corrections" were performed. Not explicitly noting the nature of these "estimates" might mislead an evaluator (but hopefully not a researcher, student, policymaker, or juror) that these rates have the same empirical status as those reported by Hanson, which make up the rest of Wollert's "recalibrated" table.

In support of the contention that a Paraphilia Not Otherwise Specified, Nonconsent (PNOSN) is either nonexistent or occurs as a negligible base rate, making its reliable detection impossible, Wollert (2007c, Study 2) performed something that has the form of a research project, but one that would it inadmissible for fulfillment of any graduate-level research requirement. Wollert provided several vignettes describing PNOSN to four masters-level clinicians and one doctoral-level clinician working under his supervision in an outpatient sex-offender clinic. The vignettes, he states, were provided because there is no criteria set for PNOSN. He then asked the participants to provide their subjective "priors," that is estimates of the frequency of occurrence of this kind of clinical syndrome, based on their experience. The "study," based upon the information from five clinicians, found that the average estimated rate of occurrence of PNOSN was 5% with a standard deviation of 5%. The setting of this study, an outpatient clinic, is the least likely place to find individuals with PNOSN, and no one respectful of sampling issues would admit to applying estimates from this kind of setting to an SVP sample, even if the estimates were unbiased by the participants' likely familiarity with Wollert's views on the subject. It is unclear that participants would abstract the same criteria from the vignettes, and the approach overlooks the work of Doren (2002) and others toward specifying PNOSN. This study has correspondences to several positions described in Table 3.2, notably positions SB1, SB4, BA4, BA5, and XS2, although the reader will be able to draw other correspondences as well.

In a highly informal exercise (one that I would not deem adequate to be called research, but that is very similar to the Wollert effort described here), this author queried six doctoral, licensed SVP evaluators about their estimates of percentage of individuals with PNOSN, and obtained a whopping average of 43% (range of 25% to 70%) of those evaluated. True, these were evaluators in employment of an SVP program who had some knowledge of the investigator's views on the subject as the "investigator," and the evaluators were under the investigator's administrative supervision. These same biasing factors were present in Study 2 of Wollert's presentation (2007c). The difference in estimates in these two "studies" shows the fatal flaw of subjective priors, as well as a cavalier attitude toward knowledge generation on the part of one of the founding members of the school of SVP Bayesians.

An Honest Bayesian Game Is Loaded in Favor of Commitment

This chapter section shows that alternative prior assumptions as reasonable or more reasonable than those offered by the SVP Bayesians can result in Bayesian analyses steering civil commitment in a very different direction from the SVP Bayesians trying to sail. Modern probability theory has its origins in logical and mathematical attempts to increase success in games of chance, especially games with a fixed sample space (limited number of possible outcomes) such as exactly 52 cards in fixed categories, dies whose sides determine fixed outcomes, etc. (Hájek & Hall, 2002). Pascal's Wager stretches this model to include such things as the number of lives that would have to be wagered to profitably cover the bet that God exists. Pascal limited the sample space to two outcomes at the end of life: oblivion and eternal life (in either damnation or salvation). Pascal's answer was that three lives cover the bet (Hájek, 2008). Probabilities all ride on how you define the practical enterprise as a game, describe its sample space, relevant risks (excluding others; for example, Pascal did not consider Limbo, Purgatory, Nirvana, or Satori as possible outcomes), and prior probabilities. But life, and even diagnostic work, has much richer sample spaces. As Hegel put it, "The tree of life is greener than the tree of thought"

Donaldson and Wollert (2008) cite Mossman (2006), who rightly censured applying estimates to an individual who is not similar to or represented by the standardization population. We know that subjects of SVP evaluations are not randomly drawn offenders from the population of known sex offenders. They are "cherry picked" for risk by review boards who consider their scores on risk instruments, detailed criminal histories, including criminal conduct for each offense, prison comportment, etc. We should agree with Mossman (2006), by concluding that to the extent that actuarial instruments misrepresent SVP candidates, the most likely direction of the misrepresentation is that of underestimating their risk. By similar logic (which is not endorsed here) the reasonable Bayesian prior relevant to an assessment for commitment status would be the rate of trials ending in commitment in that state, meaning an expectation of commitment of .8 or higher in most states. Disconfirmation of this commitment baseline prediction would require significant countervailing indications. Whether you take the base rate of offending related to a test score or the rate of commitment in the class of respondents to commitment petitions, the dice are loaded in favor of commitment, if you want to play the Bayesian game.

There is another important statistical dilemma that the radical form of Bayesianism can answer. In civil commitment assessment, we rely on the observed recidivism rates associated with actuarial risk assessment scores to determine an anchor point for risk. If it is conceded that the prognostic effectiveness of these instruments or any imaginable instruments are impacted by decreasing offense rates (Wollert, 2006, Table 2, Direct Application 3), what conclusions and actions should be taken as the result of this realization? The fact of the dropping rates begs the question of whether the state should be required to unleash the dragon periodically to show that the dragon still has the propensity to devour children and maidens. Among the many factors contributing to the drop of sex offender recidivism rates in the United States are policy-driven interventions such as longer sentences, improved community supervision, greater community awareness and sensitivity to the potential for sexual abuse and violence, access to improved treatment, and incapacitation due to civil commitment. Should we undo all of these factors for the sake of observing a base rate that might be more reflective of the internal propensities of assessed offenders? Bayesianism allows us to posit a prior expectation of what the base rate would be if this web of extensive social engineering were to be unraveled. One reasonable prior would be to use the base rate for reoffending in, say, 1985, or some other year prior to these extensive changes, and evaluate our actuarials and our cases accordingly.

Clearly, Bayesianism, which allows such machinations as described in the previous paragraph, should not be the only game in town; but if it is, the only sensible recommendation is not to play at all, because the house always wins in the long run. It is a game that forensic examiners do not have to play. Clinical psychology and psychiatry have developed methods for application of practical reasoning informed by science and humanistic philosophical and ethical principles, such as the literature on established practice in the five noble traditions cited at the onset of this chapter. This tried-and-true tradition is a safer bet than eccentric applications in twenty-first-century America of "new discoveries" from eighteenth-century England.

Conclusion and Recommendations

One of the goals of this chapter is to alert the legal bar, the courts, and editorial boards of journals that a fairly systematic attempt at revolution is taking place, so that that the usual outposts can be duly manned with a little extra vigilance, and that the usual suspects are greeted at the border with an appropriate level of circumspection. SVP practice and policy domains are already crowded with self-styled heroes on both sides of the divide, between defenders of these statutes and the professional practices that support them, and those that would dismantle such laws. To the extent that any insights or observations offered here appear to take on the fervor of one wanting to save the day, the fervor is fueled by the conviction that if philosophical notions and pseudoscience are allowed to pose as communally established science and to pass the usual gatekeepers of our forums for truth-seeking with minimal to no questioning, all sides contending with the SVP dilemma will be done a major disservice. Disturbingly, one hears at practice conferences psychologists from both sides claiming that "the fix is in" on certain journal editorial boards for or against SVP commitment, insinuating that, to an appreciable extent, the decision to publish or decline to publish is related to the submission's position, either stated or by implied by the approach taken.

Of course, the two viable methods (and sets of assumptions) of Bayesian and frequentist statistics can lead to convergence in observations and conclusions, or they can lead to remarkable differences. There are situations that recommend one approach over the other. To evaluate the preferred approach in an application, beyond technical questions, reasonable social and moral questions are: What are the costs of an error? Who will pay the cost? How will the error and costs be justified to the world? In risk assessment of civil commitment respondents, there are costs to be bear whatever the outcome. When the assessed risk due to psychopathology is sufficiently high, the law requires the offender to bear the cost of restricted freedom and often coerced treatment. Society bears other costs for this decision, such as the cost of apparent compromise to ideals of individual liberty and a just-deserts model of justice administered to an agent responsible for his or her volitional behavior rather than restricting liberty for long-term risks due to pathological mental states or actuarially assessed propensities. When the assessed risk due to psychopathology is not sufficiently high, society bares the risk of releasing a high-risk offender and may experience the cost of new victims and new insults to public faith in criminal justice, mental health expertise, and the entirety of the social compact.

Our scientific and professional institutions have a special responsibility in performing boundary work (Gieryn, 1983) demarking science from other enterprises and differentiating domains of knowledge. This boundary work not only enables the orderly advancement of knowledge, but it makes it reasonable for consumers of science, including forensic experts and the courts, to rely on publication as an important criterion for acceptance of information as scientifically credible. Regarding knowledge and expertise claims ultimately presented in legal proceedings, this credentialing function of peer reviewed journals is all the more powerful because of

Daubert v. Merrill Dow Pharmaceuticals, Inc. (1993) and other decisions that endowed the court with the power to determine the validity of proffered expert evidence. Evaluating the veracity of scientific and expert claims, either generally or within in a certain field, is not usually within the specific training of judges, and judges may not be able to accurately make these determinations (Kovera & McAuliff, 2000). *Daubert* explicitly suggested that the courts consider whether or not the scientific claims considered for admission into evidence were vetted through publication in peer-reviewed journals. However, once scientific evidence has been admitted, opposing expert witness testimony contradicting or correcting the views previously presented may be not only ineffective in correcting the knowledge base of jurors, but may undermine the perception of the credibility of expert witnesses in general (Levett & Kovera, 2008).

Our journals have the responsibility to provide science consumers with the best odds of making these cost-benefit decisions by providing clear, reliable information. Given the lack of rigor, balance, fairness, and discipline that are found in recent SVP Bayesian publications in respectable journals, it appears fair to conclude that some of our gatekeepers have been asleep while on duty, or have just given in by dent of the persistence of the SVP Bayesian true-believers, or have become converts themselves. A more generous explanation is that the journals that have published the most problematic SVP Bayesian articles are either policy or clinical research journals. Perhaps authors submitting mathematical proofs or new assessment models, albeit carrying policy and clinical implications, should be referred to journals specializing in technical methodological and assessment issues, such as *Psychological Methods* and *Psychological Assessment*.

Because the ability of science consumers to rely on publication as a criterion for acceptance has been undermined by the publication of seriously flawed writings of SVP Bayesians without contextual commentary, and that these publications have not as yet been followed by sufficient systematic published rebuttal and contradiction, several stop-gap recommendations are offered. It is recommended that triers of fact who must consider the admissibility or credibility of Bayesian expertise or arguments might be encouraged to consider the concerns identified in *Regina v. Adams*, which could be restated as: Does the argument or method rest on subjective assumptions that are obscured by complexity and scientific trappings? Is the trier of fact being asked to understand and use a complicated formula to evaluate evidence in place of the usual process of practical reasoning? Is it being advocated that each piece of evidence be weighed separately from other evidence, preventing consideration of the chain of evidence as a whole? Is a method or formal logic being advanced toward the purpose of displacing common sense and practical reasoning, and interrupting rather than aiding the ability of jurors to understand and discuss the evidence and its relevance to the issues at hand?

In addition to these considerations, the categories of Table 3.2 can be used to analyze expert claims related to Bayes's Theorem and probability for the types of knowledge assertions being made. Two kinds of claims can be detected by non-clinicians, including attorneys who have become familiar with established practice in SVP evaluations and clinicians who are intermittent readers of scientific and professional journals in this area. Such informed nonexperts can recognize Strong Bayesianism, which can be fairly typified as subjective and philosophical in nature. If the expert is asked to clearly identify the assumptions of applications, and the source of the assumption are made as explicit as possible, a non-expert may be able to evaluate whether the assumptions are minimal to the analysis and if the quality of evidence for considering the assumptions as widely accepted. Idiosyncratic methods are probably not easily identified by individuals without relevant clinical and research training and experience in evaluation practice. The main advantage to typologies like Table 3.2 is to draw attention that assertions that are different in kind are often made regarding Bayes's Theorem and its applications and ideological extensions. Assertions and methods can be different in relevance and objective veracity (and most probably in admissibility as recognized, relevant and reliable). The presented typology can also be used to consider the perspective of knowledge destruction (Bonta & Andrews, 2006), that is, to consider the possibility that the function of the Bayes's Theorem–related assertion is to deter truth finding. A final practical recommendation rests on common sense and common law practice: In a preliminary assessment of a Bayes's Theorem–related assertion, the reputation and possible motivations of the individual or research team making the assertion is usually of considerable, but not definitive value for beginning a search for blind spots, overemphasis, or intentional distortion of issues or facts.

Notes

1. It is possible that an expert could forgo psychodynamic explanations if the mental abnormality predominates risk prediction—that is, if either if a specific diagnosis was found to be so correlated with risk exceeding the statutory threshold that the diagnosis alone provided a sufficient causal nexus. The strongest candidates for this are co-occurring combinations such as narcissistic personality disorder and pedophilia, exclusive type.

2. There is a third school of statistics, fiducial statistics, developed by Fisher. Fiducial statistics has been typified as Bayesian statistics with frequentist prior.

3. This is another way of saying they were realists but others would say they are Platonist, whereas Bayesianism has much in common with the Sophists, such as Gorgias, who argued for subjectivism.

4. The belief that probability is sufficient for action, since certainty in knowledge is unattainable.

5. The doctrine that knowledge is restricted to the conscious self and its sensory states.

6. Harris and Rice (2007) showed that although Wilson approximation applied inappropriately to an individual score by Hart, Michie, and Cooke (2007) resulted in unacceptably wide confidence intervals, applying an exact method in the same fashion would result in a confidence interval of zero for the highest VRAG category.

7. Although see Harris and Rice (2007) for an empirical critique showing that Mossman's base rate adjustments overcorrect.

8. Harris and Rice (2007) have pointed out that this presumption is no longer relevant when the subjects of an evaluation are persons previously convicted of sexual violence.

9. Harris and Rice (2007) stated the point most succinctly: "Actuarial methods embody Bayesian logic in that risk estimates are based on data about the base rate and are revised based on the relationship of individual characteristics and the base rates. Actuarial instruments also provide revised estimates based on the unique and incremental contribution of each predictive characteristic (Hanson, 2003), consistent with Bayesian inference" (p. 1652).

References

Andrews, D. A., & Bonta, J. (2006). *The psychology of criminal conduct* (4th ed.). Cincinnati, OH: Anderson Publishing.

Beech, A. R., Fisher, D. D., & Thornton, D. (2003). Risk assessment of sex offenders. *Professional Psychology: Research and Practice, 34*, 339–352.

Cox, C. & Mouw, J. T. (1992). Disruption of the representativeness heuristic: Can we be perturbed into using correct probabilistic reasoning? *Education Studies in Mathematics*, 23, 163–178.

Daubert v. Merrill Dow Pharmaceuticals, Inc. (1993). 113 S. Ct. 2786.

Dawid, A. P. (1987). The difficulty about conjunction. *The Statistician, 36*, 91–97.

Dawid, A. P. (2002). Bayes's theorem and weighing evidence by juries. In R. Swinburne (Ed.), *Bayes's theorem* (pp. 71–90). Oxford, UK: Oxford University Press.

Dawid, A. P. (2005). Statistics on trial. *Significance, 2*, 6–8.

Donaldson, T., & Wollert, R. (2008). A mathematical proof and example that Bayes's Theorem is fundamental to actuarial estimates of sexual recidivism risk. *Sex Abuse: A Journal of Research and Treatment, 20*, 206–217.

Doren, D. M. (2002). *Evaluating sex offenders*. Thousand Oaks, CA: Sage.

Doren, D. M., & Epperson, D. (2001). Great analysis, but problematic assumptions: A critique of Janus & Meehl (1997). *Sexual Abuse, 13*, 45–51.

Fergusson, D. M., Fifield, J., & Slater, S. (1977). Signal detectability theory and the evaluation of prediction tables. *Journal of Research in Crime and Delinquency*, 14, 237–246.

Gigerenzer, G. (1991). How to make cognitive illusions disappear: Beyond "heuristics and biases." *European Review of Social Psychology, 2*, 83–115.

Gigerenzer, G., & Selten, R. (2001). *Bounded rationality: The adaptive toolbox*. Cambridge, MA: MIT Press.

Gieryn, T. F. (1983). Boundary-work and the demarcation of science from non-science: Professional ideologies of scientists. *American Sociological Review, 48*, 781–795.

Griffin, D., & Brenner, L. (2004). Perspectives on probability judgment calibration. In D. J. Koehler & N. Harvey (Eds.), *Blackwell handbook of judgment and decision making* (pp. 177–199). Malden, MA: Blackwell Publishing.

Hájek, A. (forthcoming). Pascal's Wager. In E. N. Zalta (Ed.), *The Stanford encyclopedia of philosophy* (Fall 2008 Edition). Retrieved September 11, 2008, from http://plato.stanford.edu/archives/fall2008/entries/pascal-wager/.

Hájek, A., & Hall, N. (2002). Induction and Probability. In P. Machamer & M. Silberstein (Eds.), *The Blackwell guide to the philosophy of science* (pp. 149–172). Malden, MA: Blackwell Publishers.

Hanson, R. K. (2008). Declaration of Dr. R. K. Hanson, submitted February 2, 2008, In re the Detention of William Davenport, Franklin County Superior Court.

Harris, A. J. R., & Hanson, R. K. (2004). *Sex offender recidivism: A simple question* (Corrections User Report No. 2004-03) Ottawa: Public Safety and Emergency Preparedness Canada.

Harris, G. T., & Rice, M. E. (2007). Characterizing the value of actuarial violence risk assessments. *Criminal Justice and Behavior, 12*, 1638–1658.

Hart, S. D., Michie, C., & Cooke, D. J. (2007). Precision of actuarial risk assessment instruments: Evaluating the "margin of error" of group v. individual prediction of violence. *British Journal of Psychiatry*, *190*, 260–265.

Howson, C., & Urbach, P. (1993). *Scientific reasoning: The Bayesian approach* (2nd ed.). Chicago, IL: Open Court.

Jackson, R. L., & Hess, D. T. (2007). Evaluation for civil commitment of sex offenders: A survey of experts. *Sex Abuse: A Journal of Research and Treatment, 19*, 425–448.

Jackson, R. L., & Richards H. J. (2008). Evaluations for the civil commitment of sexual offenders. In R. L. Jackson (Ed.), *Learning forensic assessment* (pp. 183–209). New York: Routledge/Taylor & Francis Group.

Jackson, R. L., Rogers, R., & Shuman, D. (2004). The adequacy and accuracy of sexually violent predator evaluations: Contextualized risk assessment in clinical practice. *International Journal of Forensic Mental Health, 3*, 21–35.

Janus, E. S., & Meehl, P. E. (1997). Assessing the legal standard for sex offenders: A comparison of three actuarial scales. *Psychology, Public Policy, and Law, 3*, 33–64.

Kahneman, D. (2011). *Thinking, fast and slow*. New York: Farrar, Straus and Giroux.

Keynes, J. M. (1923). *A tract on monetary reform*. London: Macmillian.

Kovera, M. B., & McAuliff, B. D. (2000). The effects of peer review and evidence quality on judge evaluations of psychological science: Are judges effective gatekeepers? *Journal of Applied Psychology, 85*, 574–586.

Kuhn, T. S. (1962). *The structure of scientific revolutions*. Chicago: University of Chicago Press.

Kusch, M. (2001). "A general theory of societal knowledge"? Aspirations and shortcomings of Alvin Goldman's social epistemology. *Studies in the History of Philosophy of Science, 32*, 183–192.

Lakatos, I. (1978). *Mathematics, science, and epistemology*. Cambridge, UK: Cambridge University Press

Levett, L. M., & Kovera, M. B. (2008). The effectiveness of opposing expert witnesses for educating jurors about unreliable expert evidence. *Law and Human Behavior, 32*, 363–374.

Lynch, M., & McNally, R. (2003). "Science," "common sense," and DNA evidence: A legal controversy about public understanding of science. *Public Understanding of Science, 12*, 83–103.

Martinson, R. (1974). What works? Questions and answers about prison reform. *The Public Interest, 35*, 22–54.

Meehl, P. (1955). Antecedent probability and the efficiency of psychometric signs, patterns, or cutting scores. *Psychological Bulletin, 52*, 194–216.

Meehl, P. E. (1977). Specific etiology and other forms of strong influence: Some quantitative meanings. *Journal of Medicine and Philosophy, 1*, 33–53.

Meehl, P. E. (1978). Theoretical risks and tabular asterisks: Sir Karl, Sir Ronald, and the slow progress of soft psychology. *Journal of Consulting and Clinical Psychology, 46*, 806–834.

Meehl, P. E., & Rosen, A. (1955). Antecedent probability and the efficiency of psychometric signs, patterns, and cutting scores. *Psychological Bulletin, 52*, 194–216.

Mossman, D. (2006). Another look at interpreting risk categories. *Sexual Abuse, 18*, 41–63.

Mossman, D. (2008). Analyzing the performance of risk assessment instruments: A response to Vrieze and Grove (2007). *Law and Human Behavior, 32*, 279–291.

Mossman, D., & Sellke, T. (2007, July). Avoiding errors about "margins of error." *British Journal of Psychiatry*; Electronic letter in response to Hart, Michie, & Cooke, 2007.

Prentky, R. A., Janus, E., Barbaree, H., Schwartz, B. K., & Kafka, M. P. (2006). Sexually violent predators in the courtroom: Science on trial. *Psychology, Public Policy and Law, 12*, 357–393.

Packard, R. L., & Levenson, J. (2006). Revisiting the reliability of diagnostic decisions in sex offender civil commitment. *Sexual Offender Treatment, 1*. Retrieved December 19, 2006, from http://www.sexual-offender-treatment.org/50.0.html.

Popper, K. R. (1959). The propensity interpretation of probability. *British Journal for the Philosophy of Science, 10*, 25–42.

Reichenbach, H. (1938). *Experience and prediction*. Chicago: University of Chicago Press.

Sober, E. (2002). Bayesianism—its scope and limits. *Proceedings of the British Academy, 113*, 21–38.

Swets, J. A. (1988). Measuring the accuracy of diagnostic systems. *Science, 240*, 1285–1293.

Swets, J. A., Dawes, R. M., & Monahan, J. (2000). Psychological science can improve diagnostic decisions. *Psychological Science in the Public Interest, 1*, 1–12.

Tversky, A., & Kahneman, D. (1974). Judgment under uncertainty: Heuristics and biases. *Science, 185*(4157), 1124–1131.

Waller, N. G., Yonce, L. J., Grove, W. M., Faust, D., & Lenzenweger, M. F. (2006). *A Paul Meehl reader: Essays on the practice of scientific psychology*. Mahwah, NJ: Lawrence Erlbaum Associates.

Wenger, E. (1998). *Communities of practice: Learning, meaning, and identity*. London: Cambridge University Press.

Wenger, E. (2004). Knowledge management is a donut: shaping your knowledge strategy with communities of practice. *Ivey Business Journal*, January 2004.

Williams, D. (2001). *Weighing the odds: A course in probability and statistics*. Cambridge, UK: Cambridge University Press.

Wollert, R. (2006). Low base rates limit expert certainty when current actuarial tests are used to identify violent predators: An application of Bayes's Theorem. *Psychology, Public Policy, and Law, 12*, 56–85.

Wollert, R. (2007a). Poor diagnostic reliability, the Null-Bayes Logic Model, and their implications for sexually violent predator evaluations. *Psychology, Public Policy, and Law, 13*, 167–203.

Wollert, R. (2007b, August). Validation of a Bayesian method for assessing sexual recidivism risk. Presented at the 115th Annual Convention of the American Psychological Association, San Francisco, CA.

Wollert, R. (2007c, October). A re-specification of Hanson's updated Static-99 experience table that controls for the effects of age on sexual recidivism in a sample of young offenders. Presented at the Convention for the Association for the Treatment of Sex Abusers in San Diego, CA.

CHAPTER FOUR

Sexually Violent Predators and State Appellate Courts' Use of Actuarial Tests in Civil Commitments

Frances P. Bernat, Jacqueline B. Helfgott, and Nicholas Godlove

In the late twentieth century, popular culture and public sentiment converged to create a moral panic over sexual predators. Films on violent offending brought to the public conscious the term "predator." Public distress increased as predatory crime stories heightened attention to heinous offenses committed by persons like Earl Shriner and Wesley Dodd in Washington State and Richard Allen Davis in California. Public pressure was placed on the states to do something about violent recidivism. State legislatures responded to the public outcry by enacting laws to civilly confine offenders who could be deemed violent predators. The transfer of the use of the term "predator" from pop culture to law coincided with the exponential accumulation of research in the area of psychopathy, sexual deviancy, and violent crime. Research in psychology and criminology, particularly in the areas of life-course criminology (Moffitt, 1993) and psychopathy (Hare, 1993), supports the notion that a small subgroup of offenders commit the majority of offenses (Lussier &

Healey, 2010). Psychopathy is believed to be one of the more robust indicators of chronic offending and violent recidivism (Douglas, Vincent, & Edens, 2006).

Civil Commitment of Sexually Violent Predators

State Laws and Sexually Violent Predators

States with sexually violent predator (SVP) laws are concerned with protecting the public from individuals whose mental abnormality affects their ability to control their sexual impulses and volitional behaviors. In general, these laws are a revival of the old "sexual psychopathy" laws of the early 1900s because they reflect a conceptual connection between psychopathy and sexual deviancy. Some states (e.g., Minnesota) still use the terms "sexual psychopathic personalities" and "sexually dangerous persons" in their modernized versions of the early-twentieth-century sexual psychopath statutes. SVP laws can extend an offender's commitment past his or her criminal sentence through civil commitments. In 1990, Washington was the first state to respond to public pressure by reviving its old sexual psychopath laws and enacting a SVP civil commitment statute (R.C.W. §71.09 et seq.). The Washington SVP law involves an end of criminal sentence review. The state prosecuting attorney or attorney general petitions a court for a probable cause hearing to determine whether or not the offender meets the legal definition of sexually violent predator; which, according to the state, is "any person who has been convicted of or charged with a crime of sexual violence and who suffers from a mental abnormality or personality disorder which makes the person likely to engage in predatory acts of sexual violence if not confined in a secure facility" (R.C.W. §71.09.020). If probable cause exists, then a court will hold a full hearing to determine if civil commitment should be ordered. The length of civil commitment is indefinite, but an offender may be released from confinement to the community or to less restrictive community custody. Such release is based upon a further finding that the offender participated in treatment and that the offender made treatment gains evidencing a reduced likelihood of risk to the public's safety.

In 1994, Kansas became the second state to enact a SVP civil commitment statute. Kansas, like the state of Washington, relied on theory and research on sexual violence and treatment amenability of predatory offenders to create its SVP statute. Kansas's statute defines a SVP as "any person who has been convicted or charged with a sexually violent offense and who suffers from a mental abnormality or personality disorder which makes the person likely to engage in the predatory acts of sexual violence" (Kan. Stat. Ann. § 59-29a01). By 2011, 21 states had civil commitment statutes for sexually violent offenders.[1] The state laws vary in terms of the processes used to determine if a person is a SVP, the burden of proof needed to find that a person is a SVP, the processes used to release a person from civil confinement, and where a person may be held as a SVP. In almost all states with a SVP law, the individual is held in a secure inpatient mental health facility.[2] These civil commitments are based on the state's assertion that in order to protect the public from violent sex offenders who cannot control their behavior, involuntary civil commitment must take place.[3]

Psychopathy and the Prediction of Dangerousness

The state's need to predict with some degree of certainty if a person is a violent predator means that it needs robust indicators of future dangerousness. One primary tool, though not originally developed for the purpose of risk assessment, has been the Psychopathy Checklist–Revised (PCL-R). The PCL-R is a valid and reliable measure of psychopathy, a strong predictor of general and violent recidivism, and a determinant of high criminogenic offender risk (Gacono, 2000; Hare, 1996, 2003; Hare & Neumann, 2006; Harris, Rice, & Cormier, 1991; Hart, 1998; Hemphill, Templeman, Wong, & Hare, 1998; Hodgins, 1997; Laurell & Dåderman, 2005; Litwack & Schlesinger, 1998; Salekin, Rogers, & Sewell, 1996; Serin & Amos, 1995; Simourd & Hodge, 2000). The prediction of who is a sexually violent recidivist can be a difficult one to make (Rogers & Jackson, 2005; Wollert & Waggoner, 2009). Milloy (2003) studied recidivism among 89 Washington State sex offenders who were released from prison but not civilly confined. Of the offenders in his study who were recommended for civil commitment but for whom a civil commitment process was not initiated, over half (57%) were convicted of new felony offenses; of these recidivists, 40% committed a violent crime and 29% committed a felony sex offense.

Robert Hare's research on the PCL-R produced the first big successes in violence risk prediction (1991, 1998, 2003). The PCL-R is 20-item checklist measuring two factors: personality traits, and behavioral symptoms. A score of 30–40 is generally associated with primary psychopathy, a score of 20–29 with secondary psychopathy, and 0–19 with the absence of psychopathy. Factor 1 is positively correlated with clinical ratings of psychopathy, prototypical ratings of narcissistic and histrionic personality disorder, and self-report measures of Machiavellianism and narcissism, and is negatively correlated with measures of empathy and anxiety

(Hare, 1991; Harpur, Hare, & Hakstian, 1989; Hart & Hare, 1997). Factor 2 is positively correlated with criminal behaviors, socioeconomic background, self-report measures of socialization and antisocial behavior, and diagnosis of APD (Hare, 1991; Harpur et al., 1989; Schopp & Slain, 2000).

There has been extensive discourse and debate regarding whether psychopathy is a categorical or a dimensional construct (Edens & Petrila, 2006). Some researchers suggest that PCL-R scores above 30 reflect a categorical condition characterized by cognitive deficit, while scores below 30 reflect a dimensional construct (Wallace, Schmitt, Vitale, & Newman, 2000). Others suggest that psychopathy be viewed along a hypothetical continuum for the purpose of treatment (Meloy, 1988). The notion of psychopathy as a taxon and the idea that a particular score on the PCL-R or other actuarial measures is indicative of a distinctive personality type or chronically violent offender subtype has important implications for the use of actuarial tools like the PCL-R in both the civil and criminal courts. To determine if an offender is a violent predator, courts are frequently admitting an offender's PCL-R score as evidence of mental illness and an inability to control one's sexual impulses. While not all sexually violent predators meet the criteria for primary or prototypical psychopathy (i.e., PCL-R score above 30), many have a high number of psychopathic personality traits. Recent research suggests that PCL-R items cluster in four (rather than two) factors: Interpersonal, affective, lifestyle, and antisocial (Hare & Neumann, 2006) with subsets of PCL-R items associated with each. The decomposition of psychopathy into factors—affective/interpersonal and impulsive/antisocial—has led to an "explosion of meaningful external correlates" with growing evidence that the risk for reactive violence is related to low levels of restraint associated with impulsivity factor (Kamphuis & Emmelkamp, 2005, p. 171).

Other actuarial tools such as the Violence Risk Appraisal Guide (VRAG), the Level of Service Inventory–Revised (LSI-R) and Sex Offender Risk Appraisal Guide (SORAG) have also been used to predict dangerous offending. These tools have imbedded within them some components of the PCL-R, and the success of these measures in predicting dangerousness may be due to their PCL-R psychopathy measures (Gendreau, Goggin, & Smith, 2002). The PCL-R, VRAG, LSI-R, and other forensic assessment instruments are used by the courts and departments of corrections in Canada and the United States to make critical pretrial detainment, correctional management, and release decisions (Girard & Wormith, 2004). Some actuarial instruments developed in the last 15 years are used with other specialized populations such as wife assaulters, young offenders, and sex offenders.

These specialize tools include the Rapid Risk Assessment for Sexual Offender Recidivism (RRASOR), the Structured Anchored Clinical Judgment–Minimum (SACJ-Min), the Minnesota Sex Offender Screening Tool (MnSOST-R), the Sexual Violence Risk–20 (SVR-20), and the Static 99. These risk assessments are based on statistical measures rooted in the criminal history, offending behavior patterns, and mental illness diagnosis of offenders (Hanson, 2005) (see Table 4.1).

Each of these instruments represent a new wave of theoretically derived and empirically validated risk assessment tools, but they have grave implications for criminal justice practice. Violent risk assessment research shows that no single variable or constellation of variables can prove the root cause of violence. It is the combination of psychopathy, sexual deviancy, and predatory behavior that puts SVP offenders at an extremely high risk for sexual reoffense. Additionally, tools used to measure a person's propensity toward violence can produce an unacceptable level of false positives (Monahan et al., 2001). Viljoen, McLachlan, and Vincent (2010) indicate that actuarial tools were deemed valid and reliable from studies that used graduate students as raters. They argue that there is, at present, limited research on the real-world settings that would verify that the tools have interrater reliability and validity among clinicians. In addition, while some researchers have argued that clinical judgments should be completely replaced with actuarial methods of criminal dangerousness (Quinsey, Harris, Rice, & Cormier, 1998), clinicians may be reluctant to rely solely on the actuarial measures since they provide "probalistic" measures of future dangerousness and cannot pinpoint specific individual risk alone (Petrila, 2008). Consequently, the justice system is faced with the challenge of making critical public safety decisions that depend on a science that might be imperfect in order to comport with state laws which authorize SVP civil commitments.

The Clash of Legal and Medical Models

In *Kansas v. Hendricks* (521 U.S. 346, 1997), the U.S. Supreme Court recognized the inherent disagreement between the law and psychology. The two fields utilize different definitions on what constitutes mental illness and what to do about it. The Court found that the legal community seeks retribution and incapacitation for mentally ill offenders, but the psychiatric community seeks treatment and rehabilitation. In *Hendricks*, the Court was asked to determine the constitutionality of a state law civilly confining habitually mentally ill sex offenders. The *Hendricks* inmate was diagnosed with paraphilia and personality disorder. The Court stated that

Table 4.1 Actuarial Tests Used to Diagnose Sexually Violent Predators

Psychopathy Checklist–Revised (PCL-R) Hare (1991, 2003)	A 20-item checklist designed to measure the clinical construct of psychopathy. Consists of Factor 1 items reflecting interpersonal/ affective features and Factor 2 items reflecting antisocial/lifestyle features. Each of the 20 items is scored on a 0- to 2-point scale. The score is the sum of the 20 items with total score range from 0 to 40 points. Items scored based on interview with offender and institutional file information.
Violence Risk Appraisal Guide (VRAG) (Quinsey, Harris, Rice, & Cormier, 1998)	A 12-item scale for male offenders who have committed serious, violent (including sexual) offenses. Items include: lived with both biological parents, elementary school maladjustment, history of alcohol problems, marital status, criminal history score for nonviolent offenses using, failure on prior conditional release, age at time of offense, victim injury, female victim, meets DSM-III criteria for personality disorder, meets DSM-III criteria for schizophrenia, PCL-R score). Scored based on review of a comprehensive psychosocial history including information gathered from third parties and review of records. Gives statistical probability from zero to 100% that an offender will violently or sexually violently recidivate.
Sex Offender Risk Appraisal Guide (SORAG) (Quinsey, Harris, Rice, & Cormier, 1998)	A 14-item scale for male offenders who have committed sexual offenses. Items include items on the VRAG + phallometric test results, number of previous convictions for sexual offenses, history of sex offenses only against girls under 14. Scored based on review of a comprehensive psychosocial history including information gathered from third parties and review of records. Gives statistical probability from zero to 100 percent that an offender will violently or sexually violently recidivate.
Level of Service Inventory–Revised (Andrews & Bonta, 1995, 2001, 2003)	A 54-item instrument that includes a range of risk factors associated with criminal conduct. The 54-items on the LSI-R are answered with

Table 4.1 (Continued)

	a Yes/No or 0–3 rating and measure offender risk, needs, and responsivity factors. The content of the LSI-R reflects the recidivism literature, professional opinions of community corrections officers, and the social learning theory of criminal behavior.
Historical, Clinical, Risk–20 (HCR-20) (Webster, Douglas, Eaves, & Hart, 1995, 1997)	A 20-item instrument that includes 10 historical items (e.g., severity and frequency of previous violence, young age at first violent incident, history of serious, acute mental illness, psychopathy assessed by the PCL-R, prior supervision failure), 5 clinical items (e.g., lack of insight, negative attitudes, active symptoms of major mental illness), and risk management items (lack of personal support, stress, exposure to destabilizers).
Sexual Violence Risk–20 (SVR-20) (Boer, Hart, Kropp, & Webster, 1997)	A 20-item scale developed specifically for assessing risk of sexual violence. Variant of the HCR-20. Items include psychosocial adjustment items (e.g., sexual deviation, victim of child abuse, psychopathy, major mental illness), sexual offense items (e.g., multiple sex offense types, physical harm to victim in sex offenses, escalation in frequency or severity of sex offenses, and future plans items (lacks realistic plans, negative attitude toward intervention).
Rapid Risk Assessment for Sexual Offender Recidivism (RRASOR) (Hanson, 1997)	A 4-item instrument designed to measure sex offender recidivism. Items include prior sex offenses, age at release from period of incarceration, victim gender, and relationship to victim. The score is the sum of the four items with total score range from 0 to 6 points.
Structured Anchored Clinical Judgment-Minimum (SACJ-Min) (Thornton; see Prentky & Burgess, 2000)	A 9-item clinical rating scale including: male victim, never married, noncontact sex offenses, stranger victims, any current sex offense, any current nonsexual violent offense, any prior nonsexual violent offense, and four or more prior sentencing occasions.

(continued)

Table 4.1 (Continued)

Minnesota Sex Offender Screening Tool (MnSOST-R) (Epperson, et al., 2003)	A 16-item scale developed for the Minnesota Department of Corrections. Items include: Number of sex-related convictions, length of sex offending history, number of different age groups victimized, age at release from institution, drug alcohol abuse, sex offender treatment while incarcerated, chemical dependency treatment while incarcerated.
Static-99 (Hanson & Thornton, 1999)	A 10-item scale combining items from the RRASOR and SACJ-Min. Items 1–5 are coded using archival data. Items 6–10 are coded using all available information including self-report, collateral reports, and victim statements.
Sex Predator Risk Assessment Screening Instrument (English, 1999, 2006)	Comprised of four parts: Defining sexual assault crimes, relationship to victim, sex offender risk scale, mental abnormality (as measured by a 30+ score on the PCL-R or 18+ on the Psychopathy Checklist: Screening version or 85+ on MCMI-3 narcissistic, antisocial, and paranoid scales.
Self-Appraisal Questionnaire (Loza & Green, 2003)	A 72-item self-report risk-need measure designed to cover predictive content areas demonstrated to be reliable and valid for the assessment and prediction of post-release offending. Items are true/false items and make up eight subscales: Criminal Tendencies, Antisocial Personality Problems, Conduct Problems, Criminal History, Alcohol and/or Drug Abuse, Antisocial Associates, Anger, and Validity subscales. The items in the Anger scale are not included in the total score of the due to the controversial relationship between anger The number of items used in the prediction of recidivism is 67 out of the total number of the 72 SAQ items. The Validity subscale can be used to validate offenders' truthfulness in responding to the SAQ's items.
Abel Assessment for Sexual Interest (Abel et al., 1994; Helfgott, 2008, pp. 463–465)	Computerized test used to identify sexual interest by presenting slides of nude people in different age ranges.

civil commitments of sex offenders will be lawful if a mentally ill offender cannot control his sexual impulses. Since *Hendricks*, states can use general mental illness diagnoses—e.g., personality disorder, mental abnormality—to serve as the classification catalyst that triggers sexual predator civil commitments.[4] In short, *Hendricks* necessitates that states seeking civil commitment of sexual repeat offenders must show, first, that a sex offender suffers from a mental illness, and second, that he or she cannot control sexual impulses (Elco, 1998).

Despite *Hendricks*, the long-term and perhaps indefinite civil commitment of offenders has generated much litigation by individuals who argue that they do not fit the legal definition of a sexual predator. A major source of the litigation is the difference in opinion between the legal and medical communities on what constitutes "mental illness" as the precursor to the civil commitment of sexual predators (Cunningham & Reidy, 2002; DeMatteo & Edens, 2006; Gendreau et al., 2002; Sparks, 2008). As Wilson (1998) notes:

> [S]tate legislatures have historically been left the task of determining which particular terms will be adopted by their civil commitment statutes, and also how such mental health terms will be defined in a legal context. The states have chosen a variety of terms and very often, those terms do not comport with psychiatric definitions. Because the terms used to define the requisite mental disorder within the sex predator statutes serve a legal and not a medical function, there is no reason for courts to place an undue emphasis upon how the psychiatric community would define such illness. (p. 368)

Due to the accepted use of actuarial tools in the field of psychology, courts have generally accepted the admission of the PCL-R and other actuarial tests to diagnose an offender's mental illness (DeMatteo & Edens, 2006). Jackson and Richards (2007a) found in their sample of Washington State SVP commitments that the most common Axis I diagnosis was "paraphilia" (specifically pedophilia) and that "psychotic disorder" was rarely diagnosed. They also found that the most common Axis II diagnosis was Antisocial Personality Disorder. Additionally, 28 percent of sexually violent predators for whom a PCL-R score was available received a score of 30 or above (generally considered to be indicative of primary or severe psychopathy).

Problematically, clinicians can vary in the PCL-R scores that they generate. According to Murrie, Boccaccini, Johnson, and Janke (2007), an expert's PCL-R score can be influenced by an allegiance to the party bringing them to testify, showing allegiance to either the prosecution or defense team. Their findings suggest that PCL-R scores can be more subjective than has been previously believed of actuarial tests. To date, research has shown that when the construct of psychopathy and PCL-R scores are introduced in court, this information is most likely to have a negative impact on the offender. A high PCL-R score is more likely to be considered an aggravating factor in sentencing decisions and as indicative of dangerousness in civil commitment decisions (Lyon & Ogloff, 2000; Edens, 2001; Edens & Petrila, 2006; Zinger, 1995).

SVP laws continue to generate both substantive and procedural due process challenges (Miller, 2010). To make a determination about future dangerousness, courts routinely rely on both clinical and actuarial tool assessments. Some legal scholars assert that the use of psychiatric actuarial tools, while better than clinical assessments, are still tenuous when determining a particular offender's future dangerousness (Beecher-Monas & Garcia-Rill, 2006; DeMatteo & Edens, 2006; Edens, Buffington-Vollum, Kelen, Roskamp, & Anthony, 2005; LaFond, 2000). The state's duty to protect citizens is weighed against the state's legal responsibility to use scientific tools that meet legal standards of admissibility. The question remains, are actuarial tests or clinical assessments the best tools to guide SVP civil commitments?

State Appellate Courts and Expert Testimony Predicting Sexual Recidivism

Method

A case law search was conducted using both Lexis/Nexis and WestLaw databases to identify state appellate court cases. The case search was limited to decisions rendered after 1990 when recent SVP laws were enacted. We used the queries that would be likely to generate case law on the issue of the necessity to civil commit sex offenders such as "sexual predator and civil commitment," "sexually violent predator and PCL-R," as well as other actuarial tests (e.g., Static 99). Only cases in which the ultimate issue was whether or not the offender would be classified as a sexually violent predator were included in the study. Because it takes several years for litigation to reach the appellate courts and most states did not enact their SVP laws until the late 1990s or early 2000s, it is not a surprise that the majority of cases used in this study were decided after 2000. The search produced a total of 107 state appellate court cases decided between January 1994 and June 2011 in 20 states.[5] The majority of the state appellate court opinions came from three states: California, Ohio, and Minnesota. Other state appellate court decisions included in this study were from Arizona, Florida, Illinois, Iowa, Kansas, Missouri, Minnesota, New Hampshire, New Jersey, North Dakota, Pennsylvania, Rhode Island, South Carolina, Texas, Virginia, Washington, and Wisconsin.

Each appellate case was read and coded by one of the authors in accordance with measures and factors associated with SVP adjudications. The cases were then reread and recoded by that same author several times by one of the authors in order to ensure reliability and validity of the measures recorded for each decision. The variables included in this study include: offender characteristics and criminal history, offense characteristics, victim-offender relationship, mental illness diagnosis, clinical and actuarial SVP assessments, treatment history, legal standards regarding the burden of proof, and the appellate court's holding.

Results

Case Variables and Legal Outcomes Burden of Proof

A critical point of analysis for any court is the quantum of proof a state must meet in order to establish that a person is a sexual predator. To initiate the SVP civil commitment process in states that initiate commitments after the conclusion of an offender's prison sentence or for parole revocation or continued mental health confinement, state laws provide that a preliminary probable cause hearing be held. If there is probable cause to believe that a person is a SVP or if the state initiates SVP hearings at the conclusion of a criminal trial, then the state will hold a full commitment hearing. In the full civil commitment process, many states require that the state prove that the person is either a SVP beyond a reasonable doubt (Arizona, California, Illinois, Iowa, Kansas, Massachusetts, South Carolina, Texas, Washington, and Wisconsin) or by clear and convincing evidence (Florida, Minnesota, Missouri, Nebraska, New Hampshire, New Jersey, North Dakota, Pennsylvania, and Virginia).

In the cases included in this study, 62% (n = 63) of the cases utilized the clear and convincing standard. In 18% (n = 19) of the cases, the quantum of proof was beyond a reasonable doubt, in 9% (n = 10) of the cases the appeal came from the preliminary probable cause determination, and in 2% (n = 2) of the cases, the quantum of proof was by a preponderance of evidence. In 3% (n = 3) of the cases, the offender stipulated to being a sexual predator at his criminal trial for the sex offenses, which then initiated the civil commitment process. In these three cases, the state court refused to reopen the inquiry as to whether the offender was a sexual predator and proceeded with an analysis as to the future dangerous potential of the offender. It is not clear why in our study there were more cases from jurisdictions utilizing a clear and convincing standard; we speculate that since the standard is not as high as beyond a reasonable doubt that offenders felt that the diagnosis as a SVP was not as strong as in those states where the burden of proof was beyond a reasonable doubt. In California, however, a state with a beyond-a-reasonable-doubt quantum of proof, we analyzed a large number of appellate cases. This litigation might be attributable to two factors: there are a large number of SVP civil commitments in California (D'Orazio, Arkowitz, Adams, & Maram, 2009), and at trial, the California courts often heard testimony from several clinicians who proffered conflicting results.

Ultimate Appellate Court Outcomes

In virtually every case, a male offender was challenging a lower-court determination that he[6] be civilly confined or continued to be confined as a SVP. The state appellate court cases primarily addressed four issues regarding SVP civil commitments: could the person be identified as a sexual predator (79%, n = 85), should the person be discharged from sexually violent predator status (11%, n = 10), should the person be recommitted as a sexually violent predator (5%, n = 5), or other (e.g., parole discharge or probable cause consideration; 6%, n = 6).

The ultimate decision in the large percentage of cases by the appellate court was to affirm the lower court's determination, but in 9% of the cases (n = 10), the appellate court reversed and remanded the lower-court determination for further proceedings. In some of these reversals, the appellate court believed that some procedural error had occurred that should be corrected. In other reversals, the court determined that the offender's civil commitment might be justified although the trial court did not find the person to be a violent predator. In terms of SVP disposition, in 96% (n = 104) of the cases, it was determined that the individual was a sexually violent predator and should be civilly committed. In 3% (n = 3) of the appeals, the court determined that the state did not meet its burden of proof and the individual should *not* be given a sexual predator label. Thus, there appears to be grave deference to the state in its ability to civil confine sex offenders who pose a danger or who might pose a danger if released from custody.

Mental Illness Diagnosis

A point of controversy raised on appeal is whether the state must be proven that the offender suffers from a specific mental illness. In regard to sexual offending, a question exists as to whether the offender needs to have an Axis I diagnosis of paraphilia or Axis II diagnosis of personality disorder, or if any combination of diagnoses can meet the legal definition of mental abnormality or mental illness. In the cases studied here (see Table 4.2), if the appellate courts discussed the mental illness

Table 4.2 Sexual Predator Case Characteristics

Offender Characteristics:	
Gender	99% male (n = 106)
Mental Illness	44% diagnosed as pedophile/paraphilia/psychopath (n = 47) 23% offender has mental illness, not clearly identified (n = 23) 6% no history of mental illness (n = 6)
Treatment History	16% failed to complete treatment program (n = 17) 13% had treatment for mental illness (n = 14) 10% did not participate/refused treatment program (n = 11) 3% treatment not available to offender (n = 3)
Sex Offense History	41% past rape convictions (n = 44) 29% past rapes or sex crimes acknowledged, no conviction (n = 31) 7% stipulated that he is a sexual predator (n = 8)
Other Criminal History	35% violent crime history (n = 38) 22% violent and property crime history (n = 24) 3% property crime history (n = 3)
Sexual Fantasies	24% admit to having sexual fantasies (n = 26)
Sex Abused as Child	9% admit being sexually abused as a child (n = 10)
Age Discussed	35% old age argued to be a mitigation factor by offender (n = 35) 8% young age argued to be an aggravating factor by state (n = 9) 7% age discussed as a criterion used in the evaluation (n = 8)
Offense Characteristics:	
Victim Characteristics	43% multiple child victims (n = 46) 27% child victim (n = 29) 26% female adult victim (n = 28) 14% multiple female adult victims (n = 15) 7% multiple victims/ adult and child (n = 8)
Type of Rape	52% child victims violated position of trust (n = 56) 21% weapon used or threatened (n = 23) 10% cruelty/extreme cruelty shown (n = 11) 2% no finding of cruelty/ extreme cruelty (n = 2)

diagnosis, they usually found the offender to have a paraphilia, most often pedophilia (44%, n = 47), or a personality disorder (23%, n = 23). Because state laws do not require a particular type of mental illness to be proven, state prosecutors could show that an offender suffered from a generalized finding of mental illness in order to meet this threshold measure. In *Hale v. State of Florida*, 891 So. 2d 517 (2004), both mental health experts did not have a specific diagnosis (one determined Hale had a personality disorder with antisocial functions, and the other expert deemed Hale to have an unspecified personality disorder), the court nonetheless affirmed civil commitment since the offender was found to be a sexual predator.

In general, the appellate courts did not discuss the degree to which a mentally ill offender completed or received any treatment for his mental illness. In those cases where treatment was discussed, an offender's failure to complete treatment or refusal to engage in treatment was viewed negatively (26%, n = 27). When an offender received or completed treatment for his sexual offending behavior, the courts did not find this factor to be enough evidence to establish the offender as no longer a threat to the public. In this regard, if the offender sexually violated one or more children (70%, n = 75), or the sex assault was extremely deemed to be excessively violent or cruel (41%, n = 43) civil commitment was deemed warranted. For example, in *In the Matter of the Care and Treatment of Berg*, 342 S.W. 3d 374 (2011), the appellate court affirmed the civil commitment of the offender despite some testimony by an expert (brought by the offender) that civil commitment should not be ordered. The offender's expert witness argued that the offender was not a predator despite the fact that the offender groomed child victims for sexual assault and suffered from "paraphilia." The court, however, relied on other testimonial evidence provided by the state's expert witnesses that even with a "low" or "medium-low" actuarial score, the offender's offense history, predilection to young boys, failure to complete therapy, addition to drugs and alcohol, and other factors made him a dangerous predatory who was likely to recidivate. In *People v Roberge*, 62 P.3d. 97 (2003), the offender's repeated convictions for forcible rapes showed that he was substantially likely to reoffend.

Court's View of Offenders and the Theory That They Age Out of Offending Behavior

In a few cases, age was argued by the defense to be a protective factor to show that a person may or may not offend as they grow older. When an offender was older, he usually claimed that because of old age, he would never reoffend sexually. He argued that either he has aged out of crime or has not sexually offended for a while, and thereby can establish a diminished capacity for sex offending in the future. The appellate courts have not agreed, on the whole, with these assertions. Clinical assessments of sexual predators, according to the courts, have shown that sex offenders continue to violate on victims who fit their profile regardless of age. In this regard, the courts stated that offenders had been kept from children while they are incarcerated had no opportunity to offend. The courts agreed with clinicians that the actuarial tests do not adequately assess the offender's future threat to children once they are released from custody. In this regard, an offender's admission to having been a victim of child sexual abuse themselves or fantasizing about sexual acts led courts to find they would likely sexually reoffend despite an advanced age.

Mental Health Testimony in Civil Commitment Cases

Use of Experts' Views in Appellate Cases

The appellate courts very rarely overturned a lower-court ruling that an offender should be civilly confined as a sexual predator. In some states, it is expected that only one expert provide information to the court on behalf of both the state and offender; in other states, offenders can proffer experts who disagree with the state's SVP determination. As Table 4.3 shows, in the majority of cases utilized in this study (58%, n = 62), two or more experts provided testimony; and in 43% (n = 46) of these cases, there was conflicting expert testimony as to whether the offender should be civilly confined as a SVP. In California, for example, appellate courts analyzed the conflicting testimony from experts; the number of experts who testified at the civil commitment hearing ranged from two to eight. The courts found that the clinical assessments of the experts who favored civil commitment to be more definitive evidence than the actuarial test scores when conflicting evidence was presented. In a recent California case, *Moore v. Superior Court of Los Angeles*, 237 P.3d 530 (2010), the appellate court affirmed a trial court order of civil commitment on the

Table 4.3 Expert Testimony in SVP Civil Commitment Cases

Expert testimony discussed in the appellate case:
Only one expert testimony discussed: 25% (n = 27)
Two experts' testimony discussed: 30% (n = 32)
Three or more experts' testimony discussed: 28% (n = 30)
Conflicting opinions presented from the experts in cases with more than one expert:
Yes: 57% (n = 31)
No: 43% (n = 23)

basis of the state's expert testimony despite the offender's experts' assertions that a civil commitment hearing should not proceed when the offender was incompetent to participate. In *Moore*, the California Supreme Court, in balancing the rights of the offender with the need to protect the public, concluded that due process was not violated by the process since the commitment hearing was a civil, not a criminal, proceeding.

Actuarial Tests and SVP Hearings

A range of forensic assessment measures were used in the sexual predator cases, including clinical predictions and PCL-R, Static 99, RRasor, MnSOST-R, VRAG, SORAG, SVR-20, and the ABLE Assessment for Sexual Interest scores (Table 4.4). Not all actuarial tests were used, but some clinical assessments were based on more than one instrument. We categorized the high and low ranges based upon actually reported scores (and their associated meaning according to the actuarial test used). If the actual score was not reported, then we utilized the terminology given in the court's opinion as to whether a person is deemed a "low-risk" or "high-risk" offender. Thus, actuarial test scores may have ranged from low to high and the appellate courts nonetheless affirmed commitment of an offender because they found clinical judgments arguing for civil commitment to be persuasive. The courts noted that the psychiatric testimony was necessary to determine if a person was to lose their liberty or be released into the community.

In a majority of the cases in this study, the courts discussed in some detail the salient characteristics of the clinical or actuarial assessments that informed their decision. Actuarial tests were used to inform the court about the likelihood of future recidivist behavior; see, for example, *In the Matter of the Detention of Thorell et al.*, 72 P.3rd 708 (2003). In some cases, the courts noted that these clinical assessments were supported by actuarial scores on the PCL-R (34%) and the Static 99 (39%). Some experts indicated that their assessments were based on the use of two or more actuarial scores; some of these scores denoted a high risk of reoffending and others a lower risk for reoffending. In such cases, the courts depended on the clinical assessments which favored commitment. For example, in *In re the Detention of Betsworth*, 711 N.W.2d 280 (2006), the Iowa appellate court stated that the psychologist who opined that the offender was a SVP used three actuarial assessments that had scores ranging from moderate risk to high risk for reoffense. The court majority in *Betsworth* affirmed the civil commitment even though the offender's mental incapacity was due to an organic brain disorder that is not amenable to treatment. In California, where the courts regularly had several expert opinions and a

Table 4.4 Range of Actuarial Scores Indicated in SVP Civil Commitment Cases

Actuarial Test Discussed in Appellate Case	Totals (may be more than 100% since more than one tool may have been discussed)	Low Score	Low-Medium Score	Medium Score	Medium-High Score	High Score
Clinical	78 73%	10 9%		4 4%	23 21%	41 38%
Static-99	40 39%	2 2%	6 6%	7 7%	11 10%	14 13%
PCL-R	36 34%	3 3%	6 6%	2 2%	8 7 %	17 16%
MnSOST-R	26 24%	2 2%	1 1%	1 1%	5 5 %	17 16%
RRASOR	15 14%	4 4%		3 3%	6 6 %	2 2%
VRAG	7 7%	1 1%		1 1%	3 3%	2 2%
SVR20	6 6%				3 3%	3 3%
SORAG	5 5%					5 5%
ABLE assessment	4 4%	1 1%	1 1%	1 1%	1 1%	1 1%

number of actuarial test scores with conflicting results, the appellate courts were not likely to side with an offender and release the person because he "might" be a danger. Thus, when conflicting testimony or actuarial results existed, the appellate courts held that the state met its burden of showing that an offender could be a danger to the public and upheld civil confinement.

Discussion

Practitioners and courts like actuarial risk tools because they have adequate predictive validity and can provide easy and cost-effective outcome measures (Lieb, 2000; Loza & Loza-Fanous, 2003; Quinsey et al., 1998). Walsh and Walsh (2006) in their study of federal and state American courts, found that the PCL-R was introduced in nine different types of cases: sexual predator commitments, parole decisions, capital sentencing decisions, determinations of guilt, transfers of a juvenile to adult court, sentence enhancements and mitigations, competency determinations, termination of parental rights, and civil commitments in general. Lyon and Ogloff (2000) also found that the PCL-R has been introduced in a range of cases including product negligence, child custody, juvenile waiver hearings, witness credibility, and capital sentencing.

Our findings show that the appellate courts made their determinations to uphold civil confinement primarily on clinical assessments of dangerousness. Even when conflicting testimony about an offender's risk scores existed, the court affirmed civil commitment on the basis that the person could be a risk to the community. This finding is consistent with national studies that have shown that psychologists, themselves, continue to rely heavily on clinical rather than actuarial prediction of dangerousness. Our findings are also consistent with the findings of Jackson and Richards (2007b, p. 321) that offenders placed in SVP units may be more "psychiatrically compromised and at higher risk than average sex offenders." The offenders in this study, and in Jackson and Richards's sample, were more likely to offend against children and suffer from pedophilia. In most of these cases, the offender had a history of multiple sex offender victims, and many did not participate in or successfully complete treatment programs.

Psychosexual evaluations in which an offender exhibited some form of cruelty to the victim during the sexual offense also justified civil commitment. Such cruelty could establish someone to be a predator if the offender engaged in both vaginal and anal intercourse, if the defendant used a weapon, if the offender did not exhibit remorse for the offense, or if the offender continued to fantasize about rape. Other factors that are used to justify commitment included the offender's age, general mental health diagnosis, and criminal history (long history of violent or property crime). High PCL-R scores (above 30), together with a clinical assessment of predatory behavior that is unabated because of the offender's criminal history and demographic background, were regularly used justify involuntary confinement. Even when low scores are found, clinical assessments are enough to satisfy a SVP civil commitment if offender history, clinical diagnosis, rape fantasies or other indicia of continued violent propensity exists.

Conclusion

At a time when violent crime rates in the United States were declining in the 1990s, popular crime literature contributed to a growing fascination and disgust with chronic criminal offenders whose reoffending behavior was not abated with age or incarceration. In order to protect the public, states began to follow the lead of Washington State and enact sexually violent predator legislation. These laws allow for the incapacitation of mentally ill offenders who are deemed to be sexual predators. A sexual predator determination could confine offenders indefinitely or until such time as they no longer pose a danger to others. To date, most of the studies that have examined the introduction of PCL-R testimony in the courts have involved a general overview of cases or have focus on capital sentencing (e.g., Edens, 2001). This study looked at the nature of testimony on the PCL-R in conjunction with other forensic assessment measures in order to analyze appellate cases from state appellate jurisdictions with SVP laws. This chapter attempted to fill the gaps in the literature by assessing the use of PCL-R and other actuarial tests in SVP civil commitment cases.

The empirical link between psychopathy and violent recidivism led to the development and use of forensic assessment tools to predict future dangerousness (Viljoen, McLachlan, & Vincent, 2010). According to Hare (1998, p. 205), "Indices of psychopathy are rapidly becoming a routine part of assessment batteries used to make decisions about competency, sentencing, diversion, placement, suitability for treatment, and risk for recidivism and violence." These assessment tools have been accepted by courts analyzing whether states can civilly confine individuals as sexual predators. In our study, we found that many of the SVP offenders exhibit common features. Many SVP offenders have criminal histories that reflect sexual offending against children or excessive violence in the rape of women. Many suffer from mental illness that was not adequately treated, if at all; and many are specifically diagnosed as being a psychopath or pedophile. If the scientific community and the legal community are in agreement, it is in the need to protect people from violent rapists who do not take responsibility for their offending behavior and continue to pose some threat to the community.

We were primarily concerned with the use of the PCL-R and other actuarial tools in civil commitments of sexually violent predator cases and conducted our search within these parameters. We found that actuarial tests did not play as critical a role in the civil commitment decisions as we had anticipated. We thought that as the PCL-R and other risk tools took on statistical reliability, appellate courts would find them to be more useful or place more weight on the risk scores than on a clinical assessment. Our findings were to the contrary; courts were more likely to support confinement on the basis of a clinical assessment of dangerousness despite the use, misuse, or nonuse of the PCL-R and other tests for sexual or psychopathic recidivism. The appellate courts in our study relied heavily on clinical assessments that an offender posed a future danger to reoffend, even if actuarial measures showed a low risk for recidivism. Expert testimony was not always conclusive on the issue of whether a person was a SVP who could not control their sexual offending behavior. Some actuarial tools gave an offender a low-risk score and other tools gave him a high-risk score for reoffense. Courts were willing to overlook the mixed results from the actuarial tests when at least one expert testified that the offender was a high-risk sexual predator offender. With at least one expert clinical assessment that a person was a SVP, appellate courts did not overturn lower court decisions to civilly commit the offender.

Appellate courts in our study upheld application of SVP laws to particular offenders because the laws were enacted to protect the public. They relied more heavily on clinical assessments because actuarial tests are still being scientifically developed, and the courts did not wish to release someone who could sexually violate more children or engage in very violent rapes. Our study's findings are consistent with observations by Garland (2001) and others (Harcourt, 2007) suggesting that actuarial prediction of dangerousness serves an underlying expressive rather than rational function. Our findings suggest that the courts may be inclined to affirm civil commitments. Even if the evidence is contradictory, they err on the side of protecting the public.

This study's results, while instructive, need to be understood within the limitations of our research. We located only 107 cases, but most of these cases came from three states. Some state laws are fairly recent, and more civil commitment appeals are likely to occur. Because civil commitment is based on measures that are predictive, offenders subject to civil confinement might continue to challenge their loss of freedom. Future research should examine the degree to which actuarial predictors serve as "smoke and mirrors" to disguise expressive sanctions as rational-legal decisions.

Notes

1. Arizona (Ariz. Rev. Stat. §36-3701 et seq.), California (Cal. Welf. & Inst. Code §6600 et seq.), Florida (Fla. Stat. §394.910 et seq.), Illinois (725 Ill. Comp. Stat. 205/1 et seq. and 207/1 et seq.), Iowa (Iowa Code §229A), Kansas (Kan. Stat. Ann. §59-29a01), Louisiana (La Rev Stat Ann §15:560.2(I), Massachusetts (Mass. Gen. Laws ch. 123A §1 et seq.), Minnesota (Minn. Stat. §253B), Missouri (Mo. Rev. Stat. §632.480 et seq.), Nebraska (Neb. Rev. Stat. §71-1201 et seq.), New Hampshire (N.H. Rev. Stat. §135-E), New Jersey (N.J. Stat. §30.4-27 et seq.), New York (N.Y. C.L.S. Mental Hyg. §10.01 et seq.), North Dakota (N.D. Cent. Code §25-03.3 et seq.) Pennsylvania (42 Pa. Cons. Stat. §6401 et seq.), South Carolina (S.C. Code Ann. §44-48 et seq.), Texas (Tex. Health & Safety Code Ann. §841), Virginia (Va. Code Ann. §37.1 et seq.), Washington (Rev. Code Wa. §71.09 et seq.), Wisconsin (Wis. Stat. §980.01 et seq.); one state, Ohio rescinded its civil commitment law. For a discussion of these laws and the questions still raised about civil confinement of SVPs see: James, Thomas and Foley (2007).

2. In Texas, SVPs are handled as outpatients because the state determined that it would be cost prohibitive to civilly confine these persons within secure facilities.

3. Schopp and Slain (2000) argue that SVP civil commitment laws are at odds with the purposes of the civil and criminal law if they provide first for offender punishments in prison and then civil confinement. In this regard, they suggest that if a psychopath cannot conform to conventional social norms through criminal sanctions when a SVP status shows that they are not amenable to penal sanction.

4. At issue in the *Hendricks* case was whether or not pedophilia could be considered a "mental abnormality" and whether it was constitutionally permissible to civilly commit an individual for a condition if there is no known treatment. The U.S. Supreme Court in *Seling v. Young*, 531 U.S. 250 (2001) was asked to consider the commitment of Andre Brigham Young. Young was a civilly committed resident of the Washington State Special Commitment Center (SCC) for sexually violent predators who sued the superintendent of the SCC for failing to provide adequate treatment and for the punitive nature of his civil confinement. The court upheld Young's civil commitment but remanded the case for the District Court to determine whether the conditions at the Center rendered the Act punitive as applied to Young. In *Kansas v. Crane*, 534 U.S. 407 (2002), the U.S. Supreme Court determined that absolute volitional impairment need not be shown. See, for example, Sarkar (2003) for a discussion of these cases.

5. Official cases are those that have been recorded in the state's reporter system. Unofficial cases are those that are not recorded in a state's reporter system,

and litigants cannot use them as precedent, but these cases are legal outcome decisions from an appellate court. If an official court reporter citation is not noted, and a reference is provided to a WestLaw number, then the case is an unofficial decision.

6. In only one appellate case was the offender a woman.

References

Abel, G. G., Lawry, S. S., Karlstrom, E. M., Osborn, C. A., & Gillespie, C. F. (1994). Screening tests for pedophilia. *Criminal Justice and Behavior, 21*, 115–131.

Andrews, D. A., & Bonta, J. (1995, 2001, 2003). *The Level of Service Inventory–Revised*. North Tonawanda, NY: Multi-Health Systems

Beecher-Monas, E., & Garcia-Rill, E. (2006). Genetic predictions of future dangerousness: Is there a blueprint for violence? *Law and Contemporary Problems, 69*, 301–341.

Boer, D. P., Hart, S. D., Kropp, P. R., & Webster, C. D. (1997). *Manual for the Sexual Violence Risk-20: Professional guidelines for assessing risk of sexual violence*. Vancouver, British Columbia, Canada: The Mental Health, Law, and Policy Institute.

Cunningham, M. D., & Reidy, T. J. (2002). Violence risk assessment at federal capital sentencing: Individualization, generalization, relevance, and scientific standards. *Criminal Justice and Behavior, 29*, 512–537.

DeMatteo, D., & Edens, J. F. (2006). The role and relevance of the Psychopathy Checklist–Revised in court: A case law survey of U.S. courts (1991–2004). *Psychology, Public Policy, and Law, 12*, 214–241.

D'Orazio, D. M., Arkowitz, S., Adams, J., & Maram, W. (2009). *The California sexually violent predator statute: History, description and areas for improvement*. California Coalition on Sexual Offending.

Douglas, K. S., Vincent, G. M., & Edens, J. F. (2006). Risk for criminal recidivism: The role of psychopathy. In C. J. Patrick (Ed.), *Handbook of psychopathy* (pp. 533–554). New York: Guilford Press.

Edens, J. F. (2001). Misuses of the Hare Psychopathy Checklist–Revised in court: Two case examples. *Journal of Interpersonal Violence, 16*(10), 1082–1093.

Edens, J. F., Buffington-Vollum, J. K., Keilen, A., Roskamp, P., & Anthony, C. (2005). Predictions of future dangerousness in capital murder trials: Is it time to "disinvent the wheel?" *Law and Human Behavior*, 29, 55–86.

Edens, J. F., & Petrila, J. (2006). Legal and ethical issues in the assessment and treatment of psychopathy. In C. J. Patrick (Ed.), *Handbook of psychopathy* (pp. 573–588). New York: Guilford Press.

Elco, J. E. (1998). *Kansas v. Hendricks*, 117 S. Ct. 2072 (1997). *Duquesne University Law Review*, 36, 471–491.

English, K. (1999, 2006). Adult Sex Offender Risk Assessment Screening Instrument. Colorado Division of Criminal Justice; Office of Research and

Statistics. Retrieved October 2, 2007, from http://dcj.state.co.us/ors/pdf/docs/svp1a.PDF.

Epperson, D. L., Kaul, J. D., Huot, S., Goldman, R., & Alexander, W. (2003). Minnesota Sex Offender Screening Tool–Revised (MnSOST-R) Technical Paper: Development, validation, and recommended risk level cut scores. Retrieved January 19, 2012, from http://www.psychology.iastate.edu/~./old%20accounts/dle/TechUpdatePaper12-03.pdf.

Gacono, C. B. (Ed.). (2000). *The clinical and forensic assessment of psychopathy: A practitioner's guide*. Mahwah, NJ: Lawrence Erlbaum Associates.

Garland, D. (2001). *The culture of control: Crime and social order in contemporary society*. Chicago: University of Chicago Press.

Gendreau, P., Goggin, C., & Smith, P. (2002). Is the PCL-R really the "unparalleled" measure of offender risk? A lesson in knowledge cumulation. *Criminal Justice and Behavior, 29*(4), 397–426.

Girard, L., & Wormith, J. S. (2004). The predictive validity of the Level of Service Inventory–Ontario Revision on general and violent recidivism among various offender groups.' *Criminal Justice and Behavior, 31*, 150–181.

Hanson, R. K. (2005). Twenty years of progress in violence risk assessment. *Journal of Interpersonal Violence, 20*(2), 212–217.

Hanson. K. R., & Thornton, D. (1999). Static 99: Improving actuarial risk assessments for sex offenders. Public Works and Government Services Canada User Report. No. J2-165/1999. Retrieved from http://courtdiagnostic.com/Static%2099-02.pdf.

Harcourt, B. E. (2007). *Against prediction: Profiling, policing, and punishing in an actuarial age*. Chicago: University of Chicago Press.

Hare R. D. (1991, 2003). *Manual for the Psychopathy Checklist–Revised*. Toronto, Ontario, Canada: Multi-Health Systems.

Hare R. D. (1993). *Without conscience: The disturbing world of psychopaths among us*. New York: Pocket Books.

Hare, R. D. (1996). Psychopathy: A clinical construct whose time has come. *Criminal Justice and Behavior, 23*(1), 25–54.

Hare R. D. (1998). Psychopaths and their nature: Implications for the mental health and criminal justice systems. In T. Millon, E. Simonsen, E. Birket-Smith, & R. D. Davis (Eds.), *Psychopathy: Antisocial, criminal, and violent behavior* (pp. 188–212). New York: Guilford Press.

Hare, R. D., & Neumann, C. S. (2006). The PCL-R assessment of psychopathy: Development, structural properties, and new directions. In C. J. Patrick (Ed.), *Handbook of psychopathy* (pp. 58–88). New York: Guilford Press.

Harpur, T. J., Hare, R. D., & Hakstian, R., (1989). Two-factor conceptualization of psychopathy: Construct validity and assessment implications. *Psychological Assessment: A Journal of Consulting and Clinical Psychology, 1*, 6–17.

Harris, G. T., Rice, M. E., & Cormier, C. A. (1991). Psychopathy and violent recidivism. *Law and Human Behavior, 15*(6), 625–637.

Hart, S. D. (1998). Psychopathy and risk for violence. In D. J. Cooke, A. E. Forth, & H. D. Hare (Eds.), *Psychopathy: Theory, research and implications for society* (pp. 355–373). New York: Kluwer Academic Publishers.

Hart, S., & Hare, R. D. (1997). Psychopathy: Assessment and association with criminal conduct. In D. M. Stoff, J. Breiling, & J. D. Maser (Eds.), *Handbook of antisocial behavior* (pp. 22–35). New York: John Wiley & Sons.

Hemphill, J. F., Templeman, R., Wong, S., & Hare, R. D. (1998). Psychopathy and crime: Recidivism and criminal careers. In D. J. Cooke, A. E. Forth, & H. D: Hare (Eds.), *Psychopathy: Theory, research and implications for society* (pp. 375–399). New York: Kluwer Academic Publishers.

Hodgins, S. (1997). An overview of research on the prediction of dangerousness. *Nordic Journal of Psychiatry, 51*(Suppl. 39), 33–38.

Jackson, R. L., & Richards, H. J. (2007a). Diagnostic and risk profiles among civilly committed sex offenders in Washington state. *International Journal of Offender Therapy and Comparative Criminology, 51*, 313–323.

Jackson, R. L., & Richards, H. (2007b). Evaluations for the civil commitment of sex offenders. In R. Jackson (Ed.), *Learning forensic assessment* (pp 183–209). Mahwah, NJ: Lawrence Erlbaum Associates.

James, N., Thomas, K. R., & Foley, C. (2007). Civil commitment of sexually dangerous persons: CRS Report for Congress. Washington, DC: Congressional Research Service.

Kamphuis, J. H., & Emmelkamp, P. M. (2005). Twenty years of research into violence and trauma. *Journal of Interpersonal Violence, 20*(2), 167–174.

LaFond, J. Q. (2000). The future of involuntary civil commitment in the U.S.A. after *Kansas v. Hendricks*. *Behavioral Sciences and the Law, 18*, 153–167.

Laurell, J., & Dåderman, A. M. (2005). Recidivism is related to psychopathy (PCL-R) in a group of men convicted of homicide. *International Journal of Law and Psychiatry, 28*, 255–268.

Lieb, R. (2000). Social policy and sexual offenders: Contrasting United States' and European policies. *European Journal on Criminal Policy and Research, 8*, 423–440.

Litwack, T. R., & Schlesinger, L. B. (1998). Dangerous risk assessments: Research, legal, and clinical considerations. In A. K. Hess & I. B. Weiner (Eds.), *Handbook of forensic psychology* (pp. 171–217). New York: John Wiley & Sons.

Loza, W. & Green, K. (2003). The self-appraisal questionnaire. *Journal of Interpersonal Violence, 18*, 781–797.

Loza, W. & Loza-Fanous (2003). More evidence for the validity of the Self-Appraisal Questionnaire for Predicting Violent and Nonviolent Recidivism: A 5-year follow-up. *Criminal Justice and Behavior, 30*(6), 709–721.

Loza, W., & Loza-Fanous, A. (1999). The fallacy of reducing rape and violent recidivism by treating anger. *International Journal of Offender Therapy and Comparative Criminology, 43*, 492–502.

Lussier, P., & Healey, J. (2010). Searching for the developmental origins of sexual violence: Examining the co-occurrence of physical aggression and sexual behaviors in early childhood. *Behavioral Sciences and the Law, 28*, 1–23.

Lyon, D. R., & Ogloff, R. P. (2000). Legal and ethical issues in psychopathy assessment. In C. B. Gacono (Ed.), *The clinical and forensic assessment of psychopathy* (pp. 139–173). Mahwah, NJ: Lawrence Erlbaum Associates.

Meloy, J. R. (1988). The psychopathic mind: origins, dynamics, and treatment. Northvale, NJ: Jason Aronson.

Milloy, C. (2003). Six-year follow-up of released sex offenders recommended for commitment under Washington's sexually violent predator law, where no petition was filed. Olympia, WA: Washington State Institute for Public Policy.

Miller, J. A. (2010). Sex offender civil commitment: The treatment paradox. *California Law Review*, *98*, 2093–2128.

Moffitt, T. E. (1993) Adolescence-limited and life-course-persistent antisocial behavior: A developmental taxonomy. *Psychological Review, 100*, 674–701.

Monahan, J., Steadman, H. J., Silver, E., Appelbaum, P. S., Clark Robbins, P., Mulvey, E. P., . . . Banks, S. (2001). *Rethinking risk assessment: The MacArthur Study of Mental Disorder and Violence*. Oxford, UK: Oxford University Press.

Murrie, D. C., Boccaccini, M. T., Johnson, J. T., & Janke, C. (2007). Does interrater (dis)agreement on psychopathy checklist scores in sexually violent predatory trials suggest partisan allegiance in forensic evaluations? *Law and Human Behavior*. doi:10.1007/s10979-007-9097-5 (uncorrected journal proof)

Petrila, J. (2008). Because they do terrible things: Fear, science, and the erosion of civil liberties in sexually violent predator proceedings. *Journal of Psychiatry and Law, 36*, 359–387.

Prentky, R., & Burgess, A. (2000). *Forensic management of sexual offenders*. New York: Kluwer Academic/Plenum.

Quinsey, V. L., Harris, G. T., Rice, M. E., & Cormier, C. A. (1998, 2006). *Violent offenders: Appraising and managing risk*. Washington DC: American Psychological Association.

Rogers, R., & Jackson, R. L. (2005). Sexually violent predators: The risky enterprise of risk assessment. *Journal of the American Academy of Psychiatry and the Law, 33*, 523–528.

Salekin, R. T., Rogers, R., & Sewell, K. W. (1996). A review and meta-analysis of the psychopathy checklist and psychopathy checklist-revised: Predictive validity of dangerousness. *Clinical Psychology: Science and Practice, 3*, 203–215.

Sarkar, S. P. (2003). From *Hendricks* to *Crane*: The sexually violent predator trilogy and the inchoate jurisprudence of the U.S. Supreme Court. *Journal of the American Academy of Psychiatry and the Law, 31*, 242–248.

Schopp, R. F., & Slain, A. J. (2000). Psychopathy, criminal responsibility, and civil commitment as a sexual predator. *Behavioral Sciences and the Law, 18*, 247–274.

Serin, R. C., & Amos, N. L. (1995). The role of psychopathy in the assessment of dangerousness. *International Journal of Law and Psychiatry, 18*(2), 231–238.

Simourd, D. J., & Hodge, R. D. (2000). Criminal psychopathy: A risk-and-need perspective. *Criminal Justice and Behavior, 27*, 256–272.

Sparks, K. (2008). Differences in legal and medical standards in determining sexually violent predator status. *Law & Psychology Review, 32*, 175–188.

Viljoen, J. L., McLachlan, K., & Vincent, G. M. (2010). Assessing violence risk and psychopathy in juvenile and adult offenders: A survey of clinical practices. *Assessment, 17*, 377–395.

Wallace, J. F., Schmitt, W. A., Vitale, J. E., & Newman, J. P. (2000). Experimental investigations of information-processing deficiencies in psychopaths: Implications for diagnosis and treatment. In C. B. Gacono (Ed.), *The clinical and forensic assessment of psychopathy: A practitioner's guide* (pp. 87–109). Mahwah, NJ: Lawrence Erlbaum Associates.

Walsh, T., & Walsh, Z. (2006). The evidentiary introduction of psychopathy checklist-revised assessed psychopathy in U.S. courts: Extent and appropriateness. *Law and Human Behavior, 30*, 493–507.

Wilson, L. A. (1998). Comment: No longer free to offend: Involuntary civil commitment statutes for sexual predators create the basis for a uniform act. *Northern Illinois University Law Review, 18*, 351–386.

Webster, C. D., Douglas, K. S., Eaves, D., & Hart, S. D. (1997). *HCR-20: Assessing risk for violence* (version 2). Burnaby, British Columbia, Canada: The Mental Health, Law, and Policy Institute of Simon Fraser University.

Wollert, R., & Waggoner, J. (2009). Bayesian computations protect sexually violent predator evaluations from the degrading effects of confirmatory bias and illusions of certainty: A reply to Doren and Levenson. *Sexual Offender Treatment, 4*, 1–23.

Zinger, I. (1995). The misuse of psychopathy in Canadian court proceedings. *Issues in Criminological and Legal Psychology, 24*, 157–159.

CHAPTER FIVE

Actuarial Prediction in Determinate-Plus Sex Offender Release Decisions

Jacqueline B. Helfgott and Beck M. Strah

Introduction

In 2001, the Washington state legislature enacted Determinate-Plus Sentencing for sex offenders convicted of certain sex offenses who are subjected to an indeterminate life sentence with discretionary release by the Indeterminate Sentence Review Board (ISRB). Determinate-Plus Sentencing widened the net for sex offenders in Washington State, allowing for indeterminate confinement of sex offenders who did not fall under the scope of Three Strikes, Two Strikes, and Sexually Violent Predator Laws previously enacted in 1993, 1996, and 1990, respectively.

Little is known about the factors that influence Indeterminate Sentence Review Board decisions since the adoption of the Determinate-Plus Sentencing legislation. Previous research suggests that parole board decision-making is influenced by offender blameworthiness, public safety, and practical constraints and consequences (Huebner & Bynum, 2006) and that actuarial measures are superior to clinical judgment in predicting recidivism (Beech & Ford, 2006; Bengston & Langstrom, 2007; Zagar, Busch, Grove, & Hughes, 2009).

The purpose of this study is to determine factors that influence Indeterminate Sentence Review Board decisions to release Determinate-

Plus Sentencing sex offenders with focus on the use of actuarial tests in release decisions. When there is disparity between factors that offenders believe affect release decisions and factors parole boards consider, offenders become confused, angry, and less likely to conform to institutional requirements (West-Smith, Pogrebin, & Poole, 2000). When sex offenders are denied release, they and their attorneys want to know how to better prepare for ISRB hearings and have questions regarding factors hindering their release, such as how actuarial tests are being used in release decisions, what other factors are being used (e.g., expressions of remorse and accountability), and what factors explain consecutive release denials in situations where sex offenders have completed treatment. The present study seeks to provide partial answers to these questions.

The study examines 688 Determinate-Plus Sentencing cases reviewed by the Washington State Indeterminate Sentencing Review Board from 2003 to 2010 to determine the relationship between offender characteristics and release decisions. Research questions include: What is the profile of a determinate-sentencing plus case that results in release? What role do actuarial scores play in release decisions? What role does offender expression of remorse play in release decisions? And, does completion of sex offender treatment influence release decisions? Additional factors including nature of crime, victim type, actuarial risk scores, expression of empathy and remorse, completion of treatment, offender accountability, and victim impact are examined. Implications for parole decision-making, sentencing policy, and offender reentry are discussed.

Literature Review

Parole and Indeterminate Sentence Review Decision Making

Decision-making in the field of parole and indeterminate sentence review has become more crucial to the state of our prison system than ever before; imprisonment rates for sex offenders have grown faster than for any other crime, and research has demonstrated that sex offenders serve a larger part of their sentence than offenders committing nonsexual crimes (Huebner & Bynum, 2006; Sample & Bray, 2003). Though parole and indeterminate sentencing boards hold set parameters for release, these decisions are not applied consistently; instead, they may often rely on the background of the individual board member, their feelings toward the offense, and the institutional behavior, crime severity, victim input, mental illness, incarceration length, criminal history, and treatment sought by the inmate (Caplan, 2007).

The literature casts little reference to indeterminate sentence review decision-making though holds focus on the decision making handled by parole boards. Huebner and Bynum (2006) assert that parole decision-making is influenced by interplay of legal and extralegal factors, balancing offender blameworthiness, public safety, and organizational constraints or consequences. To further deconstruct this premise, the role of offender blameworthiness within parole decision making refers to the pressure asserted by the victims and communities upon the parole board in making their decision; further, research has demonstrated that this extralegal factor *does* hold a sway over parole decisions, particularly through victim impact testimony (Parsonage, Bernat, & Helfgott, 1992). In focusing on the public safety aspect of parole decisions, the parole board must take into consideration the protection of the community through the assessment of risk; the general focus of the correctional system itself (Feeley & Simon, 1992). Finally, the organizational constraints and consequences of parole decisions embody the political and financial problems of the correctional system, as prison crowding, changes in state correctional resources and policies, and political agendas may shape and greatly impact release decisions to be made (Huebner & Bynum, 2006).

As the topic of sex offender release remains a controversial societal issue, with laws and safeguards placed in attempts to protect communities (e.g., Megan's Law, Adam Walsh Child Protection and Safety Act, sex offender registration and notification laws), release for this offender subset presents special challenges for the decision makers. Possibly due to this extremely negative public perception of sex offenders, parole boards have demonstrated lower levels of sex offender release in recent years; in 1990, 47% of sex offenders eligible for parole were released, whereas the overall offender population held a 68% of release when eligible for parole. Even more recently, in 2004, only 13% of parole-eligible sex offenders were granted release, whereas the rest of the eligible correctional population had a release rate of 48% (Huebner & Bynum, 2006).

Though most states currently do not have indeterminate sentencing boards in place, past research has demonstrated that the officials of these boards have been most likely influenced by the seriousness of the index offense, the offender's demonstration of accountability regarding the offense, and the length of the sentence. Extralegal factors taken into consideration by these boards most likely to affect release decisions have historically been the nature of the offense, time served, prior offenses, institutional infractions received, and age of the offender (Carroll & Burke, 1990; Carroll & Payne, 1977; Huebner & Bynum, 2006, Wilkins, Gottfredson, Robinson, & Sadowsky, 1973).

Regardless of societal controversy, sex offenders have been demonstrated to have lower rates of recidivism than other offenders (Langan & Levin, 2002) though they are eight times less likely to be paroled (Turpin-Petrosino, 1999). Langan, Schmitt, and Durose (2003) have estimated this rate of recidivism at 5.3% within three years of release from prison. Further, not all types of sex offenders exhibit the same characteristics in recidivism, as research has suggested rapists have a significantly higher rate of reoffense than child molesters (Song & Lieb, 1994).

Actuarial Instruments Used in Release Decisions

The utilization of actuarial instruments within the context of release decisions holds a primary focus upon the variable of recidivism, in evaluation of an offender's potential to return to society. Within the last 20 years, these tools have provided perhaps our most significant advancement in sex offender assessment, in that they have allowed society a tool that has demonstrated predictive abilities in recidivism among adult male sex offenders (Barbaree, Langton, & Peacock, 2006). These instruments are comprised of items selected and weighted, based upon their empirical relationship with offender recidivism, often sharing like and overlapping variables *pertaining to* age, gender, sexual offense history, length of time in cohabitating intimate relationships, and whether the victims were strangers (Barbaree et al., 2006; Craissati & Beech, 2005). These instruments contain similar items (e.g., Static-99 contains all four items utilized by RRASOR) as a result of the developers mining data from the sex offender literature for variables demonstrated to be empirically significant in predicting probabilistic estimates of risk, which serve as an indication as to the percentage of offenders with like scores that would expectedly reoffend within a period of opportunity (Seto, 2005). These actuarial scales (e.g., RRASOR, Static-99, and MnSOST-R) have demonstrated reliability in their predictions, holding up against cross-validations in several studies (Allan, Dawson & Allan, 2006; Barbaree et al., 2006; Langton et al., 2007; Seto, 2005).

Though these tests are not to be the sole deciding factor in release decisions, the Washington State ISRB considers these tests to be indicators to initially examine when an offender is attempting to qualify for release. In reviewing the accuracy of violence and sexual violence risk assessment tools utilized in empirical studies, Quinsey, Harris, Rice, and Cormier (1998) suggest that the accuracy of such actuarial tools is 69% or higher.

While these actuarial tools may lend confidence and support to officials concerning the potential release of sexual offenders, they are not without their weaknesses. First, these actuarial tools are limited by their ability to predict in that they are only able to predict further reconvictions with further accuracy, not individual behaviors. Undisclosed offenses and allegations of offenses are not taken into account within the context of these tools, and as a large figure of sex offenses remain unreported, this may lead to leniency and inaccuracy within the tool itself (Craissati & Beech, 2005). Additionally, the differing instruments are considered of equal value in their predictive abilities; this may raise problematic issues, should the use of multiple instruments provide dissimilar outcomes as to the individual offender's potential for release (Barbaree et al., 2006).

As sex offenses differ greatly from other patterns of specialized offending, the study of these offenders becomes vitally important; surmising a greater understanding of these offenders and the risks that are presented to society with their release. With particular concern to sex offenders, Quinsey, Rice, and Harris (1995) conducted a longitudinal study held over the course of 59 months, examining a sample of 178 offenders convicted of rape or child molestation. Within this sample, 28% were convicted of new sex offenses within the 59-month period, while 40% were arrested, convicted, or sent to a psychiatric facility after committing a violent or sexual offense. Of the measures utilized by actuarial tools, the results of this study suggested that the presence of psychopathy and prior sexual offenses as measures within actuarial tools served as the greatest predictors of sexual reoffense. Other studies have suggested critical predictors of recidivism in sex offenders such as social inadequacy, sexual interests, anger/hostility, pro-offending attitudes (Allan, Grace, Rutherford, & Hudson, 2007), victim and offender age (Huebner & Bynum, 2006), childhood difficulties and trauma (Craissati & Beech, 2005), completion of sex offender treatment programs, levels of sexual deviancy, prior sexual offenses, offenses with strangers or male victims, young age at first sexual offense and index offense, cohabitation status, and general criminological factors (Beech & Ford, 2006; Hanson & Bussiere, 1998; Hill, Habermann, Klusmann, Berner, & Briken, 2008; Langton, et al., 2007; Stadtland et al., 2005).

As a heavily weighed factor reviewed by parole and indeterminate sentence review boards, potential for recidivism and further criminal behavior is crucial for analysis in examination of this topic. Though clinical assessment and actuarial testing tap into important facets of offending history and assess potential risk of future offending, the diagnoses and assessment scores do not always result in certain release for the offender. However, these instruments combined, in addition to the judgment of the board, illustrate a clearer picture of an offender's capacity for release and reintegration into society, of which the utmost importance rests on the offender's capacity to reoffend and impart further damage to society.

Though the potential for sexual recidivism may present paramount concern to the families and communities to which sex offenders are released, this is not often the case. In a meta-analytic review of 34 studies, Hanson et al. (2002) reported that only 10% to 15% of sex offenders are identified as having committed another sex offense within four to five years following release.

Prison Programs and Sex Offender Treatment

Sex offender treatment programs (SOTP) can also factor into the decisions of parole or indeterminate sentence release decisions and are frequently featured as a measure within some of the actuarial tools (e.g., MnSOST-R, WSSORLCT) utilized in assessing release for sex offenders. SOTP generally consists of cognitive-behavioral treatments, behavioral programming, written assignments, group therapy, and adjunct classes that may be considered helpful to individuals undergoing SOTP (e.g., Stress and Anger Management, Alcoholics Anonymous) (McMurran & Theodosi, 2007; Washington State Indeterminate Sentence Review Board, personal communication, April 11, 2011).

Hanson et al. (2002) examined the effects of treatment on offender release, conducting a large-scale review of sex offender treatment outcome studies. The results of research suggested that treatment has a significant positive effect on the reduction of sexual recidivism, reducing the likelihood of reoffense from 17% down to 10%. However, this figure accounts solely for the offenders that have *completed* treatment, as research has suggested greatly differing results for offenders who have begun and subsequently dropped out of treatment (Hanson & Bussiere, 1998). Beech and Ford (2006) also examined the benefits of offender treatment, though in high-risk/high-deviance sex offenders. Their results indicated that of all the offenders within their sample that had left the SOTP having responded to treatment, none of these offenders were reconvicted for sexual offenses at follow-up periods at two and five years. Conversely, offenders who had *not* engaged in SOTP were 17% likely to be reconvicted of sexual offenses over a two-year period, and 42% over a five-year period (Beech & Ford, 2006).

As offenders that have completed treatment are less likely to reoffend, offenders that drop out of treatment are at greater risk of recidivism. Hill et al. (2008) found in a meta-analysis of 61 follow-up studies of sex offenders, that *not* completing treatment was a predictor of sexual recidivism—though research has not been clear as to whether non-completion of treatment actually lends to *increased* risk of reoffending over no treatment at all

(Hanson et al., 2002; McMurran & Theodosi, 2007; Stadtland et al., 2005). Rates of treatment completion for sex offenders in prisons is shown to be generally high, approximating 91%, while offenders in community settings attempting treatment are more likely to fail, with treatment completion rates approximating 50% to 66% (McMurran & Theodosi, 2007).

Actuarial Instruments Used in Washington State

Actuarial instruments are used in Washington State at key decision points in the criminal justice process from sentencing through release. At the different points—sentencing, facility assignment and institutional custody level, release, civil commitment eligibility, community notification risk assignment, post-release supervision—specific agencies are designated to conduct the assessment (e.g., private treatment providers at sentencing, Department of Corrections for facility assignment, IRSB for release decisions) (Washington State Institute for Public Policy, 2008). The actuarial instruments used include a set of standardized and validated instruments that produce quantitative scores that suggest risk for reoffense. The tests rely on empirically derived or empirically guided risk factors for criminal outcomes and produce a score that suggests level of risk for individuals with certain characteristics. The factors incorporated in the tests may be static (do not change over time; e.g., age of first sexual offense, personality) or dynamic (change over time; e.g., antisocial attitudes, awareness of offense cycle). Most standard instruments assess static factors to a greater extent than dynamic factors. Different batteries of tests are used at the different points in the process, and there have been changes or omissions over time.[1]

Currently the actuarial tests used by the ISRB in release decisions are the Minnesota Sex Offender Screening Tool–Revised (MnSOST-R), Washington State Sex Offender Risk Level Classification Tool (WSSORLCT), Rapid Risk Assessment for Sexual Offender Recidivism (RRASOR), and Static-99. Risk-level scores from these tests were incorporated as independent variables in the present study. Each of these tests will be further described in detail as follows.

Minnesota Sex Offender Screening Tool (MnSOST-R)

The Minnesota Sex Offender Screening Tool (MnSOST-R) is a 16-item scale developed for the Minnesota Department of Corrections. This instrument was developed to assess risk of recidivism among adult males having committed at least one sexual offense. However, this instrument holds a limitation not found in the other actuarial instruments utilized in this study, in that its use is intended only for nonrelated victims, thus rendering its use null in cases of incest offenses.

Items comprising the MnSOST-R include: Number of sex-related convictions, length of sex offending history, number of different age groups victimized, age at release from institution, drug or alcohol abuse, sex offender treatment while incarcerated, chemical dependency treatment while incarcerated. Actuarial scores of the MnSOST-R can range from −14 to 30; among these scores, 3 and lower is considered of low risk to reoffend, 4–7 of moderate risk to reoffend, and scores of 8 and higher are regarded as individuals of high risk to reoffend (Langton, Barbaree, Seto, Peacock, Harkins & Hansen, 2007).

Washington State Sex Offender Risk Level Classification Tool (WSSORLCT)

The Washington State Sex Offender Risk Level Classification Tool (WSSORLCT) was developed by the Washington Institute for Public Policy (1999). Items include factors that had constituted the MnSOST-R 1995 version and four "notification considerations" that had not been a part of the standard MnSOST-R. This test was utilized by the Washington State Indeterminate Sentencing Review Board in review of release decisions until 2009, when its use was discontinued due to lack of funding. Though this test contained items that had been examined in MnSOST-R, the test was not validated during its period of use (Washington State Indeterminate Sentencing Review Board, personal communication, April 11, 2011). Conversely, the RRASOR, Static-99, and MnSOST-R were demonstrated to reliably predict recidivism outcomes in offenders as designed, no significant differences were found among these instruments in their accuracy of determining recidivism (Langton et al., 2007).

Rapid Risk Assessment for Sexual Offender Recidivism (RRASOR)

The Rapid Risk Assessment for Sexual Offender Recidivism (RRASOR) is a four-item instrument designed to measure sex offender recidivism. Items include prior sex offenses, age at release from period of incarceration, victim gender, and relationship to victim. The score is the sum of the four items with total score range from 0 to 6 points (Langton et al., 2007). This test was utilized by the Washington State Indeterminate Sentencing Review Board in review of release decisions until 2009, when its use was discontinued due to lack of funding. However, the items examined within the RRASOR can be found within the Static-99, which is still utilized in decision making by the Washington State ISRB (Washington State Indeterminate

Sentencing Review Board, personal communication, April 11, 2011). Although a noted overlap of variables between the RRASOR and Static-99 tests exists, no attempt to *combine* these actuarial scales has resulted in a statistically significant advantage over the single actuarial scale (Seto, 2005).

Static-99

The Static-99 is a 10-item scale combining items from the RRASOR and Structured Anchored Clinical Judgment (SACJ-Min) actuarial predictive instruments (Allan, Dawson & Allan, 2006). Items 1–5 are coded using archival data (e.g., age, cohabitation with romantic partner for two years, current convictions regarding nonsexual violence, prior nonsexual violence, and prior sex offenses). Items 6–10 are coded using all available information including self-report, collateral reports, and victim statements (e.g., reporting of unrelated victims, stranger victims, male victims, prior sentencing dates, and convictions for noncontact sex offenses). This instrument uses the results of scoring to generate four categories of risk; low, low-medium, medium-high, and high, and has been validated through use on several diverse samples of offenders (Craissati & Beech, 2005).

Method

Sample

The data utilized in this study was collected from 688 case files of Washington's Indeterminate Sentence Review Board (ISRB). The subjects detailed within each case file consisted of incarcerated sexual offenders, sentenced in Washington State under Determinate-Plus, appearing before the ISRB for a release hearing between 2003 and 2010. Case files are comprised of information concerning each individual offender for each individual hearing. Each case file contains information pertaining to the offender (e.g., age, offense, infractions received while incarcerated, treatment received during incarceration), information pertaining to the offense (e.g., victim age, nature of the crime, length incarcerated, minimum sentence imposed), and information on the release eligibility of each offender (e.g., actuarial scores assessing risk, the board's assessment of the offender's risk of recidivism based upon the evidence provided and meeting with the offender).

The sample encompassed 688 case files representing 434 sex offenders, many of which came before the board on more than one occasion. Data was obtained from the ISRB through public records request and provided to researchers through a defense attorney who represents clients under ISRB review. Of the offender sample, 259 offenders appeared before the

ISRB for a release hearing on one occasion, 122 on two occasions, 31 on three occasions, 19 on four occasions, 2 on five occasions, and 1 offender on six occasions. The sample was comprised of 685 males (99.6%) and 3 females (0.4%), with an offender age range of 18 to 79 ($M = 37$, $SD = 12$). Victims ranged in age from 1 to 82 ($M = 12$, $SD = 9$). The majority of the offender sample (59.7%) had committed sex offenses prior to the immediate offense, offenses primarily pertaining to child molestation (39.1%), assault with sexual motivation (26.9%), and rape (18.5%).

In the majority of index offenses, ($n = 269$, 39.1%) Child Molestation was the crime type for which the offender was convicted. This statistic is followed by Assault with sexual motivation ($n = 184$, 26.9%), Rape ($n = 127$, 18.5%), Indecent Liberties ($n = 27$, 3.9%), other sexual offenses (e.g., kidnapping, incest, luring, indecent exposure, exhibitionism) ($n = 35$, 5.1%), Burglary with sexual motivation ($n = 27$, 3.9%), and Communication with a Minor for Immoral Purposes ($n = 18$, 2.6%), and other offenses.

Sex offender "levels" of risk as assigned by law enforcement were divided between Level 1 (38.3%), Level 2 (30.7%), and Level 3 (30.9%), and the mean minimum sentence of offenders was 51.82 months, while mean time served was 40.78 months (see Table 5.1).

Following the release hearing for each offender, the ISRB made a release decision based upon the preponderance of the evidence and took action in one of three ways: (1) release the offender; (2) release the offender with conditions; and (3) find the offender not releasable and add further months of incarceration to their minimum term.

Independent Variables

Various data was extracted from each individual case file with particular regard to offense, offender, and release eligibility–related variables. Independent variables were included based on the extent to which they were factors identified in the literature associated with parole and indeterminate sentence release decisions and/or were factors of concern to defense attorneys and offenders as they prepared for ISRB review.[2]

Offense variables included: Offense type and severity, minimum sentence imposed (in months), length of time the offender had been incarcerated for the offense (in months), the victim type (family, acquaintance, stranger, or other), the victim age (in years), designation whether the victim was a minor, a narrative explaining the nature of the crime, whether the offender exhibited empathy, and whether or not the offender admitted the crime.

Offender variables included: Name, case number, number of infractions committed while incarcerated, infractions received, number of times

Table 5.1 Sample Characteristics

Sample Characteristics (N = 688)		
	M	*SD*
Offender Age (years)	36.98	12.02
Victim Age (years)	12.02	9.41
Minimum Sentence (months)	51.82	38.67
Time Served (months)	40.78	22.29
Number of times before ISRB	1.53	0.82
	Frequency	***Percentage***
Gender		
Male	685	99.60%
Female	3	0.40%
Crime Type		
Child Molestation	269	39.10%
Assault with Sexual Motivation	184	26.90%
Rape	127	18.50%
Indecent Liberties	27	3.90%
Burglary with Sexual Motivation	27	3.90%
Communication with a Minor for Immoral Purposes	18	2.60%
Other	35	5.10%
Sex Offender Level		
I	263	38.30%
II	211	30.70%
III	212	30.90%

the offender had appeared before the ISRB for release hearings, age (years), mental health issues, chemical dependency, whether the offender had received treatment while incarcerated (e.g., mental health treatment, anger management workshops), whether the offender had participated in and completed the sex offender treatment program (SOTP), and the number of prior sex offenses committed.

Release eligibility related variables included: Actuarial test scores assessing offender risk (e.g., Minnesota Sex Offender Screening Tool Revised [MnSOST-R], Washington State Sex Offender Risk Level Classification Tool [WSSORLCT], Rapid Risk Assessment for Sexual Offender Recidivism [RRASOR], and Static-99), the board's assessment as to whether the offender was more likely than not to reoffend, and sex offender level as designated by law enforcement. These actuarial tests were utilized to provide the ISRB an indication of dangerousness to appraise. Let it further be noted that use of RRASOR and WSSORLCT actuarial tests was discontinued in 2009 due to lack of funding (Washington State Indeterminate Sentencing Review Board, personal communication, April 11, 2011).

Among the independent variables noted, the "key independent variables" utilized for analysis were: Type of offense/victimization that occurred; likelihood of reoffense (e.g., determined more likely than not or not more likely than not to reoffend); sex offender treatment programs completed while incarcerated; prison programs completed while incarcerated; mental illness diagnosis; history of sex offenses; time served in prison; chemical dependency history; known/unknown victims; victim age; offender age; minimum months of sentence; rated sex offender level (e.g., I–III); actuarial risk scores as taken from RRASOR, Static-99, WSSORLCT and MnSOST-R; institutional infractions noted; whether the victim was a minor; crime type (e.g., sexual assault, rape, molestation); number of times before ISRB; offender's admission of the offense; offender's expression of remorse/empathy toward the victim; and notation of victim impact.

Dependent Variable

This study was conducted as an exploratory analysis of the factors that facilitate release for sex offenders in Washington State. The dependent variable holding the primary focus of this study was the board's decision to release or not release, a decision made by the ISRB based upon the preponderance of evidence presented (e.g., clinical assessments, actuarial assessments, index offense narratives, victim statement, offender remorse, offender's participation in treatment).

Analyses (Correlation, Multivariate Logistic Regression Analysis)

Analyses were performed to address two research questions: (1) What factors are associated with the Washington State ISRB decisions for Determinate-Plus Sentencing sex offenders; and (2) What is the profile of a Determinate-Plus Sentencing case that results in release?

Initially, each independent variable was entered into correlation with the dependent variable (release) as to determine the strength of the relationship between each of the "key independent variables" and the dependent variable. Though "likelihood of reoffense," describing the board's determination based on variables of likelihood that the offender will reoffend was originally within this category, it was not utilized within the following binary logistic regression analysis due to being tautological.

Examining the correlation strength of independent variables, the variables that had a significant ($p < .05$) correlation to the dependent variable were then entered into a binary logistic regression analysis, with released/not released as the dependent variable.

Results

Correlation Results

The variables most strongly correlated with ISRB Determinate-Plus sex offender release decisions were ISRB determination of "Likelihood of Reoffense" (n = 682, r = −.87, p < .00),[3] WSSORLCT score (n = 639, r = −.43, p < .00), sex offender risk level classification (n = 687, r = −.42, p < .00), MnSOSTR (n = 678, r = −.39, p < .00), RRASOR (n = 621, r = −.36, p < .00), and Static-99 scores (n = 668, r = −.36, p < .00), whether or not the offender had completed sex offender treatment, number of prior sex offenses (n = 688, r = .35, p < .00), victim type (nonstranger/stranger) (n = 688, r = −.17, p < .00), institutional infractions (n = 596, r = −.15, p < .00), completion of prison programs (n = 688, r = .13, p < .00), mental illness diagnosis (n = 688, r = −.13, p < .00), victim age (n = 568, r = −.11, p < .00), sentence length (n = 683, r = −.09, p < .01), and offender age (n = 685, r = −.07, p < .05) (see Table 5.2).

It was hypothesized that offender expression of remorse and accountability would be positively associated with ISRB decision to release. Offender admission of offense was not significantly correlated with ISRB decision to release (n = 506, r = −.01, p < .75); however, offender expression of remorse was significant at < .10 level (n = 360, r = .09, p < .08) that may warrant further examination of a possible relationship between offender remorse and release decisions.

Logistic Regression Results

The logistic regression model presented in Table 5.3 shows that when controlling for other variables, the strongest predictor of parole release was completion of sex offender treatment program (Exp(B) = 32.783, p < .00) followed by offender age (Exp(B) = .955, p < .00), prior sex offenses (Exp(B) = .305, p < .00), sentence length (Exp(B) = .983, p < .00), WSSORLCT score (Exp(B) = .936, p < .01), mental illness diagnosis (Exp (B) = .789, p < .01), and sex offender level (Exp(B) = .559, p < .04). Variables approaching significance were infraction history (Exp(B) = .86, p < .10) and completion of prison programs (Exp(B) = 1.729, p < .10) (see Table 5.3).

Table 5.2 Factors Correlated with ISRB Decision to Release

Variable	N	R	P
Likelihood of reoffense*	682	−0.868	0.000
WSSORLCT*	639	−0.431	0.000
Sex Offender Level*	687	−0.418	0.000
MnSOSTR*	678	−0.389	0.000
RRASOR*	621	−0.362	0.000
Static-99*	668	−0.358	0.000
SOTP Completed*	688	0.348	0.000
Prior Sex Offenses*	688	−0.334	0.000
Victim Type (non-stranger/stranger)*	688	−0.170	0.000
Institutional Infractions*	596	−0.150	0.000
Prison Programs Completed*	688	0.133	0.000
Mental Illness Diagnosis*	688	−0.127	0.001
Victim Age*	568	−0.112	0.008
Minimum Sentence (months)*	683	−0.091	0.017
Offender Age*	685	−0.074	0.052
Chemical Dependency	688	−0.073	0.056
Expression of Remorse	360	0.092	0.081
Time Served	679	−0.046	0.229
Crime (Sexual Assault/Rape)	688	−0.029	0.451
Minor Victim	653	−0.028	0.479
Admission of Crime	506	−0.014	0.755
Number of Times before ISRB	688	−0.004	0.917

*p < .05

Scores on the MnSOSTR (Exp(B) = .961, $p = .32$), RRASOR (Exp(B) = .844, $p = .45$), and Static-99 (Exp(B) = 1.030, $p < .84$) were not significantly associated with the ISRB decision to release in the regression model. Multicollinearity issues are apparent given that these instruments measure highly overlapping concepts (mostly static risk factors). These actuarial tools are highly correlated with each other and with ISRB release in the bivariate analysis. Table 5.4 shows the correlation matrix showing the relationship between MnSOSTR, RRASOR, Static-99, and WSSORLCT.

Profile of the Determinate-Plus Sex Offender Most Likely to Be Granted ISRB Release

The results suggest that the Determinate-Plus sex offender most likely to be granted release by the ISRB is a younger offender who has served a shorter sentence, successfully completed sex offender treatment, scored

Table 5.3 Results of Logistic Regression Model of Factors Considered in ISRB Decision to Release ($N = 688$)

Variable	B	SE	Wald	df	p	Exp(B) Lower	95% C.I. for EXP (B) Upper	
Completed Sex Offender Treatment*	3.482	.418	72.03	1	.000	32.783	14.454	74.351
Offender Age*	−.046	.013	12.29	1	.001	.955	.931	.980
Prior Sex Offenses*	−1.186	.350	11.47	1	.001	.305	.154	.607
Minimum Sentence*	−.017	.006	9.15	1	.002	.983	.972	.994
WSSORLCT*	−.066	.022	8.65	1	.003	.936	.896	.978
Mental Illness Diagnosis*	−.237	.086	7.613	1	.006	.789	.666	.934
Sex Offender Level*	−.581	.276	4.434	1	.035	.559	.326	.961
Completed Prison Programs	.547	.332	2.715	1	.099	1.729	.901	3.316
Institutional Infractions	−.151	.094	2.594	1	.107	.860	.716	1.033
Victim Age	−.020	.017	1.470	1	.225	.980	.948	1.013
RRASOR	−.170	.223	.583	1	.445	.844	.545	1.305
MnSOST-R	−.040	.041	.958	1	.328	.961	.886	1.041
Victim Type (stranger/non-stranger)	−.186	.435	.184	1	.668	.830	.354	1.946
Static-99	.030	.151	.040	1	.842	1.030	.767	1.385
Constant	6.283	.858	53.631	1	.000	535.635		

*$p < .05$

Table 5.4 Correlation Matrix for Actuarial Tests used in ISRB Release Decisions

		MnSOSTR	STATIC-99	RRASOR	WADOCRISK
MnSOSTR	Pearson Correlation	1	.678**	.576**	.761**
	Sig. (2-tailed)		.000	.000	.000
	N	678	666	619	636
STATIC99	Pearson Correlation	.678**	1	.821**	.727**
	Sig. (2-tailed)	.000		.000	.000
	N	666	668	621	625
RRASOR	Pearson Correlation	.576**	.821**	1	.660**
	Sig. (2-tailed)	.000	.000		.000
	N	619	621	621	620
WADOCRISK	Pearson Correlation	.761**	.727**	.660**	1
	Sig. (2-tailed)	.000	.000	.000	
	N	636	625	620	639

**Correlation is significant at the 0.01 level (2-tailed).

lower on the WSSORLCT, has no indication of a specific mental illness diagnoses, and has a lower sex offender level classification. Results also suggest that completion of prison programs and lower number of infractions may also be a characteristic of the Determinate-Plus sex offender most likely to be granted release.

Discussion

If the data generated by the data analyses were to be compiled to create a profile of the Determinate-Plus sex offender most likely to be granted release by the Washington State ISRB, the offender would have: Completed SOTP, received a classification as a lower level sex offender (e.g., Level I), scored lower on the WSSORLCT, been convicted of fewer/no prior sex offenses, be of a relatively young age, completed a shorter sentence, and have no indication of mental health diagnosis. Bivariate analyses also suggest that expression of remorse may play a role and suggests that further examination of the relationship between offender remorse and release decisions is warranted.

The results suggest that Determinate-Plus ISRB release decisions are primarily based on factors associated with public safety (e.g., sex offender level, actuarial risk score), as well as factors empirically associated with recidivism (e.g., SOTP, prior sex offenses, mental illness diagnosis, sentence length). Of the differing factors weighed against one another, Completion of Sex Offender Treatment was demonstrated to be the strongest predictor of release by ISRB.

Several of the findings are worth exploring further. Research suggests that there is an inverse relationship between age and sexual recidivism risk where younger offenders pose a greater risk of reconviction than older offenders, which has led to the development of actuarial tests that identify offenders under age 25 as posing the greatest risk (Craig, 2008). However, the results here show that age was inversely related with ISRB decision to release, which means that Washington State ISRB decisions were made in the favorable direction for younger rather than older offenders. Similarly, sentence length was also inversely related to release decisions, suggesting that the shorter the sentence, the more likely the decision to release. It could be speculated that older offenders who have been confined for long periods of time are perceived by the ISRB as posing a greater risk or are less amenable to change and reentry success. This discrepancy between known correlates of recidivism risk (i.e., age) and the relationship between age, sentence length, and the relationship between these factors and other variables needs to be further explored.

The finding that offender admission of guilt was not significantly related to ISRB release decisions, but that offender expression of remorse approached significance highlights the need for further research on the role of offender remorse and accountability release decisions. Previous studies have found that extra-legal variables (Drury & DeLisi, 2010) and victim impact testimony (Parsonage, Bernat, & Helfgott, 1992) can impact criminal justice decision-making.

Offenders coming up for release have expressed concern that they will not adequately be able to convey remorse and, when they are denied parole, are left to wonder if this was a factor. Presser (2003) found that conventional culture and structural arrangements in correctional contexts facilitate a dynamic that allows male prisoners to avoid feeling remorse by neutralizing their violence, but that offenders who are afforded the opportunity to talk about their actions can promote their own rehabilitation and help all parties to an offense. Other studies have found that expression of offender remorse and accountability are central components of victim and community healing (Helfgott et al., 2000; Helfgott, Lovell, & Lawrence, 2002; Lovell, Helfgott, & Lawrence, 2002). The number of cases in which this variable was able to be recorded in the present study was small (360 cases, 52% of the total sample) and with the trend toward significance ($p < .10$), there is some indication that further examination of the role of offender expression of remorse in release decisions is warranted.

The multicollinearity of the actuarial tests used in ISRB decisions found in the present study is an ongoing issue in risk prediction. The results here suggest (as has been found in other studies) that the WSSORLCT, RRASOR, MnSOSTR, and Static-99 are measuring overlapping constructs. The overlapping nature of forensic assessment measures used to evaluate offender risk to predict dangerousness has been well documented and discussed. Research is mixed regarding whether or not using multiple measures of latent constructs adds validity when they are used together. Some studies have found that despite high correlation between the scales, they may add incremental validity when used together, and that incremental validity is enhanced when specific combinations of tests are used with subtypes of offenders (e.g., general, violent, sex offenders) and suggest that decision makers should select the best test or tests to fit the population and jurisdiction (Serin, 2005). There is currently no scientific consensus concerning which is the "best" instrument for the prediction of sexual recidivism, and different instruments may be better or worse for specific decisions in specific jurisdictions. However, some studies have found that tests do not add incrementally to one another in the prediction of sexual recidivism and suggest that the use of multiple instruments is an unnecessary hassle. Given these mixed results, it is likely that an averaging approach would be the optimal method of combining the findings of the multiple scales (Babchishin, Hanson, & Helmus, 2011).

In addition to issues of multicollinearity, there are a number of limitations in the study findings. First, the sample involved Determinate-Plus sex offender cases under review by the Washington State Indeterminate Sentence Review Board. This is a specialized sub-offender population that was not caught under the "net" of previous Washington State legislation designed to enhance public safety including Three Strikes, Two Strikes for sex offenders, and civil commitment of sexual predators. The results found here on release decisions for this population of offenders in a state that has the particular history that Washington does with respect to the evolution of sex offender legislation and sentencing may not be generalizable to other populations in other states with different legislative histories and parole and indeterminate sentence review processes. Second, changes over time in the actuarial tests used by the Washington State ISRB (dropping the LSI-R in 2008 and the WSSORLCT in 2009) make it difficult to examine the combination of specific actuarial tests over time. Third, lack of information in the available data regarding extralegal variables such as offender expression of remorse and accountability and victim and community impact and/or expression of community sentiment regarding public safety issues related to a particular offender's release made it difficult to determine the impact of these variables on release decisions in the present study.

The findings of the present study are promising, as they suggest that sex offenders may hold some control over their own release through their behaviors, as dynamic factors such as SOTP, institutional behavior, admission of crime, and infraction history are found to be significantly related to Determinate-Plus sex offender ISRB release decisions. However, not all factors associated with release are controllable by the offender, as some factors during an offender's incarceration are static and will not be able to be changed by the offender themselves (e.g., age, severity of crime, mental health diagnosis). These results may lend importance in both providing information for ISRB regarding future release decisions as well as informing sex offenders coming up for release of the obstacles they may face ahead. Further research is needed on the role of specific static and dynamic factors in release decisions, on the different actuarial tests used, and the weight given to additional dynamic factors such as offender expression of remorse in sex offender release decisions. Examination of the relationship between offender expression of remorse, traditional factors used in offender release decisions, and different actuarial tests with different types of offenders is an important direction for future study.

Acknowledgments

The authors would like to thank Brad Meryhew for the inspiration for and assistance with this study and to the Washington State Indeterminate Sentence Review Board for their assistance in accessing data and clarifying questions about ISRB process.

Notes

1. The LSI-R was used by Washington State Department of Corrections from 1999 to 2008 and was dropped because research showed the test had low to moderate predictive accuracy for Washington State offenders. In August 2008, the LSI-R it was replaced with a static risk assessment instrument with a separate offender needs assessment to capture dynamic factors developed with the assistance of the Washington State Institute for Public Policy (see Washington Institute for Public Policy, 1999, 2006a, 2006b, 2008, 2010). ISRB use of RRASOR and WSSORLCT was discontinued in 2009 due to lack of funding (Washington State Indeterminate Sentencing Review Board, personal communication, April 11, 2011).

2. In the development stage of the study design, the first author participated in a discussion with a group of approximately 30 sex offenders confined in a Washington State correctional facility who had completed sex offender treatment and had been previously denied release by the ISRB, and a defense attorney whose client caseload predominantly consists of incarcerated sex offenders. Several of the independent variables included in the study (e.g., actuarial test scores, expressions of remorse and accountability) were specifically included to address questions raised by offenders and the attorney in this and other discussions.

3. The Likelihood of Offense variable was the ISRB determination of whether or not the offender was "more likely than not" to reoffend if released based on the totality of information. Thus, it was expected that this variable would be the most strongly correlated with the decision to release since in some respects, the relationship is tautological. However it was included in the correlation analysis as an indicator of the totality of factors to determine the extent to which who were not determined to be more likely than not to reoffend were denied release.

References

Allan, A., Dawson, D., & Allan, M. M. (2006). Prediction of the risk of male sexual offending in Australia. *Australian Psychologist, 41*, 60–68.

Allan, M., Grace, R. C., Rutherford, B., Hudson, S. M. (2007). Psychometric assessment of dynamic risk factors for child molesters. *Sex Abuse, 19*, 347–367.

Babchishin, K. M., Hanson, R. K., & Helmus, L. (2011). The RRASOR, Static-99R and Static-2002R all add incrementally to the prediction of recidivism among sex offenders 2011-2012. Corrections Research User Report. Ottawa: Public Safety Canada. Document No: PS3-1/2011-2E-PDF.

Barbaree, H. E., Langton, C. M., & Peacock, E. J. (2006). Prediction of the risk of male sexual offending in Australia. *Australian Psychologist, 41*, 60–68.

Beech, A., & Ford, H. (2006). The relationship between risk, deviance, treatment outcome and sexual reconviction in a sample of child sexual abusers completing residential treatment for their offending. *Psychology, Crime, and Law, 12*(6), 685–701.

Bengston, S., & Langstrom, N. (2007). Unguided clinical and actuarial assessment of re-offending risk: A direct comparison with sex offenders in Denmark. *Sex Abuse, 19*, 135–153.

Caplan, J. M. (2007). What factors affect parole: A review of empirical research. *Federal Probation, 71*(1), 16–19.

Carroll, J. S., & Burke, P. A. (1990). Evaluation and prediction in expert parole decisions. *Criminal Justice and Behavior, 17*, 315–332.

Carroll, J. S., & Payne, J. W. (1977). Crime seriousness, recidivism risk and causal attributions in judgments of prison term by students and experts. *Journal of Applied Psychology, 62*, 595–602.

Craig, L. A. (2008). How should we understand the effect of age on sexual recidivism? *Journal of Sexual Aggression, 14*(3), 185–198.

Craissati, J., & Beech, A. (2005). Risk prediction and failure in a complete urban sample of sex offenders. *Journal of Forensic Psychiatry and Psychology, 16*, 24–40.

Drury, A.J. & DeLisi, M. (2010). Past Is Prologue: Prior Adjustment to Prison and Institutional Misconduct. *The Prison Journal*, 90(3), 331–352.

Feeley, M. M., & Simon, J. (1992). The new penology: Notes on an emerging strategy of corrections and its implications. *Criminology, 30*, 449–474.

Hanson, R. K., & Bussière, M. T. (1998). Predicting relapse: A meta-analysis of sexual offender recidivism studies. *Journal of Consulting and Clinical Psychology, 66*(2), 348–362.

Hanson, R. K., Gordon, A., Harris, A. J. R., Marques, J. K., Murphy, W., Quinsey, V. L., & Seto, M. C. (2002). First report of the collaborative outcome data project on the effectiveness of psychological treatment for sex offenders. *Sexual Abuse: A Journal of Research and Treatment, 14*, 169–194.

Helfgott, J. B., Lovell, M. L., & Lawrence, C. F. (2002). Citizens, Victims, and Offenders Restoring Justice: Accountability, healing, and hope through storytelling and dialogue. *Crime Victims Report, 6*, 3–4+.

Helfgott, J. B., Lovell, M. L., Lawrence, C. F., & Parsonage, W. H. (2000). Results from the pilot study of the Citizens, Victims, and Offenders Restoring Justice

Program at the Washington State Reformatory. *Journal of Contemporary Criminal Justice*, *16*, 5–31.

Hill, A., Habermann, N., Klusmann, D., Berner, W., & Briken, P. (2008). Criminal recidivism in sexual homicide perpetrators. *International journal of offender therapy and comparative criminology*, *52*, 5–20.

Huebner, B. M., & Bynum, T. S. (2006). An analysis of parole decision making using a sample of sex offenders: A focal concerns perspective. *Criminology, 44* (4), 961–990.

Kerbs, J., Jones, M., & Jolley, J. M. (2009). Discretionary decision making by probation and parole officers: The role of extralegal variables as predictors of responses to technical violations. *Journal of Contemporary Criminal Justice, 25* (4), 424–441.

Langan, P. A., & Levin, D. J. (2002). Recidivism of prisoners released in 1994. Washington, DC: U.S. Department of Justice, Bureau of Justice Statistics.

Langan, P. A., Schmitt, E. L., & Durose, M. R. (2003). Recidivism of sex offenders released in 1994. Washington, DC: U.S. Department of Justice, Bureau of Justice Statistics.

Langton, C. M., Barbaree, H. E., Seto, M. C., Peacock, E. J., Harkins, L., & Hansen, K. (2007). Actuarial assessment of risk for reoffense among adult sex offenders: Evaluating the predictive accuracy of the Static-2002 and five other instruments. *Criminal Justice and Behavior, 34*.

Lovell, M. L., Helfgott, J. B., & Lawrence, C. F. (2002). Citizens, Victims, and Offenders Restoring Justice: Social group work bridging the divide. In S. Henry, J. East, & C. Schmitz (Eds.), *Social work with groups*. New York: Haworth Press.

McMurran, M., & Theodosi, E. (2007). Is treatment non-completion associated with increased reconviction over no treatment? *Psychology*, *Crime & Law, 13*, 333–343.

Parsonage, W. H., Bernat, F., & Helfgott, J. B. (1992). Victim impact testimony and Pennsylvania's parole decision-making process. A pilot study. *Criminal Justice Policy Review, 6*, 187–206.

Presser, L. (2003). Remorse and neutralization among violent male offenders. *Justice Quarterly, 20*(4), 801–825.

Quinsey, V. L., Harris, G. T., Rice, M. E., & Cormier, C. A. (1998). *Violent offenders: Appraising and managing risk*. Washington, DC: American Psychological Association.

Quinsey, V. L., Rice, M. E., & Harris, G. T. (1995). Actuarial prediction of sexual recidivism. *Journal of Interpersonal Violence, 70*, 85–105.

Sample, L. L., & Bray, T. M. (2003). Are sex offenders dangerous? *Criminology and Public Policy,* 3(1), 59–82.

Seto, M. C. (2005). Is more better? Combining actuarial risk scales to predict recidivism among adult sex offenders. *Psychological Assessment, 17*, 156–167.

Song, L., & Lieb, R. (1994). *Adult sex offender recidivism: A review of studies*. Olympia, WA: Washington State Institute for Public Policy.

Stadtland, C., Hollweg, M., Kleindienst, N., Dietl, J., Reich, U., & Nedopil, N. (2005). Risk assessment and prediction of violent and sexual recidivism in sex offenders: Long-term predictive validity of four risk assessment instruments. *Journal of Forensic Psychiatry & Psychology, 16*, 92–108.

Turpin-Petrosino, C. (1999). Are limiting enactments effective? An experimental test of decision making in a presumptive parole state. *Journal of Criminal Justice, 27*, 321–332.

Washington State Institute for Public Policy (1999). Washington State Sex Offender Risk Level Classification Tool. Document No. 05-12-1205. Olympia, WA: Washington State Institute for Public Policy. Retrieved from http://www.wsipp.wa.gov/rptfiles/05-12-1205.pdf.

Washington State Institute for Public Policy (2006a, January). Sex offender sentencing in Washington State: Sex offender risk classification and recidivism. Document No. 06-01-1204. Olympia, WA: Washington State Institute for Public Policy.

Washington State Institute for Public Policy (2006b, February). Sex offender sentencing in Washington State: Predicting recidivism based on the LSI-R. Document No. 06-02-1201. Olympia, WA: Washington State Institute for Public Policy.

Washington State Institute for Public Policy (2008, June). Risk assessment instruments to predict recidivism of sex offenders: Practices in Washington State. Document No. 08-06-1101. Olympia, WA: Washington State Institute for Public Policy.

Washington State Institute for Public Policy (2010, January). Washington's Offender Accountability Act: Final report on recidivism outcomes. Document No. 10-01-1201. Olympia, WA: Washington State Institute for Public Policy.

West-Smith, M., Pogrebin, M. R., & Poole, E. D. (2000). Denial of parole: An inmate perspective. *Federal Probation, 64*(2), 3–10.

Wilkins, L. T., Gottfredson, D. M., Robinson, J. O., & Sadowsky, A. (1973). *Information selection and use in parole decision-making*. Hackensack, NJ: National Council on Crime and Delinquency.

Zagar, R. J., Busch, K. G., Grove, W. M., & Hughes, J. R. (2009). Can violent (re) offense be predicted? A review of the role of the clinician and use of actuarial tests in light of new data. *Psychological Reports, 104*, 247–277.

SECTION II

Law Enforcement and Public Safety

CHAPTER SIX

Crisis Intervention and Police Interactions with Individuals with Mental Illness

Elizabeth Neidhart

Encounters with persons with mental illness (PwMI) have always been a reality for law enforcement officers; a reality that has expanded exponentially in recent years with a significant increase in this population who are now living within the community (Bittner, 1967; Lamb, Weinberger, & DeCuir, 2002; Thompson, Reuland, & Souweine, 2003). As a function of their charge to be peacekeepers, to protect the safety and welfare of the populace at large, and *parens patriae* doctrine, their responsibility to assist and shield from harm those who for whatever reason are less than able, police have long sought for the best manner in which to manage situations which involve individuals experiencing mental health crises (Lamb et al., 2002; Teplin, 2000). Law enforcement personnel in essence are the gatekeepers, the frontline decision-makers who must make discretionary judgments as to whether the behavior exhibited by an individual with apparent mental illness primarily warrants routing them through the criminal justice system or the mental-health system (Lamb et al., 2002; Menzies, 1987; Teplin, 2000). It is estimated that between 7% and 10% of law enforcement contacts involve some aspect of mental illness (Deane, Steadman, Borum, Veysey, & Morrissey, 1999) and officers more and more find themselves playing this role of "street-corner psychiatrist," essentially not only having to assess criminal culpability but also to quickly evaluate an individual's mental health condition and to try to determine how and where those who are experiencing mental health crises will be best served (Borum, 2000; Cordner, 2000; Lamb & Weinberger, 2005; Lamb et al., 2002; Menzies, 1987).

Full Circle—from Institution to Society and Back

How society has approached the issue of individuals with mental illness has varied throughout history driven at least in part by our level of understanding and perception of the nature of mental disorders (Anderson, 1997). Earlier in the twentieth century, those suffering from mental illnesses were closeted away in formal state-run psychiatric institutions; however, beginning in the 1960s, attitudes about mental illness began to shift (Morrissey & Goldman, 2007). Advances in the development of psychotropic medications, and increasing concern over rising patient-care costs, institutional conditions, and civil rights issues, all served to foster a belief that people would be better served through community mental health clinics as opposed to formal psychiatric institutions (Mechanic & Rochefort, 1990; Morrissey & Goldman, 2007). As such, this period saw a move in society toward the deinstitutionalization of those with mental illness.

Changes in the legal code also were enacted in the years that followed that gave individuals greater control over their inclination toward receiving or not receiving psychiatric treatment (*O'Connor v. Donaldson*, 1975; Teplin, 1984). Furthermore, beginning in California in 1969 with the Lanterman-Petris-Short Act, states began to legislate more stringent commitment guidelines making involuntary civil commitment of the mentally ill much more difficult to impose barring a credible and imminent threat of self-harm or harm to others (Lamb & Weinberger, 2005; Lamb, Weinberger & Gross, 2004).

Recognizing the rights of those who were mentally ill to be a part of the community, empowering them to be more in charge of their lives, and attempting to reduce the stigma attached to mental illness, all seem to be positive moves on the part of an enlightened, progressive society. Numerous psychiatric institutions were closed or downsized, and funding that had originally been designated for institutional care was to be redirected into the community to provide outreach services that would help those with mental illness (Mechanic & Rochefort, 1990).

However, in most cases, funding for these services never materialized or did not meet the increased needs of the population (Matheson et al.,

2005). Cutbacks in funding for mental health treatment in the 1980s exacerbated the situation (Teplin, 1984). What actually resulted from all these changes was a splintered and confusing array of mental health care facilities that lacked cohesion and that failed to provide the service and treatment integration that was needed for those who were now residing in the community (Grob, 2005).

Assumptions were made concerning the shift from institutional care to community care despite scant empirical evidence, and that also failed to acknowledge the reality of much of the population who would be released (Grob, 1992). Grob suggests that the purported benefits of community clinic care were based on the assumptions that those who were to be released from institutional care would (1) have a home to go to; (2) have supportive family or guardians; (3) not be impeded in their rehabilitation by the organization of the household; and (4) not prove to be an undue burden on the family, when in actuality, the majority of those living in institutional care in 1960 had no families to go to, and as a result, many upon release became homeless. This failure to address the needs of those who were mentally ill, socially marginalized, and impoverished inevitably resulted in their further marginalization, victimization, and often an exacerbation of their mental illness (French, 1987). Mechanic and Rochefort (1990) suggest that there is growing consensus that deinstitutionalization may be seen as "one of the era's most stunning public policy failures," rather than the great progressive movement that it was originally intended to be (p. 302).

The ensuing reality became that there was an influx of mentally ill and often unstable individuals into a society that was ill prepared to effectively deal with their special needs (Schanche, 2002). Lack of mandatory monitoring meant that many individuals were not getting proper attention, treatment, or medication, often resulting in their experience of psychotic episodes and crisis situations (Mechanic & Rochefort, 1990). Unmedicated and unmonitored, surrounded by a public who often viewed them as dangerous and unstable, many who were experiencing severe mental health crises found themselves in recurrent encounters with law enforcement personnel (Lamb & Weinberger, 2005). The ramping up of the war against drugs along with a growing intolerance for public order violations in the 1980s and 1990s also brought many PwMI who were homeless and addicted into the purview of the police (Lurigio, Smith & Harris, 2008). Ultimately, many of these individuals who might have been much better served by treatment in mental health facilities ended up arrested and incarcerated, often on a repetitive basis (Lamb et al., 2004; Teplin, 2000).

Police Discretion and Incident Outcomes

Though an unintended effect of the changing mental health environment, the significant and disproportionate growth of incarcerated individuals with mental illness led some to characterize this as essentially amounting to the criminalization of the mentally ill (Abramson, 1972; Teplin, 1983, 1984, 2000). Whether or not the police excessively use arrest as the disposition of choice in their encounters with PwMI is an area of debate within the research community. Some studies indicate that in similar situations, persons who were exhibiting signs of mental illness had a higher probability of being arrested than those who did not, whereas several other studies did not find statistical evidence that would support the "criminalization hypothesis," finding conversely that officers seem to view mental illness as a mitigating factor in their dispositional decisions (Bittner, 1967; Bonovitz & Bonovitz, 1981; Engel & Silver, 2001; Novak & Engel, 2005; Teplin, 1984).

Situational Influences

This issue of discretionary decision-making is an inherent part of policing as officers are continually faced with interpreting and applying broad legal concepts to very specific situations incorporating an array of varying factors, only one of which is the aspect of mental illness (Walker & Katz, 2005). Walker and Katz (2005) suggest that police discretion in any interaction may be influenced by situational factors surrounding the incident; organizational factors encompassing departmental policy and the culture of the organization itself; as well as environmental factors such as the political culture of the area. Although law enforcement departmental policies will at times outline directives for officers as to how to respond in situations involving PwMI, research suggests that often there are no specific guidelines governing the appropriate management of PwMI, and without clear guiding principles, there is room for ambiguity as to when a behavior is to be considered criminal and when it is to be considered psychiatric (Cooper, McLearan, & Zapf, 2004; Ruiz & Miller, 2004).

Situational factors, such as the seriousness of the incident, the dynamics of the incident, and as to who is involved and where it takes place, all clearly play a large role as to what dispositions are available or are perceived as available to the responding officers (Patch & Arrigo, 1999; Teplin & Pruett, 1992). Morabito (2007) describes these factors influencing officers' decisions to arrest PwMI as "horizons of context"—scenic, temporal, and manipulative, and which encompass the characteristics of the community, the offender, the officer, and the incident (p. 1582). Sometimes the gravity of the incident clearly mandates an arrest regardless of the mental status of the offender; but in other situations, officers may opt to arrest, may attempt to try to resolve the situation at the scene, or alternatively, may seek hospitalization for the individual depending on the circumstances (Cooper et al., 2004; Teplin, 2000). For instance, Teplin and Pruett (1992) found that officers may opt to arrest a person with mental illness in circumstances where they perceive that the individual's problem behavior is likely to persist or exceeds what the public will continue to tolerate. Teplin and Pruett also suggest that arrest may occur when PwMI have co-occurring disorders, such as alcohol or other substance abuse, that would likely make it difficult to obtain mental health services for them, due to limitations and restrictions of the parameters of certain facilities (i.e., sites that may only treat individuals with mental illness or only those with substance abuse issues).

Individual Influences

Individual officer characteristics such as attitudes and attributions can also play a part in dispositional decisions. Despite working in an era governed by a community-policing philosophy, there are still some officers who adamantly believe that police responsibilities should not include having to respond to mental health emergencies (Borum, 2000). Even for those officers who accept this reality as being part of their job, personal views toward those with mental illness may also factor into discretional actions. Watson, Corrigan, and Ottati (2004b) found that although officers' preexisting knowledge of an individual's mental illness did not have a significant effect on their response to them as a suspect in a situation, it did, however, affect their perception of perceived credibility when it came to the mental health status of PwMI in the role of being a victim or witness. This issue of discounted credibility would seem to be a concern in light of the fact that that there is a substantial amount of criminal victimization of PwMI (Hiday, Swartz, Swanson, Borum, & Wagner, 1999).

Watson et al. (2004b) also found that officers who were angered and attributed responsibility for the situation to the subject were less likely to take action to help the subject. In a similar study, Watson, Corrigan, and Ottati (2004a) established that officers tended to perceive those with schizophrenia as being more dangerous but also less responsible and more deserving of assistance. Further complicating the issue is the fact that individuals with severe mental illness are often the ones who are the least likely to perceive themselves in need of psychiatric treatment and thus may be more resistant to a hospitalization disposition (Elbogen, Mustillo, Van Dorn, Swanson, & Swartz, 2007).

Mental Health Training Influences

Another factor affecting officers' discretionary decision-making in these situations is a dearth of knowledge regarding mental illness and its associated behaviors, and, despite the frequency of encounters between law enforcement and PwMI, many officers receive little, if any, specialized training in this area beyond what may be covered in their police academy education (Vermette, Pinals, & Appelbaum, 2005). However, research also indicates that officers do view their interactions with individuals undergoing mental health crises as representing a fairly significant problem (Borum, Deane, Steadman, & Morrissey, 1998). Concern over the limited amount of training that officers receive in mental health issues was noted in several studies, with officers indicating that they perceived education on the topic of mental illness to be an important matter for their job (Bittner, 1967; Borum, 2000; Cooper et al., 2004; Handberg & Pilchick, 1980; Vermette et al., 2005).

Although officers may be legally empowered to coercively bring offenders with apparent mental illness to the hospital, meeting the stringent involuntary hospitalization criteria once there can be difficult; and police officers are ever present to the reality that mental health providers may disagree with their assessment of the individual, potentially refusing to provide treatment, wasting officers' time, and leaving them to find another way to effectively deal with the situation (Bittner, 1967; Green, 1997; Handberg & Pilchick, 1980; Steadman et al., 2001). Bittner (1967), in his formative study of law enforcement discretion in dealing with emergency mental illness situations, noted that many officers were often reluctant to bring these individuals to mental health facilities preferring to engage in what he referred to as "psychiatric first-aid" (p. 288). Police officers acknowledged that recognizing mental illness was not their area of expertise and as such were hesitant, barring extreme situations, to essentially adjudge that individuals were mentally ill (Bittner, 1967).

Officers' fundamental lack of training in the recognition and understanding of mental illness and any specialized response that such encounters might require can be problematic from a safety standpoint as well (Lamb et al., 2002; Teplin, 2000). As Teplin (2000) states, "Many mental disorders are associated with a number of disconcerting symptoms. Although some symptoms, such as verbal abuse, belligerence, and disrespect, are not themselves against the law, such behaviors may provoke an officer to respond more punitively" (p. 12). Approaching individuals undergoing extreme mental disturbance from a traditional police perspective can at times exacerbate the situation, escalating violence levels and creating environments rife with the potential for injury to both officer and civilian (Teplin, 2000).

Mental Health System Structural Influences

The presence of reliable and structured support avenues within the mental health system that are able to respond in an effective manner also plays a part in officer discretion (Bittner, 1967). Several studies have indicated that an additional consideration that may have influenced officers' dispositional decisions in the past is the knowledge that mental health providers would at times quickly release the individual with mental illness back into the community, a "revolving-door scenario," creating frustration for the officers and the potential for a probable repeat of the situation (Bittner, 1967; Olivero, 1990; Rogers, 1990). Furthermore, officers who did bring individuals to mental health facilities often found themselves spending inordinate amounts of time waiting for processing in hospital emergency rooms, which was perceived as an ineffective use of their time (Bittner, 1967). Even in cases where mobile mental health crisis care was available, the lengthy time spent waiting for these limited services to respond to the situation was perceived as unproductive (Steadman et al., 2001).

Consequently, lacking specialized expertise to defuse the situation, with a dearth of mental health services available, stringent commitment requirements, and confronted with often hostile and violent individuals, arrest could often appear to be the most viable and appealing option for officers (Teplin, 2000). Choosing to process these individuals through the criminal justice system rather than the mental health system resulted in seemingly efficient processing. Teplin (2000) notes that, "the criminal justice system may have become the default option for dealing with individuals who cannot or will not be treated by the mental health system" (p. 12). An arrest allowed officers to return to the streets quickly with the knowledge that mental health evaluation and care would be somewhat provided by services at the jail, and the case could be closed from the officer's standpoint (Matthews, 1970; Teplin, 1984).

The Search for Alternatives

Though there is some difference of opinion as to whether those with mental illness are truly disproportionately arrested, there does seems to be a mounting consensus, in the research community and both the law enforcement and mental health systems, that the substantial number of PwMI in the jail and prison population is a growing and urgent problem (Laberge & Morin, 1996; Lamb et al., 2004; Perez, Leifman, & Estrada, 2003; Thompson et al., 2003). The Bureau of Justice Statistics reports that in mid-2005, over half of the jail and prison inmate population have some form of mental health problem (James & Glazer, 2006). This translates to approximately 705,600 of inmates in state prisons, 70,200 in federal prisons, and 479,900 in local jails—or 56% of state prisoners, 45% of federal prisoners, and 64% of jail inmates (James & Glazer, 2006).

In an effort to turn this tide and to find a more humanitarian, treatment-oriented, and cost-effective way of dealing with interactions between those with mental health problems and law enforcement, many communities have begun to look for alternative solutions. These exist in the form of diversion programs at varying junctures of the criminal justice process and can involve a variety of innovative methods linking officer training and collaborative efforts between law enforcement, mental health providers, parole and probation officers, and the courts (Borum, 2000; Deane et al., 1999; Hartford, Carey, & Mendonca, 2006; Olivero, 1990; Perez et al., 2003; Reuland, 2004; Steadman, Morris, & Dennis, 1995).

Pre-arrest diversion programs come in an array of types with police departments that do have a specialized response falling into three types of categories: *police-based specialized police response*, which involves officers who are specifically trained to respond to calls involving issues of mental health; *police-based specialized mental health response*, which involves mental health workers who are hired by the police as non-sworn civilian officers to respond to those calls involving issues of mental health; and *mental-health-based specialized mental health response*, which involves implementing mobile mental health crisis teams who respond to police calls for assistance in dealing with individuals with mental health issues (Deane et al., 1999). Post-arrest diversion programs exist in some communities in the form of specialized Mental Health Courts, which oversee treatment plans and supervise individuals with mental health issues who have been arrested but who agree to participate voluntarily, and who must stringently adhere to court-mandated conditions in order to avoid incarceration (Criminal Justice/Mental Health Consensus Project, 2003). Other communities utilize diversion clinicians from the mental health system who do a post-booking screening of arraignment lists looking for known clients with mental health issues who then may intercede on their behalf with the courts in an attempt to get treatment; others use trained correctional officers who assess each individual for mental health issues before they are to appear in court (Lattimore, Broner, Sherman, Frisman, & Shafer, 2003). Several locales use a multimodal approach with diversion programs available at both the pre-arrest and post-arrest junctures that can serve to accommodate PwMI in differing situations (Neidhart, 2008; Sirotich, 2009).

Evolution of the Crisis Intervention Team (CIT)

Research suggests that the most well-known and most prevalent type of diversion program currently found in the United States is a pre-arrest, police-based specialized police response program called the Crisis Intervention Team (CIT) (Compton, Bahora, Watson & Oliva, 2008; Watson, 2010). The CIT program was first developed in Memphis in 1988 after a public outcry following the fatal shooting of a young man with a history of mental illness in 1987 by Memphis police officers, and was a combined endeavor between law enforcement and the mental health community largely based on suggestions emanating from the Memphis chapter of the National Alliance on Mental Illness (Memphis Police CIT Program, n.d.; Vickers, 2000). The CIT program involves the use of specially trained police officers who are dispatched to situations which are identified as incidents involving issues of mental illness. The goals of the Memphis CIT were to quickly respond to and manage crisis situations involving those with mental illness, to minimize or eliminate injury to officers and civilians, and to find appropriate services that would care for and treat the needs of the individual and hopefully result in reduced recidivism (Memphis Police CIT Program, n.d.; Vickers, 2000).

The "Memphis Model," as it has come to be known, is a collaborative effort on the part of the police, mental health providers, and the community, with its core being a cadre of patrol officers who volunteer for 40 hours of training in recognizing the signs and stages of mental illness, how to interact effectively and safely with those with mental health issues, and learning the special skills of "active listening" and the vocal and physical movements that can help defuse an intense situation (Memphis Police CIT Program, n.d.; Reuland & Cheney, 2005). Although participation is voluntary, applicants are screened and selected based on their demonstrated skills in such areas as communications and problem solving. In addition, CIT officers in Memphis receive a small financial stipend. These specially trained officers perform standard patrol functions but are also dispatched to situations that appear to be incidents involving issues of mental illness (CIT, n.d.; Memphis Police CIT Program, n.d.).

As part of the Memphis CIT program, police dispatchers were also trained to better identify and recognize situations involving potential mental health issues, thus enabling them to request a response from the appropriately trained police personnel (Bower & Pettit, 2001). Additionally, a single-point drop-off center was established where all individuals with mental health issues could be brought by officers, and which had a no-refusal policy and an expedited processing system that would allow officers to return to duty as quickly as possible, ideally within 15–20 minutes (CIT, n.d.). This center served to then evaluate the individuals in crisis and provided services or linkage to services to assist them (Vickers, 2000).

CIT Program Challenges

Reuland and Cheney (2005) note that certain barriers exist in implementing and maintaining police-based specialized response programs such as CIT. They found that funding, staff attitudes, staffing shortages, and sharing information between agencies are all significant issues faced by these programs. Additionally, they note the challenges presented by the rapid changes in mental health treatments, which require ongoing training for officers, the logistics of program management, fewer community resources due to funding cuts, and the need to maintain staff interest in the program. Underlying program effectiveness is also impacted by structural, political, and human resources considerations (Schwarzfeld, Reuland, & Plotkin, 2007). CIT program success is heavily dependent on the level of adaptive change that occurs within these frameworks, both internal and external to the law enforcement organization.

Structural Factors—Internal and External

Structural organization plays a key role in CIT program effectiveness. Success of CIT programs depends not only on considerations of law enforcement organizational structure, but also on the structural makeup of the mental health organizations with which they partner. Internally, law enforcement organizations are structured in a top-down (vertical) hierarchy, with power theoretically concentrated with the chief at the apex and line officers at the bottom tier (Roberg, Novak, & Cordner, 2005). However, the fundamental nature of their jobs provides officers with a great deal of discretionary power in how they resolve situations (Bittner, 1967). The end result is that, regardless of program edicts from higher up in the police organization, individual officer decisions and attitudes will inevitably impact CIT program success.

In theory, some of the past obstacles that may have kept officers from opting for hospitalization (i.e., long ER waits, revolving door processing, etc.) should no longer be an issue in light of the CIT's collaborative partnership with mental health providers. However, old habits die hard, and training aside, officers may be reluctant to give up their traditional method of handling these situations. Handberg and Pilchick (1980) observe that patterns of police behavior that have developed in response to certain problems are often difficult to change. This is an adaptive change that requires a shift in both officer mind-set and behavior for program effectiveness. The structural placement of CIT patrol officers thus places them in a critical position to influence program effectiveness.

Externally, though the CIT program is located in the law enforcement system, it is also heavily reliant on lateral networking with the mental health system. Borum, Deane, Steadman and Morrissey (1998) suggest that the mental health and social service infrastructure that exists will greatly affect "the conceptualization of problem-solving approaches to mental disturbance calls" (p. 403). Consequently, structure of the organizations with which CIT partners will inevitably impact program effectiveness. It is essential that the necessary services to assist and treat those with mental health issues are also in place. Fragmentation of services can be problematic; as Lurigio and Swartz (2000) note there is a critical need for mental health services for offenders with comorbid disorders of substance addiction.

One key factor in the success of CIT programs appears to be officer access to a 24-hour-a-day, one-stop crisis center, with a no-refusal policy and efficient processing where those individuals that appear to be undergoing mental health crises can be brought (Borum et al., 1998; Steadman et al., 2001). Deane et al. (1999) found that officers' perceptions of program effectiveness were significantly impacted by whether or not they had access to such a drop-off facility. Steadman et al. (2001) suggest that such an arrangement addresses the past difficulties officers perceived about utilizing mental health services as a dispositional alternative to incarceration. For rural communities this can present a significant challenge, as the establishment of a central receiving facility in less-populated areas may not be feasible (Compton et al., 2010).

Steadman et al. (2001) also found that two additional important considerations are the establishment of legal foundations so that the dedicated crisis response site can handle those individuals who may also have pending criminal charges, as well as the provision of effectual linkage to follow-up community services subsequent to hospitalization. This was particularly true in the cases where individuals had co-occurring disorders and also having nontraditional case workers was found to be valuable (Draine & Solomon, 1999; Steadman et al., 1999).

Political Factors

The effectiveness of a CIT program is also significantly affected by political constraints as it exists in a political arena internally, within the law enforcement organization itself, and also externally, within a broader "public policy ecosystem" (Bolman & Deal, 2003, p. 231). It is no doubt externally politically expedient for a community to have a CIT program from a public policy perspective; having such a program signifies to the community at large that there is concern over and commitment to better addressing the needs of individuals with mental illness. However, the internal political situation within law enforcement is also an important factor in the success of the CIT program; a commitment to the program at the higher levels is essential not just in terms of "endorsing the program and authorizing staff training," but "through visible and practical changes in how the agency partners with the community and realigns internal processes" (Schwarzfeld et al., 2007, p. 9). The success of the program is thought to depend on fidelity to all aspects of the overall CIT model; officer training alone will not suffice without the concomitant changes internally and externally that the CIT program requires (Munetz, Morrison, Krake, Young, & Woody, 2006). For example, if dispatch personnel are not adequately trained in identifying calls with a mental illness component and fully understand their department's policies on these calls, then the effectiveness of the CIT program is somewhat compromised regardless of officer training, as the trained officer may never be sent to the incident (Compton et al., 2010). Without such a comprehensive and integrated approach, the program risks being merely window dressing, a CIT program in name only.

Despite the fact that law enforcement agencies are hierarchical, as noted, those on the lower echelons wield a great deal of discretionary power. Their structural positioning also has political repercussions for CIT program success. Bolman and Deal (2003) observe that successful organizational change first requires "mapping of the political terrain" to appreciate how the status quo functions (p. 207). If the status quo for officers has been to arrest PwMI, then CIT program success is going to depend on shifting that perspective within the whole department, not just for those officers who are CIT-trained. Although CIT officers may support the goals of the program, the reality is that non-CIT officers may at times also respond to incidents involving mental health issues. From a political standpoint, their willingness to call in CIT officers will depend on their adaptive belief in the value and goals of the CIT program and of the concept of jail diversion as a whole. Reuland (2004) observes that some officers believe that jail diversion is not consistent with traditional policing principles. The degree of adaptation and support given by these officers will notably have an impact on CIT program success.

This belief in and support of the program goals also has external political implications, with several studies concurring that the nature and quality of the community partnerships and alliances formed between law enforcement and the mental health providers play an integral part of the road to success for a CIT program (Borum et al., 1998; Munetz et al., 2006; Reuland & Cheney, 2005; Steadman, Deane, Borum, & Morrissey, 2000). How effectively trained the CIT police officers are becomes a moot point without a true collaborative partnership with those in the mental health community. This requires overcoming the idea of historically divergent views and abandoning preconceived attitudes of the other. Draine and Solomon (1999) note that police officers may be concerned that the diversion process allows individuals to dodge punishment, while those in the mental health community may perceive the same process positively as helping individuals get into treatment. Draine and Solomon suggest that these incompatible views can be resolved by focusing on the process as avoiding imprisonment, but not necessarily evading accountability and criminal charges.

Steadman et al. (2001) suggest that mutual respect and understanding of differences and commonalties is a key principle of success, finding that mental health providers often hold a stereotypic view of the police or have unrealistic expectations of them. Altering this mind-set is once again an adaptive change that training alone cannot achieve. Reuland (2004) suggests the importance of achieving mutual understanding of the "limitations and abilities," and "roles and responsibilities" of each partner (p. 30). Teller, Munetz, Gil, and Ritter (2006) posit that the organizations may be seeking complementary yet different outcomes; the police may be primarily focused on improving safety and reducing injury to officers and civilians, whereas mental health providers may be more interested in reducing inappropriate incarceration of those with mental illness. Steadman (1992) suggests that a key component to effective interactions may be the use of "boundary spanners," positions that can bridge the criminal justice and mental health systems. Support for this idea is also found in other more recent studies and is one of the recommendations of the Criminal Justice/Mental Health Consensus Project (2003), a national effort to improve interactions between the criminal justice system and individuals with mental illness (Hartford et al., 2006; Thompson et al., 2003). Overcoming political obstacles, mutual distrust, and establishing common ground are all essential for CIT program success.

Furthermore, Reuland and Cheney (2005) find that political issues such as funding and sharing information between agencies are both significant issues faced by CIT programs. Reuland and Cheney note the logistical difficulties posed by cross-jurisdictional programs. For example, since it is essential for certain mental health services to be in place for CIT success, cutbacks in federal funding of these services will have an understandable impact on CIT program effectiveness.

Wolff (1998) observes that a lack of clear boundaries and guidelines on both sides can make effective cross-system coordination problematic. Similarly, Wolff finds that there is a scarcity of information exchange between the organizations, which creates "information bottlenecks" (p. 141). Additionally, privacy laws may limit accessibility to some information. For example, the police may be unable to access an individual's mental health background because of confidentiality laws such as the Health Insurance Portability and Accountability Act (HIPAA) (Reuland & Cheney, 2005). This lack of information can make the officer's on-site assessment more difficult and in turn have an impact on the effectiveness of the CIT program.

Human Resource Factors

There are human resources considerations that impact CIT program success as well. Training alone is likely not the only factor in an improved outcome, in that the officer's interest, attitudes, and skills are all important considerations (Hails & Borum, 2003). Hails and Borum (2003) observe that research and experience have established that not all officers are equally skilled in responding to mental health emergencies. The CIT programs "identify officers with the greatest interest, most amenable attitudes, and best interpersonal skills, then provides them with intensive training and deploys them specifically as a first-response to these specialized calls" (Hails & Borum, 2003, p. 59). Officer interest in the CIT program is evidently a factor in program success, and Reuland (2004) suggests that voluntary participation in CIT is a key principle. A CIT program that attempts to direct or mandate participation on a nonvoluntary basis may be in some sense, setting itself up for failure. Finding the right people, who not only are eager but who also exhibit the necessary skills and temperament, is an important factor for CIT program success. Yet, mental health training for law enforcement officers is not a panacea, and even with training, not all officers will be equally skilled or effective in dealing with individuals with mental illness (Borum, 2000; Dupont & Cochran, 2000; Hails & Borum, 2003).

Evaluating CIT Program Effectiveness

The perceived success of the Memphis CIT program, now more than 20 years after its inception, has been exceptional, and it is now considered the premier CIT program in the country (Lurigio et al., 2008; Reuland, 2004). As a result, CIT programs and partnerships with the mental health system are evolving and expanding exponentially, nationally and internationally, with an estimated 300-plus programs currently reported within communities in the United States and with several states implementing the CIT program on a statewide basis (Compton et al., 2008; Morrissey, Fagan, & Cocozza, 2009; Munetz et al., 2006).

Positive Program Outcomes

Many of the current CIT programs are essentially still in their infancy, and empirical evidence relating to their efficacy is in many cases just beginning to materialize. Initial studies from programs such as those in Memphis, Albuquerque, Salt Lake City, and others suggest that implementation of the CIT programs has resulted in encouraging findings (Bower & Pettit, 2001; Memphis Police CIT Program, n.d.; Reuland & Cheney, 2005; Salt Lake City Police Department CIT History, n.d.; Teller et al., 2006; Vickers, 2000). Reuland and Cheney (2005), in research conducted for the Police Executive Research Forum, compiled data from 29 law enforcement agencies with police-based specialized response programs for comparison purposes. Many of the findings suggest positive outcomes but are also relatively anecdotal, reflecting somewhat intangible concepts such as improved relationships and increased respect between law enforcement, mental health providers, mental health consumers and their families, the community at large, and the media, as well as an increase in officers' confidence in dealing with individuals with mental illness. They found that the statistical data available to date, though limited, suggest a significant reduction in injuries to both officers and civilians involved in "mental disturbance" calls; reductions in arrests of mentally ill individuals, in SWAT team calls, and in officer time spent on mental health calls; and a reduction in criminal recidivism.

Specifically, initial findings from the Memphis CIT program indicated a dramatic decrease in injuries in incidents involving PwMI, both to officers (50%) and civilians, and a substantial reduction in callouts of their hostage negotiation teams and their TACT (Memphis equivalent of SWAT) team for these situations (Dupont & Cochran, 2000; Vickers, 2000). It is possible that other factors may be contributing to these decreases (e.g. increased use of less lethal weapons), and as such, it is not possible to attribute the decrease purely to the implementation of CIT (Personal communication, S. Cochran, April 2007). However, the timing and degree of the decrease, in addition to the fact that other cities have reported similar findings after implementing CIT programs, adds credence to the role that CIT plays in reducing the need for these costly police responses (Dupont & Cochran, 2000). Furthermore, the number of referrals to the emergency psychiatric service center by law enforcement doubled in the four years following Memphis' implementation of CIT (Dupont & Cochran, 2000).

In addition, although more anecdotal than empirical, CIT officers in Memphis report feeling well prepared as a result of their specialized training in responding to mental health emergencies, better prepared than their non-CIT counterparts acknowledge feeling (Borum et al., 1998). Interestingly, the majority of officers in Memphis, both CIT and non-CIT, also rated their program as highly effective in minimizing the time spent on mental health calls, meeting the needs of individuals with mental illness, keeping them out of jail, and preserving the safety of the community (Borum et al., 1998). Memphis's ability to have a one-stop mental health facility that is always available and that accepts all cases is most likely the biggest factor in this positive response (Borum et al., 1998).

Results from a study of the Salt Lake City CIT program indicate a reduction in criminal recidivism by individuals with mental illness, reductions in officer injuries, and improved relationships between law enforcement and mental health providers since its inception (Salt Lake City Police Department CIT History, n.d.). This study also found that less than 1% of those individuals who were taken to the hospital were deemed to actually not need hospital care, suggesting that their CIT officers seem to be effective at evaluating individuals with mental illness and making appropriate dispositional decisions. Strauss et al. (2005), in their study of the Louisville CIT program, found that, as was the case in Salt Lake City, the CIT-trained officers appear to be effective in identifying those who are in need of mental health treatment and are making appropriate dispositional decisions in referring them for evaluation and treatment in a hospital environment.

The city of Albuquerque noted a decrease in officer shootings in incidents involving mental illness despite a growing urban population since the inception of their CIT program (Bower & Pettit, 2001). As well, similar to Memphis, their data indicate a 58% decrease in special weapons and tactics (SWAT) callouts for such incidents (Bower & Pettit, 2001). Albuquerque also reported a reduction in arrests of the mentally ill and a concurrent increase in the number of these individuals that were taken to mental health facilities for professional care (Bower & Pettit, 2001).

The CIT program in Akron, Ohio, began in May 2000 and since its inception, there has been an increase in the number of police calls involving mental illness as well as an increase in the number of individuals brought to mental health facilities by CIT officers (Teller et al., 2006). Additionally, the number of individuals who have gone to the hospital on a voluntary basis has also increased, which would seem to suggest that the communication skills that CIT officers learn may be helpful in persuading those with mental illness of the need for them to obtain treatment (Teller et al., 2006).

Preliminary data from the CIT program in Miami and Miami Beach also show a significant decrease in the number of individuals with mental illness who were arrested as well as a reduction in both use of force and injuries related to law enforcement encounters with these individuals (Perez et al., 2003).

This limited use of force by CIT officers is also evident in the results of a recent study in Las Vegas (Skeem & Bibeau, 2008). Skeem and Bibeau (2008) found that the majority of cases handled by CIT officers were related to suicide crises and, in most cases, involved limited violence potential; however, even in cases where the prospective for violence was heightened, CIT officers used force in only 15% of these cases. Skeem and Bibeau also note that CIT officers in the Las Vegas study resolved the majority of incidents (74%) through the disposition of hospitalization and arrested in only 4% of the cases. They note that this arrest rate of individuals with mental illness is comparable to the findings in other CIT programs (Dupont & Cochran, 2000; Steadman et al., 2000; Teller et al., 2006) and lower than the 14% rate that Teplin (2000) suggests in her study of traditional police encounters with PwMI.

In addition to the improved confidence and comfort level that CIT officers appear to experience from their specialized training (Borum et al., 1998), Compton, Esterberg, McGee, Kotwicki, and Oliva (2006) find that officers experience shifts in knowledge and attitudes toward those with schizophrenia after CIT training. Compton et al. note that subsequent to their CIT training, officers report an enhanced understanding of schizophrenia, with improved attitudes regarding the aggressiveness of these individuals and greater support for obtaining treatment for them. Considering the earlier findings of Watson et al. (2004a) regarding officers' attitudes toward those with schizophrenia, these current results suggest that the specialized training CIT offices receive is helpful in reducing stigmatizing perceptions and as such may be helpful in improving law enforcement encounters with schizophrenic individuals.

Research results of a study of the Chicago CIT program suggest that CIT-trained officers in this locale referred more individuals to mental health services than non-CIT officers (Watson, 2010). Overall, Watson (2010) did not find a significant difference in terms of use of force applied in interactions with PwMI between CIT and non-CIT officers, but did find a reduced use of force in districts where there were high numbers of CIT-trained sergeants. Watson posits that this may be indicative that officers who work in these areas, whether they were CIT-trained or not, may get greater support from their superiors for responding to PwMI in a certain manner, in essence what could be seen as a positive diffusion of CIT's de-escalation techniques.

CIT and Comparative Pre-Booking Diversion Programs

Alternative programs have been developed in other cities that aim for the same goals of jail diversion and mental health assistance as the CIT program but through a different means. In terms of response capability, a comparative analysis of the three types of programs suggests that although the latter two programs (non-sworn community service officers and mobile-crisis teams) were very effective in handling the crisis situations at the scene, there were staffing and time constraints (Steadman et al., 2000). Steadman et al. (2000) find that the limited number of civilian officers can mean sometimes a low availability of qualified personnel and consequently a limited response capability, especially on all shifts at all times. They find a similar situation occurs with mobile-crisis units, where the results suggest that the response time for these units to arrive at the scene can be frustrating for officers and, as a consequence, officers may be less inclined to utilize them. On the other hand, the CIT program and its inherent structure allowed officers to efficiently respond and process these cases (Steadman et al., 2000).

In terms of dispositional outcome, Steadman et al. (2000) in their study found that arrest rates across all three types of programs were relatively low; however, the CIT program had the lowest arrest rate, with only 2%

of the incidents resulting in arrest. Steadman et al. found that in all three programs, more than half of the outcomes resulted in some sort of treatment option with the CIT program using this option 75% of the time. These results suggest that all three programs seem to be achieving the goal of jail diversion; however, the downtime for officers in the non-CIT programs could be seen as problematic in that, if it is too extended, it may potentially affect which dispositional outcome officers choose based on previous research findings (Bittner, 1967).

In regards to police perceptions of these three types of programs, fewer officers from the non-CIT programs reported feeling confident and well prepared to interact with people with mental illness (Borum et al., 1998). Borum et al. (1998) find that the officers from the site with a CIT program perceived their program as highly effective in meeting its goals overall and viewed the mental health system as helpful. Even Non-CIT officers from this site evaluated the program similarly, although their perceptions of the mental health system were slightly less positive. Officers from the other sites perceived their programs as effective at achieving some of its goals but differed significantly from the CIT officers in their evaluation of whether the program helps to minimize the time officers must spend on these calls. They also tended to perceive the mental health system as being less helpful. As Borum et al. (1998) note, the particular CIT program in this study (Memphis) has a one-stop drop-off psychiatric center with a no-refusal policy that officers can utilize 24/7. This factor clearly affects the amount of downtime officers must spend on each incident, which ultimately affects their attitudes and potentially their dispositional choices. Other research supports that this type of specific response site is a key factor in program success (Reuland & Cheney, 2005; Steadman et al., 2001).

Cautions and Criticisms of CIT Research

The CIT program clearly has an abundance of enthusiastic supporters as is evidenced by its rapid development and expansion across the nation; but what is less evident, some researchers point out, is any hard and fast evidence from rigorous and generalizable studies that would genuinely substantiate that the program is truly a worthwhile investment for a community from an outcome or a financial perspective (Compton et al., 2008; Geller, 2008; Morrissey et al., 2009). Critical reviews of the current research on CIT programs across the United States conclude that most studies to date have been beleaguered with methodological constraints such as small sample sizes, lack of control groups, lack of multivariate analyses, and limited generalizability, compounded by the often-different CIT program goals and makeup of the law enforcement and mental health systems found in different communities (Compton et al., 2008; Geller, 2008; Sirotich, 2009; Watson, 2010). Watson (2010) points out that at least some of these constraints are a factor of not being able to control aspects of research in this area, such as the voluntary nature of CIT training, the way officers are dispatched, and the way police data on PwMI are or are not recorded. But the fact remains that at present, at least from an empirical standpoint in light of the shortcomings and limitations of the current research, there is little in the way of solid evidence that would validate an assertion that the CIT program is or is not an effective program, or is the best choice of diversion program for a community, or that would warrant a community rushing to jump on the CIT bandwagon, however altruistic the motivation.

Sellers, Sullivan, Veysey, and Shane (2005) urge the importance of assessing the needs of police and mental health agencies specific to each community before incorporating any type of specialized response model. Sellers et al. replicated the methodology of the earlier three-program study by Steadman et al. (2000), but incorporated a fourth site with no specialized response program or training but with a law enforcement emphasis toward treatment rather than arrest for individuals with mental illness. They obtained similar and sometimes better results when compared to the specialized response programs. They posit that similar results may be obtained by having an implicit understanding between the law enforcement and mental health systems and that a specialized response program and structure may just not be possible or necessary in every locale.

Similarly, in terms of officer training, Fyfe (2000) maintains that officers should be taught techniques and strategies for interacting with individuals with mental illness; however, he does not necessarily advocate having a specialized response team for these situations. Fyfe suggests that all officers can be taught the necessary skills in a relatively short period of time and should be held accountable for following these guidelines, but he maintains that as is the case with medicine, "no specialty should be created unless its members can perform their task significantly better than can generalists" (p. 347).

Problematic Benchmarks for Program Evaluation

Training

In terms of judging the efficacy of CIT officer training, Geller (2008) posits that since CIT officers self-select for the program, any differences found in post-training incident handling or officer attitudes might well be attributed to the different core-type of officer involved rather than the direct result of CIT training, a self-select bias that has the potential to affect study results. He also notes that as different localities may have very different core relationships between law enforcement personnel and mental health providers, differing state or municipal legal policies, and differing availability of hospital and community services, etc., that it may be the absence or presence of certain of these factors that have a significant impact on program outcomes regardless of officer training.

Disposition—Arrest or Hospitalization

One of the goals of CIT has been as a diversion program to keep PwMI from being arrested; therefore, one area that has often been looked at for evaluation is the arrest and hospitalization rates of PwMI by CIT-trained officers versus non-CIT-trained officers. However, using this to assess efficacy fails to account for the fact that many officers, CIT or non-CIT, are responding to calls involving PwMI that may involve suicidal ideations or other types of crisis situations where arrest is not a potential outcome of the situation, as no criminal behavior has occurred; therefore, diversion is also not occurring. An exploratory study in Seattle looked at the element of probable cause in police interactions with PwMI and found that approximately 25% of the total hospitalization outcomes could be considered as actually constituting diversion, incidents where some criminal charge could potentially have been levied (Neidhart, 2008). CIT- and non-CT-trained officers were found to be about equal in the percentage of these cases. Assessing all hospitalization outcomes equally becomes problematic from an evaluation standpoint, as not all hospitalizations are diversions (Compton et al., 2008; Neidhart, 2008).

Likewise, is comparing CIT and non-CIT arrest rates a good indicator of program efficacy? The numbers themselves do not necessarily tell the whole story. In terms of actual arrest rates, some research has indicated lower CIT arrest rates, but study results from Akron, Seattle, and Chicago did not find that CIT officers arrested less often (Neidhart, 2008; Teller et al., 2006; Watson et al., 2010). But what does that mean? Is there potentially some other factor also influencing incident outcome? Are CIT officers because of their mental health training possibly being dispatched to the more challenging cases where there is perhaps less room for discretion and thus diversion? In these particular locales where CIT arrest rates were not lower than non-CIT, is the coexistence of a post-arrest diversion program in the form of Mental Health Court in these communities possibly influencing dispositional outcome results? In other words, are officers in these jurisdictions possibly opting to arrest some PwMI instead of hospitalizing them, because they believe they will be more likely or better able to obtain mental health services through another diversion route, such as when it is mandated by a court? Are those being arrested more likely to be repeat offenders? Research needs to delve deeper into these questions if we are to understand what is transpiring and why.

Differing Community Characteristics

Another issue that is raised is how to adequately evaluate and/or compare CIT programs when not all communities have stayed true to the "Memphis Model" in their program implementation (Compton et al., 2008). Some CIT programs provide officer stipends, some do not, some programs emphasize dispatcher training, some do not; some have a formalized arrangement for a one-stop drop-off facility with a no-refusal policy, other communities may not or may just have a non-formalized memorandum of understanding in place with the hospitals and mental health providers. Although there is clearly a perception of the CIT program as effective, and the results to date are certainly promising, it is still not at all apparent whether there is one aspect that is the most crucial or essential, or whether efficacy is truly dependent on an interplay between all or several components.

CIT and the Road Ahead

Interacting with PwMI is, and will continue to be, an ongoing reality for law enforcement officers, whether or not they perceive it as a justifiable part of their job (Miller, 2006). As such, continuing to find ways to enhance their response to these individuals, in a manner that recognizes the special circumstances of the situations, acknowledges the need for alternative approaches, and maintains the safety of all involved parties, is of paramount concern. The development of jail diversion programs such as CIT and others has been a promising step forward in this quest. Although the CIT concept is being widely implemented, and initial evaluative studies do seem to suggest that the program yields at least some positive results, as of yet concrete empirical evidence of its efficacy remains limited. As Hartford et al. (2006) note, thus far there is no clarity in the literature on pre-arrest jail diversion programs as to best practices, optimal staffing, funding and virtually no generalizable data to guide decision-making processes on "policy, planning, or training" (p. 850).

Conducting methodologically sound research in criminal justice in a real-world environment has its challenges, and there are numerous data limitations to overcome. However, the reality is that we live in a society that increasingly demands evidence-based practices, especially when it comes to allocating the diminishing funding available for any programs in today's economy. The popularity of a program or a perception of success should not be enough; it needs to be backed by systematic evidence of its effectiveness. In that light, there seems to be a consensus that there is a critical need for much more formal, rigorous, and generalizable research on the CIT program and other jail diversion programs in order to truly substantiate which model components are essential, identify program strengths and weaknesses to allow for improvement, develop meaningful assessment standards, understand how other community factors may influence its effectiveness, and assess its impact on PwMI, those it was designed to help (Compton et al., 2008; Morrissey et al., 2009; Watson et al., 2010). If we have learned anything from the failure of deinstitutionalization, it should be important for us to take the time to validate the assumptions we are making; to consider all the factors, influences, interactions, and variables; and to recognize that the answer may not come in a one-size fits all category for every community.

Finally, it is important to remember that independently, neither the mental health system nor the law enforcement system can sufficiently meet the needs of those suffering from mental illness; it is not merely about keeping those individuals out of jail that matters, but about getting PwMI the support they need. A true collaborative effort between the criminal justice and mental health systems is needed, one that can address the issue of public safety while also considering the special circumstances of those coping with mental illness. But no amount of law enforcement training will suffice if the necessary concomitant mental health structures and support personnel are not available to respond. In essence, much of the effectiveness of a cross-boundary program like CIT comes down to dollars and cents, and to the question of how high a priority addressing the issue of PwMI truly is to our society.

References

Abramson, M. F. (1972). The criminalization of mentally disordered behavior: Possible side-effects of a new mental health law. *Hospital and Community Psychiatry, 23*, 101–105.

Anderson, M. (1997). Mental illness and criminal behaviour: a literature review. *Journal of Psychiatric and Mental Health Nursing, 4*, 243–250.

Bittner, E. (1967). Police discretion in emergency apprehension of mentally ill persons. *Social Problems, 14*, 278–292.

Bolman, L. G., & Deal, T. E. (2003). *Reframing organizations: Artistry, choice, and leadership* (3rd ed.). San Francisco, CA: Jossey-Bass.

Bonovitz, J. C., & Bonovitz, J. S. (1981). Diversion of the mentally ill into the criminal justice system: The police intervention perspective. *American Journal of Psychiatry, 138*, 973–976.

Borum, R. (2000). Improving high risk encounters between people with mental illness and the police. *Journal of the American Academy of Psychiatry and the Law, 28*, 332–337.

Borum, R., Deane, M., Steadman, H. J., & Morrissey, J. (1998). Police perspectives on responding to mentally ill people in crisis: Perceptions of program effectiveness. *Behavioral Sciences and the Law, 16*, 393–405.

Bower, D. J., & Pettit, G. (2001). The Albuquerque police department's crisis intervention team: A report card. *FBI Law Enforcement Bulletin*. Retrieved March 3, 2007, from http://www.au.af.mil/au/awc/awcgate/fbi/crisis_interven.pdf.

Compton, M. T., Bahora, M., Watson, A. C., & Oliva, J. R. (2008). A comprehensive review of extant research on Crisis Intervention Team (CIT) programs. *Journal of the American Academy of Psychiatry and the Law, 36*, 47–55.

Compton, M. T., Broussard, B., Hankerson-Dyson, D., Krishan, S., Stewart, T., Oliva, J. R., & Watson, A. C. (2010). System- and policy-level challenges to full implementation of the Crisis Intervention Team (CIT) model. *Journal of Police Crisis Negotiations, 10*(1–2), 72–85. doi:10.1080/15332581003757347777.

Compton, M. T., Esterberg, M. L., McGee, R., Kotwicki, R. J., & Oliva, J. R. (2006). Crisis intervention team training: Changes in knowledge, attitudes, and stigma related to schizophrenia. *Psychiatric Services, 57*, 1199–1202.

Cooper, V. A., McLearan, A. M., & Zapf, P. A. (2004). Dispositional decisions with the mentally ill: Police perceptions and characteristics. *Police Quarterly, 7*, 295–310.

Cordner, G. W. (2000). A community policing approach to persons with mental illness. *Journal of the American Academy of Psychiatry and the Law, 28*, 326–331.

Criminal Justice/Mental Health Consensus Project. (2003). Council of State Governments. Retrieved October, 20, 2007 from www.consensusproject.org.

Crisis Intervention Team (CIT). (n.d.). Memphis Police Department Website. Retrieved May 10, 2007 from http://www.memphispolice.org.

Deane, M. W., Steadman, H. J., Borum, R., Veysey, B. M., & Morrissey, J. (1999). Emerging partnerships between mental health and law enforcement. *Psychiatric Services, 50*, 99–101.

Draine, J., & Solomon, P. (1999). Describing and evaluating jail diversion services for persons with serious mental illness. *Psychiatric Services, 50*, 56–61.

Dupont, R., & Cochran, S. (2000). Police response to mental health emergencies: Barriers to change. *Journal of the American Academy of Psychiatry and the Law, 28*, 338–344.

Elbogen, E. B., Mustillo, S., Van Dorn, R., Swanson, J. W., & Swartz, M. S. (2007). The impact of perceived need for treatment on risk of arrest and violence among people with severe mental illness. *Criminal Justice and Behavior, 34*, 197–210.

Engel, R. S., & Silver, E. (2001). Policing mentally disordered suspects: A reexamination of the criminalization hypothesis. *Criminology, 39*, 225–252.

French, L. (1987). Victimization of the mentally ill: An unintended consequence of deinstitutionalization. *Social Work, 32*, 502–505.

Fyfe, J. J. (2000). Policing the emotionally disturbed. *Journal of the American Academy of Psychiatry and the Law, 28*, 345–347.

Geller, J. L. (2008). Commentary: Is CIT today's lobotomy? *Journal of the American Academy of Psychiatry and the Law, 36*, 56–58.

Green, T. (1997). Police as frontline mental health workers: The decision to arrest or refer to mental health agencies. *International Journal of Law and Psychiatry, 20*, 469–486.

Grob, G. N. (1992). Mental health policy in America: Myths and realities. *Health Affairs, 11*, 7–22.

Grob, G. N. (2005). Public policy and mental illnesses: Jimmy Carter's presidential commission on mental health. *Milbank Quarterly, 83*, 425–456.

Hails, J., & Borum, R. (2003). Police training and specialized approaches to respond to people with mental illness. *Crime and Delinquency, 49*, 52–61.

Handberg, R., & Pilchick, S. (1980). Police handling of mental patients: Crisis intervention requirements and police behavior. *Criminal Justice Review, 5*, 66–73.

Hartford, K., Carey, R., & Mendonca, J. (2006). Pre-arrest diversion of people with mental illness: Literature review and international survey. *Behavioral Sciences and the Law, 24*, 845–856.

Hiday, V. A., Swartz, M. S., Swanson, J. W., Borum, R., & Wagner, H. R. (1999). Criminal victimization of persons with severe mental illness. *Psychiatric Services, 50*, 62–68.

James, D. J., & Glazer, L. E. (2006). Mental health problems of prison and jail inmates. *Bureau of Justice Statistics–Special Report*. Retrieved May 10, 2007, from http://www.nami.org/Content/Microsites140/NAMI_Austin/Home130/Whats_New57/DOJ_Study1/DOJ_Mental_Illness_Prison.pdf.

Laberge, D., & Morin, D. (1996). The overuse of criminal justice dispositions: Failure of diversionary policies in the management of mental health problems. *International Journal of Law and Psychiatry, 18*, 389–414.

Lamb, H. R., & Weinberger, L. E. (2005). The shift of psychiatric inpatient care from hospitals to jails and prisons. *Journal of the American Academy of Psychiatry and Law, 33*, 529–534.

Lamb, H. R., Weinberger, L. E., & DeCuir, W. J. (2002). The police and mental health. *Psychiatric Services, 53*, 1266–1271.

Lamb, H. R., Weinberger, L. E., & Gross, B. H. (2004). Mentally ill persons in the criminal justice system: Some perspectives. *Psychiatric Quarterly, 75*, 107–126.

Lattimore, P. K., Broner, N., Sherman, R., Frisman, L., & Shafer, M. S. (2003). A comparison of prebooking and postbooking diversion programs for mentally ill substance-abusing individuals with justice involvement. *Journal of Contemporary Criminal Justice, 19*, 30–64. doi:10.1177/1043986202239741.

Lurigio, A. J., Smith, A., & Harris, A. (2008). The challenge of responding to people with mental illness: Police officer training and special programmes. *The Police Journal, 81*, 295–322. doi:10.1358/pojo.2008.81.4.431.

Lurigio, A. J., & Swartz, J. A. (2000). Changing the contours of the criminal justice system to meet the needs of persons with serious mental illness. *Criminal Justice, 3*, 45–108.

Matheson, F. I., Creatore, M. I., Gozdyra, P., Moineddin, R., Rourke, S. B., & Glazier, R. H. (2005). Assessment of police calls for suicidal behavior in a concentrated urban setting. *Psychiatric Services, 56*, 1606–1609.

Matthews, A. (1970). Observations on policy and procedures for emergency detention of the mentally ill. *Journal of Criminal Law, Criminology and Police Sciences, 61*, 283–295.

Mechanic, D., & Rochefort, D. (1990). Deinstitutionalization: An appraisal of reform. *Annual Review of Sociology, 16*, 301–327.

Memphis Police Crisis Intervention Team (CIT) Program. (n.d.). *National Alliance on Mental Illness*. Retrieved February 27, 2007, from http://www.nami.org.

Menzies, R. J. (1987). Psychiatrists in blue: Police apprehension of mental disorder and dangerousness. *Criminology, 25*, 429–453.

Miller, L. (2006). *Practical police psychology: Stress management and crisis intervention for law enforcement*. Springfield, IL: Charles C. Thomas.

Morabito, M. S. (2007). Horizons of context: Understanding the police decision to arrest people with mental illness. *Psychiatry Services, 58*, 1582–1587.

Morrissey, J., Fagan, J., & Cocozza, J. (2009). New models of collaboration between criminal justice and mental health systems. *American Journal of Psychiatry, 166*(11), 1211–1214.

Morrissey, J., & Goldman, H. (2007). Care and treatment of the mentally ill in the United States: Historical developments and reform. *Annals of the American Academy of Political and Social Science, 484*, 12–27.

Munetz, M. R., Morrison, A., Krake, J., Young, B., & Woody, M. (2006). Statewide implementation of the crisis intervention team program: The Ohio model. *Psychiatric Services, 57*, 1569–1571.

Neidhart, E. (2008). Managing those in crisis: A yearlong analysis of incidents handled by the Seattle police department (Unpublished master's thesis). Seattle University, Seattle, WA.

Novak, K. J., & Engel, R. S. (2005). Disentangling the influence of suspects' demeanor and mental disorder on arrest. *Policing, 28*, 493–512.

O'Connor v. Donaldson, 422 U.S. 563 (1975).

Olivero, J. M. (1990). Police linkage with community mental health centers in the management of criminal justice-mental health. *Journal of Police and Criminal Psychology, 6*, 8–13.

Patch, P. C., & Arrigo, B. A. (1999). Police officer attitudes and use of discretion in situations involving the mentally ill. *International Journal of Law and Psychiatry, 22*, 23–35.

Perez, A., Leifman, S., & Estrada, A. (2003). Reversing the criminalization of mental illness. *Crime and Delinquency, 49*, 62–78.

Reuland, M. (2004). A guide to implementing police-based diversion programs for people with mental illness. *Police Executive Research Forum*. Delmar, NY: GAINS Technical Assistance and Policy Analysis Center for Jail Diversion.

Reuland, M., & Cheney, J. (2005). Enhancing success of police-based diversion programs for people with mental illness. *Police Executive Research Forum*. Delmar, NY: GAINS Technical Assistance and Policy Analysis Center for Jail Diversion.

Roberg, R., Novak, K., & Cordner, G. (2005). *Police & society* (3rd ed.). Los Angeles, CA: Roxbury.

Rogers, A. (1990). Policing mental disorder: Controversies, myths and realities. *Social Policy and Administration, 24*, 226–236.

Ruiz, J., & Miller, C. (2004). An exploratory study of Pennsylvania police officers' perceptions of dangerousness and their ability to manage persons with mental illness. *Police Quarterly, 7*, 359–371.

Salt Lake City Police Department Crisis Intervention Team (CIT) History. (n.d.). Retrieved March 2, 2007, from http://www.ci.slc.ut.us.

Schanche, D. (2002). Mental illness history comes full circle. *The Macon Telegraph*. Retrieved May 25, 2007, from http://www.accessmylibrary.com/coms2/summary_0286-5953417_ITM.

Schwarzfeld, M., Reuland, M., & Plotkin, M. (2007). Improving responses to people with mental illnesses: The essential elements of a specialized police-based program. *Bureau of Justice Assistance–Special Report*, 1–11. Retrieved December 20, 2007, from http://ncmhr.org/downloads/ImprovingResponsesToPeopleWithMI.pdf.

Sellers, C. L., Sullivan, C. J., Veysey, B. M., & Shane, J. M. (2005). Responding to persons with mental illness: Police perspectives on specialized and traditional practices. *Behavioral Sciences and the Law, 23*, 647–657.

Sirotich, F. (2009). The criminal justice outcomes of jail diversion programs for persons with mental illness: A review of the evidence. *Journal of the American Academy of Psychiatry and the Law, 37*, 461–472.

Skeem, J., & Bibeau, L. (2008). How does violence potential relate to crisis intervention responses to emergencies? *Psychiatric Services, 59*, 201–204.

Steadman, H. J. (1992). Boundary spanners: A key component for the effective interactions of the justice and mental health systems. *Law and Human Behavior, 16*, 75–87.

Steadman, H. J., Deane, M. W., Borum, R., & Morrissey, J. (2000). Comparing outcomes of major models of police responses to mental health emergencies. *Psychiatric Services, 51*, 645–649.

Steadman, H. J., Deane, M. W., Morrissey, J. P., Westcott, M. L., Salasin, S., & Shapiro, S. (1999). A SAMHSA research initiative assessing the effectiveness of jail diversion programs for mentally ill persons. *Psychiatric Services, 50*, 1620–1623.

Steadman, H. J., Morris, S. M., & Dennis, D. L. (1995). The diversion of mentally ill persons from jails to community-based services: A profile of programs. *American Journal of Public Health, 85*, 1630–1635.

Steadman, H. J., Stainbrook, K. A., Griffin, P., Draine, J., Dupont, R., & Horey, C. (2001). A specialized crisis response site as a core element of police-based diversion programs. *Psychiatric Services, 52*, 219–222.

Strauss, G., Glenn, M., Reddi, P., Afaq, I., Podolskaya, A., Rybakova, T., ... El-Mallakh, R. S. (2005). Psychiatric disposition of patients brought in by Crisis Intervention Team police officers. *Community Mental Health Journal, 41*, 223–228.

Teller, J. L., Munetz, M. R., Gil, K. M., & Ritter, C. (2006). Crisis intervention team training for police officers responding to mental disturbance calls. *Psychiatric Services, 57*, 232–237.

Teplin, L. A. (1983). The Criminalization of the mentally ill: Speculation in search of data. *Psychological Bulletin, 94*, 54–67.

Teplin, L. A. (1984). Criminalizing mental disorder: The comparative arrest rate of the mentally ill. *American Psychologist, 39*, 794–803.

Teplin, L. A. (2000). Keeping the peace: Police discretion and mentally ill persons. *National Institute of Justice Journal*, 8–15.

Teplin, L. A., & Pruett, N. S. (1992). Police as streetcorner psychiatrist: Managing the mentally ill. *International Journal of Law and Psychiatry, 15*, 139–156.

Thompson, M. D., Reuland, M., & Souweine, D. (2003). Criminal justice/mental health consensus: Improving responses to people with mental illness. *Crime & Delinquency, 49*, 30–51.

Vermette, H. S., Pinals, D. A., & Appelbaum, P. S. (2005). Mental health training for law enforcement professionals. *Journal of the American Academy of Psychiatry and the Law, 33*, 42–46.

Vickers, B. (2000). Memphis, Tennessee Police Department's Crisis Intervention Team. *Bulletin from the Field, Practitioner Perspectives, Bureau of Justice Assistance*. Retrieved March 2, 2007, from http://ojp.usdoj.gov/BJA.

Walker, S., & Katz, C. (2005). *The police in America: An introduction* (5th ed.). New York: McGraw-Hill.

Watson, A. C. (2010). Research in the real world: Studying Chicago police department's Crisis Intervention Team program. *Research on Social Work Practice, 20*, 536–543. doi:10.1177/1049731510374201.

Watson, A. C., Corrigan, P. W., & Ottati, V. (2004a). Police officers' attitudes toward and decisions about persons with mental illness. *Psychiatry Services, 55*, 49–53.

Watson, A. C., Corrigan, P. W., & Ottati, V. (2004b). Police responses to persons with mental illness: Does the label matter? *Journal of the American Academy of Psychiatry and Law, 32*, 378–385.

Watson, A. C., Ottati, V., Morabito, M., Draine, J., Kerr, A., & Angell, B. (2010). Outcomes of police contacts with persons with mental illness: The impact of CIT. *Administration and Policy in Mental Health, 37*, 302–317. doi:10.1007/s10488-009-0236-9.

Wolff, N. (1998). Interactions between mental health and law enforcement systems: Problems and prospects for cooperation. *Journal of Health Politics, Policy, and Law, 23*, 133–174.

CHAPTER SEVEN

The Elements of Hostage (Crisis) Negotiation

Lisbeth Eddy and Stanley W. Patrzalek

Hostage (crisis) negotiation has evolved to become one of law enforcement's most effective nonlethal tools. With an estimated 10,000 people taken hostage each year in the United States (Kennedy, 2010) the presence of trained negotiators is a welcomed addition to most police departments. This contention is further supported by an analysis of the Federal Bureau of Investigation's (FBI) Hostage Barricade Database System (HOBAS). Data examined from 2002 to 2003 showed that approximately 82% of reported hostage and barricade incidents were resolved without death or injury (Van Hasselt et al., 2005). This highly successful and nonviolent resolution of hostage and barricade incidents has repeatedly demonstrated its value to the law enforcement community.

The aim of this chapter is to examine the unique and often complex world of hostage (crisis) negotiation. It is important to keep in mind that aside from the traditional role of hostage negotiations, negotiators have adapted their skills to be effectively utilized to intervene in a number of crisis situations, such as high-risk suicide attempts, mood-disordered or psychotic subjects, domestic incidents, prison and jail riots, mental health warrants, high-risk warrants, debriefing in crisis incidents, stalking incidents, violence in the workplace, and school violence (McMains & Mullins, 2010; Noesner & Webster, 1997).

The historical shift in terminology from "hostage" negotiation to "crisis" negotiation will be explored in the forthcoming sections, but for now, a brief introduction into the evolution of twenty-first-century hostage (crisis) negotiation is worth elucidating. When the art of hostage negotiation was being developed in the early 1970s, it was in response to a very specific problem, that being: how can law enforcement mitigate the risk and injury to *all* persons involved during a hostage-taking incident? As negotiator skill sets were identified and developed for this purpose, it was not long before law enforcement agencies recognized that trained hostage negotiators were useful in other situations as well. Initially, what appeared to evolve was the majority of critical incidents facing law enforcement–involved subjects motivated primarily by emotional needs, exhibiting mainly expressive behaviors (Noesner & Webster, 1997). As data made its way to the FBI, it was clear that traditional trained hostage negotiators were performing a more general "crisis" negotiation function.

Accordingly, the following sections summarize the many facets of crisis negotiation. The majority of this work draws upon the expertise and unique personal experience of Lisbeth Eddy, a former law enforcement officer who is a graduate of the FBI national hostage negotiator-training program and a 29-year veteran as a crisis negotiator with the Seattle Police Department. In addition, the personal experiences offered in this chapter are framed by the scholarly work of those who have made major contributions to the understanding and evolution behind the "art and science" of crisis negotiation.

Historical Antecedents of Hostage Taking and Hostage Negotiation

The history of hostage taking and intervention strategies is rich in anecdotal evidence and as old as recorded history itself. The frequent use of hostages has been demonstrated in political and military venues throughout the world. Recounting biblical times, the Book of Genesis 14:12–16 gives the first recorded account of the liberation of a hostage by use of force. When Abraham's nephew Lot was taken captive by the armies of four kings, Abraham assembled a 318-man reaction force and successfully rescued his nephew (Grubb, 2010; Van Zandt, 2006). Moving forward in history, the Roman Empire quashed revolts in Italy, Spain, and Gaul by requiring the vanquished tribes to give hostages as a guarantee of their future obedience (Rush & Hanser, 2007). In addition, pirates captured Julius Caesar in the year 75 BCE where Caesar negotiated a ransom for his own release and subsequently had his kidnappers killed (Van Zandt, 2006). The Crusades offer another historical example of hostage taking as a means of guarantee in political and military encounters. In coordinating the end of the siege of Acre in 1191, Christian forces met for a negotiated surrender with the Muslim garrison on July 4. The Muslim garrison gave hostages as a guarantee they would return to the parley so that they may leave to consult Saladin regarding the Crusader terms (Kosto, 2003). As Saladin rejected the Crusaders' initial terms, the Muslim garrison within a week of negotiations surrendered on their own accord. As a representative from the Crusaders entered the city to raise the Crusaders' banners, a hostage was given to ensure his safe passage (Kosto, 2003).

In early American history, President Thomas Jefferson in 1805, attempted to rescue 307 American sailors being held for ransom by the Barbary pirates of Tripoli. President Jefferson refused to pay the ransom, citing reasons that it would only encourage the other Barbary States to take American hostages. After failed negotiations with the Barbary pirates, President Jefferson was convinced that the best course of action was to assemble a reactionary force to rescue the hostages and lay siege to the city of Tripoli. The Barbary pirates countered the American threat with a threat of their own to kill all the American hostages. After several days at an impasse, President Jefferson agreed to pay $60,000 in ransom for the American hostages (Rush & Hanser, 2007). During World War II, Nazi Germany would take hostages in retaliation for acts of sabotage and assassination. In one such incident, during the Nazi occupation of Czechoslovakia in 1942, 10,000 Czechoslovakian hostages were taken by the Nazis and randomly executed in reprisal for the attempted assassination of a high-ranking Nazi official (Rush & Hanser, 2007). In that same year, Nazi Germany also took two million French hostages after the division of France in order to ensure the compliance of the French people (Grubb, 2010). Thus far, the events discussed comprise only a brief historical snapshot of hostage incidents but nonetheless have been influential in the evolution and development of hostage-taking intervention strategies.

The development of modern hostage-negotiation strategies can be attributed to several incidents; however, one incident is often cited as the impetus for change in the way law enforcement agencies have developed and employed negotiation strategies. The incident occurred in 1972 during the Olympic Games in Munich, Germany, and is commonly known as the "Munich Massacre" (Grubb, 2010; Rush & Hanser, 2007; Vecchi, Van Hasselt, & Romano, 2005). During this incident, 11 Israeli hostages, 5 Palestinian hostage takers, and 1 police officer were killed when negotiations failed and Munich police attempted to rescue the hostages. In dealing with this situation, no specifically trained hostage negotiator was available. Instead, several police and government officials representing West German, Israel, U.S., and Arab interests attempted to negotiate the release of the Israeli hostages without success, resulting in mass casualties (Rush

& Hanser, 2007). Following this debacle, international law enforcement agencies began scrutinizing the lack of effective intervention strategies for hostage situations and began to explore new techniques, which could be employed during these situations. Since then, several models of negotiation have been developed for use in hostage situations, rooted primarily on problem-solving approaches to response, management, and resolution of these incidents (Grubb, 2010; Vecchi et al., 2005).

In light of the Munich tragedy, law enforcement agencies in the United States began rethinking and evaluating the "hard" or tactical approach taken to managing high-conflict incidents. Among the first to evaluate their effectiveness was the New York City Police Department (NYPD). Utilizing the talents of Harvey Schlossberg, a detective with a PhD in psychology, and Lieutenant Frank Boltz, they developed tactics that led to the resolution of high-conflict incidents with the primary aim of minimizing the loss of life as experienced in the Munich tragedy (McMains & Mullins, 2010). Schlossberg and Boltz stressed three primary principles that the reader will engage throughout this chapter:

1. The importance of containing and negotiating with the hostage taker in a hostage incident.
2. The importance of understanding the hostage taker's motivation and personality in a hostage situation.
3. The importance of slowing an incident down so time can work for the negotiator.

Due to the pioneering efforts of Schlossberg and Boltz, the NYPD established the first hostage negotiation program in the country emphasizing the "soft" negotiation approach rather than the "hard" or tactical approach (McMains & Mullins, 2010). Upon request by the NYPD, the FBI was asked to review their curriculum for hostage negotiation. Shortly afterward, obviously inspired by the NYPD curriculum, the FBI developed a national training program for police officers who wanted to learn about hostage negotiation (McMains & Mullins, 2010). Today it is estimated that 70% of trained police negotiators have been trained directly or indirectly using the FBI curriculum (McMains & Mullins, 2010).

Hostage and Non-Hostage Incidents

Hostage taking is typically defined as the "holding of one or more persons against their will with the actual or implied use of force" (Van Hasselt et al., 2005, p. 22). Other definitions position hostage taking as "a person held and threatened by a subject or subjects to force the fulfillment of substantive demands made on a third party" (Van Zandt, 2006, p. 260). Furthermore, the elements of hostage taking are broken down into "instrumental" versus "expressive" needs of the specific incident. Traditionally, instrumental hostage taking has been defined as an attempt to achieve some particular goal or societal change. Expressive hostage taking has been defined as being motivated by internally felt emotions and impulses (Wesselius & DeSarno, 1983). Further research has clarified the understanding of "instrumental" versus "expressive" needs in the context of hostage versus non-hostage situations. Under a hostage situation, the hostage taker is motivated by instrumental or tangible reasons and relies upon the needs of the police or other authorities to meet specific demands (e.g., ransom, transportation, money, release of political prisoners). In these events, the hostage is used as leverage to obtain other substantive goals (Noesner & Webster, 1997; Vecchi et al., 2005). In a non-hostage situation, a person is taken captive for expressive or intangible reasons in which he or she does not need the police or other authorities. In situations like these, the subject is in a highly emotional state, (e.g., anger, jealousy, frustration, despair), and the captive is likely to become a victim or homicide-to-be. (Vecchi et al., 2005). Working within this framework of instrumental versus expressive situations, we can define the role of hostage negotiation as not always involving hostages. Early efforts had focused on hostage negotiators responding to terrorist hostage situations motivated by political or religious ideologies. The 1980s marked a clear shift among negotiators in the types of incidents that were of a greater concern to law enforcement, which involved emotionally disturbed individuals, trapped criminals, and domestic incidents (Grubb, 2010; McMains & Mullins, 2010). Research conducted at the time revealed "less than 18% of the incidents dealt with by negotiators over a five year period in 15 of the largest U.S. cities actually involved hostages" (Grubb, 2010, p. 343). In light of this shift, law enforcement began to employ crisis intervention principles and suicide intervention to a broad range of policing issues. Through the incorporation of psychologically based crisis intervention techniques (e.g., rapport-building, active listening skills, empathy), the approach widely known as hostage negotiations is now widely referred to as "crisis negotiation" to reflect a broader strategy in conflict resolution (McMains & Mullins, 2010; Van Hasselt et al., 2005).

Negotiating the release of a hostage(s) or even dealing within the broad spectrum of crisis situations is unequivocally the most psychological law enforcement discipline. Crisis negotiation emphasizes the "slowing down" of an incident, allowing the subject to vent feelings (anger, frustration, anxiety) and, in turn, defusing a negative emotional state (Van Hasselt & Romano, 2004). While the academic literature offers a rich history and theoretical framework for which negotiation "methods" have been found to be successful, it is difficult to convey the esoteric nature and dynamics of crisis negotiation from the outside looking in. As a seasoned negotiator, author Lisbeth Eddy offers an insider's view in the following sections, giving us a more personal understanding of the experiences of a crisis negotiator.

Behind the Lines with Lisbeth Eddy

I attended my first, FBI-sponsored hostage negotiators' training with the Seattle Police Department in February 1981. During the early 1980s, the art of hostage negotiation was still a relatively new concept for our department. To say the least, the training mesmerized me. We watched videos, listened to recordings, and learned about Stockholm syndrome. We listened to agents and officers share ideas that they had used in hostage situations, which resulted in a peaceful outcome. The training course was detailed and fascinating, and as a newly minted hostage negotiator, I was anxious to put my acquired knowledge to work.

Within a month of attending the class, I was working in the South Precinct of the Seattle Police Department. A police lieutenant walked in, saw me, and asked, "you went to that hostage negotiator training didn't you?" "Yes," I stated. He said, "well, come on . . . we have a guy barricaded in an apartment building with a firearm, and he is threatening to kill himself, and anyone who tries to interfere." As we were headed that way, I asked him if other negotiators had been called. He stated, "No, we have you." I tried to explain to him that our training as negotiators is based on the team concept, and that I would like to have other negotiators requested to respond as well. He stated that we would get there first, and then see if that could be arranged.

We arrived, and passed underneath the yellow tape that kept the public from entering our perimeter, and found the command post. The subject was barricaded in a third-floor apartment, located in a residential neighborhood. I was initially taken to a room across the street from the subject, where I could see that he had broken out a big glass window. He appeared to be under the influence, or suffering from some form of psychosis. The subject continually kept pointing the gun out the window, and placing it in his mouth, and generally waving it all around. I was handed a bullhorn. I realized that "bullhorning," from the location I was in, was not very safe and probably not going to be effective, so I requested to be moved into the building where the subject was.

I was relocated to a position just down the hall from the subject's door. I learned his name, and began to call to him. His initial reaction was to scream back, not making a lot of sense. Eventually, a second negotiator did arrive, and the two of us worked to try to calm the man and learn as much as we could about him from neighbors and from persons who knew him. After several hours of negotiating, he did settle down, and he eventually agreed to come out, without any use of force. To our advantage, whatever influence he was under might have dissipated, allowing his cognitive reasoning ability to return.

What I realized that day was how relevant my training was to this situation. In order to affect behavior change in almost any barricade/hostage situation, part of the strategy is to contain the situation, slow things down, and try to get the subject to a place where he can begin to reason again.

A Standard Hostage Taker Typology

What causes a person to engage in hostage taking/barricaded subject behavior? Social scientists, law enforcement, and the FBI's Crisis Negotiation Unit (CNU) have been studying this question for years. Researchers have learned that the reasons and motivations are variegated, making it difficult to determine the etiology of this kind of behavior. However, there are some general types of barricade/hostage situations that law enforcement officers often encounter. Several typologies exist that categorize hostage takers into one of several types and even subtypes (Grubb, 2010; Rush & Hanser, 2007). Having an established typology of hostage takers is often a useful tool and first step in coordinating the type of responses necessary (e.g., negotiations strategy, tactical team responses, etc.) to ending a crisis situation. As an FBI-trained hostage negotiator, I have experience with the standard FBI model that classifies hostage takers into four distinct classifications or typologies.

Trapped Criminal

The trapped criminal rarely plans on taking hostages but feels forced to do so in the event of a planned robbery, burglary, or some other crime in which something went wrong. The perpetrator(s) often find themselves "cornered." Seeing no way out of their dilemma, they often take innocent bystander(s) as their potential hostages. Trapped criminal hostage takers are generally the most rational and predictable to negotiate with because they are motivated by a will to survive and do not want to be arrested. They can often be convinced not to make things difficult, and alternative ideas are offered to them as "rewards" for cooperating with authorities.

The Prison Inmate

The prison inmate planning an escape may deliberately include hostages in the escape plan as leverage for getting out. These types of situations are potentially volatile because the potential escapee has nothing to lose. Other situations may involve hostage taking in an attempt to demand better conditions or other concessions. One historic example of this was the 1991 takeover of the "Alpha Unit" at the Talladega Federal Correctional Institution. Cuban detainees fighting deportation took 11 hostages, prompting a 10-day standoff that ended with armed agents storming the unit and taking control back from the inmates.

Terrorist

Terrorist or politically motivated hostage takers desire to make a statement to the rest of the world. Their agenda is to gain the attention of both media and government and garner some type of international recognition for their cause. The terrorist hostage taker generally has a strong commitment to a cause or ideology. Often these situations can be the hardest to deal with, as they are not motivated by freedom or even by staying alive in some cases. Some of the subjects involved in this kind of case have already made up their minds, and they are prepared to die. Recall the 1985 abduction of journalist Terry Anderson by Hezbollah, which was aimed at driving U.S. military forces from Lebanon during the Lebanese Civil War.

Mentally Disturbed

The fourth and final category can best be described as the mentally disturbed hostage taker. This category normally concerns the psychopathic/antisocial individual, the paranoid schizophrenic, the inadequate individual, and the depressed individual. Often, domestic violence situations can elicit some type of mental irrationality. As one example, a domestic violence situation may have started out as the subject being trapped in his house by law enforcement, but then the subject's behavior becomes threatening to others as he attempts to sort out his issues and possibly consider suicide.

Not all hostage-taking incidents fit into one specific category. Often, the conditions will be a combination of the above, or start out as one type and become another. For the negotiator doing the work, the type of situation they are dealing with might not become clear for several hours into the negotiation.

The Negotiation Team Structure

As mentioned earlier, the art of crisis negotiation was researched and further developed by the FBI, and the structure of the negotiation team soon took shape. This is not a one-person job, as Hollywood movies might portray. No single negotiator could engage in this very strenuous activity without the support of a versatile and well-trained team. There is a clear strategy involved with the structure of a negotiation team as explained in more detail below.

The *key communicator*, the one in the "hot seat," is described as the primary negotiator. This is the position that most negotiators aspire to be. It is probably the most demanding, physically and emotionally, and yet is one of the most satisfying. This negotiator communicates directly with the subject. This negotiator is not a decision maker, and should not be in a leadership position. The key is to relate to the subject at his level and submit all requests through the supervisor. Equate this to the car salesman stating, "I'm not sure I can do this for you, but let me talk to my manager." This negotiator must do his or her best to convince the subject that he or she is important (but not too important) and, whatever the subject's needs/demands are, must go through this negotiator. Most importantly, this negotiator must demonstrate a willingness to employ active listening techniques and should appear nonjudgmental and nonthreatening to the subject.

The next position on the team is that of a "secondary" or *coach negotiator*. This negotiator should (ideally) be able to hear both sides of the conversation between the subject and the primary. This negotiator, because he or she is not actively engaged in the communication with the subject, has the task of listening carefully to specific words used by the subject, and developing ideas that can be used to encourage the subject into making the right choices. This negotiator will screen all ideas that come from the rest of the team, including the team leader, and determine the appropriate time to introduce the new information to the primary negotiator for consideration.

One extremely important but less glorious position on the team is that of the "scribe," or *note taker*. Ideally, this team member would also be able to hear both sides of the conversation. This member has the task of writing down, as closely as possible, the key points of the conversation. Some things that are said can be very critical, and must be written down verbatim whenever possible. The scribe should be experienced enough to recognize what statements are critical and need to be written down. When the team is not actively engaged in negotiations with the subject, they are strategizing and need to be able to review what has been said. The team must be able to review specific statements, especially if they are threats, whether they are general threats or threats to a specific individual. Also, after hours and hours of negotiations, reviewing a transcript can show changes in the subject's demeanor that negotiators may not have picked up on during the conversation.

The *team leader* of the negotiation team is the supervisor of the group. Usually, this is one of your most experienced negotiators. Often, this team leader will be a sergeant or a first-line supervisor; but that is not necessary, as long as they have the experience and the respect of the team and the command staff managing the situation. The team leader has the task of assigning the positions on the working team. The team leader has the responsibility of determining the strategies of the negotiations. That might involve making a decision regarding what gender of negotiator should be primary, or if/when to switch out negotiators. The team leader has the responsibility of communicating with the "on scene" commander and the tactical team commander about how the negotiations are progressing. The tactical team commander and the scene commander will often consult with the team leader about the threat assessment of the subject, and if any threats made are likely to be carried out. This is a huge responsibility. Clearly, when reviewing a crisis situation, the best predictor of future behavior is past behavior; but there are no absolutes. The team leader must convey their position regarding threatening behavior, based on the situation at hand, and what training, experience, and research has shown regarding hostage takers' threats and actions.

Other positions on the team include the *interviewer/intelligence gatherers*. The more a negotiator knows about their subject, the better the chance of finding "common ground," or a "hook." This would be a bit of information that causes the subject to open up and start thinking that maybe staying alive, and coming out, might be better than the other options presented. The team members assigned to this task will run computer checks and contact and interview relatives, friends, neighbors, employers, and, if there are any, escaped or released hostages. They gather the relevant information and provide it to the team leader and the secondary negotiator for their review. The team leader and the secondary negotiator will consult with the primary negotiator when he or she is not actively communicating, or they will pass notes if they need to provide pertinent, specific information as soon as possible.

As an added bonus, when the negotiation team has the luxury of a full contingent, they would include a member whose job is to write down important information on a whiteboard, or full-size sheets of paper that can be hung up in the negotiations area. That makes the key information readily available for review by any team member. Also, if the team has the added benefit of a full-time technical support person (e.g., to keep phones operational, ensure power, etc.), this is a huge bonus. This can be an instrumental position on the team, but one that is often overlooked.

Benefits of a Team Psychologist

The FBI and most major police departments highly encourage the use of a psychologist when conducting operations with a hostage taker or barricaded subject. A psychologist can contribute to the work of the negotiation team by clarifying the nature and attitudes of the subject and the psychological aspects of the hostage or barricade situation (Bailes, 2004). Psychologists never speak to the subject but may use several different methods to analyze the subject, such as reviewing criminal records, hospitalization records, and reports from family and friends as well as documents, drawings, or statements that the subject has issued before or during the incident. Furthermore, the psychological intervention by a psychologist can be very beneficial under a number of situations—for example, the subject has a history of mental health problems, the situation was resolving then deteriorated, the incident becomes protracted, or there is a child involved so every resource is made available to the scene commander (Bailes, 2004). It is important to clarify that the psychologist should never be the negotiator and should serve only in an advisory role. In addition, the psychologist should never be expected to provide "exact" predictions about the likelihood of dangerous behavior occurring, although pressure to do so may exist (Bailes, 2004). The psychologist should have exposure to the working environment and nuances of police work. Ideally, they should have spent some time riding with police officers and being around the police culture. They should research past situations involving hostage takers and barricaded subjects, and they should train regularly with the negotiation and tactical teams.

I recall one incident in particular, where a man who was either under the influence of some type of drug or having a psychotic break had crashed his car into the garage door of an apartment building. Moments later, he was seen by a neighbor across the street, breaking a window and climbing inside a ground-level apartment. Police responded and were talking to him through the door, which he now had barricaded. He was making threatening statements, and he indicated that he had a weapon and would hurt police if they tried to come in. After my arrival, I reviewed the information that had been gathered, and interviewed a friend of the subject's. The information indicated to me that his threats were probably just "bravado." I reviewed my assessment with the team psychologist, and he concurred. I consulted with the scene commander, and offered our opinion that if the tactical team performed a forced entry to extract him, he would likely just roll over and allow himself to be handcuffed. The tactical team did make entry, and as soon as they were in the door, the subject threw up his hands, turned around, and dropped to his knees. In the end, the tactical team was impressed with our assessment, and it did a lot to support our credibility with them.

Setting the Stage to Negotiate

When a hostage or barricade incident presents itself, a proper response and setup protocol is not only necessary, but also a critical first step in setting the stage to negotiate. The initial responding officer(s) are tasked with ensuring the containment of the scene and taking measures to ensure everyone's safety. Usually, once the situation is determined to be an actual hostage or barricade subject incident, the tactical team and negotiation team will be called out. In some instances, if a responding officer is already talking with the subject, the negotiation team leader will often assign a negotiation team member to "coach" that officer until an appropriate time is determined to turn the helm over to a trained negotiator. Other factors to keep in mind concern the gender or maturity of the negotiator in order to maximize cooperation from the subject—for example, utilizing a male negotiator in cases of hostage taking under domestic violence conditions, or using a more mature-sounding male negotiator in incidents involving older military veterans.

During a hostage or barricade incident, the subject must be isolated and contained in one place and a perimeter established to keep unauthorized persons out. This might be inside a building, perhaps a specific room; or it could be outside in a play yard, or on a city street. Once the situation is contained, law enforcement can establish some form of reliable communication with the hostage taker, such as a line phone, cell phone, pager, or even a bullhorn as illustrated earlier. Establishing communication is critical because the sooner communication can be established with the subject, the higher the chances of a peaceful resolution. Research has shown that during a crisis incident, the first 15–45 minutes is considered the most dangerous time next to surrender or tactical assault, because this is the time when confusion and panic are likely to be greatest (Miller, 2007).

As the situation is being contained, controlling the subject's environment is also essential in setting the stage to negotiate. Law enforcement should consider turning off the power and water, and shutting down outside lines to where the subject is contained. Keep in mind that shutting down the phones is more difficult to do nowadays, with the proliferation of cellular phones over traditional landlines; however, it can be done. Ultimately, the goal is to eliminate the subject's knowledge of what is happening outside and create some discomfort that can eventually be used as a bargaining piece for negotiators. In addition, hostage negotiators have been known to create environmental anxiety for the subject by disturbing the senses by employing loud noises, such as sirens, banging, or loud music. In some protracted incidents, negotiator tactics have been quite creative. Tactics have included frying bacon and blowing the aroma toward the subject's location. In other instances, where the subject can see the negotiator, comforting items have been used, such as sipping hot coffee on a cold day or perhaps an iced beverage on a very hot day. These initial techniques are used to arouse the subject's senses, hopefully leading toward some form of compliance.

If official contact has not already been established during a hostage or barricaded incident by responding officers, the lead negotiator will initiate contact with the subject by saying something as simple as, "Hello, my name is . . ." Keep in mind that negotiators should never use first names or titles of subjects. If the negotiator knows the subject's name, they usually refer to him or her formally, as in Mr. or Mrs., etc., and ask permission to use the subject's first name or some other preferred nickname.

Following the introduction, the negotiator should state that they are there to help. The most common first statement by a negotiator, after introductions, is usually something along the lines of "Are you OK?" or "Can you tell me what's going on?" or "I am really confused about what's happening." The negotiator needs to be prepared for a variety of responses, such as hanging up the phone, threats, obscenities, outrage, screaming, or even possibly cooperation. Negotiators must take a deep breath and remind themselves to remain thick-skinned and settle in for a long haul.

It is important in the process that the negotiator not be too authoritative. The first contact with the subject should be seen as checking on their well-being, and determining what their needs are. Cooperation will develop more quickly if they see the negotiator as being on their side and not "ordering them" as to what they need to do. Generally, the negotiator will play down the needs and importance of the hostages or victims. Any damage/injury that the subject has caused should be downplayed. If the subject inquires as to the condition of someone they may have hurt or killed, the negotiator should explain that they do not know, but that they will try to find out that information.

Often negotiators will start working with subjects, making statements that the subject can readily agree with. If the negotiator can demonstrate that the subject is in agreement with many of the statements the negotiator makes, the subject may begin to see the negotiator as being "mostly right." This is where the note taking and the record of the subject conversation can be valuable. If the negotiator can refer the subject back to something he or she said, or agreed to earlier, the subject has a hard time backing away from that statement, and is likely to become more compliant because they had committed to that statement earlier.

The negotiator can briefly inquire as to how any hostages are doing, but it is best to not refer to them as hostages. Refer to them as people, or men, women, or children, but refrain from placing too much importance on them. If the subject does not feel comfortable talking about hostages, then the negotiator should not push him. The negotiator wants to appear to be empathic to the subject's situation. The subject may wish to bring up matters that the negotiator does not consider relevant, but let them go ahead and talk about it because the negotiator's job is to *actively listen* at this point.

Defining Active Listening

Negotiation teams have an elaborate "toolbox" of techniques and strategies to gain compliance in various hostage or non-hostage situations. However, regardless of which techniques a negotiator chooses to go with, all processes are going to begin with demonstrating good active listening. Active listening poses no threat to an individual's self-image, it can help a subject become less defensive, and it can be the impetus for developing a positive relationship that will lead to behavioral change and, ultimately, crisis resolution (Noesner & Webster, 1997; Vecchi et al., 2005).

Furthermore, the hostage taker or person in crisis is going to subscribe to beliefs and ideas that are often radically different from those of the negotiator. It is imperative that negotiators avoid intimidating, demeaning, lecturing, criticizing, and evaluating the subject (Noesner & Webster, 1997). If the negotiator adapts such negative behavior, the negotiator will not be able to focus on actively listening to what the hostage taker or person in crisis is saying (McMains & Mullins, 2010). Simply put, focus on the message and not the messenger.

So how does a negotiator demonstrate that they are really listening? By engaging in the following primary and supplemental active listening skills:

Primary Active Listening Skills

Paraphrasing is when you take something the subject just said and briefly restate it to him in your own words. A good paraphrase is concise, it summarizes the essence of the meaning, the main point is the focus, and it is focused on facts (McMains & Mullins, 2010).

Emotion labeling is a comment back to the subject, using a word to label what you believe they are feeling. Even if you misidentify an emotion, this effort at least demonstrates to the subject that you are trying to understand the situation, which tends to defuse emotionality (Vecchi et al., 2005). An example of emotional labeling is, "You sound really frustrated with that," or "I hear anger in your voice."

Mirroring is a response in which the negotiator mirrors back the last few words of what the subject just said such as: "OK, so you got mad" or "So you broke the window." Mirroring helps to ensure that the discussion focuses on the subject rather than on the negotiator, thereby remaining in the subject's frame of reference (Vecchi et al., 2005).

Summarizing is a response that can be used to summarize the main facts and feelings that the subject has expressed over a relatively long period (McMains & Mullins, 2010). Furthermore, you also want to make sure you have received the information accurately. You can start by saying: "So, let me make sure I understand this so far." This is a good technique to slow someone down, without making the subject angry, and shows that the negotiator is demonstrating that they are really trying to "get it."

Supplemental Active Listening Skills

Minimal encouragers can be demonstrated in face-to-face communication by nodding the head, facial expressions, or other nonverbal behaviors. In communication over the telephone, or through a closed door, they must make these indicators audible. Saying things such as "okay," "sure," "uh-huh," "go on," "yeah," etc., demonstrates you are hearing and not interrupting, just acknowledging.

Effective pauses are used to allow time for the subject to reflect on what he is saying and to encourage the subject to fill the empty or blank space with additional communications or information (McMains & Mullins, 2010). Good negotiators are not afraid of silence. On the flip side, if the negotiator is involved in suicide intervention and the subject is not talking at all, it might be important to continue trying to insert thoughts and ideas that might break up the suicidal thought process of the subject.

Open-ended questions should be asked; avoid asking the subject "yes" or "no" questions. Open-ended questions encourage the subject to contribute more information and help to describe to the negotiator what they are going through. Open-ended questions typically start with "what" or "when" or statements, such as "Tell me more." "Why" statements are usually avoided, as they tend to be perceived as interrogatory (Vecchi et al., 2005).

"I" messages involve the negotiator expressing his or her emotions in response to the subject. When trying to support someone else in a communication, if "you" statements can be avoided, they should be. Starting a statement with "you" always sounds accusatory. Negotiators try to begin statements with things like: "I am trying to understand" or "I am confused about" or "I am struggling to see what you meant by that."

When initially employing active listening, it is recommended that the negotiator use the core group (i.e., paraphrasing, emotional labeling, mirroring, summarizing) until the negotiator has determined effective "hooks." The supplemental group should be used as needed to enhance the effectiveness of the core elements (Vecchi et al., 2005).

Gaining Trust

Negotiators should present themselves as someone who can be trusted and relied upon. Many times there are simple, safe things that the negotiator can accomplish to build rapport. This might be as simple as having the lights or heat turned on or turning down music or some distracting noise. Keep in mind that some of these opportunities to establish rapport may have been intentionally created as illustrated earlier. However, these things need to be cleared with the scene commanders. In addition, there is a certain amount of subliminal suggestion that can occur with the negotiation process. One technique when talking to the subject is to frequently refer to "when you come out" instead of "if you come out." This demonstrates the positive influence the negotiator is trying to convey and sends the message that they are working as a team to reach a resolution. Another commonly used tactic is reciprocity. This method also aids in gaining the trust of the subject. Negotiators will offer up some concession to be made, but there has to be something offered in return. This could be a promise from the hostage taker to not harm anyone, in return for the negotiator turning off the bright lights, for example. Sometimes, it can be something more significant, like asking a subject to release a hostage in return for water, or food, or cigarettes. The common axiom among hostage negotiators is, do not give something up unless you get something in return. However, it is commonly understood that sometimes, in the early stages, negotiators will make some concession in the interest of demonstrating good faith, and that they can be counted on to get things done.

It is important when communicating with the subject to have them clarify things that they say in order to avoid miscommunications, as well as to buy time. This is especially imperative when dealing with a possibly suicidal subject. If they say something like, "My wife won't have to worry about me anymore, she'll be alone soon enough," you should go ahead and ask, "Does that mean you are going to kill yourself?" It should be established immediately, that you are not afraid of talking about suicide, and they should not be afraid of discussing it with you, if that is what they are thinking.

A Cautionary Note

The public often asks why law enforcement does not permit family members, friends, clergy, or other trusted civilians to talk with the subject. Often hostage takers wish an audience of their family or loved ones. Other times, having the family or loved ones might make the situation worse, as their presence could embarrass the subject. There might be times when a third party could be invited to participate in the negotiation process. Usually, they are kept in an advisory role. This is because the subject needs to see the negotiator as his way out. However, with much coaching, interviewing, and preparation, a third party could be successfully used, the caveat being that the negotiator must use extreme caution with this practice.

I recall learning a valuable lesson when I was a young negotiator. We had a subject who was being evicted from his apartment. On eviction day, the landlord was at his door with the police. There was no answer upon knocking, and the landlord used his key to enter the apartment. The subject was seated about 10 feet inside the room, with a loaded rifle sitting across his lap. He then raised the rifle and pointed it toward the officers and the landlord. The officers and landlord chose to back out and call for assistance. As the standoff ensued, the subject's family showed up at the scene, asking to talk with him, explaining that they could convince him to come out. After about 10 hours of negotiating, we agreed to let his ex-wife, with whom he was supposedly on good terms, speak with him. She began by just telling him to come out and "man up." He softly and repeatedly told her it was none of her business and to go away and leave him to his business. She got frustrated after a few minutes, and blurted out, "Oh, fuck it! Just shoot him!" Obviously, after hours of talking with the subject, that was not really the message we had hoped to convey to him. Eventually, any lost ground due to this "judgment call" was made up in the end upon his peaceful surrender. The lesson I learned from this situation was that when you decide to let an untrained person in as a third-party negotiator, you take a big risk in how they might affect the outcome of the situation.

Dealing with Demands and Buying Time

When dealing with subject's demands, pay close attention to their motives and behaviors. What demands are being communicated? Does the negotiator find the demands are *instrumental* or *expressive*? If the demands are instrumental, the negotiation strategies are structured around buying time and increasing realism and rationality in the subject. The goal is to have the subject recognize that their expectations are unreasonable and assist them in seeing the value of surrender.

When the demands are more expressive in nature, it can indicate a more difficult negotiation process. These are the instances in which subjects wish to make a display out of their own suicide, or perform a suicide/homicide in front of an audience. These are very difficult cases to deal with because they are most often motivated by strong emotions and impulses. In other words, there is little that can be offered up as a possible goal to be obtained; or a possible solution to these situations. More time must be spent listening, and supporting, and waiting for the subject to work through to a point where their problem-solving skills become clearer. The negotiator must be careful to not promise anything that cannot be delivered.

There are some specific types of behavior that could indicate that a subject is acting in a manner that is expressive in nature. Some examples might include a history of violent past behavior, the subject calling 911 on himself or choosing a target that he knows (i.e., ex-girlfriend/wife, boss, coworker, etc.). Keep in mind that if the subject initiated contact with law enforcement after committing a criminal act, it could be an indicator of the subject's desire to engage with law enforcement, and the phenomenon of "suicide by cop" becomes a variable to be considered. However, the presence of these indicators does not mean the situation cannot be resolved peacefully; it could just mean that the road ahead is going to be a long one.

If the subject is communicating freely, and making specific demands, that is a good thing. In this case, it is mostly a matter of time. The negotiator needs to stay engaged and assure the subject they are part of the planning process, and a resolution will be forthcoming. In an effort to buy more time, the negotiator can use certain techniques. For example, if the subject asks for food to be sent in, the negotiator can exploit this request by asking the subject what kinds of food; and perhaps discussing that some of the hostages might have certain dietary restrictions or food allergies and maybe it might be wise to verify, before a decision on food can be made. Subsequently, if pizza is ordered, for example, a discussion can follow on whether it should come from a specific vendor (e.g., Papa John's or Domino's) A logical progression could then include discussions on the type of crust, toppings, etc. One strategy utilized by negotiators to buy time has been to send in the makings for sandwiches, which also has the added benefit of creating a situation in which the hostage taker and hostage(s) ended up working together to construct the sandwiches. This situation is ideal because it allows the hostage taker to identify with and humanize the hostage(s).

The strategy of buying time in a hostage situation is meant to wear down the hostage taker and allow law enforcement more time to strategize. With the passage of time, many things take place: basic human needs increase, anxiety and emotions decrease, and rationality goes up. Rapport develops between the negotiator and the hostage taker, and the hostage taker's expectations are reduced. After an amount of time (which is different with every situation), the hostage taker will often acquiesce to releasing hostages or perhaps agreeing to surrender. Often, as time goes by, their demands have been reduced from a helicopter and a million dollars to a cigarette and a beer.

Negotiable versus Nonnegotiable Demands and the Art of Saying "No"

Traditionally, hostage-taker demands are divided between negotiable demands and nonnegotiable demands. Of course, the situation will dictate how much of a demand should be provided and how much should be negotiated without being paid off. The courts (see *United States v. Crosby*, 1983) have given latitude in negotiations by determining that such "contracts" between a hostage taker and negotiator are considered a product of duress and that a contract under duress is unenforceable under law (Becker, 2009). Within the same vein, there is no obligation to provide the hostage taker Miranda warnings prior to or during negotiations. Anything developed during the negotiations may be included during trial without fear of exclusion for Miranda violations (see *United States v. Mesa*, 1980). In order for Miranda rights to apply, two elements must be present—custody and interrogation. Neither is present during a hostage situation (Becker, 2009).

One question that always comes up when I am training new negotiators is the question about saying "no" to the demands presented by hostage takers or barricaded subjects. Like the salesperson on a showroom floor, the negotiator really does not want to say "no" right away to anything because this sets an adversarial relationship right from the beginning. With that said, before considering which demands are negotiable or nonnegotiable, it is important to remember that each hostage situation is unique and the general guidelines governing hostage-taker demands are just "guidelines." Traditionally, negotiable demands have included food, cigarettes, drinks, and media coverage. Additionally, transportation and money can also be "negotiable" even if there is no intent to give in to these demands. Money may also be given to the hostage taker as a show of good faith and to obtain the release of hostages (Becker, 2009; McMains & Mullins, 2006). When I first entered hostage negotiations, alcohol was considered a nonnegotiable demand. However, times have changed, and experience has shown that in some circumstances, alcohol is negotiable. The rationale behind this is simple—the hostage taker may be an alcoholic. Without moderate amounts of alcohol to calm the hostage taker, he may become nervous, paranoid, irritable, and agitated, causing irrational behavior that may harm the hostages at the slightest provocation (McMains & Mullins, 2006). Keep in mind if the negotiator decides to go this route, it is usually at the direction of a consulting psychologist (Becker, 2009).

Regardless of how the incident plays out, there is a list of demands that are considered nonnegotiable. The negotiator should make a best practice to not discuss nonnegotiable demands because it has the ability to worsen the situation. If a hostage taker believes that at some point he or she will receive drugs, and then if the offer is reneged, this could damage the development of trust and rapport, anger the hostage taker, or lead to the hostages being harmed (McMains & Mullins, 2006). Items that are traditionally considered by law enforcement to be nonnegotiable include weapons, drugs, release of prisoners, and exchange of hostages.

Weapons are never negotiated, because a weapon gives the hostage taker the perception of having power. The negotiator, if presented with such a demand, should make clear that weapons are nonnegotiable. In contrast to alcohol, drugs are never negotiated because they may produce paranoia and psychotic episodes, thus reducing rationality and increasing unpredictability and violent behavior. Request for release of prisoners is very rare in the United States and, if demanded, can be resolved with some ease if the negotiator stays persistent. Finally, the exchange of hostages should not be considered for the simple reason of giving the hostage taker power and control and impeding the development of the Stockholm syndrome by allowing the hostages to become faceless "objects" that have no human value. In other words, if hostages are traded, the new hostages are less likely to be seen as "people" to the hostage taker and more likely to be seriously injured (McMains & Mullins, 2006).

The point of this section is to avoid saying "no" directly and instead buy time and entertain the request to pacify and wear down the subject. For example, the negotiator's response even to the most unreasonable of requests is likely to be something such as, "I can check on that for you, but I don't think that is going to happen. But what else can we look at?" That starts the subject thinking of possible ideas that would allow him to exit this situation feeling that he had some part in the decision-making process.

The Stockholm Syndrome

Negotiators need to be aware of the positive and negative aspects of a psychological syndrome known as the Stockholm syndrome. The Stockholm syndrome developed from an incident that occurred in 1973 in Stockholm, Sweden. For several days, two bank robbers held four hostages until the police ended the incident using tear gas without sustaining any casualties. Following the resolution of the situation, authorities were stunned when the hostages showed enormous sympathy toward the two hostage takers and animosity toward the police (McMains & Mullins, 2010). Furthermore, the victims refused to testify at the hostage takers' trial and even raised money for their legal defense fund. Several months after the incident, a former hostage became engaged to one of the hostage takers (McMains & Mullins, 2010). The interactions and subsequent bonding between the hostage taker and hostages during and after the incident promoted research into the phenomenon of what is now known as the Stockholm syndrome (Vecchi, 2009). Basically, the Stockholm syndrome is an emotional reaction taken by people in a hostage situation and is an attempt, at least initially, to survive (McMains & Mullins, 2010). However, as the situation progresses, the Stockholm syndrome becomes less of a survival mechanism and more of a coping and adaptation response, and can have an empathetic component as the hostage learns more about the hostage taker (McMains & Mullins, 2010). There are three widely accepted indicators of the Stockholm syndrome (Vecchi, 2009):

1. Positive feelings by the hostage(s) toward the hostage taker(s)
2. Positive feelings by the hostage taker(s) toward their hostage(s)
3. Negative feelings by the hostage(s) toward the police and authorities trying to win their release

In most incidents, a relationship to some degree is going to take place between the hostage taker, hostage(s), and negotiator after many hours of working together. The negotiation team needs to pay close attention to the indicators of the Stockholm syndrome developing. While in most hostage situations the encouragement and development of the Stockholm syndrome can be beneficial to the safety and/or survival of hostages, in other cases it can cause serious problems for law enforcement, as they cannot trust hostages to commit to a plan or to tell law enforcement officers true and valid information upon their release. Finally, building a close, positive relationship is key. The hostage taker must believe in and trust that the negotiator is truly doing everything in their power to resolve the incident (McMains & Mullins, 2010). However, and as unique as it may seem, the team leader must be cognizant in making sure that the primary negotiator has not developed too close an identification with the subject, as this too can compromise the operation.

The Surrender Ritual

The negotiation team must remember to structure the surrender ritual and resolution of the crisis carefully and know when to utilize a tactical response, if necessary (Miller, 2007). However, once the subject has accepted the terms of the negotiation and the surrender process begins, it is still not over. Sometimes, the discussion of surrender can last several hours. Many times, the subject needs to feel like they "save face" by doing one more thing that made them feel like they were still in charge. It might be something as simple as "I want to wear my red shirt," or "OK, I'll come out, but don't handcuff me in front of the neighbors." Most of these requests are usually benign in nature and can be worked out, but only with the approval of the on-scene commander and tactical team commander. Remember, the surrender process is a collaborative process between the negotiator and subject in which solutions and alternatives have to be suitable to both (Vecchi, 2009). Next, the negotiation team must prepare the tactical team for the subject's exit. As mentioned earlier, three especially dangerous periods exist in a hostage crisis: (1) the first 15–45 minutes of the hostage taking, (2) the surrender of the subject(s), and (3) tactical assault to rescue the hostages. During the surrender of the subjects(s), hair-trigger emotions, ambivalence, and lack of coordination between the subjects(s) and crisis team members can cause an otherwise successful resolution to go bad (Miller, 2007). It is imperative that the negotiation team communicates to the subject(s) very clear and precise instructions, such as from which door he must exit; and that upon his exit, he must follow all the verbal commands of the officer who greets him. Negotiators will constantly remind the subject that only by following their commands can they ensure his safety.

Unfortunately, there are going to be situations in which all reasonable attempts to peacefully resolve the crisis by negotiation have failed. Violence against the hostage(s) may have taken place or may be imminent. In these cases, tactical assault to rescue the victims and or apprehend the subject becomes necessary, carrying with it the highest risk of possible casualty, injuries, and violence.

Regardless of the outcome, hostage and barricaded incidents take their toll on everyone. Post-incident support and advice may be sought addressing the stress reactions and support needs of perpetrators, hostages, family, and police personnel (Bailes, 2004). As a basic rule, individuals who have been traumatized should be referred to their general practitioner or local mental health professional if they require specialist help. However, if needed and on a limited basis, the negotiation team psychologist could be involved in debriefing or critical stress management planning afterwards for groups of police officers or individuals (Bailes, 2004).

Since my early years as a young negotiator, many things have changed in the field of hostage (crisis) negotiation. Technology has advanced and rules have evolved, but the fundamentals have remained the same. I am often asked what it takes to be a good negotiator. The most commonly expected answer is "a gift of gab." In fact, the very opposite is true. Being a good negotiator requires good listening skills above all else. However, a successful negotiator is not only an excellent active listener; he or she is also patient, able to show empathy and not pass judgment. He or she must believe that all situations are negotiable and must be willing to invest the time and effort it takes to reach a positive outcome. A good negotiator does not give up on the process. Adhering to these basic skills, I believe, is still one of the best investments that can be made by law enforcement in a crisis situation.

Conclusion

Law enforcement professionals utilize a wide range of knowledge and skills to manage the many critical situations they are called upon to face. Although knowledge and skills derived from psychologically based techniques apply to many aspects of law enforcement, this relationship is most apparent in the world of hostage (crisis) negotiation (Soskis & Van Zandt, 1986). As detailed in this chapter, the negotiator relies on self-knowledge, familiarity with stress and psychopathology, interviewing skills, active listening, empathy, rapport, and the keen ability to redefine seemingly insoluble problems for the person in crisis, in what is surely one of the most spectacular "talking cures" ever invented (Soskis & Van Zandt, 1986).

The literature and personal insight brought to our attention in this work did not rise like a phoenix from the ashes, but rather developed from a long history of strategies and techniques by law enforcement practice and academic research. With this said, a symbiotic relationship must continue between scholar and negotiator, allowing for the effective transference of knowledge. Without such a relationship, we would not have made the life-saving advances in crisis negotiation we see today. In addition, the negotiation community benefits highly from what we refer to as "cop scholars." For example, several of the references utilized in this chapter are from authors who have "real-world" experience as negotiators and hold advanced degrees in the social and medical sciences. This type of "expertise" adds immeasurable depth and insight to the negotiation literature and law enforcement community.

In the end, there is no one-size-fits-all model for effective crisis negotiation. Every situation is unique and demands a combination of strategies and techniques specifically tailored for the crisis at hand. To be most effective, recommendations for future and current negotiators would include blending theory with field experience to develop strategies that are flexible and adaptable to the person in crisis. Until human behavior can be predicted with absolute certainty, the best we can do is to continue to study crisis situations when they occur, and continue to learn from each incident in a way that preserves crisis negotiation as law enforcement's most effective nonlethal tool.

References

Bailes, G. (2004). Sieges, the police ... and a psychologist? *Psychologist, 17*(7), 380–383.

Becker, R. F. (2009). *Criminal investigation* (3rd ed.). Sudbury, MA: Jones and Bartlett Publishers.

Grubb, A. (2010). Modern day hostage (crisis) negotiation: The evolution of an art form within the policing arena. *Aggression and Violent Behavior, 15*, 341–348.

Kennedy, B. P. (2010). Behavioral analysis in hostage negotiation. *Behavior Analysis Digest International, 22*(2), 5–6.

Kosto, A. J. (2003). Hostages during the first century of the Crusades. *Medieval Encounters, 9*(1), 1–31.

McMains, M. J., & Mullins, W. C. (2006). *Crisis negotiations: Managing critical incidents and hostage situations in law enforcement and corrections* (3rd ed.). Cincinnati, OH: Anderson Publishing.

McMains, M. J., & Mullins, W. C. (2010). *Crisis negotiations: Managing critical incidents and hostage situations in law enforcement and corrections* (4th ed.). Cincinnati, OH: Anderson Publishing.

Miller, L. (2007). Negotiating with mentally disordered hostage takers: Guiding principles and practical strategies. *Journal of Police Crisis Negotiations, 7*(1), 63–83.

Noesner, G. W., & Webster, M. (1997). Crisis intervention. *FBI Law Enforcement Bulletin, 66*(8), 13–19.

Rush, J., & Hanser, R. (Eds.). (2007). *Homeland security: Responding to the threat.* Boston, MA: Pearson Custom Publishing.

Soskis, D. A., & Van Zandt, C. R. (1986). Hostage negotiation: Law enforcement's most effective nonlethal weapon. *Behavioral Science and the Law, 4*(4), 423–435.

United States v. Crosby, 713 F.2d 1066 (5th Cir. 1983).

United States v. Mesa, 638 F.2d 582 (3rd Cir. 1980).

Van Hasselt, V. B., Flood, J. J., Romano, S. J., Vecchi, G. M., de Fabrique, N., & Dalfonzo, V. A. (2005). Hostage-taking in the context of domestic violence: Some case examples. *Journal of Family Violence, 20*(1), 21–27.

Van Hasselt, V. B., & Romano, S. J. (2004). Role-playing: A vital tool in crisis negotiation skills training. *FBI Law Enforcement Bulletin, 73*(2), 12–17.

Van Zandt, C. (2006). *Facing down evil: Life on the edge as an FBI hostage negotiator.* New York: Putnam.

Vecchi, G. M. (2009). Conflict and crisis communication: Workplace and school violence, Stockholm Syndrome, and abnormal psychology. *Annals of the American Psychotherapy Association, 12*(3), 30–39.

Vecchi, G. M., Van Hasselt, V. B., & Romano, S. J. (2005). Crisis (hostage) negotiation: Current strategies and issues in high-risk conflict resolution. *Aggression and Violent Behavior, 10*, 533–551.

Wesselius, C. L., & DeSarno, J. V. (1983). The anatomy of a hostage situation. *Behavioral Sciences and the Law, 1*(2), 33–45.

CHAPTER EIGHT

Criminal Profiling: Empirical Evidence on Skills and Accuracy*

Richard N. Kocsis

Criminal profiling, or more simply "profiling," is the technique of analyzing behavior patterns of a crime, or series of crimes in order to primarily construct a descriptive template of the probable offender(s) (Kocsis, 2009). Although the concept of profiling has expanded into new spheres such as predicting an offender's area of residence (e.g., Canter & Larkin, 1993; Rossmo, 2000), the bulk of profiling literature largely remains concerned with the identification of an offender's characteristics such as their age, sex, and marital and employment status (Kocsis, 2006). The oft-cited role of profiling is as an investigative aid (Holmes & Holmes, 1996; Vorpagel, 1982) with a constructed profile typically serving to guide an investigation either by matching the profile with a pool of suspects, or by offering a compilation of descriptors from which potential suspects may be identified for investigation.

Unlike other mainstream forensic techniques such as fingerprinting or facial identity kits, the origins of profiling stem from the investigation of atypical crimes that usually feature a psychologically aberrant offender whose motives appear outside typical criminological patterns and police

---

*This chapter is a revised version of the manuscript originally published as: Kocsis, R. N. (2003). "Criminal psychological profiling: Validities and abilities?" *International Journal of Offender Therapy and Comparative Criminology*, 47(2), 126–144.

investigative procedures (Fisher, 1993; Geberth, 1981). Indeed, the genesis of profiling as a technique seems inextricably linked with the concept of the serial sexual murderer. The investigation of possibly one of history's first serial killers, the Whitechappel murderer (aka "Jack the Ripper"), involved the consultation of psychiatrist Dr. Thomas Bond to provide the police investigation with some description of the potential offender based upon the behaviors exhibited in the crimes (Rumbelow, 1988). Other historical subjects of criminal profiles include the Mad Bomber of New York, and the Boston Strangler (Brussel, 1968; Frank, 1966). Although now advanced by progress in various disciplines, the fundamental concept of interpreting behaviors to determine attributes of the probable offender(s) remains essentially the same to this day.

Despite the long history of psychological analysis in assisting some form of criminal investigation (now contemporaneously termed "profiling") and its popular renown over other forensic techniques, surprisingly little empirical scrutiny has been undertaken to examine the validity of profiling vis-à-vis correspondence between a profile and the actual perpetrator (Oleson, 1996). Indeed, the bulk of material cited in support of the accuracy, and thereby validity, of profiling consists of largely anecdotal accounts found in true crime memoirs (e.g., Britton, 1997; Douglas & Olshaker, 1995; Ressler & Shachtman, 1992) or in professional journals (e.g., Douglas & Burgess, 1986; Vorpagel, 1982). A number of studies have shown that police are often happy with or request profiling services in their investigations (e.g., Copson, 1995; Jackson, Van Koppen, & Herbrink, 1993), and at times these consumer satisfaction studies appear to be offered as evidence to support the accuracy of profiling (Ainsworth, 2001; Gudjonson & Copson, 1997; Stevens, 1997; West, 2001).

The purpose of this chapter is to contribute to the empirical knowledge of the effectiveness of criminal profiling. The conclusions offered in this chapter combine the research of Kocsis, Irwin, Hayes, and Nunn (2000), Kocsis, Hayes, and Irwin (2002), and Kocsis (2004) with some additional original data included in the analysis. These results provide some comparative and empirically based understanding of the level of accuracy and types of information profilers appear more proficient in while seeking to identify the constituent skills that contribute to effective profiling.

Past Empirical Examinations of Profiling

Possibly the first empirically based study investigating the accuracy of profiling was undertaken by Pinizzotto and Finkel (1990). This research involved the details of a closed rape and murder case being given to various small groups (consisting of six subjects in each). The respective groups were trained profilers, police detectives, clinical psychologists, and students. Each group was assigned the same profiling exercises and asked to identify the likely offender. The details of the perpetrators of both offenses were known, thus providing the "correct" profile as a criterion for quantitative analysis. This research was composed of six small studies that included exercises that involved the linguistic measurement of the produced profiles, a prioritization exercise of potential suspects, and an exercise to measure the recollection of case information. However, of most relevance in the study conducted by Pinizzotto and Finkel was an exercise that involved administering two 15-item multiple-choice questionnaires to each participant in each of the groups. These questionnaires were designed to objectively elicit from each of the participants predictions concerning the characteristics of the probable offender for both the rape and murder case. This study, as a consequence, served as the first quantitatively based demonstration of profiling accuracy. Unfortunately, however, the results of Pinizzotto and Finkel's (1990) study were far from unequivocal in demonstrating the accuracy of profilers. No significant differences were found amongst any of the groups involving the number of correct predictions in the murder case. Indeed, the sampled profilers were unable to predict the characteristics of the murderer any better than any of the compared groups, and indeed, their mean score was found to be the lowest amongst the four groups.

Slightly better results however, emerged with respect to the sexual assault case. First, the profilers were found to significantly outperform a categorization of non-profilers that combined the scores of the detectives, psychologists, and students. Additionally, a law enforcement categorization of profilers and detectives surpassed the non-law-enforcement categorization of psychologists and students. Finally, a categorization of all professional groups—that is, the combination of profilers, detectives, and psychologists—surpassed the nonprofessional students. When examining the specific items of information in which profilers excelled, it was found that they consistently identified items concerning age, education, and the vehicle condition of the offender, as well as the nature of the relationship between the victim and the offender.

New Empirical Research

More recent endeavors in empirically testing the accuracy and therefore validity of profiling have been akin to the approach adopted by Pinizzotto and Finkel (1990) by presenting information to participants about a crime where the offender's characteristics were already known. The individual findings from each of these studies are reported in Kocsis et al. (2000, 2002, 2004). The design of each study was similar to that of Pinizzotto and Finkel (1990) in that it involved a solved arson or murder case. Next, all the case materials for each of the crimes that had been available to investigators prior to the respective perpetrator's apprehension were assembled and summarized. Accompanying each of these case packages was a 33-item multiple-choice questionnaire that was designed to elicit an objective description of the probable offender.[1] As both of the cases had been solved, the responses to the questionnaires could be objectively scored for accuracy against the known details of the convicted offender. Thus, these studies sought to examine the correlates of accuracy vis-à-vis the characteristics of the person writing the profile.

What skills or special aptitudes might be useful in constructing an accurate profile? With the exception of Hazelwood, Ressler, Depue, and Douglas (1995), the literature is largely silent on this matter. Generally four principal attributes emerge as being essential to effective profiling. The first skill identified by Hazelwood et al. (1995) is an appreciation of the criminal mind and entails an ability to understand the type of person who committed any given crime. The second prescribed skill is that of investigative experience, and in the opinion of Hazelwood et al. (1995, p. 119), "No amount of education can replace the experience of having investigated crimes." The third skill is a capacity for objective and logical analysis; that is, the profiler must possess an ability to think logically without being diverted by personal feelings about the crime. The fourth nominated skill is the psychic-like faculty of intuition.[2] The various studies by Kocsis et al. sought to empirically examine the relevance of each of these skills to effective profiling.

To emulate the skills of objective reasoning, investigative experience, behavioral knowledge, and intuition for the purpose of the studies, participants were recruited who predominantly demonstrated each of these skills. Consequently, a sample of 20 self-declared psychics was selected to demonstrate the capacity for intuition. To garner a group of individuals who possessed skills in logical and objective reasoning, a combined sample of 85 university science sophomores was obtained over all three studies. For some representation of an understanding of the human psyche and appreciation of behavior, a combined sample of 36 psychologists was assembled from the first two studies.

Clearly, the most obvious group of individuals who are inherently representative of investigative experience is police personnel. However, due to Hazelwood et al.'s (1995) description of investigative experience as a *quintessential* skill for effective profiling, particular focus was placed on the empirical documentation of this skill. For this reason, numerous samples were obtained to account for a range of both quantitative and qualitative possibilities concerning the inherent attributes likely to stem from such experience. The fundamental notion of investigative experience involves quantitative notions of exposure. Presumably, Hazelwood et al. (1995) consider that the more criminal investigative experience an individual has had, the more likely they are to be proficient profilers. Consequently, to account for such quantitative differences, three samples of police personnel were recruited to optimally examine any role of quantitative differences in investigative experience. To represent the novice capabilities derived from only minimal experience, a combined sample was obtained of 50 police recruits who had just commenced their training as police officers. As a contrast to the recruits, two samples of experienced police personnel were obtained. One combined sample comprised of 88 general police personnel who possessed a substantial amount of experience but not necessarily with respect to the investigation of crimes in any specialized area relevant to the case information. The second combined sample consisted of 26 specialist detectives who also possessed a significant amount of experience, but this experience was sourced specifically in the investigation of crimes akin to the presented cases (i.e., murder and arson).

Another important aspect of investigative experience involves a qualitative dimension. Thus, it is not merely experience in the investigation of crime alone that is relevant, but specific experience in the investigation of crimes presented for profiling. To take account of this factor, the previously mentioned samples of general police versus specialist detectives were relied upon. However, to further explore this issue, an additional group of 12 non-police specialists was also introduced. This group comprised of arson investigators from fire brigades. This group of 12 personnel possessed a substantial amount of specialized experience in the investigation of arson offenses akin to the specialist detective, and thus possessed a qualitative investigative experience different from that of a police officer.

As the pivotal issue of this research is the empirical assessment of accuracy in profiling, a combined sample of 11 profilers was assembled during the course of all three studies. Thus, the profiler group was expected to provide a demonstration of their capabilities that would serve as a criterion against which to compare the performance of the other groups.

Finally, to act as a control condition for all of the previously mentioned groups, a combined sample of 120 unskilled participants was obtained during the course of all three studies. These individuals did not possess skills akin to any of the previously described groups. Furthermore, these control participants were not given any case information for the crimes and were instructed to complete the multiple-choice questionnaire simply by speculating about what they believed were the characteristics of the "typical" murderer or serial arsonist. This control condition, therefore, afforded an empirical demonstration of what could be achieved on the questionnaire simply by guesswork and reliance upon stereotypical notions of a murderer or serial arsonist.

As the purpose of this chapter is to present a holistic impression of the data from all three of the previous studies, as well as to incorporate additional data not previously utilized, a procedure was undertaken to make the scores comparable across all studies prior to combining the data. Both Kocsis et al. (2000, 2002) used a homicide case, whereas Kocsis (2004) used an arson case. Given that these are different crimes, and the questions on the profiling task were different, it is not necessarily the case that getting, say, 15 questions correct on the homicide profiling task equates to the same accuracy as getting 15 correct on the arson profiling task. To make the scores comparable prior to pooling the studies, the accuracy scores were first standardized within crime type by converting the scores to z scores (i.e., deviations from the study mean in standard deviation units). After this transformation, an accuracy score of one, for example, corresponds to performance one standard deviation above the mean, where the mean is in reference to the performance of all participants completing the profiling task for that particular crime ($n = 335$ for homicide and $n = 95$ for arson). Converting the scores to this common metric makes them comparable across studies. Table 8.1 summarizes the combined analysis of the data sets from all studies as well as the additional data.

The Performance of Profilers

The fundamental aim of this analysis was to undertake an empirical examination of the capabilities of profilers with specific regard to whether they could produce a more accurate profile of an unknown offender by way of holistic comparison to the other sampled groups from the combined previous studies. From the limited sample of 11 profilers, some affirmative indication emerged to the effect that the sampled profilers were capable of outperforming the other tested groups. In particular, the profilers surpassed all of the compared groups in the total number of correct predictions as shown in Table 8.1. Although in no way claiming to be

Table 8.1 Mean Profile Accuracy, Standardized within Crime Type (Standard Deviations in Parentheses)

	Accuracy Measure				
Group	Total Correct	Physical Characteristics	Cognitive Responses	Offense Behaviors	Social Habits/ History
Psychologists ($n = 36$)	0.16 (1.13)	0.50 (0.74)	−0.30 (1.09)	0.33 (0.95)	−0.10 (1.10)
Profilers ($n = 11$)	0.82 (1.32)	0.56 (0.69)	0.34 (1.14)	0.34 (1.07)	0.49 (1.08)
Science Students ($n = 85$)	0.31 (0.87)	0.40 (0.84)	−0.18 (0.98)	0.10 (0.98)	0.37 (0.94)
Specialist Detectives ($n = 25$)	−0.43 (1.09)	0.17 (0.85)	−0.37 (1.05)	−0.22 (0.95)	−0.47 (0.91)
Psychics ($n = 20$)	−0.14 (0.87)	−0.38 (1.07)	0.19 (0.96)	0.05 (0.77)	−0.18 (1.15)
Non-Police Specialists ($n = 12$)	0.12 (0.90)	0.48 (0.90)	−0.40 (1.01)	−0.23 (1.11)	0.35 (0.67)
General Police ($n = 85$)	0.07 (0.90)	0.19 (0.81)	0.07 (0.88)	−0.08 (1.01)	0.00 (0.93)
Police Recruits ($n = 50$)	0.17 (1.03)	0.22 (0.97)	0.15 (1.04)	−0.26 (1.00)	0.24 (1.05)
Stereotype Controls ($n = 120$)	−0.36 (0.92)	−0.73 (0.95)	0.15 (0.98)	0.02 (1.01)	−0.28 (0.92)

statistically representative, the current sample of 11 profilers does nonetheless represent the largest empirical sample currently available involving individualized group comparisons[3] to inform the scientific and law enforcement communities on the issue of proficiency.

This positive result, however, does show some incongruity, as individual profilers were not uniformly superior in their performance. Indeed, the profiler group demonstrated the second-highest degree of statistical variation amongst any of the sampled groups. This finding suggests that there is a clear potential for variation in abilities amongst profilers. Simply because an individual is labeled and/or professionally engaged in profiling does not necessarily mean they are accurate in their predictions or that their accuracy is uniform from one case to another.

The Skill of Investigative Experience

Quite possibly, the most prominent claim concerning the requisite skills for profiling involves investigative experience. This skill is presumably only acquired by police personnel and is viewed as a prerequisite (Hazelwood et al., 1995). The importance of this skill is visible in the recruitment, training, and policies of policing agencies that often prefer to select police personnel with such experience over other potential individuals who lack investigative experience but may possess other useful skills. Given the stated importance of investigative experience, it would therefore be a logical assumption to expect individuals with such experience to demonstrate superior performance over the other sampled groups lacking in such experience, with the possible exception of the profilers.

Unfortunately, the combined data fails to support the asserted importance of investigative experience as the key skill necessary for proficient profiling. Indeed, police personnel and the non-police specialist investigators demonstrate poor performance across all of the measures in comparison to most of the other groups. More remarkable is that when our examination focused upon the three police groups, the virtual reverse of Hazelwood et al.'s (1995) observation was observed. Senior police officers with the most investigative experience performed the worst, generalist police with a moderate amount of experience demonstrated a modest position in performance, while police recruits with no investigative experience performed the best (Kocsis et al., 2002).

What could possibly explain the poor performance observed in the police groups and furthermore the negative relationship between profiling accuracy and investigative experience? At the outset it must be recognized that profiling is a discrete task in which police personnel are not routinely trained or that they engage in (Geberth, 1996; Stevens, 1997). That is, police personnel are generally not trained to be profilers and thus may not necessarily possess any pertinent skills or experience specific to the task of profiling. However, given police personnel's exposure to crime and the criminal justice system, it would perhaps be natural to expect that these activities would have some influence upon their reasoning when attempting to construct a criminal profile.

One possible explanation may lie with the prevailing educational standards of each of the police groups. That is, each of the sampled police groups may represent not only the degree of experience, but also the recruitment and education criteria of their time. The observed trend may therefore be a reflection of historical changes in criteria for recruitment that may select individuals better suited to the presented profiling task.

Another possible explanation may lie in considering the effects of experience on the cognitive processes of police personnel. Social psychology has long studied the authoritarian personality and its manifestations in police culture and behaviors. Although speculative, perhaps experience in the investigation of crime may actually generate various erroneous heuristic assumptions about crime and criminal behavior that are manifested in the observed results (Chapman & Chapman, 1969).

Perhaps a more pertinent question to emerge from the overall results of the police groups is not why senior detectives performed so poorly, but rather, why the police recruits performed so well in comparison. Although the above-mentioned issues of generation difference and/or heuristics may assist in answering this conundrum, another explanation may lie not in the differences of the recruits, but rather in their similarities to other groups. This point will be explored further in our examination of the science sophomores.

Science Sophomores and the Capacity for Logical and Objective Reasoning

Quite possibly the most surprising finding to emerge from the combined data in Table 8.1 comes from the performance of the sampled psychologists and especially the science sophomores. Following the profilers, the science sophomores and psychologists appear to be the next most proficient groups. This result was also observed in the initial study by Kocsis et al. (2000) and has generally remained consistent throughout each of the subsequent studies (Kocsis et al. 2000, 2002; Kocsis, 2004). Given the long-standing association between the profiler concept and the behavioral sciences, the superior performance of the psychologist was not entirely unanticipated (Drukteinis, 1992; Rappaport, 1988; Turco, 1990). The truly remarkable result however, lies in the high performance of the science sophomores who possessed no particular knowledge or skills in behavioral science, psychology, psychiatry, or criminal investigation. Indeed, across most of the scales, the science sophomores actually surpassed the sampled psychologists making them, arguably, the most proficient group after the profilers. Furthermore, the science sophomores demonstrated the least amount of group variance, indicating that their performance is consistent with some form of element or factor common to their group. There are a number of important implications to arise from this trend, which critically serves to inform our understanding of criminal profiling.

At the outset, the findings give further impetus to considering the actual importance of investigative experience to profiling. What, however, does appear to be the crucial skill necessary for proficient profiling? The initial findings of Kocsis et al. (2000) indicated psychologists had a slight numerical lead on the sampled science sophomores. The data taken over all three previous studies and now combined within this study reverses this trend. To best understand this phenomenon, the author believes that the answers lie in the similarities between these two groups rather than their differences. That is, although psychologist participants possessed a degree of training and understanding of human behavior, they are also orientated with a capacity for logical and objective thinking akin to the science sophomores. Were the insights garnered from psychological training of significant importance, it would be expected that the psychologists would demonstrate some degree of superiority over the science sophomores. Indeed, aspects of this hypothesis, to some degree, are demonstrated by the performance of the police recruits. Unlike their predecessors, the specialist detectives, general police, or even the non-police specialists, the current sample of police recruits are selected and trained under a university diploma qualification. Previous generations of police personnel were primarily educated under a paramilitary system, whereas the sampled recruits were primarily educated via a university program designed to foster critical thinking, analysis, and expression (Aik & Edmonds, 1986; Winterowd & Winterowd, 1997). Thus, the common element amongst the profilers, psychologists, science sophomores, and police recruits may be sourced in the respective participants having engaged in some form of higher education that encourages skills such as critical thinking.

Psychic Detectives: Are They Better Than Bartenders?

Finally, some review must also be made of the performance of the psychics, the intuitive skill they represent, and the proficiencies of the various groups in their predictions beyond what could be merely achieved through guesswork. The final factor is particularly pertinent to the control groups who answered the questionnaires without the benefit of case information, for their performance is an indication of what could be predicted simply by speculation and/or the cognitive social stereotype of the typical murderer or arsonist. Again, an interesting pattern emerges that is congruent with the higher education/critical thought hypothesis. All participants who possess some higher educational background demonstrated a degree of superiority over the stereotype controls. The groups without such an educational background, however, tended to demonstrate poor performance that appears to be relative to that of the stereotype controls. The most pronounced of these groups were the psychics and the specialist detectives.

There are a number of issues that arise from this first factor that further serve to inform our understanding of profiling. One of the earliest criticisms of profiling was its description as "hit and miss and no better than what the average bartender could predict" (Campbell, 1976, p. 213). Although colloquial in expression, Campbell had identified a key issue in not only questioning the accuracy of profilers, but also whether this degree of accuracy represents anything beyond common knowledge or what the local bartender might be expected to surmise. The present findings go some way toward demonstrating that profilers can produce quantitatively more accurate predictions than what might reasonably be achieved through guesswork or common knowledge, which a lay person or bartender may be expected to possess.

Although not directly related to the topic of profiling, the concept of psychics assisting in police investigations in a similar fashion to a profiler is not unusual (Lyons & Truzzi, 1991; Reiser, Ludwig, Saxe, & Wagner, 1979; Wiseman, West, & Stemman, 1996). Indeed, some texts describe the use of psychics in a similar context to profiling (e.g., Geberth, 1981, 1996). The combined data suggest little support for the use of psychics in accurately generating the characteristics of an unknown offender. Additionally, given the apparently poor performance of the psychic group in comparison to the control group, the importance of intuitive thinking in the construction of profiles appears limited. Indeed, this aspect of intuition may be observable in the specialist detectives who predominantly came from more senior generations of police officers and who may have relied on the colloquial "gut instinct" to inform their views regarding the likely offender.

Limitations and Directions for the Future

Further empirical investigation into the validity and underlying skills of criminal profiling is undoubtedly still warranted. It is quite disappointing to consider that, despite the popularity of profiling, very little in the way of genuinely original data-driven research testing the capabilities of profilers has been published in scholarly mediums beyond the studies conducted by Kocsis and colleagues and the work by Pinizzotto and Finkel (1990). However, replication and development of similar studies may not be the most viable option for further exploring the subject of profiling due to the apparent difficulties in obtaining the cooperation of participants. Indeed, the combined data covered by this manuscript was collected from three consecutive studies that spanned a period of approximately six years and yet was only able to achieve an accumulative total of 11 profilers.

Regrettably, it seems that alternative avenues may be needed to explore the efficacy of profiling to overcome such logistical impediments. Perhaps one of the most feasible ways of facilitating such empirical research may be via the utilization of participants who have demonstrated similar proficiency to the sampled profilers. From the present findings, the most likely groups could be science sophomores or psychologists. Both of these groups have consistently demonstrated strong performance in comparison to the sampled profilers and are likely to be a readily available source of data. Indeed, it is quite possible that the utilization of such proxy samples may help to remedy the tardy scientific development that seems to plague this topic (Oleson, 1996).

Alternate approaches to studying profiling are also warranted as they may have the effect of circumventing the methodological limitations of the present research. Although the present research provides much needed objective measures for profiling accuracy, this work only examines profiling performance within the context of a multiple-choice questionnaire. Thus, the studies collectively impose various recognition and response parameters that are not encountered in the actual investigative application of the profiling technique (Kocsis, 2006). Another possible shortcoming of these studies is the possibility that the observed results are actually representations of idiosyncratic artifacts of the utilized cases in each of the experiments. That is, some atypical feature of a particular case used in these experiments may have potentially skewed the results. Although the study by Kocsis (2004) provides some evidence to guard against this contingency Pinizzotto and Finkel (1990) consider this rationale as one of the most viable explanations for the poor performance of the sampled profilers in their homicide case exercise. The substantial logistical difficulties that would be encountered in obtaining a sufficiently diverse representation of cases and then administering them to a suitably large sample once again highlight the need for more innovative research designs in the future.

One final issue worthy of consideration is whether there may also be some variation in intelligence across the sampled groups. This issue was first identified in referees' comments on the paper by Kocsis et al. (2000) and was then more explicitly considered in the study by Kocsis et al. (2002) with the administration of the 16PF intelligence scale (IPAT, 1993). In the latter analysis, no significant differences emerged between any of the sampled groups on the 16PF intelligence scale. Nonetheless, given the high statistical variance within the profiler group and the low variance in the science sophomore group, perhaps further exploration of this issue is indeed warranted via the administration of a thorough IQ instrument testing for covariance with participants' performance. Unfortunately, due to logistical constraints, a thorough measure of IQ was not capable of being feasibly incorporated into the undertaken research.

Conclusions

Although nowhere near enough, a small amount of empirically based data has emerged to support the validity of a profiler's capacity to accurately describe the characteristics of an unknown offender. Accompanying this new evidence, however, is a number of unexpected findings that challenge some of the existing preconceptions concerning the constituent skills required for effective profiling. Possibly the most notable is the apparent importance of logical and objective reasoning and the seeming unimportance of investigative experience. The implications of these findings should hopefully serve to guide future recruitment and training methods of personnel selected to work as profilers in support of criminal investigations. With more empirically based evidence, the reputation of profiling may move beyond a stylized art and toward a more replicable science akin to other forms of forensic tools that are presently subjected to judicial scrutiny.

The findings of some studies into the profiling technique have been previously misinterpreted and utilized as evidence to support a variety of unsubstantiated policy initiatives and/or policing organizational plans (Ainsworth, 2001; Stevens, 1997; West, 2001). Consequently, it must be clearly recognized that although some promising measure of empirical support has emerged for the accuracy of professional profilers, these conclusions say nothing about the utility of these profiles in assisting criminal investigations. The present findings are only pertinent to the issue of accuracy. These findings do not necessarily imply that the information contained within such profiles would consistently prove to be of any definitive utility in assisting a police investigation in actually apprehending an offender. Most anecdotal accounts of profiling do not describe profiles as identifying and thereby leading to the apprehension of an offender. Rather, in retrospect, the predictions contained in profiles are interpreted as matching the offender who is apprehended typically through normal investigative procedures (Britton, 1997; Brussel, 1968; Douglas & Olshaker, 1996; Egger, 1984; Jeffers, 1992; Kennedy & Whitaker, 1992; Shears, 1996). Indeed, a survey of police agencies that had used a profiling service found that although 46% of the profiles were deemed to be of some benefit to the investigation, only 17% were considered to be of any assistance in the actual identification of the suspect (Pinizzotto, 1984). Consequently, the issue of profiler input and therefore utility in actually assisting a criminal investigation is still one requiring consideration.

A more comprehensive picture is now beginning to emerge regarding the likely skill and accuracy of profilers. Although at a disappointedly slow rate, the practice of profiling is developing some measure of empirical evidence to support its validity. With further development, including the publication of theoretical principles capable of replication, the scientific rigor of profiling as a technique should improve immeasurably.

Notes

1. Full details of these case booklets and questionnaires can be found in Kocsis et al. (2000) and Kocsis (2004).
2. A more comprehensive discussion of the rationale underpinning each of these skills and the identification of participants for these skills can be found in Kocsis et al. (2000).
3. The author uses these terms to reflect the nature of this analysis as involving individual comparisons of all sampled skill-based groups against each other rather than any form of merged analysis wherein differing groups are collapsed into a dichotomous categorisation such as being either a profiler or nonprofiler. Readers may refer to Kocsis et al. (2008) and Kocsis (2010) for the limitations of such methods.

References

Aik, K. C., & Edmonds, S. (1986). *Critical thinking: Selected topics for discussion and analysis*. Singapore: Longman Publishers.

Ainsworth, P. (2001). *Offender profiling and crime analysis*. London: Willan Publishing.

Britton, P. (1997). *The jigsaw man*. London: Bantam Press.

Brussel, J. (1968). *Casebook of a criminal psychiatrist*. New York: Bernard Geis.

Campbell, C. (1976, May). Portrait of a mass killer. *Psychology Today, 9*(12), 110–119.

Canter, D., & Larkin, P. (1993). The environmental range of serial rapists. *Journal of Environmental Psychology, 13*, 63–69.

Chapman, L. J., & Chapman, J. P. (1969). Illusory correlation as an obstacle to the use of valid diagnostic signs. *Journal of Abnormal Psychology, 74*, 271–280.

Copson, G. (1995). *Coals to Newcastle: A study of offender profiling*. Police Research Group, Special Interest Series. UK: Home Office.

Douglas, J. E., & Burgess, A. W. (1986). Criminal profiling: A viable investigative tool against violent crime. *FBI Law Enforcement Bulletin, 55*(12), 9–13.

Douglas, J. E., & Olshaker, M. (1995). *Mindhunter*. London: Heinemann.

Douglas, J. E., & Olshaker, M. (1996). *Unabomber*. New York: Pocket Books.
Drukteinis, A. M. (1992). Serial murder: The heart of darkness. *Psychiatric Annals, 22*, 532–538.
Egger, S. A. (1984). A working definition of serial murder and the reduction of linkage blindness. *Journal of Police Science and Administration. 12*, 348–357.
Frank, G. (1966). *The Boston strangler*. New York: New American Library.
Fisher, A. J. (1993). *Techniques of crime scene investigation* (5th ed.). New York: Elsevier.
Geberth, V. J. (1981). Psychological profiling. *Law and Order, 29*(2), 46–52.
Geberth, V. J. (1996). *Practical homicide investigation: Tactics, procedures and forensic techniques* (3rd ed.). Boca Raton, FL: CRC Press.
Gudjonson, G. H., & Copson, G. (1997). The role of the expert in criminal investigation. In J. L. Jackson & D. A. Bekerian (Eds.), *Offender profiling: Theory, research and practice* (pp. 61–76). Chichester, UK: Wiley.
Harrower, M. (1998). *Applying psychology to crime*. London: Hodder & Stoughton.
Hazelwood, R. R., Ressler, R. K., Depue, R. L., & Douglas, J. C. (1995). Criminal investigative analysis: An overview. In R. R. Hazelwood & A. W. Burgess (Eds.), *Practical aspects of rape investigation: A multidisciplinary approach* (2nd ed., pp. 115–126). Boca Raton. FL: CRC Press.
Holmes, R. M., & Holmes, S. T. (1996). *Profiling violent crimes: An investigative tool* (2nd ed.). Thousand Oaks, CA: Sage.
IPAT. (1993). *The 16-personality factor questionnaire*. Illinois: Institute for Personality and Ability Testing.
Jackson, J. L., Van Koppen, P. J., & Herbrink, C. M. (1993). *Does the service meet the needs? An evaluation of consumer satisfaction with specific profile analysis and investigative advice as offered by the scientific research advisory unit of the National Criminal Intelligence Division (CRI)*, The Netherlands: NISCALE Report NSCR 93-05.
Jeffers, H. P. (1992). *Profiles in evil*. London: Warner Bros.
Kennedy, L., & Whitaker, M. (1992). *Granny killer: The story of John Glover*. Sydney: HarperCollins.
Kocsis, R. N. (2004). Psychological profiling of serial arson offenses: An assessment of skills and accuracy. *Criminal Justice and Behavior. 31*(3), 341–361.
Kocsis, R. N. (2006). *Criminal profiling: Principles and practice*. Totowa, NJ: Humana/Springer.
Kocsis, R. N. (2008). Taking stock of accuracy in criminal profiling: The theoretical quandary for investigative psychology. *Journal of Forensic Psychology Practice, 8*(3), 244–261.
Kocsis, R. N. (2009). *Applied criminal psychology*. Springfield, IL: Charles C. Thomas.
Kocsis, R. N. (2010). Criminal profiling works and EVERYONE agrees. *Journal of Forensic Psychology Practice, 10*(3), 224–237.

Kocsis, R. N., Hayes, A. F., & Irwin, H. J. (2002). Investigative experience and accuracy in psychological profiling a violent crime. *Journal of Interpersonal Violence, 17*(8), 811–823.

Kocsis, R. N., Irwin, H. J., Hayes, A. F., & Nunn, R. (2000). Expertise in psychological profiling: A comparative assessment. *Journal of Interpersonal Violence, 15*, 311–331.

Lyons, A., & Truzzi, M. (1991). *The blue sense: Psychic detectives and crime*. New York: Warner.

Oleson, J. C. (1996). Psychological profiling: Does it really work? *Forensic Update, 46*, 11–14.

Pinizzotto, A. J. (1984). Forensic psychology: Criminal personality profiling. *Journal of Police Science and Administration, 12*(1), 32–40.

Pinizzotto, A. J., & Finkel, N. J. (1990). Criminal personality profiling: An outcome and process study. *Law and Human Behavior, 14*, 215–233.

Rappaport, R. G. (1988). The serial and mass murderer: Patterns, differentiation, pathology. *American Journal of Forensic Psychiatry, 9*(2), 39–48.

Reiser, M., Ludwig, L., Saxe, S., & Wagner, C. (1979). An evaluation of the use of psychics in the investigation of major crimes. *Journal of Police Science and Administration, 7*, 18–25.

Ressler, R. K., & Shachtman, T. (1992). *Whoever fights monsters*. London: Simon & Schuster.

Rossmo, D. K. (2000). *Geographic profiling*. Boca Raton, FL: CRC Press.

Rumbelow, D. (1988). *The complete Jack the Ripper*. London: Penguin.

Shears, R. (1996). *Highway to nowhere*. Sydney: HarperCollins.

Stevens, J. A. (1997). Standard investigatory tools and offender profiling. In J. L. Jackson & D. A. Bekerian (Eds.), *Offender profiling: Theory, research and practice*. Chichester, UK: Wiley.

Turco, R. N. (1990). Psychological profiling. *International Journal of Offender Therapy and Comparative Criminology, 34*, 147–154.

Vorpagel, R. E. (1982). Painting psychological profiles: Charlatanism, coincidence, charisma or new science. *Police Chief, 3*(8), 156–159.

West, A. G. (2001). From offender profiler to behavioural investigative advisor: The effective application of behavioural science to the investigation of major crime. *Police Research and Management, 5*(1), 95–108.

Winterowd, W. R., & Winterowd, G. R. (1997). *The critical reader, thinker and writer* (2nd ed.). San Francisco: Mayfield.

Wiseman, R., West, D., & Stemman, R. (1996). An experimental test of psychic detection. *Journal of the Society of Psychical Research, 61*, 34–45.

CHAPTER NINE

Linkage Analysis of Serial Murder Cases Involving Prostitute Victims

C. Gabrielle Salfati

Introduction

The key questions in the area of linking serial murder are whether we can link crime scenes to each other and thereby identify a series, while also identifying different series from one another. One of the key approaches has been to focus on the type of victim that the offender targets. One of the groups of particular focus has been that of vulnerable victims.

Egger suggests (2003, cited in Quinet, 2011) that 65% of serial murder victims are female, and nearly 78% of female victims of serial murderers are prostitutes. As a subgroup of vulnerable victims, they therefore present a highly targeted group. When street prostitutes as a group are looked at in general, figures show that homicide is the second-leading cause of death amongst prostitutes in Canada (Lowman & Fraser, 1995). Being a street prostitute in the United States makes a woman 18 times more likely to be murdered than non-prostitute women of similar demographics (Potterat et al., 2004). Prostitute homicides are also some of the most difficult to solve, with figures in the United Kingdom suggesting that 10 years on, 69% were still unsolved (Kinnell, 2001). An important question regarding violence against prostitutes is whether it takes place due to opportunity and availability, whether prostitutes represent specific targets to the offender, or whether there is another consistent pattern to the selection of victims. Understanding what the consistency is between victims is key to understanding the link between prostitute homicides and non-prostitute homicides, particularly within the series itself.

This chapter aims to connect the literature on linking serial murder with the literature on behavioral consistency, with a specific focus on series that involve prostitute victims either exclusively or as part of a mixed-victim series, to further discuss possible underlying patterns to offender victim targeting.

Linking Serial Homicide

The key questions in the area of linking are whether we can link crime scenes to each other, and thereby identify a series, while also identifying different series from one another. Specifically, what behaviors may be the most reliable to focus on when we make this determination? So, what do we mean by consistency, and how might this be displayed?

It is of crucial importance, however, that before we even start looking at linking and consistency patterns in an offender's "series," we clearly define what a series is (Salfati, 2008a, 2011). Salfati and Taylor (2006) make the additional important point that much of the criminological literature conceptualizes legally separate crimes, based on interpretations of crime seriousness rather than any criminological or psychological measurement—e.g., sexual homicide and rape are seen as two crimes set apart by very different psychological mechanisms and motivations. As a consequence, research adhering to such legal distinctions accepts a restricted perspective for examining patterns in offenders' behavior and may consequently overlook important similarities and differences across the various forms, e.g., sexual violence. In order to fully understand crimes such as sexual violence, it is necessary to extend beyond a research perspective shaped by legal classifications and instead identify the actual psychological variations in crime scene actions that will differentiate between sexually violent offenses.

Salfati and Taylor's study analyzed a sample of 37 sexual homicides and 37 rapes determining whether these two types of offending were specialized types of crime, or whether they were on a sexual assault continuum. They first identified key behaviors of sexual assault crime scenes and, secondly, compared these in terms of their relative importance in sexual homicide and rape offenses. Their analysis indicated that offender-victim interactions in sexual homicide and rape were predominantly distinguished by the degree of violence, so that behaviors associated with each type of offense were found to occur in two discrete points along a single continuum. Their study clearly highlighted the need to understand criminal behavior beyond its primary legal definitions, by looking at it in relation to the psychological meaning it may have to the offender. Salfati (2008a) points out that this becomes especially important when we look at the progression of an offender's crime development, and attempt to understand the consistency pattern, i.e., in cases where an offender progresses from sexual assaults, to rapes, to sexual homicides. Each one of these crimes is a separate legal crime type, but psychologically, the offender is committing a series of sexual assaults that shows psychological consistency. However, the offender is also showing development and change as well as escalation in both physical invasion of the victim and escalation in violence.

Before we test whether an offender is consistent, however, a number of recent studies (Bateman & Salfati, 2007; Salfati, 2011; Salfati & Bateman, 2005) have made the argument stressing the need to define the point of focus we start from in making this determination. Notably, we must define whether we look at the individual behavior (i.e., "binding" or "gagging"), or whether we look at the psychological type of behavior, or what we also call a theme (i.e., "controlling"). Salfati (2011) provides an illustrative example based on psychological types of rapes originally developed by Canter and Heritage (1990). The example outlines a hypothetical situation in which a number of rapes have been committed and have been linked, because in each case, the offender used the single identifying behavior of gagging his victim. In addition, another rape has occurred where the offender bound the victim. By using a single behavior to focus on, only one series has been identified, and has also excluded us from linking the one rape to the series of rapes.

Canter and Heritage (1990) show that there is a subgroup of offenders whose primary psychological theme is one of control, and these offenders will engage in a certain subset of behaviors that physically demonstrate this psychological theme. By moving from the individual to the thematic, we can expand the unit of analysis from the descriptive to the psychological, and thereby increase our chances of linking. This becomes important when the individual level of analysis is affected by the situational factors, e.g., the offender may bind the victim in situations where she tries to run away, yet gag her in situations where she screams. In both situations, although the individual behaviors are different, they both illustrate the offender attempting to control the situation. The offender possesses a variety of offending behaviors with the same function, which are used in a different context. Therefore, relying on psychological themes establishes context-victim connections that are typically ignored in offender-focused approaches when analyzing behavior.

Recent work (e.g., Horning, Salfati, & Labuschagne, 2012; Salfati, Horning, Sorochinski, & Labuschagne, 2012) has corroborated this by showing the usefulness of looking at the victim targeting as a focus in modeling offender behavior, and linking serial crimes. In this way we use our understanding of the interpersonal interaction between the offender and victim to learn more about the offender. We also identify different offender characteristics depending on what actions the offenders display.

Bateman and Salfati (2007) state that researchers and practitioners until very recently did not explain in detail how they link crimes, so the validity of their statements is left untested. Indeed, much of this early literature was not supported by empirical studies, but instead was a collection of theoretical and practice-led papers that proposed patterns. Although this wealth of experience provides a great basis for understanding behavior, a detailed examination and definition of linking and behavioral consistency needs to be developed and empirically tested.

Salfati and Bateman (2005) and Bateman and Salfati (2007) provide the first two studies in the linking literature that focus specifically on the methodological and theoretical differences between the individual behavioral-unit approach and the thematic approach.

Linking Using Individual Behaviors

One focus in the theoretical literature on linking has been on what has been termed "signatures" (for details regarding the literature in this area, see Bateman & Salfati, 2007). Douglas and Munn (1992) define signature as the "calling card" left by the offender that is unique to the offender's pattern of behaviors throughout their offenses. For example, this signature may be related to the ritualistic acts committed by an offender, perhaps to fulfill a specific fantasy. They explain that the signature aspect of the violent offense is a constant behavior performed by an offender during his offenses but that it may evolve and become more developed throughout the offense series. Unfortunately, as Bateman and Salfati (2007) highlight, early research in this area did not explain in detail how these conclusions were arrived at, so that the validity of their statements is left untested. Bateman and Salfati explain that the idea behind using individual behaviors is that an investigator should be able to look at a crime, in this case a homicide, and identify individual crime scene behaviors that are unique to a particular offender. From here, if a second homicide occurs, the investigator can look to see whether these same individual behaviors exist in the new homicide and if so, can infer that there is a strong possibility that the two homicides in question are linked. But they highlight that much of the literature on signatures is not backed up by empirical studies to provide the basis for making these links. A detailed examination and definition of what a signature consists of needs to be more fully developed, as well as an empirical testing of its inherent ability to account for consistency across an offender's series.

Bateman and Salfati (2007) go on to provide the first empirical study looking at the methodological and theoretical concept of signatures, by looking at how signatures may be used to link cases of serial homicide. This tests the psychological idea of consistency across time, i.e., (1) do offenders display what has been defined as signature behaviors, and if so, what do these consist of? And (2), do they display them consistently across their series, providing justification for using these behaviors to link individual crimes? They looked at 90 serial homicide series, with five offenses in each, and identified six behavioral categories from the literature on signatures and serial homicide: body disposal behaviors; forensic awareness behaviors; mutilation behaviors; weapons used; theft behaviors; and sexual behaviors. Each one of these categories in turn contained a diverse number of objectively defined and physically observable behaviors from the crime scene adhering to the description of the category. An 80% consistency criterion was used, meaning that an offender was only deemed consistent if he employed an individual behavior in four out of five crime scenes. The results from Bateman and Salfati (2007) showed that there were inherent difficulties in using individual behaviors to identify consistency patterns across a series, and consequently to link cases. Serial homicide offenders did not show consistency in their use of the same crime scene behaviors, nor did this consistency increase when behaviors were looked at as general groups—i.e., the offenders showing the use of any kind of sexual behavior, any kind of body disposal behavior, etc. This study provided the first in a wave of empirical testing that questions current theories in the literature on serial homicide, which have suggested that signatures or specific key behaviors are not only obvious, but key in understanding the consistency in an offender's behavior across their crimes. The study also highlighted the importance in identifying which of these key behaviors is more indicative of the offender and their psychology, rather than behaviors that change depending on the situation, such as the environment, the interaction with the victim, and through learning and maturation.

Linking Using Behavioral Type

As highlighted previously, the other side of the consistency debate is the "psychological theme"–based approach. Using a type or theme approach allows investigators and researchers to examine "pools" of offending behaviors that all encompassed the same psychological meaning rather than simply examining the individual behaviors displayed throughout the course of the crime (Canter, 1994; Salfati, 2000). This may be more effective because offenders may use different behaviors due to situational factors, but these different behaviors may belong to the same theme of offending style. In this case, using the theme-based approach rather than a signature or individual behavior approach would help to alleviate the problem of finding inconsistency in behaviors due to the situation dependency of behaviors.

Salfati and Bateman (2005) provided the first empirical study focusing on developing methodological benchmarks for the theme-based approach to serial homicide offenses. The authors based their work on a framework originally used to classify single homicides (e.g., Salfati, 2000; Salfati & Canter, 1999), into two types, notably expressive and instrumental, which they also found held serial homicides. They then went on to test the consistency with which offenders offended according to the same theme across their series (the idea being that by focusing on themes, more of the situational factors could be factored out than by looking at individual behaviors alone). Results from this study showed that although this general homicide classification was more productive in analyzing consistency than single behaviors, consistency levels were still not high. In addition, they showed that the differences in results depended on which criterion of stringency they employed for testing consistency. Their study highlighted the importance of providing clear guidelines for how cases are allocated to theme, and how cases are linked, and the guidelines that they provided have since been found to be the most useful to date (see Trojan & Salfati, 2008, for a full discussion). Using the most stringent classification criterion, only 13% of cases demonstrated a consistency in dominance, i.e., where each of the three crime scenes showed not only a dominant theme, but the same dominant theme across the series. One of the issues the study highlighted was that the individual behaviors that make up each theme still need to be refined to factor out behaviors that are more dependent on the situation than on the offender's psychology. The study therefore highlighted the importance of further investigating the nature of individual behaviors themselves so that the understanding of the consistency and stability of these can be fed back into a more thematic model.

Other follow-up studies have been done looking into some of these issues in greater detail. Specific features that have been found useful to help tighten the reliability of models have focused in on the victim of these crimes. Salfati, Horning, Sorochinski, and Labuschagne (2012), using a sample of serial homicides from South Africa consisting of 30 offenders with a total of 283 victims and 235 crime scenes, showed that the level of interaction with the victim may be influential to the stability or instability of offending patterns across the series. They based their classification of each crime scene on the Victim as Object/Vehicle model (see Horning, Salfati, & Labuschagne, 2012, for details). Victims as Object involved situations where the primary focus was on instrumental gains, interaction with the victim throughout the phases of the crime was limited, and victims included males and live females. Victims as Vehicle (where the victim was a conduit through whom the offender could realize their specific psychological needs, the interaction was extensive and victims tended to be vulnerable).

When looking at the consistency levels with which offenders engaged in victim-defined crime scene actions, these were much higher (50%) than those previously reported by Salfati and Bateman (2005) due to both refinements in the data collection (see Salfati, 2011, Homicide Profiling Index) and selection of more reliable behaviors. The analysis showed that using this model, almost two-thirds of the cases showed a dominant Victim as Vehicle theme. A lower percentage of offenders used the Victim as Object theme. However, many of those that began with this theme remained consistent. Conversely, offenders who engaged in the Victim as Vehicle theme remained less consistent as the series progressed. These results, they suggest, may indicate that an offender's focus and involvement with the victim may be influential in consistency patterns. This lends an additional level of complexity to the analysis and definition of consistency, by incorporating change as possibly being part of a consistency pattern (Salfati, 2008a). Testing this alongside looking at further refining more salient behaviors for linking they suggest may help us in disentangling this question.

When the stability of individual victim features were looked at as a whole in relation to consistency level as the series progressed, the decrease in consistency was even more marked, from 60% when looking at the first two crime scenes in a series, to 25% when looking at the first four crime scenes in a series. Most of the individual victim features (couples, live victims, vulnerable victims) which were key in defining each of the victim-based types (Object/Vehicle) were also in and of themselves not stable as the series progressed. Offenders tended to consistently target vulnerable victims in the beginning of the series; however, as the series progressed, offenders changed pattern and there was a substantial decrease in procuring vulnerable victims. Salfati et al. (2012) concluded that it may be in the beginning that offenders are operating in their comfort zone and target these types of victims because they are easily accessible, and then offenders may become bolder or more experimental in their victim selection as the series continues. These are all patterns they recommend need to be explored further as we move forwards in elucidating victim-focused consistency patterns in serial homicide.

These results from the analysis of individual components of each theme, however, support the original conclusions made by Bateman and Salfati (2007), who also found very low levels of consistency when focusing on individual isolated features, and who recommended that moving from an individual behavior focus to a theme- or type-based focus, would be more useful as it would be able to factor in behavioral change due to the situation or interaction with the victim. Another possible explanation to change patterns as the series moved forward, Salfati et al. (2012) suggest, may be that offenders changed interaction patterns (both thematically and in terms of length of offense) in response to the type of victim selected, and this should also be explored in more depth. Results therefore suggest again that thematic stability or instability across the series may be due to the type of victim targeted, and the question remains whether identifiable patterns may be determined based on these changing features as the series develops.

Prostitute Victims and Serial Homicide

Vulnerable victims have been found to feature highly in serial murders in the United States. Egger (2003, cited in Quinet, 2011) suggests that 65% of serial murder victims are female and nearly 78% of female victims of serial murderers are prostitutes. As a subgroup of vulnerable victims, they therefore present a highly targeted group.

Quinet (2011), in a survey of serial homicide from 1970 to 2009, found that of cases with female victims only, 32% involved prostitute victims. She additionally suggested that the proportion of cases involving prostitute victims has dramatically increased by decade, despite the decline in serial murder cases overall between the 1980s and the 2000s. She reports the proportion of cases involving female prostitute victims as 16% during the 1970s, 30% during the 1980s, 46% during the 1990s, and 69% from 2000 to 2009. In addition, her analysis showed that offenders remained active an average of 9.3 years in the 1970s, declining almost by half to 5.1 by the 1980s, 3.2 by the 1990s, and 2.2 years by 2000–2009. However, further analysis also showed that for each decade, the average length of time that offenders were active was longer for cases involving prostitute victims.

When prostitute victims are murdered, figures suggest that in at least 35% of cases, a serial offender will be involved (Brewer, Dudek, et al.,

2006). Recent U.S. figures have also suggested that approximately one-third of serial murders involve prostitutes (Quinet, 2011). The question that remains is whether offenders who target prostitutes *only* target prostitutes—i.e., whether serial offenders specialize in terms of the type of victim they target.

Salfati, James, and Ferguson (2008) show that in a large proportion (14 out of 19) of offenders who had previous violent convictions, 6 involved a pre-conviction for at least one murder. With figures as high as these, they suggest that it is likely that a prostitute will come into contact with clients with violent pre-convictions on a relatively regular basis. Indeed, in one prostitute homicide case in their study, the victim had had sex with a client who had previous convictions for attempted murder and serious sexual assaults on women, in the same night as she was killed by another client who also had previous convictions for attempted murder. The evidence thus suggests that men who assault prostitutes have convictions for assaulting other women as well, which suggests that violence against prostitutes may be considered as part of a continuum of violence against women more generally, and not just against prostitutes specifically.

This now needs to be further investigated and analyzed to test the assumption that offenders are consistent in their behaviors at one level and across situations and is the first step in being able to make inferences about the nature of prostitute serial homicides, and the specific characteristics of the offenders responsible for these crimes.

Key Questions

One of the biggest questions remains whether violence against prostitutes has to do with opportunity and availability, or because they are prostitutes, i.e., whether violence against prostitutes is sexual or theft-motivated (both behaviors of which have been associated with instrumental homicides; see Salfati, 2000), or whether they represent specific targets to the offender. And ultimately, it is key to understand the link between prostitute homicides and non-prostitute homicides, particularly within the series itself. Indeed, there may be an assumption that the murder of a prostitute is a sexually motivated offense, but this may not be the case. As in the case of rape, it may not be simply just a matter of sex, but rather an exertion of power.

Salfati et al. (2008b) specifically aimed to look at this issue in an attempt to further understand the nature of the sexual and nonsexual violence in prostitution homicides by comparing them to sexual and nonsexual homicides of non-prostitute women. In particular, their study focused on the issue of whether prostitute homicides can be conceptualized as persons against whom the offender vents their anger, victims who are available and vulnerable, or victims who provide an outlet for the offender to obtain sex or theft, or what could also be seen as the offender targeting victims within the interpersonal model structure of Victim as Persons, Vehicle, and Object—i.e., they compared the difference between the idea that it may be the ease of availability and increased opportunity that makes prostitutes more prone to attack, or the idea that it may be *type* of female victim that they are.

It is sometimes difficult to distinguish between sexually and non-sexually motivated homicide. One homicide may have an overtly sexual element to it, whereas another may show no such evidence but may still be motivated by sexual drives. In some cases it may even be that sexual behaviors are observed, but that the crime was not sexually motivated. In some cases, it is the offender's control of the victim, and in turn their pain and humiliation, that becomes linked to the offender's sexual arousal. Another difficulty may arise when a sexual assault, a rape for example, culminates in the victim's death purely because the offender wants to eliminate a potential witness and not because the offender gains any sexual arousal from the killing itself (Keppel & Walter, 1999; Schlesinger, 2007).

Series Composition of Prostitute Serial Homicide Offenders—Answering Some Questions

The data used for this study[1] was accessed through the Homicide Incidents Tracking System (HITS), from the Attorney General's Office in Seattle, Washington. Nineteen series were identified that had at least one prostitute victim. In total there were 19 offenders, and 106 victims. Of the 19 series, 8 series (42%) were composed of prostitute victims only, and 11 series (58%) were mixed, containing both prostitute victims and non-prostitute victims, thus clearly showing that not all offenders specialize in terms of targeting specifically prostitute victims. Salfati et al. (2011) show that specific victim subtype does not provide the focus for consistency. Instead, they suggest that it is overall psychological defined victim type that helps look at consistency, notably victim as object and victim as person.

The question that is raised at this point is thus whether there is a deeper underlying psychological theme that underlies the type of victim targeted. Salfati (2009) in a summary of the literature on violence and homicide against street prostitutes, summarized two key trends in the literature, notably the sexual element that is often associated with these cases, or the element of vulnerability.

Comparing prostitute (N = 16) and non-prostitute (N = 90) victims in the current study on sexual assault that could be measured from the information in the case file, 43% of prostitutes and 44% of non-prostitutes were sexually assaulted. The results thus indicate that overt sexual assault does not provide a distinguishing factor between the actions of the offender during the crime.

When the sexual element is looked at to determine whether it provides the element of consistency that ties the different types of victims together, the analysis showed that, of the 19 series, 2 series included prostitute victims who were all sexually assaulted, 5 series included prostitute victims who were not sexually assaulted, and 11 series included mixed victim types (prostitutes and non-prostitutes) and a mix of sexual assaults and no sexual assaults. The dominant trend thus again points away from using specific elements at the crime in order to understand any element of consistency that may be present.

Salfati (2008) suggests that by adding the element of time into the analysis, a more in-depth analysis can be done to look at how an offender's behavior changes across a series in a more consistent way in terms of how he chooses his victims and what behaviors he engages in, in terms of psychological processes such as experimentation, escalation, and development. All features that authors have spoken about as being key in understanding the influencing factors on consistency and change over an offender's series across time (see Bateman & Salfati, 2007; Canter, 2000; Salfati & Bateman, 2005). In this way, consistency may be determined an offender's apparent inconsistent pattern (Salfati, 2008a).

Prostitute Killers

Understanding something about the offenders who target these victims, and what differentiates them in terms of consistency patterns and victim choice, may add another level to understanding prostitute murders. A number of studies have highlighted the key role clients have in the violence perpetrated toward street workers, with 62%–81% of the violence being committed by clients (Church, Henderson, Barnard, & Hart, 2001; Farley & Barkan, 1998; Lowman, 2000). Similar figures can be seen in homicides (62%–64%), and 35% of prostitute homicides can be attributed to having been committed by serial homicide offenders, with approximately one-third of these serial offenders being identified as clients (Brewer, Dudek, et al., 2006).

In a book by Kinnell (2008), the nature of clients was looked at in more detail, gleaning an interesting picture that allows a more in-depth understanding of the possible issues at play when prostitutes are attacked by clients. Kinnell highlights that attackers are commonly described as "clients," but when the details of these cases are examined, a high proportion of this violence comes from those who do not actually pay; and since the definition of a client is payment for sexual services, these attackers are therefore not clients, even though they may have approached the sex worker as if they were clients, or pretending they were clients, or engaging in initial con-behaviors to suggest they were clients.

Kinnell (2008) in one study looked at the suspects in 139 offenses, of which 70% approached the street worker in the guise of a client. About half of these were nonpayers. They refused to pay and became violent as soon as payment was requested. About a quarter of these nonpayers also robbed the victim. In an overview of 118 cases where the sex workers were killed, Kinnell (2008) observed that of those for whom working method was known, 78% were street workers. The suspect was identified in 94 cases. Of the cases where the information was available, it was assumed that 65% of the offenders approached as a client. This is similar to numbers from Canada (Lowman, 2000) and the United States (Brewer, Dudek, et al., 2006). The assumption that offenders approached as clients is based on the belief that the victims were "at work"; but based on her work on nonfatal attacks, where 30% of attackers did not exhibit any client behaviors even though the victims were at work, Kinnell suggests that the same pattern may be present in murders, although she states that we cannot test this since the victim is deceased, and they may have approached in some other guise or simply attacked the victim. Kinnell (2008) based on her observations, concludes that paying for sex may not be the link to violence; instead, it is *not* paying that is. The explosions of anger that erupt when the sex worker insists on payment, she suggests, indicate that the problem is not that these men believe that paying for sex gives them the right to command women to obey their sexual demands or to inflict violence on them, but they are insulted by the suggestion that they can only get sexual compliance if they pay, that they have the right to "take" sex from these women, and that refusing to pay asserts that right and demonstrates their power. The interplay between the sexual element of the crime and the vulnerability is thus an issue that needs to be examined in greater detail to elucidate the interaction of the two during the crime.

Serial Offenders

Kinnell (2008) reports that 45% of the suspects in her sample were charged with attacks on more than one sex worker. Client suspects were not typical clients in that they had a much higher level of previous convictions, and overall, those with previous convictions were likely to be repeat offenders. These figures are consistent with other studies (Brooks-Gordon, 2006; Brewer, Dudek, et al., 2006).

Kinnell (1993, cited in Brooks-Gordon, 2006) stated that the high proportion of attacks ascribed to clients has led to assumptions that a high proportion of clients are violent. However as Brooks-Gordon (2006) shows, most clients are nonviolent, and the majority of violence is committed by a small proportion of offenders. Based on her study, she therefore concluded that information about attackers suggest that many are serial offenders. Similar conclusions have been reached by other researchers (e.g., Brooks-Gordon, 2006).

Salfati et al. (2008) report that prostitute homicide offenders were the least likely to have previous nonviolent offenses (20%), compared to sexual (41%) and nonsexual, non-prostitute homicide offenders (81%). Prostitute homicide offenders also had significantly more pre-convictions for sexual offenses compared to nonsexual and, to a lesser extent, sexual homicide offenders. They also reported that significantly more prostitute homicide offenders (69%) had also spent time in prison than both nonsexual (27%) and sexual (29%) non-prostitute homicide offenders. The relationship between previous criminal behavior and current behavior (i.e., whether sexual or nonsexual) therefore remains unclear. What is clear however, is that offenders who target prostitutes have a history of violence and sexual assault, sometimes against non-prostitutes.

In accord with the general literature on violence against prostitutes, Salfati et al.'s (2008) study also shows that in a large proportion (14 out of 19) of offenders who had previous violent convictions, 6 involved a pre-conviction for at least one murder. With figures as high as these, they suggest that it is likely that a prostitute will come into contact with clients with violent pre-convictions on a relatively regular basis. Indeed, in one prostitute homicide case in their study, the victim had had sex with a client who had previous convictions for attempted murder and serious sexual assaults on women, in the same night as she was killed by another client who also had previous convictions for attempted murder.

In an extensive national search of media sources, Brewer, Dudek, Potterat, Muth, Roberts, and Woodhouse (2006) and Brewer, Muth, Dudek, Roberts, and Potterat (2006) compared clients who assaulted, raped, and/or killed prostitute women, with clients arrested for patronizing prostitutes in the same jurisdictions and time periods, on observable characteristics easily assessed by police during an investigation. Violent clients were less likely to have a precious criminal history of miscellaneous other (nonviolent, non-property, non-sex, non-patronizing) offenses. Men with a criminal history of violent and/or rape offenses comprised a pool that included 40% of prostitute killers (47% of serial prostitute killers). In addition, meaningful proportions of clients arrested for patronizing in two jurisdictions had less money in their possession than the price they had agreed to pay for sex or carried weapons at the time of arrest, suggesting a potential for violence in client's interactions with prostitutes, a result that is consistent with Kinnell's more recent 2008 study showing that most "clients" intended non-payment prior to approaching street workers.

In another study by Kinnell (2004, cited in Brooks-Gordon, 2006) of 73 homicides of sex workers showed that 71% were street workers. Of the 46 cases where a suspect was known, 52% approached their victim as a client, while 42% had previous or subsequent convictions for violence, including rape, and homicide both against sex workers and non-sex workers, and against both men and women. Of the (22 out of 35) cases where an offender was identified in Kinnell's (2006) study, 49% had previous convictions for homicide or other violent offenses. The majority (19 out of 22) of these offenders with previous criminal convictions for violence were clients. Through additional case studies, she further showed that those who kill sex workers do not only target that group, but often targeted non-sex workers, which again stresses the important issue of understanding the elements that relates to the consistency in victim target.

Conclusions

The key question in the area of linking outlined at the start of this chapter was whether we can link crime scenes to each other, and thereby identify a series, while also identifying different series from one another. Specifically, the questions were raised regarding what factors may be the most reliable to focus on when we make this determination, and where our focus needs to be. As this chapter has outlined, linking is not a straightforward process. Consistency in victim targeting, which has been the emphasis of this chapter, is one of the foci that are being explored in the literature. Our specific focus in this chapter has been on prostitute victims due the sheer number who fall victim to serial homicide offenders. What the literature and the analysis has highlighted, however, is that offenders do not always only target prostitutes in their series, and few specialize. This goes against much of the belief in the field that offenders are behaviorally consistent and display key signatures and victim preferences. It is therefore key to understand what psychological factors may link these victims to each other so that consistency may be looked at beyond the individual variable toward a more psychological understanding of the patterns that offenders display throughout their series in terms of their development and change.

Note

1. Early findings of this study were originally presented by C. G. Salfati at the American Society of Criminology in 2008.

References

Bateman, A., & Salfati, G. (2007). An examination of behavioral consistency using individual behaviors or groups of behaviors in serial homicide. *Behavioral Science and the Law, 25*, 527–544.

Brewer, D. D., Dudek, J. A., Potterat, J. J., Muth, S. Q., Roberts, J. M., & Woodhouse, D. E. (2006). Extents, trends, and perpetrators of prostitution related homicide in the United States. *Journal of Forensic Science, 51*(5), 1101–1108.

Brewer, D. D., Muth, S. Q., Dudek, J. A., Roberts, J. M., & Potterat, J. J. (2006). *A comparative profile of violent clients of prostitute women*. Unpublished report. Seattle, WA: Interdisciplinary Scientific Research.

Brooks-Gordon, B. (2006). *The price of sex: Prostitution, policy and society*. Cullumpton, Devon, UK: Willan Publishing.

Canter, D. V. (1994). *Criminal shadows*. London: HarperCollins.

Canter, D., & Heritage, R. (1990). A multivariate model of sexual offence behaviour: Developments in "offender profiling." *Journal of Forensic Psychiatry, 1*, 185–212.

Church, S., Henderson, M., Barnard, M., & Hart, G. (2001). Violence by clients towards female prostitutes in different work settings; questionnaire survey. *British Medical Journal, 322*, 524–525.

Douglas, J. E., & Munn, C. M. (1992). Modus operandi and the signature aspects of violent crime. In J. E. Douglas, A. W. Burgess, A. G. Burgess, & R. K. Ressler (Eds.), *Crime classification manual* (pp. 259–268). New York: Lexington Books.

Farley, M., & Barkan, H. (1998). Prostitution, violence and post-traumatic stress disorder. *Women and Health, 27*(3), 37–49.

Horning, A. and Salfati, C. G., & Labuschagne, G. (under review). South African Serial Homicide: A Behavioral Typology Based on Offender Victim Relationship. *Special Issue on Serial Homicide in South Africa*.

Keppel, R. D., & Walter, R. (1999). Profiling killers: A revised classification model for understanding sexual murder. *International Journal of Offender Therapy and Comparative Criminology, 43*(4), 417–437.

Kinnell, H. (1993). *Prostitutes' exposure to rape: Implications for HIV prevention and for legal reform*. Paper presented to *VII Social Aspects of AIDS conference*. South Bank University, London, June.

Kinnell, H. (2001). Violence against sex workers. Response to Church et al. (2001). *British Medical Journal, 322*.

Kinnell, H. (2002). *Violence against sex workers in London: The London Ugly Mugs List*. October 2000 to February 2002. Unpublished paper.

Kinnell, H. (2004). Violence and sex work in Britain. In S. Day & H. Ward (Eds.), *Sex work, mobility and health in Europe* (pp. 179–197). London: Kegan Paul.

Kinnell, H. (2006). Murder made easy: The final solution to prostitution? In R. Campbell and M. O'Neill (Eds.), *Sex work now* (pp. 141–168). Cullompton, Devon, UK: Willan Publishing.

Kinnell, H. (2008). *Violence and sex work in Britain*. Cullompton, Devon, UK: Willan Publishing.

Lowman, J. (2000). Violence and the outlaw status of (Street) prostitution in Canada. *Violence against Women*, 6(9), 987–1011.

Lowman, J., & Fraser, L. (1995). *Violence against persons who prostitute: The experience in British Columbia*. Retrieved from http://mypage.uniserve.ca/~lowman/.

Potterat, J. J., Brewer, D. D., Muth, S. Q., Rothberg, R. B., Woodhouse, D. E., Muth, J. B., . . . Brody, S. (2004). Mortality in a long-term open cohort of prostitute women. *American Journal of Epidemiology, 159*(8), 778–785.

Quinet, K. (2011). Prostitutes as Victims of Serial Homicide: Trends and Case Characteristics from 1970–2009. *Homicide Studies*, *15*(1), 74–100.

Salfati, C. G. (in press). Research methods in offender profiling research. In B. Rosenfeld & S. Penrod (Eds.), *Research methods in forensic psychology* (Chap. 7, pp. 122–135). New York: John Wiley & Sons.

Salfati, C. G. (2000). The nature of expressiveness and instrumentality in homicide. *Homicide Studies, 3*(4), 265–293.

Salfati, C. G. (2007, November). *Prostitutes: Vulnerable or sexual targets of serial homicide?* Paper presented at the Annual American Society of Criminology Conference, Atlanta, GA.

Salfati, C. G. (2008a). Linking serial crimes. In J. Fossi & L. Falshaw (Eds.), *Issues in forensic psychology*. British Psychological Society, Division of Forensic Psychology Publications, Vol. 8.

Salfati, C. G. (2008b, March). *Prostitute victims of serial homicide: Investigative concerns*. Paper presented at the Academy of Criminal Justice Sciences, Cincinnati, OH.

Salfati, C. G. (2009). Prostitute homicide: An overview of the literature and comparison to sexual and non-sexual female victim homicide. In D. Canter, M. Ioannou, & D. Youngs (Eds.), *Safer sex in the city: The experience and management of street prostitution* (pp. 51–68). The Psychology, Crime and Law Series. Aldershot, UK: Ashgate.

Salfati, C. G. (2011). Serial crime: The psychology of behavioral consistency and applications to criminal careers and linking. In M. DeLisi and K. M. Beaver

(Eds.), *The life-course of antisocial behavior: Aggression to delinquency to crime* (pp. 201–210). Boston, MA: Jones & Bartlett.

Salfati, C. G. (2012) The Homicide Profiling Index. Retrieved February 16, 2012, from http://web.jjay.cuny.edu/~gsalfati/index_files/research.htm.

Salfati, C. G., & Bateman, A. (2005). Serial homicide: An investigation of behavioral consistency. *Journal of Investigative Psychology and Offender Profiling, 2* (2), 121–144.

Salfati, C. G., & Canter, D. V. (1999). Differentiating stranger murders: Profiling offender characteristics from behavioral styles. *Behavioral Sciences and the Law, 17*, 391–406.

Salfati, C. G., Horning, A., Sorochinski, M., & Labuschagne, G. (2012) South African serial homicide: Consistency in victim target and behaviors across series. *Special Issue on Serial Homicide in South Africa. Journal of Investigative Psychology and Offender Profiling.*

Salfati, C. G., James, A. R., & Ferguson, L. (2008). Prostitution Homicides: A Descriptive Study. *Journal of Interpersonal Violence, 23*, 3.

Salfati, C. G., & Taylor, P. (2006). Differentiating sexual violence: A comparison of sexual homicide and rape. *Psychology, Crime and Law*, *12*(2), 107–126.

Schlesinger, L. B. (2007). Sexual homicide: Differentiating catathymic and compulsive murders. *Aggression and Violent Behavior*, *12*, 242–256.

Trojan, C., & Salfati, C. G. (2008). Methodological considerations of determining dominance in multi-dimensional analyses of crime scene behaviors and offender characteristics. Special Issue: Debates and Critiques within Investigative Psychology (D. V. Canter, Ed.) *Journal of Investigative Psychology and Offender Profiling, 5*(3), 125–146.

CHAPTER TEN

Profiling Psychopathic Traits in Serial Sexual Homicide: A Case Study of the Personality and Personal History of the Green River Killer, Gary Leon Ridgway

Loren T. Atherley

Introduction

Psychopathy is believed to be a definitive personality trait. Previously, sex offenders of all kinds have been identified as primary psychopaths, when in actuality their motivation stems from a paraphilic disorder. The sex offender as primary psychopath (see Hare, 2003) is a contradiction; motivated by a libidinal need, these offenders profit emotionally from the pain, suffering, and subjugation of their prey. If our understanding of psychopathy is accurate, the psychopathic offender cannot recognize the emotion in order to profit from it. Nowhere is the duplicitous[1] nature of this condition more apparent than in the offense behavior of the serial homicide offender.

This case study highlights the shared ancestry of psychopathy and violent paraphilia identifying psychopathy as a lesser, enabling trait in the pathology of one of America's most notorious sexual predators, Gary L. Ridgway, the Green River Killer (GRK). Whereas only a few years ago, this killer would have been labeled a psychopath, this case study reveals psychopathy to be the vehicle by which this personality conveyed his paraphilic desires to fruition.

In the summer of 1982, the King County Sheriff's Office (then the King County Police) began recovering the nude bodies of young women deposited in Washington State's Green River. Few people could have predicted the prodigious nature of this killer's ability. As more and more bodies were discovered, the Green River Taskforce (GRTF) was formed from local and state law enforcement agencies in an attempt to manage the mounting case load. In late 1983, the taskforce formally requested the help of the FBI to profile the Green River Killer (GRK).

Today, developments in our understanding of the dynamics of personality disorder and paraphilia have opened a window on the life and offense behavior of the GRK to include the role of psychopathy and its physical manifestations in the commission of sexually motivated crimes. Indeed, when this case was being investigated, it was a natural assumption, a reflex, to relate serial killer and psychopath as interchangeable and synonymous. The GRK, in fact, illustrates the profound paradoxical nature of this relationship and distinctness of violent paraphilia from primary psychopathy. Paraphilia, secondary psychopathy, and catathymia (see Meloy, 1988) define the offense behavior of the GRK.

Background

Psychopathy

The psychopath is characterized by an inability to empathize, a "defect in affect" (Hare, 1993) which serves to disassociate the offender from the emotional consequences of their actions. A term that has replaced the archaic sociopathy, psychopathy is most closely related to the Axis II, Cluster B disorders in the American Psychological Association, DSM-IV, and can be further broken into primary psychopathy, secondary psychopathy, and non-psychopathic. Current research suggests this emotional dysfunction is the result of biological deficiency as predispositional factors in combination with an excess of hard stimuli to permanently engrain the pathology as early as age 36 months (Blair, Mitchell, & Blair, 2008; Meloy, 1988).

The primary psychopath is human nature's true predator—self-preserving, criminally versatile, and motivated by profit. Beginning in the 1980s, Dr. Robert Hare formally established the construct with the Psychopathy Checklist–Revised (PCL-R)[2] designed to evaluate personality along a well-defined continuum in an effort to "identify these individuals in order to minimize the risk they pose to others" (Hare, 1993). Hare's PCL-R identifies two types of psychopaths, primary and secondary. The psychopath is motivated by pecuniary gain or prestige and suffers most severely from the emotional deficit described above. Secondary psychopathy is considerably more insidious. These offenders are perceptive of emotion but can choose not to empathize, allowing them to profit from the emotional feedback of pain, terror, or fear manifested in the behavior of their victims. A primary psychopath is incapable of recognizing these emotions and thus is unable to reap the emotional harvest.

Violent Paraphilia: A Common Ancestry

Within the pathology of the serial killer is a confluence of behavioral psychodynamics. The erotophonophiliac is the worst-case scenario of biological deficiency, environmental factors, and sexual defect to produce violent paraphilia enabled by psychopathic mechanisms. The factors that predispose a personality to psychopathy also facilitate the disassociation and social languish that later develop into the violent sexualized fantasy. If fantasy provides the motivation, psychopathy is the catalyst by which the offender is able to offend.

Hickey's (1997) trauma-control model explains how acute trauma in a susceptible personality translates into violent paraphilia. According to Hickey (1997), it is the presence of "predispositional factors" that defines the risk of violent paraphilia. Mental illness, personality disorder, and brain functionality are all predispositional factors that affect a person's ability to cope with trauma. If trauma takes place in the "formative years" when a personality is still developing, and without adequate support structures to assist in coping, that personality is at risk of developing a paraphilia.

Arrigo and Purcell (2001) integrate two formative models of paraphilic development to show how fantasy manifests itself in action and evolves to explain serial aggression or homicide in an "integrative conceptual schema" (p. 19). The model proposed by Arrigo and Purcell (2001) suggests an integration of Burgess's (1986) motivational model and Hickey's (1997) trauma-control model of paraphilic development. Where Burgess (1986) and Hickey (1997) mirror each other on topic of fantasy development, Hickey (1997) expands upon the theory, proposing a "feedback loop" that "generates new and sustaining[s] existing fantasies" (Arrigo & Purcell, 2001, p. 19). This feedback and conditioned reinforcement of existing fantasy deviance promotes the escalation or development of serial homicide offense behavior.

Sex and aggression become linked in the brain for these personalities, and to attain sexual arousal is to sponsor aggression and vice versa. Suffering from libidinal deficiencies that develop into fully formed sexual dysfunction in early puberty, the disordered libido seeks to satisfy its need for sexualized stimuli through other systems of arousal. Utilizing a fight-or-flight reflexive system in place of traditional sexual arousal, violence, anger, hatred, and power beget sexual gratification on a neurochemical level through adrenaline rather than nitrous oxide. Biological mechanisms in the brain of the serial killer, driven to satisfy our need for arousal, engage in a cross-referencing of arousal mechanisms (Myers, Husted, Safarik, & O'Toole, 2006; Purcell & Arrigo, 2006).

Predation and Catathymia: Complementary Motivations

The majority of homicides are motivated by affective, rather than predatory aggression. According to Meloy (2000), only 1% of homicides are serial, and only a fraction of those are purely motived by predation. Helfgott (2008) suggests, "it could be argued that no crime is purely predatory" (p. 176). However prevalent, it certainly is true that the majority of serial homicides are motivated by some degree of predatory aggression and violence. To that end, it is logical to examine a crime scene or series of scenes for evidence of either affective or predatory aggression. For example, the offender's knowledge or understanding of their actions as wrong may prompt them to engage in a certain degree of forensically aware countermeasures to evade detection, such as wearing gloves. An affectively motivated killer may not be directly aware of the illicit nature of their behavior and thusly may not leave such signs of premeditation. Academically and practically, we hold these two motivational structures to be exclusive of one another.

The compulsive/catathymic model of aggression (Meloy, 2000) is comprehensive and adequately explains most violence. Though a well-developed typology, couched in valid psychological theory, the compulsive/catathymic delineation fails to address the motivation of the GRK. A cursory observation of the complexity of the human behavior would suggest that human aggression cannot be expressed in a simple bifurcated model. In fact, Dr. Michael Stone (2009) uses 22 separate categories to express the breadth of violent motivation and readily admits his typology does not cover every permutable calculation. Understanding psychopathy as a component of personality is critical to understanding the complex motivational structure of the serial sexual offender.

The GRK presents as a motivational paradox. An analysis of the life of Gary Ridgway suggests an abundance of predispositional factors and formative trauma sufficient to support the formation of violent paraphilia. A retrospective analysis of his offense behavior yields evidence of both predatory and affective aggression working in concert to satisfy the specific paraphilic needs of the offender. These two modes of aggression are indicative of murder motivated by violent paraphilia (catathymia) and facilitated by psychopathic (predatory) mechanisms.

Method

The following case study was developed in 2010 as research for a master's thesis.[3] The study was conducted in two phases in which the subject was profiled from case evidence and archived audio/video recordings of interviews with the subject. This profile, including a PCL-R score, was compared with the profile inferences of the original investigation to determine if advances in the understanding of serial homicide offense behavior, psychopathy, and violent paraphilia would have been more effective at identifying the GRK. This thesis was signed in approval in June 2010.

Case Study

In December 2003, as part of a plea agreement to avoid the death penalty, Gary Leon Ridgway was sentenced for the aggravated murder of 48 women and remanded to the custody of the Washington State Department of Corrections. Prior to this time he was held at a location near the King County Airport, Boeing Field, where the GRTF debriefed him. From June to December 2003, Ridgway recounted detailed information sufficient to recover several missing persons suspected to be victims of the GRK. In addition to corroborating what was already known about the GRK, Ridgway spoke with a forensic psychologist retained by his defense and a representative of the FBI BAU-2 to shed light on the development of the GRK.

Personal History

Gary L. Ridgway is a white male who was an active serial killer between 1982 and 2003. This offender has a history of contact with law enforcement for prostitution-related offenses and an unprosecuted history of petty theft and public disorder offenses. There are not obvious signs that Ridgway is mentally ill by DSM-IV, Axis I diagnoses standards; however, he does suffer from a complex of DSM-IV, Axis II, Cluster B, personality disturbances most closely resembling secondary psychopathy.[4] Ridgway is currently held at the Washington State Penitentiary in Walla Walla, Washington. Prior to incarceration, he was employed in a nonprofessional, "blue-collar" occupation. During his offense career, Ridgway was geographically stable, although he demonstrated a capacity for brief periods of mobility, outside of his activity space, as necessary to avoid detection or mislead the investigation.[5] He is of below-average intelligence, with an IQ of between 82 and 87 (Prothero & Smith, 2006) and has no formal education beyond high school. Gary Ridgway has military experience (U.S. Navy, noncombat) and received an honorable discharge.[6] He has been married several times and sought long-term relationships with women.[7] Though incarcerated, Ridgway has not ceased his offense career; he was merely interrupted and, if released, will continue to offend.

Criminal History

The GRK's official criminal history contains a few prostitution-related offenses and 48 convicted counts of aggravated murder; however, the unofficial criminal career of Gary L. Ridgway is far more extensive. In addition to stalking, vandalism, arson, and cruelty to animals, at age 15, Ridgway assaulted a younger boy with a knife, nearly killing him. As an adult, Ridgway had a long history of petty theft for which he was never caught. Inarguably, the GRK is most accomplished as a homicide offender; but as predicted by the FBI profilers (FBI, 1987), Ridgway appeared before a judge on two separate occasions for prostitution-related offenses and was contacted a number of times, without citation, for soliciting.

Like many personality-disordered children and adolescents, the GRK exhibited conduct-disordered behavior as a child. Though there are no charged or adjudicated offenses related to juvenile delinquency or conduct, Ridgway admits to an extensive list of antisocial behaviors in this study's sample of interviews. In addition to generalized comments about vandalism and arson, three major offenses are indicated and explained in detail. Cruelty to animals (specifically, the suffocation of a cat in the family's cooler), the stalking of girls on their way home from school, and the life-threatening assault on a young boy when Ridgway was 15 years old.

Typology

The GRK is a hedonistic serial killer, lust subtype; this offender "realizes sexual gratification through the homicide, making it an eroticized experience" (Holmes & Holmes, 2009, p. 121). This type of offender is process-oriented; consequently, offense behavior is prolonged and may take "some time to complete" in order for the paraphilic processes, evidenced by the presence of necrophilia at body recovery sites, to be realized. This portion of the analysis draws on the theories outlined in the literature review pertaining to psychopathy, trauma and fantasy, self-medication/self-soothing, and serial homicide offense behavior.

Fantasy and Violent Paraphilia

As discussed previously, personality, paraphilia, and compulsive behaviors are formed between birth and puberty, and are reinforced in adolescence through pornography, autoeroticism, and substance abuse. Gary L. Ridgway exhibits deficiencies in cognitive and emotional processing consistent with the biological precursors discussed as risk factors for personality disturbances such as psychopathy and antisocial personality disorder. Background investigations conducted by Ridgway's defense reveal significant environmental disturbances during these formative years of personality development. The interaction between biological predeterminate factors, which undercut coping and environmental challenges to healthy development, paves the way for violent paraphilia (Arrigo & Purcell, 2001).

Mary Rita Ridgway is described as an unrelenting force, domineering, and a potentially inappropriate sexual role model. When Marcia, Ridgway's second wife, met Mary Rita for the first time in 1973, she noted that "she did not believe that she was Ridgway's mother because she was wearing a lot of makeup, tight cloths, and to her, looked like a prostitute" (Prothero & Smith, 2006, p. 64). In addition to dressing provocatively, Mary Rita Ridgway was an overbearing and often belligerent force in Ridgway's life. When Gary struggled in learning to read, she called him stupid, and when he wet the bed, she paraded him naked in front of his brothers, causing further humiliation (Prothero & Smith, 2006). Compounding the sexual confusion stemming from improper attachment and puberty (Meloy, 2000), Mary Rita would often clean Gary's genitalia wearing only an open bathrobe after he wet the bed, and when Gary became erect, Mary Rita mocked and shamed him. As a result, Gary Ridgway learned to hate the promiscuous sexual object presented in the form of his mother. Not able to fight back against her frustrating and humiliating behavior, Ridgway fantasized about reasserting dominance, which artificially reinforced his self-esteem.

As Ridgway entered his teenage years, his personality disturbance deepened. During the interviews with GRTF, Ridgway indicated that his mother would often sunbathe in a two-piece swimsuit in their backyard.

Gary would masturbate while fantasizing about his mother, fully aware that those feelings are not conventional or appropriate for a mother/son relationship. The confusing mix of sexual arousal and humiliation formed a unique set of compulsive needs. As Gary entered high school, he became more comfortable in social situations and even dated girls who attended his high school. Unfortunately, the impact of Mary Rita Ridgway's repeated assaults on Gary's self-esteem and sexuality left a lasting impression on his personality and, ultimately, the development of violent paraphilia (Hickey, 1997). No longer content to act out his fantasies in his mind, Ridgway engaged in pathological play (discussed further below), or simulated surrogate dominance of his mother.

By Ridgway's mid-teenage years, his fantasy had developed into an obsessive need to dominate the object of his personal humiliation. Pathological play behavior in killing small animals, committing petty vandalism, and assaulting a younger boy served as a proving ground for his first offense. It is not uncommon for marginal personalities who have been subjected to sexual humiliation to be impotent in conventional sexual encounters. This, combined with the depressed autonomic nervous system of a psychopath, resulted in Gary L. Ridgway developing a sexual need for totally submissive sexual partners, later manifested as necrophilia (Stein, Schlesinger, & Pinizzotto, 2010). Presented with an object symbolic of his mother's domineering and promiscuous nature, Ridgway seeks to completely dominate and control that object. Though Ridgway is capable of achieving orgasm conventionally, total psychosexual satisfaction does not come without the act of killing, for which Ridgway receives a second orgasm-like experience and postmortem sexual intercourse. In addition to this primary fantasy, which constitutes the primary motivation for the Green River murders, Ridgway had secondary fantasies. Throughout his interviews, Ridgway discusses these fantasies, including one in which he mounts and displays a female corpse by inserting a fencepost into her vagina. It is unclear whether Ridgway attempted to manifest this fantasy in reality.

Pathological Play

Domination of small animals is not uncommon for budding serial homicide offenders. As discussed above, much of the antisocial behavior exhibited by offenders is an attempt to artificially inflate their self-image. In dominating a smaller animal, a child may be acting out sadistic fantasies or, in the GRK's case, fantasies of domination in the face of his mother's unrelenting psychological abuse (discussed further below) and the ensuing inadequacy and frustration felt by Ridgway. While discussing his childhood with FBI psychologist Mary Ellen O'Toole, Ridgway describes general animal cruelty (killing birds and shooting dogs with a BB gun); however, the most telling offense, detailed in this phase of the interviews, is his use of an "ice chest" to suffocate a cat. This very passive-aggressive act of violence against a cat is indicative of his offense behavior later in life in form and symbol. Not only is he causing death by asphyxiation, his preferred method of death with human victims, but he is doing so in a way that removes him from the process. This would seem to indicate that his intention was domination of another living thing rather than sadistic pleasure; otherwise, he would have watched the cat asphyxiate.

In the same interview, July 18, 2003, Ridgway indicates that he occasionally followed girls as they walked home from school. This stalking behavior is remarkably similar to the voyeuristic and extremely passive behavior exhibited by another sexually motivated offender, the *Power Reassurance* type rapist (Holmes & Holmes, 2009). These personalities have great difficulty relating to women even though they believe their sexual acts are in some way desired by their victims; I do not believe Ridgway operated under this delusion. In the mind of the power reassurance offender, their victim is the focus of a prolonged and intense fixation; however, I believe Ridgway was attempting to establish a normal sexual relationship but, for reasons discussed later, was unfamiliar with the prosocial interactions on which most conventional relationships are predicated. Nonetheless, Ridgway describes following girls on their way home from school, and though he was never caught, he planned for the eventuality by devising an excuse that would seem plausible enough to relieve him of suspicion if caught; again, indication that he understood his behavior to be aberrant but proceeded anyway.

Most disturbing of the GRK's juvenile delinquent behavior was a serious assault that occurred when he was 14 or 15 years old. In discussing his childhood with Dr. O'Toole, Ridgway indicates casually, alongside comments about breaking windows with rocks and setting fires, that he stabbed a boy on the playground at school. Previously he vehemently denied having ever used a knife with any of his victims, stating that he disliked blood. Ridgway recounted the event as follows: "Uh, it was down by . . . where I used to go to school, and a boy was playin'. I stabbed him in the side and . . . uh, didn't kill him . . . that's what I took my ag—gression [out] on. I couldn't take it out on my mom. I had to take it out on my animals and . . . and the kids" (Prothero & Smith, 2006, p. 411). Following this casual admission, detectives from the GRTF tracked Ridgway's stabbing victim, now an adult living in Southern California, with a clear memory of the events surrounding his assault. The victim confirmed Ridgway's story, adding only that after stabbing him, Ridgway said to the boy, "You're gonna die," laughed, and added "I always wanted to feel what it would be like to kill somebody" (Prothero & Smith, 2006, p. 469). Thus, pathological play is the experimental behavior by which a serial killer tests the limits of what they can get away with and cautiously approaches the threshold to their first kill.

First Offense Behavior

Gary L. Ridgway did not begin his offense behavior in a way that would be recognizable as the GRK. In fact, Ridgway committed his first homicide perhaps as many as 10 years prior to the beginning of the Green River series. Sometime in 1972, Ridgway recalls picking up a hitchhiker between the Kenworth Plant on East Marginal Way, Seattle, and his residence in Maple Valley, Washington. He believes he may have picked up this woman following a union meeting and had sex with her in the front seat of his truck. He recalls strangling her either before or after intercourse and transporting the body, still in the front seat, to a location along "Empire Way," where he disposed of her by pushing her body out of the vehicle and driving off. Ridgway recalls being panicked and wishing to leave as quickly as possible (Green River Taskforce, 2003).

As is typical of first-offense behavior in serial homicide offenders, the full signature and modus operandi (MO) of the recognizable series can be absent to a certain degree. Jeffrey Dahmer committed his first homicide at the age of 17, nearly a decade before his series began (Benecke, 2005). Serial killers often experience a period closely following puberty, referred to as pathological play, which often culminates with a first offense. This offense is primarily experimental and the product of thousands of hours spent fantasizing; as a result, the full paraphilic nature of the homicide may not be readily apparent. The scope of this study has not yielded any corroborative evidence to support Ridgway's claims; however, the information was unsolicited and not material to the plea agreement that spared his life. Therefore, Ridgway had no reason to embellish, though he admits it would not be unusual for him to do so without reason.

Offense Behavior

Modus operandi is generally defined by the offender's need to evade detection while adequately fulfilling their desires. Following Ridgway's first offense in 1972, he studied serial killers in books, newspapers, and magazines to learn from their mistakes. Over the course of nine years, Gary L. Ridgway, a man with an IQ in the low to mid 80s, developed a sophisticated set of rules and procedures designed to evade detection and prolong his offense career. Between 1972 and 2003, the GRK abducted, had sex with, strangled, and engaged in necrophilia with 78 victims in and around King County, Washington. The first bodies were found in the Green River; however, following the widely publicized efforts of the King County Police to "sting" the killer in stakeouts similar to those used to catch the Atlanta Child Murderer, the GRK's MO changed dramatically. Since 1983, bodies attributed to the GRK have been located in heavily wooded areas immediately adjacent to major highways throughout south and central King County and the Seattle-Tacoma International Airport. The bodies were often lightly disguised by foliage and often indicated anthropological and pathological evidence of postmortem sexual behavior.

Living less than a mile from the target-rich environment of Pacific Highway South, Gary L. Ridgway sometimes killed as often as twice a week for nearly three years. Like many serial killers, Ridgway was a creature of habit and began his pre-offense ritual by hunting for a victim. Age, race, and appearance were ancillary to the availability of a target that could be solicited without witnesses. Rule number one of the GRK was to never pick up a victim if a witness could on-view the abduction. Before becoming the GRK, Ridgway was an accomplished patron of prostitutes. Stemming from his experiences in the military, prostitutes were willing subjects he could use for sex, the GRK frequented areas he was familiar with in his "dating"[8] behavior. Either before work or immediately following work, the GRK would troll these areas for potential victims, and upon selecting a victim, the GRK would approach the prostitute and solicit her in a date. The terms of the transaction would be set and, barring the presence of witnesses, the victim would enter his vehicle.

With a willing victim in his vehicle, the GRK would ask a series of questions to assess the viability of the prostitute as a suitable victim. The second rule of the GRK was he would only kill prostitutes while "working women" were not suitable victims because he viewed them as honest people. He often identified his mother as a working woman, which presents an interesting dichotomy given his mother is also the source of his sexual desire to dominate and kill prostitutes for her provocative qualities. Ridgway and his victim would travel to a previously agreed upon outdoor location, or in some instances his residence off Military Road, near Interstate 5.

Upon arriving at the agreed-upon location for the date, Ridgway would request the victims to disrobe. If the weather was nice, he would take a blanket he kept in his truck and laid it on the ground where the sex act would begin. Ridgway preferred fellatio to achieve an erection prior to engaging in vaginal intercourse in the missionary position. Depending on the situation, Ridgway would be in varying stages of dress. Sometimes he kept his shirt on, unbuttoned, but would generally remove his pants as they inhibited movement during the kill, which he learned from a failed attempt in October 1982. After engaging in vaginal intercourse in the missionary position for a period of time, Ridgway would request vaginal intercourse in the "doggy style" position.

As Ridgway approached climax, if outdoors, he would often indicate to his victim that someone was approaching and they were in danger of being discovered. As the victim would raise her head to look, he would apply the carotid restraint or a ligature to her neck. Usually a brief struggle ensued, during which Ridgway used his legs to stabilize the torso while applying continuous pressure to achieve asphyxiation; at this point, Ridgway's behavior is rewarded as he achieves a secondary orgasm or similar psychosexual release. Once the victim lost consciousness, Ridgway employed a variety of techniques to continue starving the brain of oxygen until death was complete: he continued to hold manual pressure, or apply a ligature, and in some cases, actually stood on the neck of his victims.

Once the victim was deceased, the GRK carried out disposal of the body with a high degree of forensic awareness. Following the first murder in 1972, Ridgway went to considerable effort to engage in an independent study of serial killers, their flaws, and successes. Following the homicidal act, Ridgway stripped the bodies of all clothing and jewelry and clipped their fingernails to control for trace and DNA[9] evidence. The GRK was aware that stripped of potential sources of evidence, and absent a witness to their abduction, there was little evidence to tie him to the nameless victims discarded in the woods.

In the act of discarding his victims, Ridgway placed them in *clusters* so he could more easily recall their location for future visits. After transporting the body to a selected disposal site, immediately accessible by major highways, Ridgway would pull over to the side of the road, unload the body, and place it just off the shoulder of the road. He then moved his vehicle several hundred feet away, to misdirect any attention from passersby or law enforcement investigating an abandoned vehicle, and returned to drag the body into the woods. Ridgway discovered bodies moved more easily on their back, feet first so he could use their ankles, just above the foot, for secure holds. Once placed in an acceptable location, the GRK would go about camouflaging the body. Tracker Joel Harden made the observation that the GRK is "calm" and does not rush in his examination of movements around the Star Lake Cluster (Baird, Eakes, McDonald, Goodhew, & O'Donnell, 2003).

Up to this point, the discussed behavior of the GRK has been driven by a desire to evade detection. These elements are MO characteristics and can change from victim to victim. In some cases, not all, Ridgway preferred to dig a shallow grave to disguise his victims; while in others, they were left in illegal trash dump sites and disguised by sheets of plastic or plywood. Additionally, the GRK's choice of location varied with regard to the level of risk associated with using the same location. In cases where he felt one site was getting more use than another, he may have changed his MO to a different disposal site to evade detection; nonetheless, the fact that these bodies were clustered, by his own admission, so he could remember where he placed them suggests elements of signature. What need did Ridgway serve in revisiting the bodies?

Crime Scene Deviations

Most serial killers maintain a consistent MO, which only deviates in when an offender has a need to mitigate a particular risk of detection. In reviewing the *Prosecutors Summary of the Evidence*, it is clear that several victims do not fit the MO of the GRK. Two stand out as examples of the mix of predators and affective aggression in the GRK's profile. The deaths of Carol Christiansen and Patricia Yellowrobe were departures from the norm for Ridgway. The manner in which these bodies were treated, postmortem, is wholly inconsistent with the GRK and suggests ulterior motives.

The first five victims of the GRK were disposed of in the city of Kent, Washington, in or on the banks of the Green River. Bodies were discovered weighted down by heavy rocks near the banks accessible from adjacent roads. In August 1982, the GRK shifted his offense behavior and began disposing of bodies in heavily wooded areas referred to as "cluster sites." As mentioned before, Ridgway had a remarkable sense of forensic awareness and took extreme measure to remove potential sources of trace evidence. Also mentioned was his reliance on true crime novels and media accounts of serial killers and how they were caught. Ridgway's shift in post-offense, disposal MO is a direct result of monitoring the investigation and mitigating potential risk of detection.

Ridgway likely got the idea to dispose of his victims in a river from the Atlanta Child Murder, Wayne Williams. Ridgway believed that disposing of his victims in water would wash away trace evidence that could be linked to him (Baird et al., 2003). Ironically, disposing of the bodies in cool water preserved DNA evidence, which was later used to convict him. While Ridgway was not necessarily aware of the trace evidence preserved by the water, he was aware that the FBI staked out Wayne Williams and apprehended him following an attempt to dispose of a victim (Douglas & Olshaker, 1995). Ridgway was likely alerted to the presence of a surveillance team on and around the Green River by the local CBS affiliate news channel KOMO 4, which televised the efforts of law enforcement to catch the GRK disposing of a victim at the Green River (Guillen, 2007). Sensing an increased risk of detection, Ridgway opted to dispose of victims in wooded, remote outdoor scenes. During interviews with the taskforce, Ridgway suggested he would have killed many more had he been able to dispose of the bodies more effectively (Baird et al., 2003).

Carol Christiansen was last seen leaving her place of work, the Barn Door Tavern, around 2:30 a.m. on May 3, 1983; she was the 22nd victim of the GRK. Several inconsistencies are present in this case. First, Christiansen was not a prostitute; she worked as a waitress, and she was a "woman" rather than a "lady." While Ridgway was known to victimize some hitchhikers, he knew Christiansen personally from the Barn Door. Second, most of the GRK victims were found many months after they were carefully hidden in heavily wooded cluster sites. As such, there was little evidence of posing or postmortem behavior, beyond necrophilia, present. Christiansen was found just five days after her disappearance, fully clothed and deliberately posed. She was laying on her back with an empty bottle of wine across her stomach, ground sausage on her hands, and two trout laid across her upper torso. A ligature had been used to strangle her, and it was still around her neck.

Ridgway admitted to killing Christiansen and posing her body to throw off the investigation, which it did. There was speculation following the recovery of Christiansen that she was even a Green River victim. Some speculated that she may be the product of a religious zealot's ritual murder or that the GRK may himself be religiously motivated (Rule, 2004). The GRTF detectives pushed Ridgway to remember more about his encounter with her, but he only stated that it was an effort to mislead the investigation. A review of this murder, in context, would suggest that she represented a catathymic release for Ridgway. He abducted her as she walked home from work and took her to his house on Military Road. Ridgway killed her at the house and transported the body to a wooded area in Maple Valley. After posing the body, he left her relatively unmolested. In interviews, Ridgway admitted to intimate knowledge of Christiansen; not only was he familiar with her at her place of work, but he also knew where she lived and could, 20 years after the fact, recall the color of the trailer she lived in. A DNA sample was recovered and was matched to Ridgway. The deviation present in the Christiansen MO suggests an attempt to serve an ulterior motivation rather than the need to mitigate a risk.

Sometimes necessity prompts a shift in MO. In the early morning of August 6, 1998, Patricia Yellowrobe's body was discovered in the middle of the road behind All City Wrecking, in Southpark, a suburb in south Seattle. Her body was fully clothed, and there was no apparent sign of fatal injury. Additionally, there was no sign of vaginal or anal intercourse and only a small amount of spermatozoa were recovered, not enough to produce a viable DNA profile. Yellowrobe had an extensive history of drug and alcohol abuse and was not considered to be a victim of the GRK until Ridgway admitted to her killing in interviews with the GRTF.

Yellowrobe represents a departure from the GRK's MO; Ridgway states this anomaly is due to being "rusty" because he had not killed in an extended period of time. The killing of Yellowrobe was motivated by a mix of predatory and affective aggression. It is apparent from toxicology reports that Yellowrobe was intoxicated and was probably on the verge of losing consciousness during her encounter with the GRK. Ridgway stated that "I just didn't wanna pay for somebody just layin' around" (Green River Taskforce, 2003), and he became enraged and strangled her. Initially, Ridgway states he intended to kill Yellowrobe in the manner he had killed 47 other victims, but later contradicts himself with the statement indicated above. Whether Ridgway intended to kill Yellowrobe when he picked her up to "date" is suspect; however, Ridgway did admit, several times, to becoming enraged when hurried or otherwise unsatisfied with the service provided by his prostitute and that rage prompted a kill. The crime scene evidence (e.g., departure from the MO: finding the body clothed, discarded in plain sight on a busy road) indicates this murder was catathymic killing, while the disposal may have simply been an anomaly of convenience.

Ridgway's behavior suggests he feels no personal attachment for his victims other than a sense of possession or personal property. While the victims themselves represent nothing more than "garbage," and in interviews, Ridgway suggests he was doing King County a favor by taking prostitutes off the street. The wholly detached attitude toward his victims as objects rather than people is perhaps why he did not engage in any postmortem mutilation or experimentation with trophy taking as indicated by Holmes and Holmes (2009) as standard with the lust killer type. For a brief time, just as Ridgway is engaged in the struggle to asphyxiate, prior to loss of consciousness, his victims represent his mother; past this point, they are just objects to be discarded.

Signature

It is not uncommon for a marginalized personality to be functionally or psychologically impotent in conventional sexual encounters. Therefore, these personalities often resort to necrophilia as post-offense behavior. Necrophilia is a signature behavior; in other words, while not necessary to effect a kill, necrophilia is significant for its psychosexual value, which is unique to the offender (Stein, Schlesinger, & Pinizzotto, 2010).

Necrophilia is a strong element of fantasy and paraphilic motivator for the GRK. Several lesser signature elements appear to support the need for postmortem sexual intercourse. Some of the victims were found with triangular rocks lodged in their vaginas. When asked to explain the significance of these rocks, Ridgway states they were placeholders, deliberately inserted to keep other people from engaging in necrophilia with *his* victims (Green River Taskforce, 2003). Furthermore, the need to cluster the bodies, and the use of place markers such as fallen trees, mileposts, or guardrails to remember where those bodies were located, were all done so the GRK could revisit the bodies for postmortem coitus (Green River Taskforce, 2003). However, necrophilia stands as *the* significant signature element of the Green River murders.

The GRK's offense behavior betrays this complexity of motive with relation to ritual and signature. Whereas the FBI interpreted the GRK's choice of prostitutes as victims of opportunity, there is a potentially obscured but equally possible alternative. Meloy (2000) refers to a phenomenon known as *catathymia*, whereby the offender transfers feeling of rage for a familiar figure to a stranger and acts upon those feelings, most typically in a manner referred to as *displaced matricide*. While it may be a Freudian cliché to suggest that the GRK's offense behavior was motivated by a desire to injure his mother, interviews conducted with Ridgway suggest that his choice of victim was a deliberate attempt to strike back at an overbearing and provocative maternal figure suggesting the MO disguised his signature.

In this way the GRK similarly embodies the problematic and perhaps overly simplistic nature of bifurcated typologies, particularly the compulsive/catathymic model. Just as Wuornos and Yates seem to have dual or overlapping motivations, Ridgway killed prostitutes for reasons of convenience and with a desire to destroy the tormenting figure of his promiscuous mother. This conclusion would seem to suggest either a fundamental flaw in the bifurcated typology or an unreasonable expectation of exclusivity for all offense types. Perhaps a motive can serve a dual purpose, and it is necessary to acknowledge that reality when profiling a series.

Gary Leon Ridgway is not a primary psychopath; in fact, he rates low on Hare's scale as a secondary psychopath. Yet his stalking and killing behavior indicate a level of predation generally reserved for the callous, even sadistic upper secondary and primary psychopaths. Failure to correctly identify personality traits central to the pathology of the GRK depends largely on our misunderstanding of the role of psychopathy in homicidal pathology. While the methodical manner in which the homicides were conducted, up until the act of killing itself, suggests predatory aggression, a close examination of Ridgway's pathology reveals a distinctly catathymic mode of aggression. The GRK utilizes psychopathy to overcome the immense, emotional gravity of his crimes against women so that he may satisfy the psychosexual needs of his specific paraphilic set. Ridgway did not kill because he is a psychopath; rather, because he is a psychopath, the GRK was able to kill to effect another goal, the complete and total domination of a maternal surrogate.

Ridgway shares a host of risk factors with psychopaths and other serial killers. In combination with relatively low intelligence, Ridgway shows social and emotional intelligence deficits that suggest some form of emotional impairment leading to dissociative disorders (e.g., psychopathy). Additionally, the subject has developed violent sexual paraphilias and extreme hatred toward prostitutes and sexually provocative female figures. While no acute trauma is evident in Ridgway's background, it is clear his mother was distant, overbearing, and a considerable source of consternation and low self-esteem sufficient enough to be a traumatic influence.

Psychopathy

More than antisocial tendencies, psychopathy represents cognitive rational unique to violent offenders and is a primary measure of this study. Gary L. Ridgway is not a primary psychopath, scoring on the low end of the secondary range. A prime example of psychopathy manifested in Ridgway's personality is his attorney's characterization of his dialectic style, like a flea on an electric hotplate. Hare (1993) and others describe the psychopath's interpersonal skills as well versed in multiple topics, but suggest that a deeper examination of their familiarity in any given subject reveals a shallow or flawed understanding. Prothero indicates that Ridgway could tell and appreciate jokes, and although research on psychopathy suggests these personalities learn to mimic the appropriate response, they do not truly understand the nuances of many personal interactions.

On a functional level, Ridgway's behavior most closely resembles a secondary psychopath. The GRK employs many of the cognitive and disassociative attributes of a psychopath to be a more successful killer. Ridgway does have a PCL-R score that was generated for his defense; however, given the stigmatic nature of this kind of branding, the score was kept private and unavailable for public disclosure.

PCL-R, 2nd Edition Scores

The 20 items contained within the PCL-R scoring criteria are grouped into the two factors of aggressive narcissism and antisocial lifestyle. The aggressive narcissism component of psychopathy is almost completely absent in Ridgway. He is neither glib nor superficial and demonstrates a quality described by one of the researchers as "pathetic." Below, each of the 20 items is explained in detail along with some paraphrased comments pertaining to each of the items. The scores provided are those of the lead researcher and reflect the total score developed for statistical analysis (see Table 10.1).

Psychopathy Discussed

With a score of 21, Ridgway ranks in the 43rd percentile of psychopathic male offenders in North America. Given that serial killers, especially lust killers, those exhibiting some degree of sadism, feed on the emotional reactions of their victims, a rating of secondary psychopathy is not surprising. The primary psychopath does not possess the emotional awareness or processing ability to recognize, or be motivated by, any emotion other than greed rendering catathymic aggression impossible. Hervey Cleckley (1988) proposed in the primary psychopath "we are dealing here not with a complete man at all but with something that suggests a subtly contracted reflex machine which can mimic the human personality perfectly" (p. 369). Since Cleckley, we have discovered that a careful observer can readily spot the artifice of a psychopath; secondary psychopaths, on the other hand, have a dimensionally limited capacity for emotional processing and therefore, a presumably enhanced capacity for mimicry at points along that scale.

This human personality to which Cleckley (1988) refers is most readily present in how we relate to others. Factor 1 items, or "interpersonal factors," render an extremely narcissistic and aggressive personality in the primary psychopath. As a secondary psychopath, Ridgway employs these affective characteristics to use people around him for emotional gain. All of Ridgway's marital relationships have been characterized by some

Table 10.1 Complete Raters Scores

Items	LRATER Total	JRATER Total	MRATER Total
Glibness and/or Superficial Charm	0	1	1
Grandiose Sense of Self-Worth	1	1	1
Pathological Lying	2	2	2
Conning or Manipulation	2	1	1
Lack of Remorse or Guilt	2	2	2
Shallow Affect	2	2	1
Callousness, Lack of Empathy	2	2	2
Failure to Accept Responsibility for One's Own Actions	1	0	0
Parasitic Lifestyle	0	0	0
Poor Behavioral Controls	1	1	1
Lack of Realistic Long-Term Goals	0	0	0
Impulsivity	1	1	1
Irresponsibility	0	0	0
Juvenile Delinquency	1	2	2
Early Behavioral Problems	1	1	2
Need for Stimulation, Boredom	0	0	0
Revocation of Conditional Release	0	0	0
Sexual Promiscuity	2	2	2
Criminal Versatility	2	2	2
A History of Many Short-Term Marital Relationships	1	1	1
Final Score	21	21	21

LRATER, JRATER, and MRATER are coded rater identifiers.
Final score compiled as an average of all three raters (not all three raters rated the same).

dependency or another. His first wife was naïve when they married, but being forced to live on a military budget with her husband overseas, she became more independent and eventually left Ridgway for another man. Similarly, his second wife was overweight when they met. Ridgway claims as she lost weight and began to consider herself more attractive, she withdrew from her dependent relationship and began flirting in the taverns and bars they frequented on social occasions. Eventually, this manifested as a source of conflict between them, leading to the inevitable separation. His final marital relationship, beginning in 1985, which happened to coincide with a dramatic reduction in offense behavior, has been described in personal communications with the researcher as dependent[10] and even needy. Ridgway lacks a grandiosity and self-importance which are hallmarks of the primary psychopath. As a result, his marital relationships failed until he met a dependent personality he was capable of dominating. Ridgway scores in the 82nd percentile on Factor 1 traits in North American male offenders (Hare, 2003).

With regard to Factor 2, social deviance items, Ridgway ranks in only the 16th percentile of male offenders in North America. Apart from a penchant for petty theft, Ridgway confined his deviant lifestyle behaviors to serial homicide. Primary psychopaths are known to offend, reoffend, and continue doing so until they are caught. In correctional settings, these offenders are more likely to be refused conditional release and may attempt to escape. Furthermore, they generally lack the cognitive ability to accept the reality of the causal relationship between their confinement and their actions, preferring instead to blame their predicament on someone or something else (Hare, 1993, 2003). Apart from a few interactions with law enforcement and the courts for prostitution, Ridgway has no criminal history of serious offense. This relatively low score, given the seriousness and heinous nature of his crimes, highlights the fundamentally secondary nature of psychopathy in the GRK's personality.

Summary

Though able to coldly and brutally murder 78 women, Gary L. Ridgway, like so many serial killers, led a double life as a seemingly normal guy. He dated women, engaged in appropriate marital relationships, had a steady job, and integrated into society with little outward display of discomfort. Ridgway is not an aggressive narcissist as characterized by the disorder. Rather, psychopathy is a tool by which he was able to carry out his violent paraphilic desires. Splitting, or identifying prostitutes as garbage, allowed the GRK to kill with relatively little intrapsychic conflict, even as they plead for their lives.

It requires 10 minutes or more of constant pressure on the carotid arteries of the neck to achieve death by asphyxia (Spitz, 2006). Strangulation, as manner of death, is indicative of extreme motivation on the part of the offender, as there are easier ways to kill. Combined with an analysis of victimology, it can be readily inferred the GRK has targeted personal rage toward promiscuous female forms. The fact that this act was profitable enough to be repeatable suggests the offender has some capacity for emotional recognition. Use of models pertaining to the development of serial killer pathology indicates these murders are an attempt to dominate and destroy a surrogate for the overbearing maternal force at the heart of this personality's violent paraphilia (Hickey, 1997; Holmes & Holmes, 2009) and are incongruous with the motivations of a primary psychopath.

The GRK is both a predatory and catathymic actor. The role of psychopathy (predatory) in this killer's pathology is to facilitate the sexual (catathymic) motivation. A conventionally affected personality would be unable to simultaneously ignore and profit selectively from the intense emotionality of the act of killing another person. This complex interplay of motivation and facilitating psychological factors, I believe, is generalizable through the erotophonophiliac community.

Conclusion

As a serial killer, Gary L. Ridgway was tremendously successful; a combination of forensic awareness and selective self-control enabled the GRK to evade detection and kill unimpeded for nearly two decades. Ridgway was constantly in search of another victim; on his way home from work, before work, and on the weekends, he would cruise the prostitution neighborhoods in search of his next kill. Once he located a lady ("women" was a term reserved for hard-working, honest people), he lured them with the promise of money and strangled them until they died. Following the act, Ridgway would discard their bodies in clusters so he could remember where they were located and revisit the fresh corpse to engage in necrophilia sex. Once the body was too far decomposed for sex, the GRK moved on to select a new victim and the cycle repeated.

Gary Ridgway killed for a combination of compulsive or predatory reasons and catathymia. For this type of offender, emotion is central to the motivation structure of the kill. Psychopathy is used as a means of neutralizing the conflict, which would inhibit a normally affected personality. In this way, psychopathy clearly identified as a facilitator of the behavior, a means by which the offender can effect the kill.

Implications for Criminal Profiling and Investigations

Understanding the role of psychopathy and offense motivation is critical to understanding the serial homicide offender. Previously, psychopathy was thought to be such a domineering factor in personality as to overshadow catathymic motivation. It is important to note that in lesser psychopathic pathologies, the personality is defined by how the offender relates to the emotion they do process. Sexual motivation requires a tacit understanding of the baser, prominent emotional features embodied by our emotional extremes, fear, anger, and pain; however, for the offender to profit from these emotional outputs, they must first override the intrapsychic conflict inherent in the infliction of pain. This is the role of psychopathy in serial homicide.

The investigators involved in the Green River Murders were presented with a methodical, predatory, sexually motivated killer. With few leads to identify the killer, it was apparent that the GRK was very careful and very proficient in abducting, killing, and disposing of his victims. This predatory behavior is the hallmark of the psychopathic portion of Ridgway's personality. What happened peri- and postmortem reveals the true offense motivation of the GRK. Functionally impotent with a live, reactive female, Ridgway craved the catathymic release of the act of strangling his maternal surrogate and libidinal satisfaction not achievable through sexual contact with a live woman. Displaced matricide and unresolved oedipal motivations are why the Green River Killer murdered 78 women in and around King County; psychopathy is the means by which the intrapsychic conflict was neutralized to enable the behavior.

Notes

1. "Duplicitous—marked by deliberate deceptiveness especially be pretending one set of feelings and acting under the influence of another." Retrieved March 14, 2011, from http://freedictionary.com.

2. The PCL-R was developed by Hare to evaluate personalities on 20 separate criteria across three factors—interpersonal, affective, and lifestyle.

3. Available at the Seattle University Lemieux Library, "Profiling Ridgway: A Retrospective Analysis of Criminal Profiling through the Green River Killer Investigation."

4. No record of a PCL-R score for Ridgway was found in the course of researching this topic. Indicators of secondary psychopathy were identified through review of case history, personal history and review of more than 30 hours of interview footage.

5. In the spring (March or April) of 1984, fearing the GRTF was closing in, Ridgway transported partial remains of several victims to Tigard, Oregon. Ridgway deposited these skeletal remains in a drainage ditch near the offices of Allstate Insurance, partially out of spite over a settlement from a recent vehicle accident (Green River Taskforce, 2003).

6. Fearing he would be drafted, Ridgway joined the U.S. Navy in 1969 and was stationed in the Philippines on a supply ship. Ridgway was never engaged in combat operations; however, he regularly told friends and family about participating in clandestine combat operations and that he was shot at (Prothero & Smith, 2006).

7. Since his incarceration, Ridgway corresponds regularly with as many as 18 women, nearly exclusively (Prothero, 2009).

8. Date is a term used in reference to the transaction between a prostitute (trick) and a John.

9. Though in its infancy during the mid-1980s, Ridgway was aware of the potential evidence lodged under a victims fingernails and mentions DNA specifically. It is unclear whether this awareness was present at the time of offense or if he became aware of it after being presented with the evidence against him.

10. The source of these personal communications will not be published here but can be produced upon request of the researcher.

References

Arrigo, B. A., & Purcell, C. E. (2001). Explaining paraphilias and lust murder: Toward an integrated model. *International Journal of Offender Therapy and Comparative Criminology*, 45(1), 6–31.

Baird, J. B., Eakes, P. A., McDonald, B. M., Goodhew, I. M., & O'Donnell, S. P. (2003). *Prosecutors summary of evidence*. Seattle, WA: King County Prosecuting Attorney.

Blair, J., Mitchell, D., & Blair, K. (2008). *The psychopath: Emotion and the brain*. Malden, MA: Blackwell Publishing.

Burgess, A W., Hartman, C. R., Ressler, R. K., Douglass, J. E., McCormack, A. (September 1986). Sexual homicide: A motivational model. *J Interpers Violence*, *1*(3), 251–272.

Cleckley, H. (1988). *The mask of sanity* (5th ed.). Augusta, GA: Emily S. Cleckley.

Douglas, J., & Olshaker, M. (1995). *Mindhunter: Inside the FBI's elite serial crime unit*. New York: Simon & Schuster.

Douglas, J., Ressler, R., Burgess, A., & Hartman, C. (1986). Criminal profiling from crime scene analysis. *Behavioral Science and the Law*, 4(4), 401–421.

Federal Bureau of Investigation, U.S. (1987). *Letterhead memorandum: Greenmurs, Major Case #77, Kidnapping*. Washington, DC: Author.

Green River Taskforce (Director). (2003). *State of Washington v. Gary L. Ridgway 01-1-10270-9 SEA: GRTF Interviews* [Motion Picture].

Guillen, T. (2007). *Serial killers: Issues explored through the Green River murders*. Pearson Prentice Hall.

Hare, R. D. (1993). *Without conscience: The disturbing world of psychopaths among us*. New York: Pocket Books.

Hare, R. D. (2003). *Hare Psychopathy Checklist–Revised (PCL-R)* (2nd ed.). North Tonawanda, NY: Multi-Health Systems.

Helfgott, J. (2004). Primative defenses in the language of the psychopath: Considerations for forensic practice. *Journal of Forensic Psychology Practice*, 4(3).

Helfgott, J. (2008). *Criminal behavior: Theories, typologies, and criminal justice*. Thousand Oaks, CA: Sage Publications.

Hickey, E. W. (1997). *Serial murderers and their victims* (2nd ed.). Belmont, CA: Wadsworth.

Holmes, R., & Holmes, S. (2010). *Serial murder* (3rd ed.). Thousand Oaks, CA: Sage Publications.

Khantzian, E. J., Suh, J. J., Ruffins, S., Robins, C. E., & Albanese, M. J. (2008). Self-Medication Hypothesis: Connecting affective experience and drug choice. *Psychoanalytic Psychology*, 518–532.

McClellan, J. (2007). Animal cruelty and violent behavior: Is there a connection. *Journal of Security Education*, 29–45.

Meloy, J. R. (1988). *The psychopathic mind: Origins, dynamics and treatment*. Lanham, MD: Rowman & Littlefield.

Meloy, J. R. (2000). The nature and dynamics of sexual homicide: An integrative view. *Aggression and Violent Behavior*, 1–22.

Myers, W., Husted, D., Safarik, M., & O'Toole, M. (2006, July). The motivation behind serial sexual homicide: Is it sex, power, and control or anger? *Journal of Forensic Science, 51*(4), 900–907.

Prothero, M. (2009, March). Attorney at law. (L. T. Atherley, Interviewer).

Prothero, M., & Smith, C. (2006). *Defending Gary: Unraveling the mind of the Green River killer*. San Francisco, CA: Jossey-Bass.

Purcell, C., & Arrigo, B. (2006). *The psychology of lust murder: Paraphilia, sexual killing, and serial homicide*. New York: Elsevier.

Rule, A. (2004). *Green River running red*. New York: Pocket Books.

Spitz, W. U. (2006). Asphyxia. In W. U. Spitz & D. J. Spitz (Eds.), *Medicolegal investigation of death: Guidelines for the application of pathology to crime investigation* (4th ed., pp. 783–845). Springfield, IL: Charles C. Thomas.

Stein, M. L., Schlesinger, L. B., & Pinizzotto, A. J. (2010). Necrophilia and sexual homicide. *Journal of Forensic Sciences*.

Turvey, B. (1999). *Criminal profiling: An introduction to behavioral evidence analysis*. San Diego, CA: Academic Press.

USDOJ FBI, R. D. (2009, August 18). Personal communication, subject: "GREENMURS (MAJOR CASE #771)" (L. T. Atherley, Interviewer).

CHAPTER ELEVEN

Forensic Psychological Evaluations for Behavioral Disorders in Police Officers: Reducing Negligent Hire and Retention Risks

Ronn Johnson

Introduction

Most states and municipalities have codes that specify physical and psychological standards for hiring all public safety and other criminal justice personnel. Agencies throughout the United States also use mission and vision statements to define an officer's perceived roles Police officers are the face of the criminal justice system. Criminal justice personnel licensed by the authority to carry a weapon are usually required to undergo physical and psychological evaluations as part of the hiring process (Dantzker, 2011; Johnson, 2012). One of the objectives of the psychological evaluation is to identify any history or presence of a behavioral disorder, misconduct pattern, and/or job-relevant psychopathology. These factors could subsequently function as the basis for complaints and/or legal action related to negligent hire or retention. This chapter covers the psychological issues that require special attention in the process of evaluating these individuals (pre-employment or fitness for duty).

Purpose of Psychological Screening of Police Officers

Psychological evaluation of police and other public safety employees who carry weapons is not a simple mental status exam or standard clinical evaluation, in part because people with a current Axis I mental disorder rarely apply for these jobs. It is also not a usual employment exam. It is the job of the psychological screener to recommend those applicants who are most suitable for developing police job competencies (Decker, 2006; Rostow & Davis, 2004). This psychological screening task is at least partially achieved by documenting stress resilience in the anticipated face of future psychological risk demands. Although officers who will be the greatest liabilities (i.e., problem officers) can usually be identified within the first six years of service, police service tenure generally lasts for 25 to 30 years from hiring to pension. Problem officers tend to display early onset of difficulties, with high frequency, and long duration of problematic behaviors (Harris, 2009). However, because pension and other benefits are tied to department, municipality, or state, problem officers are unlikely to leave as they might another job, while union rules and legal interventions prevent most firings. So once an applicant is hired, this is likely to be a 30-year marriage for the department. The psychological examiner must keep in mind that the purpose of the exam is to evaluate and document the applicant's inability to manage the essential functions of this job under usual job and personal stresses long into the future. The evaluation is also not strictly a forensic evaluation in that it is not about evaluating culpability or responsibility at a particular time in the past. However, it *is* a forensic psychological evaluation in the sense that the evaluator must document evidence of the ability to cope under stress, as a defense against potential future claims of negligent hiring, possibly occurring years later. Relevant legal statutes must also be met (Gutman, Koppes, & Vodanovich, 2010). The evaluator must find ways to reveal and document indicators of past patterns and coping methods that would likely lead to unacceptable actions or compromise behavioral and interpersonal control and judgment. The behavioral concerns must be assessed with awareness that an officer, over many years, is subjected to stresses associated with ordinary personal or job events—work rules, schedules, discipline, relationships with peers, superiors, citizens, or unsettling family situation, personal and economic life events (Hickman, Fricas, Strom, & Pope, 2011; Johnson & Scott, 2010; Pasillas, Follette, & Perumean-Chaney, 2006).

While the more salient traumas of policing, death, abuse, and human tragedy are likely to be cited as the cause of an officer's "stress," these are often less individual than system issues. Where systems deal with traumatic events effectively, most officers prove to be relatively resilient (Koch, 2010). As one officer said of a shooting, "I know I signed up for this but I never expected to have to shoot anyone, but I did exactly what I was trained to do, how I was trained to do it, and knew exactly what I was doing and why."

Even a few vulnerable officers can randomly moderate stress with timely system interventions. Although usual job stress that is particularly difficult for less mature officers is the top-down military structure of the job, which is, in fact, a nonmilitary job environment (Huddleston, Stephens, & Paton, 2007; Johnson, 2012). The night wardens in the Middle Ages established the idea that the job of the police is to "keep the peace," not fight an enemy. This calls for great restraint under pressure and causes significant stress. As one naïve young police officer, understandably anxious when approaching car windows to write minor tickets, said after receiving too many citizen complaints, "Well no one told me I wasn't supposed to yell back." Here, too, system management is an issue. Top-down support is needed in a top-down structure. On the other hand, "problem officers" are usually individuals who are vulnerable because of long-standing, well-established personality patterns that make it difficult for them to cope with usual life and work stresses that affect everyone—issues such as schedules, overtime, shifting assignments, and usual life events (Huddleston et al., 2007).

A properly trained police psychological examiner usually spends a considerable amount of time in advance of an interview crafting evaluee-specific questions, reviewing department supplied records, studying history forms, application, and test results—at minimum. To an untrained person, it may seem impossible to elicit and document these important vulnerabilities in a time-limited interview (30 minutes minimum). Or worse, one might erroneously assume that an examiner must spend a long time in a face-to-face interview in order to render an empirically based opinion of an applicant. Applicants are usually young people, under age 25, with limited life history and barely fully myelinated frontal lobes! It is easy to dismiss family and school events as juvenile, but past misconduct and test-based vulnerabilities must be fully explored—not just for seriousness as it relates to the position at hand, but to understand the applicant's attitudes, ability to understand their own motivations, and ability to learn from prior experiences, not just in words but in actions. One major assessment point in the psychological screening is determining the extent to which an applicant or incumbent officer is anticipated to be able to handle the two types of police stress (operational and managerial)

(Biggam, Power, MacDonald, Carcary, & Moodie, 1997; Kop, Schaufeli, & Euwema, 1999; McCreary & Thompson, 2006).

It is important to be detailed in discussing issues; important to notice how the applicant handles their dismissal of minor past missteps; important to appraise their retrospective judgment about personal problems and relationships, even those minor ones of adolescence; important to notice their discussion of how they evaluate past coping, and how they manage discussions of the current testing and interview (Johnson, 2011). Interview responses usually reveal and can be used to document an applicant's ability, over time, to cope with usual life and work stresses and to maintain both mental and behavioral control while under police stress demands (Huddleston et al., 2007). A behavioral disorder can refer to one significant act or a pattern of events, past or present, that reflect poor judgment, thinking, and/or reasoning. Such disorders suggest vulnerability to stress and problematic post-hire malfunctioning on or off duty. Although a mental disorder has no definition that specifies precise boundaries, several recognized professional sources purport to measure clinical signs (e.g., distress, dysfunction, dyscontrol, inflexibility, and/or irrationality syndromal patterns) (APA, 2000).

The Psychological Interview Process

Who

Most of these evaluations are performed by licensed psychologists with well-documented training, appropriate professional associations or affiliations, and supervision in police psychology. In some venues, codes require a specific level of certification and/or experience. Some larger venues have permanent staff who perform evaluations ongoing (Dantzker, 2011).

What

In almost all states, some psychological screening is a required part of the hiring process of anyone who will be licensed to carry a weapon in the performance of job duties. The process of evaluation and reporting may be defined in the state code or may be left to the examiner to determine. Almost all states require testing as part of the process, and most require that at least two recognized psychological tests, validated for police psychology purposes, be administered. Some examiners use only testing to screen, then perform an interview only when they believe the testing raises issues. However, most states specify that a face-to-face interview is required. One practice of this writer is that testing should never be used as the sole basis for making an evaluation decision (Johnson,

2011). In most venues, testing is considered valid for 12 months. Departments differ as to whether and when a disqualified applicant can reapply. An applicant recycling through after a psychological disqualification must be able to provide clear and convincing evidence that he or she has done something substantial to address and correct the issues related to the original bypass or disqualification. It is recommended that at least an 18-month window be used as the waiting period before reapplying or participating in another pre-employment psychological evaluation (Johnson, 2011).

In California, screening requires use of the POST (Peace Officer Standards of Training). Many venues and examiners, though not covered under the law, adhere to those standards. The POST was initially developed for consistency in evaluating peace officers. In 2006, the POST Commission approved the issuance of the "Psychological Screening Dimensions" for use in the pre-employment psychological evaluation of peace officers. The new set of 10 validated peace officer psychological attributes was developed from an extensive job analysis. Each of the 10 psychological dimensions includes a behaviorally based definition and a list of associated positive and counterproductive peace officer behaviors (e.g., adaptability/flexibility, avoidance of substance abuse, conscientiousness/dependability, integrity/ethics impulse control/attention to safety, stress tolerance, and judgment, etc.). The use of POST Psychological Dimensions subsequently occurs after the testing, review of documents, and a face-to-face interview as well as a second evaluation for those initially found psychologically not qualified. Some venues and examiners throughout the country elect to use the POST standards and process because it provides a degree of uniformity.

Why Do Psychological Evaluations for Police?

The psychological screening is "not" performed for the purpose of "screening in" what is theoretically thought to be the "best" individuals, but to "screen out" those with confirmed psychological issues (behavioral disorder) that would, over time, interfere with their performing the essential functions of their job and dealing with the predictable stresses the job entails. The "Rule Out" as opposed to "Rule In" approach is the standard of practice in the psychological screening of police officers (Johnson, 2012; Lowman, 1989; Sanders, 2008). The Rule Out approach demonstrates that individuals with at least some history of a behavior disorder are more likely than not to experience difficulties or involve themselves in misconduct while trying to consistently fulfill all the duties of a police officer (Johnson & Marek, 2012).

It is the department that establishes guidelines for who to screen "out." In larger venues this may be done by civil service exams, where the highest grades as well as legal preferences for special populations such as veterans and diverse candidates may result in an applicant pool that is not specifically selected to meet the job demands. In smaller venues the screening may be simply the choice of the chief. In others, a board of municipal leaders and/or superior officers who guide the selection based on community needs or officer experience does the initial selection. Some departments use standardized behavioral, nonmedical screening psychological questionnaires such as the Inwald Personality Inventory to guide the initial selection of candidates.

A civil investigation is usually conducted by the department as part of the screening process, prior to any conditional offer. These reports may contain information that, while not a basis for a legal disqualification, must be explored as a basis for further psychological evaluation. These might include medical issues a background investigator or detective cannot pursue, or questions about the applicant's handling of major or even minor events. It is essential that the screener thoroughly review those documents, explore those issues during the psychological screening evaluation, and, when indicated, request further evaluation by the background investigators or detectives (Anderson, Dyson, Burns, & Taylor, 2008).

When Do Psychological Screenings Take Place?

The psychological screening is a medical examination that cannot legally begin before the candidate has been given a conditional job offer. At that point, the candidate can be asked for any and all medical history and documents needed for the exam. Since time is important, it is the job of the applicant to secure the relevant and required documents requested by the department. Some agencies use a screening check list covering past life, work, educational, legal, relationship, physical, and mental medical history to assure that they are aware of and obtain all medical history and documents (Borum, Super, & Rand, 2003).

Under the Genetic Information Nondiscriminatory Act of 2008 (GINA), no police-hiring authority can use an individual's genetic information when making hiring, firing, job placement, or promotion decisions. If any is accidentally provided, the venue must prove it was not used in any hiring or future promotional decision. At the same time, the screener must be alert to historical trauma that can be activated in vulnerable individuals under the stressful demands of any psychologically strenuous training or work experience (Resnick, 2008). PTSD and mTBI are relevant factors for evaluating OEF/OIF Veterans who now represent a sizable number of applicants.

Since the psychological exam is costly, some venues schedule it after the physical screening to save on cost. Others find it useful to do it first, since more candidates are eliminated by psychological screening than because of physical limitations, thus reducing the total cost for physical exams. Although modifications in public safety jobs are necessarily limited, potential modifications must be considered in any evaluation (Sherman & Longworthy, 1982).

Stress from Diverse Police Work Settings

This section identifies some of the diverse settings and stressful demands associated with police work. It includes case scenarios that reflect the types of problematic job-relevant behaviors, stress vulnerability, and psychiatric diagnoses reflected in behaviors of some applicants in pre-employment second- and third-opinion evaluations. It explores those incidents in the light of our understanding not of mental disorders such as depression, anxiety, etc. (see DSM-V), but in the light of the personality structure that underlies what can be referred to as behavioral disorders. Stress is not a *reason* for a behavior disorder, but a *precipitant* in vulnerable individuals. In fact, stress tolerance and the ability to maintain mental function and reasonable behavior in the face of disturbing, anxiety-provoking—i.e., stressful—events encountered by police officers is the reason for psychological screening of behavioral disorders (Martelli, Waters, & Martelli, 1989; Martin, McKean, & Veltkamp, 1986; Railings, 2002; Violanti, 1996). Huddleston et al. (2007) found that daily organizational stressors such as resources issues (e.g., insufficient resources, unreliable equipment, lack of financial resources), activity issues (e.g., irregular meal times, shift work interfering with other activities), workload and administration issues (e.g., paperwork) are good predictors of psychological distress in police officers.

Behavioral Disorders

A behavior disorder includes not only minor misbehavior, but a significant single event, history, or pattern of misconduct—a history of misconduct that is assessed as likely to interfere with performance under the stressful demands of a police officer. The behavior disorder is expected to, more likely than not, raise questions about the individual's ability, especially under stress, not simply to maintain mental function, cognition, affect, and mood, but also to assess a situation, read-react, anticipate and solve problems, make accurate judgments, organize reasonable responses, understand their reasoning in making split-second decisions, and take responsibility for difficulties that arise (Johnson, 2011). Therefore, in evaluating applicants, psychological evaluations must give considerable weight to how the applicant handles and now presents minor family and relationship issues. Even minor behavioral problems connected to intoxicant use are troublesome, since these problems reflect on the quality of judgment for a safety-sensitive position. Alcohol is a concern with police officers; therefore, a person attempting to enter this occupation with preexisting alcohol difficulties would represent a significant negligent hire risk. Relationship issues can arise. For example, an applicant who made threatening phone calls to a romantic competitor and had to be brought to legal authorities several times by the same victim would represent a risky hire. During the psychological interview, this applicant gave as evidence of his ability to change the fact that he had then signed up for military service, but did not acknowledge that he had done that at the suggestion of the court.

Assessment standards must be higher when evaluating police applicants than for other public safety, civilian (security and other non-sworn positions) or military personnel (e.g., MPs). The duties of an armed security guard, military police officer, or correctional officer working in a special inmate unit are not comparable to a police officer. Even during active military, the threat is clearer, while peer and supervisor support is stronger. Driving a truck, carrying a rifle, operating equipment/radio, firefights, patrolling villages, and receiving an honorable discharge is laudable, but the demands and stresses are distinctly different from a police officer. One veteran police psychiatrist asked an overly aggressive ex-sergeant applicant if he understood that, "In the military they give you a gun and tell you to shoot people, and in the police department they give you a gun and tell you not to shoot."

In civilian policing, as in no other occupation, events shift from boring to traumatic in an instant. For example, when a suicide is completed, police officers are usually the first responders. They perform the immediate tasks—securing the scene, talking with distressed family, and investigating. They must deal with the unedited experience, and then be quickly dispatched to the next call (Johnson, 2012).

On-duty violence, physical threats, gang violence, and anticipation of terrorist attacks are interspersed with tedious shift work (Violanti & Aron, 1994). They must remain vigilant during long periods of boredom and deal with shifting duty hours that result in the perception that one is never really off duty (Gershon, Lin, & Li, 2002; Martin, McKean, & Veltkamp, 1986; Martelli, Waters, & Martelli, 1989; Railings, 2002; Violanti, 1996; Violanti & Aron, 1994).

An investigation by Brough (2004) found that police work predicted psychological stress (i.e., mood symptoms and interpersonal impairments) different from that of firefighters and paramedics. For example, on scenes an officer often knows little or nothing about citizens they come into contact with day-to-day in the midst of crises. Correctional officers at least have the added benefit of working in a structured setting, where they know the inmates that they come into contact with as part of a scene management team. However, police officers must also manage the termination of a pursuit chase or explosive event where the unexpected surge of adrenaline-fueled emotions can lead to the use of excessive force (Anderson et al., 2008).

In the face of these disturbing events and emotions, police officers must be perceived as stable and in charge (i.e., command presence), must secure compliance from citizens, and must establish effective cooperative relationships with firefighters, EMTs, dispatchers, and sometimes other law enforcement personnel in a way that does not cause them to be viewed as off-putting or rude. They cannot allow stressful situations or hostile responses to precipitate the use of excessive force, rough or disrespectful language, or otherwise abuse their authority. Police officers must be perceived as fair and credible—on or off duty—across racial and ethnic groups. Seron, Pereira & Kovath (2004) found that blacks rate police misconduct significantly higher than their white counterparts.

In the face of these kinds of perceptions, officers without strong administrative support may have to carry out routine duties under vacillating direction to enforce or not enforce routine laws. They may be vulnerable to justified or unjustified negative media attention. They sometimes must carry out routine duties under political pressure and still present as consistent, stable and professional (Dantzker, 2005).

An applicant's explanation of even a minor alcohol-related event, of fights, or of failures can provide insight into and document their ability to not be drawn into or cover up wrongdoing on the part of fellow officers. An interviewer who explores seemingly minor missteps found in past incidents and infractions can reflect the difference between meddling and becoming complicit. Patterns of reasoning and behavior are well established by adolescence and change only with effort (Jacobs, 2011).

A psychological interview is an ideal place to elicit and document the presence or absence of an applicant's effort to outgrow patterns of avoidance, blaming, and denying. An examination of problematic personal information can uncover blaming, a particularly toxic behavioral disorder characteristic (inaccuracies in data provided, persistent inconsistencies in information reported, evasiveness, history of lying, claiming to be a private person to avoid disclosures, lack of forthrightness, or failure to make full disclosures). Logical and hard to change, blaming not only alters judgment and reasoning, but obstructs the ability to experience distress and shame and gets in the way of behavioral change. For example, an officer was fired after he passed out offensive photos he said were given to him by a training instructor. In fact, the photos were part of a training course, the point of which was a discussion of handling and control of offensive materials; the photos were clearly marked, "Return to the instructor before leaving the class."

A unique area of police stress is the rapid shift from work to family and life. There are few comparable occupations (Gershon et al., 2002; Kop & Euwema, 2001; Violanti & Aron, 1994). The nexus between work and off-duty stresses can be, "reciprocal or recursive, with problems in one area leading to problems in the other area and vice-versa" (Slate, Johnson & Colbert, 2007)." Therefore, an applicant or incumbent officer's past is especially relevant because of the vulnerability to miscues and negligence. Police personnel are known to take their job stress home with them, resulting in dysfunctional impact on their contacts with their families (Kerley, 2005; Violanti, 2005; Wester & Lyubelsky, 2005). An off-duty officer received a 10-day suspension for violating the department's policy after he pulled his service revolver on a youth who accidentally struck his personal car during a snowball fight game. It is important in screening to evaluate the individual's ability to place psychological boundaries between their personal life and demands of the job (Pasillas et al., 2006).

Gender and race may also function as stress factors since police work is still predominantly a white male occupation. (Violanti, O'Hara, & Tate, 2011). In the context of terrorism, officers must work equably and establish working trust relationships with diverse populations and unaccustomed cultures (Mythen & Walklate, 2006; Poynting & Mason, 2008; Spalek & McDonald, 2010). They must be able to develop trust relationships within groups that play key roles in relation to gathering community intelligence often required for antiterrorism and counterterrorism efforts (Demos, 2007; Hillyard, 1993, 2005; Virta, 2008).

Female officers experience a subset of gender-specific stressors: acceptance by males, paucity of role models, and persistent issues of being "in charge" of home and child care (Herrington, 2002; Morash & Haarr, 1995; Rabe-Hemp, 2008). As one woman officer said in defense of her spouse, "He'll do anything I ask around the house and he is always glad to take care of the kids but I have to do all the thinking about it."

Prejudice and ignorance make essentially normal mental vulnerability shameful and threatening, creating barriers to readily available and not especially complex forms of stress reduction and self-management. Disappointingly, however, these self- and group-imposed barriers prevent at-risk officers from seeking treatment and prevent peers from alerting others to an officer at risk. Not surprisingly, suicide is sometimes a terrible consequence of the unmanaged demands (Violanti, 2005; Huddleston et al., 2007). For example, a police officer who shot his wife multiple times before shooting himself had, that day, run a marathon that he referred to as a form of "stress relief." Friends of the officer were aware of both moodiness related to the recent suicide of his son and financial pressures stemming from two bankruptcies. Although aware of his distress, the friends and colleagues expressed disbelief that he would ever do anything like that.

Intoxicant-Use Patterns and Police Stress

Alcohol dependence and misuse is a significant problem, regardless of department size or location (Violanti, Slavin, et al., 2011). It is not surprising. When the dismissal of mental problems is pervasive, alcohol is usually the self-prescribed cop "medication" for problems with mood and sleep—and is likely, over time, to biologically enhance both the mood and sleep disturbance. Ballenger et al. (2010) found that in a large sample of urban police officers, 18.1% of males and 15.9% of females reported experiencing adverse consequences from alcohol use, and 7.8% of the sample met criteria for lifetime alcohol abuse or dependence. Careful assessment of alcohol use is essential during the psychological interview. Applicants and incumbent officers are quite aware of their alcohol-related patterns, and those difficulties can be denied, distorted, minimized, or misrepresented. Any DUI/DWI is known to predict future problems (Ballenger et al., 2010). Juvenile arrests for alcohol-related events are often dismissed during an evaluation, at times rightly so, but careful exploration of the circumstances—how the individual handled it, how they actually now understand it, should take place since that reflects the applicant's later reasoning and judgment. And any history of problematic drinking, integrity, or difficulty resolving relationship issues are negligent hire risks that no department should be forced to absorb, because such history reinforces concerns about a behavior disorder.

To summarize, the psychological evaluation process is essentially the assessment of risk, based on a pattern of behavior that can predict the sequelae of job-relevant problem behavior. The later emergence of the psychological problems, highlighted by past relevant history (no matter when it occurred) and uncovered as a result of some egregious act (or inaction) by a police officer (on or off duty) could function as the basis for lawsuit alleging a negligent hire or retention, often years later. Such acts from an officer represent vulnerability and pose an increased risk for both citizens and department liability. The shooting of Immigration Customs Enforcement (ICE) agents involved an on-duty dispute that resulted in the death of one officer. An undercover Border Patrol Agent, shot and killed a female after he jumped on the hood of her car. The female in question had no known criminal records. The department and the examining psychologist, even years after the initial hire, must be able to convincingly defend opinions for what was known or should have been known regarding all the officers involved in the aforementioned cases. Previous psychological reports of all the officers involved will be reviewed for any job-relevant psychopathology pertinent to these cases.

In 2012, one East Coast department had several police officers face federal charges after they were accused of depriving Latinos of their rights, in a pattern of excessive force against undocumented immigrants, harassment, intimidation, and unlawful searches. They were also accused of harassing and intimidating people, including advocates, witnesses, and other officers, who tried to investigate or report misconduct or abuse the officers committed. The charges were sustained in the face of the fact that several of the officers involved in this case were decorated veterans in the department. But their status as decorated veterans, with awards for military policing, reputation as good family men, honorable military service discharge, and work in military policing, did not equate with and should not necessarily have been seen as qualifiers for civilian police work. In fact, this case reinforces the need to use a police psychology standard of practice of "rule out" as opposed to a "rule in" approach when performing psychological evaluations of applicants (Johnson, 2011; Lowman, 1989). No laundry list of positives (i.e., rule in) can be used to offset negatives contained in the history or testing. Even in the face of the prior history, the additional history of minor indicators of undue aggression, braggadocio in the military, and a spotty high school record, though remote, need to be rigorously explored to elicit the applicant's reasoning, judgment, and maturation. This probing is essential, because in the face of later misdeeds, any problematic history will be exposed during any subsequent legal proceedings, making it almost impossible to defend or restore the credibility of the officers for later infractions.

For example, an off-duty officer shot and killed his girlfriend with his service revolver. The family sued the city for negligent hire, based on the fact that the pre-employment psychologist failed to follow up on an alcohol incident that occurred when the officer, then 12 years old, imbibed a six-pack of beer on one occasion. The psychologist, as per department policy, had only notes that revealed the single pre-adolescent binge drinking episode. No psychological report was written documenting that the juvenile alcohol incident was explored and the reasoning through which it was dismissed. The jury awarded the family a third of a million dollars, stating that the city was at least partially at fault for the death of the girlfriend. In fact, even if there had been a report outlining the psychologist's reasoning for dismissing the incident as problematic, drinking at an early age, at 12 or 14, is a well-known indicator of significant alcohol vulnerability (Masten, Faden, Zucker, & Spear, 2008).

In the same vein, an examiner must explore and document reasons for dismissing common issues, such as uneven academic performance or money mismanagement issues. For example, the way an applicant or incumbent officer handles financial problems can reflect difficulty with problem solving and distracting stress. It can signal concerns including poor judgment, inability to anticipate problems, distractibility, and other possibilities that can arise in a nonjudgmental discussion. In fact, the police psychologist should document the applicant's insight, increased maturity, improved reasoning, thinking, and quality of judgment.

Even a young officer must find a way to proceed fairly when other officers are not. For example, how should a young officer manage traffic stops in an area where nearly half or a third of the drivers pulled over by certain officers for minor violations were Latino, and the number of Latinos pulled over by certain squads were "extraordinarily high"? And when other officers are accused, they must report evidence as accurately as they are able.

Just a history of youthful difficulty resolving personal relationship and family tensions, intoxicant misuse, and decisions that negatively impact finances could form the basis for a negligent hire legal case. This is especially true when negative events put the officer's entire history under increased review. Psychologists evaluating applicants (i.e., first, second or third opinions evaluators) and incumbent officers in fitness evaluations must provide clear and convincing documentation (i.e., not rule in data) of the reasons for dismissing past difficulties with behavior, reasoning, judgment, or acts of irresponsibility.

Psychological testing or empirically based rating systems may or may not reflect high risk. The examiner's documentation must reflect his or her reasoning for accepting or rejecting negative test results that conflict with their conclusions, even if their decision is based on a single event or only a few of incidents that reflect, nonetheless, a pattern consistent with unwanted traits or a frank behavior disorder. There is no empirical basis to refute problematic psychological test data of police applicants by using non-elevated or low test scores (Johnson, 2012). For example, psychological tests tend to show that officers later rated as having more problems with citizens showed higher levels of impulsivity, antisocial attitudes, cynicism, suspiciousness, and anxiety on prior testing. However, these tendencies may not be borne out either by history or even by the officer's later career path. In either accepting or countervening test results, the examiner must document the reasoning and evidence that led to their decision.

Evidence of an applicant's behavioral maturity may be hard to elicit from a 22-year-old, but in the end, the past is prologue in evaluating behavioral disorders even in young adults (Johnson, 2011). An applicant once gave a valid history of terrible poverty and abuse as the reason for his youthful arrest for soliciting prostitutes, "living on the streets." Six months into the job, he was the object of several complaints from prostitutes that he abused his authority by demanding sexual favors to avoid arrest. There were also several female motorists who filed complaints that he would promise to tear up citations if they would provide their home numbers.

Patterns of thinking, responding, and coping are quite well established by young adulthood, and change only with great effort over a lifetime. Decisions about the presence or absence of a behavior disorder can and must be based on a detailed review of youthful life events and the applicant's assessment of them, their meaning, and consequence. The evaluator must consider quality of judgment and reasoning such as the ability to plan and anticipate consequences, the ability to fairly assess one's role in a situation, to maintain mood, to control behavior, and to fairly accept responsibility. Such self-imposed growth-maturing efforts reflect and can document the presence or absence of a behavior disorder, if included in an evaluator's report.

In documenting the presence or absence of a behavior disorder, the examiner must apply professional judgment in identifying psychologically relevant behavioral evidence that can be convincingly defended. These are not appeals to a layperson-perceived acceptable rationale for opinions. The validity and accuracy of the examiner's opinions in the end are based on their qualifications (i.e., education, training, professional development activities, and supervision) plus review and analysis of the reasonably available data that could withstand scrutiny by qualified external examiners. Each of these three components—qualification, analysis, and clear and convincing documentation—are necessary to sustain validity in the face of informed external critiques. For example, in reviewing the qualifications of one opposing expert, it was noted that, "A review of Dr. Phil Windchime's curriculum vitae revealed that his last involvement with professional development activities was in the 1980s. He has had been using the Personality Assessment Inventory (PAI) for several years in outside (OE) psychological screening of police applicants but only in the last six months did he claim to have attended some unnamed training on the use of this test. Dr. Windchime reported consulting with a colleague when he needed help with the PAI. The colleague was later reported to be a master's level student supervised by Dr. Windchime." In one hearing, he offered evidence from an article that he secured from WebMD to support his applicant evaluation conclusions.

It is also difficult for unqualified professionals to take seriously or understand how what they assess as the youthful indiscretions and seemingly benign behavioral outcomes could result in a psychological opinion for an applicant or incumbent offer who presents as "normal." Few applicants come into the evaluation process or subsequent appealing hearing with their "hair on fire" or displaying overtly bizarre behavior. Applicants and incumbent officers can come across at appeal hearings and outside evaluations as calm and seemingly reasonable people and, given these superficial characteristics, elicit unconscious positive countertransference reactions from others. These thin-veneer first impressions are positive stereotypes that confuse the real, psychologically relevant issues that were assessed during the psychological screening evaluation. In other words, outside evaluators, the opposing attorney, and, occasionally, hearing officers mistake the cooperative and subdued presentation by the applicant or incumbent officer as a sign of their suitability for the position in question. The documentation of an applicant's behavioral disorder must include compelling insights about the relatively minor events in the individual's background report and history, testing, presentation, and disclosures or lack thereof during the psychological interview. Outside evaluators hired by an appellant may attempt (mistakenly) to use a "rule in" approach, a litany of accomplishments or letters of support, to justify a positive recommendation, which ignores the psychologically relevant signals reflected in minor but persistent behavioral disorder indicators. As previously stated, in evaluating relatively minor events that nonetheless reflect behavioral disorders, "What's past is prologue" (Shakespeare, *The Tempest*).

The most challenging demand for examiners writing the report is integrating data from several sources (Gacono & Hutton, 1994; Meloy, 1991; Sattler, 2001). Given the complexity of these psychological judgments, the report must make a clear and convincing case for dismissing negative test, stress, other vulnerabilities, or worrisome history data. For example, an examiner conducting an outside evaluation (OE report) cannot merely point to unrelated low test results as a means for dismissing other problematic history or test data. The report must pull together and integrate what can seem like an unending stream of raw data (Harvey, 1997; Weddig, 1984; Whitaker, 1994) and craft it in a way that allows a diverse group of decision makers to read and understand the recommendations. The report must offer sufficient justification as to what behavior is expected in response to specific kinds of relevant stresses. The report must offer a clear rationale as to why problematic behavior in various areas could be dismissed as psychologically relevant. One question the report writer may have to explain is why it is reasonable to err on the side of public safety, as opposed to an individual's right to a job. One reason is that departments do not need to "settle on marginal at best candidates" when there is no shortage of more suitable applicants.

There are ample cases that justify the need to err on the side of public safety concerns. For example, a correctional officer applicant won a psychological disqualification appeal to be hired. At issue was that, while in high school, she was arrested for selling drugs to classmates on campus. While youthful drug use is common, selling is always a serious sign of behavioral disorder vulnerability. The officer was later arrested for selling the drug PCP. In the investigation, it emerged that she had, while working as a CO, smuggled drugs into inmates at a substance abuse facility where she had been assigned. Another applicant was psychologically disqualified at the pre-employment screening for a DUI that took place four years prior to his application with a police department. The DUI-citing officer smelled alcohol as he approached the applicant's vehicle. He could also smell alcohol on the breath of the applicant as he questioned him. The applicant denied imbibing alcohol to the officer. The same applicant's psychological testing raised concerns about alcohol and integrity.

Departments or municipalities should expect that they will have to absorb the loss of public trust or liability awards for negligent hire or retention. For that reason, recommendations should have a reasonable degree of psychological certainty. In practical terms, an examiner's opinions boil down to whether there is sufficient evidence to support a decision. In a small number of these cases, an examiner could decide that there is justification for concerns about an individual, but not enough evidence to substantiate a negative recommendation to the department or hiring authority. These ambiguous or "wobbler" cases are usually handled by requesting a second- or third-opinion evaluation (Johnson & Scott, 2010).

It does not matter if it is a second- or third-opinion psychological evaluation. The conclusions of the evaluation must be communicated in writing and sometimes orally defended in front of a municipal board, civil service commission, court, or other appellant body, or defended in a lawsuit. Thus, not only the decision, but the report is a major product of the police psychologist's work (Guller, 2010). It must present an accurate and an exhaustive identification and integration of relevant findings as well as an understandable presentation of how conclusions and recommendations were reached. It must be written as if it is likely be read by everyone including the applicant, or in open court years later after distressing negative events have led to litigation and post-hire issues of credibility, quality of judgment, conscientiousness, and instability (Johnson & Marek, 2012).

Conclusions

Police work is a stressful occupation. Psychological evaluations in police psychology and public safety play a valuable role in addressing issues related to negligent hire and retention. Examiners may be advised to think of their report as being read years later after some high-profile incident. These evaluations can have a lasting impact, as reflected in subsequent screening out of applicants showing instability, poor judgment, intoxicant abuse tendencies, and other undesirable behavioral characteristics thought to be incompatible with successful functioning as peace officers. Police psychologists conducting pre-employment or fitness-for duty evaluations cannot assume everyone referred is being forthright and fully truthful.

There is sufficient cause to believe that an individual being evaluated would have sufficient motivation (securing or maintaining employment as a police officer) to be less than truthful during a psychological interview. A common issue in this regard is for the police psychologist to consider whether the inconsistency was willful lying or the product of simple forgetting (the defense of which the applicant almost always invokes). Inconsistency in an applicant's disclosures does raise integrity sensibilities. In addition, inconsistencies raise concerns about accuracy, attention to details, and ability to report. Police officers must provide credible (consistent) information during a trial. Some applicants or incumbent officers may feel provoked by the sensitive probing by a skilled police psychologist. The perception of provocation is usually confused with the evaluee's discomfort over having someone review the most negative portions of their personal history. The psychological interview is not designed to provoke reactions in those being evaluated, but there are individuals who struggle to manage the internal stress they experience. In this case, a reasonable question would be: If they cannot manage the stress from a gray-haired psychologist, how could they manage the accumulative stress of the job of a police officer?

As previously stated, the past is prologue. The examiner is under no professional obligation to weigh strengths as opposed to weaknesses, as it undermines the "rule out" approach, which is the standard of practice. Even the most undesirable evaluee has potential "rule-in" characteristics. Whether a pre-employment, special unit, or fitness-for-duty evaluation, the calculus of making decisions (bypass, DQ, letter grade, or not suitable) can be aided by spending considerable time establishing a foundation in the report that culminates in an integration section or I-section (Johnson, 2011). Police psychologists must make continuing efforts to developing competencies related to performing these sometimes complex, intensive, and multifaceted evaluations.

Appendix A

Objectives of the Psychological Evaluations of Police Applicants and Incumbent Officers

- To assess the level of psychological functioning as reflected in affective state, mental coping with stress, and quality of judgment
- To assess for previous psychologically relevant issues and behavioral disorder factors and relationship to the position in question
- To formulate a summary of the negligent risk factors associated with the person being evaluated
- To offer a clear rationale for the opinions and recommendations offered to the department or hiring authority
- To adhere to the standard of practice by using a "rule out" as opposed to "rule in" approach in rendering opinions or recommendations

Key Differences between Fitness-for-Duty and Pre-Employment Psychological Evaluations

The IACP provides a useful guide that explains the differences between pre-employment and fitness for duty evaluations (IACP, 2009). These evaluations required informed consent. They are also intrusive and stressful.

Pre-employment psychological screenings (PEPS):

- Pre-employment psychological screenings are always conducted on initial hires
- They are limited in their scope (psychological screening)

- Typically require use of at least two standardized objective personality tests (stability and suitability)
- Require a psychological interview lasting at least 30 minutes
- Requires a review of records provided by the department
- Requires the examiner to state in unambiguous language a firm and unambiguous psychological conclusion as to whether or not the applicant Meets, Does not Meet, Pass or Does not Pass, or assign a recognized rating designation (grade or number) that clearly informs the hiring authority their opinion regarding the applicant
- Guided by department, jurisdiction, or state guidelines related to the evaluation and recommendation

Fitness-for-duty evaluations (FFDE):

- Takes place on incumbent officer referred by the hiring authority or designee because of some concern about an officer's behavior
- Are intrusive and psychologically stressful
- Must address all the referral questions raised by the department, hiring authority, or designee
- Requires the use of assessment or evaluation tools that are specifically related to some aspect of the referral questions
- Are often comprehensive, and the length of the report and time involve vary depending on the issues in the case
- Should include interviews of readily available informants with caveats related to confidentiality and informed consent
- Requires the examiner to state in unambiguous language whether or not the evaluee is fit, not fit, fit with modifications, or conditions for returning (retention) to full duty

Appendix B

Semi-Structured Psychological Interviews

A semi-structured clinical interview is often conducted as part of any comprehensive psychological evaluation and assessment of PEPS or FFDEs. It is important to remember that each person being evaluated may require several hours of professional psychological work. In advance of the interview, there is a review of reasonably available records, history, application materials, testing results, previous reports, employer evaluations, personal references, available medical records, and background information that can take hours. Some of the applicant information may be assessed as anecdotal when it comes to rendering the final psychological opinions or recommendations. Crafting additional questions for psychological interview probes can also consume a great deal of time for properly trained forensic examiners working in these contexts. At a minimum, the PEPS interview should last a minimum of 30 minutes. The face-to-face time of the psychological interview should not be used as the only gauge of evaluating the appropriateness of the psychological screening, although the relevant scope of the issues addressed should be a variable used to determine the adequacy of the psychological interview (Johnson, 2011). FFDEs usually require longer interviews involving the officer referred and relevant collateral or third-party interviews (TPI).

The semi-structured psychological interview is where behavioral observations are used as part of the mental status examination section of the report. These are usually not stress interviews, but examinees should be informed in advanced that the interview can be stressful. Probes in personal areas can be viewed as highly intrusive but necessary as long as they are justifiable as job-relevant and do not violate GINA (Johnson, 2012; Johnson & Marek, 2012).

The psychological interview in this police psychology context is designed to review information relevant to a variety of areas associated with the applied-for position. Some of these assessment areas include: prior medical and psychiatric history, prior intoxicant use patterns, financial, driving record, tolerance for boredom, emotional reactivity, accountability-responsibility, maturity, legal authority contacts, employment, developmental issues, and stressful life events. An examiner must assess for the capacity to handle the stressful demands of the job in question, relationship history, self-assessment, psychological coping skills, disability status, and motivational factors for the position in question. Most importantly, the psychological interview also affords the qualified psychological examiner the opportunity to evaluate an individual's quality of judgment, thinking, reasoning, and ability to assess self in the situation (Johnson, 2012).

Psychological Testing in PEPS and FFDEs

IACP (2009) guidelines recommend that at least two psychological tests be used during evaluations. Because of the variations in referral questions for FFDEs, an examiner may use other psychological instruments to address the concerns raised by the department. No test or combination of test results should be used in isolation as the basis for opinions or recommendations related to the individual evaluated (Johnson, 2012). It is beyond the intent of this chapter to perform an exhaustive review of all the tests frequently used in this context of police psychology. In general, the APA ethical codes spell out considerations that should be made when deciding on the use of various testing tools. In this police psychology context, several instruments have been used for these types of evaluations.

- MMPI-2
- MMPI2-RF
- 16-PF
- Inwald Personality Inventory (IPI)
- California Psychological Inventor (CPI)
- Personality Assessment Inventory (PAI)

Several of the aforementioned instruments have law enforcement normative data that would be useful in rendering opinions in this type of police psychology and public safety work (Johnson, 2011).

Format of Police and Public Safety Psychological Reports

I. Introduction (referral questions; descriptive header, informed consent, sources of information)
II. Relevant History (past biopsychosocial history; previous reports, history of the FFDE incident and its aftermath)
III. Collateral or third party interviews (if appropriate)
IV. Mental Status Examination
V. Psychological Test Results
VI. Psychological findings
VII. Conclusions (including negligent risk assessment factors and rating)
VIII. Opinions and Recommendations (responses to evaluation questions; unambiguous recommendation to the department or hiring authority)

Problems with FFDE and PEPS Reports

Tallent (1993) identified some of the concerns associated with psychological reports. Some of these included:

- Complex (meaningless) words that are often used to add length to the report
- Report not frequently enough written in lay language
- The clinician's lack of true understanding of the assessment findings
- Language that is so vague and unclear that it cannot be falsified or considered wrong
- Psychologists too often fail to demand clear referral questions

Johnson (2012) reported that police psychology and public safety reports also have problems. Some of these report issues include:

- Mistaken use of "Rule in" versus standard of practice "Rule out" approach
- Failure to make a unambiguous recommendation at the end of the report
- Offering interpretive opinions on low test results as mitigators for problematic elevations
- Stating findings or opinions contained in other reports without offering a clear rationale for challenging the opposing opinions found other data or reports (reporting but no empirical evidence to refute them)
- Using anecdotal information provided by collaterals as equivalent to more scientifically based information
- Using self-serving statements by the examinee to challenge negative information
- Failing to sufficiently probe examinee or accepting as face valid information they provide
- Overreliance on computer-generated test interpretation as opposed to examiner's opinions
- Accepting and reporting evaluee statements as face valid or assuming self-exculpatory information is accurate and truthful
- Paucity of a relevant evidence-based foundation for the opinions and recommendations contained in the report

Officers rated as having more problems with citizens showed higher levels of impulsivity, antisocial attitudes, idiosyncratic thinking, cynicism, suspiciousness, and anxiety on vulnerabilities highlighted by worrisome psychological test results. An examiner has to explain how this examinee would be dealing with the stress of give and take exchanges with citizens and other job tasks.

References

American Psychiatric Association (APA). (2000). *Diagnostic and statistical manual of mental disorders* (4th ed., text rev.). Washington, DC: Author.

Anderson, J. F, Dyson L., Burns, J., Taylor, K. (1998). Preemployment screening and training could reduce excessive force litigation cases. *J Police Crim Psychol, 13*, 12–24.

Ballenger, J. F., Best, S. R., Metzler, T. J., Wasserman, D. A., Mohr, D. C., Liberman, A., ... Marmar, C. R. (2010). Patterns and predictors of alcohol use in male and female urban police officers. *American Journal on Addictions, 20*, 21–29. ISSN:1055-0496 print/1521-0391; online doi:10.1111/j.1521-0391.2010.00092.x.

Bersoff, D. N. (1995). *Ethical conflicts in psychology*. Washington, DC: American Psychological Association.

Biggam, F. H., Power, K. G., Macdonald, R. R., Carcary, W. B., & Moodie, E. (1997). Self-perceived occupational stress and distress in a Scottish police force. *Work Stress, 11*, 118–133.

Borum, R., Super, J., & Rand, M. (2003) Forensic assessment for high-risk occupations. In A. Goldstein & I. B. Weiner (Eds.), *Handbook of psychology, volume 11: Forensic psychology*. Hoboken, NJ: Wiley.

Brough, P. (2004). Comparing the influence of traumatic and organizational stressors on the psychological health of police, fire, and ambulance officers. *International Journal of Stress Management, 11*(3), 227–244.

Dantzker, M. L. (2005). *Understanding today's police* (4th ed.). Monsey, NJ: Criminal Justice Press.

Dantzker, M. L. (2011). Psychological preemployment screening for police candidates: Seeking consistency if not standardization professional psychology. *Research and Practice, 42*(3), 276–283.

Decker, K. P. (2006). Introduction to fitness for duty evaluations in law enforcement personnel. In K. P. Decker (Ed.), *Fit, unfit or misfit: How to perform fitness for duty evaluations in law enforcement professionals* (pp. 3–31). Springfield, IL: Charles C. Thomas.

Demos. (2007). *The activist police force*. London: Author.

Gacono, C. B., & Hutton, H. E. (1994). *The Hare PCL-R: Clinical interview schedule (Adult form)*. Clinical Interview Schedule (Adult form). Unpublished manuscript.

Gershon R. R., Lin, S., & Li, X. (2002). Work stress in aging police officers. *Journal of Occupational Environmental Medicine, 44*, 160–167.

Guller, M. (2010). Who is qualified to provide expert testimony on the psychological fitness for duty of a police officer? A guide for agencies, lawyers and hearing officers. *Journal of Police Criminal Psychology, 25*, 67–74. doi:10.1007/s11896-009-90658.

Gutman, A., Koppes, L. L., & Vodanovich, S. J. (2010). *EEO law and personnel practices* (3rd ed.). New York: Taylor & Francis.

Harris, C. J. (2009). Exploring the relationship between experience and problem behaviors: A Longitudinal analysis of officers from a large cohort. *Police Quarterly, 12*(2), 192–213. doi: 10.1177/1098611108327314.

Harvey, V. S. (1997). Improving readability of psychological reports. *Professional Psychology: Research and Practice, 28*(3), 271–274.

Herrington, P. (2002). Advice to women beginning a career in policing. *Women Criminal Justice 14*, 1–13.

Hickman, M. J., Fricas, J., Strom, K. J., & Pope M. W. (2011). Mapping Police Stress. *Police Quarterly, 14*(3), 227–250. doi:10.1177/1098611111413991.

Hillyard, P. (1993). *Suspect community: People's experience of the Prevention of Terrorism Acts in Britain*. London: Pluto Press.

Hillyard, P. (2005). *"The War on Terror: 'Lessons from Ireland'", Essays for Civil Liberties and Democracy in Europe. European Civil Liberties Network*. http://www.ecln.org/essays/essay-1.pdf.

HM Government, "Countering International Terrorism: the United Kingdom's Strategy" (Cm 6888 London TSO 2006), p. 1 para. 5 and p. 5 para. 22.

Huddleston, L., Stephens, C., & Paton, D. (2007). An evaluation of traumatic and organizational experiences on the psychological health of New Zealand police recruits. *Work, 28*, 199–207.

Jacobs, D. (2011). *Analyzing criminal minds: Forensic investigative science for the 21st century*. Santa Barbara, CA: Praeger.

International Association of Chiefs of Police (IACP). (1998). Standards of conduct. Alexandria, VA: IACP National Law Enforcement Police Center. Arlington VA. Retrieved March 6, 2012 from http://www.theiacp.org/psych_services_section/.

International Association of Chiefs of Police (IACP), Police Psychological Services Section. (2009). *Fitness for duty evaluation guidelines*. Arlington, VA. Retrieved March 6, 2012, from http://www.theiacp.org/psych_services_section/.

Johnson, R. (2011, September 29). *Cultural and ethical issues in delivering services in a forensic psychology setting*. Paper presented at the 20th Annual Patton State Hospital Forensic Psychology Conference, San Bernardino, CA.

Johnson, R. (2012). *Writing forensic psychological reports for police officer applicants: First responders in the war on terrorism*. Paper presented at the 64th annual scientific meeting of the American Academy of Forensic Sciences. Atlanta, GA.

Johnson, R., & Marek, B. (2012). *Professional and ethical issues in outside forensic psychological evaluations of police officers*. Paper presented at the 28th Annual Meeting of the American College of Forensic Psychology, San Francisco, CA.

Johnson R., & Scott, M. (2010). *Forensic ethical and risk assessment factors in law enforcement pre-employment psychological evaluations: Race matters*. Paper presented at the American College of Forensic Psychiatry 26th Annual Symposium, San Francisco, CA.

Kerley, K. R. (2005). The costs of protecting and serving: Exploring the consequences of police officer stress. In K. Copes (Ed.), *Policing and stress*. Englewood Cliffs, NJ: Prentice Hall.

Koch, B. J. (2010). The psychological impact on police officers of being first responders to completed suicides. *Journal of Police Criminal Psychology, 25*, 90–98. doi:10.1007/s11896-010-9070-y.

Kop, N., Schaufeli, W., & Euwema, M. (1999). Burnout, job stress and violent behaviour among Dutch police officers. *Work Stress, 13*, 326–340.

Kop, N., & Euwema, M. C. (2001). Occupational stress and the use of force by Dutch police officers. *Criminal Justice Behavior, 28*, 631–652.

Lowman, R. L. (1989). *Pre-employment screening for psychopathology: A guide to professional practice*. Sarasota, FL: Professional Resource Exchange.

Martelli, T. A., Waters, L. K., & Martelli, J. (1989). The police stress survey: Reliability and relation to job satisfaction and organizational commitment. *Psychological Reports, 64*, 267–273.

Martin, C. A., McKean, H. E., & Veltkamp, L. J. (1986). Post-traumatic stress disorder in police working with victims: A pilot study. *Journal of Police Science and Administration, 14*(2), 98–101.

Masten, A. S., Faden, V. B., Zucker, R., & Spear, L. P. (2008). Underage drinking: A developmental framework. *Pediatrics, 121*, S235–S251. doi:10.1542/peds.2007-2243A.

McCreary, D. R., & Thompson, M. M. (2006). Development of two reliable and valid measures of stressors in policing: The operational and organizational police stress questionnaires. *International Journal Stress Management, 13*, 494–518. doi:10.1037/10725245.13.4.494

Meloy, R. (1991). Discussion of "dangerous mentally disordered criminals: unresolvable societal fear?" (Letter to the editor). *Journal of Forensic Sciences, 36*, 1279–1280.

Morash, M., & Haarr, R. N. (1995). Gender, workplace problems, and stress in policing. *Justice Quarterly, 12*, 113–140.

Mythen, G., & Walklate, S. (2006). "Criminology and Terrorism." *British Journal of Criminology, 46*(3), 379–398.

Pasillas, R. M., Follette, V. M., & Perumean-Chaney, S. E. (2006). Occupational stress and psychological functioning in law enforcement offers. *Journal of Police and Criminal Psychology*, 21(1), 41–53.

Poynting, S., & Mason, V. (2008). The new integrationism, the state and Islamophobia: Retreat from multiculturalism in Australia. *International Journal of Law, Crime and Justice, 36*(4), 230–246.

Rabe-Hemp, C. (2008). Survival in an "all boys club": policewomen and their weight for acceptance. *Policing International Journal Police Strategic Management, 31*, 251–270.

Railings, M. (2002). The impact of offending in police officers. *Issues in Forensic Psychology, 3*, 20–40.

Resnick, D. (2008, August 22). GINA—a big step toward personalized medicine. *Mass Tech High*.

Risdon, N., Slate, R. N, Johnson & W. W., & Colbert, S. S. (2007). Police stress: A structural model. *Journal of Police & Criminal Psychology*, 22:102–112. DOI 10.1007/s11896-007-9012-5.

Rostow, C. D., & Davis, R. D. (2004). *A handbook for psychological fitness-for-duty evaluations in law enforcement*. New York: Haworth Clinical Practice Press.

Sanders, B. (2008). Using personality traits to predict police performance. *Policing: An International Journal of Police Strategies and Management, 31*(1), 129–147.

Sattler, J. M. (2001). *Assessment of children: Cognitive applications* (4th ed.). San Diego, CA: Author.

Seron, C., Pereira, J., & Kovath, J. (2004). Judging police misconduct: "Street-level" versus professional policing. *Law and Society Review, 38*(4), 665–710.

Shapiro, D. L. (1991). *Forensic psychological assessment*. Boston, MA: Allyn & Bacon.

Sherman, L., & Longworthy, R. (1982). Measuring homicide by police officers. In J. Fyfe (Ed.), *Readings on police and deadly force* (pp. 12–46). Washington, DC: Police Foundation.

Spalek, B., & McDonald, L. Z. (2010). Anti-social behaviour powers and the policing of security. *Social Policy and Society, 9*(1), 123–133.

Tallent, N. (1993). *Psychological report writing* (4th ed.). Englewood Cliffs, NJ: Prentice Hall.

Texas Department of Public Safety. (2010). Retrieved May 12, 2010, from Texas Department of Public Safety: http://www.txdps.state.tx.us/index.htm.

Violanti, J. M. (1996). Trauma. stress, and police work. In D. Paton & J. M. Violanti (Eds.), *Traumatic stress in critical occupations: Recognition, consequences, and treatment* (pp. 87–112). Springfield, IL: Charles C. Thomas.

Violanti, J. M. (2005). Dying for the job: Psychological stress, disease, and mortality in police work. In K. Copes (Ed.), *Policing and stress*. Upper Saddle River, NJ: Prentice Hall.

Violanti, J. M., & Aron, F. (1994). Ranking police stressors. *Psychological Report, 75*, 824–826.

Violanti, J. M., O'Hara, A. F., & Tate, T. T. (2011). *On the edge: Recent perspectives on police suicide*. Springfield, IL: Charles C. Thomas.

Violanti, J. M., Slaven, J. E., Luenda, E., Burchfie, C., Burchfiel, C. M., Andrew, M. E., & Homish, G. G. (2011). Police and alcohol use: A descriptive analysis and associations with stress outcomes. *American Journal of Criminal Justice, 36*, 344–356. doi:10.1007/s12103-011-9121-7.

Virta, S. (2008). Community policing meets new challenges. In S. Virta (Ed.), *Policing meets new challenges: Preventing radicalization and recruitment* (pp. 15–41). Finland: University of Tampere Department of Management Studies, CEPOL.

Weddig, R. R. (1984). Parental interpretation of psychoeducational reports. *Psychology in the Schools, 21*, 477–481.

Wester, S. R., & Lyubelsky, J. (2005). Supporting the thin blue line: Gender sensitive therapy with male police officers. *Professional Psychology: Research and Practice, 36*(1), 51–58

Whitaker, D. (1994). *How school psychology trainees learn to communicate through the school psychological report* (Unpublished doctoral dissertation). University of Washington, Seattle, WA.

SECTION III

Criminal Law and the Courts

CHAPTER TWELVE

Competency to Stand Trial: Legal Foundations and Practical Applications

Stacey L. Shipley

Introduction

Competency to stand trial is the most commonly raised and adjudicated competency. Other competency issues addressed by the courts include competency to waive the right to an attorney, competency to plead guilty, competency to testify, competency to confess, and competency to be sentenced and executed. Psychologists answering psycho-legal questions for the courts or those concerning psychology and the legal system have an obligation to be well versed in mental health law and the relevant literature.

The idea of competency to stand trial (CST) or competency to proceed has a long history, beginning in English common law. This allowed for an arraignment, trial, judgment, or execution of an alleged capital offender to be stayed if he or she "be(came) absolutely mad" (Hale, 1736, cited in Silten & Tullis, 1977, p. 1053). Mossman et al. (2007, p. S4) define competency to stand trial as "the legally determined capacity of a criminal defendant to proceed with criminal adjudication. Jurisdictional statutes and case law set out the criteria for competence to stand trial." It should also be noted that the terms "adjudicative competency" can be used interchangeably with CST. The precise meaning of competency assumes different forms, however, depending on the context for which it is addressed. In general, there is long-standing agreement that an individual should not be subjected to the processes of the legal system if he or she is unable to understand the nature and purpose of those proceedings and be able to participate meaningfully in their defense. The issue of trial competency can be raised by the defendant, the judge, the prosecuting attorney, and most typically the defense attorney. The laws addressing a defendant's competency to proceed to trial are to protect the due process rights of that individual (e.g., right to a fair and speedy trial; right to confront one's accusers). Our criminal justice system affords us the opportunity to be physically and mentally present to face our charges and accusers in a court of law in order to preserve the dignity and fairness of our criminal justice system. The adversarial nature of this system makes putting an incompetent defendant on trial comparable to a fight "in which the defendant, like a small boy being beaten by a bully, is unable to dodge or return the blows" (*Frith's Case*, 1790, as cited in Golding, 2008, p. 76).

This chapter is intended to be an introduction to CST and provides a brief overview of the historical context, relevant case law, key elements of the CST interview, sources of evidence, opinion formulation, and written report. There are many unique and important areas related to CST that are either described briefly or that are beyond the scope of this chapter (e.g., juvenile fitness to proceed, intellectually disabled defendants). The implications for forensic psychology, policy analysis, and practice are also briefly discussed. High-profile cases such as Ted Kaczynski (the Unabomber), Colin Ferguson (Long Island Railroad Massacre), and most recently Brian David Mitchell have created significant debate regarding issues related to CST.

Brian David Mitchell was alleged to have kidnapped Elizabeth Smart from her bed in 2002, and his case was in legal limbo for a number of years due to the conflicting expert opinions about his CST. This case will be used to demonstrate many of the core issues of adjudicative competency. The information in the case vignette is summarized from a number of public records sources, particularly Judge Atherton's and Judge Kimball's decisions regarding CST in district and federal court, respectively, which included aspects of the competency evaluations completed by the various experts.

Brian David Mitchell

In 2002, Brian David Mitchell (then age 48) kidnapped Elizabeth Smart at age 14 by knifepoint from her Salt Lake City home. Mitchell, a drifter and self-described prophet who called himself Emmanuel, had done some handyman work at the Smarts' home. In March 2003, nine months later,

Mitchell and his now-estranged wife Wanda Barzee were arrested after they were spotted walking on a suburban street with Elizabeth Smart. At the age of 21, Elizabeth Smart testified in Mitchell's competency hearing in October 2010, and indicated that she was taken by Mitchell out into the vast woods behind her family home. He subsequently performed a ceremony he claimed married them and then raped Elizabeth. She was held captive for nine months in both Utah and California and was sexually assaulted by Mitchell on a daily basis. After his arrest, he was referred for a CST evaluation for bizarre beliefs and his unwillingness to discuss issues with his defense counsel. Mitchell claimed to receive revelations from God that he felt compelled to act upon. However, at his later competency hearings and trial, witnesses, particularly Elizabeth Smart and Wanda Barzee, as well as other lay witnesses, testified that Mitchell's actions were manipulative and his alleged revelations occurred when he needed them to justify his actions for self-gratification. There was significant debate regarding the presence and extent of delusions potentially affecting his CST.

Mitchell was found incompetent to stand trial by Salt Lake City district judge Judy Atherton on July 26, 2005. At the initial competency hearing, Dr. Jennifer Skeem, a forensic psychologist, diagnosed Mitchell with delusional disorder, indicating that he was out of touch with reality, experienced religious delusions, and was unable to rationally assist counsel in preparing a defense or understand the legal proceedings against him. In her 2004 report, Dr. Skeem wrote that Mitchell believed "he would be held in jail for seven years until a day of judgment when he would be rescued by God and reunited with Smart and his now-estranged wife, Wanda Barzee." Regarding whether or not Mitchell experienced religious delusions, which was central to the court's finding of incompetency, key points from Judge Atherton's final holding include: "delusional disorder . . . are not merely the logical outcomes of choices made by someone with extreme religious beliefs . . . lacks the capacity to realistically determine what is in his own best interests . . . Therefore, the court concludes that Defendant is incompetent to proceed to trial." Mitchell was committed to a forensic hospital in Salt Lake City. Later, Judge Atherton denied a request to involuntarily medicate Mitchell. On December 18, 2006, he was again found incompetent to stand trial.

Mitchell was indicted in federal court in 2008 on charges of kidnapping and unlawful transportation of a minor across state lines. New testimony was included in the federal competency hearing to include expert witness testimony, primarily Dr. Michael Welner, a forensic psychiatrist, as well as numerous lay witnesses, including Elizabeth Smart and individuals who cared for Mitchell in the Utah state hospital. The issue of having laypersons, including the alleged victim, testify at a competency hearing was hotly contested. The federal competency hearing began on October 2009, with Elizabeth Smart giving early testimony, and continued throughout November and December 2009.

In 2008, Dr. Richart DeMier, a court-appointed forensic psychologist from the U.S. Medical Center for Federal Prisoners in Springfield, Missouri, diagnosed Mitchell with schizophrenia, paranoid type. He said he believed Mitchell had a factual understanding of the legal proceedings but not a rational understanding, and opined that he was incompetent to stand trial. According to court testimony, Dr. DeMier reported, "I think his delusional beliefs, they are not possible . . . I think that it is a bizarre belief that he has been ordained and appointed by God . . . to battle the Antichrist." He further indicated that it was not a belief in the end of days that made Mitchell's beliefs delusional, but rather "his insertion of himself personally into that belief that he's a savior . . . There's a lack of a rational understanding of what's going on." In his competency evaluation, Dr. DeMier wrote that Mitchell "is preoccupied with these well-entrenched beliefs, they appear to have caused him significant distress, and they have led to a drastic decline in his ability to function effectively in society." Dr. DeMier indicated that Mitchell was not capable of making rational decisions about his criminal defense due to religious delusions such as the belief that he is going to be miraculously delivered from prison by God in two years' time. During his testimony at the competency hearing, Dr. DeMier indicated that he did not believe Mitchell was malingering, or faking an illness to avoid prosecution, adding that most patients who malinger try to exhibit symptoms not consistent with the illness they are trying to fake. Dr. Skeem also testified in the 2008 hearing, although she deferred to the more recent evaluation of Dr. DeMier. She continued to diagnose Mitchell with a delusional disorder and opined that he remained incompetent.

Dr. Michael Welner, a forensic psychiatrist, concluded that Mitchell's diagnoses were pedophilia and antisocial and narcissistic personality disorders. Dr. Welner indicated that Mitchell was not psychotic or delusional and described him as having psychopathic and sadistic personality traits. Judge Kimball indicated in his ruling that he agreed with Dr. Welner regarding Mitchell's malingering or feigning symptoms of mental illness to avoid responsibility for his conduct. Dr. Welner described Mitchell as an "effectively misleading psychopath" who was able to manipulate mental health professionals and others. Dr. Welner was critical of other mental health professionals, suggesting they did not adequately research

Mitchell's purported religions to include the Latter-day Saints' movements or Mormonism in order to put into context the importance and relatively common acceptance of revelations, prophesies, and prophets. In other words, Dr. Welner reported that beliefs that were being interpreted as delusional were not bizarre within the subculture of the aforementioned religions. His conclusions focused on Mitchell's twisting of religious beliefs to manipulate others, stating, "Lust trumped religion." In Dr. Welner's conclusions, he equated Mitchell's behavior to that of pedophile Catholic priests who "routinely and dramatically distort their relationship with God" to rationalize the sexual misconduct. A criticism of Dr. Welner's findings include interpreting all of Mitchell's thoughts and behaviors as a result of an extremely malignant and often prejudicial combination of personality characteristics (i.e., antisocial, narcissistic, psychopathic, and sadistic).

On March 1, 2010, a federal judge ruled that Mitchell was competent to stand trial, making it possible for him to move forward with facing charges almost eight years after kidnapping Elizabeth Smart. U.S. district judge Dale Kimball wrote in a 149-page ruling that Mitchell "does not presently suffer from a mental disease or defect that impedes his rational and factual understanding" of the proceedings against him. The ruling came after a 10-day competency hearing held for Mitchell in 2009, in which experts who testified split in their opinions about Mitchell's competency.

During many court proceedings, Mitchell had to be removed from court because he would break into song, disrupting proceedings. These actions and others were viewed by Dr. Welner and ultimately Judge Kimball to be volitional acts. Judge Kimball wrote, "The court agrees with Dr. Welner that Mitchell's singing in court is a contrivance to derail the proceedings and create the false impression that he is unable to control his behavior." The following are excerpts from Judge Kimball's published ruling (2010, pp. 132–133):

> Finally, Mitchell has demonstrated not only callousness and a profound lack of empathy, but also sadistic behaviors. He served his step-daughter her pet rabbit for dinner and later gloated over having tricked her into thinking it was chicken. (Tr. at 1082; Gov't Ex. 17f.) . . . Mitchell's sadism was also evident in his dehumanizing treatment of Elizabeth . . . All of these qualities, along with others detailed in Dr. Welner's report, support the conclusion that Mitchell is not psychotic, but a psychopath. . . . Indeed, Dr. DeMier conceded the possibility that Mitchell is a psychopath and agreed that he displays many of the traits typical of psychopathy, including grandiosity, lying, sadistic behavior, 14 parasitic lifestyle, lack of remorse

> and lack of responsibility. (Tr. at 1624–27.) While disagreeing with the ultimate conclusion, Dr. DeMier candidly acknowledged, "You can construct an explanation by which many of his behaviors are explained by psychopathy." (Tr. at 1628.)
>
> The outcome of this proceeding does not turn on whether Mitchell's personality disorder is best classified as psychopathy or some other variation of Antisocial or Narcissistic Personality Disorder. Both Dr. Welner and Dr. Gardner agree that Mitchell meets the diagnostic criteria for both Antisocial Personality Disorder and Narcissistic Personality Disorder. (Gov't Ex. 5 at 42–44; Gov't Ex. 20 at 120 & 142–44.) The evidence shows that Mitchell's behaviors do not fit a diagnosis of delusional disorder or schizophrenia, but are entirely consistent with a personality disorder. Mitchell's extreme beliefs, painting himself in a prominent religious role is an attempt to gain power and authority. They are not delusional because he has voluntarily employed those beliefs for his own self-interested purposes. After weighing the evidence presented, the court agrees with the psychiatric expert opinion that Mitchell does not suffer from a psychotic mental illness but rather one or more personality disorders.

In November 2010, Wanda Barzee, then age 64, pleaded guilty in federal court to kidnapping and unlawful transportation of a minor for her part of Elizabeth Smart's abduction. Her plea deal with prosecutors included her agreement to cooperate in the state and federal cases against her estranged husband. Brian David Mitchell's criminal trial on federal kidnapping charges began on November 8, 2010, and after only a five-hour deliberation, the jury rejected the insanity plea and returned guilty verdicts on both counts on December 10, 2010.

Literature Review

To allow criminal court hearings or a trial to proceed while the defendant is psychologically incapacitated would prevent that individual from making decisions affecting their liberty. Melton, Petrila, Poythress, and Slobogin (2007) estimated that there are around 60,000 competency cases annually, with 20% to 30% of those cases resulting in the defendant being found incompetent to stand trial. Research suggests that about 10% to 15% of defense attorneys question his or her client's competency to stand, but only raise the question in half of those cases (Grisso, 2003). The increasing number of felony arrests results in rising numbers of competency referrals. Rogers and Johansson-Love (2009) describe the assessment of CST as "the most common pretrial focal point" in forensic psychology or psychiatry (p. 452).

The legal definition of CST was put forth by the Supreme Court in *Dusky v. United States* (1960). The *Dusky* standard requires the individual to have (1) "sufficient present ability to consult with a lawyer with a reasonable degree of rational understanding" and (2) "rational as well as factual understanding" of the general proceedings (*Dusky v. United States*, 1960, p. 402). However, the *Dusky* court was silent about what conditions may make a person incompetent to stand trial (*Dusky*, 1960). The *Dusky* court's attention was on defendant's "ability," not "willingness." The ambiguity of *Dusky* leaves the very definition and evaluation of CST in many jurisdictions vague and open to interpretation. Some legislatures and courts have attempted to develop guidelines for evaluators, but ample opportunities for variance remain.

Aspects of *Dusky* can be found in virtually every state's competency standard (Grisso, 2003). Some courts and legislatures (e.g., Texas) have provided direction to evaluators but there is no uniform way to interpret *Dusky* (Roesch, Zapf, & Golding, 1999). In Texas, defendants are presumed competent and are found competent unless proved incompetent by a preponderance of the evidence. The due process rights of the defendant are paramount to the fairness of the process. Being a rational and meaningful participant in one's defense is essential.

Clinicians who undertake answering psycho-legal questions for the trier of fact are required to work within the scope of their competence. The defendant's mental status and functional capacities specific to adjudicative competency are examined in a competency to stand trial evaluation. The importance of education and training for clinicians working in the forensic arena has gained greater attention over the past two decades; yet, some states continue to not mandate specialized forensic training (Roesch et al., 1999; Mossman et al., 2007). Forensic experts are frequently called upon to assess for CST and to address the standards set forth in *Dusky v. United States* (Rogers, Grandjean, Tillbrook, Vitacco, & Sewell, 2001). In *U.S. vs. Timmins* (9th Circuit, 2002), the court ruled that when offering an opinion about a defendant's competence to stand trial, evaluators must be careful to closely scrutinize the independent decision making abilities of the defendant. The case demonstrated the necessity of utilizing a mental health expert to assist in a competency determination in part because "a lawyer is not a trained mental health professional capable of accurately assessing the effects of paranoid delusions on the client's mental process" (Osinowo & Pinals, 2003, p. 261). On the other hand, Melton et al. (2007) discuss the perils of courts relinquishing their role in making the ultimate decision on competency issues to experts. Specifically, they state, "Presumably, conclusory reliance on diagnosis or unsubstantiated opinion will exacerbate the tendency on the part of the courts and lawyers to avoid investigating the competency issue; this abdication in turn will ill serve defendants, who deserve a legal, not a clinical determination of competency" (p. 136).

Competency versus Sanity

Competency to stand trial is often confused with sanity, despite being independent legal constructs. While competency focused on the defendant's present capacities, sanity is an evaluation looking back and centering on the defendant's state of mind at the time the alleged offense was committed. Criminal trials occur several months and sometimes years after a crime occurred. As a result, an individual who is currently competent to stand trial may still qualify as legally insane at the time of the offense. Conversely, an individual who does not qualify for legal insanity may be presently incompetent to stand trial. A competency evaluation centers on a patient's current mental state and abilities and, as a result, typically does not require as much collateral information as a sanity evaluation, which is retrospective (Mossman et al., 2007). A sanity revaluation requires the evaluator to do their best to recreate or determine from a variety of sources the defendant's state of mind at the time of the crime.

The outcome for those found insane or incompetent are vastly different. Typically, the defendant found legally insane or not guilty by reason of insanity (NGRI) faces a legal commitment, and this is the disposition of their legal situation. The NGRI individual may spend an indeterminate amount of time in a psychiatric hospital or until treatment providers and most importantly the court of jurisdiction determine that they no longer pose a significant risk of harm to others due to their symptoms of mental illness and can return to the community. When someone is found incompetent to stand trial, the disposition of their case is put on hold, and they have yet to be tried or convicted of their charge(s). The restoration of trial competency is central to their treatment. Skills such as being able to rationally and factually assist his or her attorney in preparation of a defense and being capable of rationally understanding his or her charges are the focus. If delusions or perceptual disturbances are impairing these abilities, treating these symptoms is an important part of restorability. Admission to a forensic psychiatric hospital is the most typical outcome when the defendant's incompetence is considered restorable with treatment (Grisso, 2003). A trained, forensic clinician at the admitting facility, who is not involved with the defendant's treatment, will conduct another competency to stand trial evaluation, when the defendant's treatment gains suggest he or she may be ready to return to court for another competency hearing.

Authors recommend that sanity and competency be conducted separately and that sanity evaluations are not conducted on incompetent defendants (Arrigo & Shipley, 2005; Melton et al., 2007; Mossman et al., 2007; Roesch et al., 1999). Some state laws prohibit performing a sanity evaluation on a defendant who has been evaluated and recommended to be incompetent to stand trial; for example, the Texas Code of Criminal Procedure Article 46B.025 addressing competency evaluations states: "(c) An expert's report may not state the expert's opinion on the defendant's sanity at the time of the alleged offense, if in the opinion of the expert the defendant is incompetent to proceed." If a defendant is thought to be incompetent or incapable of rationally participating in their defense or legal proceedings, moving forward with an evaluation that could likely impact the ultimate disposition of their case is at the least ill advised.

Raising the Question

Raising the issue of competency to proceed to trial creates an opportunity for a delay in the process (Roesch et al., 1999). In *Pate v. Robinson* (1966, p. 385), the U.S. Supreme Court ruled that a suitable hearing on CST must be held whenever there is a "bona fide doubt" about a defendant's competency. This is a low threshold and suggests that in order to protect all defendants' rights to a fair trial, many competent defendants may have to go through an evaluation to prevent the prosecution of a defendant who is incompetent to stand trial (Mossman et al., 2007). When issues are raised by any party regarding CST, almost invariably the motions are granted by the courts, primarily to avoid a due process violation.

The Role of Mental Illness

The mere presence of mental illness does not equate to incompetency. Whether or not symptoms of the mental illness significantly impact the defendant's capacity to function as a defendant is the issue in CST (Arrigo & Shipley, 2005). A psychiatric diagnosis does not equal incompetence, which is a legal construct. Psychiatric diagnosis may "play a role in the legal process but it is not always a sine qua non in the resolution of a legal matter (Slovenko, 2002, p. 421). The court must consider whether or not a mental illness or intellectual or developmental disabilities preclude a criminal defendant's understanding or ability to participate in the trial process. The defendant's capacity to have a factual and rational understanding of both pretrial and trial procedures is critical (Grisso, 2003; Melton et al., 2007; Wolber, 2008).

For example, a diagnosis or symptoms of psychosis do not necessarily mean that a defendant is incompetent. It would be critical to ascertain the nature of the symptoms and if they would impact the individual's capacities such as being able to rationally understand their charges, work with their attorney, or prepare a defense. Do symptoms of psychosis (e.g., auditory hallucinations, delusions) intermingle with issues related to their case and the court system? For example, if a defendant experiences delusions that include the belief that his attorney is part of a government conspiracy to incarcerate him in order to steal all of his inventions, property, and money, he is unlikely to be able to rationally work with that attorney in preparing a defense. The evaluator must consider if inappropriate behavior is volitional or driven by mental illness. One might have to examine if they are confronting a delusion or an overvalued idea. Is there an atypical report of symptoms? Consistency across interviews? Consistency across situations? The specific demands and circumstances of each individual case must be considered by the evaluator when formulating their opinion on CST. Consider the following excerpt from Judge Kimball's final holding regarding Brian David Mitchell's CST in federal court (Kimball, 2010, pp. 134–135):

> *B. Do Mitchell's Personality Disorders Impact His Competency to Stand Trial?*
>
> Expert testimony at the competency hearing established that, unlike psychoses, personality disorders do not impair a person's ability to accurately interpret reality. (Tr. 629–630.) Individuals with personality disorders "have the ability for a rational and factual understanding of the issues they face but may make very maladaptive choices, based on their interpretation of the world." (Tr. 630–31.) In this case, the experts agree that Mitchell's personality disorders would not be a basis for a finding of incompetency. (Tr. 632, 816, & 1879.)
>
> Mitchell's personality disorders do not detach him from reality or affect his rational ability to understand the world around him. They are merely maladaptive personality traits that lead to poor decisions. These are not competency limiting because they are voluntary decisions. Mitchell's condition has not dramatically changed over time. Unlike someone suffering from actual delusions, who cannot control his actions, Mitchell selectively uses his belief system to achieve his own self-interested purposes. After his plea negotiations with the State broke down, Mitchell's decision not to participate in "a corrupt system" and not to be "judged of man" appears to be consistent with his personality disorders. His refusal to participate is a reaction to his loss of power over the situation and it is the only way he knows to exert power over the process . . .

> *C. Even if Mitchell has Mental Disease or Defect, Does He Have the Requisite Competency Abilities?*
>
> Even if the Court were to accept the defense experts' opinion that Mitchell suffers from a psychotic mental illness, the evidence demonstrates that Mitchell nonetheless possesses the requisite competency abilities. As both Dr. Skeem and Dr. DeMier readily acknowledged, a person suffering from delusional disorder or schizophrenia may still be competent to stand trial. (Tr. at 1601 & 1812.) "That a defendant suffers from some degree of mental illness or disorder does not necessarily mean that he is incompetent to assist in his own defense." *United States v. DeShazer*, 554 F.3d 1281, 1286 (10th Cir. 2009); *see also United States v. Vamos*, 797 F.2d 136 ("It is well-established that some degree of mental illness cannot be equated with incompetence to stand trial."). 1146, 1150 (2d Cir. 1986)

Similarly, a diagnosis of mental retardation does not necessarily mean that person is incompetent to stand trial. *Dusky* does not require that a mental disorder be present in order to find a defendant incompetent, but some state legislatures have done so. Texas statute indicates the evaluator must consider "whether the defendant has a diagnosable mental illness or is a person with mental retardation" and "the impact of the mental illness or mental retardation, if existent, on the defendant's capacity to engage with counsel in a reasonable and rational manner (Art. 46B.024)."

Godinez v. Moran (1993) established that the states may adopt criteria for competence that are more structured than *Dusky*. It also interpreted *Dusky* as requiring a defendant to have decision-making capacities related to CST (e.g., whether or not to testify, what type of defense to put forward, etc.). This certainly impacts the types of questions forensic evaluators need to ask to form an opinion regarding CST.

Examples of how the three prongs of *Dusky* are examined include: (1) *Factual understanding*—conditions such as brain damage, dementia, mental retardation, severe depression, and thought disorders are the most likely to potentially impact this area (Mossman et al., 2007). Asking follow-up questions is important to ensure that a defendant is not just parroting answers without a conceptual understanding. (2) Rational understanding—the evaluator has to determine whether symptoms impact the reality-based understanding of their legal situation, perceptions and decisions regarding it, as well as their logical participation in that process (e.g., a delusion that one is married to someone famous may not impact their rational competence; whereas, a delusion that one is the president of the United States and believes he can issue his own pardon and not face trial would). (3) Ability to assist counsel—addresses the defendant's ability versus willingness to assist their counsel or the average attorney. A choice to not participate does not render one incompetent. The defendant needs to be capable of providing rational information to the attorney regarding defense strategy, cross-examining witnesses, considering the attorney's advice, considering plea options in consultation with their attorney, and the like. Rogers and Shuman (2005, p. 154) note that a number of defendants "make poor, emotionally based decisions that do not accurately capture the potential risks and benefits," but their faculties are not compromised by mental disorders. In *Drope v. Missouri* (1975, p. 171), the Supreme Court enhanced the capacity to consult with one's attorney requirement in *Dusky*, stating that a defendant must be able to "assist in preparing his defense." Moreover, this case indicated that "a trial must always be alert to circumstances suggesting a change that would render the accused unable to meet the standards of competency to stand trial."

In the United States, the Sixth Amendment established a defendant's right to be represented by attorneys. However, U.S. law does not require criminal defendants to use lawyers in criminal proceedings (Mossman et al., 2007). In *Faretta v. California* (1975), the Supreme Court held that the right to self-representation is implicit in the structure of the Sixth Amendment. A knowing and intelligent decision to represent oneself is required, and the defendant must be competent to waive the right to counsel. However, legal knowledge is not essential, and those proceeding pro se are commonly referred to as having "a fool for a client." A number of courts have held that active mental illness should not, alone, prevent someone from proceeding pro se. Nonetheless, courts have a responsibility to preserve the integrity of judicial process.

Conducting the CST Evaluation

Statutes or case law provide that information gleaned during a competency evaluation cannot be used in the guilt/innocence phase of a criminal trial unless a defendant places their mental state into evidence either at trial (e.g., sanity defense) or sentencing (*Estelle v. Smith*, 1981; Golding & Roesch, 1988; Mossman et al., 2007). Whether a court can convict a defendant based on information obtained in a competency evaluation became the subject of *Estelle v. Smith* (1981) and *Buchanan v. Kentucky* (1987). In *Estelle v. Smith*, the defendant had been convicted of murder and then faced sentencing before the jury that found him guilty. Based on a pretrial competency evaluation, the competency evaluator testified that Smith lacked remorse, was untreatable, and was at very high risk of committing future acts of violence, and the jury subsequently imposed the death penalty. Ultimately, a federal district court vacated the death sentence, after determining that the trial court made a constitutional error in allowing the psychiatrist's testimony based on the pretrial competency evaluation at the penalty phase. The Supreme Court upheld the finding. In *Buchanan v. Kentucky*, the Supreme Court expressly limited the protections described above to situations in which the defendant did not initiate the mental health evaluation or attempt to introduce psychological evidence at trial. When the defense raises the issue, the prosecution can use information this psychological evidence in rebuttal.

The forensic evaluator will need to review relevant history, conduct a mental status examination, and, most importantly, evaluate competence-related capacities. The relevant police reports should be thoroughly reviewed prior to beginning the interview, as well as prior competency evaluations (if applicable) to determine what led to the initial finding of incompetency. The evaluator should gather and review all the information needed prior to confronting any inconsistencies such as previous mental health history, treatment records, and criminal history.

At the start of a CST interview, the evaluator should provide a forensic warning or inform the defendant of the purpose and potential consequences of evaluation, who will get a copy of the report, and the overall limits to confidentiality (e.g., no doctor-patient confidentiality; may have to testify; information cannot be used in guilt/innocence phase except under conditions described above). The defendant's understanding of the nature and consequences of the evaluation should be assessed; for example, having him or her paraphrase the information provided to them. The evaluator should be familiar with the legal literature related to CST to ensure that the competency evaluation and the reports prepared for court be in accord with both the spirit and the letter of the law (Arrigo & Shipley, 2005; Grisso, 2003; Melton et al., 2007; Mossman et al., 2007).

When evaluating someone's CST, you are assessing their abilities related to their specific charge or each of their multiple charges. A criminal defendant with conspiracy to commit capital murder charges will have to function within a far more complex legal arena than the defendant with a misdemeanor trespassing charge. An inquiry into the defendant's awareness of the charges and ability to describe the specific allegations should be open-ended and phrased in a way that does not assume guilt in the alleged offense; for example, "What is the prosecution alleging that you did?" "What have you been accused of doing?" The defendant has to be capable of providing a rational, relatively consistent, coherent account of the offense to defense counsel (Mossman et al., 2007).

A lack of information about the charges does not equal incompetence. When a defendant claims no knowledge of the charges or other elements of court facts or procedures, providing brief tutorials about these concepts is not only allowed, but expected to determine if the defendant can benefit from instruction and demonstrate their ability to work appropriately with that information. To distinguish between ignorance and incapacity to learn, you can use various methods involving teaching and testing the patient within the course of the interview (Arrigo & Shipley, 2005; Melton et al., 2007; Mossman et al., 2007). For example, the evaluator should educate the defendant about facts of the case from the police report and then have the defendant describe them back in their own words. Melton et al. (2007) suggest that clinicians should avoid following a rigid, test-like series of questions, and defendants only need a basic understanding of underlying concepts; therefore, it is okay if they cannot provide a precise legal definition of terms. When a defendant is reluctant to discuss information regarding their charges, hypothetical inquiries like what is used in some of the forensic assessment tools (e.g., the MacCAT-CA) may be useful (Melton et al., 2007). Moreover, a number of legal findings have held that amnesia does not equal incompetence (e.g., *Missouri v. Davis*, 1983; *Montana v. Austed*, 1982; *Morrow v. Maryland*, 1982; *Ritchie v. Indiana*, 1984; *Wilson v. United States*, 1968). These decisions support the view that evaluators cannot reach a finding of incompetency based upon mental state alone, independent of the facts of the legal case (Mossman et al., 2007).

Additionally, an evaluation of CST is examining information relevant for a defendant's functioning in the courtroom, such as: ability to consult with one's attorney; the capacity to engage in appropriately self-protective behavior; capacity to engage in rational, independent decision making; ability to learn and apply new information effectively; capacity to pay attention to legal proceedings; the defendant's degree of impulse control and ability to maintain appropriate behavior; knowledge and rational understanding of the various legal strategies and plea options; etc. Although symptoms of mental illness (e.g., delusions, hallucinations) do not necessarily equal incompetence, it is quite common for individuals to be rationally incompetent based on their symptoms, while their factual understanding remains intact.

CST evaluations do not require a detailed social history. Brief histories, particularly describing prior mental health treatment, may be needed if significant impairments in functional abilities related to trial competency are present in order to help provide linkage to your conclusions and to help form preliminary diagnostic impressions about restorability (Melton et al., 2007). The ultimate decision on CST belongs to the court, either a judge or jury depending upon the jurisdiction. Evaluators inform the court by offering for adjudication an opinion about whether or not the defendant is CST. More often than not, the court concurs with the evaluator. Once found incompetent, the trial is postponed or the charges are dismissed, usually without prejudice and a defendant's right to refuse treatment is more restricted (Roesch et al., 1999; Mossman et al., 2007).

Psychological Tests and Competency Evaluations

An evaluator must consider if there is a need for formal psychological testing. What question needs to be answered? Can the capacities be directly observed? More information is not always better if the information is not valid for the issue at hand. The forensic evaluator has to consider whether or not the norms and psychometric properties are a good fit. A wrongly used psychological test or forensic assessment tool can lead to incorrect conclusions.

Very few forensic assessment tools have been specifically designed for CST evaluations. However, there are criticisms that the reliability and validity of instruments have not been sufficiently tested and cannot be used with confidence in the courtroom (Weiner, 2003). These instruments typically do not delve into the case-specific issues that are often at the core of a defendant's lack of rational competency. The quality of forensic evaluations must sustain cross-examination, be consistent with standards of forensic practice, and be supported by relevant evidence. A study that examined the use of psychological testing in CST evaluations found that 70% of the evaluations did not describe any relationship between testing data and CST (Skeem, Golding, Cohn, & Berge, 1998). The remaining 30% only provided ambiguous claims related to symptoms identified by testing and broad impairment in CST. Intellectual testing was only occasionally related to capacities relevant to competency. Finally, these authors found that objective, neuro-psychological, and projective test data were almost never associated with CST (Skeem et al., 1998).

Administration of conventional psychological tests (e.g., MMPI-2) is unlikely to be a relevant or cost-efficient means of gathering information in most competency cases (Melton et al., 2007); however, in a limited range of cases, when specific issues need explored such as malingering, testing may be useful (e.g., TOMM, SIRS, VIP, etc.). Additionally, if incompetency is suspected based on interview data related to potential cognitive/intellectual deficits, cognitive testing may be useful to corroborate the degree of intellectual disabilities or to assess the ability to consider alternatives and process information in a structured situation (Melton et al., 2007).

A structured CST interview specifically designed around the relevant law and psycho-legal question at hand is the preferred method of many forensic evaluators. This type of targeted interview more closely approximates the attorney client interaction as it is tailored to the defendant's case. This well-structured, case-specific competency interview can provide invaluable information about ability to participate in a meaningful interchange with their attorney (Arrigo & Shipley, 2005). The evaluator must provide the linkage between the information or evidence described and the opinion on adjudicative competence, and, if relevant, describing any steps to be taken to compensate for difficulties a defendant may have.

Overall, research indicates use of standard forensic assessment instruments are, at best, screening instruments. The studies endorsing the use of these tools caution evaluators to understand the instrument's limitations. The assessment of CST should go beyond the data that can be gathered by these tools. The following provides a brief overview of two of the second-generation measures that use relatively standardized interview formats to examine *Dusky*-related abilities (Melton et al., 2007).

The *MacArthur Competence Assessment Tool–Criminal Adjudication* (MacCAT-CA) was a product of the MacArthur Adjudicative Competence Project (Poythress, Nicholson, Otto, et al., 1999). It is a 22-item test that takes 30 to 45 minutes to administer and includes a hypothetical case and questions surrounding it. Moreover, it addresses a defendant's beliefs about his or her own case in one section of the test. Its validity, reliability, and ease of administration are good compared to other measures of adjudicative competence (Otto et al., 1998). Strengths include derivation from psycho-legal theory of competence, assessment of multiple psycho-legal abilities, assessment of the capacity to assimilate new information, standardized administration, objective criterion-referenced scoring, and availability of normed data for the purpose of comparison (Mossman et al., 2007). Weaknesses include its focus on understanding factual rather than rational aspects; limited focus on the complexity of the defendant's case; a lack of formally addressing potential malingering and claims of amnesia, and those with severe thought disorders, major concentration problems, or serious memory impairment likely will be unable to complete an assessment with the instrument (Mossman et al., 2007).

The *Evaluation of Competency to Stand Trial–Revised* (ECST-R) is a more recently developed tool by Rogers, Tillbrook, and Sewell (2004). It is a semi-structured interview with 46 items total. There are 18 items and three scales that speak to factual and rational understanding of criminal proceedings and consulting with counsel. There are also five scales for consideration of atypical presentation or feigning, considering rare symptoms and symptom severity (Rogers & Johansson-Love, 2009). Rogers and Johansson-Love (2009) describe the ECST-R's strong psychometric properties as compared to the MacCAT-CA. It should be noted that likely due to the relative newness of this instrument, most of the peer-reviewed articles available that examine the ECST-R are authored by one or more of its designers. Mossman et al. (2007, p. S43) note that evaluators "should not overvalue the information that they provide . . . should interpret results of testing in light of all other data obtained from clinical interviews and collateral sources." Regarding forensic assessment tools, Golding (2008, p. 76) indicates "competency cannot be reduced to a precise set of operational definitions (like a score of such-and-such on a test, or the presence of a given symptom or diagnosis), but is by its nature open-textured . . . this is one of the main reasons why various proposals to operationalize competency, by means of nomothetic tests, often produce unsatisfactory or incomplete results."

Malingering

A diagnosis of malingering can have long-standing, negative connotations, and an opinion that a defendant is feigning or exaggerating can adversely affect his or her treatment in ensuing criminal proceedings (Mossman et al., 2007). The true extent of feigning or exaggerating symptoms in order to be found incompetent is unknown (Hall & Poirier, 2001). Cornell and Hawk (1989) reported that out of 314 consecutive admissions to the Michigan Center for Forensic Psychiatry for pretrial evaluations, 8% were diagnosed by staff as malingering. Grisso (1988) indicates that faking for incompetency typically includes either faking for behaviors directed toward mental disorder and those aimed at specific competency abilities. These specific competency abilities can include things such as: knowing the nature and process of the court proceedings; appreciating the possible consequences of the various legal options, and the ability to cooperate with one's attorney. Malingering can result in a finding of incompetence with recommendation for continued observation and treatment (Hall & Poirier, 2001). The DSM-IV-TR (APA, 2000) recommends that malingering should be strongly suspected when an individual is: involved in a forensic evaluation, has an antisocial personality disorder, is being uncooperative with assessment or treatment, or there is a significant discrepancy between a person's reported distress and objective findings.

According to Hall and Poirier (2001), the majority of criminal defendants, including those with extensive criminal backgrounds, are cooperative with evaluations and do not try to exaggerate or minimize psychopathology. There are also occasions when the accused attempts to not cooperate (i.e., refusing to be interviewed or tested) in order to disrupt part or all of the evaluation. In these instances, the evaluator must determine if a lack of cooperativeness is volitional and for secondary gain or if it is stemming from a genuine symptom such as paranoia and delusional thinking. If a defendant is cooperative in the interview initially and then stops cooperating mid-evaluation, capacity versus willingness is again the issue. When a defendant will not cooperate with the evaluation, the evaluator must rely heavily on collateral sources (e.g., records, observations, collateral interviews). According to Hall and Poirier (2001), if methods are unavailable or are inconclusive, the defendant should be presumed competent to stand trial and returned to court as uncooperative. Regarding Brian David Mitchell, Judge Kimball wrote in his decision (2010, p. 135):

> The court finds that his statements and conduct are voluntary and not the manifestations of a psychotic mental disease or defect.
>
> Furthermore, Mitchell's involvement with his lawyers has been similarly selective based on his own self interests . . . The evidence shows that he has the ability to participate when it is in his interest to do so. Mitchell's decision not to participate in the process does not render him incompetent.
>
> Accordingly, the court finds that Mitchell's personality disorders do not affect his ability to rationally understand the proceedings against him or his ability to consult with his lawyers with a reasonable degree of rational understanding.

Potential sources of evidence to support a diagnosis of malingering include: direct observation; psychological testing and/or specialized instruments for detecting malingering; medical, psychological, jail, and hospital records; and interviews with family, friends, police, jail staff, hospital staff, and others who have had contact with the defendant (Mossman et al., 2007). If a defendant is facing serious legal charges or is facing mandatory sentencing for multiple offenses, his or her motivation to malinger and avoid or delay prosecution would be much greater.

In at least two federal cases, a precedent has been set for malingering to be viewed as obstruction of justice, resulting in longer sentences. In these cases, the appellate courts have held that deliberate efforts to feign mental problems can be grounds for imposing a longer prison term under federal sentencing guidelines (Mossman et al., 2007). In *U.S. v. Greer* (1998), a defendant's sentence was enhanced by 25 months as a result of his malingering, which was determined to be a willful attempt to obstruct justice. In *U.S. v. Binion* (2005), a sentencing enhancement was added based on the finding that the defendant was malingering, and this was upheld in federal appeals court. This poses ethical questions for evaluators regarding what issues must be covered in the informed consent process (e.g., that a finding of feigning by the court may be considered obstruction of justice and lead to a harsher sentence).

The Written Report

Because competency evaluations typically do not result in courtroom testimony, a written report usually is the evaluator's primary work product (Mossman et al., 2007). The report's primary audience is made up of attorneys and judges rather than mental health professionals, so it is important to use jargon-free language. Offer your opinion and carefully explain the reasoning process behind the opinion. In some jurisdictions, evaluators are barred from expressing ultimate-issue opinions, while in others it is allowed or even directed. The report should clearly describe how conclusions regarding the presence of mental illness are linked to the functional capacities involved in trial competency. Reports should be free of gratuitous comments about defendants' behavior, need for incarceration, violence risk, or lack of remorse (Mossman, et al., 2007).

CST evaluations become court documents, and unnecessary information should be excluded from the report. According to Rogers and Shuman (2005, p. 168), "Psychosocial history is, at best, only peripheral to the current . . . assessment of competency to stand trial . . . Past information may be irrelevant to the referral issue and represent an ethical violation in its unnecessary violation of privacy." If there is medical or other personal information that is not directly relevant to adjudicative competency, do not include it (e.g., HIV status). The report should be a standalone document, which provides or reproduces the data needed to support the opinions that the evaluator expresses. In a quality report, the psychological data should be linked to the legal issue with a clearly articulated chain of reasoning. Inconsistencies should be explained. Even when the law prevents the information gleaned from the competency evaluation from being raised by the prosecution at trial or sentencing, be careful about what information you include.

Restoration of Trial Competency

The Supreme Court ventured to address the question of how long an incompetent defendant could be hospitalized in *Jackson v. Indiana* (1972). Prior to *Jackson*, incompetent defendants were often held in psychiatric facilities for periods longer than what would have been allowed if tried and convicted. Subsequently, the prosecution would, at times, raise the issue of competency to essentially confine the individual without the benefit of trial (Wrightsman, Nietzel, & Fortune, 1994). In *Jackson v. Indiana* (1972), the Supreme Court held that confinement indefinitely based upon one's incompetency to stand trial created a more stringent standard for release than those committed under civil statutes, constituting a violation of the Fourteenth Amendment's equal protection clause and the right to due process.

The Court's decision in *Jackson* placed restrictions on the time afforded to the states to treat a defendant found incompetent to stand trial (IST) and restore his or her competence. The *Jackson* decision set the stage for states to make individual decisions affecting commitments, specifically setting limits on their lengths. The *Jackson* decision indicated that if treatment could not restore a defendant to competence, the state must either initiate civil commitment proceedings or release the defendant. *Jackson v. Indiana* (1972) defined the parameters of this limitation as "a reasonable period of time necessary to determine whether there is a substantial probability that [the defendant] will attain the capacity [competence] in the foreseeable future (pp. 737–738). The Supreme Court's *Jackson* decision was their first to place legal restrictions on the commitment times for those found IST. Despite its imprecise or vague description, the *Jackson* decision ultimately required forensic evaluators to address whether or not those defendants found to be IST have a substantial probability of regaining competency in the foreseeable future with treatment (Hubbard, Zapf, & Ronan, 2003). Carbonell, Heilbrun, and Friedman (1992) found that clinicians were wrong in predicting the treatment outcomes of 85% of defendants who ultimately were not restored to competence. According to Hubbard et al. (2003), forensic examiners are relatively poor at predicting which defendants will regain competency due to the infrequency of nonrestorability. You need only give estimates of potential restorability and time frames in a CST evaluation. Evaluators should exercise caution in providing feedback to courts concerning the likely success of competency restoration. Evaluators must consider restoration issues: requirements for inpatient versus outpatient, the role of medications in competency restoration, and the likelihood to restore in the foreseeable future.

Mossman et al. (2007) suggests the evaluator consider the following factors: (1) whether the ICST results from a treatable disorder or deficit as opposed to a static and relatively irreversible (or even degenerative) condition such as dementia; (2) a defendant's previous psychiatric treatment and responses to treatment; and (3) a defendant's particular symptoms and current scientific knowledge about how well those symptoms respond to treatment. The two most common causes of incompetency to stand trial are psychosis and mental retardation (Grisso, 2003; Mossman et al., 2007; Nicholson & Kugler, 1991). Except for an irreversible condition (e.g., a severe head injury) or a mental disorder that has proven treatment resistant, most defendants are restorable (Melton et al., 2007).

Since psychosis is the very frequent cause of impairments resulting in adjudicative incompetency, the need for psychotropic medications in their treatment for restoration is common. In *Sell v. U.S.* (2003), the Supreme Court limited the right of a lower court to order involuntary psychiatric medication with the singular purpose of restoring a criminal defendant who is incompetent to trial competency. Specifically, the court held that medication is medically appropriate only when it is necessary and likely to restore the defendant to competency, unlikely to have side effects that interfere with the defendant's ability to assist counsel in conducting a defense, and less intrusive treatments are unlikely to achieve substantially the same results. In 2005, after being found incompetent to stand trial in Utah District Court and committed to a forensic hospital, Judge Atherton denied a request to involuntarily medicate Brian David Mitchell. In Judge Kimball's written holding regarding Mitchell (2010, p. 137):

> During the state proceedings, Mitchell expressed an understanding of and particular interest in the involuntary medication hearing. Mitchell's social worker noted that Mitchell " 'asked pertinent questions about medication hearings without religious overtones.' " (Gov't Ex. 20 at 47.) Mitchell and his father discussed the application of new involuntary medication legislation. (*Id.*) Mitchell also asked another patient how his medications made him feel because it was likely that he would be forced to take medications. (Tr. at 141–42.) Mitchell even had the foresight to ask his treatment team whether his singing in court would cause the judge to order him involuntarily medicated. Mitchell showed "an awareness of the consequence of his singing in a court proceeding and how it could have broader legal ramifications." (Tr. at 910.)

Clinical and Policy Implications

The prevalence of adjudicative competency in the forensic arena and the importance of related implications for forensic clinicians cannot be understated. Psychological or psychiatric expert opinions regarding CST are typically greatly valued and relied upon by the trier of fact. If all parties (e.g., judge, defense attorney, prosecution) stipulate regarding the determination of the defendant's competence or incompetence, and if there is agreement regarding the results of the forensic evaluation, a formal competency hearing is unnecessary (Grisso, 2003). Thus, the mental health expert has the potential to significantly influence the future of the defendant being examined for CST. Involuntary medication to restore competency has significant policy implications. The administration of psychiatric medications may greatly help to restore a defendant's competency, but whether or not the restoration of CST is a justifiable reason to forcibly administer medications to defendants is debated by some. Do government interests in bringing the individual to trial override civil liberties, and what are the guidelines? These can vary by jurisdiction.

Suggestions for Future Research

What constitutes a competent individual? Given individual differences and the unique requirements of each legal situation, evaluators must consider these nuances alongside a somewhat ambiguous legal standard. Research on defendants not restorable to competency could be beneficial in helping to better understand the most relevant characteristics that contribute in order to better classify and predict restorability.

According to Pinals (2005, p. 104), "Overall, competency restoration literature supports that between 80 [and] 90% of all defendants with mental illness will be able to be restored to competence, and generally this restoration has been achieved in a period of less than six months." Continued research is needed on the accuracy of predicting restorability in CST evaluations and on the most efficacious interventions for restorability for the diverse types of criminal defendants.

References

American Psychiatric Association (APA). (2000). *Diagnostic and statistical manual of mental disorders* (4th ed., text rev.). Washington, DC: Author.

American Psychological Association. (2002). Ethical principles of psychologists and code of conduct. *American Psychologist, 57*, 1060–1073.

Arrigo, B. A., & Shipley, S. L. (2005). *Introduction to forensic psychology: Issues and controversies in law, law enforcement, and corrections* (2nd ed.). San Diego, CA: Elsevier/Academic Press.

Bardwell, M. C., & Arrigo, B. A. (2002). Competency to stand trial: A law, psychology, and policy assessment. *Journal of Psychiatry and Law, 30*(2), 147–269.

Bullock, J. L. (2002). Involuntary treatment of defendants found incompetent to stand trial. *Journal of Forensic Psychology, 2*(4), 1–33.

Carbonell, J. L., Heilbrun, K., & Friedman, F. L. (1992). Predicting who will regain trial competency: Initial promise unfulfilled. *Forensic Rep, 5*, 67–76.

Coles, E. M., & Veiel, H. O. F. (2001). Expert testimony and pseudoscience: How mental health professionals are taking over the courtroom. *International Journal of Law and Psychiatry, 24*(6), 607–625.

Cornell, D. G., & Hawk, G. L. (1989). Clinical presentations of malingerers diagnosed by experienced forensic psychologist. *Law and Human Behavior, 13*, 375–383.

Golding, S. L. (1992). Studies of incompetent defendants: Research and social policy implications. *Forensic Reports, 5*, 77–83.

Golding, S. L. (2008). Evaluations of adult adjudicative competency. In R. L. Jackson (Ed.), *Learning forensic assessment* (pp. 75–108). New York: Taylor and Francis Group.

Golding, S. L., & Roesch, R. (1988). Competency for adjudication: An international analysis. In D. N. Weisstub (Ed.), *Law and mental health: International perspectives* (Vol. 4, pp. 73–109). New York: Pergamon.

Grisso, T. (1988). *Competency to stand trial evaluations: A manual for practice*. Sarasota, FL: Professional Resource Exchange.

Grisso, T. (2003). *Evaluating competencies: Forensic assessments and instruments* (2nd ed.). New York: Kluwer Academic/Plenum.

Hall, H. V., & Poirier, J. G. (2001). *Detecting malingering and deception: Forensic distortion analysis* (2nd ed.). Boca Raton, FL: CRC Press.

Hubbard, K. L., Zapf, P. A., & Ronan, K. A. (2003, April). Competency restoration: An examination of the differences between defendants predicted restorable and not restorable to competency. *Law and Human Behavior, 27*(2), 127–139.

Melton, G., Petrila, J., Poythress, N., & Slobogin, C. (2007). *Psychological evaluations for the courts: A handbook for mental health professionals and lawyers* (3rd ed.). New York: Guilford Press.

Mossman, D., Noffsinger, S. G., Ash, P., Frierson, R. L., Gerbasi, J., Hackett, M., . . . Zonana, H. V. (2007). AAPL practice guideline for the forensic psychiatric evaluation of competence to stand trial. *Journal of the American Academy of Psychiatry and the Law, 35*(4), S3–S72.

Nicholson, R., & Kugler, K. (1991). Competent and incompetent criminal defendants: A quantitative review of comparative research. *Psychological Bulletin, 109*(3), 355–370.

Osinowo, T. O., & Pinals, D. A. (2003). Competence to stand trial. *Journal of the American Academy of Psychiatry and the Law, 31*(2), 261–264.

Otto, R. K., Poythress, N. G., Nicholson, R. A., Edens, J. F., Monahan, J., Bonnie, R. J., . . . Eisenberg, M. (1998). Psychometric properties of the MacArthur Competence Assessment Tool–Criminal Adjudication (MacCAT-CA). *Psychological Assessment, 10*, 435–443.

Pinals, D. (2005). Where two roads met: Restoration of competence to stand trial from a clinical perspective. *New England Journal of Civil and Criminal Confinement, 31*, 81–108.

Poythress, N. G, Nicholson, R, Otto, R. K., Edens, J. F., Bonnie, R. J., Monahan, J., & Hoge, S. (1999). *Professional manual for the MacArthur Competence Assessment Tool–Criminal Adjudication (MacCAT-CA)*. Odessa, FL: Psychological Assessment Resources.

Roesch, R., Zapf, P. A., & Golding, S. L. (1999). Defining and assessing competency to stand trial. In I. B. Weiner & A. K. Hess (Eds.), *Handbook of forensic psychology* (2nd ed., pp. 327–349). New York: John Wiley & Sons.

Rogers, R., Grandjean, N., Tillbrook, C. E., Vitacco, M. J., & Sewell, K. W. (2001). Recent interview-based measures of competency to stand trial: A critical review augmented with research data. *Behavioral Sciences and the Law, 19*(4), 503–518.

Rogers, R., & Johansson-Love, J. (2009). Evaluating competency to stand trial with evidence-based practice. *Journal of the American Academy of Psychiatry and the Law, 37*(4), 450–460.

Rogers, R., & Shuman, D. W. (2005). *Fundamentals of forensic practice: Mental health and criminal law*. New York: Springer.

Rogers, R., Tillbrook, C. E., & Sewell, K. W. (2004). *Evaluation of Competency to Stand Trial—Revised (ECST–R) and professional manual*. Odessa, FL: Psychological Assessment Resources.

Silten, P. R. & Tullis, R. (1977). Mental competency in criminal proceedings. *Hastings Law Journal, 28*, 1053, 1058–1065.

Skeem, J. L., Golding, S. L., Cohn, N. B., & Berge, G. (1998). The logic and reliability of evaluations of competence to stand trial. *Law and Human Behavior, 22*, 519–547.

Slovenko, R. (2002). The role of psychiatric diagnosis in the law. *Journal of Psychiatry and Law, 30*(3), 421–444.

Texas Code of Criminal Procedure Ann. Art. 46B.025 (2006). Retrieved March 15, 2011, from http://www.statutes.legis.state.tx.us/docs/CR/htm/CR.46B.htm.

Tillbrook, C., Mumley, D., & Grisso, T. (2003). Avoiding expert opinions on the ultimate legal question: The case for integrity. *Journal of Forensic Psychology Practice, 3*(3), 77–87.

Weiner, I. B. (2003). Prediction and postdiction in clinical decision making. *Clinical Psychology: Science and Practice, 10*(3), 335–338.

Weiss, M. (1997). A legal evaluation of criminal competency standards. *Journal of Contemporary Criminal Justice, 1*(3), 213–223.

Wolber, G. (2008). The unrestorable incompetent defendant: Length of attempted restoration and factors contributing to a decision of unrestorable. *American Journal of Forensic Psychology, 26*(3), 63–77.

Wrightsman, L., Nietzel, M., & Fortune, W. (1994). *Psychology and the legal system* (3rd ed.). Pacific Grove, CA: Brooks/Cole.

Cases

Buchanan v. Kentucky, 483 U.S. 402 (1987).

Daubert v. Merrell, 509 U.S. 579, 591 (1993).

Drope v. Missouri, 420 U.S. 162 (1975).
Dusky v. United States, 362 U.S. 402 (1960).
Estelle v. Smith, 451 U.S. 454 (1981).
Faretta v. California, 422 U.S. 806 (1975).
Frith's Case, 22 Howes' State Trials 307, 318 (1790).
Godinez v. Moran, 509 U.S. 389 (1993)—U.S.S.C.
Jackson v. Indiana, 406 U.S. 715 (1972).
Missouri v. Davis, 653 S.W.2d 167, Mo. Sup. Ct. (1983).
Montana v. Austed, 641 P.2d. 1373 Mont. Sup. Ct. (1982).
Morrow v. State, 423 A.2d 251, Md. Ct. Spec. App. (1980).
R. v. Frith, 22 St. Tr. 307 at 318 (1790).
Ritchie v. Indiana, 468 N.E.2d 1369, Ind. Sup. Ct. (1984).
Sell v. U.S., 539 U.S. 166 (2003).
United States v. Binion, 132 Fed. Appx. 89, 8th Circuit (2005).
United States v. Greer, 158 F. 3d 228, 5th Circuit (1998).
United States v. Timmins, 9th Circuit (2002).
Wilson v. United States, 391 F.2d 460, D.C. Cir. (1968).

Brian David Mitchell Case Information Sources

Atherton, J. S. (2005). Findings and conclusions re: Defendant's competency to proceed to trial. Case No. 031901884, pp. 1–60. Retrieved from http://www.utcourts.gov/media/news/archives/State%20v.%20Mitchell—Ruling%20on%20Competency%20to%20Proceed.pdf.

Kimball, D. A. (2010). Memorandum decision and order determining competency. Case 2:08-cr-00125-DAK Document 236 Filed 03/01/2010, pp. 1–149. Retrieved from http://i.cdn.turner.com/cnn/2010/images/03/01/determinig.competency.pdf.

CHAPTER THIRTEEN

Insanity Defense

Arthur J. Lurigio and Lauran Babchuk

Basic understandings of insanity appeared centuries before its instantiation as a legal concept. The origins of the insanity defense purportedly lie in the ancient Code of Hammurabi (c. 1800 BCE) (Hermann, 1997). The written source of religious authority in Orthodox Judaism, the Talmud, contains a passage that portends the legal prongs of modern formulations of insanity: "A deaf mute, an idiot, and a minor are awkward to deal with, as he who injures them is liable [to pay], whereas if they injure others they are exempt" (Platt & Diamond, 1965, p. 358). Varying degrees of responsibility in judgments of guilt (criminal law) and liability (civil law) have been incorporated into the legal decision-making process as well as in widely accepted attributions of culpability (Heider, 1958; Shaver, 1985). Hence, the insanity defense is fraught with broader legal conceptualizations and commonsense notions of blameworthiness, and "represents a necessary conflict between two fundamental American values: justice for criminals and compassion for the ill" (Melville & Naimark, 2002, p. 554).

As we discuss in this chapter, the insanity defense has been a highly controversial and hotly contested legal strategy, and the subject of legal wrangling since its introduction in British common law in the nineteenth century (Melville & Naimark, 2002). Legal scholars, legislators, and jurists have yet to reach consensus on the definition of insanity or on the legal standards and the exculpatory criteria that must be satisfied in order to proffer the insanity defense successfully (Hermann, 1997). Moreover, the public harbors numerous misconceptions about the meaning and use of insanity as a legal defense (Borum & Fulero, 1999). Insanity cases have often attracted the public's attention. The media's coverage of such cases has served only to fuel the debate about the legitimacy of the defense and has created even more confusion about its rightful place in American jurisprudence.

This chapter is divided into five sections. The first section discusses the legal concepts that constitute the foundation for the insanity defense. It also describes an offshoot of the insanity defense, known as "guilty but mentally ill." The second section explains the evaluation of defendants who plead insanity and describes standardized assessment tools that clinicians have employed to gather information for constructing expert testimony about the mental status of a defendant at the time of the alleged offense. The third section provides an historical overview of the legal standards that define insanity and its use as a defense in criminal trials. The fourth section presents some of the more recent and prominent insanity cases in the United States. These cases have influenced public opinion about the insanity defense, and one has significantly altered the legal standards and criminal procedures pertaining to the insanity defense. The fifth section explores mock jury studies in addition to widespread myths and misconceptions about the insanity defense and interpretive constructs that affect judgments in such cases.

Basic Concepts and Standards

NGRI

Not Guilty by Reason of Insanity (NGRI) is an affirmative criminal defense by which defendants argue that they should be freed from criminal liability for breaking the law because they were legally "insane" at the time that the alleged crime was committed. A defendant must enter a plea of NGRI at arraignment (Hermann, 1997). As we discuss below, the definition of "insanity" has varied across times and jurisdictions. In general, the insanity defense assumes that people with serious mental illness or mental defects are either unable to recognize the consequences or the wrongfulness of their criminal actions, or lack the ability to resist the compulsion to commit a crime as the result of delusions, hallucinations, or other cognitive impairments (Wrightsman, Greene, Nietzel, & Fortune, 2002). As such, the insanity defense is predicated on the concept of criminal responsibility or *mens re*, which means "guilty mind."

The failure to prove intent in a criminal case generally leads to a finding of not guilty or a conviction on a lesser charge (e.g., involuntary manslaughter, instead of murder). Defendants who are found NGRI or not responsible by reason of insanity, as it is sometimes called, are acquitted because a judge or jury decided that a mental disorder rendered them unable to form the requisite intention to commit a crime or to engage in purposeful criminal behavior. The Latin phrase *actus non facit reum nisi mens sit rea* ("the act will not make a person guilty unless the mind is also guilty") captures the essence of the insanity defense (Huss, 2009).

The legal definition of "insanity" differs from the medical definition of "mental illness." Indeed, insanity is a legal rather than a psychiatric concept (Fradella, 2008). The presence of a mental disorder is insufficient legal justification to relieve a defendant from responsibility for an illegal act. The majority of defendants who plead NGRI have been diagnosed with a mental illness or developmental disability, but insanity is neither a symptom of a psychiatric disorder nor a psychiatric disorder in itself (Fradella, 2008; Hermann, 1997).

Simply put, insanity is not the same as mental illness (Halleck, 1987). The term "insanity" is found nowhere in the American Psychiatric Association's *Diagnostic and Statistical Manual of Mental Disorders*, which is the classification system used widely by mental health professionals to assess the nature and severity of mental illness. Most people with mental illness who commit crimes fail to meet the legal criteria for insanity, and no specific category of mental illness is associated with the insanity defense. Overall, the definition of most serious mental illnesses includes impairment in functioning; nonetheless, the forensic definition of insanity requires a highly specific type and level of impairment delineated by legal, not clinical, criteria (Huss, 2009; Moriarty, 2001).

Various legal standards define insanity and specify the evidence and the level and burden of proof needed for a successful insanity defense. These definitions differ among state statutes and between state and federal statutes. Some states prohibit the insanity defense yet allow defendants to adduce evidence that speaks to their state of mind during the commission of a crime (Borum & Fulero, 1999). Since 1950, the specification of the insanity defense has changed five times in the federal statutes alone (Wrightsman et al., 2002).

Although the elements of proof vary by jurisdiction, for the insanity defense to be persuasive, the defense must prove that the defendant either committed the crime without comprehending that the act was illegal or was unable to understand its consequences because of a mental disorder. Therefore, defendants who invoke the insanity defense are required to undergo a thorough psychiatric history and mental status examination, which can be initiated by the state or defense. The evidence must demonstrate that the mental disorder interfered with the defendant's ability to distinguish right from wrong at the time of the offense. In other words, insanity acquittees lack the mental capacity to realize that a wrongful act was committed or to appreciate that the act was wrongful (Hermann, 1997).

Several states allow defendants to argue that they understood their behavior was criminal but were unable to control it; this is the "irresistible impulse" defense. This defense permits judges and juries to decide that defendants are not "criminally responsible" for their actions even though their acts would be a crime in the absence of a mental disorder that compelled them to commit the act. Diminished responsibility (or diminished capacity) also can be employed as a mitigating factor in cases other than those that proffer the insanity defense (Elliott, 1996). For example, jurisdictions accept inebriation or drug intoxication as a mitigating factor, although such conditions alone are legally insufficient as an insanity defense (Fradella, 2008).

Any defendant can invoke the insanity defense for any type of crime. A trial in which the insanity defense is invoked must involve the testimony of forensic psychiatrists or psychologists who present opinions about the defendant's state of mind at the time of the offense. However, mental health practitioners are prohibited from offering direct opinions on the issue of whether a defendant was actually insane or not, which is known as the "ultimate issue" prohibition. If a defendant is willing to plead guilty or is found guilty at trial, numerous jurisdictions have an alternative to the NGRI sentencing option referred to as either Guilty but Mentally Ill (GBMI) or Guilty but Insane (Moriarty, 2001).

Several characteristics are common among defendants who are found NGRI. First, they are likely to have a criminal history similar in length and severity to that of other convicted felons. In other words, the criminal records of insanity defendants are neither more nor less severe than those of other felony defendants (Boehnert, 1989). Second, like other felony defendants, those who plead NGRI successfully are from impoverished backgrounds (Nicholson, Norwood, & Enyart, 1991). Third, most insanity acquittees are diagnosed with severe mental illness and have lengthy psychiatric histories that include hospitalizations (Nicholson et al., 1991). Fourth, most insanity acquittees have been previously found to be incompetent to stand trial (Boehnert, 1989). Fifth, men and women insanity acquittees are similar with respect to their criminal and psychiatric histories (Heilbrun, Heilbrun, & Griffin, 1988). Sixth, most insanity acquittees are unemployed white men in their early 20s or early 30s (Wrightsman, Nietzel, & Fortune, 1998).

GBMI

The GBMI verdict has been adopted in at least 14 states, including Alaska, South Carolina, Georgia, Illinois, South Dakota, and Michigan, which was the first state to enact a GBMI statute (Bartol, 1993). A common feature of these insanity standards involves defendants' lack of appreciation for the wrongfulness of their actions. If the insanity requirements are met, defendants are exculpated due to their inability to comprehend fully the legal ramifications or wrongfulness of their behaviors (see above). In contrast, a verdict of GBMI is still a finding of guilty. GBMI defendants are deemed to have possessed the capacity to appreciate the wrongfulness of their actions. In simple terms, the GBMI verdict has three manifest elements: the defendant is found guilty of a crime; the defendant is believed to have a mental illness; and the defendant is found legally sane (Huss, 2009).

The GBMI verdict was intended to reduce the number of NGRI verdicts by providing juries with an intermediate verdict or sentencing compromise—less culpable than denoted by a guilty verdict but more culpable than denoted by a NGRI verdict—in difficult cases in which the evidence regarding the defendant's crime-related mental status is ambiguous (Melville & Naimark, 2002). Yet, studies have shown that when the option of GBMI is available to jurors, they are more likely to find a defendant GBMI rather than guilty or NGRI, a phenomenon known as "verdict-shifting" (Roberts & Golding, 1991). The GBMI verdict was also instituted as a sentencing option in order to increase the likelihood that people with mental illness would receive mental health services in the correctional system. However, research indicates that people found GBMI were no more likely to participate in psychiatric treatment while incarcerated than those found NGRI or guilty (Borum & Fulero, 1999).

Although a GBMI verdict acknowledges that defendants were mentally ill at the time of the crime, the finding does not lessen the degree of culpability or responsibility associated with their actions. In fact, defendants found GBMI generally receive harsher sentences than do those who are found "only" guilty of committing an offense (Callahan, McGreevy, Cirincione, & Steadman, 1992). As such, the verdict could be used to circumvent the ethical conflicts inherent in the insanity defense, thereby leading unwittingly to harsher punishments (e.g., longer sentences) for GBMI defendants than those found simply guilty (Melville & Naimark, 2002).

The GBMI verdict also has been criticized for its complexity. "If regular insanity instructions are confusing to jurors, the GBMI verdict only adds to the confusion by introducing the very difficult distinction for juries to make between mental illness that results in insanity and mental illness that does not" (Wrightsman et al. 2002, p. 326). Furthermore, GBMI offenders are more stringently supervised following release from prison than are non-GBMI offenders convicted of the same types of crime (McGraw, Farthin-Capowich, & Keilitz, 1985). For these and other reasons (e.g., its presence as a sentencing option raises the threshold for insanity), the GBMI option has been criticized by legal professionals and mental health advocates, such as members of the National Alliance for the Mentally Ill, the American Psychiatric Association, the American Psychological Association, and the American Bar Association (American Psychiatric Association, 1983; Borum & Fulero, 1999; Roberts, Sargent, & Chan, 1993).

Evaluations of Insanity

Insanity Assessment Tools

Clinical psychologists have few valid or reliable tools to employ in gathering information to support or refute the insanity defense. Among the tools that have been developed for insanity evaluations are the Rogers Criminal Responsibility Scales (R-CRAS; Rogers, 1986) and the Mental Status Examination at the Time of the Offense (MSE; Slobogin, Melton, & Showalter, 1984). The R-CRAS is a well-known standardized assessment tool for insanity evaluations (Rogers & Cavanaugh, 1981). The tool consists of 25 psychological and situational scales to determine if the standards of insanity have been met. The tool includes five subscales that measure organicity (brain disease caused by lesions or structural defects), psychopathology, and cognitive and behavioral control, which are rated from 0 to 6 (0 = no information and 6 = the highest level of clinical significance).

Following the administration of the subscales, the forensic examiner uses a decision model to render an opinion about a defendant's level of criminal responsibility or culpability. The R-CRAS has fairly high interrater reliability (kappa reliability coefficient of 0.73). The tool is successful in differentiating among defendants found by the courts to be legally sane or insane. Furthermore, the R-CRAS also has been employed to establish the validity of the insanity construct (Rogers, Wasyliw, & Cavanaugh, 1984).

As its name suggests, the MSE assesses a defendant's level of psychological functioning at the time of the alleged criminal act. Specifically, the MSE seeks to detect the presence of a "significant mental abnormality," defined as "any diagnostic category representing a disorder which, if present at the time of the offense, might form the basis for a legal defense" (Slobogin et al., 1984, p. 308). The MSE is used early in the legal process in order to save court time and resources.

The MSE examines a defendant's psychiatric history, the nature of the alleged offense, and the defendant's present mental state. The false negative rate for the MSE is very low, indicating that the instrument is accurate in identifying defendants as legally sane who are actually found as such by the courts (Slobogin et al., 1984). However, the tool is best used only as a supplemental guide for the collection of information in a more comprehensive assessment of insanity (Zapf, Golding, & Roesch, 2006). In general, apart from the factors included in the R-CRAS and the MSE, insanity evaluation reports encompass the following information: psychiatric and substance use history, the results of a mental status examination and psychological testing, the use of psychiatric medication, previous diagnoses, and the defendant's and others' descriptions of the alleged offense (Borum & Grisso, 1996).

CST

Assessments of competency to stand trial (CST) and insanity focus on different legal issues and on the state of mind of a defendant at different times (Fradella, 2008). CST requires that defendants understand the charges against them, comprehend their right to plead guilty or not guilty, participate meaningfully in the mounting of their own defense, and follow the progress of their case through the court process. Clinical evaluations of competency must examine defendants' present mental state on the basis of the aforementioned dimensions and at the time of the trial. Defendants found incompetent to stand trial must be restored to competency by being treated for their psychiatric disorders. Trial proceedings are halted until a clinician can testify that competency has been restored, and if so, it is presumed that the trial can continue with the defendant's understanding of the court process and engagement in the formulation of a defense (Hermann, 1997).

In contrast, evaluations of insanity focus on the defendant's state of mind in the past; that is, at the time the alleged offense was committed. CST has no bearing on insanity. However, as we noted above, competency must be established before the court can turn its attention to the insanity defense. In short, "competence refers exclusively to the defendant's mental abilities at the time of the proceeding, whereas insanity relates to the defendant's mental state at the time the offense was committed" (Wrightsman et al., 1998, p. 312).

Legal Standards

The belief that it is immoral to punish people who are not responsible for their actions has been embraced since antiquity. For example, in the Roman Empire, tribunals could find people *non-compos mentis* (without mastery of mind), thereby freeing them from any responsibility for their criminal actions. The Roman concept of "mastery of mind" is the basis for *mens rea* or "guilty mind" (Borum & Fulero, 1999; Costanzo, 2004).

The first formal legal standard pertaining to insanity is known as the "wild beast standard," which was incorporated into English common law in 1724 following the case of *Rex v. Arnold.* The case involved a defendant who shot and attempted to kill a British lord (Gerald, 1997). The judge in the case (Judge Tracy) pronounced that insanity requires an individual to be so afflicted that he or she has no understanding and memory and no realization of "what he is doing any more than an infant, a brute, or a wild beast" (Platt & Diamond, 1965, p. 360). *Rex v. Arnold* was the first case to conceptualize insanity as a cognitive or mental defect (Perlin, 1994).

The M'Naghten Rule

The court can apply a number of different legal rules in making a determination of insanity (Elliott, 1996). The oldest is the M'Naghten Rule. In 1843, in Great Britain, Daniel M'Naghten made an attempt on the life of Prime Minister Robert Peel, but in the process shot and killed Edward Drummond, Peel's secretary. M'Naghten apparently suffered from paranoid schizophrenia and held the prime minister and the Tory Party responsible for all the imagined suffering and torment in his life (Moran, 1981). To the shock of the nation, M'Naghten was found not guilty on the grounds that he was insane when he attempted to kill the prime minister. A public outcry compelled the House of Lords to establish strict standards for the insanity defense (Dalby, 2006). Thus, the M'Naghten Rule was implemented.

The M'Naghten Rule states that a person may be "insane" if "at the time of the committing of the act, the party accused was laboring under such a defect of reason, arising from a disease of the mind, as not to know the nature and quality of the act he was doing, or, if he did know it, that he did not know what he was doing was wrong." Critics of the M'Naghten

Rule assailed its inordinate focus on a defendant's cognitive abilities and underscored the difficulties in ascertaining a defendant's "knowledge" of wrongfulness when the crime was perpetrated. The absence of attention to a defendant's emotional and behavioral control in the M'Naghten Rule led its detractors to call for an expansion of the insanity standard (Elliott, 1996). The M'Naghten Rule is regarded as the most stringent of the modern insanity standards and therefore the least likely to result in an acquittal on the basis of insanity (Huss, 2002; Weiner, 2004).

Irresistible Impulse Test

In the 1887 case of *Parsons v. State*, the Alabama Supreme Court ruled that the insanity defense must involve not only assessments of defendants' ability to distinguish right from wrong (the knowledge prong of the defense) but must also consider their ability to control their compulsions (the volitional prong of the defense). The court's ruling stated that even though the defendant in the case could differentiate right from wrong, "the duress of such mental disease that he had [caused him to lose] the power to choose right from wrong" and that "his free agency was at the time destroyed," and thus "the alleged crime was so connected with such mental disease in the relation of cause and effect, as to have been a product of it solely." As the result of the *Parsons* case, the Irresistible Impulse Test became an appendage and corrective to the M'Naghten Rule in several states. The test was also subjected to criticism stemming from the difficulty of differentiating an uncontrolled from an uncontrollable act—the latter being the standard needed to satisfy the test—and the narrowness of the impulse criterion (Elliott, 1996; Hermann, 1997).

The Durham Rule

Originally adopted in New Hampshire in 1871, the Durham Rule or "product test" was prescribed by the U.S. Court of Appeals for the District of Columbia Circuit in 1954. It states that "an accused is not criminally responsible if his unlawful act was the product of mental disease or defect." The Durham Rule was designed to simplify the M'Naghten and Irresistible Impulse Tests by inserting objective clinical diagnoses into the core of evidence in insanity cases (Gerald, 1997).

Monte Durham was charged with "housebreaking and petit larceny" in 1951 (Weiner, 1985, p. 9). Durham had a history of mental illness and suicide attempts, which had led to a discharge from the U.S. Navy and several psychiatric hospitalizations. The trial judge ignored this history and forbade Durham from entering a NGRI plea. He was subsequently found guilty of breaking and entering. In 1954, the Court of Appeals for the District of Columbia overturned the conviction and instituted the Durham Rule, also referred to as the Product Rule (Gerald, 1997).

Since the 1970s, jurisdictions have generally rejected the Durham arguments because of their ambiguity, overemphasis on "mental disease or defect," and undue weight on the testimony of psychiatrists and psychologists. The Durham Rule is problematic because forensic examiners can disagree as to whether a defendant has a mental disorder and over the specific nature of the diagnosis. Similarly, the determination of whether a crime was the "product" of mental illness can be approached from a range of perspectives, including a highly narrow view that the crime would never have occurred without the mental illness, to the very broad view that the defendant's entire life history should be considered in the calculus of an insanity claim (Huss, 2002). By 1972, all states except New Hampshire had abandoned the Durham Rule (Elliott, 2006).

The American Law Institute's Model Penal Code Test

The M'Naghten Rule was gradually replaced in most jurisdictions by the American Law Institute's (ALI) standards, known as the ALI Test, which were included in the Model Penal Code (1962). Broader than the M'Naghten Rule and the Irresistible Impulse Test, the ALI Test's proof of insanity states that people suffering from a mental disease or defect are not responsible for their actions if they lack the substantial capacity to appreciate the criminality of their conduct or to conform their conduct to the requirements of the law, which includes both the cognitive and volitional aspects of insanity. The mental defect must be a diagnosable medical condition. With the incorporation of this element, the ALI Test captured all three elements of its predecessors: the right-versus-wrong distinction of M'Naghten, the lack of control of the Irresistible Impulse Test, and the mental disease or defect required by Durham (American Law Institute, 1985). As stated in the Moral Penal Code (1962):

> A person is not responsible for criminal conduct if a the time of such conduct as a result of mental disease or defect he lacks substantial capacity either to appreciate the criminality (wrongfulness) of his conduct or to conform his conduct the requirements of the law. (Section 4.01)

Emerging from the ALI Test, more stringent rules were passed to delineate that people with certain psychiatric diagnoses, such as substance use and personality disorders, could still be held legally responsible for their criminal behaviors because their level of functioning and their ability to make decisions was not sufficiently impaired to reach the insanity threshold (Halleck, 1987; Insanity Defense Working Group, 1983). The ALI Test was eventually superseded by Congress with the passage of the Insanity Defense Reform Act of 1984.

The Brawner Rule

On September 8, 1967, after several hours of drinking alcohol, Archie W. Brawner and his friends were involved in several altercations at a party in an apartment building. When Brawner left the party, he was bleeding and injured. He returned to the party with a gun and an intention "to kill or be killed." One witness testified that Brawner said, "[I'm] going to get my boys" and come back, and that "someone is going to die tonight." After Brawner returned to the apartment, he shot through the door, killing a man named Billy Ford. Brawner was arrested a few minutes later, several blocks away from where the shooting had occurred. The arresting officer testified that Brawner spoke lucidly and appeared sober. The expert witnesses, called by both defense and prosecution, all agreed that Brawner was suffering from an abnormality of a psychiatric or neurological nature (epilepsy) (471 F.2d 969: *United States of America v. Archie W. Brawner*, Appellant).

In *U.S. v. Brawner*, the D.C. Circuit Court of Appeals (*United States v. Brawner*, 471 F.2d 969 (1972)) established the Brawner Rule, which replaced the short-lived Durham Rule by arguing that the ruling's requirement that a crime must be a "product of mental disease or defect" placed the question of guilt on expert witnesses and undermined the jury's role in determining guilt (Garrison, 1998; Slovenko, 1994). Under Brawner, juries were allowed to decide the "insanity question" by weighing all the evidence presented in the case. Basing its ruling on the ALI's Model Penal Code, the court declared that for a defendant to be found NGRI, the defendant must "lack substantial capacity to appreciate that his conduct is wrongful or lack substantial capacity to conform his conduct to the law."

The Insanity Defense Reform Act

The Insanity Defense Reform Act, passed by Congress in 1984 in response to the verdict in the John W. Hinckley trial (see below) and codified at 18 U.S.C. § 17, states that a person accused of a crime can be judged NGRI if "the defendant, as a result of a severe mental disease or defect, was unable to appreciate the nature and quality or the wrongfulness of his acts." After the Hinckley verdict, Congress and several states passed laws designed to toughen standards in insanity defenses. Instead of requiring prosecutors to prove a defendant's sanity, the act mandated defense attorneys to carry the burden of persuading a judge or jury that their clients are insane by clear and convincing evidence. In summary, the Insanity Defense Reform Act mirrors the M'Naghten Rule except that it requires a defendant to suffer from a severe mental defect, and it places the burden on the defendant to prove this by offering clear and convincing evidence (higher than the preponderance of the evidence standard required of the defendant by most states following the M'Naghten Rule) (Elliott, 1996).

Infamous Insanity Cases of the Twentieth Century

The passage of the Insanity Defense Reform Act stemmed in part from the public's misperception that the insanity defense is used often and successfully. As we discuss in section five, several surveys of the general public have uncovered these misperceptions (e.g., Bower, 1984; Hans & Slater, 1983). Furthermore, a handful of highly publicized insanity cases, tried in the past 60 years, have reinforced these inaccurate beliefs. The most notorious case involved the shooting of President Ronald Reagan (Caplan, 1984).

John W. Hinckley Jr. attempted to assassinate President Reagan on March 10, 1981, while cameras were recording the president's exit from a hotel in Washington, D.C. Hinckley's attorney conceded that his client planned the attack, stalked the president, bought a gun and special bullets for the occasion, and fired the weapon from a crouched position. To support Hinckley's insanity claim, his psychiatrists testified that their client could neither "appreciate" the wrongness of his actions nor have the ability to control his actions because of his diseased mind. Similarly, his defense attorneys argued that his actions arose from his obsession with actress Jodie Foster and the movie *Taxi Driver*. They also argued that his apparent planfulness in his attempt to kill the president was actually the result of his disturbed adherence to a fictitious movie script, which was constructed from his psychotic thoughts and beliefs (Caplan, 1984). In their words, "a mind that is so influenced by the outside world is a mind out of control and beyond responsibility" (Winslade & Ross, 1983, p. 188).

To bolster the insanity defense, Hinckley's attorneys introduced expert testimony indicating that the defendant suffered from schizophrenia as well as the results of a CAT scan showing abnormalities in Hinckley's brain consistent with such a diagnosis. Judge Barrington Parker instructed the jury to apply the federal law in the case, which placed the burden of proof on the prosecution and elevated the standard of proof to beyond a reasonable doubt. The law or penal code of the District of Columbia, however, would have placed the burden of proof on the defense and set the standard of proof at a lower threshold (clear and convincing evidence).

After four days, the jury found Hinckley NGRI. During debriefing sessions, the jurors reported that the judge's instructions were pivotal in their arrival at the verdict. When faced with conflicting evidence about Hinckley's mental state, the jurors concluded that the prosecutors failed to prove the defendant's sanity beyond a reasonable doubt (Wrightsman et al., 2002). A firestorm of public outrage ensued (Caplan, 1984).

Other successfully proffered but less controversial insanity cases include the case of Anthony Kiritsis, who kidnapped and threatened to kill the mortgage banker who was in the process of foreclosing on his property, and Edward Gein, who was convicted of the murders of two women in the 1950s near Plainfield, Indiana. Gein confessed to robbing graves and using the parts of corpses in order to recreate the image of his dead mother (Wrightsman et al., 2002). Seemingly disturbed defendants can be found guilty even though the evidence in their cases appears to support the insanity defense. For example, Herbert Mullin murdered 13 people in the early 1970s in an area surrounding Santa Cruz, California. He chose his victims randomly and claimed to hear voices that ordered him to kill. Expert witnesses diagnosed him with schizophrenia. The jury found him guilty of two counts of first-degree murder and eight counts of second-degree murder (Lunde & Morgan, 1980).

The Jeffrey Dahmer case is certainly one of the best-known cases of a failed insanity defense, receiving exhaustive media coverage and the attention of numerous documentarians. Dahmer confessed to murdering and dismembering 15 young men over the course of 10 years, some of whom he cannibalized or whose remains he preserved as remembrances of their sexual encounters. Dahmer's purported motivation for killing his victims was to render them as slaves or "zombies" who would be under his absolute control for the purpose of sexual gratification. Although his extreme sexual paraphilia and cannibalism were indicative of a severe mental disturbance, the members of the jury found him sane. They decided that he appreciated the wrongfulness of his criminal actions because he took deliberate steps to hide his crimes, which also meant that he could control his actions. These facts nullified his insanity defense. In the jurors' view, Dahmer's actions were not the result of an inability to comport himself in accordance with the law (Davis, 1995).

Other notorious killers whose insanity pleas were rejected include Jack Ruby, who was sent him to prison for shooting Lee Harvey Oswald, the assassin of President John F. Kennedy. John Wayne Gacy was convicted of killing and burying in a crawl space 33 young boys in Chicago. Sirhan Sirhan was convicted of the assassination of Senator Robert Kennedy. The court also rejected the insanity defense of David Berkowitz, New York's "Son of Sam" murderer, who claimed that he was commanded to kill by a demon that possessed his neighbor's dog (Wrightsman et al., 2002).

A Pennsylvania jury found millionaire John DuPont GBMI in the murder of a wrestling coach. Lawyers for Unabomber Theodore Kaczynski argued that he was insane, but Kaczynski resisted such a defense and pleaded guilty. Lee Boyd Malvo and Andrea Yates are other examples of high-profile, highly dramatic, and media-worthy cases that have used the insanity defense. Lorena Bobbitt argued that she was temporarily insane when she severed her husband's penis with a kitchen knife. A Virginia jury agreed, and she was released after three months of psychiatric evaluation (Reznek, 1997).

Insanity Myths and Public Perceptions

As we have noted throughout this chapter, the insanity defense has prompted vociferous debate among lawyers, clinicians, and the general public. Most people believe that defendants exploit the insanity defense as a "legal loophole" to escape punishment for serious criminal charges. They also believe that defendants use the insanity defense more frequently than they actually do; insanity defense cases are usually profiled in the media, leading to the misperception that such cases are common (Jeffrey & Pasewark, 1983; Perlin, 1996; Reznek, 1997). In fact, the insanity plea is used in fewer than 1% of all criminal cases and is successful in only 26% of those; "this means that of the nine insanity pleas raised in every 1,000 cases, only two will be successful (Wrightsman et al., 2002, p. 321). NGRI success rates vary from state to state, but overall, the more insanity cases are heard in a state, the lower the acquittal rate (Silver, Cirincione, & Steadman, 1994).

Rarely do NGRI acquittees walk free. In almost all such cases, a verdict of an NGRI leads to a lengthy term in a secure treatment center until mental health officials determine that the defendant poses no further danger to others. For some, that could be the equivalent of a life sentence. A successful NGRI defense typically results in a long and often indeterminate commitment to a psychiatric facility, especially for the commission of a violent crime (Rodriguez, LeWinn, & Perlin, 1983; Silver, 1995). In addition, insanity acquittees are incarcerated for longer than defendants convicted of non-NGRI felonies (Braff, Arvanites, & Steadman, 1983). These disparities were challenged by the Supreme Court in *Foucha v. Louisiana*, which held that states must release defendants who are no longer deemed mentally ill and dangerous (Huss, 2002).

Research has shown that the public believes that three types of defendants are successful in proffering the insanity defense: "mad killers," who are unable to control their murderous impulses and behaviors; "crafty cons," who deceive jurors by feigning mental illness in order to convince them of their inability to control themselves; and "desperate defendants," who see the insanity defense as their only hope for acquittal in light of overwhelming evidence against them (Sales & Hafemeister, 1984). However, analyses of insanity cases provide little support for these beliefs. For example, most defendants who plead NGRI are diagnosed with a severe mental disorder and below-normal intelligence (Silver et al., 1994). Such cognitive impairments and limitations hamper their ability to be "crafty," and few defendants have the ability to fool forensic examiners by feigning mental illness (Boehnert, 1989; Melton, Petrila, Poythress, & Slobogin, 1987).

One study reported that 77% of insanity acquittees suffered from a psychotic disorder, serious depression, mental retardation, or organic brain disease; only 1% were identified as malingerers (Cochrane, Grisso, & Frederick, 2001). In another investigation, nearly 90% of insanity acquittees were diagnosed with a psychotic disorder or other type of major mental illness (Cirincione, Steadman, & McGreevy, 1995). The belief that insanity acquittees are more dangerous to the public than non-NGRI offenders also has no empirical support. Their recidivism rates are comparable to those of non-NGRI felons, and they are less likely to recidivate than non-NGRI when they receive treatment for their mental illness (Kravitz & Kelly, 1999; Nicholson et al., 1991). Finally, contrary to public perceptions, the insanity defense is invoked for a wide range of crimes, not just murder. For example, a study of insanity cases in eight states found that, among NGRI acquittees, the chargers were as follows: 14% murder, 38% assault, 12% other violent crime, 7% robbery, 18% property crime, and 10% minor crime (Callahan, Steadman, McGreevy, & Robbins, 1991).

Insanity Studies and Kelman's Conceptualization of Jury Decision-Making

Numerous studies have examined juror's decision-making strategies and dispositions in insanity cases by employing a mock jury paradigm in which research participants deliberate and judge ersatz cases. For example, one such study explored jurors' construals of insanity (Finkel & Handel, 1989). Participants read four cases and were asked to render and explain their verdicts (i.e., guilty or NGRI). The explanations were categorized into general and specific insanity constructs (e.g., defendant motive, control, planfulness). Different constructs were applied to each of the four cases. The mock jurors provided several reasons to explain their verdicts, which were consistent with the constructs that they had chosen in each case. The variety of constructs applied to each case suggests that the jury's decision-making process in insanity cases is more complicated and less rigid than generally thought. The results also suggest that jurors evaluate the insanity defense based on complex case features that depart from the legal standards of insanity.

Another study involved two experiments investigating jurors' understanding of insanity defense standards (Ogloff, 1991). In the first, participants were presented with varied insanity standard instructions. Three independent variables were manipulated: insanity standards (ALI, M'Naghten, or no instructions); burden of proof (defendant or prosecution), and standard of proof (preponderance of evidence, clear and convincing evidence). After participants had watched a video clip of a trial reenactment, they were asked to judge the defendant as guilty of first-degree murder, guilty of second-degree murder, guilty of voluntary manslaughter, or NGRI. No significant differences were found among the conditions, suggesting that insanity test and burdens as well as levels of proof have no effects on a jury's decisions.

In the second experiment, researchers explored mock jurors' understanding of jury instructions and explored their beliefs about the importance of case features in insanity determinations. Participants performed poorly on a free-recall task that tested their comprehension of the legal standards for insanity. Moreover, no significant differences were found among experimental groups' beliefs about the important elements for reaching an NGRI verdict. Findings suggested that jurors base their decisions on lay interpretations of insanity rather than on legal standards; they appear to apply their own personal beliefs and perceptions about insanity in rendering verdicts (Ogloff, 1991).

The effects of the GBMI option on the dynamics of jury decision-making also have been investigated in mock jury paradigms (Roberts & Golding, 1991). In one such study, participants were presented with vignettes that varied on three independent variables: delusional content (self-defense or non-self-defense), planfulness of the crime (planful or non-planful), and judicial instructions (only NGRI instructions or NGRI instructions supplemented with GBMI instructions). The presence of the

GBMI verdict created a shift that decreased the number NGRI and guilty verdicts. Cases involving a lesser degree of planfulness resulted in a greater number of NGRI verdicts. The GBMI verdict option also led participants to perceive that the defendant possessed a greater degree of culpability. Furthermore, participants' responsibility construals were influenced by defendant characteristics. The mock jurors' attitudes about the insanity defense suggested that these differences are at least as important as the legal aspects of the proceedings in rendering attributions of responsibility; however, the results of the study neither supported nor contradicted the assertion that GBMI is a compromise verdict.

The concept of insanity gains its legitimacy from the legal code and is viewed as an objectively and rationally determined verdict. Nonetheless, actual deliberations of the insanity defense depart from strict interpretations of the law and incorporate factors that are mutable, subjective, and nonlegal in nature, including psychological theories, perspectives, and decision-making strategies. Such counterintuitive approaches question the degree to which rationality guides legal decisions in insanity cases.

Based on the provocative arguments presented in his well-respected, influential writings, Kelman (1981) asserts that determinations of insanity are "un-rational" and influenced by "interpretive construction." He contends that the law strives to embody reason and objectivity, but is inherently flawed by limitations in human judgments and decision making. Through an analysis of interpretive constructs (i.e., time framing, accounts, intent, and defendant characteristics), Kelman contends that powerful factors "unconsciously" affect jury decision-making in insanity. Many aspects of these interpretive constructs are grounded in psychological theory and research, and lead to a heuristically informed conceptualization of the insanity defense.

Time Framing

The first interpretive construct is time framing. Shifting the time frame can change juror's perspectives regarding criminal incidents and affect the outcome of an insanity trial. The decision maker is responsible for imposing the time frame. Is it appropriate to restrict the time frame to only the occurrence of the criminal act or should the time frame include events that precede or follow the incident? Time framing is relevant to the insanity defense because it determines whether the defendant's medical history or current psychiatric assessments will be incorporated into an examination of the defendant's state of mind at the time of the alleged crime. Applying a broad time frame to an insanity defense case allows forensic experts to provide testimony about factors that could affect a defendant's state of mind before and after the alleged offense; such expert testimony can change jurors' decisions (Ogloff, 1991).

Experts are limited in their assessments of a defendant's state of mind at the time of the crime; they can make only retrospective judgments about an incident that occurred months or even years before the examiner's evaluation. Experts are barred from commenting on a defendant's precise state of mind owning to "ultimate issue or opinion" constraints. However, assessment tools, such as the MSE, which we discussed earlier in this chapter, attempt to evaluate a defendant's mental state during the incident. The determination of insanity hinges upon hypothesized mental functioning within a precisely delimited, previous time period; yet much of the evidence and arguments in insanity cases are based on a considerably broader time frame.

Another issue associated with extending the time frame involves hypothesizing about the future. One myth about the insanity defense is that it is raised in cases that involve only violent crimes—a misconception that is fueled by media coverage of rare and dramatic cases (Perlin, 1995). If operating under such an assumption, jurors might be concerned about the possibility of the defendant committing violent acts in the future. When this misguided belief is tied to another insanity misconception (e.g., that NGRI defendants are quickly released), jurors might eschew the NGRI verdict out of fear that the defendant will be released early and pose a danger to society (Perlin, 1995).

Accounts

The choice to disjoin or unify accounts of the case is the second interpretive construct. A decision must be made about whether all the relevant facts embody a single incident or separate incidents. Time framing is related to this interpretive construct; choice of time frame determines which accounts are deemed relevant to the case. A broader time frame encompasses more accounts, and the categorization of these accounts influences attributions of causality. The perceived causal chain of events dictates the causal inferences that can be drawn. Unifying or disjoining accounts directly affect this progression, resulting in various opinions regarding causal links. In insanity cases, a pivotal issue is whether the cause of the crime can be attributed to the defendant's mental illness or free will.

Unifying accounts attenuate the causal relationship between mental illness and the alleged offense. Disjoining the same accounts leads decision makers to infer causal links among independent elements of the incident. This view fosters the interpretation that mental illness was the proximate cause of the offense and benefits the NGRI defendant by supporting the argument that the criminal act was attributable to mental illness.

Intent

The third interpretive construct addresses intent and how broadly or narrowly the act is defined. A narrow interpretation of intent assumes that the defendant committed only the specific criminal act in question. Alternatively, a broad interpretation assumes that the same criminal act is one in a broader category of intended actions. A broad view of intent encompasses a wider range of defendant actions or motivations, lessening the degree of intention directed at a particular goal or act, and viewing the acts as instances of a more generalized intention.

A common argument in insanity cases is that defendants could not intend to act in the manner they did as mental illness robbed them of their free will (Martin & Weiss, 2010). By employing a narrow definition of intent, the prosecution could argue that a defendant failed to appreciate the moral wrongfulness of their actions or might have thought that their actions were morally justified, but they still intended to commit the act. An example of this argument can be found in the case of Andrea Yates, who claimed to have genuinely believed that murdering her children was the (morally correct) will of God. She intended to engage in these actions in order to fulfill a powerful moral obligation. However, soon after the murders occurred, she called 911, and her communications to the emergency operator suggested that she was aware that murdering her children was wrong. The prosecution argued that Andrea Yates possessed *mens rea*, and therefore she failed to meet the insanity standard (i.e., her mental illness did not diminish her responsibility for the act) (Huss, 2002).

Advances in neuroscience might contribute to determinations of criminal responsibility by "[focusing] on the extent to which [brain scan evidence] could be used to reduce responsibility, not to establish it" (Aharoni, Frank, Sinnott-Armstrong, & Gazzaniga, 2008, p. 149). Neuroscience research is relevant to the insanity defense in its explorations of how intentionality can be inferred from images of the living brain. Such evidence could demonstrate how deficiencies in functioning are related to the appreciation of wrongfulness, a basic prong of the insanity defense. Experts warn against the possibility of abusing neuroscientific evidence, such as making claims that are unsupported by laboratory findings (Aharoni et al., 2008). The potential for neuroscience research to inform court decisions suggests the need to bridge the gap between legal and scientific concepts and to explore further the use of scientific evidence in insanity cases.

Views of the Defendant

The view of a defendant is the fourth interpretive construct. Defendants can be considered as representatives of a larger group based on their age, ethnicity, and gender. Defendants also can be judged by the specific traits or idiosyncrasies that differentiate the individual from others. An example of a broad view of a defendant would be categorizing the individual according to the schema of an "insane" person, rather than focusing on the defendant's individual characteristics. The adoption of this perspective perpetuates the stereotypes and myths associated with insanity as a legal defense (Perlin, 1995). An even broader view would be to classify the defendant as an "average" person. Holding the defendant to the "reasonable person standard" lowers the saliency of the unique mental capacities or aberrations of the defendant, which is a disadvantage for defense attorneys seeking to characterize the defendant as exempt from this standard of accountability.

Adopting a narrow view of the defendant focuses on individual traits and characteristics. Clinical assessments are employed as a vehicle for presenting evidence that the defendant is a member of the "legally insane population." As mentioned above, an insanity designation allows defendants to escape the broader standards of criminal responsibility that are applied to a "reasonable person." When defendants are found NGRI, their culpability is removed.

Summary

The insanity defense is rooted in ancient beliefs and proto-legal practices that recognized the need to consider the accused individual's state of mind during the commission of a crime when rendering decisions about culpability. This basic principle serves as the foundation for the insanity defense and is incorporated in some fashion into the primary legal standards that determine whether a defendant is NGRI. Insanity is an elusive and variegated concept. Modern legal standards related to the insanity defense differ among states and between state and federal statutes as well. These differences affect the degree to which the insanity defense can be successfully proffered. These standards have been repeatedly refined in order to increase their stringency or to tie them more closely to legal (e.g., the burden and standard of proof) and/or clinical concerns (e.g., the effects of mental illness on thinking, understanding, and behavioral control).

Predicated on the wild beast test and focused on cognitions (i.e., the defendant's mental capacity to comprehend), the M'Naghten Rule is the prototype for most modern standards of insanity. M'Naghten requires a lack of understanding of the act or its consequences in order to lead to a NGRI verdict. In response to critiques claiming M'Naghten's overemphasis on cognitive formulations, the irresistible impulse test was incorporated into existing M'Naghten standards as well as other legal formulations of insanity. Stemming from the insanity criteria adopted in New Hampshire, the Durham Test was decidedly clinical in its orientation, judging insanity on the basis of whether the crime was a direct product of psychiatric illness. Durham was assailed due to its inordinate dependence on expert witness opinions about vague judgments (i.e., the defendant's "state of mind"). The ALI legal standards (the Brawner Rule) were crafted to incorporate elements of M'Naghten, the Irresistible Impulse Test, and the Durham (Product) Rule.

Throughout history, case precedents have been the impetus for the creation, revision, and codification of insanity standards. Public outcries over insanity acquittals have also spurred the revision of insanity standards. Other than M'Naghten, Hinckley was the most influential case in terms of raising the standards and changing the criminal procedures pertaining to insanity trials. The outcome of the Hinckley trial triggered and intensified public misconceptions of insanity verdicts. The insanity defense is used sparingly and usually rejected. Most NGRI acquittees are seriously mentally ill and serve longer terms of confinement than non-NGRI convicted felons; the former are no more likely than the latter to recidivate or commit violent crimes.

The backlash following the Hinckley acquittal led Congress to pass the Insanity Defense Reform Act, which returned the standards to the strict and narrow M'Naghten Rule, shifted the burden of proof to the defense, and increased the standard of proof to clear and convening evidence. The GBMI verdict is an option that recognizes that defendants can be mentally ill yet culpable in legal terms for their criminal behaviors. The addition of GBMI appeared to complicate the decision-making process without reducing the number of NGRI cases and without providing jurors with a viable, meaningful, intermediate option between guilty and NGRI. As reported in the findings of mock jury research—a paradigm employed to simulate juror decision-making in insanity cases—the rendering of NGRI and GBMI verdicts are more complicated and subjective than previously understood.

In conclusion, despite its firmly entrenched, age-old position in criminal law and procedure, the insanity defense remains mostly misunderstood and presents serious challenges to the jurors and judges who are entrusted with the task of deciding the fate of insanity defendants. These challenges are inherent in attempts to comprehend the unfathomable effects of brain diseases on complicated human judgments and behaviors. The law too is complicated on these questions, and the interface of criminal responsibility and psychopathology is still mostly *terra incognito*, especially for most jurors who lack knowledge and sophistication in either arena. As illustrated by the rugged history of insanity cases, there might never be an easy remedy to untangle the complexities of the NGRI verdicts and no easy way to sate the public's fascination with lurid criminal cases or alleviate their unfounded distrust and fear of NGRI acquittees.

References

Aharoni, E., Funk, C., Sinnott-Armstrong, W., & Gazzaniga, M. (2008). Can neurological evidence help courts assess criminal responsibility? Lessons from law and neuroscience. *Annals of the New York Academy of Sciences, 1124*, 145–160.

American Law Institute (1985). *Model penal code and commentaries* (official draft and revised comments). Sec. 4.01. Philadelphia, PA: Author.

American Psychiatric Association. (1983). *Statement on the insanity defense*. Arlington, VA: Author.

Bartol, A. (1993). *Before and after Hinckley: Evaluating insanity defense reform*. New York: Guilford Press.

Boehnert, C. (1989). Characteristics of successful and unsuccessful insanity pleas. *Law and Human Behavior, 13*, 31–40.

Borum, R., & Fulero, S. M. (1999). Empirical research on the insanity defense and attempted reforms: Evidence toward informed policy. *Law and Human Behavior, 17*, 157–166.

Borum, R., & Grisso, T. (1996). Establishing standards for crimianl forensic reports: An empirical analysis. *Bulletin of the American Academy of Psychiatry and the Law, 24*, 297–317.

Bower, B. (1984). Not popular by reason of insanity. *Science News, 126*, 218–219.

Braff, J., Arvanites, T., & Steadman, H. J. (1983). Detention patterns of successful and unsuccessful insanity defendants. *Criminology, 21*, 439–448.

Callahan, L. A., McGreevy, M. A., Cirincione, C., & Steadman, H. J. (1992). Measuring the effects of the guilty but mentally ill (GBMI) verdict: Georgia's 1982 GBMI reform. *Law and Human Behavior, 16*, 447–462.

Callahan, L. A., Steadman, H. J., McGreevy, M. A., & Robbins, P. C. (1991). The volume and characteristics of insanity defense pleas: An eight-state study. *Bulletin of the American Academic of Psychiatry and Law, 19*, 331–338.

Caplan, L. (1984). *The insanity defense and the trial of John W. Hinckley Jr*. Boston, MA: Godine Publishing.

Cirincione, C., Steadman, H. J., & McGreevy, M. A. (1995). Rates of insanity acquittals and the factors associated with successful insanity pleas. *Bulletin of the American Academy and the Law, 23*, 399–409.

Cochrane, R. E., Grisso, T., & Frederick, R. I. (2001). The relationship between criminal charges, diagnoses, and psychological options among federal pretrial defendants. *Behavioral Science and the Law, 19*, 565–582.

Costanzo, M. (2004). *Psychology applied to law*. Belmont, CA: Wadsworth.

Davis, D. A. (1995). *The Jeffrey Dahmer story: An American nightmare*. New York: St. Martin's Press.

Dalby, J. T. (2006). The case of Daniel M'Naghten: Let's get the story straight. *American Journal of Forensic Psychiatry, 27*, 17–32.

Elliott, C. (1996). *The rules of insanity: Moral responsibility and the mentally ill offender*. New York: SUNY Press.

Finkel, J. N., & Handel, S. F. (1989). How jurors construe "insanity." *Law and Human Behavior, 13*, 41–59.

Fradella, H. F. (2008). *Forensic psychology: The use of behavioral science in civil and criminal justice*. Mason, OH: Cengage.

Garrison, A. H. (1998). The history of the M'Naghten insanity defense and the use of posttraumatic stress disorder as a basis of insanity. *American Journal of Forensic Psychology, 16*, 39–88.

Gerald, R. (1997). The evolution of the insanity defense: Welcome to the twilight zone of mental illness, psychiatry, and the law. *Journal of Contemporary Criminal Justice, 13*, 224–243.

Halleck, S. (1987). *The mentally disordered offender*. Washington, DC: American Psychiatric Press.

Hans, V. P., & Slater, D. (1983). John Hinckley Jr. and the insanity defense: The public's verdict. *Public Opinion Quarterly, 47*, 202–212.

Heider, F. (1958). *The psychology of interpersonal relations*. New York: Wiley.

Heilbrun, K. S., Heilbrun, P., & Griffin, N. (1988). Comparing females acquitted by reason of insanity, convicted, and civilly committed in Florida: 1977–1984. *Law and Human Behavior, 12*, 295–312.

Hermann, D. H. J. (1997). *Mental health and disability law*. Eagen, MN: WestLaw.

Huss, M. T. (2009). *Forensic psychology: Research, clinical practice, and applications*. Malden, MA: Wiley-Blackwell.

Insanity Defense Working Group. (1983). American Psychiatric Association statement on the insanity defense. *American Journal of Psychiatry, 22*, 2949–2950.

Jeffrey, R. W., & Pasewark, R. A. (1983). Altering opinions about the insanity plea. *Journal of Psychiatry and Law, 11*, 29–40.

Kelman, M. (1981). Interpretive construction and the substantive criminal law. *Stanford Law Review, 33*, 591–673.

Kravitz, H. H., & Kelly, J. (1999). An outpatient psychiatry program for offenders with mental disorders found not guilty by reasons of insanity. *Psychiatric Services, 50*, 1597–1605.

Lunde, D. T., & Morgan, J. (1980). *The die song: A journey into the mind of a mass murderer*. New York: Norton.

Martin, E., & Weiss, K. J. (2010). Knowing moral and legal wrong in an insanity defense. *Journal of the American Academy of Psychiatry and the Law, 38*, 286–288.

McGraw, B., Farthin-Capowich, D., & Keilitz, I. (1985). The guilty but mentally ill plea and verdict: Current state of knowledge. *Villanova Law Review, 30*, 117–191.

Melton, G. B., Petrila, J., Poythress, N. G., & Slobogin, C. (1997). *Psychological evaluations for the court*. New York: Guilford Press.

Melville, J. D., & Naimark, D. (2002). Punishing the insane: The verdict of guilty but mentally ill. *Journal of the American Academy of Psychiatry and Law, 30*, 553–555.

Moran, R. (1981). *Knowing right from wrong: The insanity defense of Daniel McNaughtan*. New York: Free Press.

Moriarty, J. C. (2001). *The role of mental illness in criminal trials: The insanity defense*. New York: Routledge.

Nicholson, R. A. (1999). Forensic assessment. In R. Roesch, S. D. Hart, & J. R. Ogloff (Eds.), *Psychology and law: The state of the discipline* (pp. 122–173). New York: Kluwer Academic/Plenum.

Nicholson, R. A., Norwood, S., & Enyart, C. (1991). Characteristics and outcomes of insanity acquittees in Oklahoma. *Behavioral Sciences and the Law, 9*, 487–500.

Ogloff, J. R. P. (1991). A comparison of insanity defense standards on juror decision-making. *Law and Human Behavior, 15*, 509–531.

Perlin, M. (1995). The jurisprudence of the insanity defense. *Journal of Legal Medicine, 16*, 453–459.

Perlin, M. L. (1994). *The jurisprudence of the insanity defense*. Durham, NC: Carolina Academic Press.

Perlin, M. L. (1996). Myths, realities, and the political world: The anthropology of insanity defense attitudes. *Bulletin of the American Academy of Psychiatry and the Law, 24*, 5–26.

Platt, A. M., & Diamond, B. L. (1965). The origins and development of the "wild beast" concept of mental illness and its relation to theories of criminal responsibility. *Journal of the History of Behavioral Sciences, 1*, 355–367.

Reznek, L. (1997). *Evil or ill?* New York: Routledge.

Roberts, C. F., & Golding, S. L. (1991). The social construction of criminal responsibility and insanity. *Law and Human Behavior, 15*, 349–376.

Roberts, C. F., Sargent, E. L., & Chan, A. S. (1993). Verdict selection processes in insanity cases: Juror construals and the effects of guilty but mentally ill instructions. *Law and Human Behavior, 17*, 261–275.

Rodriguez, J., LeWinn, L., & Perlin, M. L. (1983). The insanity defense under siege: Legislative assaults and legal rejoinders. *Rutgers Law Journal, 14*, 397–430.

Rogers, R. (1986). *Conducting insanity evaluations*. New York: Van Nostrand.
Rogers, R., & Cavanaugh, J. L. (1981). Rogers criminal responsibility assessment scales. *Illinois Medical Journal, 160*, 164–169.
Rogers, R., Wasyliw, O. E., & Cavanaugh, J. L. (1984). Evaluating insanity: A study of construct validity. *Law and Human Behavior, 8*, 293–303.
Sales, B. D., & Hafemeister, T. (1984). Empiricism and legal policy on the insanity defense. In L. A. Teplin (Ed.), *Mental health and criminal justice* (pp. 253–278). Newbury Park, CA: Sage.
Shaver, K. G. (1985). *The attribution of blame: Causality, responsibility, and blameworthiness*. New York: Springer-Verlag.
Silver, E. (1995). Punishment or treatment? Comparing the lengths of confinement of successful and unsuccessful insanity defendants. *Law and Human Behavior, 19*, 375–388.
Silver, E., Cirincione, C., & Steadman, H. J. (1994). Demythologizing inaccurate perceptions of the insanity defense. *Law and Human Behavior, 18*, 63–70.
Slobogin, C., Melton, G., & Showalter, S. R. (1984). The feasibility of a brief evaluation on mental state at the time of the offense. *Law and Human Behavior, 8*, 305–321.
Slovenko, R. (1994). *Psychiatry and criminal culpability*. New York: John Wiley & Sons.
Weiner, B. A. (1985). The insanity defense: Historical development and present status. *Behavioral Science and the Law, 3*, 3–35.
Weiner, B. (2004). On responsibility inferences and the perceived moral person. *International Journal of Existential Psychology and Psychotherapy, 1*, 66–73.
Winslade, W. J., & Ross, J. W. (1983). *The insanity plea*. New York: Scribner's.
Wrightsman, L. S., Greene, E., Nietzel, M. T., & Fortune, W. H. (2002). *Psychology and the legal system* (5th ed.). Belmont, CA: Wadsworth.
Wrightsman, L. S., Nietzel, M. T., & Fortune, W. H. (1998). *Psychology and the legal system* (4th ed.). Pacific Grove, CA: Brooks/Cole.
Zapf, P. A., Golding, S. L., & Roesch, R. (2006). Criminal responsibility and the insanity defense. In I. B. Weiner & A. K. Hess (Eds.), *The handbook of forensic psychology* (pp. 332–363). New York: Wiley.

CHAPTER FOURTEEN

The Psychology of Criminal Behavior and Sentencing

Olaoluwa Olusanya

Modern theories to explain criminal behavior are diverse and include biological theories (Mednick, Gabrielli, & Hutchings, 1987; Raine, Buchsbaum, & LaCasse, 1997; Wilson & Herrnstein, 1985), psychological theories (Blackburn, 1992; Caspi et al., 1994; Eysenck, 1977, 1998; Farrington, 1994) and sociological theories (Agnew, 1985, 1992; Bursik, 1984; Bursik & Webb 1982; Cohen, 1955; Cloward & Ohlin, 1960; Merton, 1938; Wolfgang & Ferracuti, 1967). All of these theories are based on the positivist tradition (Greene et al., 2007; Vold et al., 2002, p. 27). In addition, to some extent these theories interact and overlap each other, but each has its own identity. The present chapter is however concerned with psychological perspectives on criminal behavior—that is, the assumption that personality traits are associated with criminal behavior (Blackburn, 1992; Caspi et al., 1994; Farrington, 1994; Eysenck, 1977, 1998). This chapter shall also focus on sentencing. In this respect, there are five main purposes of sentencing: punishment, crime reduction, reform and rehabilitation, public protection, and reparation. The use of risk/needs instruments is the dominant approach to offender sentencing (Andrews & Bonta, 2006). The risk/need model focuses primarily on utilitarian goals of sentencing (Hannah-Moffat, 2010, p. 9). These goals seek to reduce the crime level by preventing reoffending and protecting the community (Andrews & Bonta, 2006).

However, it can be maintained that psychological theories of criminal behavior also reflect retributive aims. This is because, the process of working to change the faulty thinking patterns that lead an individual to criminal behavior often beings with the admission of wrongdoing or guilt, and the commitment to changing his ways. Here the criminal is said to suffer the "pain of remorse." As stated by Meyer (2005), "[l]ike retribution, remorse is a boomerang of the crime. The offender gets his own law thrust back upon himself, to experience for himself the pain of the crime."

Finally, the forthcoming discussion is divided into several main parts. The first section will focus on the term "criminal behavior" and will discuss problems of definition. This approach is important because identifying a universal definition is a prerequisite for differentiating between criminal actions and noncriminal actions. It follows that in the absence of a common definition of "criminal behavior," the fact that someone does something "wrong" does not necessarily mean that he is a criminal—one man's criminal is another man's law-abiding citizen. The second section will discuss competing models of criminal behavior. In this respect, the rational actor assumption, a derivative of the classical school of criminology as conceptualized by Beccaria (1764/1986) undergirds the criminal law's approach to criminal behavior. From this perspective, fear of punishment is viewed as a sufficient disincentive to crime. In contrast, the positivist school has attempted to find scientific objectivity for the measurement and quantification of criminal behavior. The assumption here is that dealing with the offense rather than treating the offender will result in a failure to address criminogenic needs—that is, those areas that are found to be strong predictors of criminal behavior, such as antisocial attitudes and beliefs, procriminal associates, temperament and impulsiveness, familial-marital-dysfunctional relationship, and alcohol and other drug use. In the third section, two contrasting models of sentencing are examined: the determinate sentencing model—a fixed-term sentence pronounced by a judge—and the indeterminate sentencing model—the prison term imposed after conviction for a crime, which does not state a specific period of time or release date. The final section presents an integrated framework for cognitive-behavior modification.

Criminal Behavior: Problems of Definition

Defining criminal behavior[1] is a prerequisite for distinguishing between criminal actions and noncriminal actions. Therefore, acts such as murder, rape, robbery, aggravated assault, burglary, larceny-theft, motor vehicle theft, and arson should be "repulsive to all people at all times and in all places." However, a number of obstacles impede efforts to define criminal behavior—these include cultural variation, logical inconsistency of crimes, and measurement and normative judgment (Greer & Hagan, 2001, p. 208).

In addition, Greer, and Hagan (2001) have identified seven approaches to delimiting "much of sociology's response to crime and deviance" (p. 208). They are:

1) A legal-consensus definition
2) A socio-legal definition
3) A cross-cultural definition
4) A statistical definition
5) A labeling definition
6) A human rights definition
7) A utopian definition

It is beyond the scope of this chapter to examine all of these approaches; however, this section offers a relatively brief discussion of the legal-consensus definition and the cross-cultural definition.

From the perspective of a legal-consensus definition, criminal behavior is an act that violates criminal law and may consequently be punishable through criminal proceedings. As stated by Glanville Williams, "a crime is an act capable of being followed by criminal proceedings having a criminal outcome." Another definition of crime is that provided by Tappan: "an intentional act in violation of the criminal law, committed without defence or excuse and penalised by the state" (quoted in Greer & Hagan, 2001, p. 208).

However, the legal-consensus definition has several shortcomings (Greer & Hagan, 2001, p. 208). For instance, as pointed out by Greer and Hagan (2001, p. 208), one of the main limitations of the legal-consensus definition is that "being legally called a criminal depends on being caught and convicted. This sampling process results in not only a narrowly defined but also a non representative collection of subjects for study."

The above statement highlights a major flaw in trait-based approaches. In this respect a number of research efforts claimed to have found an association between the personality traits identified by Eysenck (1998)—that is, psychoticism, extraversion, and neuroticism (PEN)—and repeat and chronic criminal offending (1977, 1998). Eysenck and Gudjonsson (1989) maintained that delinquents could be characterized by a homogeneous high PEN profile. From this perspective criminality was interpreted as an individual failing or defect (Rafter, 2006, p. 46). However, to the extent that being labeled a criminal is subject to luck (or possibly to other factors such as race) in not being caught and convicted, is it fair to divide people into piles of good people or bad people? After all, as stated by Cole and Smith (2007), "[s]elf-report studies, in which people are asked to report on their own criminal behavior, have shown that nearly everyone has committed a crime, although most are never caught" (p. 24; see, e.g., Elliott et al., 1985). Also as pointed out by Zhang, Benson, and Deng (2000), "[o]fficial statistics are often thought to reflect police activities and therefore tend to underestimate the 'true' level of crime. Even when serious crimes are involved (such as armed robbery, burglary, and auto theft) chances of ever being detected are still slim, about 2 out of every 10 violations" (p. 284). It follows that those who carry the label "CRIMINAL" could simply be viewed as "unsuccessful" offenders instead of bad people.

Finally, the cross-cultural definition is a second approach that deserves consideration. The cross-cultural definition postulates that "some conduct norms are *invariant* across *all* cultural groups" (Greer & Hagan, 2001, p. 209). However, according to Phillipson (1971), the temporal and cultural relativity of "crime" ensures that "there is no one behavioral entity which we can call crime, there is no behavior which is always and everywhere criminal" (p. 5). It follows that the position of acts such as maternal infanticide, rape, prostitution, use of cocaine, incest, and murder and the law varies widely, reflecting different social norms and structures and social costs and benefits. For instance the act of infanticide is viewed as one of the most terrible crimes in the United States. "A woman convicted of infanticide in the U.S. judicial system may face a long prison sentence or even the death penalty" (Spinelli, 2004, pp. 1549–1550). In contrast, in the United Kingdom and in 29 other countries, it is treated as a relatively minor crime. The UK Infanticide Act 1938 made infanticide a less severe crime than it had been previously and mandated sentences of probation and psychiatric treatment for women who were found guilty (Spinelli, 2004).

Competing Models of Criminal Behavior

The Classical Model

The classical school of criminology focuses on the criminal act and not on the criminal. Its origins can be traced to the works of social contract theorists such as Rousseau, Beccaria, Bentham, Feurbach, and Maudsley, who refuted the notion of a necessary connection between law and morality (see generally, Cavender, 1981).

In addition, the social contract theory as derived from the works of Hobbes, Montesquieu, Rousseau, Rawls, and Beccaria presupposes that each one of us is an active contracting party. In other words, we are autonomous, rational, and able to act as moral agents. Individuals who fulfill these requirements give up some personal liberties in exchange for certain kinds of protection of stability (see Cavender, 1981). Thus, from the perspective of the classical school, the decision to engage in crime is based on the anticipated balance of pain and pleasure (Jeffery, 1956, p. 663). Emphasis is therefore placed on the free will of criminals and on making punishment proportional to the objective harm caused by the crime.

However, the main limitation of the classical school is its rigidity. For instance, Cesare Becarria "argued that all people who violated a specific law should receive identical punishments regardless of the circumstances surrounding the case, such as age, sex, wealth, and state of mind" (Jeffery, 1956, p. 663). Beccaria's statement is symptomatic of the weakness in the classical approach. As pointed out by Friedman et al. (2009), "[s]entences aimed at punishment without an understanding of the different types of ... offenders and their potential for successful treatment fail to promote the goals of sentencing set forth in 18 U.S.C. § 3553(a)."

Furthermore, Beccaria's ideology appears to influence judicial decision-making to some extent. In this respect, it has been maintained that judges have eschewed attempts to integrate psychological research with relevant legal analysis (see e.g., Jones, 2003, 1034–1035). In addition, Hall (1960), for instance, is of the opinion that behavioral science is incompatible with criminal law. He made the following relevant statement in this respect:

> [Psychiatry] purports to be rigorously scientific and therefore takes a determinist position. Its view of human nature is expressed in terms of drives and dispositions which, like mechanical forces, operate in accordance with universal laws of causation. On the other hand, criminal law ... is not a theoretical science whose sole concern is to understand and describe what goes on. It is, instead, a practical, normative science which, while it draws upon the empirical sciences, is also concerned to pass judgment on human conduct. (pp. 1121–1122)

Finally, the main explanations for forgoing the breadth and complexity essential to theoretical perspectives on blame, responsibility, and punishment in favor of practical perspectives centered on freewill concepts that are approachable and decipherable as exemplified by the classical school are that the latter approach allows for "easy administration of justice, solves any tension that might exist between deterministic science and normative criminal justice theory" (Jones, 2003, p. 1036) and provides rationalization for the infliction of punishment on an offender.

The Positivist Model

Psychological models of crime and criminal behavior are a legacy of the positivist school of criminology or the Italian school of criminology which was founded by Cesare Lombroso, Enrico Ferri, and Raffaele Garofalo (Falcón Y Tella & Falcón Y Tella, 2006, p. 183).

In addition, the positivist school of criminology gained prominence during the late nineteenth century and encouraged new methods for studying crime. These new techniques involved the scientific study of the mind, the body, and the environment of the offender. The focus shifted from the crime to the criminal. Therefore, contrary to the basic tenets of classicism—namely, that individuals have the ability to make certain choices on their own—the positivist school posited that factors causing crime are often well beyond the individual's control.

Perhaps the central question here is the following: Do individuals differ in terms of their propensity for criminal behavior? Disagreement among researchers exists about the mechanisms that produce behavioral continuity. Three contrasting perspectives have emerged (Piquero, Farrington, Nagin, & Moffitt, 2010). Criminal propensity theories emphasize the persistence of individual differences in the likelihood of committing criminal acts (Nagin & Paternoster, 1991, 2000). In this respect, Gottfredson and Hirschi (1990) have advanced the "persistent heterogeneity" explanation. According to this explanation criminal behavior is largely ingrained and unchangeable. From this perspective, static factors that are associated with future offending place the offender at a serious disadvantage as they are unchangeable and are bound to history.

In contrast to the above views are state-dependent theories (Nagin & Paternoster, 1991, 2000) postulating that life events can have a strong causal effect on future behavior (Sampson & Laub, 1993). State-dependent theories "are dynamic in that they both allow for a causal effect of prior on future behavior and are compatible with the idea that changes in life circumstances can affect one's proclivity to offend." (Paternoster, Dean, Piquero, Mazerolle, & Brame, 1997, p. 234).

Yet a third perspective has been to incorporate both persistent-heterogeneity and state-dependence factors—in other words, a mixed model. This new perspective "ascribes importance to both heterogeneity and state-dependence processes, with the exposition of two distinct offender groups, adolescence-limited and life course–persistent offenders, for whom the persistent-heterogeneity and state-dependence processes play out differently" (Ousey & Wilcox, 2007).

Furthermore, psychological theories of criminal behavior are more closely aligned with mixed models that ascribe importance to both heterogeneity and state-dependence processes. In addition, the psychology of criminal behavior addresses the thought processes that result in deviant acts and the motivations that drive them. In this respect, two processes are distinguishable: cognition processes view criminal behavior as emanating from faulty thinking patterns. Examples of such faulty thinking patterns include deficits in self-control, problem solving, social perspective taking, and critical thinking (McCann, Ivanoff, Schmidt, & Beach, 2007, p. 135). From this perspective, changing the way offenders think is the key to changing their criminal behavior (e.g., Sweet & Loizeaux, 1991, p. 161).

In contrast, social learning processes hold that an individual learns criminal behaviors from watching and imitating the antisocial behavior of offenders and receiving their approval (Bandura, 1969; Meichenbaum, 1977). In addition, an individual's level of moral disengagement can be affected by the social structures within which the person operates, such as family (Patterson, 1984, 1986) and friends (Dishion, Capaldi, Spracklen, & Li, 1995). Thus individuals can learn that " 'It's OK to steal if [they] need money' and 'It's okay to steal something if that's the only way [they] could ever get it' " (Esbensen & Weerman, 2005, p. 22). It follows that through repeated, negative, reinforcements, individuals' cognitions and sentiments become habitual. Also, once habitual patterns of behavior are well learned, they become very hard to change.

Contrasting Sentencing Models

Over the past 20 years, there has been a lack of focus in U.S. federal government policy on judicial sentencing authority. Federal government policy on judicial sentencing authority has oscillated between the policy of sentencing discretion and that of mandatory sentencing guidelines. Finally, in this section, federal government policy on judicial sentencing authority is divided into three periods: before the enactment of the Sentencing Reform Act (SRA; 1984); during the period when the SRA took effect (1984–2004); and post *Booker* (2005).

Indeterminate Sentencing (Pre-1984)

Prior to the Sentencing Reform Act (1984), judges had broad discretion to impose sentences in federal cases. Between 1880 and 1899, seven states passed indeterminate sentencing laws (Nagel, 1990, 894). From 1900 to 1911, another 21 states followed suit. By the 1960s, every state in the nation gave judges wide discretion to determine the appropriate sentence under an indeterminate sentencing system (Nagel, 1990, 894).

In addition, under the rehabilitation model, indeterminate sentencing granted judges the power to impose any sentence from probation to the statutory maximum applicable to the offense of conviction. The original philosophy of indeterminate sentencing structures was that most criminals could be rehabilitated, and that this goal required an individualized approach to sentencing and sentencing flexibility.

However, unfettered judicial discretion resulted in unacceptably wide variations in sentences imposed on different convicted offenders for the same crime. One explanation for these variations is that judges based their sentencing decisions on whatever information they deemed relevant and were able to shape the outcome of a case based on personal biases. By the 1970s, criticism of indeterminate sentencing began to grow. Judge Frankel, a former federal district judge in New York, became one of the foremost critics of the indeterminate sentencing system (1973). He maintained that the indeterminate sentencing systems produced disparities in sentencing and that the variance was attributable to the primary judge effect (1972, p. 54) what he termed as "character, bias, neurosis, and daily vagary" (1973, p. 21).

Furthermore, rehabilitation theory, a corollary of indeterminate sentencing, faced a myriad of issues and problems in the late 1970s that led to its demise as the dominant ideology. These issues included claims attributed to Martinson's report, that corrections was not rehabilitating offenders and the discriminatory treatment of minority offenders who were treated unfairly under indeterminate sentencing structures (MacKenzie, 2006, p. 58). In relation to the discriminatory treatment of minority offenders, earlier findings of studies on judicial discretion exercised at sentencing suggested that extra-legal variables such as race (Green, 1961, 1964), gender (Nagel & Weitzman, 1971), and socioeconomic status (Hagan, Nagel, & Albonetti, 1980) exerted a significant and rather strong direct impact on sentences. However research findings on the effects of race, gender, and socioeconomic status on sentencing have been inconsistent. For example, in relation to race, Bernstein, Cardascia, and Ross (1977) found that black defendants receive less severe sentences than white defendants at sentencing. In terms of gender, other studies have found that women are sentenced more harshly than males, especially when they violate traditional sex-role expectations as well as expectations for law-abiding behavior (e.g., Bernstein et al., 1977, p. 379). Also in relation to the issue of socioeconomic status, other research (e.g., Burke & Turk, 1975) failed to find a significant effect of socioeconomic status on sentence severity.

Another related problem is the problem of bias in racial differences in DSM diagnosis. For instance, several studies show that African American inmates tend to be assigned more severe mental health diagnoses in comparison to whites even when they exhibit similar symptoms (Strakowski, Shelton, & Kolbrener, 1993; Strakowski et al, 1996). Minsky and colleagues (2003) found that African Americans were diagnosed as having a disorder in the schizophrenic disorders spectrum more frequently than did Latinos and European Americans. The study also found that Latinos were disproportionately diagnosed as having major depression, despite the fact that significantly higher levels of psychotic symptoms were self-reported by Latinos. They attributed the higher rates of depression in Latinos to "cultural variances in characteristic symptom clusters typically used by clinicians as a template for assigning a diagnosis in a treatment setting (p. 643). Also, Neighbors, Jackson, Campbell, and Williams (1989) have maintained that the clinicians' different interpretations of symptoms exhibited by blacks and whites could result from sociocultural distance between clinicians and minority patients.

The other major issue raised in Martinson's report (1974) was that corrections were not rehabilitating offenders. Martinson evaluated 231 studies of treatment programs conducted between 1945 and 1967 (Cullen & Gendreau, 1989). From this research, Martinson arrived at the conclusion that "with few and isolated exceptions the rehabilitative efforts that have been reported so far have had no appreciable effects on recidivism" (1974, p. 25). In addition, it should be noted that escalating crime rates, accompanied by a groundswell of public opinion against the perceived leniency of the rehabilitative ideal, also contributed to the decline of the rehabilitative model (Friedman, 1993, p. 305).

It followed that by the mid-1970s, several states and the federal government abandoned indeterminate sentencing. The treatment era ended, largely because of widespread disenchantment with the rehabilitation model. A number of states abolished release on parole and replaced the indeterminate sentence with a determinate sentence. Retributive justice became the primary goal.

Presently indeterminate sentencing has reincarnated itself under a new name—risk-based sentencing (Andrews & Dowden, 2006). According to

Tonry (1999, p. 5), "[r]isk-based sentencing is in some ways a reconceptualization of indeterminate sentencing, but with the key difference that individualized assessments of risk are seen as being as much a means to achieve public safety as to facilitate offender rehabilitation."

There are two basic approaches to the risk assessment of violence or any other form of human behavior—clinical prediction and actuarial prediction. Clinical prediction draws on factors such as intuitive reasoning, previous experience, and judgment. In cases involving violence, this prediction is usually provided by a psychiatrist, and psychologists, but also by parole board members or judges. The factors considered important in assessing risk in a clinical assessment vary from case to case and lack temporal stability. These risk factors comprise of antisocial attitudes that are supportive of crime, personal demographic variables, and mental disabilities (Mann, 1995; Sutton, 1994). Combined, these individual-level characteristics give a picture of the offender and influence decisions about the potential risk and harm an offender may pose upon release. The U.S. Supreme Court has recognized the clinical method as a constitutionally valid measure for assessing risk (Litwack, Kirschner, & Wack, 1993).

In contrast to clinical prediction, actuarial prediction provides explicit rules for combining risk factors into specific probability estimates. The U.S. criminal justice system relies heavily on actuarial tools for assessing violence risk. For instance, in relation to parole decision-making examples of actuarial risk-assessment tools that have been relied upon include the Base Expectancy Score (Gottfredson & Bonds, 1961), the Level of Supervision Inventory (Andrews, 1982), the Salient Factor Score–Revised (Hoffman, 1983), and the Statistical Information on Recidivism (SIR) scale (Nuffield, 1989).

In addition, actuarial data can be used to identify a group of persons to be considered for possible civil commitment, For example, in *Kansas v. Hendricks*, the Supreme Court in 1997 upheld a sexually violent predator statute, which constitutes a form of civil commitment for certain former felons. By associating sexually violent behavior with mental illness, the Kansas Sexually Violent Predator Act is used to continue the confinement of certain sex offenders after they have finished serving their prison sentences.

Finally, in the sentencing phase of capital murder cases, psychiatric experts rely on an actuarial instrument, the Psychopathy Checklist–Revised (PCL-R), which is used to differentiate those who will be violent in the future from those who will not, to support expert testimony that a defendant will be a "continuing threat to society," even if incarcerated for the remainder of his or her life (Bersoff, 2002).

Mandatory Sentencing (1984–2004)

In 1984, under the Sentencing Reform Act (SRA), mandatory federal sentencing guidelines replaced judicial discretion, thereby heralding the switch from indeterminate to determinate sentencing schemes. In addition, Congress passed the Federal Sentencing Guidelines Act in 1984 to achieve two goals. The first goal was to ensure honesty in sentencing (U.S. Sentencing Guidelines Manual § 1A1.3, 2009). This concerns parole. Prior to the implementation of the federal sentencing guidelines, defendants could be released on parole, in some cases, after only one-third of the imposed sentence had been served. The SRA eliminated parole for federal prisoners and limited early release from prison for good behavior.

Furthermore, the second goal of the SRA was to reduce the huge disparities in sentencing (U.S. Sentencing Guidelines Manual § 1A1.3, 2009). This was achieved through the use of determinate sentencing. In addition, determinate sentencing schemes involve the setting of a fixed penalty for the commission of a criminal offense. Such schemes unduly limit judicial discretionary power to sentence offenders; therefore, judges lose control over sentencing and cannot apply discretion given the particular facts of a case. Moreover, the mechanics of the determinate sentencing process are as follows: "a jury finds facts that support a conviction. That conviction, in turn, authorizes the imposition of a sentence within a specified range, established either by statute or administrative guideline" (*United States v. Fruchter*).

It follows that, under the SRA, neither federal nor state judges can deviate from sentencing guidelines except when there are aggravating or mitigating circumstances that are not adequately covered in the guidelines. After making such departures from the guidelines, judges must justify them in writing. Moreover, the main purposes of determinate sentencing are retribution, deterrence, and incapacitation. Determinate sentencing is philosophically opposed to the rehabilitation model. As stated by Bunzel (1995): "The penal philosophy associated with determinate sentencing inescapably conflicts with the rehabilitative model: "There is room for punishment [i.e., retribution] ... in the treatment [i.e., rehabilitation] approach, but little room for treatment ... in the punitive approach' " (p. 950).

Starting with retribution, the fact that these guidelines aim to ensure the imposition of specific and identical sentences on defendants who violate the same law provides evidence of its retributive goal. As stated by Lowenthal (1993): "Determinate sentencing's principal goal has been the elimination of unwarranted disparity, with legislatures seeking proportional punishment for different offenses and consistent punishment for similar crimes" (p. 63). In terms of the incapacitative goal of determinate sentencing, the following theoretical explanation had been advanced by Roche (1999) citing Sherman et al. (1998): "The way mandatory sentencing attempts to prevent known offenders from offending is simple enough: 'for as long as offenders are incarcerated they clearly cannot commit crimes outside of prison.' "

Furthermore, since determinate sentencing aims to ensure that offenders who commit similar crimes should serve similar sentences, it accords relative importance to the goals of deterrence. This view is based on the assumption that if an offender knows there is a swift and severe punishment awaiting him if he commits the same offense, it may be reason enough for him to desist from reoffending in the long term as a result of fear. Thus fear of similar punishment acts as a motivator to desist from crime again (Akers, 2000; Gabor & Crutcher, 2002).

However, even though specific deterrence theorists maintain that recidivism would decline as the severity of the sanction increased (see, e.g., Dejong, 1997), studies into the deterrent effect of the Three Strikes law, which are based on aggregated crime data at three different levels (city, council, or state), have presented mixed and contradictory results (Chen, 2008). For instance, some studies have shown that the two- and three-strikes provisions of California's law resulted in significant deterrent effects on murder, assault, robbery, and burglary rates (Shepherd, 2002). In contrast, other studies found that the laws have resulted in an increase in homicides as offenders facing strikes sentences seek to evade law enforcement authorities or eliminate witnesses (Kovandzic, Sloan, & Vieraitis, 2002).

Moreover, the introduction of harsh determinate sentencing schemes, such as mandatory minimum sentences for drug offenses, "three strikes" statutes, and a panoply of other "get tough on crime" initiatives, have been controversial. More specifically, determinate sentencing schemes have had a devastating and disparate effect on African Americans and have resulted in racialized mass incarceration (Bobo & Thompson, 2010). For instance, it is widely accepted that Black Americans have been disproportionately affected by the war on drugs because African Americans tend to use crack more than powder cocaine; white Americans, on the other hand, are more likely to use powder cocaine (Bobo & Thompson, 2010, p. 335). However, the law does not equalize powder cocaine and crack cocaine. Previously under the mechanism known as the "100-to-1 drug ratio," crack cocaine was given 100 times the weight of powder cocaine. As a result, approximately 85% of defendants convicted of crack offenses in federal court were African American (USSC, 2002, pp. 102–103). Thus the severe sentences required by the 100-to-1 ratio were imposed primarily upon African American offenders. (Free, 1999, p. 514).

However, the assumption that African Americans are more likely to commit drug offenses is unsupported by empirical evidence. In this respect, drawing on statistics from the Office of National Drug Control Policy, Goldberg (2010) has maintained that "Whites use more than 70% of all illegal drugs, yet Blacks are seven times more likely to be sentenced to prison" (p. 86).

Furthermore, Three Strikes laws have been a source of great debate since their inception. Three Strikes laws are a type of selective incapacitation. These laws are defended under an incapacitative rationale because it is argued that these individuals are more likely to commit future crimes, so they should be held for longer periods of time. There is evidence that selective incapacitation has disproportionately affected African Americans and Hispanics (Ehlers, Schiraldi, & Lotke, 2004). Ehlers and his colleagues (2004) found that Three Strikes law had a racially disproportionate impact. Under the law, African Americans third strikers were 12 times more likely to be convicted and Latino third strikers were 40% more likely to be convicted compared to their Caucasian counterparts.

Moreover, it is important to note the contributions of psychology to the policy of selective incapacitation. Psychological theory predicts that individuals scoring low on Agreeableness and Conscientiousness, high on Extraversion, and a combination of low and high on Neuroticism would be classified as high-risk offenders (Lynam, Caspi, Moffitt, Loeber, & Stouthamer-Loeber, 2007). Furthermore, underlying this approach are typological theories that stress qualitative individual differences between offenders. These theories are based on the assumption that a large category of offenders engage in criminal activity only during adolescence, and only a small group of offenders persist in crime and remain criminally active far into adulthood. In addition, these theories postulate that distinct causal mechanisms are responsible for the criminal behavior of each group (see, e.g., Moffitt, 1993). From this perspective, life-course-persistent offenders differ from lower-level offenders on a range of characteristics. "They have an earlier onset, longer duration and higher offending frequency, and they also differ on social characteristics and psychological measures." (Skarðhamar, 2009, p. 863)

However, one problem for typological theories is that the argument that high-rate offenders are fundamentally different from other people relies on the "Big Five" model of personality (e.g., Heaven, 1996). The "Big Five" Personality Dimensions have been used to account for variance in reoffending. In this respect, only a few studies have examined the relationship between the Big Five and criminal recidivism (Corff & Toupin, 2009). For example, a study by Van Dam and colleagues (2005) involved a group of young male offenders in a juvenile detention centre in the Netherlands. The study explored the relationship between PEN profiles, delinquency, and recidivism in this sample of offenders. The aim of the study was to test Eysenck's hypothesis that delinquents score high on three basic Dimensions: Psychoticism, Extraversion, and Neuroticism (PEN model). Results from cluster analysis showed that only a small group of offenders had high scores on all three PEN dimensions. They concluded that the PEN profiles were not able to differentiate between recidivists and nonrecidivists. Similarly, Corff and Toupin (2009) concluded from their comparison of persistent juvenile delinquents and normative peers with the Five-Factor model that there was no significant difference between the groups (p. 1107).

In addition, there are several limitations of the Big Five-Factor Model of Personality. A thorough evaluation of these limitations is beyond the scope of this article (see Prinz, 2009, pp. 121–122). It suffices at this point to draw attention to criticisms of this model by McAdams (1992) who refers to this model as "essentially a 'psychology of the stranger' providing information about persons that one needs to know when one knows nothing else about them." According to McAdams (1992), a major limitation of the model lies in its "disregard of the contextual and conditional nature of human behavior and experience."

Furthermore, aside from limitations of taxonomy, selective incapacitation also faces limitations in terms of actuarial prediction of future criminal behavior. Those who favor the policy of selective incapacitation maintain that recidivism rates can be predicted and explained by a prior criminal record (see, e.g., Irish, 1989). They also argue that a prior criminal record provides a justification for increasing the penalty. However this viewpoint belies the fact that other factors such as type of offense, gender, race, education level, marital status, and employment status are all significantly associated with recidivism. For instance, Mears, Wang, Hay, and Bales (2008) found that the effects of race remained after controlling for individual-level risk factors for recidivism, including prior criminal record, educational background and incarceration profile (p. 313). This raises obvious ethical issues arising from increasing the punishment of those who belong to minority racial groups, the unemployed, the young, or those who grew up in a single-parent family (Sapir 2008, p. 260).

Finally, the ineffectiveness of "get tough on crime" policies has led to the realization that punitive correctional practices do not appear to have much overall deterrent effect on either habitual offenders or potential offenders from committing future crimes. In short, "there is no evidence that punitive correctional programs either reduce recidivism or produce other positive gains for offenders (Cullen & Gendreau, 2000, 161). In addition, the cost of deterring these crimes greatly exceeds the benefits to the state. For instance "The nonpartisan California Legislative Analyst's Office estimates that the state's Three Strikes policy currently costs approximately $500 million per year to implement, with expenses expected to escalate dramatically in the long run, even if the prison population does not expand further, due to aging of the inmate population and corresponding growth in medical expenses" (Chen, 2008, p. 364). These factors paved the way for the shift from retributive fixed sentencing toward rehabilitative indeterminate sentencing.

Mixed Determinate/Indeterminate Sentencing System Post *Booker* (2005–Present)

Until 2005, the United States Sentencing Guidelines were mandatory, and, except for extremely unusual circumstances, federal judges had no choice but to impose a sentence from within the Guideline range. In *United States v. Booker* (2005), a five-justice majority found that mandatory federal sentencing guidelines violated defendants' Sixth Amendment right to trial and rendered them advisory. *Booker* marked a departure from the "all or nothing" approach to sentencing. It resulted in the coexistence of judicial discretion and mandatory sentencing. "Accordingly, a post-*Booker* sentencing court has more options than a pre-*Booker* court. It can sentence within the Guidelines range, depart from the Guidelines as before, or apply a variance under § 3553(a)" (Brody, 2011, p. 2139).

Furthermore, it has become clear that the "all or nothing" approach to sentencing cannot succeed, since no monolithic sentencing system could possibly reduce recidivism effectively. For instance, in the subsequent quarter century since Martinson's critique, research has shown positive effects of offender treatment, and studies have confirmed the effectiveness of treatment in reducing recidivism (Cullen & Gendreau, 2000). In addition, offender treatment outcome studies in the context of meta-analysis reveal that some correctional interventions have achieved substantial reductions in recidivism (Cullen & Gendreau, 2000).

Finally, there is presently an increasing acknowledgment of the need to develop a more integrative approach to sentencing. Some states such as Maine have led the way in developing a more integrative approach to sentencing. These states rely on a mixed determinate/indeterminate sentencing system. Maine's "mixed determinate/ indeterminate sentencing system marks clear constitutional boundaries for sentencing judges while simultaneously ensuring the individualization of each defendant's sentence" (Gallini & Shults, 2006, p. 29). This means that it is able to ensure an individualized offender-oriented approach while at the same time prevent unwarranted sentencing disparities. Also in Washington State, "Determinate-Plus" sentencing is adopted for sex offenders convicted of certain sex offences who are subject to a life sentence in prison with discretionary release by the Indeterminate Sentencing Review Board. Determinate-Plus offenders are sentenced to both a determinate minimum and an indeterminate maximum sentence, where the maximum term of incarceration will be the statutory maximum for the offence (Barnoski, 2006).

Psychological Theories of Offender Rehabilitation

Presently there has been a shift toward rehabilitation in many Western correctional systems (Gendreau, 1996). In terms of understanding offender behavior change, three psychological theories have strong explanatory value (Birgden, 2002). The first is Festinger's (1957) cognitive-dissonance theory. According to this theory, individuals seek to ease or eradicate the discomfort of inconsistent beliefs and/or behavior by changing their beliefs (Draycott & Dabbs, 1998). The second is the concept of self-efficacy, which is rooted in Bandura's social cognitive theory. This concept affects cognition, emotion and behavior. Bandura (1992) stated that self-efficacy continues to grow throughout life as people acquire new skills, experiences, and understanding. A third theory is that of decisional balance, which involves weighing the pros and cons of changing (Janis & Mann, 1985).

Furthermore, the Stages of Change Model (SCM), also known as the Transtheoretical Model of Change (Prochaska & DiClemente, 1982), has been offered as a general explanatory model that captures the constructs of cognitive dissonance, self-efficacy, and decisional balance. In addition, this section extends the SCM to explain the process of changing offender behavior. The SCM was originally developed in the late 1970s and early 1980s by James Prochaska and Carlo DiClemente to explain how smokers were able to give up their habits. At present, it has become one of the most influential models of behavior change, particularly in the area of addictive behavior (e.g., Prochaska, Norcross, Fowler, Follock, & Abrams, 1992) and has been widely applied to the area of offender rehabilitation (Williamson, Day, Howells, Bubner, & Jauncey, 2003). According to Petrocelli (2002), the SCM is an "empirically derived multistage sequential model of general change" (p. 23). DiClemente and Prochaska (1982) identify a broad cycle of change with five distinct stages of change: precontemplation, contemplation, preparation, action, and maintenance.

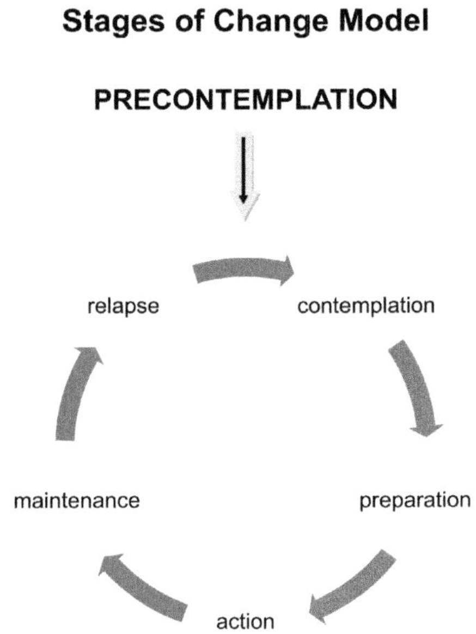

Figure 14.1 Stages of Change Model. (Adapted from Velasquez et al., 2001; Miller and Rollnick, 1991, 2002)

Furthermore, within the criminal justice context, the rehabilitation of offenders is essentially coerced (Birgden, 2002, p. 283) and involves a mixture of retribution, prevention, and protection (Slobogin & Fondacaro, 2000). Thus, efforts within the criminal justice system, such as legal sanctions, rehabilitation efforts, and interactions with agents (Prochaska & Levesque, 2002) constitute essential mechanisms for promoting movement through the stages. Finally, the sections below provide a detailed description of these stages and the processes associated with each (Velasquez et al., 2001; Miller and Rollnick, 1991, 2002).

Stages 1 and 2—Remorse

Remorse is a positive motivator to change criminal attitudes, values, and beliefs (Salekin, Salekin, Clements, & Leistico, 2005, p. 347). Remorseful offenders generally have significant motivation to enter into treatment and they believe that treatment is likely to have a positive effect (Salekin et al., 2005, p. 347).

Furthermore, lack of remorse is one of the so-called core personality traits of psychopathy. This is supported through research by Rogers and Cruise (2000), who administered psychometrics to a variety of offender samples and found that 83% engaged in a denial of criminality.

Table 14.1 Stages of Change Model as Applied to the Rehabilitation and Sentencing of Offenders (Adapted from Velasquez et al., 2001; Miller and Rollnick, 1991, 2002).

Stage	Issues	Mechanisms for Promoting Movement through the Stages	Sentencing Objectives
1. Precontemplation	Denial and minimization	Forced participation in treatment	Retribution/ rehabilitation
2. Contemplation	Acknowledgment of wrongdoing	Voluntary participation in treatment	Retribution/ rehabilitation
3. Preparation	Intention to change	Cognitive-behavioral therapy	Rehabilitation
4. Action	Active involvement in making changes.	Cognitive-behavioral therapy	Rehabilitation
5. Maintenance	Maintaining the changes made	Cognitive-behavioral therapy	Rehabilitation
6. Termination	Desistance from crime and discovery of agency	Reintegration into society	Crime prevention and community safety

In comparison, slightly more than 34.9% of non-psychopaths were high on this dimension. According to the *Diagnostic and Statistical Manual of Mental Disorders*, 4th edition, text revision (DSM-IV-TR), antisocial personality disorder (ASPD) replaces psychopathy as a diagnosis (Lykken, 1995). Both PCL-R-defined psychopathy and DSM-IV-TR antisocial personality disorder are known to be associated with abnormalities in psychological components associated with processing moral judgment, such as lack of empathy and remorse, or with affective dysregulation. However, it has been argued that the DSM-IV ASPD criterion set provides an inadequate representation of psychopathy. This is suggested in part by its differential correlation with the two commonly identified factors of the PCL-R (Lilienfeld, 1994). It is worth emphasizing that PCL-R is often differentiated with respect to two correlated factors. The first factor consists of core psychopathic traits, including superficiality, grandiosity, and lack of remorse for behaviors (Rogers et al., 2000). The second factor is typically explained by antisocial behavior manifested by failing to conform to societal norms (Rogers et al., 2000). Hare (2003) has stated that "research that uses a DSM diagnosis of [ASPD] taps the social deviance component of psychopathy but misses much of the personality component. Whereas such component is measured by the PCL-R" (p. 92). Nevertheless, it is acknowledged in DSM-IV that the PCL-R items not included within the criterion set for ASPD will at times improve the validity of the assessment of ASPD. As stated by the American Psychiatric Association (2000, p. 703):

> Lack of empathy [and other core psychopathic traits] . . . are features that have been commonly included in traditional conceptions of psychopathy that may be particularly distinguishing of the disorder and more predictive of recidivism in prison or forensic settings where criminal delinquents or aggressive acts are likely to be non-specific.

Moreover, the early stages of sentencing focus on the need for an offender to admit responsibility for the offense—in other words, remorse. In this respect, the presence or absence of remorse or apology can positively or negatively affect perceptions of the defendant. In federal court, for example, the expression of remorse is treated as a permissible factor that may warrant a downward departure in an offender's sentence. In *United States v. Hammick*, 36 F.3d 594, 600 (7th Cir. 1994), it was observed that "a fundamental principle underlying the acceptance of responsibility reduction" is "that in the absence of evidence of sincere remorse or contrition for one's crimes, a guilty plea entered for the apparent purpose of obtaining a lighter sentence does not entitle a defendant to a reduction for acceptance of responsibility."

Finally, "in a capital sentencing proceeding, assessments of character and remorse may carry great weight and, perhaps, be determinative of whether the offender lives or dies [depending on the seriousness of the offense]" (*Riggins v. Nevada*, 504 U.S. 127, 144 (1992); Kennedy, J., concurring in the judgment). For instance, PCL-R Factor 1 traits such as remorselessness and superficial emotional responsiveness are widely assumed to have a prejudicial effect on laypersons (Gunn, 1998; Helfgott, 1997; for a contrary view, see Guy & Edens, 2003).

Stages 3, 4, and 5—Cognitive-Behavioral Treatment

In stages three, four, and five, treatment becomes a main focus. Moreover, cognitive-behavioral treatment's (CBT) primary aim is to assist offenders in carrying out intended behaviors, not to influence intentions. Therefore, offender readiness for participation is key to responsivity (Howells, 1998). Generally offenders who score high on precontemplation and low on contemplation and action are low in readiness to change, and those high on contemplation and action and low on precontemplation are high in readiness to change (Williamson et al., 2003, p. 305; for a contrary view, see Polaschek & Ross, 2010, p. 109).

In addition, precontemplators usually attend treatment due to external pressure and are therefore at greatest risk of falling out of treatment programs. As stated by Olver and Wong (2011): "The failure to complete treatment is a common problem in psychotherapy research and practice. Often the highest risk, highest need individuals are those most likely to dropout, a finding that extends to violent offenders, domestic batterers, sex offenders, and psychopathic offenders."

Furthermore, cognitive-behavioral approaches have become prevalent in correctional settings (Dodson & Khatri, 2000). The phrase cognitive-behavioral has been described as "an unwieldy conjunction of two unlikely sounding complementary parts" (McGuire, 2000, 15). It follows that key to CBT is the belief that using both cognitive therapy and behavioral therapy is more effective than just one of these types.

On the one hand, cognitive therapy assumes that maladaptive, or faulty, thinking patterns cause criminal behavior (Fabiano, Porporino, & Robinson, 1991). Cognitive therapy interventions seek to achieve one common goal from different perspectives—that is, to correct faulty thinking patterns that help maintain patterns of criminal offending. This can be achieved by: "teaching new cognitive skills, such as self monitoring, self-awareness, interpersonal perception, knowledge" (Wikström & Treiber, 2008, p. 28; see also Landenberger & Lipsey, 2005; Meichenbaum, 1995; Wilson, Bouffard, & MacKenzie, 2005).

In addition, cognitive therapy has been used to treat anger in offenders. In the case of offenders, there is an assumption that they have a tendency to make riskier, more impulsive decisions than the general population in hot cognition settings because of their relative inability to regulate strong emotions and urges. In this respect, Barratt et al. (1997) have contended that although insufficient by itself, impulsivity—along with anger, poor verbal information processing, social-problem skills, and parietal lobe dysfunctions—plays an important role in impulsive aggression (to Komarovskaya, Loper, & Warren, 2007, p. 1501).

In contrast to cognitive therapy, behavior therapy is based on the notion that the social environment affects criminal behavior (Clear, Cole, & Reisig, 2008, p. 354). Furthermore, teaching offenders new prosocial skills to replace the antisocial ones like fighting, stealing, using drugs, or lying is a central aspect of this approach. This is achieved through behavioral rehearsal, modeling, and token economies. It is therefore worth briefly explaining at least one of these behavioral methods (Sweet &

Loizeaux, 1991)—that is, token economies (Ayllon & Azrin, 1968). In this respect, Pearson, Lipton, Cleland, and Yee (2002) have defined token economy as: "[a] reinforcement system in which offenders/inmates who perform specific behaviors satisfactorily ... are rewarded with tokens, which can later be exchanged for privileges" (p. 481). A token economy is therefore a form of behavior modification designed to increase desirable behavior and decrease undesirable behavior with the use of tokens.

In addition, a series of classic experiments exploring some aspects of chimpanzee social behavior using token economy confirmed the efficacy of this approach. The chimps were first trained to put poker chips into a "chimp-o-mat" vending machine. Each chip dispensed a few grapes or raisins. Once the animals had learned to exchange tokens for food, they would learn new tasks to earn the chips. To maintain the value of the token, the chimps were occasionally allowed to use the "chimp-o-mat" (Coon & Mitterer, 2008, p. 231).

Finally, token economies have received a fair amount of criticism on ethical and broader, moral grounds. Kassirer (1974), for instance, pointed out that "[t]oken economies and other programs of contingency management necessitate deprivations. These deprivations might be so severe as to be invalid under the eighth amendment (p. 255). Also, programs involving token economies have been labeled as "brainwashing" and "lobotomy" (Geller, Johnson, Hamlin, & Kennedy, 1977). In addition, to the the extent that it represents a form of positive reinforcement, token economies have been criticized on the ground that "it is inequitable to reward antisocial individuals for doing what is minimally expected of most citizens" (Marlowe, 2006, 131).

Stage 6—Desistance from Crime and Discovery of Agency

One of the core constructs of the SCM is self-efficacy. Self-efficacy is seen as one of the main social-cognitive variables that change across the stages. Self-efficacy is typically low in early stages and increase when individuals move on to the later stage (Sutton, 2005). In the SCM, confidence in the ability to change the risk behavior (Velicer et al., 1998) and temptation to continue the risk behavior (Prochaska, Redding, & Evers, 1997) influence the self-efficacy concept.

In addition, Day, Bryan, Davey, and Casey (2006) in their research found that the themes that differentiate desisters from persisters are: "a stable and positive sense of self, an optimistic perception of personal control over one's destiny; a desire to be productive and to give something back to others and the next generation; and valuing life satisfaction (contentment, happiness, interpersonal relations)" (p. 481).

Furthermore, in many ways, this last stage encapsulates the two stages discussed above. For instance, both empathy and guilt (Tangney, 1995) and self efficacy (e.g., Bandura, 1986) are positively correlated with prosocial behavior. Therefore, one would expect that high levels of empathy and self-efficacy will increase the chances of desistance from crime, and that low levels of empathy and self-efficacy will decrease the chances of desistance from crime.

Finally, it is important to stress that the key to helping offenders discover their own agency is to work "with offenders not on them." As stated by McNeil (2009): "[I]f desistance is about discovering agency, then interventions need to encourage and respect self-determination; this means working with offenders not on them" (p. 28). In this respect, Hayles (2006) has criticized the risk assessment model for treating "the offender as an object of criminal justice strategies" (p. 74). According to Hayles (2006), "[m]uch of the work undertaken with offenders pays little genuine deference to their personal goals and ambitions" (p. 73).

Conclusion

This chapter focused mainly, although not exclusively, on the role of psychological theory and diagnoses on sentencing. It addressed the following key questions: How did the use and misuse of psychological theory and diagnoses contribute to the adoption of determinate sentencing policies? What role does psychological theory and diagnosis play in determinate sentencing? How and why were indeterminate sentencing policies maintained despite the adoption of determinate sentencing? What role does psychological theory and diagnosis play in indeterminate sentencing?

It is clear from the above that psychological theories of criminal behavior are not aligned with any specific form of sentencing and punishment ideology. They have been equally supportive of both determinate and indeterminate sentences. For instance, the theory of life-course-persistent antisocial behavior underlies the adoption of Three Strikes legislation based on the notion that a small group of offenders is responsible for a large proportion of crime. At the same time, psychological theories are intrinsic to the dominant penology of individualized diagnosis and treatment. As stated earlier, the original philosophy of indeterminate sentencing structures was that most criminals could be rehabilitated, and that this goal required an individualized approach to sentencing and sentencing flexibility.

Furthermore, it has become clear that the "all or nothing" approach to sentencing cannot succeed, since no single sentencing system could possibly reduce recidivism effectively. There is presently an increasing acknowledgment of the need to develop a more integrative approach to sentencing.

Some states such as Maine and Washington State have led the way in developing a more integrative approach to sentencing. These states rely on a mixed determinate/indeterminate sentencing system. For instance, Maine's "mixed determinate/indeterminate sentencing system marks clear constitutional boundaries for sentencing judges while simultaneously ensuring the individualization of each defendant's sentence." This means that it is able to ensure an individualized offender-oriented approach while at the same time prevent unwarranted sentencing disparities.

Moreover, as was evident in the above discussion, the specter of discrimination has reared its ugly head in psychological theory and diagnoses. Specifically, the use and misuse of psychological theory and diagnoses has been evident across all sentencing schemes. In relation to determinate sentencing schemes, this has been dramatically exemplified by the reliance on selective incapacitation as a crime control strategy. Specifically, the Three Strikes law has a disproportionate effect on African Americans. While in terms of indeterminate sentencing schemes, some studies on judicial discretion exercised at sentencing suggested that extralegal variables such as race, gender, and socioeconomic status exerted a significant and rather strong direct impact on sentences. Another related problem that was identified above is the problem of bias in racial differences in diagnosis.

Finally, it was emphasized above that there has been a shift toward rehabilitation in many Western correctional systems (Gendreau, 1996). This has important implications for the role of psychological theory and diagnoses in modern-day correctional practices. As is evident from the above discussion, the Stages of Change model was extended to explain offender rehabilitation and sentencing in the context of the criminal justice system.

Note

1. The terms "criminal behavior" and "deviant behavior" are used interchangeably and herein refer to "only those situations in which behavior is in a disapproved direction, and of sufficient degree to exceed the tolerance limit of the community" (Clinard, 1963, p. 22).

References

Agnew, R. (1992). Foundation for a general strain theory of crime and delinquency. *Criminology, 30*, 47–66.

Agnew, R. (1985). A revised strain theory of delinquency. *Social Forces, 64*, 151–167.

Akers, R. L. (2000). *Criminological theories: Introduction, evaluation, and application* (8th ed.). Los Angeles, CA: Roxbury Publishing.

American Psychiatric Association. (2000). *Diagnostic and statistical manual of mental disorders* (4th ed., text rev.). Washington, DC: Author.

Andrews, D. A. (1982). The Level of Supervision Inventory (LSI): The First Followup. Toronto: Ontario Ministry of Correctional Services.

Andrews, D. A., & Bonta, J. (2006). *The psychology of criminal conduct* (4th ed.). Newark, NJ: LexisNexis.

Andrews, D. A., & Dowden, C., (2006). Risk principle in case classification in correctional treatment: A meta analytic investigation. *International Journal of Offender Therapy and Comparative Criminology, 50*, 88–100.

Ayllon, T., & Azrin, N. (1968). *The token economy: A motivational system for therapy and rehabilitation*. New York: Appleton-Century Crofts.

Bandura, A. (1969). *Aggression: A social learning analysis*. Englewood Cliffs, NJ: Prentice Hall.

Bandura, A. (1986). *Social foundations of thought and action: A social-cognitive theory*. Englewood Cliffs, NJ: Prentice-Hall.

Bandura, A. (1992). Self-efficacy mechanism in psychobiologic functioning. In R. Schwarzer (Ed.), *Self-efficacy: Thought control of action* (pp. 355–394). Washington, DC: Hemisphere.

Barnoski, R. (2006). Sex offenders in Washington State: Key findings and trends. Olympia, WA: Washington State Institute for Public Policy, Document No. 06-03-1201.

Barratt, E. S., Stanford, M. S., Felthous, A. R., & Kent, T. A. (1997). The effects of phenytoin on impulsive and premeditated aggression: A controlled study. *Journal of Clinical Psychopharmacology*, 17(5), 341–349.

Beccaria, C. (1986). *On crimes and punishments* (D. Young, Trans.). Indianapolis, IN: Hackett. (Original work published 1764)

Benson, M. L., Fox, G. L., DeMaris, A., & Van Wyk, J. (2000). Violence in families: The intersection of race, poverty, and community context. *Families, Crime and Criminal Justice,* 2, 91–109.

Benson, M., & Fox, G. (2003). Concentrated disadvantage, economic distress, and violence against women in intimate relationships. *Final report for National Institute of Justice*, grant number 98-WT-VX-0011. Washington, DC: U.S. Department of Justice, National Institute of Justice, 2004, NCJ 199709.

Bernstein, I. N., Cardascia, J., & Ross, C. E. (1979). Defendants' sex and criminal court decisions. In R. Alvarez, K. G. Lutterman, and Associates, *Discrimination in organizations*. San Francisco, CA: Jossey-Bass.

Bersoff, B. N. (2002). Some contrarian concerns about law, psychology, and public policy. *Law & Human Behavior, 26*(5), 565–574.

Birgden, A. (2002). Dealing with the resistant criminal client: a psychologically-minded strategy for more effective legal counseling. *Criminal Law Bulletin, 38*, 225–243.

Blackburn, R. (1992). *The psychology of criminal conduct*. Chichester, UK: Wiley.

Bobo, L. D., & Thompson, V. (2010). Racialized mass incarceration: Poverty, prejudice, and punishment. In H. R. Markus & P. Moya (Eds.), *Doing race: 21 essays for the 21st century*. New York: Norton.

Brody, F. (2011). Extracting compassion from confusion: Sentencing noncitizens After *United States v. Booker*. *Fordham Law Review, 79*, 2129–2172.

Bunzel, S. M. (1995). The probation officer and the federal sentencing guidelines: Strange philosophical bedfellows. *Yale Law Journal, 104*(4), 933–966.

Burke, P. J. & Turk, A. T. (1975). Factors Affecting Postarrest Dispositions: A Model for Analysis. *Social Problems* 22(3), 313–332.

Bursik, R. (1984). Urban dynamics and ecological studies of delinquency. *Social Forces, 63*, 393–413.

Bursik, R., & Webb, J. (1982). Community change and patterns of delinquency. *American Journal of Sociology, 88*, 24–42.

Cavender, G. (1981). Philosophical justifications of determinate sentencing. *American Journal of Jurisprudence, 26*, 159–177.

Caspi, A., Moffitt, T. E., Silva, P. A. Stouthamer-Loeber, M., Krueger, R. F., & Schutte, P. S. (1994). Are some people crime-prone? Replications of the personality-crime relationship across countries, genders, races and methods. *Criminology, 32*, 163–195.

Chan, W. (1997). Legal equality and domestic homicides. *International Journal of the Sociology of Law, 25*, 203–229.

Chen, E. Y. (2008). Impacts of "Three Strikes and You're Out" on crime trends in California and throughout the United States. *Journal of Contemporary Criminal Justice, 24*, 345–370.

Clear, T. R., Cole, G. F., & Reisig, M. D. (Eds.). (2008). *American corrections*. Belmont, CA: Wadsworth.

Clinard, M. B. (1963). *Sociology of deviant behavior*. New York: Holt, Rinehart & Winston.

Cloward, R. A., & Ohlin, L. E. (1960). *Delinquency and opportunity*. New York: Free Press of Glencoe.

Cohen, A. K. (1955). *Delinquent boys*. New York: Free Press of Glencoe.

Cole, G. F., & Smith, C. E. (2007). *Criminal justice in America* (5th ed.). Belmont, CA: Wadsworth Publishing.

Coon, D., & Mitterer, J. O. (2008). *Introduction to psychology: Gateways to mind and behavior* (12th ed.). Belmont, CA: Wadsworth.

Corff, Y. L., & Toupin, J. (2009). Comparing persistent juvenile delinquents and normative peers with the five-factor model of personality. *Journal of Research in Personality, 43*(6), 1105–1108.

Cullen, F., & Gendreau, P. (1989). The effectiveness of correctional treatment: Reconsidering the "nothing 'works' debate." In L. Goodstein & D. L. Mackenzie (Eds.), *American prison: Issues in research and policy* (chap. 3). New York: Plenum.

Cullen, F., & Gendreau, P. (2000). Assessing correctional rehabilitation: Policy, practice, and prospects. In J. Horney (Ed.), *Criminal justice 2000: Policies, processes, and decisions of the criminal justice system* (pp. 109–175). Washington, DC: National Institute of Justice.

Day, A., Bryan, J., Davey, L., & Casey, S. (2006). The process of change in offender rehabilitation programmes. *Psychology, Crime and Law, 12*(5), 473–487.

Dejong, C. (1997). Survival analysis and specific deterrence: Integrating theoretical and empirical models of recidivism. *Criminology, 35*, 561–576.

DiClemente, C., & Prochaska, J. (1982). Self change and therapy change of smoking behavior: A comparison of processes of change in cessation and maintenance. *Addictive Behavior*, 7, 133–142.

Dishion, T. J., Capaldi, D., Spracklen, K. M., & Li, F. (1995). Peer ecology of male adolescent drug use. *Development and Psychopathology, 7*, 803–824.

Dodson, K., & Khatri, N. (2000). Cognitive therapy: Looking backward, looking forward. *Journal of Clinical Psychology, 56*, 907–923.

Draycott, S., & Dabbs, A. (1998). Cognitive dissonance 1: An overview of the literature and its integration into theory and practice in clinical psychology. *British Journal of Clinical Psychology, 37*, 341–353.

Ehlers, S., Schiraldi, V., & Lotke, E. (2004). *Racial divide: An examination of the impact of California Three Strikes laws on African Americans and Latinos.* Retrieved from http://www.justicepolicy.org/images/upload/04-10_TAC_CA RacialDivide_AC-RD.pdf.

Elliott, D. S., Huizinga, D. & Ageton, S. S. (1985). *Explaining delinquency and drug use*. Beverly Hills, CA: Sage.

Esbensen, F. A., & Weerman, F. M. (2005). Youth gangs and troublesome youth groups in the United States and the Netherlands; a cross-national comparison. *European Journal of Criminology*, 2(1), 5–37.

Eysenck, H. J. (1977). *Crime and personality* (3rd ed., rev.). London: Routledge & Kegan Paul.

Eysenck, H. J. (1998). Personality and crime. In T. Millon, E. Simonsen, M. Birket-Smith, & R. D. Davis (Eds.), *Psychopathy: Antisocial, criminal, and violent behavior* (pp. 40–49). New York: Guilford Press.

Eysenck, H. J., & Gudjonsson, G. H. (1989). *The causes and cures of criminality*. New York: Plenum.

Fabiano, E. A., Porporino, F. J., & Robinson, D. (1991). Canada's cognitive skills program corrects offenders faulty thinking. *Corrections Today, 53*, 102–108.

Falcón Y Tella, M. J., & Falcón Y Tella, F. (2006). *Punishment and culture: A right to punish?* (P. Muckley, Trans.). Leiden: Martinus Nijhoff, 2006.

Farrington, D. P. (Ed.). (1994). *Psychological explanations of crime*. Aldershot, UK: Dartmouth.

Ferraro, K. (2003). The words change but the melody lingers: The persistence of battered woman syndrome in criminal cases involving battered women. *Violence against Women, 9*, 110–129.

Festinger, L. (1957). *A theory of cognitive dissonance*. Evanston, IL: Row, Peterson

Frankel, M. E. (1972). Lawlessness in sentencing. *University of Cincinnati Law Review, 41*, 1–54.

Frankel, M. E. (1973). *Criminal sentences: Law without order*. New York: Hill & Wang.

Free, M. D. (1999). Minorities as perpetrators and victims of crime. In L. R. Kurtz & J. E. Turpin (Eds.), *Encyclopedia of violence, peace, and conflict*. San Diego, CA: Academic Press.

Friedman, I., Pimentel, R., Supler, K. W., & Weiss, R. (2009, December). Sexual offenders: How to create a more deliberative sentencing process. *The Champion*. Retrieved from http://www.iannfriedman.com/images/uploads/sentencing-process-for-sex-offenders-NACDL.pdf.

Friedman, L. (1993). *Crime and punishment in American history*. New York: Basic Books.

Gabor, T., & Crutcher, N. (2002). *Mandatory minimum penalties: Their effects on crime, sentencing disparities, and justice system expenditures*. Ottawa, Ontario: Justice Canada.

Gallini, B. R., & Shults, E. Q. (2006). Herding bullfrogs towards a more balanced wheelbarrow: an illustrative recommendation for federal sentencing post-Booker. *Journal of Legislation, 33*, 1–31.

Geller, E. S., Johnson, D. F., Hamlin, P. H., & Kennedy, T. D. (1977). Behavior modification in a prison: Issues, problems, and compromises. *Criminal Justice and Behavior, 4*(1), 11–43.

Gendreau, P. (1996). Offender rehabilitation: what we know and what needs to be done. *Criminal Justice and Behavior, 23*, 144–161.

Goldberg, R. (2010). *Drugs across the spectrum*. Belmont, CA: Wadsworth, Cengage Learning.

Gottfredson, D. M., & J. A. Bonds. (1961). A manual for intake base expectancy scoring. San Francisco: California Department of Corrections, Research Division.

Gottfredson, M. R., & Hirschi, T. (1990). *A general theory of crime*. Stanford, CA: Stanford University Press.

Green, E. (1961). *Judicial attitudes in sentencing*. London: MacMillan.

Green, E. (1964). Inter- and intra-racial crime relative to sentencing. *Journal of Criminal Law, Criminology, and Police Science, 55*(3), 348–358.

Greene, E., Heilbrun, K., Fortune, W. H., & Nietzel, M. T. (2007). *Wrightsman's psychology and the legal system* (6th ed.). Belmont, CA: Wadsworth/Thomson Learning.

Greer, S., & Hagan, J. (2001). Crime as disrepute. In S. Henry & M. Lanier (Eds.), *What is crime?* (pp. 207–226). Lanham, MD: Rowman and Littlefield.

Gunn, J. (1998). Psychopathy: An elusive concept with moral overtones. In T. Millon, E. Simonsen, M. Birket-Smith, & R. Davis (Eds.), *Psychopathy: Antisocial, criminal and violent behavior* (pp. 32–39). New York: Guilford Press.

Guy, L. S., & Edens, J. F. (2003). Juror decision-making in a mock sexually violent predator trial: Gender differences in the impact of divergent types of testimony. *Behavioral Sciences and the Law, 21*(2), 215–237.

Hagan, J., Nagel (Bernstein), I. H., & Albonetti, C. A. (1980). The differential sentencing of white-collar offenders in ten federal district courts. *American Sociological Review, 45*, 802–820.

Hall. J. (1960). *General principles of criminal law* (2nd ed.). Indianapolis, IN: Bobbs-Merrill.

Hannah-Moffat, K. (2010). *Actuarial sentencing: An "unsettled" proposition*. University at Albany Symposium on Sentencing. Retrieved from http://www.albany.edu/scj/documents/Hannah-Moffatt_RiskAssessment_000.pdf.

Hare, R. D. (2003). *The Psychopathy Checklist–Revised technical manual* (2nd ed.). Toronto, Ontario, Canada: Multi-Health Systems.

Hayles, M. (2006). Constructing safety: A collaborative approach to managing risk and building responsibility. In K. Gorman, M. Gregory, M. Hayles, & N. Parton (Eds.), *Constructive work with offenders*. London: Jessica Kingsley.

Heaven, P. C. L. (1996). Personality and self-reported delinquency: Analysis of the "Big Five" personality dimensions. *Personality and Individual Differences, 20*(1), 47–54.

Helfgott, J. B. (1997, March). *The popular conception of the psychopath: Implications for criminal justice policy and practice*. Paper presented at the Annual Convention of the Academy of Criminal Justice Sciences, Louisville, KY.

Hoffman, P. B. (1983). Screening for risk: A revised Salient Factor Score (SFS-81). *Journal of Criminal Justice, 11*, 539–547.

Hoge, R. D., & Andrews, D. A. (1996). *Assessing the youthful offender: Issues and techniques*. New York: Plenum.

Howells, K. (1998). Cognitive behavioral therapy for anger, aggression and violence. In N. Tarrier and A. Wells (Eds.), *Treating complex cases: The cognitive behavioral therapy approach* (pp. 295–318). Chichester, UK: Wiley.

Howells, K., Day, A., & Wright, S. (2004). Affect, emotions and sex offenders. *Psychology, Crime and Law, 10*, 179–195.

Howells, K., Day, A., Williamson, P., Bubner, S., Jauncey, S., Parker, A., & Heseltine, K. (2005). Brief anger management programs with offenders: outcomes and predictors of change. *Journal of Forensic Psychiatry and Psychology, 16*, 296–311.

Hudson, B. (2002). Gender issues in penal theory and penal policy. In P. Carlen (Ed.), *Women and punishment: The struggle for justice* (pp. 21–46). Cullompton, UK: Willan Publishing.

Irish, J. F. (1989). *Probation and recidivism: A study of probation adjustment and its relationship to post-probation outcome for adult criminal offenders*. Mineola, NY: Nassau County Probation Department.

Janis, I. L., & Mann, L. (1985). *Decision-making: A psychological analysis of conflict, choice, and commitment* (2nd ed.). New York: Free Press.

Jeffery, C. R. (1956). The structure of American criminological thinking. *Journal of Criminal Law, Criminology and Police Science, 46*, 658–672.

Jones, M. (2003). Overcoming the myth of free will in criminal law: The true impact of the genetic revolution. *Duke Law Journal, 52*, 1031–1053.

Kassirer, L. B. (1974). Behavior modification for patients and prisoners: Constitutional ramifications of enforced therapy, *Journal of Psychiatry and Law, 2*(3), 245–302.

Komarovskaya, I., Loper, A., & Warren, J. (2007). The role of impulsivity in antisocial and violent behavior and personality disorders among incarcerated women. *Criminal Justice and Behavior, 34*, 1499–1515.

Kovandzic, T. V., Sloan, J. J., & Vieraitis, L. M. (2002). Unintended consequences of politically popular sentencing policy: The homicide promoting effects of "Three Strikes" in U.S. cities (1980–1999). *Criminology and Public Policy, 1*(3), 399–424.

Landenberger, N., & Lipsey, M. (2005). The positive effects of cognitive-behavioral programs for offenders: A meta-analysis of factors associated with effective treatment, *Journal of Experimental Criminology, 1*(4), 451–476.

Laws, D. R., & Ward, T. (2010). *Desistance from sex offending: Alternatives to throwing away the keys*. New York: Guilford Press.

Lilienfeld, S. O. (1994). Conceptual problems in the assessment of psychopathy. *Clinical Psychology Review, 14*, 17–38.

Litwack, T., Kirschner, S., & Wack, R. (1993). The assessment of dangerousness and predictions of violence: Recent research and future prospects. *Psychiatric Quarterly, 64*(3), 245–271.

Lowenthal, G. T. (1993). Mandatory sentencing laws: Undermining the effectiveness of determinate sentencing reform. *California Law Review 81*, 61–123.

Lykken, D. T. (1995). *The antisocial personalities*. Mahwah, NJ: Lawrence Erlbaum Associates.

Lynam, D. R., Caspi, A., Moffitt, T. E., Loeber, R., & Stouthamer-Loeber, M. (2007). Longitudinal evidence that psychopathy scores in early adolescence predict adult psychopathy. *Journal of Abnormal Psychology, 116*, 155–165.

MacKenzie, D. L. (2006). *What works in corrections: Reducing the criminal activities of offenders and delinquents*. New York: Cambridge University Press.

Mann R. E. (1995). Reducing the risk of sexual reoffending. Paper presented at the Institute for the Study & Treatment of Delinquency Annual Residential Conference Managing Risk: Achieving the Possible at University of Nottingham, UK.

Marlowe, D. B. (2006). Depot naltrexone in lieu of incarceration: A behavioral analysis of coerced treatment for addicted offenders. *Journal of Substance Abuse Treatment, 31*, 131–139.

McCann, R. A., Ivanoff, A., Schmidt, H., & Beach, B. (2007). Implementing dialectical behavior therapy in residential forensic settings with adults and juveniles. In L. A. Dimeff & K. Koerner (Eds.), *Dialectical behavior therapy in clinical practice: Applications across disorders and settings* (pp. 112–144). New York: Guilford Press.

McGuire, J. (2000). *An introduction to theory and research: Cognitive-behavioral approaches*. HM. Inspectorate of Probation Report. London: Home Office. Available at http://www.justice.gov.uk/inspectorates/hmi-probation/docs/cogbeh1-rps.pdf.

McAdams, D. P. (1992). The five factor model in personality: A critical appraisal. *Journal of Personality, 60*, 329–361.

McNeill, F. (2009). What works and what's just? *European Journal of Probation, 1* (1) 21–40.

Mears, D. P., Wang, X., Hay, C., & Bales, W. D. (2008). Social ecology and recidivism: Implications for prisoner reentry. *Criminology, 46*, 301–340.

Mednick, S. A., Gabrielli, W. F., Jr., & Hutchings, B. (1987). Genetic factors in the etiology of criminal behavior. In S. A. Mednick, T. E. Moffitt, & S. A. Stack, *The causes of crime: New biological approaches*. Cambridge, UK: Cambridge University Press.

Meichenbaum, D. (1977). *Cognitive-behavioral modification: An integrative approach*. New York: Plenum Press

Meichenbaum, D. (1995). Cognitive-behavioral therapy in historical perspective. In B. Bongar & L. Beutler (Eds.), *Comprehensive textbook of psychotherapy: Theory and practice* (pp. 140–158). New York: Oxford University Press.

Merton, R. K. (1938). Social structure and anomie. *American Sociological Review, 3*, 672–682.

Meyer. L. R. (2005). Eternal remorse. In A. Sarat (Ed.), *Toward a critique of guilt: Perspectives from law and the humanities* (Studies in Law, Politics and Society, Vol. 36, pp. 141–15). Amsterdam: Elsevier.

Moffitt, T. E. (1993). Adolescent-limited and life-course-persistent antisocial behavior: A developmental taxonomy. *Psychological Review, 100*, 674–701.

Nagel, I. H. (1990). Structuring sentencing discretion: The new federal sentencing guidelines. *Journal of Criminal Law and Criminology, 80*, 883–943.

Nagel, S., & Weitzman, L. (1971). Women as litigants. *Hastings Law Journal, 23*, 171.

Nagin, D. S., & Paternoster, R. (1991). On the relationship of past to future participation in delinquency. *Criminology, 29*(1), 163–187.

Nagin, D. S., & Paternoster, R. (2000). Population heterogeneity and state dependence: State of the evidence and directions for future research. *Journal of Quantitative Criminology, 16*(2), 117–145.

Neighbors, H. W., Jackson, J. S., Campbell, L., & Williams, D. (1989). The influence of racial factors on psychiatric diagnosis: A review and suggestions for research. *Community Mental Health Journal, 25*(4), 301–311.

Olver, M. E., & Wong, S. (2011): Predictors of sex offender treatment dropout: Psychopathy, sex offender risk, and responsivity implications. *Psychology, Crime and Law, 17*(5), 457–471.

Martinson, R. (1974). What works?—Questions and answers about prison reform. *Public Interest, 35*, 22–54.

Minsky, S., Vega, W., Miskimen, T., Gara, M., & Escobar, J. (2003). Diagnostic patterns in Latino, African American, and European American psychiatric patients. *Archives of General Psychiatry, 60*(6), 637–644.

Nuffield, J. (1982). Parole decision making in Canada: Research towards decision guidelines. Ottawa, Ontario: Ministry of Supply and Services Canada.

Oum, R. E., & Lieberman, D. (2007). Emotion as cognition: An information processing view of the mind. In K. D. Vohs, R. F. Baumeister, & G. Loewenstein (Eds.), *Do emotions help or hurt decision making? A hedgefoxian perspective* (pp. 133–154). New York: Russell Sage.

Ousey, G. C., & Wilcox, P. (2007). The interaction of antisocial propensity and life-course varying predictors of delinquent behavior: Differences by methods of estimation and implications for theory. *Criminology, 45*, 313–354.

Paternoster, R., Dean, C. W., Piquero, A., Mazerolle, P., & Brame, R. (1997). Generality, continuity, and change in offending. *Journal of Quantitative Criminology, 13*, 231–266.

Patterson, G. R. (1984). Siblings: Fellow travelers in a coercive system. In R. J. Blanchard & D. C. Blanchard (Eds.), *Advances in the study of aggression* (Vol. 1, pp. 173–215). New York: Academic Press.

Patterson, G. R. (1986). The contribution of siblings to training for fighting: A microsocial analysis. In D. Olweus, J. Block, & M. Radke-Yarrow (Eds.), *Development of antisocial and prosocial behaviors* (pp. 235–260). Orlando, FL: Academic Press.

Pearson, F. S., Lipton, D. S., Cleland, C. M., & Yee. D. S. (2002). The effects of behavioral/ cognitive-behavioral programs on recidivism. *Crime and Delinquency*, *48*(3), 476–496.

Petrocelli, V. J. (2002). Processes and stages of change: Counseling with the transtheoretical model of change. *Journal of Counseling and Development, 80*(1), 22–30.

Phillipson, M. (1971). *Sociological aspects of crime and delinquency*. London: Routledge & Kegan Paul.

Piquero, A. R., Farrington, D. P., Nagin, D. S., & Moffitt, T. E. (2010). Trajectories of offending and their relation to life failure in late middle age: Findings from the Cambridge study in delinquent development. *Journal of Research in Crime and Delinquency, 47*(2), 151–173.

Polaschek, D. L. L., & Ross, E. C. (2010). Do early therapeutic alliance, motivation, and change readiness predict therapy outcomes for high risk violent prisoners. *Criminal Behavior and Mental Health, 20*, 100–111.

Prinz, J. (2009). The normativity challenge: Cultural psychology provides the real threat to virtue ethics. *Journal of Ethics*, 13: 117–144.

Prochaska, J. O., & DiClemente, C. C. (1982). Transtheoretical therapy: toward a more integrative model of change. *Psychotherapy: Theory Research and Practice, 19*, 276–288.

Prochaska J. O., Redding, C., & Evers, K. (1997). The transtheoretical model of behavior change. In K. Glanz, F. M. Lewis, & B. K. Riner (Eds.), *Health behavior and health education: Theory, research and practice* (2nd ed., pp. 60–84). San Francisco, CA: Jossey-Bass.

Prochaska, J. O., Norcross, J. C., Fowler, J., Follock, M. J., & Abrams, D. B. (1992). Attendance and outcome in a worksite weight control program: Processes and stages of change as process and predictor variables. *Addictive Behavior, 17*, 35–45.

Prochaska, J. O., & Levesque, D. A. (2002). Enhancing motivation of offenders at each stage of change and phase of therapy. In M. McMurran (Ed.), *Motivating offenders to change: A guide to enhancing engagement in therapy* (pp. 57–73). New York: John Wiley & Sons.

Rafter, N. (2006). H. J. Eysenck in Fagin's kitchen: The return to biological theory in 20th-century criminology. *History of the Human Sciences, 19*(4), 37–56.

Raine, A., Buchsbaum, M., & LaCasse, L. (1997) Brain abnormalities in murderers indicated by positron emission tomography. *Biological Psychiatry, 42*, 495–508.

Roche, D. (1999). Mandatory sentencing. *Trends & Issues, 138*. Canberra: Australian Institute of Criminology. http://www.aic.gov.au/documents/C/1/E/%7BC1EFCBE4-7FCE-4B22-8BB9-AFD965E2E536%7Dti138.pdf.

Rogers, R., Salekin, R. T., Hill, C., Sewell, K. W., Murdock, M. E., & Neumann, C. S. (2000). The Psychopathy Checklist: Screening Version: An examination of criteria and subcriteria in three forensic samples. *Assessment, 7*, 1–15.

Rogers, R., & Cruise, K. R. (2000). Malingering and deception among psychopaths. In C. B. Gacono (Ed.), *The clinical and forensic assessment of psychopathy: A practitioner's guide* (pp. 269–284). Mahwah, NJ: Lawrence Erlbaum Associates.

Salekin, R. T., Salekin, K. L., Clements, C. B., & Leistico, A. R. (2005). Risk-sophistication-treatment inventory. In T. Grisso, G. Vincent, & D. Seagrave (Eds.), *Mental health screening and assessment in juvenile justice* (pp. 341–356). New York: Guilford Press.

Sampson, R. J., & Laub, J. H. (1993). *Crime in the making*. Cambridge, MA: Harvard University Press.

Sapir, Y. (2008). Against prevention? A response to Harcourt's against prediction on actuarial and clinical predictions and the faults of incapacitation. *Law and Social Inquiry, 33*(1), 253–264.

Shepherd, J. (2002). Fear of the first strike: The full deterrent effect of California's two- and three-strikes legislation. *Journal of Legal Studies, 31*, 159–201.

Sherman, L., Gottfredson, D., MacKenzie, D., Eck, J., Reuter, P., & Bushway, S. (1998). *Preventing crime: What works, what doesn't, what's promising: A report to the United States Congress*. Retrieved from https://www.ncjrs.gov/pdffiles/171676.PDF.

Skarðhamar, T. (2009). Reconsidering the theory on adolescent-limited and life-course persistent antisocial behavior, *British Journal of Criminology, 49*, 863–878.

Slobogin, C., & Fondacaro, M. (2000). Rethinking deprivation of liberty: possible contributions from therapeutic and ecological jurisprudence. *Behavioral Sciences and the Law, 18*(4), 499–516.

Sorenson, J., & Pilgrim, R. (2006). *Lethal injection capital punishment in Texas during the modern era*. Austin, TX: University of Texas Press.

Spielberger, C. D. (1991). *State-Trait Anger Expression Inventory* (Rev. research ed., professional manual). Odessa, FL: Psychological Assessment Resources

Spinelli, M. G. (2004). Maternal infanticide associated with mental illness: Prevention and the promise of saved lives. *American Journal of Psychiatry, 161* (9), 1548–1557.

Stark, E. (1995). Re-presenting woman battering: From battered woman syndrome to coercive control. *Albany Law Review, 58*, 973–1026.

Strakowski, S. M., Shelton, R. C., & Kolbrener, M. L. (1993). The effects of race and comorbidity on clinical diagnosis in patients with psychosis. *Journal of Clinical Psychiatry, 54*(3), 96–102.

Strakowski, S. M., Flaum, M., Amador, X., Bracha, H. S., Pandurangi, A. K., Robinson, D., & Tohen, M. (1996). Racial differences in the diagnosis of psychosis. *Schizophrenia Research, 21*(2), 117–124.

Stubbs, J., & Tolmie, J. (2008). Battered women charged with homicide: Advancing the interests of Indigenous women. *Australian and New Zealand Journal of Criminology, 41*(1), 138–161.

Sutton, J. (1994). Learning to better predict the future: National Parole Board risk-assessment training. *Forum on Corrections Research*, 6(3), 20–22.

Sutton, S. (2005). Stage theories of health behavior. In M. Conner & P. Norman (Eds.), *Predicting health behaviors* (2nd ed., pp. 223–275). Maidenhead, UK: Open University Press.

Swan, S. C., & Snow, D. L. (2006). The development of a theory for women's use of violence in intimate relationships. *Violence against Women, 12*, 1026–1045.

Sweet, A., & Loizeaux, A. (1991). Behavioral and cognitive treatment methods: A critical comparative review. *Journal of Behavioral Therapy and Experimental Psychiatry, 22*, 159–185.

Tangney, J. P. (1995). Shame and guilt in interpersonal relationships. In J. P. Tangney, & K. W. Fischer (Eds.), *Self-conscious emotions: The psychology of shame, guilt, embarrassment, and pride* (pp. 114–139). New York: Guilford Press.

Tonry, M. (1999, September). The fragmentation of sentencing and corrections in America. In *Sentencing and Corrections, Issues for the 21st Century*, no. 1. Washington, DC: U.S. Department of Justice, National Institute of Justice, NCJ 175721.

United States Sentencing Commission (USSC). (2002, May). *Report to Congress: Cocaine and Federal Sentencing Policy IV*. Retrieved June 18, 2009, from http://www.ussc.gov/Legislative_and_Public_Affairs/Congressional_Testimony_and_Reports/Drug_Topics/200205_RtC_Cocaine_Sentencing_Policy/200205_Cocaine_and_Federal_Sentencing_Policy.pdf.

United States Sentencing Commission (USSC), Guidelines Manual §1A1.3 (Nov. 2009)

Van Dam, C., Janssens, J. M. A. M., & de Bruyn, E. E. J. (2005). PEN, big five, juvenile delinquency and criminal recidivism. *Personality and Individual Differences, 39*(1), 7–19.

Velicer W. F., DiClemente, C. C., Prochaska, J. O., Abrams, D. B., Emmons K. M., & Pierce, J. P. (1995). Distribution of smokers by stage in three representative samples. *Preventive Medicine 24*, 401–411.

Vold, G. B., Bernard, T. J., & Snipes, J. B. (2002). *Theoretical criminology* (5th ed.). New York: Oxford University Press.

Wikström, P. O., & Treiber, K. (2008). *Offending behavior programmes: Source document*. London: Youth Service Board.

Williamson, P. J., Day, A., Howells, K., Bubner, S., & Jauncey, S. (2003). Assessing offender readiness to change problems with anger. *Psychology Crime and Law*, 9(4), 295–307.

Wilson, D., Bouffard, L., & MacKenzie, D. (2005). Quantitative review of structured, group-oriented, cognitive-behavioral programs for offenders, *Criminal Justice and Behavior, 32*(2), 172–204.

Wilson, J. Q., & R. J. Herrnstein (1985). *Crime and human nature: The definitive study of the causes of crime*. New York: Simon & Schuster.

Wolfgang, M., & Ferracuti, F. (1967). *The subculture of violence*. London: Social Science Paperbacks.

Zhang, S., Benson, T., & Deng, X. (2000). A test–retest reliability assessment of the international self-report delinquency instrument. *Journal of Criminal Justice*, *28*, 283–295.

Cases

Riggins v. Nevada, 504 U.S. 127, 144 (1992).

United States v. Booker, 543 U.S. 220 (2005).

United States v. Fruchter, 411 F.3d 377, 384 (2d Cir. 2005). Retrieved from http://ftp.resource.org/courts.gov/c/F3/411/411.F3d.377.02-1552.02-1561.02-1542.02-1474.02-1451.html.

United States v. Hammick, 36 F.3d 594, 600 (7th Cir. 1994).

CHAPTER FIFTEEN

Mental Health Court: One Approach for Addressing the Problems of Persons with Serious Mental Illnesses in the Criminal Justice System

Matthew W. Epperson, Kelli E. Canada, and Arthur J. Lurigio

Introduction

Persons with Serious Mental Illnesses in the Criminal Justice System

Since the 1960s, the policy of deinstitutionalization has resulted in a massive downsizing of large state-run psychiatric institutions (the "asylum" was a relic of the nineteenth century). The overarching goals of this paradigm shift were to reduce the stigmatization of persons with serious mental illnesses (PSMI) and to integrate mental health services into community settings. These changes have undoubtedly led to service and policy innovations in mental health treatment, but they also had unbidden, harmful consequences. For example, PSMI have increasingly been brought into contact with criminal justice professionals at every stage of the criminal justice process.

The disruptive public behavior of PSMI often leads to arrest because of a paucity of community-based services (e.g., housing) and psychiatric care, or police might be unaware of these service options (Teplin, 2000). PSMI are a vulnerable population, and protecting and treating them is a challenge for jail and prison administrators. Beyond specific forensic categories (e.g., guilty but mentally ill), sentencing alternatives for PSMI can be quite limited. Standard correctional programs or traditional case management strategies rarely fit this population, and probation and parole officers must struggle to locate scant services and treatments for PSMI sentenced to community supervision (Lurigio & Swartz, 2000). PSMI experience symptoms that can interfere with their abilities to adhere to the conditions of release and to achieve successful reintegration and reentry into the community (Council of State and Local Governments, 2002).

Serious criminal behavior, which can be related to their untreated psychiatric and substance use disorders, can cause other PSMI to enter the criminal justice system. Many individuals with chronic mental illnesses have either not fully accessed community services available to them or have fallen victim to service gaps in their local communities. The number of homeless PSMI has also grown significantly in the last 20 years (Baumohl, 1996; Padgett, Gulcur, & Tsemberis, 2006). The transinstitutionalization of PSMI has resulted from the lack of accessible and affordable mental health care in this country. PSMI are now more likely to be treated in a jail or prison than in a psychiatric facility (Council of State and Local Governments, 2002; Lamberti, 2007).

This progression of events has led to a disproportionate number of PSMI involved in the criminal justice system. Although statistics vary based on methodology and definitions, most studies cite that between 7% and 18% of individuals arrested, incarcerated in jails and prisons, or under court supervision have a serious mental illness (Broner, Lattimore, Cowell, & Schlenger, 2004). Despite variations in statistics, researchers consistently report that rates of serious mental illness in the correctional population are in fact much higher than those in the general population (Diamond, Wang, Holzer, Thomas, & Cruser, 2001; Ditton, 1999). An estimated one million PSMI are arrested and booked in the United States each year (Morrissey, Meyer, & Cuddeback, 2007), which has resulted in jails becoming the largest de facto inpatient psychiatric facilities in the nation (Slate & Johnson, 2008).

The presence of a mental disorder among justice-involved individuals complicates the supervision and custodial responsibilities of the criminal justice system. PSMI who are incarcerated in jail or prison require costly treatment and pose a burden on correctional supervision. They also spend more time incarcerated and are more likely to be victimized while incarcerated than those without serious mental illnesses (Ditton, 1999; James & Glaze, 2006). PSMI on probation or parole supervision are highly likely to violate the terms of their supervision, placing them at heightened risk of reincarceration (Skeem, Emke-Francis, & Louden, 2006). This penetration of offenders with mental illnesses into deeper levels of criminal justice involvement has implications for public safety, public health, and public spending (Prins & Draper, 2009).

One Response to the Problem: Mental Health Court

Growth in the number of PSMI entering the criminal justice system has demanded the development of specialized programs. Professionals from many quarters (advocates, researchers, and legal scholars) have recommended that criminally involved PSMI be treated justly, fairly, and humanely at each point of interception in the criminal justice process (arrest, detention, sentence, incarceration, and reentry) (Lurigio & Swartz, 2000). In the past 20 years, a variety of jail diversion efforts have been implemented for PSMI, including pre-booking strategies, law enforcement training, and enhanced linkages to community treatment settings. The actual criminalization of PSMI for minor criminal behaviors, for example disorderly conduct, has been reduced by police and court programs that divert these individuals from the criminal justice system and into the mental health system (Lurigio, Smith, & Harris, 2008). Despite these diversionary efforts, substantial numbers of PSMI continue to appear before the judiciary. The court's failure to recognize the association between psychiatric illness and criminal activity may have contributed to the repeated cycling of PSMI through the criminal justice system (Bernstein & Seltzer, 2003; Lurigio & Swartz, 2000). In response, stakeholders in the criminal justice system sought to address the issue by creating a specialty court, known as "mental health court." The development and growth of mental health courts (MHCs) has been spurred on by two converging legal trends: therapeutic jurisprudence and the drug court movement.

Therapeutic Jurisprudence

First appearing in the law literature in the late 1980s, the term therapeutic jurisprudence arose in the field of mental health law. Therapeutic jurisprudence is defined as "the study of the extent to which substantive rules, legal procedures, and the roles of lawyers and judges produce therapeutic or anti-therapeutic consequences for individuals involved in the legal process" (Hora, Schma, & Rosenthal, 1999, p. 440). Therapeutic jurisprudence is a conceptual framework for examining a variety of legal subjects, including the criminal court system's response to the behavioral health care problems and needs of PSMI. Using social scientific theories and methodologies, therapeutic jurisprudence also explores the harmful and healthful effects of legal decisions on people's lives. Since its introduction, legal scholars from a wide variety of disciplines have applied the concept of therapeutic jurisprudence in order to understand and foster the psychological well-being of participants in the legal process and to address the emotional and social problems of legal consumers. The concept of therapeutic jurisprudence encourages the court to be problem-solving, proactive, and results-oriented in its responses to cases, and it assumes that punishment should be reserved for only people that "deserve" punishment (Schneider, Bloom, & Heerema, 2007). Therapeutic jurisprudence was the driving concept behind an umbrella of "problem-solving courts," which emerged to address offender recycling problems that have not improved with the traditional judicial model (Winick, 2002). The most prevalent and widely known application of therapeutic jurisprudence via a problem-solving court model is the drug treatment court.

Drug Treatment Court

Beginning in 1989, drug treatment courts (or "drug courts") introduced treatment principles into the criminal justice process for defendants with substance use disorders. Led by a judge, drug treatment court staff work as a team to develop a treatment plan. In exchange for agreeing to participate in mandatory drug treatment, offenders have their charges dismissed or reduced, or they receive other incentives (Hartley & Phillips, 2001). In its first two decades of operations, drug courts have grown to more than 2,000 nationwide, giving legitimacy to the concept of a problem-solving court that focuses on the needs and characteristics of the offender and causes of criminal behavior (Dorf & Fagan, 2003). The drug treatment court model has transformed specialized criminal courts from adversarial and legalistic to a more therapeutic and rehabilitative approach, thus laying the foundation for MHCs (Fulton-Hora, 2002).

MHC Model

Following the development and proliferation of drug treatment courts, the first MHC in the nation was implemented in Broward County, Florida, in 1997. Hundreds of MHCs are now operating across the country (Council of State Governments Justice Center, 2009). The numerous jurisdictions that have implemented MHCs tailor their program to meet the local needs of their community; thus, the design of MHCs often reflects the availability of resources, funding sources, and political exigencies at the local level. Because of variability among localities, no single MHC model fits all. However, the general working definition of a MHC is a court with a specialized docket for certain defendants with mental illnesses (Council of State Governments Justice Center, 2008; Redlich, Steadman, Monahan, Robbins, & Petrila, 2006). MHCs move beyond traditional court approaches to crime and punishment by examining the causes of behavior and offering assistance to address those causes. Mental health courts are voluntary; they divert consenting individuals from trial and possible incarceration to monitored community-based treatment as a condition of program participation (Boothroyd, Poythress, McGaha, & Petrila, 2003; Nochomovitz & Hickman, 2008; Redlich, 2005). Such courts also directly supervise clients, requiring them to attend regular status hearings in the presence of a judge and rewarding and sanctioning them to encourage compliance with court-ordered conditions of release (Redlich et al., 2006). Mental health courts also strive to provide an alternative to hospitalization, reduce the number of individuals being incarcerated for low-level crimes, and afford better access to treatment than what is currently provided in jails (Nochomovitz & Hickman, 2008).

Mental health courts vary on their eligibility criteria, including types of charges and mental illness diagnoses accepted, as well as plea requirements and the referral process; nonetheless, they are united by a problem-solving approach that emphasizes linking defendants to effective treatment (Council of State Governments Justice Center, 2009). Court researchers and practitioners have identified 10 essential components of a MHC: (1) planning and administration; (2) target population; (3) timely participation identification and linkage to services; (4) terms of participation; (5) informed choice; (6) treatment supports and services; (7) confidentiality; (8) court team; (9) monitoring adherence to court requirements; and (10) sustainability (Council of State Governments Justice Center, 2008).

MHC Operations and Policies

Participant Eligibility

The client eligibility criteria of MHCs differ, even though most of them pursue common goals related to the reduction of recidivism and the provision of behavioral health care services. In many MHCs, individuals are identified as possible MHC participants within days after arrest. Screening processes vary as some jails have mental health workers who screen people for mental illnesses whereas others access a database that identifies people who have used mental health services or received disability income for a mental illness in the recent past. MHCs also identify potential participants through referrals from a number of sources, including public defenders, private lawyers, jail staff, and defendant family members. A defendant can also request consideration for the program (Steadman, Redlich, Griffin, Petrila, & Monahan, 2005).

The basic eligibility requirement for participation in a MHC is a diagnosis of mental illness. Each individual court has other, more specific eligibility requirements. For example, the National Survey of Mental Health Courts (NAMI, TAPA Center, GAINS Center, & Consensus Project, 2005) found that one-third of the courts admitted to the program only defendants with an Axis I diagnosis (acute symptoms that need treatment). People with developmental disabilities (mental retardation) rarely participate in MHCs (fewer than 10%) and even fewer (only 3%) admit defendants with a primary Axis II diagnosis (personality disorder). According to the national survey, some courts use the severity of the psychiatric disorder to determine eligibility for admission rather than an Axis I or Axis II diagnosis. For example, approximately 25% of MHCs admit only offenders with a "severe and persistent mental illness." Another 4% of the courts expressly defined the following diagnostic categories as constituting a severe and persistent mental illness: schizophrenia, schizoaffective disorder, bipolar disorder, and major depression (NAMI et al., 2005).

Besides diagnosis, a few MHCs consider other factors relating to an individual's mental illness. For instance, 8% of surveyed courts limit participation to defendants whose mental illness contributed directly to the offense for which they were charged. A small percentage (4%) of courts base eligibility on the availability of treatment for the defendant; others also consider the "treatability" of the defendant and the defendant's willingness to take medication as part of the treatment plan (NAMI et al., 2005).

After an individual is identified as having a mental illness, the MHC staff collaboratively reviews the current charges and history of violence in order to make a determination of MHC eligibility. Many MHCs restrict participation to people with nonviolent, misdemeanor charges; a smaller portion of such courts accepts people with felony charges. Increasingly, courts are accepting a combination of misdemeanor and felony charges or individuals with felonies only (Erickson, Campbell, & Lamberti, 2006; Redlich, 2005). Redlich and colleagues (2005) reported that many of the first-generation MHCs accept only defendants with misdemeanors.

The second generation of MHCs is more likely to accept individuals with felonies and violent charges. Specifically, according to the National

Survey of Mental Health Courts, more than one-fourth (27%) of the courts admit only defendants with misdemeanor charges, fewer than half (46%) admit only defendants with nonviolent misdemeanor or felony charges, and a very low percentage (3%) admit defendants with felony charges only. A low percentage of MHCs (5%) evaluate for admission defendants who have been charged with any type of offense (NAMI et al., 2005).

Some authors have suggested that MHCs should accept only felony charges and individuals with misdemeanors should be diverted from the courts altogether (Fisler, 2005; Redlich et al., 2005). However, court policies on eligible charge types are often fueled by the public's faulty perception that all or most people with mental disorders are violent and in order to ensure community safety, only individuals with misdemeanors should be diverted to MHCs and community treatment (Fisler, 2005). The public's perception of community safety might also influence the courts' refusal to accept individuals with a history of violent crimes.

Meeting the criteria for MHC eligibility is only the first step in program admission. Defendants must also be deemed competent to stand trial in order to participate in the court's proceedings. Competency is a requirement to be admitted into MHC, but no subsequent evaluations are conducted to ensure that clients are competent throughout the process of program participation and therefore able to render decisions about case planning or to participate in court hearings (Stafford & Wygant, 2005). Moreover, little is known about clients who were denied access to a MHC program because of incompetence. What proportion of such defendants has been denied entry? What are their characteristics and their outcomes in the court and supervisory process? (Stafford & Wygant, 2005). Allowing a mentally compromised defendant to participate in MHC violates the principles of therapeutic jurisprudence. Such defendants are unable to competently opt out of participation in a program that subjects them to punitive and restrictive rules and regulations.

MHCs often treat individuals who would have otherwise been sentenced to incarceration or standard probation with no opportunities to receive specialty services. Most clients must initially consent to participate in mandatory treatment, which supplies the leverage needed to serve clients who are difficult to engage in the community supervision process. Typically, MHC participants have failed previous treatment episodes and have records of incarceration. The combination of court mandates and the support of the MHC team can help clients benefit from services and complete the program successfully (Lurigio, Lyons, Braude, & Jantz, 2008).

The decision to accept or reject an individual for MHC participation is made by a team of court staff, including the judge, state prosecutor, public defender, caseworkers, probation officers, court administrators, and treatment providers who have specialized knowledge of mental health issues (Bazelon Center for Mental Health Law, 2003; Griffin, Steadman, & Petrila, 2002). This team approach is also utilized to expedite the transfer of eligible individuals out of the jail and into the MHC program. Several jurisdictions with MHCs report that they have significantly reduced the total days PSMI spend in jail compared with the number of days that PMSI spend in jail in jurisdictions with only traditional courts (Christy, Poythress, Boothroyd, Petrila, & Mehra, 2005). In the courts studied by Griffin and colleagues (2002), participants were identified and referred to the MHC within 24 to 48 hours after arrest. Depending on the court, researchers have found that the processing of eligible participants ranges from 1 to 47 days with acceptance rates ranging from 20% to 100% (Steadman et al., 2005).

Rejection from MHCs is typically due to mental health status, prior arrests, or individual preference for a traditional court disposition (Steadman et al., 2005). Other reasons for exclusion include offense types such as child abuse, first-time offenses, chronic offenses, sex offenses, and offenses in which a firearm was used in the commission of a crime. Several MHCs also exclude persons with driving under the influence and domestic violence charges, because their district has specialty courts for defendants convicted of those offenses. Individuals who are rejected from the MHC are removed from the court's docket and typically redirected to the traditional court. Defendants can also decline to participate in the MHC for a variety of reasons.

Plea Arraignments

MHCs' policy regarding plea arraignments varies by court. Many MHCs require a guilty or no contest plea to participate (Bernstein & Seltzer, 2003). After graduating from MHC, charges are often dismissed. Courts generally subscribe to one of three plea models: (1) *pre-adjudication*, in which guilty pleas are required but the case is not adjudicated at the onset; (2) *post-plea-based*, in which convictions are rendered but sentences are not imposed; or (3) *probation-based*, in which sentences to probation are imposed but jail is deferred (Griffin et al., 2002; Redlich et al., 2005). Critics argue that requiring a guilty plea without trial or using a guilty plea as leverage is an obstacle to community integration (i.e., felony convictions may restrict housing and benefit eligibility) (Bernstein & Seltzer, 2003) and a violation of due process (Haimowitz, 2002; Seltzer, 2005). Redlich and colleagues (2005) found that the second generation of MHCs is more likely to employ a post-plea arraignment, which means referrals for potential participants occur later in the criminal justice process.

Treatment Planning

Upon diversion from jail to the MHC, a hearing is arranged for new participants. Case hearings are designed to be an informal venue for defendants, judges, the MHC staff, community treatment providers, and, on occasion, participants' family members, to engage in a dialogue. Boothroyd and colleagues (2003) compared hearings in traditional courts and MHCs. They found that defendants in MHC are encouraged to speak and interact with the judge, whereas defendants in traditional courts speak very little. During case hearings, the judge spoke about half the time while the defendant spoke about 33% of the time. The remaining commentary came from attorneys, MHC staff, and treatment providers. The researchers also found that during hearings, court personnel and defendants discussed defendants' understanding of the goals and voluntary nature of the court (but only in 16% of cases), as well as issues related to the defendant's mental health history and current needs (Boothroyd et al., 2003). Redlich (2005) cautions that because of the informal nature of the courts, due process is especially vulnerable to be violated.

In many MHCs, during the initial hearing, participants and staff agree on treatment specifications and probation conditions. Treatment of some type is required in nearly all MHCs (Erickson et al., 2006). In some cases, participants are already linked with a mental health treatment provider; in these instances, the court will likely recommend that the participants return to or remain in treatment. The MHC team can also make new recommendations or ask a community mental health provider to develop a treatment plan. In addition, courts can make recommendations but ask participants to follow up with agencies on their own (Boothroyd et al., 2003). Many courts recommend medication as the only treatment (Bernstein & Seltzer, 2003; Petrila, 2004).

Treatment Monitoring

As we indicated above, court supervision is an integral component of MHC participation; it ranges from contacts "as needed" to weekly or even more frequent appearances before the court (Griffin et al., 2002). The researchers identified three models of MHC supervision. In the first model, the MHC staff refers clients to community treatment and requires them to report to the court on a regular basis. For example, the Broward County MHC treatment team is equipped to initiate treatment directly because they have access to a 24-bed, inpatient sector housed on the grounds of a state hospital. It is a residential program with small cottages that house participants of the courts. Psychiatrists visit to manage medication, employment services are available, and transportation is provided

(Mikhail, Akinkunmi, & Poythress, 2001). Despite having access to this resource, Broward County relies on local social service providers to treat and monitor participants (Boothroyd, Mercado, Poythress, Christy, & Petrila, 2005).

In the second model, the mental health treatment and court staff supervise participants collaboratively (Griffin et al., 2002). For example, in San Bernardino and Santa Barbara MHCs, teams of mental health treatment staff and probation officers work together to supervise participants (Griffin et al., 2002). In this model, community treatment providers supply the courts with progress reports on their clients. In the third model, only MHC staff supervise clients. Of the MHCs surveyed by Redlich and colleagues (2005), 50% had community treatment providers monitor participants, roughly 38% had court staff or probation officers monitor participants, and 25% had both parties monitor participants. Newer MHCs tend to adopt a model of treatment monitoring in which the MHC staff provides all or nearly all of the supervision (Redlich et al., 2005). Regardless of who supervises participants, the judge is generally at the center of both treatment and supervision (Goldkamp & Irons-Guynn, 2000).

Length of Probation

The length of supervision for MHC clients also varies greatly among courts. For example, MHCs can limit the length of supervision to the state's maximum sentence for the crime (Griffin et al., 2002). Others mandate supervision from three months to open-ended periods of supervision (NAMI et al., 2005). As Watson and colleagues (2000) stated, "State law specifies and limits which crimes may be the basis for an order of probation or supervision imposed without a conviction" (Watson, Luchins, Hanrahan, Heyrman, & Lurigio, 2000, p. 481). In 40% of courts surveyed, supervised treatment is longer in the MHC than the jail sentence would be in a traditional court (Bernstein & Seltzer, 2003). Many courts have no written policies for the potential length of supervision, and it is unclear what is required for graduation from MHC (Bernstein & Seltzer, 2003; Erickson et al., 2006; Seltzer, 2005). In other courts, charges are dropped only after clients have successfully completed mandated treatment. Critics argue that the courts often inadequately define participant "success" (Seltzer, 2005).

Rewards and Sanctions

As reported in a survey of MHCs, the failure to participate in mandated services or to adhere to the conditions of supervision can lead to the imposition of a range of sanctions, such as requiring more services (36%) and increasing the frequency of supervision (27%) (Bazelon Center, 2003).

The courts surveyed also placed non-adherent clients in jail (64%) or removed clients from the program (18%). Similarly, the National Survey of Mental Health Courts (NAMI et al., 2005) found that violations of court mandates can lead to detention in jail (60%) or a modification of treatment plans (39%). Other sanctions for violating the conditions of MHC supervision can include verbal warnings, written essays, curfews, electronic monitoring, and more frequent reporting to probation officers. Defendants who wish to transfer to traditional criminal court after they have agreed to participate in MHC could face penalties—a practice reported by 56% of the MHCs in a national survey (Bazelon Center, 2003).

To increase compliance with court-ordered mandates, MHCs use a wide range of sanctions, including detention in jail, which is used more often in courts that accept clients convicted of felonies than in those that accept clients convicted of misdemeanors (Redlich et al., 2006). Redlich and colleagues (2006) surveyed a sample of MHCs and found that 8% never use jail as a sanction, whereas 2% use it in most of their cases. Redlich and colleagues (2005) also noted that the second generation of MHCs is using jail as a sanction more regularly compared to the first generation of MHCs.

Just as sanctions are used as punishment for failure to comply with the conditions of probation, rewards are used to recognize participants for adhering to probation and treatment requirements. MHCs use rewards when participants comply with treatment plans, remain drug-free and sober, and obey probation and court mandates. Rewards include being called first in court, applause, verbal praise and public recognition of accomplishments, fewer court appearances, fewer urine analyses, overnight passes to visit family, fewer restrictions on freedom, and ultimately, graduation from MHC.

MHC Participants

The demographic characteristics of MHC participants typically reflect the client population of the courts and the communities they serve. Compared with the composition of the jail population, persons referred to MHCs tend to be older, white women diagnosed with schizophrenia, schizoaffective disorder, and bipolar disorder (Steadman et al., 2005). Conversely, other studies suggest that nonwhite, homeless individuals committing multiple crimes in the past 12 months are the most common MHC participants (McNiel & Binder, 2007). Although most MHC participants have an Axis I diagnosis, some MHCs may accept participants with a head injury or developmental disabilities (Bernstein & Seltzer, 2003; Erickson et al., 2006).

All MHCs report that participation is voluntary. As we discussed above, eligible individuals must be able to consent to the process and conditions of MHC (Goldkamp & Irons-Guynn, 2000). Research on competency is sparse and has produced mixed results (Erickson et al., 2006). In studies that investigated enrolled participants, researchers reported that individuals with greater insight into their illness have a better understanding of the MHC (Redlich, Hoover, Summers, & Steadman, 2008), are more likely to enter the courts, and experience less coercion in treatment than eligible individuals with less insight (Redlich, 2005). Some research suggests that individuals with schizophrenia were, on average, more impaired than individuals with other diagnoses (Steadman et al., 2005); other research found no distinct differences on demographic characteristics or diagnoses between individuals deemed incompetent or competent (Stafford & Wygant, 2005).

Redlich and colleagues (2008) studied competency in MHCs using the Dusky standard, which asserts that individuals must have a factual and rational understanding of the MHC and its processes. Mental health court personnel must ensure that clients are provided with sufficient information to make a decision about participation, that decision making is voluntary and without any coercion, and that clients are competent enough to make their own treatment decisions (Redlich et al., 2005). Studies on the voluntary nature of MHCs conclude that some individuals do not know MHCs are voluntary. Specifically, in a study conducted by Redlich et al. (2008), roughly 60% of surveyed MHC participants reported that they were unaware that the process was voluntary. Many participants reported that someone other than themselves made the final decision to participate.

Although researchers conclude that the majority of participants seem to make "knowing, intelligent, and voluntary" decisions, they note that clients are often limited in their knowledge regarding the voluntary nature of participation, their right to transfer out of the program, the requirements of graduation and length of treatment, and the potential disadvantages of MHC participation (Redlich et al., 2008). Seltzer (2005) further cautions that individuals are making decisions about participating in MHCs under great stress, and courts do not always honor the right of clients to opt out of the MHC process at any time.

Most of the defendants accepted for participation in a MHC are diagnosed with schizophrenia, schizoaffective disorder, bipolar disorder, and major depression (Steadman et al., 2005). As the NAMI survey found, the majority of MHCs also report that a significant number of participants have a co-occurring substance use disorder (NAMI et al., 2005). This population of individuals often has complicated symptoms. When MHC clients experience more severe symptoms, such as psychotic episodes, the court is likely to continue its authority over clients, compelling them to adhere to treatment. Despite their focus on clients' mental health problems, MHCs operate mostly in accordance with criminal proceedings. Stafford and Wygant (2005) conclude that "a number of defendants with major mental illness and misdemeanor charges lack the capacity to waive the constitutional rights and make the informed decisions necessary to participate in mental health court. Therefore, the goals underlying both the legal and service-providing aspects of MHCs may sometimes be conflicting" (p. 257).

Funding MHC

The Law Enforcement and Mental Health Project Act, sponsored in the Senate by Mike DeWine (R-Ohio) and in the House of Representatives by Ted Strickland (D-Ohio), was signed into law by President Bill Clinton in November 2000. The law authorized funding for the county-level implementation of MHCs. Congress appropriated $5 million and $4 million in fiscal years 2002 and 2003, respectively, for seed money to support the implementation of MHC programs. However, no such funds were allocated in fiscal year 2004 by the House of Representatives or by the Commerce, Justice, State, and Judiciary Appropriations Subcommittees of the Senate.

With limited federal funding, MHCs rely on competitive federal and state grants to help support administrative costs and personnel (Council of State Governments Justice Center, 2008). Many MHC development grants have been awarded under the Mentally Ill Offender Treatment and Crime Reduction Act (MIOTCRA), which was signed into law by President Bush in 2004 and was reauthorized by Congress in 2008. This law created the Justice and Mental Health Collaboration Program and authorized a $50 million grant program to be administered by the Department of Justice. Additionally, some courts utilize county funds through sales tax, grants, and other county-based funding sources to support the program.

The Current State of Mental Health Court

Researchers have distinguished between the "first generation" of MHCs, which were created in roughly the first five years of MHC operations, and second-generation courts, which were created since 2002 (Redlich et al, 2005). Although there are many overlapping characteristics between first- and second-generation MHCs, Redlich (2005) note that the second generation of MHCs are more likely to accept persons with felony or violent offenses; employ post-plea adjudication models; use jail as a sanction; and utilize court personnel or probation for supervision. MHCs rely on state and federal grants and local funding sources to support operation of the courts. Given the current budget restriction at all three levels of government, it is unclear whether MHCs will continue to proliferate at the same pace as they have over the past decade.

Effectiveness of MHC

The number of MHCs has increased rapidly in their first 14 years of operation, with approximately 250 in operation and many in the planning stages (Council of State Governments Justice Center, 2009; Steadman, Redlich, Callahan, Robbins, & Vesselinov, 2011). After 14 years of operations, researchers continue to investigate the impact of MHCs on the judicial system, community, and participants. Mental health court outcome research focuses on recidivism rates, symptom reduction, quality of life, and service utilization. Researchers have identified promising preliminary outcomes for individuals who participate in MHCs. For example, MHCs appear to reduce recidivism among their participants (Christy et al., 2005; Council of State Governments Justice Center, 2008; Gurrera, 2005; Herinckx, Swart, Ama, Dolezal, & King, 2005; Sarteschi, Vaughn, & Kim, 2011; Trupin & Richards, 2003).

In a recently published meta-analysis of 18 outcome studies, MHCs were associated with reduced criminal recidivism with an average effect size of −0.54 (Sarteschi et al., 2011), especially among program graduates. Mental health court graduates were 3.7 times less likely to be arrested than nongraduates (Herinckx et al., 2005). Graduates also reported significantly more days to new arrest than nonparticipants (McNiel & Binder, 2007; Trupin & Richards, 2003). Moore and Hiday (2006) attribute this success to individuals' receipt of a "full dose" of MHC.

Not only do MHCs appear to reduce recidivism, they also seem to reduce the severity of future criminal activity, at least during the year following participation (Cosden, Ellens, Schnell, Yamini-Diouf, & Wolfe, 2003; Gurrera, 2005; Moore & Hiday, 2006). Among MHC participants who are rearrested, their crimes are likely to be nonviolent offenses or parole violations (Cosden et al., 2003; Gurrera, 2005; McNiel & Binder, 2007). MHC participants also reported a decrease in violent acts during MHC probation. The same sample of MHC participants reported fewer violent acts during the eight-month follow-up period, compared with a matched sample of traditional court participants (Christy et al., 2005).

MHCs have also been found to enhance the quality of life for participants. In a meta-analysis, MHC participants, on average, were more likely than non-MHC participants to report significant improvements in quality of life—i.e., overall state of health and fulfillment of family, occupational, and social obligations (Sarteschi, 2009). Preliminary research also suggests greater service utilization among MHC participants. In one investigation, MHC participants increased their service use by 62% in the eight months following MHC participation compared with the eight months prior to participation. Service utilization was also higher for MHC participants compared with non-MHC participants with mental health disorders (Boothroyd et al., 2003). Interestingly, in this study, researchers found no significant relationship between the treatments recommended during MHC hearings and the services that MHC participants actually utilized in the follow-up period (Boothroyd et al., 2003). In other words, the treatment plans recommended by MHC staff are not always utilized by MHC participants after the initial hearings. Clients' failure to seek services might be due to the lack of availability of community services, participants' treatment preferences, or a disconnection between the MHC staff and community treatment providers.

Nearly all MHCs strive to reduce the psychiatric symptoms of their participants. However, no current studies have shown that MHCs are achieving this goal (Boothroyd et al., 2005). One of the few studies that measured psychiatric symptoms actually found that participants' symptoms worsened over time in both traditional courts and MHCs. Researchers noted that although individuals were engaged in treatment, no record of the type and quality of service was ever examined. This preliminary analysis suggests that treatment and MHC participation alone might not be sufficient to reduce symptoms (Boothroyd et al., 2005).

Limitations of Current MHC Research

Although research on MHCs has reported mostly positive outcomes, these studies have several limitations, which temper conclusions about the effectiveness of MHCs. Most studies of MHC have employed weak research designs. For example, few investigations are prospective or include random assignment to either MHC or another program. Additionally, many MHC studies select only MHC graduates, which is likely to introduce selection bias and therefore overstate the overall effectiveness of MHC.

Perhaps the most significant weakness in extant MHC effectiveness research is the lack of an appropriate comparison group. Nearly every MHC effectiveness study employs "treatment as usual" as a control group, or no comparison group at all. Even the most recently published, and arguably the most scientific, multisite study of MHCs utilized regular court processing for a comparison condition (Steadman et al., 2011). Given the large body of literature demonstrating deleterious outcomes for PSMI who receive "treatment as usual" through the criminal justice system, it is not surprising that specialized programming, such as MHC, has a relatively positive impact when compared to standard interventions. Lastly, the current state of MHC research does not address whether MHC is more or less effective than competing models for serving PSMI in the criminal justice system, such as diversionary programs for jail detainees or specialized mental health units for probationers.

Criticisms of MHC

Several criticisms have been leveled at the concept of MHC and at MHC operations. For example, Seltzer (2005) and others have argued that the implementation of MHCs is a misguided attempt to fix the structural problems of the mental health system. The development of a MHC in a particular jurisdiction guarantees no improvement in the availability or quality of mental health services to all PSMI in the area and could restrict access to treatment for criminally involved PSMI who are ineligible for or decline to participate in MHC (Council on State and Local Governments, 2002), which, some suggest, contributes to the criminalization of PSMI (Bernstein & Seltzer, 2003). Hence, by virtue of their connection to the court system, MHC participants gain better access to scarce treatment resources, restricting non-MHC participants from timely access to services (Stefan & Winick, 2005).

Wolff (2002) cautions that the depletion or reallocation of funding for MHCs could have anti-therapeutic effects by limiting the availability of services for other PSMI in need. Furthermore, Seltzer cautions against the use of jail as a sanction for noncompliance in MHCs. Using drugs is an illegal behavior, but exhibiting symptoms of a mental disorder is not (Bernstein & Seltzer, 2003). Participants of MHCs who commit a crime but do not meet the requirements for involuntary commitment should not be forced to take medication or enter into mandatory treatment (Bernstein & Seltzer, 2003). Advocacy groups, such as the Bazelon Center (2003), would argue that the MHC process is violating a person's right to self-determination by applying sanctions to treatment noncompliance.

The goals, structure, and operations of MHCs have not been clearly and consistently defined. MHCs evolved from drug treatment courts but have not adopted the precise, or single-program model that typifies most drug courts; in contrast, each MHC has its own rules and procedures (Bazelon

Center, 2003). Nonetheless, consistency among similar jurisdictions would be quite useful, even though no single model for MHCs would necessarily fit all court systems (Watson, Hanrahan, Luchins, & Lurigio, 2001), This inconsistency has resulted in fewer resources being available for operations and less research being conducted on the effectiveness of MHCs compared with drug treatment courts (Steadman, Davidson, & Brown, 2001).

Critics argue that MHCs are too restrictive (Nochomovitz & Hickman, 2008) and accept only the "good risk" clients (Wolff, 2002). Wolff (2002) estimates that MHCs divert from incarceration only 10% to 20% of eligible PSMI in order to minimize the likelihood of bad outcomes through a restrictive court selection process. This criticism addresses both the issue of "creaming" among potential MHC participants, as well as concerns about the overall penetration of MHCs into the larger population of PSMI involved in the criminal justice system.

Critics also have focused on the supervision standards of MHCs. One study found that in 40% of courts surveyed, supervised treatment was longer in the MHC than a jail sentence would be in a traditional court for the same type of offense (Bernstein & Seltzer, 2003). Many courts have no written policies for length of supervision, and the meaning of successful completion or graduation is unclear (Seltzer, 2005; Bernstein & Seltzer, 2003; Erickson et al., 2006). Charges can be dropped after "successful" completion of MHC, but few courts clearly define what is meant by "successful" (Seltzer, 2005). Seltzer (2005) suggests that eligible participants of MHCs should receive a contract that clearly states length of supervision and potential sanctions for noncompliance. Some MHCs do provide individuals with an advocate to assist them through the supervisory process (Seltzer, 2005).

Although not a criticism that applies exclusively to MHC, a growing body of literature is providing an alternative narrative to the "criminalization" hypothesis (i.e., the primary reason for the overrepresentation of PSMI in the criminal justice system is untreated symptoms of mental illness). This critique suggests that mental illness is not the principal cause of criminal justice involvement for most PSMI. Rather, many of the primary risk factors for criminal involvement are shared by PSMI and non-PSMI in the general population and may in fact be more prevalent among PSMI. (Skeem, Manchak, & Peterson, 2011). These criminogenic risk factors include poverty and other forms of social disadvantage (Draine, Salzer, Culhane, & Hadley, 2002; Fisher, Silver, & Wolff, 2006); living in communities with heavy concentrations of substance use, unemployment, and crime (Fisher & Drake, 2007); undiagnosed and untreated trauma histories (Wolff, Blitz, & Shi, 2007); and proximate risk factors, such as expressing antisocial thinking styles and having criminal associates (Andrews, Bonta, & Wormith, 2006; Gendreau & Goggin, 1997). Therefore, remedial programs such as MHC, which focus primarily or wholly on linking clients with mental health services as the sole means to reduce criminal recidivism could fail to address a wider array of potential risk factors for future criminal involvement.

Recommendations

MHC Program Recommendations

The experiences of trail-blazing suggest that MHCs' success is dependent on a number of essential elements, such as staffing (Bernstein & Seltzer, 2003). In their operational history, MHCs function best when adopting a team approach in order to broker treatment and other services for PSMI. Core members of the team should include representatives from the mental health system who are experts in diagnoses and treatment and knowledgeable about how to locate and obtain mental health services. The cross-training of MHC staff members in one another's respective areas enhances levels of program effectiveness and productivity. Specifically, the mental health staff in MHCs should be trained in criminal justice policies and procedures, and the court staff in MHCs should be trained on mental health policies and procedures (Bureau of Justice Assistance, 2000).

MHC participants must be able to avail themselves to multilayers of services. Clients' service needs can vary significantly as a function of the severity of their psychiatric disorders, the length of their histories of treatment, and extensiveness of their social support networks. Hence, participants' treatment plans should be comprehensive, flexible, and tailored to their specific risk, needs, and responsivity. Solidified early in the MHC implementation process and with the full cooperation and approval of mental health authorities at the state and county levels, MHCs should establish and clarify their relationships with the professionals in the program who conduct assessments, engage in case planning, deliver treatment, and provide relapse prevention services. Such relationships expand clients' access to a variety of services.

More effective and available treatments for mental illness can stem the tide of criminalizing PSMI, keeping greater numbers of mentally ill persons off ever-expanding court dockets and out of overcrowded jails (Massaro, 2004; Petrila, Ridgely, & Borum, 2003). Undeniably, mental health services for criminally involved PSMI are viewed widely as the key to addressing the problem of PSMI in the criminal justice system at every step in the process (Council of State and Local Governments, 2002). Further, mandatory treatment is the centerpiece of most criminal justice–based programming for PSMI (Draine, Wilson, & Pogorzelski, 2007). However, mental health services are not a sufficient condition for reducing criminalization and recidivism. Layers of service should include both standard mental health treatment and a wider array of support services to address criminogenic risk factors at numerous levels. In particular, criminally involved PSMI often suffer from multiple psychiatric morbidities, especially co-occurring substance use disorders that put them at higher risk for continued criminal activity and violence and make it more difficult for them to succeed in criminal justice programming (Lurigio, 2009). Furthermore, the provision of stable and supportive housing is a key element in ensuring that MHC participants will have a chance to receive entitlement benefits as well as to reside in a consistently stable and safe environment (Broner et al., 2004).

Persons with serious mental illnesses should volunteer for participation in the MHC programs and provide their informed and competent consent to all aspects of program participation. In general, MHC procedures should be neither more coercive nor oppressive nor more likely to undermine a client's chances for affordable housing, gainful employment, or accessible health care services than standard criminal court procedures (Bazelon Center, 2003).

An attorney with a background in mental health should be assigned when potential MHC defendants initially enter the system in order to protect their rights, to help them understand court procedures, and to act as their advocate (Bazelon Center, 2003). For example, a guilty plea could result in the creation of future barriers for PSMI. This decision should be negotiated only with the advice of an expert attorney who can help the client comprehend the ramifications of pleading guilty (Griffin et al., 2002).

To increase the impact of MHCs, several aspects of the mental health and court systems must be addressed. The successful implementation of MHC depends on greater access to a wide range of services, including housing, drug treatment, and educational programming (Denekla & Berman, 2001). Community-based treatment and resources for MHC participants are imperative (Bazelon Center, 2003; Watson et al., 2001). The failure of the community to provide appropriate mental health treatment for PSMI led, in part, to the development of MHCs (Bureau of Justice Assistance, 2000). Therefore, an integral component of MHC is the availability of community-based treatment programs (Bazelon Center, 2003). However, most jurisdictions have created few, if any, new services for

PSMI; thus, mandatory participation in those services does not guarantee that such programs will be available and accessible in the community (Steadman, Davidson, & Brown, 2001). In addition, to ensure that MHC services match clients' needs, program personnel must collaborate with community treatment providers. MHC protocols should be manualized, containing clearly stated eligibility criteria and standard operating procedures.

Future MHC Research

In a comprehensive article outlining recommendations for MHC research, Wolff and Pogorzelski (2005) suggest that a better comparison group for MHC evaluations would consist of the clients of another specialized criminal justice program designed for PSMI. This sentiment was echoed by an advisory group of MHC experts convened by the Council of State Governments Justice Center (2009), who stressed the importance of studying MHCs and other court interventions that might have a greater system-wide reach, and allowing policy makers to choose between several options. However, to our knowledge, no MHC evaluation in the literature has compared MHC participants to an alternative specialized criminal justice approach for PSMI.

Steadman (2005) suggests that MHC studies with appropriate comparison groups are difficult to conduct because they are expensive and few communities have an alternative model to a MHC. He also notes, however, that such studies are essential for ensuring that empirical knowledge about MHC grows (Steadman, 2005). Furthermore, a mixed-methods approach to evaluation of MHCs and other court programs is suggested, in order to integrate qualitative observations by program staff and clientele into quantitative analyses. Lastly, MHC proponents have encouraged not only studying if a program works, but for whom, and under what conditions (Steadman, 2005; Council of State Governments Justice Center, 2009; Steadman et al., 2001).

Conclusion

In a relatively short period, MHCs have become one of the most dominant strategies for addressing the overrepresentation of PSMI in the criminal justice system. Mental health courts provide a compelling example of collaboration among the judiciary, members of the mental health treatment community, and PSMI stakeholders. Research on MHCs demonstrates that such programs hold promise for effectively reducing recidivism and increasing service utilization, but further research is needed to fully ascertain the costs and benefits of MHC compared with alternative models for supervising PSMI under the court's jurisdiction. Although MHCs have grown at a rapid rate over the past 14 years, most experts agree that MHCs will have the capacity to reach only a small proportion of the overall population of PSMI who are involved in the criminal justice system.

Along with the further development and research of MHC programs, other alternative and complementary programs should continue to be examined, such as specialized probation units (Skeem & Louden, 2006), pre- and post-booking jail diversion programs (Draine, Blank, Kottsieper, & Solomon, 2005), crisis intervention teams (Teller, Munetz, Gill, & Ritter, 2006), and other specialty programs. Hence, specialized programs for PSMI are needed at every interception point of the criminal justice process (Munetz & Griffin, 2006). As such, MHC should be viewed as only one important component of a range of clinical and structural interventions that can help better address the wide-ranging and serious service needs of PSMI involved in the criminal justice system.

References

Andrews, D. A., Bonta, J., & Wormith, J. S. (2006). The recent past and near future of risk and/or need assessment. *Crime and Delinquency, 52*(1), 7–27.

Bazelon Center for Mental Health Law. (2003). Criminalization of people with mental illness: The role of mental courts in system reform. *Jail Suicide/Mental Health Update, 12*, 1–11.

Baumohl, J. (1996). *Homelessness in America*. Westport, CT: Greenwood Publishing Group.

Bernstein, R., & Seltzer, T. (2003). The role of mental health courts in system reform. *University of the District of Columbia Law Review, 7*, 143–162.

Boothroyd, R. A., Mercado, C. C., Poythress, N. G., Christy, A., & Petrila, J. (2005). Clinical outcomes of defendants in mental health courts. *Psychiatric Services, 56*(7), 829–834.

Boothroyd, R. A., Poythress, N. G., McGaha, A., & Petrilla, J. (2003). The Broward mental health court: Process, outcomes, and service utilization. *International Journal of Law and Psychiatry, 26*(1), 55–71.

Broner, N., Lattimore, P. K., Cowell, A. J., & Schlenger, W. E. (2004). Effects of diversion on adults with co-occurring mental illness and substance use; Outcomes from a national multi-site study. *Behavioral Sciences & the Law*, 22, 519–541.

Bureau of Justice Assistance. (2000). *Emerging judicial strategies for the mentally ill in the criminal caseload: Mental health courts*. Washington, DC: U.S. Department of Justice. Retrieved October 30, 2012, from https://www.ncjrs.gov/html/bja/mentalhealth/contents.html.

Christy, A., Poythress, N. G., Boothroyd, R. A., Petrila, J., & Mehra, S. (2005). Evaluating the efficiency and community safety goals of the Broward County mental health court. *Behavioral Sciences & the Law, 23*(2), 227–243.

Cosden, M., Ellens, J. K., Schnell, J. L., Yamini-Diouf, Y., & Wolfe, M. M. (2003). Evaluation of a mental health treatment court with assertive community treatment. *Behavioral Sciences and the Law, 21*(4), 415–427.

Council of State and Local Governments. (2002). *Criminal justice–mental health consensus project report*. New York: Author.

Council of State Governments Justice Center. (2008). *Mental health courts: A primer for policymakers and practitioners*. New York: Council of State Governments.

Council of State Governments Justice Center. (2009). *Mental health courts: A guide to research-informed policy and practice*. New York: Council of State Governments.

Denekla, D., & Berman, G. (2001). *Rethinking the revolving door: A look at mental illness in the courts*. Washington, DC: State Justice Institute.

Diamond, P. M., Wang, E. W., Holzer, C. E., Thomas, C., & Cruser, D. A. (2001). The prevalence of mental illness in prison. *Administration and Policy in Mental Health, 29*(1), 21–40.

Ditton, P. (1999). Mental health and treatment of inmates and probationers. *Bureau of Justice Special Report*, NCJ 174463.

Dorf, M., & Fagan, J. (2003). Problem-solving courts: From innovation to institutionalization. *American Criminal Law Review, 40*(4), 1501–1512.

Draine, J., Blank, A., Kottsieper, P., & Solomon, P. (2005). Contrasting jail diversion and in-jail services for mental illness and substance abuse: Do they serve the same client? *Behavioral Sciences and the Law, 23*(2), 171–181.

Draine, J., Salzer, M. S., Culhane, D. P., & Hadley, T. R. (2002). Role of social disadvantage in crime, joblessness, and homelessness among persons with serious mental illness. *Psychiatric Services, 53*, 565–573.

Draine, J., Wilson, A., & Pogorzelski, W. (2007). Limitations and potential in current research on services for people with mental illness in the criminal justice system. *Journal of Offender Rehabilitation, 45*, 159–177.

Erickson, S. K., Campbell, A., & Lamberti, S. (2006). Variations in mental health courts: Challenges, opportunities, and a call for caution. *Community Mental Health Journal, 42*(4), 335–344.

Fisher, W. H., & Drake, R. E. (2007). Forensic mental illness and other policy misadventures. Commentary on "Extending assertive community treatment to criminal justice settings: Origins, current evidence, and future directions." *Community Mental Health Journal, 43*(5), 545–548.

Fisher, W. H., Silver, E., & Wolff, N. (2006). Beyond criminalization: Toward a criminologically informed framework for mental health policy and services research. *Administration and Policy in Mental Health & Mental Health Services Research, 33*(5), 544–557.

Fisler, C. (2005). Building trust and managing risk: A look at a felony mental health court. *Psychology, Public Policy, and Law, 11*(4), 587–604.

Fulton-Hora, P. (2002). A dozen years of drug treatment courts: Uncovering our theoretical foundation and the construction of a mainstream paradigm. *Substance Use and Misuse, 37*, 1469–1488.

Gendreau, P., & Groggin, C. (1997). Correctional treatment: Accomplishments and realities. In P. Van Voorhis, M. Braswell, & D. Lester (Eds.), *Correctional counseling and rehabilitation* (3rd ed., pp. 271–279). Cincinnati, OH: Anderson.

Goldkamp, J. S., & Irons-Guynn, C. (2000). Emerging judicial strategies for the mentally ill in the criminal caseload: Mental health courts in Fort Lauderdale, Seattle, San Bernardino, and Anchorage. Bureau of Justice Assistance NCJ: 182504.

Griffin, P. A., Steadman, H. J., & Petrila, J. (2002). The use of criminal charges and sanctions in mental health courts. *Psychiatric Services, 58*(10), 1285–1289.

Gurrera, M. M. (2005). *An evaluation of a mental health court: Process, procedure, and outcome.* Retrieved from Dissertations and Theses database (AAT 3269390).

Haimowitz, S. (2002). Law and psychiatry: Can mental health courts end the criminalization of persons with mental illness? *Psychiatric Services, 53*(10), 1226–1228.

Hartley, R. E., & Phillips, R. C. (2001). Who graduates from drug courts? Correlates of client success. *American Journal of Criminal Justice, 26*(1), 107–119.

Herinckx, H. A., Swart, S. C., Ama, S. M., Dolezal, C. D., & King, S. (2005). Rearrest and linkage to mental health services among clients of the Clark County mental health court program. *Psychiatric Services, 56*(7), 853–857.

Hora, P., Schma, W., & Rosenthal, J. (1999). Therapeutic jurisprudence and the drug court movement: revolutionizing the criminal justice system's response to drug abuse and crime in America. *Notre Dam Law Review, 74*, 439–555.

James, D. J., & Glaze, L. E. (2006). Mental health problems of prison and jail inmates. Washington DC: U.S. Department of Justice.

Lamberti, J. S. (2007). Understating and preventing criminal recidivism among adults with psychotic disorders. *Psychiatric Services, 58*, 773–781.

Lurigio, A. J. (2009). Comorbidity. In N. A. Piotrowski (Ed.), *Encyclopedia of psychology and mental health* (pp. 439–442). Pasadena, CA: Salem Press.

Lurigio, A. J., Lyons, T., Braude, L., & Jantz, I. (2008). Exercising therapeutic jurisprudence in an urban felony court: The Cook County Mental Health Court Program. *Executive Exchange, 24*, 8–17.

Lurigio, A. J., Smith, A., & Harris, A. (2008). The challenge of responding to people with mental illness: police officer training and special programs. *The Police Journal, 81*(4), 295–322.

Lurigio, A. J., & Swartz, J. A. (2000). Changing the contours of the criminal justice system to meet the needs of persons with serious mental illness. In J. Horney (Ed.), *NIJ 2000 Series: Policies, processes, and decisions of the criminal justice system* (Vol. 3, pp. 45–108). Washington, DC: National Institute of Justice.

Massaro, J. (2004). *Working with people with mental illness involved in the criminal justice system.* Delmar, NY: National Gains Technical Assistance and Policy Analysis Center for Jail Diversion.

McNiel, D. E., & Binder, R. L. (2007). Effectiveness of a mental health court in reducing criminal recidivism and violence. *American Journal of Psychiatry, 164*(9), 1395–1403.

Mikhail, S., Akinkunmi, A., & Poythress, N. (2001). Mental health courts: A workable proposition? *Psychiatric Bulletin, 25*(1), 5–7.

Moore, M. E., & Hiday, V. A. (2006). Mental health court outcomes: A comparison of re-arrest and re-arrest severity between mental health court and traditional court participants. *Law and Human Behavior, 30*(6), 659–674.

Morrissey, J., Meyer, P., & Cuddeback, G. (2007). Extending assertive community treatment to criminal justice settings: Origins, current evidence, and future directions. *Community Mental Health Journal, 43*(5), 527–544.

Munetz, M., & Griffin, P. (2006). The use of the sequential intercept model as an approach to decriminalization of people with serious mental illness. *Psychiatric Services, 57*, 544–549.

NAMI, TAPA Center, GAINS Center, & Consensus Project. (2005). *Survey of mental health courts.* Retrieved October 30, 2012, from http://www.nami.org/Template.cfm?Section=Grading_the_States_2009&template=/ContentManagement/ContentDisplay.cfm&ContentID=83635.

Nochomovitz, L., & Hickman, F. J. (2008). Mental health, mental health courts, and minorities. In S. Loue & M. Sajatovic (Eds.), *Determinants of minority mental health and wellness.* New York: Springer New York.

Padgett, D. K., Gulcur, L., & Tsemberis, S. (2006). Housing first services for people who are homeless with co-occurring serious mental illness and substance abuse. *Research on Social Work Practice, 16*(1), 74–83.

Petrila, J. (2004). Emerging issues in forensic mental health. *Psychiatric Quarterly, 75*(1), 3–19.

Petrila, J., Ridgley, M. S., & Borum, R. (2003). Debating outpatient commitment: Controversy, trends, and empirical data. *Crime & Delinquency, 49*, 157–172.

Prins, S. J., & Draper, L. (2009). *Improving outcomes for people with mental illnesses under community corrections supervision: A guide to research-informed policy and practice.* New York: Council of State Governments Justice Center.

Redlich, A. D. (2005). Voluntary, but knowing and intelligent: Comprehension in mental health courts. *Psychology, Public Policy, and Law, 11*(4), 605–619.

Redlich, A. D., Hoover, S., Summers, A., & Steadman, H. J. (2008). Enrollment in mental health courts: Voluntariness, knowingness, and adjudicative competence. *Law and Human Behavior.* doi:10.1007/s10979-008-9170-8.

Redlich, A. D., Steadman, H. J., Monahan, J., Petrila, J., & Griffin, P. A. (2005). The second generation of mental health courts. *Psychology, Public Policy, and Law, 11*(4), 527–538.

Redlich, A. D., Steadman, H. J., Monahan, J., Robbins, P. C., & Petrila, J. (2006). Patterns of practice in mental health courts: A national survey. *Law and Human Behavior, 30*, 347–362.

Sarteschi, C. M. (2009). Assessing the effectiveness of mental health courts: A meta-analysis of clinical and recidivism outcomes. Retrieved on November 11, 2009, from http://etd.library.pitt.edu.

Sarteschi, C. M., Vaughn, M. G., & Kim, K. (2011). Assessing the effectiveness of mental health courts: A quantitative review. *Journal of Criminal Justice, 39*, 12–20.

Schneider, R. D., Bloom, H., & Heerema, M. (2007). Mental Health Courts: Decriminalizing the mentally ill. Toronto, Ontario, Canada: Irwin Law.

Seltzer, T. (2005). Mental health courts: A misguided attempt to address the criminal justice system's unfair treatment of people with mental illnesses. *Psychology, Public Policy, and Law, 11*(4), 570–586.

Skeem, J. L., Emke-Francis, P., & Louden, J. E. (2006). Probation, mental health, and mandated treatment: a national survey. *Criminal Justice and Behavior, 33* (2), 158–184.

Skeem, J. L., & Louden, J. E. (2006). Toward evidence-based practice for probationers and parolees mandated to mental health treatment. *Psychiatric Services, 57*(3), 333–342.

Skeem, J. L., Manchak, S., & Peterson, J. K. (2011). Correctional policy for offenders with mental illness: Creating a new paradigm for recidivism reduction. *Law and Human Behavior, 35*(2), 110–126.

Slate, R. N., & Johnson, W. W. (2008). *The criminalization of mental illness: Crisis and opportunity for the justice system*. Durham, NC: Carolina Academic Press.

Stafford, K. P., & Wygant, D. B. (2005). The role of competency to stand trial in mental health courts. *Behavioral Sciences & the Law, 23*(2), 245–258.

Steadman H. J. (2005). *A guide to collecting mental health court outcome data*. New York: Council of State Governments.

Steadman, H., Davidson, S., & Brown, C. (2001). Mental health courts: Their promise and unanswered questions. *Psychiatric Services, 52*, 457–458.

Steadman, H. J., Redlich, A. D., Callahan, L., Robbins, P. C., & Vesselinov, R. (2011). Effect of mental health courts on arrest and jail days: A multisite study. *Archives of General Psychiatry, 68*(2), 167–172.

Steadman, H. J., Redlich, A. D., Griffin, P., Petrila, J., & Monahan, J. (2005). From referral to disposition: Case processing in seven mental health courts. *Behavioral Sciences and the Law, 23*(2), 215–226.

Stefan, S., & Winick, B. J. (2005). A dialogue on mental health courts. *Psychology, Public Policy, and Law, 11*(4), 507–526.

Teller, J. L. S., Munetz, M. R., Gill, K. M., & Ritter, C. (2006). Crisis intervention team training for police officers responding to mental disturbance calls. *Psychiatric Services, 57*, 232–237.

Teplin, L. A. (2000). *Keeping the peace: Police discretion and mentally ill persons*. Washington, DC: National Institute of Justice.

Trupin, E., & Richards, H. (2003). Seattle's mental health courts: Early indicators of effectiveness. *International Journal of Law and Psychiatry, 26*(1), 33–53.

Watson, A., Hanrahan, P., Luchins, D., & Lurigio A. (2001). Mental health courts and the complex issue of mentally ill offenders. *Psychiatric Services, 52*, 477–481.

Watson, A., Luchins, D., Hanrahan, P., Heyrman, M., & Lurigio, A. (2000). Mental health courts: Promises and limitations. *Journal of the American Academy of Psychiatry and Law, 28*, 476–482.

Winick, B. J. (2002). Therapeutic jurisprudence and problem solving courts. *Fordham Urban Law Journal, 30*, 1055–1104.

Wolff, N. (2002). Courts as therapeutic agents: Thinking past the novelty of mental health courts. *Journal of American Academy of Psychiatry and the Law, 30*, 431–437.

Wolff, N., Blitz, C. L., & Shi, J. (2007). Rates of sexual victimization in prison for inmates with and without mental disorders. *Psychiatric Services, 58*(8), 1087–1094.

Wolff, N., & Pogorzelski, W. (2005). Measuring the effectiveness of mental health courts: Challenges and recommendations. *Psychology, Public Policy, and Law, 11*(4), 539–569.

CHAPTER SIXTEEN

Mental State at the Time of the Offense Forensic Psychological Evaluation: Teresa Lewis Death Penalty Case

Ronn Johnson

Teresa Wilson Bean Lewis was the first woman to be given a death sentence in Virginia in almost a century (*Lewis v. Commonwealth of Virginia*, 2004). The case fueled considerable controversy due to a number of forensic psychological factors that included gender, personality, and IQ.

The Circuit Court of Pittsylvania County sentenced Teresa Lewis to death for two counts of capital murder. An earlier case, *Atkins v. Virginia* (2002), seemed to set a contradictory precedent, when the court ruled that to impose the death penalty on someone classified as mentally retarded would constitute cruel and unusual punishment. Opponents of the Lewis ruling argued that since her low IQ score of 72 fell within the same range for mental retardation, she too should have been spared the death penalty. Today the case remains a forensic training platform in criminal psychology. Teresa Lewis was the only woman on death row in Virginia prior to her execution. She was sentenced to death by lethal injection for using sex and money to arrange for the murders of her husband and stepson in October 2002. Lewis sought to profit from a $250,000 life insurance policy that her stepson had taken out as a U.S. Army reservist in anticipation of his deployment to Iraq.

The first part of this chapter explores the issue of forensic psychological training competencies. Attention will also be devoted to psychocultural factors as a critical prerequisite for working with these types of forensic cases. Then, the chapter addresses the relevant forensic psychological factors that arose as a result of the Atkins and Lewis cases, including the question of whether the death penalty should be imposed on a mentally retarded inmate. The chapter compares definitions of mental retardation: clinical and legal, as defined by various state legislatures. Assessment practices in forensic psychology are examined, as well as controversies over current practices and standards regarding the assessment of IQ. Implications and suggestions for criminologist and forensic psychologists are presented. Finally, trends in relevant research are explored.

Forensic Psychological Training Competencies

Training is recognized as effective if the trainee is able to apply clinical and scientific skills to solve problems related to a forensic psychological matter. This expertise usually addresses areas related to assessment, treatment, and consultation (Marczyk, DeMatteo, Kutinsky, & Heilbrun, 2008). The history of forensic psychology can be traced to the work of Hugo Munsterberg (1908), which identified roles that psychologists could assume as experts in various court cases. Probably the most notable of all of these was the work of Carl and Mamie Clark (Guthrie, 1990). Their research involved using dolls to examine children's attitudes about race. The Clarks testified as expert witnesses in *Briggs v. Elliott*, one of the cases rolled into *Brown v. Board of Education* (1954). The Clarks' forensic work played a major role in the ruling of the U.S. Supreme Court decision that that racial segregation in public education was unconstitutional (Guthrie, 1976).

The works of the Clarks and Munsterberg delineate a trail of contributions where psychologists have provided services to the legal system (see Bartol & Bartol, 2006, and Otto & Heilbrun, 2002, for comprehensive summaries). Otto and Heilbrun (2002) detail early examples of training in action, achieved through interactions between psychologists and the incarcerated adult or juvenile offenders they provided with clinical services. Other early activities of psychologists providing services within the criminal justice system included psychological fitness testing of law enforcement personnel and the pretrial evaluation of criminal offenders (Bartol & Bartol, 2006; Johnson & Scott, 2010). These early efforts helped to solidify the relationship between psychologists and the legal system.

Evaluating law enforcement personnel, criminal offenders, and civil litigants has now become commonplace (Melton, Petrila, Poythress, & Slobogin, 2007). The U.S. Court of Appeals for the District of Columbia Circuit decision in *Jenkins v. United States* (1962) held that appropriately qualified psychologists could testify in court as experts in psychiatric disorders, and that psychological measures could be introduced in court to support their expert opinions, expanding the interactions of psychological practitioners within the courts. Following this decision, the use of psychologists as expert witnesses in judicial proceedings has increased dramatically, with thousands of forensic evaluations conducted each year on a variety of psycho-legal issues (Otto & Heilbrun, 2002).

It is generally understood that forensic psychology is a cross-disciplinary specialty area that combines law with psychology research and practice (Weiner & Hess, 2006), but there is less agreement regarding the precise definition and scope of forensic psychology. At its basic level, forensic psychology can be conceptualized as the application of the science and profession of psychology to questions and issues relating to the law and the legal system. This is the definition of forensic psychology adopted by the American Board of Forensic Psychology (ABFP, 2006). Although most practitioners would likely agree, at least in principle, with the core components of this definition, there is considerable disagreement over the scope of forensic psychology and what activities (i.e., research, assessment, and treatment) and roles should appropriately be considered the exclusive province of forensic psychology. The specialty training in forensic psychology primarily occurs at the postdoctoral level (Otto & Heilbrun, 2002). Minimum training required includes:

- Core knowledge in at least one major area (e.g., clinical, developmental, experimental, cognitive)
- Ethical-legal professional codes and guidelines—e.g., *Ethical Principles of Psychologists and Code of Conduct* (American Psychological Association, 2002)—and forensic research and practice—e.g., *Specialty Guidelines for Forensic Psychologists* (Committee on the Revision of the Specialty Guidelines for Forensic Psychology, 2006).
- Research methods and advanced statistics
- Legal knowledge: structure of the legal system, sources of law, legal research, relevant civil and criminal case law, and criminal and civil procedures relevant to forensic practice
- Guidelines for expert witness testimony and case preparation
- Standards for admissibility of expert opinions and testimony
- Use of forensic assessment tools and techniques

- Knowledge of psychopathology from developmental, sexual orientation, ethnoracial, and gender standpoints
- Awareness of evidence-based practices and consultation

Forensic criminal psychology cases require core competencies (Fouad et al., 2009) and the Competency Assessment Toolkit (Kaslow et al., 2009). Psychocultural factors emerge in forensic psychology work and must be included during training (Johnson & Scott, 2010). A sharper focus on biopsychosocial factors would reinforce this foundational forensic training competency. The Teresa Lewis case illustrates that psychocultural factors already influence the conceptualization and operationalization of the competencies relevant to the practice of forensic mental health, and need to be expressly examined in the context of criminal psychology.

Psychocultural Factors in Criminal Psychology Cases

The evidenced-based integration of individual and cultural diversity as a foundational forensic is strengthened by changing demographics, ethical codes, and research—all pointing for the need for this competency (Sue & Sue, 2003). Professional references and other publications used in guiding the work of those in the criminal justice field have only recently attempted to embrace this diversity, and often do not sufficiently or meaningfully cover the subject (Giannet, 2003). Bronfenbrenner's Ecological Model (Forrest, Miller, & Elman, 2008) describes how enmeshed systems and components guide the development of individuals in training. This model suggests that mainstream cultural values (i.e., white, middle-class, male, heterosexual, and able-bodied, among others) impact the approach and conceptualizations used by forensic psychologists. A desirable goal would be to re-craft the training model to ensure it encompasses a wide range of psychocultural influences.

The training process must "examine how dominant culture values (macro) influence interactions with and assessment of trainees from diverse backgrounds (micro and macro), and how macrosystemic notions of diversity and power impact the ability to balance their roles as gatekeeper and educator (Forrest et al., 2008, p. 187). Death penalty cases such as *Lewis v. Virginia* offer the best training, practical, real-life platforms where trainees' core competencies can be assessed through their study of the inherent criminal psychology issues.

Teresa Lewis Case: Forensic Psychology Perspective

The role of mental health status in death penalty cases has been controversial for decades, encompassing topics such as mental illness, IQ and mental retardation, cultural considerations, and the effects of domestic violence. The September 2010 execution of Teresa Lewis in Virginia highlighted the mental competency argument. Lewis's lawyers insisted to the end that she should not be sentenced to death for her involvement in the murders of her husband and stepson because she was borderline mentally retarded with an IQ equivalent to a 13-year-old (Gold, 2010). According to *The Washington Post*, Governor Robert McDonnell denied clemency because Lewis had never been officially diagnosed as "mentally retarded as defined by Virginia law." But was the state's argument psycho-legally viable if cultural influences, demographic factors, and appropriateness of IQ tests in general were taken into consideration? In addition to intelligence level and competency to stand trial, what other forensic mental health issues could be used as mitigators in life or death penalty cases?

Public outcry over the Lewis case continued from the time she was sentenced until her execution. Some advocates argued that she was given an unfair sentence because she was a woman (Leonard, 2010). The actual triggermen in the murder-for-hire scheme against her husband and stepson both received life sentences. Proponents of the discrimination argument theorized that because so few women were ever involved in such heinous murder crimes, when one did come along, she was judged much more harshly than if a man had committed the same crime. In other words, women who step out of their societal role are considered particularly dangerous and evil (Leonard, 2010).

Elizabeth Rapaport (1991) presented an alternate view of death penalty ideology that still resonates today. She found that women were far less represented on death row than men. This, she concluded, was not attributed to women receiving an undeserved lenient hand in sentencing, but rather due to the fact that most women capital offenders lacked two major criteria for receiving the death penalty: a prior criminal record, and commission of a crime that was particularly brutal or serious. She identified a third prong for the few women that were sentenced to death: relative culpability (Rapaport, 1991). Of these categories that seem relevant to death penalty sentencing, the third is most open to interpretation by juries and judges. It seems, then, that Lewis receiving the death penalty may have been debatable only on this last point, considering that the first two prongs were found satisfied (*Lewis v Commonwealth of Virginia*,

2004). This brings us to a discussion of her culpability in the planning and execution of a murder-for-hire scheme. Rapaport (1991) cautions that women are often stigmatized into two categories of culpability: the dominated, manipulated tagalong to a more powerful male, and the manipulator of a male counterpart, using him to take the brunt of the action and fault for the crime. Perhaps the biggest issue of contention with this determination in the Lewis case is her questionable mental capacity.

Mental State at the Time of Offense Forensic Psychology Issues

A forensic evaluation of the mental state of the accused at the time of the offense (MSO) is designed to provide psychological mitigators used in the defense of the accused. In the Teresa Lewis case, the question is whether such an evaluation would uncover clear and convincing evidence to support the opinion that she had mental disease or mental defect at the time of the offense that contributed to the offense for which she was charged. A strong evidence-based link must be made between mental disease and the offending behavior (Applebaum & Gutheil, 1991; Gutheil, 1999). The forensic psychological data is not always linear. That is, all of the information collected may not correlate with the act to which the accused has been charged. There are two primary forensic psychological matters that must be considered in this regard. First, one must have confidence that the forensic psychological opinion rendered in the MSO evaluation is based on the credible (i.e., reliable and valid) data sources. That is, would this data meet the Frye or Daubert standards? What are the state mental disease or defect standards? For example, in evaluating Ms. Lewis directly, to what extent has there been consistency in her clinical presentation and psychologically relevant statements? In this case, has she developed symptoms or displayed behaviors since the time of incarceration that could undermine her integrity (malingering) with regard to how she might want to portray herself (i.e., in a way that benefits her case)?

A second daunting issue revolves around the extent to which a forensic psychological foundation can be crafted from her past that would offer mitigators that would withstand close scrutiny from opposing counsel. For example, are there developmental, ethnoracial, environmental life history issues, psychosocial stressors, or physiological factors that would offer an explanation for the actions of the accused? A somewhat controversial forensic psychological concern is the extent to which the accused was able to exercise some degree of control or restraint over the very behavior that resulted in offense to which they are now charged (Resnick, 2000). A psychological diagnosis of a mental disorder may be used in some aspect of a criminal psychology case even though it does not always answer all of the forensic psychological questions.

The Diagnostic Statistical Manual (DSM-V) is the most widely used diagnostic tool in the United States. Use of the DSM-V is problematic in some criminal psychology case because the presence of a diagnosis does not equate with the legal definition of mental disease, mental defect or whatever legal requirements set forth by a particular statement. For example, the DSM-IV-TR states, "the clinical diagnosis of a DSM-IV mental disorder is not sufficient to establish the existence for legal purposes of a mental disorder, mental disability, mental disease or mental defect" (American Psychiatric Association, 2000).

The forensic assessment insights obtained from the DSM-V may be significantly augmented by using a biopsychosocial framework. A biopsychosocial framework in cases such as Teresa Lewis allows a forensic examiner to provide multiple opinions in the case that can be used by the trier of fact. In this instance, there were biological, psychological, and/or ethnoracial-social factors that provide a foundation that are aimed at addressing the Daubert or other state criteria. With the caveat of the reliability and validity of Internet and media sources, and the information in this case, there are several observations. A forensic psychological examination includes a review of relevant academic, mental health, legal contacts, medical records, and interviews with Ms. Lewis as well as third-party interviews. The specific MSO evaluation issues of the Teresa Lewis case center around information available through public sources allowed some of the following findings to be identified.

1. Teresa Lewis may have been convincingly viewed as operating with intent by recruiting the men to kill her husband and son.
2. She offered insurance gifts, money, and sex in exchange for the murders.
3. Men were motivated to receive the insurance money after the deaths.
4. She was a person who had a history of mental instability and whose intellectual functioning made her more vulnerable to being duped or manipulated by others.
5. Teresa Lewis had a history of contact with DSS and removal of her children for abuse-neglect issues.
6. Court records reveal psychiatric evaluations, and DSS reports reveal some concern about her ability to remain consistently compliant with intervention plans aimed at family restoration.
7. Psychological testing providing conflicting IQ estimates that fuel concerns about methods used by the examiners and malingering issues in the accused.

8. A dependent personality disorder or traits could fuel a tendency for Ms. Lewis to get involved in distorted or imbalanced relationships where they require constant assistance and reassurance from others.
9. Use of a biopsychosocial framework when there are co-occurring disorders, a forensic psychologist can reliably assign the contributions of each diagnostic entity to the defendant's functional impairments at the time of the offense. After all, it is only those impairments attributed to a personality disorder that would not be permitted to nullify criminal responsibility under the alternative assertion for this debate. Impairments attributed to another diagnosis may be considered for nullification of criminal responsibility; therefore, it is critical that clinicians be able to reliably differentiate among diagnoses and reliably attribute functional impairments to each of them. In such complicated situations, it may not be possible as a matter of science to reliably parse out the relative contributions of each diagnostic entity, particularly if asked to do so in the "point in time" analysis of a defendant's mental status at the time of a specific offense. In practice, it is often difficult to confidently parse out the relative contributions of co-occurring diagnoses even in much simpler situations.
10. The children were removed from Lewis's custody in September 1996, after the behavior of the youngest child raised concerns that he had been sexually abused. Further investigation demonstrated that both Ervin and Shakela showed physical, emotional, and behavioral indications of long-term sexual abuse.
11. Lewis's brother and his girlfriend lived with the family at the time the children were removed, and some evidence indicated that the brother sexually abused the children. All three children were found to be neglected and abused, as they were also subjected to physical abuse and neglect.
12. The finding of abuse suffered by the children was not contested. The record demonstrates that the children had special needs due to their history of abuse. They required a highly structured environment and cooperation among their counselors, caregivers, and teachers. Their counselor, Mary Elizabeth McGhee, testified that she was concerned for their welfare if they were in an environment of inadequate supervision or structure.
13. Dr. Susan Rosebro conducted two parent competency evaluations of Lewis, one in March 1998 and one in September 1998. The reevaluation was done after Lewis completed both the parenting and the sexual abuse classes and participated in individual counseling.
14. Dr. Rosebro noted that, despite the instruction Lewis had received, she failed to respond appropriately when asked what behavior might indicate a child was sexually abused. Rosebro also observed that, when Lewis discussed with the children the sexual abuse that had occurred, Lewis minimized what had occurred, rephrased the children's complaint, and failed to acknowledge any responsibility for not protecting the children. Dr. Rosebro met with the children and expressed concern about Lewis's ability to protect them.

Case Discussion

Teresa Lewis, a woman assessed as having "borderline mental retardation," was executed in Virginia for being identified as the "mastermind" behind the murder of her husband and stepson. The men who actually carried out the killing received life prison sentences.

Matthew Shallenberger and Rodney Fuller shot and killed Julian Lewis and his adult son Charles Lewis in their home in the early hours of October 30, 2002. On May 15, 2003, Teresa Lewis pleaded guilty to capital murder for her role in the killings, a plea that meant she would be sentenced by a judge rather than a jury. Prosecutors claimed that she had lured Shallenberger and Fuller with sex, gifts, and a promise to share life insurance proceeds to commit the murders. Fuller received a life sentence in return for a guilty plea and his cooperation, and the judge, "in good conscience," said he could not sentence Shallenberger to a harsher sentence than Fuller received.

A psychologist tested Teresa Lewis prior to her plea and found that she had an IQ (intelligence quotient) of 72, indicating that her intellectual function was in the "borderline mental retardation" range. Post-conviction investigations raised additional evidence of her mental disabilities. A second psychologist, selected by the state, assessed her IQ at 70. Other mental health experts diagnosed her with dependent personality disorder and an addiction to painkillers before the crimes, that all raised doubts as to her somehow being designated as the "mastermind." Perhaps the forensic psychological evidence could have been more persuasive in a jury as opposed to a bench trial with regards to the IQ issues.

In contrast, Shallenberger's IQ was scored at 113 (and Fuller's at 68). In an interview conducted by Lewis's defense team in 2004, Shallenberger said that he had "manipulated the whole thing," and that the murders had been his idea. According to an investigator for the defense, Shallenberger informed him that "as soon as he met Teresa, he sized her up as someone who was not too bright and could be easily manipulated." The investigator asserted that Shallenberger said that, while he had committed the crime for the proceeds from the life insurance policies he assumed the victims would have, "he and Teresa never specifically talked about money, about the insurance, or about Teresa 'paying' him for any killing." Separately, in a letter to a friend obtained by the lawyers, Shallenberger wrote that "the only reason I had sex with [Teresa Lewis] was for the money—to get her to 'fall in love' with me so she would give me the insurance money." Also in 2004, Fuller said that "it seemed to me that Mrs. Lewis would do just about anything Shallenberger asked her to do," and that "Shallenberger was definitely the one in charge of things, not Mrs. Lewis."

Several of the above findings raise considerable concern about Teresa Lewis's cognitive capacity to function as an adequate parent when it came to making decisions to care for or protect her children.

Intelligence Quotient and Testing

The *Atkins* case (2002) provided that no one classified as mentally retarded could receive the death penalty; however, it left the definition of mental retardation up to the individual states to determine. Most of these state definitions derive from either the American Association on Intellectual and Developmental Disabilities (formerly the AAMR) classification or the American Psychological Association (APA) classification contained in the DSM-IV-TR (Duvall & Morris, 2006).

The AAMR created its most recent definition in 2002, which states: "Mental retardation is a disability characterized by significant limitations both in intellectual functioning and in adaptive behavior as expressed in conceptual, social, and practical adaptive skills. This disability originates before age 18" (2002, p. 1). This definition is unique in that it acknowledges a three-part designation for adaptive functioning. In contrast, the APA (2000) defines mental retardation as: "A. Significantly sub-average intellectual functioning: and IQ of approximately 70 or below on an individually administered IQ test. B. Concurrent deficits or impairments in present adaptive functioning (i.e., the person's effectiveness in meeting the standards expected for his or her age by his or her cultural group) in at least two of the following areas: communication, self-care, home living, social/interpersonal skills, use of community resources, self-direction, functional academic skills, work, leisure, health, and safety. C. The onset is before age 18 years" (APA, 2000, p. 49). The definitions of adaptive functioning are likewise varied: the AAMR defines significant limitations in adaptive behavior as: "performance that is at least two standard deviations below the mean of either (a) one of the following three types of adaptive behavior: conceptual, social, or practical, or (b) an overall score on a standardized measure of conceptual, social, and practical skills" (AAMR, 2002, p. 14). This places much more of an emphasis on concrete testing of adaptive functioning than does the DSM-IV-TR definition, which reads: "how effectively individuals cope with common life demands and how well they meet the standards of personal independence expected of someone in their particular age group, sociocultural background, and community setting" (APA, 2000, p. 42). The problems that arise from having so many definitions of the key concepts in MR assessments are evident in the constant debates that occur in *Atkins* cases.

Reviewing the literature, the most prevalent themes revolving around the death penalty are the idea of IQ, what constitutes mental retardation, and ethical implications for mental health professionals. In 2002, the decision of *Atkins v. Virginia* found that executing mentally retarded offenders was unconstitutional because it violates the prohibition of "cruel and unusual punishment," under the Eighth Amendment of the Constitution (Meyer & Weaver, 2006, p. 228). The ruling of *Atkins v. Virginia* left the responsibility to the individual states to determine their own description of what constituted mental retardation. Definitions and standards vary amongst the states. As Brodsky and Galloway (2003) put it, "No single consistent measurement device, no gold standard, is utilized across different institutions with different populations" (p. 7). Bonnie and Gustafson (2007), however, identified the commonalities between the standards of the AAMR and the APA.

The literature reveals conflicting arguments, supporting or denouncing the use of both standards. Ellis (2003) notes that although using IQ cutoff scores may seem to be easier and faster, there are potential problems with this practice since other testing-related factors have an impact on the outcome. He emphasizes the importance of ensuring that an experienced mental health professional considers more than just a score alone, but also the limitations of functioning in everyday life, the type of test, normed populations, etc. Duvall and Morris (2006), along with Cunningham and Tassé (2010) would agree with Ellis's (2003) position.

An individual and the group he or she is being compared to must share similar traits. Brodsky and Galloway (2003) contend that comparing lower-IQ offenders to the national norms is more beneficial than comparing them to inmates. They reach this conclusion because the data from comparison groups of inmates are often derived from "brief group-administered screening tests of intelligence, and are of arguable use with individuals of low IQ" (p. 6). They further emphasize that norms that represent the general population are also applicable to correctional populations. What Brodsky and Galloway (2003) fail to overlook, however, are a couple of extremely important factors. Bonnie and Gustafson (2007) follow APA's ethical guideline of selecting assessments or tests in which the sample contains similar traits to that of the individual being tested (2010), including "sensory, motor, linguistic, cultural, and behavioral factors" (p. 828), because to do otherwise would be unethical. In addition, some IQ tests are not representative of the general population, nor are all scales appropriate for the individuals that need to be tested. For example, Bonnie and Gustafson (2007) point out that though the Stanford-Binet and Wechsler scales are the most widely known and used measurements of IQ, these tests are not appropriate for those with language impairments. Now, while language would not be the sole determining factor of mental retardation, it is one small factor amongst many that can culminate in a diagnosis of low IQ or mental retardation. However, let it be noted that though death sentences are appealed and sometimes overturned, the resulting executions are irreversible, so comprehensive accuracy must be assured in death penalty cases.

Ellis (2003) suggests that one way to avoid the limitations of IQ tests in mental retardation death penalty cases is for states to base their decisions on the working definitions of AAMR and/or APA to "ensure that the individual in not merely a poor test-taker, but rather is a truly disabled individual" (p. 8). Ellis (2003) goes on to say that no matter which definition courts employ, a mentally retarded defendant will meet the qualifications. As with any other suggestion, however, his theory does not go without criticism. One argument that is fairly prevalent revolves around the requirement that onset of mental retardation occur before the age of 18. Bonnie and Gustafson (2007) call attention to the fact that some, as adults, "Acquire deficits in intellectual functioning and adaptive behavior that may be equivalent in severity" (p. 822) to that of mental retardation. Traumatic brain injury (TBI) is one example. This is important to be aware of since, contrary to Ellis's (2003) above statement that all mentally retarded persons would qualify, many states, in fact, do not include this aspect in their working definitions of mental retardation or mental disorders (Mulford, Repack, Mulvey, Woolard, & Portwood, 2004) and therefore could potentially put someone at risk for the death penalty. Furthermore, the National Disability Rights Network (2007) declared that it does not make sense to exempt some from the death penalty, while others who in fact might have been mentally affected at the time of the offense are still subjected to it; after all, "Both groups of defendants are impaired by brain-based disorders that they have not chosen to have" (p. 7). Bonnie and Gustafson (2007) propose that states adopt language in a current Kansas law that replaces developmental onset of the cognitive disability to instead encompass all those with "significant limited intellectual functioning and deficits in adaptive behavior" (p. 822).

Another consideration about the age-of-onset clause that Ellis (2003) notes as important is the malingering aspect. He states:

> The issue of malingering [. . .] has not proven to be a practical problem in the assessment of individuals who may have mental retardation [due to age of onset in childhood]. There are no reports in the clinical literature

> indicating that this is a practical problem in the assessment of individuals who are thought to have mental retardation. (p. 10)

Though his stance on the topic may seem as if it holds some weight to it, the truth is that there is cause to consider the possibility of malingering along with the subject being frequently addressed in the literature. First, any time there is to be such a large gain for an individual (in capital punishment cases, it would be the sentence of life instead of death), some amount of malingering, whether significant or minuscule, should be considered and accounted for. Brodsky and Galloway (2003) make an important point of mentioning that just because a defendant malingers does not mean that deficits in intellectual functioning are not there. They further accentuate that without a malingering assessment, detection based on clinical interviews alone is not likely to occur. Griffin, Normington, May, and Glassmire (1996), and Greiffenstein, Baker, and Gola (1994) (as cited in Brodsky & Galloway, 2003) provide statistics that 20%–40% of individuals claiming some type of cognitive impairment are malingering.

Second, Ellis (2003) also fails to consider cultural and socioeconomic factors. The adaptive functioning theory implies that individuals suffering from mental retardation must be diagnosed by the age of 18. However, as we have seen in the case of *Atkins v. Virginia*, it is possible for youth to essentially slip through the cracks and undiagnosed. In low socioeconomic cultures, there may not be access to the appropriate services or money to pay for them. Although it is mandatory for schools to pay for these services if a parent or guardian suspects abnormal cognitive functioning in their child, there is an assumption that all parents or guardians notice the problems, are competent enough, care enough, or are emotionally available to advocate for their child. Tobolosky (as cited in Bonnie & Gustafson, 2007) emphasizes that the *diagnosis* need not take place before the age of 18 due to the factors mentioned above, but that only *evidence* of deficits before age 18 are necessary. Nonetheless, what would distinguish between "general lack of motivation" (Meyer & Weaver, 2006, p. 227) as was the case of Daryl Atkins in *Atkins v. Virginia*, and legitimate mental retardation?

Mental State at the Time of The Offense (MSO)

Just as mental retardation is a significant circumstance that may result in the lesser sentence of life in prison rather than the death penalty, mental illness and life history can be mitigating factors in capital punishment cases like *Lewis v. Virginia*. The idea that capital offenders should be treated as unique individuals was sparked by the 1976 decision of *Woodson v. North*

Carolina (Fabian, 2003). This decision was an automatic sentencing of a man to death for first-degree murder without regard to criminal history, character, or other circumstances that may have affected his actions. *Lockett v. Ohio* set the precedent that issues such as mental illness, post-traumatic stress disorder (PTSD), abuse during childhood, or other cultural influences must be considered by the jury (Fabian, 2003). For the purposes of this chapter, only mental disorder or illness shall be mentioned when discussing mitigating factors. Mental illness not only affects the historical actions of defendants, but also directly affects how they participate in trials. Blume and Leonard (as cited by Fabian, 2003) point out that the diagnosis or presence of mental illness can influence whether a confession is made and how the confession occurred (forced or voluntary), as well as feelings, thoughts, and behaviors during the trial process. Along with this, competency to stand trial, criminal responsibility, and the effects of domestic violence are also included in this section.

Meyer and Weaver (2006) define criminal responsibility as "the state of the defendant's mind at the time of the alleged crime," and competency to stand trial as "the defendant's psychological state at the time of the trial" (p. 114). While both are important mitigators, Meyer and Weaver (2006) note that assessing and evaluating the defendant's functioning as close to the time of offense as possible prevails over their functioning at the time of the trial. Though these standards are fairly concrete, there is no consensus about the definite exclusion of mentally disordered individuals from the death penalty amongst the states. According to Winick (2009), several professional organizations in this field contend that a defendant's mental illness at the time of the offense should be determined on a case-by-case scenario, and not be placed in a category. Along with Winick (2009), Hessick (2008) maintains that mitigating factors like mental illness are justified and crucial in how a jury convicts and sentences a defendant, while Dershowitz (as cited in Kirchmeier, 2005) asserts that the trend of defendants claiming adverse histories carries with it serious and negative implications for public safety and freedom. Though these authors make valid points, they (along with some of the other literature reviewed) fail to define or provide an example of what constitutes a "serious mental illness." The American Bar Association, American Psychiatric Association, American Psychological Association, National Alliance on Mental Illness, and Mental Health America (as cited by Winick, 2009, p. 818) provides a list of criteria as:

> Mental illness that significantly impaired their capacity to: Appreciate the nature, consequences or wrongfulness of their conduct, b. Exercise rational

judgment in relation to the conduct, or c. Conform their conduct to the requirements of the law.

Life-history interviews are a powerful tool for evaluating whether mental illness exists or not. Wattendorf and Hadley (2005), and Brooks-Gunn, Duncan, and Aber (1997), insist that assessing for the presence of mental health problems are so important in life history investigations that mental health experts should research "at least three generations prior for genetic history, familial medical conditions, substance abuse, vulnerability to mental illness, and exposure to environmental toxins." To accurately identify behavioral norms, the life history should also include cultural aspects and racial identity as well as the views of the defendant's community and family that they identify with, (Dudley & Blume, 2008). Hicks (2004) offers compelling statistics on the higher prevalence of diagnoses to African American males and adolescents compared to other racial groups. He attributes this to the possibility that clinicians could be biased, but stresses the importance of ethno-racial considerations so that individuals are not compared to groups of people that do not share cultural commonalities with them. Furthermore, Dudley and Blume (2008) suggest that, "The failure of mental health systems to accommodate cultural needs and responses helps explain why many capital clients have medical and mental conditions that were not identified prior to their arrest" (p. 968). Another area for forensic psychological probing is related to "the battered spouse syndrome" in capital punishment cases. There is essentially no literature to support it as an evidentiary reason (Blowers & Bjerregaard, 1994).

What is available, nevertheless, is the abundance of literature on cultural and ethical considerations, and implications for professionals in the field. Touched upon throughout the chapter, these matters are a significant aspect in the push for forensic mental health services to become more culturally focused. According to the U.S. Department of Health and Human Services (as cited in Dudley & Blume, 2008, p. 978), "Institutions in general, and the field of mental health in particular, have been slow to recognize the needs and perspectives of non-white, non-mainstream patients." To emphasize the idea of norms when comparing groups on behavior, functioning, etc., Dudley and Blume (2008) reiterate that, "It is critical to select appropriate research that is based on a cohort of people who are most like the defendant" (p. 984). All too often, minority cultures have been deemed as wrong or bad when they do not fit into the box that they are place in, or do not follow the standards set forth by the majority group. As training mental health professionals, it is our responsibility and ethical obligation to advocate for our clients when issues similar to these arise (APA, 2010).

Another ethical issue that the literature emphasizes is the need for competent mental health professionals. With such responsibility as another being's life in our hands, it is of the utmost importance that mental health experts in the forensics field actually know and understand their responsibilities, or take active measures to become trained and competent in a certain area. Although Ellis (2003) acknowledges that courts will often require the assistance of a psychiatrist, he also points out that most often they are unavailable or too expensive, thereby requiring the help of a trained, experienced clinician instead. This is an important implication, since it suggests that clinicians in the field need to know more than just what is required of them, but also need to be aware of issues affecting other professions or departments.

As the research shows, there is no definitive, concrete solution to problems surrounding forensic mental health and its impact on the death penalty. Because of our federal system it seems likely that there will always be disagreement amongst the various states, as well as the various professional organizations involved concerning the issues of mental retardation or low IQ, mental illness, other mitigating factors, and the cultural and ethical implications that must be considered. One thing that may be certain, however, is that the consistent presence of crime in our society creates an ongoing opportunity for mental health professionals to challenge issues in forensic mental health in order to best serve clients in the criminal justice system.

Adaptive Functioning and Criminal Behavior

In 2007, Young, Boccaccini, Conroy, and Lawson conducted a phone survey of 13 psychologists and 7 psychiatrists in Texas who had each performed a mental retardation assessment in capital cases at least once. They reported their experiences with the assessment practice as well as their opinions about how to incorporate measures of adaptive functioning. Young et al. (2007) concluded that although the AAMR suggests using standardized measures of adaptive functioning, there was no standard practice for using these tests. Evaluators also disagreed about the use of criminal behavior as an indicator of impaired adaptive functioning, some arguing that it showed significant adaptive functioning, others arguing that it instead showed the possibility of another mental deficiency or disorder such as antisocial personality disorder (Young et al., 2007). While these findings seem to indicate that there is a lack of consensus among professionals on how to provide a standard psychological assessment, the demographic of the study was rather limited and may only be representative of professionals operating in Texas. The author provides the opinion that, given the controversy over these issues, professionals conducting assessments in cases like Teresa Lewis should be knowledgeable about the variables and be prepared to discuss why they are or are not taking certain variables into account in their reports. This raises the question: Is this the best that can be done?

In an analysis of various state legislative requirements for psychological testing and varying definitions of mental retardation, Duvall and Morris (2006) show similar indications that while there may be some overlapping concepts, there is nothing resembling a consensus. They also point out that there is often a conflict between the APA Code of Ethics and state legislative practices and requirements for assessment. Some states, such as Arizona, require that more than one assessment be conducted to prove mental capacity of a defendant, giving rise to such issues as inflation of scores because of practice effects and test-retest effects. Duvall and Morris (2006) argue that because of effects like these that render test results inaccurate, psychologists should be conscious that this is not an advised practice as delineated in the APA, and thus they should adhere to their own code of ethics, refusing to administer such tests within the legal system. Duvall and Morris recommend that if psychological ethics conflict with state laws, the ethics code is the priority to be followed (2006). This, however, could potentially put other, less competent people in the position of evaluators of mental status, and does not seem to address a solution for the inconsistency between the law and the APA's ethical standards. Perhaps a better practice would be to include the limitations and possible invalidities of the testing process in a psychological report, which then would give the courts the final decision of how the assessment should be used.

A subset of issues results from the practice of forensic mental health assessment for mental retardation, in that most definitions for MR include some mention of adaptive functioning. Marc Tassé (2009) presents a comprehensive discussion of some of the more salient issues that follow the assessment for adaptive functioning, including standardized instruments, self-reporting, selection of respondents, and clinical judgment. A common concern among these issues is the availability of reliable information. While the tests for assessing adaptive functioning are professionally accepted as valid, the question arises whether a single test alone can serve as an indicator of low functioning. Instead of simply relying on a single behavioral test, Tassé (2009) recommends that information be sought through three methods: testing, interviews of respondents who have seen the individual interact in a variety of settings, and a review of all available records of the individual. Professionals need to be aware of pitfalls when gathering this information. For instance, respondents may provide biased information, as could individuals who are asked for a self-report. Additionally, there is the problem of clinical competency of the evaluator. If one hires a professional that has experience working with people with mental disabilities, it is likely that individual will lack competency in the forensic arena; and the opposite might be true of a forensic mental health professional. If standards for diagnosing MR in the forensic arena are not established and consistent with assessment practices in other areas, we run the risk of allowing professionals to use two different standards of diagnosis: one clinical, and one forensic (Tassé, 2009). This prediction seems a little premature, however, since the tools and principles used are the same in both contexts and should be governed by the same ethical principle of thoroughness. For the Teresa Lewis case, school records, job performance history, traumas, and medical and other cognitively oriented data sources may offer a more accurate index of her intellectual functioning around the time of the incident and therefore how it might have impacted her judgment.

One of the greatest impediments to optimal forensic reporting is the imposition by courts of a specific IQ cutoff point for MR. Most courts that delineate a number set the bar at 70—at or below which individuals are not eligible for the death penalty, above which they are. This brings up a question Tassé (2009) raised: is a single test score properly indicative of a person's intellectual functioning? In an effort to synthesize a reliable set of data to show whether IQ score alone is sufficient for determining MR of defendants, Ceci, Scullin, and Kanaya (2003) gathered IQ test data from a large sampling of school children in the United States. They chose 1,011 students for the synthesis, all of whom tested on the cusp of MR at one point, and then within 48 months were either given the same IQ test again or given an updated and re-normed version. The hypothesis was that, given rising IQ scores over time (Flynn, 2006), scores for those taking the re-normed version would be lower, and there would be a great variance in scores from the previous test. This was shown to be true, as a full 38% of students who originally tested on the cusp fell below the cutoff for MR on their second testing with the updated version (Ceci et al., 2003). The indication from this data is that IQ test score can vary drastically depending on whether an updated version of the test is administered or an old version. Implications for this can be dramatic, especially in the forensic field, in which a defendant's life could depend on the score.

Ceci et al. (2003) conclude that because of this significant change in test scores, IQ score alone should be insufficient to establish MR and thus to determine eligibility for the death penalty. Indeed, it seems that a solid cutoff point would pose a significant problem for a test that is best interpreted within a range of scores.

Forensic Psychological Testing for IQ

Of relevance is not only which dated version of a test is administered, but also which test in particular is given. Giving the same test more than once is not recommended, as it can produce a practice effect and raise an individual's score. To avoid this effect, practitioners may give more than one type of test, for instance, the WAIS and then the Stanford-Binet. In an article on the IQ differences between the WAIS and SB tests, Silverman et al. (2010) call attention to these differences as problematic in the forensic arena. Using a sample size of 74 adults who had been diagnosed with MR, Silverman et al. examined IQ scores on various intellectual tests to determine if there was indeed a substantial difference in scores depending on the type of test administered. While admittedly not perfect, each test that was examined, particularly the Stanford-Binet and WAIS tests, was accepted within the field as a valid tool for measuring intellectual functioning. The concluding data indicated that between the two tests, there was a substantial difference in scores, with all individuals scoring higher on the WAIS than the SB (Silverman et al., 2010). The results of this study give clear and convincing evidence that there is a less-than-acceptable difference in test scores, especially for tests that are routinely given in *Atkins* cases. Silverman et al. (2010) suggest that increased attention and effort needs to be given to discovering the reasons for this discrepancy as well as to the validity of each test.

As far as the implications in criminal psychology, the difference in test scores would mean that a defendant could be significantly aided by taking the Stanford-Binet instead of the WAIS, as his IQ score would be lower, possibly even so much lower that he could avoid the death penalty. However, Silverman et al. (2010) deny psychologists using this as a justification for providing the SB over the WAIS, as this type of practice is unethical and leads to questions of motivation and competence of supposedly unbiased evaluators. A better idea for practice would be to use several tests, all different, and use them only once. With a range of scores available, professionals could collaborate and develop a much more appropriate diagnosis. However, this still does not address the problems inherent in the use of IQ cutoff in courtrooms by triers of fact. Forensic psychology experts may be able to provide a layperson explanation of the concept of "true score" and other relevant psychometric terms. That is, Teresa Lewis's IQ scores may have been consistent with the concept of a band where the "true score" may actually be with a reasonable degree of statistical certainty.

In a similar cutoff score finding, David Cooke and Christine Michie (2010) reported significant variations in test scores for the Hare Psychopathy Checklist–Revised. They found the precision of specific numerical scores to be much less accurate than previously thought. In addition, the variation of scores above and below the cutoff was much greater than anticipated for one of the most trusted tests in forensic psychology. The indication is that these limitations of accuracy and precision apply to any test identically applied in the field of forensics, namely, any tested group statistic that is then applied to an individual (Cooke & Michie, 2010). Thus, they caution clinicians against reliance upon such tests as a means of diagnosis or prediction in any individual case. In any forensic assessment case, Cooke and Michie (2010) suggest a practice that states fail to address in legislation: collaboration between forensic professionals in evaluations to produce consensus diagnoses rather than mean scores. While the data from their study provide an important insight into testing validity, it is based on adult males, and therefore more research is needed to address the validity of such testing practices in diverse populations.

Flynn Effect (FE) and IQ

One major contributor in the field of IQ testing has been James Flynn. In his 2006 article titled "Tethering the Elephant," Flynn addresses the importance in capital cases of taking into account the phenomenon by his own name: the Flynn Effect. This effect is roughly categorized as "IQ gains over time" (Flynn, 2006), and can be understood to indicate that IQ test scores will often depend on the norms against which the score is compared. Flynn indicates that an individual's IQ score will be represented inaccurately if the test she took was normed before the time it was administered. By comparing IQ scores from different WISC and WAIS tests against scores of the norms on each test in its current and outdated forms, Flynn (2006) shows that the average IQ gain is 0.3 points per year over time. This, he recommends, is the standard gain that should be applied to all IQ test scores in order to give an accurate measurement against the sample norm. Ignoring this standard gain becomes a "flight from reality" (p. 175) and results in largely unreliable and misrepresentative test scores. As Flynn points out, this turns death sentencing into a matter of chance. The difference between a defendant who receives the death penalty and one who does not may be little more than the year each took an intelligence test and how outdated the test was from its original sample.

While the Flynn Effect (FE) has gained recognition over the years, controversy over its accuracy and application continues today. However, Flynn asserts that we are faced with two options: adjust IQ scores for obsolescence of the samples, or accept that the scores we have can be inaccurate and misleading (Flynn, 2006). When the cutoff number presents a life-or-death scenario, inaccurate assessments and test scores are unacceptable. Flynn's opinion does advocate for a change in the current standard of practice but does not capture accurately what that practice entails. Hagan, Drogin, and Guilmette (2008) took the opportunity to review current practice and report on the status of the Flynn Effect in clinical settings. They conducted a survey to find out if it was common practice to adjust scores for the FE. They conducted several studies, two interviewing individuals familiar with IQ test administration and training, and one surveying current textbooks, intelligence tests, and government testing practices for evidence of using the FE as justification to adjust IQ scores. Ninety-four percent of school psychologists surveyed never adjusted IQ scores, even in light of the FE, and only 2% of graduate educators reported teaching the adjustment practice to their students.

Written materials also advocated strict adherence to testing manuals and scoring practices, never advocating score adjustment for the FE. It is obvious from this study that while the FE may be a known theory, it still has not been incorporated into standard psychological practice, and using it to justify adjustments in scores may actually be contrary to accepted ethical, legal, and professional guidelines. Hagan et al. (2008), however, make no suggestions regarding the adjustment of scores. They imply only that psychologists who do accept forensic positions of assessment keep in mind all pertinent variables for test validity and accuracy in their reports. While this study shows that there is no standard accepted use of the FE, it does not address either implications of the effect or whether psychologists should integrate it into their practice.

In direct critique to the study administered by Hagan et al. (2008), Cunningham and Tassé (2010) argue in an article addressing adjustment of IQ scores for the FE that the forensic arena is indeed different from the clinical arena, and thus affords a different consideration than accepted standard clinical practice. The main difference for Cunningham and Tassé (2010) lies in the fact that in capital cases, the score for an individual could mean life or death as in the Teresa Lewis case, and thus has a greater implication than, for instance, an IQ score for a schoolchild. When considering whether or not score adjustment for the FE should be the normative practice in forensic cases, Cunningham and Tassé (2010) argue that the standard should be based on current scientific research and data as opposed to current trends in clinical practice. Important to their case is the idea that clinical practice and training often lag behind currently available empirical data. To emphasize the point, they use the example of blood-letting in past centuries, a practice that was continued long after scientific data disproved its beneficence. The standard, they state, should be that "best science illuminates best practice" (p. 418), and that forensic usage of the FE to adjust test scores is not only acceptable, but recommended in light of current scientific data. This argument seems logical, but also biased. Would a parent with a child on the borderline of MR agree that the stakes are less important for proper diagnosis of her son than for a convicted felon? Although the educational environment allows for subsequent IQ testing as a child moves through his or her formal academic experiences, minimal forensic psychological options exist for an inmate put to death by lethal injection assuming that a rigid IQ cutoff score was weighted more heavily.

To assume that the stakes of a test should dictate the accuracy with which its score is presented is unreasonable. A thorough assessment should be made and the most accurate testing practices should be applied in any field of psychology, no matter what the stakes of the outcome. Hagan, Drogin, and Guilmette (2010) provide a similar argument in a rebuttal article wittily titled, "Science Rather Than Advocacy When Reporting IQ Scores." They argue that not only is adjusting IQ scores against best practice, but that it is not actually supported by enough scientific data to be justified. While Hagan et al. (2008, 2010) and Cunningham and Tassé (2010) are in agreement over the existence of the FE, Hagan et al. (2010) assert that there is not enough reliability in it to determinably say how much any given *individual's* test score should be adjusted. Indeed, it goes back to the research of Cooke and Michie (2010), who concluded that it was inadvisable to apply group data trends to individual cases. Rather, the score shift should be acknowledged for what it is: proof that there is a range of IQ scores valid for any individual. By "correcting" the IQ score to reflect the FE (Cunningham and Tassé, 2010, p. 418), practitioners not only assert that there is a single correct score, but that they know the direction and type of error with enough certainty to change the evidence in a case. As Hagan et al. (2010) point out, this practice ignores all other possible reasons for score ranges, including age of test takers, administration miscues, and test-taker effort and attention. One standard that both parties agree on, however, is that any inconsistencies in test scores should be reported to the court, along with a discussion of the available theories that address the range of scores available.

Controversies such as these show why it is necessary to keep up with current forensic practices and to establish a standard among them. Setting such a standard proves a challenge, however, because the forensic field of mental health is both constantly changing and also intricately connected to a very slowly changing field: that of law. The two fields stand in dichotomy, as law is a field with an extremely old foundation, whereas forensic psychology is only recently reaching recognition as a scientific field. In an article on education and training in forensic psychology, DeMatteo, Marczyk, Krauss, and Burl (2009) note some of the challenges forensic psychology doctoral programs have faced since their inception in 1973. The biggest challenge, they state, is the lack of a model curriculum or standard educational model. As the number of students interested in forensic psychology continues to rise, so does the number of programs offered; and yet they still face a lack of consensus on the role of their graduates in practice and the scope of the forensic psychology field (DeMatteo et al., 2009). The recommendation from DeMatteo et al. (2009) is to avoid producing specialists and rather focus the degree programs on giving students standard competence in a variety of areas. This recommendation seems appropriate, as it will allow students to be generally competent practitioners but still leave room for them to be flexible with their ever-changing field.

Kathleen Heide and Eldra Solomon (1997) provide an insider's glimpse of some of the roles a forensic psychologist can prepare to assume in the field. They assert that mental health professionals are hired to evaluate a range of questions: a defendant's mental state at the time of the crime, his remorse afterward, his status as mentally retarded, and the likelihood that he poses a continued risk to society. This information is important to both the prosecution and the defense, and a mental health professional could be hired by either side to evaluate and report this information (Heide & Solomon, 1997). Something of particular interest is a point that has been mentioned in other articles: that mental health professionals often will correspond with other professionals (including numerous other psychologists) to gain the most accurate understanding of the defendant's behavior (Heide & Solomon, 1997). This indicates that while there a standard for practice may not yet exist in the forensic application of mental health testing, collaboration and consensus is a valued aspect of prevailing practice.

Since the issue of MR in capital cases is so complex, Gregory Olley (2009) presents an article directed toward those experts who may desire to become involved in assessing these cases. He presents a view of those borderline cases of MR that typify *Atkins* decisions that indicates how complex it is to assess mild MR accurately. Of particular significance in providing an accurate diagnosis is not just IQ scores, but also a behavioral history, evidence of impairment in adaptive functioning, information about typical community functioning and day-to-day living, as well as the nature of personal social relationships of the individual. These considerations show a knowledge of the various definitions of MR (AAMR, 2002; APA, 2000) and the importance of considering multiple factors rather than just a single test score (Ceci et al., 2003; Cooke & Michie, 2010; Silverman et al., 2010; Tassé, 2009). Because the knowledge required making an accurate diagnosis is so extensive, Olley (2009) suggests that it is imperative for the expert to be experienced with persons having MR as well as having trained sufficiently in the process of forensic psychology. Training should address the significant standards for expert testimony, the difference between a diagnosis of MR and a hearing for competency to stand trial, and a working knowledge of the characteristics that make individuals with MR prone to false confessions and waiving of their *Miranda* rights (Olley, 2009). This opinion acknowledges the increasing need for professionals trained in forensic psychology as well as MR assessment to take part in the court process for sentencing. It underscores the fact that forensic psychology is a developing field with many changing roles that professionals need to be prepared to fulfill.

A few well-versed and highly experienced authors contribute to the discussion of the future of forensic psychology and assessment. The first, Kirk Heilbrun and Stephanie Brooks (2010), present a "Proposed Agenda for the Next Decade." They cite the progress that forensic psychology has seen over the years, including greater recognition of research imperatives, increased attention in books and journals, and increased sources of authority for standard practice (Heilbrun & Brooks, 2010). They acknowledge the need for codifying forensic practice guidelines and for developing a standard of practice that can be enforced by authoritative organizations. Included in these guidelines, they recommend collaboration with international professionals to develop a practice that is more globally and culturally accurate (Heilbrun & Brooks, 2010). This particular recommendation is advisable, since working with diverse populations and considerations of cultural diversity have been recently added priorities in all related fields of psychology. Unique to their perspective, however, is the recommendation of public outreach, to be conducted in the hope of gaining more social recognition for the value of forensic work. This recommendation too is beneficial, although Heilbrun and Brooks (2010) do not delineate specific ways in which this is to be accomplished. Perhaps this is wise, as they can leave the specific details of such outreach to proper organizations and eager students. Certainly such recognized guidelines would need to meet Daubert standards but would be instructive in cases such as that of Teresa Lewis.

The second authoritative duo which detail suggestions for future forensic practice is MacVaugh and Cunningham (2009). They provide 20 recommendations for practice standards, to educate forensic persons, and to spark discussion of the most relevant issues for the future. They assert common points that have arisen elsewhere in forensic assessment literature, namely that reporting of MR should be done in thorough fashion, indicating limitations of tests, score ranges, and a diverse assessment of all available information. Cunningham and Tassé (2010) agree that since IQ scores are often imprecise, they should not be the single factor in determining intellectual functioning of an individual. They also caution against using clinical judgment improperly; first impressions are not scientific data, and are often mistaken. In order for clinicians to provide an assessment true to their ethics and standards of practice, they need to use every available resource, including clinical interviews, third-party interviews, tape recordings of defendants, old school records, and prior criminal histories. In the case of Teresa Lewis, the history of noncompliance with child protective service family restoration plans may have particular relevance in assessing her cognitive competencies and especially function. Of impending importance to both above-mentioned authorities is the lack of consensus in how to reconcile known legal standards to clinical assessments (Cunningham & Tassé, 2010; Heilbrun & Brooks, 2010), and how to ensure that there is eventually a standard of practice for these types of cases. Both parties provide excellent recommendations for the future practice of forensic psychology, especially with regard to the sensitive issue of mental retardation and the death penalty.

Implications for Criminal Forensic Psychology Training and Practice

The forensic mental health issues that plagued the Teresa Lewis case are not singular to her debate. The issues found therein, namely what to do with IQ cutoff scores and borderline mentally retarded individuals, are widespread among the field of forensic psychology for several reasons. There are an increasing number of the accused who are affected by cognitive deficits and oftentimes mental health disorders that significantly interfere with reasoned judgment. As a consequence, the burden often falls upon forensic psychologists to provide evaluations that clarify the exact nature of these difficulties. Unfortunately, the differences in defining and tools available to evaluate these individuals pose a major challenge. As a consequence, misdiagnosis or misclassification can lead to serious consequences in a decision made by the triers of fact. By integrating into practice some of the considerations discussed here, forensic psychologists can help ensure that an accurate diagnostic opinions are rendered.

The contribution to the legal system by default requires a translation of neuroscience research findings into language that attorneys, jurors, and judges can easily understand. In this regard, forensic psychological reports can be crafted in a manner that explains the entire process and evidence-based results. Training must be geared to instilling a culturally-responsive forensic psychological approach to cases like *Lewis v. Virginia*.

Previous data has indicated a need for research in intelligence test validity, application of the Flynn Effect, developing measures of adaptive functioning, and creating a standard of practice for professionals who must face these issues. Where we stand now, there is no non-debatable answer to whether or not the death sentence was warranted for Teresa Lewis. What we can acknowledge is that professional consensus on these matters needs to be pursued rigorously and is likely to be the subject of much discussion in the future.

References

American Association on Mental Retardation. (AAMR). (2002). *Mental retardation: Definition, classification, and systems of supports* (10th ed.). Washington, DC: Author.

American Board of Forensic Psychology. (ABFP) (2006). Specialty Guidelines for Forensic Psychology. Washington, DC: Author.

American Psychiatric Association. (APA). (2000). *Diagnostic and statistical manual of mental disorders* (4th ed., text rev.). New Delhi, India: Medical Publishers (P) Ltd.

American Psychological Association. (2010). *Ethical principles of psychologists and code of conduct*. Washington, DC: American Psychological Association.

Applebaum, P. S., & Gutheil, T. G. (1991). *Clinical handbook of psychiatry and the law* (2nd ed.). Baltimore: Williams and Wilkins.

Atkins v. Virginia, 536 U.S. 304 (2002).

Bartol, C., & Bartol, A. (2006). History of forensic psychology. In I. B. Weiner & A. K. Hess (Eds.), *The handbook of forensic psychology* (3rd ed., pp. 3–27). Hoboken, NJ: Wiley.

Blowers, A. N., & Bjerregaard, B. (1994). The admissibility of expert testimony on the battered woman syndrome in homicide cases. *Journal of Psychiatry and Law, 22*, 527–560.

Bonnie, R. J., & Gustafson, K. (2007). The challenge of implementing *Atkins v. Virginia*: How legislatures and courts can promote accurate assessments and adjudications of mental retardation in death penalty cases. *Law Review*, University of Richmond.

Brodsky, S. L., & Galloway, V. A. (2003). Ethical and professional demands for forensic mental health professionals in the post-Atkins era. *Ethics and Behavior, 13*(1), 3–9.

Brooks-Gunn, J., Duncan, G., & Aber, J. L. (Eds.) (1997). *Neighborhood poverty II: Policy implications for studying neighborhoods*. New York: Russell Sage.

Ceci, S. J., Scullin, M., & Kanaya, T. (2003). The difficulty of basing death penalty eligibility on IQ cutoff scores for mental retardation. *Ethics and Behavior, 13*(1), 11–17.

Cooke, D. J., & Michie, C. (2010). Limitations of diagnostic precision and predictive utility in the individual case: A challenge for forensic practice. *Law and Human Behavior, 34*, 259–274.

Cunningham, M. D., & Tassé, M. J. (2010). Looking to science rather than convention in adjusting IQ scores when death is at issue. *Professional Psychology: Research and Practice, 41*(5), 413–419.

DeMatteo, D., Marczyk, G., Krauss, D. A., & Burl, J. (2009). Educational and training models in forensic psychology. *Training and Education in Professional Psychology, 3*(3), 184–191.

Dudley, R. G., & Leonard, P. B. (2008). Getting it right: Life history investigation as the foundation for a reliable mental health assessment. *Hofstra Law Review, 36*(3), 963–988.

Duvall, J. C., & Morris, J. (2006). Assessing mental retardation in death penalty cases: Critical issues for psychology and psychological practice. *Professional Psychology: Research and Practice, 37*(6), 658–665.

Ellis, J. W. (2003). Mental retardation and the death penalty: A guide to state legislative issues. *Mental and Physical Disability Law Reporter*.

Fabian, J. M. (2003). Death penalty mitigation and the role of the forensic psychologist. *University of Alabama Law and Psychology Review, 27*.

Flynn, J. R. (2006). Tethering the elephant: Capital cases, IQ, and the Flynn Effect. *Psychology, Public Policy, and Law, 12*, 170–189.

Forensic Specialty Council. (2011). *Speciality Guidelines for Forensic Psychology*. Retrieved 01 November, 2012 from http://www.ap-ls.org/aboutpsychlaw/SGFP_Final_Approved_2011.pdf.

Forrest, A. R., Abdelhamid, R. F., & Carninci, P. (2009). Annotating non-coding transcription using functional genomics strategies. *Briefings in Functional Genomics and Proteomics, 8*(6), 437–443. Retrieved from http://www.ncbi.nlm.nih.gov/pubmed/19833699.

Forrest, L., Miller, D. S., & Elman, N. S. (2008). Psychology trainees with competence problems: From individual to ecological conceptualizations. *Training Ideas and Research You Can Use: VISTAS 2011* 10 *and Education in Professional Psychology*, 2, 183–192. doi:10.1037/1931-3918.2.4.183.

Fouad, N. A., Grus, C. L., Hatcher, R. L., Kaslow, N. J., Hutchings, P. S., Madson, M., . . . Crossman, R. E. (2009). Competency benchmarks: A developmental model for understanding and measuring competence in professional psychology. *Training and Education in Professional Psychology, 3*(4), S5–S26. doi:10.1037/a0015832.

Giannet, S. (2003). Cultural competence and professional psychology training: Creating the architecture of change. *Journal of Evolutionary Psychology, 24*, 117–128.

Gold, M. (2010, September 23). Virginia executes Teresa Lewis for role in slayings in husband, stepson in 2002. *The Washington Post*. Retrieved from http://www.washingtonpost.com/wp-dyn/content/article/2010/09/23/AR2010092306827.html.

Greiffenstein, M. F., Baker, W. J., & Gola, T. (1994). Validation of malingered amnesia measures with a large clinical sample. *Psychological Assessment, 6*, 218–224.

Griffin, G. A. E., Normington, J., May, R., & Glassmire, D. (1996). Assessing dissimulation among Social Security disability income claimants. *Journal of Consulting and Clinical Psychology, 64*, 1425–1430.

Gutheil. T. G. (1999). A confusion of tongues: Competence, insanity, psychiatry and the law. *Psychiatric Services, 50*, 767–773.

Guthrie, R. (1976). *Even the rat was white*. New York: Harper and Row.

Guthrie, R. (1990). Mamie Phipps Clark. In A. O'Connell & N. Russo (Eds.), *Women in psychology*. Westport, CT: Greenwood Press.

Hagan, L. D., Drogin, E. Y., & Guilmette, T. J. (2008). Adjusting IQ scores for the Flynn Effect: Consistent with the standard of practice? *Professional psychology: Research and practice, 39*, 619–625.

Hagan, L. D., Drogin, E. Y., & Guilmette, T. J. (2010). Science rather than advocacy when reporting IQ scores. *Professional Psychology: Research and Practice, 41*(5), 420–423.

Heide, K. M., & Solomon, E. P. (1997). Mental health professionals in forensic arenas. *Journal of Police and Criminal Psychology, 12*(2), 35–41.

Heilbrun, K., & Brooks, S. (2010). Forensic psychology and forensic science: A proposed agenda for the next decade. *Psychology, Public Policy, and Law, 16* (3), 219–253.

Hessick, C. B. (2008). Why are only bad acts good sentencing factors? *Boston University Law Review, 88*(1109), 1110–1163.

Hicks, J. W. (2004). Ethnicity, race, and forensic psychiatry: Are we color-blind? *Journal of the American Academy of Psychiatry and the Law, 32*(1), 21–33.

Jenkins v. United States, 307 F.2d 637 (D.C. Cir. 1962).

Johnson, R. & Scott, M. (2010, October). *Physical Disorders Presenting with Psych Symptons*. Paper presented at the International Association of Chiefs of Police (IACP) 117th Annual Meeting, Law Enforcement and Technology Conference, Police Physicians Section Meeting, Orlando, FL.

Kaslow, N. J., Grus, C. L., Campbell, L. F., Fouad, N. A., Hatcher, R. L., & Rodolfa, E. R. (2009). Competency assessment toolkit for professional psychology. *Training and Education in Professional Psychology, 4*(Suppl.), S27–S45.

Kirchmeier, J. L. (2005). A tear in the eye of the law: Mitigating factors and the progression toward a disease theory of criminal justice. *Law Review*, University of Oregon.

Leonard, T. (2010, September 20). Is it because Teresa Lewis's a woman she's to be executed by lethal injection? *Daily Mail* (United Kingdom). Retrieved December 17, 2010, from World News Mail Online database.

Lewis v. Commonwealth of Virginia, 267 Va. 302 (2004).

MacVaugh, G. S., & Cunningham, M. D. (2009). *Atkins v. Virginia*: Implications and recommendations for forensic practice. *Journal of Psychiatry and Law, 37*, 131–187.

Marczyk, G., DeMatteo, D., Kutinsky, J., & Heilbrun, K. (2008). Training in forensic assessment and intervention: Implications for principles-based models. In R. Jackson (Ed.), *Learning forensic assessment* (pp. 3–31). New York: Routledge (Taylor & Francis Group)

Melton, G., Petrila, J., Poythress, N., & Slobogin, C. (2007). *Psychological evaluations for the courts: A handbook for mental health professionals and lawyers* (3rd ed.). New York: Guilford Press.

Meyer, R. G., & Weaver, C. M. (2006). *Law and mental health: A case-based approach*. New York: Guilford Press.

Mulford, C. F., Repack, N. D., Mulvey, E. P., Woolard, J. L., & Portwood, S. L. (2004). Legal issues affecting mentally disordered and developmentally delayed youth in the justice system. *International Journal of Forensic Mental Health, 3*(1), 3–22.

Munsterberg, H. (1908). *On the witness stand: Essays on psychology and crime*. New York: Doubleday.

National Disability Rights Network. (2007, March). Talking points: Mental disabilities and the death penalty. Retrieved 01 November 2012 from http://www.napas.org/en/issues/criminal-justice.html.

Olley, G. J. (2009). Knowledge and experience required for experts in Atkins Cases. *Applied Neuropsychology, 16*, 135–140.

Otto, R. K., & Heilbrun, K. (2002). The practice of forensic psychology: A look toward the future in light of the past. *American Psychologist, 57*, 5–18.

Rapaport, E. (1991). The death penalty and gender discrimination. *Law and Society Review, 25*(2), 367–383.

Resnick, P. J. (2000). *American Academy of Psychiatry and Law forensic review course syllabus*. Annual Meeting of the American Academy of Psychiatry and the Law, Baltimore, MD.

Silverman, W., Miezejeski, C., Ryan, R., Zigman, W., Krinsky-McHale, S., & Urv, T. (2010). Stanford-Binet and WAIS IQ differences and their implications for adults with intellectual disability (aka mental retardation). *Intelligence, 38*, 242–248.

Sue, D. W. & Sue, D. (2003). *Counseling the culturally diverse: Theory and practice*. New York: John Wiley & Sons.

Tassé, M. J. (2009). Adaptive behavior assessment and the diagnosis of mental retardation in capital cases. *Applied Neuropsychology, 16*, 114–123.

Wattendorf, D. J., & Hadley, D. W. (2005). Family history: The three generation pedigree. *American Family Physician, 72*(3), 441–448.

Weiner, I. B., & Hess, A. K. (Eds.). (2006). *The handbook of forensic psychology* (3rd ed.). Hoboken, NJ: Wiley.

Winick, B. J. (2009). The Supreme Court's evolving death penalty jurisprudence: Severe mental illness as the next frontier. *Boston College Law Review, 50*(3), 785–858.

Young, B., Boccaccini, M. T., Conroy, M. A., & Lawson, K. (2007). Four practical and conceptual assessment issues that evaluators should address in capital case mental retardation evaluations. *Professional Psychology: Research and Practice, 38*(2), 169–178.

About the Editor and Contributors

The Editor

Jacqueline B. Helfgott is Professor and Chair of the Criminal Justice Department at Seattle University. She has a PhD and MA in Administration of Justice with a graduate minor in psychology from Pennsylvania State University and a BA from the University of Washington in Psychology and Society & Justice. Her research interests include criminal behavior, psychopathy, correctionsand offender reentry, and victim impact in criminal justice decision-making. She is author of *Criminal Behavior: Theories, Typologies, and Criminal Justice* (Sage Publications, 2008). Her work has been published in journals including *Journal of Police and Criminal Psychology*, *Journal of Forensic Psychology Practice, International Journal of Offender Therapy and Comparative Criminology, Criminal Justice and Behavior, International Review of Victimology*, and the *Encyclopedia of Prisons and Correctional Facilities* and the *Encyclopedia of Street Crime in America*. She has been involved in research and service in correctional settings since 1987. From 1997 to 2000, she was principal investigator on a project funded by the Soros Open Society Institute's Center on Crime, Communities and Culture that involved development, implementation, and evaluation of *Citizens, Victims, and Offenders Restoring Justice (CVORJ)*, a prison-based encounter program at the Washington State Reformatory. Her current/forthcoming work includes *No Remorse: Psychopathy and Criminal Justice* (Sage Publications) and coauthor of *Success on the Streets: Creating Opportunities for Offender Reentry* (Lynne Rienner Publishers) and applied research evaluating the Seattle Police Crisis Intervention Team/Mental Health Practitioner Pilot Project. She has served on the Advisory Board for the Washington State Department of Social and Health Services Special Commitment Center at McNeil Island that houses civilly committed sexually violent predators and currently serves on the Board of Directors for Interaction Transition (a nonprofit, ex-offender transition agency) and the Virginia Mason Separation and Loss (support services for family members following violent death).

The Contributors

Loren T. Atherley holds a master's degree in criminal justice from Seattle University, where he conducted thesis research on behavioral profiling and serial sexual homicide, the Green River Killer and the offender Gary L. Ridgway. A former national park ranger, he has worked in the National Incident Management System (NIMS) for fire and Search and Rescue (SAR) incidents since 2003. Additionally, Mr. Atherley has consulted on criminal and accident investigations, behavior, incident management, disaster response and a national child abduction case for law enforcement agencies throughout the region, including the Social Security Administration Office of the Inspector General, the Washington State Department of Corrections joint Seattle Police Department Neighborhood Corrections Initiative, the King County Sheriff's Office, the Stevens County Sheriff's Office, and the Grays Harbor County Sheriffs Office. He resides in the Seattle area and works in aviation safety management and accident investigation for one of the oldest private aviation operators in the world.

Lauran Babchuk is a PhD candidate and research assistant at Loyola University in Chicago.

Frances P. Bernat is Professor and Chair of the Public Affairs and Social Research Department at Texas A&M International University, and is a member of the emeritus faculty at Arizona State University. She holds both a PhD and a JD. She is the current editor of *Women and Criminal Justice* and has served on various professional organization committees for both the Academy of Criminal Justice Sciences and the American Society of Criminology. Her research interests are criminal law, women and youth in the criminal justice system, and contemporary practices in the criminal justice system. She is the author of *Human Sex Trafficking* and a coauthor of *Criminal Procedure Law: Police Issues and the Supreme Court.*

Eddy Brand is an Associate Professor in the Department of Child Psychiatry at Leiden University Medical Center in Leiden, the Netherlands.

Ruud Bullens has been working as a Professor at the Free University of Amsterdam (Child and Juvenile Forensic Psychology). He has published many articles and books in the field of juvenile and adult sex offenders. Currently he is working as a senior consult/therapist at De Waag, forensic psychiatric outpatient clinic in Amsterdam, and he is also Director of the Diagnostic Expertise Centre in Amsterdam (a center for forensic personality assessment).

Kelli E. Canada is a doctoral candidate at the University of Chicago, School of Social Service Administration. She received her bachelor of arts degree in psychology from DePauw University and her master of science in social work from Columbia University. Prior to pursuing her doctorate, Ms. Canada worked in Chicago as a clinical social worker in psychiatric rehabilitation, and she continues to work as a clinical social worker with older adults. Ms. Canada has published research on serious mental illnesses, treatment, mental health courts, and crisis intervention teams.

Lisbeth Eddy graduated with a BA in speech communications from the University of Washington, in 1976. She was hired as a Seattle Police officer in 1979. She worked many assignments as an officer, including patrol, training, and communications. In addition to these assignments, she was chosen to be trained as a hostage negotiator in 1981 andmaintained her status as a hostage negotiator for her entire career. In 1992, she was promoted to sergeant and became the team leader for the SPD hostage negotiations team. As a sergeant, in addition to supervising the hostage negotiations team, Ms. Eddy worked in patrol, internal investigations, domestic violence and her final assignment was as the coordinator/supervisor for the (1998) Crisis Intervention Team comprised of officers trained to better deal with mentally ill offenders. She has guest lectured at the University of Washington and Seattle University, retired from the Seattle Police Deparment in 2010, and is currently contracted with the Washington State Criminal Justice Training Commission to consult and assist with the King County–wide CIT training.

Matthew W. Epperson is an Assistant Professor in the School of Social Service Administration at the University of Chicago. His primary area of interest is intervention research on co-occurring problems of HIV, substance abuse, mental illness, and criminal justice involvement. Dr. Epperson is currently conducting research funded by the National Institute of Justice, which entails a comparative evaluation of court-based programs for persons with mental illnesses in the criminal justice system in Cook County, Illinois, as well as a study of the implementation of a specialized mental health caseload within the New Jersey Department of Probation. Dr. Epperson received his PhD with distinction from the Columbia University School of Social Work, a MSW from Grand Valley State University, and a BS in sociology and criminal justice from Central Michigan University. Before joining the faculty of the University of Chicago, he completed a postdoctoral fellowship at the Center for Behavioral Health Services and Criminal Justice Research at Rutgers University. Dr. Epperson has over 15 years of post-masters clinical and administrative social work experience in mental health, substance abuse, and criminal justice settings.

Nicholas Godlove received his JD from the University of California at Davis. He recently served as a federal court clerk for the District Court in Anchorage, Alaska. He is the coauthor of *Criminal Procedure Law: Police Issues and the Supreme Court*. He currently teaches Imperatives of Proof at Arizona State University and is a member of the California State Bar Association.

Ronn Johnson is an Associate Professor in the clinical mental health program at the University of San Diego. His forensic and research interests include women death penalty, mental state at the time of the offense, police psychology, PTSD, and terrorism.

Richard N. Kocsis is a consultant medicolegal psychologist in private practice. Over his career, Dr. Kocsis has produced five books (his latest text entitled *Applied Criminal Psychology*) and is the author/coauthor of approximately 100 scholarly publications (articles, book chapters, etc.) on topics such as criminal profiling, serial violent offenders, and forensic psychological practice. He has served as an expert consultant to law enforcement, emergency, and prosecution agencies as well as various law firms. In addition to his clinical and forensic work, he has held various academic positions in the areas of forensic psychology and criminology. In 2000, he was awarded the Australian Museum's prestigious Eureka Prize for critical thinking in recognition of his scientific research in the area of criminal profiling.

Arthur J. Lurigio, a psychologist, is Associate Dean for faculty in the College of Arts and Sciences, and a Professor of criminal justice/criminology and of psychology at Loyola University Chicago, where he is also a member of the Graduate Faculty and Director of the Center for the Advancement of Research, Training, and Education (CARTE). In 2003,

Dr. Lurigio was named a faculty scholar, one of the highest honors bestowed on senior faculty at Loyola University Chicago. Dr. Lurigio's research is focused primarily in the areas of offender drug abuse and dependence, drug treatment services, mental disorders and crime, co-occurring disorders, AIDS prevention, community corrections, police-community relations, criminal victimization, and victim services. In recognition of the overall contributions of his research to practices in the fields of psychology and criminal justice, Dr. Lurigio was conferred the University of Cincinnati Award in 1996; the Hans W. Mattick Award in 2003; the Champion for Recovery: Excellence in Research Award in 2009; the University of Illinois: Distinguished Contributions to Criminal Justice Research and Practice Award in 2010; and the American Psychological Association's Distinguished Career Award in 2010.

J. Reid Meloy is a diplomate in forensic psychology of the American Board of Professional Psychology, and consults on criminal and civil cases throughout the United States and Europe. He is a Clinical Professor of Psychiatry at University of California, San Diego, School of Medicine, and a faculty member of the San Diego Psychoanalytic Institute. He is a fellow of the American Academy of Forensic Sciences and is past president of the American Academy of Forensic Psychology. He has received a number of awards from various professional organizations and is chairman of Forensis, Inc., and Forensis Europa, Inc., two nonprofit, public benefit corporations devoted to forensic psychiatric and psychological research (http://www.forensis.org). Dr. Meloy has authored or coauthored over 200 papers published in peer-reviewed psychiatric and psychological journals, and has authored, coauthored or edited 10 books. His first book, *The Psychopathic Mind* (Aronson, 1988), was an integration of the biological and psychodynamic understanding of psychopathy, His most recent edited book, *Stalking, Threatening and Attacking Public Figures* (Oxford University Press, 2008), led to a commissioned study for the National Academy of Sciences on threats toward public figures published in March, 2011 (http://www.nap.edu). Dr. Stephen White and he created the WAVR-21 (Specialized Training Services, 2007), the first scientifically based structured professional judgment instrument for workplace targeted violence assessment. His forthcoming edited book with Dr. Jens Hoffman, *The International Handbook of Threat Assessment*, will be published by Oxford University Press in 2013. Dr. Meloy is also a consultant to the counterintelligence division of the FBI and intermittently teaches at the Behavioral Analysis Units in Quantico. He is a member of the Fixated Research Group for the United Kingdom's Home Office concerning threats to the Royal Family and British political figures, and also teaches for the Netherlands National Police. He has been a technical consultant to the television program *CSI* since its inception in 2001.

Eva Mulder is an Associate Professor in the Department of Child Psychiatry at Leiden University Medical Center in Leiden, the Netherlands.

Elizabeth Neidhart received her BS specializing in forensic psychology, and later her master's degree in criminal justice, from Seattle University, specializing in the areas of research and evaluation. She is currently involved in consulting work as a criminal justice researcher and analyst. Her main area of interest is the intersection of criminal justice and psychology and her research has primarily focused on policy related criminal justice/mental health issues. At the municipal level, she has studied the use of the Crisis Intervention Team (CIT) model in law enforcement, chiefly focusing on outcomes of its use within the Seattle Police Department. At the state level, she has participated in research as part of a larger multiagency task force study examining existing state policies and practices regarding sex offender risk assessment for offenders leaving the Department of Corrections. Her work centered on investigating the efficacy of structured risk assessment tools for sex offenders in Washington State in an effort to assess best practices policy and to inform issues relating to community management and public safety concerns.

Olaoluwa Olusanya earned his PhD in law in 2004 via collaboration between Humboldt University, Berlin, Germany, and the University of the Western Cape, South Africa. He received his LLB from Buckingham University, UK, in 1997 and earned his LLM degree at the University of Cape Town, South Africa. He is currently Lecturer (Assistant Professor) in the Department of Law and Criminology at the University of Wales Aberystwyth. His primary research interests are focused on the intersection of social cognitive science and criminal culpability/deviance and criminal law/criminal justice across multiple contexts genocide, race, and military veterans in the criminal justice system. His most recent work has appeared or is forthcoming in *New Criminal Law Review, Psychiatry, Psychology and Law, Critical Criminology, The Journal of Human Behavior in the Social Environment*, and *Criminal Justice Studies: A Critical Journal of Crime, Law, and Society*. His most recent book (coedited with Roelof Haveman) is *Sentencing and Sanctioning in Supranational Criminal Law*, Antwerp: Oxford: Intersentia, October 2006.

Stanley W. Patrzalek is a master's candidate at Seattle University in the Department of Criminal Justice. He received his bachelor of arts degree in law and justice from Central Washington University. Stanley's research interests include terrorism, crisis negotiation, police interrogation, criminological theory, offender profiling, and the intersection of technology and forensic science. Future research will explore the culture of martyrdom through a content analysis of the last will and testament of suicide bombers with emphasis on the personal and emotional significance of their statements.

Henry Richards received his doctorate from Loyola University of Chicago. His doctoral internship was conducted under the auspices of NIMH at St. Elizabeths Hospital in Washington, D.C., where his internship and postdoctoral studies focused the assessment and treatment of NGRI patients. He was later contracted by the Department of Justice to review the status of care of all White House cases at St. Elizabeths Hospital. He directed clinical services at Patuxent Institution, Maryland, and was executive director of the Special Commitment Center, McNeil Island, Washington. His publications are in the areas of addiction, psychopathy and other personality disorders, and sexual offending. He currently cochairs the Washington State Public Safety Review Panel, which advises the state hospitals and courts regarding the risk posed by potential releases of patients found NGRI for felonies. His forensic practice is in Seattle, Washington, where he is on the adjunct faculty of the University of Washington, and Seattle University.

C. Gabrielle Salfati is currently Professor of psychology at John Jay College of Criminal Justice, where she is the Director of the Investigative Psychology Research Unit (IPRU). She has a PhD in investigative psychology (University of Liverpool, UK, 1998) and is part of the first group of people who emerged within the new field of investigative psychology, and was instrumental in its development as an international research field on the empirical analysis of violent criminal behavior, in particular the advancement of the science of offender profiling. Her main areas of expertise relate to the methodology of research in offender profiling and linking serial crimes, specifically with a focus on homicide and violent sexual crimes. This work is being developed within an international framework through collaboration with major research centers and law enforcement agencies internationally. She has presented and published widely both nationally and internationally on her work, and provides training to law enforcement and crime analysts internationally. She has served as the elected vice president of the Homicide Research Working Group (HRWG), is a fellow of the International Association of Investigative Psychology, and associate editor on a number of academic journals including the *Journal of Investigative Psychology and Offender Profiling*, *Homicide Studies*, and the *International Journal of Offender Therapy and Comparative Criminology*.

Stacey L. Shipley obtained her doctorate in clinical/forensic psychology from California School of Professional Psychology in Fresno, California. She is the Director of psychology at North Texas State Hospital, the only maximum-security forensic hospital in Texas. She specializes in the areas of forensic and clinical assessment, violence risk assessment, and evaluating and treating maternal filicide offenders and offenders with severe mental illness. She serves as a consulting expert witness and conducts assessments of competency to stand trial and sanity. She is trained in the investigation and evaluation of violent crimes and offenders, serial crimes, linkage analysis, and threat communications. She has published in the areas of psychopathy, homicide, women and crime, maternal filicide, forensic case formulation for sexual offenders, and serial murder and serial rape typologies. Dr. Shipley is the first author of *Introduction to Forensic Psychology: Court, Law Enforcement, and Correctional Practices* (3rd ed., in press) with Elsevier/Academic Press.

Beck M. Strah received his master's degree in criminal justice from Seattle University, where he conducted research on sexual offenses and indeterminate sentencing decisions in Washington State, and has presented research in regional and national conferences. Mr. Strah received his bachelor of arts degree in psychology from the University of Alaska Anchorage, and has worked for the Snohomish County Sheriff's Office since 2009, assisting in law enforcement operations. He currently resides in the Seattle area and works for the Snohomish County Sheriff's Office as a custody deputy.

Faye S. Taxman is a Professor in the Criminology, Law and Society Department and director of the Advancing Correctional Excellence Center at George Mason University. Dr. Taxman is recognized for her work in the development of the seamless systems of care models that link the criminal justice with other service delivery systems as well as reengineering probation and parole supervision services. She has active "laboratories" with her nearly 20-year agreement with the Maryland Department of Public Safety and Correctional Services; she has been a PI of one of the National Institute on Drug Abuse's research centers in the Criminal Justice Drug Abuse Treatment Studies (CJ-DATS) network. She has received numerous awards, including a fellow of the Academy of Experimental Criminology and the Distinguished Scholar from the American Society of Criminology's Division on Sentencing and Corrections.

Hjalmar J. C. van Marle, psychiatrist, MD, and PhD, is Professor in forensic psychiatry at the Faculty of Medicine as well as the Faculty of Law, Erasmus University Rotterdam. Furthermore, from 2002 he is working as a forensic psychiatrist–psychotherapist at the forensic outpatient clinic "De Dok" in Rotterdam, and he is registered as an expert witness at the Courts of Justice. Formerly he was working as a psychiatrist, chief of staff and medical superintendant, respectively, of the maximum security hospital Dr. S. van Mesdagkliniek in Groningen (1979/1982/1984–1990), and of the forensic observation centre the Pieter Baan Centrum in Utrecht (1990–1996). From 1996 to 2003, he was appointed as a psychiatric advisor of the Ministery of Justice, as well as of the Prof. W. P. J. Pompekliniek in Nijmegen. From 1991 to 2003, he was professor in forensic psychiatry at the University of Nijmegen. From 1992 to 2002, he was also working as a psychotherapist at the Dr. H. van der Hoeven tbs-hospital in Utrecht. From 2002 to 2009, he was chairman of the Research Program of the Forensic Psychiatric Centre of Expertise in Utrecht; until now the chair of the International Scientific Committee of this Centre. His research concerns aggression and psychopathy in schizophrenic patients, cognitive distorsions in child molesters and neuropsychological functioning in mentally disordered offenders. He is member of the editorial board of *International Journal of Offender Therapy and Comparative Criminology*, *Forensische Psychiatrie und Psychologie*, the *International Journal of Forensic Health*, the (Dutch) *Journal of Psychiatry*, and Psychiatrienet.nl.

Index

Note: page numbers followed by f or t refer to Figures or Tables

AAMR. *See* American Association on Intellectual and Developmental Disabilities
Abel Assessment for Sexual Interest, 94t, 102
Active listening, 182–84
Actuarial risk assessment instruments (ARAIs): list of, 92t–94t; prediction of violence and, 342; in release of sex offender decisions, 116–21; risk prediction and, 59–60, 69–70; serious juvenile defenders and, 7–8, 10–14; SVP hearings and, 102–4. *See also specific tests*
Adaptive functioning, 402–3, 408–11. *See also* Mental retardation
African Americans: indeterminate sentencing and, 340–41; mandatory sentencing and, 344–45; police work and, 262, 265
Age factors, 100–101, 129–30
Alcohol use, 260, 263, 265
ALI Test, 316–17
American Association on Intellectual and Developmental Disabilities, 402–4, 408
American Law Institute (ALI) Test, 316–17
Amnesia, 294
Antisocial personality disorder (ASPD), 46, 350–51
ARAIs. *See* Actuarial risk assessment instruments (ARAIs)
Atherton, Judy, 284, 301
Atkins v. Virginia (2002), 393, 402–3, 405, 416

Barefoot v. Estelle (1983), 7
Barzee, Wanda, 283, 286
Baxstrom v. Herold (1966), 6–7
Bayesianism: cab problem and, 54–58; categorizing positions on, 66t–67t; civil commitment and, 68–72, 74, 78–79; in courtroom cases, 62–65; frequentist statistics versus, 58–62; overview, 44; recommendations for use, 79–82; sexually violent predator considerations and, 44, 65, 68–77; subjectivist philosophy of, 47. *See also* Bayes's Theorem
Bayes's Theorem. *See also* Bayesianism: cab problem and, 54–58; categorizing positions on, 66t–67t; evidence evaluation and, 64; knowledge destruction techniques and, 47; probability calibration and, 61; sexually violent predator considerations and, 68–69; truth-finding and, 82; validity of, 44; Woollert and, 70–76
Becarria, Cesare, 337
Behavioral disorders, 259–63. *See also* Criminal behavior
Behavioral genetics, 49–50

Behavior modification, 49
Berkowitz, David, 320
Big Five Personality Dimensions, 345–46
Biopsychosocial frameworks, 399–400
Blaming, 262
Bobbitt, Lorena, 320
Boltz, Frank, 172
Boston Strangler, 196
Brawner, Archie W., 318
Brawner Rule, 318
Briggs v. Elliott, 394
Bronfenbrenner's Ecological Model, 396
Brooks, Stephanie, 416–17
Brown v. Board of Education (1954), 394
Buchanan v. Kentucky (1987), 292–93
Burden of proof, 97–98
Buying time, 187

Caesar, Julius, 170
Christiansen, Carol, 242–43
CIT. *See* Crisis intervention teams (CIT)
Civil commitment: legislation and, 140; sexually violent predator evaluations and, 43–44, 68–72, 74, 78–79; sexually violent predators (*see* Sexually violent predators)
Clark, Carl and Mamie, 394
Classical school of criminology, 336–38
Classification of Violence Risk (COVR), 12
Clinical and Actuarial Prediction (Meehl), 42
Clinical judgment, 14
Clinical prediction of violence, 342
Coach negotiators, 177
Code of Hammurabi, 307
Cognitive-behavior treatment (CBT), 351–52
Cognitive-dissonance theory, 348
Community mental health care, 140–42, 368–69. *See also* Mental health courts
Competency to stand trial (CST): Brian David Mitchell and, 282–86; clinical and policy implications, 301–2; conducting the evaluation, 292–95; definition and overview, 281–82; delays and, 289; future research, 302; insanity defense and, 313–14; literature review, 286–88; malingering and, 297–99; mental illness and, 289–92; psychological tests and, 295–97; restoration of, 299–301; sanity versus, 288–89; written reports, 299
Compulsive/catathymia, 232–33, 244
Controlling behaviors, 213–14
Costs and benefits, 15
COVR. *See* Classification of Violence Risk (COVR)
Criminal behavior: adaptive functioning and, 408–11; classical model of, 336–38; definitions of, 334–36; positivist model of, 338–39
Criminal profiling. *See* Profiling
Criminal responsibility, 308, 312, 325–26, 328, 406
Criminogenic needs, 8–10
Crisis intervention teams (CIT): cautions and criticisms of, 157–60; challenges of, 148–53; effectiveness of, 153–57; evolution of, 147–48; future prospects, 160–61
Crisis negotiation, 173. *See also* Hostage (crisis) negotiation
Cross-cultural definition of criminal behavior, 336
Crusades, 170–71
CST. *See* Competency to stand trial (CST)
Cultural values, 396, 405, 407–8

Dahmer, Jeffrey, 319
Dangerousness, 3, 6–7, 89–91
Daubert v. Merrill Dow Pharmaceuticals, Inc. (1993), 81
Davis, Richard Allen, 87
Death penalty cases, 292, 393–94, 396, 408, 412–13
Decisional balance, 348
Deinstitutionalization, 140–41, 367
DeMier, Richart, 284–86, 291
Determinate-Plus Sentencing case study: actuarial instruments used in release decisions, 116–18, 119–21; discussion, 129–32; method, 121–25; parole and indeterminate sentence review decision making, 114–16; prison programs and sex offender treatment, 118–19; results, 125–29. *See also* Determinate sentencing
Determinate sentencing, 343–47. *See also* Determinate-Plus Sentencing case study
Diagnostic and Statistical Manual of Mental Disorders (DSM): antisocial personality

disorder and, 350–51; in criminal cases, 399; insanity and, 309; mental retardation and, 402–4, 409; racial bias and, 341
DiClemente, Carlo, 348
Displaced matricide, 244
Diversion programs, 146–47. *See also* Crisis intervention teams
Dodd, Wesley, 87
Drope v. Missouri (1975), 292
Drug treatment courts, 370
DuPont, John, 320
Durham, Monte, 315–16
Durham Rule, 315–16
Dusky v. United States (1960), 287, 291
Dynamic factors, 8–10

ECST-R. *See* Evaluation of Competency to Stand Trial–Revised (ECST-R)
Effective pauses, 183
Emotion labeling, 183
Erotophonophilia, 231
Estelle v. Smith (1981), 292–93
Ethical issues, 407–9
Evaluation of Competency to Stand Trial–Revised (ECST-R), 296–97
Expert testimony, 101–2
Extra-statistical positions (XSs), 65

Fantasy deviance, 231–32, 235–36
Faretta v. California (1975), 292
FBI hostage negotiation program, 172, 175
Federal Sentencing Guidelines Act (1984), 343
Ferguson, Colin, 282
Fitness-for-duty evaluations (FFDE), 270–74
Flynn, James, 412–13
Flynn Effect (FE), 412–17
Ford, Billy, 318
Forensic psychology: psychocultural factors and, 396; Teresa Lewis case (*see* Lewis, Teresa Wilson Bean); training competencies, 394–96, 417–18
Forensic risk assessment: criminogenic needs/dynamic models of, 8–10; future considerations, 15–16; overview, 4–5; prediction of dangerousness, 3, 6–7; psychodynamic model of, 5–6; statistical model of, 7–8; structured clinical judgment models, 10–11; tools for, 11–16. *See also* Risk assessment
Foster, Jodie, 318
FPJ. *See* Juvenile Forensic Profile (FPJ)
Frequentism, 58–62
Fuller, Rodney, 401

Gacy, John Wayne, 320
GBMI. *See* Guilty but Mentally Ill (GBMI)
Gein, Edward, 319
Gender: indeterminate sentencing and, 340–41; police work and, 262–63
Genetic Information Nondiscriminatory Act of 2008 (GINA), 258
Godinez v. Moran (1993), 291
Green River Killer. *See* Ridgway, Gary Leon
Guilty but Insane, 310
Guilty but Mentally Ill (GBMI), 310–12, 323–24

Hale v. State of Florida (2004), 100
Hanson, Karl, 76
Hare, Robert, 89, 230. *See also* Psychopathy Checklist–Revised (PCL-R)
HCR-20. *See* Historical/Clinical/Risk Management–20 (HCR-20)
Heilbrun, Kirk, 416–17
Hinckley, John W., 317–19
Hispanics. *See* Latinos
Historical/Clinical/Risk Management–20 (HCR-20), 11–12, 93t
Homelessness, 141, 368
Homicide Incidents Tracking System (HITS), 220
Hostage (crisis) negotiation: active listening and, 182–84; behind-the-scenes view of, 173–75; definition and overview, 172–74; demands and buying time, 186–89; evolution of, 170; gaining trust, 184–85; historical overview, 170–72; hostage taker typology, 175–77; negotiation team structure, 177–79; setup protocol, 180–82; Stockholm syndrome and, 189–90; surrender ritual, 190–91; team psychologists, 179–80; untrained third parties and, 185–86

ICT. *See* Iterative Classification Tree (ICT)
Idiosyncratic methods (IMs), 65
I messages, 184
Incompetent to stand trial (IST), 300–301, 310
Indeterminate sentence review, 114–16
Indeterminate Sentence Review Board (ISRB), 113–14, 116, 119–32
Indeterminate sentencing (pre-1984), 340–42
In re the Detention of Betsworth (2006), 102
Insanity defense: American Law Institute Test, 316–17; Brawner Rule, 317; competency to stand trial and, 313–14; Durham Rule, 315–16; guilty but mentally ill, 310–12; historical legal standards, 314; history and overview, 307–8; insanity assessment tools, 312–13; Insanity Defense Reform Act, 317–18; irresistible impulse test, 315; Kelman on jury decision-making, 323–26; M'Naghten Rule, 314–15; myths and public perceptions, 320–21; not guilty by reason of insanity, 308–10; studies of, 321–23; twentieth century cases, 318–20
Insanity Defense Reform Act (1984), 317–18
Instrumental versus expressive demands, 186–87
Intelligence quotient and testing, 402–5, 410–17
Intent, 325–26
Interviewer/intelligence gatherers, 178–79
In the Matter of the Care and Treatment of Berg (2011), 100
In the Matter of the Detention of Thorell, et al. (2003), 102
Irresistible impulse defense, 310, 315
IST. *See* Incompetent to stand trial (IST)
Iterative Classification Tree (ICT), 12

Jackson v. Indiana (1972), 299–300
Jack the Ripper, 196
Jefferson, Thomas, 171
Jenkins v. United States (1962), 395
Jury decision-making, 321–26
Juvenile Forensic Profile (FPJ), 24
Juvenile offenders. *See* Serious juvenile offenders

Kaczynski, Ted, 282, 320
Kahneman, Donald, 42
Kansas v. Hendricks (1997), 91, 95, 342
KDTs. *See* Knowledge destruction techniques (KDTs)
Kennedy, John F., 320
Kennedy, Robert, 320
Key communicators, 177
Kimball, Dale, 285, 290, 298, 301
Kiritsis, Anthony, 319
Knowledge destruction techniques (KDTs), 45–48
Kuhn, Thomas, 44, 48

Lanterman-Petris-Short Act, 140
Latinos, 341, 345
Law enforcement: investigative experience and profiling, 202–3; persons with mental illness and, 139–40, 142–45, 367–69 (*see also* Crisis intervention teams; Mental health courts); psychological evaluations of police officers (*see* Psychological evaluations of police officers)
Law Enforcement and Mental Health Project Act (2000), 379
Legal-consensus definition of criminal behavior, 335–36
Level of Service Inventory–Revised (LSI-R), 12–13, 90, 92t–93t
Lewis, Charles, 401
Lewis, Julian, 401
Lewis, Teresa Wilson Bean: adaptive functioning and criminal behavior, 408–11; case details, 393–94, 401–2; Flynn Effect and IQ, 412–17; forensic psychology perspective, 397–98; implications for training and practice, 417–18; intelligence quotient and testing, 402–5, 411–12; mental competency, 397–98; mental state at the time of the offense, 398–400, 405–8
Lewis v. Commonwealth of Virginia (2004), 393, 396, 405
Life-history interviews, 407
Linkage analysis, 212–18
Listening skills, 182–84
Lockett v. Ohio (2003), 406

Long Island Railroad Massacre, 282
Lot, 170
LSI-R. *See* Level of Service Inventory–Revised (LSI-R)

MacArthur Competence Assessment Tool-Criminal Adjudication (MacCAT-CA), 296–97
Mad Bomber of New York, 196
Malingering, 297–99, 405
Malvo, Lee Boyd, 320
Mandatory sentencing (1984–2004), 343–47
McGhee, Mary Elizabeth, 400
Meehl, Paul, 41–43, 48–50, 68, 74
Memphis Model, 147
Mens rea, 314
Mental health courts (MHCs): criticisms of, 382–84; current state of, 379–80; development of, 369–70; effectiveness of, 380–82; funding, 379; future research, 386; length of probation, 376; overview, 370–71; participant characteristics, 377–79; participant eligibility, 371–74; plea arraignments, 374; recommendations, 384–86; rewards and sanctions, 376–77; treatment planning and monitoring, 375–76
Mental illness: competency to stand trial and, 289–92; insanity versus, 309; life-history interviews and, 407; police officer attitudes and knowledge, 142–45; programs for, 140–42; trial behaviors and, 406–7. *See also* Mental health courts; Persons with mental illness (PwMI); Persons with serious mental illnesses (PSMI)
Mentally Ill Offender Treatment and Crime Reduction Act (2004), 379
Mental retardation, 291, 301, 397, 402–5, 409–17. *See also* Adaptive functioning
Mental state at the time of the offense (MSO), 398–400, 405–8
Mental Status Examination at the Time of the Offense (MSE), 313–14
Mexican Americans. *See* Latinos
Mild traumatic brain injury (MTBI), 258–59
Minimal encouragers, 183
Minnesota Sex Offender Screening Tool (MnSOST-R), 74, 91, 94t, 119–20
Miranda warnings, 187
Mirroring, 183
Missouri v. Davis (1983), 294
Mitchell, Brian David, 282–86, 290–91, 298, 301
Mixed determinate/indeterminate sentencing, 347–48
Mixed model of criminal behavior, 339
M'Naghten, Daniel, 314
M'Naghten Rule, 314–15, 318
MnSOST-R. *See* Minnesota Sex Offender Screening Tool (MnSOST-R)
Model Penal Code, 316–17
Modem probability theory, 78
Montana v. Austed (1982), 294
Morrow v. Maryland (1982), 294
MSE. *See* Mental Status Examination at the Time of the Offense (MSE)
MSO. *See* Mental state at the time of the offense (MSO)
MTBI. *See* Mild traumatic brain injury (MTBI)
Mullin, Herbert, 319
Munich Massacre, 171–72
Munsterberg, Hugo, 394

National Disability Rights Network, 404
Nazi Germany, 171
Necrophilia, 244
Negotiable versus nonnegotiable demands, 187–89
Neuroscientific evidence, 325–26
New York City Police Department (NYPD), 172
NGRI. *See* Not guilty by reason of insanity (NGRI)
Non-compos mentis, 314
Nonproblematic Applications (NAs), 65–67
Note takes, 177–78
Not guilty by reason of insanity (NGRI), 288, 308–10, 311, 320–21. *See also* Insanity defense
Nothing Works paradigm, 45
Null-Bayes Logic Model, 70–74

OEF/OIF Veterans, 259
Olley, Gregory, 416

Open-ended questions, 184
Oswald, Lee Harvey, 320

Paraphilia, violent, 231–32, 235–36
Paraphilia Not Otherwise Specified Nonconsent (PNOSN), 77
Paraphrasing, 183
Parole, 114–16, 343
Parsons v. State (1887), 315
Pascal's Wager, 78
Pate v. Robinson (1966), 289
Pathological play, 236–38
PCL-R. *See* Psychopathy Checklist–Revised (PCL-R)
Peace Officer Standards of Training (POST), 257
Peel, Robert, 314
People v. Roberge (2003), 100
PEPS, 270–71
Persons with mental illness (PwMI), 139: in the criminal justice system, 367–69; crisis intervention teams and (*see* Crisis intervention teams [CIT]); diversion programs, 145–47; hostage taking and, 176–77; police interactions with, 139–40, 142–45; services for, 140–42, 145. *See also* Persons with mental illness (PwMI), crisis intervention teams and; Persons with serious mental illnesses (PSMI)
Persons with serious mental illnesses (PSMI): in the criminal justice system, 367–69; criminogenic risk factors, 383–84; drug treatment court and, 370–71; mental health services for, 384–86; therapeutic jurisprudence and, 369–70. *See also* Mental health courts; Persons with mental illness (PwMI)
Plea arraignments, 374
PNOSN. *See* Paraphilia Not Otherwise Specified Nonconsent (PNOSN)
Police. *See* Law enforcement
Positivist school of criminology, 338–39
POST. *See* Peace Officer Standards of Training (POST)
Posttraumatic stress disorder (PTSD), 258–59
Predation, 232. *See also* Sexually violent predators
Predispositional factors, 231
Pre-employment psychological screenings (PEPS), 270–74
Prison inmates, 176
Probability, 54–58
Probation, 376
Prochaska, James, 348
Profiling: current research, 197–200; definition and overview, 195–96; future considerations, 205–7; investigative experience and, 202–3; past empirical examinations of, 196–97; profiler accuracy, 200–201; psychic detectives and, 204–5; science sophomore skills, 203–4
Prostitutes: clients and, 221–22; linking crime scenes, 212–18; overview, 211–12; serial offenders and, 222–24; sexual versus nonsexual motivations, 219–21; statistical overview, 218–19
Psychics, 204–5
Psychodynamic analyses, 49
Psychodynamic model, 5–6
Psychological evaluations of police officers: behavioral disorders, 259–63; fitness-for-duty versus pre-employment evaluations, 270–71; intoxicant-use patterns, 263–69; objectives of, 270; in PEPS and FFDEs, 270–74; psychological interview process, 256–57; purpose of, 254–56; rationale for, 257–58; semi-structured interviews, 271–72; timing of, 258–59
Psychological theme approach, 215–18
Psychologists on hostage negotiation teams, 179–80
Psychometric assessment, 49
Psychopathy: DSM and, 350–51; Green River Killer and, 229–31, 245–48; prediction of dangerousness and, 89–91; serial homicide offenders and, 249–50
Psychopathy Checklist–Revised (PCL-R): Green River Killer and, 246–48; overview, 11, 92t; primary and secondary psychopaths, 230–31; sentencing and, 342; in SVP hearings, 102, 104–5; test score variations in, 412; violence risk prediction and, 89–90
Psychosis, 290, 301

PTSD. *See* Posttraumatic stress disorder (PTSD)
PwMI. *See* Persons with mental illness (PwMI)

Rapid Risk Assessment for Sexual Offender Recidivism (RRASOR): overview, 93t; predictions of dangerousness and, 91; in SVP hearings, 102; use in release decisions, 120–21
R-CRAS. *See* Rogers Criminal Responsibility Scales (R-CRAS)
Recidivism: mental health courts and, 380; serious juvenile offenders and, 21–24, 33–36; by sex offenders, 100–101, 116–18, 129–30
Regina v. Denis John Adams, 63–64
Regina v. Sally Clark, 63
Rehabilitation, 340–42, 348–54
Reichenbach, Hans, 74
Remorse, expressions of, 130, 349–51
Responsivity principle, 9–10
Rex v. Arnold (1724), 314
Ridgway, Gary Leon: catathymia and, 232–33; crime scene deviations, 241–43; criminal history, 234; fantasy and violent paraphilia, 235–36; first offense behavior, 238; modus operandi, 238–41; pathological play, 236–38; personal history, 233–34; predation and, 232; psychopathy and, 229–31, 245–48; signature, 244–45; typology, 235; violent paraphilia and, 231–32
Ridgway, Mary Rita, 235–36
Riggins v. Nevada (1992), 351
Risk assessment, 4–5. *See also* Forensic risk assessment
Risk-based sentencing, 341–42
Risk principle, 9
Ritchie v. Indiana (1984), 294
Rogers Criminal Responsibility Scales (R-CRAS), 313–14
Rosebro, Susan, 400
RRASOR. *See* Rapid Risk Assessment for Sexual Offender Recidivism (RRASOR)
Ruby, Jack, 320
Rule out versus rule in approach, 258, 264, 270, 274

SACJ-Min. *See* Structured Anchored Clinical Judgment–Minimum (SACJ-Min)
Sanity, 288–89
Schlossberg, Harvey, 172
SCM. *See* Stages of Change Model (SCM)
Selective incapacitation, 345–46
Self-Appraisal Questionnaire, 94t
Self-efficacy, 348, 353–54
Sell v. U.S. (2003), 301
Semi-structured clinical interviews, 271–72
Sentencing: intermediate (pre-1984), 340–42; mandatory (1984–2004), 343–47; mixed determinate/indeterminate, 347–48; of sex offenders: Washington State, 113, 119, 131
Sentencing Reform Act (1984), 340, 343
Serial homicide: Gary Leon Ridgway and (*see* Ridgway, Gary Leon); prostitute victims (*see* Prostitutes)
Serious juvenile offenders: case study, 23–36; classification of, 21–23; recidivism and, 21–24, 33–36
Sex Offender Risk Appraisal Guide (SORAG), 90, 92t, 102
Sex offenders: parole of, 114–21; recidivism and, 100–101, 116–18, 126–30; sentencing of, 113, 119, 131
Sex offender treatment programs (SOTP), 118–19
Sex Predator Risk Assessment Screening Instrument, 94t
Sexually violent predator evaluations (SVPEs): Bayesianism and, 44, 47, 65, 68–77; civil commitment and, 43–44, 68–72, 74, 78–79; controversy in, 48–54; frequentism and, 58–62; knowledge destruction techniques and, 45–48. *See also* Sexually violent predators
Sexually violent predators: actuarial tests, 92t–94t; characteristics of, 99; expert testimony and recidivism predictions, 96–105; legal versus medical models, 91, 95–96; psychopathy and prediction of dangerousness, 89–91; state laws and, 88–89. *See also* Sexually violent predator evaluations (SVPEs)
Sexual Violence Risk–20 (SVR-20), 93t, 102

Shallenberger, Matthew, 401–2
Shriner, Earl, 87
Signatures, 214–15, 244–45
Sixth Amendment, 292
Skeem, Jennifer, 283–84, 291
Smart, Elizabeth, 282–86
Social contract theory, 337
Social learning processes, 339
SORAG. *See* Sex Offender Risk Appraisal Guide (SORAG)
SOTP. *See* Sex offender treatment programs (SOTP)
Stages of Change Model (SCM), 348–54
Stanford-Binet scales, 404, 411
State-dependent theories of criminality, 338–39
State laws on sexually violent predator laws, 88–89
Static 99, 76, 94t, 102, 121
Statistical model, 7–8. *See also* Actuarial risk assessment instruments
Stockholm syndrome, 189–90
Strangulation, 248. *See also* Ridgway, Gary Leon
Stress, of police officers: behavior disorders and, 259–63; intoxicant-use and, 263–69; psychological evaluations and, 254–59, 270–74
Structured Anchored Clinical Judgment–Minimum (SACJ-Min), 91, 93t
Structured clinical judgment models, 10–11
Summarizing, 183
Surrender process, 190–91
SVPEs. *See* Sexually violent predator evaluations (SVPEs)
SVR-20. *See* Sexual Violence Risk–20 (SVR-20)

TBI. *See* Traumatic brain injury (TBI)
Team leaders, 178
Terrorists, 176
The Paul Meehl Reader (Meehl), 41
Therapeutic jurisprudence, 369–70
Thinking, Fast and Slow (Kahneman), 42
Three Strikes laws, 344–47
Time framing, 323–24
Token economies, 352–53
Training competencies, 394–96, 417–18
Trait-based approaches, 335–36
Transtheoretical Model of Change, 348–54
Trapped criminals, 175–76
Trauma-control model, 231
Traumatic brain injury (TBI), 404
Treatment, 375–76. *See also* Rehabilitation

Unabomber, 282
Unifying/disjoining accounts of cases, 324–25
United States of America v. *Archie W. Brawner* (1972), 318
United States v. *Booker* (2005), 347
United States v. *DeShazer* (2009), 291
United States v. *Fruchter*, 343
United States v. *Hammick* (1994), 351
United States v. *Vamos* (2009), 291
U.S. v. *Binion* (2005), 298
U.S. v. *Greer* (1998), 298
U.S. v. *Timmins* (2002), 287

Verdict shifting, 311
Victim as Object/Vehicle model, 217
View of the defendant, 326
Violence Risk Appraisal Guide (VRAG): overview, 92t; predictions of dangerousness and, 90; in SVP hearings, 102; validity of, 11
Violence Risk Scale (VRS), 13
VRAG. *See* Violence Risk Appraisal Guide (VRAG)
VRS. *See* Violence Risk Scale (VRS)

Washington State Sex Offender Risk Level Classification Tool (WSSORLCT), 120
Wechsler scales, 404, 411
Welner, Michael, 283–86
What Works principles, 21, 33, 36, 45–46
Wild beast test, 314
Williams, David, 62
Williams, Wayne, 241–42
Wilson v. *United States* (1968), 294
Wollert, Richard, 70–77
Woodson v. *North Carolina* (2003), 405–6
WSSORLCT. *See* Washington State Sex Offender Risk Level Classification Tool (WSSORLCT)

Yates, Andrea, 320, 325
Yellowrobe, Patricia, 243